APPLYING PSYCHOLOGY IN BUSINESS

Applying Psychology in Business

The Handbook for Managers and Human Resource Professionals

Edited by

John W. Jones
London House/SRA, Inc.

Brian D. Steffy
Franklin and Marshall College

Douglas W. Bray
Development Dimensions International

LEXINGTON BOOKS
An Imprint of Macmillan, Inc.
NEW YORK

Maxwell Macmillan Canada
TORONTO

Maxwell Macmillan International
NEW YORK   OXFORD   SINGAPORE   SYDNEY

Lexington Books
An Imprint of Macmillan, Inc.
866 Third Avenue, New York, N.Y. 10022

Maxwell Macmillan Canada, Inc.
1200 Eglinton Avenue East
Suite 200
Don Mills, Ontario M3C 3N1

Macmillan, Inc. is part of the Maxwell
Communication Group of Companies.

Printed in the United States of America

printing number

2 3 4 5 6 7 8 9 10

Library of Congress Cataloging-in-Publication Data

Applying psychology in business : the handbook for managers and human
resource professionals / edited by John W. Jones, Brian D. Steffy,
Douglas W. Bray.
p.   cm.
ISBN 0-669-15838-0 (alk. paper)
1. Personnel management—Psychological aspects.   2. Psychology,
Industrial.   I. Jones, John W. (John Walter), 1953–
II. Steffy, Brian D.   III. Bray, Douglas Weston.
HF5549.A8953   1990
658.3'001'9—dc20   86-46357
                                                         CIP

CONTENTS

CONTRIBUTORS

Steven Arneson
University of Tulsa

Ross E. Azevedo
University of Minnesota

Thomas E. Backer
Human Interaction Research Institute

Melany E. Baehr
London House/SRA, Inc.

Bruce N. Barge
University of Minnesota

Richard W. Beatty
Rutgers University

Terry A. Beehr
Central Michigan University

Gary Behrens
London House/SRA, Inc.

Andrew G. Billings
Rohrer, Hibler, and Replogle, Inc.
Stanford University Medical Center

James A. Breaugh
University of Missouri, St. Louis

Meg Bond
University of Lowell

Barbara K. Brown
Purdue University

Michael J. Burke
New York University

James N. Butcher
University of Minnesota

William C. Byham
Development Dimensions International

Michael A. Campion
Purdue University

Mo Cayer
New York University

Stephen M. Colarelli
Central Michigan University

Steven F. Cronshaw
University of Guelph, Ontario

Deborah F. Crown
University of Colorado, Boulder

Peggy Crull
City University of New York

René V. Dawis
University of Minnesota

Donald T. DeCarlo
TransAmerica

C. William Deckner
Vanderbilt University Medical Center
Education Corporation of America

Michael Duane
Mercy College of Detroit

Ann D'Ercole
New York State Psychiatric Institute

Loren E. Falkenberg
University of Calgary

Charles H. Fay
Rutgers University

Hubert S. Feild
Auburn University

Laurence S. Fink
George Mason University

Anne Fuehrer
Miami University

Dee Gaeddert
National Information Systems, Inc.

Sidney Gael
NYNEX Corporation

Robert Gatewood
University of Georgia

Stephen G. Glasscock
Vanderbilt University Medical Center
Education Corporation of America

Donald L. Grant
University of Georgia

FOREWORD

Can more reliable and honest workers be selected? Are there some really good ways to make hiring and promotion decisions about supervisors and managers? How should performance appraisals be designed and carried out? What are the keys to success in the design of a compensation and reward system? How do you decide what should be in a training program? Are there different leadership styles that are effective in different situations? How can you motivate your workers to be more service oriented?

These and hundreds of other questions managers ask psychologists are answered in this handbook. Jones, Steffy, and Bray have brought together a group of authors to write in a highly readable fashion about the best tactics and techniques applied psychologists have developed for helping organizations deal with these sorts of questions.

What is particularly interesting in this handbook is that the authors of the chapters tell you not only *what* to do to solve particular problems, but the evidence that supports the approaches recommended. Thus, the *Handbook* authors present their recommendations and suggestion bolstered by the accumulated scientific research. And this scientific research in applied psychology has been growing at an impressive rate. This is perhaps true because of the often-demonstrated link between the application of applied psychology principles and practices and organizational effectiveness. Apparently managers in organizations are anxious to discover what does and does not work!

As the reader of the *Handbook* will see, applied psychologists invariably check out their practices and procedures in real organizations against real world problems prior to promoting them as solutions. In this way, for example, applied psychologists have shown how useful appropriately developed selection and training programs can be (they save organizations huge sums of money through improved productivity and lowered turnover, for example). What is important about this handbook, then, is that principles and procedures that are appropriate, that *work,* are emphasized so that managers and consultants seeking potential solutions can know what to try and what to avoid.

It is easy to get carried away with the amount of important information in this book. But just a quick glance at the table of contents will reveal the breadth and depth of issues covered. We are very pleased that Jones, Steffy and Bray took on this massive effort and we are very pleased to have it in our Series.

Benjamin Schneider
Arthur P. Brief

PREFACE

Managers are typically well versed in the principles that have served them well: finance, accounting, and economics. Finance and accounting in particular have contributed to the efficient management of financial, material, energy, and technological resources. But managers typically are not as well versed in the principles and practices related to the management of human resources. Although they carefully parent nonhuman resources, managers often do not appreciate the economic payoff of personnel practices and policies based on psychological principles. Just as plant facilities, machinery, materials, and monies possess an asset value that can be cultivated, so too do employees have an asset value than can be increased through the application of psychological principles and practices.

This book was written to provide professional managers, consultants, and students of management with a comprehensive overview of these principles and practices. Among the topics addressed are the conceptual, legal, and ethical foundations of applied psychology, the practice of recruitment, selection and internal staffing, procedures for appraising and rewarding performance and managing careers, and programs designed to improve the quality of work life and decrease job stress and counterproductive behaviors such as accidents and injuries.

Although the book focuses on psychological applications for profit-centered organizations, the principles and practices discussed are readily applied to not-for-profit and government organizations. The emphasis is practice, not theory, though we recognize that all practices are theoretically based, governed by empirical analysis and legal guidelines. Our intent was to produce a useful resource for practitioners—a book that addresses a wide range of human resource issues work organizations regularly confront. The contributors to this book—corporate, consulting, and academic behavioral scientists, who are members of leading professional organizations, including the Society for Industrial and Organizational Psychology, the American Psychological Association, and the Academy of Management—are experts in both the theory and application of applied psychology.

The *Handbook* is divided into nine parts. Part I, Foundations of Applied Psychology, contains seven chapters that provide a broad overview of the strate-gic role of applying psychology to work organizations. They examine the role of experimental and field research in making business decisions and the role of consultants and ethical considerations in applying psychological principles and practices in organizations. Chapter 7 highlights how organizations can use psychological products and services to increase their competitive posture into the next century.

Part II, Applied Measurement and Legal Guidelines, discusses basic principles for validating psychological tests, treatments, and practices. The chapters suggest ways for conceptualizing, measuring, and communicating the economic impact of psychologically based interventions. One chapter examines how computer software can improve the efficiency and effectiveness of employment testing practices; the others cover legal considerations in individual assessment and selection.

Part III, Analyzing Jobs, provides an overview of job analysis, the foundation of all other personnel activities in organization. The chapters are meant to assist managers in selecting and designing alternative forms of job analysis. Since different job analysis techniques are applied to different job classifications and occupations, we have included chapters for nonmanagerial, administrative, executive, and professional jobs. The part concludes with a chapter on exemplary forms of job analysis employed by organizations.

Part IV, Staffing with the Best, contains chapters that cover topics ranging from an overview of the role of selection, the role of recruitment, realistic job previews, and identifying successful recruiters, to assessment practices in identifying individual differences. Other chapters outline an array of employment selection practices, including forms of assessing management potential, mental abilities testing, biographical information, structured interviewing, and screening for substance abuse.

Part V, Assessment, Advancement, and Reward, focuses on issues of performance appraisal, promotion decisions, assessment centers, compensation, and reward. Particular attention is paid to designing assessment and appraisal programs in the light of measurement principles and tested procedures for implementation. The chapters on compensation and reward are written as a tutorial for practitioners unfamiliar with the basic psychological and human resource principles that underlie their design and administration. The part also offers a more detailed account of how to implement merit programs, since pay-for-performance programs are strongly rooted in psychological theories of motivation and incentives. The final chapter updates readers on the employment-at-will controversy. Typically applied psychologists focus on decisions to select individuals for a job and then decisions on mobility through the job system. Little attention has been paid to exits, another form of mobility. We hope that this chapter will encourage more attention on in this area.

Part VI, Career Development and Training, examines the role of psychological assessment in career planning and development. Among the topics and issues addressed are career pathing, mentoring, executive derailment, and outplacement counseling. The chapters on training discuss how to assess when training is most likely to be effective and how to evaluate the effectiveness of training programs.

Part VII, Optimizing the Organization, the largest in the *Handbook*, covers a wide range of topics in organizational behavior. This part begins with a discussion of work-adjustment theory and its implications for employee-centered developmental practices. The next two chapters discuss one of the currently most popular organizational topics, climate and culture. The next four chapters focus on leadership and participative management practices. Subsequent chapters address issues of job design, employee and customer surveys, the organizational effects of computer-automated technology, performance withdrawal, the use of temporary employees, and the prevention and control of sexual harassment.

Part VIII, *Dealing with Workplace Stress,* consists of nine chapters that look at the deleterious impact of excessive and chronic job stress on both employees and their organizations. Most of the chapters outline procedures, policies, and practices for preventing and managing stress. Some of the organizationally sponsored programs reviewed include employee assistance, substance abuse, physical fitness, and merger stress management programs. An additional chapter reviews emerging legal rights of employees relating to adverse consequences of workplace stress.

Part IX, Managing Safety and Security, addresses the personality characteristics of accident-involved employees and using psychological testing to identify high-risk applicants and employees. A comprehensive review of other safety management programs is provided in subsequent chapters, including how to employ disability management and rehabilitation counseling services. The remaining chapters review programs and policies for controlling security-risk employees—for example, employees who steal and engage in other types of counterproductivity.

We hope that you find the *Handbook* a useful resource. Numerous individuals must be credited with the completion of this ambitious project. Foremost, we thank our contributors for writing original chapters for the book. We also thank our colleagues and associates who constantly encouraged and assisted us—particularly the staff at Franklin and Marshall College, London House, Inc., and Development Dimensions International. We extend our appreciation for the guidance and constructive criticism offered by the series editors, Benjamin Schneider and Arthur P. Brief, as well as Robert Bovenschulte at Lexington Books. Finally, we thank our spouses, children, and other family members for their encouragement and support.

PART I

FOUNDATIONS OF APPLIED PSYCHOLOGY

1 APPLIED PSYCHOLOGY IN BUSINESS: A MULTILEVEL OVERVIEW

Benjamin Schneider

Several months ago I was on an airplane from Washington, D.C., to San Diego. The person next to me struck up a conversation, and, given that I was otherwise unoccupied, I struck back. One topic followed another, as will happen, and soon we were speaking about our respective jobs. Mine, I indicated, was as a professor and a consultant in the field of industrial and organizational (I-O) psychology. "Pretty impressive title for a field," he said. "What the heck is it? Is it how people are hired and trained to do their work? How leaders manage people? How people work together in teams? Why organizations look and feel the way they do when I visit them?"

After holding up my hand to slow him down, I noted that I/O psychology is really applied psychology in business and that it addressed each of those issues. I also noted that what really made the field interesting was thinking about those issues simultaneously because, in real organizations, they occur simultaneously. "In fact," I said, "if managers fail to consider all of those issues at the same time, their organization can't really be very effective."

"Tell me more. We have a long trip," was his reply.

In what follows, I have tried to recapture what I told my fellow traveler. It has come out a bit neater here than it did then, but the goal is the same: to present an overview of I/O psychology that captures the multilevel human complexity of organizations. This complexity is really a function of the fact that human behavior exists at many levels in organizations: individual, interpersonal, team, and organizational. To show this complexity, I examine each of these levels separately and conclude by integrating them to show why one organization can look, feel, and be more effective than another. As is obvious from the length of this *Handbook,* I certainly cannot begin to summarize all of the ways psychology has been able to help business think about its human components and function more effectively. In this overview, I introduce some of the many ways in which psychologists work in organizations to improve organizational functioning and, thereby, organizational effectiveness.

ORGANIZATIONS AS ONIONS

Prior to detailing the different levels at which psychologists have worked, it will be helpful to present an overview of what organizations look like to me, an applied psychologist. In brief, I think of organizations as onions; they are layers upon layers of phenomena internal to the workings of the organization. Their roots extend to the larger environment from which they draw nourishment, and they are exposed to the external world from which they draw resources and provide output.

Like onions, organizations are living systems surrounded by environments that can have dramatic effects on their growth and development. Also like onions some parts of organizations are closer to the environment than others, yet all layers are required to function interdependently for the whole to flourish. Each layer of the onion encompasses other layers and is dependent upon those other layers; the different layers are all functioning simultaneously and interactively. There is no such thing as an independent layer in an onion or in an organization, and there is no such thing as only one layer functioning at a time. Indeed, the boundaries between layers are highly permeable. The layers need to be highly permeable to each other for each layer to help the other and for the onion to

I was helped in preparing this chapter by comments on earlier versions from Eric Braverman, Art Brief, Harold Goldstein, Paul Hanges, Katherine Klein, Purnima Mathur, and Joe Schneider. Errors of logic, interpretation, or fact remain mine.

profit from its relationships with the larger environment in which it exists and with which it interacts.

The fact that organizations, like onions, are in constant contact with and sometimes almost totally dependent on the relationships they have with the larger environment in which they function is important to remember. This does not mean that organizations cannot control their internal workings. It does mean that the success of organizations is a function of the extent to which they are effective in dealing with the larger environment. Different kinds of onions grow better in different kinds of soil because of the fit of the kind of onion to the environment in which it grows. This is true for organizations as well.

Some people, unfamiliar with the full range of the application of psychology in business, may have a narrow view of what applied psychologists in business actually do. Some may have the view that personnel selection is the province of psychologists, while others may think of attitude or culture surveys as what most psychologists do. In different organiza-tions executive-management consulting is seen as the applied psychologist's role, while across the street psychologists are dealing with the design of job enrichment programs as a vehicle for improving the quality of work life and productivity. Some organizations would never promote individuals to a supervisory job without using I-O psychologists to train them in interpersonal and team-building skills, while competitors in the same industry employ psychologists to design executive succession plans and change the culture of their organization from one of efficiency to one of service.

Thus, applied psychologists have developed principles and methods for dealing with human behavior at all of these levels: people as individuals, people as interpersonal entities (in leadership and team roles), and people as the key to understanding the way organizations look and behave. Here I review some of the issues at each of these levels to provide a flavor for the techniques and findings contained in the *Handbook.*

THE INDIVIDUAL IN THE ORGANIZATION

Psychologists have paid most attention to individuals in organizations, including selecting and training them, appraising and motivating them, and assessing their work attitudes and work commitment. All of this is done with the goal of strengthening individuals' contributions to organizational effectiveness. These contributions can be in the form of raw productivity, lower levels of turnover, higher levels of quality, and/ or better levels of cooperation among individuals.

What is unique about applied psychologists, compared to other psychologists, is this focus on the contributions of individuals to organizational effectiveness. This notion of contributions is called "the criterion" by applied psychologists. By "the criterion" they mean the standard of excellence or the goal that is to be achieved. So, for example, we study individual differences in abilities not just because we are interested in the range of individual differences or the bases of skills. We study them to establish a relationship or connection between individual differences in abilities and criteria or goals that are important for organizational effectiveness. Once those relationships are established, the information can be used to make more valid hiring decisions, design superior training programs, institute more motivation goal-setting and reward systems, and design organizational policies and practices that may yield improved retention of valuable employees.

In fact, as will be clear to the reader of the *Hand-book,* quite a lot is known about how to select, train, motivate, and retain employees who are more likely to promote organizational effectiveness. Studies even exist showing the utility, in bottom-line dollars, of these procedures. The studies show that investments in selection, training, reward systems, and goal setting are invariably paid back in less than one year, and, in addition, they yield impressive improvements in effectiveness over time. Obviously periodic attention needs to be paid to such programs to monitor their continued effectiveness, but Wayne Cascio (1982), for example, has made it clear that investments in these programs compound over time to produce high returns on investment (ROI).

Applied psychologists' focus on individuals is logical given that they are, after all, psychologists. This focus, of course, has a particularly American flavor, wherein the individual is the center of thinking about work performance. In contrast to America, other cultures, such as Japan and the Scandinavian countries, promote work effectiveness through more interpersonal (team, group) work.

But in America, the data are very clear that when the kinds of programs applied psychologists have developed for understanding, predicting, and motivating individuals are instituted in organizations, some of the best ROI is from these individually based procedures: selection, training, reward systems, and goal setting.

The problem is that, like all other good things, there is no quick fix. Selection and training programs require extensive and intensive job analysis information prior to the design of effective programs. For selection, the design of effective programs rests on a few basic principles. First, through job analysis identify the competencies (knowledge, skills, abilities, and other characteristics, or KSAOs) the job requires. Second, get as close to the assessment of those competencies as possible in the hiring process. If these two principles are not followed closely, the procedure will likely lack validity and be open to legal challenge if the hiring process reveals adverse impact for protected groups.

This principle of getting as close as possible to the competencies required by the job in the hiring process reveals why research evidence shows that the typical interview is not a particularly valid selection process. That is, since the typical interview only taps into some verbal skills and vague motivations about what people say they want to do in the future, relevance to the job for which they are being hired is questionable. Some advances in interview design, especially those called "situational interviews" (Latham, Saari, Pursell & Campion, 1980) show how getting close to the actual job and the job situation can yield valid interviews.

In fact, the most fundamental principle of personnel selection programs is that they should be validated, that is, proved to be effective. When programs that seem to look and feel right are subjected to scientific validation, they just might not be right.

As with personnel selection, the starting point with training is job analysis, and the ending point is validation. For some reason, perhaps because of legal challenges to them, selection programs are more likely to be subjected to validity tests than are training programs. Failure to validate a training program is analogous to neglecting to check a new computer system's accuracy for billing prior to using it to prepare bills for clients. Even so, nonvalidated training programs are the norm rather than the exception.

The design of reward systems requires elaborate research to identify the kinds of rewards and the procedures for distributing rewards that are likely to work best given the particular kinds of employees to be served by the system. There is good evidence to

suggest that what is being rewarded needs to be carefully monitored in organizations. Thus, Steven Kerr (1988) has shown that the behaviors managers say they are rewarding (e.g., quality of performance) are different from the behaviors employees say are being rewarded (e.g., volume of productivity). His research shows that employees do what they get rewarded for doing, not what management says is being rewarded.

Not only do some managers fail to reward the behavior they say they want, but they try to keep employees from speaking about the wages they do receive. It is clear, however, that trying to keep wages and salaries a secret is silly since the information always leaks. Managers try to do this especially when newly hired people to a job are paid higher wages than experienced persons due to such factors as labor shortages. The combination of attempts at secrecy and disparity yields anger among existing employees.

The point is that it is critical that the reasons or purposes for putting these selection, training, or reward systems in place must be specified. Is the goal increased productivity, increased quality, improved service, improved retention of employees, fewer accidents, or something else? Unless these goals are defined and clarified up front and the goals are bought in to by management and those putting the systems into place, procedures for selecting, training, and rewarding employees will yield unsatisfactory results. This is true because ambiguity and disagreement about the goals a system should yield will make someone unhappy with the goals the system produces.

In fact, the role of goals in human behavior at work has been very well documented. Evidence presented by Edwin A. Locke and Gary P. Latham (1984) shows that superior performance is likely when people have specific, challenging goals and receive feedback on their performance as they work toward goal accomplishment.

Now, while the evidence is clear for the utility of these individually based procedures for improving organizational effectiveness, the research also clearly shows that a focus only on individuals at work ignores other potentially important layers of influence. Thus, it would be as if we put all of our faith for what an onion will become in the seed and ignored the environment in which the seed develops and the many layers of development that occur.

INTERPERSONAL ENTITIES AT WORK

Applied psychologists know a lot more about the behavior of individuals at work than they know about how interpersonal relationships function at

work. This is because of the tendency always to think about people as individuals rather than as interpersonal entities.

By interpersonal entity I refer to, for example, ice-skating pairs dancers compared to single skaters. The pair is an entity just like the individual is an entity. Pairs dancing cannot be judged or appreciated by focusing on one or the other of the partners; it is the entity that must be judged on how it behaves as a whole.

Every organization is defined by the patterns of interpersonal behavior that exist there. Thus, if no interpersonal behavior occurs in a setting, it cannot be an organization. The very concept of organization implies coordination, interaction, mutuality of effort, and common purpose, none of which is possible without interpersonal interaction.

At the simplest level, people interact as superior and subordinate or as coworkers. These interactions have known characteristics, including the roles of power, leadership, cooperation, competition, and morale. Note how each of these words would be useless in describing an individual's behavior; the words all connote a frame of reference, and that frame of reference is other people. In this section of the chapter I first discuss leadership and then groups.

Leadership

It is an interesting paradox that most of the early studies of leadership focused only on the traits of leaders, ignoring the impact of others and the situation. In contrast, it is largely agreed now that leadership is highly situational in nature. This means that a given person may be a leader in one situation but not in another. The example frequently used is Winston Churchill who, both before and after World War II, was not considered much of a leader, but during the war he was *the* acknowledged leader. What is critical to note is that the war made Churchill, not others, leader. Obviously it is what was in Churchill as a person and what was in the war as a situation that yielded Churchill the leader. The point, and it cannot be overly emphasized, is that leadership is quite situational in nature. Leadership is an area in which we can observe a real crossing over of layers of the onion. One layer, the individual, interacts with another layer, the situation, to produce the phenomenon we call leadership. Consider some examples. Start-up high-tech companies require different kinds of leaders than cash cow companies; YMCAs will find leadership in different kinds of people than the success stories in Silicon Valley; and an AT&T in the monopoly era required a different style of leadership from the era of divestiture.

An additional point is that people are not infi-

nitely flexible. Thus, when situations change, the leader may also have to change. Churchill was unable to be a leader both before and after the war; he was not infinitely flexible. This principle of finite flexibility means that theories of leadership that promote a prescription for how to be an effective leader in all situations are probably wrong. Leadership training programs that promote a best way to effectiveness are probably wrong. And leadership programs that tell people how to behave as a leader as they encounter many different kinds of situations are wrong. People have finite flexibility.

In fact, some research by Barry Staw (Staw & Ross, 1984) and by Bernard M. Bass (1985) suggests that a certain rigidity or consistency in style, vision, and goals is associated with being seen as a leader. Without this consistency it appears that followers experience ambiguity and uncertainty and, thus, fail to lock on to the leader's vision.

It may be obvious from the above, but it needs saying: leadership is a characteristic people attribute to a person based on observations of that person in interaction with others. The attributions made about the leader are based on some or all of the following kinds of observations: (1) the leader is able to get others, willingly or unwillingly, to do his or her bidding; (2) in the absence of the leader, the behavior of people is disorganized, tentative, and uncertain; and (3) especially in times of stress or crisis, followers look to the leader for guidance and direction.

Observations of these kinds, of course, do not answer the question of why certain people in certain situations are able to function in these ways. At present we do not know much about which kinds of people in which kinds of situations result in those people being leaders. What we do know, however, is that leadership is an interpersonal situation and that to speak of this or that person as being a "natural" leader is to miss the point. The phrase must at least be that he or she is a "natural leader *in such and such situation.*"

Teams

Most work in organizations occurs in teams or groups. In spite of this, most American corporations, especially compared to Japanese and Scandinavian corporations, fail to select people, train people, and reward people for teamwork; the focus has been on the individual. Perhaps because of this, applied psychologists have not been consistent in their interests in teams at work, with considerable work having been done in the 1950s, sporadic work until the mid-

1980s, with a somewhat increased interest since, most likely due to American business's increasing interest in teams.

Thus it is becoming clear that teams can function effectively when the team is composed of people who are fairly similar, but not identical, in their attitudes and perceptions; people who are individually of high ability and complement other team members' abilities; and people who are predisposed to working in teams. Teams composed of these kinds of people need to be supported by the larger environment with the necessary tools, equipment, and knowledge to function effectively. In addition, if the team can have early success experiences, this appears to generate a kind of momentum that promotes a sense of efficacy in the team so that future successes are even more likely. George Shea and Richard Guzzo (1987) speak of groups that are "potent"; they have a sense of themselves as being competent and effective. Their research shows that these efficacious groups outperform groups that lack this sense of potency.

Organizations like Xerox, GE, AT&T, Westinghouse, and others have found that groups can be very effective when issues like those identified above are managed by the organization. In addition to the group composition and resource issues, these organizations create an expectation that the way to succeed is through team effort, and it is teams that are rewarded and supported. A pleasant outcome of the team approach is strengthened commitment to the team and, thus, to the organization.

This is especially true when group members are offered opportunities to participate in decisions that affect the group. These decisions include those regarding work schedules, who will work at which tasks, how tasks should be designed for maximum performance *and* for maximum job enjoyment, and specification of the resources needed by the group (in terms of physical resources and staff, for example) to function optimally. There is a growing body of literature showing that managers fear participation by their subordinates in decision making because they feel it dilutes their power in the group. The evidence, however, as Arnold Tannenbaum (1968) has shown, reveals that participation increases the total power in a group. This means that managers do not lose power so much as subordinates gain power, creating more total power in a group. People like Richard Hackman (1986) have argued that groups can self-manage when they are empowered to behave autonomously if they are provided with appropriate resources and sufficient independence to make important decisions.

It has been known in the research literature for at least fifty years, since the famous Hawthorne studies, that teams matter at work. Those studies revealed how groups can both restrict and enhance productivity. Numerous laboratory studies in the 1950s showed, additionally, how team members communicate with each other, how they castigate people who are "different," and how leaders emerge in groups. Indeed, Robert Bales (1950) showed the ebbs and flows of group development, documenting the typical cycles that groups move through as they become a smoothly functioning unit. The lesson from Bales's work is that simply putting people in a room and expecting them to function smoothly is silly; groups take time to form, as anyone who has participated in team sports knows.

Perhaps the most important point to make about teams is that norms evolve over time for the kinds of behavior that are appropriate for team members to display. These norms determine the kinds of behaviors most likely to be observed in a team. Further, these norms get established relatively early in a team's life, so it is important to get groups off to a good start by paying careful attention to group composition, the presence of needed resources, and early success. The last is frequently a problem in organizations that use teams only when a crisis emerges and the team does not have sufficient time to establish itself as a team; time to deal with the crisis, not time to build a team, is of the essence. Those are precisely the conditions under which a team is least likely to succeed, so it is no wonder that teams in those organizations are reputed to be ineffective.

What *is* an effective group is a difficult question to answer in the abstract, and, in the absence of an answer, it is difficult to understand and/or predict the conditions that will increase group effectiveness. Thus, is a group effective when its members are happy with the group experience, when the group produces a high volume of products, when the group has few products returned to it to correct defects, when the group functions harmoniously, when there is low turnover from the group, and/or when the leader of the group obtains a promotion?

Clearly group effectiveness, like individual effectiveness, has many facets. The important point is that organizations must be clear about the criteria of effectiveness or goals against which they will judge groups prior to emphasizing the importance of groups for long-term organizational effectiveness.

In the 1980s, the study of groups added an interesting dimension. This concerns the study of what has come to be called "intergroups." The study of intergroups is about how individuals are really members in many groups and how any one individual can embody the attributes of the numerous groups of which he or she is a member. Thus, females can be a member of a group called *females,* the group called *whites,* the group called *mothers,* the group called *daughters,* and the group called *managers.* Any one woman may simultaneously belong to all of those groups, *and others may interact with her as if she had all of the stereotypical attributes of all of the members of all of those groups.*

Researchers like Clayton Alderfer (1987) show, for example, that black women managers are behaved to differently from white women or white male managers. These differences suggest that being black and/or being female determine how people are behaved toward more than does the attribute manager. Indeed, Alderfer has shown that, within an organization, there can be conflict between different individuals based on these kinds of intergroup attributes. Obviously this kind of conflict can be a constraint on individuals' working together effectively. This is especially true because of the subtlety with which intergroup conflicts can get played out in organizations.

For example, other things being equal (e.g., in an application for a job that includes a resume with sex identified but all other information the same), women are less likely to be offered a job, will be offered a job at lower pay, or will be slotted into "female" (staff rather than line) jobs more than males. Rosabeth Kanter (1977) notes that males, who typically may make these decisions, rarely realize that the sex of the applicant affects their decision. Rather, they tend to attribute their decisions to differences in competency or some other nongender-related characteristic.

Another, less subtle, indicator of intergroup conflict in organizations concerns team members who speak about other teams and their members in "we-they" terms, a characteristic of intergroup tension. For example, union-management relationships are frequently clouded by attributions each party makes about the other, especially during negotiations. Here the individual union representative and the individual management representative embody the stereotypes each may hold about the members of the other group. Unless and until these stereotypes are broken and the parties can deal with each other as individuals, harmony in union-management negotiations will not occur. When harmony occurs, union-management cooperation can exist, as it has, for example, at Ford Motor Co. (e.g., Banas, 1988) and the outcome for both parties to the corporation can be positive.

A final point about groups is that they, like individuals, exist in a larger context and are subject to larger context phenomena; groups are another layer of activity in organizations. As another layer, groups need to be viewed not only in isolation but in interaction with other layers. Thus, groups have an impact on the individual members of the group, and, simultaneously, groups interact with the larger context in which they are immersed. For example, leader-member relationships in a group may be partially determined by such external factors as shared intergroups, mutual acquaintances, previous jobs held in the same organization, and so on. Or an individual's desire to remain a member of a group may result in his or her engaging in some behavior that is inconsistent with what he or she would do in another context. The important point to note here is that attempts to explain the behavior of individuals in the workplace require attention to a lot more than that individual's own attributes — answers to why a person does what he or she does can also be found in examining the nature of that person's interpersonal relationships. This fact cautions against making an easy, individually focused attribution about why individuals and groups behave as they do toward each other and demonstrates the need to keep an open mind to alternative explanations.

Summary

From the discussion it becomes clear that interpersonal entities at work exist at a number of different levels: leader-member relationships, work team relationships, and intergroup relationships. The last may involve very large numbers of people (e.g., union people versus management people) or two individuals who behave toward each other based on their intergroup attributes (a union negotiator and a management negotiator). Group and intergroup issues at work are far more important, and frequently more subtle, than is typically recognized. Further, the issue of leadership requires a situational focus because any one person cannot be infinitely flexible. The leader in one particular situation may not be a leader in another situation. Therefore, leadership selection and training must take into account the situation(s) in which the leader must lead because specification of a general personality profile of a leader is not possible and plainly does not make sense.

THE ORGANIZATIONAL LAYER

To this point my focus has been on the basic human elements of organizations: individuals and individuals in interaction with each other. It is patently obvious, of course, that individual and interpersonal behaviors occur in a larger organizational context; however, we frequently ignore the obvious.

Psychologists who consult with organizations are often amazed at the failure of managers and executives to identify the pervasive effect of organization-level practices and policies on the behavior that occurs in their organization. Executives usually attribute problems to not getting people with the right skills or problems motivating people to be more productive. Organizational diagnoses by psychologists invariably reveal that the policies and practices that pervade the organization at all levels can account for a large proportion of the problems executives identify.

These policies and practices can conveniently be summarized by the words *climate* and *culture*. Climate and culture energize and direct the behavior toward certain activities and away from others. For example, some organizations have policies and practices that emphasize the quality of working life because the founder of the corporation believed that an investment in human capital was morally and ethically right. Such organizations may have relatively generous policies about pregnancy leave, child care, the availability of loans for emergencies, a team- or even company-wide profit-sharing plan, and a practice of involving all levels of employees in decisions that have an effect on their day-to-day work world.

People who work in these kinds of organizations might describe the climate as being "benevolent" or "like a family." And they may attribute this family feeling to the "guy who founded the place." Because of this kind of feeling in the workplace, people may treat each other more cordially and helpfully, there are likely to be more teams and work group approaches to production and service, and commitment to the organization is likely to be high and turnover low.

Applied psychologists believe that organizational policies and practices communicate more information and communicate it more directly to employees than all forms of printed or verbal communication combined. The rule here is that behavior talks.

What happens is that people do a kind of mental collating of the policies and practices under which they work and pull together different policies and practices to form a message. In the example mentioned about the organization that had pervasive practices regarding the quality of work life, all of the policies and practices combine to yield the family feeling.

An example of how a policy decision by management can have pervasive influences on workers' lives and organizational functioning concerns the implementation of new technology. Organizations always implement new technology, but the managers who cause this to happen can frequently ignore the human consequences of these technological changes. A subfield of applied psychology, sociotechnical systems, is concerned with the ways technology and humans interact.

The sociotechnical systems idea came out of research in England by Eric Trist and his colleagues (Trist & Bamforth, 1951). They documented what happens in a coal mine when new technology changed the ways workers are asked to carry out their jobs. In this case, the means of mining coals was changed from a method in which small teams of miners, each with different skills (blasters, cutters, loaders), mined a particular seam of coal. The new technology created large teams of miners with each team having a specialized function (e.g., a team of blasters), the work became machine paced rather than team paced, and much of the coal-removal process was mechanically, not team, handled.

The result was a severe drop in productivity at the coal mine as the result of the development of a norm of low productivity. This norm was a result, in turn, of the large teams being difficult to supervise and a breakup of teams that had developed close interpersonal relationships from working in a team where each member had his own competencies and productivity followed through a complementarity of competencies.

This study, although accomplished many years ago, reveals the ways a decision by management to institute a new policy can have unintended consequences for the way people feel about their work and the effectiveness of work teams and the total organization. It shows how technological issues at the level of management decisions cannot be divorced from the other layers of organizational functioning. Other management policies can also have unintended negative consequences. For example, a new policy about documenting travel expenses can ripple through an organization, yielding a perception on the part of employees that management does not trust workers. Changes in health benefits and who pays for them can yield the perception that management does not care about workers and their families. Indeed, the list is essentially endless. The point is that the management of organizations must consider the intended as well as the unintended consequences of the implementation of new policies, whether those policies have to do with technology, expense accounts, health benefits, or something else.

In contrast to the implementation of new policies or systems, some of the policies and practices of organizations are carried out in sometimes unknowing, quite subtle, ways. For example, the organization in which the "family" feeling is created may have over time evolved recruitment and selection procedures that unknowingly keep out noncooperative types of people. Or when people first are hired, the organization may assign a "buddy" to the newcomer to help him or her get socialized to the new setting. Finally, in training, cooperation and teamwork may be emphasized as "the way we do things around here." Thus, what happens is that the layers of organizational life we discussed earlier, like selection, training, and interpersonal interactions, combined with organizational policies regarding profit sharing, pregnancy leave, and child care, all collate to form the image people have of their work organization. This kind of mental arithmetic—of adding up the kinds of things that happen to and around people—yields the pervasive message psychologists call climate and culture.

Climate and culture can emphasize different goals; they can send different messages. One company can send the message by its policies and practices that the volume of productivity is critical and that quality is secondary. Another organization can send the message that service excellence is what will be rewarded, supported, and expected. A third might send the message that innovation is the key to success. These messages are sent by all of the policies and practices of the organization that surround employees. Indeed, some organizations may be able to get across multiple messages, such as service excellence *and* innovation. The critical issue is that merely by carrying out the daily life of an organization, management established policies and practices, and the choices that are made about them send messages to employees. Note that the policies and practices are not at all those that are announced or formal; it is what management *does,* not what it *says,* that is important.

This kind of complexity makes it difficult for managers to know what to do in their own organizations after reading books like *In Search of Excellence* by Peters and Waterman (1982). Those books show how specific companies have clarified their priorities through their practices and policies. However, in any particular organization, the priorities may be different, or they may be ordered differently. Thus, the challenge for management is to identify priorities and establish individual (selection and training), group (providing time for group development), and organizational (implementation of technology) practices and policies that will send the desired messages. If this is not done, it will never be clear what kind of onion you want to be *or even if you want to be an onion.* In the absense of a clear specification of goals and priorities for those goals, it is not possible to send consistent messages to organizational members. Inconsistent messages will yield ambiguity and uncertainty accompanied by an inability to achieve coordinated effort.

In order to avoid this ambiguity, executives need to answer questions like the following:

- What messages about the importance of quality do we want to send to our employees?
- What messages do we want to send to employees about their value as human resources?
- What messages do we want to send to consumers about the reliability of our products and our willingness to stand behind them?
- What messages do we want to send to the larger environment in which we operate about our concern for that environment?

Note that the questions are worded, "*What* messages . . . ," not, "Do we want to send messages?" Management will send messages; the question is, What will they be?

Fortunately there exist some excellent recent examples of organizations that have asked and answered these kinds of questions and have been able to change themselves in ways that have produced organizational effectiveness. SAS (Scandinavian Air Systems), for example, was an airline beset by financial malaise and declining international traffic. Jan Carlzon (1987), as chief executive officer, made a commitment to reverse this pattern and to do it through an emphasis on exceptional service *at every step of the process of contact between the consumer and the airline.* Once he had made the commitment to exceptional service, the challenge became one of operationalizing that commitment through explicit attention to all layers of SAS's practices and policies. The details of Carlzon's approach, and the effectiveness of his efforts are recorded in his book, *Moments of Truth.*

Not only service organizations, like airlines, but manufacturing organizations, too, can become redirected. Consider the redirection of the Ford Motor Company to a company known for producing quality products at a profit from a car company that had become a producer of poorly designed, poorly produced, unreliable automobiles. This organizational transformation also began with a decision to make a commitment to quality, indeed to adopt quality as a strategy for organizational success. The adoption of this strategy was followed by a series of tactical decisions, primary of which was the realization that without union-management cooperation, the new strategy would not succeed. More specifically, executives at Ford reached the conclusion that without front-line involvement and commitment, the strategy could not succeed; without the union's buy-off, front-line employee involvement was not possible. Some of the details of Ford's efforts in this process are outlined in a fascinating chapter by Paul Banas (1988), Ford's internal consultant to the transformation process.

Obviously SAS and Ford did not undergo transformation based only on their human resources policies and practices; messages to employees get sent through many policies and practices. At SAS, large investments were made in modernizing all kinds of equipment, not only aircraft equipment. At Ford, investments were made in computer-aided design (CAD) and computer-aided manufacturing (CAM), and a new spirit of acceptance was generated for unusual and new designs for the cars themselves.

I choose to focus on human resources practices because this is a *Handbook* on applied psychology that concerns human resources in the workplace. However, production and service effectiveness require more than investments in selection, training, team building, and so forth; they require all kinds of systems support (Katz & Kahn, 1978). These include, obviously, equipment and supplies, manufacturing and production efficiencies and effectiveness, sales and marketing excellence, wise financial planning and investment, and so forth. However, especially in more labor-intensive service and manufacturing organizations, increased attention to human resources can pay rich dividends. In one study, for example, David Bowen and I (Schneider & Bowen, 1985) have shown that employee reports on how they are treated as human resources (e.g., the career programs they have, the training they receive, and the quality of the supervision they have) are related to the kind of service *consumers* say they receive when they are served by those employees. This kind of find-

ing makes clear the relationship between what happens inside the organization and how the external world of which the organization is a part receives the goods or services produced. The SAS and Ford cases reveal a similar phenomenon: internal transformation leads to the external world's having a different perception of what the organization stands for and can do.

I chose to speak about Ford and SAS because they represent total organization *turnarounds*, the challenge faced by most organizations in an increasingly competitive international marketplace. What these organizations show is how much is possible through the systematic application of relatively straightforward practices and policies. The point is that when the kinds of practices and policies applied psychologists know about are directed at clearly defined goals, organizational success will occur. It will not occur overnight (SAS and Ford had been at it for a decade when this chapter was written). How long change will take will vary by how long the organization has been in its current state, how real the need for change is perceived to be, and how complex the change effort is. By complexity of change I mean that change can occur simply in small pockets of an organization (e.g., a change in training), or it can occur more complexly by having change simultaneously in every facet of the organization (Schneider, 1990). The shorter the time in the current state, the more need for real change is felt, and the more complex the intervention for change, the quicker change will occur.

Think of it this way. Your organization is an onion that has existed in a particular kind of environment, but the environment has changed. You wake up to this change one day and realize that continued growth and success are possible only through internal transformation. This transformation will require getting all the layers to change the way they have been doing things and, simultaneously, to change the nature of the relationships between layers. Since your onion is an ongoing system, it must simultaneously carry on its day-to-day behavior *and* change to new and different ways of behaving. The change must be coordinated with other layers so the change is synchronized and does not yield confusion and the desire on the part of organizational members to return to the "good old days" of certainty.

CONCLUSION

We were getting near touchdown in San Diego, and he obviously wanted to ask me a question: "Why does it have to be so darn complex? Is this why they pay those CEOs of big companies so much money; they have to juggle all of these things at once?"

"Yup," was my insightful reply.

Organizations are effective to the extent that the activities that go on in them are coordinated and directed at the accomplishment of effective environmental functioning and growth. Effectiveness thus requires specification of what is required to be effective in a particular environment and mechanisms for coordinating efforts in those directions.

I have outlined in this chapter some of the activities requiring coordination and direction if an organization is going to be effective. I have stressed the multiple levels or layers at which activities occur. In addition, I have emphasized the idea that all of these levels are behaving simultaneously, sending messages to the people in the organization about where they should be directing their energies. Finally, I have noted that organizational change requires commitment to all of these levels, that organizational transformation is slow but that organizational transformation is possible.

As we touched down, it occurred to me that getting an airplane from Washington, D.C., to San Diego would have made a good example of all of the organizational layers and levels that need to function simultaneously for an effective outcome: all the hiring and training that gets done, the various teams that need to function smoothly, the kind of leadership required to direct attention to safety, and all of the reward systems, not to speak of information and operations management systems, that all must mesh across layers to bring that plane in safely and on time.

REFERENCES

Alderfer, C.P. (1987). An intergroup perspective on group dynamics. In J.W. Lorsch (Ed.), *Handbook of organizational behavior.* Englewood Cliffs, NJ: Prentice-Hall.

Bales, R.F. (1950). *Interaction process analysis: A method for the study of small groups.* Cambridge, MA: Addison-Wesley.

Banas, P.A. (1988). Employee involvement: A sustained labor/management initiative at the Ford Motor Company. In J.P. Campbell (Ed.), *Productivity in organizations.* San Francisco: Jossey-Bass.

Bass, B.M. (1985). *Leadership and performance beyond expectations.* New York: Free Press.

Carlzon, J. (1987). *Moments of truth.* Cambridge, MA: Ballinger.

Cascio, W.F. (1982). *Costing human resources: The financial impact of behavior in organizations.* Boston: Kent.

Hackman, J.R. (1986). The psychology of self-management in organizations. In M.S. Pallak & R.O. Perloff (Eds.), *Psychology and work.* Washington, DC: American Psychological Association.

Kanter, R.M. (1977). *Men and women of the corporation.* New York: Basic Books.

Katz, D., & Kahn, R.L. (1978). *The social psychology of organizations* (2d ed.). New York: Wiley.

Kerr, S. (1988). Some characteristics and consequences of organizational rewards. In F.D. Schoorman & B. Schneider (Eds.), *Facilitating work effectiveness.* Lexington, MA: Lexington Books.

Latham, G.P., Saari, L.M., Pursell, E.D., & Campion, M.A. (1980). The situational interview. *Journal of Applied Psychology, 65,* 422–427.

Locke, E.A., & Latham, G.P. (1984). *Goal setting: A motivational technique that works.* Englewood Cliffs, NJ: Prentice-Hall.

Peters, T.J., & Waterman, Jr., R.H. (1982). *In search of excellence: Lessons from America's best-run companies.* New York: Harper & Row.

Schneider, B. (1990). Creating service-oriented organizations: Simultaneous and sequential models for change. In D.E. Bowen, R.B. Chase, & T.G. Cummings (Eds.), *Service management effectiveness.* San Francisco: Jossey-Bass.

Schneider, B., & Bowen, D.E. (1985). Employee and customer perceptions of service in banks: Replication and extension. *Journal of Applied Psychology, 70,* 423–433.

Shea, G.P., & Guzzo, R.A. (1987). Groups as human resources. In K.M. Rowland & G.R. Ferris (Eds.), *Research in personnel and human resources management* (vol. 5). Greenwich, CT: JAI Press.

Staw, B.M., & Ross, J. (1984). Commitment in an experimenting society: An experiment in the attribution of leadership from administrative scenarios. *Journal of Applied Psychology, 65,* 249–260.

Tannenbaum, A.S. (1968). *Control in organizations.* New York: McGraw-Hill.

2 PSYCHOLOGICAL RESEARCH IN BUSINESS

Douglas W. Bray

In the modern world, policies and practices, whether industrial, governmental, or educational, depend on the continuous pursuit of knowledge. Unlike past societies in which decisions were made on the basis of hunch, superstition, or untested assumptions, ours seeks to proceed as rationally as possible, aided by as much relevant data and tested theory as can reasonably be obtained. Although such research was originally the province of the physical sciences, the importance of applying the scientific method to the study of human resources is now clear. We no longer believe that because all people are persons, they are therefore personnel experts.

Research on the human aspects of organizations is not the exclusive province of psychology. Max Weber, a sociologist, developed the concept of the Protestant ethic many years ago, a concept still invoked in discussions of work motivation. The historic Hawthorne studies of group and individual factors in productivity were conducted from an anthropological point of view. Nevertheless, since this is a book concerned with psychology in business, our attention will be focused on that field.

This book is not about psychology in general. As its title states, it is about applying psychology. Readers may wonder why, then, chapters on research are included. One obvious reason is that the manager may be urged to support research by others in the company, by a consultant retained by the organiza-

tion, or by an academic psychologist seeking a research site. The manager will have to evaluate such proposals. Much more important, however, is the fact that conducting research can make applied psychology much more effective.

Suppose, for example, that a company decides to start a management assessment center, having learned that this method has improved the quality of management in other firms. No doubt an assessment program could be started without any research, and some benefit might result. Since such programs are expensive, however, it would be more sensible to do a preliminary study to see whether the assessment center should be directed at selection or development, or both, and which level of management should be the target of the effort.

Psychological research important to business is conducted by university-based psychologists, consultants, and psychologists employed full time in business. Over the years, such researchers have produced a large body of knowledge useful to the manager. This knowledge provides the basis for many of the chapters in this book, although promising but incompletely tested theory is also represented. Some areas have been much more thoroughly researched than others. The manager will find a vast literature on personnel selection, for example, but less on the effectiveness of methods for improving the quality of work life.

AIMS OF RESEARCH

Psychological research is conducted for a number of different purposes. A distinction is often made between basic research and applied research. Basic research seeks to add to psychological knowledge by exploring an area, such as human learning, or by testing hypotheses, such as that learning is greatly expedited by knowledge of results, without any use for the findings in mind. Some basic researchers may not be interested in developing applications of their

findings but expect that their work will be useful to others some day.

Applied research may be conducted to find the causes of practical problems and to test methods of resolving problems, including the evaluation of the results of remedial action. It should be noted that basic and applied research can be conducted either in a laboratory setting or in the outside world. Naturally, however, most work in business will be of an applied nature. Applied research, if well done, often contributes to the science with which basic research is also concerned.

Even though much knowledge is already available, excellence in managing human resources will nearly always be advanced by additional research within the organization itself. Exceptions are cases in which a problem and its causes are clear and experience elsewhere provides a likely solution. After the breakup of the Bell system, for instance, telephone customers became confused as to which service problems should be handled by the local telephone company and which by AT&T. As a result, many became short-tempered and hard to deal with. Regional telephone companies experienced an upsurge of customer complaints about poor treatment by those they reached when calling to report trouble. One of these companies contracted to have a behavior modeling training program designed to train such employees.

Since a behavior modeling approach to similar problems had often been used in other companies, as reported elsewhere in this book, no preliminary research was necessary. Even so, follow-up fact finding was done to measure the reduction in customer complaints.

In many other cases, however, the cause of a problem will not be clear. An important function of research, therefore, is to seek the cause or causes of organizational problems. Some problems may surface in operations. Less than optimal productivity, too many product defects, and falling sales are examples. Investigation of such problems is not, of course, the sole province of human resources researchers. Specialties such as industrial engineering and marketing are relevant, and it may turn out that the root of a problem does not lie in human resources at all. In other cases, however, people will be a significant factor. Productivity and quality problems may involve poor motivation. Sales problems may be due to a lack of skill in the sales force.

In addition to being possible contributors to operational inadequacies, human resources problems may manifest themselves directly. Excessive turnover, absenteeism, evidence of unusual stress, and numerous grievances are examples. Such symptoms are expensive in their own right and may also have a negative effect on operations. Research into causes is again called for.

Signals that research is needed may thus appear on either the operational or human side of the organization. There are also two areas of underlying causes that may be at work: characteristics of members of the organization and the organizational environment in which they are embedded. Poor-quality output (an operational symptom) may be the result of poor

employee motivation for quality or too heavy an organizational emphasis on high production quotas. Excessive turnover of entry-level managers may be due to their lack of managerial skills and motivation or because they face unchallenging work and poor supervision.

Determining the cause of a problem sometimes points the way to a solution. If inadequate employee performance, for example, is found to be due to poor skills and employees have the aptitude for acquiring such skills, a training program would be strongly suggested. Research, however, may not clearly indicate the needed intervention. Experience in dealing with similar problems elsewhere and expert judgment may have to be relied on.

Since problems may be traced to either individual or organizational factors, interventions will be aimed at changing people or changing the organization in some way, or both. The principal interventions that focus on individuals are training and selection. Training is an effort to improve the knowledge and skills of current job holders. Selection seeks to improve the quality of those employed or advanced by screening in those with greater aptitude, skills, or motivation. Efforts to change aspects of the organization range from those that are narrowly focused, such as installing a merit pay plan, to those that are very broad indeed, such as trying to revamp the whole culture of an organization.

Those who work on the organizational rather than the personnel side may also seek to change individuals, particularly with respect to motivation and attitudes. Job enrichment, work teams, and participative management, for example, are undertaken in the belief that the work will not only be better done but that the motivation of those who work under the new conditions will be increased.

The discussion thus far may have suggested that unless the causes of organizational problems are clear, research should always precede action. This is not the case. One simple reason for this is that it would not be feasible to support the amount of research that would be required to investigate everything. The human resources manager must judge the seriousness of the problems facing the organization in order to allocate resources for research, which will necessarily be limited.

Researching problems may not always be required since organizations are not completely unique. The same problems may well arise in similar organizations for similar sets of reasons. This is why an experienced consultant can be useful. A reasonable diagnosis may be arrived at without more than some simple fact finding.

Once the cause of a problem is identified, remedial intervention is called for. An intervention may be directed at organizational personnel, at aspects of the organization itself, or both. Many interventions, such as assessment centers, behavior modeling training, performance appraisal systems, and productivity programs, are available off the shelf from outside vendors. Such programs, as well as many others, may also be custom made either by in-house specialists, if available, or by consultants.

Even while a program is being decided upon, plans should be made for follow-up research to evaluate the success of the intervention. The uninitiated might expect that this goes without saying, but the truth of the matter is that rigorous study of program outcomes is a rarity. It is perennially surprising that organizations spend a great deal of money on programs and devote much management time to them without doing a serious follow-up. Yet a recent dissertation (McAllaster, 1987), which tracked the history of three well-known management training programs in one company, concluded that whether training was accomplishing organizational goals was a nonissue and that few companies are serious about program evaluation.

Planning evaluation right from the outset is important not only because it makes it more likely that evaluation will actually take place. It may be that a before-and-after intervention design is called for or that some individuals or groups will deliberately not be involved in order to constitute a control group. Evaluation research holds a number of pitfalls, and using professionals in its design is essential.

These points may be illuminated by considering a specific piece of research I directed some years ago. The marketing department at AT&T requested that the personnel research section develop and validate an assessment center for selecting communication consultants, an important sales job. The reason for the request was the conviction that too many of those being brought into this job lacked good potential for the work.

Note that marketing did not ask the psychologists to dig into the problem of poor sales performance. Was the overall performance of the sales staff really unsatisfactory? If so, was this due to poor sales skills, a poor incentive system, or ineffective supervision? If skills were at fault, was this because of lack of aptitude or inadequate training? In other words, marketing did not ask to have its problem researched. It was convinced that it had identified the major factor in less-than-optimal sales results.

Requests for assistance from researchers often come in this form and are usually difficult to modify. Operating people frequently want action and will not tolerate the delay that preliminary research would

introduce. Furthermore, they may resent having their judgment questioned. In any case, psychologists may have to go work a little further downstream than they might think best.

The first step in the process of designing a communications consultant assessment center was the identification of the qualities, now called "dimensions" in assessment center work, critical in performance of the job. These were arrived at through interviews, the observation of training for the job, and actual customer visits with well-rated communications consultants. Twenty dimensions were isolated, such as oral presentation, oral defense, flexibility, and persistence (Bray & Campbell, 1968). Whether to call such dimensional job analysis "research" is debatable. Some might describe it more in terms of sophisticated fact finding. Here it was an essential step in an undertaking that, overall, certainly was research.

Once the dimensions were agreed on, assessment exercises to elicit behavior relevant to the dimensions were selected or devised. Some were borrowed from the AT&T management assessment centers, which had been in operation for some time. Others were devised or revised for this new center. Putting together the assessment center was not a research undertaking. It was developing an intervention, often one aspect of a research undertaking. Once the center was pretested, a group of sales managers was trained to be assessors and went to work evaluating 142 persons just employed or assigned as communications consultants by various telephone companies in the Bell system.

Validation of the assessment center had been planned from the beginning. Care was taken, therefore, that no reports were made of how any assessee was evaluated. Approximately six months after assessment, an evaluation of on-the-job performance was made by a field review team from AT&T that went out on sales calls with those who had been assessed. The reviewers had no knowledge of how those they were observing had been rated at assessment. Each participant was rated as either meeting or not meeting field review standards.

This was, of course, the heart of the research. The crucial question was how strongly assessment ratings were related to later field performance ratings. The results were strongly positive. Of those rated acceptable or more than acceptable by the assessors, 68 percent met performance review standards as compared to only 24 percent of those rated less than acceptable or unacceptable. The marketing department moved ahead to make assessment a standard step in the communications consultant employment process.

INTERORGANIZATIONAL RESEARCH

Research has an important role to play in analyzing the human resources components of organizational problems and in evaluating human resources programs. Not all research, however, need be in response to specifically defined problems. One can use research to uncover hidden weaknesses. Most organizations do not know, for example, how their human resources compare with those in other companies. This should be a matter of concern because even if the firm is doing well, it might do even better with more capable and motivated people. Surprisingly enough, however, research across organizations is rare.

One example of such research is in the area of employee attitudes and morale. A number of companies that make periodic surveys of such matters have joined together in the Mayflower Group. They have agreed to include a set of common items in their questionnaires so that they can compare their standing on a confidential basis with the rest of the group. This can not only reveal the extent of a problem, if there is one, but can serve as a baseline for testing the effects of attitude improvement efforts.

The possibility of achieving a more intensive look at managers across organizations was demonstrated by the Inter-organizational Testing Study Ann Howard and I conducted as part of our AT&T research on managers. In this study, eight businesses and two government agencies participated in the testing of middle-aged middle managers and an equal number of young beginning managers—about 400 of each in total. Ability tests, motivational questionnaires, and attitude scales were among the measures used. Each organization was provided with the results for the other companies (not individually identified) to compare with its own.

One example of the many insights such comparisons provided was the difference in one organization between the mental ability test scores of young and older managers. In the typical organization, the scores of older managers would be a little higher since scores on such tests increase somewhat with age and experience. In the company in question, the older managers scored substantially lower than the young group and than older managers in other organizations. Several explanations were possible, but the one top management thought most likely, and most worrisome, was that the company was losing the brighter managers early in their careers.

AN EXAMPLE OF BASIC RESEARCH

Work at AT&T also provides an unusual example of long-term basic research in a business context. In 1956, I was given the opportunity to initiate an ambitious longitudinal study of managers, the Management Progress Study. AT&T's purpose was to study the careers of managers as they unfolded, not only to examine the development of managerial ability but to learn what effects on the managers themselves life in a large corporation might produce. The company expected, of course, that the study would yield findings of practical value in the development of managers, but the fact that no specific problems were posed and support was generous allowed the research to be extremely broad gauged. Perhaps even more remarkable, the company's commitment to the research lasted over thirty years (Howard & Bray, 1988).

The accumulation of the very large body of Management Progress Study data over the years provides answers to questions not originally thought to be objectives of the research. Howard (1986) recently used the data to investigate the relationship of college experiences such as major, grades, and extracurricular activities to success in management. Her finding—that liberal arts majors excelled more than technical and business graduates—plays a large role in the current reemphasis on such an educational background. This, as well as other unexpected uses of the study data, illustrates the value of broad research undertakings. Other Management Progress Study findings are reported by Howard in chapter 46.

The examples provided are those of organizations as the prime movers in initiating research, but this is not always the case. University-based industrial-organizational psychologists often seek opportunities for themselves or their graduate students to do studies in their areas of interest. Companies are frequently approached to participate, and it is not unusual for them to find that the research would be worth supporting.

SELECTING RESEARCHERS

However the organization comes to consider a research undertaking, a qualified researcher will be needed. Since human resources managers may not have such a person on their staff, they must turn to outside human resources experts. Some of these will be found at universities; others will operate as individual consultants or as members of consulting firms. The manager will have a wide choice, and, unfortunately, there is no sure way for the uninitiated to identify the consultant or firm best suited for the project the organization has in mind. It may be helpful, however, to review some of the distinctions among areas of consultant specialization.

One major distinction is between those who focus on personnel and those who are more concerned with the organization. Personnel psychologists often conduct research into and prescribe procedures for selection for employment and advancement. These may include testing, assessment centers, and appraisal plans, among other activities. Some consulting firms are strongest in the training area, including training needs analyses, the development of training, including train-the-trainer capabilities, and follow-up studies of training effectiveness.

Consultants who are more concerned with the organization are often involved in projects such as organizational development, job enrichment, work teams, participative management, and culture change.

They may use techniques that ask individuals to respond, such as attitude surveys, but their intent is to use the results for interventions in the organization rather than decisions about the individual. Such consultants may also use training to further organizational change, such as training supervisors in participative management skills.

A further complication is that a consultant may be able to provide or develop excellent action programs without being at all expert in research. There are at least two dangers here: the consultant may propose adopting a program with no preliminary research or may conduct mediocre research. Managers would be well advised to ask for examples of research the consultant has conducted and to get the views of other firms for which the consultant has worked.

It should be emphasized, however, that there are consultants with excellent research skills who do much less research than they would like. They find that companies spend their personnel dollars on training or organizational change programs rather than on research. Although this may not always be a grievous error, there is no doubt that corporations waste much money on programs that do not address the organization's true needs and whose effectiveness is never validated.

GUIDELINES FOR SUCCESSFUL RESEARCH

Psychological research in industry should not be thought of in terms of the old, somewhat mythical, physical science model. There the researchers, working pretty much in isolation from the organization, make a discovery that promises to be useful. A developmental phase may then occur utilizing the discovery to design a practical application. The organization then puts the new method into use. Few of the ultimate users have been involved in the whole process.

This is not a satisfactory model for human resources research. Organizations usually resist change in personnel practices and in their way of operating much more strongly than technological changes. It is important, therefore, to involve members of the organization to the greatest possible extent. Some may help plan the research; others may serve as interviewers, trainers, test administrators, or some other func-

tion appropriate to the study. Research plans and progress should be widely communicated.

Research instruments vary tremendously in their complexity and cost, and the researcher is often confronted by a difficult choice between covering large numbers and reaching a valid and deep understanding of the issue under investigation. Trying to do things as cheaply as possible often leads to the use of ad hoc questionnaires widely administered. Yet other methods, such as well-designed and -conducted interviews, focus group discussions, and simulations would yield richer information about such areas as motivations and attitudes.

Several points should be kept in mind in confronting such a dilemma. It is not necessary to involve all members of large groups in a particular piece of research on order to reach valid conclusions. Much less than 100 percent samples will normally suffice.

Working with smaller numbers makes it possible to use more intensive methods. Nevertheless, if comparisons must be made among many subgroups, such as departments, locations, and levels of management, the number of participants needed will increase dramatically. A compromise solution is to use questionnaires for a large number but to supplement them with other approaches, involving far fewer participants, to enrich understanding and verify the validity of the questionnaire results.

Some researchers, however, rarely consider anything but the questionnaire. They seem to believe that a thirty-minute form will generate the knowledge required for actions to reduce turnover, increase productivity, eliminate managerial stress, or improve morale. But we should be cautious of the quick fix in improving organizational effectiveness. Analogously, quick, superficial studies will not yield much of value.

There is a distinction to be made between good research design and good research instruments. It is not unusual for a researcher to be expert in laying out research in terms of control groups, before-and-after measurements, sophisticated statistical treatments, and so forth but squander such talents by using trivial measures of the variables under study. It is just this situation that makes some published research of little weight.

Better research requires at least a modest organizational commitment, which, unfortunately, is often difficult to obtain. I was surprised at the number of large companies that rejected the opportunity to participate in the Inter-organizational Testing Study. My colleagues and I contacted about 150 firms, of which only 10 finally took part, even though all test supplies and analyses were to be underwritten by AT&T. A major stumbling block was the fact that 80 managers would have to spend half a day being tested. Because

of this, many organizations passed up the rare chance to see how their managers compared with those elsewhere in motivation, attitudes, and mental ability.

Organizational changes stimulated by research are not limited to those central to the research. Merely conducting research may induce change. When AT&T started the Management Progress Study, its intention was to learn about the growth of managers, not how to select them. Yet when the researchers observed that a surprising number of the college recruits they studied did not appear to have much management potential, attention was focused on college recruiting. More rigorous methods, including better recruiter training and mental ability testing, were instituted.

Better data can often be obtained if information on individuals is not available to management. This will usually be an acceptable plan, since management is interested primarily in group results, not individual responses. Nevertheless, researchers will often need to be able to identify individuals so that correlations essential to the research can be determined. If, for example, a research question is whether negative feelings about immediate bosses lead to early termination, individual data would be necessary to match supervisors and subordinates.

Researchers should have no problem in using individual data while protecting research participants. This is particularly true if the researchers are from outside the organization, but it may also be true for internal staff. Human resources groups in several large companies have established their trustworthiness over a number of years and have little difficulty in getting excellent cooperation from most participants, even when sensitive information is involved. Researchers must have clear and explicit backing from upper management for such confidentiality.

CONCLUSION

The manager who applies psychology in business may do so, often to the advantage of his or her company, without supporting any research in connection with the application. Some problems are ubiquitous, and methods of dealing with them have been developed and validated. It is not necessary to research the same intervention again and again. Unless this situation clearly prevails, however, research will clarify the exact nature of the problem, help to indicate a promising remedy, and evaluate the effectiveness of the attempted cure.

A manager considering psychological research should:

Evaluate the seriousness of problems that appear to have their roots in the personnel or organizational area, decide whether the causes are unclear enough to require research, and apportion available research resources accordingly.

Consider the possibility of intercompany research and research comparing departments and locations to uncover hidden personnel and organizational problems.

Ensure that research plans and activities are shared widely.

If possible, select action programs (interventions) that research elsewhere has shown to be effective.

Be sure that plans for evaluating the effectiveness of the action program, once adopted, are made before the program is put into effect.

Choose consultants to conduct research or design action programs carefully, ascertaining their demonstrated competence in psychological research and applied psychology.

REFERENCES

Bray, D.W., & Campbell, R.J. (1968). Selection of salesmen by means of an assessment center. *Journal of Applied Psychology, 52,* 36–41.

Howard, A. (1986). College experiences and managerial performance. *Journal of Applied Psychology, 71,* 530–552.

Howard, A., & Bray, D.W. (1988). *Managerial lives in transition: Advancing age and changing times.* New York: Guilford Press.

McAllaster, C.M. (1987). *Assessing vendor produced off-the-shelf programs in a specific company environment.* Ph.D. dissertation, Columbia University.

3 RESEARCH-BASED BUSINESS DECISIONS

Charles H. Fay

Much of a manager's time, whether planning, staffing, directing, or controlling, is devoted to making decisions. Most managerial activity is, in fact, decision making, and, as one author points out, "more than anything else, competence in this activity differentiates the manager from the non-manager and, more important, the effective manager from the ineffective manager" (Harrison, 1981, p. 1). Since decision making is a primary factor in managerial success, managers should learn to make the best decisions possible. There are several guidelines that can help managers improve their own decision-making capability:

1. Decision making is a process characterized by the interdependency of its participants and takes place under conditions of uncertainty. Since decision-making success affects careers, most managers seek to reduce uncertainty by gathering information relevant to the decision.

2. There are several ways of knowing information; the scientific method is most likely to produce information relevant to the decision.

3. The research-based decision cycle can be divided into eight discrete stages. In stage 1, managers react to symptoms through a series of problem definition activities that result in a model of the problem.

4. Models are useful in that they force the manager to think systematically about the problem, suggest information gaps, provide safe and economic means for testing out ideas, provide a framework for organizing information and establishing decision policies, and provide a basis for developing empirical knowledge about the problem.

5. Through the use of the scientific method, the manager can develop a research design to test the model.

6. The result of the test is data, which must be interpreted and communicated to appropriate participants in the decision.

7. Participants then make the decision. The cycle does not end here, for the decision results must be evaluated and controlled, again making use of guidelines provided by scientific method.

8. A significant aspect of evaluation is the tracking of the symptoms that engendered the decision cycle initially. If they do not improve, the research-based decision cycle begins again.

DECISION MAKING AS A PROCESS

Managerial decision making is a process. Simon (1977) points out that popular images of decision making personified by the decision maker "at the moment of choice, ready to plant his foot on one or another of the routes that lead from the crossroads," are false because they "ignore the whole lengthy, complex process of alerting, exploring, and analyzing that precede that final moment, and the process of evaluating that succeeds it." Metadecisions (decisions about the decision process itself) may be lost in organizational history; they are so embedded in the process that no current organizational member thinks about them at all. They are simply the rules of the game. Lenin once noted that the historian of an organization shaped its destiny; by interpreting (and distorting) its past, the historian provided precedents to determine its future.

THE INTERDEPENDENCY OF DECISION MAKERS

A third factor of importance is the organizational nature of the decisions being made. There is a good deal of talk today about the need for participative decision making. In fact, most decisions in organizations have always been participative in the sense that most managers are dependent on peers and subordinates to call their attention to situations requiring decisions, to provide information relating to the decision problem, to suggest alternatives, and to implement the decisions made even though the choice of the alternative may be jealously held by the autocratic manager. The interdependency of managers in the modern organization has been well documented (Sayles, 1964); that this interdependency extends to decision making has been noted also (Sayles, 1964, p. 218; Simon, 1977, pp. 115–119; Ebert & Mitchell, 1975, chap. 12).

THE IMPACT OF DECISION MAKING ON CAREERS AND ORGANIZATIONS

Making decisions is important to the careers of the individuals involved and the organization itself. Decision making in organizations is the ultimate basis for success, and careers rise and fall depending on the goodness of the decisions managers make. Whole organizations have collapsed when faulty decisions have been made.

THE INFLUENCE OF UNCERTAINTY ON DECISION MAKING AND THE CONSEQUENT NEED FOR INFORMATION

Almost all decisions made in organizations are made under conditions of uncertainty: what Congress may do, what will happen to the economy and interest rates, whether a product will gain consumer acceptance, how long a piece of machinery will continue to operate, or the probability that some other event will or will not occur at some future time. Decision makers often require more information than they have about their problem. What options are available, for example? What are the most likely consequences of a set of actions?

To summarize, decision making in organizations:

1. Is the activity that differentiates the manager from the nonmanager and the effective manager from the ineffective manager.

2. Is a process that takes place over time. The actual choice point itself may be one of the less important parts of that process.

3. Is a process characterized by the interdependency of its participants.

4. Strongly affects the careers of decision makers and the success of organizations.

5. Is characterized by the uncertainty in which the process is embedded.

6. Requires information-collecting activities on the part of decision makers.

THE RELATION BETWEEN BUSINESS RESEARCH AND DECISION MAKING

The problem managers face is how to make a good decision. Academics and practitioners have attacked this problem in one of two ways, for the most part. A great quantity of empirical research has been done on how decisions are actually made by individuals and groups, both in and out of business organizations (Ebert & Mitchell, 1975; MacCrimmon & Taylor, 1976). This work, which is largely descriptive, focuses on the psychological factors that influence the decision-making process.

Much of this work suggests that actual managers become aware of problems, seek information, and make decisions under conditions of bounded rationality (Cyert & March, 1963; Simon, 1976). March and Simon (1958) define the concept as follows: "This, then, is the general picture of the human organism that we will use to analyze organization behavior. It is a picture of a choosing, decision-making, problem-solving organism that can only do one or a few things at a time, and that can attend to only a small part of the information recorded in its memory and presented by the environment."

Another body of work has been prescriptive; it has offered advice on how to make better decisions. Much of the prescriptive work has also concentrated on psychological factors but in addition has looked at economic and technical factors.

This chapter is also prescriptive; it is premised on the observation that, in business organizations, the quality of decisions is likely to be most influenced by the applicability and quality of the data on which they are based. The information used by business to make its decisions should come from business research. Research-based decisions (that is, decisions based on data properly conceptualized, gathered, and analyzed) are likely to be better than decisions based on other grounds.

In looking at business research and its place in the decision-making process, a limitation must be placed on the kind of research meant by business research. Specifically, this chapter examines research that bears on finance, marketing, accounting, production, personnel and industrial relations, management and policy, legal environments, and international business. All of these are applied fields, and thus the primary research interest is applied research.

Thus, for example, I do not pursue here the methodology or problems of basic, or even applied, chemical research. Some data resulting from chemical research may be used in the decision-making process, but most managers will have to rely on the expertise of the chemist when such information is required. Similarly most managers will not be doing basic research in psychology even though the results of such research are certainly useful to decision makers in personnel and industrial relations or management. On the whole, research in the natural sciences and technology and product development is beyond the scope of this chapter.

The research technology of the social sciences is much more germane to the needs of managers, though the academic emphasis on the laboratory experiment does not hold much appeal to most management decision makers. The philosophy underlying research in both the social and physical sciences—the scientific method—is, of course, the basis for business research as well as the pure and applied research in the natural and social sciences.

If proper research is to be conducted as the basis for better decisions, there have to be rules of the game. At the heart of these rules are some assumptions about the proper ways of knowing (Kerlinger, 1973).

Ways of Knowing

A decision maker can have data or knowledge in four ways. The method of knowing has strong implications for the value of the data and the goodness of decisions based on the data.

Tenacity. The first of these ways is to know through tenacity. That is, something is known to be true because the believer has heard it so often and has accepted it for so long that the acceptance itself reinforces the truth of the data. Many male managers, for example (and a number of female managers too), believe that women are not capable of being first-line supervisors, and much of the strength of this belief lies in the length of time it has been believed. A manager who has hiring decisions to make and makes those decisions on the basis of data "known" through tenacity is likely to get results that are not beneficial to the organization or to his or her career. Actually, anything known through the method of tenacity is of value only to one who so knows it; a second party, on hearing the information for the first time, cannot know it to be true through this method. In terms of organizational decision making, then, tenacity is an impractical method of knowing because it provides no basis for transfer of data.

Authority. A method that does provide a basis for transfer of data is, in fact, knowing because of the source of the data. This is the method of authority. The method of knowing through authority of the source can best be exemplified by considering the *Harvard Business Review* syndrome (Wallace, Crandall & Fay, 1982). Most managers have known at least one senior executive who has ordered the installation of some program or other after reading about the success of such a program in the *Harvard Business Review* or other prestigious business magazine. Typical programs installed because of knowledge gained by authority have included job enrichment, management objectives, PPBS (planning, programming, budgeting systems), and sensitivity training. It is not that the programs and information proffered by authority are inherently wrong, for all of the programs noted have worked for some organization at some time. Rather, it is that the applicability of most data depends on the circumstances. This is particularly the case when dealing with anything as complex as any of the programs noted. Still, in the end many of the data used by organizations are known by authority. In many cases we have no other choice.

Intuition. A third way of knowing, perhaps even more popular in business than knowing through authority, is the method of intuition. Anything known because it "stands to reason" is known by intuition. Thus, a manager who decides that all jobs in the organization should be as specialized as possible (so that relatively unskilled workers may be hired and trained to do one simple set of tasks) in order to maximize efficiency makes this decision because it "stands to reason" that specialization leads to efficiency and (by implication) the efficient organization is the effective organization. The fact that other managers may reason differently can cause significant problems in an organization. What is intuitive to one manager may be counterintuitive to another, and this system provides no means of settling disputes.

The unifying characteristic of these three ways of knowing is the central role of the knower: in all these systems the quality of the information relies on the goodness of the knower. Unfortunately, we are not all perceptive enough to recognize such goodness. If organizations are to develop information that will maximize the quality of decisions that must be made, they must "know" in some fashion that is independent of the knower.

Scientific Method. The fourth way of knowing differs from the previous three in its attempt to divorce the knowing from the knower. This is the method of science. Scientific method provides a way of knowing not dependent on the knower. It explicitly rests on the idea that there is a reality that exists independent of the opinion we may have of it (Kerlinger, 1973). The whole process of scientific method has as its goal the getting at this reality so that regardless of who follows the process, the end result will be substantially the same.

The device scientific method uses to achieve this objectivity is the check. Throughout the process of developing knowledge, the researcher committed to the scientific method attempts to build in checks, where what is being discovered may be disproved. The process is scientific only insofar as it is "capable of being tested by experience, . . . it must be possible for an empirical scientific system to be refuted by experience" (Popper, 1965).

This does not mean that intuition has no role in good decision making. The value of intuition in a portion of the research process is well documented. Thus, in defining problems and generating possible explanations of phenomena, intuition can be helpful. Intuition can also be very limiting if the decision maker confines his or her efforts to that technique. Even when intuition does enter the process, a scientific approach to testing that which is intuited is a necessary check.

THE RESEARCH-BASED DECISION CYCLE

Research-based decision making may be viewed as a cyclical process consisting of eight stages. Four of these stages are states of nature. The other four stages are complex reactions by management decision makers to these states of nature. Briefly, the first stage of the cycle consists of symptoms of a problem. The manager reacts to these symptoms by a series of problem definition activities, which culminate in a model of the problem. The chief characteristic of the model is that it allows the manager to state explicit relationships between various aspects of the problem and, possibly, with other variables of interest. Given the model, the manager can embark on the next stage by developing a research design to determine whether the relationships proposed in the model are supported by objective tests. The result of this testing is the fifth stage of the cycle, which is a set of data. Data alone, however, are of little use in making a decision; they must be interpreted and communicated to interested parties. At this point, the decision is made. The final stage of the cycle, the evaluation and control stage,

Figure 3–1. The Decision Cycle

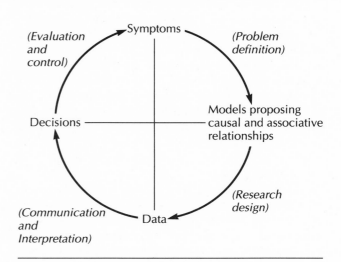

Source: Charles H. Fay and Marc J. Wallace, Jr., *Research-Based Decisions* (New York: Random House, 1987), p. 11. Used by permission.

occurs as the manager determines whether the problem prompting the decision cycle in the first place has been alleviated. This evaluation and control process places the decision maker back at the beginning of the cycle, with an awareness of symptoms. If the problem has not been solved (that is, the symptoms still exist), the decision cycle begins anew. A diagram of the decision cycle is shown in figure 3–1.

MOVING FROM SYMPTOMS TO MODELS: PROBLEM DEFINITION

Managers are trained in and used to dealing with symptoms. If you were to talk with a manager about her operations, the chances are that she would describe her day in terms of problems she has dealt with or is facing. Unless a manager can move from being aware of symptoms to models proposing causal and associative relationships, however, she will be limited to decisions that are not based on research. Indeed, a great many decisions are based on nonscientific methods of knowing outlined previously (for example, tenacity, authority, and intuition). Thus, many decisions are based on simple authority ("when E.F. Hutton speaks . . . "), tenacity ("no one has ever done it any other way in our industry"), or intuition ("I've got this gut feeling . . . "). The problem with these methods of knowing as bases for decision making is they are not consistent or systematic, they do not indicate why the decision should be made, and they do not provide an understanding of the phenomena under consideration sufficient to allow the decision maker to generalize his or her knowledge to new but similar situations or to recognize situations that are different enough to warrant a different decision.

Many decisions often arouse the decision maker's interest beyond wanting to know what mechanical steps to take in making the decision. Thus, the home builder may not only need to know that interest rates are climbing and mortgage money drying up but may be interested in knowing what factors are associated with and predict movement of interest rates. Indeed, he or she may become interested in the problem out of a desire to be able to predict the downturn of interest rates and loosening of mortgage money in order to be ready with new homes ahead of the competition. As soon as a decision maker begins to worry about causes, he or she has made a fundamental step toward a scientific basis for knowing rather than the nonscientific bases.

The home builder has taken the first step in research-based decisions by defining the nature of the problem. In effect, he or she is turning attention away from symptoms and their documentation to models that propose causal and associative relationships that explain the symptoms he or she is facing. In the process of defining the problem, the decision maker attempts to identify not only the variables defining the problem but also looks for other variables in the situation that are influencing that variable (hence, for example, the builder's interest in finding variables that predict interest rate movements). Problem definition as a first step in decision making results in a model. Models help focus the problem facing the manager by abstracting from reality. As the third stage of the decision cycle, they highlight the most important aspects or characteristics of the problem relevant to the decision that must be made.

These models may be either causal or associative. In looking at an increase in accident rates in a company, for example, a manager would consider the most likely sources of the increase: new equipment, new employees, changes in hours worked, or any other probable cause of the problem. The model constructed by the manager not only specifies possible causes of the problem under consideration but also specifies how the relationship works. Thus, if changes in hours worked are thought to be a probable cause of increased accident rates, the model would be likely to specify that increased hours make for more tired and less aware workers with increased carelessness and accident rates as the result. This type of model would be considered a causal model since it shows cause-and-effect relationships. Causality and the study of causal relationships require rigorous controls if results are to be acceptable (Campbell & Stanley, 1963).

Associative models might also be developed. It might be observed that as accident rates went up, unexcused absenteeism levels for employees also rose. These two phenomena would be associated with each other, but it would be hard to picture either "causing the other." In fact, work hour changes might lead to both. Study of association also requires rigor, for as Simon (1969) has remarked, the world is like some great spider web: all events, things, and time periods are caught in the same web and thus are more or less closely associated. Spurious relationships may be observed where none really exists. They appear because of the way we go about getting our information, because of the relationship of each variable with a third variable not under consideration, or because of random error.

Regardless of whether a causal or associative model is under consideration, it redefines the problem in terms of dependent variables (the characteristic constituting the problem—for example, sales, profit, turnover rates, performance), independent variables (other characteristics in the system believed to have an impact on the dependent variable—for example, employee behavior, wage rates paid, advertising budget, machines employed), and the relationships proposed to exist among the variables (for example, turnover rate is negatively associated with wage rate).

Types of Models

Models are extremely useful tools for the decision makers. They can take many forms (Kaplan, 1964).

An *iconic model* is a physical representation of the real thing, often scaled down in size. An architect's clay mockup of a building or a model plane in a wind tunnel are examples of iconic models.

An *analogue model* is a representation that stands in for the real thing and uses properties other than features of the system itself to represent the phenomenon. Thus a relief map may use colors to represent elevation, or a designer may use colors to represent the function to be carried out in a given area of a floor space.

A *symbolic model* is one that employs symbols to represent characteristics of the system. Such symbols may include language (for example, an announcer's description of an event that has taken place) or may involve diagrams. In fact, the decision cycle represented in figure 3–1 is a symbolic model. The boxes represent events in the decision process, and the arrows represent the appropriate sequencing of these events.

A *mathematical model* is a highly sophisticated symbolic model that employs the rules of mathematics in representing the real world. Mathematical models can involve algebra, geometry, or calculus.

Advantages of Models

Decision theorists have long known that models have a number of distinct advantages for decision makers (Kaplan, 1964). Models force the decision maker to be explicit about the way the problem is perceived. There is less room for sloppy or confused thinking when modeling. The very act of systematically considering the impact of one variable on another forces one to make one's logic consistent while thinking about a problem. The explicitness of the model may

suggest information gaps in the decision maker's knowledge about a problem. The act of modeling may often define information needs and questions to be answered before a decision is made.

Models also have what philosophers like to call *heuristic* value. That is, they suggest questions (or hypotheses) to be investigated that will expand our knowledge about phenomena. In addition, models are effective and efficient ways of organizing the decision maker's knowledge about a problem.

Finally, models provide a safe and economical way of testing out policies and procedures. A mathematical model, for example, allows the planner to simulate the effect of making a change in one variable on other variables without actually making the change.

It is not often easy to make the transition from stage 1 (symptom identification) to stage 2 (modeling the problem). Practicing managers are oriented toward action; they want to take whatever pragmatic steps are necessary to resolve the problem. Modeling, in contrast, is a contemplative activity that raises a number of questions that must be resolved before any action is taken to address the problem. The skilled decision maker learns to make some very subtle but critical shifts in the way questions are asked in order to move from symptoms to model. The question, "Why did our sales revenues decline last quarter?" becomes, "What characteristics influence the sales of our organization?" The question, "How can I reduce turnover?" becomes, "What employer and employee characteristics are predictive of the likelihood of leaving employment?" Note the critical shift in focus between the first question and the second question in each case. The first question has been called a *management* question (Emory, 1980). The management question is a statement or recognition of a problem. It does not contain within itself any hint of understanding the sources of the problem or what steps the manager might take to resolve it. The second question is a *research* question. The research question addresses the issue of cause and effect directly. It is stated in terms of critical variables and relationships. If the research question is successfully answered, the manager will have understanding with regard to the sources of the problem and direction with regard to actions that might be taken to resolve it.

The Importance of Theory

Research questions lead to the construction of a model relevant to the manager's problem. At this point, the manager might draw upon theory and bodies of knowledge relevant to the problem to suggest variables and relationships to study. Problems of profit, for example, are addressed in numerous economic and financial theories. Problems of turnovers are addressed by at least three theories in the fields of personnel and industrial relations and organizational behavior. In both cases, substantial empirical investigation has been done on these theories, and bodies of knowledge have developed concerning profit and turnover phenomena. The manager's best bet at this point is that the problems addressed by these theories and the findings of such research will provide some insight about the situation under consideration. Indeed, the knowledge may be sufficiently complete and impressive to use as a basis for decision. The manager may judge that the situation addressed in the theory and subsequent research is so much like the current one that it is safe to conclude that they are the same and make decisions based on the body of knowledge. Similarly, in diagnosing a given disease, a physician decides that this set of symptoms is sufficiently similar to warrant administering a drug that previous research has demonstrated to be effective. In this case, therefore, the decision maker can go directly to the decision.

In other situations, however, theory is not well enough developed or the body of knowledge not well enough documented to afford bypassing the research step. In this case, the decision maker must design research that addresses the questions raised by the model directly. The research will be suggested by the model itself. If the model has been sufficiently well developed, the manager will have an explicit model that identifies and defines each variable and relationship to be studied as part of the problem. There are two definitions of variables and one of relationships that the model must include.

Initially, each variable must be defined conceptually. Loosely speaking, conceptual definitions are akin to the definition one might find in a good dictionary, with an explicit statement of the nature of the variable. In addition, a conceptual definition will suggest other parts of the model to which the variable is expected to be related and should contain some general implications for measuring the variable.

An operational definition of the variable will define the variable in terms of a specific set of measurement operations. Thus, a manager might define conceptually a "satisfied" worker as one who is likely to do this not do that or who feels a certain way about the employing organization. An operational definition might consist of a specific fifty-item true-false questionnaire given to workers under specific circumstances; "satisfied" might consist of answering "true" to forty-five or more of the questions.

Relationships are defined in terms of explicit propositions or hypotheses about predicted relationships observed between the operationally defined variables present in the model. The hypothesis "satisfied workers will have lower turnover rates" might translate to "workers in unit A who score above 45 on a specific questionnaire will not be fired or quit voluntarily at the same rate as workers in unit A scoring below 30 on the specific questionnaire." (Note that layoffs, transfers, and promotions are not considered in this hypothesis.)

MOVING FROM MODELS TO DATA: RESEARCH DESIGN

Unless a decision maker takes a model and tests it against reality, there will not be a scientific basis for knowing whether the model provides a sound basis for making choices. Earlier it was pointed out that while decision makers could rely on a number of unscientific bases for knowing their situation (authority, tenacity, and intuition), scientific method is different from these bases and is better for developing information with which to make decisions.

Scientific method is the only method that demands a decision maker to test a model against reality and to risk the failure of predictions based on the model. In this step, the decision maker designs and executes a research effort (research design) that results in data that either deny or support the model. This single quality—the capability of a model being denied by empirical data (the real world)—is the sin-

gle factor distinguishing scientific method from nonscientific bases for knowing about the world.

The Criterion of Falsifiability

Karl Popper (1965) has defined the boundary between science and nonscience as the criterion of falsifiability. According to this standard, a model is scientific only if its hypotheses (its predictions) can be denied by actual data if they are wrong. The criterion of falsifiability (the ability to be proved wrong) has had a major impact on the way research is done, whether in physics or marketing. Indeed, this standard leads to a special mode of thinking among those doing research (Ackoff, 1953).

The first impact has been a tradition of skepticism. Unlike an attorney doing everything to prove a point in courtroom debate, researchers are their own worst enemies. They play devil's advocate to their ideas and set up very tough tests for them. A second impact has been the skeptic's desire to divorce the knowledge from the knower. This has led to an avoidance of tenacity, intuition, and authority as ways of knowing. To do this researchers have developed a tradition of empiricism. Briefly, empiricism requires that all ideas or hypotheses be tested against the real world through experience, observation, or experiment. Ideas (no matter how logical they appear) are not treated as sound until they have withstood the test of real-world data. Thus, a manager's idea that consumers will purchase more of a product if the price is lowered is not accepted until an actual test of the idea is made. One outcome of empiricism is the requirement that decision makers derive and express their ideas first and then test them against the data. It is considered a violation of the rule to gather data first and then draw inferences from them. While hindsight may be useful in framing hypotheses for future research, scientists require that explicit predictions be made about the data before they are actually collected and examined.

During the last several decades, researchers have developed a number of rules and guides that ensure that investigations will adhere to the criterion of falsifiability. Taken together, these rules constitute a concern with research method. "Method," in the case of research method, refers to the approach to answering questions (Campbell & Stanley, 1963; Cook & Campbell, 1979) rather than specific tools (a survey or a computer) or techniques (laboratory experiment or specific statistical analysis). In fact, research method guides the manager in determining which tools and techniques might be useful in specific situations.

Figure 3–2 illustrates this concern. Rules of method override questions of what technique or what tool to use in answering a manager's question. Thus, it is foolhardy for a manager to address a problem by saying, "Let's use the computer on this problem [a mere tool]," or "I think we should use multiple linear regression on this problem [a statistical technique]." Methods issues must be resolved and decided upon before one can logically and effectively choose what techniques and what tools will be appropriate in answering the manager's question. Emory (1980) points out that many researchers lose their effectiveness when they become technique bound; that is, they come to rely on a specific tool or technique to answer every question, whether appropriate or not.

Many fields abound with technique and theory-bound research. Some managers have come to rely too heavily on the questionnaire as a tool for gathering empirical data. Thus, instead of defining the problem first and letting that dictate whether a questionnaire would be appropriate they let a commitment to questionnaires dictate the way they formulate research questions. Economists, on the other hand, can sometimes go off the deep end with what appears to the layperson to be arcane and often heroic assumptions about reality in order to salvage the internal logic of their models.

Many organizational development managers have operated so long on the theory that people want to be (in Maslow's terms) self-fulfilled and have a need to participate in all aspects of all decisions that they cannot accept that some workers are quite content to work on an assembly line or at a typewriter, be told what to do, and take no part in any decision.

Bad decisions based on reliance on technique are common. The greatest error of this kind in recent memory is the introduction of the "new" Coke. The soft drink industry has become technique bound by addiction to the taste test as a basis for determining consumer preferences for soft drinks. Although the majority of tasters presumably preferred a sweeter cola, taste was clearly not the only factor in determining buyer behavior. Marketers at Coke clearly did not formulate the appropriate research questions in this case.

Figure 3–2. Consecutive Levels of Research Design

Consecutive Levels of Research Design

Exploratory Designs — Initial
Gain familiarity with a phenomenon

Case Study
Confirm ideas about major features of a phenomenon through analysis and documentation of specific instances

Taxonomic Designs
Design and validation of measures
Establishment of construct validity

Descriptive Designs — Level of Knowledge
Estimation of distributions
Establishment of norms

Associate Designs
Test hypotheses about relationships

Experimental Designs
Test hypotheses about the effects of empirical operations — Advanced

Source: Charles H. Fay and Marc J. Wallace, Jr., *Research-Based Decisions* (New York: Random House, 1987), p. 17. Used by permission.

Aside from adverse consequences for specific companies, being technique, tool, or theory bound can seriously set back a field of inquiry. Research has demonstrated, for example, that progress in building knowledge in such fields as organizational behavior, finance, marketing, and personnel and industrial relations has slowed when managers or researchers think first of techniques and then allow them to dictate the research question rather than the opposite. Because many managers do not have an understanding of research method, they have particular problems when confronted by subordinates or consultants who are trained researchers. It may be difficult for the manager to recognize that the researcher is pushing for use of a particular set of techniques when they are not appropriate to the research question. Managers who are grounded in research methods can avoid such situations.

Research method deals with three specific concerns in assuring that a research design is scientific: (1) inference process, (2) concepts and definitions, and (3) hypotheses.

Inference Processes: Deduction and Induction

Inference is the thought process by which one reaches a conclusion. A manager, for example, might begin with a model of the relationship between price and quantity. Economic models suggest that if price is lowered, greater quantities of the item will be demanded. The manager reasons that the general model fits the specific business and situation and concludes, "If I lower the price of my product, I will sell more of it." This sequence of reasoning is called *deduction*. It begins with a general principle, theory, or idea and narrows to a prediction about what one would expect about a specific situation.

Contrast this with the manager who keeps detailed accounts of every transaction at the checkout counter. He notes one day that blue beach balls outsold red beach balls by a factor of two to one. From this fact he concludes, "Blue products sell better than red products." This sequence of reasoning is called *induction*. It begins with a specific observation and concludes with a general theory of principles.

Neither deduction nor induction alone is sufficient to satisfy the criterion of falsifiability and, therefore, neither is scientific by itself. Deduction alone is weak because it is not empirical. A manager can deduce logically consistent ideas about the real world all day long, but until they are tested, they are completely useless as guides for decisions. Induction alone

suffers from equally important weaknesses. Specifically, two people can look at the same fact and draw two completely different conclusions. The data alone cannot specify which is the correct interpretation. Further, in a more technical sense, induction is subject to sampling error. That is, what is observed in any single situation is a function both of real phenomena and error in the observation. Reliance solely on induction maximizes the impact of this kind of error.

Managers should note that the rule of scientific method demands an interplay between deduction and induction in the design of research. Thus, logically consistent models of the phenomenon must be built. Predictive hypotheses (propositions) must be logically derived from the model. Deductive inference predominates during this phase. The hypotheses, further, must be tested against the data. Inferences are then made from the data back to the model. This is an inductive mode of inference. In practice there is a back-and-forth interplay of deduction and induction. A marketing group wishing to expand a product line might initially develop a product deductively. In running a test market or in plotting consumer reaction to a product prototype, the group might draw inferences from the interplay of consumer preferences and consumer characteristics to redesign two products from the prototype to appeal to different market segments. A second test of the two products would then be set up on the basis of deductive logic.

Theories and models are continuously being revised and retested as knowledge accumulates during the process of research. Indeed, most people who conduct or work with research agree that no theory is ever finally demonstrated to be a rock-hard truth. There is always the possibility that subsequent empirical findings will lead to a revision and improvement of a theory.

Concepts and Definitions

Concepts and definitions are critical matters in scientific research. A concept is simply an idea or notion. Business concepts usually involve specific variables of interest to managers. Profit is a concept. Sales, gross revenue, job satisfaction, time value of money, promotion, discounted cash flow, and channels of distribution are all concepts commonly expressed in the functional areas of finance, human resource administration, and marketing.

A definition communicates the concept to another person. Without definitions, the manager could not communicate with others in the organization. Definitions can take several forms: ostensive, conceptual, and operational.

Ostensive definitions, the simplest form, consist of "pointing to" an example or instance of the concept. Thus, a manager might point to a lounging employee and say, "Now, that's a lazy worker!"

Conceptual definitions employ symbols to represent the concept. A narrative description of some concept would constitute a verbal conceptual definition. The use of mathematical symbols would constitute a mathematical conceptual definition.

An *operational definition* is the technique employed to measure a concept and gather data about it. A paper-and-pencil IQ test is an operational definition of the concept of intelligence. A questionnaire is (all too) often employed as an operational definition of the concept of job satisfaction.

Conceptual and operational definitions are of key importance in scientific research method. Conceptual definitions should be complete enough to leave no doubt as to the nature of the concept being defined. This becomes a very difficult task when a scientist is proposing a new concept. Indeed most scientists strive to develop *constructs* in their definitions (Cronbach & Meehl, 1955; Schwab, 1980). A construct is a very special type of conceptual definition that has the following qualities:

1. The concept is related to other concepts (for example, we might propose that the concept of consumer preference should be related to the concept of consumer choice).

2. The concept is defined as distinct from other concepts. Thus not only does the definition specify what other concepts it should be related to but also how the concept is different from other concepts.

3. The concept is accompanied by instructions for actually measuring it empirically (the operational definition).

Operational definitions allow managers conducting research to be scientific in their investigations. An operational definition can take a variety of forms depending on the characteristic being measured. A ruler (straight edge marked off in standard distances) is an operational definition of length. Twenty multiple-choice questions on a questionnaire may constitute an operational definition of preferred product attributes. Frequently, human resource administrators and line managers use the interview technique as an operational definition of a job applicant's performance potential. A hallmark of scientific method in research design is to take extreme care in establishing conceptual and operational definitions as explicitly as possible. In addition, pretesting of operational definitions is frequently done to help ensure that the measurements specified in the operational definition are accurate and error free.

Hypotheses

The hypotheses is probably the single most critical element in scientific research. Hypotheses are tight, predictive statements, derived deductively from models and tested empirically against the data to see if the event or state predicted actually occurs. There are three major types of hypotheses: descriptive, comparative, and deductive.

Descriptive hypotheses are stated in definitional form. They predict that a variable will take on a given value. Thus, a manager might predict, "Our sales will be $4 million this year."

Comparative hypotheses make comparisons between people, organizations, products, or objects. Thus a marketing manager might predict, "Red Chevrolets will be more attractive to young drivers than black Chevrolets."

Relational hypotheses are a form of comparative hypotheses that is most frequently used in business research. They are particularly useful to managers because they deal directly with critical relationships. Thus, a manager might propose that "sales volume will be positively related to advertising expenditures."

Hypotheses are important for several reasons:

1. They link the models to the real world. They are bridges between the world of theory and the world of reality.

2. They capture the manager's problem and define it in a way that will provide practical answers to critical questions.

3. They define exactly what steps must be taken to answer the manager's questions. In fact, well-stated hypotheses will leave no doubt as to what steps must be taken in designing a research project.

What is a good hypothesis? Developing good hypotheses is more of an art than science; intuition and experience both have a role. Unfortunately, there are few guidelines that can be provided in the way of management steps to develop effective hypotheses. The skill can be developed only through actual practice. However, good hypotheses do tend to be characterized by three qualities:

1. They are tight and explicit: "Sales will increase by 15 percent this year" is far more effective than "Sales might increase."

2. They are defined in terms that are of immediate use to the manager. "Employees who see a direct connection between performance and pay increases will respond to the incentive, while those who do not see the connection will not respond," is far more useful then "Employees who are in touch with organizational contingencies will tend to respond according to appropriate modalities."

3. They are stated before the fact. "I predict that sales will increase by 15 percent if we increase our advertising" is far more effective than, "If

you had only asked me, I could have told you that advertising would increase sales."

The application of scientific method to business problems has made a revolutionary contribution to the practice of management in this century. In research design intuition, authority, and tenacity have been replaced by scientific method. The result is that contemporary managers have increased their capacities to improve decisions. General models and bodies of knowledge have vastly improved the decisions made in all functional areas of business.

MOVING FROM DATA TO DECISIONS: COMMUNICATION AND INTERPRETATION

When the research design is implemented, the product is data. These data may be in many different forms: stacks of questionnaires returned from a survey, a log of events in a manager's day, a computer tape or sales records kept in the accounts receivable department, or something else.

Regardless of how the data are stored, while still in raw form they are of very little practical use to the decision maker. A major problem with raw data is sheer magnitude. Computer experts, for example, like to talk of "bits" of information. A bit of information is an independent unit of information that must be stored, retrieved, and analyzed as a unit. A market survey that asks 1,000 people 100 things generates 100,000 (1,000 × 100) bits of information that must be dealt with. If we were to ask for ten years of such information, we would have to deal with 1 million (100,000 × 10) bits of information.

A second problem with raw data is interpretation. Frequently the data in raw form do not immediately indicate information of direct relevance to the manager's decision problem. Thus, the empirical finding that the standardized beta coefficient emerging from a linear regression between sales volume and advertising volume is .88 and positive may not be of immediate significance to the marketing manager. Nor will an $R^2 = .95$ mean much to the typical manager. However, a statistician would look at these results and conclude that there is a strong positive relationship between the amount of advertising volume and sales volume and that 95 percent of the variation in sales among the companies studied can be attributed to variation in their advertising volume and he or she (depending on organizational constraints) would recommend that if the sales manager

wants to increase sales, the store's advertising volume should be increased.

A necessary third step in research-based decisions, therefore, is interpretation and communication of the data emerging from research. Before decisions can be made, according to the model in figure 3–1, the relevance of the data to the decision must be defined. Managers use a number of techniques and tools to help in the interpretation and communication of data, such as data aggregation and use of descriptive and inferential statistics.

Data Aggregation

Data aggregation, or summation, allows the decision maker to deal meaningfully with millions of bits of information. Thus, the sales manager for a chain of 1,000 retail outlets may find it necessary to aggregate (or total) sales data for all 1,000 outlets. In other cases there may be a need to aggregate by regions or cities.

Descriptive Statistics

Descriptive statistics allow the decision maker to summarize data so that answers to the following questions are possible: (1) what were the extreme values in the data? (2) what were the most typical or common values in the data? (3) how much variation was there in the data? How different or similar were the observations from each other? (4) How much covariation was there in the data; that is, were there strong or weak relationships between variables of interest?

Inferential Statistics

Inferential statistics allow the decision maker to test the hypotheses generated from initial models and decide in a systematic way whether to accept or reject them. The sales manager, for example, may have begun with the hypothesis that advertising volume is positively associated with sales volume. The technique of statistical inference allows the manager to accept or reject that hypothesis on the basis of the data with an estimate of the risk of being in error. Thus statistical inference allows for either rejection of the hypothesis with a known risk that the hypothesis is actually correct or acceptance of the hypothesis with a known risk that the hypothesis is actually incorrect.

Once the data emerging from research have been communicated and interpreted, the manager is ready to make a decision. It is useful to consider the process of a decision as structuring a decision because of the critical elements involved in a decision:

1. The decision rule guiding one's choice.

2. The way information is factored into the decision.

3. The values or managerial goals at stake in the decision.

When approaching decisions, managers should be careful to decide the nature of the decision situation (individual or institutional) and structure the decision accordingly. They should be aware of the tools for making decisions derived from classical decision theory and, where appropriate, make use of decision support systems to aid in the process.

In addition to the decision rules chosen, managers should be careful to note that decision making in actual practice often occurs within groups, and this circumstance presents critical challenges. Group phenomena can create what are called process losses in the decision process. Problems with group decisions include the time involved, lower levels of individual member effort in the decision, and the problems associated with "groupthink" (Janis, 1972). Managers must recognize the need to coordinate within and between groups in order to achieve consensus in group decisions.

RETURNING FROM DECISIONS TO SYMPTOMS

This discussion of research-based decisions began with symptoms, and the final stage in the model returns to the same symptoms. Effective decision makers constantly monitor their decisions. Once choices are made, effective managers gather data with respect to the symptoms that originally prompted the decisions. Through the processes of evaluation and control, they track the variables defining their problems. If sales were down and the manager decided to boost advertising volume, she or he keeps track of sales in a controlled fashion following the decision. In effect, evaluation and control are similar to the empirical test of hypotheses accomplished by research design in the earlier analysis of the manager's problem. If symptoms respond in the predicted direction, the decision is confirmed, and managers usually establish policies and procedures to be repeated in similar circumstances. If symptoms do not respond as predicted, the research cycle begins again and is repeated until the symptoms are brought under control.

SUMMARY AND IMPLICATIONS

Decision making and research are closely allied. Decision making has been defined as a core activity of managers—indeed the single activity that defines the difference between managers and nonmanagers. Success and failure in decision making influence both organizations and individual managerial careers directly.

Research is the major process by which good information for decisions is generated. In almost all cases, research based on the scientific method is the preferred method of generating information (over tenacity, authority, or intuition). It is imperative, therefore, that managers—decision makers—become familiar with the rules and steps by which research is conducted.

The research-based decision cycle provides a framework for managers to think about the process of generating information so they can make better decisions. A number of guidelines for making better decisions can be derived from a consideration of the cycle:

1. Avoid jumping to action when confronted with problems in operations.
2. Step back from the problem and develop some preliminary models of the situation. Define the problem in terms of the dependent variable; then ask what other variables might be influencing it.
3. Make as explicit a statement of the problem as possible with the model. Hypotheses or propositions should be as explicit and specific as possible.
4. Test hypotheses empirically. Hypotheses must be stated in a way that will allow them to be dis-

proved by the data if the underlying model is wrong.

5. Be careful in the interpretation of data. The standard rules of statistical inference should be used to determine the confidence that can be placed in results. Time should be taken to translate these results into something meaningful in the context of the decision situation.
6. Audit, monitor, and control decisions and the decision process. The choice of a decision alternative is only the middle of the process. Follow-up is needed. Did the desired result occur? If not, what other factors have been missed or not considered? Researchers must be ready to repeat the research cycle as many times as necessary.

REFERENCES

Ackoff, Russell L. (1953). *The design of social research*. Chicago: University of Chicago.

Campbell, Donald T., & Julian C. Stanley (1963). *Experimental and quasi-experimental designs for research*. Chicago: Rand McNally.

Cook, Thomas D., & Donald T. Campbell (1979). *Quasi-experimentation: design and analysis issues for field settings. Slokie, IL: Rand McNally.*

Cronbach, Lee J., & P.E. Meehl (1955). *Construct validity in psychological tests. Psychological Bulletin*, 281–302.

Cyert, Richard M., & James G. March (1963). *A behavioral theory of the firm*. Englewood Cliffs, NJ: Prentice-Hall.

Ebert, Ronald J., & Terence R. Mitchell (1975). *Organizational decision processes*. New York: Crane, Russak.

Emory, C. William (1980). *Business research methods* (rev. ed.). Homewood, IL: Richard D. Irwin.

Harrison, E. Frank (1981). *The managerial decision-making process* (2d ed.). Boston: Houghton Mifflin.

Janis, Irving L. (1972). *Victims of groupthink*. Boston: Houghton Mifflin.

Kaplan, Abraham (1964). *The conduct of inquiry*. New York: Chandler Publishing Company.

Kerlinger, Fred N. (1973). *Foundations of behavioral research* (2d ed.). New York: Holt, Rinehart, and Winston.

MacCrimmon, Kenneth R., & Ronald N. Taylor (1976). Decision making and problem solving. In *Handbook of industrial and organizational psychology*. Edited by Marvin D. Dunnette. Chicago: Rand McNally.

March, James G., & Herbert A. Simon (1958). *Organizations*. New York: John Wiley & Sons.

Popper, Karl R. (1965). *The logic of scientific discovery*. New York: Harper and Row.

Sayles, Leonard (1964). *Managerial behavior: Administration in complex organizations*. New York: McGraw-Hill.

Schwab, Donald P. (1980). Construct validity in organizational research. In Barry Staw, ed., *Research in organizational behavior*. Greenwich, CT: JAI Press.

Simon, Herbert A. (1976). *Administrative behavior*, 3rd ed. New York: Free Press.

Simon, Herbert A. (1977). *The new science of management decision* (Rev. ed.). Englewood Cliffs, NJ: Prentice-Hall.

Simon, Julian (1969). *Basic research methods in social science*. New York: Random House.

Wallace, Marc J., Jr., N. Fredric Crandall, & Charles H. Fay (1982). *Administering human resources*. New York: Random House.

4 CONSULTING SKILLS FOR ORGANIZATIONAL RESEARCH

Marc B. Sokol

Most organizational field research requires some, if not a great deal of, cooperation from members of the organizations we seek to study. The relationship between researcher and the site can serve as context for initial entry, data collection, and even validation of the findings. In this chapter, I focus on some of the consulting skills that contribute to effective organizational research. I also suggest that the organizations we study can be thought of as environmental landscapes: once polluted by insensitive research strategies, they can become inhospitable to future research activity.

I propose that organizational research, in both the short and the long term, can be improved by paying greater attention to the following themes:

1. Sensitivity to the site when selecting research methods is important.

2. Support (or reactivity) toward research builds over time.

3. Internal researchers are more likely than external researchers to feel the effects of site insensitivity.

4. The relationship between the researcher and the organization continues to develop throughout each study.

5. Researchers should be trained to manage their research relationships better with and within organizations.

SENSITIVITY TO THE SITE WHEN SELECTING RESEARCH METHODS

Research methods should be appropriate to the site as well as to the content of the study. Consider the following four anecdotes:

> While prefacing her presentation of a recently completed study, one researcher noted her enthusiasm at actually finding a site in Boston that had not been studied before.

> Another researcher describing the context of a study indicated the moderate adjustments he had to make after realizing that the managers of the site he was to study were not only familiar with the basic tenets of contemporary organizational development but were eager to discuss with him the significance of Chris Argyris's latest book.

During the entry phase of one project, employees remarked to the researcher that a professor from the same university was once there before. It turned out that the employees remembered this professor from when he had study conducted almost twenty years ago.

> Upon asking the managers of one office how their staff might respond to a questionnaire, the response was, "That's the last thing we need—another form to fill out. If you want to learn something about what we do, come spend a day or two with us."

These anecdotes illustrate my central theme: many people in the organizational settings that we seek to study have become familiar with the basic principles of organizational behavior and have already had some experience with the activities of researchers. Commensurate with their experience, it is likely that people have certain assumptions and biases concerning who we are, whose interests we serve, and how we

I am grateful to my many colleagues from AT&T and the University of Maryland for their comments on an earlier draft of this chapter.

carry out the work we do. These beliefs may facilitate, but also may inhibit, the way we go about conducting research. Just as research methodology must be chosen appropriately to the content of the study (Burke, 1982), research methods must also be appropriate to the history of research in each setting.

How often are the diagnostic lenses of researchers clouded with respect to site readiness for (or resistance to) various research methodologies? The consequences can range from a study quickly becoming pigeonholed by participants as just another academic exercise (and not worthy of serious time or response), to unexpectedly jeopardizing the researcher's entry in the research setting, to polluting the site from being a future research environment. A common blind spot of researchers at the point of organizational entry is to overlook the sophistication and prior research exposure of a field site.

Consider, for example, the trade-offs between surveys and interviews as research methodologies (Beer, 1981). Surveys are seemingly a more economical approach to gathering data reliably from a large number of employees. In many settings, however, a survey is viewed as another event in an unending series of administrative interruptions. Is it any wonder that optional completion of a lengthy survey often will have a limited response rate? In the same setting, however, an employee may gladly devote the same amount of time to participating in an interview. This is not to say that a more labor-intensive interview method should always be pursued. Rather, what may be necessary is to spend more time developing commitment among employees to survey participation (for example, see Alderfer & Brown, 1972, on the construction of the empathic questionnaire).

SUPPORT (OR REACTIVITY) TOWARD RESEARCH BUILDS OVER TIME

Subject reactivity to research instrumentation, as well as research involvement, is well documented as a potential threat to validity (Cook & Campbell, 1979). Goldstein (1986a) also notes that evaluation efforts within organizations cannot afford to ignore the concerns of those people who are directly affected by the conduct of the study. Recently he has suggested that as professional field researchers, we also need to study the so-called threats to validity rather than just attempting to control for such threats through more sophisticated research designs (Goldstein, 1986b).

It is important to recognize that research participants' feelings of reactivity are not necessarily rooted in their appraisal and experience of individual studies. Rather, reactivity to participation in a particular study is likely to be rooted in prior exposure to and beliefs about other studies that have already been conducted. Employees who feel that they have been "burned" or "ripped off" by one researcher are not likely quickly to trust the next person wanting to conduct a survey or "just ask a few questions." In some ways, it is like a watering hole: if someone pollutes it, the effects may be felt by others who wish to enter at a later date.

As an illustration of this point, Denison (1986) recently noted the need for him as a researcher to respect the privacy (at particular times during the workday) of those he sought to interview. A lack of sensitivity to such dynamics might have destroyed his credibility as an empathic interviewer (no matter how carefully phrased the questions might have been) and

even jeopardized his maintaining sufficient entry within the research setting. One can also see from this example how the biases of research participants might tend to develop over time when such interactions are not handled with sensitivity.

On a different level, consider the limited trust that unions place in organizational researchers. Even though the quality of the relationship between unions and industrial psychologists has recently improved (Klein, 1986), the dominant perception of our profession by unions has been based upon their experience of us as clipboard-carrying, stopwatch-bearing "tools of management" (Argyris, 1977). Is it any wonder that many organizational researchers repeatedly encounter the assumption that we are conducting time-and-motion studies for "management"?

Among the many components of organizational culture, there will exist normative myths and assumptions concerning the permissible extent of open reflection on individual and organizational processes. Moreover, it is not unreasonable to speculate that as the members of a work unit or organization become exposed to organizational research, a climate for research participation begins to develop. Techniques to assess such attitudes would serve as a valuable diagnostic tool for the organizational researcher.

Institutional support for organizational research represents the flip side of participant reactivity. In settings where organizational members have had a series of positive experiences participating in research (or where they perceive high potential payoff from being studied), entry and the choice of site-appropriate research methods may be easy tasks. Furthermore these sites may be well suited for the exploration and refinement of alternative data collection strategies. Toward this end, some companies routinely establish short-term task forces, through which representatives of the target group(s) to be studied may influence the selection and planning of appropriate data collection strategies (Neumann, 1986).

Returning to the metaphor of a research site as a watering hole, just as a researcher's insensitivity might pollute a setting over time, the opposite is also possible: a polluted research site may be cleaned up. The requirements, however, include some particularly valuable resources—time, commitment, and allowing research participants a greater voice in the conduct of research (Torbert, 1981).

INTERNAL RESEARCHERS ARE MORE LIKELY THAN EXTERNAL RESEARCHERS TO FEEL THE EFFECTS OF SITE INSENSITIVITY

Most organizations are small enough communities such that researcher credibility is an outcome of a long-term relationship-building process. Like the internal consultant, the internal researcher must be sensitive to the history of the setting. In fact, internal researchers are more likely than external researchers to be sensitive to the political ramifications of their activities. For the internal researcher, the prospect of alienating one group or another can have long-term consequences. In contrast, external researchers, because they tend to study multiple organizations, are somewhat less affected by the consequences of their insensitivity within any one organization. This is not to say that external researchers choose to act insensitively. Rather, because they are not truly members of the organization and tend to have a short-term relationship with the setting, they may not become aware of the impact of their actions.

The internal or external research role may also be thought of as stereotyped positions on a continuum of the relationship between the researcher and the setting. External researchers who maintain long-term relationships with an organization are likely to be extremely aware of fluctuations in their acceptance within the organization. Similarly, it is clearly possible that the internal researcher working within a large corporation or a decentralized company may be sufficiently apart from the various parts of the organization. For all intents and purposes they act as an external researcher who carries a corporate banner. Under such circumstances it is particularly important that the researcher monitor his or her credibility throughout different segments and subgroups of the organization.

Just as the adoption of an innovation can be affected by persons who take on roles of product champion or assassin, the work of a researcher can be facilitated or inhibited by champions and assassins.

Every research project therefore should be viewed (especially by the internal researcher) as an additional opportunity for relationship building to take place within the organization.

Again, the fundamental concern for choosing site-sensitive research methods, whether the researcher is internal or external to the organization, is the face validity of the method relative to the immediate goals of the research and the perceptions of the research participants. An internal researcher, presumably having a better sense of history within a setting than would an external researcher, should have a strong feeling for what will and what will not be accepted. In any event, both the internal and the external researcher should be prepared to pose a range of questions that permit assessment of appropriate research methods.

A variety of diagnostic questions can be generated from the discussion. Some have been discussed by other authors (Nadler, 1977; Smith, 1978) as components of the entry-contracting phase of action research. The answers to the following questions should help design field research efforts that generate less reactivity or, at a minimum, sensitize the researcher to likely occurrences to research resistance:

Has a similar study taken place in this setting in the past?

What percentage (and subgroups) of current staff participated in the study?

What methods were used? What was the reaction to this type of data collection method?

Would some data collection methods seem more invasive (or more appealing) than others? How can particular data collection methods be made to seem less invasive (or more appealing)?

Would a "sliding contract" (requiring separate agreements of research involvement) from each of the various participating groups be more appropriate than only securing top-down support for data collection procedures?

What anxieties are likely to exist over confidentiality of the data to be collected?

What types (and level of detail) of feedback are desirable, necessary, or should be avoided in this setting?

To what extent have research results been put to use in the past? How?

Moreover, the process of asking these questions should contribute to a relationship-building process between researchers and the sites we seek to study.

THE RELATIONSHIP BETWEEN THE RESEARCHER AND THE ORGANIZATION CONTINUES TO DEVELOP THROUGHOUT EACH STUDY

Increased support of organizational research requires more than a list of diagnostic questions. The relationship between the researcher and the organization is a dynamic one and evolves from entry through exit.

Figure 4–1 illustrates how the conditions of organization entry in part establish a dynamic relationship between researcher and members of the research setting. Over the course of any study, the researcher and the organization initiate various actions and respond to each other. This will occur around fundamental issues such as consensus over (and support of) research goals, willingness to participate, appropriateness of specific research methods, confidentiality, and feedback. The outcome of the relationship may set the tone for eventual use of the research findings, as well as the desire to continue or discontinue the research relationship. The interactions between the researcher and members of the setting also contribute toward development and modification of an organizational climate with respect to research activity in this setting.

This climate, in turn, becomes part of the conditions of organizational entry to be encountered by the next researcher to approach the setting.

Entry

During the entry phase of figure 4–1, three relationship dimensions are highlighted. Site history of research encompasses the collective experience of the organization with organizational behavior intervention and research. This may revolve around certain methods of data collection (e.g., the survey), the perceived value of prior research efforts, and even the action of specific researchers or research teams. Researcher image, the second facet of entry, reflects the role and alliances that the researcher portrays to the organization (e.g., expert versus collaborator). Current organizational events, the third facet, reflect the current pressures inside and outside the organiza-

Figure 4–1. Researchers and the Organization: An Evolving Relationship

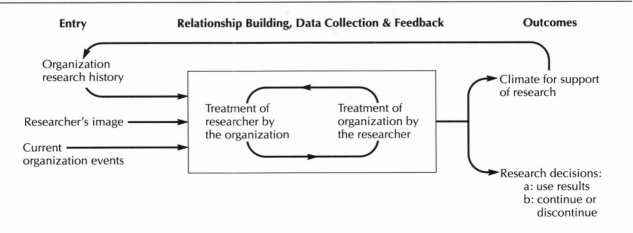

tion. These may be the very reason that the researcher has been able to obtain entry (e.g., heightened concern for quality awareness) or may overshadow the research objectives (e.g., the dramatic impact of a full-scale employee walkout).

Relationship Building

The second phase of figure 4–1 emphasizes the dynamic interaction between the researcher and the organization. The researcher may have little control over organizational events and prior history of research in the setting. His or her response to initial defensiveness within the organization, however, as well as a willingness to invest time to forge research partnerships with organizational members and an ability to develop a psychological contract surrounding research objectives, data collection procedures, and feedback, will largely influence how the researcher and the organization continue to treat each other over the course of a study.

Outcomes

Above and beyond the actual quality of the findings, the relationship that has developed between the researcher and the organization may influence the extent to which research results are implemented within the setting, as well as the desire to continue or discontinue the relationship. Another outcome is the effect of the relationship between researcher and the setting on the climate for support of (and participation in) future research.

As a conceptual model, figure 4–1 makes the case that researchers first must be aware of the conditions surrounding their entry into each research setting. Second, the research activity occurs within the context of a dynamic relationship between researcher and members of the organization. Third, this relationship will color how the research results are viewed within the organization and, of longer-term consequence, how organizational research and researchers continue to be perceived within this setting. Table 4–1 provides examples of actions that are expected to increase support for organizational research. The research endeavor is again presented as one of the researcher's entry, relationship building, and exit.

Table 4–1.
Increasing Support for Organizational Research

Entry	Explore overlap between goals of the researcher and the organization
	Assess general climate around organizational research
	Inquire about history of research and use of various methods in the setting
	Discuss anticipated use of data and feedback to the organization
Relationship-building issues	Clarify the researcher's objectives and role with various subgroups and departments
	Permit some participation in data collection decisions (how, when, where, by who)
	Identify norms that may conflict with data collection (privacy, work priorities, routing hierarchies)
	Monitor/document organizational events (reorganizations, crises, etc.) and adjust data collection as appropriate
Exit	Provide feedback to the organization (how delivered, how much, to whom, when)
	Conduct exit interviews (how were the research findings and the process received within the organization?)
	Close out with key participants/supports (in person, by letter, or by telephone)

TRAINING RESEARCHERS TO MANAGE THEIR RESEARCH RELATIONSHIPS WITH AND WITHIN ORGANIZATIONS

For the most part, site sensitivity has been overlooked as a component of training in research methods. It is surprising that among the extensive listings of information to collect during diagnosis (Levinson, 1972), there is no mention of research history or of appropriateness of various data collection methods for the particular setting.

Walter Nord, in a recent discussion of contemporary organization development (1986), suggests that as a profession, we need to examine the Jungian shadow side of ourselves more closely (that is, to confront that side of ourselves we typically try to overlook). Mirvis and Berg's (1977) well-known book, *Failures in Organizational Development,* is a good example of the learning that can arise through careful reflection of unsuccessful change efforts. In similar fashion, as organizational field researchers we should dare to ask ourselves and our clients where we make mistakes and where we place our own needs to gather data far above the requirements of building a strong relationship with the site.

Among the recent trends in our profession are an increased interest in consultancy training (Lundberg, 1986) and an elaboration of qualitative methodologies for field research (Berg & Smith, 1985; Denison, 1986). Both trends represent a clear recognition that consultative skills are necessary to function effectively in the field. These ideas can, and should, be incorporated into the training of all field researchers, not just to a subset of special interest groups. The effective management of field research requires that the choice of research designs go hand in hand with the development of a consultation relationship. This is not a minor issue. Just as the consultant does not necessarily possess strong research skills, the possession of research skills does not necessitate any particular degree of consultation skill.

Daft's (1983) contention that the "craft of research" is developed over many years should not keep us from attempting to teach the consultative skills that are prerequisites for effective field research. The management of field research is a topic that can be systematically addressed during the training of researchers, drawing from the organizational experience of researchers in psychology, organizational behavior, and sociology.

Alderfer and Brown (1972), for example, discuss the empathic questionnaire, an approach of soliciting survey participation after some initial relationship building between researcher and research participant has occurred. Alderfer (1981) also details how research entry, data collection, and feedback necessarily differ between overbounded and underbounded organizational settings. These lessons should be applicable to all field researchers, irrespective of a qualitative or quantitative orientation.

As a final note, graduate courses in organizational diagnosis illustrate efforts to convey the multidisciplinary knowledge that can be applied to training in the management and conduct of organizational field research. One model for this can be derived from Berg (1980), who describes an apprenticeship model for training in clinical field research. Within this model, Berg argues for the connection of (1) individual self-scrutiny, (2) the capacity to develop and manage field relationships, and (3) the quality of the research with respect to data collection and interpretation. It is through just such a training process that we may begin to understand how the motivations and biases of researchers influence their relationships with field settings and how these dynamics ultimately come to affect the research that we pursue.

SUMMARY

Researchers tend to overlook the site history of previous organizational research and the appropriateness of various data collection methods in the settings we seek to study. This can affect the conduct of research during a study, as well as the willingness of the members of a site to participate in future research studies.

By exploring the research site's prior history of research participation, as well as the appropriateness of various data collection strategies, additional relationship building between the researcher and the site participants can take place during the course of a study.

The management of field research is a topic worthy of systematic examination and training. Our capacity to make use of the consultative skills necessary for field research not only affects us during our individual research studies but also affects us collectively as a profession.

REFERENCES

Alderfer, C. (1981). The methodology of diagnosing group and intergroup relations in organizations. In H. Meltzer & W. Nord (Eds). *Making organizations humane and productive.* New York: Wiley.

Alderfer, C., & Brown, L. (1972). Designing an empathic questionnaire for organizational research. *Journal of Applied Psychology, 56,* 456–460.

Argyris, C. (1977). Problems and new directions for industrial psychology. In M. Dunnette (Ed.), *Handbook of industrial and organizational psychology.* Chicago: Rand McNally.

Beer, M. (1981). *Organizational change and development: A systems view.* Santa Monica, CA: Goodyear.

Berg, D. (1980). Developing clinical field skills. In C. Alderfer & C. Cooper (Eds.), *Advances in experimental social research* (vol. 2). New York: Wiley.

Berg, D., & Smith, K. (1985). *Clinical methods for social research.* Beverly Hills, CA: Sage.

Burke, W. (1982). *Organization development: Principles and practices.* Boston: Little, Brown.

Cook, T., and Campbell, D. (1979). *Quasi-experimentation: Design and analysis issues for field settings.* Chicago: Rand McNally.

Daft, R. (1983). Learning the craft of organizational research. *Academy of Management Review, 8,* (4), 539–546.

Denison, D. (1986). *Using emotion in organizational diagnosis: Lessons from a team of surgical nurses.* Presentation at the annual meeting of the Academy of Management, Chicago.

Goldstein, I. (1986a). *Training in organizations: Needs assessment, development and evaluation* (2d ed.) Monterey, CA: Brooks/Cole.

Goldstein, I. (1986b). *Values and interventions: How and where are we looking?* Presidential address, American Psychological Association, Division 14, Washington, DC.

Klein, K. (1986). *Unions and I/O psychologists: Working for, with or against each other?* Symposium presented at a meeting of the American Psychological Association, Washington, DC.

Levinson, H. (1972). *Organizational diagnosis.* Cambridge: Harvard University Press.

Lundberg, C. (1986). *Enhancing the teaching-learning of consultancy: Practices and issues.* Symposium presented at the annual meeting of the Academy of Management, Chicago.

Mirvis, P., & Berg, D. (1977) *Failures in organizational development and change.* New York: Wiley Interscience.

Nadler, D. (1977). *Feedback and organizational development.* Reading, MA: Addison-Wesley.

Neumann, D. (1986). Personal communication.

Nord, W. (1986). *New paths and unexpected bedfellows in OD's future.* Presentation at the annual meeting of the Academy of Management, Chicago.

Smith, K. (1978). *Multiple entry and the sliding contract.* Unpublished manuscript, University of Maryland.

Torbert, W. (1981). A collaborative inquiry into voluntary metropolitan desegregation. In P. Reason & J. Rowan (Eds.), *Human inquiry: A sourcebook of new paradigm research.* New York: Wiley & Sons.

5 ETHICAL ISSUES IN APPLYING PSYCHOLOGY IN ORGANIZATIONS

Rodney L. Lowman

Bill Gaither was a psychologist employed by the Eratco Corporation to screen candidates for managerial selection and promotion. A rejected candidate for selection asked for feedback on the results of his psychological testing, which constituted the primary basis for his being rejected. Because of Eratco's policy of not allowing the release of such information, Gaither refused. The unsuccessful candidate filed an ethics complaint with both the state agency regulating the practice of psychology in Dr. Gaither's state and with the American Psychological Association, potentially jeopardizing the psychologist's license to practice.

Marthena Miller, Ph.D., directed Supreme Corporation's employee assistance program (EAP). Sam Hill, a Supreme employee with a drinking problem, was referred to the EAP in lieu of dismissal because of the deterioration of his work performance due to his inability to control his drinking. Sam's manager called Dr. Miller to find out how he was doing and whether he could safely return to work. Dr. Miller refused to discuss Sam's case with the supervisor, even to indicate whether Sam had come to see her. In fact, she had asked Sam for permission to talk with his supervisor, but he had refused to sign a written release form allowing her to communicate with the supervisor. Dr. Miller's refusal to discuss the case angered the manager, who vowed to do what he could to cut the funding of the EAP and to see if a way might be found to get Sam to resign.

Both of these cases illustrate the complexity of practicing psychology in organizational settings and ways in which the ethical guidelines of psychologists may potentially conflict with the policies or preferred practices of employers. In the first case, the corporate policy conflicted with the ethical standard of psychologists that requires that psychologists "respect the client's right to know the results, the interpretations made, and the bases for their conclusions and recommendations" (Ethical principles of psychologists, 1981, p. 637) when conducting psychological assessments. While it can be debated what constitutes the client in a case like this, the psychologist cannot ignore a responsibility to persons being assessed.

In the second case, the psychologist had an ethical obligation not to release information that was appropriately regarded as confidential. The relevant ethics principle states: "Psychologists have a primary obligation to respect the confidentiality of information obtained from persons in the course of their work as psychologists. They reveal such information to others only with the consent of the person or the person's legal representative, except in those unusual circumstances in which not to do so would result in clear danger to the person or to others" (Ethical principles, 1981, pp. 635–636).

Managers who wish to ensure a high level of ethical practice by psychologists in their employ benefit by being familiar with the basic ethical principles that govern the practice of psychology. While there are times when the practices and culture of employers and of psychologists may conflict, it must be remembered that ethical standards are generally of considerable value to the organization using psychological services because they help to set a high standard of practice and to define and differentiate a profession. Because ethical standards are both *regulatory* (directive of what must or must not be done) and *aspirational* (identifying goals to which professionals can aspire but perhaps never quite reach), ethics principles both control and inspire. On the regulatory side, there are serious consequences associated with psychologists' failure to follow ethical guidelines, so managers need to be aware of the principles by which their behavior is guided.

GUIDELINES AND STANDARDS FOR ETHICAL BEHAVIOR

In applying psychology in organizational or employment contexts, psychologists are governed by a variety of standards and principles.

Basic Principles

Basic ethical tenets apply to all psychologists who are members of the American Psychological Association (APA) and, by their formal incorporation into most of the state laws governing the practice of psychology, to most licensed or certified psychologists, regardless of whether they are members of the APA. (Legislative definition and control of the activities of psychologists occurs largely at the state level. There is considerable variability in these laws as they relate to the practice of psychology in organizational contexts. See, for example, Howard & Lowman, 1982, 1985.) Periodically revised (a revision is taking place as of this writing), the APA ethical standards specify, in ten principles, the basic rules governing the practice of psychology. The most recent version of the APA ethical principles is published in the *American Psychologist* (see, for example, Ethical principles, 1981). Copies of these principles can also be obtained from the APA in Washington, D.C. An example of one of these principles concerns competence (Principle 2), which, among other things, specifies: "Psychologists recognize the boundaries of their competence and the limitations of their techniques. They only provide services and only use techniques for which they are qualified by training and experience" (Ethical principles, 1981, p. 634).

Unfortunately, the current ethical standards for psychologists were primarily developed for psychology practiced in one-on-one relationships and do not always clearly indicate how the principles apply to complex situations in which third parties are involved (e.g., evaluating a candidate for selection when the "client" is the organization). In certain cases the well-intentioned psychologist must exercise considerable judgment in applying the ethical principles to organizational contexts.

It is also important to note that ethical standards are guiding principles, but they must be applied by practitioners to specific situations and decisions. This inevitably involves judgment and analysis. Also available to assist in this application are technical standards and case material, which help to demonstrate how generic ethical principles are best translated into practice. Several relevant documents are listed here.

Technical Standards

Standards for Educational and Psychological Testing. Since applications of psychology in organizations often involve the use of psychological tests, managers need to be aware of some of the standards that govern the use of psychological tests. This is important because, in conducting psychological assessments, it is an ethical requirement that psychologists utilize established scientific procedures and observe the relevant APA standards. One such set of guidelines is the *Standards for Educational and Psychological Testing* (1985), jointly published by the APA, the American Educational Research Association, and the National Council on Measurement in Education. Under continuous review, the most recent edition of this document was published in 1985. A separate chapter in this document, "Employment Testing," identifies issues important in the application of psychological testing in industry.

Principles for the Validation and Use of Personnel Selection Procedures: 2d ed.[1] These standards, published by the Society for Industrial and Organizational Psychology of the APA, specify scientific principles considered acceptable for use of psychological tests in personnel selection.

Standards for Providers of Psychological Services. This document outlines specialty standards as they relate to the practice of industrial-organizational psychology (American Psychological Association, Committee on Professional Standards, 1981).

Case Material

Several other sources of information are available to assist in the process of translating APA ethical standards into practice in organizational settings. A recent casebook (*Casebook on Ethical Principles*, 1987) by the APA presents many examples of unethical behavior and how the APA Ethics Committee dealt with the behavior. In addition, the Society for Industrial and Organizational Psychology has published a casebook (Lowman, 1985) showing how the APA ethics standards apply to a variety of specific cases involving the practice of many different aspects of psychology in organizations.[2] In addition, several articles have appeared that address the application of APA ethics to questions of personnel psychology (London & Bray, 1980; Eyde & Kowal, 1987; Eyde

& Quaintance, 1988) and to organizational issues (Lowman, 1986; Mirvis & Seashore, 1979; Walton & Warwick, 1973).

Consequences of Unethical Behavior

Thus, the practice of psychology is governed by a variety of standards, rules, and guidelines. The consequences for ignoring these or acting contrary to ethical principles can be severe. Complaints of unethical behavior by a psychologist can result in a review by the relevant ethics committee at the state regulatory level or at the national levels by the APA. A variety of negative sanctions can be applied against a psychologist by such bodies, including censure, stipulated resignation from APA, expulsion, and (through state regulatory bodies) delicensure. Since these are measures that have serious implications for the future livelihood of the psychologist, it is important that managers understand the principles governing the practice of psychology and know which standards may create ethical dilemmas or misbehavior.

Obviously, psychologists can be unethical in grossly inappropriate ways or in ways that are much more complex and open to debate. Psychologists who lie, misrepresent their training, or practice outside their areas of training or specialty clearly are not behaving appropriately by the standards of virtually all professions, not to mention the expectations of the public at large about what constitutes ethical behavior.

On the other hand, there are more subtle and complex ways in which psychologists may risk charges of unethical behavior and in which managers may, by applying their own cultural standards or expectations to the psychologist, unwittingly encourage unethical behavior. For example, highlighting the positive aspects and minimizing the negative aspects of a product might be a firmly entrenched value for a sales organization; to hide or ignore limitations of a psychologist's work can constitute unethical behavior. Or again, to "make do" with inadequate resources may be an organizational reality in many parts of a corporation. Yet a psychologist who ignores requirements of validity or ethics due to such factors risks charges of ethical malfeasance.

AREAS OF POTENTIAL CONFLICT BETWEEN PSYCHOLOGISTS AND ORGANIZATIONAL EMPLOYERS

It is not possible, in a brief presentation, to cover all the rules and guidelines to which adherence by psychologists is expected and required. To assist in thinking conceptually and preventively about the ethical risks faced by employers of organizational psychologists, this section will present several common themes and illustrate ethical constraints and typical conflicts that arise in applying these standards in industry. Each of these areas represents a potential conflict of cultures, which can give rise to difficulties between psychologists and business organization.

Scientific versus Entrepreneurial Cultures

The profession of psychology is a science-based discipline. The essence of science is the pursuit of the discovery of truth. This means that scientific professions value the open pursuit of knowledge, wide distribution of research findings, deciding differences of opinion on the basis of empirical findings and knowledge, and the openness to questioning, challenge, and repudiation of any of its findings or conclusions so long as

commonly accepted rules of empirical evidence are followed. Scientists are taught to be skeptical about their own and others' research findings, to communicate clearly the limitations and deficiencies of their findings, and to present services to the public in a manner that emphasizes objectivity and minimizes self-serving one-sidedness. That these objectives and values are never fully achieved in scientific professions such as psychology does not keep them from being highly prized and protected values.

Entrepreneurial values are somewhat different. While both science and commerce value "success" (achievement of desired goals), the definition of goals varies widely between the two domains. In the world of business, though goals vary with the type of enterprise, they typically include commercial success, protection of the organization, and subordination of personal needs and interests to those of the larger group. If a new product or process is discovered by employees of an organization, the intent is generally to profit from that creation rather than sharing it with those in competing firms in the broader interests of "truth." Similarly, in offering a product or service, a firm typically emphasizes the positive aspects and when required by law to point out defects (such as the health consequences of cigarettes) does so in a manner that minimizes the potential negative impact to the organization.

To assume that a psychologist is just another employee, bound by primary loyalty to an employer rather than to a profession, ignores the reality of the differences in cultures that a professional brings to the organization. Employers should understand that most psychologists, especially those who practice in organizational settings, have been carefully trained in scientific standards and values and that these will at times necessarily conflict with commercial ones. However, because psychology is typically (though not always) applied to internal concerns rather than external ones (e.g., the selection of employees versus the marketing of a product), there may be less difficulty than might be anticipated. In the matter of internal issues, the organization is well advised to create a culture in which the exposure of faults, limitations, and difficulties is encouraged rather than ignored. Many industrial-organizational psychologists have been trained to evaluate critically, and the organizational climate should encourage them to do so, not just as an issue of professional ethics but also as something that is of potential value to the organization.

The norms and values of commerce and psychology potentially collide when the psychologist is expected to adhere to organizational norms that are in direct conflict with those of the scientific world. For example, to ask a psychologist not to provide feedback when requested by a nonselected applicant on the grounds that this information belongs to the company that employs the psychologist ignores the psychologist's obligations to people who are assessed (see "Conducting Individual Assessments" case, Lowman, 1985, pp. 12–14). To insist that a psychologist write a report that ignores limitations on the validity of a selection device developed by the organization to hire new managers asks the professional to violate both ethical and scientific standards and norms. To require a psychologist to misrepresent the actual capability of an organization to perform a particular service also violates ethical norms and standards.

Prior Competency versus Pragmatic On-the-Job Learning

In many industrial settings, managers are expected to learn on the job. This means that they may have had no prior experience in managing a particular function or task, but, by use of generic managerial skills, they are expected to learn the function quickly and to administer it competently thereafter. While this may be a customary procedure in business, if such a standard is applied to the practice of psychology, it can result in pressures to behave unethically. Psychologists should never be asked or expected to perform duties outside their areas of competency without providing ethically appropriate means of acquiring the desired skills. For example, an industrial-organizational (I-O) psychologist might need additional training and supervision to be competent in evaluating selected aspects of personality as part of an executive assessment program if (as is typical) the I-O psychologist had no prior training in personality assessment. Supervision by a psychologist trained in this specialization might be needed for a period of some time until relevant competencies were mastered. On the other hand, to ask an I-O psychologist with no training in clinical or counseling psychology to provide assistance to impaired executives would severely stretch the limits of competency. Without substantial retraining in the clinical or counseling speciality, the I-O psychologist would risk an ethics charge or malpractice suit; the employer might also be sued if the advice given by the psychologist in counseling individual employees or their family members led to adverse consequences.

An analogy to medicine is relevant. Few executives would ask or expect their cardiologists to perform neurosurgery on them. To request a psychologist on their staff to practice outside areas of training or competency is equally inappropriate. The limitations on competencies of psychologists who practice in the work setting need to be respected. Managers must ensure that psychologists neither practice nor are encouraged to practice outside their specialties even though at times it may appear expedient to do so. Adequate resources should be provided to ensure that the psychologist is able to obtain needed training or supervision to meet professional standards of good professional practice.

Protection of Client versus Employer "Rights"

Because loyalty to and protection of the perceived interests of the employer are generally regarded as desirable characteristics by work organizations, these institutions may have little regard for protecting the interests of parties regarded as external to the organization. Additionally, when there are conflicts between employees and members of the managerial hierarchy of the organization, it may be expected that company officials will take the side of the organization, while the psychologist's ethical standards may require neutrality.

Applicants for jobs provide an illustration of these concerns. For many private sector employers, applicants for jobs may be screened utilizing psychological assessment devices and notified only if they are hired. In the United States, applicants for jobs are generally afforded little legal protection unless they fall into a protected category (e.g., racial minorities) or it can be demonstrated that the manner in which personnel selection decisions were made was arbitrary or otherwise discriminatory. Especially for higher-level positions, companies generally have considerable latitude in how they make decisions about selections or promotions. There are often implicit pressures at the managerial level that keep individuals who might otherwise protest a selection decision from filing formal charges or complaints lest they be branded as a troublemaker and opportunities for future jobs restricted. Thus, in many settings, unsuccessful candidates for selection or promotion are provided little information about the reasons for nonselection or the rationale behind the particular selection methods used.

In contrast, psychologists cannot escape their ethical obligations to protect the interests of those with whom they work, even when someone else is paying for their services. This means that the psychologist has an ethical obligation to protect the legal and civil rights of individuals with whom they work. Asking a psychologist to violate a job applicant's legal or civil rights requires the psychologist to risk an ethical violation.

The Fiduciary Relationship versus Control

Psychologists must be sensitive to both the implicit and explicit possibilities of undue pressures to require employees to participate in psychological activities. While almost everyone would agree that it is inappropriate to force a college student to participate in a professor's psychology experiment when the student feels it would be harmful or undesirable to do so, in business and industry, protection of the rights of human subjects may be more lax. For example, negative sanctions may arise when an employee elects not to participate in a study where inclusion of all employees is expected.

While psychologists have an ethical obligation to "fully inform consumers as to the purpose and nature of an evaluative, treatment, educational or training

procedure, and they freely acknowledge that clients, students, or participants in research have freedom of choice with regard to participation" (Ethical principles, 1981, p. 636), in practice there may be pressures that make this difficult to apply. In this context, "research" may include not just test validation efforts but collection of attitudinal data from employees or even field-testing a new data collection form. Generally, employees respond positively when the purpose of a study is explained to them, their rights are protected, and they have the opportunity not to participate should that be their preference. However, in authoritarian organizations, the employer may be so ingrained in telling employees what to do that the psychologist's insistence on voluntary participation in psychological activities may be met with resistance. As an example of some of the ways in which workers can be pressured to participate, in a psychological study conducted in a hospital in which participation was supposed to be voluntary, a psychologist overheard the chief nurse telling her key nursing staff that she wanted a "good showing" of participation and that the nursing staff was expected to take part in the study. While a vocal employee might be direct enough to protest, the subtle pressures to participate, or the perceived consequences of nonparticipation, might seriously threaten the right of employees not to participate in the study.

Another complicated example involving psychologists' obligation to protect the welfare of those with whom they work concerns the case of the would-be employees for sensitive positions who refuse to have psychological evaluations done prior to being considered for a job, often on the basis of this being an irrelevant invasion of their privacy. The company may have a legitimate right to rule out from certain jobs individuals whose psychological problems place them at high risk for problems on the job (such as police or nuclear power plant operators), even though the validity of commonly used measures for this purpose is less than ideal (see Lowman, 1987). On the other hand, the psychologist must deal cautiously with the would-be employee who does not wish to be so screened or who is ruled to be an unacceptable psychological risk. Ideally, an alternative selection methodology could be available for persons with legitimate reasons for wanting not to participate. However, allowing alternative means of evaluation may confound validity or result in more than one standard being applied to a job applicant pool. Clearly, acting in such a manner that the interests of both company and potential assessee are protected requires considerable forethought.

RECOMMENDATIONS

1. *Become familiar with psychologists' ethical guidelines.* Managers responsible for overseeing the functions of psychologists in organizational contexts should familiarize themselves with the APA's *Ethical Principles,* which is readily obtained from the APA. The document is only six pages and will familiarize the manager with the basic ethical guidelines to which psychologists must adhere.

2. *When in doubt, don't.* If there is ambiguity about how the ethical standards apply in a particular situation, it is better to seek outside guidance than to proceed with a practice of questionable ethicality. The APA's Ethics Committee can be contacted directly if there is doubt about how the principles apply in a case. To ask questions after the fact places both the psychologist and the organization in a potentially inappropriate situation. It is better to think through the ethical issues prior to rather than after the commission of an ethically ambiguous act.

3. *Develop methods for encouraging ethical behavior.* First, encourage dialogue on ethical issues and concerns. Organizational life is increasingly complex. Many of the issues that arise in practice were not thought of when the *Ethical Principles* were created or last revised. By being aware of the ethical standards of psychologists, managers can also become sensitive to ways in which they may be creating conflict for the psychologists they employ or use as consultants. The manager should encourage an open dialogue on ethical issues and make sure that the psychologist is encouraged to raise any ethical concerns about a proposed course of action before it is undertaken. Legitimizing the discussion of controversial areas or practices can go a long way to preventing unethical behavior.

Another valuable suggestion in this area is provided by the *Ethical Principles* themselves. In recognizing that there will at times be difficult conflicts between the reality of an immediate situation and the demands of the ethical code, they specify: "When conflicts of interest arise between clients and psychologists' employing institutions, psychologists clarify the nature and direction of their loyalties and responsibilities and keep all parties informed of their commitments" (Ethical principles, 1981, p. 636). Psychologists should take the responsibility for confronting ethically conflictual situations and making their position clearly known.

Second, encourage members of the organization to report suspected violations of ethical standards. Organizations should make it easy for managers, employees, job applicants, or other interested parties to make complaints about alleged unethical or questionable behavior. In so doing, the organization communicates to relevant parties that it holds its psychologist employees to the same high standards that the profession of psychology does and so both discourages any unethical practices but also encourages the raising of possible ethical conflicts or concerns. Should there be problems with potentially unethical behavior in such a system, it may be identified early enough that appropriate action can be taken to prevent further difficulties.

Managers themselves should report clearly unethical behavior on the part of psychologists if they have been unable to stop or prevent it. This can be done through the state regulatory body if the psychologist is licensed or through the APA's Ethics Committee for all members of that body. Ethics committees are expected to investigate all complaints impartially and reach a decision about the appropriateness of the psychologist's actions. Obviously, it is better to have no behavior occurring that would violate ethical guidelines; indeed, the vast majority of psychologists practice ethically and never are accused of unethical behavior. However, when such behavior does occur, it should be reported so it can be stopped.

Third, develop an organizational or company code of ethics. Often violations of ethical standards in organizational settings occur because some member of the firm acts in a manner contrary to implicit normative rules. There is no ethics code for managers comparable to that of psychologists, and many employers have not developed an ethics code for their own organization. Thus, the appropriate behavior of managers is less well defined than that of psychologists. Conflicts between psychologists and managers may therefore arise because a manager superior to the psychologist in the organizational hierarchy does not understand the required behavior of psychologists or may understand it and reject the standards as inappropriate or irrelevant to their organizational context. Such managers may themselves be acting in ways that violate desired company norms or standards, yet in the absence of written ethical guidelines and enforcement mechanisms, the manager may proceed unchecked. Explicit statements about ethical expectations are potentially valuable in these and other situations and may assist companies in ensuring high levels of ethical behavior by all members of the organization.

The development of a dialogue and definition of what constitutes ethical behavior by managers within a competitive framework has a potentially salutary effect on everyone. Moreover, the very act of thinking through a code of ethics requires focus on what is appropriate behavior and what should be done in the event of noncompliance or conflicts. Even in today's increasingly litigious environment, ethical problems anticipated, debated, and discussed may be legal and ethical problems avoided.

A FINAL (GOOD) EXAMPLE

Because so much of what constitutes ethical violations brings forth the negative in professional practice, it may be instructive to close with a positive example of a conflictual situation handled in an appropriate manner.

Bill Signet, chief executive officer of Bethesda Products International, asked his company's psychologist to do something that, unknown to him, constituted a possible ethics violation. In a recent business magazine Signet had read about the value of personality tests in predicting executive behavior. The article suggested the use of projective tests such as the inkblot test to divine the hidden secrets of executives and thereby to manage them more effectively. The company psychologist, Marissa Richardson, discussed the limitations of this method and her own lack of training in this area. Used to getting his own way, Signet asked Richardson to present him with a plan for implementing projective testing in for future managers.

To support her case, Dr. Richardson reviewed the literature on the specific measure in which the executive had interest and noted the scarcity of supporting validity evidence for its intended use. She recommended that personality testing might be considered as part of the preemployment testing process but that it needed to be carefully chosen and valid for the specific purpose. She presented Signet with a detailed report outlining the merits of each of three possible personality measures, including the one Signet wanted, and demonstrated that the alternatives had a superior validity record to the "inkblot test" the executive had read about. She further stated that the administration and interpretation of personality tests was outside her areas of competence and outlined the additional resources that would be needed to allow inclusion of the measures as part of the firm's assessment battery. Finally, she noted the specific requirements for validity in employment testing to which the measures would be subject and the specific ethical principles that would need to be met.

While recognizing the elaborate work that had been done by his psychologist, Signet was nevertheless persistent. Because Signet refused to accept Dr. Richardson's recommendations, she suggested contacting the ethics committee of the state and national psychological associations to present the conflict to them for their recommendations. Signet reluctantly agreed to abide by the results of this consultation since he did not want to lose Richardson or to jeopardize her license or career. Both committees agreed that the proposed plan to use the unvalidated inkblot test for this purpose raised serious concerns of ethics and professional practice and recommended that the psychologist act in accordance with the guidelines of the profession in following her recommendation not to use the test as part of a standard battery. There was, of course, no objection to the use of a personality measure or even to the use of the instrument in question if appropriate validation research were undertaken but rather to the use of the measure as if its validation had already been established. Moreover, the expectations of the manager were overly optimistic, quite at odds with the status of the few available research findings in this area. The belief that the use of this one test would provide great insights into potential executives' on-the-job behavior was at odds with available validation research. Moreover, the committees noted that the psychologist acknowledged having had no training or experience in the use of the test in question; acquiring the minimal experience level might take years of supervised training, something to which the manager seemed oblivious.

CONCLUSION

Ethical principles restrict practice, but they also guide and protect it. It is for the protection of consumers of psychological services that ethical guidelines are most relevant. Often there is no conflict between ethical guidelines and the practice of psychology in organizations. The presence of the ethics in these cases helps to ensure a high level of practice and to protect the organization against those who do not adhere to the required standards.

In other cases, there is conflict between the ethical requirements of psychologists and the norms, values, or standards of persons in the organization. Some of these conflicts result from differences and inconsistencies in cultural values and expectations. In such cases it is to the advantage of the organization and the protection of the psychologist to ensure that a forum exists for the expression of conflicts and disagreements and that steps are taken preventively to ensure sound and ethical practice.

NOTES

1. Copies may be ordered from the Society for Industrial/Organizational Psychology, 617 East Golf Rd., Suite 103, Arlington Heights, IL 60005.

2. Copies may be ordered from the Society for Industrial/Organizational Psychology, Department of Psychology, University of Maryland, College Park, MD 20742.

REFERENCES

American Psychological Association. Committee on Professional Standards (1982). Specialty guidelines for the delivery of services by industrial/organizational psychologists. *American Psychologist, 37,* 698–701.

Casebook on ethical principles of psychologists (1987). Washington, DC: American Psychological Association.

Ethical principles of psychologists (1981). *American Psychologist, 36,* (6), 633–638.

Eyde, L.D., & Kowal, D.M. (1987). Computerised test interpretation services: Ethical and professional concern regarding U.S.A. producers and users. In L.D. Eyde (Ed.), *Computerised psychological testing.* London: Erlbaum.

Eyde, L.D., & Quaintance, M. (1988). Ethical issues and cases in the practice of personnel psychology. *Professional Psychology, 7,* 295–306.

Howard, A., & Lowman, R.L. (1982). Licensing and industrial/organizational psychology. *Industrial/Organizational Psychologist, 19* (3), 10–18.

Howard, A., & Lowman, R.L. (1985). Should industrial/organizational psychologists be licensed? *American Psychologist, 40* (1), 40–47.

London, M. & Bray, D.W. (1980). Ethical issues in testing and evaluation of personnel decisions. *American Psychologist, 35,* 890–901.

Lowman, R.L. (Ed.) (1985). *Casebook on ethics and standards for the practice of psychology in organizations.* College Park, MD: Division 14, American Psychological Association.

Lowman, R.L. (1986). The ethical practice of consultation: Not an impossible dream. *Consulting Psychologist, 13* (3), 466–472.

Lowman, R.L. (1987). *Ethical issues in the selection of nuclear power plant operators.* Paper presented at the annual meeting of the American Nuclear Society, Dallas.

Mirvis, P.H., & Seashore, S.E. (1979). Being ethical in organizational research. *American Psychologist, 34,* 766–780.

Walton, R.E., & Warwick, D.P. (1973). The ethics of organization development. *Journal of Applied Behavioral Science, 9,* 681–698.

6 MANAGING TO FIT YOUR COMPETITIVE STRATEGY

Susan E. Jackson, Randall S. Schuler

In order to grow and prosper, a firm must gain and retain a advantage over its competitors. One way to gain a competitive advantage is via strategic initiative. MacMillan (1983) defines strategic initiative as the ability of a company or business unit to capture control of strategic behavior in the industry in which it competes. When one firm gains the strategic initiative, competitors in the industry are cast into playing a reactive role. They must find ways to respond that enable them to reduce the advantage gained by the competitor who has seized the initiative. According to MacMillan's view, then, firms that gain a strategic advantage control their own destinies, at least for as long as it takes competitors to close the strategic gap.

A competitive advantage facilitates growth, profitability, and, ultimately, survival (Porter, 1985). In order to gain competitive advantages, firms develop and implement various strategies. There are many possible competitive strategies available to firms, and many typologies have been used to describe them. In this chapter, we focus on the three strategies of innovation, quality enhancement, and cost reduction to illustrate how corporate-level strategic choices can affect choices related to human resource management.

First, we briefly describe these three competitive strategies. Then we describe several types of behaviors that are needed from employees in order to implement these different strategies successfully. We also explain how managers can diagnose the behavioral demands implied by the specific strategies for their firms. Finally, we describe how various human resource management practices can be used to elicit the behaviors needed for the three competitive strategies of innovation, quality enhancement, and cost reduction.

THREE COMPETITIVE STRATEGIES

Innovation

One way to beat the competition is to offer unique products that no one else can offer, thereby differentiating your firm from competitors. Pursuing this strategy requires innovation. Ideas for new products and/or services must be generated, and the products must be made available to consumers before they can be copied by competitors. This is the essence of entrepreneurship. An innovation strategy often implies high R&D costs, which must be offset by relatively high prices. Fortunately, truly unique and innovative products typically command high margins.

Low Cost

An alternative way to beat the competition is by offering low-cost products and/or services. Firms that pursue this strategy wait for products developed by others to appear on the market. They then copy these products, producing and selling them at rock-bottom prices. To be successful with the cost reduction strategy, firms must be vigilant in keeping production costs as low as possible. Economies of scale and market share should both be maximized.

Quality Enhancement

A third way to compete is to offer top quality. Like uniqueness, quality is something people are willing to pay extra for, especially when quality products are scarce. As the experience of the U.S. auto industry shows, offering the best-quality products and services is a sure way to gain market share quickly, especially when competitors are focusing on other concerns.

BEHAVIOR PROFILES TO FIT COMPETITIVE STRATEGIES

During the past few years, the concept of strategic human resource management has gained popularity. As our descriptions of three different competitive strategies reflect, strategy formulation has generally emphasized decisions about what types of products or services to offer and what types of customers to serve. The focus is not on decisions about how to manage employees. So what does it mean to manage to fit your competitive strategy?

Managing to fit your competitive strategy refers to making decisions about staffing, appraisal, compensation, training, and development based upon the imperatives of the competitive strategy. The basic assumption is that different competitive strategies require fundamentally different types of work forces. For example, some of the employee attitudes and behaviors that could stimulate the creative breakthroughs needed in a firm pursuing an innovation strategy would be disastrous in a firm pursuing a cost-cutting strategy. When innovation is the goal, false starts and dead-end ideas are accepted as costs related to progress; these are the same costs that must be eliminated to be successful in pursuing a low-cost strategy.

Table 6–1 illustrates several dimensions of attitudes and behavior managers need to consider when evaluating whether there is a match between the behaviors and attitudes needed to implement their strategy and those encouraged by their management practices. We refer to these as role attitudes and behaviors to emphasize that they are at a somewhat more general level of abstraction than the skills and abilities needed to do particular jobs.

In essence, the profile of role attitudes and behaviors defines the corporate culture for the firm. Next we describe three different profiles that fit the three competitive strategies of innovation, cost reduction, and quality enhancement.

Role Attitudes and Behaviors for the Innovation Strategy

The role attitudes and behaviors needed from employees in order to innovate have been described in detail by authors calling for renewal of the entrepreneurial spirit in U.S. industry, as well as by those who have studied the unique characteristics of entrepreneurs (e.g., Pinchot, 1984; Brandt, 1986; Drucker, 1985). They include creativity, cooperativeness, a longer-term focus, risk taking, a willingness to as-

Table 6–1
Role Attitudes and Behaviors for Competitive Strategies

Repetitive, Predictable	Creative, Innovative
Short-Term Focus	Long-Term Focus
Cooperative & Interdependent	Autonomous & Independent
Low Concern for Quality	High Concern for Quality
Low Concern for Quantity	High Concern for Quantity
Low Risk Taking	High Risk Taking
High Concern for Process	High Concern for Results
Desire Low Responsibility	Desire High Responsibility
Inflexible to Change	Flexible to Change
Comfortable with Certainty and Stability	Tolerant of Ambiguity and Uncertainty
Narrow Skill Application	Broad Skill Application
Low Job Involvement	High Job Involvement

sume responsibility, flexibility, and tolerance for ambiguity and uncertainty. The reasons these characteristics are important becomes clear when considering what the process of innovation is like.

The process of innovation has been carefully observed and recorded by many researchers, so a great deal is known about how it occurs. By its nature, innovation requires moving into unknown territories. In some cases, getting to the new territory means advancing current technical knowledge. Such innovations are most likely to be developed by creative people with high levels of expertise in their field of interest. This is because "the innovation process is knowledge intensive, relying on individual human intelligence and creativity. New experiences are accumulated at a rapid pace, the learning curve is steep" (Kanter, 1985). According to Drucker, a big mistake "is believing that money can be used in lieu of good people. It's very common when it comes to the question of how you staff that people will say, 'We can't spare Joe for the new. What he's doing is so important, we can't take him off it.' The result is that companies staff with people they can spare. That is the quickest way to kill something—the combination of poor people and a generous budget" (Rutigliano, 1986).

In other cases, the new territory involved represents an intersection between two or more knowledge bases. Such innovations are likely to be developed by teams of experts working together on a common project. Thus, innovation also requires people who are willing to collaborate and cooperate with each other. These can be facilitated by a firm's performance appraisal and compensation practices. For example, the use of group-level criteria for performance appraisal and compensation is instrumental in creating synergy among corporate entrepreneurs. "The right places are the integrative environments that support innovation, and encourage the building of coalitions and teams to support and implement visions" (Kanter, 1983).

New discoveries are often made through a process of trial and error. One consequence is that many errors will be made, and some of them will be costly in terms of time and/or money. Therefore, innovation requires that employees be willing to take risks. Relying upon trial-and-error methods also means that the rate at which progress will occur on a project is difficult to predict in advance, a fact that both product developers and their managers must learn to cope with. They need to adopt a long-term orientation and learn to tolerate ambiguity and uncertainty.

Consistent with there being a significant time span before results are realized, organizations need to establish long-term financial arrangements to compensate employees. Employee stock ownership plans (ESOPs) and profit-sharing plans ensure that employees will be compensated in accordance with the performance of a newly developed product or service. Conversely, firms that are interested in encouraging employees to assume responsibility for risky projects must recognize that short-term failures should have only short-term impacts on compensation.

Role Attitudes and Behaviors for the Low-Cost Strategy

The desire of early U.S. manufacturers to produce large quantities of goods that could be sold at low prices fueled the industrial revolution. This was accomplished through scientific management, which involved breaking jobs down into simple tasks that could be performed after only a little training and selecting people with the skills needed for these highly specified jobs. Pay was based on results rather than number of hours worked to encourage employees to be as productive as possible. In general, the goal was to maximize efficiency and minimize labor costs.

Today, minimizing costs is again a high priority for many U.S. industries. In many cases, firms that had allowed other concerns to take priority during times of economic expansion are now realizing they must cut costs significantly to compete effectively in a global marketplace. If labor represents a large portion of their total costs, then it is natural that these firms have begun to look for ways to reduce labor costs.

The general principle of job simplification is still behind many current efforts to minimize costs, especially in much of the service sector. As described later, job simplification has been a cornerstone in the successful cost-minimization efforts of United Parcel Service. The banking industry provides another illustration; the introduction of automated electronic tellers has decreased the variety of tasks now performed by human tellers. When job simplification is used as a route to reduced labor costs, the behaviors needed from employees become more repetitive (unlike the creativity needed for innovation).

Other more direct methods of cost reduction are common as well. For example, work force reductions and pay cuts have been the popular methods for lowering manufacturing costs in many industries, including steel, airlines, automobiles, appliances, and textiles. During periods of steady growth and expansion, many firms increased both the size of their work force and the size of their compensation packages, with little consideration for how they would cope with an economic downturn. Consequently, employees developed a feeling of security and the expectation that they could continue working for the same company as long as they continued to perform adequately. E.I. Du Pont de Nemours & Company is typical in this respect. According to chairman Richard E. Heckert,

> At the beginning of the 1980's, we staffed up for the anticipated increase in business activity that was supposed to accompany the economic growth forecast by economists. But the first five years of the 1980s were relatively flat, and we ended up considerably overstaffed. Compounding the problem of poor economic growth was the exchange rate problem—until the dollar began to ease.... Consequently, we had excess employees because of circumstances beyond our control. We knew we had to do something, but we also knew we had to be creative and humane in doing it. (Staff, 1987, p. 24)

Du Pont eventually cut its worldwide staff by 35,000 people through a combination of voluntary termination incentives, an early retirement opportunity program, natural attrition, and divestitures.

The pain of massive layoffs and failed attempts to use two-tier pay systems has taught employers the importance of remaining flexible with respect to work force commitments. Many companies are now relying more on temporary employees, part timers, and subcontractors, who have minimal expectations for a long-term commitment. (For an interesting example of how one firm in the energy business is restructuring its work force to include fewer permanent employees, see DeLuca, 1988.)

Given such practices, it is appropriate for employees to adopt a short-term orientation, especially in comparison to the longer-term orientation appropriate for firms pursuing an innovation strategy. Also, when reducing costs is the top priority, employees are usually encouraged to focus on results and emphasize quantity of output. By implication, experimentation and risk taking are discouraged because they often result in costly "errors."

Role Attitudes and Behaviors Needed for the Quality Strategy

Xerox chief executive officer David Kearns defines quality as "being right the first time every time." In order to accomplish this goal, manufacturing employees must be ever vigilant in perfecting production processes to reduce the probability of turning out defective parts. Service employees must be responsive to the needs of their clients and customers. Like a cost-cutting approach, a results orientation is appropriate, but the priority is quality first and quantity second.

The results of using such a strategy can be impressive. Seattle-based Nordstrom is a good example. The rapidly expanding billion-dollar department store chain has successfully competed in a low-margin industry by providing high-quality service that meets its customers' exacting standards. Employees are drilled in the dogma, "The customer is always right." Apparently management is right here, with the result being sales per square foot of space that about double the industry average.

Often quality improvement means changing the processes through which goods are produced and by which services are delivered. Because the pursuit of quality is an ongoing process, minor changes are likely to be continually called for, and major changes may be frequent. Thus employees are needed who are comfortable with change and flexible enough to adapt to it, even when the changes result in fundamental shifts in the nature of employees' jobs.

Many firms recognize that improving quality requires employees who are truly committed to this goal and who are willing and able to help achieve it. To achieve improved quality, these organizations rely on employee problem-solving groups, such as quality circles, because they know employees are in the best position to diagnose and solve quality-related problems. Thus, the pursuit of a quality enhancement strategy often requires employees who are able to cooperate with each other and who exhibit a concern for process as well as for results.

ASSESSING NEEDED EMPLOYEE ATTITUDES AND BEHAVIORS

Our discussion is intended to illustrate a few major differences in role behaviors and attitudes associated with three competitive strategies. Table 6–1 provides a more complete list of role behaviors and attitudes to consider when managing to fit your competitive strategy.

We still have not begun to describe what firms should do with their human resource management practices based upon these differences in needed role behaviors and attitudes. Before making decisions about which human resource management practices are appropriate for each competitive strategy, all needed role behaviors and attitudes should be carefully considered. This process may be time-consuming, but it is an essential step. If fact, it will become the foundation that supports and guides future decisions.

Clearly, the process of clarifying the ideal profile of employee attitudes and role behaviors is not a task

that can be accomplished by isolated personnel managers. It requires active input from line and staff managers from various functions and levels in the organization. Only after determining the profile of attitudes and behaviors needed to support your competitive strategy is it possible then to make effective choices about how to manage people. In other words, the profile serves as a blueprint of what type of work force you want to create. Human resource management practices are your tools. The challenge is to select the right tools for the job of building an effective work force.

Next, we review briefly the variety of management tools available. Then we describe three illustrative examples of how three firms, each pursuing different strategies, have used human resource management practices to build and shape their work forces to match their strategies.

HUMAN RESOURCE MANAGEMENT CHOICES

Schuler (1987) emphasizes that there is not one best way to manage human resources; instead there are many alternative human resource management tools to choose from. Whether the choice a firm makes is effective will depend upon the competitive strategy of the firm. The key is to choose human resource management practices that support your objectives.

Table 6–2 summarizes many of the choices to be made. The choices are organized into five "menus," with each menu reflecting one aspect of human re-

source management (planning, staffing, appraising, compensating, and training and development). Notice that the choices to be made within each menu fall along a continuum. The choices are fairly self-explanatory, so we will not review them all here. Instead we will focus on the selection menu as an example. A detailed discussion of the choices can be found in Schuler (1987).

Recruiting Sources

The first staffing decision is, "Where to recruit?" One choice is to rely upon the internal labor market, which means recruiting primarily from within the department where a job opening exists or from other departments in the firm. Alternatively, a firm might rely upon the external labor market as its primary source of labor, filling job openings primarily by bringing new employees into the firm.

Internal recruitment is appropriate if a long-term commitment is desired because internal promotions provide important rewards. However, a possible drawback of internal recruitment is that new ideas are less likely to be brought into the firm, so creativity may suffer.

Career Paths

In general, broad career paths are appropriate for firms that need employees who are generalists, and narrow career paths are appropriate for firms that wish to encourage specialization. Both broad and narrow career paths can encourage skill acquisition, especially if combined with a policy of promotion from within.

Narrow career paths encourage employees to become technical experts and discourage employees from acquiring the range of skills that would ensure their flexibility and hence adaptability in times of major organizational change. Broad career paths, which are characterized by promotions across functional boundaries, encourage employees to become local experts for the firm as a whole and discourage maintenance of technical competencies.

The appropriate time frame for evaluating career progress is likely to be much longer for broad career paths than for narrow ones. In the short run, promotions may be quicker within narrow career paths, but in the long run opportunities for advancement may end at a lower level within the firm.

Table 6–2
Human Resource Management Menus

Planning Choices

Informal	Formal
Short Term	Long Term
Job Simplification	Job Enrichment
Low Employee Involvement	High Employee Involvement

Staffing Choices

Internal Sources	External Sources
Narrow Paths	Broad Paths
Explicit Criteria	Implicit Criteria
Limited Socialization	Extensive Socialization
Closed Procedures	Open Procedures

Appraising Choices

Behaviorial Criteria	Results Criteria
Purposes: Developmental, Remedial, Maintenance	
Short-term Criteria	Long-Term Criteria
Individual Criteria	Group Criteria

Compensating Choices

Low Base Salaries	High Base Salaries
Internal Equity	External Equity
Few Perks	Many Perks
Standard, Fixed Package	Flexible Package
No Incentives	Many Incentives
Short-Term Incentives	Long-Term Incentives
No Employment Security	High Employment Security

Training and Development

Short Term	Long Term
Narrow Application	Broad Application
Productivity Emphasis	Quality of Work Life Emphasis
Unplanned, Spontaneous	Planned, Systematic
Individual Orientation	Group Orientation

Selection Criteria

The criteria used for selecting employees to fill a job opening are a critical aspect of any staffing system. These criteria can range from explicit to implicit. Explicit criteria send clear messages to employees about which skills and achievements will be rewarded. These messages help motivated employees channel their energies in ways that increase their promotability. However, the price of clarity may be a loss in flexibility.

Explicit criteria send messages that tell employees how to prepare themselves for jobs as they exist in the company. But the skills needed for today's jobs may not be the same as those needed for tomorrow's jobs. Relying upon implicit criteria is one way to encourage employees to develop diverse sets of skills (rather than only those needed to do a particular job that currently exists).

Socialization

The amount of effort firms invest in socializing new job incumbents varies tremendously. Intensive socialization is called for when a firm's strategy depends upon employees who predictably follow prescribed procedures and/or employees who are psychologically committed to the goals of the firm. However, extended socialization and orientation can be expensive. In addition, intensive socialization practices may stifle creativity and risk taking if they communicate the message that there is one best way of doing things.

Openness

Open staffing procedures imply that employees are informed about available positions within the firm, usually through job postings. Job postings can serve many functions: they can increase the size of the applicant pool, which should make it easier to find a qualified person; they can inform employees about the skills needed for advancement, as well as the general availability of opportunities within the firm; and they increase the level of employee participation and involvement in the process. In offering more openness, however, the decision-making process slows down.

But as with each of the choices we have discussed, there are also benefits associated with the alternative choice. For example, by not posting openings, managers may feel more comfortable bringing in new talent from outside the firm. In addition, they may be able to make decisions more quickly if they are not compelled to leave a vacancy open the length of time required to give insiders a chance to apply. Finally, closed procedures can keep the pool of applicants small, thereby limiting the costs associated with evaluating applicants.

CASE EXAMPLES

Innovation at Frost, Inc.

Frost, Inc. is located in Grand Rapids, Michigan.[1] The firm manufactures overhead conveyor trolleys used for assembly line work in the auto industry. President Chad Frost worried about being dependent upon one cyclical industry and made several attempts to diversify his business. Several such attempts failed because engineers could not design new types of products, production people could not make them, and sales people could not sell them. Describing the inflexibility of his work force, Frost commented, "We had single-purpose machines and single-purpose people, including single-purpose managers."

To increase their flexibility, Frost decided to automate the production system. In addition to adding new machinery, they designed and built an automated storage-and-retrieval inventory control system. This would eventually be sold as one of their products. The increase in available computer equipment that resulted from automation of the factory floor also made it possible to automate the front office completely, which reduced indirect labor costs.

Frost clearly set out to pursue an innovation strategy. In the process, he adopted several human resource management practices that would support needed employee attitudes and behaviors and facilitate the change in strategy. For example, Frost realized early on that he needed his employees to identify with the new company and adopt a long-term perspective. To encourage this he gave each worker ten shares of closely held stock and set up a 401(d) plan for employees to make additional stock purchases. In addition, both a standard corporate profit-sharing plan and a discretionary profit-sharing plan were established.

To be successful, Frost needed to strike a balance between encouraging employees to focus on productivity results versus the manufacturing process. To encourage productivity, Frost instituted a quarterly bonus based upon company-wide productivity. By making the quarterly bonus dependent on company-wide productivity, Frost encourages cooperation and acceptance of interdependence. Cooperative attitudes and an open atmosphere are further supported by elimination of most executive perks, a reduction in the levels of hierarchy from eleven to four, and offices that have no doors. Forty terminals scattered throughout the facility give all employees access to the company's mainframe computer (only payroll information is off-limits).

A "celebration fund" was also established. Managers can tap this fund at their discretion. The effect is that managers have a resource for immediately rewarding exemplary behaviors, making it easy for them to communicate clearly that creativity and innovation are appropriate for the firm's new strategy. The creativeness of the rewards being given provides evidence that employees are receiving the message; they range from dinner with Chad Frost to belly-dancing performances at the office.

We have argued that an important component of an innovation strategy is getting employees to broaden their skills, assume responsibility, and take risks. To encourage skill development, Frost pays for extensive training programs offered by the company and by local colleges. Acquiring new skills is a prerequisite for advancement in the firm.

The case of Frost, Inc. illustrates how one firm used staffing practices, compensation, and training to develop a work force that could successfully implement an innovation strategy. The following case illustrates how the use of very different human resource management practices can support a low-cost strategy.

Keeping Costs Low at United Parcel Service

In an industry where "a package is a package," United Parcel Service (UPS) succeeds by a low-cost strategy. According to Larry P. Breakiron, senior vice-president of engineering, "Our ability to manage labor and hold it accountable is the key to success" (Machalaba, 1986).

To keep costs low, UPS uses work standards and work simplification, which is the key to its efficiency and productivity. Its methods date back to the 1920s, when founder James E. Casey hired the pioneers of time and motion study to measure the amount of time UPS drivers spent on various tasks during their workdays. UPS engineers cut away the sides of UPS trucks so they could watch how the drivers performed. These studies were used to establish work standards.

When inefficiencies were identified, the engineers eliminated them. During the day, employees engage in highly repetitive, short-term behaviors. Because specialists are used to identify the best way to accomplish tasks, employees do not participate in decisions about how to change their jobs. The result has been enormous improvements in employee efficiency, which translates into lower costs for UPS and lower fatigue for the employees.

Time and motion studies conducted by more than 1,000 industrial engineers are used by UPS to establish highly specified, efficient job behaviors. To ensure that efficient behaviors are maintained, UPS closely monitors the performance of its workers. In return for complying with the company's standards, UPS drivers, all of whom are Teamsters, earn salaries that are above those of drivers at most other companies. In addition, employees who perform adequately are assured of job security.

Honda's Quality Enhancement Strategy

An example of how human resource management practices can support a quality enhancement strategy is provided by Honda of America's plant at Marysville, Ohio. This plant, with a work force of approximately 4,500, produces cars of comparable quality to those built in Japan. The company has fewer layoffs and lower inventory rates than competitors, and sales have continued to grow while those of other U.S. manufacturers have faltered. How do they do it?

Honda knows that the delivery of quality products depends on the predictable and reliable performance of employees. This means absenteeism, tardiness, and turnover must all be minimized. To ensure reliability from its employees, Honda uses extensive employee socialization, which includes employees' spouses. Honda knows that new employees will experience fatigue during their first weeks on the job because their assembly line jobs require a variety of activities. Honda believes that if spouses are oriented to the demands and the needs of the company, they can decrease the probability of absenteeism and tardiness. Job security discourages turnover.

The importance of reliable attendance is further communicated to employees by clear rewards. For example, associates (employees) who have perfect attendance for several weeks receive special attendance bonuses. Attendance also influences the semi-annual bonuses, which are usually paid each spring and autumn.

In addition to reliability, Honda's human resource management practices encourage employees to adopt a long-term perspective and to be flexible in the face of change. Employment security, a policy of promotion from within, and constant formal and informal training programs facilitate these role attitudes and behaviors. Performance appraisals also support the training objectives, being developmental in focus rather than evaluational. Team leaders are trained to spot and remove performance deficiencies as they occur.

Cooperation and interdependence are fostered at Honda by an egalitarian management system. There are only four levels of hierarchy between associates on the plant floor and the plant manager. All associ-

ates wear identical uniforms, embossed with their first names. Parking spaces are unmarked. There is one cafeteria for everyone, and the modern health and sports facility is open to everyone. Except for a small shift differential, all entry-level associates are paid the same.

These human resource management practices encourage all employees to regard themselves as part of a collective enterprise. Without this underlying attitude, the flexible work hours, the air-conditioned plant, and the advanced automation would not be enough to sustain commitment and identification with the plant's high quality standards.

IMPLEMENTING THE FRAMEWORK

Our description of Frost, UPS, and Honda are intended as illustrations of how human resource management (HRM) practices can be used to encourage and support the attitudes and behaviors needed to implement three different competitive strategies. However, we do not wish to suggest that there is only one set of HRM practices found in organizations that are using each strategy. It is likely that a variety of practices will be found; some may even be contrary to those described here. This is because HRM practices are affected by many things besides a firm's competitive strategy. For example, its practices may reflect the values of top management, the laws of the land, what the competitors are doing, or what society values.

Consequently, to get to the point of tailoring HRM practices to a firm's competitive strategy, managers need to ask several questions. These questions can be clustered into three major groups. The first set of questions are those related to selecting which competitive strategy the organization should pursue; addressing these questions is beyond the scope of this chapter. The second set of questions are those that should be explored as the organization considers whether major changes are needed in the ways they are managing people, and whether the time is right for beginning the change process. The following questions belong to this second set:

1. What are your current HRM practices? Before thinking about change, you need to assess what *is*. When considering what your company does currently, table 6–2 may be helpful.

2. What are the determinants of your current HRM practices? Are there critical pieces of history in the firm that should be considered before trying to change current practices?

3. What is your competitive strategy? Because larger firms are often quite complex, it is possible that different units or divisions of the firm have different strategies.

4. What types of behaviors and attitudes are needed from employees for this strategy to be implemented? This is where you should find table 6–1 helpful.

5. Do any of your current practices need to be changed? If changes are needed, how can can they be accomplished? Will top management support the change?

6. Assuming top management sees the power behind your arguments for needed changes, what is the best way to proceed? If your firm has a participative culture, a great deal of employee involvement may be called for. Obviously, to proceed here you need to have a good handle on the current organizational culture.

7. Are you and your firm ready for change? Is everything frozen? Do things need to be unfrozen before going onward? Do you have the time and the money? To make extensive changes, a great deal of management time is necessary. A cost-benefits analysis may be appropriate. Are you able to conduct one?

Answering these questions is absolutely necessary before going ahead with the formulation and implementation of a plan for matching human resource management practices to a firm's competitive strategy. If, having considered these questions, you and your organizational colleagues decide to begin efforts designed to improve the alignment of your human resource management practices and your competitive strategy, then the process of implementing change can begin.

Elsewhere, we have explained in detail the steps involved in an organizational change process designed to align human resource management practices with strategic business needs (Schuler & Jackson, 1988; Schuler, 1989). Much of this change process involves a reorientation in the way both line managers and the human resource (HR) department staff view the HR department's role in the organization. One aspect of the new perspective needed is for the HR department to think of line managers as their customers—customers whose needs should be assessed are met to the extent possible. Line managers must, in turn, be willing to communicate their needs and be cooperative recipients of the services HR can offer. We use the term *customerization* to describe the reorientation and transformation that result in HR practices' becoming more closely tied to strategic business needs. Briefly, the steps involved in customerization are:

Step 1: Information gathering. The HR department gathers information from line managers. The focus during this step is on having line managers answer three questions: (1) "What are you—the customer—getting right now from the HR department?" (2) "What would you ideally like to be getting?" and (3) "How can you work together to change and improve the situation?"

Step 2: Developing agendas. Both the HR department and line managers develop action agendas, which lay out their visions of what changes are needed in the short term and in the longer-term future. During this step, goals and objectives are clarified.

Step 3: Implementing the action agendas. The HR

and line managers work together to prioritize their joint goals and come to agreement about what changes are needed in order for both parties to achieve the goals, who specifically will have what responsibilities for various aspects of the change process, and how and when the efforts at change will be evaluated. In many ways, step 3 involves developing a contract stating why, what, how, and when changes are to occur.

Step 4: Evaluating and revising the agendas. As each element of change is completed, it is important to evaluate the results using the criteria agreed to during step 3.

Organizations are dynamic systems, and they face a constantly changing environment. Consequently, change efforts such these should be viewed as fluid and ongoing. At the very least, fine tuning will be necessary as the firm tailors and adapts its competitive strategy to the environment. In some cases, however, major changes in competitive strategy may signal the need for a complete overhaul of the human resource management system. Such changes are extremely complex. They require extensive planning (see Jackson & Schuler, in press) and can take years to implement (see Banas, 1988). Thus, effective realignment efforts must begin as soon as a change in competitive strategy has been decided upon.

It is clear that to be successful in achieving large-scale HR changes designed to facilitate a firm's competitive strategy, an HR department must have the support and cooperation of line managers who understand the logic of how competitive strategies can affect decisions related to the design of HR systems.

NOTE

1. These three case descriptions are adapted from Schuler & Jackson (1987).

REFERENCES

Banas, P.A. (1988). Employee involvement: A sustained labor/management initiative at Ford Motor Company. In J.P. Campbell et al., *Productivity in organizations.* San Francisco: Jossey-Bass.

Brandt, S.C. (1986). *Entrepreneuring in established companies.* Homewood, IL: Dow Jones–Irwin.

DeLuca, J.R. (1988). Strategic career management in non-growing, volatile business environments. *Human Resource Planning, 11,* 49–62.

Drucker, P.F. (1985). *Innovation and entrepreneurship.* New York: Harper & Row.

Jackson, S.E., & Schuler, R.S. (in press). The state of human resource planning: Challenges for industrial/organizational psychologists. *American Psychologist.*

Kanter, R.M. (1983). Change masters and the intricate architecture of corporate culture change. *Management Review* (October), 18–28.

Kanter, R.M. (1985). Supporting innovation and venture

development in established companies. *Journal of Business Venturing* (Winter), 47–60.

Machalaba, D. (1986). United Parcel Service gets delivery done by driving its workers. *Wall Street Journal* (April 22), 1, 23.

MacMillan, I.C. (1983). Seizing competitive initiative. *Journal of Business Strategy,* 43–57.

Pinchot, G., III (1984). Entrepreneurship: How to top corporate creative energies. *Mainstream, 1* (2).

Porter, M.E. (1985). *Competitive advantage.* New York: Free Press.

Rutigliano, A.J. (1986). Managing the new: An interview with Peter Drucker. *Management Review* (January), 38–41.

Schuler, R.S. (1987). Human resource management practice choices. *Human Resource Planning* (March), 1–19.

Schuler, R.S. (1989). A case study of the HR department at Swiss Bank Corporation: Customerization for organizational effectiveness. *Human Resource Planning 11,* 241–253.

Schuler, R.S., & Jackson, S.E. (1987). Linking competitive strategies with human resource management practices. *Academy of Management Executive, 1* (3), 207–219.

Schuler, R.S., & Jackson, S.E. (1988). Customerization. *Personnel* (June), 35–44.

Staff of AMA Human Resources Periodicals (1987). Highlights of AMA's 58th Annual Human Resources Conference: Restructuring for competitive advantage. *Personnel* (October), 24–34.

7 EFFECTIVE ORGANIZATIONS IN THE TWENTY-FIRST CENTURY

Stephen M. Colarelli, Terry A. Beehr

What will effective organizations look like in the next century? These are questions that should engage anyone who has a stake in an organization. Although it is tempting to speculate about novel, utopian forms of organizations in the next century, we weave no such fantasies. An effective organization in the twenty-first century will be essentially the same as an effective organization in the twentieth century or, for that matter, in the first century B.C. What changes are the problems, technologies, and social contexts.

This chapter has three objectives: to describe the functions essential for effective organization, to present critical trends that will affect organizations in the future, and to suggest how organizations can prepare for these changes in order to stay effective in the next century.

WHAT IS AN EFFECTIVE ORGANIZATION?

Organizational effectiveness can be conceptualized in a number of ways (Daft, 1983, pp. 80ff.; Goodman & Pennings, 1977). We view organizational effectiveness as a three-tiered hierarchy (table 7–1). The levels in the hierarchy are survival, sustained viability, and higher values.

Survival

The first level is survival. Organizations that survive are more effective than those that perish. Survival of any living system is based on whether the system takes in as much or more energy (resources) than it uses (cf. Yuchtman & Seashore, 1967). For example, organisms that burn more energy than they take in starve; organizations that spend more money than they make go bankrupt. Organizations that use as much energy as they take in lead a precarious, hand-to-mouth existence. It is only when organizations take in more resources than they use—when they have slack—that they become capable of attaining higher levels of effectiveness. Slack resources give organizations the time and resources to think, experiment, make mistakes, train their people, and renew

Table 7–1
Components of Organizational Effectiveness

Survival	Does the organization take in as many or more resources than it uses?
Sustained viability	Adaptation to the environment Goal attainment Integration Cultural pattern maintenance
Higher values	Does the organization benefit its community and society? Does it advance civilization? Are its leaders civilized men and women? Do its leaders support higher values?

their energies. However, a word of caution is due here. Slack resources are necessary but not sufficient for attaining higher levels of effectiveness. Resources need to be used intelligently.

Sustained Viability

The next level of effectiveness is sustained viability. This level of effectivenes is based on an organization's performing four functions (Parsons, 1951): adapting to its environment, developing and attaining goals,

We thank Lawrence Brunner, Department of Economics, Central Michigan University, for economic references, ideas, and stimulating conversation.

integrating internal components, and developing and maintaining cultural patterns.

To obtain resources, an effective organization must adapt to its environment. The first step is to define its environment—which segments have the resources? It also monitors its environment and creates environments—that is, it alters its environment to become more munificent, manageable, or predictable. Table 7–2 shows how nonadaptive organizations quickly lose their dominant positions.

Goal attainment depends first on the development of appropriate goals. Such goals are based on a realistic assessment of the organization's needs, capabilities to fulfill those needs, and an accurate assessment of the availability of resources. Organizations also need means for developing strategies to achieve goals and means for implementing strategies. Methods for achieving goals include organizing internal components and directing individual behavior. Organizing includes structuring organizations, designing jobs, and allocating resources. Directing human behavior includes selection, training, development, and motivational programs (figure 7–1).

Table 7–2
Ten Largest Industrial Firms, 1909–1984

Rank		Firms
1909	1984	
1	15	U. S. Steel Corp. (now USX Corp.)
2	1	Standard Oil Co. (New Jersey) (now Exxon)
3	84	American Tobacco Co. (now Americand Brands)
4	a	International Mercantile Marine Co.
5	a	Anaconda Co.
6	79	International Harvester Co. (now Navistar)
7	a	Central Leather Company
8	a	Pullman Inc.
9	a	Armour & Co.
10	a	American Sugar Refining Co.

Source: Bach (1987, p. 405). Reprinted with permission of *Fortune,* © 1984 Time Inc. All rights reserved; and the Brookings Institution.
a No longer in top 100 firms.

Figure 7–1. Mechanism for Goal Attainment

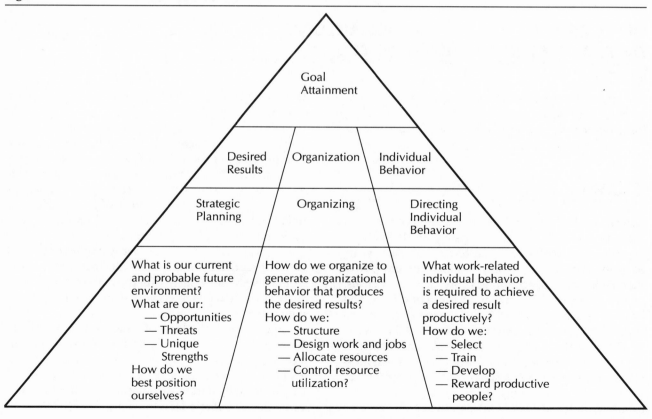

Source: Colarelli, Meyer & Associates, Inc., St. Louis, Missouri. Reprinted with permission.

Integration is the processes by which collaboration, cooperation, and communication take place among diverse organizational components. It is "creating and maintaining 'solidarity,' despite the emotional strains involved in the processes of goal attainment and the manner of sharing the fruits of cooperation" (Morse, 1961, p. 114). Primary mechanisms for achieving integration are values, structures, and policies that promote communication and cohesion.

Cultural pattern maintenance involves "restoring, maintaining, or creating the energies, motives, and values of the cooperating units" (Morse, 1961, p. 114). Effective organizations maintain a reasonable degree of cultural continuity. Organizations that remain effective pass on functional cultural patterns. They develop, transmit, and maintain appropriate beliefs, values, motives, and norms as long as they are useful to survival (Schein, 1985).

Higher Values

At the highest level, organizational effectiveness involves the promotion of higher values. These are values that go beyond producing the products that are responsible for organizational survival. Higher values include contributions to education, the arts, literacy, health, the environment, and community life. Indications of the promotion of higher values include: How does an organization benefit its community and society? Does it advance civilization? Are its leaders civilized men and women? Do its leaders support higher values?

Some argue that the business of business is to create wealth; the promotion of higher values is the purview of government, foundations, universities, and other nonprofit organizations. We disagree. Business organizations exist within a larger social and cultural context. The quality of society influences the quality of business enterprise. Businesses that want a high-quality work force contribute money, time, and talent to education; those that desire civilized employees contribute to cultural life; and support of ethical politics by business promotes stable political life. In the short term, contributing to higher values may have little effect on an organization's well-being. However, over the long term, it is in business organizations' best interest to promote a healthy, civilized society.

CHANGES FACING ORGANIZATIONS IN THE TWENTY-FIRST CENTURY

In applying psychology to business in the next century, areas of particular importance are the work force, jobs, unions, government regulations, economic issues, and social trends.

The Work Force

Education. The overall level of education of the work force in the United States is rising. In 1959, 15.5 percent of the work force had fewer than eight years of schooling; in 1979, only 4.4 percent had fewer than eight years of schooling (Bureau of the Census, 1980). In 1959, 9.6 percent of the work force had bachelor's degrees; in 1984, the percentage increased to 20.9 (Bureau of Labor Statistics, 1985). Since 1981–1982, the number of women earning bachelor's degrees has surpassed that of men (Center for Education Statistics, 1987). Significant proportions of women are also earning professional degrees—for example, in 1983–1984, 30 percent of all master's degrees in business administration were earned by women.

Fewer college graduates are receiving degrees in liberal arts, while increasing numbers are graduating in technical and professional fields (Center for Education Statistics, 1987). While the production of technicians may have short-term benefits, the same cannot be said for the long term. The half-life of scientific and technical information is short and getting shorter, while the analytical and communication skills learned in a liberal arts curriculum last a lifetime. Howard (1986) found that managers with liberal arts backgrounds were more successful throughout a period of thirty years than managers with degrees in business or engineering.

Even though the level of education is increasing, many indicators point to a decline in the quality of secondary education in the United States. Approximately 57 percent of seventeen-year-olds in school are functionally illiterate or marginally literate (Committee for Economic Development, 1985). This is in stark contrast with Japan—America's strongest economic competitor—where high school completion and literacy are the highest in the world—nearly 100 percent (Committee for Economic Development, 1985). The marginally literate high school students of today portend a poorly qualified work force for tomorrow.

Diversity. The twenty-first century will see increasing diversity in the work force, particularly in the managerial, technical, and professional occupations. In 1972, the percentages of women who were managers, attorneys, and accountants were 18, 4, and 22, respectively. In 1985, these percentages increased to 36, 18, and 44 (Bureau of the Census, 1978, 1986). Similarly, the percentage of minorities entering the ranks of the managerial, professional, and technical work force is increasing. There has always been ethnic diversity in the semiskilled and unskilled labor force, as it is the source of jobs for newly arrived immigrants. Changes are occurring, however, in the skilled work force, with more women and minorities entering the skilled trades.

The ethnic composition of the population of the United States will be different in the twenty-first century. The minority segments of the population will grow, while the percentage of whites will decline. For example, in 1960, 10 percent of the population was black, and 87 percent of the population was white. By the year 2000, the percentages are projected to change to 13 and 83, respectively (Bureau of the Census, 1986).

Aging of the Work Force. The work force is aging. In 1960, 9 percent of the work force was over sixty-five; it is estimated that 13 percent of the work force will be over sixty-five in the year 2000. In 1960, 55 percent of the work force was under thirty-five; in the year 2000, that percentage will have dropped to forty-seven (Bureau of the Census, 1986).

Women in the Work Force. The single most significant change in the composition of the work force may be the influx of large numbers of women. In 1950, 34 percent of the employable female population were working outside the home. In 1985, the percentage leaped to 55 percent. In 1960, 19 percent of married women with children under six were employed; in 1986, the percentage increased to 54. While participation of women in the work force is not new (during World War II, much of the industrial work force was female), the large proportion of women who will be permanent members of the work force is unique in the history of Western industrialized countries. Many

women may also advance into positions of considerable authority, which has not been the case in the past.

Jobs

Jobs in the twenty-first century will have three prominent features. With a shift toward a service economy, fewer workers will be dealing with machines and more workers will be dealing with people. The age of high technology and information also means that work will become increasingly complex and specialized. Finally, the rapid emergence of new types of jobs and changes in extant jobs will become commonplace. Changes in jobs and the aging of the work force also portend multiple careers and frequent retraining for the average worker.

Unions

Traditional strongholds of union membership, manufacturing and transportation, will continue to decline in the twenty-first century. On the other hand, the unionization of government employees, lower-level professionals, and service employees should rise (Bureau of the Census, 1986).

Middle and lower-level managers may unionize. With frequent mergers, buy-outs, and downsizing, the wholesale firing of managers—once considered taboo—is becoming commonplace. Eighty-hour weeks and corporate loyalty no longer ensure career progress; middle management status no longer guarantees job security. Blocked mobility occurring simultaneously with rising expectations (a product of increased education) is a recipe for disillusionment and hostility. Disillusioned managers may turn to unions for leverage to gain the rewards they expect.

Government Regulations

Government will play an increasing role in the regulation of business in the twenty-first century, despite the current swing toward conservatism and protestations from the business community about government interference. History shows a trend of increasing government regulation of business, with business losing the majority of its battles with government (Levitt, 1968). With an increasingly interdependent polity, government is needed to mediate disputes; it responds to social and political problems through the creation of laws, which tend to be cumulative. Government, not business, is a prime architect of political values, which are embodied in law. With the growing political, educational, and economic enfranchisement of the common person, expectations for social and economic rights will continue to rise. Government regulation of business should also increase in health, safety, equal employment opportunity, and job security; government policy may also encourage business to participate in employee stock ownership plans (ESOPs).

The Economy

The Service Economy. A service is a product whose value depends on the quality of how it is mediated from the seller to the buyer. By 1984 the service sector was responsible for "74 percent of all nonfarm jobs . . . and 69 percent of all national income" (Heskett, 1986, p. 3). The transition to the service economy has two important implications for the manager. The first is that human talent will become the prime ingredient for competing in the marketplace. Since the value of service is determined primarily by how it is mediated to the customer, highly developed skills are crucial for day-to-day performance. The second implication is that the ability to deal effectively with people will become a critical skill for the majority of the work force in a service economy.

The Global Economy. The next century will usher in a global economic order. The transition has already begun. In 1960, $4 billion in U.S. assets were abroad, and $2 billion in foreign assets were in the United States; in 1986, $29 billion in U.S. assets were abroad, and $69 billion in foreign assets were in the United States (Council of Economic Advisers, 1987). The global economy portends unprecedented economic and social interdependencies among the community of nations, competition among organizations from different countries, and the increasing dominance of multinational corporations. Managers who understand foreign cultures and who can deal effectively in an international environment will have a strong advantage.

Technology. Technological advances will be a hallmark of the twenty-first century, and three will be particularly important for managing: the computer, communication systems, and robotics. The computer enables managers to process more information more efficiently. However, the computer poses two threats: information overload and succumbing to the mystique of the computer (assuming that the information must be high quality because it was generated by a sophisticated machine). Managers without a sense of priorities and values will be no better off with a computer than they would be with an abacus. Communication technology is and will continue to enable managers to communicate more widely, more often, and more efficiently with their work force and customers. Robotics will come into its own in the twenty-first century. Many manufacturing jobs once performed by human hands will be done by robots. This offers the potential for freeing humans from hazardous and repetitive work.

The Size of Organizations. Partly because of mergers, the trend is for large manufacturing firms to increase in numbers of employees as well as share of assets and sales (Bach, 1987). On the other hand, the number of small businesses is also increasing (Bureau of the Census, 1977, 1986). With the largest organizations dominating major markets, these markets will be less competitive. Innovative small businesses—with their ability to respond quickly to changing conditions and generate innovations—should survive. Medium-sized firms may face the greatest threats to survival.

Social Trends

A number of social trends will also affect the psychology of work and organization, including changes in family life, attitudes about work and organizations, religious attitudes, geographic mobility, and the consumer ethic.

The Family. Profound changes are occurring in the American family. The birthrate per 1,000 women in 1950 was 118; the corresponding number in 1984 was 65. The composition of the household has also changed. At the turn of the twentieth century, an extended household was common. In the mid-twentieth century, a nuclear family was common. In the late twentieth century, the single-parent family is commonplace. Births to unmarried women rose from 5.3 to 21 percent of all births from 1960 to 1984. The percentage of divorced individuals tripled from 1970 to 1985—from 4.3 to 13.1 percent (Bureau of the Census, 1986). What are some of the implications for work organizations of a changing family structure? More women, including women of childbearing age and women with young children, will be full-time members of the work force. The pool of good managers may shrink. Better managers typically come from larger families, where they learn to deal with many people and work in a team (Kotter, 1982). Also, will children with a tenuous family life develop the self-confidence necessary to perform successfully throughout their working careers? Will infants and preschoolers from families where both parents work full time receive the cognitively challenging attention that maximizes mental growth? Will children of single, economically disadvantaged females have access to the services (music lessons, private tutors), activities (athletics, trips to museums or plays), and products (books, magazines, chemistry sets, musical instruments) that foster intellect and character?

Geographical Mobility. Geographic mobility is increasing. Fixed ties to communities may lessen in the next century. With fewer ties to a community and to a geographical location, individuals may look more to their workplace for a sense of identity, as Durkheim (1893/1964) predicted almost 100 years ago. A sense of community will come from colleagues at work rather than neighbors or religious brethren. Increased geographical mobility therefore may work to the advantage of locally established elites and to the disadvantage of migratory workers of all stripes, including professionals and managers. Individuals who stay put, develop business relationships, and thoroughly learn an environment are in a better position to control local resources and thus have power over more migratory individuals.

Rising Expectations about Work Life. While most people still work to survive, the advent of unemployment insurance, severance pay, unions, relatively full employment, and a stable economy have created a wider psychological gap between work for survival and work for psychological rewards. People will therefore expect a better quality of work life from their employers. Yet not all difficult, dangerous, and meaningless work will be automated. Employers may turn more to overseas (third world) labor markets and alien laborers in the United States to do the type of work that an educated and sophisticated work force refuses to do.

Religion. In one way or another, business (and political) organizations benefit from religion—primarily as a source of values (the Protestant work ethic, respect for authority, morality). Yet religiosity and church attendance are in decline in the United States (Bureau of the Census, 1986). Less religiosity among the population suggests that management will need to turn to other sources for higher values and will need other sources to inculcate functional values in their employees.

Paradox of a Consumer Society. Consumers are essential to economic growth in industrial and postindustrial economies, but a society with a consumer mentality does not have the values and drive of a producer society (McCraw, 1988). To ensure the existence of a productive cadre, organizations may manage the values of their employees to create a two-tier society, such as the Eloi and the Morlocks in H.G. Wells's novel, *The Time Machine*. The elite, producer class would be spartan, ambitious, thoughtful, and productive. The consuming class could be relied upon to get routine work done, but its primary function would be to consume and fuel the economy.

IMPLICATIONS FOR ORGANIZATIONAL EFFECTIVENESS IN THE TWENTY-FIRST CENTURY

Effective organizations will respond to changing conditions to ensure the performance of the four functions essential to organizational effectiveness. In the twenty-first century, this will require a focus on leadership, the structure of executive work, organizational design, and mechanisms for talent development and organizational socialization.

Leadership

Many executives are disappointed with the current quality of business leadership in America. In a survey of nearly 4,000 of its readers, the *Harvard Business Review* (1987) reported that 92 percent of those surveyed believe that U.S. competitiveness is declining, and "almost 90% place the burden on the shoulders of U. S. managers" (p. 25). The responsibility for organizational effectiveness rests with an organization's leadership. What qualities will be demanded of men and women who can effectively lead organizations in the twenty-first century? The next century will demand business leaders who are liberally educated, civil, and courageous.

Liberally Educated Leaders. In the next century, organizations will face increasing foreign competition, diversity in the workplace, government regulation, and specialization in the work force. Leaders with a broad perspective will manage best in such an environment. Leaders who have a liberal arts background—

in history, politics, literature, foreign affairs—will best understand foreign cultures and perspectives, work most effectively with a diverse array of customers, colleagues, and subordinates, and view their organizations in a historical and systems context.

A liberal arts education prepares individuals to see trends and not just facts, to look forward and backward, to deal with nonquantifiable problems (Weeden, 1987), and communicate with a diverse constituency. One of the qualities that has contributed to the success of many executives is their ability to communicate—to talk with anyone about anything. Interacting with a diverse constituency helps leaders with integration and goal achievement. For example, smooth interaction among top managers is instrumental in effective strategy formulation (Miller, 1987).

One of the greatest leaders of all time, Julius Caesar, was a literature "major." Literature was a key ingredient in the education of ancient Rome's ruling class because "literature [is] 'a representation of our manners in the characters of others and [is] a vivid picture of our daily life' " (Kahn, 1986, p. 33).

Civility. In the industrial age when labor was inexpensive, unskilled, and uncivilized, fear was a fairly effective motivator. In the twenty-first century, labor will be educated, expensive, professional, and gentle. In this environment civility will be a critical ingredient in managing employees. When asked what how he managed his climb to the top, IBM chairman John Akers (Byrne, 1984, p. 246) said: "by being nice to everybody."

Courage. Courageous leaders have a clear vision for themselves and their organization and can pursue that vision relentlessly. Ultimately, the success of any organization depends on its ability to exploit the environment to garner resources. This demands courageous leaders, and some suggest that this is precisely what American business is lacking (Hornstein, 1986). The changes in the twenty-first century therefore call for heroic leaders who challenge human capacities and boldly face their environments. Such leaders are men and women with a clear sense of mission and the ability to evolve and effect bold plans.

The Structure of Executive Work

To manage effectively, managers need time to think. Unfortunately, busyness (working eighty-hour weeks, constantly on the move, never-ending meetings) has become a benchmark of toughness in twentieth-century business life. The frenetic manager who spends almost no time thinking, reading, writing serious material, or planning has become glorified in the academic (Mintzberg, 1973) and popular management literatures. American managers seem to believe that "busier is better." Yet thinking, reflection, and planning are the keys to effective action, especially with the complexity of work and technology and the world economy. This is not to say that action is inappropriate: thoughtful action is more appropriate than thoughtless action.

Organizations that dominate in the twenty-first century will be those that value and reward clear thinking. Effective organizations will structure executive work so that managers, especially those at higher levels, have time to think. Outstanding leaders know the importance of giving themselves time to think, relax, and renew their energies. Three of the modern world's most influential leaders—John D. Rockefeller, Sr., Winston Churchill, and Ronald Reagan—structured their work to ensure sufficient time for thought, rest, and renewal. John D. Rockefeller did not "work with health-wreaking intensity. . . . 'Ever since I was married,' he said in 1917, 'I have made it a practice to lie down in the afternoon and take a brief nap' " (Nevins, 1940, p. 233). Churchill's afternoon naps are legendary (Brendon, 1984, P. 165), as are Ronald Reagan's eight-hour workdays and regular vacations (Weisman, 1984).

Organizational Structures and Processes

Five types of organizational structures and processes will characterize effective organizations in the twenty-first century: (1) contingency organizing, (2) participative decision making, (3) work organizations becoming total institutions, (4) increasing emphasis on research and development (R&D), and (5) linking human resource programs to corporate strategy.

Contingency Organizing. Adaptation to the environment depends on effective information processing (Galbraith, 1973) and focusing energy on high-priority goals. Thus, effective organizations will be flexible in their approach to organizing, developing structures contingent upon strategic objectives and the complexity of their environments.

Participative Decision Making. As the economy and organizations become more knowledge based, vital knowledge will be located throughout all levels of the organization. Participative decision-making mechanisms will be necessary to ensure that good decisions are made. In addition to its effect on the quality of decisions, participation helps maintain the morale of an educated work force. Finally, participation by employees will be an important counter-control to poor decisions. Counter-control provides checks on the quality of decisions made at the top and keeps power from deteriorating into brutality. Traditionally, counter-control came from influential stockholders, boards of directors, and market forces. In the twenty-first century, a source of counter-control will be an educated work force. The degree of participation of employees in decisions affecting their work lives has increased over the past 200 years. Effective organizations in the twenty-first century will not resist this trend but will work with it and use it to their benefit.

Work organizations as Total Institutions. Effective organizations in the twenty-first century will become total institutions involved in the nonfinancial needs of their employees. Because of the continuing breakdown of social institutions, work organizations will take up the slack with, for example, day care and preschool facilities for working parents and health care and wellness programs for all employees.

Research and Development. With the increasing importance of science and technology to the economy and to organizational competitiveness, R&D must be given more priority. The importance of this is aptly summarized by one manager's comments to the *Harvard Business Review* survey on competitiveness: "I believe that the winner will be the country which educates and demands the most of its engineers and scientists and which has the foresight to utilize the funds for R&D" (1987, p. 26).

The global economy and the growth of knowledge put a premium on innovation. As a result, effective organizations in the twenty-first century will also concentrate R&D efforts on production innovation and on ways to mobilize human resources to increase productivity (Hage, 1988).

Linking Human Resource Programs to Strategy. Because of the importance of human resources to productivity in the next century, effective organizations will routinely integrate human resource technologies and planning with corporate strategy. Just as an organization's financial plans are linked to overall corporate strategy, plans for the acquisition, development, and movement of human resources will become essential components of corporate strategy (Rousseau, 1988).

Talent Development and Organizational Socialization

The core technology of the next century will be talented people. Developing talented employees takes years. This will occur through increased involvement of the business sector in public education, more on-the-job training, and career development programs.

Increasing Business Involvement in Public Education Systems. A literate work force will be the most important economic resource in the twenty-first century. It will be in business's self-interest to take a leading role in improving public education in primary and secondary schools (Committee for Economic Development, 1985). Good education takes money and sound management to ensure that resources are used effectively.

On-the-Job Training. Training in organizations is already big business and will become bigger and more important in the next century. Jobs are likely to change rapidly, and to stay competitive, employers will have to ensure that employees continually update their skills. Moreover, as the human element becomes critical to productivity, training will be as important to productivity in the twenty-first century as machine maintenance was during the early twentieth century. Training systems in effective organizations will be integrated into all business functions, will be part of the work experience, and will be part of every manager's job—a critical management responsibility.

Career Development. As human talent becomes important to organizational effectiveness, career development programs will grow in stature. Developing human talent takes time and careful planning. Moreover, career development programs will be useful in attracting and keeping good people. Talented individuals want to work in organizations that make a commitment to developing skills throughout a career.

Mechanisms for Socialization. According to a recent *Harvard Business Review* (1987) survey, the deterioration of traditional values—on the part of both management and employees—is an important cause for America's declining competitiveness. As one manager said: "[The] decline of competitiveness is due not only to economic reasons but also to deep social issues like the breakdown of pride in self, family, and society. Only when you have these can you make quality products and be competitive in the long run" (p. 26).

Socialization programs in organizations will become instrumental in inculcating values into the work force in the twenty-first century. Cultural systems that develop work values congruent with the changing business environment will be important to organizational effectiveness (see, for example, Schneider & Rentsch, 1988). In addition, business schools will play an increasingly important role. While business schools have traditionally taught hard business skills, they will increasingly focus on the socialization of students and liberal arts. Many business schools are adding subjects such as international relations, world civilizations, foreign languages, communication, manners, and ethics to their M.B.A. curricula (Main, 1989). A recent study by Dreher, Dougherty, and Whitely (1985) suggests that the value of a graduate business education may have as much to do with socialization as with acquiring functional skills.

CONCLUDING REMARKS

Organizations that dominate in the twenty-first century, will—like effective organizations in all previous periods of history—be those that adapt to their environment, develop and achieve realistic goals, integrate internal components, and maintain functional cultural patterns.

To do so rests upon an organization's ability and willingness to monitor its external and internal environments, anticipate changes, and set and pursue appropriate objectives. Managers who take the time to think, ponder the future, and anticipate trends will be the managers who are best prepared for the twenty-first century.

REFERENCES

Bach, G.L. (1987). *Economics.* 11th ed. Englewood Cliffs, NJ: Prentice-Hall.

Brendon, P. (1984). *Winston Churchill: A biography.* New York: Harper & Row.

Bureau of the Census (1977). *County business patterns 1974.* Washington, DC: U.S. Government Printing Office.

Bureau of the Census (1978). *Statistical abstract of the United States 1978* (99th ed.). Washington, DC: U.S. Government Printing Office.

Bureau of the Census (1980). *Social indicators III.* Washington, DC: U.S. Government Printing Office.

Bureau of the Census (1986). *County business patterns 1984.* Washington, DC: U.S. Government Printing Office.

Bureau of the Census (1986). *Statistical abstract of the United States 1987* (107th ed.). Washington, DC: U.S. Government Printing Office.

Bureau of Labor Statistics (1985). *Handbook of labor statistics.* Bulletin 2217. Washington, DC: U.S. Government Printing Office.

Byrne, J.A. (1984). Be nice to everybody. *Forbes,* (November 5), 244–246.

Center for Education Statistics (1987). *Digest of education statistics 1987.* Washington, DC: U.S. Government Printing Office.

Committee for Economic Development. (1985). *Investing in our children.* New York: Author.

Council of Economic Advisers (1987). *Economic report of the President.* Washington, DC: U.S. Government Printing Office.

Daft, R.L. (1983). *Organization theory and design.* St. Paul, MN: West.

Durkheim, E. (1893/1964). *The division of labor in society.* New York: Free Press.

Dreher, G.F., Dougherty, T.W., & Whitely, B. (1985). Generalizability of MBA degree and socioeconomic effects on business school graduates' salaries. *Journal of Applied Psychology, 70,* 769–773.

Galbraith, J. (1973). *Designing complex organizations.* Reading, MA: Addison-Wesley.

Goodman, P.S., & Pennings, J.M. (Eds.). (1977). *New perspectives on organizational effectiveness.* San Francisco: Jossey-Bass.

Hage, J. (1988). The new rules of competition. In J. Hage (Ed.), *Futures of organizations* (1–24). Lexington, MA: Lexington Books.

Harvard Business Review (1987). Competitiveness survey: HBR readers respond. *Harvard Business Review* (May–June), 24–27.

Heskett, J.L. (1986). *Managing in the service economy.* Boston: Harvard Business School Press.

Hornstein, H.E. (1986). *Managerial courage: Revitalizing your company without sacrificing your job.* New York: Wiley.

Howard, A. (1986). College experiences and managerial performance. *Journal of Applied Psychology, 71,* 530–552.

Kahn, A.D. (1986). *The education of Julius Caesar.* New York: Schocken.

Kotter, J.P. (1982). General managers are not generalists. *Organizational Dynamics,* (Spring), 5–19.

Levitt, T. (1968). Why business always loses. *Harvard Business Review* (March–April), 81–89.

McCraw, T.K. (Ed.). (1988). *America versus Japan: A comparative study.* Boston: Harvard Business School Press.

Main, J. (1989). B-schools get a global vision. *Fortune* (July 17), 78–86.

Miller, D. (1987). Strategy making and structure: Analysis and implications for performance. *Academy of Management Journal, 30,* 7–32.

Mintzberg, H. (1973). *The nature of managerial work.* New York: Harper & Row.

Morse, C. (1961). The functional imperatives. In M. Black (Ed.), *The social theories of Talcott Parsons* (100–152). Carbondale, IL: Southern Illinois University Press.

Nevins, A. (1940). *John D. Rockefeller.* New York: Scribner's.

Parsons, T. (1951). *The social system.* New York: Free Press.

Rousseau, D.M. (1988). Human resource planning for the future. In J. Hage (Ed.), *Futures of Organizations* (245–266). Lexington, MA: Lexington Books.

Schein, E.H. (1985). *Organizational culture and leadership.* San Francisco: Jossey-Bass.

Schneider, B., & Rentsch, J. (1988). Managing climates and cultures: A futures perspective. In J. Hage (Ed.), *Futures of organizations* (181–203). Lexington, MA: Lexington Books.

Weeden, E.T. (1987). In a multidimensional world, humanists think multidimensionally. *Chronical of Higher Education,* (September 2), B-4.

Weisman, S.R. (1984). Can the magic prevail? *New York Times Magazine,* (April 29), pp. 38–56.

Yuchtman, E., & Seashore, S.E. (1967). A system resource approach to organizational effectiveness. *American Sociological Review, 32,* 891–903.

PART II

APPLIED MEASUREMENT AND LEGAL GUIDELINES

8 THE DOLLAR PRODUCTIVITY IMPACT OF HUMAN RESOURCE INVESTMENTS

Brian D. Steffy

Personnel specialists have become interested in measuring the dollar-productivity value of personnel practices and policies (Brief, 1984; Cascio, 1982; Dunnette & Fleishman, 1982; Flamholtz, 1985; Fitz-Enz, 1984; Werther, Ruch & McClure, 1986). For purposes here, *productivity* is defined as the act of creating economic value to, or the asset value of, the firm (Kendrick, 1984; Kopelman, 1986). Personnel investments potentially increase a firm's value if the personnel expenses incurred in some base period lead to an incremental increase in the future service value of employees, assuming that the revenue flows associated with the change in service contributions exceed the costs of generating those revenues (Flamholtz, 1985).

According to personnel psychology, personnel programs affect a firm's economic value because they increase the acquisition and retention of better-performing individuals, hence securing greater future service potential of employees. Economists and accounting theorists, however, not operating from an individual level of analysis but at the level of the firm or market, caution that increases in firm-specific economic value may not necessarily follow increases in human performance (Viren, 1979). These literatures account for influences not typically entertained by personnel psychologists. For example, both labor economists and accountants suggest that economic value is principally embodied not in individuals but in the job (Flamholtz, 1985; Joll et al., 1982; Thurow, 1975; Viren, 1979), its value defined by the wages and other labor costs (opportunity costs) required to obtain some base rate of "successful" job performance. Individuals do not possess economic value, but a service contribution, or *use value,* which the firm "rents" and which enacts the value embodied in the job. But because individuals differ in their productive capacity, some employees may enact higher or lower values relative to the expected economic value of successful performance. That is, individuals' use values vary around this expected job value. Following this logic, personnel activities are productive to the degree to which they result either in an upward shift of the distribution of individuals' use values above the base rate of success or result in a modification of performance variance such that there is a truncation of the distribution below the expected value. From this perspective it is also possible to speculate as to what institutional and market factors may enhance or constrain the human asset creation potential of personnel activities. For example, it is suggested that the value-additive potential is anchored by the job's marginal revenue product (MRP) and the potential for variance in individual use values. These constraints, as well as others, will be more fully discussed in later sections.

This chapter will focus on efforts to measure the monetary impact of personnel activities that have surfaced in labor economics, accounting, and industrial psychology. To date, each discipline has remained largely parochial (Bemmels, 1984). Labor economics and accounting typically ignore individual differences but favor an analysis of aggregate market and institutional behavior (Kendrick, 1984). Personnel psychology, on the other hand, has typically ignored the institutional and market factors that constrain payoff. This chapter rejects a parochial perspective and emphasizes a multidisciplinary approach to productivity modeling, or what Wallace (1983) calls a "vertical synthesis" of the individual, job, institutional, and market levels of analysis. To accomplish this, four approaches to human productivity conceptualization and measurement are discussed: firm-specific human capital, human resource accounting, behavior costing, and utility analysis. Productivity indexes are not addressed; although these output-input ratios provide an audit of the "efficiency" of the personnel function, they fail to provide a dollar interpretation of the effects of specific programs. The intent of this chapter is not to provide a comprehensive review of all productivity measures but to draw from various disciplines so as to provide a broad framework from which new directions in model building and empirical research can be construed. Before discussing the four approaches, I outline a sample of measurement issues that have surfaced across a number of these approaches and facilitate an analysis of the strengths and limitations of each approach, as well as suggesting where research attention may be required: (1) the purpose of measurement, (2) the representation of time-related phenomena, (3) the problem of dollar valuation, and (4) the feasibility and face validity of measurement.

MEASUREMENT ISSUES

Purpose of Productivity Measurement

The purpose of productivity measurement refers to its alternative uses. For example, personnel managers may want to communicate their economic contributions in the form of financial statements, an external use. Of concern here are the certainty, reliability, and verifiability of measurement outcomes. It follows, however, that if information is used by the public, then public accounting standards must exist to ensure accuracy and uniformity (Flamholtz, 1974; Dittman, Juris & Resvine 1976). A second purpose is for internal decision making or for estimating the future net benefits to the firm of personnel investments (e.g., Cronshaw & Alexander, 1985). It follows that if estimates are obtained for managers, then public accounting standards need not apply, and any means of measuring dollar value is sufficient as long as management feels that measurement facilitates the useful ranking of the monetary impact of alternative investments. Also, productivity measurement may be used to evaluate the economic implications of research results, for example, the dollar payoff of a behavioral intervention on job safety or the economic losses due to an affirmative action policy.

Time-Related Factors

Three time-related issues may arise. The first concerns the length in time that economic value arising from some personnel intervention is assumed to accrue. Do benefits accrue only as long as the individual is in a particular job, or does their accrual generalize across organizational tenure? Perhaps some other length can be assumed. A related issue is the shape of the dollar payoff schedule. Is it constant over tenure, or is some alternative payoff schedule more representative? Perhaps a training program, because its effects may not be readily transferable to the firm, might result in high initial cash flows but decline over time. In contrast, perhaps the productivity effects of a performance appraisal program may increase as employees adjust to its usage and recognize its importance.

A third concern is the measurement of system dynamics (Boudreau & Berger, 1985; Ledvinka, Scarpello & Gatewood, 1985; Steffy & Werling, 1985). In evaluating "future service potential," measurement may require some means for forecasting the number of employees treated over successive years, as well as their expected length of stay in various service states throughout the heterogeneous job system. That is, future service potential, while it is a function of the effectiveness of the personnel treatment, is also a function of the probability of treated employees' remaining in the job, moving to another service state, or leaving the firm (Flamholtz, 1985). It may also be possible to evaluate the impact of a multifaceted personnel treatment system where different selection, training, and other programs are employed in different jobs, or service states, as well as the impact of changing productivity parameter values and their relationships over time. Later sections discuss modeling strategies for measuring these effects.

Representing and Valuating Dollar Productivity

A subtle issue is how to quantify the dollar value of future productivity changes arising from personnel activities; some dollar-value metric, or *valuation base,* is required. Accounting theory suggests two concepts of valuation (Barton, 1974; Craswell, 1978; Resvine, 1978); ex-ante concepts and ex-post concepts. Ex-ante valuation reflects the investor's subjective expectation of the relative contribution of an investment to changes in the overall economic value of the firm. The economic contribution of a personnel practice would therefore be operationalized by

> estimating the firm's future earnings, discounting these earnings to determine the firm's present value, and allocating a portion of this present value to the human resource [intervention] based upon [its] relative contribution. (Friedman & Lev, 1974, p. 243)

Measurement of a personnel treatment's relative contribution, however, can be problematic, because changes in the value of the firm over time can be ascribed to both human and nonhuman (material, technological, capital) production inputs (Flamholtz, 1985; Friedman & Lev, 1974). It is possible to employ standard costing procedures to determine that proportion of changed asset value attributable to a personnel intervention (see Ogan, 1976; Roche, 1965), but such approaches can be very complex and time-consuming (Cronbach & Gleser, 1965), especially in capital-intensive firms where labor inputs constitute a fraction of the production function and in cases where production outputs attributed to labor are intangible and not easily priced (Flamholtz, 1985).

Assuming that ex-ante valuation, though ideal, may not be feasible, accounting theory suggests that ex-post measures be employed as a conservative *surrogate,* or proxy, valuation base (Barton, 1974; Resvine, 1978). While ex-ante valuation reflects the "pure profit" potential of a personnel investment, ex-post valuation reflects an entity's or event's direct relative economic contribution to the firm as currently valuated by the owner, in this case "renter," of the asset. Thus, valuation is based not on future expectations but on the actual cost of acquiring the service potential, the break-even point from the investor's perspective. Such valuation assumes that costs incurred in labor reflect management's willingness to forgo alternative asset acquisitions; hence, value obtained is equivalent to the value sacrificed (Sterling, 1970). As will be expanded upon later, it is possible to estimate that portion of service value obtained through personnel activities that exceeds the break-even point. This can be accomplished if we assume that the impact of the activity is a continuous, linear function of the expected value of economically successful performance.

Two ex-post measures are applicable in a personnel context: replacement cost and those based upon the market's current valuation (wages) of a particular level of performance in a job. In replacement cost, the costs incurred in recruiting, selecting, compensating, and training reflect the expected value of successful job performance (Flamholtz, 1985). Compensation and replacement cost valuations should be relatively similar, though the more inefficient the firm is, the greater (and more artificial) is the assessed value. Some accounting theorists therefore support using current market valuation, also suggesting that current market valuation is objective, relatively reliable, verifiable, and speaks the common language of relative worth (Barton, 1974; Edwards & Bell, 1961; Resvine, 1978; Sterling, 1970). For purposes that will be relevant later, it is important to note that, barring market imperfections, all valuation bases, ex ante and ex post, will be equivalent, even in the short run. It is only under imperfect market conditions that divergence, particularly in the short run, of dollar values using alternative bases occurs (Dittman, Juris & Resvine, 1976).

Feasibility and Face Validity

Another issue is the feasibility of measurement. For instance, can the firm keep track of the many costs and benefits accumulated subsequent to personnel treatments? In some cases the measurement program may itself bear little utility because of the time and costs required in managing the data system. Further, what is the face validity of measurement to management, who may perceive approaches other than simple productivity ratios as too complex and ill conceived? Perhaps there exists a trade-off between face validity and the capacity for a measurement model to provide enough detail of real-world processes to facilitate good investment analysis.

ALTERNATIVE APPROACHES TO MEASURING THE PRODUCTIVITY VALUE OF PERSONNEL ACTIVITIES

Following is an overview of four measurement approaches. Table 8-1 summarizes some of the principal attributes of each of the four models, especially how each approach addresses measurement issues. For ease of presentation, all mathematical definitions are confined to figure 8-1.

Firm-Specific Human Capital

Firm-specific human capital (FSHC) is defined as the net present value of income stream to the firm attributable to human resource investments (Hashimoto,

1981; Mangan, 1983). FSHC is more a theoretical construct than a measurement scheme. That is, this literature suggests no means for measuring the magnitude of economic effectiveness of a personnel activity. This can be accomplished only through analysis at the level of the individual. The notion of FSHC is valuable, nevertheless, because it provides a framework in which most of the other approaches are conceptually embedded. In particular, it sheds light on the valuation issue and brings attention to the market and institutional constraints on the economic effectiveness of personnel activities.

To illustrate under what conditions value creation

Figure 8–1. Mathematical Definitions of Four Models for Measuring the Dollar Impact of Personnel Practices

A. Firm-Specific Human Capital Theory: The firm increases its human capital when the marginal economic contribution of employees exceeds the marginal labor costs of generating increased product.

Model

$$MRP_{t, t+n} > W_{t, t+n} + R_t + S_t + T_t + O_t,$$ where W, R, S, T, and O are interactive over time.

Terms

$MRP_{t, t+n}$ = the summed marginal revenue product of labor between some initial point in time, t, and some later point in time, $t + n$.

$W_{t, t+n}$ = the summed wage costs between t, and $t + n$.

R, S, T, O = recruiting, selection, training, and other labor costs incurred at t.

Additional Modeling Components

Substitution effects of nonhuman capital for human capital.
Union effects on all variables in the model.
Effects on R, S, T, and O of economies of scale in the practices.

B. Human Resource Accounting: Human asset creation occurs when personnel practices and policies increase the net present value of the firm.

Model (Adapted from Flamholtz (1985), Ogan (1976), and Lau and Lau (1978)).

$$\sum_{t=1}^{T} \sum_{j=1}^{J} (1 + r)^{-t} (S_t j)(V_t j) > I_c,$$ where $S_t j = (S_t i_1)(Pj/i) + E_t j$

Terms

T = the time horizon of interest, expressed in years, t.
J = the number of hierarchically arranged jobs between which personnel move over time; i is the source job and j is the target of mobility.
(Pj/i) = the square transition matrix consisting of the probability rates of moving between i and j (which also includes an absorbing, or exit, state) between $t - 1$ and t.
$S_t j$ = the number of employees predicted to be in job j at t.
$S_t i_1$ = the number of employees currently in the source job, i.
$E_t j$ = the number of hirees in year t brought into j to fill vacancies created by exits, promotions out, demotions out, and labor force expansion.
$V_t j$ = the expected dollar value of service contribution of an employee in j at t.
r = the discount rate.
I_c = the labor costs associated with changes in the service value of employees.

Additional Modeling Components

Specific procedures for defining I_c and $V_t j$.
Depreciation procedures.

is possible, it is instructive to portray the conditions in which it is not. Assume an industry consisting of profit-maximizing firms facing purely competitive labor markets where both a homogeneous demand for (employees are perfectly substitutable) and supply of (current and potential employees are equal in productive capacity) labor exist. Assuming this, variance in individuals' use value within jobs would not exist, and wages would equal the marginal revenue productivity of employees (Joll et al., 1983). Internal labor markets would be absent, and wages would constitute the only labor cost. It follows that since individual differences would not matter, any personnel investment would be economically irrational. In most

C. Behavior Costing: Value is added to the firm when savings are accrued due to a decrease in service costs subsequent to a personnel activity abatement of counterproductive behaviors.

Model

$$SC_t < SC_{t+n}$$
$$\text{where} \quad SC = A + 1 + T + L + E$$

Terms

SC_t and SC_{t+n} = service costs associated with labor between t and $t + n$.

$A, I, T, L,$ and E = financial losses due to accidents, insurance costs, turnover, theft, and other inefficiencies and counterproductive behaviors.

Additional Modeling Components

Expansion of factors contributing to service costs.

D. Utility Analysis: The dollar contribution of personnel practices and policies to the firm.

Model

D1: (Adapted from Boudreau, 1983a; utility model for selection practice):

$$\Delta U_s = (N)(T) \; (R_{x,\,sv})(\bar{Z}_x)(SD_{sv}) \; - \; (R_{x,\,sc})(\bar{Z}_x)(SD_{sc}) \; - \; C$$

D2: (Adapted from Boudreau, 1983b; utility model for selection practice):

$$\Delta U_s = \sum_{k=1}^{F} \sum_{t=1}^{k} \; (N_{a_t} - N_{s_t}) \; (r_{x,\,sv})(\bar{Z}_x)(SD_{sv}) \; - \; (r_{x,\,sc})(\bar{Z}_x)(SD_{sc}) \; - \; \sum_{k=1}^{F} (C_{sk}).$$

Terms

ΔU_s = the incremental dollar-valued utility of using predictor x.

F = the number of future periods (years) of interest to management.

N = (in equation D1) the number of employees selected.

N_{a_t} = the number of treated employees subtracted from the work force in t.

N_{s_t} = the number of treated employees subtracted from the work force in t.

$r_{x,\,sv}$ = the validity coefficient between the predictor and service costs, sc.

SD_{sv} = the estimated standard deviation of service value of productivity in the applicant population.

SD_{sc} = the estimated standard deviation of service costs in the applicant population.

$\bar{Z}_x$ = the averaged standardized predictor score among selectees.

C = (in equation D1) the cost of selecting N employees.

K = the future periods in which costs and benefits occur.

t = the future period in which employee flows occur.

T = (in equation D1) the expected tenure of selectees.

C_{sk} = the cost of selecting N_{ak} employees added in period K.

Additional Modeling Components

Effects of taxes and discounting (Boudreau, 1983a).
Can be generalized to other personnel practices.
Human asset model (Boudreau and Berger, 1985).

situations, however, a firm faces, at least in the short run, both a heterogeneous demand for and supply of labor. Variance in use values (and wages) within jobs exists, and internal labor markets, operationalized through personnel practices and policies, emerge as a decision tool for controlling labor costs and positively affecting individual use values. An efficient firm will attract and retain high-performing individuals by setting competitive pay rates and investing in a mix of personnel programs to a point where the internal rate of return equals some desired rate of interest (Thurow, 1970). Thus, firms might profit by engag-

Table 8–1
Outline of Alternative Approaches to Productivity Measurement

Approach	Source	Level of Analysis	Concept of Productivity	Purposes
Firm specific	Labor economics	Market institution	Increase of marginal productivities	Theoretical construct
Human resources accounting	Accounting	Institution	Increase of human asset value	External reporting
Behavior costing	Organizational behavior	Program	Cost savings	Cost accounting
Utility analysis	Industrial psychology	Individual	Effectiveness of personnel activity investments	Internal investment analysis research

ing in recruitment programs that decrease selection ratios and increase the number of competent applicants; selection programs that identify within applicant pools individuals bearing the greatest productive capacity and requiring the least training outlays; training programs that increase marginal productivities; and allocation provisions promising advancement potential and employment security, thus providing a disincentive for voluntary turnover, which could prematurely terminate payoff schedules. Given heterogeneity, there also no longer exists an equivalence of wages and marginal revenue product (Becker, 1975). The mean compensation value of a group of employees, however, may still approximate the economic value of expected successful job performance (Thurow, 1970; Doeringer & Piori, 1971). That is, FSHC theory suggests that compensation levels may be a valid surrogate of expected productivity value.

Personnel activities, however, even when they positively affect performance, may not be value additive (Muckler, 1982). As mentioned earlier, the magnitude of productivity effects is anchored by the economic value embodied in the job where treatment occurs and the variance in use values possible in the job. Other constraints on value creation addressed here include those due to the costs incurred in changing service values and the interdependency of those costs and those due to exogenous forces occurring in the labor market.

The Interdependency of Labor Costs. Human capital theorists two decades ago pointed out that investments in training may be associated with changes in wage, selection, and turnover costs. Specifically, this literature distinguishes along a continuum between two forms of training: general and specific (Becker, 1975). General training is provided to employees who do not possess the required mix of human capital attributes for successful job performance. Through general training, human capital values, as well as the firm's use values, are simultaneously enhanced and as a result, though the potential for asset creation exists, so are the conditions for turnover, since trained employees can market their heightened productive capacities. Given the uncertainty of future service potential, the firm will still engage in training but transfer the cost to trainees through a reduction in wages. Once training is over, wages are increased to regain some equivalence between wages and productivity value (Becker, 1975). Asset creation is therefore possible if decreased wages offset the cost of training and, once training is completed, marginal productivity value exceeds wage costs. These conditions may be stringent, since competitive and union wage pressures may prohibit the necessary temporary reduction in

Valuation Bases	Model Contributions	Feasibility/ Face Validity	Applications
Opportunity cost (compensation)	Conceptual basis for productivity measurement Constraints on asset creation	Not relevant/ Intuitive notion of how decisions made	Not relevant
Compensation Replacement cost Net Benefits Stochastic	Valuation thoery System dynamics Financial considerations	Moderate/Moderate to Low	Overall asset value of employees (Flamnoitz, 1985)
Not relevant	Avoids valuation problem Cost perspective	Moderate/Moderate	Turnover/absenteeism sick leave, smoking (Cascio, 1982) Attitudes (Mirvis & Lawler, 1977)
Cost accounting Net benefits Sales value Compensation Rational estimation	Captures individual differences Measures effectiveness of treatment	Moderate/Moderate to Low	Selection (e.g., Schmidt et al., 1979) Recruitment (e.g., Boudreau and Rynes 1985) Mobility (e.g., Steffy Werling 1985) Turnover (e.g., Boudreau and Berger, 1985) Training (e.g., Hunter et al., 1982) Performance appraisal (e.g., Cascio, 1982)

wages. Further, training costs may be too large to compensate for through reduced wages and later increased marginal productivity (Dittman, Juris & Resvine, 1976; Joll et al., 1983). The potential for asset creation is increased, however, if the firm has (or purchases) economies of scale in training and if the performance effects of training are large and persistent over time.

Specific training more readily leads to asset creation because individual use values are increased but not their human capital values. Trained individuals therefore are not provided an incentive to leave the firm, but since benefits flow primarily to the firm, there is also no incentive for individuals to bear the cost of training through reduced wages. Therefore, the firm must pay both competitive wages and bear the training costs, meaning that if any asset creation is to occur, the marginal productivities of employees in the posttraining period must increase enough to offset the inequality between labor costs (wages and training) and productivity value during training (Dittman, Juris & Resvine 1976). Economies of scale in training (OJT) and effectiveness of training will also increase the potential for asset creation.

This discussion can be generalized to other cost interdependencies as well. Assuming that the firm knows that point where marginal revenues equal marginal costs, any personnel investment that leads to increased productivity value may decrease the need for other personnel investments. Recruitment and selection, for example, may be viewed as a process of identifying where applicants reside within the applicant queue where the distribution is defined according to required training outlays (Thurow, 1975). Further, a firm's competitive posture in the external labor market regarding wages will ultimately determine the distribution of human capital attributes of members of the applicant pool, the quality of those selected, the rejection rate of top selectees given offers (Murphy, 1986), the degree of general training required, and the composition of the terminating cohorts. Selection, training, and appraisal programs may also affect the level of costs associated with counterproductive behaviors such as accidents, stress, and theft.

Exogenous Effects. As pointed out by Boudreau (1983a), tax and discount rates will ultimately constrain the assessed present value of a personnel investment by as much as 15–20 percent. Asset creation may also be constrained (or enhanced) by other factors not under management's control. First, applicant population characteristics such as availability of candidates with the necessary human capital attributes will determine the composition and distributional characteristics of the applicant population (Boudreau

& Rynes, 1985). This, in turn, will determine the effectiveness of recruitment and selection. Second, labor market, regulatory, and union pressures may push wage levels upward. Third, equal employment opportunity policies, specifically in regard to preferential treatment, may preclude hiring applicants who require the least general training outlays or may encourage the internal selection of employees with less ability (Steffy & Ledvinka, 1986). Fourth, provisions regarding the feasibility and cost of overtime may determine the attractiveness of internal and external selection investments (Joll et al., 1983). On the other hand, research suggests that unions may enhance human asset creation by decreasing turnover, increasing productive efficiency, and providing a social framework for getting greater economies of scale and effectiveness out of personnel treatments (Freeman & Medoff, 1984).

Human Resource Accounting

Human resource accounting (HRA) is a method for systematically measuring the asset value of employees, as well as asset creation attributable to personnel activities (Friedman & Lev, 1974; Lau & Lau, 1978). It is less theoretically driven, given that accounting is more a tradition slowly evolving in response to practical measurement problems. Since the mid-1970s, interest in HRA has waned, speculated to be due to the fact that its purpose has been principally to report human assets in financial statements, thus mandating compliance with stringent public accounting standards (Craft & Birnberg, 1976; Flamholtz, 1985; Tsay, 1978). According to these standards, to qualify as an asset, treated employees must be shown to have a certain, accurately valued, and verifiable service potential of more than a year beyond the investment period (Dittman, Juris & Resvine 1976; Flamholtz, 1985). Material resources, because they can be bought, controlled, and sold, possess a fairly certain, reliable, and verifiable value to the firm. Except for slave economics, however, future human resource services cannot be controlled and guaranteed. Employees can vary their use value and terminate their services at any time. Given these constraints, advocates of HRA developed measurement strategies to circumvent these obstacles. Specifically, they developed model components to estimate the future service potential of treated employees, or the forecasted length of dollar payoff and valuate dollar productivity according to sound accounting and economic principles.

To appease critics who argued that accountants cannot claim human resources as assets because their future service life is so uncertain, HRA researchers attempted to measure directly the level of uncertainty of future service life (Flamholtz, 1974, 1985; Friedman & Lev, 1974; Lau & Lau, 1978; Morse, 1973; Sadan & Auerbach, 1974). These researchers developed what they call a stochastic valuation model (figure 8–1), which, when applied to the evaluation of the value-additive potential of personnel treatments, enables the estimation of expected service life with knowledge of the degree of estimate error. To accomplish this, Markov models are employed to measure "system dynamics." That is, expected service life in the job, assuming that the length of payoff is job specific (a conservative estimate), is a function of the probability of remaining in the job over successive years. Conversely stated, expected job tenure is a function of the probability of promotion or demotion to some other service state in the hierarchically arranged job classification system (Bartholomew, 1982; Grinold & Marshall, 1977). The greater is the probability of moving, the less is the expected service life. Transition probabilities, in turn, are triggered by vacancies created by labor force expansion and exit rates (Stewman, 1975). Assuming that exit rates are constant, we should therefore find that labor force growth leads to lower expected service life on some jobs, while the converse is true under conditions of contraction (Steffy & Werling, 1985). Therefore, assuming a fixed-size labor force, the value-additive potential of a training program administered in each service state is a linear function of the number trained in each service state, the expected tenure of each trained cohort (a function of system dynamics), the effectiveness of each program, and the service, or asset, value of employees in each job.

Regarding the valuation issue, HRA argues that value is embodied in the job and that the level of asset creation attributable to a personnel investment is ideally measured according to ex-ante concepts, meaning that changes in service values and service costs attributed to human production inputs be specifically estimated to determine the contribution of the treatment to the firm's profits (Flamholtz, 1985). HRA, recognizing that ex-ante valuation may not be feasible, suggests that ex-post concepts may have to be employed as surrogate measures. For example, both compensation value (Flamholtz, 1974; Lev & Schwartz, 1971; Sadan & Auerbach, 1974) and replacement cost (Flamholtz, 1985) have been used.

Behavior Costing

According to behavior costing, the productivity value of personnel activities lies in their ability to decrease expenses associated with dysfunctional behaviors such as turnover, absenteeism, and accidents (Cascio, 1982; Macy & Mirvis, 1976; Mirvis & Lawler, 1977). Specifically, cost accounting procedures evaluate reductions in the costs of counterproductive behaviors subsequent to the personnel intervention. This is operationally feasible because records of cost-related behaviors are often maintained in personnel records.

Behavior costing may be advantageous to other approaches in that asset values do not have to be estimated, only the concrete costs associated with "loss" behavior and their subsequent changes. But while behavior costing may seem feasible and practical, it is limited in a number of respects. First, it deals with only one facet of the income equation, the reduction in costs. It fails to define the economic gains made possible through heightened use value. Second, it is limited in that many employee behaviors do not have concrete costs associated with them. When, for example, behavior costing has been extended to estimate the dollar value outcomes of less tangible behaviors (affects, attitudes), problems have arisen (Mirvis & Lawler, 1977). Then existence of a strong causal relationship between an affect or attitude and cost-related behaviors is not certain. A simple equation of the cost behavior model is outlined in figure 8–1.

Utility Analysis

Utility analysis, as it is advanced by psychometricians, measures the economic contribution (asset creation value) of specific personnel activities as their effectiveness in identifying and modifying individual behaviors, hence the future service value of employees. Early utility models focused exclusively on the economic contribution of selection practices (e.g., Brogden, 1946; Cronbach & Gleser, 1965). Here, selection utility is measured as a continuous linear function of (1) increased predictor validity, (2) better recruitment practices that lead to lower selection ratios and a greater number of competent candidates, (3) the economic value of expected criterion performance of randomly selected prescreened applicants, (4) the number treated, and (5) their expected tenure. Program costs should be subtracted to assess the practice's marginal utility (Cronbach & Gleser, 1965).

Recent revisions to this model have addressed some of the measurement issues outlined earlier (see figure 8–1). Modifications have been made to (1) evaluate alternative procedures of dollar valuation, (2) generalize the scope of the model beyond selection utility, (3) explain the interdependency of productivity effects of sequentially administered treatments on the same cohort, and (4) incorporate the effects of system dynamics.

Dollar Valuation. Perhaps the most problematic issue in utility analysis is that of valuating SD_y, the standard deviation of the criterion distribution in dollars (Boudreau, 1983a). The utility literature refers to this as a problem of estimation (Bobko, Karren & Parkington, 1983; Schmidt et al., 1979). I, however, distinguish between problems of estimation and problems of valuation. The former refers to technical issues of quantifying dollar value along a continuous scale once a valuation base is chosen. The valuation problem is a qualitative one. As noted earlier, ideally, we might want to employ ex-ante measures, but often surrogate measures based upon ex-post concepts may have to be employed. This problem, defined by accountants, describes the predicament in which utility analysis seems to be entrenched.

Some utility models have drawn upon ex-ante concepts of valuation. For example, standard costing procedures have been used systematically to cost out all human and nonhuman costs associated with changing sales value (the value of goods and/or services as paid by the consumer) to define profits (Brogden & Taylor, 1950; Roche, 1965). The procedure then employs performance rates to determine the economic contribution of personnel inputs to profits relative to material, technological, and capital inputs. This amount of "relative contribution" is then used as a base for SD_y valuation. Another procedure, outlined by Boudreau (1983a), subtracts from sales value variable human and nonhuman costs (service costs) associated with changes in service value over time to obtain the net benefits of the personnel treatment. In cases where the personnel treatment results in a decrease in service costs, this savings would be added to service value. Boudreau (1983a) also suggests that the standard deviation of net benefits be further corrected to reflect the effects of discounting and taxes, thus accounting for exogeneous effects on asset creation. This net benefits approach, which is defined in figure 8–1, resembles cost accounting procedures, especially in capital-intensive firms where accounting for all the nonhuman variable costs could be quite complex. Boudreau's (1983a) method, however, does not operationally specify the proportion of human effort in the overall production function. While he accounts for the relative proportion of human and nonhuman costs, he fails to account for the relative contribution of human inputs to sales value.

Ex-post measures have also been proposed. Two alternative approaches to valuation are based on the market's assessment of the employee's current value, or compensation. According to Hunter and Schmidt

(1982), the standard deviation of dollar criterion performance can be estimated as 40–60 percent of annual salary. Here, the average pay for employees in a job reflects that job's base-level economic contribution to the firm, and 40 percent of the salary is the additive (or subtracted) value of one standard deviation of service contribution value. Another method proposed by Cascio and Ramos (1986) employs a pay-based valuation procedure that breaks down each job into its constituent tasks, and the dollar value of each task is then determined by approportioning the job's pay (equivalent to the job's MRP) across tasks according to the weighted importance of each task. Dollar values are then assigned to individuals by weighting task-specific dollar values according to the individual's evaluated performance on the tasks (via a behaviorally anchored rating scale). SD_y is then derived from this empirical distribution.

Another alternative to complex ex-ante valuation is based upon a global estimation procedure, actually a decision science technique called "probability encoding" (Huber, 1974). Probability encoding is a subjective estimation process typically employed in situations where objective data cannot feasibly be obtained (Watson, 1981). It has been used extensively in utility analysis (Bobko, Karren & Parkington 1983; Burke & Frederick, 1984; Schmidt et al., 1979; Weekly et al., 1985). Assuming a normal distribution of individual use values within a job, the procedure asks estimators to assign a dollar value to the employee who is the average performer, or at the fiftieth percentile of performance, as well as the dollar value of members at the fifteenth and eighty-fifth percentiles.

The procedure is problematic, however, in that sometimes a valuation base may not clearly emerge. Schmidt et al.'s (1979) instructions regarding the valuation base to employ in framing subjective judgments read: "In placing an overall dollar value on this output the yearly value to the company of output produced, it may help to consider what the cost would be of having an outside firm provide these products and services" (p. 621). Though the intent of the instructions is to facilitate the subjective estimation ex-ante income (yearly value to company of output produced), the instructions suggest a valuation base similar to replacement cost, an ex-post concept. Weekly et al. (1985) make the instructions even more abstract by dropping the latter part of this instruction, asking estimators to valuate "the yearly value to the company of the output produced" (p. 123). Researchers note, however, that many estimators independently employ ex-post concepts (salary) in valuating the relative economic contribution of employees to the service value of the firm (Bobko, Farren & Parkington 1983; Weekly et al., 1985).

Recently, utility research has empirically evaluated the equivalence of estimates derived from alternative valuation bases, including alternative forms of probability encoding (Bobko, Farren & Parkington, 1983; Burke & Frederick, 1984; Weekly et al., 1985; Eulberg, O'Connor & Peters, 1985). Results regarding the convergence of alternative valuation procedures have been mixed. This is not surprising given that the accounting and economics literatures suggest that the convergence within and between ex-ante and ex-post measures is a function not only of the innate attributes of each approach, but of market and institutional conditions under which the bases are used (Barton, 1964). Specifically, when product and labor markets are competitive, when there exists increasing homogeneity in the demand for and supply of labor, and when there occur no changes in material and technological inputs, only then are ex-ante and ex-post valuations equivalent (Resvine, 1978; Sterling, 1970). Under conditions of monopoly and heterogeneity, divergence occurs, the same conditions that give rise to personnel functions. Here, compensation paid no longer equals net benefits, and, in general, the cost of anything purchased will not equal its market value (Sterling, 1970). This implies that future research on the equivalence of alternative valuation bases be conducted with the knowledge that the capital intensiveness of the firm, the level of labor competition, and the degree to which the internal labor market drives a wedge between productivity value, wages, and replacement costs may moderate the degree of equivalence between alternative bases. If convergence does occur, it most likely does so cumulatively over the long run (Sterling, 1970). To date, however, research has been cross-sectional at a single point in time.

Other issues in SD_y valuation revolve around factors that determine the variance of dollar performance, thereby influencing the potential effect size of a personnel treatment. Briefly, we might expect that variance in dollar performance is narrower in jobs governed by piece-rate reward systems and in jobs where teamwork and cooperation are required. Further, the variance in dollar performance may vary according to race, sex, and age groups. For instance, disadvantaged groups characterized by lower human capital values may have greater variance in use value than advantaged groups, suggesting that the marginal utility of a personnel treatment might be greater for disadvantaged groups.

The Interdependency of Utilities of Sequentially Administered Personnel Treatments. The utility model has been expanded to evaluate the economic effects of not only selection practices but the effects of training

(Schmidt, Hunter & Pearlman, 1982), performance appraisal and feedback (Landy, Farr & Jacobs, 1982), recruitment (Boudreau & Rynes, 1985), turnover (Boudreau & Berger, 1985), and equal employment policies (Steffy & Ledvinka, 1986). The impact of rejections of hiring offers has also been evaluated (Murphy, 1986). These studies evaluate the economic impact of a single treatment, though from the firm's perspective, it may be more realistic to evaluate the impact of an array of treatments sequentially administered to a cohort of employees. Such an analysis may be complex, since "the utility of any component will generally affect the likelihood of additional value from other components" (Landy, Farr & Jacobs 1982, p. 29). That is, assuming a cohort recruited, selected, trained, and appraised, early treatments will most likely decrease the variance of use values, thus decreasing the potential for strong productivity effects in subsequent treatments. In economic terms, marginal costs in later treatments may increase due to diminishing potential marginal returns. FSHC theory suggests that, assuming relatively fixed wages, firms will engage in that strategic mix of personnel practices that minimizes labor costs. To date, utility analysts have not defined a dynamic model of the composite utility of sequentially administered personnel treatments.

System Dynamics. As in HRA, utility analysts have recognized that to measure the incremental effects of personnel treatments on employees' future service values and costs, we need specifically to account for labor force mobility (Boudreau, 1983b; Boudreau & Berger, 1985; Steffy & Werling, 1985). As shown in figure 8–1, Boudreau (1983b) outlines a descriptive model that accounts for the effects of turnover on the net size of the treated cohort. The model also represents the treatment of new cohorts over successive years. Boudreau and Berger (1985) expand on this model by representing the simultaneous effects, over successive years, of external selection and random or nonrandom turnover on the dollar productivity of retained employees. This model, is in fact, a human asset model in that its focus is on the "absolute utility" of current employees and not only the value added through personnel treatments.

These models fail, however, to provide a means for specifically forecasting cohort sizes and the expected tenure of those treated. To accomplish this, we need a means of forecasting the flows of employees as they move into, through, and out of a job system consisting of hierarchically arranged service states, each possessing its required treatments. As suggested, the HRA literature suggests a means of accomplishing this.

NEW DIRECTIONS IN MODELING THE DOLLAR-PRODUCTIVITY IMPACT OF PERSONNEL ACTIVITIES AND ASSOCIATED RESEARCH QUESTIONS

The four approaches discussed provide a foundation for a multidisciplinary model of the economic impact of personnel activities. Utility analysis measures changes in individual's use value as a continuous, linear function of the measured effectiveness of those activities. FSHC theory provides the framework for evaluating the impact of institutional and market forces on the extent to which increases in individual use value lead to actual asset creation, as well as a framework for conceptualizing the valuation issue. HRA, developed not so much from a theoretical framework but out of the practical necessity of developing measurement strategies to estimate human asset values as specified by stringent public accounting standards, provides suggestions as to how to measure employee "future service potential" through modeling system dynamics, as well as guidelines for choosing among alternative valuation bases. Behavior costing facilitates the analysis of cost savings accrued through personnel treatments that inhibit counterproductive behaviors. Such analysis is complemen-

tary and mathematically additive to utility analysis, which typically focuses more on the positive effects of functional (selection, training) treatments on service values and costs.

At this point the measurement issues addressed earlier are outlined in the light of the overview of the four modeling approaches. New directions for model building are pointed out, as are research questions associated with an integrative conceptual framework. Specific research questions are outlined in table 8–2.

Time-Related Issues

Utility analysts define the length of dollar payoff as a function of the expected tenure of treated employees, though they do not propose whether tenure should be job or organization specific or according to some other interval of time, HRA, on the other hand, borrowing from FSHC theory, suggests that the productivity effects of a treatment will not generalize much

Table 8-2
Research Questions Associated with an Integrated Conceptual Model

Time-Related Issues

1. Does the length of the dollar-payoff schedule extend across job tenure, organizational tenure, or some other time period such as tenure within job class?

    a. Does the length vary according to the type of personnel treatment?

    b. Does the length vary according to the job (or job class) or industry where the treatment was employed?

    c. What organizational factors influence the length of dollar-payoff? For example, do factors such as social climate, situational constraints on behavioral change, and labor-management relations influence the length of payoff?

2. What is the shape of the dollar-payoff schedule? Is it uniform, inclining, declining, or curvilinear?

    a. Does the shape of the payoff schedule vary according to the type of personnel treatment and the job where implemented?

    b. What organizational factors influence the direction and magnitude of the payoff schedule? To what extent do budgetary constraints and social pressures that suppress individual differences shape the payoff schedule?

System Dynamics

3. What is the impact of alternative mobility structures (reflected in transition rates) on the potential for human asset creation?

4. What is the impact of affirmative action policies on the utility of personnel treatments?

5. What is the magnitude of impact of seniority rules on the utility of internal selection practices?

6. What is the differential economic impact of alternative termination and layoff procedures?

7. What impact do unions have on reducing mobility costs such as turnover costs?

Dollar Valuation

8. Does the variance in dollar-performance change according to types of occupations and jobs? For example, are jobs requiring cooperation and teamwork characterized by low variance in performance, and do the social influences present in such jobs constrain the capacity for personnel treatments to lead to performance changes?

9. Is the variance in dollar-performance less in unionized jobs than nonunionized ones?

10. Does the magnitude of variance differ in different race, sex, and age groups? If so, which groups possess greater variance?

11. Does the convergence of alternative valuation bases differ according to the competitive structure of the industry where measurement is taking place?

12. Using protocol analysis, what are the bases that individuals employ when rationally estimating ex ante valuation? Are they employing ex post concepts?

Constraints on and Enhancements to Asset Creation

13. Is greater marginal utility gained from specific training as compared to general training?

14. What characterizes the firm that gets greater economies of scale in training? For example, are firms that have been training longer obtaining less costly training? Does the quality of management-labor relations contribute to obtaining economies of scale? Does the length of time the company engages in training improve the effectiveness of the treatment? How do unions affect the effectiveness of treatment?

15. What is the direction and magnitude of the relationship of wage, recruitment, selection training, and appraisal costs? Given various levels of effectiveness of each type of treatment, how does it specifically affect the economic impact of subsequent treatments?

16. What is the impact of wage and equal employment opportunity regulation on the economic impact of personnel treatments? To what extent do costs associated with compliance offset the monetary gains associated with personnel investments?

17. To what extent do wage pressures arising from unions and external labor markets offset the marginal utility of personnel treatments?

18. To what extent do early personnel treatments affect the potential for marginal utility of later treatments? Is there a diminishing function whereby later investments require increasing marginal costs to obtain decreasing marginal revenues?

    a. To what extent do compensation policies, especially individual-and group-based incentive plans, reduce the potential for dollar-performance changes?

    b. Can we determine the impact of selection practices on the economic impact of training practices?

beyond the job for which the treatment occurred (Flamholtz, 1985). Given, however, that individual progression along a job ladder is defined according to the clustering of similar skills, it makes sense that, while effects may not extend across organizational tenure, effects may extend to all jobs within the job class. Further research needs to clarify the length of dollar payoff and the possible mediating effects of type of treatment, type of job, and organizational policies such as those defining job design and career lines.

To date, utility analysts have also assumed that, given no turnover, the "effect size" of a treatment is constant across the length of the productivity effect. Is the assumption realistic, and what is the direction and magnitude of a nonuniform payoff? How does the payoff curve of the treated group compare to the asset-value curve of the untreated group? Do the direction and magnitude of the payoff schedule vary according to type of treatment and job or organizational forces than influence the motivation and ability to change performance behaviors?

System Dynamics

From a practical measurement perspective, the use of stochastic flow, or Markov, models in HRA is advantageous because they provide the skeletal structure for representing both a heterogeneous job system with different treatments and productivity values and constituent mobility linkages. They also facilitate the practical forecasting of the future service potential of treated employees. Current mobility models found in the utility literature are descriptive (see Boudreau & Berger, 1985). Markov models have been criticized, however, because the probability of movement is not a function of job vacancies arising from labor force expansion and attrition of current supply. Instead, transition rates, determined from archival data, are assumed to be stationary over time. Further, they assume that all current and potential employees are homogeneous in productive capacity (Grinold & Marshall, 1977; Heneman & Sandver, 1976). The validity of these models for long-term forecasting has also been questioned, (Steffy & LeDvinka, 1986). To compensate for these deficiencies, Markov-renewal models have been employed (Ledvinka, Markos & Ladd, 1982). These models differ in that transition probabilities are not assumed to be stationary but vary according to vacancies (Stewman, 1975). The advantage of incorporating renewal processes is that future service potential is estimated as a function of labor force demand and attrition. Given these forces,

it is possible to forecast both the number of internal moves and the number of hirees required to meet demand. Therefore, assuming treatments with both external and internal selection, it is possible to forecast the number undergoing various treatments in each job each year. The model also has been shown to be more valid than the simple Markov model (Stewman, 1978; Bartholomew, 1982; Zanakis & Maret, 1980).

By modeling system dynamics, it is also possible to address the impact of allocation policies on asset creation. For example, given labor-force demand (or contraction) and attrition rates, what mix of internal selection with training and external recruitment-selection brings the largest rate of return? Second, what is the impact of affirmative action policies on selection and training utility (see Steffy & Ledvinka, 1986)? What is the economic impact of manipulating quit rates? Employing semi-Markov analysis (see Bartholomew, 1982), what is the impact of alternative policies regarding seniority versus merit-based internal selection?

Dollar Valuation

This chapter suggests that the valuation issue should be addressed in the light of two concepts of valuation, ex ante and ex post, with the latter base acting as a potential surrogate for the former. It is also suggested that valuation and system dynamics are closely intertwined. That is, future service valuation is uncertain and ultimately stochastic (Flamholtz, 1985; Friedman & Lev, 1974; Lau & Lau, 1978), thus affecting the dollar value of a treatment. This chapter also suggests that future utility research on the convergence of alternative valuation bases should account for the moderating effects of economic and institutional forces on the potential convergence of alternative valuation bases. Other research on valuation might address the relative cost and complexity of each valuation procedure relative to its convergence with other approaches. If compensation seems reasonable, it may be most practical to use this. HRA and FSHC provide theoretical support for using this surrogate.

Constraints on Human Asset Creation

Table 8–2 also summarizes the numerous potential constraints on human asset creation suggested by an economic, accounting, and psychological perspective. To date, none of these questions has been empirically examined. Categorically, the potential for human asset creation resulting from a personnel treatment is a function of: (1) the economic value of the job where the treatment effects take place; (2) the potential for variance in individual use values, which may be a function of job and technology types, the presence of a union, and whether the treatment has been preceded by other treatments; (3) the interdependency of labor costs, such that one type of personnel investment affects the level of cost associated with other personnel activities (for example, the effect of training on wages); and (4) the impact of exogeneous influences that may be outside the control of management.

REFERENCES

Bartholomew, J. (1982). *Stochastic modeling*. New York: Wiley.

Barton, A.D. (1974). Expectations and achievements in income theory. *Accounting Review, 47*, 664–681.

Barton, A.D. (1978). Surrogates in Income Theory: A reply. *Accounting Review, 51*, 160–162.

Becker, G. (1975). *Human capital*. New York: National Bureau of Economic Research.

Bemmels, B. (1984). *An integrated approach to productivity measurement*. Ph.D. dissertation, University of Minnesota.

Bobko, P., Karren, R., & Parkington, J.J. (1983). Estimation of standard deviations in utility analysis: An empirical test. *Journal of Applied Psychology, 68*, 170–176.

Boudreau, J.W. (1983a). Economic considerations in estimating the utility of human resource productivity improvement programs. *Personnel Psychology, 36*, 551–576.

Boudreau, J.W. (1983b). Effects of employee flows on utility analysis of human resource productivity improvement programs. *Journal of Applied Psychology, 68*, 396–406.

Boudreau, J., & Berger, C. (1985). Decision-theoretic utility analysis applied to employee separations and acquisitions. *Journal of Applied Psychology, 70*, 581–612.

Boudreau, J., & Rynes, S. (1985). Role of recruitment in staffing utility analysis. *Journal of Applied Psychology, 70*, 354–366.

Brief, A.P. (1984). *Productivity research in the behavioral and social sciences*. New York: Praeger Publishers.

Brogden, H.E. (1946). On the interpretation of the correlation coefficient as a measure of predictive efficiency. *Journal of Educational Psychology, 37*, 65–76.

Brogden, H.E., & Taylor, E.K. (1950). The dollar criterion—applying the cost accounting concept to criterion construction. *Personnel Psychology, 3*, 133–154.

Burke, M.J., & Frederick, J.T. (1984). Two modified procedures for estimating standard deviations in utility analysis. *Journal of Applied Psychology, 69*, 482–489.

Cascio, W. (1982). *Costing human resources: The financial impact of behavior in organizations*. Boston: Kent.

Cascio, W.F., & Ramos, R.A. (1986). Development and application of a new method for assessing job performance in behavioral/economic terms. *Journal of Applied Psychology, 71*, 20–28.

Craft, J.A., & Birnberg, J.G. (1976). Human resource accounting: Perspectives and prospects. *Industrial Relations, 15*, 2–12.

Craswell, A. (1978). Surrogates in accounting. *Abacus, 14*, 81–93.

Cronbach, L.J., & Gleser, G. (1965). *Psychological tests and personnel decisions*. Urbana: University of Illinois Press.

Cronshaw, S.F., & Alexander, R.A. (1985). One answer to the demand for accountability: Selection utility as an investment decision. *Organizational Behavior and Human Decision Processes, 35*, 102–118.

Dittman, D.A., Juris, H.A., & Resvine, L. (1976). On the existence of unrecorded human assets: An economic perspective. *Journal of Accounting Research, 14*, 49–65.

Doeringer, P.B., & Piore, M.J. (1971). *Internal labor markets and manpower analysis*. Lexington, MA: Lexington Books.

Dunnette, M.D. (1982). Critical concepts in the assessment of human capabilities. In M.D. Dunnette & E.A. Fleishman (Eds.), *Human capability assessment*. Hillsdale, NJ: Lawrence Erlbaum Associates.

Dunnette, M.D., & Fleishman, E.A. (1982). *Human capability assessment*. Hillsdale, NJ: Lawrence Erlbaum Associates.

Edwards, E.O., & Bell, P.W. (1961). *The theory and measurement of business income*. Berkeley: University of California Press.

Eulberg, J.R., O'Connor, E.J., & Peters, L.H. (1985). *Estimates of the standard deviation of performance in dollars: An investigation of the influences of alternative sources of information*. Academy of Management meetings, Dallas, presented paper.

Fitz-Enz, J. (1984). *How to measure human resource management*. New York: McGraw-Hill.

Flamholtz, E.G. (1974). *Human resource accounting*. Encino, CA: Dickinson.

Flamholtz, E.G. (1985). *Human resource accounting*. San Francisco: Jossey-Bass.

Freeman, R.B., & Medoff, J.L. (1984). *What do unions do?* New York: Basic Books.

Friedman, A., & Lev, B. (1974). A surrogate measure of the firm's investment in human resources. *Journal of Accounting Research, 12*, 235–250.

Grinold, R.C., & Marshall, K.T. (1977). *Manpower plan-*

ning models. New York: Elsevier North-Holland.

Hashimoto, M. (1981). Firm-specific human capital as a shared investment. *American Economic Review, 71,* 475–482.

Heneman, H.G., III, & Sandver, M.G. (1976). Markov analysis in human resource administration. *Academy of Management Review, 2,* 535–542.

Huber, G.P. (1974). Methods for quantifying subjective probabilities and multi-attribute utilities. *Decision Sciences, 5,* 430–458.

Hunter, J.E., & Schmidt, F.L. (1982). Fitting people to jobs: The impact of personnel selection on national productivity. In M.D. Dunnette & E.A. Fleishman (Eds.), *Human capability assessment.* Hillsdale, NJ: Lawrence Erlbaum Associates.

Joll, C., McKenna, C., McNabb, R., & Shorey, J. (1983). *Developments in labor market analysis.* London: George Allen & Unwin.

Kendrick, J.W. (1984). *Improving Company Productivity.* Baltimore: John Hopkins University Press.

Kopelman, R.E. (1986). *Managing productivity in organizations.* New York: McGraw-Hill.

Landy, F.J., Farr, J.L., & Jacobs, R.R. (1982). Utility concepts in performance measurement. *Organizational Behavior and Human Performance, 30,* 15–40.

Lau, A.H., & Lau, H. (1978). Some proposed approaches for writing off capitalized human resource assets. *Journal of Accounting Research, 16,* 80–102.

Ledvinka, J., Scarpello, V., & Gatewood, R. (1985). Impact of human resource management of productivity and minority employment. *National Science Foundation Proposal.*

Lev, B., & Schwartz, A. (1971). On the use of economic concept of human capital in financial statements. *Accounting Review, 71,* 103–112.

Macy, B.A., & Mirvis, P.H. (1976). A methodology for assessment of quality of worklife and organizational effectiveness in behavioral-economic terms. *Administrative Science Quarterly, 21,* 212–226.

Mangan, J. (1983). The intra-organizational flow of labour services. In J. Edwards, C. Leek, R. Loveridge, R. Lumley, J. Mangan, & M. Silver (Eds.), *Manpower planning.* New York: John Wiley and Sons.

Mirvis, P.H., & Lawler, E.E. (1977). Measuring the financial impact of employee attitudes. *Journal of Applied Psychology, 62,* 1–8.

Morse, W. (1973). Toward a model for human resource valuation: A comment. *Accounting Review, 50,* 131–140.

Muckler, F.A. (1982). Evaluating productivity. In M.D. Dunnette & E.A. Fleishman (Eds.), *Human capability assessment.* Hillsdale, NJ: Lawrence Erlbaum Associates.

Murphy, K.R. (1986). When your top choice turns you down: Effects of rejected offers on the utility of selection test. *Psychological Bulletin, 99,* 133–138.

Myers, M.S., & Flowers, V.S. (1974). A framework for measuring human assets. *California Management Review, 16,* 5–16.

Ogan, P. (1976). A human resource value model for professional service organizations. *Accounting Review, 51,* 302–320.

Oi, W.Y. (1983). Heterogeneous firms and the organization of production. *Economic Inquiry, 21,* 147–171.

Pagano, A.M., & Verdin, J. (1983). An approach to measuring quality of output in service organizations. In *Academy of Management Proceedings,* Dallas.

Resvine, L. (1978). Surrogates in income theory: A comment. *Accounting Review, 51,* 156–159.

Roche, W.J. (1965). The Cronbach-Gleser utility function in fixed treatment employee selection. In L.J. Cronbach & G.C. Gleser (Eds.), *Psychological tests and personnel decisions.* Urbana, IL: University of Illinois.

Rosenbaum, J.E. (1984). *Career mobility in a corporate hierarchy.* New York: Academic Press.

Sadan, S., & Auerbach, L.B. (1974). A stochastic model for human resources valuation. *California Management Review, 4,* 24–31.

Schmidt, F.L., Hunter, J.E., McKenzie, R.C., & Muldrow, I.W. (1979). Impact of valid selection procedures on work-force productivity. *Journal of Applied Psychology, 64,* 609–626.

Schmidt, F.L., Hutner, J.E., & Pearlman, K. (1982). Assessing the economic impact of personnel programs on workforce productivity. *Personnel Psychology, 35,* 333–346.

Schneider, B. (1985). Organizational behavior. *Annual Review of Psychology, 36,* 573–611.

Schoenfeldt, L.F. (1984). The status of test validation research. In B. Plake (Ed.), *Social and technical issues in testing.* Hillside, NJ: Lawrence Erlbaum Associates.

Sibson, R.E. (1976). *Increasing employee productivity.* New York: AMACON.

Spetzler, C.S., & Staehl von Holstein, C. (1975). Probability encoding in decision analysis. *Management Science, 22,* 340–358.

Steffy, B.D., & Ledvinka, J. (1986) *The trade-offs between minority mobility and employee productivity under five definitions of "fair" employee selection.* Academy of Management meetings, Chicago, presented paper.

Steffy, B., & Werling, S. (1985). Incorporating human resource planning models into utility analysis to determine the long-term economic impact of selection and training. In *Academy of Management Proceedings,* 279–283.

Sterling, H. (1970). *Accounting theory.* New York: Wiley.

Stewman, S. (1975). An application of the job vacancy chain model to a civil service internal labor market. *Journal of Mathematical Sociology, 4,* 37–39.

Stewman, S. (1978). Markov and renewal models for total manpower systems. *Omega, 6,* 341–351.

Thurow, L. (1970). *Investment in human capital.* Belmont, CA: Wadsworth.

Thurow, L.C. (1975). *Generating inequality: Mechanisms of distribution in the U.S. economy.* New York: Basic Books.

Tsay, J.J. (1978). Human resource accounting: A need for relevance. *Management Accounting, 23,* 33–19.

Viren, M. (1979). *Human capital and wage differentials in a dynamic theory of the firm.* Helsinki: Societas Scientiarum Fennica.

Vough, C.F., & Asbell, B. (1979). *Productivity: A practical program for improving efficiency.* New York: AMACON.

Walker, J.W. (1980) *Human resource planning.* New York: McGraw-Hill.

Wallace, M.J. (1983). Methodology, research, practice, and progress in personnel and industrial relations. *Academy of Management Review, 8,* 6–13.

Watson, H.J. (1981). *Computer simulation in business.* New York: Wiley.

Weekly, J. Frank, B., O'Conner, E., & Peters, L. (1985). A comparison of three methods of estimating the standard deviation of performance in dollars. *Journal of Applied Psychology, 70,* 122–126.

Werther, W.B., Ruch, W.A., & McClure, L. (1986). *Productivity through people.* St. Paul, MN: West.

Zanakis, S., & Maret, M. (1980). A Markov chain application to manpower supply planning. *Journal of Operations Research Society, 31,* 1095–1102.

9 BASIC VALIDATION PRINCIPLES IN PERSONNEL PSYCHOLOGY

Mary L. Tenopyr

Validation in employment settings is a process of investigation undertaken to determine the worth of a selection procedure. Validation, although treated in some earlier books as a simple subject, is a complex process. It is not a procedure easily carried out by someone not trained in personnel psychology and definitely should not be undertaken by someone unfamiliar with the applicable government guidelines, case law, and professional standards. Nevertheless, the manager whose education and experience is in other areas can and should comprehend the concepts underlying validation and its consequences.

VALIDITY DEFINED

In an employment context, basically validity is the degree of accuracy of inferences made on the basis of results of a selection procedure, be it a test, an interview, or any other means of judging a person's suitability for employment or advancement. One should never speak of the validity of a test, interview, or application blank but of the validity of the conclusions one draws from using the test or other procedures.

If you are going to use a selection procedure in an employment context, you should be able to conclude that the selection procedure gives you better employees than you would get if you did not use the procedure. For example if you implement a spelling test for hiring secretaries, the validity question is, "How much better are my new secretaries than those I got before I started to use the test?"

There are some special things to note about validity. First, it is not an all-or-none affair. There are various degrees of validity. A large range of validities is possible, depending upon the selection procedure, the nature of the job, and the range of qualifications in the applicant pool. In some situations the same selection procedure may be more valid than in other situations.

Despite the fact that a range of validities is possible, it is common to speak of a test or other procedure as being valid or not valid in a given situation. When someone uses the term *valid* so categorically, he or she usually means that the degree of validity in a particular instance is above a predetermined floor. This floor is usually determined by the laws of probability. Just as a "true" unadulterated coin when tossed ten times may come up heads six times and tails four times, a small degree of validity can occur by chance when there is no validity at all. When someone speaks of a test as being valid for a given purpose, it is usually the same as saying that the validity is greater than is likely to have occurred by chance. That is, the validity is above the "chance floor." It is also important to note that the "chance floor" is much higher when a small sample of people is studied than it would be were a large group (1,000 or so) studied. With a small sample, one must have a greater degree of validity in order to say that a test or other procedure is valid. This is just another way of saying that you have to base your validation work on large samples in order to draw firm conclusions. This makes validation work more difficult for the small employer, but with careful validation work, it is possible to do validation studies on relatively small samples. In many cases, however, the smaller employer is advised to use other procedures, which will be described later in this chapter.

No test or other selection procedure is equally valid for all purposes. For example, a mechanical comprehension test may be highly valid for selecting machinists but will probably have low validity for selecting typists. Some (Schmidt, Hunter & Pearlman, 1981) would argue, however, that general mental ability tests are valid for selecting people for all jobs. However, there are still debates on this issue.

ASPECTS OF VALIDITY

It is common to speak of three aspects of validity, each of which involves different validation procedures: criterion-related validity, content validity, and construct validity. These three aspects have been sorted out mainly to provide a shorthand way of talking about validity. The three are really inseparable in concept, and each often is involved at different stages of the validation process for the same selection procedure.

Criterion-Related Validity

Criterion-related validity typically involves evidence that there is a relationship between scores on a selection procedure (predictor or predictors) and scores on one or more measures of job success (criterion or criteria). The relationship is usually shown in mathematical form. The mathematics are concerned with the degree to which people who score high on the test also do well on the job and vice versa. The summary statistic most commonly used to show the degree of this relationship is the coefficient of correlation, which is a unit-free index number (not a proportion) that can be anywhere from -1.00 to $+1.00$. A $+1.00$ indicates a perfect relationship (the top scorer on the test was the best job performer); the second-best scorer was the second-best performer, and so on. Such perfect relationships rarely, if ever, occur in employee selection. A -1.00 indicates a perfect inverse relationship (the worst scorer was the best performer). Again, such a perfect inverse relationship is highly unlikely to occur. In fact, in employee selection the only time that relationships that are even slightly negative occur is when one of the two things correlated has an inverse scale. This can occur with inverse scales like error rates. For example, a negative correlation might occur between error rates and performance ratings, where the person who has a low error score is a good performer. A zero coefficient of correlation indicates a pure random relationship.

There are two general types of criterion-related validation study: the predictive and the concurrent. These are not always distinguishable in practice, but they will be discussed separately. In a predictive study, tests, interviews, or other selection procedures are administered to job applicants, and the results are not used in the selection of employees. Later the employer follows up on the job applicants and obtains measures of their performance. The test results and performance measurement results are subjected to statistical analysis, and the coefficient of correlation (validity coefficient) between the two is calculated. In a concurrent study, employees are administered the tests or other procedures, and performance measures are gathered at about the same time. The mathematics are essentially the same as with a predictive study. There are advantages and disadvantages to both methods (predictive and concurrent), but either method is professionally acceptable (Society for Industrial and Organizational Psychology, 1987).

Content validity refers to the result of building validity into a selection procedure. A test, interview, or other selection procedure is said to be content valid if the content of the procedure is a sample of the content of the job.

Content Validity

Content validity is most appropriately applied to work sample tests, job knowledge tests, performance appraisals, and experience and education requirements. However, in any selection procedure, no matter what aspect of validity is used to justify it, it is important that there be the right content. Establishing content validity requires an analysis of the job or jobs for which a selection procedure is to be designed. The job analysis should show the tasks performed and, in addition, may include documentation of the knowledges, skills, and abilities necessary to perform those tasks.

After the job analysis is done, a sample of tasks, knowledges, skills, or abilities is taken as a basis for developing the selection instrument. This sample need not cover the whole job but may represent a carefully defined part of the job. For example, a typist may do a number of tasks, such as typing, answering telephones, and processing mail. The employer may choose only a portion of the job as the basis for a selection procedure. Commonly only the typing content of the job is chosen for development of a content-valid test. This is not to say that selection cannot be improved by adding clerical aptitude tests, which can be justified by a criterion-related study.

The whole procedure of sampling from the job analysis data is complicated. In deciding how to sample the job tasks, it is important to note that there is no requirement that a selection procedure developed on the basis of content have perfect validity. That requirement is not made in criterion-related validation. The important consideration is that there be a justifiable rationale for whatever sampling is done.

Some recommend random sampling (Wigdor &

Green, 1986). However, there are often good reasons to avoid random sampling, which may select tasks that are problematic to include in the selection procedure. For example, a job may involve operating an expensive piece of equipment. Obviously one does not risk damage to that equipment by allowing job applicants to operate it. Nor does the employer give tests that pose a risk to the safety of the job applicant or others. Also the matter of expense has to be taken into account. Employers usually seek the most cost-effective way of selecting employees. Random sampling may select some tasks on which performance is very expensive to measure.

Again, it is not necessary to measure performance on all tasks involved in the job, nor is it necessary to do random sampling of tasks. After the sampling, the selection procedure should be developed carefully. It is possible to do a good job of task sampling and then prepare a selection procedure that measures something not related to task performance. For example, it is possible to write a test in which the writing is so complicated or confusing that the test measures reading ability more than anything else. Also, it is possible to write a test so carelessly that examines can get items correct when they do not know the right answers.

Performance appraisals are particularly problematic procedures. One may sample tasks and develop rating forms so that they represent well what is done on the job yet through inadequate training of raters or neglect of other important administrative matters produce, in fact, ratings that have little to do with actual performance.

Work samples involving equipment also can present problems. The same manufacturer's equipment, such as a machine, may function differently from testing location to testing location. Also, a piece of equip-

ment may wear with use so that later test scores are not comparable with those obtained earlier when the equipment was new.

There have been many debates about the acceptability of content validation for justifying broad traits. In general, it is probably best to get additional evidence beyond content to justify broad traits like intelligence, reasoning ability, or drive (Tenopyr, 1977).

Construct Validity

Construct validation is the third aspect of general validation. A close analogy may be drawn between a construct and a trait. The word *construct* is used because the traitlike concept it represents has been constructed. Constructs like sociability, anxiety, or spatial visualization have no reality; they are conceptualizations.

Construct validation in an employment situation is a relatively complex process. First, you must gather a variety of evidence to support the contention that the selection procedure you intend to use is a measure of a given construct. The evidence may take a number of forms, and no one piece of evidence stands alone. The judgment that a selection procedure represents a construct is based upon the preponderance of the evidence. After this is done, the next step is to prove that the same construct is related to successful job performance or other important job behavior, such as attendance. There is no simple prescription for preparing a case to justify construct validity, so none is presented here. Attempting to conduct construct validation is probably better left to experienced professionals in industrial psychology.

PRACTICALITIES OF VALIDATION

The smaller employer has particular problems in validating selection procedures. He or she may not have sufficient employees in any one job or group of jobs to do meaningful criterion-related validation studies. Furthermore, the employer may not have access to the type of professional expertise needed to conduct validation work properly. In cases like these, the employer may have several options.

One option is to join in a consortium with other employees to do validation work. A number of trade associations and other groups have joined together to do collective validation studies. This approach has the advantage of providing sufficiently large numbers of

people in similar jobs so that adequate criterion-related studies may be done. Consortia also provide the means for sharing the cost of professional expertise.

Another approach for the small employer is to rely on the results of a technique known as meta-analysis (Hunter & Schmidt, 1989). This procedure mathematically cumulates the results of previous validation studies done by others. Results of these meta-analyses are available in the published psychological literature (Pearlman, Schmidt & Hunter, 1980). Results for some types of job are better than those for other jobs. Also, there are often problems in adapting others' results to the employers' exact situation. Consequently, again, it is advisable for the employer to seek professional guidance.

Much has been said in this chapter about the need for professional advice. There are a number of publications with which the employer should be familiar. The most important of these is the Uniform Guidelines on Employee Selection Procedures (Equal Employment Opportunity Commission, Civil Service Commission, Department of Labor & Department of Justice, 1978). These guidelines are the concerned government agencies' positions on validation. The employer whose selection procedures are being legally questioned will undoubtedly face these guidelines. There is a major problem with those guidelines. As they are not revised frequently, they may not reflect the current status of either the case law or the professional literature. Furthermore, professional developments have often outpaced case law.

Other documents that should be of interest to the employer are *Standards for Educational and Psychological Testing* (American Educational Research Association, American Psychological Association, & National Council on Measurement in Education, 1985) and *Principles for the Validation and Use of Personnel Selection Procedures* (Society for Industrial and Organizational Psychology, 1987). The *Standards* pertain to tests used in a variety of circumstances, including the fields of education and mental health, and parts are not applicable to personnel selection. The *Principles,* on the other hand, provide readable guidance directly relevant to the personnel selection situation.

There are no fixed rules for selecting an expert to advise on the validation process. In general, persons with Ph.D.s specialized in industrial psychology or psychological measurement are to be preferred. Not all persons who are psychologists are qualified to advise on personnel selection even though these persons may have worked in business. For example, many organizational development specialists and clinical psychologists do not have the basic qualifications to advise in this area. If a psychologist is offering his or her services as a consultant, the employer should be certain that the individual meets the appropriate state licensing or certification requirements necessary to offer psychological services to the public legally.

A local university's psychology department is a good place to start in the search for a consultant. Also, the American Psychological Association regularly publishes a directory of psychologists. Psychologists are listed by locality and by the divisions of the association to which they belong. Industrial psychologists typically belong to Division 14 of the American Psychological Association. Division 14 is the Society for Industrial and Organizational Psychology. However, neither membership in the division nor the whole American Psychological Association is a guarantee of qualifications in the area of personnel selection. The directory is usually available in public and university libraries.

In choosing a psychologist, one should prefer one who has experience in preparing legal cases to defend personnel selection procedures. A past appearance on the witness stand in an employee selection case is also desirable. In making arrangements with an outside consultant, there should be a clear understanding about what the psychologist's role will be in the event of legal challenge to the selection procedures he or she develops or recommends.

Although validation has legal aspects, it is important for the employer to recognize that validation of selection procedures is just plain good business. There is no advantage, and there may be considerable costs, in using employee selection procedures that do not select better employees. The whole purpose of using personnel selection procedures like interviews and tests is to improve the work force. It is obvious that selecting better employees contributes to the bottom line. Also there is a voluminous literature supporting this contention (Schmidt, Hunter, McKenzie & Muldrow, 1979.) An employer generally cannot improve personnel selection without the aid of validation research and development.

SUMMARY

Validation results of the application of personnel selection procedures is a worthwhile business practice. There are a number of related approaches to validation that may be used. Although the basic concepts of validation are rather straightforward, employers should seek professional guidance in the actual conduct of validation.

REFERENCES

American Educational Research Association, American Psychological Association, & National Council on Measurement in Education (1985). *Standards for educational and psychological testing.* Washington, DC: American Psychological Association.

Equal Employment Opportunity Commission, Civil Service Commission, Department of Labor, & Department of Justice (1978). *Adoption by four agencies of Uniform Guidelines on Employee Selection Procedures. Federal Register, 43,* 38290–38315.

Hunter, J.E., Schmidt, F.L., & Hunter, J.E. (1980). Validity generalization results for tests used to predict job proficiency and training success in clerical occupations. *Journal of Applied Psychology, 65,* 373–406.

Schmidt, F.L., Hunter, J.E., McKenzie, R., & Muldrow, T. (1979). The impact of valid selection procedures on workforce productivity. *Journal of Applied Psychology, 64,* 609–626.

Schmidt, F.L., Hunter, J.E., & Pearlman, K. (1981). Task differences as moderators of aptitude test validity in selection: A red herring. *Journal of Applied Psychology, 66,* 166–185.

Society for Industrial and Organizational Psychology, Inc. (1987). *Principles for the validation and use of personnel selection procedures.* (3d ed.). College Park, MD: Author.

Tenopyr, M.L. (1977). Content-construct confusion. *Personnel Psychology, 30,* 47–54.

Wigdor, A.K., & Green, B.F., Jr. (Eds.) (1986). *Assessing the performance of enlisted personnel: Evaluation of a joint-service research project.* Washington, DC: National Academy Press.

10 VALIDITY GENERALIZATION: IMPLICATIONS FOR PERSONNEL SELECTION

Michael A. McDaniel

The productivity of a business's work force is a major determinant of the success or failure of an enterprise. To increase the productivity of human capital, personnel psychologists have invested great effort in the development of methods for selecting capable employees from a pool of applicants. As part of this effort, much research has been conducted on the relationship between mental ability and job performance. The use of mental ability testing in personnel screening became widespread during World War I with the testing of almost 2 million military recruits. While this program was primarily experimental and had little impact on the staffing of the military during the war, it led to a substantial increase in the use of testing in the postwar years as personnel psychologists applied their skills in the civilian sector (Wigdor & Garner, 1982). By the middle of this century, large amounts of validity data had been accumulated in the research literature. Early attempts to summarize this research yielded disappointing results. Validities appeared to be situationally specific. Ghiselli summarized the findings:

> A confirmed pessimist at best, even I was surprised at the variation in findings concerning a particular test applied to workers on a particular job. We certainly never expected the repetition of an investigation to give the same results as the original. But we never anticipated them to be worlds apart. Yet, this appears to be the situation with test validities. (1959, pp. 397–398)

Thus there was widespread pessimism regarding the generalizability of test validity across different situations. This belief that the validity of personnel selection measures was situationally specific encouraged employers to conduct a validity study in each new application of the test.

POPULATION PARAMETERS AND SAMPLE STATISTICS

An important concept in understanding validity generalization research is the distinction between population parameters and observed or sample statistics. A *population* validity coefficient expresses the true relationship between a selection procedure and a measure of job performance. It is the population coefficient that describes the true value of a test in predicting job performance. One conducts a validity study in an attempt to estimate this population validity coefficient. The *observed* validity coefficient obtained in a validity study is a distorted estimate of the population validity coefficient. A major source of distortion in the observed validity coefficient is sampling error. The smaller is the sample size, the greater is the distortion. This error causes the observed validity coefficient to be randomly higher or lower than the population validity coefficient. Since the number of persons available to participate in a validation study is small (usually under 100), sampling error will play havoc with the observed validity coefficient.

While sampling error distorts the observed validity coefficient in a random fashion, measurement error causes the observed validity coefficient to underestimate the population correlation. All measurement involves some degree of error. In validity studies, the major source of measurement error that distorts observed validity coefficients is inaccuracy in the measurement of the job performance criteria. To the extent to which the criterion is measured with error, the observed validity coefficient will underestimate the population validity.

SITUATIONAL SPECIFICITY AND VALIDITY GENERALIZATION

The situational specificity position holds that situation-specific moderators (between-job task or behavior differences) cause a selection procedure to be valid in one setting but not another. This position is supported to the extent that variability in validity coefficients (correlations between an employee's score on a selection procedure and the employee's job performance) from one setting to another cannot be accounted for by alternative explanations (such as statistical and methodological artifacts). Validity generalization may be defined in several ways (Pearlman, 1982). Using the most conservative definition, the validity of a test is held to be generalizable when the population validities are the same in all applications of the test. By a second definition, validity may be generalized when most of the population validities are greater than a minimum useful validity. This second definition permits some variability in the population distribution. This variability may be due to situational or other moderators or from uncorrected statistical-methodological problems in the data, but this remaining variance is sufficiently small to allow the measure to be valid for the vast majority of its applications.

The assumptions of situational specificity and the related lack of generalizability of validity across settings came under serious question as a result of a series of studies by Schmidt, Hunter, and their associates (Schmidt, Hunter & Urry, 1976; Schmidt & Hunter, 1977). Schmidt et al. (1976) began the assault on the situational specificity hypothesis by documenting that sample sizes available for most validity studies have limited statistical power. This means that validity studies based on small samples (for example, 100 people) are likely to yield inconclusive and uninterpretable results. Schmidt and Hunter (1977) continued their argument by postulating that situational specificity was illusory, and the appearance of situational specificity was due to several methodological and statistical artifacts such as sampling error and measurement reliability that caused observed validity coefficients to bounce about from one study to another.

EVIDENCE FOR VALIDITY GENERALIZATION OF COGNITIVE ABILITY MEASURES

In their refutation of the situational specificity hypothesis, Schmidt and Hunter (1977) cited several sources of statistical and methodological artifacts that produce variance in observed validity coefficients, thus giving the false impressions of situational specificity and the lack of validity generalization. Some of these artifacts also reduce the size of the observed validity coefficients. They supported their argument by demonstrating that artifactual sources of variance were responsible for about half of the observed variance in four sets of validity coefficients. A flurry of studies then demonstrated that most of the variance in the validities of mental ability measures is due to these artifacts, with sampling error being the major source of artifactual variance (Callender & Osburn, 1981; Pearlman, 1982; Pearlman & Northrop, 1978; Pearlman, Schmidt & Hunter, 1980; Schmidt, Gast-Rosenberg & Hunter, 1980; Schmidt, Hunter & Caplan, 1981; Schmidt, Hunter & Pearlman, 1981; Schmidt, Hunter, Pearlman, & Shane, 1979). These studies also demonstrated that statistical artifacts reduced the size of the observed validity coefficients and thus underestimated the true value of selection procedures in screening applicants.

The ideas presented by Schmidt and Hunter (1977) were expanded and more formally presented in their 1982 book (Hunter, Schmidt & Jackson; see Hunter & Schmidt, 1989, for a revision of this classic text) on metaanalysis. Metaanalysis is a collection of methods that facilitate the development of accurate conclusions about the magnitude and direction of correlation coefficients based on a body of past studies. Validity generalization is an application of metaanalysis. Glass (1976) introduced the term *metaanalysis* and developed several useful procedures. Schmidt, Hunter and their associates (Hirsh, Schmidt, Hunter & Pearlman, 1985; Schmidt & Hunter, 1977; Schmidt, Gast-Rosenberg, et al., 1980) have developed additional procedures that extend and complement Glass's initial effort. Procedures yielding comparable results have been developed by Callender and Osburn (Callender & Osburn, 1980, 1981; Callender, Osburn & Greener, 1979) as well as by Raju and Burke (1983).

The validity generalization research conducted by

Schmidt, Hunter, and others has demonstrated that measures of mental ability are valid predictors of performance in all jobs (Schmidt & Hunter, 1981). Most validity generalization studies have focused on the validity of mental ability tests for specific occupational groups, including clerical occupations (Pearlman, 1979; Pearlman, Schmidt & Hunter, 1980), science and health aid/technicians (Lilienthal & Pearlman, 1983), petroleum occupations (Callender & Osburn, 1981; Schmidt, Hunter & Caplan, 1981), psychiatric aides (Distefano & Pryer, 1984), law enforcement occupations (Hirsh, Northrop & Schmidt, 1986), apprentice and helper-trainee positions (Northrop, 1986), computer programmers (Schmidt, Gast-Rosenberg & Hunter, 1980), retail industry positions (Schmidt, Hunter, Pearlman & Caplan, 1981), supervisors (Shane, 1978), and semiprofessional occupations (Trattner, 1985).

Other researchers have examined the extent of validity generalization across occupations (Gandy, 1986; Gutenberg, Arvey, Osburn & Jeanneret, 1983; Hunter, 1983; McDaniel, 1986; Pearlman, 1982). Several of these studies examined the relationship between the cognitive complexity requirements of the job and the level of test validity. For example, Hunter (1983) demonstrated that the validity of cognitive

and psychomotor abilities (e.g., finger dexterity, coordination) depends on the cognitive demands of an occupation. The validity of cognitive measures is highest for the most complex jobs. Conversely, psychomotor tests are most valid for the least complex jobs. Hunter used this relationship to determine the optimal weights for a battery of cognitive and psychomotor tests for occupations at any level of complexity.

The U.S. Employment Service, an agency of the Department of Labor, has used Hunter's research in the scoring of the General Aptitude Test Battery (GATB) (U.S. Department of Labor, 1970). The U.S. Employment Service provides an invaluable service to the private sector by testing thousands of persons each year and referring those most likely to succeed to companies in need of personnel. Based on Hunter's research (1983), the U.S. Employment Service is able to score optimally the GATB for any of the 12,000 occupations in the U.S. economy. Thus, the GATB can be validly used to select employees for any occupation. Madigan and coworkers (1986) describe how the U.S. Employment Service is applying validity generalization knowledge in an applicant screening program that promotes employee productivity while fostering racial balance in the work force.

ADVANTAGES OF VALIDITY GENERALIZATION

The validity generalization research conducted to date provides compelling evidence for the validity of professionally developed measures of cognitive ability. Cognitive ability measures predict performance in all occupations. This is not to say that the validity of a cognitive ability test is constant across occupations. Cognitive tests are more valid for some occupations (e.g., more complex jobs) than others. The important point is that cognitive ability tests will provide a good level of prediction for all jobs. The use of valid screening tools can result in massive dollar savings through increased work force productivity (Hunter & Schmidt, 1982). Furthermore, validity generalization diminishes the need for conducting validity studies on cognitive ability measures in one's own company. Such studies can be costly. In addition, cognitive ability measures have been demonstrated to be fair to minorities in that they do not underpredict the performance of minority persons (see Wigdor & Garner, 1982, for a summary of this literature). (Additional discussion of the fairness of cognitive ability measures is presented in chapter 25.)

An important consideration for employers in using evidence generated by any research approach is the professional acceptance of the research. *Principles for the Validation and Use of Personnel Selection Procedures* (American Psychological Association, Division of Industrial and Organizational Psychology, 1986) is the primary set of professional guidelines accepted by personnel psychologists. These principles acknowledge the substantial contributions that validity generalization research has made to the personnel field and consider the application of knowledge gained from validity generalization studies to staffing decisions as acceptable practice. Specifically, the principles state, "To the extent that validity generalization is available, researchers may rely on it to support the use of selection instruments" (p. 17).

Employers should be aware that the cognitive ability measures summarized in validity generalization research are professionally developed measures of cognitive ability. Test development is a highly specialized area. Employers should not attempt to develop their own measure of cognitive ability without the assistance of a competently trained psychometrician. Given the expense entailed in developing a cognitive ability measure and the relative inexpense of commercially available tests, employers may wish to obtain a cognitive ability measure from a test vendor. Descriptions of such measures are available in product catalogs distributed by test publishers.

VALIDITY GENERALIZATION EVIDENCE FOR OTHER SELECTION PROCEDURES

While the bulk of validity generalization research has addressed mental ability measures, substantial validity generalization research has been conducted for other common selection measures. Both Gaugler and associates (1987) and Lowenberg and associates (1985) have applied validity generalization methods to the extensive literature on assessment centers. While the studies differ in important respects, both sets of researchers reported substantial support for the validity of assessment centers.

McDaniel, Schmidt, and Hunter (1988a) examined the validity generalization of several methods of evaluating training and experience. These applicant screening methods are formal approaches to assessing the value of an applicant's training, education, and experience as summarized on resumes, applications, or other documents. These screening methods vary in the type of information reviewed and the manner in which it is evaluated. Due to the limited number of primary validity studies on such measures, the conclusions drawn from this study are tentative. The results indicated that the validity of the most commonly used method of training and experience assessment (the point method) was very low. In the point method, an applicant receives points according to the type and amount of job experience, education, and training he or she possesses. This is a very credentialistic approach to screening applicants and is similar to less formalized approaches used in public sector employment offices. In contrast to the credentialistic point approach, the behavioral consistency method (Schmidt, Caplan, Bemis, Decuir, Dunn & Antone, 1979) requires applicants to describe their achievements in job-related areas that differentiate superior from minimally acceptable employees. The McDaniel et al. (1988a) study indicated that the behavioral consistency method shows substantial validity.

McDaniel (1986) and McDaniel, Schmidt, and Hunter (1988b) applied validity generalization methods to evaluate the validity of length of job experience as a predictor of job performance. These studies found length of job experience to be most valid when the applicant pool had limited amounts of job experience. When the applicant pool consisted of persons with substantial amounts of job experience, the length of job experience proved less valuable as a predictor of job performance.

Both Wiesner and Cronshaw (1988) and McDaniel and associates (1986) used validity generalization methods to summarize the value of the employment interview. Both studies indicated that structured interviews have higher validities than unstructured employment interviews. In contrast to the unstructured interview, structured interviews tend to have a fixed set of questions asked of each applicant, the interviewer has a clear idea of what constitutes a correct answer, and an interviewer has a formalized scoring procedure for the interview. Wiesner and Cronshaw (1988) reported that employment interviews based on job analyses yielded the highest validities. That is, interviews that were focused on important aspects of the job are substantially better than those interviews constructed without a thorough review of the demands of the job. However, McDaniel et al. (1986) noted that the validity evidence reported in their study was based on employment interviews that were probably better conducted than most other employment interviews. Thus, the validity evidence reported by Wiesner and Cronshaw (1988) and McDaniel et al. (1986) probably overestimates the value of the employment interview as typically conducted.

Dye, Reck, and McDaniel (1989) conducted a major review of the validity of written job knowledge measures. These measures are paper-and-pencil tests that measure technical information specific to an occupation. For example, a job knowledge test for the selection of accountants would measure knowledge of accounting principles and practices. Job knowledge measures were shown to be very good predictors of job performance. The usefulness of the measures was highest when the knowledge topics measured by the test were very similar to the knowledge demands of the job. The measures were more useful for complex jobs than for less complex jobs.

SUMMARY

The seminal work of Schmidt and Hunter (1977) laid the groundwork for a large research effort to determine the generalizability of the validity of many personnel selection procedures. Over the last decade, an enormous volume of research has been conducted in this area. Professionally developed cognitive ability measures have received the most attention. The results are clear: cognitive ability measures are valid predictors of job performance for all occupations. Businesses that are not using cognitive ability measures to screen personnel are losing money through the selection of a less than optimal work force. Researchers have also addressed the validity generalizability of other selection procedures. In general, these studies have supported the usefulness of most personnel selection procedures. Based on this growing body of cumulative knowledge in personnel selection, employers may now confidently choose the selection procedure with the highest validity for their occupations.

REFERENCES

American Psychological Association. Division of Industrial and Organizational Psychology (1986). *Principles for the validation and use of personnel selection procedures* (3d ed.). Berkeley, CA: Author.

Callender, J.C., & Osburn, H.G. (1980). Development and test of a new model for validity generalization. *Journal of Applied Psychology, 65,* 543–558.

Callender, J.C., & Osburn, H.G. (1981). Testing the constancy of validity with computer-generated sampling distributions of the multiplicative model variance estimate: Results for petroleum industry validation research. *Journal of Applied Psychology, 66,* 274–281.

Callender, J.C., Osburn, H.G., & Greener, J.M. (1979). *Small-sample tests of two validity generalization models.* Paper presented at the meeting of the American Psychological Association, New York City.

Distefano, M.K., & Pryer, M.W. (1984). Meta-analysis of the validity of a verbal ability selection test with psychiatry aides. *Psychological Reports, 54,* 676–678.

Dye, D.A., Reck, M., & McDaniel, M.A. (1989). *Moderators of the validity of written job knowledge measures.* Paper presented at the Fourth Annual Conference of the Society of Industrial and Organizational Psychology, Inc.

Gandy, J.A. (1986). *Job complexity, aggregated subsample, and aptitude test validity: Meta-analysis of the GATB data base.* Washington, DC: U.S. Office of Personnel Management, Office of Staffing Policy.

Gaughler, B.B., Rosenthal, D.B., Thornton, G.C., & Bentson, C. (1987). Meta-analysis of assessment center validity. *Journal of Applied Psychology, 72,* 493–511.

Ghiselli, E.E. (1959). The generalization of validity. *Personnel Psychology, 12,* 397–402.

Glass, G.V. (1976). Primary, secondary and meta-analysis of research. *Educational Researcher, 5,* 3–8.

Gutenberg, R.L., Arvey, R.D., Osburn, H.G., & Jeanneret, P.R. (1983). Moderating effects of decision-making/information-processing job demands on test validities. *Journal of Applied Psychology, 68,* 602–608.

Hirsh, H.R., Northrop, L.C., & Schmidt, F.L. (1986). Validity generalization results for law enforcement occupations. *Personnel Psychology, 39,* 399–420.

Hirsh, H.R., Schmidt, F.L., Hunter, J.E., & Pearlman, K. (1985). *An improved method for estimating the standard deviation of the distribution of true validities.* Paper presented at the 93d Annual Convention of the American Psychological Association, Los Angeles.

Hunter, J.E. (1983). *Test validation for 12,000 jobs: An application of job classification and validity generalization to the General Aptitude Test Battery (GATB).* Washington, DC: U.S. Department of Labor, Employment and Training Administration, Division of Counseling and Test Development.

Hunter, J.E., & Schmidt, F.L. (1989). *Methods of meta-analysis.* Newbury Park, CA: Sage.

Hunter, J.E., Schmidt, F.L., & Jackson, G.B. (1982). *Meta-analysis: Cumulating research findings across studies.* Beverly Hills, CA: Sage.

Lilienthal, R.A., & Pearlman, K. (1983). *The validity of federal selection tests for aid/technicians in the health, science, and engineering fields* (OPRD-83-1). Washington, DC: U.S. Office of Personnel Management, Office of Personnel Research and Development. (NTIS No. PB 80. 102 650).

Lowenberg, G., Faust, B.D., Loschenkohl, G.H., & Conrad, K.A. (1985). Meta-analyses demonstrating validity generalization for managerial assessment center dimensions. In H.R. Hirsh (Chair), *Meta-analysis of Alternative Predictors of Job Performance.* Symposium presented at the 93d Annual Convention of the American Psychological Convention, Los Angeles.

McDaniel, M.A. (1986). *The evaluation of a causal model of job performance: The interrelationships of general mental ability, job experience, and job performance.* Ph.D. dissertation, George Washington University.

McDaniel, M.A., & Schmidt, F.L. (1985). *A meta-analysis of the validity of training and experience ratings in personnel selection* (OSP-85-1). Washington, DC: U.S.

Office of Personnel Management, Office of Staffing Policy. (NTIS No. PB 86 109 618/AS)

McDaniel, M.A., Schmidt, F.L., & Hunter, J.E. (1988a). A meta-analysis of methods for rating training and experience in personnel selection. *Personnel Psychology, 41*, 283–314.

McDaniel, M.A., Schmidt, F.L., & Hunter, J.E. (1988b). Job experience correlates of job performance. *Journal of Applied Psychology, 73*, 327–330.

McDaniel, M.A., Whetzel, D., Schmidt, F.L., Hunter, F.L., Hunter, J.E., Maurer, S., & Russell, J. (1986). New research on the validity of employment interviews. In M.A. McDaniel (Chair), *New research in validity generalization.* A symposium presented at the International Personnel Management Association Assessment Council Annual Conference, San Francisco.

Madigan, R.M., Scott, K.D., Deadrick, D.L., & Stoddard, J.A. (1986). Employment testing: The U.S. Job Service is spearheading a revolution. *Personnel Administrator, 31*, 102–112.

Northrop, L.C. (1986). *Validity generalization results for apprentice and helper-trainee positions.* Washington, DC: U.S. Office of Personnel Management, Office of Staffing Policy.

Pearlman, K. (1979). *The validity of tests used to select clerical personnel: A comprehensive summary and evaluation* (TS-79-1). Washington, DC: U.S. Office of Personnel Management, Personnel Research and Development Center. (NTIS No. PB 80 102 650)

Pearlman, K. (1982). The Bayesian approach to validity generalization: A systematic examination of the robustness of procedures and conclusions. Ph.D. dissertation, George Washington University. *Dissertation Abstracts International, 42*, 49609A.

Pearlman, K., & Northrop, L.C. (1978). *An analysis of criterion-related validity evidence relevant to Test 650* (TM-78-7). Washington, DC: U.S. Civil Service Commission, Personnel Research and Development Center. (NTIS No. PB 298406)

Pearlman, K., Schmidt, F.L., & Hunter, J.E. (1980). Validity generalization results for tests used to predict training success and job proficiency in clerical occupations. *Journal of Applied Psychology, 65*, 373–406.

Raju, N.S., & Burke, M.J. (1983). Two new procedures for studying validity generalization. *Journal of Applied Psychology, 68*, 382–395.

Schmidt, F.L., Caplan, J.R., Bemis, S.E., Decuir, R., Dunn, L., & Antone, L. (1979). *The behavioral consistency method of unassembled examining* (TM-79-21). Washington, DC: U.S. Office of Personnel Management, Personnel Research and Development Center.

Schmidt, F.L., Gast-Rosenberg, I., & Hunter, J.E. (1980). Validity generalization: Results for computer programmers. *Journal of Applied Psychology, 65*, 643–661.

Schmidt, F.L., & Hunter, J.E. (1977). Development of a general solution to the problem of validity generalization. *Journal of Applied Psychology, 62*, 529–540.

Schmidt, F.L., & Hunter, F.L. (1981). Employment testing: Old theories and new research findings. *American Psychologist, 36*, 1128–1137.

Schmidt, F.L., Hunter, J.E., & Caplan, J.R. (1981). Validity generalization results for two occupations in the petroleum industry. *Journal of Applied Psychology, 66*, 261–273.

Schmidt, F.L., Hunter, J.E., & Pearlman, K. (1981). Task difference moderators of aptitude test validity in selection: A red herring. *Journal of Applied Psychology, 66*, 166–185.

Schmidt, F.L., Hunter, J.E., Pearlman, K., & Caplan, J.R. (1981). Validity generalization results for three occupations in the Sears Roebuck Company. Unpublished manuscript.

Schmidt, F.L., Hunter, J.E., Pearlman, K., & Shane, G.S. (1979). Further tests of the Schmidt-Hunter Bayesian validity generalization procedure. *Personnel Psychology, 65*, 643–661.

Schmidt, F.L., Hunter, J.E., & Urry, V.W. (1976). Statistical power in criterion-related validation studies. *Journal of Applied Psychology, 61*, 473–485.

Shane, G.S. (1978). *The Schmidt-Hunter approach to validity generalization: An application to supervisory selection.* Ph.D. dissertation, George Washington University.

Trattner, M. (1985). *Estimating the validity of aptitude and ability tests for semiprofessional occupations using the Schmidt-Hunter interactive validity generalization procedure* (OSP-85-3). Washington, DC: U.S. Office of Personnel Management, Office of Staffing Policy. (NTIS PB 861 694 63/AS)

U.S. Department of Labor. U. S. Employment Service (1970). *General Aptitude Test Battery, Section III: Development.* Washington, DC: U.S. Government Printing Office.

Wiesner, W.H., & Cronshaw, S.F. (1988). A meta-analytic investigation of the impact of interview format and degree of structure on the validity of the employment interview. *Journal of Occupational Psychology, 61*, 275–290.

Wigdor, A.K., & Garner, W.R. (1982). *Ability testing: Uses, consequences, and controversies. Part I: Report of the committee.* Washington, DC: National Academy Press.

UTILITY OF PERSONNEL DECISIONS

Nambury S. Raju, Michael J. Burke

The financial impact of human resource services such as personnel selection, evaluation, and training programs has been receiving a great deal of attention lately. The reason for this added attention is at least twofold: the need to justify the financial contribution of activities performed in the name of human resource management to the bottom line or overall profit picture of an organization and recent methodological developments that make the determination of the financial value of human resource activities such as personnel selection and training quite feasible. The purpose of this chapter is to describe some of the available procedures for determining the utility of personnel selection and organizational intervention programs and illustrate their application.

UTILITY ANALYSIS MODELS

Suppose an organization wants to develop and implement a selection program for the job of a clerk-typist. Typically, the person in charge of developing the selection program analyzes the job of a clerk-typist, identifies potential selection procedures, and validates the usefulness of the selection procedures for hiring clerk-typists. Personnel selection procedures generally consist of aptitude, achievement, and/or personality tests, and their usefulness for selection is typically expressed in terms of a correlation (or validity) coefficient, which expresses the degree of linear relationship between a set of selection procedures and performance on the job under consideration. In absolute terms, the correlation coefficient varies between 0 and 1; the higher the correlation coefficient is, the greater is the predictive value of a selection program. While the size of the correlation coefficient tells one, in statistical terms, the usefulness of a selection program, it does not yield, in a straightforward manner, information about the financial impact of a selection program. The need for financial information was well recognized by psychologists, especially by Brogden who, in 1949, presented a method for assessing the financial impact of a selection program (Brogden, 1949). The pioneering work of Brogden is still the basis for much of the utility analysis conducted by industrial-organizational (I-O) psychologists and human resource professionals today.

Brogden's Utility Model

Brogden showed that an estimate of the dollar value or utility (ΔU) of hiring N_s applicants based on their personnel selection test scores (X) rather than selecting them at random can be assessed by

$$\Delta U = N_s \, r \, SD_Y \, \overline{X}_s - C \qquad (11.1)$$

where r is the correlation between the personnel selection procedure and job performance, SD_Y is the standard deviation of the dollar value of employee job performance (assuming all applicants were on the job), $\overline{X}_s$ is the mean test score (expressed in a standard score form with mean and standard deviation equal to 0 and 1, respectively) of those newly hired, and C is the total cost of the selection program. Brogden's initial presentation did not contain C, but its inclusion was later suggested by Cronbach and Gleser (1965).

Several significant aspects of the utility equation are worth noting. First, the greater is the number of new hirees, the greater is the utility. The question of how many to hire for a given job depends upon the business needs of an organization, as it should be. No manager will be able to hire more people than the organizational needs dictate. Therefore, the quantity N in equation 11.1 is not one that a personnel psychologist or human resources specialist can manipulate to increase the utility of a selection program. However, there are other quantities in the equation that one can manipulate to increase the utility of a selection program, as we shall soon show.

The next quantity in equation 11.1 is r, which is the correlation between personnel selection procedure scores and job performance and is often referred to as the validity coefficient. According to equation 11.1, the higher the validity coefficient is in absolute terms, the greater is the utility associated with the selection program under consideration. In practice, most validity coefficients are 0.40 or lower, with only a few exceeding 0.60. The importance of this observation is that even though the utility of a selection program can be increased by raising the validity coefficient, substantial increments in validity coefficients are often hard to come by. Problems concerning the consistency of applicant responses to personnel selection procedures and the consistency of scores on job performance measures (such as the reliability of supervisory ratings) as well as the complex nature of job performance itself (Smith, 1976) have limited I-O psychologists' ability to raise the level of validity coefficients significantly.

The next quantity in equation 11.1 is the standard deviation (SD_Y) of the dollar value of applicants. This is the most difficult quantity to estimate. Strictly speaking, one needs information about the dollar value of the performance of each and every employee to compute SD_Y. Complex and time-consuming cost accounting procedures are generally needed to determine accurately the dollar value of an employee. Until very recently, this problem of estimating SD_Y has discouraged many investigators and human resource professionals from assessing the dollar value of selection programs and other organizational interventions. Recently, several simpler methods have been proposed, and they are currently being used for estimating SD_Y. These developments, in part, explain the current interest in utility analysis among I-O psychologists and human resource specialists. The new methods for estimating SD_Y will be discussed in some detail in the next section.

The next component or term in equation 11.1 is $\overline{X}_s$, which is the mean score for the new hirees on the selection procedure. Typically, the top-scoring applicants are hired, thereby making $\overline{X}_s$ as high as possible, which, in turn, will make total utility as high as possible. That is, the greater is the mean score for the new hirees, the greater is the total utility. The mean score depends upon not only who is hired but also on how many are hired and the size of the applicant pool. For example, hiring the two top-scoring individuals from a pool of ten applicants will yield a higher mean predictor score than hiring the five top-scoring individuals from the same applicant pool (except when the five top-scoring individuals all have the same selection procedure score). Also, other things being equal, hiring the top twenty individuals from a pool of fifty will probably result in the same mean predictor score as hiring the top forty individuals from a pool of one hundred applicants, the reason being that the same proportion of individuals is hired in each case. For a fixed number of job openings, a larger applicant pool is very likely to result in a greater mean predictor score (and, therefore, greater total utility) than a smaller applicant pool.

The last term in equation 11.1 is C, which is the total cost associated with the implementation of a selection program or an organizational intervention. Needless to say, some programs cost more than others. For example, an assessment center is generally more expensive than a typical test-based selection program. Also, the bigger the applicant pool is, the greater is the cost associated with a selection program. This last aspect is not necessarily undesirable because, as noted above, the bigger the applicant pool is, the greater is the mean predictor score for the top-scoring new hires.

Having presented in detail some of the major variables that contribute to the total utility of a selection program or organizational intervention, let us turn to a discussion of some of the currently popular procedures for estimating SD_Y.

Estimation of SD_Y

Recently Schmidt, Hunter, McKenzie, and Muldrow (1979) proposed practical alternative for estimating the SD_Y parameter. This procedure avoids the complex, often time-consuming cost accounting procedures. This procedure estimates the dollar value to the organization of the goods and services produced by the average employee and those produced by an employee at the eighty-fifth percentile. Assuming that the dollar value of employees is normally distributed, Schmidt et al. suggest that the difference between the values associated with the fifteenth and eighty-fifth percentiles be used as an estimate of SD_Y. Their procedure also calls for estimating the dollar value of an employee at the fifteenth percentile, which is then used to obtain a second estimate of SD_Y. The two SD_Y estimates are averaged to obtain the final estimate of SD_Y. In their 1979 study with computer programmers, Schmidt et al. obtained the dollar value of the average employee from supervisors who were supplied the following instructions:

> Based on your experience with agency programmers, we would like for you to estimate the yearly value to your agency of the products and services produced by the average GS 9–11 computer programmer. Consider the quality and quantity of output typical of the average programmer and the value of this output. In placing an overall dollar value on this output, it may help to consider what the cost would be of having an outside firm provide these products and services. (1979, p. 621)

Similar instructions were also used for gathering dollar value data for employees at the eighty-fifth and fifteenth percentiles. Other procedures with apparently greater face validity have been developed for estimating SD_Y (see Cascio, 1982; Cascio & Ramos, 1986; Hunter & Schmidt, 1982). These later procedures use salary as the common valuation base.

Extensions to Brogden's Model

Utility Analysis of Intervention Programs. The success of an organization depends not only on hiring the right people but also on correctly placing these people and properly managing them. As to the management of employees, training for such things as technical and nontechnical skills, performance appraisals and feedback, and management by objectives plays a significant role in maintaining the well-being of an organization. The model of Brogden is not directly applicable to these intervention programs. In order to apply Brogden's model to these organizational interventions, some modifications to it recently have been proposed by Schmidt, Hunter, and Pearlman (1982) and Landy, Farr, and Jacobs (1982). The Schmidt et al. (1982) modification still uses equation 11.1 for estimating the dollar value of an organizational intervention except that the correlation coefficient (r) is replaced by a quantity known as the effect size (d). The effect size is simply the difference in job perfor-

mance between the average trained and untrained employee expressed in standard deviation units of the untrained group. The Landy et al. (1982) extension is similarly defined.

Boudreau's Extension of Brogden's Model. In reviewing Brogden's model for selection, Boudreau (1983a) identified three economic concepts (variable costs, taxes, and discounting) that he felt were left unaccounted for in that model. The omission of these factors, according to Boudreau, can upwardly bias Brogden's estimates of utility. Previous utility studies dealt exclusively with the "value of sales" (Cascio & Silbey, 1979) or the "value of products and services" (Schmidt et al., 1979) and therefore misrepresented the financial benefit of a selection program to the organization. According to Boudreau,

> First, when variable costs rise (or fall) with productivity (e.g., incentive or commission-based pay, benefits, variable raw material costs, variable production overhead), then a portion (V) of the gain in product sales value will go to pay such costs (or will be reflected in additional cost savings). Second, when the organization faces tax liabilities, a portion (TAX) of the organization's profit (sales less variable cost) will go to pay taxes rather accruing to the organization. Third, where costs and benefits accrue over time, the value of future costs and benefits must be discounted to reflect the opportunity costs of returns foregone because costs incurred earlier and benefits received later cannot be invested for as many periods. (1983a, p. 397)

Boudreau's utility formulas are given in Boudreau (1983a). It should be emphasized that Boudreau's formulation deals with contribution to profit, whereas Brogden's formulation concentrates on the increase in output as sold. Therefore, Boudreau's selection utility is generally smaller than Brogden's utility. Both utilities are useful in practice, each for a different purpose. Boudreau (1983b), Boudreau and Berger (1985), and Boudreau and Rynes (1985) have extended Boudreau's initial work by incorporating the flow of employees in and out of the work force and the effects of recruitment activities.

EXAMPLES OF UTILITY ANALYSES

In this section we will review two utility analyses; one will concern evaluating the dollar impact of a managerial selection program, and the second is an evaluation of the economic utility of a corporate man-

agerial training program. Although our examples are chosen for managerial selection and training programs, results concerning the dollar utility of selection and training programs over and above their costs can be generalized to other job groups (such as clerical and scientific/professional) as well. In addition, we will demonstrate, in the form of a summary table, possible gains from the use of validated personnel selection procedures with respect to several occupations where SD_Y has been estimated.

A Personnel Selection Example

Burke and Frederick (1986) were recently interested in evaluating the dollar impact (contribution to profit) of a managerial assessment center used for selecting district-level sales managers at a large national manufacturing company. The job of district-level sales manager at this organization involves organizing and directing sales teams' efforts to major grocery, drug, and mass merchandiser accounts. These sales teams consist of sales representatives, sales merchandisers, and account managers.

The candidates for the assessment center were area sales representatives (one level below district sales manager). As of 1983 (the year the utility analysis was conducted), 132 area sales representatives had been assessed. The assessment center consisted of a series of exercises that evaluated an area sales representative's potential to succeed in a district sales management position (in terms of their ability to plan and organize, make decisions, tolerate stress, demonstrate sensitivity, and so forth).

The company undertook the utility analysis to obtain an estimate of the economic impact of the assessment center for selecting district sales managers as compared with their previously used interviewing selection program. Prior to discussing the utility analysis, let us consider the expanded utility equation, which allows for a comparison of two selection procedures and incorporates economic concepts such as taxes, discounting, and variable costs (Boudreau, 1983a):

$$\Delta U =$$
$$N_s\left[\sum_{t=1}^{T} (1/(1+i)^t)SD_Y(1+V)(1-TAX)(r_1-r_2)\overline{X}_s\right] -$$
$$(C_1-C_2)(1-TAX)$$

(11.2)

where

ΔU = total estimated dollar value of replacing one selection procedure (11.1) with another procedure (11.2) after variable costs, taxes, and discounting,

N_s = the number of employees selected,

T = the number of future time periods,

t = the time period in which a productivity increase occurs,

i = the discount rate,

SD_Y = the standard deviation of job performance in dollars,

V = the proportion of SD_Y represented by variable costs,

TAX = the organization's applicable tax rate,

r_1 = the validity coefficient for one selection procedure,

r_2 = the validity coefficient for an alternative selection procedure,

$\overline{X}_s$ = the mean standard score on the selection procedure of those selected (this is assumed to be equal for each selection procedure),

C_1 = the total cost of the first selection procedure,

C_2 = the total cost of the alternative selection procedure.

Although the assessment center had been in operation for seven years at the time of the utility analysis, a value for T of four years was used, since this was the average time (tenure) for the 29 (N_s in equation 11.2) district sales managers who had been selected from the pool of 132 assessed area sales representatives. A primary objective of the utility analysis at the organization was to compare the estimated dollar value of selecting 29 managers with the assessment center with what the economic gain would have been if 29 sales managers were selected by an interviewing program.

The company employed an interdisciplinary approach when estimating the various components of equation 11.2. For instance, values of V and TAX were provided by the accounting and tax departments, respectively. These values were .05 for V and .49 for TAX. V was considered as the proportion of dollar sales volume as compared with operating costs. Since there was a positive relationship between combined operating costs (such as salary, benefits, supplies, and automobile operations) and sales volume, a value for V of $-.05$ was used in equation 11.2. In addition, the value for the discount rate, i, of .18 was based on examination of corporate financial documentation. The accounting department also provided the figure for C_1 (the total cost of the assessment center): $263,636. Based on 29 selected individuals, the cost of selecting one district sales manager was computed to be about $9,091. The estimated total cost to select 29 sales managers by the previously used one-day interviewing program was $50,485 (the value for C_2 in equation 11.2). Let us now turn to the final four components of equation 11.2: r_1, r_2, $\overline{X}_s$, and SD_Y.

The validity coefficient for the assessment center (r_1) for predicting job performance was found to be .59, whereas the validity for the interviewing program (r_2) was estimated to be .16. The mean score on the assessment center ($X{****}_s$) was determined to be .872. This value was assumed to be the same for both the assessment center and interviewing program. Also, based on the inputs of a group of regional-level sales managers (one level above the job of district sales manager), the value of SD_Y was estimated to be approximately $30,000.

Placing the previous values into the utility analysis equation would result in a dollar value of approximately $316,460. This value represents the estimated present value, over a four-year time period, to the organization from the use of the assessment center in place of an interviewing program to select 29 sales managers. Although the cost of the interviewing program is only about one-fifth of the assessment center cost, the estimated dollar gain from the use of the assessment center instead of the interviewing program is substantial. This result is primarily due to the greater predictive effectiveness (higher validity coefficient) of the assessment center.

Considering the same economic conditions and time period as discussed above ($T = 4$, $i = .18$, $V = .05$, $TAX = .49$), one could estimate the dollar impact of various types of selection procedures for other jobs, assuming one has knowledge of the validity (r) of a selection procedure for these jobs, SD_Y for the jobs, and cost of the selection procedure. Two other possi-ble examples of the dollar impact of validated selection procedures, based on the above assumptions and SD_Y values obtained from the personnel selection literature are reported in table 11-1. As shown in table 11-1, the estimated gains in dollars from the use of an ability test battery in place of an interviewing program for selecting computer programmers and insurance salespersons are $626,661 and $1,566,255, respectively. These examples once again highlight the differential impact of validated personnel selection procedures on the organization's bottom line.

An Organizational Intervention Example

Although research on the economic utility of personnel selection programs has been enlightening, more recently advances have been made in the utility analysis of organizational interventions (see Schmidt, Hunter & Pearlman, 1982). The following is an example of an evaluation of the economic value of a managerial training program.

In illustrating the value of utility analysis for estimating the dollar worth of a training program, use is made of a hypothetical example. Suppose there are 200 managers of computer programmers in a large data processing company and that half are assigned randomly to a leadership training course while the other 100 managers continue their jobs as usual and serve as a comparison group. The cost of the leadership training course is $500 per manager. Each manager supervises a unit of approximately 10 computer programmers. The outcome variable is the number of error-free computer programs produced by each unit. Assume that after the training, the t-test for the difference in number of error-free programs between the

Table 11-1
Examples of Economic Impact of Validated Selection Procedures

Job/Selection Procedure	r	SD_Y	N_s	$\overline{X}_s$	C	U^a	U^b
Computer programmer							
Ability test battery	.53	$10,413	100	1.17	$50	$842,136	$626,661
Interviewing program	.14	$10,413	100	1.17	$150	$215,475	
Insurance salesperson							
Ability test battery	.53	$52,308	50	1.17	$50	$2,119,020	$1,566,25
Interviewing program	.14	$52,308	50	1.17	$150	$552,765	

Note: The validity coefficients (r's) were obtained from Hunter and Hunter (1984). N_s is the number of individuals selected for a job. The average standard score on the selection procedure ($\overline{X}_s$) of 1.17 was based on the value obtained from Hunter and Hunter's results for a selection ratio of .3. The SD_y for the computer programmer was obtained from Schmidt, et al. (1979) and the SD_y for the insurance sales job was obtained from Bobko, Karren, and Parkington (1983).

[a]This change in utility represents the estimated gain from using a particular type of selection procedure over random selection.

[b]This change in utility represents the estimated gain from using the ability test battery in place of the interviewing program for the respective job under consideration.

group receiving the training and a comparison group is statistically significant. The important question is: What is the dollar value of this difference between the two groups resulting from the training to the data processing company?

Since the t-statistic does not provide a direct answer to this question, we must determine the average gain in performance due to the leadership training in standard score units and then convert this statistic to dollars. The following equation permits us to make such an estimation of the economic value of the training program:

$$\Delta U = [\sum_{t=1}^{T} (1/(1+i)^t) \, N \, SD_Y \, d_t \, (1+V)(1-TAX)] - NC(1-TAX) \tag{11.3}$$

where

ΔU = the dollar value of the training program after taking into account discounting, variable costs, and taxes,

T = the number of years' duration of the training effect on performance,

N = the number trained,

d_t = the difference in job performance between the average trained and untrained employee in standard deviation units,

SD_Y = the standard deviation of job performance in dollars of the untrained group,

C = the cost of training per trainee, and the other terms are as defined in equation 11.2.

Since we have already discussed how most components of this equation can be estimated, let us see how parameter d_t in equation 11.3 is estimated in our

example. The performance mean (average number of error-free programs) of the trained group was 55, whereas it was 50 for the untrained group. The standard deviation of the number of error-free programs for both groups was 10. The observed gain in performance in standard score units is:

$$d_t = \frac{55 - 50}{10} = .5.$$

Furthermore, let us assume that the effect of training will last three years.

Since we are concerned here with a management position and do not have available an estimate of SD_Y for computer programming managers, we might consider a percentage of mean salary as a conservative estimate of SD_Y. Recently, evidence has been provided to support the assertion that SD_Y for a given job falls between 40 and 70 percent of yearly salary (Hunter & Schmidt, 1982). Thus, with knowledge of the mean annual salary for a group of individuals in a job, we can estimate SD_Y to be conservatively 40 percent of this value. For example, a mean computer programming manager salary of $33,000 would yield an SD_Y estimate of $13,200. Using this value for SD_Y, the previous values for the training components (.5 for d_t and 3 for T), as well as the previously noted economic values in the selection utility examples ($i = .18$, $V = .05$, and $TAX = .49$), we are now ready to calculate the dollar value of the training program. By placing these values back into equation 11.3, we would find that the estimated present dollar value of the managerial training program is $669,767. In addition to this example, Godkewitsch (1987) has provided examples of the financial utility of various methods of managerial training. In sum, the economic impact of successful organizational interventions such as training programs on the bottom line of the company can be substantial.

CONCLUSION

The discussion focused on using decision-theoretic utility equations to make estimates of the dollar utility of various personnel programs. It is not necessary, however, to express the gains from personnel programs in terms of dollars. As discussed by several personnel researchers (Burke & Pearlman, in press; Bobko, Karren & Kerkar, 1987; Schmidt & Hunter, 1983; Raju & Burke, 1986), one can employ other metrics such as percentage increase in performance or measured performance when using decision-theoretic utility equations to estimate utility gains from person-

nel programs. Regardless of how utility gains are expressed, a number of questions remain concerning the completeness of the equations in modeling personnel contexts as well as questions relating to the accuracy of SD_Y estimates. Although we look forward to research addressing these questions, there is sound evidence that no matter how SD_Y is estimated with current procedures or to what extent utility equations are expanded, one will invariably obtain an SD_Y value that leads to correct decisions in a utility analysis. That is, Boudreau (1984) has shown that it may not always be necessary to obtain exact or even approximate SD_Y estimates in order to make accurate decisions regarding alternative personnel programs. Instead of estimating the level of expected utility for each alternative program, he suggests focusing on the identification of "break-even" values (minimum SD_Y values necessary for utility gain to meet the costs associated with a personnel program) that are critical to making decisions. While break-even analysis offers a useful framework for practical decision making in many situations, we also encourage efforts toward improving the accuracy with which we can estimate the utility of personnel and human resource programs. To this end, the work of personnel researchers such as Ledvinka and Ladd (1987), Raju, Burke, and Normand (1987), and Steffy and Maurer (1988) related to developing new utility analysis equations, advocating interdisciplinary utility analysis efforts, and focusing on improving the communication of utility analysis results is encouraged.

REFERENCES

Bobko, P., Karren, R., & Kerkar, S.P. (1987). Systematic research needs for understanding supervisory-based estimates of SD_Y in utility analysis. *Organizational Behavior and Human Decision Processes, 40,* 69–95.

Bobko, P., Karren, R., & Parkington, J.J. (1983). Estimation of standard deviations in utility analyses: An empirical test. *Journal of Applied Psychology, 68,* 170–176.

Boudreau, J.W. (1983a). Economic considerations in estimating the utility of human resource productivity improvement programs. *Personnel Psychology, 36,* 551–576.

Boudreau, J.W. (1983b). Effects of employee flows on utility analysis of human resource productivity improvement programs. *Journal of Applied Psychology, 68,* 396–406.

Boudreau, J.W. (1984). Decision theory contributions to HMR research and practice. *Industrial Relations, 23,* 198–217.

Boudreau, J.W., & Berger, C.J. (1985). Decision-theoretic utility analysis to employee separations and acquisitions. *Journal of Applied Psychology, 70,* 581–612.

Boudreau, J.W., & Rynes, S.L. (1985). Role of recruitment in staffing utility analysis. *Journal of Applied Psychology, 70,* 354–366.

Brogden, H.E. (1949). When testing pays off. *Personnel Psychology, 2,* 171–183.

Burke, M.J., & Frederick, J.T. (1986). A comparison of economic utility estimates for alternative SD_Y estimation procedures. *Journal of Applied Psychology, 71,* 334–339.

Burke, M.J., & Pearlman, K. (in press). Personnel recruitment, selection and classification. In J.P. Campbell (Ed.), *Frontiers in industrial/organizational psychology* (vol. 2). San Francisco: Jossey-Bass.

Cascio, W.F. (1982). *Costing human resources: The financial impact of behavior in organizations.* Boston, MA: Kent.

Cascio, W.F., & Ramos, R.A. (1986). Development and application of a new method for assessing job performance in behavioral/economic terms. *Journal of Applied Psychology, 71,* 20–28.

Cascio, W.F., & Silbey, V. (1979). Utility of the assessment center as a selection device. *Journal of Applied Psychology, 64,* 107–118.

Cronbach, L.J., & Gleser, G.C. (1965). *Psychological tests and personnel decisions.* Urbana, IL: University of Illinois Press.

Godkewitsch, M. (1987). The dollars and sense of corporate training. *Training, 5,* 79–81.

Hunter, J.E., & Hunter, R.F. (1984). Validity and utility of alternative predictors of job performance. *Psychological Bulletin, 96,* 72–98.

Hunter, J.E., & Schmidt, F.L. (1982). Fitting people to jobs: Impact of personnel selection on national productivity. In M.D. Dunnette and E.A. Fleishman (Eds.), *Human performance and productivity,* vol. 1: *Human capability assessment.* Hillsdale, NJ: Lawrence Erlbaum Associates.

Landy, F.J., Farr, J.L., & Jacobs, R.R. (1982). Utility concepts in performance measurement. *Organizational Behavior and Human Performance, 30,* 15–40.

Ledvinka, J., & Ladd, R.T. (1987). *Computer simulation of multiple-job systems and its application to utility analysis.* Unpublished manuscript, University of Georgia.

Raju, N.S., & Burke, M.J. (1986). Utility analysis. In R.A. Berk (Ed.), *Performance assessment: Methods and applications.* Baltimore: The Johns Hopkins University Press.

Raju, N.S., Burke, M.J., & Normand, J. (1987). *A new model for utility analysis.* Unpublished manuscript, Illinois Institute of Technology.

Schmidt, F.L., & Hunter, J.E. (1983). Individual differences in productivity: An empirical test of estimates derived from studies of selection procedure utility. *Journal of Applied Psychology, 68,* 407–414.

Schmidt, F.L., Hunter, J.E., McKenzie, R.C., & Muldrow, T.W. (1979). The impact of valid selection procedures on work force productivity. *Journal of Applied Psychology, 64,* 609–624.

Schmidt, F.L., Hunter, J.E., & Pearlman, K. (1982). Assessing the economic impact of personnel programs on workforce productivity. *Personnel Psychology, 35,* 333–347.

Smith, P.C. (1976). Behaviors, results, and organizational effectiveness: The problems of criteria. In M.D. Dunnette (Ed.), *Handbook of industrial and organizational psychology* (745–775). Chicago, IL: Rand McNally.

Steffy, B.D., & Maurer, S.D. (1988). The dollar-productivity impact of the human resource function: Conceptualization and measurement. *Academy of Management Review, 13,* 271–286.

12 COMPUTERIZED ADAPTIVE TESTING

C. David Vale

Twenty years of empirical research has shown that computerized adaptive testing (CAT) offers some significant advantages over conventional methods of testing. In particular, CAT should have a practical appeal to the practitioner of personnel testing. A number of studies have demonstrated that it can reduce testing time by a factor of at least 50 percent without sacrificing measurement quality (Knapp & Pliske, 1985; McBride, Corpe & Wing, 1987; Moreno, Wetzel, McBride, & Weiss, 1983). Now that computers capable of administering adaptive tests are almost as prevalent as office typewriters, it is time to consider seriously adaptive tests as a viable new form of testing for employee selection, training evaluation, and career counseling applications.

The objectives of this chapter are to provide a conceptual overview of CAT, detail what is required to implement an adaptive test, and describe a few practical implementations of CAT to illustrate its utility. In line with these objectives, this chapter is divided into three parts. The first discusses the concepts that underly CAT, including item response theory (IRT). Although theoretical research in CAT can require a substantial knowledge of mathematics, such knowledge is not necessary for a conceptual understanding of or the practical implementation of CAT. In this section the basics of both CAT and IRT are described in a completely nonmathematical way. A number of technical terms are introduced, but these too are described in a nontechnical way; the purpose of their introduction is to assist you in reading other articles on CAT.

The second section discusses what is required to implement an adaptive test. This discussion is limited to the technical issues; organizational issues relevant to computerization are not discussed. The final section describes a few practical implementations of CAT. Although few implementations have been documented to date, the few that have present some practical information regarding the utility of CAT.

BASIC CONCEPTS

Described in its most basic terms, CAT is a testing procedure in which the difficulty of the test is tailored to the ability of the examinee. It works from a pool of test items that all measure an important trait. The pool contains more items than anyone is likely to answer. The CAT administration strategy is to select from the pool those items that are most useful in estimating the examinee's ability level. This strategy is implemented by giving difficult items to examinees of high ability and easy items to those of low ability.

This simple concept is complicated by the fact that the examinee's level of ability is unknown when testing begins. The test must thus adapt to provisional estimates of the examinee's ability during the course of testing to select a tailored subset of test items from a larger item pool. This estimate improves during the course of testing, as does the quality of item selections.

There are a number of ways in which item selection can be accomplished. Many of the early techniques branched from one item to another in a mechanical strategy. One, for example, ordered items from easy to difficult and, starting in the middle of the list, branched to the next more difficult one after each correct response and to the next less difficult one after an incorrect response. Most of these early branching strategies have been abandoned, however, and replaced with better methods based on IRT (Hambleton & Swaminathan, 1985; Lord, 1980). The item-selection component of an adaptive test is still often referred to as the branching strategy, however, even though few current procedures do any real branching. Comprehensive reviews of various strategies of CAT are available (e.g., Weiss, 1985). Most of the non-IRT strategies are of historical rather than technical interest, however.

Item response theory refers to a family of mathematical models that relate an examinee's level on an underlying trait (such as ability) to observable item responses. The concept of one or more hypothetical, underlying, unobservable (latent) traits is basic to all item response theories. Such a trait is simply a graded continuum of some psychological characteristic on which people vary. (From this point on, I will use "ability" in place of "trait level" and will use the corresponding concepts of "difficulty," and so on. The IRT models are generally applicable to all psychological traits, but CAT applications to date have been primarily in the ability domain. Limiting the discussion to ability makes description easier.) Most item response theories used in CAT express the scale of ability to be standard, with a mean of zero and a variance of one. I will use this scale for discussion here.

Item Response Functions

All item response theories express the probability of an item's response as a function of the underlying trait and item parameters. If we restrict our discussion to dichotomously scored (right-wrong) items, the probability of a response as a function of ability takes on either an S- or a Z-shaped curve. Correct responses take on the S shape, with the probability of observing a correct response increasing as the level of ability goes up. Incorrect responses exhibit a Z shape, with the probability of observing one going down as ability goes up. These functions are properly called item response functions or (less frequently) response likelihood functions. The curves that correspond to correct responses are also called item characteristic curves. Figure 12–1 shows an item response function for a correct response (solid) and one for an incorrect response (dashed).

The actual shape of the item response function is mathematically specified. Two shapes are frequently found in the literature: logistic and normal ogives. Visually they look very similar. Mathematically they act somewhat differently. Practically the logistic function is easier to work with than is the normal function and gives results that are intuitively more pleasing. Thus, it is more popular.

But more important than the exact shape of the item response functions are the item parameters that modify the shape of the curves. The most general model in popular use has three parameters that index the difficulty of the item (b), its capacity to discriminate among different levels of ability (a), and its proneness to guessing (c). These item parameters completely determine the shape of the item response

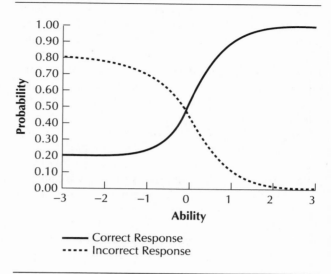

Figure 12–1. Item Response Functions

functions. Differences in difficulty cause the curve to be positioned differently to the right or left. Differences in discriminating power change the slope of the curve. Differences in proneness to guessing change the asymptotes at the left side of the curve.

Likelihood Functions and Trait Estimation

Given the item parameters, the corresponding item response function expresses the probability of observing a type of response (e.g., right or wrong) as a function of ability. This fact can be used to infer the examinee's level of ability from a set of item responses.

Intuitively, you might choose as a good estimate of ability that value that corresponded to the highest probability of the observed response occurring. Another way of expressing this is that you would select the level of ability that had the highest likelihood, given the observed response (the one with the maximum likelihood). Unfortunately, this approach does not work well with a single item because the ability level corresponding to the highest likelihood will be positive or negative infinity. Fortunately, most tests are longer than one item.

The concept applies similarly to tests of several items. By the features of IRT, a test likelihood function can be obtained by simply multiplying the response likelihood functions together. When you multiply several of them together, assuming some items have been answered correctly and others incorrectly, the curve has a maximum at a more reasonable value. As before, the maximum-likelihood estimate of ability is the level of ability corresponding to the highest point of the test likelihood function. Figure 12–2 shows the item likelihood functions and the resulting test likelihood function for a particular pattern of responses to a three-item test; the examinee answered two easy items correctly and missed a difficult one.

Sometimes, however, you do not want to put unlimited faith in the test data. For example, the estimate is still infinite if the examinee answers all of the items correctly and an ability estimate of infinity is probably a bit generous. An alternative to the maximum-likelihood approach to scoring is the Bayesian approach. The Bayesian approach admits to some degree of prior belief regarding permissible values of ability (that it follows a standard normal distribution, for example).

A Bayesian scoring approach introduces this prior belief as another likelihood function in the system of item likelihood functions. If, for example, a standard normal distribution reflects the prior belief, a standard normal probability density function is introduced into the system; the test likelihood function is multiplied by this probability density function. The result is a Bayesian posterior likelihood function. Ability can be estimated from this function in the same manner as before. The estimate that is the value of ability corresponding to the highest value of the Bayesian posterior function is called the Bayesian modal estimate (because the highest point of the distribution corresponds to the mode). Figure 12–3

Figure 12–2. Likelihood Functions

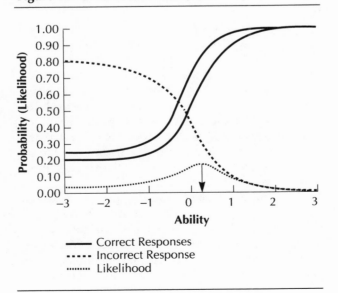

Figure 12–3. Bayesian Estimation

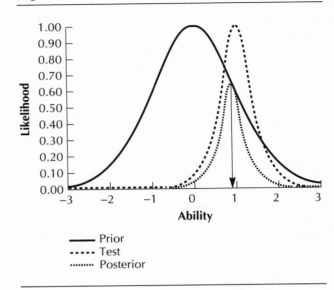

shows a Bayesian posterior likelihood function. Note that the ordinates of the likelihood plot have been doubled (scaled likelihood functions retain all of their essential properties) to make it easier to see.

If we care to, we can compute a mean and variance of this Bayesian posterior distribution. The mean is an alternative estimate of ability. The square root of the variance corresponds to an individual standard error of measurement for the person being tested.

Adaptive Testing Concepts

The best test will have the smallest standard error for each person tested. If we plan to administer only a finite number of items, the best test design is one that will make the standard error (the posterior variance) as small as possible for any given test length. We know, both intuitively and from psychometric theory I will discuss shortly, that the utility of items for shrinking the standard error varies from person to person (from ability to ability). Difficult items are more efficient for capable people, and easy items are more efficient for less capable people.

Say, for example, that we can administer a test consisting of only a single item. Assume that we have some idea of an examinee's level of ability before we start (e.g., that he or she was sampled from a population in which ability levels are normally distributed with a mean of zero and a variance of one). We could evaluate every item in our pool to see which one would produce the smallest standard error after administering an item. We do this by evaluating the standard error that would result from a correct response and the standard error that would result from an incorrect response and then taking a weighted average of them. This is called preposterior analysis, and the item chosen is the most efficient single-item test that we could administer.

As a result of administering this one-item test, we would have one of two possible estimates of ability. We could use this estimate, and its corresponding standard error, as the basis of a new "prior" and select a second item to administer. These two items would constitute the best two-item test that could be constructed, given the examinee's response to the first item and the original prior information. Note that we would have two different tests, differing in their difficulty and the ability levels for which they were appropriate. Or we could say we had an adaptive test, a test that tailored its difficulty to the ability level of the examinee based on the responses of the examinees to the items.

We could continue with this process until the standard error of measurement for the examinee we were testing got sufficiently small, until we had administered a predetermined number of items, or until the time we had for testing ran out.

This "full Bayesian" procedure for selecting items is computationally intensive. A full search and evaluation of a large pool is still too time-consuming for implementation on most microcomputer-based testing systems. As an alternative, selection on the basis of a statistic called item information is an approach that is computationally much easier and loses little measurement efficiency.

The item information function is a function similar to the item response function. Instead of giving a probability of a response as a function of ability, however, it provides psychometric information as a function of ability. Psychometric information is the reciprocal of the square of the expected standard error of measurement that would result from administering an item; higher information results in better measurement.

As shown in figure 12–4, information functions appear graphically as curves with single peaks. Each item has its own information function. Its peak is near the difficulty level of the item. The height of that peak goes up as the discriminating power of the item increases and goes down as the probability of answering the item correctly through guessing increases.

A test also has an information function. Recall that the test likelihood function was obtained by multiplying the item response likelihood functions together. The test information function is obtained by adding the item information functions together. Intuitively an information function is useful because it shows where, along the ability continuum, a test or an item measures most accurately.

The item information function provides an alternative technique for selecting items. Instead of evaluating the expected posterior variance and picking the item with the lowest one, we can select the item that has the highest information at the estimated level of ability. Since, for each item, information is a function of only the level of ability, it is feasible to preselect items for discrete ranges of ability and put these selections in a table. Thus no computations need be done to select the items when the test is administered; even the most anemic microcomputer can do it.

The Practical Application of These Concepts

From this information, we are now ready to summarize what is involved conceptually in administering an adaptive test. The process normally starts with some notion (prior belief) regarding the distribution of ability. This initial prior is used to select the first item from the pool of items based either on a full Bayesian preposterior analysis or by selecting the item that provides the most psychometric information at the initial estimate of ability. After obtaining a response to the item, the estimate of ability is updated, as is its standard error, and a new item is selected on the basis of the estimate and administered. This process repeats until the test terminates. When the test has terminated, the final estimate of ability can be taken as the test score.

Figure 12–4. Information Functions

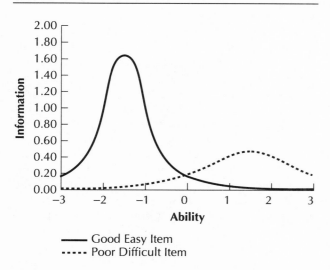

— Good Easy Item
····· Poor Difficult Item

IMPLEMENTING AN ADAPTIVE TEST

There are a number of steps common to the development of both conventional and adaptive tests. To develop a conventional test, for example, you must specify the domain of content, write the items, pretest the items, select items for the final test, and validate the final test, possibly by correlating scores on it with some external criterion. The development of an adaptive test proceeds through essentially the same five steps, although there are some notable differences.

Specifying the content domain may be as simple as writing a description of the trait the items are to tap or as detailed as a formal content plan listing, describing, and weighting a number of content elements. An important difference between specification for adaptive and conventional tests, however, is that the elements in the specification must be considered interchangeable. IRT assumes that the content domain that encompasses the items is unidimensional. (Multidimensional IRT models exist but are more complicated to explain and often impractical to implement.) That is, it assumes that all the items measure the same thing. What it means to measure the same thing is a matter of degree. To measure the same thing, a test would have to consist of replications of a single item, a rare and practically useless test. This degree of unidimensionality is not required, however. Conceptually, two things are required in the specification of a unidimensional pool. First, you must believe that all that is interesting in the test can be summarized in a single score. This means that you would be unwilling to interpret subsets of items as meaning something different from the information that could be obtained from the total score. Second, you must believe that no content balancing within the domain is necessary. In other words, it cannot matter to you which items were used to compute the score.

For example, a test measuring knowledge of business mathematics might be considered unidimensional even though it contained items assessing skills with percentages, decimals, and fractions. You should not consider it so, however, if you have a desire to compute subscores for the three areas. You should also not consider it unidimensional if you feel that to obtain a fair and accurate measure of skill in business mathematics you have to administer a reasonable balance among the three areas. In fact, you are likely to find that percentage items are more difficult than decimal items and that a person who does poorly on decimals will not get the opportunity to try any percentage items. This is not to suggest that you cannot have adaptive tests that measure the three skills independently. But you will not have a single adaptive test that does this. You will have three.

The second major difference between conventional and adaptive test development will show up when you pretest the items. In conventional testing, the pretest is usually conducted on a small number of examinees, and its purpose is to weed out the items that are too easy, too difficult, or do not correlate well with total scores. Pretesting for an adaptive test is replaced by item calibration. Item calibration is the effort that provides the data you will need to estimate the item parameters. Unlike conventional pretesting, calibration usually takes a large number of subjects. Five hundred is probably a minimum. Two thousand is a more desirable sample size. Having fewer than a hundred examinees for a conventional item analysis can result in a suboptimal choice of items for the final test. Having too few examinees for item calibration can result in poorly estimated item parameters, which can in turn result in inaccurate scores. The computations are also different. Conventional item analysis can be done by hand. Item calibration can take a few hours on a computer.

A third difference comes in constructing and administering the final form of the test. The final form of a conventional test consists of a fixed set of items, usually administered in a fixed order and scored by counting the number of items answered correctly. The final form of an adaptive test is chosen during the course of testing. There may be as many final forms as there are examinees, and since they all differ in difficulty, the number-correct score has almost no relation to ability.

Of course, there is also the issue of computerization. Conventional tests are usually administered in printed form. Adaptive tests are almost always administered on a computer. This means that the items must be entered into the computer and the computer must be programmed to select the proper items, administer them to the examinee, and score them using an IRT-based scoring method. It is unlikely that you would undertake the programming of a system to administer an adaptive test yourself. In addition to being sufficiently familiar with the mathematics and statistics of IRT and CAT, you would have to be sufficiently familiar with computers to develop all of the software to implement the mathematics and statistics and to present the items. Fortunately, there are two alternative approaches available. The first is to enlist the assistance of a consulting firm with experience in the development of CAT and CAT computer systems.

At present, several major test publishers and a number of smaller firms have this capability. The second alternative is to develop your test using an authoring system. The most widely used such system is the MicroCAT Testing System (Assessment Systems Corporation, 1989), which provides all of the capabilities required to implement adaptive tests on IBM and IBM-compatible personal computers.

A FEW CAT IMPLEMENTATIONS

Although research in CAT has been under way for over twenty years, the first practical implementations of the technology began only in 1985. Since that time, several implementations have been reported. I will discuss just two in moderate detail here.

The first implementation to become operational was the Computerized Adaptive Screening Test (CAST; Sands & Gade, 1983; Knapp & Pliske, 1985), a test for use by military personnel recruiters. All enlisted personnel for all branches of the U.S. armed services are selected using a single battery of tests, the Armed Services Vocational Aptitude Battery (ASVAB). The ASVAB, which currently consists of nine subtests measuring both general abilities and specific knowledge, is summarized for basic selection purposes in a qualifying score called the AFQT. The score an applicant obtains on the AFQT determines which branches of the armed services he or she is eligible for, as well as which enlistment bonuses can be extended. It is important for the recruiter to be able to predict how high an AFQT score an applicant will obtain in order to determine which enticements may be available.

This need was initially met with a paper-and-pencil test given by the recruiters to predict AFQT performance. This test contained 20 vocabulary items and 15 arithmetic items. It correlated approximately .8 with the AFQT, which was considered adequately predictive, but required up to 45 minutes of supervised administration time, which was considered too long.

The CAST was developed from a pool of 78 vocabulary and 225 arithmetic items. These items have been used for CAT experimentation and were calibrated and ready for incorporation into a CAT test. The resulting test, which also correlated approximately .8 with the AFQT, required the examinee to answer 10 vocabulary items and 5 arithmetic items. The time required was about 15 minutes on the average.

The CAST was a dramatic success for CAT. With relatively little effort, testing time was cut to approximately-one third of its original duration, and no loss in prediction occurred. Its developers had two advantages, however, which are not usually available to CAT test developers. First, they had a pool of items that had already been calibrated, thus eliminating what is usually a substantial effort. Second, computer equipment was already in place for other aspects of the recruiting function. Thus the issue of how to automate the process at thousands of recruiting stations across the country had already been addressed and solved. These observations are not meant to detract from the success of the effort but are important factors to note.

A much larger effort is currently in progress to develop a CAT version of the ASVAB itself (McBride, 1982; Wiskoff & Schratz, 1988). The ASVAB is currently administered to nearly 1 million applicants each year in almost one thousand sites, most of them in the continental United States. The current paper-and-pencil ASVAB has several problems, which were outlined by Wiskoff and Schratz (1988): (1) the ASVAB takes too long to administer—up to 4 hours; (2) it has poor precision for applicants that are of either low or high ability; (3) being a paper-and-pencil test, it is subject to breaches in security such as theft, compromise, and coaching; (4) it is difficult to maintain standardization of administration across all administration sites; and (5) it is a massive, time-consuming effort to revise the battery since new materials have to be shipped to so many sites. Computerized adaptive administration is intended to remedy all of those problems.

The CAT-ASVAB project was one of the first CAT implementation projects to get started, beginning in the late 1970s. The fact that it is still not operational is due primarily to the magnitude of the effort and the thoroughness with which it is being conducted. The number of administrations per year and the number of sites at which they occur speak to the magnitude of the effort. The thoroughness of the effort can be seen from the amount of applied research that has been done by the armed services. For example, most of what is known about the effects of medium of administration has been funded by the armed services (e.g., Kiely, Zara, & Weiss, 1986). Furthermore, the item development effort required was massive (Prestwood, Vale, Massey, & Welsh, 1985).

Part of the delay, however, was also due to a few false starts in the effort. In the early 1980s, neither the hardware nor the software required for the implementation was available off the shelf. The armed services decided to procure custom-developed hardware and software on a contractual basis. Unfortunately, in the early 1980s it was not apparent that the microcomputer boom would be as great as it ultimately became. By the time the initial designs of the CAT-ASVAB hardware equipment were completed, off-the-shelf hardware was available that met the requirements nearly as well at a fraction of the cost. The CAT-ASVAB implementation was recently pilot tested using commercially available hardware and software written in-house by personnel at the Navy Personnel Research and Development Center in San Diego.

The operational implementation of the CAT-ASVAB, when it occurs, will be tremendously significant to the field of CAT. The important research that it has spawned aside, the CAT-ASVAB will be the first major use of CAT for personnel selection and placement. Its overall success will illustrate the benefits of CAT in the selection of personnel. It shortcomings

will illuminate areas that need greater care in future CAT implementations.

In addition to these two major CAT implementations, two smaller-scale commercial CAT implementations are worthy of note. First, the Computerized Placement Tests published by Educational Testing Service (Ward, 1988; Ward, Kline, & Flaughter, 1986) comprise a battery of four adaptive tests that assess skills in reading comprehension, sentence construction, arithmetic, and elementary algebra. In typically less than 1$\frac{1}{2}$ hours, this battery obtains sufficient information to allow two- and four-year colleges to assign incoming students properly to basic English and math courses.

The second is the DAT Adaptive, an adaptive version of the Differential Aptitude Tests published by the Psychological Corporation (McBride, Corpe & Wing, 1987). The DAT assesses basic skills and abilities in eight areas. While the original DAT takes approximately 3$\frac{1}{2}$ hours, the adaptive version can be administered in less than 2 hours.

CAT IN SUMMARY

Computerized adaptive testing offers some significant advantages over conventional testing. Probably the major advantage is efficiency, which was predicted by theory and has been demonstrated in practice: CAT can achieve the measurement quality of a conventional test with typically about half as many items. Additionally, CAT can provide better measurement at the extremes of ability than can conventional tests, which must focus their measurement precision at levels where most of the people are.

Other advantages of CAT are not even psychometric in nature. For example, security is increased because rarely will a specific test be administered more than once to the same or a different examinee. This feature is of apparent importance to military testing. Test disclosure laws make it important for commercial tests, too.

CAT is not without its price, however. Two costs must be considered: the cost of development and the cost of computerization. A computer for test administration currently costs about $1,000 to purchase and $200 per year to keep running. Assuming it can be

used 1,000 hours per year and amortized over five years, the cost per hour is 40 cents, or 80 cents per 2-hour test. This is probably a small price to pay for saving 2 hours of an examinee's time.

Development costs are substantial. To get a calibration sample of 500 examinees for each item, pilot administration time will be equivalent to about 1,500 to 2,000 test administrations. Thus, the time savings available in a CAT test will begin to show up only after approximately 3,000 to 4,000 operational administrations. CAT tests should obviously not be used for small applications. Of course, this analysis is not relevant for a commercial adaptive test that someone else has already developed.

In summary, CAT tests are efficient to administer but inefficient to develop. Thus, CAT is appropriate for applications where the quantity of use is sufficient to justify the expense of implementation. Ultimately, the use of CAT tests will be widespread. For the next few years, however, CAT tests will be developed primarily by large companies, consortia of smaller companies, and test publishers.

REFERENCES

Assessment Systems Corporation (1989). *User's manual for the MicroCAT testing system.* St. Paul, MN: Author.

Hambleton, R.K., & Swaminathan, H. (1985). *Item response theory: Principles and applications.* Boston: Kluwer-Nijhoff.

Kiely, G.L., Zara, A.R., & Weiss, D.J. (1986). *Equivalence of computer and paper-and-pencil Armed Services Vocational Aptitude Battery tests* (AFHRL-TP-86-13). Brooks AFB, TX: Air Force Human Resources Laboratory.

Knapp, D.J., & Pliske, R.M. (1985). *Preliminary report on a national cross-validation of the computerized adaptive screening test (CAST)* (Working Paper 85-15). Alexandria, VA: U.S. Army Research Institute for the Behavioral and Social Sciences.

Lord, F.M. (1980). *Applications of item response theory to practical testing problems.* Hillsdale, NJ: Erlbaum.

McBride, J.R. (1982). *Computerized adaptive testing project: Objectives and requirements* (Technical Note 82-22). San Diego: Navy Personnel Research and Development Center.

McBride, J.R., Corpe, V.A., & Wing, H. (1987). *Equating the computerized adaptive edition of the Differential Aptitude Tests.* Paper presented at the Annual Convention of the American Psychological Association, New York, August.

Moreno, K.E., Wetzel, C.D., McBride, J.R., & Weiss, D.J. (1983). *Relationship between corresponding Armed Services Vocational Aptitude Battery (ASVAB) and computerized adaptive testing (CAT) subtests* (Report No. 83-27). San Diego: Navy Personnel Research and Development Center.

Prestwood, J.S., Vale, C.D., Massey, R.H., & Welsh, J.R. (1985). *Armed Services Vocational Aptitude Battery: Development of an adaptive item pool* (AFHRL-TR-85-19). Brooks AFB, TX: Air Force Systems Command.

Sands, W.A., & Gade, P.A. (1983). An application of computerized adaptive testing in U.S. Army Recruiting. *Journal of Computer-Based Instruction, 10,* 87–89.

Ward, W.C. (1988). The College Board computerized placement tests: An application of computerized adaptive testing. *Machine-Mediated Learning, 2,* 271–282.

Ward, W.C., Kline, R.G., & Flaughter, J. (1986). *College board computerized placement tests: Validation of an adaptive test of basic skills* (RR-86-29). Princeton, NJ: Educational Testing Service.

Weiss, D.J. (1985). Adaptive testing by computer. *Journal of Consulting and Clinical Psychology, 53,* 774–789.

Wiskoff, M.F., & Schratz, M.K. (1988). Computerized adaptive testing of a vocational aptitude battery. In R.F. Dillon & J.W. Pellegrino (Eds.), *Testing: Theoretical and applied perspectives.* New York: Praeger.

13 FAIRNESS IN PERSONNEL SELECTION

Steve Wunder, C. Paul Sparks

This chapter is an overview of the legal developments that have led to our current understanding of the concept of fairness in personnel selection. It is also a synopsis of one major company's efforts to be fair to its applicants and employees in its selection decisions and at the same time avoid serious interference in the conduct of its business through careful attention to regulations promulgated to effect equal employment opportunity.

In order to follow the description of these developments and efforts, the reader must understand the company's definitions of both selection and fairness. *Selection is the act of choosing a particular individual instead of some other individual from a group of individuals for some specified treatment associated with the administration of the personnel function.* This action may have positive consequences for the individual. Hiring, promotion, entry into a training program, or a salary increase come readily to mind. The action may also have negative consequences for the individual. Involuntary termination, layoff, demotion, disciplinary action, unfavorable assignment, and unwanted premature retirement are examples. *Fairness in personnel selection occurs when uniform application of standards, procedures, rules, and policies has the same result for each individual, without regard to classification by sex, race, ethnic group, national status, religion, age, handicap, or other legally protected status.* Put another way, it is not required by law that selection programs be error free. To the contrary, the law often favors methods that result in more errors (for example, subjective methods such as interviews favored over objective methods such as tests). What is legally mandated is that those errors not be borne disproportionately by protected groups of candidates.

Returning to our first definition, the act of selection occurs after some process has been used to evaluate the competing individuals. Available processes have become increasingly constrained. First and foremost are the many limitations imposed by statutory law, presidential order, and guidelines of the agencies established for their administration. Courts have generally upheld the legitimacy of the agencies' guidelines and have even embellished them in directing employers to perform in very specific ways. Professional organizations such as the American Psychological Association and the Society for Industrial and Organizational Psychology have published principles of good practice with respect to selection. While these publications have no legal standing, they have been used by legislative bodies and the courts as a proper expression of the state of the art. Employers must also consider constraints imposed by contractual agreements with employee unions and by pacts made with advocate organizations representing minority groups, women, the handicapped, and others. Employers must be concerned with political actions that may be taken against a company whose policies or results are found offensive to some group. Equally important are the demoralizing effects such policies or results may have on the company's own work force. In either instance, no company can afford a climate of ill will.

The organizations involved in this synopsis were multiple U.S. entities of Exxon Corporation, the world's largest energy company. The psychologists involved were those of the Personnel Research group, supervised for many years by the first author and later by the second author. Personnel selection practices at Exxon are reviewed for illustrative purposes only and not to imply that the Exxon procedures are the ideal ones. The basic problem was the development, maintenance, and evaluation of systems for personnel administration that would satisfy legal and quasilegal requirements of the various regulatory agencies concerned with equal employment opportunity.

In 1964 Congress enacted a civil rights act. Title VII of that act dealt with employment and included the soon to be noteworthy Tower amendment:

> Nor shall it be an unlawful employment practice for an employer to give and to act upon the results of any professionally developed ability test provided that such test, its administration or action upon the results is not designed, intended, or used to discriminate because of race, color, religion, sex, or national origin.

The act also created an independent executive agency, the Equal Employment Opportunity Commission (EEOC), to interpret and enforce the act.

In 1965 President Lyndon Johnson issued Executive Order (EO) 11246, amended later by EO 11375, to include a bar against sex discrimination. The equal employment opportunity clause of the executive order then read:

> The contractor [doing business with the federal government] will not discriminate against any employee or applicant for employment because of race, color, religion, sex, or national origin. The contractor will take affirmative action to ensure that applicants are treated during employment without regard to their race, color, religion, sex, or national origin.

EO 11246 was only one more in a series that had been initiated by Franklin D. Roosevelt. It was not even the first to specify affirmative action. However, it was the most powerful. Responsibility for its enforcement was placed in a cabinet position, the Department of Labor, and penalties for violation were specified in considerable detail. Further, the EO provided that violations would not be illegal per se. Rather, they would be interpreted as noncompliance with a contract for goods or services executed between the organization and the federal government. Additionally, violation by even a single unit of a multiunit organization could result in a finding of noncompliance for the entire organization. The potential for penalties was awesome. For example, a finding of noncompliance in a small gasoline storage terminal could jeopardize an oil company's right to bid on federal oil lease acreage. While this situation enormously complicated the task of the company's psychologists and personnel managers, it also ensured top management's attention to the problem.

In the early days of EO 11246 enforcement was spread across several federal government agencies, such as the Atomic Energy Commission and the Department of the Interior. Frequently, a company contracting with the government in more than one line of business would experience contradictory findings between two compliance agencies when the facts of their compliance reviews were fundamentally the same. For example, on one occasion, two adjacent Exxon units were simultaneously lauded and criticized even though they utilized essentially identical personnel practices. In recent years the government has consolidated its compliance under one agency, the Federal Office of Contract Compliance Programs (OFCCP). This has done much to reduce confusion surrounding compliance with EO 11246. Even so, there remains some inherent conflict between the objectives of employers and government enforcement agencies, and thus their respective definitions of fairness. Employers typically consider fairness to be to maximize employment of women and minorities *in the context of seeking the best-qualified employee.* This often results in "underutilization" of women or minorities even though they were treated identically to men or nonminorities. The agencies, on the other hand, define fairness as being *"fully utilized"* or, as it is sometimes referred to, "getting the numbers right." It is easy to see how there exists such a persistent discrepancy between fairness as defined by the government and by employers. A prime example dealt with preemployment inquiries. A summary of applicant data by sex and by race-ethnic group was necessary for federal compliance (to aid in determining degree of utilization). Yet employers were forbidden to use application form data for this purpose, since fairness in this instance was to be sex and race neutral. To solve this dilemma, the company developed an applicant registration card filled in at the time of the application but kept physically separate from any information that might be used by the persons involved in evaluating applicants or making employment decisions.

In 1966 the EEOC issued its first guidelines on employee selection. Included as an appendix was the recommendation by a panel of psychologists that any tests used for selection should be validated. The OFCCP issued a more extensive order in 1968, again emphasizing the need for test validation. In companies such as Exxon, which had historically validated its tests to ensure their usefulness from a business standpoint, these new developments caused little consternation. At Exxon the first validation study had been carried out at one of our refineries in 1937, and the effort had been constant since that time. Other validation studies had been carried out during the 1950s for a wide variety of occupations: all of the refinery and chemical plant job classifications, secretarial and clerical positions, petroleum products salespersons, service station dealers, first-line supervisors, and management personnel. A matrix of job families and validation studies was developed, and projects were established to fill in the remaining gaps. However, an unanticipated problem arose, one that cast doubt on the current value of the earlier studies and created perplexing problems in the conduct of new ones.

Since the cessation of hostilities in Korea, the petroleum industry had been in a protracted economic slump due to lack of product demand. This, of course, worked its way back to exploration and producing activities and to various administrative and support operations. The company had attempted to minimize the impact on its workers through use of normal attrition, early retirement, training and cross-training, and a moratorium on hiring. Eventually, however, new hires were needed, and the programs put in place in the 1950s were put to the test. Putting it bluntly, they broke down. Comparison of the employee characteristics of the 1950s with applicant characteristics of the 1960s showed dramatic differences. For example, refinery and chemical plant employees of the 1950s had an average of 10.5 years of formal schooling, while the applicants of the 1960s had an average of 13.5 years. Petroleum products general salespersons were now college recruits instead of employees chosen from lower-level jobs. A graphic representation of the length of employee service made about 1965 would have resembled a Bactrian camel in almost every company function. A professionally defensible validation study based upon an aggregation of two such disparate groups was determined to be infeasible. On the other hand, use of only the short-service group was also infeasible because of the insufficient numbers of people in almost every job classification. The decision was made to collect test and other information on applicants, compare and contrast them with those hired, and follow the new hires until their job performance could be reliably and validly evaluated. At the same time programs were put in motion to study the tests themselves to find differences in score or item characteristics, if any, that differentiated among examinees by race or ethnic group and, later, by sex. The driving force behind this detailed, methodical examination of applicants and tests was to determine if there were any inadvertent characteristics in either that could render the selection tests invalid or unfair to any subgroup of applicants. One finding that began to be all too apparent was that minorities and nonminorities showed a very reliable, consistent difference in their respective performances on preemployment tests. An effort was begun to understand the meaning of this finding for test validity and fair treatment of applicants of both sexes and all racial and ethnic groups.

Meanwhile, EEOC was beginning to investigate charges that employers had discriminated unfairly, particularly with respect to race and/or national origin. A pattern began to form. As Shaeffer (1973) defined it retrospectively,

> Employers soon learned that their original ideas about how the Equal Employment Opportunity Commission would function were mistaken. It was true that members of the commission's investigative staff came into companies only in response to individual charges of discrimination. But contrary to expectations, they did not limit themselves to investigating the specific complaint that brought them in. Instead they asked for many records and insisted on touring many areas seemingly unrelated to that particular complaint. (p. 8)

The definition of fairness adopted by the EEOC became increasingly based on the adverse effect any selection procedure might have on protected classes. Employers were often found guilty of discrimination if a single nonprotected class person could be found who was given more favorable treatment under similar conditions than the protected class complainant. A typical case would be one where a minority employee was fired for excessive absenteeism. If any nonminority employees could be found who had as many or more absences than the complainant and were not terminated, the implication was that the employer was unfairly discriminating. The company's psychologists were actively involved in rebutting many such cases, particularly where there was an entire group or class of employees involved, resulting in a need for detailed statistical analyses of the comparative treatment of protected class and nonprotected class individuals.

Knowing that EEOC investigations of charges and OFCCP compliance reviews ranged far afield, Personnel Research began to adopt a strategy of looking for areas that might be challenged. Often we would act as "devil's advocate," mimicking the kind of statistical and other types of investigations that agencies and plaintiffs' experts would be likely to conduct. The purpose of these exercises was, of course, to target areas of potential vulnerability for action before the potential could become reality. For example, on several occasions, the statistical technique of multiple regression was used to investigate fairness of the compensation administration program, at both the individual and organizational levels. Statistical models of the compensation system would be developed using such legitimate correlates of pay as job performance, amount of time in pay classification, experience, and level in the organization. These "predictors" would be mathematically weighted to maximize their correlation with the "criterion" of salary. Then, an additional predictor would be added to the model: employee sex and/or ethnic group. If the addition of this predictor significantly improved the model's correlation with pay, the implication could be drawn that sex-ethnic group, above and beyond the legitimate predictors of pay, was associated with pay—not a very desirable state of affairs. On the other hand, if addition of sex-ethnic group to the model did not significantly change the predictive strength of the equation, it could be concluded that this illegitimate variable was not a factor in salary administration. At the individual level of analysis, the statistical model could be applied to each employee, thus generating a *predicted* salary for each person. This could then be compared with each person's *actual* salary. Where large discrepancies were found, investigations could be launched to ascertain why the discrepancies existed and, if indicated, action taken.

It was noted earlier that the large gap between less experienced employees and more experienced in the 1960s precluded using a concurrent test validation strategy. Therefore, the company decided to use a predictive validation strategy and to follow up on new hirees as they completed their formal training programs. The company was aware that the EEOC and OFCCP frequently viewed training, particularly textbook or knowledge training, as just another hurdle that would impede minorities' progress. To ensure the fairness of the training criterion and to combat the agencies' (in our opinion) erroneous perception of the purpose of using training success as a criterion, a program was initiated to establish the close relationship between the content of what was contained in the training program with the content of the actual job. In other words, the "content validity" of training was the objective; to demonstrate the fairness of making personnel decisions (such as promotion or termination) based upon performance in training. An example of the kind of procedure followed was a technician training program for our refineries and chemical plants. The first step was a training needs analysis of each operations, maintenance, and laboratory job. Care was taken to distinguish between those things "nice to know" and "need to know." Training needs were then grouped according to knowledge and skill cores. Examples were refrigeration, compressors, pumps, heat transfer, fluid flow, welding, and electric motors. A given core subject might be unique to just one job (perhaps electrician), but most were of significance to a number of jobs. Modules were constructed for the conduct of training in each core subject, and mastery tests (both written and/or performance, as appropriate) were designed. To ensure, and to demonstrate to any complaining parties, that no artificially high hurdles to minorities' success were being presented by the training program, the mastery tests were tried out on a representative sample of experienced workers in the jobs for which the new hirees were to be trained. A standard of 90 percent of the sample attaining 90 percent correct responses was set as appropriate evidence of the job relatedness and fairness of the training program. The program has been

extremely successful; it has successfully undergone several compliance reviews and withstood a number of complainants' challenges. Reflective of the success of this and other efforts to establish training success as a legitimate selection criterion, the first author was later invited to prepare an article on success in training as a criterion for test validation (Sparks, 1981). The basic proposition was that any measure of employee performance, if it were shown to be tied in content very closely to the content of the actual job, could be considered manifestly fair. This notion has been applied not only to training program design but also to the development of performance appraisals for various job groups based upon thorough analyses of the jobs themselves prior to construction of the appraisal forms.

While much progress had been made in understanding and complying with the legal requirements of validity and fairness, the late 1960s through the late 1970s were periods of great uncertainty for employers, company psychologists, EEO lawyers, and consultants. Additional EEOC guidelines on religious discrimination, sex discrimination, and national origin discrimination and OFCCP orders on affirmative action simply muddied the waters. Employers and their psychologists began to put pressure on the enforcement agencies to open themselves up to greater participation in rule-making by the employers and psychologists having to comply with their guidelines. The secretary of labor responded by creating an Advisory Committee on Selection and Testing in 1968. The first author was one of nine psychologists appointed to that committee. Industry associations such as the American Petroleum Institute (API) developed programs to inform their memberships of methods to comply with legal fairness requirements. API appointed a Subcommittee on Selection Techniques, its general purpose being to develop informational and resource materials to assist the petroleum industry in dealing with some of the complex issues involved in achieving equal employment opportunity. The subcommittee, composed of five company psychologists, oversaw the publication of (1) a manual to interpret the various federal guidelines and orders relating to equal employment opportunity, (2) a manual to describe how to validate employee selection techniques, and (3) a compilation of validity studies relevant to the petroleum industry. Member companies used these documents as reference pieces and as training materials for personnel and EEO specialists. They were even used by EEOC as training materials for their investigators.

Beginning in the mid-1960s and extending into the late 1970s was the concept of *differential validity*. The earliest definition, stated simply, was that tests are valid for nonminorities but not for minorities. Later this definition was replaced with a more sophisticated formulation: that tests might be valid for both groups but are significantly less valid for minorities than for nonminorities. By the late 1970s this concept had been thoroughly debunked, but in the meantime its appeal with the enforcement agencies and testing critics was great. The revised guidelines of EEOC and even the revised orders of OFCCP required separate statistical analyses by race-ethnic group and by sex in the reporting of validity studies. In essence, the requirement was for (at least) two validation studies within each overall study. Further, in all but the largest employers, the limited number of minority persons available made such efforts technically infeasible. Even very large companies in capital-intensive industries, such as Exxon, often found themselves unable to obtain sufficient data to perform such "differential validity" analyses adequately. For many companies the burden (and additional expense) was too much to continue their testing programs, and they simply dropped them.

An offshoot of the specious concept of differential validity was the concept of *test bias,* which says that tests are unfair to protected classes since they predict a lower level of job performance than the members of the protected group will actually achieve. As with differential validity, the appeal for test critics was compelling, and a requirement for test bias (also referred to increasingly as "test fairness") analyses was included in the federal guidelines still in effect today. The psychological profession, after a period of debate about the proper methodology for assessing the presence of test bias, finally landed on one that uses regression lines to examine for systematic underprediction of protected groups' job performance. The increasingly clear answer to the question of test bias is this: it rarely occurs, and when it does, it tends to work to the *favor* of the protected group by somewhat overpredicting their job performance, a quite counterintuitive result in the minds of many and one that is still not fully recognized by the enforcement agencies and other critics of testing.

In March, 1971 the U. S. Supreme Court handed down its first decision involving preemployment testing (*Griggs v. Duke Power Co.*) The gist of the decision is contained in these words:

> Nothing in the Act [the Civil Rights Act of 1964] precludes the use of testing or measuring procedures; obviously they are useful. What Congress has forbidden is giving these devices and mechanisms controlling force unless they are demonstrably a reasonable measure of job performance. . . . What Congress has commanded is that any tests used must measure the person for the job and not the person in the abstract. [And also] Con-

gress directed the thrust of the Act to the consequences of employment practices, not simply the motivation.

Included elsewhere in the decision was a statement to the effect that the guidelines of the enforcing agency were entitled to *"great deference"* and a footnoted citation to the 1970 EEOC guidelines. For employers who had not validated their selection devices, *Griggs v. Duke Power* provoked much anxiety, since an unvalidated test could be construed to be measuring "the person in the abstract." Even companies like Exxon, with a long history of validating their selection materials, had to evaluate their positions since many of the validation practices of the past could have been swept away with *Griggs.* Criteria such as rationally derived and global order-of-merit lists came under new scrutiny. The decision was made to underpin performance criterion measures with job analyses to ensure that the criteria our tests were predicting were themselves validly and fairly job related.

At this point, a few words are warranted concerning fairness and performance appraisal. Whereas technical solutions exist relative to test fairness, nothing of that nature exists where appraisals are concerned. There are two major approaches to ensuring fairness in appraisal. The first is to underpin every appraisal form with a thorough job analysis. This makes certain that the areas upon which each employee's performance are judged are related to the job and not to factors tangentially related to the actual requirements of the job. The other area is rater training, which focuses on observing and assessing behavior on the job accurately. In 1984 Exxon embarked on a corporate-wide effort to train all supervisors in doing just that in conjunction with the introduction of a new performance appraisal based on the analysis of over 3,000 sampled positions across the corporation. The training employed lecture material coupled with workbook and videotaped exercises designed to hone the observation and assessment skills of performance appraisers.

In 1973, another landmark decision was handed down by the Supreme Court in *McDonnell Douglas Corp. v. Green.* The key words were:

> The complainant in a Title VII trial must carry the initial burden under the statute of establishing a prima facie case of racial discrimination. This may be done by showing (i) that he belongs to a racial minority; (ii) that he applied and was qualified for a job for which the employer was seeking applicants; (iii) that, despite his qualifications, he was rejected, and (iv) that, after his rejection, the position remained open and the employer continued to seek applicants from persons of complainant's qualifications.

Interpreted literally, black applicant A meets the minimum formal qualifications stated in an employment ad or other advisory. He is rejected, and the organization employs white applicant B, who is processed later against the same qualifications. Black A has grounds for a charge of discrimination. Because of situations like this, the company's psychologists recommended that employing authorities make no decision on hiring or rejecting until all eligible candidates for an opening had been completely processed. In the case of field and plant operations, this sometimes meant that a projection of future vacancies was necessary, with those employed being placed in a utility position until a job opened up. The rationale was that it was easier to defend selection of one or a few from many than it was to establish acceptable reasons for a series of individual hiring or rejecting decisions.

In 1972 the Congress had enacted the Equal Employment Opportunity Act, actually an amendment to the Civil Rights Act of 1964. The EEOC gained many privileges under the act, but the most important feature for practitioners was the creation of the Equal Employment Opportunity Coordinating Council (EEOCC). Membership was specified as being the chairman of the EEOC, the chairman of the Civil Service Commission, the secretary of labor, the attorney general, and the chairman of the Commission on Civil Rights, or their designees. The mission of the EEOCC included elimination of the conflict, competition, duplication, and inconsistency among the agencies. No leadership role was designated, no staff was authorized, and no budget was provided. The council tried valiantly against almost impossible odds. The first issue tackled was the development of uniform guidelines on employee selection procedures to replace the three that were then in effect. The first draft effort was considered so unacceptable to the psychologists of the business community and their managements that a group was formed, composed of psychologists and lawyers from leading corporations. The group's purpose was to provide constructive criticism and input to the agencies drafting the guidelines. As a result of these efforts, all of the participating agencies, save the EEOC, were able to reach agreement on a new set of guidelines. The EEOC simply republished its 1970 guidelines, so employers were still left with two different sets of federal guidelines to contend with. It was not until 1978 that the EEOC finally came into line with the other agencies with the publication of the current federal Uniform Guidelines on Employee Selection Procedures. These guidelines represent nearly a decade and a half of debate over employee selection, most of it centering around what is and is not fair (discriminatory). By the time they were published, the Uniform Guidelines required twenty-six pages of small print in the *Federal Register* followed by another sixteen pages of interpretive material—all to interpret section 703(h) of the Civil Rights Act of 1964 (the Tower amendment), a fifty-three-word statement that said it was not illegal to use a "professionally developed ability test."

About this time increasing momentum developed to employ more women in the higher-paying blue-collar jobs that had traditionally been held almost exclusively by men. Generally, the jobs had high physical demands, and managers were reluctant to evaluate many women as being capable of performing them. Paradoxically, a strong affirmative action effort was encouraging more women to apply for these jobs. Two avenues were explored in Exxon. First, all physically demanding tasks were studied to see if demands could be reduced by the installation of special mechanized equipment. Second, a research program was initiated to develop a physical abilities test battery. Going into the project, it was clear that physical tests, particularly those involving strength, were likely to have considerable adverse effect on women. At the same time, it was recognized that there was a pressing need to do a better job, not of screening out women but of screening in the *right* women—those who could do the job. Realistically, we also knew that the more pronounced was the adverse effect, the heavier would be the burden of showing the validity and fairness of the tests. An intensive analysis of the physically demanding components of the jobs led to our being able to plot a profile for each job in terms of the kinds and degrees of physical abilities required for successful performance. Then, based upon these profiles, tests were designed to measure those abilities where the demand was high. A predictive criterion-related validation study was carried out against a performance evaluation criterion measure developed specially for this project and based upon the physical ability job analysis. Very strong validities were found, and statistical test fairness analyses disclosed no evidence of unfairness to women. Despite these satisfying results, we were still concerned about the possibility of indirect influences on the fairness of the tests. Subsequent studies were made of the general physical activity levels of men and women applicants, and of test-taking technique, as possible explanatory factors for the male-female differences on the strength tests. None of these studies yielded positive results, but while we were not able to learn anything that we could use to mitigate adverse impact, our level of comfort that the tests were, in fact, fair to women was raised.

Because of the need to acquire adequate samples of employees in appropriate jobs, almost all validation research had been conducted in large organizational units. Concern was increasingly expressed about the use of selection tests in units where no local validation studies were available. The Uniform Guidelines (1978) provide that evidence of validity in one unit of a multiunit organization may be transported to other units, provided that similarity of the job(s) can be demonstrated. Since a profile of job tasks and duties was generally available for most of the jobs for which validity studies had been performed, a program for matching these profiles with those in units unable to perform their own validation studies was undertaken for the purpose of establishing the "transportability" of the validity to the new location. Methods using multivariate analysis of variance were developed to compare the profiles of the jobs in the two locations. Our experience has been that, while these methods are quite sensitive to differences in jobs, we have yet to find an instance where transportability has not been supported.

Related to our rather casual observation that locations (and therefore, test validities) were more similar to one another than we might have expected is the rapidly developing concept of "validity generalization" or, as it has come to be known in some quarters, "metaanalysis." The basic theory is that, contrary to (earlier) prevailing wisdom, validity is not situation specific and that most of the observed differences in validity statistics across employee populations, plants, and so on are the result of such statistical artifacts as small samples, differences in criterion and/or predictor reliability, and restriction in range on the predictor (see Schmidt and Hunter, 1977). In the petroleum industry, the American Petroleum Institute, pooling data from fourteen companies, sponsored a validity generalization study of selection tests in common use in the industry. Results showed a high degree of generalizability, and thus transportability, of these test. A technical report on the study later appeared in the

Journal of Applied Psychology (Schmidt, Hunter, & Caplan, 1981). While Exxon did not halt its efforts in the test validation area by any means, the developing data base of transportability and validity generalization results increases our confidence that those tests do, in fact, have broad applicability. This has allowed us to concentrate our efforts on the development and validation of new test batteries rather than continually revalidating existing batteries.

As one reads this document it generally appears as a somewhat logical progression: thrust, parry, counterthrust, as EEO pressures increased and as the company was able to meet expanding requirements. The continuing tension between employers' and enforcement agencies' conceptions of fairness is epitomized by an exchange between the first author and a compliance reviewer. The compliance reviewer, reflecting his view of the meaning of fairness said, "My job is to get more blacks into that refinery," and the author, reflecting his, replied, "And my job is to see that they don't come in through a revolving door and go right back out." Clearly, the most valid selection device is, in our view, the most fair. Still, the enforcement agencies and courts have often not seen fairness in that light. A major concern is the attitude of the federal courts. They have been willing to grant great deference to the regulations and interpretations of the enforcement agencies. But the courts have also been willing to give credence to a body of professional evidence such as that provided by psychologists through research reports, standards, and principles published to guide practitioners. At the same time, a large body of case law on the proper use of selection standards has been developed. It may ultimately become the job of psychologists to analyze legal precedents in preference to conducting new research. We hope not.

REFERENCES

Griggs v. Duke Power Co. (1971). 401 U.S. 424.

McDonnell Douglas Corp. v. Green (1973). 411 U.S. 792.

Shaeffer, R.G. (1973). *Nondiscrimination in employment: Changing perspectives, 1963–1972.* New York: The Conference Board.

Schmidt, F.L., & Hunter, J.E. (1977). Development of a general solution to the problem of validity generalization. *Journal of Applied Psychology, 62,* 529–540.

Schmidt, F.L., Hunter, J.E., & Caplan, J.R. (1981). Validity generalization results for two job groups in the petroleum industry. *Journal of Applied Psychology, 66,* 261–273.

Sparks, C.P. (1981). Success in training as a criterion for test validation. *Journal of Policy Analysis and Information Systems, 5,* 31–41.

U.S. Equal Employment Opportunity Commission (1970). Guidelines on employee selection procedures. *Federal Register, 35,* 12333–12335.

U.S. Equal Employment Opportunity Commission, U.S. Civil Service Commission, U.S. Department of Labor, & U.S. Department of Justice (1978). Adoption by four agencies of uniform guidelines on employee selection procedures. *Federal Register, 43,* 38290–38315.

EMPLOYMENT TESTING AND THE LAW IN THE UNITED STATES

James C. Sharf

In the era in which *competitiveness* has become a household buzzword and the pressures on employment officials to hire productive employees are greater than ever, the dilemma that faces management is that traditional sources of preemployment information have lost much of their perceived usefulness to employment decision makers.

This loss of usefulness is due to a number of reasons. (1) Although universally used, measures of educational achievement have become less and less meaningful as a consequence of grade inflation. (2) Recommendations and letters of reference from prior employers are less and less likely to accomplish more than merely confirming dates of prior employment because of employers' liability concerns. And, as if this loss of useful information to employment decision making is not enough, (3) employers are finding it increasingly difficult to discharge nonproductive employees as management's prerogative known by the term "employment at will" is eroded in the courts; an employer is simply not able to rely on hiring an individual and firing that person for whatever reason when on-the-job training fails to ensure productive behavior.

Out of necessity, employers have had to seek alternatives to measures of academic achievement, letters of recommendation, and probationary employment in deciding who to hire. The good news is that employment testing is strategically positioned and is increasingly becoming a major employment tool permitting organizations to attain a competitive edge by hiring more productive workers than has ever been

possible through the use of more traditional sources of preemployment information (Lee, 1988). As the National Research Council of the National Academy of Science noted in 1982 with regard to employment testing (Wigdor & Garner, 1982): "the committee has seen no evidence of alternatives to testing that are equally informative, equally adequate technically, and also economically and politically viable."

As Wunder and Sparks note in chapter 13, the precedent of case law on the proper use of employment testing is well established and although admittedly complex, this precedent has been thoroughly described in a number of sources (Ballew, 1987; Bersoff, 1981; Booth & Mackay, 1980; Gold, 1985; Ledvinka & Schoenfeldt, 1978; Lerner, 1979; Potter, 1986; Schlei & Grossman, 1983.

Rather than looking over our shoulder to describe the precedent of employment testing law, this chapter provides the opportunity to highlight three strategic testing practices likely to be of the greatest consequence for virtually every employer in both the public and private sectors: (1) the use of cognitive ability testing for employment purposes without having to conduct a full-blown validity study, a breakthrough in employment testing known as "validity generalization" (2) the use of "race norming" to reduce the adverse impact that would result if testing results were used without regard to an applicant's race, color, religion, sex, or national origin (Linn, 1982); and (3) the 1989 Supreme Court *Atonio* decision defusing the adverse impact definition of employment discrimination.

VALIDITY GENERALIZATION

The well-recognized proponents of the generalizability of cognitive ability tests for employment purposes are Schmidt and Hunter (1981). Writing in the Oc-

tober 1981 issue of *American Psychologist,* they announced their breakthrough conclusions to the profession in the following statement:

> Professionally developed cognitive ability tests are valid predictors of performance on the job and in

The opinions expressed are those of the author and not official policy of the U.S. Office of Personnel Management.

training for all jobs . . . in all settings . . . [and] cognitive ability tests are equally valid for minority and majority applicants and are fair to minority applicants in that they do not underestimate the expected job performance of minority groups.

Note 1, added by the *American Psychologist* editors, states:

> The cognitive ability tests referred to throughout this manuscript are professionally developed, objective tests of verbal ability, quantitative ability, mechanical comprehension, spatial ability, and inductive and deductive reasoning that are widely used in personnel selection in industry and government.

Schmidt and Hunter's conclusions were a breakthrough in that they rejected the historical presumption (Albright, Glennon & Smith, 1963; Ghiselli, 1966; Guion, 1965; that validity findings were specific to the situation in which the validity study had been conducted and that validity evidence was similarly presumed to be specific to the population subgroup for whom the validity evidence had been developed. Tenopyr (1981), an internationally recognized employment testing expert, recognized Schmidt and Hunter's conclusions as "one of the more noteworthy contributions to the field of personnel psychology . . . [but that it] probably will have little impact on events in the real world for some time." The time, if not upon us, is fast approaching.

VALIDITY GENERALIZATION IN THE UNIFORM GUIDELINES

The Uniform Guidelines on Employee Selection Procedures (1978) are the federal fair employment standard adopted by the Equal Employment Opportunity Commission (EEOC), the Department of Justice, the Department of Labor, and the Civil Service Commission (now the Office of Personnel Management). Although the Uniform Guidelines are likely to be revised in the near term, they do not preclude utilizing validity generalization—that is, the use of validity evidence conducted elsewhere in lieu of a local validation study.

Section 7(B) of the Uniform Guidelines states:

> Use of criterion-related validity evidence from other sources. Criterion-related validity studies conducted by one test user, or described in test manuals and the professional literature, will be considered acceptable for use by another user when the following requirements are met:
>
> (1) Validity evidence. Evidence from the available studies meeting the standards of section 14(B) below clearly demonstrates that the selection procedure is valid;
> (2) Job similarity. The incumbents in the user's job and the incumbents in the job or group of jobs on which the validity study was conducted perform substantially the same major work behaviors, as shown by appropriate job analyses both on the job for which the selection procedure is to be used; and
> (3) Fairness evidence. The studies include a study of test fairness for each race, sex, and ethnic group which constitutes a significant factor in the borrowing user's relevant labor market for the job or jobs in question.

Schmidt, Hunter, and Caplan (1981) claim that all three Uniform Guideline 7(B) requirements can usually be met for the following reasons: (1) the first requirement is met based on the cumulative weight of validity study evidence typically conducted at the organizational level but analyzed across organizational studies utilizing the metaanalysis research design; (2) validation studies "always examine major work behaviors"; and (3) the generally accepted principles and practices of personnel psychology now recognize that tests are fair in that they do not underpredict minority job performance. This last point was echoed in the 1982 National Research Council report on ability testing, which noted (Wigdor & Garner, 1982):

> Predictions based on a single equation (either the one for whites or for a combined group of blacks and whites) generally yield predictions that are quite similar to, or somewhat higher than, predictions from an equation based only on data for blacks. In other words, the results do not support the notion that the traditional use of test scores in a prediction equation yields predictions for blacks that systematically underestimate their actual performance. If anything, there is some indication of the converse, with actual criterion performance being more often lower than would be indicated by test scores of blacks. Thus, in the technically precise meaning of the term, ability tests have not been proved to be biased against blacks; that is, they predict criterion performance as well for blacks as for whites.

GENERALLY ACCEPTED PRINCIPLES AND PRACTICES OF PERSONNEL PSYCHOLOGY

The generally accepted principles and practices of personnel psychology include the *Principles for the Validation and Use of Personnel Selection Procedures* (1987) and the *Standards for Educational and Psychological Testing* (1985). The *Principles,* which articulate the wisdom of the specialty of industrial-organizational psychology, note with regard to validity generalization that

> classical psychometric teaching has held that validity is specific to the research study and that inability to generalize is one of the most serious shortcomings of selection psychology. Current research has shown that the differential effects of numerous variables are not so great as heretofore assumed; much of the difference in observed outcomes of validation research can be attributed to statistical artifacts. It now seems well established from both validity generalization studies and cooperative validation efforts that validities generalize far more than once supposed.

> Validity generalization is a demonstration that a selection procedure or kind of selection procedure permits valid inferences about job behavior or job performance across given jobs or groups of jobs in different settings.

> Validity generalization [is defined as] evidence that the results of validity studies obtained in one or more studies may be appropriately applied to other situations involving the same or similar jobs.

The *standards,* while written primarily from the perspective of educational measurement, nevertheless recognize validity generalization, but in somewhat more qualified terms:

> When adequate local validation evidence is not available, criterion-related evidence of validity for a specified test use may be based on validity generalization from a set of prior studies, provided that the specified test-use situation can be considered to have been drawn from the same population of situations on which validity generalization was conducted.

PLAINTIFFS' BAR'S CRITICISM OF VALIDITY GENERALIZATION

Without a doubt, it is clear that the plaintiff's bar views validity generalization (VG) as a broadside attack on the *Griggs* standard of employment discrimination. In testimony before the Subcommittee on Employment Opportunities of the House Committee on Education and Labor in December 1984, the Lawyers' Committee for Civil Rights Under Law made their objections to VG quite clear based on their testimony as follows (Robinson & Seymour, 1984):

> For some years, the officials of the U.S. Office of Personnel Management responsible for developing the government's job tests have been pushing a new theory called "validity generalization." Based entirely on reviews of the published results of large numbers of validation studies, without any check of such studies to determine whether the studies reviewed had been performed in accordance with professional standards, and largely ignoring the likelihood that developers do not publicize their failures, they have concluded that the validity of tests is not limited to the particular jobs for which studies have been done, or to the particular situations in which the tests were used, and that the findings of validity are not even limited to the tests that were studied.

> If this "validity generalization" approach is accepted, there would be no more need for any employer to perform any study of the validity of a test which operates to exclude minorities or women at a disproportionately high rate. Validity would always be presumed, and it would necessarily follow that *no employer could ever lose a testing case.*

> We are concerned that the Department of Labor's U.S. Employment Service—which provides the funds for State Employment Services and develops tests for their use in deciding which applicants for referrals to employers should be classified as qualified to perform particular types of jobs—may be considering adoption of the "validity generalization" approach in its developments of tests. While its validation studies have been of poor quality in the past, it might not even make a stab at performing such studies in the future. If the Department of Labor's Office of Contract Compliance Programs follows suit, the

present standards applicable to government contractors would dissolve. . . .

Until now, the EEOC has been a firm bulwark against any notion that validity could simply be presumed. However, the Commision has recently decided to undertake a review of the Uniform Guidelines. The scope of the review suggests strongly that what the agency actually has in mind is a number of drastic limitations, including . . . the adoption of the validity generalization approach.

U.S. EMPLOYMENT SERVICE'S USE OF VALIDITY GENERALIZATION

Since 1947, the U.S. Employment Service (USES) has produced over 500 criterion-related studies of the validity of the General Aptitude Test Battery (GATB), making it in all likelihood one of the most studied tests in use anywhere. To date there have been no adverse court rulings against use of the GATB, and in fact the *Pegues v. Mississippi State Employment Service* (1980) decision specifically permitted the validity evidence of the GATB to be transported from one location to another. Certainly for most private sector employers, the USES's GATB administered through state employment service offices will increasingly become a pragmatic means of obtaining valid information identifying the best candidates available for virtually any entry-level job.

Today, forty-two state employment services operating under the USES funding umbrella use validity generalization established by Hunter (1980) to make job referrals to nearly 12,000 jobs based on a candidate's GATB scores. According to the U.S. Department of Labor, the use of validity generalization is "based on the premise that: 1) there is a linear relationship between GATB scores and job performance; 2) GATB scores can be used to predict performance in all 12,099 jobs in the *Dictionary of Occupational Titles;* and 3) there is no differential prediction (i.e., the GATB is equally valid in predicting job performance for majority and minority group members)" (Quigley, 1987).

To avoid adverse impact in GATB referrals, state employment services utilize so-called within-group percentile conversions, which are the equivalent of separate ranking for nonminorities, blacks, native Americans, and Hispanics. Employment services give a single list of referrals to employers with racial and national origin percentages paralleling the composition of the work force for those groups. (For lower-level jobs having no or low educational requirements, the work force typically resembles the racial and national origin composition of the labor market.)

Typically, when a company places a job order, the state employment service sends two to three times as many candidates as the company has openings. Consequently, the employer receives a single referral list containing nonminorities, blacks, native Americans, and Hispanics in proportions reflecting the work force for these groups. The company usually has sufficient flexibility to ensure that there is no "bottom-line" adverse impact in the selections made. Of relevance on this point is Hunter's showing that using separate rankings for minorities and nonminorities reduces test utility by about 15 percent compared to the optimum strategy of top-down hiring (Hunter & Hunter, 1984).

To the extent that a company's use of a state employment service makes the within-group percentile conversions in effect a pass-fail component of the employer's overall selection procedure, however, such a use could serve as the basis for a Title VII lawsuit (Potter, 1987).

DEPARTMENT OF JUSTICE CHALLENGES WITHIN-GROUP PERCENTILE CONVERSIONS

In November 1986, Assistant Attorney General Brad Reynolds wrote to the director of the USES questioning the legality of the separate ranking by race methodology as constituting an illegal classification and segregation under the U.S. Constitution and Title VII (*Daily Labor Report*, 1987). Since then, an agreement has been reached by the Department of Justice and Department of Labor under which the VG program will continue and the Justice Department will forgo initiating any litigation against state employment service offices using the program. In February 1987, the Department of Labor announced that the USES's use of validity generalization for interpreting and implementing GATB scores was to be investigated by a blue ribbon panel at the National Research Council of the National Academy of Science and was being undertaken primarily in response to Justice Department concern that the use of separate scoring systems for minorities may result in "reverse discrimination."

To make sure that VG is fair to minority groups, conversions from composite scores to percentiles are computed within ethnic groups. Separate conversion tables have been developed for blacks, Hispanics, native Americans, and nonminorities. This practice, known as in-group conversion, is what prompted a letter of concern to the Department of Labor from Assistant Attorney General Brad Reynolds. The civil rights concern over the technique, according to Reynolds, centers on whether separate scoring dis-

criminates against nonminorities and if doing away with it discriminates against minorities. The associate solicitor for civil rights at the Labor Department has insisted that they are not backing away from VG and are trying to do everything they can, including spending money on the National Research Council study, but they cannot ignore the legal issues.

According to the deputy assistant secretary of labor, " 'The issues should have been discussed up front' before VG became so popular and widely used . . . Now," he said, "it looks as though the department is stepping back from its position, but this is not the case." "When we come out [of the study], we will have a system we can defend, or if not, we will know why not and know what we have to deal with" (*Daily Labor Report*, 1987)).

NATIONAL RESEARCH COUNCIL SUPPORTS VALIDITY GENERALIZATION AND RACE NORMING

In May 1989, the National Research Council (NRC) issued its long-awaited report on the merits of the validity generalization claims made for the GATB and the way in which race norming was being used by state employment service offices to implement GATB referrals. The NRC found that the GATB is a valid predictor of job performance for most jobs handled by the employment service and generally supported Schmidt and Hunter's conclusions that the GATB is more reliable than any other single selection procedure including interviews, educational background, skills, and job experience. Concluded Hartigan, co-author of the report, "We probably cannot afford not to use" the GATB (*Daily Labor Report*, 1989).

The more controversial recommendation in the NRC report was the conclusion that there was a scientific rationale for race norming, although the authors cautioned that they were offering advice "on aspects of the problem that lend themselves to scientific analysis" but not making conclusions about the legality of race-conscious scoring methods (*Daily Labor Report*, 1989, p. A-5). As could have been expected in an area of public policy as controversial as this, the recommendations regarding the scientific rationale for race norming did not meet with universal concurrence (Holden, 1989).

SUPREME COURT REWRITES THE *GRIGGS* RELIANCE ON ADVERSE IMPACT STATISTICS

The timing of the NRC GATB report preceded by a week the most significant Title VII Supreme Court decision since *Griggs v. Duke Power* Co. in 1971. The consequence of the Supreme Court decision in *Wards Cove Packing Company v. Atonio* was to disarm the use of the adverse impact statistical trigger of *Griggs,* which had been interpreted by lower courts to read an equality of employment results premise into Title VII. Essentially only days after issuing the report, the legal rationale of the NRC's race norming recommendations to reduce adverse impact was removed, at least as a statistical presumption, as shown

in the following excerpts from the Court's majority opinion in *Antonio:*

> The Court of Appeals' theory, at the very least, would mean that any employer who had a segment of his work force that was—for some reason—racially imbalanced, could be hauled into court and forced to engage in the expensive and time-consuming task of defending the "business necessity" of the methods used to select the other members of his work force. The only practicable option for many employers will be to adopt racial quotas, insuring that no portion of his work force

deviates in racial composition from the other portions thereof; this is a result that Congress expressly rejected in drafting Title VII. *Watson.* The Court of Appeals' theory would "leave the employer little choice . . . but to engage in a subjective quota system of employment selection. This, of course, is far from the intent of Title VII. *Albemarle.*

[Regarding] the question of causation in a disparate-impact case . . . The law in this respect was correctly stated by Justice O'Connor's opinion last Term in *Watson:*

> We note that the plaintiff's burden in establishing a prima facie case goes beyond the need to show that there are statistical disparities in the employer's work force . . . the plaintiff is in our view responsible for isolating and identifying the specific employment practices that are allegedly responsible for any observed statistical disparities. *Watson*

[A] Title VII plaintiff does not make out a case of disparate impact simply by showing that, "at the bottom line," there is racial *imbalance* in the work force.

[Plaintiffs] will also have to demonstrate that the disparity they complain of is the result of one or more of the employment practices that they are attacking here, specifically showing that each challenged practice has a significantly disparate impact on employment opportunities for whites and nonwhites. To hold otherwise would result in employers being potentially liable for "the myriad of innocent causes that may lead to statistical imbalances in the composition of their work forces." *Watson*

Some will complain that this specific causation requirement is unduly burdensome on Title VII plaintiffs. But liberal civil discovery rules give plaintiffs broad access to employers' records in an effort to document their claims. Also, employers falling within the scope of the Uniform Guidelines on Employee Selection Procedures are required to "maintain . . . records or other information which will disclose the impact which its test and other selection procedures have upon employment opportunities of persons by identifiable race, sex, or ethnic group[s.]" This includes records concerning "the individual components of the selection process" where there is a significant disparity in the selection rates of whites and nonwhites.

If, on remand, respondents meet the proof burdens outlined above, and establish a prima facie case of disparate impact with respect to any of petitioners' employment practices, the case will shift to any business justification petitioners offer for their use of these practices [emphasis added].

This phase of the disparate-impact case contains two components: first, a consideration of the justifications an employer offers for his use of these practices; and second, the availability of alternate practices to achieve the same business ends, with less racial impact. *Albemarle*

Though we have phrased the query differently in different cases, it is generally well-established that at the justification stage of such a disparate impact case, *the dispositive issue is whether a challenged practice serves, in a significant way, the legitimate employment goals of the employer. The touchstone of this inquiry is a reasoned review of the employer's justification for his use of the challenged practice . . . There is no requirement that the challenged practice be "essential" or "indispensable" to the employer's business for it to pass muster . . . "* [emphasis added].

In this phase, the employer carries the *burden of producing evidence of a business justification for his employment practice. . . . "The ultimate burden of proving that discrimination against a protected group has been caused by a specific employment practice remains with the plaintiff* AT ALL TIMES." *Watson. . . .* We acknowledge that some of our earlier decisions can be read as suggesting otherwise. But to the extent that those cases speak of an employer's "burden of proof" with respect to a legitimate business justification defense, they should have been understood to mean AN EMPLOYER'S PRODUCTION—BUT NOT PERSUASION—BURDEN. The persuasion burden here must remain with the plaintiff, for it is he who must prove that it was "because of such individual's race, color," etc., that he was denied a desired employment opportunity.

Finally, if on remand the case reaches this point, and respondents cannot persuade the trier of fact on the question of petitioners' business necessity defense, respondents may still be able to prevail. To do so, respondents will have to persuade the factfinder that "other tests or selection devices, without a similarly undesirable racial effect, would also serve the employer's legitimate (hiring) interest[s];" by so demonstrating, respondents would prove that "[petitioners were] using [their] tests merely as a "pretext for discrimination." *Albemarle.* If respondents, having established a prima facie case, come forward with alternatives to petitioners' hiring practices that reduce the racially-disparate impact of practices currently being used, and petitioners refuse to adopt these alternatives, such a refusal would belie a claim by petitioners that their incumbent practices are being employed for nondiscriminatory reasons.

Of course, any alternative practices which respondents offer up in this respect must be equally effective as petitioners' chosen hiring procedures in achieving petitioners' legitimate employment goals. Moreover, "[f]actors such as the cost or other burdens of proposed alternative selection devices are relevant in determining whether they would be equally as effective as the challenged practice in serving the employer's legitimate business goals" *Watson.* "Courts are gener-ally less competent than employers to restructure business practices," *Furnco;* consequently, the judiciary should proceed with care before mandating that an employer must adopt a plaintiff's alternate selection or hiring practice in response to a Title VII suit.

LEGAL PRECEDENTS: VALIDITY GENERALIZATION

Based on the precedent of case law as of winter 1990 (appendix 14–A), personnel measurement has thus far been successful in explaining the generally accepted principles and practices of personnel psychology that support transporting and generalizing validity evidence. Personnel measurement has not been as successful, however, in convincing courts that there is an adverse productivity consequence to using test results in other than a linear, rank-order manner without regard to a candidate's race, color, religion, sex, or national origin.

Prior to *Atonio,* employers frequently had chosen the pragmatic alternative of using an applicant's race, color, religion, sex, and/or national origin in order to balance the numbers by selecting members of groups against some numerical quota and thus avoiding disparate impact based on differences in group selection rates. While this may have been a pragmatic solution under *Griggs* for employers to avoid the regulatory hassle and the explicit threat of litigation based on the *Griggs* disparate impact definition of discrimination, such a pragmatic approach had not gone without notice in the scientific community. According to an earlier report issued by the National Research Council (Wigdor & Garner, 1982):

> After 15 years of enforcement activity ... it is now being recognized that there has been a dramatic shift in government policy from the requirement of equal treatment to that of equal outcome. Bureaucratic and judicial interpretation of Title VII has turned increasingly toward a notion of equality based on group parity in the work force or what has come to be called a "representative work force." This policy makes the redistributive impulse in Title VII much more immediate, and it is accompanied by a good deal of tension and confusion inside and outside of government as to rights, obligations, and permissible social costs.

Given the repeated failure of tests and other modes of selection to withstand challenge (under Title VII), as well as the pressure from the compliance authorities to achieve a representative work force, it seems probable that many employers will quietly begin to select on the very bases that Title VII disallows (race, color, sex, or national origin) but now for the purpose of eliminating the work force imbalances that made them vulnerable to litigation.

We find little convincing evidence that well-constructed and competently administered tests are more valid predictors for one population subgroup than for another: individuals with higher scores tend to perform better on the job, regardless of group identity.

The practice of using quotas to select the relatively better qualified applicants within various population subgroups—race norming—is a political solution that is not supported by the generally accepted principles and practices of personnel psychology. To the contrary, personnel psychology recognizes that the rule, not the exception, is that for valid tests, there is a linear relationship between test performance and job performance (*Principles,* 1987):

> In usual circumstances, the relationship between a predictor and a criterion may be assumed to be linear. Consequently, selecting from the top scorers on down is almost always the most beneficial procedure from the standpoint of an organization if there is an appropriate amount of variance in the predictor. Selection techniques developed by content-oriented procedures and discriminating adequately within the range of interest can be assumed to have a linear relationship to job behavior. Consequently, ranking on the basis of such scores is appropriate.

The validity of the testing process should not be compromised in the effort to shape the distribution of the work force.

What is of primary importance is that the integrity of the information being used in the selection process be maintained. At present, the conflict between competing goals is having the effect of eliminating useful tests along with those that make little or no contribution to hiring decisions. Productivity and equity would be far better served by shifting the burden of balancing interests from tests to the decision rule that determines how test scores and other selection criteria will be used.

CONCLUSIONS

While this chapter has focused on validity generalization and the law rather than on employment testing in general, the choice was purposeful. This is because I believe that employers will increasingly rely on the U.S. Employment Service's use of the GATB as well as other tests of general cognitive ability to identify the most productive applicants in their labor market.

Since the Supreme Court's 1989 *Atonio* majority has disarmed the adverse impact statistical trigger based on *Griggs,* the focus of Title VII is likely to return to the more basic issue of equal employment opportunity rather than the litigious preoccupation with equality of employment results. While the civil rights bar can be expected to propose new legislation restoring the *Griggs* "business necessity" burden of proof on employers, it remains to be seen whether Congress will be willing to rewrite the civil rights promise of equal employment opportunity—the clear intent of the Civil Rights Act of 1964. What is increasingly clear, however, is that employers' legitimate concern with work force quality is resulting in a renaissance of employment testing.

APPENDIX A: LEGAL PRECEDENT OF VALIDITY GENERALIZATION CASE LAW

Friend v. Leidinger, 446 F. Supp. 361 (E.D. Va. 1977), *aff'd,* 588 F.2d 61 (4th Cir. 1978):

> The dispute in guidelines deals with whether Fire Fighter B-1(M) Test used by the [Richmond] bureau had been properly validated. A part of the validation study was done in California and plaintiffs objected to a study not conducted in Richmond. However, *plaintiffs* have shown no difference in the duties of a fireman in the 55 areas of California, where the test was validated, from the duties of a Richmond fireman. *To requie local validation in every city, village and hamlet would be ludicrous* [emphasis added].

Pegues v. Mississippi State Employment Service, 488 F. Supp. 239 (N.D. Miss. 1980), *aff'd in part and rev'd in part,* 699 F.2d 760 (5th Cir.), *cert. denied,* 464 U.S. 991 (1983).

> Empirical research has demonstrated that validity is not perceptibly changed by differences in location, differences in specific job duties or applicant populations. Valid tests do not become invalid when these circumstances change. Plaintiffs' allegation that validity is specific to a particular location, a particular set of tasks and to a specific applicant population or in other words, that a valid test in one set of circumstances is not valid in circumstances not perfectly identical is not true.

Samuel Cox v. Consolidated Rail Corporation and *Lawton Frazier v. Consolidated Rail Corporation and United Transportation Union,* No. 83-0514 & 85-0845, slip op. (District of Columbia, August 26, 1987).

> That [content valid] study was properly "transported" and utilized in evaluating Conrail's written and oral testing procedures, and buttresses the conclusion that Conrail's Engineer Training Program was content valid.... [The expert] supported his conclusions by what is known as validity generalization. This is a proper and accepted practice of generalizing the validity of one program by reference to a study made of another, similar program.

Equal Employment Opportunity Commission v. Atlas Paper Box Company, No. CIV-1-83-251, slip op. (E.D. Tenn., January 30, 1987).

> [The expert] testified that the Wonderlic test is a good measure of cognitive ability—mathematical reasoning, verbal skills, and spatial aptitude. He testified that the test is fair to minority applicants and better than any other predictor of success on the job such as level of training, previous work record, or the impression made in the interview. He testified that the validation studies made at other companies and on other groups of workers have indicated that the Wonderlic is a valid test for all types of clerical work. The more complex the clerical task, the higher the correlation was between a good score on the Wonderlic and successful performance on the job.
>
> While no formal validation study was performed at Atlas itself, it is obvious that any attempt to validate the Wonderlic test on a clerical work force as small as the one at Atlas would have been statistically meaningless. Much evidence was offered to show that the use of a cognitive ability test as an applicant screening device is more reliable than any other single predictor of job success.

The Court is satisfied that Atlas effectively rebutted the *prima facie* case and that there was nothing to suggest that the use of the Wonderlic test was a mere pretext for racial discrimination.

Although this testimony *was not actually contradicted,* Dr. Richard S. Barrett, an industrial psychologist, questioned the appropriateness of generalizing between other validation studies and the work situation at Atlas.

In *Atlas,* EEOC's industrial psychologist testified only on the factual issue of adverse impact and did not offer any opinion regarding on the VG claims at issue.

(See also: *Bruckner v. Goodyear Tire and Rubber Co.,* 339 F. Supp. 1108 (N.D. Ala. 1972), *aff'd per curiam,* 476 F.2d 1287 (5th Cir. 1973) (supporting transporting validity evidence); *Rivera v. City of Wichita Falls,* 665 F.2d 531, 538 at n. 10 (5th Cir. 1982) (supporting transporting validity evidence for police cadets); Van Aken v. Young, 541 F. Supp. 448 (E.D. Mich. 1982) *aff'd* 750 F.2d 43 (1983) (rejecting validity generalization); *Brunet v. City of Columbus,* 642 F. Supp. 1214 (S.D. Ohio 1986) *appeal dismissed without opinion,* 826 F.2d 1062 (6th Cir. 1987, *cert. denied* 108 S.Ct. 1593 (1988) supporting transporting validation study for firefighters).

REFERENCE

Albright, L.E., Glennon, J.K., & Smith, W.J. (1963). *The use of psychological tests in industry.* Cleveland, OH: Howard Allen. American Educational Research Association, American Psychological Association, & National Council on Measurement in Education (1985). *Standards for educational and psychological testing.* Washington, DC: American Psychological Association.

Ballew, P.J. (1987). Courts, psychologists, and the EEOC's Uniform Guidelines: An analysis of recent trends affecting testing as a means of employee selection. *Emory Law Journal, 36,* 203.

Bersoff, D. (1981). Testing and the law. *American Psychologist, 36,* 1047.

Booth W.B. & Mackay W.F. (1980). Legal constraints on employment testing and evolving trends in the law. *Emory Law Journal, 29,* 121.

Comment (1987). Courts, psychologists, and the EEOC's Uniform Guidelines: An analysis of recent trends affecting testing as a means of employee selection. *Emory Law Journal, 36,* 203.

Daily Labor Report (1987). Justice Department challenge of job validation technique prompts new study. February 9, A6-8.

Equal Employment Opportunity Commission v. Atlas Paper Box Company (1987). No. CIV-1-83-251, slip op. (E.D. Tenn., January 30).

Friend v. Leidinger, (1977). 446 F. Supp. 361 (E.D. Va.), *aff'd,* 588 F.2d 61 (4th Cir. 1978).

Ghiselli, E.E. (1966). *The validity of occupational aptitude tests.* New York: Wiley.

Gold, M. (1985). Griggs' folly: An essay on the theory, problems, and origin of the adverse impact definition of employment discrimination and a recommendation for reform. *Industrial Relations Law Journal, 429.*

Guion, R.M. (1965). *Personnel testing.* New York: McGraw-Hill.

Hunter, J.E. (1980). Test validation for twelve thousand jobs: An application of job classification and validity generalization analysis to the General Aptitude Test Battery (GATB). Washington, DC: U.S. Employment Service, U.S. Department of Labor.

Hunter, J.E., & Hunter, R.F. (1984). Validity and utility of alternative predictors of job performance. *Psychological Bulletin, 96,* 72–98.

Ledvinka, J., & Schoenfeldt, L. (1978). Legal developments in employment testing: Albemarle and beyond. *Personnel Psychology, 31,* 1.

Lee, C. (1988). Testing makes a comeback. *Training, 25* (12), 49–59.

Lerner, B. 1979). Employment discrimination: Adverse impact, validity, and equality. *Supreme Court Review, 1979, 17.*

Linn, R. (1982). Ability testing: Individual differences, prediction, and differential prediction. In Wigdor A.K. & Garner W.R. (Eds.), *Ability testing: Uses, consequences, and controversies.* Washington, DC: National Academy Press.

Pegues v. Mississippi State Employment Service, (1980). 488 F. Supp. 239 (N.D. Miss.), *aff'd in part and rev'd in part,* 699 F.2d 760 (5th Cir.), *cert. denied,* 464 U.S. 991 (1983).

Potter, E. (1986). *Employee selection: Legal and practical alternatives to compliance and litigation* (2d ed.). Washington, DC: National Foundation for the study of Equal Employment Policy.

Potter, E. (1987). Study of validity generalization testing program of the U.S. Employment Service. *Equal Employment Advisory Council Memorandum 87-26,* March 5, Washington, D.C.

Quigley, A.M. (1987). *Validity generalization, the U.S. Employment Service, and the courts.* Inglewood, CA: California Test Development Field Center, U.S. Department of Labor.

Robinson, W.L., & R. T. Seymour (1984). Testimony of the Lawyers' Committee for Civil Rights Under Law on recent efforts of the Administration to alter the effect of Title VII of the Civil Rights Act of 1964, before the Subcommittee on Employment Opportunities of the House Committee on Education and Labor, pp. 10–14.

Samuel Cox v. Consolidated Rail Corporation and Lawton Frazier v. Consolidated Rail Corporation and United Transportation Union (1987). No. 83-0514 & 85-0845, slip op. (District of Columbia, August 26).

Schlei, B., & Grossman, P. (1983). *Employment discrimination law* (2d ed.). Washington, DC: Bureau of National Affairs.

Schmidt, F.L., & Hunter, J.E. (1981). Employment testing: Olld theories and new research findings. *American Psychologist, 36,* 1128–1137.

Schmidt, F.L., Hunter, J.E., & Caplan, J.K. (1981). Validity generalization results for two job groups in the petroleum industry. *Journal of Applied Psychology, 66,* 261–273.

Society for Industrial and Organization Psychology, Inc. (1987). *Principles for the validation and use of personnel selection procedures* (3d ed.). College Park, MD: Author.

Tenopyr, M.L. (1981). The realities of employment testing. *American Psychologist, 36,* 1120–1127.

Wards Cove Packing Company v. Atonio, (1989). 109 S.Ct. 3115.

Widgor, A.K. & Garner, W.R. (1982). *Ability testing: Uses, consequences, and controversies.* Washington, DC: National Academy Press.

15 EMPLOYMENT TESTING AND THE LAW IN CANADA

Steven F. Cronshaw

This chapter will discuss theoretical, professional, and legal issues that industrial psychologists and personnel managers must be conversant with when they decide to develop or use employment tests in Canada. More specifically, I will examine the status of the following five technical concepts within the respective domains of theory, professional practice, and law: job analysis, test reliability, test validity, test utility, and test bias-fairness. I judge these five concepts to be critical for informed, responsible, and productive use of employment testing in Canada. If industrial psychologists and personnel managers in Canada properly apply these key five concepts when developing and using employment tests, they will go a long way toward ensuring that their selection decisions yield substantial productivity gains for their sponsoring organizations. In addition, these selection decisions will be fair to groups protected under human rights legislation.

HOW EXTENSIVELY ARE EMPLOYMENT TESTS USED IN CANADA?

Before discussing the five technical concepts, it is important to establish the extent to which Canadian organizations utilize major types of employment tests. If such tests are widely used for personnel selection in Canada, it becomes all the more necessary to clarify the professional and legal standards which apply to them. Fortunately, Thacker and Cattaneo (1987) recently conducted a large-scale survey that addressed this question. They mailed a survey of organizational practices in selection and performance appraisal to 2,500 Canadian personnel managers and received back 581 completed questionnaires. Thacker and Cattaneo reported results on how frequently Canadian organizations utilize four major types of employment tests in selection (where "employment tests" refer to standardized paper-and-pencil measures of psychological variables commonly used in personnel selection). These four types of employment tests are listed in table 15–1 along with percentages representing the frequency with which each type of test is used across all sizes of Canadian organizations.

Even if some allowance is made for nonresponding companies, which comprised about 75 percent of the total sample (noting that these companies might use employment testing to a lesser extent than the companies that responded to the survey), it is clear that many Canadian organizations utilize employment tests in selection. This is particularly true for the aptitude test category, which includes measures of verbal, numerical, spatial, and manual aptitude. The Thacker and Cattaneo study therefore demonstrates that employment tests are an important complement to other commonly used selection predictors such as

The author acknowledges the useful comments on this chapter supplied by the following graduate students enrolled in his course on personnel selection and performance appraisal during the winter semester of 1988: Chuck Evans, Jean Douglas, Mary Kenny, and Mary Simpson. The author can be contacted through the Graduate Program in Industrial/Organizational Psychology, Department of Psychology, University of Guelph, Guelph, Ontario, Canada N1G 2W1.

Table 15–1
Type and Frequency of Test Use in Canadian Organizations

Type of Test	Percentage of Organizations Surveyed Using Test Type in Selection
Aptitude tests	43.7
Personality inventories	20.5
Interest inventories	14.2
Honesty tests	1.0

Source: Adapted from Thacker and Cattaneo (1987).

application blanks and interviews (Cronshaw, Corriveau & Jain, 1987; Thacker & Cattaneo, 1987). However, it should also be noted that large organizations utilize employment tests more frequently than do small organizations (Thacker & Cattaneo, 1987).

This disparity in test use between small and large organizations is to be expected given that large organizations have more resources to hire and support the personnel specialists who are trained in the development and use of employment tests.

FIVE KEY TECHNICAL CONCEPTS IN EMPLOYMENT TESTING

This chapter will review the status of five key technical concepts in employment testing within three knowledge or jurisdictional domains. For the purposes of clarity, the status of each concept within the three respective domains is summarized in table 15–2. As this chapter progresses, each entry in the table is discussed. First, however, the technical concepts (listed along the top of the table) and the knowledge-jurisdictional domains (listed along the left side of the table) will be defined to ensure that all readers have a common understanding of the terminology used throughout this chapter.

Job analysis is the process of obtaining information about jobs, including work activities engaged in as well as the knowledge, skills, abilities, and other individual difference characteristics (KSAOs) required to perform the job. Personnel specialists have traditionally viewed job analysis as a basic and necessary step in the development and use of employment tests. *Test reliability* refers to the extent to which test scores are influenced by error of measurement. Reliability is an important property of any employment test because, as testing experts agree, adequate test reliability is an absolute prerequisite for test validity. *Test validity* refers to whether the inferences made from test scores are appropriate, adequate, and defensible. In other words, the scores from an invalid employment test cannot be depended on to make decisions about which applicants to accept or reject during the selection process. *Test utility* represents the benefits accruing to the organization from employment testing. Often this test utility is expressed in terms of dollar productivity improvements in the selectee group over random selection or an alternative predic-

tor (Cascio, 1987). *Test bias/fairness* establishes whether an employment test equivalently measures the same trait or attribute over two or more subgroups of people (bias) and whether the test is used in a manner that balances the legitimate interests of the job applicant, organization, and larger society (fairness).

Lest these five concepts seem too "theoretical" or "academic," the purpose served by each concept will now be stated in nontechnical terms. *Job analysis* ensures that the characteristics measured by the test are related to higher job performance. *Test reliability* is an index of whether the testing instrument itself is capable of measuring the performance-related characteristics identified in the job analysis. *Test validity*, which is predicated on the assumption that the test is reliable, demonstrates that inferences drawn from the test scores (e.g., that higher-scoring applicants will perform better on the job) are reasonable and defensible. Test validity in turn forms the basis of *test utility*, which translates the job performance prediction achievable by employment testing into indexes of organizational benefit. These indexes (e.g., increases in dollar productivity, payroll savings) are more familiar to managers outside the personnel function than are psychometric concepts such as validity. These managers can then use the utility data to make personnel decisions producing the greatest possible benefits for the organization (e.g., the manager might decide to discontinue use of an employment test with negative dollar utility). Finally, *test bias/fairness* directly tackles the question of how well employment testing serves human rights goals. Investigations of test bias and fairness demonstrate whether perfor-

Table 15–2
The Status of Key Technical Concepts in Employment Testing

Knowledge or Jurisdictional Domain	Job Analysis	Job Reliability	Test Validity	Test Utility	Test Bias/Fairness
Theoretical	+	+	+	+	+
Professional	+	+	+	+	−
Legal	+	+	+	?	+

Note: +: the concept is addressed within the respective domain at preset; −: the concept is not now addressed within the domain; ?: the concept has an uncertain status within the domain and so requires clarification.

mance-related individual characteristics are measured equivalently by employment test for different groups (e.g., men verses women) and, if not, how so-called biased employment tests can be used "fairly" to balance the interest of both the organization and those job applicants who are protected under human rights legislation. From a more general perspective, it should now be obvious that the five interrelated concepts comprise an integrated approach for solving the most formidable problems facing the practitioner who utilizes employment tests. That is why these five concepts form the underpinning of this chapter.

Before we discuss the theoretical, professional, and legal status of each technical concept, it is also necessary to define each of these three knowledge/jurisdictional domains (which are listed along the left margin of Table 15–2) in order to ensure that everyone has a common understanding of what these domains represent. First, it is assumed that the *theoretical* domain encompasses the existing research and empirical literatures of industrial psychology and personnel management. Statements based in this domain will reflect the current research published in the major American and Canadian journals of industrial psychology and personnel management such as *Personnel Psychology* and the *Canadian Journal of Administrative Sciences*. Second, it is assumed that the *professional* domain is defined by the professional standards on employment testing promulgated in the *Guidelines for Educational and Psychological Testing* developed by the Canadian Psychological Association (1986). Given that psychologists are the major proponents of paper-and-pencil testing, the *Guidelines* are as close to a state-of-the-art professional pronouncement on employment testing as is possible. However, the fact that the *Guidelines* are emphasized here does not imply that other professional groups have ignored testing issues. For example, the Canadian Guidance and Counselling Association has published *Guidelines for Ethical Behaviour* (1981), which recommend basic standards of test use. These professional groups should be commended for such work. Nonetheless, the *Guidelines* will be used to define the professional domain of employment testing because they represent a detailed document produced by the professional group that is most centrally involved with employment testing in Canada.

The third domain (the *legal* domain) is primarily defined in three ways: (1) by human rights codes in all Canadian provinces and in the federal jurisdiction, (2) by policy statements on employment discrimination from human rights commissions across Canada, and (3) by the accumulated weight of human rights tribunal and court decisions dealing with personnel

selection and employment testing. It should be noted that human rights commissions in Canada have not codified legal requirements for employment testing as was done in the Uniform Guidelines on Employee Selection Procedures developed by four federal government departments in the United States (Equal Employment Opportunity Commission, Civil Service Commission, Department of Labor & Department of Justice, 1978). As well, no human rights code in Canada specifically mentions employment testing (or any other assessment procedure used in selection for that matter). As a consequence, the work of interpreting what employment testing practices are permissible in Canadian organizations has been left to human rights tribunals and courts, and even here only one decision has involved scrutiny of employment tests on technical grounds (*Action Travail des Femmes v. Canadian National,* Decision of the Tribunal under the Canadian Human Rights Act, 1984; hereafter referred to as the *CN* decision). However, employment testing complaints have been heard under other legal jurisdictions (including a provincial labor boards and civil service appeal boards), and in the future the frequency of litigation involving employment testing will almost certainly increase in all jurisdictions.

It is notable that human rights commissions in Canada have not followed the lead of U.S. agencies in issuing employment testing standards. While this approach may seem unduly conservative to some, technical shortcomings in the American Uniform Guidelines have caused some intractable problems for organizations and courts in the United States (such as the application of the "four-fifths rule" for determining adverse impact of an employment test; see Boardman, 1979). In my opinion, issuance of quasi-legal guidelines by governmental agencies in Canada will create as many problems as they solve. Human rights commissions in Canada have instead relied on tribunals and courts to develop testing standards on an ad hoc basis as plaintiffs and defendants pit their expert witnesses against each other in employment discrimination cases. They will probably continue to rely on this approach for the foreseeable future.

It should be apparent that the theoretical, professional, and legal issues are interrelated. Professional documents such as the Guidelines are based on the work of psychological researchers, though these documents typically lag behind the latest theoretical developments. In turn, tribunals or judges could in the future draw upon professional standards when making decisions about employment testing matters (for example, about whether an employment test is valid pursuant to establishing a bona-fide occupational requirement). Or, as in the *CN* decision, legal authorities may rely primarily on the testimony of experts in industrial psychology who have in-depth knowledge of current research and theory in employment testing. Conversely, legal concerns will increasingly prompt research psychologists and management scientists to initiate investigations into such areas as test bias. In short, the theoretical, professional, and legal issues in employment testing discussed in this chapter are closely related and will converge to an even greater extent in the future.

THE THEORETICAL STATUS OF FIVE CONCEPTS IN EMPLOYMENT TESTING

(Each of the cells in table 15–2) will now be examined in more detail, starting first with the theoretical status of each employment testing concept. Theoreticians in industrial psychology and personnel management generally consider job analysis to be essential to valid employment testing. The reasoning usually proceeds along the following lines: There are a potentially very large number of human attributes (KSAOs) that contribute to improving job performance in the thousands of jobs across the Canadian economy. If job analysis is not used to discover which individual attributes determine performance for the particular job under study, the choice of an employment test from among the thousands available becomes a chancey proposition indeed. Even if an organization is developing an employment test in-house (rather than purchasing an existing test from a test publisher or consultant), a job analysis is essential because the test developer must know what KSAOs to assess in the test. In sum, the theoreticians are worried less about whether a job analysis should be done (because they usually assume that it is essential) than about which job analysis method is most suited to getting the information needed for a particular application of employment testing.

The state of job analysis research is sufficiently rudimentary that few firm principles are available to practitioners who wish to choose the "right" method of job analysis for a specific application. Of the various job analytic methods available (for example, task inventories, structured questionnaires, critical incidents), practitioners may often find that individual or group interviews are the most flexible means of obtaining the detailed job information needed. These interview data might be supplemented with occupational information from the Canadian Classification and Dictionary of Occupations (CCDO) (Employment and Immigration Canada, 1985). Regardless of the job analytic method used however, the practitioner must necessarily identify the KSAOs' underlying effective job performance if the employment test eventually used is to be validated.

Having made the point that detailed job analyses are a necessary prerequisite to valid employment testing, a possible exception to this general rule must be noted. Two researchers (John Hunter of Michigan State University and Frank Schmidt of the University of Iowa) have found that tests of certain basic abilities (such as, general cognitive ability) may predict job performance well across a wide range of jobs. As a consequence, researchers such as Pearlman (1980) have maintained that a job analysis need only be detailed enough to ensure that the job under study belongs to a more general set of jobs within which the test predicts criteria of success such as job performance. It should, however, be recognized that this recommendation applies to some ability tests only under specific circumstances and that in all other cases detailed job analyses should be conducted before any employment test is developed or used.

The theoretical status of test reliability is clear: reliability is a necessary prerequisite to the use of any employment test. However, testing theorists are more equivocal on how reliability should be estimated. Some theorists have become dissatisfied with the "classical test theory" on which much of employment test reliability is based. They have proposed alternative models of reliability, of which "generalizability theory" is the most comprehensive and influential (Cronbach, Gleser, Nanda, & Rajaratnam, 1972). The conceptual and technical differences between these theories are highly significant for a theoretician, yet this revolution in reliability estimation may go relatively unnoticed by the practitioner except for changes in terminology (for example, the use of the term "generalizability coefficient" instead of "reliability coefficient"). But whatever the theoretical elaborations on the concept, reliability will remain a key concept in employment testing.

Test validity is probably the most important concept in all of psychological measurement. Consequently, a great deal has been written on how employment test scores should be validated, and numerous validation studies are reported in the industrial psychology literature. As with reliability, theoreticians agree that employment test scores must be validated for the use intended. However, they agree less well on how this validation should be carried out. For example, some theorists (Guion, 1978) argue that the content validation strategy recommended by many psychologists is not a form of validation at all but is a type of test construction strategy. In other words, even if theorists believe that test validation is essential, they do not always agree on how validation should be carried out.

The concept of test utility has been with us for at least five decades (Taylor & Russell, 1939) and reached its most refined state in a seminal book by Cronbach and Gleser (1965). In general terms, test utility represents the benefits accruing to an organization from using an employment test where those benefits can be expressed in dollar terms or even in terms of capital budgeting indexes derived from capital budgeting theory (Cronshaw & Alexander, 1985). While the theory of test utility is well advanced, the applications of these ideas in personnel decision making have lagged far behind the theory for many years because personnel managers had great trouble in estimating the values of key inputs to the utility equations. In the past ten years, enough progress has been made in solving these measurement problems to spark considerable interest among practitioners in estimating test utility. There is little doubt that utility analyses will gain increased acceptance as time goes on.

Finally, it is well established that test bias and fairness are important concepts in the theoretical literature, even if theorists often disagree on which test bias and fairness models they would like to adopt. For example, test bias (at least as it pertains to employment tests) can be variously viewed as differential validity, predictive bias, or item bias. In addition, test bias and fairness concepts are complex and technically difficult. Because they are so complex, they are notoriously difficult to translate into operational terms for practitioners, who may have limited knowledge of statistics and psychometric theory. Therefore, even though they have important theoretical status, relatively few practitioners are fully conversant with these ideas.

In summary, extensive theoretical literature exists to support the use of all five technical concepts in employment testing. However, research on employment testing is always in a state of flux. As a result, professionals who apply this research may incorporate the core of the generally accepted research findings into professional standards that promote competent and consistent application of employment testing principles in organizations across the country. This is, of course, the major purpose of the Canadian *Guidelines*. We will therefore move on to consider the professional status of job analysis, test reliability, test validity, and test utility as promulgated in the *Guidelines*.

THE PROFESSIONAL STATUS OF FIVE CONCEPTS IN EMPLOYMENT TESTING

Job analysis is specifically recommended in the *Guidelines* as a requirement where content evidence of test validity is collected. The requirement reads as follows: "Content validation should be based on a clear definition of the content domain of interest. For job selection, classification, and promotion, the characterization of the domain should be based on an analysis of job characteristics relevant to the proposed test use" (Guideline 11.4, p. 60). The *Guidelines* do not specifically discuss the function of job analysis in the collection of other types of validity evidence. However, this should not be taken as evidence that job analysis is unimportant in these other situations (note that the theoretical literature clearly outlines the important role of job analysis in all types of validation).

The *Guidelines* contain an entire section, along with ten detailed testing standards, on *test reliability*. The practitioner's responsibilities for test reliability are best summarized by the following excerpt from the *Guidelines*:

Typically, test developers and publishers have the primary responsibility for obtaining and reporting evidence concerning reliability and errors of measurement adequate for the intended uses. The typical user generally will not conduct separate reliability studies. Users do have a responsibility however, for determining that the available information regarding reliability and measurement error is relevant to their intended uses and interpretations and, in the absence of such information, for providing the necessary evidence. (p. 17)

Although organizations using employment tests do not necessarily incur a responsibility for collecting reliability data, they should have sufficient knowledge about testing matters to evaluate critically reliability data reported in test manuals written by the test developer or publisher. Where such data are not available, the employment test should not be used.

The *Guidelines* state that test validity is "the most important consideration in test evaluation" (p. 8). According to this document, validity refers to "the appropriateness, meaningfulness, and usefulness of the specific inferences made from test scores" (p. 8). Test validation, on the other hand, refers to the means by which evidence is collected to support such inferences. An example of an inference that might be made on the basis of employment test scores is as follows: that higher test scores in the population of job applicants are associated with improved job performance. If the process of test validation yields the necessary evidence to support this inference, we might conclude that the test is "valid" (further noting that the test will produce benefits for the organization in terms of higher worker productivity among hiree groups selected by the test). As the reader can easily see, test validity is indeed an indispensable concept in employment testing.

A brief description of the ways that an organization can collect validity evidence will help to clarify how personnel managers and industrial psychologists can support an inference of validity for an employment test. *Content-related evidence* is collected by demonstrating that the items or questions on an employment test are representative of the critical knowledge, skills, or behaviors required in the job. This type of evidence is often obtained during the process of developing achievement tests. *Criterion-related evidence* is obtained by showing that the scores on the employment test are related in a systematic way to one or more "success criteria." An example of a success criterion that is of great importance to any organization is individual job performance. Usually the systematic relationship between test scores and the success criterion is expressed quantatively in terms of a correlation coefficient or similar type of statistical index. *Construct-related evidence* is accumulated through a series of investigations that attempt to show that an employment test measures a psychological characteristic of interest. Furthermore, this "characteristic of interest" must be an important determinant of job performance or some other success criterion. A good example of a psychological characteristic associated with job performance across a wide range of jobs is *general cognitive ability* (Hunter & Hunter, 1984), otherwise known as intel-

ligence. There are numerous fine nuances to validation theory that cannot possibly be covered in this brief chapter. The reader is referred to general sources in the psychological literature for further background on this technical concept (e.g., Ghiselli, Campbell, & Zedeck, 1981).

Test utility is only briefly dealt with in the *Guidelines*. The *Guidelines* state that the utility of a correct selection decision, and the value judgments that utility determination entails, are relevant to the use of employment testing. There is no recommendation in the *Guidelines* as to the specific utility method that should be used. In effect, this leaves the choice of the type of utility analysis performed up to the "professional judgement" of the practitioner.

The CPA *Guidelines* contain no standards on test bias/fairness. However, it should be noted that the *Guidelines* do contain a section on developing tests with versions in more than one language. This section is obviously directed to those organizations that are developing English and French versions of employment tests. The methods used by psychologists to develop linguistically equivalent tests are similar in many respects to methods they use to investigate test bias. In fact, a "linguistically equivalent" employment test is by definition unbiased for the language groups studied.

The exclusion from the *Guidelines* of explicit standards of test bias/fairness creates additional ambiguity for those organizations that develop and use employment tests in Canada. However, some psychologists argue that standards on test bias/fairness are premature because no consensus yet exists among psychologists concerning which of the many models of test bias and fairness the profession should adopt. In addition, the technical complexity of test bias/fairness analyses, as well as the difficulties inherent in getting the necessary data, may put such standards beyond the capabilities of most Canadian organizations to comply. Nevertheless, human rights authorities in Canada have become concerned about bias and fairness in employment testing, so it is only a matter of time before the Canadian psychological profession will have to address these issues.

THE LEGAL STATUS OF FIVE CONCEPTS IN EMPLOYMENT TESTING

This chapter deals finally with technical concepts (see the last row in table 15–2). To accomplish this, a variety of sources were accessed, including policy statements from human rights commissions, tribunal

and court decisions, and writings of legal experts in the area of employment discrimination.

Before dealing with the legal status of each of the technical concepts, it is useful to outline in general terms the legal responsibilities incumbent on Canadian employers using employment tests. The following excerpt from a speech delivered by the former chief commissioner of the Canadian Human Rights Commission (CHRC), Gordon Fairweather (Fairweather, 1986), sums up the situation in Canada quite nicely. According to Fairweather, the employment selection process:

> begins with a job analysis in which the actual and essential tasks of the job are identified.
>
> Then comes the means to measure the skills necessary to carry out the tasks in question. In order to be selected for use, the test must satisfy criteria of validity, reliability, and fairness. (p. 5)

Elsewhere in his speech, Mr. Fairweather emphasizes that commission scrutiny of the selection process will take place only when one or more individuals protected under human rights legislation cite the employment test as discriminatory. Usually, the complaint alleges that the employment test has adverse impact on his or her protected group (that is, the test excludes from selection disproportionate numbers of applicants from the protected group). If the test has adverse impact, the commission will investigate the technical merits of the selection process used by the organization. Although Mr. Fairweather's remarks were not delivered as an official policy statement (and, as previously mentioned, the commission has no official guidelines regarding employment testing), his comments do offer some practical insights into the factors the Canadian Human Rights Commission considers when investigating employment testing in organizations. Not surprisingly, the issues of greatest concern to the commission (e.g., reliability, validity) are also prominent in the theoretical and professional domains already discussed in this chapter.

The legal status of each technical concept will now be briefly reviewed (see the last row of table 15–2 for a thumbnail sketch of the legal domain). Human rights authorities stress the primary importance of job analysis for employment tests that come under the scrutiny of human rights commissions. Besides the Fairweather speech, the Canadian Human Rights Tribunal in the landmark CN decision emphasized the need for job analysis to establish the job relatedness of employment tests used in selection. The fact that human rights authorities have readily adopted the concept of job analysis is easy to understand given the legal model followed by human rights commissions when they investigate complaints of employment discrimination. According to CHRC policy, once the complainant has established a prima facie case of discrimination (e.g., by demonstrating that application of the employment test has adverse impact against a protected group), the burden of proof shifts to the employer to show that the employment test was used for legitimate business reasons (e.g., merit) or that practice of employment testing is based on a bona-fide occupational requirement (Canadian Human Rights Commission, 1985). Either way, it is virtually mandatory that the organization collect job analysis data if it is to demonstrate successfully that the individual characteristics assessed by the employment test are necessary for job performance.

The only direct reference to test reliability in the legal domain is that made by Mr. Fairweather in his speech. However, human rights authorities have maintained that scores on employment tests must be validated if the tests are to be upheld as job related. The primary requirement of test validity was imposed by the tribunal in the CN decision, where CN was ordered to discontinue its use of the Bennett Mechanical Comprehension Test for selection for entry-level positions other than apprentice positions because the test had adverse impact against women and could not be validated. If the standard psychometric convention is accepted—that test reliability is a necessary precondition for test validity—then, logically, both reliability and validity are required of any employment test that comes under scrutiny by a human rights commission or court in Canada.

Of course, employment tests comprise only one of many assessment procedures utilized by Canadian organizations in personnel selection. According to CHRC policy, "assessment procedures" encompass a broad range of devices, including oral questions and interviews, written questions and tests, training programs, medical examinations, or any other formal or informal assessment of individual capacities (Canadian Human Rights Commission, 1985). This same policy states that such assessment procedures accurately assess an individual's capacity only if:

(a) they evaluate the extent to which the individual possesses capabilities reasonably necessary for or limitations likely to impair safe, efficient and reliable performance of the job; and

(b) such evaluations are valid. (p. 16)

Whether part (b) of the policy means that all of these assessment procedures must be validated according to the rigorous procedures recommended by industrial psychologists (as in the *Guidelines*) is unclear. Presumably, future tribunal and court decisions will establish whether "valid" in this context means that such evaluations must be "well grounded or justifiable" in the nontechnical meaning of the term or whether "valid" is synonymous with "developed and used according to principles established by the psychological profession." Cronshaw (1989), in his review of human rights decisions on the employment interview in Canada, was unable to find a single decision where an employer was required to validate an employment interview professionally. However, even if organizations are not held responsible for professionally validating nontest predictors such as the employment interview, it is firmly established in Canadian jurisprudence that they will be liable for validating employment tests to professional standards.

If an employment test is alleged to be discriminatory, the organization can argue that use of the test is a bona-fide occupational requirement (BFOQ). One important element of the BFOQ defense is proved by showing that the requirement (in this case, an employment test) is reasonably necessary for the efficient and economical performance of the job. This principle was established in the Supreme Court decision of *Ontario Human Rights Commissions et al. v. the Borough of Etobicoke* (1982). Because test utility is primarily an economic concept, this element of the BFOQ defense certainly holds out the possibility that legal authorities will give some weight to test utility data when deciding employment discrimination cases. However, this statement on the status of test utility remains speculative because, as table 15–2 illustrates, no human rights policy or legal decision exists that specifically addresses the role of test utility in establishing a bona-fide occupational requirement.

The final technical concept to be reviewed in the legal domain is test bias/fairness. The most direct statement on this issue by human rights authorities is contained within the previously cited speech by Gordon Fairweather.

Test fairness must then be determined [after studies of validity and reliability]: Does the test offer to all test takers an equal chance to show whether they have the capacity to do the work of the job? In practical terms we would ask whether the test is so constructed that each test taker has the opportunity to express his or her level of ability. (p. 5)

Importantly, these definitions correspond very closely to what psychologists mean by test bias. It is easy to see that test bias and fairness tackle human rights issues in employment testing that are simply too basic for human rights policymakers to ignore. Yet, the conceptual models and research methodologies required to deal with test bias and fairness are very complex. Furthermore, the daunting technical problems associated with test bias and fairness analyses render such analyses virtually impossible for most Canadian organizations. Only the very largest and technically sophisticated organizations can reasonably be expected to conduct such research. So Canadian personnel managers are in a dilemma: they have technical questions about test bias and fairness that are beyond their capabilities to answer, at least at the present time. As already pointed out, the psychological profession in Canada already admitted this (albeit implicitly) when standards on test bias and fairness were excluded from the *Guidelines*. Perhaps the only solution to the problem is to invest more resources in "generic" test bias/fairness research at Canadian universities and research institutes. The results of such research would be available to all test users by means of published sources, so largely obviating the need for organizations to conduct such analyses on a local basis.

CONCLUSION

The test bias/fairness issue is only the most extreme case of a more basic problem facing organizations that use employment tests in Canada. While human rights legislation has placed a greater burden on employers to use these tests properly, many organizations lag behind in their technical knowledge of how to use employment tests. Thacker and Cattaneo (1987) found, for example, that many Canadian employers do not understand very basic selection terminology, including validation concepts. The inescapable conclusion is that many Canadian employers are using employment tests without devoting sufficient attention to job analysis, reliability, validity, utility, and test bias/fairness. If so, many organiza-

tions in Canada are using their employment tests improperly, with resulting utility losses and potential for unfair discrimination against groups protected under human rights legislation.

Although many Canadian employers must improve their use of employment testing, there is still some room for optimism. As Ledvinka (1982) points out in his book on federal regulation of human resource management practices in the United States, it is possible for managers to comprehend the complex regulatory process imposed by government. Even though employment testing is relatively new to human rights authorities in Canada, these authorities have already shown some predictability in their responses to employment testing. As this chapter demonstrates, they have referred to the theoretical concepts and professional principles produced by the psychologists who develop and validate employment tests. In other words, the major legal trends affecting employment testing in Canada can be identified, even at this relatively early stage (Cronshaw, 1986, 1987,

1988). However, ongoing work is required to monitor these trends while human rights policy and case law relevant to employment testing continue to accumulate. It is to be hoped that this chapter has served as one stimulus for the extensive work required to adapt employment testing to the evolving legal environment in Canada.

REFERENCES

Action Travail des Femmes v. Canadian National (TD 10/ 84) (1984). Decision rendered by the Tribunal under the Canadian Human Rights Act, August 22.

Boardman, A.E. (1979). Another analysis of the EEOCC "four-fifths" rule. *Management Science, 25,* 770–776.

Canadian Human Rights Commission (1985). *Bona fide occupational requirement and bona fide justification: Interim policies and explanatory notes.* Ottawa: Canadian Human Rights Commission.

Canadian Psychological Association (1986). *Guidelines for educational and psychological testing.* Old Chelsea, Quebec: Author.

Canadian Guidance & Counselling Association (1981). *Guidelines for ethical behaviour.* Ottawa: Author.

Cascio, W.F. (1987). *Costing human resources: The financial impact of behavior in organizations* (2d ed.). Boston: Kent.

Cronbach, L.J., & Gleser, G.C. (1965). *Psychological tests and personnel decisions* (2d ed.). Urbana, IL: University of Illinois Press.

Cronbach, L.J., Gleser, G.C., Nanda, H., & Rajaratnam, N. (1972). *The dependability of behavioral measurements: Theory of generalizability for scores and profiles.* New York: Wiley.

Cronshaw, S.F. (1986). Employment testing in Canada: A review and evaluation of theory and professional practice. *Canadian Psychology, 27,* 183–195.

Cronshaw, S.F. (1987). Employment testing in Canada: Strategies for higher organizational productivity and human rights compliance. In S.L. Dolan & R.S. Schuler (Eds.), *Canadian readings in personnel and human resource management* (176–185). St. Paul, MN: West Publishing.

Cronshaw, S.F. (1988). Future directions for industrial psychology in Canada. *Canadian Psychology, 29,* 30–43.

Cronshaw, S.F. (1989). *Legal implications for the structured employment interview in Canada.* Paper presented at the 50th Annual Convention of the Canadian Psychological Association, Halifax, Nova Scotia, Canada, June.

Cronshaw, S.F., & Alexander, R.A. (1985). One answer to the demand for accountability: Selection utility as an investment decision. *Organizational Behavior and Human Decision Processes, 35,* 102–118.

Cronshaw, S.F., Corriveau, C.A., & Jain, H.C. (1987). *A*

15-year update on managerial recruitment and selection practices in the Canadian manufacturing industry. Unpublished manuscript, Department of Psychology, University of Guelph, Guelph, Ontario, Canada.

Equal Employment Opportunity Commission, Civil Service Commission, Department of Labor, & Department of Justice (1978). Adoption by four agencies of uniform guidelines on employee selection procedures. *Federal Register, 43* (166).

Employment and Immigration Canada (1985). *Guide to the Canadian Classification and Dictionary of Occupations* (5th ed.). Ottawa, Ont.: Minister of Supply and Services Canada.

Fairweather, R.G.L. (June 1986). *Notes for remarks to a symposium on "The Canadian Industrial-Organizational Psychologist and human rights legislation: Present and future strategies for employment testing.* Ottawa: Canadian Human Rights Commission.

Ghiselli, E.E., Campbell, J.P., & Zedeck, S. (1981). *Measurement theory for the behavioral sciences.* San Francisco: Freeman.

Guion, R.M. (1978). "Content validity" in moderation. *Personnel Psychology, 31,* 205–213.

Hunter, J.E., & Hunter, R.F. (1984). Validity and utility of alternative predictors of job performance. *Psychological Bulletin, 96,* 72–98.

Ledvinka, J. (1982). *Federal regulation of personnel and human resource management.* New York: Van Nostrand Reinhold Company.

Malik v. Ministry of Government Services et al. (1981). CHRR, Vol. 2, Decision 80, D/374-382.

Ontario Human Rights Commission et al. v. the Borough of Etobicoke (1982). CHRR, Vol. 3, Decision 164, D/781-785.

Pearlman, K. (1980). Job families: A review and discussion of their implications for personnel selection. *Psychological Bulletin, 87,* 1–28.

Taylor, H.C., & Russell, J.T. (1939). The relationship of validity coefficients to the practical effectiveness of tests in selection. *Journal of Applied Psychology, 23,* 565–578.

Thacker, J.W., & Cattaneo, R.J. (1987). *The Canadian personnel function: Status and practices.* Paper presented at the Administrative Sciences Association of Canada Conference, Toronto, Ontario, June.

PART III

ANALYZING JOBS

16 ANALYZING NONMANAGEMENT JOBS: AN OVERVIEW

P. Richard Jeanneret

The activities associated with the production of goods or the delivery of services comprise what is typically referred to as work. In most instances work is accomplished within an organization (private industry or public entity) established to achieve one or more objectives. The nature of these objectives defines the parameters of the work to be carried out and leads to the formation of specific jobs. Further, the work functions typically can be categorized as either nonmanagerial or managerial in scope. This chapter discusses the analysis of nonmanagerial jobs, but readers should recognize that certain of the information presented here applies equally to the study of managerial jobs.

This chapter is intended to serve several purposes, and, as indicated by its title, it is an overview of the job analysis process as applied to nonmanagement jobs. The first purpose is to define job analysis and the other terminology often associated with job analysis. A second purpose is to present a brief history of job analysis and its contribution to organizational functioning. This leads directly to the third purpose, which is to set forth the specific reasons for carrying out job analyses in the application of psychology to organizations.

Given a review of the background and value of job analysis, a fourth purpose of this chapter is to describe the various components of a job analysis and alternative procedures for accomplishing a study of nonmanagerial work. The final and overriding purpose for the entire chapter is to present sufficient information in order that reader's will have a foundation for the materials presented in the chapters that follow (chapters 14–17), which discuss specific job analysis procedures and results.

Because the information in this chapter is related to the broad range of situations that might be addressed by the manager responsible for the application of psychology in an organization (and hence the conduct of a job analysis), no attempt has been made to compile this information from a single case study. Rather, the information that follows has been derived from my experience in the conduct of hundreds of job analysis studies over the last twenty-four years.

DEFINITIONS

In the broadest sense job analysis can be defined simply as the study of work content. However, there are reasons to study work that, while related, have different objectives from those associated with applied psychology. For example, methods analysis as typically accomplished by industrial engineers, safety analysis completed by safety engineers, and work analysis performed for industrial medicine is closely akin to the job analysis of applied psychology, but the purposes of those analyses and the use of the results can be very different. Also, there is a discipline of applied psychology known as human factors engineering that is directly concerned with the study of work, usually for the purposes of designing equipment, facilities, and environments that are compatible with human capabilities. Again, while there is considerable compatibility between the job analysis efforts carried out in business and public organizations with the work analyses of engineering psychology, there is no attempt in this chapter to include the domain of human factors.

Job Analysis: A systematic process of collecting, organizing, analyzing, and documenting the content, requirements, and context of a collective set of work activities performed by one or more individuals. Since there is often confusion over the terms related to the collective set of work activities mentioned above, several additional definitions are presented.

Task: A specific or discrete unit of work activity that typically has a beginning and end point. Usually a task is set forth as a statement with an action verb and an object of that action (such as "types purchase orders"; "stocks automobile parts"; "files financial reports"; "operates cement mixing machine'").

Duty: A collection of related tasks that comprise a large segment of work activities. Thus a duty is a broader statement than a task, and often several tasks are subsumed under a specific duty. Examples of duties include: "prepares purchasing department documents" and "maintains automobile parts inventory program.'

Position: An organized and related group of duties and tasks to be performed by a worker.

Job: A group of positions that are nearly identical with respect to primary duties and tasks and are sufficiently similar to be included under one title. (The terms *position* and *job* are nearly identical and are often used interchangeably. As a matter of convention, some organizations use the term *position* when there is a single incumbent and the term *job* when there are multiple incumbents.)

Occupation: A general class of jobs that delineate in a generic sense the scope of activities performed by a number of workers (cook, mechanic, clerk, computer operator, electrician, nurse).

Job Analyst: A job analysis is typically carried out by an individual who is referred to as a job analyst. However, a job incumbent or supervisor may often serve as the job analyst when certain job analysis procedures are undertaken. Often the incumbent or supervisor participating in a job analysis study is referred to as a subject matter expert (SME).

Returning to the initial definition of job analysis, the collective set of work activities that are analyzed includes the tasks and duties that comprise the content of a position or job. Further, the job analysis process often considers the "requirements"—expressed as the knowledge, skills, abilities, and other characteristics (KSAOs)—of the workers to carry out the tasks and duties. And finally, the job analysis procedure will usually specify the context, defined as the physical environment in which the work is performed, and sometimes may include the organizational climate and psychological demands associated with job performance. All of this information is assembled and documented by one or more job analysts.

BRIEF HISTORY

Industrial Engineering

Job analysis has its roots in the field of industrial engineering and stems directly from the turn of the century work of Frank and Lillian Gilbreth. In their efforts to increase productivity, they developed methods to study worker motions and in doing so examined jobs from the perspective of very elemental parts. These early job analysis activities eventually evolved into what is called methods analysis, often carried out by industrial engineers.

Department of Labor

Apart from the issue of productivity, another early reason for job analysis data was spearheaded by the Department of Labor. This effort was directed at organizing and codifying information about jobs in the labor force, and the responsibility for doing so was assigned to the Manpower Administration (now

the U.S. Employment Service, USES, of the Training and Employment Administration). The efforts of the USES in the early 1950s focused not only on preparing a brief summary description of job content but also on documenting job requirements. Within the framework of the USES procedures, these job requirements reflect the level of involvement of the worker with data, people, and things. These three categories of involvement are defined in terms of hierarchies of worker functions as presented in table 16–1. Each level in the hierarchies has an associated number (0–6, 8, or 7), which becomes a rating given by a job analyst to the job under study. The analyst typically assigns the highest level of involvement (the lowest numerical rating) that is required by the job for each of the three functions, which in combination describe the total level of complexity of job requirements.

The efforts of the Manpower Administration/ USES culminated in the 1965 edition of the *Dictionary of Occupational Titles* (DOT), which was subsequently revised and published as the fourth edi-

Table 16–1
Hierarchical Structure of Worker Functions

Data	People	Things
0 Synthesizing	0 Monitoring	0 Setting Up
1 Coordinating	1 Negotiating	1 Precision Working
2 Analyzing	2 Instructing	2 Operating/Controlling
3 Compiling	3 Supervising	3 Driving/Operating
4 Computing	4 Directing	4 Manipulating
5 Copying	5 Persuading	5 Tending
6 Comparingng	6 Speaking/Signaling	6 Feeding/Offbearing
	7 Serving	7 Handling
	8 Taking Instructions/Helping	

Source: U.S. Department of Labor (1972).

tion in 1977. Included in the DOT for each specific job title is a nine-digit code number. The first three digits define the occupational category, division, and group of the job; the second three digits reflect the involvement with data, people, and things as described. The last three digits identify specific occupations or jobs within the six-digit code groups. A representative example of the USES occupational classification of the job Automobile Mechanic, taken from the 1977 edition of the DOT, follows:

Job Title: AUTOMOBILE MECHANIC
DOT Code: 620.261-010

Digit Representation	Code No.	Interpretation
Occupational category	6	Machine trades occupations
Occupational division	2	Mechanics and machinery repairs
Occupational group	0	Motorized vehicle and engineering equipment mechanics and repairers
Data	2	Analyzing
People	6	Speaking/signaling
Things	1	Precision working
Specific occupation sequence number	010	The first six digits of the code (620.261) are applicable to only one occupational title. The sequence number identifies specific occupational titles that otherwise have the same first six digits.

Other Job-Oriented Methods

There are several other pioneering efforts in the field of job analysis including work sponsored by the U.S. Air Force in the 1950s on the critical incident technique and in the 1960s and 1970s on task analysis, as well as the activities of the U.S. Office of Personnel Management in developing the job element method (1970s). These types of job analysis procedures emphasize the job-oriented aspects of work, with concentration on the output of jobs and the technological functions performed by incumbents.

In contrast to the job-oriented methods, there is an alternative approach to job analysis that concentrates on documenting the worker-oriented elements of jobs. In this regard "worker-oriented" elements refer to the human behaviors, characteristics, and demands that underlie the accomplishment of work activities regardless of their technological components. As a means of analyzing jobs from a behavioral perspective, a structured instrument known as the *Position Analysis Questionnaire* (PAQ) was developed by McCormick, Jeanneret, and Mecham in the late 1960s. The PAQ contains 194 elements (187 related to worker activities and 7 related to methods of worker compensation). The 187 elements are grouped into six major categories: information input, mental processes, work output, relationships with other persons, job context, and other job characteristics. Further, each element has an associated rating scale that is used by a job analyst in determining the level of involvement of the element in the job being analyzed. The rating scales used most frequently reflect either "importance to the job," "extent of use," or "amount of time." Results from the individual analyst ratings of a job are synthesized by computer processing,[1] and output is provided that presents information on job content, job requirements, job evaluation, and other relevant human resource management information. The design of the instrument and the nature of the output available from the processing of the job analyst ratings make it possible to analyze virtually any type of job with the PAQ. This versatility is complemented by the data bank of job analysis information maintained by PAQ Services, Inc., which is perhaps second only to the job analysis information retained by the USES.

Prominence of Job Analysis in Applied Psychology

Research and development in the field of job analysis, while certainly not dormant, has not received overwhelming attention by scholars and practitioners in applied psychology, in part because much of the job analysis effort was taken for granted and often seen as having little value. After all, if a company wanted to hire applicants for a job using tests, it was relatively easy to determine what one or two key requirements seem to be most important for job accomplishment. All one had to do was find the tests that measured the key requirements and put them in place, with perhaps some concern being expressed as to the level of test scores that should be required before an applicant was hired. Similar approaches could be taken with training programs, promotion tests, performance appraisal forms, and other personnel practices that require some knowledge of the jobs to which they are applied.

Another drawback to a concentrated job analysis effort has been the documentation process. Often the most usable product of a job analysis is a job description, which documents the results of the job analysis. However, job descriptions may simply rest in file drawers, become quickly outdated, are time-consuming and expensive to maintain, and thus provide little apparent return on investment. Since job analysis is synonymous with job descriptions from the perspective of many human resource professionals, the lack of support for job analysis efforts is understandable.

Regulatory and Legal Influences

With the passage of the Civil Rights Act in 1964, an increased level of importance was attributed to job analysis. This importance was derived from two sources: regulatory and legal. The regulatory source is primarily that of the Uniform Guidelines on Employee Selection Procedures issued in 1978 under the authority provided by Title VII of the Civil Rights Act. The Uniform Guidelines emphasize the need to conduct a thorough job analysis to document the job relatedness and validity of any employee selection procedure. The courts have strongly supported the fundamental principles of the Civil Rights Act and the Uniform Guidelines by first broadly interpreting the term *employee selection procedure* to apply to virtually all personnel decisions and, second, by ruling against employers' attempting to defend personnel actions alleged to be discriminatory when these actions were not supported by adequate job analysis information. Further, there is variation in past court rulings as to what is "adequate," but often the courts seem to emphasize more rigorous job analyses as being necessary as opposed to what may be viewed as rather superficial job analysis efforts.

Thus, while job analysis has had a rather lackluster history to date and often has been viewed as having little if any real value in relation to the effort required, regulatory and legal influences have created a prominence that will likely continue into the next century. As employers defend or revise existing personnel programs or initiate new human resource systems, it is clear that these employment procedures must be job related. The primary basis for establishing the job relatedness of a personnel action is a thorough job analysis. Of course, just because the job analysis is completed properly does not ensure that an employment practice will be considered legal. On the other hand, the job analysis efforts should be very valuable to an employer for the reasons discussed next.

REASONS FOR ANALYZING NONMANAGEMENT JOBS

There are numerous reasons for analyzing nonmanagement jobs, and no one reason stands out as being the most compelling. However, as of 1983 over 75 percent of the experienced civilian labor force were employed in occupations other than managerial and professional (U.S. Department of Labor, 1985). Consequently, an overwhelming proportion of the jobs in the U.S. work force are of a nonmanagerial nature, and attention to these jobs and their incumbents

requires a significant proportion of the efforts of both line managers and human resource professionals.

Statutory Reasons

One of the obvious reasons for instituting a comprehensive job analysis program has already been identified during the discussion of the regulatory and legal influences on employment practices. In today's litigious society, an organization may experience a complaint or lawsuit regarding a personnel action and immediately the employer's human resource programs become subject to scrutiny and challenge. The *Uniform Guidelines* precedent-setting legal cases, as well as the *Principles for the Validation and Use of Personnel Selection Procedures* (3d edition), serve as the standards for judging and evaluating the fairness and acceptability of the employment practice under question. All of these sources set forth the requirement that personnel actions have a foundation in job analysis.

Sometimes expert counsel is provided to organizations encouraging them never to complete job analysis studies or document work content in job descriptions. The rationale given is that if the employer has not engaged in job analysis or maintained records on job content, then this information cannot in any way be used against the employer in the event of litigation. Further, the employer supposedly will have much more flexibility in terms of human resource practices and employee obligations (e.g., employment at will). The fallacy in such reasoning is that an employer always creates some sort of track record regardless of how well or poorly documented, and in the absence of formal documents, plaintiff arguments may be developed that cannot be defended on the basis of accepted management practices. Thus, if an employer does not intend to engage in unlawful employment practices, then sound job analysis information usually will properly serve that employer in the event of ill-founded complaints or unwarranted litigation.

Operational Reasons

There are a number of operational decisions and programs that require information about the jobs involved in the operations themselves. While often these matters (e.g., work methods, standards) will be be under the purview of industrial engineers, it is also useful to consider contributions that can be made by applied psychologists.

Job Design. Underlying the operation of any organizational unit is the design of jobs whose incumbents carry out the mission of the unit. Fundamental to the design of any job, including the allocation of specific responsibilities, is an understanding of all the duties and tasks that must be accomplished. Further, the design of jobs sets the stage for most, if not all, subsequent employment practices associated with operating the organizational unit and managing its human resources.

Productivity. A key issue of the 1980s, which will likely continue into the 1990s and beyond, is the matter of worker productivity. Throughout the U.S. economy, productivity has not kept pace with costs associated with both materials and labor. Applied psychologists can make contributions to increasing productivity in a number of ways, including employee participation activities, employee selection and training programs, and effective appraisal and reward systems. Knowledge about the content of jobs is essential to any productivity enhancement effort.

Staffing/Reduction in Force. Determining how many individuals are required to staff an operating unit can be a function of both job design and productivity issues; however, even when job responsibilities are straightforward and employee efficiency is not of concern, staffing decisions must still be made on the basis of job facts. Further, when reductions in force become necessary, it is best to approach the matter first from the standpoint of what has to be done and then determining who should be retained to do it rather than making decisions in the absence of job information.

Human Resource Management

The traditional personnel functions found within organizations are presented in figure 16–1. Further, all of these functions should be rooted in information about jobs. Thus job analysis data should serve as an umbrella of information that can support and integrate various human resource programs.

Recruiting. Both the employer's recruiters as well as the prospective employees need up-to-date information about vacant jobs and their requirements.

Figure 16–1. Job Analysis as the Umbrella for All Human Resource Functions

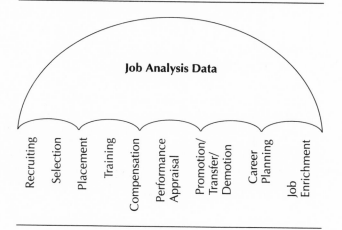

Recruiters must present realistic previews of job responsibilities to prospects, as well as have sufficient information about the job requirements so they can seek potentially qualified applicants. Similarly, potential candidates must have a clear understanding of a job in order to determine if it will match their interests and qualifications. Realistic and comprehensive information about jobs leads to less turnover and higher levels of job satisfaction, thus increasing the employer's return on employee investments.

Selection. The hiring of employees is one of the most crucial employment practices carried out by any organization. A valid selection program can support the hiring process and result in significant dollar utility to an organization. John Hunter and Frank Schmidt in 1982 estimated that there would be an increase of between $80 million and $100 million per year in material productivity if valid selection procedures were utilized throughout the economy.

The selection procedures most people think about include testing and interviewing but can include many other aspects of the hiring process, such as medical/physical examinations, application blanks, and biodata forms. All of these components of the selection process must be job related and valid, and considerable litigation has taken place since the late 1960s regarding the discriminatory results of certain employers' hiring practices. Nevertheless, research has clearly established that objective selection procedures, such as employment tests, based on solid job analysis data can be the fairest and most valuable selection procedures and, when established and implemented in the proper manner, will be upheld by the courts of law.

Placement. Closely akin to the selection process is the placement of an individual into a particular position or job assignment. While often an individual is hired for a specific job opening, there are many organizations that initially hire people into a general labor pool and then subsequently place them in specific positions as openings occur. Consequently, job analysis information is valuable for choices made at the initial hiring stage as well as for making placement decisions.

Training. The development of an employee's job knowledge and skills is often accomplished by formalized training programs. In such instances the training curricula, as well as the criteria for evaluating employee learning, should be derived from job analysis data.

Compensation. Determining the value of work to an organization is a critical step in developing a compensation plan. The internal value of work is determined by a process known as job evaluation. This process takes into consideration job analysis information and uses it to establish the internal value of jobs relative to one another. (The external values of jobs are typically determined from wage surveys.) Further, under some pay programs, additional compensation in the form of bonuses or incentive pay is available on the basis of accomplishment of specific objectives or standards. Many times these objectives or standards are set on the basis of job analysis information. Hence the fairness and effectiveness of an organization's compensation program is dependent on accurate information about the jobs themselves.

Performance Appraisal. A number of decisions can be derived from the results of an appraisal of an employee's performance, including decisions associated with placement, training, and compensation, as well as ones about promotion, transfer, demotion, and career planning. Further, appraisal of an employee's performance is probably one of the most difficult and crucial managerial functions and yet is one in which there is often considerable room for improvement. However, one thing is certain—performance appraisal will not be very effective and may not be very fair from the perspective of both the employee and the employee's supervisor unless that performance appraisal is based on sound job information. Consequently, the road to improvement in performance appraisal practices often begins with job analysis efforts, as well as comprehensive supervisor training.

Promotion/Transfer/Demotion. Decisions about the reassignment of employees, whether upward, lateral, or downward, must take into consideration information about the people as well as the jobs to which they may be assigned. Further, it may not be a simple matter of job performance. Most readers are aware of the proverbial story of promoting the most successful salesperson to sales manager, only to have the individual perform miserably in the managerial job. Potentially, this mistake could be avoided if careful attention is paid to the responsibilities and requirements of the sales manager job when making the promotion decision. Consequently, information about jobs must be carefully matched with information about employees when making promotion, transfer, or demotion decisions.

Career Planning. Closely related to the movement of employees is the matter of career planning. In such instances the organization is planning the upward mobility of workers by taking into account both employee and job facts. Thus, an attempt is made to match employee needs (interests, desired level of responsibility) with organization needs (job vacancies, critical skills required), and these latter needs must be based on job data.

Job Enrichment. Quality of work life sometimes can be improved through changes in job content and structure. Certainly job enrichment and job design are closely allied (and perhaps in the eyes of some are one in the same), and clearly both functions are concerned about jobs from a similar job analysis perspective. For example, how simple or complex are the duties and tasks? What are the working relationships between coworkers? The answers to the questions and the subsequent solutions for job design or job enrichment purposes can be derived only from factual information about the jobs.

Union Relations

For organizations with bargaining units the information obtained from job analysis usually is essential to a number of union-management issues. These include wage rates (and hence benefits), crew size or staffing levels, work rules, grievance matters, labor standards or productivity, and many other issues that may be negotiated or arbitrated. The more accurate and accepted the information is about the jobs held by the union workers, the smoother are the relations between management and union representatives.

Affirmative Action and Social Responsibility

In today's employment environment there is considerable emphasis by organizations on developing and abiding by a social conscience that extends to the communities in which they operate and to the consumers of their goods or services. Organizations want to follow employment practices that are affirmative with respect to individuals of a certain gender, religion, color, race, or national origin. Organizations wish to utilize persons who may have a certain physical or mental handicap. And organizations want to remove artificial barriers that disadvantage certain classes of workers such as women or older (over age forty) individuals. In support of the social consciences of organizations, the human resource professional must potentially answer via all of the programs previously mentioned, including those of an operational, personnel, or perhaps even a union relations function.

Summary

Job analysis is the foundation for most, if not all, human resource practices and several other managerial functions. Job analysis data are needed to identify and hire applicants, place and train new employees, and determine wage rates for jobs. Further, practices related to performance appraisal, assignment of employees from one job to another, and enriching jobs all require job information. Given the multiple purposes served by job analysis, it seems reasonable to expect that one methodology could be used to obtain the necessary information and organize it in a manner that would be useful to the practitioner. Unfortunately, such is not the case. Various job analysis methodologies have both strengths and weaknesses. The necessary components of a job analysis program are described next.

COMPONENTS OF JOB ANALYSIS

When initially determining how to proceed with a job analysis effort, at least five decisions must be made:

1. For what purpose(s) is the job analysis being conducted?
2. What types of data are to be collected?
3. What procedure will be used?
4. In what form will the information be obtained?
5. Who will conduct the job analysis?

Some answers to these questions have been explicitly stated or implied in the information presented so far in this chapter. The purposes of job analysis have been well defined in the preceding section and will not be restated here. The types of data that can be collected include:

- Work activities (duties, tasks, etc.).
- Work behaviors (coordinating, estimating, analyzing, etc.).
- Job requirements (education, training, technical skills, etc.).
- Personal requirements (interests, temperaments, physical characteristics, etc.).
- Information about the work environment (psychological demands, hazards, physical context, etc.).

Alternative Job Analysis Procedures

The procedures available to collect the job analysis information offer several alternatives that can be selected to meet the needs of the organization and yield the type of data appropriate to the purposes of the job analysis. The most useful procedures include:

- Observation of the job being performed.
- Interviews with job incumbents and/or supervisors individually or in small groups.
- Subject matter expert (SME) conferences (meetings of individuals who are very knowledgeable about the job being analyzed).
- Questionnaires, either open ended or structured in design.
- Work records such as logs or diaries of events during a work cycle.
- Critical incidents, which are examples of very good or very poor employee job performance.

There are advantages and disadvantages to each of the procedures, and several of the procedures can be combined (such as observation and interview) effectively. Further, the relevant information needs to be recorded regardless of the method, and the more structure that is provided to the recording process, the more useful (and acceptable if litigation arises) is the job analysis information. Finally, consideration should be given to the employees whose jobs are being analyzed. Generally, employees will be more comfortable with those procedures that allow them to interact with the job analyst and otherwise become part of the process.

Form of Job Analysis Data

The form of the job analysis information can be either qualitative or quantitative or a combination. Qualitative information is typically narrative and usually compiled in a job description. Quantitative information will usually be in the form of "ratings," such as rating on a scale of 1 to 5: the "importance" of performing a task (as often found on a task inventory), the "extent of use" of specific kinds of information (as rated in the Position Analysis Questionnaire), or the exact "amount of time spent" on a particular work activity (as may be recorded in a work log). Further, such ratings can be evaluated to determine the reliability of the job analysis results, a characteristic that is often overlooked when considering the value of a job analysis system. (Conceptually, reliability of job analysis data is the same as the reliability of a manufacturing process or an information processing system in that the user must be confident that the output is consistent over time and/or across operators or systems. Similarly, the reliability of job analysis data can be determined by the extent to which two or more independent analyses of the same job yield consistent findings.)

Quantitative information has the additional advantage of providing an objective basis for comparing jobs or developing statistical relationships between the job analysis results and other types of data (e.g. aptitude test scores, rates of pay). Qualitative descriptions are the more conventional forms in which job analysis results are presented and may be the easiest to understand from the point of view of the employees and line supervisors. However, such qualitative information is not easily evaluated in terms of its reliability (an essential condition if the job analysis is supporting some employee selection purpose) and may be so general in scope to be of little specific value. Consequently, a frequent complaint about qualitative job descriptions is that they are quickly outdated, expensive to maintain, and otherwise remain in file drawers, having little, if any, use in an organization.

Examples and formats for collecting and recording job analysis input are readily available, and several more widely used sources or references for such materials are listed in the bibliography to this chapter.

Who Collects Job Analysis Information

The collection of job analysis data can be accomplished by different categories of individuals, and the specific resource may depend on the procedure as well as the knowledge held by members of the organization responsible for the job analysis activity. For example, industrial engineers, industrial-organizational psychologists, or trained job analysts are usually very knowledgeable about one or more job analysis procedures. On the other hand, individuals who serve some role in a personnel function may have only a very limited background in job analysis and thus may require assistance.

Apart from the use of formally trained analysts or individuals within a personnel function, it is also possible to use job incumbents and/or supervisors directly in the job analysis process. For example, these individuals can complete questionnaires or maintain work diaries that directly document job content. Further, with some amount of guidance, incumbents and supervisors may be able to participate in more sophisticated forms of job analysis whereby these individuals not only develop job content but then analyze and formalize it using specific methods.

Finally, certain equipment can assist individuals in performing job analyses, and video cameras and various electronic recording devices have become especially useful. The major drawback is that many employees are reluctant to have recordings made of their work activities, and thus considerable resistance can develop regarding the process.

Summary

In summary, there are several decisions related to the purposes, types of data, procedures, formats, and agents that must be made before a job analysis pro-

gram can be undertaken. The most frequent scenario in industry today is likely to involve a job analyst's observing and interviewing job incumbents with the intent of collecting information on work activities, behaviors, requirements, and the environment using a semistructured format. Subsequently the information will be documented in a job description that may be used in one or more personnel and managerial functions. The major weaknesses in this scenario are that the job data are only in semistructured form and that the information is documented only in a job description. Improvements to the scenario would include the collection of data in a more structured (and perhaps more quantified) form so that they can be used more objectively and become part of a data base that is responsive to several of the purposes that are important to organizational functioning.

CONCLUDING REMARKS

Job analysis is not an end in itself but rather is a means for achieving one or more organizational purposes. Job analysis is a process that provides a data base of information about work that can be used for organizational decision making. Accordingly, the need(s) must be identified and the objective(s) clearly defined so that the job analysis process will be a valuable one. Most frequently, the needs and objectives are directly related to the management of employees, and the job analysis will form the foundation for the managerial practices or administrative systems established to meet these needs and objectives.

Job analysis is a process that requires organizational intervention. As such, it is essential that communications be developed and disseminated in a timely manner. These communications should be delivered through the typical channels and include information about the purpose, time frame, procedures, and feedback of results associated with the job analysis effort. Because it is an intervention, the job analysis process also must be sensitive to organizational functioning and climate. Hence, specific techniques and procedures would be appropriate in one organizational environment but unacceptable in others. For example, if a company thrives on extensive interaction and participation throughout all levels of employees, then using a highly formal, noninteractive

job analysis procedure would likely meet considerable resistance. Consequently, careful consideration needs to be given to the fit between the job analysis process and the environment in which it is to be applied.

It is generally accepted that there is no one best method for carrying out a job analysis study. Rather, the method selected should be appropriate for the intended purposes as well as match the organizational climate. Further, the job analysis effort should be guided by a well-conceived plan. The plan should account for such matters as schedules (to minimize operational impact), the selection of participants (employees, analysts, and possibly consultants), data collection procedures, intervention strategies (horizontal verses lateral, top down or vice versa, sampling levels, work locations), training of analysts as necessary, pilot testing of procedures, data editing and analysis, and documentation of results.

Finally, it is important to recognize that conducting an analysis of an organization's jobs provides the opportunity to respond to near-term objectives as well as to build a data base for the future. Further, that data base can be the foundation for an integrated personnel system that will yield a competitive return on the investment in the job analysis process and become state of the art in human resource management.

NOTE

[1]Computer processing is accomplished by PAQ Services, Inc., 1625 North 1000 East, Logan, Utah 84321.

REFERENCES

Bemis, S.E., Belenky, A.H., & Soder, D.A. (1983). *Job analysis: An effective management tool,* Washington, DC: Bureau of National Affairs.

Brumback, G.B., et al. (1974). *Model procedures for job analysis, test development and validation* (vol, 1). Washington, DC: American Institutes for Research.

Christal, R.E., and Weissmuller, J.J. (1976). *New comprehensive occupational data Analysis programs (CODAP) for analyzing task factor information* (AFHRL Interim Professional Paper No. TR-76-3). San Antonio, TX: Lackland Air Force Base, Air Force Human Resources Laboratory.

Cunningham, J.W., Tittle, T.C., Floyd, J.R., & Bates, J.A. (1971). *The development of the Occupation Analysis Inventory*. Raleigh, NC: North Carolina State University, Center for Occupational Education. Equal Employment Opportunity Commission, Civil Service Commission, Department of Labor, & Department of Justice (1978). Uniform guidelines on employee selection procedures. *Federal Register, 43,* 38290–38315.

Fine, S.D., & Wiley, W.W. (1971). *An introduction to functional job analysis*. Kalamazoo, MI: W.E. Upjohn Institute for Employment Research.

Gael, S. (1983). *Job analysis: A guide to assessing work activities*. San Francisco, CA: Jossey Bass.

Gael, S. (Ed.) (1988). *The job analysis handbook for business, industry, and government*. New York: John Wiley & Sons.

Hunter, J.E., & Schmidt, F.L. (1982). Fitting people to jobs: Impact of personnel selection on national productivity. In M.D. Dunnette and E.A. Fleishman (Eds.), *Human performance and productivity, vol.1*. Hillsdale, NJ: Lawrence Erlbaum Associates.

Levine, E.L., Ash, R.A., Hall, H., & Sistrunk, F. (1983). Evaluation of job analysis methods by experienced job analysts. *Academy of Management Journal, 26*(2), 339–347.

McCormick, E.J. (1979). *Job analysis: Methods and applications*. New York: AMACOM.

McCormick, E.J. (1979). Job information: Its development and applications. In D. Yoder, & H.G. Heneman, Jr. (Eds.), *ASPA handbook of personnel and industrial relations: Staffing policies and strategies*. Washington, DC: Bureau of National Affairs.

McCormick, E.J., Jeanneret, P.R., & Mecham, R.C. (1989). *Position analysis questionnaire*. Palo Alto, CA: Consulting Psychologists Press, Inc.

Primoff, E.S. (1971). *Summary of job-element principles: Preparing a job-element standard*. Washington, DC: U.S. Civil Service Commission, Personnel Measurement and Development Center.

Richardson, Bellows, Henry & Co., Inc. (1975). *Job requirements questionnaire for supervisory classifications*. Washington, DC: Author.

Sears, Victoria L. (1986). *Staffing for optimum performance*. New York: Executive Enterprises, Inc.

Society for Industrial and Organizational Psychology, Inc. (1987). *Principles for the validation and use of personnel selection procedures* (3d ed.). College Park, MD: Author.

Stone, C.H., & Yoder, D. (1970). *Job analysis*. Los Angeles, CA: California State College.

U.S. Civil Service Commission (1973). *Job analysis: Developing and documenting data—A guide for state and local government*. Washington, DC: Author.

U.S. Department of Labor (1972). *Handbook for analyzing jobs*. Washington, DC: U.S. Government Printing Office.

U.S. Department of Labor (1973). *Task analysis inventories: A method for collecting job information*. Washington, DC: U.S. Government Printing Office.

U.S. Department of Labor (1977). *Dictionary of occupational titles* (4th ed.). ed.) Washington, DC: U.S. Government Printing Office.

U.S. Department of Labor Bureau of Labor Statistics (1985). *Handbook of labor statistics*. Washington, DC: U.S. Government Printing Office, June.

U.S. Office of Personnel Management (1979). *How to write position descriptions*. Washington, DC: U.S. Government Printing Office.

Wilson, M. (1974). *Job analysis for human resource management: A review of selected research and development* (Manpower Research Monograph No. 36, Department of Labor). Washington, DC: U.S. Government Printing Office.

17 **JOB ANALYSIS METHODS: A DESCRIPTION AND COMPARISON OF THE ALTERNATIVES**

17 JOB ANALYSIS METHODS: A DESCRIPTION AND COMPARISON OF THE ALTERNATIVES

Robert Gatewood, Hubert S. Feild

Chapter 16 presented an overview of job analysis by defining the subject, pointing out its importance in complying with legal guidelines concerning human resource management (HRM) functions, and discussing the use of job analysis information in the HRM functions. The purpose of this chapter is to expand this presentation of job analysis by a discussion of the following:

1. The nature of the information that is generated through job analysis.
2. A description of the most frequently used job analysis methods.
3. A comparison of these methods in terms of ease of use by HRM staff.
4. A comparison of these methods in terms of use in various HRM functions.

INFORMATION GENERATED THROUGH JOB ANALYSIS

The development and implementation of HRM functions require the use of one or both of two types of information: the nature and characteristics of job activities and the worker attributes necessary to perform these job activities. A complete job analysis should provide both types of information.

As will become evident when we describe the various job analysis methods, information about the nature of job activities can be either qualitative or quantitative. In a qualitative form, verbal descriptions of the specific tasks that comprise the job are produced. These task statements should provide complete information about each job activity, including the action, the materials or information used, and the purpose or end result.

Quantitative data are numerical scores that indicate amounts of certain characteristics of the task or the job as a whole. The development of these numerical scores uses a defined measurement system. Scores for task statements usually take the form of ratings for such characteristics as importance or amount of time spent. When the job as a whole is scored, scores are generated from the responses of job incumbents and/or supervisors and are used to measure a general char-

acteristic usually called a job dimension or job factor. Examples of such dimensions are "verbal information provided" and "interaction with others."

Similarly, data about worker attributes can be either qualitative or quantitative. Qualitative data take the form of statements of knowledge, skill, or abilities (KSAs) and meet the following definitions (Fleishman, 1979):

Knowledge: A body of information usually of a factual or procedural nature that makes for successful performance of a task (e.g., knowledge of state workman compensation laws).

Skill: An individual's level of proficiency or competency in performing a specific task (e.g., skill in using a bank-proof machine to process fifty checks per minute without error).

Ability: A more general, enduring trait or capability an individual possesses at the time when he or she first begins to perform a task (e.g., ability to analyze loan application information to determine the financial risk to the bank).

Quantitative data are, most commonly, scores of the extent to which a knowledge, skill, or ability is needed for the performance of a task or the job in general.

Portions of this chapter are based on R. Gatewood & H.S. Feild, *Human Resource Selection* (Hinsdale, Il: Dryden Press).

Job Analysis Methods

During the seventy-plus years that job analysis has been used in HRM, many methods have been developed to collect the previously described data. It is neither possible nor useful to discuss each of these. Instead, we will present a brief summary of eight methods that we consider to be the most often used in recent years. More detailed information may be obtained from the references provided in the summary of each method.

Job Analysis Interview

One of the oldest approaches to job analysis is the use of group or individual interviews with incumbents or supervisors to collect information about both tasks and KSAs. A key assumption of the method is that interviewers are thoroughly familiar with the job being studied. Large groups may be used when it is

certain that all incumbents are performing the same major activities. Supervisory groups are usually employed in order to verify incumbent information and to provide information unavailable to employees in the job.

Certainly there are numerous approaches that could be taken in phrasing and posing questions in an interview. No one method may be suitable for all cases. Figure 17–1 presents a sample job interview schedule that asks for data in a wide variety of areas useful for characterizing a job.

The key initial step in characterizing a job with an interview procedure such as the one in figure 17–1 is the identification of critical job tasks. Once identified, each task is described in terms of KSAs required for task performance as well as environmental conditions surrounding task performance. Because of the importance of the task to the interview method, it may be helpful to review how job tasks are derived and structured with this method. Task statements are written so that each shows:

Figure 17–1. A Typical Job Analysis Interview Schedule (Abbreviated) for Use with an Incumbent

Name of Employee _____ Payroll Title _____
Job Analyst _____ Department _____

Important Job Tasks

1. Describe your job in terms of what you do.
2. How do you do it? Do you use special tools, equipment, or other sources of aid? If so, list the names of the principal tools, equipment, or sources of aid you use.
3. Of the major tasks in your job, how much time does it take to do each one? How often do you perform each task in a day, week, or month?

Knowledge, Skills, and Abilities Required

What does it take to perform each task in terms of the following:

1. Knowledge required
   a. What subject matter areas are covered by each task?
   b. What facts or principles must you have an acquaintance with or understand in these subject matter areas?
   c. Describe the level, degree, and breadth of knowledge required in these areas or subjects.

2. Skills required
   a. What activities must you perform with ease and precision?
   b. What are the manual skills that are required to operate machines, vehicles, equipment, or to use tools?

3. Abilities required
   a. What is the nature and level of language ability, written or oral, required of you on the job? Are there complex oral or written ideas involved in performing the task or simple instructional materials?
   b. What mathematical ability must you have?
   c. What reasoning or problem-solving ability must you have?
   d. What instructions must you follow? Are they simple, detailed, involved, or abstract?
   e. What interpersonal abilities are required? What supervisory or managing abilities are required?
   f. What physical abilities such as strength, coordination, or visual acuity must you have?

Physical Activities

Describe the frequency and degree to which you are engaged in such activities as: pulling, pushing, throwing, carrying, kneeling, sitting, running, crawling, reaching, climbing.

1. What the worker does, by using a specific action verb that introduces the task statement.
2. To whom or what he or she does it, by stating the object of the verb.
3. What is produced, by expressing the expected output of the action.
4. What materials, tools, procedures, or equipment are used (U.S. Civil Service Commission, 1983).

The following example demonstrates how task statements are developed from information collected in the job analysis interview.

Suppose, for example, a job analyst is reviewing the job of welfare eligibility examiner. Assume further that background and supplementary data have been obtained from the incumbent. The interviewer asks the respondent to describe his or her job using questions similar to those presented in figure 17–1. The interviewee describes the job as follows:

I interview applicants for food stamps—ask the applicants all the pertinent questions that will help to determine their eligibility. For example, are they working part time, receiving other assistance, etc.

To carry out the job I have to interpret regulations, policies, and actually make decisions about eligibility. Some applicants are referred to other assistance units. Some applicants need detailed explanations of policies at a level they can understand, to avoid their reacting unpleasantly over a decision. They also get advice about their appeal rights from me. I visit homes to evaluate a client's circumstances and make determinations. I verify what the client has said on an application: household composition, shelter arrangements, income, etc. This helps me determine whether the food stamp costs have been correctly or incorrectly determined. (U.S. Civil Service Commission, 1973, pp. 11–12)

Following these comments, the analyst then uses the task statement criteria to produce task statements representing important task activities. The goal of the process is to produce task statements that can be understood by persons unfamiliar with the job. For

---

Environmental Conditions

Describe the frequency and degree to which you encounter working conditions such as these: cramped quarters, moving objects, vibration, inadequate ventilation.

Typical Work Incidents

Describe the frequency and degree to which you do the following:
   a. Working in situations involving the interpretation of feelings, ideas, or facts in terms of personal viewpoint.
   b. Influencing people in their opinions, attitudes, or judgments about ideas or things.
   c. Working with people beyond giving and receiving instructions.
   d. Performing repetitive work or continuously performing the same work.
   e. Performing under stress when confronted with emergency, critical, unusual, or dangerous situations or in situations in which work speed and sustained attention are make-and-break aspects of the job.
   f. Performing a variety of duties, often changing from one task to another of a different nature without loss of efficiency or composure.
   g. Working under hazardous conditions that may result in violence, loss of body members, burns, bruises, cuts, impairment of senses, collapse, fractures, electric shock.

Records and Reports

What records or reports do you prepare as part of your job?

Source of Job Information

What is the principal source for instructions you receive on how to do your job (for example, oral directions or written specifications)?

Supervisory Responsibility

   1. How many employees are directly under your supervision?
   2. Do you have full authority to assign work; correct and discipline; recommend pay increases, transfers, promotions, and discharge for these employees?

Other

Are there any additional elements about your job that would help me better understand what you do? If so, please describe them.

Source: From R. Gatewood & H. Feild, *Human Resource Selection* (Hinsdale, Ill: Dryden Press, 1987), pp. 195–196.

example, the information from the interview could be rewritten as follows:

1. Asks client questions, listen, and records answers on standard eligibility form, using knowledge of interviewing techniques and eligibility criteria in order to gather information from which client's eligibility for food stamps can be determined.

From the interview response given earlier, additional tasks might include the following:

2. Determines eligibility of applicant in order to complete client's application for food stamps using regulatory policies as a guide.

3. Decides upon and describes other agencies available for client to contact in order to assist and refer client to appropriate community resources using worker's knowledge of resources available and knowledge of client's needs.

4. Explains policies and regulations appropriate to applicant's case in order to inform applicants of their status with regard to agency's regulations and policies. (U.S. Civil Service Commission 1973, pp. 7–12)

After the important job tasks have been stated, the analyst then characterizes each statement in terms of frequency of performance, KSAs required, physical activities required, environmental conditions, and other factors thought to be important to task performance. Responses to questions in the interview schedule are combined with judgments of the analyst to make these determinations for each task. An illustration may help to clarify the task characterization process. For the moment, let us reexamine the second task identified in the study of welfare eligibility examiner. The task was stated as follows: "Determines eligibility of applicant in order to complete client's application for food stamps using regulatory policies as a guide." The characterization of this task might be

Figure 17–2. Characterization of a Selected Job Task of the Job of Welfare Eligibility Examiner

Task 2:
Determines eligibility of applicant in order to complete client's application for food stamps using regulatory policies as a guide.

Task Characterization

Knowledge Required:
1. Knowledge of contents and meaning of items on standard application form
2. Knowledge of Social-Health Services food stamp regulatory policies
3. Knowledge of statutes relating to Social-Health Services food stamp program

Skills Required:
None

Abilities Required:
1. Ability to read and understand complex instructions such as regulatory policies
2. Ability to read and understand a variety of procedural instructions, written and oral, and convert these to proper actions
3. Ability to use simple arithmetic — addition and subtraction
4. Ability to translate requirements into language appropriate to laypersons

Physical Activities:
Sedentary

Environmental Conditions:
None

Typical Work Incidents:
Working with people beyond giving and receiving instructions

Interest Areas:
1. Communication of data
2. Business contact with people
3. Working for the presumed good of people

Source: U.S. Civil Service Commission (1973, pp. 13–14).

made as shown in figure 17–20. This same process is then carried out for each task statement.

Finally, the analyst should attempt to verify the data collected and the characterizations of the task statements. Verification may be obtained by reviewing the job analysis results with either the incumbents and/or their immediate supervisors.

The success of the interview as a job analysis technique depends, to a large extent, upon the skill of the interviewer. A skilled interviewer may be able to tease out job information that may go undetected by other forms of analysis. To increase the likelihood of success in using the technique, certain steps should be taken. Some suggestions are offered in the *Handbook for Analyzing Jobs* (U.S. Department of Labor, 1972) for improving the chance of success in using the interview. These suggestions address opening the interview, guiding the interview to obtain necessary information, and closing and summarizing the interview.

The Task Analysis Inventory

A task analysis inventory is a questionnaire listing a large number of tasks (100 or more is not unusual) for which respondents make some form of judgment, usually ratings. Because many different tasks may exist in any job, this type of job analysis questionnaire is typically directed toward only one job or a class of very similar jobs. Most often, the inventory is intended for use by incumbents. Nevertheless, supervisors and observers can use it assuming they are knowledgeable about the job being studied.

Figure 17–3 presents a condensed version of a typical task analysis inventory. The inventory shown is one used to analyze various tasks associated with the job of personnel analyst. Since most inventories are similar to the one exhibited, we will use it to point out two important characteristics: the *phrasing of tasks* to be rated and the use of a *rating scale* for judging the tasks. Most task inventories share these characteristics.

First, we see that the item being judged is a *task*. If we compare the phrasing of the tasks shown in figure 17–3 with those discussed in reference to the job analysis interview procedure discussed earlier, we will find that the two sets of tasks differ. For example, we see that the task statements developed previously appear to be more complex. Tasks that were identified under the interview procedure described what was done as well as the results of those actions. Work aids, materials, methods, and other requirements of a job incumbent were noted. In contrast in the task inventory example, the tasks are not as fully devel-

---

Figure 17–3. A Condensed Example of a Task Analysis Inventory for the Job of Personnel Analyst

Directions: We are interested in knowing more about your job. Below is listed a number of tasks you may perform on your job. Using the rating scales given below, rate each task as to (a) how frequently you perform it and (b) how important it is for newly hired workers in a job like yours to be able to perform this task when they first begin work. Read each task and then place your rating in the two spaces to the right of each task.

Frequency of Performance
1 = Not Performed at All
2 = Seldom
3 = Occasionally
4 = Frequently
5 = Almost All of the Time

Importance for Newly Hired
1 = Not Performed at All
2 = Somewhat Important
3 = Moderately Important
4 = Very Important
5 = Extremely Important

Task	Frequency of Performance	Importance for Newly Hired
1. Prepare job descriptions for secretarial jobs.	[ ]	[ ]
2. Check file folders for disposition of health and dental records.	[ ]	[ ]
3. Initiate request for identification cards from terminated personnel.	[ ]	[ ]
4. Describe company policies to newly hired employees.	[ ]	[ ]
5. Plan and develop training programs for newly hired clerical personnel.	[ ]	[ ]

Source: R. Gatewood & H. Feild, *Human Resource Selection*, (Hinsdale, Ill: Dryden Press, 1987), p. 203.

oped. These task statements are concerned with "what" gets done. They usually provide no information on the situation surrounding the activity.

Another important characteristic of any task inventory is the response scale used by the respondent to judge the given tasks. A response scale provides a continuum or range of options (most often consisting of five to seven steps) that a respondent can use to express his or her perceptions. Morsh and Archer (1967) have identified two general classes of rating scales used in task analysis inventories. The first class is referred to as *primary rating factors* and is used to describe an incumbent's involvement with each task. Specific factors include frequency of task performance, time spent, and degree of discretion used. The second class, *secondary rating factors*, focuses principally on the task itself rather than incumbent involvement with each task. Examples of these factors are task complexity, criticality, importance, and difficulty in learning the task.

Because most task inventories are aimed toward a specific job, they may have to be developed by the user. This process is time-consuming and often expensive. Access to previous inventories or analyses of the job in question as well as the use of technical experts in job analysis and questionnaire development are important determinants of the cost and success of the method. For those organizations committed to the development and administration of a task inventory, McCormick (1979) has summarized the major steps. Similarly, Morsh and Archer (1967) have offered a series of guidelines to be followed in preparing task statements. Only some of the major guidelines have been chosen to be presented in table 17–1. Basically, development of a task inventory should be carried out in a sequential fashion such as that outlined. There is no one best way. However, suggestions like those noted increase the chances that the resulting questionnaire will meet the objectives for which it is intended.

Once the inventory has been completed and administered, statistical analyses of the ratings can be used to isolate the most important or critical tasks of the job. These tasks, then, become the basis for the determination of appropriate KSAs. This process of

Table 17–1
Summary Guidelines for Developing Task Analysis Inventories

Sequential Steps for Developing Content of Task Inventories	Guidelines for Writing Task Items
1. Technical manuals, previous job analyses, and other job-related reports are reviewed for possible content.	*When task items are identified, they should:*
	1. Characterize activities, not skills or knowledge.
2. Technical job experts (consultants, selected incumbents/supervisors) prepare lists of tasks known to be performed.	2. Have an identifiable beginning and ending.
	3. Represent activities performed by an individual worker, not activities performed by different individuals.
3. Tasks identified are reviewed for duplication, edited, and incorporated into an initial version of the inventory. Tasks are developed subject to task-writing guidelines.	4. Have an identifiable output or consequence.
	5. Avoid extremes in phrasing activities; statement should not be too broad or too specific.
4. First draft is prepared and submitted to a panel of experts (or incumbents and/or supervisors) for review.	6. Be developed by full-time inventory writers (preferable); supervisors/incumbents should serve technical advisers.
5. Panel of reviewers adds, deletes, or modifies tasks for developing another draft of the inventory.	*When items are written they should:*
6. Steps 4 and 5 are repeated, using the same or similar panel, until an acceptable draft has been developed.	1. Mean the same thing to all respondents.
7. Task inventory is then tested on a sample of respondents to whom the final version will be given.	2. Be stated so that the rating scale to be used makes sense.
8. Appropriate modifications are made as needed.	3. Be stated so that the incumbent is understood to be the subject of the statement. The pronoun "I" should be implied. For example "(I) number all card boxes."
9. Steps 7 and 8 are repeated until a final, acceptable version is developed.	4. Be stated so that the verb is in the present tense.
	5. Use terms that are specific, familiar, and unambiguous.

Source: E.J. McCormick, "Job Information: It's Development and Applications," in D. Yoder & H. Heneman (Eds.), *ASPA Handbook of Personnel and Industrial Relations* (Washington, DC: BNA Books, 1979), p. 4065.

KSA determination is a judgmental one carried out in a similar fashion to that previously described with regard to the job analysis interview method.

The Position Analyses Questionnaire (PAQ)

The PAQ (McCormick, Jeanneret & Mecham, 1972) is a standardized, structured job analysis questionnaire containing 194 items or elements. Of this total, 187 items concern work activities, and the remaining 7 relate to compensation issues. These elements are not task statements. Rather, they represent *general human behaviors involved in work*. An analyst must decide if each of the elements applies to the job under study. If it does, then a rating scale is used to indicate the degree to which that element applies to the job.

Items on the PAQ are organized into six basic divisions or sections. These divisions and appropriate definitions are as follows:

1. *Information Input* —Where and how an incumbent gets information needed to perform the job.

2. *Mental Processes* —The reasoning, decision making, planning, and information processing activities that are involved in performing the job.

3. *Work Output* —The physical activities, tools, and devices used by the worker to perform the job.

4. *Relationships with Other Persons* —The relationships with other people that are required in performing the job.

5. *Job Context* —The physical and social contexts where the work is performed.

6. *Other Characteristics* —The activities, conditions, and characteristics other than those described that are relevant to the job (McCormick et al., 1972).

Rating scales are used in the PAQ for determining the extent to which the 194 elements are relevant to the job under study. Six different types of scales are used:

1. *Extent of Use* —Degree to which an element is used by the worker.

2. *Amount of Time* —Proportion of time spent doing something.

3. *Importance to This Job* —Importance of an activity specified by the item in performing the job.

4. *Possibility of Occurrence* —Degree to which there is a possibility of physical hazards on the job.

5. *Applicability* —Whether an item applies to the job.

6. *Special Code* —Special rating scales used with a particular item on the PAQ (PAQ Services, Inc., 1977).

Actual application of the PAQ can be thought of as a four-step sequence of activities. Although the specific steps may vary somewhat from one administration to the next, the sequence described below explains most PAQ application activities.

Selecting and Training Agents to Analyze Jobs. Various options are available for choosing agents to collect PAQ data. Either one or a combination of three groups of individuals is likely to be used from inside the organization to provide job information. These groups consist of (1) trained job analysts, (2) job incumbents, and (3) job supervisors. Job analysts will probably be the best prepared to use the PAQ. If job incumbents or supervisors are utilized, they should be individuals who know the job being studied (say, for example, six months or more job experience) and have high reading and verbal skills. (Interviewing and observational skills may also be required).

Selecting Persons to Provide Job Information. Once the type of analyst has been chosen, individuals who will provide job information must be identified. These persons are usually incumbents who have sufficient experience and know the job. Supervisors can also be employed, assuming they have had relevant and recent experience on the job in question. Three to four incumbents plus the supervisor, working independently, are suggested for completing PAQs for a given job. Since persons chosen may be describing their jobs orally, they should be willing and able to express themselves verbally.

Collecting Data. The PAQ can be completed by an analyst who has observed the job or has interviewed a selected incumbent(s) or supervisor(s). It may also be completed by an incumbent or supervisor serving as a respondent. Since the PAQ was developed to analyze a wide variety of jobs, some items will necessarily apply to some jobs and not to others. Thus, even though the questionnaire appears long, by design only one-third to one-half of the items will be answered for most jobs. Time requirements for PAQ completion may range from less than 1 hour for a trained analyst up to 3 hours for analyses involving interviews or group PAQ administration sessions.

Analyzing PAQ Data. Because empirical data are collected with the PAQ, a wide variety of analyses are available. For example, one analysis is to determine the basic nature of a job in terms of the dimensions of work activity measured by the PAQ. Several studies have found that the PAQ measures 32 specific and 13 overall dimensions of jobs. A sample of these dimensions is listed in table 17–2. It is possible to score any job analyzed in terms of these dimensions. Once scored, a profile of the job can be created. Thus, the PAQ makes it possible to depict a job quantitatively in terms of the job dimension scores.

These quantitative job data can also be used to measure important worker attributes. Initially, a list of 76 human attributes (49 of an "aptitudinal" nature and 27 of an "interest" nature) thought to be most relevant in job performance was developed by McCormick and his colleagues (Marquardt & McCormick, 1972; Mecham & McCormick, 1969). Examples of these attributes are also shown in table 17–2. A sample of psychologists was asked to rate the relevance of each of these attributes to the job elements on the PAQ. From these ratings, a median rating of the relevance of each attribute for each PAQ job element was obtained. Once PAQ job scores are iden-

tified, the attribute ratings can also be generated. These represent a profile of the attributes or specifications necessary for successfully performing a job.

Functional Job Analysis (FJA)

The key ingredient in analyzing a job using FJA (Fine and Wiley, 1971) is proper development of task statements. Once identified, these tasks are then rated by a job analyst using special sets of rating scales. The ratings provided serve as a basis for inferring worker attributes required for task performance.

When using FJA, judgments about jobs are based on at least two premises:

1. All jobs require workers to deal, in some degree, with people (clients, customers, coworkers, etc.), data (information or ideas), and things (machines or equipment).
2. The tasks a worker performs in relation to people, data, and things can be measured by rating scales.

FJA is applied by an analyst who systematically observes and/or interviews a worker about his or her job. The analyst's principal concern is with what a worker does in performing the job and not with what gets done. Application of FJA involves a sequence of activities. The major phases are described below.

Identifying Job Tasks. The fundamental unit of work under study is the task. A task represents "a fundamental, stable work element consisting of a behavior and a result," (Olson, Fine, Meyers & Jennings, 1981, p. 352).

Preparation of task statements is the most critical step in applying FJA. Much time, care, effort, and expertise must be given to wording a task statement precisely to reflect a job activity. Such explicit task statements are needed to increase the validity of inferences to be drawn about employee specifications. Thus, it is assumed that the more explicit and precise a task statement is, the more accurate are the inferences drawn about these specifications. Fine and Wiley (1977) provide details of the preparation of these statements.

The next three phases of applying FJA are used to measure the complexity of the tasks. To do so, task ratings are made using the following rating scales: Worker Functions Scales, Scale of Worker Instructions, and Scales of General Educational Development.

Table 17–2
Examples of PAQ Job Dimensions and Worker Attributes

Job Dimensions

Specific
  Interpreting what is sensed
  Using various sources of information
  Making decisions
  Using machines/tools/equipment
  Communicating judgments/related information
  Being in stressful/unpleasant environment
  Being alert to changing conditions

Overall
  Operating machines/equipment
  Performing service related activities
  Performing routine/repetitive activities

Worker Attributes

Aptitude
  Verbal comprehension
  Near visual acuity
  Selective attention

Interest
  Pressure of time
  Empathy
  Influencing people

Source: E.J. McCormick, R.C. Mecham, & P.R. Jeanneret, *Position Analysis Questionnaire Technical Manual* (System II) (Logan, Utah: PAQ Services, Inc., 1977), pp. 7–9.

Measuring Worker Functions. The Worker Functions Scales consist of separate ratings of people, data, and things. A part of the data scale is shown in figure 17–4 to provide an illustration. The data rating scale consists of six rating points or levels. Figure 17–4 contains levels 1, 4, and 6. The levels range from simple (comparing) to complex (Synthesizing) functions. In applying the data scale, a job analyst carefully reads a task statement. Definitions of each of the six levels on the scale are studied, and the level is chosen that best describes the data orientation of the task statement. The level selected reflects the *relative complexity* of the task relative to other tasks.

A second measure, orientation, which indicates the relative involvement of a worker with data, people, and things in the task, is also obtained. The measure involves assigning a percentage (usually in units of 5 or 10 percent) to each of the three functions (people, data, things) scored for a task. The sum of the three orientation scores equals 100 percent. The higher is the percentage assigned to a function, the greater is the degree of emphasis of that function in the task rated.

Measuring Worker Instructions. In addition to characterizing tasks in terms of people, data, and things, FJA also provides for measuring the degree of prescription and discretion in task performance. Prescribed aspects of tasks represent those areas in which the worker has no control over what is done. Discretionary components involve those aspects of tasks in which the worker must decide on the execution of tasks. In order to assess the degree of prescription/discretion, the Scale of Worker Instructions is used. It is similar in format and application to the Worker Functions Scales; lower levels represent high task prescription, and higher levels represent high task discretion. Where prescription is high, task performance requires little or no judgment; where discretion is high, mental effort in the form of judgment is required in performing the task (Fine and Wiley, 1977).

Measuring Worker Qualifications. The final set of rating scales is specifically directed toward the problem of determining selected worker qualifications. The Scales of General Education Development (GED) serve as a means for determining basic educational skills needed to perform a task. Thus, the GED scales assess a specific task's demands on a worker's reasoning, mathematical, and language development. The following measures compose the GED scales:

1. *Reasoning Development Scale*—concerns the problem-solving and decision-making demands of a task.

2. *Mathematical Development Scale*—focuses on the mathematical operations ranging from counting to higher mathematics required by a task.

3. *Language Development Scale*—relates to the demands of a task dealing with oral and written materials, covering from simple to complex sources of information (Fine & Wiley, 1977).

Application of these scales is identical to that discussed previously for other FJA ratings. Scores are obtained by choosing the level on a scale that best meets the task characteristics under review.

Figure 17–4. A Partial Data Function Scale of FJA

Level	Definition
	Comparing
1	Selects, sorts, or arranges data, people, or things, judging whether their readily observable functional, structural, or compositional characteristics are similar to or different from prescribed standards ("checks oil level, tire pressure, worn cables"; "observes hand signal of worker indicating movement of load").
	Analyzing
4	Examines and evaluates data (about things, data, or people) with reference to the criteria, standards, and/or requirements of a particular discipline, art, technique, or craft to determine interaction effects (consequences) and to consider alternatives.
	Synthesizing
6	Takes off in new directions on the basis of personal intuitions, feelings, and ideas (with or without regard for tradition, experience, and existing parameters) to conceive new approaches to or statements of problems and the development of system, operational, or aesthetic "solutions" or "resolutions" of them, typically outside existing theoretical, stylistic, or organizational context.

Source: From S. Fine & W. Wiley, "An Introduction to Job Analysis," in E. Fleishman & A. Bass (Eds.), *Studies in personnel and industrial psychology* (Homewood, Ill: Dorsey Press, 1974), p.11.

Threshold Trait Analysis (TTA)

TTA (Lopez, Kesselman & Lopez, 1981) assumes that each position in an organization possesses two broad aspects: the tasks or activities that must be performed and the demands or conditions under which the activities are carried out. A complete position description must contain both. Important worker traits are linked to this job information.

The TTA approach maintains that jobs and worker attributes can be grouped into five broad dimensions: physical, mental, learned, motivational, and social. Through developmental work, Lopez has translated these five dimensions into 21 job functions and 33 worker traits. Areas, functions, and traits are all specifically linked together. That is, each of the five areas is manifest in specific job functions, which, in turn, are linked to specific worker traits. Figure 17–5 presents the linkage of these three variables for one area, mental. The TTA method, therefore, is designed to identify, through responses to questionnaires completed by supervisors and incumbents, which functions and traits are important for the job under consideration and also what level of difficulty or complexity is present. To obtain this information, the following procedures are carried out.

Collecting Trait Data. A group of supervisors are assembled and given instructions in the TTA method. After receiving instructions, each independently answers various questions about the 33 traits being analyzed. A standardized questionnaire, the Threshold Trait Analysis Questionnaire, is used for this purpose. Each trait is described by five separate characteristics: relevance, significance, level, uniqueness, and practicality. Each trait is measured by the ratings obtained from the responses of supervisors.

Generating Task Statements. Task statements are also generated for the job being analyzed. To do this,

Figure 17–5. Job Functions and Traits Related to the Mental Area of the TTA

Area	Job Functions	Traits
Mental	Vigilance and Attention ⟶	Perception Memory Comprehension
	Information Processing ⟶	Problem-solving Creativity

Source: F.M. Lopez, G. Kesselman, & F.E. Lopez, "An Empirical Test of a Trait-Oriented Job Analysis Technique," *Personnel Psychology*, 24, (1981): 479–502.

trained analysts use conventional procedures, such as observation, interview, and written documents. The resulting task statements are of the general form described previously and completely describe the activities of the job. In addition work context data regarding location, individuals interacted with, types of deadlines, and so forth are also identified.

Collecting Demand Data. Third, a job inventory questionnaire, the Demand and Task Analysis Questionnaire is administered to job incumbents. This questionnaire is developed primarily from the information obtained from the job analysis. Items are briefly stated and take the form of "my position requires that I . . . " Rating scales are used to indicate such properties as significance, frequency of occurrence, and relevance of the task or demand statement to the job. An attempt is made to obtain large numbers of respondents for each job being analyzed.

The information from these three sources is then used to develop various HRM programs. Of special interest are responses to the questionnaires. Statistical analyses may be performed on responses of both supervisors and incumbants. In addition, responses of these two groups regarding such characteristics as the level and significance of traits and the demands associated with the job are compared.

Guidelines-Oriented Job Analysis (GOJA)

Developed by Biddle (1982), GOJA is a job analysis method that is designed to be a means for developing a job-related selection system based upon the content validity requirements of the 1978 Uniform Guidelines.

The actual use of GOJA can be thought of as a step-by-step process carried out by a job incumbent. Others could apply the method, but it is intended for a knowledgeable incumbent. A participant in GOJA receives a job analysis booklet that is to be completed systematically. The booklet instructs the incumbent and guides him or her through the process until all relevant job content is identified. The steps leading to the development of that part of the product are briefly described below.

Collecting Preliminary Job Data. Initially an employee provides basic data on his or her job, such as job title, job tenure, company tenure, and immediate supervisor. In addition, information is obtained about the machines, tools, and equipment used on the job, number and types of people supervised, types of supervisory tasks performed, level of supervision received, and frequency of contacts with different groups of people.

Identifying Major Job Duties. The incumbent is first required to list four to eight domains of his or her job. A domain is a broad group of job activities such as "credit analysis" or "loan documentation" for the job of a bank loan officer. Next, the duties actually performed by the incumbents for each domain are listed. Duties are defined by Biddle (1982) as a statement that "tells *what* is done, *how* and *why* it is done, and what products are obtained" (p. 15). A comparison of this definition of a duty with the definition of a task discussed earlier suggests that the two meanings are similar.

Rating of Duties. Once the associated duties have been developed, the incumbent is required to rate each duty according to frequency and importance. The frequency ratings indicate whether the duty is performed daily, weekly, monthly, quarterly, semiannually, or annually. The importance of the duties is made by using a two-step or dichotomous rating scale, for which 1 = important and 2 = critical. Critical duties are those duties in which major problems are perceived to result if they are performed poorly. Those duties that are not quite as critical to job performance are rated as important.

Identifying Knowledge and Skills. The incumbent is then asked to list the major knowledge and skills that are needed to perform the job. In doing this, respondents are first to list specific oral communication, mathematical, writing, and reading skills. After supplying information for these four general areas, the respondent is to list other, more specific skills and knowledge (such as analysis of investment data, determination of risk in loan applications, and knowledge of bank loans). For each entry, the respondent must indicate the exact domain and duty(s) that require the knowledge or skill listed. Also for each entry, it is necessary to indicate whether someone could learn the listed knowledge or skill within 8 hours or less.

Identifying Other Worker Characteristics. The next group of data concerns physical characteristics required on the job. The incumbent responds to 10 major activities (such as hearing, seeing, speaking, body movement, climbing) indicating specific examples of these activities. In addition the specific job domain(s) and duty(s) that require these physical activities must also be indicated. Finally, the respondent identifies any license, certificate, equipment, travel, or work schedule requirements of the job.

Iowa Merit Employment System (IMES)

IMES is similar to GOJA in its objectives. It is a systematic, multistep process that is designed to lead to content valid selection devices such as tests. There are, however, some important similarities and differences between GOJA and IMES. In terms of similarities, both IMES and GOJA were developed for users following a content validation model. The methods are aimed at a single job or class of jobs. Differences in the methods tend to involve the procedural steps taken in implementing the methods. For example, whereas GOJA typically involves the use of incumbents working alone or possibly in groups as analysts, IMES stresses the use of supervisors and incumbents working together in groups to identify relevant job content. In order to understand better the use of IMES, we will review the major steps taken in its application.

Job content information is collected through administration of a questionnaire called the Job Analysis Questionnaire for Selection Device Content Validation (Iowa Merit Employment Department, 1977). The questionnaire is basically a workbook to be completed by individuals serving as job agents or informants. Specifics in the application of the method can vary from one situation to the next, but the following major phases are common to most uses.

Selecting Job Agents. The first step is the identification of individuals or agents who can serve as expert informants about the job or job classes being studied. Most often these individuals are a combination of incumbents and supervisors serving in the role of subject matter experts (SMEs).

Managers supervising persons in the job being studied are initially asked to nominate individuals who can serve as SMEs. Nominations can be made on any number of criteria, but minimum qualifications such as the following might be used: the SME should work in one of the jobs or classes being studied; a chosen individual should have a minimum of six months (or, perhaps, one year) of job experience; and the SME should have demonstrated successful performance on the job. The objective is to choose approximately twelve individuals who can serve as SMEs.

Developing Job Tasks and KSAs. Once the SMEs have been chosen, they are assembled into one group with a leader. It is the leader's role to facilitate the collection and analysis of job data from the group. After a brief orientation period, SMEs are asked to generate a listing of the tasks performed on the job. The goal is to be exhaustive in task development at this point.

Task statements are almost identical in nature to those previously described. The actual editing of the job tasks according to the suggested format may be completed by the group leader or by the assembled SMEs. Essentially, the same procedures are repeated for the development of worker KSA statements.

Rating Job Tasks and KSAs. After an acceptable pool of tasks has been created, task statements are distributed to approximately sixty additional SMEs organized into groups of twelve. These SME groups are then asked to judge each task according to factors such as frequency of task performance, time spent, and criticality/significance of error. Following the rating of tasks, the SMEs are asked to review their ratings and then rank each task in terms of its importance relative to all other tasks. Similar procedures are also followed for the rating and ranking of KSA statements.

Ratings and rankings of job tasks and KSA statements are then statistically analyzed to produce, among other data, frequency distributions, means, and reliability estimates. These data are used to determine the most important tasks and KSAs.

Job Element Method (JEM)

Whereas previous methods of job analysis began with identification of tasks or basic work functions, JEM (Primoff, 1975) has a different orientation. Basically, it is a process designed to identify the characteristics of superior workers on a job. These characteristics are what Primoff calls *job elements*. Once identified, the elements are translated into more specific characteristics called subelements. The JEM involves the following steps.

Selecting a Panel of Raters. On the whole, success of the JEM depends upon judgements provided by a panel of experts. The group or panel chosen typically consists of about six incumbents or supervisors working as raters or subject matter experts. Individuals used are those who know the requirements of a job and can recognize characteristics of superior performers.

Developing Job Elements. After a panel of experts has been assembled, the next step is to develop a comprehensive list of job elements and subelements. Panel members are told that they have been brought together to identify KSAs and personal characteristics that could be used to select superior workers on the job under study. Appropriate definitions and training are provided.

Rating the Elements and Subelements. Each panel member independently rates the elements and subelements identified in the previous step. These ratings are made with respect to the element's usefulness in selecting superior employees for the job.

Once the ratings have been made, quantitative rating indexes are computed for each of the elements and subelements. Decisions as to which elements and subelements should be included in selection are based on the computed indexes.

Allocating Subelements to Elements. The indexes computed in the previous step are used to select the relevant subelements and elements describing superior performers. The next step in using JEM data is to group the elements and subelements on the basis of similarity in order to describe important dimensions of worker attributes.

Developing Job Tasks from Subelements. The final step of the job analysis is to develop task statements for each subelement. Primoff, Clark, and Caplan (1982) recommend the use of FJA to develop and characterize task statements. Once all necessary task statements have been prepared, they are rated on the FJA scales. At the conclusion of these steps, there should be a list of important elements of the job, a list of the worker qualities for each element, and a specification of the tasks that link these worker qualities to requirements of the job.

A COMPARISON OF JOB ANALYSIS METHODS

Brumback, Romashko, Hahn, and Fleishman (1974) have proposed a series of criteria that should be considered in judging the potential usefulness of methods for collecting job information. We have taken most of their considerations plus an additional one, cost of applying a method, suggested by Sistrunk and Smith (1980) and evaluated each of the methods previously described. Our evaluations are summarized in table 17–3 and are discussed below. Before reviewing our evaluations, a cautionary comment should be made. Our assessments are based principally on subjective judgements. Little objective data are available for assessing many of these techniques; the ratings shown come from our own as well as others' opinions. So, in

Table 17–3
Summary Evaluation of Eight Job Analysis Methods

Evaluation Factor	Interview	Task Inventory	PAQ	FJA	TTA	GOJA	IMES	JEM
Currently operational?	Yes	Yes	Yes	Yes	Yes	Yes	Yes	Yes
Off-the self?	No	No	Yes	In Part	In Part	In Part	In Part	In Part
Occupational versatility?	High	Moderate/ High	High	High	High	High	Moderate/ High	High
Standardization?	No	Yes	Yes	No	In Part	No	No	No
User/respondent acceptability?	High	Moderate/ High	Low/ Moderate	High	High	High	Moderate/ High	Moderate/ High
Required amount of job analyst Training?	Moderate	Low	Moderate	High	Moderate/ High	Low/ Moderate	Moderate/ High	Moderate/ High
Sample size?	Small	Large	Small	Small	Moderate	Moderate	Small	Small
Reliability?	Unknown	High	High	High	Unknown	Unknown	Moderate/ High	Unknown
Cost?	Moderate/ High	Moderate/ High	Moderate/ High	Moderate/ High	Moderate/ High	Moderate/ High	Moderate/ High	Low/ Moderate

Source: Brumback, Romashko, Hahn, & Fleishman (1974, pp. 102–107).

studying the table, the reader should be aware that different users may hold different views about these methods.

Currently Operational

Has the method been tested and refined so that it is now operational and ready for use? Each of the methods reviewed in this chapter has been tested and can be adopted for use. However, the fact that these methods are available should not be interpreted to mean that they are equally suitable for every user or purpose.

Off-the-Shelf

Is the methodological instrument involved ready-made, or must it first be designed and constructed? Only one method, the PAQ, can be considered an off-the-shelf method ready for application without requiring further data collection activities. Methods such as GOJA, JEM, IMES, PAQ, and TTA are, in part, ready for use, but additional developments are necessary. These developments consist of specifying the tasks or job elements required in a specific job.

Existing rating scales are then applied to the identified tasks or elements. Methods like the task inventory require the development of task content as well as associated rating scales for characterizing these tasks. Although it may appear that off-the-shelf measures are preferable, Brumback et al. (1974) have suggested that methods involving the determination of specific task content are more appropriate for some HRM purposes than those having ready-made content. Thus, in some situations, methods utilizing tailored measures *may* be more desirable than those incorporating preexisting measures.

Occupational Versatility

To what extent can the method be applied to a wide variety of jobs? On the whole, the various techniques can be applied to a wide variety of jobs. However, those that focus principally on tasks may be limited to jobs in which is easy to describe task content. For instance, in jobs such as managerial ones, it may be difficult to describe completely their content using typical task statements. Therefore, task-based questionnaires may not be as occupationally versatile as methods like PAQ that deal with broader worker functions.

Standardization

Are the procedures used with the method so structured that data collected from different sources at different times can be compared? Methods that use small groups of analysts in collecting job information may not have the capability of producing comparable data. For example, where different panels of subject matter experts are used to develop employee specifications for a job, such as with JEM, different lists of specifications may be developed by the different panels. In contrast, because the PAQ required job analysts to use a structured procedure for rating a specified list of work behaviors, it is the most standardized of the methods reviewed.

User-Respondent Acceptability

To what extent is the method acceptable to respondents and users of the method? Most of the job analysis methods are at least minimally acceptable. However, it seems task-based methods create problems for some respondents because of their length. In order to complete many of the data collection devices used in these methods, respondents are sometimes required to spend rather lengthy, tedious periods of time completing the appropriate materials. Most respondents would prefer briefer, easier types of measures. Levine, Ash, and Bennett (1980) showed the PAQ as receiving some of the most unfavorable ratings by users among four methods studied.

Required Amount of Job Analyst Training

How much training must a job analyst receive in order to apply the method? FJA appears to require the highest level of training. The reason is that FJA places a premium on the identification and correct preparation of task statements. In order to apply FJA correctly, training is mandatory not only in task development but in applying FJA rating scales to the specified tasks.

Methods like IMES, JEM, and TTA can also require moderate levels of analyst preparation. Since these methods employ a specific sequence of activities to be performed by an analyst, one should be totally familiar with the steps required for application. Also, these methods frequently involve group application;

thus, an analyst must also be prepared to direct group meetings and conduct group job analyses.

Sample Size

How many respondents or sources of information are required to produce dependable job analysis data? More than any other technique, the PAQ involves the fewest number of respondents, typically as few as four. JEM is also efficient in this respect, requiring approximately six to eight participants. These methods contrast with ones such as the task inventory, which may involve hundreds of respondents. The questions facing users of methods like the PAQ and JEM are how reliable these few judges are and how generalizable the results are. Careful choices should be made in selecting job analysts who are knowledgeable about the job and possess strong verbal ability.

Reliability

Will the method provide consistent, dependable results? Most of these methods can yield reliable job data. For some methods, such as the interview and GOJA, sufficient research has not been conducted to verify their ability to provide consistently reliable data. In contrast, IMES, PAQ, and TTA have established procedures for determining the extent to which analysts agree in their job assessments.

Cost

What is the estimated cost of the method? (Cost includes cost of materials, necessary training, consulting assistance, salary of job analysts, and clerical support.) In terms of direct dollar expenditures, the PAQ is probably the least expensive of all of the methods. However, there may be large expenses associated with training and data collection. JEM can also be relatively inexpensive; however, panels of job experts have to be convened on several occasions. Thus, indirect costs associated with taking key personnel from their jobs for extended periods must be considered. Task inventories can be rather expensive to develop, apply, and analyze. Because task inventories must be tailored to a job, costs will increase accordingly. Generally, the more tailored the approach is, the greater the associated costs are.

USE OF JOB ANALYSIS METHODS IN HRM

Chapter 13 described the use of job analysis information in HRM activities. As it points out, this information should be the basis for the development of HRM functions. However, as should be apparent from this chapter, the various job analysis methods are not interchangeable in terms of the specific information produced. Therefore, there are differences in the effectiveness of the various methods for use in specific HRM functions.

This issue of effectiveness has been studied by Levine, Ash, Hall, and Sistrunk (1983) and these results adapted by Holley and Jennings (1987). Specifically, Levine et al. used the ratings of ninety-three job analysts to measure the effectiveness of seven job analysis techniques for eleven HRM purposes. It is not completely clear what factors account for the differences in ratings of the job analysts among the job analysis methods. However, based on Levine et al.'s comments, it is our opinion that these differences depend upon the specificity of the information yielded by the primary data collection vehicles of each method.

Holley and Jennings used these ratings to evaluate five of the previously described methods (Task Inventory, PAQ, FJA, TTA, and JEM) on eight HRM purposes. In doing this, the mean ratings of the ninety-six analysts were modified into a dichotomous scale to indicate either below-average effectiveness or average or above-average effectiveness.

For our general purpose, we have used the dichotomous scale of Holly and Jennings to rate the three other methods described in this article (Job Analysis Interview, GOJA, and IMES). Table 17–4 contains the ratings of all eight methods. Remember that the data in this table are a mix of modified ratings of job analysts and our opinion.

The Job Analysis Interview, Task Inventory, GOJA, and IMES are highly rated on all of the HRM functions. Each of these four directly produces task and KSA statements that are specific to the job of interest. In addition, these statements are rated on such characteristics as importance and criticality. The resulting information therefore is complete and directly useful in the development of HRM functions. Other methods (JEM, PAQ, and TTA) are limited in that they do not produce task statements directly but incorporate such techniques as the interview or the task inventory to provide such information.

Table 17–4
Effectiveness Ratings of Job Analysis Methods

Purposes	Job Analysis Methods							
	Interview	Task Inventory	PAQ	FJA	TTA	GOJA	IMES	JEM
Job descriptions	+	+	0	+	0	+	+	0
Job specifications	+	+	+	+	+	+	+	+
Human resource planning	+	+	0	+	0	+	+	0
Job design	+	+	0	+	0	+	+	0
Performance appraisal	+	+	0	+	0	+	+	+
Training	+	+	0	+	0	+	+	+
Job evaluation	+	+	+	+	0	+	+	0
Legal/quasi-legal requirements	+	+	+	0	0	+	+	0

Source: Holley & Jennings (1987, p. 147). Note: +: average or above; 0: below average.

REFERENCES

Biddle, R.E. (1982) *Guidelines oriented job analysis.* Sacramento, CA: Biddle and Associates, Inc.

Brumback, G.B., Romashko, T., Hahn, C.P., & Fleishman, E.A. (1974). *Model procedures for job analysis, test development and validation.* Washington, DC: American Institutes for Research.

Fine, S.A., & Wiley, W.W. (1971). *An introduction to functional job analysis: Methods for manpower analysis* (Monograph No. 4), Kalamazoo, MI: W.E. Upjohn Institute.

Fine, S., & Wiley, W. (1977). *An introduction to functional job analysis: A scaling of selected tasks from the social welfare field.* Kalamazoo MI: W.E. Upjohn Institute for Employment Research.

Fleishman, E.A. (1979). Evaluating physical abilities required by jobs. *Personnel Administrator, 24,* 82–87.

Holley, H., & Jennings, K. (1987). *Personnel/human resource management contributions and activities.* Hinsdale, IL: Dryden Press.

Iowa Merit Employment Department (1977). *Job analysis questionnaire for selection device development.* Des Moines: Iowa Merit Employment Department.

Levine, E.L., Ash, R.A., & Bennett, N. (1980). Exploratory comparative study of four job analysis methods. *Journal of Applied Psychology, 65,* 524–535.

Levine, E.L., Ash, R.A., Hall, H., & Sistrunk, F. (1983). Evaluation of job analysis methods by experienced job analysts. *Academy of Management Journal, 26,* 339–347.

Lopez, F.M., Kesselman, G., & Lopez, F.E. (1981). An empirical test of a trait-oriented job analysis technique. *Personnel Psychology, 34,* 479–502.

McCormick, E.J. (1979). Job information: Its development and applications. In D. Yoder and H.G. Heneman (Eds.), *ASPA handbook of personnel and industrial relations.* Washington, DC: BNA Books.

McCormick, E.J., Jeanneret, P.R., & Mecham, R.C. (1972). A study of job characteristics and job dimensions as based on the Position Analysis Questionnaire (PAQ). *Journal of Applied Psychology, 56,* 347–368.

Marquardt, L.D., and McCormick, E.J. (1972). *Attribute ratings and profiles of the job elements of the Position Analysis Questionnaire (PAQ).* West Lafayette, IN: Purdue University, Occupational Research Center.

Mecham, R.C., & McCormick, E.J. (1969). *The rated attribute requirements of job elements in the Position Analysis Questionnaire.* West Lafayette, IN: Purdue University, Occupational Research Center.

Morsh, J.E., & Archer, W.B. (1967). *Procedural guide for conducting occupational surveys in the United States Air Force* (PRL-TR-67-11, AD-664-36). Lackland Air Force Base, TX: Personnel Research Laboratory, Aerospace Medical Division.

Olson, H.C., Fine, S.A., Myers, D.C., & P.G. Jennings (1981). The use of functional job analysis in establishing performance standards for heavy equipment operators. *Personnel Psychology, 34,* 352.

PAQ Services, Inc. (1977). *Job analysis manual for the Position Analysis Questionnaire (PAQ).* Logan, UT: PAQ Services, Inc.

Primoff, E.S. (1975). *How to prepare and conduct job element examinations* (TS-75-1). Washington, DC: Personnel Research and Development Center, U.S. Civil Service Commission.

Primoff, E.S., Clark, C.L., & Caplan, J.R. (1982). *How to prepare and conduct job element examinations: Supplement.* Washington, DC: Office of Personnel Management, Office of Personnel Research and Development.

Sistrunk, F., & Smith, P.L. (1980) *Critiques of job analysis methods* (vol. 2, Grant Number 78-CD-AX-0003). Washington, DC: Office of Criminal Justice Education and Training, Law Enforcement Assistance Administration.

U.S. Civil Service Commission (1983). *Job analysis: Developing and documenting data.* Washington, DC: U.S. Civil Service Commission, Bureau of Intergovernmental Personnel Programs.

U.S. Department of Labor. U.S. Training and Employment Service (1972). *Handbook for analyzing jobs.* Washington, DC: U.S. Government Printing Office.

18 JOB ANALYSIS PROCEDURES FOR HIGHER-LEVEL EXECUTIVE AND PROFESSIONAL POSITIONS

Melany E. Baehr

The successive governmental guidelines on employee selection procedures that followed the 1964 and 1972 Civil Rights Acts and the establishment of the Equal Employment Opportunity Commission in 1965 had a significant influence on industrial-organizational research. One outcome was the attention focused on the role of job analysis as a prerequisite for selection validation research and for other human resource procedures. This was very evident in the 1978 Uniform Guidelines on Employee Selection Procedures which encouraged multiunit as opposed to the job-specific validations required by the 1970 U.S. Equal Employment Opportunity Commission Guidelines and which also introduced the concept of the "transportability" of validated selection procedures. Transportability was defined as the use of properly conducted criterion validation results by an organization that had not participated in a validation when "the incumbents in the user's job and the incumbents in the job or group of jobs on which the validity study was conducted perform substantially the same work behaviors, as shown in appropriate job analyses both of the job or group of jobs on which the validity study was performed and on the job for which the selection procedure is to be used" (1978 Uniform Guidelines, excerpted from *Federal Register,* 1978, p. 38299). This clearly obviated the necessity for repeated validations. Furthermore, the Uniform Guidelines for the first time recognized not only performance criteria but also content and construct validation procedures. As in the demonstration of transportability, one essential requirement for the implementation of the two latter procedures was an accurate and definitive description of the work behaviors in the position.

During the years 1962–1982 the Human Resources Center of the University of Chicago conducted fifty-three major performance criterion validation studies for higher-level executive and nonmanagement specialist personnel (Baehr, 1984). As could be expected, the bulk of the studies (forty-four of fifty-three) were

conducted for occupations in which typically large numbers of employees performed the same functions, such as groups of first-line supervisors or a sales force. Six of the fifty-three studies were for middle management personnel, and only three were conducted at general management and vice-presidential levels. Furthermore, the latter three studies were possible only by combining the personnel at that level of functioning across all the functional departments in the organization.

It was clear that even the more flexible 1978 Guidelines did not provide a feasible approach to validations for higher-level positions where the functions performed are not immediately observable sample sizes are typically small and, at top levels, clearly similar positions may be held by no more than two or three people. The fact that successful placement in these positions is often critical for the future success of the organization led to a search for a more generalized approach to validation of selection procedures for these top-level personnel.

Many psychologists, including Guion (1976), have emphasized the necessity of general principles in establishing a science, and many approaches to generalization have been taken in the personnel field. In addition to the *Guidelines* approaches, there is the concept of validity generalization exemplified by the metaanalyses of large numbers of job-specific validations conducted by Hunter and Schmidt (Schmidt & Hunter, 1977; Schmidt, Hunter, Pearlman & Shane, 1979).

Another, less well-known approach has been called synthetic validity and later, and more appropriately, component validity Mecham & McCormick, 1969). In contrast to traditional validations, which attempt to use test measures to predict performance on the job as a whole, the object of component validity research is to predict performance on the separate, identified components of the job. This research is predicted on the assumption that the requirements of any given job component will be comparable in the case of any job in which that same component occurs. It follows that if a matrix could be established that related the separate job components to the required measurable attributes or test scores, then it would be possible to deduce the required attributes for any job with known components. This approach not only avoids the necessity of job-specific validations but even the restrictions with respect to small sample size.

The prerequisite for all of the approaches to the validation of selection procedures discussed is a viable and professionally accepted job analysis for identifying the functions performed in the positions in question. The practical and technical characteristics of a job analysis instrument that would facilitate human resource procedures for the higher-level positions in organizations could be quite clearly formulated. The first most obvious characteristic was that it should clearly differentiate among the key or bench-

mark jobs in the population of higher-level positions. Second, on the practical side, the job analysis procedure needed to be cost- and time-effective for large-scale use in industrial organizations. Third, the fulfillment of this requirement indicated that it should be implementable by job incumbents, their supervisors, or other knowledgeable organizational personnel rather than by specially trained job analysts. Fourth, the job analysis procedure needed to be useful on its own account for such organization development programs as job description and design, job clarification, and the identification of training needs. This requirement indicated that the job analysis procedure should be "work oriented" with the job descriptors related to work behavior rather than "worker oriented" with the job descriptors related to the human attributes required for successful work performance.

A REVIEW OF JOB ANALYSIS PROCEDURES

Although the requirements of work-oriented content and implementation by job incumbents indicated that the choice of relevant job analysis procedures would be fairly restricted, a rather wide-ranging review was undertaken to see if other approaches would yield important supplemental information about the job or could be adapted for use with the target population. While there are many different ways of classifying approaches to job analysis, we found it useful first to divide them into the less-structured procedures on the one hand, and, on the other hand, the structured procedures that used standard classification systems or standardized instruments as the major vehicle in the analysis. The latter were again divided on the basis of the job descriptors used in the instrument, primarily into instruments using work-oriented (behavior traits) as opposed to work-oriented (job activities) descriptors.

Less-Structured Approaches to Job Analysis

The less structured job analysis procedures can be used to elicit information about the activities performed in a job or the human attributes required for the performance of the job. Of these approaches, the most frequently used are various types of interviews with incumbents, supervisors, or others familiar with

the job; observation and analysis of the job; or actual performance of the job by the job analyst. The observation of performance is more readily applied to repetitive job cycles as found in some industrial settings or to such positions as municipal bus operator and police officer, where observation can take the form of "ride-alongs" through a tour of duty. For most higher-level staff or line executive positions, however, observation of performance on the job would be difficult to achieve, if not disruptive and inappropriate.

Interviews may be in-depth interviews conducted with individuals or conducted in a group setting with incumbents, supervisors, managers, and members of the personnel department. One variant of the group interview is "brainstorming," or the normative group process. The basic principle here is the deliberate alternation of the thought process, that is, to use the creative mind at one time and the judicial mind at another time rather than trying to think critically and imaginatively at the same time.

These procedures provide insight into the requirements of a job and a wealth of information not readily obtainable by other means. In addition, they often provide the content for the development of scales and instruments used in the more structured procedures. An example of this is the behavior observation scaling methodology based on the critical incidents technique pioneered by Flanagan (1954). The critical incident technique was an outgrowth of the Aviation Psychology Program of the U.S. Air Force in World War II, established in 1941. Through a series of studies such as the identification of the specific reasons for failure to learn to fly, identification of the specific reasons for failure of bombing missions, and a large-scale systematic effort to gather specific incidents of effective and ineffective behavior in combat, the general principles of the critical incident technique were developed. In industrial and business settings, where it has been used by a number of researchers, the technique translates into the systematic collection of critical incidents of behavior, which lead, respectively, to good or poor performance outcomes.

The technique is the basis of the "behavioral events" interviews conducted by McBer and Company (McClelland, 1978) and has also been extensively used by Dunnette and his associates. Of particular interest was a study by one of Dunnette's associates, Borman (1973), in which he constructed Behavior Observation Scales for line supervisors. He then hypothesized the behavior attributes that would be required for successful performance of each of the identified behavior dimensions and selected tests he considered to be measures of the hypothesized attributes. Finally, the tests were cross-validated against performance ratings on the identified performance dimensions and useful validities obtained for five of the six dimensions. It is conceivable that Behavior Observation Scales (BOS) could have been constructed for key occupational groups in the population of higher-level positions and the test battery or other selection procoedure used to predict BOS performance ratings. But the scales are specific to occupation and time of construction and would have required redevelopment for changes in technology or for any new jobs emerging in an expanding economy and would thus not have been cost-effective.

Structured Worker-Oriented Approaches

A review of these approaches provided valuable information on methods used to link taxonomies of work behavior and human attributes. Notable among these was the extensive work done by McCormick and his associates in the course of the development of the Position Analysis Questionnaire (PAQ) (McCormick, Jeanneret, & Mecham, 1969).

The 182 behaviorally related job activities (job elements) in the PAQ used in the development of a job taxonomy are the result of replicative factor analyses reported by Jeanneret and McCormick (1969) for

Form A of the PAQ and a later study by Marquardt and McCormick (1974a) using Form B of the PAQ for a sample of 3,700 jobs. The link between this job taxonomy and human attributes was established, again, through replicative studies with Form A (Mecham & McCormick, 1969) and Form B (Marquardt & McCormick, 1974b) and produced similar results. In the Form B study, eight to eighteen industrial psychologists rated the relevance of seventy-six human attributes to each of the job elements of the PAQ with satisfactorily high pooled reliability ratings. Thirty-seven of the seventy-six human attributes were obtained from a list produced by Theologus, Romanshko, and Fleishman (1970) as a result of efforts undertaken at the American Institutes for Research to provide a unifying set of variables for describing human task performance. The thirty-seven attributes, each with its own definition, covered human performance in the sensory, perceptual, cognitive, psychomotor, and physical areas.

There was substantial correspondence in the factorial structures obtained from the separate principal components analyses of the job element data and the attribute data. Dunnette's comments in connection with the earlier study are also appropriate here:

> The underlying similarity of the two sets of factor structures is, in a way, a kind of first requirement for concluding that fundamental similarities exist between taxonomies based on estimated importance of task elements for getting jobs done and the aptitudinal and adaptive attributes judged to be important in each of those task elements. This is an important finding, for it lays the groundwork for the further argument (basic to the concept of synthetic validity) that if a given kind of work activity, task element, or job dimension is found to be common to different jobs, then the human attributes necessary for doing those jobs ought also to be the same or similar. (Dunnette, 1976, p. 508)

The PAQ job dimension scores and attribute profiles have been related to the dimensions of the General Aptitude Test Battery (GATB) (Dvorak, 1956) and in more recent studies (McCormick, DeNisi & Shaw, 1979) to commercially used tests.

Primoff is one of the rather limited number of practioners who has implemented personnel procedures based on component validity studies. The actual procedure was called the J- (Job) coefficient (Primoff, 1955). It was developed for use by the U.S. Civil Service Commission for selecting tests for trades and industrial jobs in the federal service at a time when emergency manpower needs placed a heavy strain on the testing facilities of the commission. Primoff describes the J-coefficient as an approximation of the coefficient obtained from traditional validation procedures, a view with which Wherry (1955) concurs in his review of the coefficient. Since the 1950s there have been considerable refinements and additions to the job elements, including measures of potential and motivation (Primoff, 1969). Still later, Primoff (1972) reported the results of a study that showed that, with proper directions and definition of the elements, the job analysis could be performed by knowledgeable incumbents and supervisors (as opposed to job analysts) and that six raters were sufficient to achieve acceptable reliability.

These are important results for the objectives of the required job analysis procedure since, from the outset, it was intended that the job analysis should be conducted by organization personnel, and because after the relationships between the job analysis measures and measures of human attributes had been established, it seemed likely that component validity studies would be one approach taken in investigating the validity of the procedure.

A number of other well-developed job analysis systems should at least be briefly mentioned. One of these is Functional Job Analysis (FJA), developed in the course of research undertaken for the third edition of the *Dictionary of Occupational Titles* (DOT) (1965). The original application was to improve job placement and counseling for workers registering for employment at local employment service offices. Since then, FJA has been adapted for use in business and industrial organizations (Fine, 1974). The first step in applying FJA for a given position is the development of task statements with a strictly defined structure by job analysts. The task is then rated on ordinal scales with respect to the handling of data, people, and things. For a complete analysis, the job is also rated on additional scales of human abilities such as "general educational development," "mathematical development," and "language development."

Among other well-known job analysis procedures is an occupational classification system developed by Holland et al. (1970), based on the theory that personality types are reflected by vocational choice. In this system classifications are made with respect to six categories of jobs defined as Realistic, Investigative, Artistic, Social, Enterprising, and Conventional. Occupations are coded with respect to three of the classifications. For example, a sales position may be coded ESC, which indicates that incumbents most resemble people in the Enterprising occupations and, to a lesser extent, those in the Social and Conventional occupations. Holland et al.

describe reasonably successful attempts to link the six categories of jobs to job dimension scores on the PAQ. In a later study, an attempt was made to link the Holland and the Owens (1968) background data classification systems (Neiner & Owens, 1985). While these systems are useful for many purposes, they are clearly not geared toward job description in terms of work activities, job clarification, or job design.

Structured Work-Oriented Approaches

If a work-oriented approach is taken, a decision must be made concerning the optimal level of the specificity of the job descriptors. Specific tasks and activities can necessarily describe only single and possibly fractionated aspects of the job. Use of more generalized items is likely to describe the work behavior underlying broader job functions. Very generalized items describing work behavior are likely to shade into attributes that facilitate that bahavior. The next logical extrapolation is that jobs be described directly in terms of the human attributes required for their performance. A graphic presentation of the relationship between the degree of specificity of the job descriptor items used in structured, pencil-and-paper job analysis instruments and the range of jobs covered is given in figure 18–1, using as benchmarks some of the job analysis systems reviewed in this chapter.

The use of specific tasks as job descriptors in a job-oriented job analysis approach was typified by Morsh (1964) in his studies of positions in the U.S. Air Force. Morsh's work centered around the construction of job inventories: one, for example, to cover all levels of an airman career ladder from apprentice through journeyman and supervisor to superintendent; another for officer jobs from junior officer through company grade to staff officer. These inventories can be economically administered to large numbers of incumbents, and the resulting data can be subjected to a computerized hierarchical grouping procedure to identify and describe job types. They admirably fulfilled Morsh's objectives of facilitating training and promotion for consecutive positions in a particular Air Force career ladder. However, even if the approach were adapted to industrial occupations, the extreme specificity of the items as exemplified by "Types Air Force Form 246 (Record of Emergency Data) whenever a change occurs" would preclude its use for comparisons across functional departments.

An example of an approach with descriptors that dealt with broader job functions, determined through

Figure 18–1. Relationship between the Content of Job Descriptors and Range of Jobs Covered

Content of Job Descriptors	Single Jobs	Same Category of Job	Different Jobs
Specific			Required Attributes for Any Combination of Work Behaviors — McCormick, Jeanneret & Mecham (1969) Required Attributes Related to Tests — Primoff (1955)
General		Managers — Tornow & Printo (1976) Managers — Hemphill (1959) Supervisors — Prien (1963) Clerical — Chalupsky (1962)	
Generic	Task Inventories for U.S. Air Force Positions — Morsh (1965)		

Range of Jobs Covered

factor analysis, for a particular occupation was the research done on clerical personnel by Chalupsky (1962) and the Supervisor Position Description Questionnaire developed by Prien (1963). On an even broader level was a position description procedure for executives that employed ten factorially determined dimensions, developed by Hemphill (1959). This could be applied across companies and across business functions in a way that would make clear the similarities and differences among executive positions regardless of the company in which the positions existed.

Tornow and Pinto (1976) elaborated and considerably refined the original research conducted by Hemphill and developed the Management Position Description Questionnaire (MPDQ). Tornow and Pinto's approach was a factor analysis of MPDQ responses from 433 position incumbents, covering a wide range of managerial levels and functions, which revealed thirteen independent job factors. All positions were then compared and grouped into ten homogeneous clusters in terms of the similarities and differences in their thirteen-factor job profiles. These

clusters, which were cross-validated on a hold-out sample of fifty-six cases, form the bases of a managerial job taxonomy. Six of the ten clusters are defined in terms of their mean profiles on the thirteen position factors. The first three defined clusters represent upper, middle, and beginning management positions, and the remaining three clusters represent marketing, personnel, and legal functional departments.

While the MPDQ came the closest of the instruments reviewed to satisfying the needs of the hypothesized job analysis instrument, there was at least one way in which it did not meet the stated objectives of the instrument. First, as its name implies, the MPDQ was developed exclusively for managerial positions, while the purpose of the job analysis instrument was to cover a wider range of higher-level positions, including such nonmanagement positions as engineers, architects, lawyers, computer analysts, actuarial personnel, and sales representatives. As a result of this review, a quantitative work-oriented job analysis instrument was constructed that was suitable for the analysis of both higher-level management and professional staff positions.

DEVELOPMENT AND DESCRIPTION OF THE MANAGERIAL AND PROFESSIONAL JOB FUNCTIONS INVENTORY (MP-JFI)

The first decision to be made in the construction of this work-oriented job analysis instrument was the level of specifity of the items or job descriptors. Since the instrument was intended for use across a number of different occupations and organizational settings, it was decided to use "generic" job items that would refer to the underlying job requirements rather than the specific functions performed. For example, "the ability to make accurate sales forecasts" would almost certainly be regarded as "relevant" or "important" for sales positions and would probably be regarded as "not relevant" by most managerial and professional personnel. Yet there is some element of forecasting in many higher-level positions. Managers must judge the possible soundness of executive decisions on the basis of past results and present operating conditions. Thus, an item phrased, "the ability to predict future results on the basis of past history and experience," could be regarded as "relevant" for a number of different types of positions. The objective in writing these generic items was to maintain a fine balance between having them sufficiently general with respect to the underlying behavior required to perform the function so that they could be used across occupations but not so general or diluted that they would be equally applicable to all occupations.

The first trial instrument consisted of twelve factorially determined job function dimensions (Baehr, 1967), which were incorporated in a job analysis instrument called the Work Elements Inventory. The Work Elements Inventory received favorable comment in a review of job analysis research by Prien and Ronan (1971). However, despite its relatively successful usage record, the instrument was revised and expanded in the late 1970s in order to incorporate possible new job dimensions created by developments in the economy, by increased governmental controls of the environment, and by changes in personnel policies and practices resulting from the Civil Rights Act of 1964.

Development of the Present Form of the Job Analysis Instrument

Two hundred trial items were assembled in a pencil-and-paper format that could be machine scored. They were administered to a heterogeneous sample of 893 employees. The sample included approximately equal numbers of public and private sector employees and ranged from industrial sales representatives and other nonmanagement specialist personnel to chief executive officers.

A completely new exploratory factor analysis was performed, using a principal axis factor extraction with rotation to orthogonal (Saunders, 1962) and oblique (Hendriksen & White, 1964) solutions. The two solutions of the underlying sixteen dimensions were essentially similar, but the oblique solution was used because it yielded the clearer structure. The stability of the twelve dimensions in the preliminary form of the instrument is attested to by the fact that the original twelve dimensions all appeared again in the second analysis in spite of a ten-year time lapse, a different response technique, and a different sample of employees. The titles of the job function dimensions, with short definitions and illustrative items, are given in table 18–1. The 140 items that contributed to the job functions were randomized and presented in *Managerial and Professional Job Functions Inventory (MP-JFI)* (Baehr, Lonergan & Hunt, 1978).

Table 18–1
Expanded Definitions of the MP-JFI Dimensions

I. ORGANIZATIONAL AREA

1. *Setting Organization Objectives.* Formulating the overall mission and goals of the organization, setting short- and long-range objectives that are significant and measurable and that incorporate future predictions, evaluating alternative structures for future organizational operations (10 items).

    1. Timing major actions to take advantage of the changing factors affecting the organization.

    17. Predicting future trends on the basis of presently available information.

2. *Financial Planning and Review.* Making economic decisions and managing capital assets, establishing a budget and independent controls to ensure that the budget is met, maintaining accurate financial records using up-to-date procedures (6 items).

continued on next page

Table 18–1 *continued*

2. Making decisions on the basis of the organizations economic situation.

18. Maintaining accurate and efficient financial records.

3. *Improving Work Procedures and Practices*. Analyzing, interpreting, and evaluating operating policies within the organizational structure; ensuring that new procedures are installed smoothly (9 items).

3. Interpreting policies and rules of the organization to others.

19. Evaluating the effectiveness of organization structure for implementing procedural innovations.

4. *Interdepartmental Coordination*. Understanding and coordinating the problems and work activities of different departments within the organization, using informal communication lines as well as work committees to gain and disseminate information across the organization (7 items).

4. Knowing where to get information about the different operations in the organization.

20. Understanding the problems of other work groups and departments.

II. LEADERSHIP AREA

5. *Developing and Implementing Technical Ideas*. Originating technical ideas and designs, translating technical ideas into feasible solutions to organizational needs, leading technical projects and writing appropriate reports, helping the organization adjust to and evaluate technical changes (9 items).

5. Translating an idea into a technically operational design.

21. Preparing clear, well-organized reports.

6. *Judgment and Decision Making*. Analyzing incomplete information to make decisions, being flexible in nonroutine decisions, acting upon decisions concerning resource and work force allocation, accepting responsibility for the consequences of both one's own and one's subordinates' decisions (8 items).

6. Analyzing information needed to make decisions.

22. Taking action based on information or judgments received from others.

7. *Developing Group Cooperation and Teamwork*. Encouraging and building work group relations that will lead to better exchange of ideas, improved decision making, more open communication, higher morale, and a sense of purpose; recognizing destructive problems and conflicts within the work group (10 items).

7. Leading the way in building cooperative relationships within the work group.

23. Being alert to the level of morale in the work group.

8. *Coping with Difficulties and Emergencies*. Efficiently working under pressure; effectively handling unexpected problems, day-to-day crises, and emergency situations; quickly analyzing operation breakdowns and setting priorities for action (8 items).

8. Coping with unexpected work and production problems.

24. Recognizing priorities for action in emergencies.

9. *Promoting Safety Attitudes and Practices*. Taking responsibility for the identification and elimination of job safety and health hazards, promoting and communicating safety practices and regulations to employees, investigating possibly job-related accidents and illnesses (9 items).

9. Promoting constructive attitudes toward on-the-job safety and health.

25. Identifying and eliminating safety and health hazards in the workplace.

10. *Communications*. Monitoring and improving both external communication channels and internal upward and downward lines; developing, testing, and seeking feedback on one's own communication skills; conducting effective meetings (8 items).

10. Establishing effective processes for internal and external communication.

58. Developing interpersonal skills to facilitate communication of both facts and feelings.

III. HUMAN RESOURCES AREA

11. *Developing Employee Potential*. Evaluating employees' present performance and potential in order to create opportunities for better utilization of their abilities, examining and responding to employee dissatisfaction, assisting others in overall career development (9 items)

11. Creating opportunities for subordinates to improve their performance.

27. Rewarding good work appropriately.

12. *Supervisory Practices*. Clarifying subordinate's job functions and responsibilities, motivating employees while maintaining discipline and control, seeing that subordinates maintain established standards of performance and accepting personal responsibility for those who do not (9 items).

continued on next page

Table 18–1 *continued*

  44. Making the responsibilities of the job clear to others.
  60. Developing and maintaining effective discipline.

13. *Self-Development and Improvement.* Formulating self-improvement goals, using feedback from others to help assess one's own strengths and weaknesses, improving one's own skills by participating in developmental programs, and by assuming new positions, coordinating personal career goals with organizational need (9 items).

  13. Assessing one's own strengths and weaknesses with a view to improvement.
  45. Actively expanding the scope and responsibilities of one's own job.

14. *Personnel Practices.* Ensuring that the organization adheres to federal equal employment opportunity requirements in its employee selection procedures, keeping informed on current issues and procedures in employee selection, developing and implementing special recruiting and training programs for minority applicants (10 items).

  14. Staying informed about federal and state requirements on equal opportunity hiring.
  30. Helping to integrate members of minority groups into the work force.

IV. COMMUNITY AREA

15. *Promoting Community-Organization Relations.* Staying informed on community social, economic, and political problems and their relevance to and impact upon the organization; accepting responsibility for the ongoing relationship between the organization and the community; actively seeking information from, and disseminating information to, the community about the organization (10 items).

  15. Obtaining information regarding available community resources.
  31. Staying informed on the social, economic, and political problems in the community.

16. *Handling Outside Contacts.* Promoting the organization and its products to outside contacts and clients; handling and entertaining long-term clients, suppliers, and visitors so as to convey the organization's relationship with them; expediting customers' special requests and handling their complaints about the organization.

  32. Meeting with service agents, suppliers, or clients on a periodic follow-up basis.
  48. Making arrangements for the proper handling of important visitors.

STATISTICAL CHARACTERISTICS OF THE MP-JFI DIMENSION SCORES

Job function dimension scores were calculated by summing the importance scale values that the individual had assigned to the items selected to define a factorial dimension. The details of the operational and statistical characteristics of the job function dimension scores are given in the *Mangerial and Professional Job Functions Inventory Interpretation and Research Manual* (Baehr, 1988b). The salient information is summarized below and with greater detail in Baehr (1988a).

Reliability

Cronbach's alpha coefficients for the sixteen job function dimensions based on a sample of 882 vocationally heterogeneous individuals ranged between .48 and .93, with an average of .76. When used operationally, MP-JFI job profiles are based on composites of at least, and preferably more than, ten sets of importance ratings made by incumbents or their supervisors with respect to the job under consideration. The reliability estimates for composite profiles would, of course, be proportionately higher than for a single set of ratings made by an individual. A composite job function profile should provide a very stable operational definition of the key position.

Dimension Intercorrelations

Pearson product moment intercorrelations for the job function dimension scores were calculated. Approximately half of the coefficients (59/120) fell within the range of +.15 to −.15. This indicates that the job functions are not highly correlated but are relatively independent measures. Approximately a quarter of the remaining items (27/120) fell within the range of +.15 to +.45 and another quarter (31/120) within the range of −.15 to −.45. The implication of these results is that the MP-JFI dimensions represent identifiably different functions performed in the position.

ABILITY OF THE MP-JFI TO DIFFERENTIATE AMONG THE FUNCTIONS PERFORMED IN HIGHER-LEVEL POSITIONS

The first requirement for use of the MP-JFI for higher-level personnel was that its sixteen job function dimension scores be capable of differentiating among the functions performed by incumbents in the higher-level positions. For purposes of practical implementation and also in response to research needs, the higher-level occupations were classified by occupational specialty and level of functioning in a matrix consisting of four three-rung hierarchies composed of twelve key occupational groups (see table 18–2). Our experience has been that these occupational groups cover the majority of higher-level positions in business and industrial organizations.

The four hierarchies are the line management hierarchy, starting with first-and second-line supervisors; the professional managerial hierarchy, starting with university-trained engineers, architects, and other hard-science professionals; the traditional sales managerial hierarchy, starting with sales representatives who often hold degrees in the area of their products; and the technical hierarchy, starting with technical specialists such as programmers and computer analysts. The remaining eight key positions are the four middle-level managers and four executive managers of these personnel. It is of interest to note that three of the clusters defined by Tornow and Pinto (1976) as upper, middle, and beginning management resemble the levels of functioning in our classification matrix and that their remaining three identified clusters represent functional departments that show some overlap with the hierarchies in our classification matrix.

The ability of the MP-JFI to differentiate among the twelve key positions in the four three-rung managerial hierarchies was tested empirically through successive analyses of variance using a representative sample of 1,650 employees who had completed the final form of the MP-JFI to describe the relative importance of the functions performed in their present positions (Baehr, in press).

Significant Differences in the Importance of Functions Performed at Different Levels of Organizational Functioning

The statistical significance of the differences among the importance scores for the three occupational levels for the total group of employees (regardless of hierarchy) was determined for each of the sixteen MP-JFI factors through one-way analyses of variance. The results indicated that fourteen of the sixteen dimensions had differences across the three levels that were highly statistically significant. In order to determine whether the MP-JFI could differentiate equally well across the levels in the separate hierarchies, the one-way analyses were run separately for each hierarchy. The results indicated that thirteen of the sixteen MP-JFI dimensions had significantly different importance scores across the three levels in the line hierarchy, thirteen also for the professional hierarchy, and fourteen for the sales hierarchy. In the technical hierarchy, which is the latest and thus least well-defined hierarchy to be added to the matrix classification system, nine of the sixteen MP-JFI functions showed statistically significant differences.

In an attempt to determine which of the MP-JFI functions showed significant differentiations, the

Table 18–2
Managerial Hierarchies

Occupational Level	Line	Professional	Sales	Technical
I	Executives Vice-presidents General managers	Executives Vice-presidents General managers	Executives Vice-presidents General managers	Executives Vice-presidents General managers
II	Middle managers of Line personnel	Middle managers of professional personnel	Middle managers of sales personnel	Middle managers of technical specialist personnel
III	Supervisors (1st and 2nd line)	Nonmanagement professionals (engineers, scientists, lawyers, architects)	Sales representatives (professional sales of products or services)	Technical specialists (actuaries, accountants, analysts, programmers)

average job function scores obtained by the different occupational groups were analyzed. The results of the analysis indicated that top managerial personnel in all hierarchies consistently ascribe significantly greater importance than do entry-level personnel to the traditional top-level functions such as objective setting, decision making, and communications. On the other hand, the functions to which entry-level (Level III) personnel ascribe significantly more importance than their respective managers vary by hierarchy. For example, first-line supervisors in the line hierarchy regard supervisory practices and Personnel Practices as being two of the most important functions in their position; hard scientists and engineers in the professional hierarchy stress the Development of Technical ideas; sales representatives, understandably, stress the Handling of Outside Contacts; and technical specialists in the Technical hierarchy, which includes the financial institutions, emphasize Financial Planning and Review.

A more in-depth analysis of the important functions by hierarchy and level of functioning is given later. This preliminary analysis indicates that the MP-JFI can distinguish among the functions performed at different levels and that the differentiations are logical for the occupations involved.

Significant Differences in the Importance of Functions Performed in Different Hierarchies

An analysis of variance was also run to compare MP-JFI Importance scores across hierarchies. When the analysis was run for the total sample, regardless of level of functioning, all sixteen of the MP-JFI Importance scores showed significant differences. In order to determine at which level of functioning the significant differences occurred, the analyses were run separately at each level. The results indicated that at level III, where four different jobs were being compared (first-line supervisor, professional, sales representative, and technical specialist), all sixteen job functions had significantly different importance scores for the four occupational groups. Only seven of the sixteen job functions had significant differences at the middle management level, and at the top executive level, the number of significant differences dropped to only two out of the sixteen.

Overall, these results show an interesting decrease in the number of MP-JFI functions that differentiate across hierarchies at successively higher occupational levels. The indications are that, regardless of the functional department in which the career is started, if the employee progresses to top management levels, largely similar managerial functions are important for successful performance and that the different professional, technical, or other specialist skills the employee may have are of little consequence. The results also raised the question of whether the Level I positions in the four managerial hierarchies should be treated as a homogeneous occupational group. This would reduce the twelve occupational groups in the original occupational matrix to nine. There are, however, still differences in functions performed by the four top managerial groups, which may have practical as well as statistical significance. A final decision on the number of occupational groups to be included in the matrix must await the results of further studies.

COMMON FUNCTIONS PERFORMED BY LEVEL AND HIERARCHY

The important functions common to the hierarchies at each level were identified using the quite stringent requirement that at least one of the four occupational groups at a given level had an importance value of fifty-four or higher (on an equal-interval, standard score scale of 0 to 100) for the MP-JFI dimension and that the other groups had normalized standard score importance values of at least fifty-three or more for the dimension. This procedure will identify the functions that are both important and common to the hierarchies at each occupational level. Thereafter, to ensure that an important function was not over-looked in any hierarchy, all remaining functions at each level in each hierarchy with a normalized standard score importance value of fifty-three or larger were listed. The only exception to these rules occurs for an importance score of fifty-two for developing technical ideas, inserted in parentheses at Level III in the professional hierarchy. This score was included both because it has appeared with higher importance values in previous analyses of the data and because it was significantly higher for professionals than for executives in the hierarchy.

Common Functions at Each Level

In view of previous discussions, it is not surprising that table 18–3 shows considerable overlap in the functions performed at Level I. Indeed, the six functions with the highest importance values are common to all four hierarchies. These functions are Objective Setting, Judgment and Decision Making, Communications, Developing Employee Potential, Financial Planning, and Developing Teamwork. Intuitively, these make sense as important top-level functions in all hierarchies. In addition, a number of functions are common to two or three hierarchies, and Supervisory Practices is unique to the sales hierarchy, at the executive level.

At Level II, the first five functions listed in table 15–2 are not only common to all four hierarchies at that level but are also shared with the top executives in each hierarchy. It is important to note, however, that the importance levels for these functions are lower at Level II than they are at Level I, as shown in the "Average" column in table 15–2. A further examination of the common factors at Level II suggests that what middle managers have in common is the nurturing of employees and the smoothness of operations in the immediate work group as indicated by

such functions as Developing Employee Potential and Developing Teamwork (both common to all hierarchies), Work Procedures and Practices (common to three hierarchies), and Supervisory Practices (common to two hierarchies). In addition, coordination across functional departments is also considered important, as indicated by the fact that the Interdepartmental Coordination function is common to three hierarchies.

Level III occupational groups have only two functions common to as many as three hierarchies: Self-Development, which could be expected of this younger group of technical specialist personnel at the start of their careers, and Community-Organization Relations. The interaction with the community probably takes somewhat different forms in the different hierarchies. The most direct interaction would be that of sales representatives. In the technical hierarchy, accountants employed by accounting consulting agencies often have direct customer service and account responsibility. The more academically inclined personnel in the professional hierarchy probably represent their organizations through such activities as presentations at professional conventions and consulting with government committees. The remaining functions performed by Level III personnel are either common to only two hierarchies or are unique to each hierarchy.

TOWARD AN INTEGRATED JOB ANALYSIS–BASED HUMAN RESOURCE MANAGEMENT SYSTEM

The development of a single job data base to implement human resource management objectives in an organization is at present more a utopian concept than an achievable reality. Apart from the massive costs and time required for the completion of such a long-range project, both management personnel and a variety of professional and technical specialists must be committed to the project and believe in its eventual benefits. A more feasible approach, often followed in organizations for other human resource procedures such as wage and salary administration, would be to treat the higher-level (exempt) and lower-level (nonexempt) jobs separately.

The multiplicity of specific tasks performed in lower-level jobs (even within one specialty such as clerical occupations) makes it unlikely that they could all be covered by a single task inventory or work-oriented job analysis instrument. However, the successful performance of a bewildering number of

different tasks is determined by the possession of a finite number of human skills and abilities. It would seem to be a reasonable approach, therefore, to identify subsets of lower-level occupations that were homogeneous with respect to required skills through the use of a worker-oriented job analysis procedure such as the PAQ (McCormick, Jeanneret & Mecham, 1969). Thereafter, task inventories could be developed for each occupational subset.

In higher-level positions, the functions performed in large organizations are generally more homogeneous and fewer in number, and they decrease with upward movement in the organization. As discussed earlier, however, to be effective for both management and staff professional positions in different functional departments, the items in the job analysis instrument should reflect the underlying work behaviors. The customization of such an instrument for a particular organization still represents a considerable commit-

Table 18—3
Common Functions Performed by Level and Hierarchy

	Line		Professional	
Level I	Objective Setting	67	*Objective Setting	63
	Decision Making	56	Decision Making	56
	Communications	56	Communications	56
	Dev. Employee Potential	57	Dev. Employee Potential	55
	Financial Planning	56	*Financial Planning	53
	*Dev. Teamwork	55	Dev. Teamwork	53
	Work Practices	54		
	Comm./Org. Relations	53	Comm./Org. Relations	53
			*Interdepartmental Coord.	54
			Personnel Practices	54
	Outside Contacts	53		
Level II	Objective Setting	58	*Objective Setting	60
	Decision Making	56	Decision Making	56
	Communications	53	Communications	56
	Dev. Employee Potential	55	Dev. Employee Potential	55
	*Dev. Teamwork	55	Dev. Teamwork	53
	Financial Planning	56	*Financial Planning	53
	Work Practices	54	Work Practices	54
	Interdepartmental Coord.	57	*Interdepartmental Coord.	57
			Personnel Practices	54
	Comm./Org. Relations	53		
Level III			Self Development	53
			Comm./Org. Relations	56
			*Financial Planning	53
	*Dev. Teamwork	55		
	Coping with Emergencies	59		
			Dev. Technical Ideas	(52)[a]
			*Objective Setting	55
			*Interdepartmental Coord.	54
	Promoting Safety	60		
	Supervisory Practices	54		
	Personnel Practices	54		

[a] included because it has appeared in previous analyses
* functions common to all three levels in a hierarchy

ment, but the benefits that would accrue from the application of the instrument could be readily demonstrated. Some of the applications of a standardized work-oriented job analysis instrument are summarized below.

Job Clarification

It happens not infrequently that the composite job importance profiles for a position obtained separately from the responses of incumbents and their supervisors show significant differences. Under these circumstances, the profiled job function scores and their contributing items could serve as a vehicle for job clarification—in other words, for discussions geared toward getting agreement on job priorities. A consensus concerning job requirements will increase the accuracy of other job analysis applications such as performance appraisal.

Performance Appraisal

The simplest appraisal procedure would be to have supervisors merely rate employees on a scale of unfavorable to favorable performance on the identified important job functions. This procedure requires that

Sales		Technical		Average
Objective Setting	61	Objective Setting	63	63.5
Decision Making	56	Decision Making	56	56.0
*Communications	56	*Communications	56	56.0
Dev. Employee Potential	57	Dev. Employee Potential	55	56.0
Financial Planning	53	*Financial Planning	59	55.2
Dev. Teamwork	53	*Dev. Teamwork	53	53.5
Work Practices	54	Work Practices	54	54.0
		Comm./Org. Relations	54	54.3
		Interpersonal Coord.	54	54.0
Personnel Practices	54			
*Outside Contacts	57			
Supervisory Practices	53			
Objective Setting	55	Objective Setting	58	57.8
Decision Making	53	Decision Making	53	54.5
*Communications	53	*Communications	53	53.8
Dev. Employee Potential	59	Dev. Employee Potential	57	56.5
Dev. Teamwork	57	*Dev. Teamwork	53	54.5
		*Financial Planning	56	55.0
		Work Practices	54	54.0
Supervisory Practices	56	Interdepartmental Coord.	54	56.0
		Supervisory Practices	53	54.5
*Outside Contacts	57			
Self Development	58	Self Development	55	55.3
Comm./Org. Relations	53	Comm./Org. Relations	58	55.7
		*Financial Planning	59	56.0
		*Dev. Teamwork	53	54.0
Coping with Emergencies	53			56.0
*Communications	53	*Communications	53	53.0
*Outside Contacts	58	Outside Contacts	54	56.0
Dev. Technical Ideas	55			53.5

supervisors have a clear and common definition of the functions. An alternative procedure, which would be less subject to personal bias, would be to rate performance on the randomized items that contributed to the identified important job functions for the position. Customized performance appraisal procedures could be developed by first translating the generic MP-JFI items into specific activities performed on the job.

Identification of Training Needs

With an appropriate response mode, the job analysis instrument can be used to generate a profile that reflects (for individuals or a work group) the level of acquired skill on the various job functions. Significant differences between the importance and ability levels for a function will identify training needs.

Employee Development

When job description profiles have been systematically established for benchmark positions in the organization, an individual's developmental needs can be determined not only for the present position but for any other position for which the employee could be considered. This information would be a valuable input for succession planning programs.

Selection and Placement

Apart from the fact that job analysis is both a professional and legal prerequisite for traditional selection validation studies, it also provides a means for demonstrating the transportability of previously validated selection procedures and the basis for component validity research.

In summary, structured work-oriented job analysis procedures can be developed for higher-level personnel, which, used on their own, contribute to organizational programs of job structure and design. Used in conjunction with comparable measures of work performance, they provide quantitative and qualitative information for identifying developmental needs for individuals or groups. Finally, used in combination with validated measures of human potential, they provide a vehicle for the selection and development of the human resource and its deployment through the organization.

REFERENCES

Baehr, M.E. (in press). *A human resource management system for testing and evaluation of potential: The STEP program.* Park Ridge, IL: London House, Inc.

Baehr, M.E. (1988a). The managerial and professional job functions inventory. In S. Gael (Ed.) *Job analysis handbook for business, industry, and government* (vol. 2). New York: John Wiley & Sons.

Baehr, M.E. (1988b). *The Managerial and Professional Job Functions Inventory Interpretation and research manual.* Park Ridge, IL: London House, Inc.

Baehr, M.E. (1984). *The development and validation of the estimates of potential for successful performance (PSP) of higher-level personnel.* Park Ridge, IL: London House, Inc.

Baehr, M.E. (1967). *A factorial framework for job description.* Paper presented at the meeting of the Industrial Section, Illinois Psychological Association, Springfield.

Baehr, M.E., Lonegran, W.G. & Hunt, B.A. (1978). *Managerial and Professional Job Functions Inventory.* Park Ridge, IL: London House, Inc.

Borman, W.C. (1973). *First line supervisor validation study.* Minneapolis, MN: Personnel Decisions, Inc.

Chalupsky, A.B. (1962). Comparative factor analyses of clerical jobs. *Journal of Applied Psychology, 46,* 62–66.

Dictionary of occupational titles: vol. 1: *Definition of titles;* vol. 2: *Occupational classification* (3d ed.) (1965). U.S. Training and Employment Service. Washington, DC: U.S. Government Printing Office.

Dunnette, M.D. (1976). Aptitudes, abilities, and skills. In M.D. Dunnette (Ed.), *Handbook of Industrial-organizational psychology.* Chicago: Rand McNally.

Dvorak, B.J. (1956). The general aptitude test battery. *Personnel and Guidance Journal, 35,* 145–154.

Fine, S.A. (1974). Functional job analysis: An approach to a technology for manpower planning. *Personnel Journal,* 813–818.

Flanagan, J.C. (1954). The critical incident technique. *Psychological Bulletin, 51,* 327–358.

Gulon, R.M. (1976). Recruiting, selection, and job replacement. In M.D. Dunnette (Ed.), *Handbook of Industrial-organizational psychology.* Chicago: Rand McNally.

Hemphill, J.K. (1959). Job description for executives. *Harvard Business Review, 37*(5), 55–67.

Hendriksen, A.E., & White, P.O. (1964). Promax: A quick method of rotation to oblique structure. *British Journal of Statistical Psychology, 17,* 65–70.

Holland, J.L., et al. (1970). *A psychological classification of occupations* (Research Report No. 90). Baltimore: Center for Social Organization of Schools, Johns Hopkins University.

Jeanneret, P.J., & McCormick, E.J. (1969). *The job dimensions of "worker-oriented" job variables and of their attribute profiles as based on data from the Position Analysis Questionnaire.* (Report No. 2). Lafayette, IN: Occupational Research Center, Purdue University.

McClelland, D.C. (1978). *Guide to behavioral event interviewing.* Boston: McBer and Company.

McCormick, E.J., DeNisi, A.S., & Shaw, J.B. (1979). Use of the Position Analysis Questionnaire for establishing the job component validity of tests. *Journal of Applied Psychology, 64,* 51–56.

McCormick, E.J., Jeanneret, P.R., & Mecham, R.C. (1969). *Position Analysis Questionnaire.* West Lafayette, IN: Purdue University.

Marquardt, D., & McCormick, E.J. (1974a). *The job dimensions underlying the job elements of the Position Analysis Questionnaire (PAQ), Form B* (Report No. 4). Lafayette, IN: Occupational Research Center, Department of Psychological Sciences, Purdue University.

Marquardt, L.D., & McCormick, E.J. (1974b). *The utility of job dimensions based on Form B of the Position Analysis validation model* (Report No. 5). Lafayette, IN: Occupational Research Center, Department of Psychological Sciences, Purdue University.

Mecham, R.C., & McCormick, E.J. (1969). *The use of data based on the Position Analysis Questionnaire in developing synthetically derived attribute requirements of jobs.* Lafayette, IN: Purdue University, Occupational Research Center.

Morsh, J.E. (1964). Job analysis in the United States Air Force. *Personnel Psychology, 17,* 7–17.

Neiner, A.G., & Owens, W.A. (1985). Using biodata to predict job choice among college graduates. *Journal of Applied Psychology, 70,* 127–136.

Owens, W.A. (1968). Toward one discipline of scientific psychology. *American Psychologist, 23,* 782–785.

Prien, P. (1963). Development of a supervisor position description questionnaire. *Journal of Applied Psychology, 47,* 10–14.

Prien, E.P., & Ronan, W.W. (1971). Job analysis: Review of research findings. *Personnel Psychology, 24,* 371–396.

Primoff, E.S. (1972). *The job-element procedure in relation to employment procedures for the disadvantaged.* Washington, DC: U.S. Civil Service Commission, Bureau of Policies and Standards, Personnel Research and Development Center.

Primoff, E.S. (1969). *Use of measures of potential and motivation in a promotion examination from laborer-type positions to gardener-trainee park service.* Washington, DC: U.S. Civil Service Commission, Standards Division, Bureau of Policies and Standards, Personnel Measurement Research and Development Center.

Primoff, E.S. (1955). *Test selection by job analysis: The J-coefficient, what it is, how it works* (Assembled Test Technical Series No. 20). Washington, DC: U.S. Civil Service Commission, Standards Division, Test Development Section.

Saunders, D.R. (1962). Trans-varimax: Some properties of the ratiomax and equamax criteria for blind orthogonal rotation. *American Psychologist, 17,* 395–396.

Schmidt, F.L., & Hunter, J.E. (1977). Development of a general solution to the problem of validity generalization. *Journal of Applied Psychology, 62,* 529–540.

Schmidt, F.L., Hunter, J.E., Pearlman, K., & Shane, G.S. (1979). Further tests of the Schmidt-Hunter Bayesian validity generalization procedure. *Personnel Psychology, 32,* 257–281.

Theologus, G.C., Romashko, T., & Fleishman, E.A. (1970). *Development of a taxonomy of human performance: A feasibility study of ability dimensions for classifying human tasks* (AIR-7-26-1/70-TR-5). Washington DC: American Institutes for Research.

Tornow, W.W., & Pinto, P.R. (1976). The development of a managerial job taxonomy: A system for describing, classifying, and evaluating executive positions. *Journal of Applied Psychology, 61,* 410–413.

Uniform Guidelines on Employee Selection Procedures (1978). Adopted by the Equal Employment Opportunity Commission, the Department of Labor, The Department of Justice, and the Civil Service Commission. *Federal Register, 43,* 38290–38315.

U.S. Equal Employment Opportunity Commission (1970). Guidelines for Employee Selection Procedures. *Federal Register, 35,* 12333–12336.

Wherry, R.J. (1955). *A review of the J-coefficient* (Assembled Test Technical Series No. 26). Washington, DC: U.S. Civil Service Commission, Test Development Section, Standards Division.

19 EXEMPLARY JOB ANALYSIS SYSTEMS IN SELECTED ORGANIZATIONS

Edward L. Levine, Francis Sistrunk, Kathryn J. McNutt, Sidney Gael

The increased scrutiny accorded job analysis as a topic worthy of research studies and recent books (e.g., Gael, 1983; Levine, 1983) attests to the fact that job analysis has earned an integral role in the human resources management programs of all kinds of organizations. As Ash and Levine (1980) noted, job analysis methods serve a host of organizational purposes related to human resources management, including such purposes as job evaluation, personnel selection, performance appraisal, and the like.

The critical role of job analysis in human resource management underscores the issue of how job analysis methods may best be used by organizations to serve their various needs. At the time the study that forms the primary focus of this chapter was conceived, a definitive answer to this question was not available, and so it seemed worthwhile to study intensively the job analysis systems of a selected group of organizations. The purpose of this study, then, was to evaluate state-of-the-art job analysis systems so that an improved understanding would emerge of how such systems might best be used for human resource management. The evaluations were to be done by visiting the organizations, interviewing key staff members, and collecting organizational documents related to the job analysis system.

We did not expect that this study would provide the final answer to the question of optimal use of job analysis methods. Rather, we hoped that an investigation of the accomplishments and problems experienced by organizations with relatively successful job analysis programs would provide some guideposts for other organizations to follow.

METHOD

We took the following steps. First, after reviewing pertinent literature and using information drawn from our experience in program evaluation, we devised a comprehensive set of questions and issues that would provide us with descriptive and evaluative information about an organization's job analysis systems.

The first segment of our investigative plan covered the type of organization, its mission, the number of employees, its dollar gross or annual operating budget, and the organizational structure of its job analysis function. The next segment dealt with the job analysis function, when it started and why, what kind of planning was done at the outset, what methods are used, how information is used in human resources management, and what kinds of resources are devoted to it. The third segment covered outcomes, including issues of how the original plans worked out, problems experienced, and how the job analysis function is evaluated.

Next we located nine geographically dispersed organizations whose job analysis systems were considered to be state of the art. These nine organizations were selected on the basis of consultations with numerous job analysis experts around the country for leads on organizations that had exemplary job analysis programs. The nine organizations identified as our leading candidates for a visit all agreed to participate primarily to further knowledge and gain information about what was being done at other places. We visited the nine organizations and discussed their programs at length. We also collected and reviewed organizational literature, questionnaires, and other kinds of documents. Each site visit took from one to three days to complete. Finally, the site visits were summarized in separate confidential reports. These reports served as the raw data on which most of this chapter is based.

What kinds of job analysis programs were we looking for? Mainly, we were seeking those that could be designated as flagship programs, which would be expected to exceed the following requirements:

1. The program must have employed job analysis for at least three distinct human resource management purposes (personnel selection, performance appraisal, and job design).

2. The program must have involved at least one full-time professional (or the equivalent) in job analysis.

3. The program must have resulted in the analysis of at least ten different jobs.

In addition to these considerations, a flagship program was expected to be innovative in at least one of several ways. Of greatest interest were integrated personnel systems that relied on a common job analysis data base, as opposed to the more usual practice of analyzing jobs with different methods at different times to achieve different human resource management objectives.

We also considered organizations for inclusion in our sample on the basis of an innovative method or procedure that seemed to suit an organizational purpose very well.

Geographically, the main offices of two organizations we visited are located in the Northeast, three are located in the Midwest, one in the Southeast, one in the Southwest, and two in the Far West. The industries represented include insurance, retailing, banking, entertainment, information services and equipment, electric power generation and distribution, and the military. Six of the nine are private sector organizations, two are quasi-public utilities, and one is a public sector organization.

The number of employees in the participating organizations ranged from 1,500 to 600,000, with a median of 13,000. The number of managerial employees ranged from an estimated 500 to an estimated 100,000, with a median of 4,000. In only two organizations were a substantial proportion of employees unionized; unions were virtually or completely nonexistent in the remainder.

Annual operating budgets, revenues, or sales figures were available from seven of the nine organizations. The range was from $130 million to over $40 billion, with a median of over $2 billion. The two organizations where such figures were not available have budgets or revenues estimated to be in the billion to multibillion dollar range. All organizations in the sample save one seemed to be strong financially.

SELECTED FINDINGS THAT EMERGED FROM THE SEARCH FOR SUITABLE ORGANIZATIONS

We consulted with a number of experts throughout the country during our search for suitable organizations. Perhaps the primary finding that emerged was the dearth of job analysis functions or programs that provided a unitary data base on which all human resource applications can rely. For many organizations, the time is not yet right for such integrated personnel systems. A number of organizations in both the public and private sectors entertained the idea and even took steps to implement a program, but these efforts did not succeed or had not yet blossomed. However, there are an increasing number of organizations that are beginning to move in the direction of a universally applicable job analysis data base. There are a few consulting firms that are marketing job analysis programs that purport to be universally applicable.

We also learned of some highly ambitious job analysis efforts being mounted by consortia, such as LOMA (Life Office Management Association) and the Edison Electric Institute. These efforts are national in scope and cover a number of job cate-

gories in the industry of interest. Although we did not investigate these efforts in detail, we understand that they are based on lengthy task-based questionnaires. These questionnaires are designed to yield data that are eminently suited to computer analysis.

Indeed, it appears that these two aspects are generally associated with the most sophisticated and progressive job analysis programs. That is, such programs often rely on task inventories and feature well-developed software packages to analyze the data.

On the other hand, few were available that fell into the flagship category. In particular the Far West seemed to be anything but a hotbed of activity where job analysis is concerned. It took several weeks to locate the few organizations that might be considered as having innovative, sophisticated programs. One comment suggested why. "Many companies on the West Coast," our informant stated, "are not labor intensive. They are likely to blur structural lines and to use ad hoc task groups or teams. Labor-intensive organizations with strict divisions of work and structured salary systems need it [job analysis] more." This point probably applies to other regions as well but perhaps characterizes the Far West most because of the heavy concentration of entertainment, aerospace, and Silicon Valley companies.

It was also in the Far West where one of the more noteworthy stories about job analysis programs originated. A major company was about to embark on an extensive job analysis program. A number of experts, including industrial and organizational psychologists, were hired to implement the program. Then the manager who started the program was transferred, and the new manager dropped the program. This resulted in the layoff of the group of experts. The incident provides a key to the success of any job analysis program: job analysis efforts must have a broad base of management support to be successful.

Among our sample of nine flagship organizations, the most successful job analysis programs enjoyed broad-based management support including, but not limited to, top management support.

One final point must be emphasized before we present the results of the site visits. We are fairly confident that we did tap into the highest echelons of job analysis programs with our sample of organizations. As such, our findings are probably reflective of the state of the art in job analysis methodology as it is practiced by individual organizations. However, our findings are not necessarily representative of typical job analysis programs. We did not intend nor can we claim to have produced a set of findings that are applicable to any defined population of organization in this country.

RESULTS OF THE SITE VISITS

Since the nine organizations we studied have flagship programs, the orientation taken in the discussion of the results is one of how job analysis programs should be conducted. Thus, evaluative comments are interspersed throughout the report of results. Other organizations that wish to develop flagship programs should find useful guideposts in these results. However, though the nine organizations may have flagship programs, the programs are not without flaws. These will be underscored when and as appropriate.

Organization of the Job Analysis Function

In all nine cases, the formal job analysis program is highly centralized in the sense that it is housed in a central personnel or human resources division of the organization. The reference to a formal job analysis program is intended to distinguish more sophisticated, structured efforts from the casual job analyses that go on throughout an organization whenever a manager thinks about the kind of person needed to fill a vacancy, the kinds of tasks to include in a position, and the like.

Moreover, in eight of nine instances, there was no unit of the organization called a job analysis unit. Nor were there jobs titled job analysts in these eight organizations. In all eight organizations, part or all of the organization's job analysis function is housed in a compensation unit. Other units that house a job analysis function included a human resource planning, research, and development unit (six organizations),

training (two organizations), and organization and staffing (one organization).

This approach to organizing a job analysis function may be best for the function's survival for a number of reasons. First, job analysis may be considered overhead squared (or overhead on overhead) in the sense that it contributes only indirectly to such overhead functions as personnel selection and training. To make the function too highly visible by housing it in a freestanding unit may subject the function to harmful cost cutting or elimination when budgets grow tight.

Second, the placement of the job analysis function in a unit with a well-defined, well-regarded role in the organization provides a good measure of protection. The function can then develop and find its niche without unwarranted interference. Indeed, the strong linkage we found between job analysis and the compensation function is evidence for this. Job evaluation is a strong element in human resources, as noted in eight of the nine organizations we visited. In several instances, justification for a substantial investment in job analysis was based on the notion that an orderly approach to salary setting required job evaluation, which in turn depends on job analysis. The large expenditures on salaries made large investments in job analysis palatable.

Third, housing job analysis with an application it must serve should ensure that the information will be maximally useful. Methods can then be tailored to provide at minimum the information its organizational host requires.

Too strong a linkage between job analysis and a particular application does have its drawbacks, however. Under such conditions, job analysis data may be useful only for a particular application and no other. This may preclude the emergence of a multipurpose job analysis method that would find broad acceptance by human resource specialists in a variety of areas.

Of particular concern is the identification of job analysis primarily as a tool of compensation. Two organizations in our sample reported that their attempts to develop a multipurpose job analysis data base were harmed by the role of job analysis in a job evaluation program that caused controversy by, for example, reducing managers' control over salary setting. In our own job analysis efforts, we have often felt the need to disavow any impact of job analysis outcomes on salary in order to ensure cooperation and veridical data. This suggests that whenever an organization is contemplating a multipurpose data base, job evaluation ought to have its own separate job analysis method and data base at least initially, and it can then be incorporated into the group of applications that rely on a common method and data base at a later time. Alternatively, if compensation is the initial launching point for a major multipurpose job analysis effort, it should be made clear at the outset that the method used will serve several purposes in addition to job evaluation. Also, it should be emphasized that only portions of the information yielded by a method will play a role in job evaluation and that salary setting is a matter of company policy and, in most instances, expert judgments, not an automatic outcome of the job analysis data.

One organization in our sample attempted to alter the tradition of centralization of job analysis functions. In the context of personnel selection, this organization has put together a "how-to" manual based on job tasks and knowledge, skills, or abilities (KSAs) for managers to use in developing their own selection procedures. Early returns, based on about twenty positions analyzed, appear favorable. Managers report that they would never have used the method had they known how tedious and time-consuming it would be, but once they have used it, they will always rely on it.

Description of the Job Analysis Function

Each organization's job analysis function is a rich source of data, and it is difficult to integrate the data without losing a substantial amount of information. Perhaps we can "have our cake and eat it too" by first covering some of the commonalities—including overall trends, applications served by job analysis data, methods used, types of employees who serve as analysts, standards to be met by the data, and planning—and then presenting a more complete summary of the job analysis functions of two organizations we visited.

Overall Trends. The idea of an integrated personnel system based on a comprehensive job analysis data base is not quite ready for widespread adoption. Not one organization in our sample has yet achieved this goal. Several organizations (five in fact) have a program with the potential to accomplish this and are moving in this direction, but they had not at the time of the study gotten to the point where all human resource management applications are covered by a single job analysis data base. On the other hand, there is ample evidence to demonstrate that a multipurpose approach, designed to serve several applications, is feasible.

Two features seem to be characteristic of the most sophisticated, multipurpose approaches encountered in our sample. First, there is a highly detailed questionnaire. Second, these programs rely on elaborate software systems to analyze the data yielded by the inventories. Generally, the inventories are completely structured, dominated by work-oriented descriptors such as tasks, or worker-oriented descriptors such as are found in the Position Analysis Questionnaire (PAQ) (McCormick, Jeanneret & Mecham, 1972) and require ratings on a variety of scales such as relative time spent or importance of the task or activity. Additional item types may be tacked on to these questionnaires to render them more applicable to a greater number of purposes. These item types may cover, for example, employee attributes (e.g., abilities), responsibilities (e.g., for example decision making), or the nature of contacts with others. The most sophisticated systems tailor the inventories to particular, but still broad, subsets of jobs. These findings are similar to those mentioned earlier during the account of our search for suitable organizations.

Another general finding is that little attention is paid to job analysis methods associated with industrial engineering. Stopwatches and other equipment used to measure physical demands of jobs were not in evidence. This may have been due to the nature of the sample, which is dominated by service, as opposed to manufacturing, organizations, but may also speak to the increasing (and perhaps unfortunate) divergence of human resources and industrial engineering disciplines.

Another common practice appears to be the use of consultants. Seven of the nine organizations in our sample relied heavily on consultants at some point in the development of their job analysis function.

Applications of Job Analysis Data. The following applications are made of job analysis data or are intended in the near future by organizations in our sample: compensation/job evaluation (eight organizations); job description (eight organizations); training (seven organizations); staffing (recruitment, promotion, selection, placement, test validation) (seven organizations); performance appraisal (six organizations); career development (six organizations); work force planning (four organizations); productivity/efficiency studies (three organizations); job classification/job family development (two organizations); and job design (two organizations).

Although there is the possibility that eight of nine organizations would potentially face equal employment opportunity problems owing to their human resource programs, only four organizations cited legal problems as a consideration in their job analysis programs. However, it appears that the spectre of lawsuits or compliance audits exerts pressure on an organization to invest in a job analysis program.

The broad categories of applications subsume a number of more specific uses, some of which are relatively novel. Training includes most prominently curriculum development and needs assessment, but there was also mention of screening out employees from oversubscribed training courses by determining whether their jobs contained the elements covered in the courses. Staffing covered development of tests and other screening devices and realistic job previews, but there was also mention of outplacement by comparing a laid-off employee's job profile to jobs in the labor market and of person-job matching to facilitate a plant relocation. Career development, a relatively novel application in itself, covered the formation of career ladders and the preparation of job profiles to be compared with self-assessed person profiles.

The manner in which the data were applied was relatively straightforward and conventional. With respect to compensation, for example, job analysis results are used as the basis for expert judgment in a point-factor system or as inputs into a regression equation, which yields the job evaluation points directly.

Job Analysis Methods Used. Levine (1983) has characterized the four major building blocks of job analysis methods as (1) the kinds of job data collected, (2) the methods of data collection, (3) the sources who supply job analysis data, and (4) the manner in which the data are analyzed. The information provided by the organizations in our sample about their job analysis methods was categorized in this fashion. With respect to *kinds of job data* we found that work

activities such as tasks, worker trait requirements, job context items, and responsibilities were collected most frequently.

There was little or no emphasis on such other descriptor types as licensing and other government-mandated requirements, elemental motions or machines, equipment, tools and work aids, although some standard questionnaires, such as the PAQ, might cover such items. Again this may be a function of the types of organizations we visited.

The *method of data collection* that was overwhelmingly favored was the questionnaire or inventory. All nine organizations reported using task inventories, the PAQ, semistructured position description questionnaires for job evaluation, or some combination of these. Semistructured interviews were used by seven reorganizations, but three of these used the interviews primarily as a means to construct the questionnaires. Only two organizations relied on direct observations, while only one reported the use of diaries or actually doing the work. Group interviews, technical conferences, equipment-based methods, or the study of equipment specifications were not employed for data collection.

With respect to *sources of job data,* incumbents and/or their direct supervisors were the primary sources of job analysis data for all nine organizations. Job analysts were relied on as significant additional sources by four organizations. No instances were found in which higher-level executives, clients or customers, technical experts, or other organizations units served as significant sources of data.

Data are analyzed by computer in eight organizations, and these organizations have the capability of creating and accessing large data banks. They also can generate a variety of products such as job descriptions, job analysis summary sheets, and the like by computer. Scales to measure the relative importance of tasks or worker traits are used by all nine organizations.

Three organizations rely on or have relied on one or another of a number of well-known, commercially available methods of job analysis to provide a portion of the job analysis data they use. The remaining organizations have developed their own programs to meet most of their needs, though in some instances these homegrown systems have been adopted by numerous other organizations.

Types of Employees Who Staff the Job Analysis Function. Generally, job analysis functions are staffed by well-educated personnel. In all nine organizations, at least one major component in the organization's job analysis program is supervised by someone with a graduate degree (master's or Ph.D.), typically a Ph.D.

in industrial-organizational psychology. With few exceptions, job analysts have at least a bachelor's degree. Only four of the organizations provide significant amounts of training for job analysts. It appears that organizations are more likely to buy expertise that is already developed either from consultants or previously trained employees than to develop it in-house.

Standards to Be Met by Job Analysis Functions. The issue of what standards were to be met by the job analysis function was explored in some detail during each site visit. In only one instance were standards fully elaborated and formalized, although all organizations did subscribe to standards of one form or another. In seven cases, there were references made to process standards, which refer to a standardization of the job analysis procedure. The presence of a manual, a glossary of standard terms, or a training program for analysts was mentioned as evidence of this. Outcome standards covered the reliability or statistical quality of the data (five organizations), user acceptance of the method and its results (three organizations), review of data by personnel staff or job experts for verification purposes (two organizations), and keeping the backlog of positions to be analyzed low (one organization). Only three organizations made explicit provisions for updating job analyses on a periodic basis. However, several of the programs we studied were initiated only recently relative to the onset of this study and as a result were too new to have broached this issue.

These results suggest that establishment of standards was something of a weak spot. There certainly needs to be a greater concern for formalizing standards that deal with user acceptance. Since job analysis is so far removed from contributing to the direct output of goods and services, the acceptance of this function by key managers and consumers seems of paramount importance if a function is to be successful. The entire field of job analysis itself has been somewhat remiss in this regard, which may help explain the relative lack of formalized standards encountered in the job analysis functions we reviewed.

Planning the Job Analysis Functions. The nature of the general planning sequences that were most often encountered was as follows:

1. Compliance reviews or lawsuits engendered a job analysis program that led to plans for an integrated, multipurpose job analysis approach (one organization) or to separate programs to deal with specific applications (two organizations).

2. Problems in the area of job evaluation and compensation engendered a job analysis program that led to plans for an integrated, multipurpose approach (three organizations) or to a multipurpose effort supplemented by programs designed to meet specific needs (one organization).

3. Needs in the area of particular applications (e.g., training) led to a search for a method to meet those needs. The method proved adaptable to additional applications. These applications were added to the group of applications initially served by job analysis on an as-needed basis (one organization).

4. Specific problems in different areas led to the emergence of separate job analysis programs, and this project-by-project orientation has continued despite suggestions to integrate job analysis efforts (one organization).

Examination of these sequences suggests tentatively that legal problems will not necessarily be the best spawning ground for integrated, multipurpose job analysis programs.

The Job Analysis Functions of Two Organizations. To illustrate the kinds of job analysis functions we encountered in their entirety, two organizations' functions were selected for a more complete description. They represent different ends of a continuum. One organization provides an example of an integrated program; the other uses different methods for different applications.

The integrated program began with its primary purpose being to support a job evaluation function. Despite a shaky beginning, marked by poor planning in terms of resources and time needed to create a solid data base, the firm retained a belief in the value of job analysis and decided it wanted to ensure the success of its job analysis efforts. As a result, the firm made a substantial commitment of resources and retained a consulting firm to assist with the project. The consultant was chosen on the basis of its convenient location near corporate headquarters and reputation for expertise. It was determined at this point that although job evaluation would be the initial application served, the job analysis method used would be comprehensive enough to serve virtually all human resource management applications. Formal objectives were established between the consulting firm and the organization. A detailed questionnaire containing over 500 items was carefully developed. Incumbents rated each item on scales reflective of their importance in the incumbents' jobs. A multiple regression equation was developed to yield evaluation points, and the capacity to generate job descriptions by computer was also developed.

From this point the program was expanded by the development of additional task inventories for subsets of occupations. These inventories are machine scorable and cover areas like financial responsibility, the nature of contacts with others, and knowledge required for job performance. Technical standards require cross-validation of results and reliability. User acceptance is built in by subjecting the computer-generated job grades to management review.

Applications other than job evaluation for which the data are being or will be used include development of an assessment center, a performance appraisal system that will have generic and job-specific components, career ladders, a structured interview guide, and realistic job previews. The organization has made a commitment to achieve an integrated personnel system where virtually all applications will depend on a single job data base. This commitment has been well publicized within the organization, and a highly educated manager has been retained to ensure the full exploitation of the data base.

The organization with a differentiated program uses job analysis on an as-needed basis. There is little or no sharing of job information between groups, perhaps because the data gathered are so tailored to their applications that they are of little use for other applications. Nor is there any coordination of job analysis efforts.

Four major, distinct job analysis efforts were reviewed in this organization. One effort was designed for training needs analysis. The first step taken was to develop and verify a generic skills dictionary that would cover all the organization's jobs. The results of the survey have been provided to the appropriate training groups for their use in developing new courses.

A second effort was focused in the area of job evaluation. There was a recognized need to make salaries consistent company-wide, to get a better handle on salaries, to deal with the problems of comparable worth, and to check the proliferation of job titles. The goals of this project were to set legally defensible, equitable salaries and as a result to facilitate internal mobility of employees.

A well-known consulting firm was retained to accomplish the project, and task forces were formed to assist the firm. The method employed was based on a semistructured questionnaire completed by incumbents. Responses to the questionnaires were reviewed at several levels in the organization. Then an evaluation committee, whose members had been trained by the consulting firm, assigned points on a number of factors by reviewing the questionnaires. Job grading was checked and verified by comparison to normative data.

A third effort came about in the area of training. At the time, the organization adopted the criterion-referenced instruction (CRI) approach, and as a result there arose the need for specific, detailed task information. The goal of the task analysis is to identify the behavioral steps involved in accomplishing a task, so that resultant training courses would be job related and meaningful to trainees. The method employed relies on direct observation and interviews with incumbents. Tasks are rated on frequency and broken down into elements. Task element reports are written in a standardized CRI format. Training courses are then developed and reviewed for adequacy by subject matter experts.

The same staff member who conducts the analysis usually prepares the course. The job analysts as a group are highly educated and are trained in the standardized process of eliciting and recording tasks. The group reinforces adherence to these standards because of its dedication to the CRI approach.

A fourth program was designed to serve as the basis for a skills bank and a career development program. There was also an incipient plan to use resultant data for other applications as well. A formal schedule of responsibilities and deadline dates was established. However, resources were at a minimum due to fluctuating management support for the project.

The method used consisted of a series of interviews that served as the basis for structured questionnaires. These contained items on skills, knowledge, and tasks. Critical incidents were also requested. Analysts were highly educated with backgrounds in industrial-organizational psychology, and they set the technical standards for the project. The data were analyzed, and job profiles were written. These profiles contained requisite skills, knowledge, and typical tasks and were incorporated into a color-coded career handbook. The profiles were reviewed at two levels for accuracy.

The handbook has been used for career counseling but has not been updated since its issuance, nor has it been adopted as widely as had been hoped. The plan to use the job analysis data for other purposes was never carried out. However, the excellence of the career handbook was recognized by its receiving an award from a state professional human resources association.

Outcomes and Evaluation

We have already provided some evaluative information at various points in previous sections of this chapter. In this section, we coalesce and integrate the findings on evaluation. It must be emphasized that it is self-evaluations provided by informants that are being summarized in our sample of organizations. Evaluative comments made by us will be clearly demarcated.

Overall Trends. In no case did we encounter a full-scale program evaluation of job analysis functions. Generally, evaluations were anecdotal and not based on the results of controlled studies. The primary empirical evaluation consisted of statistical analyses of the quality of data yielded by a questionnaire. One organization did report that satisfaction with the job analysis program was explored by means of a few items on the annual morale survey.

Nor did we find any evidence that progress was being made on the quantification of the costs and benefits of job analysis functions. Quantification of benefits was not even attempted, nor were ideas forthcoming as to how they might be. Estimation of costs was possible but only in a rudimentary way.

On the other hand, every organization would support the assertion that job analysis is indispensable for an effective human resources program. It was a matter of faith that job analysis provides the foundation for the creation of human resource management products like tests and performance appraisal instruments. Indeed, at least one major component of every organization's job analysis program, or the entire program, was institutionalized to the extent that the program is a regular, ongoing feature of human resources management. Moreover, legal pressures potentially or actually exerted on all but one of the nine organizations in our sample could not be handled without the aid of their job analysis functions.

Dimensions on which success or failure of a function were based included the degree of institutionalization of a function, proportion of objectives met or exceeded, sufficiency of resources, quality and flexibility of job analysis data, degree of acceptance by organizational managers and staff members who used the results, and the extent to which an organization's program was of interest to those in other organizations.

We were surprised to find, given the flagship status of their programs, that only four of nine organizations were completely and unqualifiedly positive about their programs. The commonalities across these four organizations included centralization of the job analysis function, broad management support, investment of resources without close consideration of costs, the involvement of personnel with Ph.D.s in industrial-organizational psychology, the reliance on tailored, structured, task-based inventories whose data are computer analyzable, user-friendly software, careful quality control placed on data, and an overall objective to achieve an integrated personnel system or at least to serve a substantial number of human resource management applications with a unitary, comprehensive data base. Inventory data do appear capable of meeting the needs of selected human resource management applications, such as job evaluation, based on the results achieved in our sample.

Problems and Negative Outcomes. There was evidence that planning the job analysis function was not without its problems. A key problem mentioned by five organizations that often produced delays or caused insufficient resources to be allocated to a job analysis function was the lack of broad-based management support. This was at times the result of personnel turnover in critical management positions. In our view, failure to anticipate such mobility represents a failure in the planning of a job analysis function. Obviously, managers will move about in an organization. This should be anticipated by a suitable marketing strategy before embarking on the development of a function to ensure a broad base of knowledge about a program and a broad base of support. Continued visibility of the program should also be maintained. Then the shift of one or two managers will not cause the program to derail.

Another problem mentioned was the unsuitability of a method to the needs or characteristics of an organization. One organization mentioned that a method was too sophisticated and costly for its managers. One other organization mentioned that reports yielded by a method it uses were too heavy on statistics for its managers.

Two organizations reported that the association of a job analysis method with controversial job evaluation programs—programs that reduced an individual manager's control over salaries or that brought "skeletons out of the closet"—was a severe problem. In one case, this problem caused the organization to drop a job analysis method.

Four organizations reported serious difficulties with consultants they had retained. In one instance, the difficulty was due to the consulting firm's unwillingness to divulge its regression equation for evaluating jobs. Two organizations reported that consulting firms with which they had formed a long-standing relationship were not capable of delivering methodology that would serve all or a substantial proportion of the organization's human resource needs. One organization reported that a consulting firm had been "dragging its feet" on an expensive, long-range job analysis project.

Benefits, Successes, and Positive Outcomes. Six organizations reported that one or more components or their entire job analysis programs met or exceeded initial objectives. In six instances there was evidence that the methodology developed by an organization was of interest to other professionals. Evidence of this included presentations of papers at professional conferences, inquiries made by members of other organizations, and adoption of methods by other organizations. In one case, it was reported that over 150 other organizations had adopted the organization's methodology. In another, the organization's career handbook won an award.

All organizations reported programmatic benefits of various kinds. There were citations of more objective, legally defensible job evaluation programs, and in a more ultimate sense the evaluation programs were seen to hold down personnel costs, create more equitable salaries, and make organization-wide mobility more feasible. There were reports of more effective, legally defensible selection and performance appraisal programs. In the area of training, needs are better assessed, courses are more job related, and more of the appropriate population is reached through the use of job analysis.

Moreover, good job analysis functions made human resources management more efficient. Updating job descriptions became much quicker and easier with the aid of computers. Backlogs of job evaluation requests were reduced or eliminated. More work could be expected of the same number of people with the aid of computers and data bases that are easy to manipulate. Training courses are developed more efficiently. In fact, one organization reported that its job analysis approach saved over a half-year of an instructor's time in preparing courses. A benefit that was mentioned by only one organization but appears quite important to us is the learning that takes place when a relatively sequestered staff in the central office

has to get out to the front lines. This also forces a recognition of the special needs and problems of those who are producing the goods and providing the services.

Two organizations reported uniformly positive relationships with consulting firms. These two seem to have been successful in outlining objectives and using consultants to provide only those services that the firms were most competent to provide.

Quantification of Costs. We were able to calculate costs of job analysis functions in eight of nine organizations. The ninth organization resisted the computation of costs, saying it was not a factor in their program and was not a concern of management. It was not that the other eight were altogether willing to contemplate costs; rather, they participated in the cost computation process to be hospitable. We did find in one or two organizations some defensiveness about costs, possibly because costs may have been excessive.

In any event, cost estimates were crude and inexact. The kinds of factors that were taken into account included cost of staff time and consulting costs.

Based on these factors, annual costs for job analysis functions in individual organizations ranged from $150,000 to $4 million a year, with a median of approximately $280,000. Substantial proportions of these costs were attributable to the job evaluation function in seven of the eight organizations where costs were estimated. Though numbers are too small to allow a firm conclusion, there was evidence that the more money spent, the higher was the reported satisfaction with job analysis functions.

While these costs appear substantial, compared to annual operating budgets, gross revenues, or sales, they became rather minuscule. Expressed as a percentage of an organization's gross, the costs represented 0.01 percent to 0.2 percent, with a median of 0.015 percent. This is perhaps as it should be in the sense that an overhead function like job analysis should not command an overly high proportion of an organization's resources. On the other hand, the general lack of knowledge about costs of job analysis functions represents, in our view, a failure in planning. An organization's human resource staff should be highly knowledgeable about the costs of resources necessary to achieve its job analysis objectives.

CONCLUSIONS AND RECOMMENDATIONS

Implications for Research

There is an unfortunate lack of research on the utility of job analysis methods and functions. We need more research to build utility equations based on dollars that include the costs and benefits of using job analysis in such programs as selection and training. For example, it would be helpful to know what proportion of a training program's positive impact may be ascribed to job analysis. Perhaps, following the lead of Schmidt, Hunter, and Pearlman (1982), we could ask experts to assign, by a specially designed rating scale, a portion of the difference in the average level of achievement between trained and untrained personnel to the job analysis process. Even if this is not feasible, we should investigate the cost of job analysis programs, so that at the very least we could include a reasonable dollar figure on the fixed-cost side of the utility equation.

There is also the need to come to grips with the question of criteria by which we can judge whether a job analysis method or function is producing effective information. Ash and Levine (1980) have begun the process by looking at purposes and practicality, but we must become better informed on what represents effective information *within* purposes. For example, what are the criteria that job analysis information and functions must meet to ensure that training programs will be maximally effective?

Once we have a better idea of standards or criteria, then we would be in a better position to evaluate the effectiveness of the method that is emerging as the one of choice—the structured, task-based inventory that is tailored to homogeneous subsets of occupations (Levine, Ash, Hall & Sistrunk, 1983). Given its expense, we should probably proceed to assess this method anyway, even with the relatively rudimentary standards currently available, by resorting to experimental studies along the lines of the one conducted by Levine, Ash, and Bennett (1980).

Implications for Practice

Job analysis functions should generally be centralized and staffed by highly educated personnel, with graduate degrees in business administration and related fields. The involvement of industrial-organizational psychologists seems to be a positive factor, perhaps because their training enables them to develop and exploit a comprehensive job analysis data base. The method of choice seems to be the task-based, tailored inventory, supplemented with worker attribute information and other application-specific items, so that a variety of purposes may be served. However, should an organization of any size decide to build a function based on such inventories, it should be prepared to spend several years, and, based on cost figures drawn from our sample, to invest approximately $1 million or more to build the questionnaires, administer them, develop the software needed to process the data, analyze the data, and produce reports or other documents, with or without the aid of consultants.

When planning such a program, an organization should work to achieve a broad base of management support. Management should be primed to take the attitude that job analysis is an indispensable element in modern human resources management, and as such, all necessary costs must be absorbed. Job analysis planners, however, should have a very clear idea of what resources they will need along with their associated dollar costs.

It is premature to formulate a job analysis program model that will serve all needs at the outset. Aside from the evidence in our study that no organization has yet achieved this goal, Brumback and Palomino (1983) have articulated several reasons why this goal may not be possible to achieve. First, managers may resist because of the staff time a multipurpose, comprehensive method may require. Second, personnel specialists with responsibilities in particular areas, such as selection or job evaluation, may want to do job analysis in their own special way. Third, different applications may require information at different times. Even though a data base may be comprehensive, it may become obsolete over time. Finally, the state of current methodology may not be up to the task.

Even though the task inventory supplemented with attribute and other types of items may be an answer to the last-mentioned difficulty, it seems best to start with a small number of applications that a data base will serve and add to the list as the method gains acceptance. If possible, the initial list of applications should not include job evaluation.

Our general conclusion from this project is, not surprisingly, that job analysis is critical for human resource management. We have learned that progress has been made in improving job analysis methodology. We have also gained valuable insights into what makes a job analysis function successful.

REFERENCES

Ash, R.A., & Levine, E.L. (1980). A framework evaluating job analysis methods. *Personnel, 57, 53–59.*

Brumback, G.B., & Palomino, P.M. (1983). *Toward multi-purpose job analysis in a large public agency: Rationale, design and purpose.* Paper presented at the annual meeting of the International Personnel Management Assessment Council Conference, Washington, DC, May.

Gael, S. (1983). *Job analysis: A guide to assessing work activities.* San Francisco: Jossey-Bass.

Levine, E.L. (1983). *Everything you always wanted to know about job analysis.* Tampa: Mariner Publishing.

Levine, E.L., Ash, R.A., Hall, R., & Sistrunk, F. (1983). Evaluation of job analysis methods by experienced job analysts. *Academy of Management Journal, 26,* 339–348.

Levine, E.L., Ash, R.A., & Bennett, N. (1980). Evaluation and use of four job analysis methods for personnel selection. *Journal of Applied Psychology, 65,* 524–535.

McCormick, E.J., Jeanneret, P.R., & Mecham, R.C. (1972). A study of job characteristics and job dimensions as based on the Position Analysis Questionnaire (PAQ). *Journal of Applied Psychology, 56,* 347–368.

Schmidt, F.L., Hunter, J.E., & Pearlman, K. (1982). Assessing the economic impact of personnel programs on workforce productivity. *Personnel Psychology, 35,* 333–347.

PART **IV**

STAFFING WITH THE BEST

20 SELECTING EFFECTIVE EMPLOYEES: AN INTRODUCTION

Donald L. Grant

Selecting effective employees is crucial to the success of any organization. This brief overview sets forth the primary considerations in making selection decisions (for a comprehensive account see Gatewood and Feild, 1987.)

Though demotions, layoffs, and terminations require making selection decisions, the focus of this chapter will be on decisions involved in employing, promoting, and transferring employees and in identifying employees for special programs (for example, training). The considerations a manager should have in mind in making such selection decisions are:

What position(s) is (are) to be filled?

What are the person requirements of the position(s)?

Where can suitable applicants be found?

How should applicant qualifications be determined?

What legal constraints may be involved?

How can the outcomes be evaluated?

To obtain answers to these questions, a manager frequently will need professional help. Since early in the century, industrial-organizational psychologists have devoted much effort and study to designing and evaluating selection systems. They are well equipped to provide the assistance a manager may need in making selection decisions for his or her organization. Legal guidance also should be considered.

POSITION(S) TO BE FILLED

Frequently, only one position is to be filled, and most, if not all, organizations have routine procedures for accomplishing such. A requisition is forwarded to the personnel department, and a representative of that department proceeds to seek and screen applicants for the position. The manager submitting the requisition, may, of course, be asked to interview applicants to make a final choice, although for high-volume jobs in some large organizations (telephone operators, for example) the selection decision may be made in the employment office.

From the viewpoint of a personnel executive, however, filling many positions in an organization may be anything but routine. For that matter, it may require continuing human resource planning to adapt an organization to changing conditions (for example, growth or new technology). Such planning should be a part of or closely coordinated with overall corporate planning. The objective is to ascertain the num-

bers and kinds of people required and where they are to be placed in the organization.

According to Schneider (1976) three kinds of analyses are involved in human resource planning: organization, staffing, and job. Organization analysis provides information on changes that may be needed to adapt the organization to a changing environment. Such an analysis may indicate that jobs should be restructured or new jobs introduced to accomplish organization objectives and that people with appropriate characteristics need to be selected for the positions thus created.

Staffing analysis provides information on the people in the organization, including educational backgrounds, work experience, job training, and performance in current and previous positions. A comprehensive personnel records system can provide much of the information needed for matching people with job requirements.

ASCERTAINING PERSON REQUIREMENTS

Job analysis is required to ascertain the knowledge, skills, abilities, and other characteristics demanded of people selected for a particular job. There are many methods for obtaining such information.

The information obtained provides criteria for making selection decisions. For example, if a typist is needed, the typing skills of applicants will have to be ascertained. Usually, however, several criteria will have to be considered and the greatest weight placed on the more critical ones.

LOCATING APPLICANTS

Recruitment of applicants may be from within an organization, from sources outside the organization, or from both. The goal is to reach qualified applicants to motivate them to apply. In general, the larger the number of applicants, the more likely qualified ones are to be selected. This is referred to as the selection ratio: the number of applicants accepted divided by the number available (Gatewood & Feild, 1987). An employer seeks a low selection ratio—one in ten, for example, being preferable to five in ten. The least desirable situation, of course, arises when an employer must accept all applicants. Under such conditions there is no choice, and some proportion of below-standard performers would be expected. In addition, for affirmative action purposes, an employer would want to reach prospective applicants from groups protected by civil rights law.

Methods of recruitment are well known and include advertising, posting notices, and notifying employment agencies. An employer would want to use those methods that are appropriate to attracting relevant applicants. Knowledge of the position(s) to be filled, the local community, and appropriate methods of communication would be necessary.

DETERMINING APPLICANT QUALIFICATIONS

Once the job requirements have been ascertained and recruitment begun, a manager has a variety of methods available for evaluating applicant qualifications. To be discussed are interviewing, reference checks, psychological tests, biographical information, physical ability tests, the assessment center method, individual assessments, and performance appraisals. Regardless of the methods used, what the manager wants are valid results: accurate estimates of how effectively an applicant, if accepted, would perform.

The interview (see chapter 27) is an extensively used method for evaluating the qualifications of applicants (Bureau of National Affairs, Inc. [BNA], 1983). Much has been written about the interview, and workshops are available to train people in how to interview. Yet research by psychologists raised questions regarding its validity for making selection decisions (Arvey & Campion, 1982; Webster, 1982). The method appears limited by its subjective nature and by the need for information that an interviewer may not be able to obtain. For example, a typing test can provide more accurate information about typing skills than can questions about typing skills asked of applicants for such positions. Yet psychologists persist in seeking to improve interviewing methods (for example, Latham, Saari, Pursell, & Campion, 1980), and a recent study suggests that under conditions where an interview may be able to ascertain relevant information, the results obtained from its use can be quite valid (Arvey, Miller, Gould, & Burch, 1987).

Interviewing, of course, has multiple purposes. Information provided on an application form or in a resume can be clarified and amplified. The nature and requirements of a position can be described to an applicant, and he or she can be encouraged to ask questions about it. A supervisor seeking to fill a vacancy is given the opportunity to get acquainted with a prospective subordinate and the latter with the prospective supervisor. As a consequence of their multiple functions, therefore, interviews are conducted even though other selection methods—psychological tests, for example—may be given primary influence in making the decisions.

Reference checks also are used extensively in evaluating the credentials of applicants (BNA, 1983). Yet, as noted by Gatewood and Feild (1987), their validity is limited by the accuracy of the information obtained. Many employers may be unwilling to provide the information needed, and an applicant may be unwilling to have his or her supervisor contacted. Furthermore, where the information is obtainable, the current supervisor may have biases, pro or con, with respect to a subordinate. In some instances, for example, a supervisor may not want to interfere with a potential career opportunity for a person whose work performance has been mediocre.

Psychological tests are less frequently used in making selection decisions (BNA, 1983) and have been the objects of considerable controversy. A variety of tests are available, including mental abilities tests (see chapter 25), work sample tests (for example, typing tests), personality tests, and honesty tests. Tests are standardized and objectively scored. Extensive research indicates that many tests, especially mental abilities (Ghiselli, 1973; Schmidt & Hunter, 1981) and work sample (Asher & Sciarrino, 1974), are valid indicators of aspects of job performance, in particular the ability to learn and perform the tasks required by a job. Other kinds of tests, for example, personality and honesty, have proved less valid (Ghiselli, 1973; Sackett & Harris, 1984).

It is generally accepted that past behavior is predictive of future behavior. The truth of this belief is verified by extensive research on questionnaires designed to measure autobiographical information (Owens, 1976). Known as biodata questionnaires, they are designed like tests and objectively scored (see chapter 26). Unlike aptitude tests, which can be purchased from test publishers, biodata questionnaires must be tailored to each situation in which they are used. This requires extensive research (Thayer, 1977) and means that biodata questionnaires can be costly to develop and maintain. Their use, therefore, has been restricted to larger organizations.

Many jobs are physically demanding. Incumbents may be required to lift heavy objects, run (for example, a police officer chasing a suspect), maintain balance at great heights (for example, a construction worker), or otherwise exert themselves physically. Laws prohibiting discrimination on grounds of sex or physical handicaps have caused many employers to seek objective methods for screening applicants seeking physically demanding jobs. As a consequence, as described by Campion (1983), considerable research by psychologists and others has been conducted, and appropriate tests have been devised. To ascertain aerobic performance, for example, the bicycle ergometer, the treadmill, and the step test have been used.

The assessment center method has been of primary use in the selection of people for managerial and other higher-level positions in organizations (see chapter 24). It also is being used for selection of police officers (Tielsch & Whisenand, 1977), sales personnel (Bray & Campbell, 1968), and people for other nonmanagement positions. The method entails using a variety of techniques (for example, simulations, interviewing, and paper-and-pencil tests) and trained assessors working as a team to evaluate the potentials of applicants for a designated job.

Individual assessments also are used as aids in making selection decisions, especially for executive positions. A psychologist evaluates a candidate for a position, basing his or her evaluation on one or more sources of information (for example, interview, psychological tests). The psychologist then will report the evaluation to the organization seeking to fill the position.

Performance appraisals are not generally considered selection methods. When used, however, in making decisions regarding promotions, transfers, demotions, and terminations, they become such. Their validities for these uses are, therefore, of concern.

Decisions with respect to which method or combination of methods would be most appropriate for a job or group of jobs require consideration of a number of factors. Among these are costs, legal requirements, volume of applicant flow, estimated validity, and availability. Cost considerations arise from the fact that some selection methods are far more costly than are others; biodata questionnaires, for example, are much more costly to design than is purchasing tests from a test publisher. The volume of applicant flow can influence the efficiency of using selection methods; paper-and-pencil tests, for example, can be administered to large groups of applicants. Summaries of extensive research provide information on the comparative validities of selection methods for different kinds of jobs (for example, Schmitt, Gooding, Noe, & Kirsch, 1984), though, unfortunately, much of the desired information is never published. Finally, though most selection methods are available or can be made so, some specific methods are not; a particular test, for example, may be retained for the sole use of an employer who had it constructed.

LEGAL CONSTRAINTS

Since the passage by the U.S. Congress of the Civil Rights Act of 1964, legal considerations have played a major role in making selection decisions. Subsequent to its passage, the act has been amended, and many court decisions have made it clear to employers that discrimination against groups protected by the law has many facets. Guidance on conforming to the law can be obtained from the Uniform Guidelines on Employee Selection Procedures (1978). Interpreting the guidelines, however, may require the services of both lawyers and psychologists. In brief, the law requires that where adverse impact of a selection procedure on a group protected by the law can be demonstrated, the employer must show that the selection procedure is both job related and a business necessity. Essentially, this means that the employer must demonstrate that the procedure is valid. (See chapter 14 for a detailed discussion of the legal issues involved in the United States and chapter 15 for a discussion of relevant Canadian law.)

The consequence of civil rights legislation and subsequent case law has been to discourage the use of paper-and-pencil tests by employers. In reality, however, all selection procedures are considered "tests" by the U.S. agency set up to enforce the law, the Equal Employment Opportunity Commission (EEOC), and thus are subject to the same requirements as are paper-and-pencil tests. Furthermore, many state fair employment practices laws place limitations on what can be asked of an applicant on an application form or in an interview (Jablin, 1982).

In addition to the threat of legal action, many employers have been discouraged from the use of paper-and-pencil ability tests by the prospective costs of research needed to validate the tests and the apparent infeasibility of doing so in many situations. In recent years, however, a new concept, referred to as "validity generalization," has opened the possibility that paper-and-pencil ability tests may be used by an employer without necessitating extensive research. An employer need only demonstrate that the job(s) for which tests are desired for selection purposes are similar to the job(s) for which the tests have been demonstrated as valid. This can be accomplished by a job analysis showing that the jobs being compared are similar. (See chapter 10 for a discussion of validity generalization.)

The U.S. Employment Service (USES) is advocating the application of validity generalization through local job service offices. These offices have the General Aptitude Test Battery (GATB) available and will test applicants at no cost to the employer (Madigan, Scott, Deadrick, & Stoddard, 1986). The GATB has proved valid for large numbers of jobs; consequently, an employer is likely to find that the jobs in his or her organization are similar to many for which the GATB has proven valid.

Though civil rights law has been a major constraint on the use of some selection procedures, especially paper-and-pencil ability tests, there are other legal constraints that a manager may have to consider. The Age Discrimination in Employment Act (ADEA) is providing the legal basis for many court cases (Foley, Kleiman, & Lengnick-Hall, 1984). Decisions involving employment, promotions, transfers, demotions, layoffs, and terminations have been or can be involved in such cases. Furthermore, union contracts frequently specify upgrading procedures for employees covered by the contracts. In many instances where employees are deemed equal in ability, seniority prevails. The use of tests or other valid selection procedures may not be precluded, though a nearly successful legal challenge to the use of test in upgrading did occur (Roskind, 1980).

In making selection decisions, therefore, a manager may need legal advice. Attorneys specializing in civil rights law, labor relations specialists, and psychologists knowledgeable concerning selection procedures can provide the information needed, though more than one kind of specialist may be required to answer the questions a manager faced with a particular situation may have.

EVALUATING OUTCOMES

Three strategies for evaluating the validities of selection procedures are recognized: criterion related, content, and construct. Essentially, all three are research strategies requiring knowledge of psychological measurement, research design, and statistics.

The first of the three strategies, criterion related, involves demonstrating that scores or ratings based on a selection procedure correlate with a valid measure of job performance. The second strategy involves demonstrating that the content of the selection procedure reflects key aspects of a job—a typing test, for example, for a job requiring typing. The third strategy involves demonstrating that the selection procedure measures constructs required in performing a job. All three strategies require applications of research methods, the third requiring considerably more than the first two; consequently, its use is rare.

Principles for determining the validity of selection procedures can be found in chapter 9 and in Gatewood and Feild (1987). Application of these principles requires advanced training in industrial-organizational psychology.

A manager, however, may want information beyond that provided by determining the validity of a selection procedure. He or she may want to know whether the costs of using a particular selection procedure are offset by the benefits gained from using it. Methods for estimating the cost-benefit ratio (chapter 11) have been devised and are being used (Schmidt, Hunter, McKenzie, & Muldrow, 1979; Cascio & Ramos, 1986). Extensive research, incidentally, indicates that the use of paper-and-pencil ability tests to employ personnel for U.S. federal government agencies could produce multibillion dollar savings (Schmidt, Hunter, Outerbridge,. & Trattner, 1986).

ROLE OF PSYCHOLOGISTS

Industrial-organizational psychologists are trained in psychological measurement and in the research methods required to design and evaluate selection systems. Consequently, they can assist a manager with selection problems. Many large organizations in both the private and public sectors employ psychologists who specialize in selection work. Such psychologists also are available in consulting firms and in universities.

An industrial-organizational psychologist can assist a manager by using his or her knowledge of job analysis methods to ascertain the person requirements of a position. In addition, where validity generalization is feasible, a psychologist knows how to compare the employer's job(s) with the job(s) for which GATB or other tests have been validated. A psychologist also is familiar with a variety of selection procedures; he or she can advise on the choice of procedures and assist a manager in setting selection standards. Because of this knowledge of the principles for validating selection procedures, including the requirements of the uniform guidelines, he or she can assist a manager to avoid legal pitfalls while deferring to a lawyer on specific legal requirements, especially those involving a knowledge of case law. A psychologist also is well versed in evaluating selection procedures and in determining both their validities and utilities, the latter referring to the dollar gains from using particular selection procedures in specific situations. For that matter, the art of selection has advanced to where psychologists are capable of designing selection systems for organizations. They can therefore assist a manager with all aspects of the system, including human resource planning and recruiting along with the remaining requirements of the system.

SUMMARY

To summarize, in making selection decisions a manager should consider:

What position(s) are to be filled.

The person requirements of the position(s).

Where suitable applicants are to be found.

How applicant qualifications should be determined.

What legal constraints may be involved.

Evaluation of the selection procedures used.

Because of the technical nature and other complexities of what can be required, it is recommended that a manager consult an industrial-organizational psychologist trained in the methodologies involved.

REFERENCES

Arvey, R.D., & Campion, J.E. (1982). The employment interview: A summary and review of recent research. *Personnel Psychology, 35,* 281–317.

Arvey, R.D., Miller, H.E., Gould, R., & Burch, P. (1987). Interview validity for selecting sales clerks. *Personnel Psychology, 40,* 1–12.

Asher, J.J., & Sciarrino, J.A. (1974). Realistic work sample tests: A review. *Personnel Psychology, 27,* 519–533.

Bray, D.W., & Campbell, R.J. (1968). Selection of salesmen by means of an assessment center. *Journal of Applied Psychology, 52,* 36–41.

Bureau of National Affairs (1983). ASPA-BNA survey no. 45: Employee selection procedures. *Bulletin to Management No. 1717.*

Campion, M.A. (1983). Personnel selection for physically demanding jobs: Review and recommendations. *Personnel Psychology, 26,* 527–550.

Cascio, W.F., & Ramos, R.A. (1986). Development and application of a new method for assessing job performance in behavioral/economic terms. *Journal of Applied Psychology, 71,* 20–28.

Foley, R.H., Kleiman, L.S., & Lengnick-Hall, M.L. (1984). Age discrimination and personnel psychology: A review and synthesis of the legal literature with implications for future research. *Personnel Psychology, 37,* 327–350.

Gatewood, R.D., & Feild, H.S. (1987). *Human resource selection.* New York: CBS College Publishing.

Ghiselli, E.C. (1973). The validity of aptitude tests in personnel selection. *Personnel Psychology, 26,* 461–477.

Jablin, F.M. (1982). Use of discriminatory questions in screening interviews. *Personnel Administrator, 27*(3), 41–44.

Latham, G.P., Saari, L.M., Pursell, E.D., & Campion, M.A. (1980). The situational interview. *Journal of Applied Psychology, 65,* 422–427.

Madigan, R.M., Scott, K.W., Deadrick, D.L., & Stoddard, J.A. (1986). Employment testing: The U.S. Job Service is spearheading a revolution. *Personnel Administrator, 31*(9), 102–112.

Owens, W.A. (1976). Background data. In M.D. Dunnette (Ed.), *Handbook of industrial and organizational psychology* (pp. 609–644). Chicago: Rand-McNally.

Roskind, W.L. (1980). DECO v. NLRB, and the consequences of open testing in industry. *Personnel Psychology, 33,* 3–9.

Sackett, P.R., & Harris, M.M. (1984). Honesty testing for personnel selection: A review and critique. *Personnel Psychology, 37,* 221–245.

Schmidt, F.L., Hunter, J.E., (1981). Employment testing: Old theories and new research findings. *American Psychologist, 36,* 1128–1137.

Schmidt, F.L., Hunter J.E., McKenzie, R., & Muldrow, T: (1979). The impact of valid selection procedures on workforce productivity. *Journal of Applied Psychology, 64,* 606–626.

Schmidt, F.L., Hunter, J.E., Outerbridge, A.N., & Trattner, M.A. (1986). The economic impact of job selection methods on size, productivity, and payroll costs of the federal work force: An empirically based demonstration. *Personnel Psychology, 39,* 1–29.

Schmitt, N., Gooding, R.A., Noe, R.D., & Kirsch, M. (1984). Metaanalyses of validity studies published between 1964 and 1982 and the investigation of study characteristics. *Personnel Psychology, 37,* 407–422.

Schneider, B. (1976). *Staffing organizations.* Santa Monica, CA: Goodyear Publishing Co.

Thayer P.W. (1977). Somethings old, somethings new. *Personnel Psychology, 30,* 513–524.

Tielsch, G.P., & Whisenand, P.M. (1977). *The assessment center approach in the selection of police personnel.* Santa Cruz, CA: Davis Publishing Co.

Webster, E.C. (1982) *The employment interview: A social judgment process.* Schomberg, Ontario, Canada: S.I.P. Publications.

21 REALISTIC JOB PREVIEWS

James A. Breaugh

It has long been recognized that having high-quality employees is a key ingredient for organizational success. Given this recognition, organizations have focused considerable attention on how they select (e.g., psychological testing), motivate (e.g., performance bonuses), and develop (e.g., management seminars) their employees. Although the quality of one's work force is clearly affected by these processes, another important process, recruitment has received relatively little attention. Yet, if recruiting is done poorly, an organization may end up with a mediocre pool of applicants from which to select, job incumbents who do not value the rewards the company uses to motivate, and/or employees who have limited talent to develop. This chapter focuses on a valuable but relatively underutilized recruiting procedure, providing job applicants with realistic job previews (RJPs). In the last decade, several studies (e.g., Premack & Wanous, 1985) have shown RJPs[1] to be a cost-effective method for reducing employee turnover and increasing employee satisfaction and commitment.

To set the stage for this chapter, try to recall some of the recruiting advertisements used recently by the military. For example, the Marines are "Looking for a Few Good Men." The Army challenges you to "Be All You Can Be." Some of the common themes of military recruiting ads are esprit de corps, becoming a man, exciting work, exotic travel, getting a free education, and acquiring experiences that will enable you to get your first job in the business world. Given the sophistication of these ads (e.g., exciting soundtracks, breathtaking scenery), it is not surprising that the military has been able to fulfill its recruiting goals. However, it is also not surprising that many new recruits quickly become disenchanted with military life. In stark contrast to the ads and the recruiter's spiel, military life has its hardships. For example, recruits often find they do not receive the type of training they requested or to qualify for such training they need to enlist for more than two years. In a similar vein, they may discover that along with that exciting tour of the sea of Japan or of the Black Forest comes months of separation from family and friends. Stated simply, the recruit discovers that what he or she expected from military life was exaggerated.

Some of the results of military recruits' expectations not being met have been morale problems, a low reenlistment rate, and lawsuits claiming fraudulent advertising.

The preceding paragraph was not intended to denigrate military recruiting. Given that the United States has a volunteer army, filling thousands of positions each year (some of them quite undesirable) is critical for this nation's defense. Concerning the actions of individual recruiters, it is important to remember that their career advancement may hinge on meeting recruiting quotas. In addition, frequently the military recruiter is somewhat unfamiliar with many of the positions being filled; thus, he or she could not inform recruits of potential drawbacks of the positions even if he or she wanted to.

Although military recruitment is conducted in a more grandiose style than corporate recruitment, there are important parallels. Corporations also have positions that are difficult to fill. Company recruiters sometimes are unfamiliar with the positions they are to fill. And reward systems often tempt individuals to oversell positions.

This chapter argues that organizations need to examine carefully their recruitment approach. It suggests that employers need to move from what has been referred to as a "traditional recruitment" approach to what has become known as "realistic recruitment" (Wanous, 1980). A traditional recruitment approach is characterized by an overriding concern with quickly filling a job opening with the most highly qualified candidate available. To attract such a potential "superstar," those doing the recruiting often spend considerable time selling (overselling) the job. In contrast, a realistic recruitment approach recognizes that the most highly qualified applicant is not always the best candidate. Given this fact, the employer attempts to attract a candidate who is qualified but who also will remain with the company for a reasonable period, will be satisfied with the new position, and will be committed to the organization's objectives. Thus, the realistic recruitment approach tries to facilitate a good fit between an applicant's needs and wants (e.g., opportunity for rapid advancement) and what the job actually offers.

THE CONSEQUENCES OF UNMET EXPECTATIONS: AN EXAMPLE

Although there is substantial research (e.g., Wanous & Colella, 1989) showing that unrealistic job expectations can lead to turnover and dissatisfaction, research results often seem sterile. Therefore, to appreciate better the value of realistic recruiting, for a moment put yourself in the shoes of Greg Nelson.

> Greg, a recent graduate of the University of Michigan, is about to start a new job. Greg majored in business, graduating with an A-average. During college, he also managed to acquire impressive work experience. Given his background, Greg was attractive to many companies. During Greg's last semester, he received six job offers. Based upon what he was able to learn about these companies, Greg chose a managerial trainee position with Company X. Although the starting salary at Company X was slightly less than what the other companies offered, Greg chose the trainee position because it had other important attributes. As described to him by the campus recruiter and by Greg's new boss, the trainee position puts one on the "fast track." The trainee position was described as initially involving some selling (about 30 percent of his time), but most of Greg's time was to be spent working closely with his boss in managing the branch office. Other features of the position that Greg found desirable were its limited travel demands, its challenging assignments, and its

performance-based pay system. Next Monday, June 7, is Greg's first day of work, and he is really looking forward to it.

> It is now early October. Greg has worked as a managerial trainee for four months, and he is disillusioned. Things have not gone as he expected. Greg has been spending roughly 80 percent of his time selling. Rather than helping his boss manage the branch, Greg's boss has him writing mundane reports. Most important, Greg has come to have doubts about the promotion potential of this job. He has gotten the impression that management trainees are primarily salesmen with fancy titles. These concerns have emerged gradually. Six weeks ago, Greg discussed them with his boss. However, since then he has not noticed any changes. Frankly, Greg has begun to question the honesty of those who recruited him. Although he is not sure whether he was deliberately misled, this job certainly is not what it was described to be. Because he feels misled, Greg feels no commitment to remaining with Company X. For the last three weeks, he has been quietly contacting the other companies that made him offers. Yesterday Greg received a firm offer and he accepted it. Not only is Greg thrilled to be leaving his "trainee" position, he does not have any guilt about quitting after only four months.[2]

REALISTIC RECRUITMENT

An obvious question is whether inflated job expectations is a widespread problem. A substantial body of literature suggests that it is (e.g., "Are Your Employment Ads Misleading?" *St. Louis Post-Dispatch*, May 11, 1987; Phillips, 1987). Although the reasons for inflated job expectations may differ (e.g., naive applicants, deliberate deception by interviewers), the problem of unrealistic expectations appears to plague most recruiting efforts. Before discussing the nuts and bolts of how to develop RJPs, a proved method for increasing the accuracy of applicants' job expecta-

tions, it is important to provide an overview of why RJPs work (e.g., reduce turnover).

Why RJPs Work

Four explanations (met expectations, ability to cope, commitment to choice, and self-selection) have been offered for why RJPs work. To date, research does not clearly favor one of these over the others (Wanous &

Colella, 1989). Rather, it appears that all four factors contribute to the beneficial effects of RJPs.

The met-expectations explanation for why RJPs work is as follows. An RJP should provide applicants with detailed information about a job. This information, concerning both the desirable and the undesirable aspects of a position, generally lowers applicants' expectations so that they are more likely to be consistent with what will be encountered on the job.[3] Persons whose job expectations are met should be more satisfied with their new jobs; thus, they should be less likely to leave them voluntarily.

RJPs may also affect job satisfaction and turnover by improving the ability of new employees to cope with job demands. According to the ability-to-cope explanation, RJPs make new employees aware of problems they will encounter. New employees are thought to cope better with such problems when they do arise both because they are less disturbed by problems about which they have been forewarned and because they may have rehearsed methods for dealing with them (Breaugh, 1983).

A third explanation for why RJPs work is that they cause new employees to be more committed to their job choice. This higher level of commitment results from individuals' believing their new employer was open and honest with them; thus, they were able to make informed decisions about whether to accept a job offer. Having made informed job choices, new employees feel a greater commitment to abide by them. The Greg Nelson case provides an example of an individual lacking such a commitment to a job choice.

The self-selection explanation for RJP effects is straightforward. Having received information about both the desirable and the undesirable aspects of a job opening, an applicant should be better able to determine whether a position will meet his or her needs (for instance, is there a good person-job fit). An individual who does not see the job as meeting his or her needs is able to decline the job offer. Thus, individuals who do accept job offers are more likely to be satisfied with the job and less likely to leave it.

This overview of four explanations for why RJPs work also points out two conditions in which RJPs are likely to have the strongest effects. RJPs are more likely to have positive effects when applicants possess unrealistic job expectations and when they can realistically choose to turn down a job that does not meet their needs (e.g., the applicant has other job offers). Although RJPs work best under these conditions, one should not conclude that RJPs should be used only when applicants have unrealistic expectations and/or

the ability to turn down an undesirable job offer. Applicants react positively to RJPs under any circumstances. In particular, providing an RJP creates an initial atmosphere of trust and openness.

Implementing a Realistic Job Preview: An Example

Although a strong case has been made for utilizing realistic job previews, to this point in the chapter few details have been provided on specifically how to develop and implement RJPs. In this section, these issues are addressed.

A few years ago, a colleague and I had the opportunity to test the effects of using RJPs on subsequent employee behavior and attitudes. The study (for details, see Suszko & Breaugh, 1986) involved the position of inventory taker for a national inventory service firm. Although the job required considerable training, it did not pay well. Employee turnover was a major problem for the company. After becoming familiar with the position of inventory taker, we became convinced that many individuals did not have a good understanding of what this job entailed until they had been working for several days. For example, in exit interviews, departing inventory takers complained of being unaware of such things as the degree of travel involved, the dirty working conditions, the hostility they faced from employees working at the stores where they checked inventory, and the irregular work hours. In sum, it appeared that newly hired inventory takers had inflated expectations about what the job entailed. After several days on the job, many of them became dissatisfied and quit. Given the training involved to be an inventory taker, this turnover was very costly for the company. Based upon what we knew of this situation, we believed it was ideal for the introduction of an RJP.

Developing the RJP for the inventory taker position involved several steps. First, individual interviews were conducted with five job incumbents about their job of inventory taker. We addressed a number of topics: "Tell me about your job." "What knowledge and skills are important?" "Describe a typical day." "Tell me about specific incidents that made you feel good about working here." "Describe things that occurred while you were working that made you feel bad about your job." "Tell me about experiences that you had when you first started the job that you would not have anticipated from the training you received." Detailed notes were taken during the interviews.

Based upon the results of these interviews, lists of positive and negative job attributes were generated. These lists were examined by five additional job incumbents. This second group was asked to add any information that had been left out by the first group. Based upon the information provided by both sets of job incumbents, we felt confident that we had somewhat complete lists of the positive and the negative features of the job of inventory taker. Rather than simply providing this realistic job information to applicants in the order it was generated, we decided to try to organize it. To do this, we asked two company officials to sort the information into meaningful categories. Five categories resulted: (1) physical working conditions, (2) social relations with supervisors, clients, and coworkers, (3) hours of work, (4) duties and policies, and (5) career opportunities. Thus, the RJP we used consisted of detailed descriptions of specific critical job attributes representative of these five categories.

To test the effects of providing an RJP, we randomly assigned applicants for the job of inventory taker to one of two groups. Those in the RJP group (fifteen applicants) received a written RJP prior to their final job interview and before the extension of a job offer. These individuals also received an oral RJP as part of the training program they would undergo shortly after being hired. Those in the control group (thirteen individuals) did not receive a written RJP prior to receiving a job offer, nor was an oral RJP part of the training program they went through.

Members of both groups (who accepted job offers) went through a training program that covered such topics as standard inventory procedures, training on a ten-key calculator, standard auditing procedures, and company rules and regulations. The only difference in the training received by the RJP and the no-RJP groups occurred at the end of the training program. Those in the RJP group received an oral presentation of the information in the RJP.

In order to assess the effects of providing the RJP, we measured both employee behaviors and attitudes. In terms of behavior, we were interested in whether applicants in the RJP group were more likely to turn down a job offer (self-selection) than those in the no-RJP group. This was found to be the case. Four of the fifteen individuals in the RJP group declined job offers. In contrast, none of the thirteen applicants in the no-RJP group turned down an offer. We were also interested in the effects of providing the RJP on employee turnover. As expected, turnover was much lower for those who received an RJP than for those who had not. Seven of the eleven individuals (64 percent) in the RJP group (those who accepted job offers) were still working after three months. In contrast, only two of the thirteen individuals (15 percent) in the no-RJP group were still with the organization after three months. Providing an RJP also was found to have beneficial effects on employee attitudes. Inventory takers who received the RJP reported being better able to cope with job demands, felt the organization was more open and honest with them, and reported higher levels of satisfaction.

From this brief description of an RJP study, it should be apparent that using an RJP can have several important outcomes. In addition, it should be evident that developing and offering an RJP does not require great expertise or a great expenditure of time or money.

THE RJP PROCESS

Although developing an RJP does not require great technical expertise, it is not as easy as it may seem. In fact, the attempts of a number of companies to increase the realism of job expectations by using RJPs have failed. Given the impressive results of our inventory taker study, one might expect us to hold it up as a model for how an RJP should be developed and implemented. Such is not the case. In fact, it is likely we could have gotten even stronger RJP effects if we had considered several important RJP process factors as we developed our inventory taker RJP. In this section, we will discuss four important RJP process factors, and then we will show how a consideration of these factors can maximize the benefits of offering an RJP.

Given that research has shown that most applicants have exaggerated expectations at the time they make job choice decisions, two major objectives of a realistic recruiting program should be apparent. First, an organization needs to make sure it is not partly responsible for applicants having unrealistic expectations (recall the military advertisements). Second, whether or not it is responsible, an organization needs to do what it can to make the job expectations of prospective employees more accurate. In essence, this second objective involves changing the attitudes held by job applicants.

In an important paper, Popovich and Wanous (1982) presented a model of this attitude change process as it relates to the use of RJPs. Simply stated, Popovich and Wanous argued that in trying to change the attitudes of job candidates, four RJP process factors (the source of the RJP information, the content of the RJP, the medium used to transmit the RJP, and characteristics of the RJP recipients) need to be considered. Recently, Breaugh and Billings (1988) have suggested that RJP content is the most critical RJP process factor to attend to. Therefore, RJP content will be discussed in detail before the other three process factors are examined.

Key Properties of RJP Content

In using the term *RJP*, most authors have meant "presenting all pertinent information about the job without distortion" to job applicants. Although few would disagree with this usage, a number of writers have suggested that the actual RJPs used by organizations have not presented all pertinent information without distortion (this fact may explain why some organizations have found that their RJPs did not reduce turnover or increase job satisfaction). In order to increase the "validity" of the RJPs that are used (therefore maximizing the benificial effects of the RJP), it has been suggested that clear guidelines for developing RJPs would be useful.[4] In the remainder of this chapter, several guidelines for developing RJPs will be offered. To emphasize the importance of following these guidelines, a few examples of studies using deficient RJPs will also be briefly discussed.

In order to create RJPs that work, it is important that attention is paid to five key properties (accuracy, specificity, breadth, credibility, and importance) of the RJP content (the information actually communicated in the RJP). To develop a realistic view of what a job entails, clearly an RJP must convey *accurate* information. However, the information must be more than accurate; it must be both *specific* and *broad in scope*. Concerning specificity, if an applicant is to be able to make an informed job choice decision, the individual must receive information that is sufficiently detailed to allow such a decision. Similarly, the information conveyed in the RJP should cover a broad range of topics (e.g., job demands, reward practices, coworker relations). In addition to being accurate, specific, and broad in scope, if an RJP is to

change attitudes (or in some cases confirm already held beliefs), it must also be viewed as *credible*. Many researchers and practitioners have ignored this important property of RJP content because they have not viewed an RJP from the applicant's perspective. However, if one thinks about the RJP process, one realizes that not only is the "sent message" important, but so is the "received message." Thus, in developing an RJP, one must be aware of the credibility of the RJP content in the eyes of the applicant. The final critical property of an RJP is that it contains *important* information about the job and the organization. For the most part, information that is already known by a job candidate will not be seen as important. Thus, information transmitted in the RJP should be largely information that an applicant is lacking. Furthermore, the RJP should address aspects of the job that are of particular concern to the job candidate.

Although defining an RJP in terms of these five key properties may seem obvious, the RJPs used by numerous employers have been lacking one or more of these critical attributes. For example concerning RJP accuracy, in a report of an RJP study done with grocery store personnel, the authors noted that the RJP they used may have actually led to inflated expectations concerning supervision.[5] Concerning the specificity of RJP content, most RJPs appear to have been extremely general in nature. For example, many RJPs have been presented in booklets that could be read in 5 minutes or less. In one study, the authors tried to present a realistic picture of the job of mental health technician with a 12-minute film. A major limitation on the specificity of RJP content is due to the way the RJPs have been provided. In most studies, the same RJP was given to all applicants even though they would be working for different supervisors and in different locations. Given such usage, there is no way the RJP could be descriptive of a specific supervisor's behavior or of the work group climate in a given locale.

In addition to problems with accuracy and specificity, it appears that most RJPs, rather than being broad in scope (coverage), have been narrowly focused. For example, traditionally RJPs have focused only on factors that tend to be common across large segments of the organization (e.g., overtime policy). If one examines individual RJP studies, one finds that numerous potentially important topics have not been addressed by the RJPs. For instance, an RJP study with bank tellers did not address coworker relations. The mental health technician RJP study mentioned previously did not address supervision, promotion opportunities, or departmental politics.

We could find no RJP study that addressed such important topics as grievance procedures or layoff policies.

Concerning the fourth key property of RJP content, credibility, for the most part, it has been ignored. It appears organizations have simply assumed that their RJPs were viewed as credible recipients perceived the RJP information was accurate). Given that research has shown that those involved in recruiting employees often lack credibility, the willingness of organizations to assume RJP credibility seems unwise.

The fifth key property of RJP content is importance. Given time constraints, it is obviously impossible for an RJP to convey complete information about a position. Therefore, an RJP should focus on the most important aspects of the work situation. Generally this will be information that is currently unavailable (unknown) to the RJP recipient. At present, it is difficult to determine the extent to which RJPs have contained important information. The importance of the RJP information to the recipients has not been assessed. However, it has been suggested (e.g., Breaugh, 1983) that RJPs often provide information that is already known by job applicants, while RJPs

generally have failed to address numerous important job attributes about which applicants are likely to lack information. For example, in an RJP study with bank tellers, the RJP provided such commonly known information as "rude customers are encountered" and being a teller requires "working on your feet." In contrast, many RJPs have not focused on such important job factors as one's immediate supervisor, work group climate, or performance-reward contingencies. And even when the RJP did address an important topic such as supervision, the RJP did not focus upon a specific supervisor (e.g., his or her upward influence, tendency to delegate) but rather addressed supervision in general.

In summary, this brief review of representative RJP studies demonstrates that most RJPs have been deficient in terms of their accuracy, specificity, breadth, credibility, and/or importance. Thus, previous RJP studies have been weak tests of the potential benefits of using RJPs. The reader should not view the criticism of the studies just reviewed as being derogatory. Rather, the flaws in these studies have been cited to build a case for the more careful development and implementation of RJPs in the future.[6]

MAXIMIZING THE BENEFITS OF RJPs

Having briefly critiqued several previous efforts at providing RJPs, we can now build upon them to establish guidelines for a preferred approach to RJP development and implementation. Popovich and Wanous (1982) noted the importance of four RJP process factors (the source of the RJP, the content of the RJP, the RJP medium, and RJP recipient characteristics). Having discussed RJP content issues the five key properties), I will now examine the critical interdependence between RJP content and the other three process factors.

In order to maximize all five key properties of RJP content, multiple sources of job information need to be utilized. Only by gathering information from varied sources, (e.g., job incumbents, supervisors, personnel department employees, employee handbooks, job descriptions, former employees) can an organization create an RJP that is accurate, credible, specific, broad in scope, and with important information. Given that most applicants attach the greatest credibility to job incumbents, they should be heavily involved in developing the RJP.

Concerning RJP recipient characteristics, the most critical factor is the personal relevance of the

information presented in the RJP. To the degree the information presented is viewed as particularly relevant by the RJP recipient, he or she will be more motivated to pay attention to the information and to think actively about it. Both of these processes are important for attitude change. The personal relevance of the RJP for an applicant can be increased in several ways. Providing information that is both specific (e.g., tied to the particular job opening) and broad in scope will increase the likelihood that the RJP information will be seen as important. In addition, by having recently hired job incumbents involved in developing the RJP, important information from the perspective of a job candidate is more likely to be included in the RJP. However, given that applicants often have unique needs for information (different applicants will see different information as being important) and that time constraints limit the amount of information that can be provided, developing an RJP that offers information of high personal relevance is clearly a challenging task.

The best and most efficient way to maximize the personal relevance of the RJP information is through the RJP medium. Most RJPs have been presented via a one-way medium (e.g., a film). Unfortunately, although the use of films and booklets is quite common, their use probably has weakened the content of the RJP. For example, since typically the same booklet or film has been used for all applicants for a given position (regardless of location, supervisor, etc.), the RJP was of necessity limited in terms of specificity (e.g., "What is my boss like?"). Furthermore, because filmstrips and written materials are somewhat passive modes of communication, they do not arouse attention when compared to face-to-face conversations. Face-to-face communication is important not only because attention arousal facilitates attitude change, but because it increases message credibility, make's maximum use of the time available, and increases the personal relevance of the information to the applicant (Breaugh & Billings, 1988).

For example, in contrast to the traditional RJP booklet or film, allowing a two-way conversation enables the recruit to seek information he or she sees as important (of high personal relevance) but that may not ordinarily have been provided. Thus, if a job incumbent providing RJP information did not convey desired information on a particular job attribute (e.g., "How are salary increases determined?"), an applicant has the opportunity to request it. Similarly, if the information provided in the RJP was general in nature (e.g., "We all get along fairly well here"), a recruit can ask for greater specificity (e.g., "Do you socialize after work?"). Another advantage of two-way interchanges is that they make for the efficient use of time. For example, instead of providing the same RJP information to all applicants as is traditionally done, the RJP provider can ask the applicant whether he or she is knowledgeable about and/or interested in certain topics (e.g., maternity leave policies, tuition reimbursement). Based upon the recruit's response, the RJP provider can somewhat tailor the RJP to the applicant's needs. Another advantage of face-to-face interactions, especially off-the-record conversations with job incumbents, is that they allow for the communication of important but sensitive information that an organization may be hesitant to include in a brochure or filmstrip.

Although we have stressed the numerous advantages of using conversations with job incumbents for providing an RJP, an organization clearly is not limited to using only one method for transmitting the RJP. In fact, the best way to provide an RJP is through multiple methods (e.g., an interview with the immediate supervisor, conversations with job incumbents, a tour of the work site, participating in a work simulation, studying a job description). Each of these methods can provide an applicant with unique infor-

mation. For example, although an applicant may be told that a position involves heavy lifting and exposure to high levels of noise and dust, actually experiencing these factors (e.g., repeatedly lifting heavy crates in a work simulation, experiencing the actual level of noise and dust during a plant tour) can increase the accuracy of an applicant's job expectations.

In summary, to get maximum benefits from the use of an RJP, an employer needs to be sure that the content of the RJP has five key properties. In order to develop an RJP that possesses these five properties, an organization should draw upon multiple sources of job information in developing the RJP and present the RJP via multiple methods, some of which involve two-way interchanges.

The Timing of the RJP

In addition to following the RJP development guidelines just discussed, an organization can also increase the impact of providing an RJP by offering it at the appropriate time during the recruitment-selection process. Although most organizations appear to have given little consideration to when they provide the RJP, as will become apparent, the timing of the RJP is a crucial element of the RJP process (Wanous & Colella, 1989).

Many organizations have provided an RJP after a job offer has been extended to and accepted by a job applicant. In contrast, other employers have provided an RJP after an offer has been extended but prior to its acceptance. To determine the best time to provide an RJP, one needs to recall the four explanations for why RJPs work (met expectations, ability to cope, commitment to job choice, and self-selection). If an applicant receives the RJP prior to accepting a job offer, all four of these factors can operate. However, if the RJP is given after a job offer is accepted, it is not likely that the recipient will retract his or her acceptance, nor is it likely that the applicant will see the employer as being open and honest, thus allowing an informed job choice. Therefore, providing an RJP after a job offer has been accepted will reduce (eliminate) the effects of self-selection and commitment to choice. Thus, the impact of an RJP should be substantially reduced if it is provided after a job offer has been accepted.

Another factor to consider in deciding when to provide an RJP is the relative cost of giving the RJP in comparison to the cost of administering one's selection devices. If the RJP is relatively inexpensive to provide (e.g., a booklet), it should be given to applicants prior to the use of any selection devices. In this way, if applicants self-select out, the organization has not wasted money on administering expensive selection devices. In contrast, if the RJP is relatively more expensive to provide, it might be given after applicants have initially been screened for minimum job qualifications by an inexpensive selection device. In either case, the RJP should be given prior to the job offer's being accepted.

To this point in our coverage of the timing of an RJP, the discussion has been overly simplistic. Although most organizations have offered RJPs at one discrete point in time, this is neither necessary nor preferred. Rather, it is likely to be more efficient if an employer provides an RJP in different ways at different points in time. For example, an organization could have all applicants for a given position carefully read a detailed job description before going through any screening procedures. Having read the job requirements (e.g., mandatory overtime, weekend hours), some applicants may self-select out of consideration for the job based upon the information provided solely in the job description. Following this step, applicants might be screened by an inexpensive selection test. Those applicants who pass this hurdle might next view a videotape that presents the major job duties. Following this viewing, some other candidates may self-select out. This sequential process of providing realistic job preview information intertwined with the administration of selection devices could go on for several steps. In designing such a progression, an employer will generally keep the most expensive selection devices and RJP approaches (e.g., a face-to-face discussion with a job incumbent) for the latter stages of the sequence.

THE USE OF RJPS: CAVEATS, CONCERNS, AND MISSED OPPORTUNITIES

Although this chapter has presented strong evidence of the positive effects of providing RJPs, it should be emphasized that an RJP is not a panacea. Providing the detailed, broad-based type of RJP suggested in this chapter will be threatening to some individuals (e.g., some supervisors may resist allowing off-the-record conversations with job incumbents). In addition, individualizing an RJP (making it specific to a particular job opening) will involve some costs. Finally, for jobs with several undesirable attributes, the cost of recruiting may increase due to more applicants declining job offers. Despite these drawbacks, the use of RJPs in most situations is still recommended. For example, with regard to the costs of individualizing an RJP and the need to recruit more job applicants, these costs must be compared to the costs (e.g., the expense of training more inventory takers) resulting from the higher turnover rate that will likely result from not providing an RJP or from providing an RJP that does not address factors of high personal relevance to the applicant.

Concerning the potentially threatening aspects of an RJP, this situation must be handled carefully. A key issue is whether the RJP being presented (e.g., by job incumbents) is accurate. If it is not, actions should be taken to improve the accuracy of the RJP (e.g., utilize only job incumbents who will provide accurate job information). If, on the other hand, the information presented is accurate but largely negative, any of several actions may be appropriate. The organization can try to improve the job (e.g., enrich the job, replace an ineffective supervisor, reduce organizational politics). Alternatively, the employer can attempt to help newly hired employees cope more effectively with the negative aspects of the job (e.g., provide stress reduction workshops, provide training on dealing with the customer complaints).

In reviewing reports of RJP implementations, one quickly becomes aware that most organizations have utilized RJPs for entry-level, low-complexity positions (e.g., bank tellers, telephone operators). Although RJPs have been shown to reduce employee turnover and dissatisfaction for these types of positions, employers have been too narrow in their thinking. RJPs also are likely to be effective for higher-level and more complex jobs. For example, just because a person already works for an organization does not guarantee the individual has a realistic view of a position to which he or she may be transferred or promoted. The popular business press (e.g., "Crushed Hopes: When a New Job Proves to Be Something Different," *Wall Street Journal,* June 10, 1987) has cited several examples of individuals entering high-level positions with unrealistic job expectations. Clearly, by focusing so heavily on entry-level positions, organizations have missed an opportunity to get the benefits of using RJPs for internal transfers, promotions to higher-level positions, and external hiring for more complex positions.[7]

SUMMARY

In this chapter, a strong case has been made for the use of realistic job previews. To maximize the positive effects of providing RJPs (e.g., reduced turnover), several guidelines for RJP development and implementation have been offered. Although this chapter has advocated the use of RJPs that follow these guidelines (e.g., the RJP is given prior to a job offer being accepted), there may be some situations (e.g., due to departmental politics) in which an employer may not be able to follow the ideal RJP process suggested. Even if the recommended RJP process cannot be followed, an RJP should still be considered. In such cases, one wants to develop an RJP that reflects as many of the recommended RJP attributes as possible. The key is for the organization to do all that it can to provide a realistic picture of what the job entails. By being creative, an employer should be able to come up with a method for improving the accuracy of its applicants' job expectations. For example, the Central Intelligence Agency ("Changes at the CIA: What Once Was Censored Now Is Suggested," *Wall Street Journal,* April 2, 1982) has attempted to improve the realism of its recruits' job expectations by encouraging prospective employees to read several books critical of the agency. As a CIA spokesman stated, "We're not recommending the views, obviously, being put across by these critics, but employees should be coming in with their eyes wide open."

An RJP should not be viewed as a substitute for improving job attributes (e.g., enriching a job, making the salary more competitive). An RJP is not a panacea. However, an RJP has been shown to be a straightforward and relatively inexpensive mechanism that has important outcomes. Whether an employer uses an RJP of the type advocated in this chapter or relies on a less sophisticated approach, by instituting a realistic recruitment approach, an organization and its job candidates will likely benefit.

NOTES

1. Although RJPs have been provided in several ways (films, booklets, oral presentations), the objective of all RJPs is to provide a job applicant with relevant and accurate information about a job opening being considered. This pertinent and realistic information is designed to enable the applicant to make a fully informed job choice decision.
2. Although the preceding example is hypothetical, it is based upon actual experiences of newly hired employees (e.g., "Crushed Hopes: When a New Job Proves to Be Something Different," *Wall Street Journal,* June 6, 1987).
3. In treating the consequences of unrealistic expectations, this chapter primarily focuses on inflated job expectations. This orientation is based on the fact that research (see Wanous, 1980) has rarely found applicants to have unrealistically low expectations of what a job entails.
4. Readers interested in more detail on suggested guidelines for developing RJPs are referred to Breaugh & Billings (1988), Reilly, Brown, Blood, & Maletesta (1981), and Wanous (1989).
5. To save space, details of the studies mentioned in this section are not provided. The interested reader is referred to Breaugh and Billings (1988).
6. In fact, our inventory taker study, described earlier, also presented a deficient RJP (e.g., the same RJP was given to all applicants regardless of the supervisor to whom they would report).
7. Although theory suggests that RJPs should work for higher-level and more complex jobs, few RJP studies have been reported for such jobs (see Reilly et al., 1981). Thus, caution should be exercised in generalizing the results of RJP studies on lower-level, relatively simple jobs to more complex jobs.

REFERENCES

Breaugh, J.A. (1983). Realistic job previews: A critical appraisal and future research directions. *Academy of Management Review, 8,* 612–619.

Breaugh, J.A. & Billings, R.S. (1988). The realistic job preview: Five key elements and their importance for research and practice. *Journal of Business and Psychology, 2,* 291–305.

Carroll, P.B. (1982). Changes at the CIA: What once was censored is now suggested. *Wall Street Journal* April 2, pp. 25.

Fishman, A. (1987). Are your employment ads misleading? *St. Louis Post-Dispatch* (May 11), 10A.

Phillips, J.J. (1987). *Recruiting, training, and retaining new employees*. San Francisco: Jossey-Bass Publishers.

Popovich, P., & Wanous, J.P. (1982). The realistic job preview as a persuasive communication. *Academy of Management Journal, 7,* 570–578.

Premack, S.L., & Wanous, J.P. (1985). A meta-analysis of realistic job preview experiments. *Journal of Applied Psychology, 70,* 706–719.

Reibstein, L. (1987). Crushed hopes: When a new job proves to be something different. *Wall Street Journal* (June 10), 25.

Reilly, R.R., Brown, B., Blood, M., & Maletesta, C. (1981). The effects of realistic job previews: A study and discussion of the literature. *Personnel Psychology, 34,* 823–834.

Suszko, M.K., & Breaugh, J.A. (1986). The effects of realistic job previews on applicant self-selection and employee turnover, satisfaction, and coping ability. *Journal of Management, 12,* 513–523.

Wanous, J.P. (1980). *Organizational entry*. Reading, MA: Addison-Wesley.

Wanous, J.P. (1989). Installing a realistic job preview: Ten tough choices. *Personnel Psychology, 42,* 117–134.

Wanous, J.P., & Colella, A. (in press). Organizational entry research: Current status and future directions. In K. Rowland and G. Ferris (eds.), *Research in personnel and human resource management*. Greenwich, CT: JAI Press, Inc.

22 IDENTIFYING SUCCESSFUL RECRUITERS

Michael M. Harris, Laurence S. Fink

WHY IDENTIFY SUCCESSFUL RECRUITERS?

Identifying successful college campus recruiters has become an increasingly important concern for organizations. There are several reasons that management should be interested in the performance of their recruiters. First, many companies fill large numbers of entry-level managerial, technical, and professional positions with graduating college students. Thus, college recruiters interact with an important source of employees. Second, college recruiting entails a large investment of resources and money. Given the high costs of hiring and the fact that failure to acquire the best candidates can lead to large reductions in the value of a selection program (Murphy, 1986), it would seem imperative to have recruiters who are able to and attract and hire qualified candidates. Finally, given the intensity and scope of college recruitment conducted by many organizations, a single recruiter may affect the impressions and decisions of a large number of applicants. Therefore, a single successful or unsuccessful recruiter can have a significant impact on the achievement of an organization's recruiting goals and objectives.

MEASURING RECRUITER EFFECTIVENESS

Hard Measures

A number of suggestions have been made as to how managers might determine who the successful recruiters are in an organization. One approach involves the use of "hard" measures. Specifically, recruiters might be judged according to how many applicants they hired compared to those made offers or how many remain after a year with the company. For example, Marks (1967) used a four-factor scale to identify highly successful recruiters. The four factors he used were: "1) ratio of job acceptances to job offers made; 2) ratio of those hired who were successful (i.e., in the sense that the company was satisfied with their work performance) to the total number hired; 3) ratio of those hired who were successful and who stayed with the company for more than one year to the total hired who were successful; and, 4) ratio of offers for second interviews accepted by applicants to the total offers made to applicants for second interviews" (pp. 79–80). Rynes and Boudreau (1986) provide other indexes of recruiting effectiveness that might be applied to individual recruiters, such as meeting Equal Employment Opportunity–Affirmative Action targets or filling all vacancies.

While hard measures of recruiter performance have a tremendous appeal, there are several problems with this approach. First, decisions such as accepting or quitting a job are a function of many factors, not just the company recruiter. For example, alternative offers will have a major impact on one's choice to accept a job, as well as one's decision to quit a job. These sorts of considerations are usually well beyond the recruiter's reach. Another factor that may make identification of successful recruiters difficult is the impact of other company staff. For instance, perceptions of one's future boss may have an effect on candidate decisions to accept or decline an offer. Finally, while many companies do extensive college campus recruiting, the number of candidates actually invited for a plant trip and subsequently hired may be quite small. Thus, computation and comparison of indexes such as those used by Marks (1967) may be either impossible or meaningless for small or medium-size companies.

Soft Measures

The second approach to evaluating recruiter effectiveness has been assessment of potentially important recruiter behaviors and characteristics. Schmitt and Coyle (1976) represent one of the early applications of the "soft" approach to assessing recruiter effectiveness. They interviewed students, placement office staff, as well as others and developed a list of potentially important behaviors and characteristics of recruiters. Following this approach, successful recruiters may be identified as those who demonstrate behaviors and characteristics related to positive applicant reactions to the job, company and recruiter. A major advantage of the soft approach to evaluating recruiters is that performance should be relatively unaffected by factors not under the recruiter's control. In addition, even small companies can use this approach since it is based on applicants, as opposed to those hired or those offered jobs.

PURPOSE OF THE INTERVENTION

The purpose, then, of the intervention described here was twofold. First, we wanted to determine if in fact the college campus recruiter does have an impact on applicant perceptions of the job and company. This is, will the recruiter affect applicant perceptions of the job and company at an early stage in the hiring process? Will the recruiter have an indirect impact? Second, we wanted to determine which specific recruiter factors, if any, are related to applicant job perceptions. Specifically, is there a relationship among recruiter behavior, characteristics, gender, job function, and applicant perceptions?

INTERVENTION

Participants

The intervention was conducted at a Big Ten university campus. We approached students waiting for their campus interview at the university placement office and asked if they were interested in participating in a study on job choice. A total of 145 students agreed to participate. The students represented 35 different majors (technical areas as well as liberal arts and management) and had a mean age of twenty-two. Seventy-one percent were male. At the time of participation, the participants had an average of ten previous interviews. Thirty-three percent had prior full-time work experience. Based on these statistics, the respondents appear to be reasonably representative of Big Ten university students.

One hundred and thirty-five different recruiters were involved, from seventy-six different organizations. About half (43 percent) were from the personnel department; most (78 percent) were male. The organizations represented a wide range of public and private sector companies, ranging from Fortune 500 firms to small regional and local employers.

What Are the Important Soft Measures

Research indicates that applicants do make discriminations among recruiters regarding knowledge and preparedness, personality and behavior, interview content, and style.

Impact of Recruiter Knowledge and Preparedness. Recruiters are frequently found by applicants to be unprepared for the interview for the following reasons: (1) the recruiter has not read the applicant's resume; (2) the recruiter is not knowledgeable of what positions exist; (3) the recruiter is unaware of details of the position (Rynes, Heneman & Schwab, 1980).

Recruiter Personality and Behavior. There is evidence that recruiter personality and behavior affects applicants. For example, an enthusiastic interviewer is perceived as being younger, liking his or her job better, being more youthful, the kind of person who could be approached easily, and liked in a role as a boss. In addition, such a recruiter is perceived as showing more personal interest in the applicant, providing greater consideration, and being more intelligent.

Interview Content and Style. Recruiter interview content and style can also affect applicant perceptions of the interview and the recruiter.

With regard to interview content, applicants give higher ratings to the recruiter and the interview itself under the following conditions: (1) when the recruiter discussed the job in human terms; (2) when he or she asked about student skills, interests, and goals; and (3) when he or she indicated a concern for the needs of the students and asked questions that seemed to be related to the job.

In terms of interview style, students reacted positively to a recruiter when they had an opportunity to speak, ask questions, give personal opinions and the recruiter was attentive, asked about knowledge and experience, was ready and willing to answer questions, was friendly, and made them feel comfortable. On the other hand they disliked questions that they perceived as threatening, hostile, or pressuring. In addition, students disliked when the interviewer gave no time to the student to talk, when the interview was disorganized, and when the recruiter was unprepared, inexperienced, or spoke in a nonfluent manner.

In sum, past research suggests that college students do make discriminations between good and bad recruiters based on their characteristics, behaviors, knowledge, and interview style.

Measures Used in this Intervention

Recruiter Behaviors and Characteristics. Based on previous research, one set of questions was developed to identify candidate perceptions of recruiters. Factor analysis, a sophisticated statistical procedure, was then used to group these questions into key dimensions of recruiter behavior. We found that recruiters were seen as differing on four dimensions: personableness, competence, informativeness, and aggressiveness. The first dimension consists of such items as the degree to which the applicant felt the recruiter was thoughtful, cooperative, and socially perceptive. Competence included such behaviors on the part of the recruiter as being grammatically precise, whether he or she asked interesting and relevant questions, and the like. Informativeness included such things as: "spoke of job in great detail," "indicated kind of employee company was looking for," and "gave balanced view of company." Finally, aggressiveness was

comprised of four items: spoke forcefully, self-confident, aggressive, and persistent. All four dimensions were internally reliable. Students made ratings as to whether they agreed or disagreed the recruiter had displayed these behaviors, using a five-point scale (1 = disagree, 5 = agree).

Job and Company Characteristics. A number of measures were used to assess candidate perceptions of the job and company. A four-factor scale measuring perceptions of the job itself (e.g., "challenging work," "enjoyable work"), compensation and job security (e.g., "good salary," "job security"), work and company environment (e.g., "desirable geographic location," "boss you can work with"), and minor fringe benefits (e.g., "stock options," "private phone") was developed to measure job attributes. Students answered these items using a five-point scale (1 = not at all likely; 5 = very likely). Single questions were written to assess overall regard for the job ("Overall, how attractive is this job?") and regard for company ("How highly do you regard this company?"). Two questions were devised to determine intentions to accept job ("If you were offered this job, would you accept it?" and "If you were offered this job, would you accept it immediately?"). A single question was written to determine perceived likelihood of receiving a job offer ("How likely is it that you will be offered a job by this company?") Recruiter job function (personnel versus nonpersonnel) and gender were determined directly on the questionnaires.

Procedure

Students who agreed to participate were given a preinterview questionnaire to complete just prior to their interview. The postinterview questionnaire was completed immediately after the interview. The preinterview questionnaire consisted of questions regarding the four job factors, intentions to accept the job, and regard for job and company. The postinterview questionnaire comprised all questions from the preinterview questionnaire, as well as queries regarding recruiter behaviors, characteristics, and demographic information. Participants were given a $2 honorarium.

Results

Correlations and multiple regression analyses were used to evaluate the impact of the recruiter on applicant reactions to the job. First, we were interested in looking at the relationship between job perceptions prior to the interview and recruiter behaviors and characteristics. We found only a small relationship between ratings of recruiter behavior and characteristics and preinterview ratings of job attributes. Thus, there is little evidence that companies offering well-regarded jobs employ better recruiters than organizations with poorly perceived jobs.

Next, the relationship between recruiter demographics (recruiter gender and job function) and job attributes was examined. There was no statistically significant relationship between either gender or job function and recruiter behaviors; in addition, recruiter demographics were not significantly correlated with perceptions of the job. Thus, there was no support for a link between recruiter demographics and recruiter effectiveness.

Finally, the relationship between recruiter behaviors and characteristics and applicant reactions was examined. A hierarchical multiple regression analysis was used for assessing change in perceptions of the job and company. This strategy involves a step-by-step inclusion of relevant variables. Each step is then examined to determine whether additional variance is accounted for by the added variable or set of variables. The chief advantage of using this sophisticated analytic procedure is that any relationship between preinterview perceptions of job attributes and recruiter perceptions can be taken into account.

The results of these analyses indicated that recruiter behaviors were statistically significantly related to change in perceptions regarding job itself, compensation and job security, work and company environment, and the perceived likelihood of receiving a job offer. In terms of specific results, the data indicated that recruiter personableness and informativeness varied in tandem with perceptions regarding the job itself and work environment. Although no specific recruiter behaviors were identified with increases in perceptions of compensation and job security, on the whole there was a significant relationship. Similarly, recruiter characteristics were strongly related to regard for job and company. It is noteworthy that while recruiter competence and informativeness were the factors significantly associated with increases in regard for company, recruiter personableness and aggressiveness were related to regard for job. Moreover, aggressiveness was negatively related to increases in regard for job such that persistent and very self-confident recruiters lowered candidates' ratings of job attractiveness. Recruiter personableness was also significantly related to increases in intentions to accept a job offer. Finally, a stepwise multiple regression analysis was conducted to assess whether the recruiter has a direct effect on intention to accept the job or whether the impact of the recruiter is indirect by affecting the job attributes. We found that even when job attributes were included, the recruiter had a significant impact on intentions to accept the job. Thus, the results of this analysis indicated that the recruiter has both an indirect and direct effect on intentions to accept a job.

IMPLICATIONS AND RECOMMENDATIONS

The intervention suggests that recruiter behaviors have a significant and meaningful effect on a variety of applicant reactions to employment opportunities during the campus interview. Thus, successful recruiters would seem to make a difference as to the success or failure of a college campus recruitment program. Conversely, this intervention suggests that recruiter gender and job function have little impact on student reactions. Accordingly, companies seeking effective recruiters should not be concerned with job function or gender but the manner and style in which they interview students.

While recent research in this area (e.g., Powell, 1984; Taylor and Bergmann, 1987) suggests that the recruiter has a relatively minor role in attracting and successfully hiring college graduates, our intervention indicates that the campus interview is critical both from a student's and an organization's perspective.

Specifically, we found that the campus interview can have a large effect on students' perceptions of the company, job, and likelihood of receiving a job offer. Thus, the importance of this interview cannot be overemphasized. Perceptions and decisions based on the interview appear to lead candidates to change interests and plans to pursue employment with an organization. This point in recruitment is obviously a potentially powerful lever for implementing a successful recruitment program.

Implications for Practice

While the need for using personable, informative, competent, and nonaggressive recruiters is evident from this study, the means for providing recruiters with these skills is less clear. One mechanism for obtaining such recruiters may be through training. It seems likely that training would be useful for developing skills in competence-related matters, such as giving precise answers, asking relevant questions, and communicating information in an effective manner. Conversely, it would seem more difficult to train recruiters in intangible characteristics, such as personableness. Nevertheless, systematic training of recruiters may be a useful means of improving a recruitment program.

A second mechanism for obtaining successful recruiters may be through a selection process. Perhaps a simulation exercise wherein the candidate must interview a "college student" would be a useful way to choose recruiters. Minimally, evaluation of current recruiters using the methodology described above would be critical for developing and maintaining an effective recruitment program.

Evaluating Recruiters: A Framework

Based on the program described above, a model framework for organizations for assessing recruiter performance is as follows.

First, use a reliable, independent clearinghouse to ensure that candid information is obtained from students. University faculty or staff may be useful in this regard. It is very important that students be assured anonymity and that the study be voluntary, in accord with ethical and moral standards. Most colleges and universities have a set of guidelines that must be followed by anyone conducting surveys which involve students.

Second, develop a mechanism for tracing which recruiters interviewed which students. Some organizations require recruiters to keep careful logs as to which students they interview. This would facilitate matching of students' names to interviewers. In our study we asked students to list the names of the recruiter; approximately half complied with our request. It is unclear whether failure to record the recruiter's name was due to memory lapse or concerns about anonymity. Nevertheless, given our response rate, asking the students to provide the individuals' names may not be the ideal strategy. Companies should consider using other methods for matching students' reactions to recruiters (e.g., such as color-coded questionnaires).

Third, collect information prior to the interview. This is important for a number of reasons. First, this information will indicate a company's image on campus and how job positions are currently viewed. If these are negative, it may be worth doing more public relations activities such as job fairs. If images are too negative or inaccurate, an organization may not be getting the best or appropriate people to sign up for interviews. Second, this information will give the organization a good standard to determine if the recruiter is affecting perceptions of key job and company attributes, perceptions of likelihood of receiving a job offer, and so on.

In terms of how to collect the information, we found that many students arrive at the campus placement center approximately 15 minutes prior to their interview. This allowed sufficient time for distribution and completion of a survey. However, this process required the researcher to be present for a lengthy period of time. An alternative is for the company to distribute the questionnaire through the mail, along with a return envelope, for the applicants to complete prior to the interview. There are at least several problems with the strategy. First, some students may simply not get around to completing the survey. Others may not complete the survey until well after the interview, making a rigorous examination of the change in job perceptions induced by the interview impossible. Thus, if an organization desires to have information regarding student perceptions prior to as well as after the campus interview, it is important to have an approach whereby candidates are approached in person prior to the interview.

Another issue concerns the emotional state of job candidates at the preinterview time. Specifically, students are understandably tense at this point and may be easily distracted. Given that the average amount of time needed to complete the preinterview survey was 7 minutes, users of this intervention should keep the time issue in mind.

Fourth, collect information after the interview. Collecting information after the interview is essential in order to complete a recruiter evaluation using ratings before and after the interview. An organization should perform a number of analyses. First, ratings before and after should be compared to see if the recruiter affected key decision variables (perceptions of job attributes and company, likelihood of pursuing and taking job, and probability of receiving a job offer). Second, applicants should be asked what they now know specifically about job and company and what topics were discussed. This information is very important because it serves as a feedback mechanism for recruiters to see if they are getting specific information across to the applicant and whether they are covering the topics they intend during the interview. Finally, an organization may want to compare ratings at the end of the interview with those that the applicant provides at the beginning of a plant visit to discern if a recruiter is producing a long-term impact.

In terms of collecting the information, our experience is that the primary reason students fail to follow through, or refuse to participate to begin with, is that either a class or interview comes immediately afterward. While it is possible to provide a questionnaire with a return envelope for them to complete afterward, there may be a tendency to forget certain events or facts or to learn additional information from other sources in the meantime. Nevertheless, we found that once students agreed to participate, the vast majority of times they completed the materials immediately after the interview. In a number of cases, students seemed happy to have the opportunity to sit down and record their responses to the interview and job. Hence, our perception is that barring constraints such as a class or another interview, this step is typically not problematic.

Finally, calculate ratings for each recruiter. Change scores of job attributes and regard for job and company as well as scores on recruiter behavior factors should be calculated for each recruiter. It should be emphasized that no recruiter will be liked by every applicant. Therefore, we suggest that companies consider the average or typical applicant reaction. We also recommend that companies calculate the interrater reliability for each recruiter in order to evaluate the consistency of the recruiter's behavior.

Cautionary Remarks

Given the emphasis on change in applicant perceptions of the job and need for recruiters to be informative, there is a danger of overselling the job. That is, recruiters may be tempted to overglorify by exaggerating the actual job conditions and rewards. There is no simple solution to this problem. Obviously, it is important to emphasize to recruiters the need to be honest and to provide accurate information. Perhaps other personnel can be used to check any potentially inaccurate perceptions held by the candidate. Whatever the case, it is necessary that organizations be aware of this possible problem. Chapter 21 discusses one approach for dealing with unrealistic expectations held by candidates about the job.

CONCLUSION

The need for attracting, hiring, and retaining high-quality candidates has never been more important than it is now. We have examined one link in the process: the attraction stage. Our intervention suggests that the campus recruiter plays a vital role in this effort. We encourage organizations to conduct ongoing evaluations of recruiters to ensure the best recruiters are utilized.

REFERENCES

Alderfer, C.P., & McCord C.G. (1970). Personal and situational factors in the recruitment interview. *Journal of Applied Psychology, 54,* 377–385.

Marks, B.K. (1967). Successful campus recruiting. *Personnel Journal, 46,* 74–84.

Murphy, K.A. (1986). When your top choice turns your down: Effect of rejected job offers on the utility of selection tests. *Psychological Bulletin, 99* 133–138.

Powell, G.N. (1984). Effects of job attributes and recruiting practices on applicant decisions: A comparison. *Personnel Psychology, 37,* 721–732.

Rynes, S.L., & Boudreau, J.W. (1986). College recruiting in large organizations: Practice, evaluation, and research implications. *Personnel Psychology, 39,* 729–757.

Rynes, S.L., Heneman, H.G. III, & Schwab, D.P. (1980). Individual reactions to organizational recruiting: A review. *Personnel Psychology, 33,* 529–542.

Schmitt, N., & Coyle, B.W. (1976). Applicant decisions in the employment interview. *Journal of Applied Psychology, 61,* 184–192.

Schwab, D.P. (1982). Recruiting and organizational participation. In K. Rowland & G. Ferris (Eds.), *Human resource management* (103–125). Boston: Allyn & Bacon.

Taylor, M.S., & Bergmann, T.J. (1987). Organizational recruitment activities and applicants' reactions at different stages of the recruitment process. *Personnel Psychology, 40,* 261–285.

23 INDIVIDUAL ASSESSMENT

Ann Marie Ryan, Paul R. Sackett

Bob has been a topnotch worker for years, but will he make a good foreman? Lisa and Peter are both competent individuals. Which should be given the promotion? Maryanne is a good manager, but she needs some developing. Should resources be allocated to send her to a seminar on managerial skills, or would some other on-the-job activities serve her needs better? Mike is one of the newly hired M.B.A.s. How far is he likely to go in management, and what will best help him get there? These are questions that managers charged with personnel decision making are called upon to answer. Managers might also be asked to assess the readiness of an individual to return to work, work out a succession plan, or provide outplacement services for laid-off workers.

There are several ways psychologists can aid managers in making these decisions. First, a psychologist might be asked to develop a test battery. The psychologist would choose and evaluate the usefulness of measures of cognitive ability, personality, job knowledge, and other instruments for making the decision.

A second way psychologists might be involved in the decision-making process is in designing an assessment center. An assessment center is a process involving multiple techniques such as paper-and-pencil tests, interviews, and situational tests. Several trained evaluators, called assessors, observe the performance of the participants (assessees). This observation is separate in time from the evaluation of overall performance, which is accomplished by a pooling of assessor judgments at the end of the assessment center.

A third way psychologists might be employed is in conducting individual assessments. These services are labeled "individual assessment" because they involve one psychologist making an assessment of one individual for a personnel-related purpose. The assessment center method differs from this in that it involves a consensus decision rather than an evaluation by one psychologist.

Each of these methods is useful in different situations. When a decision situation is likely to occur often, requiring assessments of many individuals over time, as in selecting foremen, using a test battery or assessment center is most appropriate and economical. In cases such as this, a new personnel system is installed. If the situation requires evaluating a large number of people but is unlikely to occur again (as in a one-time major hiring of machinists for a new plant), a test battery may be most economical. If the decision situation occurs infrequently and/or involves assessing the capabilities of only a few individuals, individual assessments are more appropriate. If there is a need for extensive information on the development needs of individuals, the assessment center or an individual assessment is likely to yield more information than a test battery solely.

Why employ a psychologist at all in making these decisions? Managers can and do make decisions like those described above all the time. However, using methods such as the three described here has several advantages, including the formalization of the decision-making process. Additionally, the psychologist in all three instances will be attempting to connect the information used to make a decision (e.g., test scores) with what the job situation requires. The psychologist will also be instituting means to evaluate the success of the method in making good decisions.

Much has been written about developing test batteries and assessment centers, and human resource textbooks contain descriptions of what a psychologist does in these situations. However, little information is available regarding individual assessment. The purpose of this chapter is to provide an overview of individual assessment methods. We will (1) describe individual assessment services, (2) discuss how these services might be best utilized by organizations, (3) describe ways of evaluating individual assessments, (4) discuss the reactions and concerns of those assessed, and (5) discuss areas that should be considered when choosing to use psychologist in this capacity.

INDIVIDUAL ASSESSMENT PRACTICE

Ryan and Sackett (1987) surveyed industrial-organizational psychologists to find out more about what individual assessment entails. The survey returns of 163 respondents who conduct individual assessment provide some answers to questions about individual assessment practices.

What types of decisions are individual assessment services most typically used for? The most common purpose for which these psychologists conducted individual assessments was selection decisions (83.9 percent of respondents), followed by promotion decisions (75.8 percent), development (66.5 percent), career counseling (65.8 percent), succession planning (47.2 percent), preliminary employee screening (41.6 percent), outplacement of terminated employees (30.4 percent), performance assessment (17.4 percent), and back-to-work evaluations (5.6 percent).

Who typically uses individual assessments? Survey respondents indicated that client size varied greatly, from 10 to 75,000 employees and from nonprofit organizations to $40 billion in sales. Clients were drawn from fifty-three different industries, most frequently from manufacturing and banking-finance.

Who is typically assessed? The position level for which assessments were most typically conducted by those surveyed was middle management (34.0 percent, mean percentage). Assessee populations were reported as generally being white and male. Slightly fewer than half of the psychologists responding reported that they saw increasing numbers of women and minorities.

How much do these services cost? Ryan and Sackett (1987) found that prices charged varied, with the average cost being $500. Price variation was due to depth of assessment, job-salary level for which the assessment was being conducted, purpose or type of assessment, and client relationships (e.g., volume discounts).

What typically happens in these assessments? According to anecdotal evidence and the survey work of Ryan and Sackett (1987), individual assessments typically involve several hours of psychological testing and an interview conducted by the psychologist. Most assessors appear to ask for personal history information, administer ability tests and personality inventories, and conduct interviews averaging $1^{1}/_{2}$ hours in length.

What types of information does the client organization need to provide? Prior to conducting the assessment, the psychologist will want to obtain information about the job and the organization. In the survey conducted, psychologists mentioned wanting to know the organization's culture, performance expectations and standards, prevailing management style and philosophy, why the organization wants the assessment and how the information will be used, the management style or personality of the position's immediate supervisor, and the industry and structure of the organization. Additionally, survey respondents indicated they would like to have information about the particular job, such as tasks and duties; knowledge, skill, and ability requirements; job descriptions; why and how past position incumbents have succeeded or failed; working relationships and interpersonal requirements; supervisor's expectations; and the position level and general function. This information may be collected by obtaining written job descriptions; administering questionnaires to the position supervisor, incumbent, or others familiar with the job; interviewing the person contacting the psychologist; interviewing the position supervisor; and/or interviewing the position incumbent.

What is the end product the organization receives? Organizations are typically given an assessment report. Ryan and Sackett (1987) found that survey respondents most typically included development suggestions, provided a narrative description of the individual and a specific recommendation, and discussed the report with the client. Feedback is also typically offered to assessees, although that offer appears to be taken up only slightly more than half the time (51.7 percent). Feedback to those assessed typically involves developmental suggestions and a narrative of strengths and developmental needs. Only 33.6 percent of individual assessors surveyed reported allowing candidates to read the report given to the client organization.

INCORPORATING INDIVIDUAL ASSESSMENT INTO ORGANIZATIONAL DECISION MAKING

Little information exists that tells us how client organizations use the information obtained from individual assessments. Organizations may base their personnel decision entirely upon the recommendation of the psychologist. They may view the assessment report as one additional piece of information to be considered along with job performance information, recommendations of others, and interviews conducted by those within the client organization. The assessment information might be weighed more or less heavily than the other decision components. They may request the assessment so that they have justification and documentation for a decision already made.

How the assessment information is incorporated into the organization's decision-making process is the organization's choice. The decision maker should consider which relevant areas those in the organization are best suited to assess and which are better left to the psychologist. For example, the performance information the organization has about an individual may be considered an adequate reflection of that individual's job knowledge. If, however, it is felt that the performance information is biased, the psychologist can be asked to include an appropriate measure of job knowledge in his or her assessment. Another example would be an evaluation of the relevance and amount of an individual's job-related experience.

A concern of psychologists is the unethical use of the information obtained from the individual assessment. Almost 50 percent of the sample surveyed by Ryan and Sackett (1987) had turned down clients for ethical reasons, such as the client would misuse the data or the client wanted the assessment done for covert purposes.

One issue regarding the use of individual assessment information is confidentiality. *The Ethical Principles of Psychologists* (American Psychological Association 1981) notes that evaluative data concerning employees are discussed only for professional purposes and only with persons clearly concerned with the case. Psychologists are to make provisions for maintaining confidentiality in the storage and disposal of records. An individual assessment report about an employee should be clearly labeled as confidential. It should not be circulated or placed in open personnel files but viewed only by those making the decision for which the report was written.

London and Bray (1980) note that an individual has a right to be told of every potential use of assessment results. Assessees should be informed as to how the information will be used and disposed of and what safeguards will be taken to protect confidentiality.

London and Bray (1980) also note that if information collected in an assessment earlier in an employee's career is to be used later in making decisions, that information may be obsolete. The best way to determine how long an assessment report will provide useful information about an individual is by empirical evaluation. We will address this point further later but keep in mind that it is best to ask the psychologist at the time of the evaluation how long the information will be useful and to note clearly when the report is to be removed from the files and destroyed.

Using an assessment report to justify a decision that has already been made is also unethical. The *Standards for Educational and Psychological Tests* (American Educational Research Association, 1985) indicates that the assessment report should not be used to justify decisions made on another basis.

Another question regarding the use of assessment information is the extent to which the developmental suggestions made in the assessment report are followed. Many individual assessment reports will note specific areas in which the assessee should be developed if he or she is to be effective. For an organization to gain maximum use from the assessment, an attempt should be made to follow these suggestions. Additionally, it will be difficult to evaluate the accuracy of assessment predictions about an individual's performance if those predictions were contingent upon certain development activities taking place that have not occurred.

EVALUATION OF INDIVIDUAL ASSESSMENT PRACTICES

Individual assessment procedures should be empirically evaluated as part of their usage. There is a need in all personnel decision-making situations to determine whether the procedure used to make the decision is related to the outcome the organization desires. For example, does the individual assessment report really indicate who will be best in the position? Does the assessment cover the areas most in need of career development?

In many instances, individual assessment procedures are used when there are a small number of individuals being assessed in order to make a particular personnel decision (e.g., three individuals are being considered for a vice-presidency). This limits the type of evaluation an assessor can use. However, attempts should be made to collect as many relevant data as possible.

In selection situations, three types of validation strategies might be attempted. The first, criterion oriented, involves assessing the relationship between the assessment information and a criterion of interest, such as job performance. This involves computing a statistical relationship and requires a large number of assessments for the same job to obtain a meaningful calculation. In most individual assessment situations, few people are assessed for the same or highly similar positions, so this strategy is not usually feasible. However, it is probably useful for the organization to keep track of the performance of those selected and how it compares to the assessment information.

A second approach is a construct validation strategy. In this case an attempt is made to demonstrate that the measurement instruments used are actually tapping what they purport to measure. For example, does the measure of decision-making ability really tap that ability? Knowing that an ability is measured by an instrument, however, still begs the question of whether the ability is related to job performance or other criteria of interest.

The third strategy, content-oriented validation, is one that is used in most individual assessment situations. This approach involves illustrating (1) the relationship between the content of the job and the areas being assessed and (2) the relationship between these areas and the methods and instruments used to measure them. In contrast to criterion-related validation, which involves a statistical computation, this is a judgmental procedure.

Several published studies have looked at the criterion-related validity of individual assessments. For example, Hilton, Bolin, Parker, Taylor, and Walker (1955) did a preliminary study of the validity of assessments for a variety of positions (e.g., sales, engineering, accounting, supervisory) in eighteen different companies. The assessments usually consisted of paper-and-pencil tests, an interview by two psy-

chologists, and projective techniques, with one psychologist integrating the information into a report. Ratings on five scales (sociability, organizational ability, drive, overall performance and potential) were made by two psychologists who read the test results, interview notes, and final report, and their relationship to ratings on the same five scales made by one or more supervisors was examined and found to be positive.

Other studies that looked at the validity of individual assessment techniques include: Campbell, Otis, Liske, and Prien (1962); Albrecht, Glaser, and Marks (1964); Dicken and Black (1965); DeNelsky and McKee (1969); and Miner (1970). Taken together, the results of these studies indicate mixed evidence for the relationship of individual assessments for predicting criteria of interest. It is important that the client organization attempt to determine whether individual assessment procedures are valid in the situations for which they are used.

In addition to learning about the assessor's validation strategy, the organization should keep its own records regarding the effectiveness of the assessments, noting (1) the recommendation made in the report, (2) suggestions made in the report, (3) the personnel decision made, (4) action taken upon the suggestions, and (5) subsequent outcome of the decision, such as the individual's job performance and supervisory ratings on areas targeted for improvement.

Other methods of evaluating individual assessment include noting assessee reactions to the assessor and keeping track of how the assessment information is used in decision making. Periodically determining what other information would be useful to gain from the assessment will enable the assessor to accommodate the organization's needs better.

REACTIONS OF ASSESSEES

Anecdotal evidence and the survey work of Ryan and Sackett (1987) suggest that although some assessees approach the assessment with apprehension, the process does not arouse a great deal of fear and anxiety. Research is needed to investigate more fully how individuals react to being assessed.

There are several things that an organization can do to minimize the anxiety that might be associated with undergoing a psychological assessment. The first is a thorough orientation. It should be explained to those to be assessed why this is occurring and how the information will be used. Psychologists have an ethical obligation to give a full explanation of the nature and purpose of the assessment techniques they use

(APA, 1981). Before hiring an individual assessor, an organization should ascertain what type of orientation the psychologist will be giving to the assessee.

Testing can be a stressful and tiring experience for the assessee; organizations should also consider that tests that have no relationship to criteria of interest are not needed. Ensuring that all tests administered provide useful, job-related information through the validation strategies noted above will prevent unneeded stress on the assessee.

A third method of minimizing anxiety surrounding individual assessments is to provide adequate feedback to all assessees, even if the individual is not hired or promoted. Psychologists will generally provide feedback to the assessee, although sometimes this is at an additional cost to the organization. Feedback should clarify for the assessee what information led to the personnel decision made and provide suggestions for further development.

A final method of reducing negative feelings about such assessments is a clear policy regarding the use of assessments and their results. We have already noted that assessments should not be used to justify

other decisions or for purposes other than those intended. This policy should be communicated to employees along with clear guidelines regarding the types of situations that assessments might be used in. We have mentioned the need for appropriate treatment of assessment reports as confidential material. Explaining to employees how the reports will be treated in his or her files, who will have access to them, and when they will be destroyed is important.

CHOOSING AN INDIVIDUAL ASSESSOR

A recent study by Ryan (1987) looked at interrater agreement among psychologists in individual assessment. Three psychologists conducted assessments of the same three individuals who were posing as job candidates for the position of director of training and development. There was disagreement among the assessors in their recommendations for two of the candidates and in what they noted as the specific assets and limitations of each candidate. This disagreement was also found in a group of fifty other psychologists who reviewed the assessments.

The results of this study lend support to the idea that using a different individual assessment firm to conduct assessments might yield very different pictures of those being assessed. Organizations should take care in selecting an individual or firm to conduct assessments.

The most important concern in choosing an individual assessor will be the validity of the procedures used, that is, do the procedures measure what the assessor says they measure and is what is measured related to what the job requires and/or other criteria of interest (e.g., job performance, success in training). As noted, organizations should question assessors on the validity of their procedures and cooperate in any data collection deemed necessary to evaluate the procedures.

In order to ensure that the procedures utilized are job related, the assessor should conduct a job analysis. Before hiring an assessor, organizations should ask about the kinds of information the assessor typically gathers about a job and organization and how this information is obtained. There are many sources that outline specific job analysis procedures (e.g., Fine and Wiley, 1971; McCormick, 1979; Primoff, 1975; U.S. Department of Labor, 1972), and many personnel textbooks provide a general outline of what a good job analysis procedure involves.

The assessor should explain what methods he or she feels should be included in the assessment, how the inclusion of those instruments or methods was

decided upon, and the extent to which the methods have been researched either by the assessor or by others in the field. The assessor should be able to provide specific information on how the methods used match the requirements of the job for which the assessment was conducted (or the requirements of higher-level management in potential and development assessments or other areas in other types of assessments).

The client organization should also ask about the interview that the psychologist will conduct. Information should be sought on how the interview will relate to any interviews organization members will be conducting for the same purpose and the extent to which the interview questions used will be tailored to the specific assessment purpose, job, and the organization.

To ensure that assessees will be treated properly, assessors should be asked to give a step-by-step description of what the assessee will be asked to do. The orientation given to the assessee by the psychologist should be reviewed. Whether feedback will be given should be discussed and what that feedback will contain detailed.

Naturally, the client organization should be concerned about what information the assessment will yield. The assessor should be asked for a sample report for an assessment for a similar purpose. It is the organization's responsibility to make clear why the assessment is to be done, what types of information it desires to obtain, and how the information will be utilized in the decision-making process. The client organization should also ensure that there will be an opportunity to discuss the report with the assessor and that developmental recommendations will be provided.

In addition to obtaining information on the validity of the methods used, the client organization may ask further questions about how the assessor evaluates his or her practices. Specific information should be obtained on how long the report is considered valid, how long it should be kept in the files, and what, if any, other purposes the information might be used for. The assessor should provide assurances that the procedures used conform to federal guidelines in selection situations and the standards of the profession of psychology regarding testing and assessment.

If a firm of psychologists is under consideration, the organization should ask how the firm ensures standardization across all the assessors employed. Additionally, the assessor might be asked about his or her practice in general—types of clients, types of assessment services offered, assessments done similar to this one, and criteria for accepting clients.

Individual psychological assessments can be useful in personnel decision making. Organizations should be aware of what they should expect when employing such services and how best to utilize them. This can be done by determining the relationship of the assessment methods used to desired outcomes, ensuring proper attention to assessee concerns, and providing for appropriate use of assessment results.

REFERENCES

Albrecht, P.A., Glaser, E.M., & Marks, J. (1964). Validation of a multiple-assessment procedure for managerial personnel. *Journal of Applied Psychology, 48* (6), 351–360.

American Educational Research Association, American Psychological Association, & National Council on Measurement in Education (1985). *Standards for education and psychological testing.* Washington, DC: Author.

American Psychological Association (1981). *Ethical principles of psychologists.* Washington DC: Author.

Campbell, J.T., Otis, J.L., Liske, R.E., & Prien, E.P. (1962). Assessments of higher-level personnel: II. Validity of the overall assessment process. *Personnel Psychology 15,* 63–74.

DeNelsky, G.Y., & McKee, M.G. (1969). Prediction of job performance from assessment reports: Use of a modified Q-sort technique to expand predictor and criterion variance. *Journal of Applied Psychology, 53* (6), 439–445.

Dicken, C.F., & Black, J.D. (1965). Predictive validity of psychometric evaluations of supervisors. *Journal of Applied Psychology, 49* (1), 34–47.

Fine, S.A., & Wiley, W.W. (1971). *An introduction to functional job analysis: Methods for manpower analysis* (Monograph No 4.). Kalamazoo, MI: W.E. Upjohn Institute.

Hilton, A.C., Bolin, S.F., Parker, J.W., Jr., Taylor, E.K., & Walker, W.B. (1955). The validity of personnel assessments by professional psychologists. *Journal of Applied Psychology, 39* (4), 287–293.

London, M., & Bray, D.W. (1980). Ethical issues in testing and evaluation for personnel decisions. *American Psychologist 35* (10), 890–901.

McCormick, E.J. (1979). *Job analysis: Methods and applications.* New York: AMACOM.

Miner, J.B. (1970). Psychological evaluations as predictors of consulting success. *Personnel Psychology, 23,* 393–405.

Primoff, E.S. (1975). *How to prepare and conduct job element examinations.* Washington, DC: U.S. Government Printing Office.

Ryan, A.M. (1987). *An exploratory study of individual assessment practices: interrater reliability and judgements of assessor effectiveness.* Ph.D. dissertation, Bowling Green State University.

Ryan, A.M., & Sackett, P.R. (1987). A survey of individual assessment practices by I/O psychologists. *Personnel Psychology, 40* (3) 455–488.

U.S. Department of Labor (1972). *Handbook for analyzing jobs.* Washington, DC: U.S. Government Printing Office.

24 ASSESSING MANAGEMENT POTENTIAL: AN OVERVIEW

George C. Thornton III

The purpose of this chapter is to provide an overview of management assessment techniques. Management assessment is a process of determining whether individual managers possess the knowledge, skills, abilities, interests, and motivation to perform effectively in their current job or some future position. Assessment techniques include interviews, paper-and-pencil tests, background checks, management simulations (e.g., the in-basket exercise), and handwriting analysis. Assessment information can be used for making initial hiring decisions, recommending promotions, diagnosing training needs, or making placement decisions.

This overview will be in the form of a set of technical and practical issues that a manager should consider when evaluating any management assessment method. These issues have been expressed in a series of general and specific questions that the manager can ask when reading the other chapters in this part and when listening to a proposal for management assessment in an organization.

It is helpful to think of any management assessment technique as a measurement tool. In this sense, we want to know whether the technique has the technical merits of a good measuring instrument. In the jargon of the field, we want to know its psychometric properties—whether the technique measures important management abilities and aptitudes in a standardized reliable, valid, and unbiased way.

In addition, you will want to know whether the technique is practically feasible for a particular application in your organization. The best technique available will not be appropriate if it is not cost-effective and acceptable in your setting.

FADS IN MANAGEMENT ASSESSMENT

A word about fads is in order. Two types of trends can be observed in the shifting fortunes of management assessment techniques. On the one hand, some techniques remain in use long after they have been proved ineffective. At some point when the accumulated evidence shows that a procedure is not able to measure dimensions relevant to management success, it should be abandoned. On the other hand, all too often there is a rush to try out the latest thing. Human resource specialists often feel pressure to adopt the newest program because others in the industry are using it.

An alternative approach is to seek out documented evidence and determine whether the technique is technically sound and is practically appropriate for an organization. Either a tried-and-true technique or a "Johnny come lately" may be backed up with good documented evidence. Empirical evidence is better than tradition, testimony, or reputation.

The question then arises, "What is adequate evidence?" You should look for written reports that give details of the research studies that were conducted on the development of the technique and on its use in operational settings. It is standard practice to try out the technique with preliminary groups in various settings. Revisions are almost always needed. These sorts of studies are usually available in technical reports or in a test manual. Validation research on the operational version of the technique will often be published in standard professional journals or presented at professional meetings. Ask for copies of such reports.

Test developers may be reluctant to divulge certain specific information of a proprietary nature. For example, they may not freely give out the scoring formulas that state how a series of questions are weighted and combined. That is acceptable practice. But such restrictions do not preclude the developer from sharing with the general professional community the results of test development and validation studies. For example, the developer might describe how the final questions were chosen after statistical analyses of a larger pool of questions. And we might be told that the recommendations from the assessment method have been found to differentiate between highly successful and less successful managers.

In summary, as a potential user you have the right to request documented evidence of the effectiveness of any assessment technique. The proponent of the technique can be expected to have empirical evidence that supports any claim that the technique measures management skills or predicts management success.

PROFESSIONAL STANDARDS FOR VALIDATION OF ASSESSMENT TECHNIQUES

Several professional standards govern the research and development of assessment techniques. First, and most general, are the *Standards for Educational and Psychological Testing,* published by the American Psychological Association. The *Standards* provide a basis for evaluating any assessment technique by specifying the necessary technical information that test developers should provide so that users may make informed decisions about the quality of the technique. They give guidelines for the development and publication of any type of test, including the essential information that the author should disseminate.

Second, the Division of Industrial-Organizational Psychology of the American Psychological Association (1980) has published *Principles for the Validation and Use of Personnel Selection Procedures.* The *Principles* set forth standards for the conduct of personnel selection research and the application of valid selection procedures. They are intended to help managers with the responsibility to set up and implement selection procedures.

Of course, any procedures used to make decisions that influence the employment status of a person must conform to the Uniform Guidelines on Employee Selection Procedures, issued by the Equal Employment Opportunity Commission and other federal agencies (1978). The Uniform Guidelines are a codification of many accepted practices in the area of test validation in industry. Although they are in need of revision to include recent developments in the field of personnel selection research, they have been used to guide the courts in their review of fair employment practice cases.

Further standards govern the use of some specific assessment techniques. For example, the Guidelines and Ethical Considerations for Assessment Center Operations (Task Force, 1989) provides a set of guidelines developed by leading practitioners of this technique. An assessment center is a method for assessing management potential using trained management evaluators to observe candidates' behavior in several standardized situations that simulate critical components of a managerial job, such as group discussions, performance reviews, and oral presentations.

The burden of proof in determining whether the assessment technique meets these various standards rests with the developer. As a manager, you can expect a proponent to provide the information needed to evaluate the technique. The questions and issues discussed in this chapter will help you ferret out what you need to know.

LOGICAL SEQUENCE OF IDENTIFYING POTENTIAL ASSESSMENT TECHNIQUES

Standard practice in choosing a management assessment technique is to conduct a thorough job analysis (McCormick, 1979) and then identify the knowledge, skills, abilities, and other characteristics that are required for job success (Dunnette, 1976). It is then appropriate to search for a method that measures the necessary characteristics. If no existing procedure is adequate, it may be necessary to develop a new one.

Problems arise when we put the cart before the horse. That is, if we start by asking what an assessment technique can measure and then decide whether it might be appropriate for an organization, the answer is probably predetermined. We often conclude that the technique measures some characteristics necessary for the job. The technique usually appears appropriate. That sequence will often be like the child, who when given a new hammer easily finds many things to pound on—whether they need it or not.

It is far better to embed the search for an assessment technique in a broader, well-coordinated system of human resource development (Byham, 1981). The overall system would include the careful analysis of managerial duties and responsibilities, the articulation of a model of effective management in the organization, identification of success measures, and the

formulation of management development programs. Many of these concepts are discussed elsewhere in this *Handbook*.

THE VALUE OF PAST RESEARCH AND THE NEED FOR NEW STUDIES

Past research provides information about the dimensions that a technique can measure and the situations where the technique has shown validity to predict success on certain jobs. This sort of evidence should allow you to predict whether the assessment technique may be helpful for your situation. Earlier research does not, however, guarantee that the technique will work.

The extent to which past research is relevant to your new situation is a function of the similarity of the jobs, the types of success measures you wish to predict, the comparability of the job incumbents, the similarity of the applicant pools, and many other factors. It should not be assumed that the validity information from elsewhere will transfer to your situation.

Many times the prior information will transfer. When this occurs, you may be able to capitalize on the accumulation of prior studies. For some assessment techniques, validity generalization studies have been conducted. Validity generalization is a process of quantitatively combining the results of numerous studies to note trends in the data (Hunter, Schmidt & Jackson, 1982). It involves the computation of an index of the average validity of the test and an estimate of the variation in validity indexes. Certain statistical corrections are made to account for unreliability in measurement and the size of the research samples. The end result is an estimate of the "true" validity of the test and the "true" variation in these validities. Many assessment techniques show a high level of validity and little variation in validity when

they are used in different situations. In other words, the test has validity generalization. Results of some validity generalization studies will be presented later in this chapter.

It may be appropriate to conduct a research study in your own organization. Past research may not be adequate, or there may not be enough prior research to conduct a validity generalization study. When it is technically feasible to do so, your organization may need to conduct a validation study. Feasibility to do the study is a function of many considerations—the number of candidates, the practicality of obtaining adequate measures of job success, and sufficient time to conduct the study. These and other considerations are discussed in the *Principles*.

A validation study should not be undertaken lightly. If an organization cannot do a good study, no study at all should be undertaken. This principle makes sense for technical and practical reasons. A poor study is likely to demonstrate that the technique is not valid, when in fact it really is valid. In addition, a poor study is probably almost as expensive as a good one.

If a new validation study is warranted and feasible, it will take time, money, and resources. Give it your support and be patient. R&D in any field is expensive, but be confident that it is worth it. Positive results will lead to effective techniques that are defensible. Negative results will avoid the cost and harm of worthless procedures.

TECHNICAL ISSUES

Reliability

An assessment technique must provide reliable information. Reliability means that the assessment procedure provides accurate measurement (Anastasi, 1988). If the technique is reliable, the scores or recommendations will be consistent over time and across different people administering the procedure. Table 24–1 lists questions that the manager can ask to

determine if the assessment technique is standardized and reliable. These questions are relevant to the subsequent chapters in this *Handbook* and can be asked of any consultant proposing an assessment technique for your organization.

Reliability is attained through careful development and administration of the assessment technique (Nunnally, 1978). The questions must be carefully worded; the instructions must be clear and precise;

Table 24-1
Questions to Determine Reliability

General	Is this technique standardized so that it is administered consistently to all candidates? What documented evidence is there that the scores or recommendations obtained at one point in time by one assessor will be the same as those obtained at another point in time by another assessor?
Interview	Are the same questions asked of all candidates? Will two interviewers make the same recommendation after interviewing the same candidate?
Biographical information	Do people answer the questions honestly?
Personality tests	Will a person's temporary mood influence the test results? If a projective test is used, how do you avoid biases from the examiner?
Mental ability tests	Do the administrative conditions (e.g., instructions or setting) influence the results?
Work samples	Can people practice ahead of time and improve their scores?
Practical intelligence tests	Will the instructions and the expectations of the candidate influence the results?
Assessment centers	Can people practice ahead of time and improve their scores? Do the actions of other people in the exercises influence a candidate's performance? If so, how are these kept consistent?
Individual clinical assessment	Do the assessment techniques vary from candidate to candidate? How do you avoid biases on the part of the assessor?

there must be enough questions so that a candidate's lapse of memory on one question will not damage the entire results; and the entire characteristic to be assessed should be covered by a representative set of questions.

Many paper-and-pencil testing procedures provide highly reliable measurements (Anastasi, 1988). Cognitive ability tests and the answers on biographical information forms are especially reliable. The scores are usually not influenced by the person administering the technique, and the scores stay about the same from time to time. On the other hand, scores on personality tests may be highly influenced by the mood of the applicant, by the circumstances of the testing situation, or by the instructions from the examiner. The behavior of an assessee in work sample tests and assessment centers may be influenced by the behavior of other people in the exercises with whom the applicant must interact. Because work sample procedures often involve equipment, apparatus, or materials, unreliability can result if this hardware is faulty.

Unreliability can be a serious problem with the interview procedure (Arvey & Campion, 1982). A single interviewer may not be consistent over time in the questions that are asked, the interpretations of answers, or the evaluations given. More seriously, different interviewers often follow unstandardized procedures, interpret answers differently, and arrive at different recommendations given the same information. Since the background interview is an integral part of most individual clinical assessment procedures

carried out by consultants (Ryan & Sackett, 1987), these same potential sources of unreliability may affect recommendations. In addition, the executive recruiter may accumulate quite different amounts and types of information about different candidates.

Validity

The validity of a management assessment technique is the accumulated evidence that it measures attributes necessary for successful performance on the job (Binning & Barrett, 1989). Evidence includes such information as a demonstration that the test covers a representative sample of knowledge that is required for the job, research that confirms that the technique measures some aptitude or trait necessary for long-range success, or the statistical relationship of scores on the assessment technique and subsequent success on the job as demonstrated by effective performance or progress in management responsibility.

Validity in an assessment technique is attained by careful job analysis to determine the knowledge, skills, abilities, and other characteristics necessary for job success. Then some procedure is devised to observe behavior relevant to those characteristics. The assessment techniques might include some procedure for asking questions (verbally or in writing), presenting the assessee with a problem situation, or observing the assessee in lifelike situations. Finally, we have to score the responses in an accurate manner and come up with a recommendation about the candidate's suitability.

Ask for documented evidence about the validity of any techniques to assess management potential. Ask specifically for empirical studies that have been conducted with samples of people similar to your employees. Do not accept as intuitively obvious any assertion that the assessment procedure will accomplish what its proponents claim. This warning is particularly appropriate for personality tests, which often have scales with appealing titles such as "dominance" and "motivation to achieve" yet do not measure what they purport. Table 24–2 provides a set of questions that will help determine the validity of management assessment techniques.

Tests measuring intellectual reasoning abilities and the assessment center method (Hunter & Hunter, 1984) have demonstrated consistently high levels of validity over the years. Many accumulated data show that scores on cognitive tests and the overall assessment center rating predict performance and progress in management ranks. Be wary, though, of modifications of the standard techniques in these areas. Novel intelligence tests and "assessment center-like" programs may not be as valid as the standard models. Be sure to ask if the proposed method is comparable to the methods that have been researched thoroughly in the past.

Previous validation studies on the personal interview have failed to demonstrate that interviewers can accurately assess dimensions relevant to success on the job or that interviewer recommendations are consistently related to subsequent success on managerial jobs (Arvey & Campion, 1982). Furthermore, research on selection interviews has shown that interviewer evaluations may be biased against minorities and women when being considered for managerial positions (Arvey, 1979a). Ask what is being done in a new interviewing program to increase predictive validity and to overcome the biases that have plagued prior interviews.

Since the interview plays such a key role in the assessment of experienced managers as it is usually practiced by the clinical assessor and by the recruiter in a management search firm (Ryan & Sackett, 1987), your evaluation of these techniques should be based on many of these same concerns. In addition, you will want to find out how the consultant integrates information he or she has gathered and what is the basis for recommendations about the fit of a candidate with your organization. Is there any supporting evidence beyond the consultant's claim that he or she has good judgment?

Considering these special, potential problems with the interview, you should be particularly alert to any proposed assessment technique for your organization that includes the interview. You should find out what is being done differently in this application to overcome the historical problems with the interview.

Table 24–2
Questions to Determine Validity

General	What documented evidence is there that the technique measures dimensions relevant to job success and the scores or recommendations are related to evidence of subsequent management success?
Interview	How do you prevent interviewer biases from affecting the evaluation? What is the evidence that the interviewers can predict effective performance on the job?
Biographical information	How do I know that the key questions are actually related to success on the job?
Personality tests	How are the personality characteristics measured by the test related to effective management performance?
Mental ability tests	Does the test measure a single general mental ability or several separate facets of intelligence? Are differences in mental ability measured by this test related to success on the job? Is "more" actually better?
Work samples	Are the results a function of biases in the observation and judgment of the assessors?
Practical intelligence tests	Does this test measure a mental ability that is really different from general mental ability?
Assessment centers	Are the assessments just an evaluation of the observer's general impression of a good manager? How do you know you can generalize from prior research to this assessment center?
Individual clinical assessment	How do you know that we're not just measuring the assessor's idiosyncratic preferences? What's the consultant's batting average?

Fairness to Minorities, Women, and Older Candidates

Any organization wants to avoid unfair discrimination in selection decisions. Unfair discrimination is present in the following circumstance: the applicant gets a low score on the assessment technique for some reason that is unrelated to job success and is rejected; if the applicant had been hired, he or she would have been successful. In other words, it is unfair discrimination when some artificial barrier in the assessment technique, unrelated to job success, causes the applicant to get a low score or a no-hire recommendation (Avery, 1979b).

Unfair discrimination might be introduced by biased content in the questions in a test, biographical information form, or interview. It might come from prejudices held by interviewers or by assessors observing work samples and assessment centers. Biases may be introduced because of faulty assumptions about job requirements (e.g., the job requires a verbally aggressive style), because of stereotypes about minority or female applicants (e.g., women do not possess the necessary self-confidence to be verbally aggressive), or because of a faulty matching process of people and jobs. Questions to ferret out potential sources of biases are provided in table 24–3.

Many years of research into the fairness of cognitive tests in employment settings indicate the data show quite clearly that well-developed standardized tests of mental ability do not unfairly discriminate against blacks and women (Division of Industrial-Organizational Psychology, 1980). The culmination of such research has led to statements in the *Standards* and the *Principles* that it should not be assumed that well-developed cognitive tests are biased. At the same time, organizations should take care to minimize the chances of unfair treatment of minorities, women, and older candidates by giving special orientation to these candidates and by following standardized conditions in test administration.

The same types of results indicating nondiscrimination have been found for assessment centers and work sample procedures. These techniques have been demonstrated to be equally valid for blacks and whites, men and women, and younger and older candidates (Thornton & Byham, 1982).

Such evidence should not be taken carte blanche to use mental ability tests indiscriminately. Validity cannot be assumed, and any test must be used in a standardized and reliable way.

The data for other assessment techniques are not so clear. It is not possible to be so confident about the fair use of personality tests, the interview, or the assessment done by consultants who conduct individual assessments of experienced managers.

Table 24–3
Questions to Determine Fairness to Minorities, Women, and Older Candidates

General	What documented evidence is there that the technique is valid and fair for minorities, women, and older candidates—that it does not discriminate unfairly against protected classes?
Interview	Might not an interviewer be biased against certain applicants (e.g., men against women? whites against blacks? Younger against older?)
Biographical information	Would a person from a deprived early environment be at disadvantage in answering questions?
Personality tests	Might test anxiety among minorities cause them to portray a false picture of their personalities? Might women undervalue themselves and portray a weak profile?
Mental ability tests	Don't women tend to score lower on standardized tests of intelligence than men? Does the content of most intelligence tests favor white, middle-class people?
Work samples	If some candidates haven't had prior experience with the work sample material, are they at a disadvantge, even though they may be skilled?
Practical intelligence tests	Has there been any research to determine whether these tests are fair to minorities?
Assessment centers	Is it O.K. to mix blacks and whites, men and women, older and younger in the same program?
Individual clinical assessment	If the consultant is a white male, might subtle biases against minorities and females influence the information he gathers and the way he combines that information?

PRACTICAL ISSUES

Ease of Implementation and Administration

Some assessment techniques are difficult to develop but easy to administer on an ongoing basis; for others, the reverse is true; and still others are both difficult to set up and to run. These difficulties must be considered, not because they should discourage a manager from using an appropriate assessment technique but because any organization should know what it is getting into. The costs may very well justify the expense needed. The point is that if some of these techniques are to be done well, they require more work than others. If a technique is not going to be carried out properly, it should not be used at all. Table 24–4 gives some questions that uncover difficulties in implementation and use.

There are some obvious costs of implementing any assessment program. The time of human resource staff, involvement of managers and other personnel to identify job requirements, and out-of-pocket expenses for materials and space are a few. Expenses

for an outside consultant may be required if the internal staff is not fully qualified. There are also hidden costs: some techniques take a long time to develop, and losses are incurred in not implementing a more effective program.

The costs of administering an assessment program must also be considered. Direct costs include staff time, involvement of managers as assessors, and out-of-pocket expenses for facilities and materials. Indirect costs include the turmoil that can be created among participants if there are negative reactions to the procedure, a point that will be explored more fully in the next section on users' reactions.

Of course, the other side of the equation is the benefits that derive from any assessment method. Determination of economic payoff from a selection procedure can be carried out through utility analyses (Cascio, 1987b), which consider both benefits and costs, along with other factors in the selection situation.

The manager should be wary about some assessment techniques that appear deceptively easy to implement. At first it may seem easy to implement a

Table 24–4
Questions to Understand Ease of Implementation and Administration

General	What resources (people, time, space, costs) will it take to get the program started? What will it take to keep the program going?
Interview	How much time and effort does it take actually to develop the skills an interviewer needs to ask good questions, listen well, and avoid the biases in this subjective process? Do the interviewers need to be retrained periodically to maintain consistency?
Biographical information	Doesn't this approach take a lot of developmental time and effort? How many people does it take in the tryout group? Does the importance of the questions change over time, and do we need to redo the validation study?
Personality tests	How much time does it take to train people to interpret the results of personality tests? Are we going to make people "instant psychologists"?
Mental ability tests	If any of the tests are individually administered, how much training and experience does it take to be an effective examiner?
Work samples	Don't these work sample procedures take a lot of time to build? Does the content of the exercises have to be changed periodically to avoid security leaks?
Practical intelligence tests	Isn't it going too take a lot more time before these experimental procedures are ready for organizational use?
Assessment centers	How much time does it take to train the assessors adequately? Isn't each program very expensive in assessor time, facilities, and supplies?
Individual clinical assessment	How much time will it take for the consultant to get to know our organization so the assessments can be put in proper context? When key people change, does the consultant have to get to know us all over again?

program of testing mental ability or personality. Certainly numerous tests are commercially available and easily purchased. You can start tomorrow. Such ready adoption is probably not appropriate. Several steps are needed before one can be confident the tests are job related. Adequate job analyses should be done, there should be clear specification of the dimensions to be assessed, and the test should be carefully matched with job requirements. These efforts are preliminary to the validation of the tests for a particular application, if prior research does not provide adequate support.

The validation of the assessment procedure is an essential step before implementation on a regular basis. The actual processes of validating any management assessment technique are complicated and far beyond the scope of this chapter. The processes, discussed in the *Standards,* the *Principles,* and the Uniform Guidelines, include content validation, validating against measures of job success, and construct validation. All may be appropriate, and all provide different and relevant types of information about the effectiveness of an assessment technique.

The development of a biographical information form may also appear deceptively simple. It might seem simple to identify the types of background, education, and experience wanted in managerial candidates. In actuality, it can be quite difficult to pinpoint the specific experiences that differentiate among applicants and that show a demonstrable relationship with job effectiveness (Owens, 1976).

When considering work sample procedures or the assessment center method, you should recognize that start-up costs can be considerable, including the development of exercises and training assessors and staff. Ready-made exercises can be purchased, or the organization can develop custom-made exercises, possibly with the help of a consultant. The decision to make or buy depends on whether the available exercises match your needs and on volume. Ongoing costs can be substantial also when you consider the cost of managerial time of the assessors. Balanced against these costs are the benefits. Utility analyses have shown that the increased accuracy from an assessment center fully justifies the larger expense (Cascio & Ramos, 1986). In addition, assessors learn some very important skills in information gathering, evaluation of behavior, and communication as a result of serving as assessors (Lorenzo, 1984).

Reactions of Users

Any assessment technique must be acceptable in the climate where it will be used. The most technically sound and cost-effective procedure may not work in a given organization if it does not match the norms and values that prevail. The origin of these norms and values about assessment techniques may be hard to trace, but often they emanate from the basic beliefs of the corporate culture. The organization may place a heavy emphasis on training and development; it may place a high value on egalitarian treatment of individuals; a humanistic value of treating people in nonthreatening ways may exist. An antitesting posture may have originated many years ago from a chief executive officer or from an unpleasant experience with a compliance officer in the era of federal aggressiveness against tests.

The reactions of both participants who go through the assessment techniques and managers who receive and act on the results should be considered. Recruiting and selection procedures are some of the most salient contacts that candidates have with an organization, and these procedures influence perceptions of an organization (Thornton, 1989). If a candidate is treated in a perfunctory, mechanical, or disrespectful manner, the person may decline a job offer or enter the organization with negative feelings. These initial beliefs may carry forward to the employee's motivation to work and job satisfaction.

Candidates have negative reactions to assessment procedures they perceive to be irrelevant, discriminatory, or too personal. The earlier wave of polygraph testing and the recent wave of honesty testing have often met with resistance and resentment. Unless the organization takes great care to use these procedures only when they are clearly job relevant (e.g., employees are in unsupervised positions and handle large amounts of money) and to give full explanations to examinees, negative attitudes may be generated.

Personality tests often contain personal questions that many people consider an invasion of privacy. Questions that deal with religious beliefs, sexual practices, physiological symptoms, and social attitudes found their way on to personality tests because many were developed to study aberrant behavior in clinical settings. When used in employment settings, the content may be offensive. The manager would do well to fill out any test or go through any assessment procedure to experience first-hand the types of questions asked. Table 24–5 provides some questions to ask when exploring user acceptance of a management assessment technique.

On the other hand, clearly job-relevant assessment procedures meet with much more acceptance. Face validity of techniques such as work samples, the assessment center, and the interview engender more cooperation and favorable perceptions of the organization if they are conducted properly. Favorable

Table 24–5
Questions to Assess Reactions of Users

General	How will the users of the technique react, including the participants and the managers who receive the information?
Interview	Assuming that the interviews are conducted by someone outside the operating department (e.g., representatives of the human resources department), how do candidates react to such an interviewer? How do managers from the operating area feel about someone else doing the screening?
Biographical information	Don't people feel they have no chance to correct any deficiencies from their background?
Personality tests	Don't the questions delve into some personal and private information? Do managers understand the meaning of the test scores?
Mental ability tests	Do experienced candidates object to using a test to assess ability when in fact they may have proved themselves through job performance?
Work samples	How can you cover the important parts of a job in such a brief time?
Practical intelligence tests	Do candidates and operating managers understand and accept the linkage of the test to the job requirements?
Assessment centers	Isn't the assessment center a stressful experience for candidates?
Individual clinical assesment	Does the credibility of the consultant influence the acceptance of the results by candidates and managers?

Table 24–6
Questions to Assess Legal Vulnerability

General	What risk am I running that compliance agencies will object to this technique or that legal action will be taken? What has been the outcome of court cases where the technique has been challenged?
Interview	Wouldn't the organization be safer to use an informal, unscored interview?
Biographical information	Aren't some of the questions biased or discriminatory against people in protected classes?
Personality tests	Don't I need evidence of construct validity in work settings to comply with the Uniform Guidelines?
Mental ability tests	Aren't general IQ tests highly susceptible to scrutiny by compliance agencies? Hasn't the Supreme Court ruled against IQ tests?
Work samples	Isn't any novel, new, or unproved method more susceptible to challenge?
Assessment centers	If most assessors are white males, isn't this grounds for suspicion that the method may be unfair?
Individual clinical assessment	How can you defend an inherently subjective method?

reactions to the assessment procedures spread to perceptions of other aspects of the organizations.

Legal Vulnerability

Table 24–6 raises some issues relevant to the organization's legal vulnerability when using the various assessment techniques. A manager should explore whether the assessment procedure is going to elicit such adverse reaction that candidates are likely to file a complaint with a review agency, such as the Equal Employment Opportunity Commission, or seek legal redress. No one should avoid using a given technique just because of some challenge in the past, but an appreciation of risk is helpful. An organization should surely proceed to use a job-relevant assessment procedure, but it will want to be fully prepared to take special care in the development and validation of techniques that may be more highly susceptible to legal scrutiny (Cascio, 1987c).

Why are some techniques more susceptible to attack? Techniques that are more visible, less traditional, and more invasive seem to come under closest scrutiny. Paper-and-pencil tests tend to attract more attention than the normally practiced personnel interview. As discussed earlier, personality tests often ask private questions and thus raise concerns. The susceptibility does not seem related to the track record on validity: mental ability tests are probably as highly valid as assessment centers, yet the former have come under more vociferous attack in the courts.

The interview method provides a curious case. The preponderance of validity evidence shows that the interview method, as it is normally carried out in most organizations, does not have predictive validity. On the other hand, the interview has not been the subject of as much legal scrutiny as mental ability testing, which has demonstrated a long history of substantial validity. Why? The zeitgeist in recent years has been opposed to intelligence testing, whereas it seems intuitively obvious to most people that a face-to-face interview is job related and fair.

CONCLUSIONS

When a manager with responsibility over personnel assessment functions considers alternative assessment procedures for an organization, he or she should exercise some healthy skepticism yet be ready to see the value of well-validated assessment procedures. Studies of the utility of cognitive tests and assessment centers have demonstrated that the productivity gain in dollars for one year for each person selected by a more valid predictor ranges from $4,000 to $65,000 (Burke & Frederick, 1986; Schmidt, Hunter, Mckenzie & Muldrow, 1979).

There are two types of errors people often make when considering assessment programs. On the one hand, some people put too much faith in an assessment technique and abrogate their own responsibility to make difficult personnel decisions. In contrast, other people see no value in systematic measurement via the standardized procedures discussed in the ensuing chapters. This overview and the chapters that follow provide the basis to avoid either extreme position.

Several general recommendations will encapsulate the approach a manager can take when considering alternative methods of assessing management potential:

1. Ask questions about the technical merit and practical feasibility of the program and insist on written documentation to support any claims. The written documentation should include empirical validation studies carried out in actual work settings comparable to your own organization. Do not rely on testimonials from satisfied users. Although anecdotal information is helpful to understand user reactions, it is not adequate to satisfy professional standards for validation nor will it withstand the rigors of challenge in court.

2. Be prepared for the necessity of doing a validation effort in your own organization if the prior research is not adequate to support an immediate adoption and if such research is technically feasible. Validation efforts are not cheap, but utility analyses have shown that a small improvement in validity over an existing procedure will pay off handsomely. Furthermore, loss in litigation over an unvalidated test can be very costly.

3. Use a coordinated set of multiple assessment methods. Do not expect any one assessment technique to be a panacea. Recognize that no single procedure is perfectly reliable, and thus some redundancy in assessment is healthy.

4. Make sure that the assessment procedure is compatible with the overall human resource system and the organization culture. The dimensions assessed in your management assessment program should be a part of your model of successful management; information from the assessment should complement the evaluations that are obtained from performance appraisals on candidates who are current employees; assessment information can be used to help launch developmental experience in a manager's initial assignment. More generally, consider whether the method of assessment fits with values and norms regarding treatment of employees in your organization.

REFERENCES

American Psychological Association, American Educational Research Association, & National Council on Measurement in Educational (Joint Committee) (1985). *Standards for educational and psychological testing.* Washington, DC: American Psychological Association.

Anastasi, A. (1988). *Psychological testing* (6th ed.). New York: Macmillan.

Arvey, R.D. (1979a). Unfair discrimination in the employment interview: Legal and psychological aspects. *Psychological Bulletin, 86,* 736–765.

Arvey, R.D. (1979b). *Fairness in selecting employees.* Reading, MA: Addison-Wesley.

Arvey, R.D., & Campion, J.E. (1982). The employment interview: A summary and review of recent research. *Personnel Psychology, 38,* 493–507.

Binning, J.F., & Barrett, G.V. (1989). Validity of personnel decisions: A conceptual analysis of the inferential and evidential bases. *Journal of Applied Psychology, 74,* 478–494.

Burke, M.J., & Frederick, J.T. (1986). A comparison of economic utility estimates for alternative SD_y estimation procedures. *Journal of Applied Psychology, 71,* 334–339.

Byham, W.C. (1981). Applying a systems approach to personnel activities. *Training and Development Journal,* 60–65.

Cascio, W.F. (1987a). *Applied psychology in personnel management* (3d ed.). Englewood Cliffs, NJ: Prentice-Hall.

Cascio, W.F. (1987b). *Costing human resources: The financial impact of behavior in organizations* (2d ed.). Boston: Kent.

Cascio, W.F. (1987c). *Applied psychology in personnel management* (3d ed.). Englewood Cliffs, NJ: Prentice-Hall.

Cascio, W.F., & Ramos, R.A. (1986). Development and application of a new method of assessing job performance in behavioralSL>economic terms. *Journal of Applied Psychology, 71,* 20–28.

Division of Industrial-Organizational Psychology (1980). *Principles for the validation and use of personnel selection procedures* (3d ed.). Washington, DC: American Psychological Association.

Dunnette, M.D. (1976). Aptitude abilities and skills. In M.D. Dunnette (Ed.): *Handbook of industrial and organizational psychology.* Chicago: Rand McNally.

Equal Employment Opportunity Commission, Civil Service Commission, Department of Labor, & Department of Justice (1978). Uniform Guidelines on Employee Selection Procedures. *Federal Register, 43,* 38290–38315.

Gaugler, B.B., Rosenthal, O.B., Thornton, G.C. III, & Bentson, C. (1987). Meta-analysis of assessment center validity. *Journal of Applied Psychology Monograph, 72,* 493–511.

Hunter, J.E., & Hunter, R.F. (1984). Validity and utility of alternative predictors of job performance. *Psychological Bulletin, 96,* 72–98.

Hunter, J.E., Schmidt, F.L., & Jackson, G.B. (1982). *Advanced meta-analysis: Quantitative methods for cumulating research findings across studies.* Beverly Hills, CA: Sage.

Lorenzo, R.V. (1984). Effects of assessorship on managers' proficiency in organizing, evaluating, and communicating information about people. *Personnel Psychology, 37,* 617–634.

McCormick, E.J. (1979). *Job analysis: Methods and applications.* New York: AMACOM.

Nunnally, J.C. (1978). *Psychomatic theory* (2d ed). New York: McGraw-Hill.

Owens, W.A. (1976). Background data. In M.D. Dunnette (Ed.), *Handbook of industrial-organizational psychology.* Chicago: Rand-McNally.

Ryan, A.M., & Sackett, P.R. (1987). A survey of individual assessment practices by ISL>O psychologists. *Personnel Psychology, 40,* 455–488.

Schmidt, F.L., Hunter, J.E., McKenzie, R.C., & Muldrow, T.W. (1979). Impact of valid selection procedures on work-force productivity. *Journal of Applied Psychology, 64,* 609–626.

Task Force on Assessment Center Guidelines (1989). *Guidelines and ethical considerations for assessment center operations.* Pittsburgh, PA: Development Dimensions International.

Thornton, G.C. III (1989). *The effect of selection practices on applicants' perceptions of organizational characteristics.* Paper presented at conference The Individual and Organizational Side of Selection and Performance Evaluation and Appraisal, Stuttgart, West Germany.

Thornton, G.C. III, & Byham, W.C. (1982). *Assessment centers and managerial performance.* New York: Academic Press.

25 MENTAL ABILITIES TESTING IN INDUSTRY

Hannah R. Rothstein, Michael A. McDaniel

Ability tests have been an important personnel selection tool virtually since the emergence of industrial psychology in the early part of this century. These tests are used in a variety of ways in the employment setting, from screening and classifying to promoting and counseling. The focus of this chapter is on the use of a specific kind of test—that of mental or cognitive ability (popularly referred to as intelligence tests)—for the purposes of hiring and promotion. We use the terms *cognitive* or *mental ability* to refer to a person's capacity for grasping new ideas or applying previously learned principles to a new situation because we feel that the term *intelligence* has become unduly value and emotion laden.

ABILITY TESTING AND THE AMERICAN MERITOCRATIC IDEAL

Despite the criticism that tests of mental ability are used to discriminate against disadvantaged groups, we feel that the opposite is actually true. Mental ability testing is closely related to the American idea that people should be chosen for positions on the basis of talent rather than on the basis of family, connections, or of being the "right type." (See National Academy of Sciences, 1982, for a history of employment testing in America.) As Schneider and Schmitt (1986), authors of a prominent book on staffing, have noted, tests of mental ability are actually a great equalizer because they focus attention on the performance-predictive test score rather than on job-irrelevant personal attributes of the job candidate. In fact, such tests often provide the only ability and skill-related information available to the employer before a selection decision is made. Information about education or previous experience often tells little about the candidate's skills and abilities, and interviews (available only for a fraction of applicants) are subject to the idiosyncrasies of the interviewer. Schneider and Schmitt argue that objective testing has provided opportunities for many who would otherwise have been discriminated against due to prejudice, stereotypes, and ignorance.

THE USE OF TESTS IN AMERICAN INDUSTRY

An extensive survey of test use in the United States was conducted in 1975 by Prentice-Hall and the American Society of Personnel Administrators (National Academy of Sciences, 1982). They found that testing was quite popular but that organizational size was an important determinant of test use. Large and medium-sized organizations were more likely than small organizations to use tests, or other formal means of assessment, for the purposes of selection, placement, training, or promotion. The size of the employing company also determined to a large extent the source of the test (homemade versus commercially developed), the qualifications of the people involved in the testing program, and the presence of quality control checks on the adequacy of tests, with larger organizations having more effective testing programs. As a result of some changes in scientific-professional beliefs about the transportability of evidence regarding a test's value from one organization to another, we have reason to believe that tests will be used more frequently and to greater advantage by smaller firms in the future. Testing was most frequently used in the clerical occupations (such as secretarial, bookkeeping, typing, and cashiering) and more widely used in nonmanufacturing businesses such as utilities, banks, insurance, and communications companies than in the manufacturing sector. Since the number of both clerical and service positions is steadily increasing, we can expect a rise in the number of people who will be tested before hiring in the coming years. A growing number of unions appear to be using ability tests for selection into apprenticeship programs, and in several industries consortia have been formed to develop industry-wide entry and promotional testing programs. Although tests of mental ability are used less often for managerial than for nonmanagerial positions, they are frequently used with recent college graduates entering management and with managerial recruits who come from external rather than internal sources (Campbell, Dunnette, Lawler & Weick, 1970). Overall, a significant portion of the U.S. work force has taken or can expect to take a test of mental ability before being hired.

Although the popularity of mental ability tests grew between the time of their introduction in the early 1900s and the mid-1960s, a dramatic reversal of this trend occurred from the mid-1960s through at least the late 1970s. The drastic reduction in test use was caused by the introduction of equal employment opportunity legislation and federal selection guidelines, which placed many constraints on personnel activities such as hiring, promotion, and dismissal. Partly because ability tests are often the most visible, objectively scored, and well-documented part of personnel decision making and partly because they frequently result in low rates of minority hiring, they were singled out for special regulatory attention. New employment selection guidelines virtually mandated the validation of every test for every setting in which

they were used. The cost of these validation studies, plus the fear of litigation and its associated costs, caused many companies to abandon their testing program in favor of selection devices (e.g., education credentials, employment interviews) that were less valid and less objective but made adverse impact harder to demonstrate. It has been suggested by two of the top researchers in the field of personnel selection (schmidt & Hunter, 1981) that part of the decline in American productivity during the 1960s and 1970s was the result of the decline in accuracy with which employers had sorted people into jobs as a consequence of the decreased use of ability tests.

Mental ability tests do often show adverse impact against minority groups (on average, minority group members score lower than whites). However, a large body of research now shows that the tests are not unfair in that the tests do not underpredict minority group performance. Whatever aspects of cultural or other disadvantage that suppress test performance in the minority group also result in lower job performance. That is, no matter how job performance has been measured, lower average test scores are accompanied by lower average job performance for all workers, regardless of ethnic affiliation. This was also the conclusion of a blue-ribbon panel established by the National Academy of Sciences to examine ability testing (National Academy of Sciences, 1982). It is likely that any revision of the Uniform Guidelines on Employment Selection Procedures (1978) will reflect this fact. Later we will suggest how tests may be used in a manner that preserves their validity while eliminating adverse impact.

THE VALIDITY OF MENTAL ABILITY TESTS

Naive Beliefs and the Doctrine of Situational Specificity

During the initial phase of test use early in the century, it was believed that success in a wide variety of occupational tasks was related to a common core of cognitive skills and that therefore tests of general mental ability should be broadly predictive of job success. (The notion that one's performance on a test is related to performance on the job is at the core of the technical term *validity*. A test is valid to the extent that scores on the test are correlated with some non-test performance of interest.) When, however, validity studies (studies to see if, in fact, test scores are related to job performance) were done in individual organizations, it was found that the observed correla-

tion between scores on a mental ability test and performance on the same job in different organizations often varied greatly; similarly, jobs that did not seem very different from each other in the same organization oftern appeared to be very different on the basis of the relationship between test scores and job performance. The finding that observed validity coefficients varied considerably from study to study, even though the tests and jobs were the same, spawned the idea that any test had to be separately validated each time it was used for a new job or for a new organization. This belief, called the doctrine of situational specificity, was popular for about forty years and led, among other things, to the excessive validation requirements of the federal guidelines mentioned above.

The Development of Validity Generalization

During the mid-1970s, two researchers, Frank Schmidt and John Hunter, developed a new procedure for comparing the results of validity studies across organizations. Their procedure, called validity generalization (Schmidt & Hunter, 1977), provides a means of evaluating how well a test demonstrated to be valid in one setting will work in another setting and how extensively the findings of validity can be generalized to the same job across different organizations. (Chapter 10 in this book is dedicated entirely to validity generalization. Here we discuss only those findings directly relevant to tests of mental ability.) Schmidt and Hunter (1977) were able to show that validity is broadly generalizable across organizations (for the same job and type of mental ability test) and that, in fact, professionally developed tests of general mental ability had at least some degree of generalized validity (that is, are predictive of successful performance) for all jobs in the U.S. economy (Hunter, 1983). Variations in validity evident in individual studies were shown to be the result of statistical problems (e.g., random sampling error, measurement error), which are unavoidable in single small-sample studies and which severely distort validity results. These statistical problems not only cause cross-situational validities to appear variable when they are actually nearly constant but also artificially depress the average validity level. A major benefit of validity generalization is that it allows personnel researchers to control for these statistical problems and thus determine the true validity of the test. The major conclusion of the validity generalization studies is that tests of major cognitive abilities always show useful validities across the entire spectrum of jobs in the economy. In other words, a person's score on a test of mental or cognitive ability will always be predictive of (though not perfectly related to) his or her performance on the job. Validity generalization results provide strong evidence that there is no scientific need to conduct local validity studies for each job or for each organization when a professionally developed mental ability test is used as the selection instrument.

Researchers in the area of employee selection agree that validity generalizes across organizations. There is some remaining disagreement about whether the exact amount of validity is constant from situation to situation. What is important for the personnel decision maker, however, is the fact that validity generalizes, not whether it is totally constant. Thus, the practical implications of validity generalization findings will not be affected by the ultimate resolution of the question of validity constancy.

More Information on Validity Generalization Findings

Although professionally developed tests of mental ability have been shown to be usefully valid across the board, the degree of validity does vary with the complexity level or information processing requirements of the job. Hunter (1983) has shown that validities of mental ability tests are highest for high-complexity jobs, a bit lower for jobs of moderate complexity, and somewhat lower (but still quite valid) for low-complexity jobs. He also showed that tests of psychomotor ability are most valid for lower-complexity-level jobs and least valid for higher-complexity jobs. Thus, predictive validity is increased if psychomotor tests are given together with tests of mental ability and the scores on the two measures are combined. The optimal combination will depend on the complexity of the occupation. For an employer to approximate closely the actual validity of a specific type of mental ability test for a specific job in his or her organization, he or she need only identify the test type (e.g., test of general mental ability, reasoning ability) and find out the job's complexity classification, based on its code in the *Dictionary of Occupational Titles* (U.S. Department of Labor, 1970) as explained in Hunter (1983). Once the job's complexity level has been established, a list, also provided in Hunter (1983), that contains the relevant validity estimates can be consulted. This procedure would be particularly helpful if one is trying to comply with federal guidelines for test validation, since they require establishing the similarity between jobs as a precondition for generalizing validity from one situation to another.

In addition to generalized estimates of validities produced by broad-based validity generalization studies, a wide variety of tests and jobs has been individually subjected to validity generalization analysis. Specific jobs studied with this procedure include clerical occupations, sales, petroleum refinery operators, machine tenders, maintenance and laboratory technicians, power plant operators, computer programmers, first-line supervisors, apprentices in the skilled trades, law enforcement personnel, mechanical repairers, and many specific military specialties. The types of mental abilities tests that have been examined include tests of general mental ability, reasoning ability, verbal ability, quantitative ability, spatial ability, mechanical ability, and perceptual speed. (See Hunter & Hirsh, 1987, for specific references to these studies.)

Scores on the tests of mental abilities were correlated with two types of criteria for most of the jobs mentioned above: success in training programs and successful performance on the job. In the past, some personnel psychologists and other personnel decision makers have argued that the abilities that are needed to learn a job are not the same ones that are needed to perform the job after it has been learned. If this were the case, we would find that tests of ability that were related to training success were not related to job performance. Validity generalization results show that this belief is not true. The overall pattern of results was quite similar for both types of criteria. People who do well in training programs generally possess the necessary skills to do well on the job. The average validity for predicting training success, about .70 (which indicates very good predictive accuracy), is a bit higher than average job performance validity, about .55 (which indicates good predictive accuracy), but no other commonly used selection technique yields such consistently high relationships with on-the-job performance or with training success. This is particularly true for entry-level jobs, but even for higher-level jobs, cognitive ability predicts day-to-day performance nearly as well as it predicts initial learning of the job (Hunter, 1986). In addition, the massive amount of validity evidence in support of mental ability tests is far greater than that in support of any alternative predictor. We therefore strongly recommend that a test of mental ability always be part of an employee selection battery.

Does Job Experience Wipe Out the Influence of Mental Ability on Job Performance?

Some people have suggested that mental ability is important only for persons on the job a short time. With increased time on the job, they argue, job experience becomes more important than mental ability as a determinant of job performance. If this is the case, tests of mental ability should be used only at entry-level selection and would be predictive of performance only for a short time. This has important implications for the dollar-value utility of selection programs based on mental ability testing. (A general discussion of utility is presented later in this chapter.)

A recent large-scale study (Schmidt, Hunter, Outerbridge & Goff, 1988) has shown that differences in performance between high- and low-ability employees remain constant for at least five years after hiring. At all experience levels between one month and five years, employees who had scored high on a preemployment test of mental ability outperformed those who had scored low. McDaniel (1986) has found similar results extending to approximately twenty years of experience. Thus, mental ability continues to be an important contributor to job performance even for experienced workers. In part, these findings mean that tests of mental ability can be useful in making promotion as well as selection decisions.

Mental Ability Testing for Managerial Jobs

According to the most ambitious study ever conducted on managerial behavior and performance, "General intelligence tests are among the measures with the greatest potential for predicting managerial effectiveness" (Campbell, Dunnette, Lawler & Weick, 1970, p. 128). The authors of this study found that proficiency in executive and managerial jobs has been most effectively predicted by tests of mental ability, perceptual accuracy, and tests of personality and interests. In a summary of a review of the relationship between various selection devices and managerial performance, they reported that mental ability tests showed a correlation of about .25–.30 with performance, before they were corrected for the statistical distortions that produced "serious underestimate[s]" (Campbell et al., 1970, p. 167). Our estimate of the true validity of these tests for predicting managerial success is .50–.60 (good predictive accuracy), based on approximate correction for the statistical distortions. Thus, the validity of mental ability tests for managerial jobs is just about the same as their validity for other jobs. It has even been suggested that the relationship between intelligence and managerial performance rises with increases in the level of management being studied (Ghiselli, 1963), although others have disputed this finding (Korman, 1968).

UTILITY

Until recently, psychologists did not do a very good job of translating their correlation coefficients or validities into dollar and cents terms that would allow managers to see how employment testing contributed to the organization's bottom line. However, during

the past decade, a family of procedures called utility analysis has been designed to address this need. Although there are several approaches to utility analysis (Boudreau, 1983; Cascio, 1982, Hunter & Schmidt, 1983), their common conclusion is that the use of mental abilities tests can save the average company a substantial amount of money. The simplest estimates show that use of a test of mental ability as an employee selection device will nearly always save the company thousands of dollars per year per each new hiree for the entire length of service of each new employee (Hunter & Schmidt, 1983). For a medium-sized company this can mean savings of hundreds of thousands of dollars per year. The costs involved in developing or purchasing and administering a test will be quickly made up in savings due to increased productivity of the superior new employees selected. Companies not interested in increased production can maintain constant production by hiring fewer ability-tested employees, thus saving unnecessary payroll costs. Utility analysis can also be used to calculate the relative value of different selection procedures. In most cases, this sort of utility analysis will show that a test of mental ability will have a better cost-benefit ratio than any alternative test procedure (Hunter & Hunter, 1984).

The amount of savings accrued by an organization as a result of the use of a mental ability testing program will vary as a function of several factors, including the validity of the selection procedure that the test is replacing, the number of people applying for jobs relative to the number that need to be hired, and the variability of performance between good and bad performers in the current (nonmental-ability-test-selected) group of workers. Testing will save an organization the most money when it is replacing a procedure with poor validity, when the company can afford to turn down a majority of applicants, and when there is a large range of performance among the workers.

When an organization is interested in increasing productivity and meeting affirmative action goals simultaneously, the approach with the most utility is that of using the test to rank workers within racial groups and then hiring the highest-scoring persons within each racial group. For example, if an organization had ten vacancies and wished to fill five of the positions with black applicants, the employer would select the five blacks with the highest scores on the test and then select the five highest-scoring nonblack applicants. This is the procedure now being followed by the U.S. Employment Service. Unfortunately, some have objected to this procedure as a disguised quota system, and its ultimate legality has not yet been determined. The most popular alternative procedure is to use a mental ability test to screen out only the bottom 10 or 15 percent of the applicants and then to hire randomly or select on the basis of "other procedures" from the screened group. This procedure, however, results in massive productivity losses, primarily as a result of hiring less able majority group members, and often still falls short of meeting affirmative action goals.

TYPES OF MENTAL ABILITY TESTS

There are two popular types of tests of mental ability. The first type is the test of general mental ability, which is designed as a self-contained measure of all major cognitive skills. The second type is the multi-aptitude battery, which is a package of short tests of single mental abilities (such as reasoning, verbal ability, and numerical ability), which together yield a picture of general mental ability.

Although some examples of tests are presented below, the reader who is interested in information about specific tests of mental ability is referred to the Buros *Mental Measurements Yearbook* (the newest edition is the ninth, edited by Mitchell, 1986), and *Test Critiques* (Keyser & Sweetland, 1984). Both of these series contain a comprehensive list of test and quality evaluations of each measure by reputable testing experts. In addition, they contain lists of test publishers and detail how to acquire other test-related information.

Tests of General Mental Ability

A good example of an employment-oriented test of mental ability, and one of the most popular, is the Wonderlic Personnel Test (Wonderlic, 1984). The test takes 12 minutes and contains fifty items, which cover vocabulary, arithmetic reasoning, space visualization, number series, and other areas. It is meant to tap all the major cognitive skills used in most jobs. It is inexpensive, easy to administer, and has many parallel forms. It also has a Spanish version. The Wonderlic comes with extensive materials to facilitate interpretation of test scores. Norms are presented broken down by age, sex, region of the country, and education, which enable the employer to compare his or her applicants' scores to those of comparable persons. Many validity studies support the Wonderlic's predictive accuracy, and a recent court ruling

(*Cormier et al. v. PPG Industries*) indicated that the evidence for the general validity of the Wonderlic was sufficient to obviate the need for a local validity study. A very useful type of information included with the Wonderlic is expectancy tables. These show the percentage of people achieving a given test score who would be expected to be successful. The tables have been composed for many types of jobs and are based on validity studies. Other tests that are similar in content and purpose to the Wonderlic include the Adaptability Test (Tiffin & Lawshe, 1967) and the Thurstone Test of Mental Alertness (Thurstone & Thurstone, 1983).

Multiaptitude Batteries

Most multiaptitude batteries are designed to measure five to ten mental abilities that are related to job performance. Some of the most popular multiaptitude batteries include the Differential Aptitude Test (DAT) (Bennett, Seashore, & Wesman, 1982), the General Aptitude Test Battery (GATB), which is administered by most state employment services (U.S. Department of Labor, 1970), the Employee Aptitude Survey, or EAS (Ruch & Ruch, 1980), and the Basic Skills Test (Ruch, Shuh, Moinat & Dye, 1981). All of these tests have validity data to support their use and come with extensive manuals, which contain useful information about the tests.

Home-grown Tests of Mental Ability

Some organizations may prefer to develop their own tests of mental ability, in part because they can better match the subject matter of the items to the content of the job for which they will be used. While this does not increase the actual validity of the test, it sometimes increases its popularity with test takers, who feel that they can see the relationship between the test and the job for which they are applying. This apparent relationship is called face validity. If an organization wants to develop its own test, it will certainly need to hire a qualified testing consultant, and it must be large enough to support a several-hundred-employee-based validity study.

Starting a Testing Program

Any testing program, whether based on home-grown or commercial tests, should be supervised by persons with specialized training and experience. Necessary qualifications will typically include a graduate degree in psychology or psychometrics, courses and experience in the fields of selection, testing, and psychological measurement, and familiarity with applicable professional and legal standards. Standards for adequate test development and validation are presented in the *Standards for Educational and Psychological Testing* (American Psychological Association, 1985) and in the *Principles for the Validation and Use of Personnel Selection Procedures* (second edition), produced by the Society for Industrial and Organizational Psychology, Inc. (1987). This society, which is a division of the American Psychological Association, is also a reliable organization to contact for referrals to well-qualified testing consultants. Universities with programs in industrial-organizational psychology are also good sources for reputable testing and selection experts.

SUMMARY

Tests of mental ability can be useful for entry-level hiring and promotion decisions for most levels of employees (including managers). The validity of mental abilities tests has been found to be generally higher than that of other selection devices. Although the claim has been made that tests of mental ability discriminate against minorities, research has shown that test scores predict performance fairly for minority group members. Recent scientific advances have strengthened the case in favor of mental testing in industry and have also demonstrated the cost-effectiveness of these personnel screening tools.

REFERENCES

American Psychological Association (1985). *Standards for educational and psychological tests*. Washington, DC: American Psychological Association.

Bennett, G.K., Seashore, H.G., & Wesman, A.G. (1982). *The differential aptitude tests*. San Antonio, TX: Psychological Corporation.

Boudreau, J. (1983). Economic considerations in estimating the utility of human resource productivity improvement programs. *Personnel Psychology, 36*, 551–557.

Campbell, J.P., Dunnette, M.D., Lawler, E.E., & Weick, K.F. (1970). *Managerial behavior, performance and effectiveness*. New York: McGraw-Hill.

Cascio, W.F. (1982). *Costing human resources: The financial impact of behavior on organizations*. Boston: Kent.

Cormier et al. v. PPG Industries, Inc. (1983). No. 81–3485. U.S. Court of Appeals, Fifth Circuit, April 11.

Ghiselli, E.E. (1963). Managerial talent. *American Psychologist, 8*, 631–642.

Hunter, J.E. (1983). *Test validation for 12,000 jobs: Application of job classification and validity generalization to the General Aptitude Test Battery (GATB)*. Washington, DC: U.S. Department of Labor.

Hunter, J.E. (1986). Cognitive ability, cognitive aptitudes, job knowledge and job performance. *Journal of Vocational Behavior, 28*, 340–362.

Hunter, J.E., & Hirsh, H.R. (1987). Applications of meta-analysis. In I. Robertson and C. Cooper (Eds.), *International review of industrial/organizational psychology*. London: Wiley.

Hunter, J.E., & Hunter, R.F. (1984). Validity and utility of alternative predictors of job performance. *Psychological Bulletin, 96*, 72–98.

Hunter, J.E., & Schmidt, F.L. (1983). Quantifying the effects of psychological interventions on employee job performance and workforce productivity. *American Psychologist, 38*, 473–477.

Keyser, D.J., & Sweetland, R.C. (1984). *Test Critiques* (vol. 1). Kansas City: Test Corporation of America.

Korman, A. (1968). The prediction of managerial performance: A review. *Personnel Psychology, 21*, 295–322.

McDaniel, M.A. (1986). *The evaluation of a causal model of job performance: The interrelationships of general mental ability, job experience, and job performance*. Ph.D. dissertation, George Washington University.

McDaniel, M.A. (1989). Validity generalization: Implications for personnel selection. In J. Jones, B. Steffy, & D. Bray (Eds.), *Applying psychology in business: The manager's handbook*. Lexington, MA: Lexington Books.

Mitchell, J.V. (1986). *The ninth mental measurements yearbook*. Lincoln, NE: Buros Institute of Mental Measurement.

National Academy of Sciences (1982). *Ability testing: Uses, consequences, and controversies* (vol. 1). Washington, DC: National Academy Press.

Ruch, F.L., & Ruch, W.W. (1980). *Employee aptitude survey, Technical report*. Los Angeles: Psychological Services, Inc.

Ruch, W.W., Shuh, A.N., Moinat, S., & Dye, D. (1981). *PSI basic skills tests*. Los Angeles: Psychological Services, Inc.

Schmidt, F.L., & Hunter, J.E. (1977). Development of a general solution to the problem of validity generalization. *Journal of Applied Psychology, 62*, 529–540.

Schmidt, F.L., & Hunter, J.E. (1981). Employment testing: Old theories and new research findings. *American Psychologist, 36*, 1128–1136.

Schmidt, F.L., Hunter, J.E., Outerbridge, A.N., & Goff, S. (1988). Joint relation of experience and ability with job performance: Test of three hypotheses. *Journal of Applied Psychology, 73*, 46–57.

Schneider, B., & Schmitt, N. (1986). *Staffing organizations* (2d ed.). Chicago: Scott-Foresman.

Society for Industrial & Organizational Psychology, Inc. (1987). *Principles for the validation of employment selection procedures* (3d ed.). College Park, MD: Author.

Thurstone, L.L., & Thurstone, T.C. (1983). *The Thurstone Test of Mental Alertness*. Chicago: Science Research Associates, Inc.

Tiffin, J., & Lawshe, C.H. (1967). *The Adaptability Test*. Chicago: Science Research Associates, Inc.

Uniform guidelines on employee selection procedures (1978). *Federal Register, 43*, 38290–38315.

U.S. Department of Labor (1970). *Dictionary of occupational titles*. Washington, DC: Author.

Wonderlic, E.F. (1984). *The Wonderlic Personnel Test*. Northfield, IL: EF Wonderlic & Associates, Inc.

26 USING BIOGRAPHICAL DATA IN PERSONNEL DECISIONS

Bruce N. Barge

"The best predictor of a person's future behavior is the way he or she behaved in the past." This phrase is perhaps the most common rule used in attempts to understand and predict the behavior of others. In fact, it is difficult to think of a situation in which behavior would be predicted for which there was no similar previous behavior.

Biographical data (biodata) is a way systematically to collect information about a person's previous behavior in order to predict how that person might behave in the future. For example, information about how long a job applicant was employed in his or her last job or jobs might predict length of service in a future job. Also, information about how well an applicant had done previously in school might predict how well the person would do in a future job training course.

Because of the importance of these types of predictions, it has become commonplace in industry to ask job applicants to complete an application form in which questions about previous behavior are asked. The applicant's responses to the questions can then be weighted and used to predict future performance. This method of systematically collecting and weighting application blank information was the first real method of using biodata in organizations. The format and variations of it are still in wide use today.

Examples of items that may be included on an application blank or biodata form follow (the type and content of items can vary considerably depending on the user and purpose of the questionnaire):

Demographic: Age, marital status, number of children, address, home owner or renter.

Work History and Qualifications: Tenure, performance, and experience in previous job(s), education.

Personal Background: Home environment while growing up, school experiences, relationships.

Accomplishments/Activities: Awards received, offices held, organizational memberships, hobbies.

Demographic questions such as marital status or age are not often used today because of equal employment opportunity considerations.

The most frequent use of a biodata instrument is as a selection tool to aid in the screening of job applicants. Applicants can be scored on the basis of their responses to the biodata items, and the top applicant(s) can then be selected. As will be discussed in more detail later, biodata have been shown repeatedly to be excellent predictors of later job performance, job tenure, and various indicators of job adjustment or satisfaction. This is true for the entire range of occupations, from managers to manufacturing personnel.

Biodata are also useful predictors in combination with other types of information such as interviews or tests. An applicant's past behavior often provides unique and valid information that is not otherwise available. When this information is added to that of an interview or test, the quality of prediction is usually increased significantly.

Finally, biodata can be used for classification in order to place persons in the jobs for which they are best suited. A company could, for example, use biodata to divide its sales force into groups. Salespersons with one type of background might be assigned to accounts in which long-term client relations were important. Those with another type of background might be assigned to sales that involved numerous cold calls and relatively little follow-up. A diversity of employee backgrounds may make such an application of biodata highly feasible.

ADVANTAGES OF BIODATA

The use of biodata has several advantages over other types of employee selection or classification tools such as tests or interviews. Because of these advantages, biodata are extremely useful in selecting and classifying job applicants and yet avoid many problems associated with other types of assessment devices. The advantages discussed below include the validity, legal aspects, feasibility, and verifiability of biodata.

Validity

The single greatest advantage biodata possess is a well-documented history of validity in predicting criteria such as job performance, training performance, and job satisfaction or adjustment. In several recent reviews of validity studies, biodata have been shown to be the best or among the best predictors of each of these major areas of employee performance.

Ghiselli (1955, 1966, 1973) conducted an extremely thorough review of all types of applicant assessment devices and found that biodata predicted training and job performance better overall than any tests or personality measures available. This was true across several occupational groups. Similar evidence of biodata validity has been obtained in reviews by England (1971), Asher (1972), Owens (1976), Reilly and Chao (1982), and Barge and Hough (1983). These reviews also show good validity for biodata in predicting turnover, absenteeism, and substance abuse.

In addition to evidence of validity when biodata are used as a single predictor, there have been numerous studies that showed how biodata can improve validity when combined with another type of measure. For example, Harrell and Harrell (1976) combined biodata with test scores and other information and found that biodata greatly improved predictions of later career success among managers who had received their M.B.A ten years earlier. Booth, McNally, and Berry (1978) obtained similar results when biodata were added to test scores in the prediction of performance in paramedic training. Biodata have been demonstrated to have validity in classification, as when Brush and Owens (1979) used biodata to classify employees for jobs in a major oil company.

Legal Issues

An important characteristic of any employee selection device is that it meet the standards required by the U.S. Equal Employment Opportunity Commission in its Uniform Guidelines on Employee Selection Procedures (1978). The guidelines state that a selection procedure cannot be used if (1) it has adverse impact on members of a subgroup, and (2) it cannot be shown to be job related. For example, a biodata inventory would be in violation of the guidelines if members of a subgroup obtained scores on it that were significantly lower than those of the majority group and these scores were not related to later performance on the job.

In most cases, biodata inventories are related to job performance because the items are not included in the inventory unless they have already demonstrated a statistically significant relationship with performance. Such items may still have adverse impact, however, and should be avoided where alternatives exist that have less adverse impact (*Albemarle v. Moody,* 1975). In short, the ideal inventory would be both job related and have no adverse impact. Fortunately, many biodata inventories have been able to meet both of these criteria successfully.

Reilly and Chao (1982) reviewed eleven studies that reported minority versus majority racial subgroup comparisons. They concluded that the validity and fairness of biodata can be expected to hold for both groups. In the four studies they reviewed with male versus female comparisons, it was necessary to score the items differently for each sex, but when this was done, the inventories met acceptable criteria of fairness. Overall, therefore, it seems feasible to develop biodata instruments that meet legal guidelines when proper procedures are followed. Items such as age or marital status that may be objectionable or produce adverse impact should be avoided and replaced with nonobjectionable items of equal validity.

Feasibility

Another major advantage of biodata is that they are easy and inoffensive to collect. Most job applicants expect to complete an application form so they are unlikely to be surprised about or resistant to completing a brief questionnaire about their background. Usually biodata information can be gathered quickly and inexpensively, since a relatively small number of items are often sufficient to attain acceptable levels of validity. Also, a background questionnaire may be less offensive or threatening to applicants than an ability test or a personality inventory.

Verifiability

A final advantage to biodata has to do with verifying the information provided in order to determine an applicant's truthfulness in responding to questions. The responses to many biodata items can be checked, and an applicant could be eliminated from consideration if found to have falsified responses. Even if responses are not checked, applicants may respond more candidly because of the possibility of verification or because the questions refer to actual behavior rather than a general self-description. Thus, there may be less of a tendency for applicants to describe themselves in a misleading way, and the information obtained may be of higher quality.

Research on the issue of truthfulness in biodata responses is mixed, with some studies showing substantial distortion in responses and others showing quite accurate responses. It appears that persons completing a biodata form can distort their answers when motivated to do so, but the frequency with which this happens is often less than expected. A study by Haymaker and Erwin (1980) showed how a lie scale can be embedded in a biodata inventory to identify those who distort their responses; the use of this scale improved the accuracy of scores without adversely affecting validity.

SAMPLE BIODATA PROFILES

Figure 26–1 contains two sample profiles for a biodata questionnaire. These profiles supply an example of how the dimensions and scores from a biodata form might be reported for persons who had completed the inventory. Profile A is for an individual whose background and previous behavior suggests successful performance in a future job. Profile B shows a background that predicts less than ideal future performance. Biodata results can also be reported in terms of a single score if a profile is not desired or feasible.

In the example, profile A depicts an individual with a background that shows above-average achievement, adjustment, and participation in a range of life experiences and pursuits. This individual was raised in a stable home environment and did well in school, especially in extracurricular activities. Person A has been quite successful on the job and has actively pursued promotions and leadership responsibilities. Marriage, family, and leisure pursuits have received less emphasis from this person yet are still at or above average.

By contrast, profile B shows a person whose level of success and participation has been uneven. This individual grew up in a somewhat unstable home, did well in school academically, but was not involved in school activities. Person B has done fairly well on the job but has avoided leadership or group functions. Marriage and family life has been the area of most success for this person.

Again, the profiles are examples, and the actual form of score reports will differ depending on the content and purpose of the biodata questionnaire. Only those scores shown to be predictive of the criteria should be included in a profile so that decisions are based on strictly job-relevant factors. In some situations, a single overall score will be reported rather than a score profile so that individual profile scores are not overinterpreted.

Figure 26–1. Sample Biodata Profiles

Percentile	0	50	100
		Profile B	Profile A
Parental/Home Environment			
School Achievement			
School Activities			
Job Satisfaction/Stability			
Job Success/Aspirations			
Leadership/Group Participation			
Marital/Family Adjustment			
Leisure Pursuits			

BIODATA INVENTORIES AVAILABLE COMMERCIALLY

When an organization decides to begin using biodata to aid its personnel decisions, it can develop its own custom-made instrument or purchase an appropriate inventory that is commercially available. Both of these types of biodata forms are in wide use in organizations, and there are advantages associated with each. Discussed below are the major advantages of using an existing inventory from a commercial firm, as well as examples of well-researched inventories available for purchase.

A primary advantage of the existing inventory is that the purchasing organization does not have to get involved in the time, expense, and expertise associated with the development process, since this has already been completed by the vendor's research department. Second, inventories that are marketed to industry have typically been used and validated previously, so the organization has a good idea of the kind of instrument and results it is purchasing.

As examples of the kind of instruments that can be purchased, the biodata inventories available from two personnel research organizations are discussed below. These inventories have been used to predict performance in a range of jobs and organizations and have demonstrated validity in the applications for which they were developed. It is not intended that these inventories be seen as the only or the best alternatives for an organization seeking to use a biodata instrument. Again, these inventories are discussed as examples, and the organization interested in using a biodata inventory should evaluate these and other instruments according to its needs.

London House, Inc., offers two biodata instruments for sale, one intended for use with managers and professionals and the other for use with entry-level personnel. Manuals are available for both inventories and contain detailed information about the development, characteristics, and validity of the instruments. For brevity, only the inventory intended for managers and professionals is discussed below.

The Experience and Background Inventory (EBI) consists of 107 items, each of which asks a factual question concerning the individual's family, education, or work history. Responses are recorded in the inventory booklet and can be either hand scored by the organization or sent to London House for machine scoring. Results are reported on each of sixteen dimensions to form a profile of the respondent.

The EBI is the result of over twenty years of previous research and has been used for classification and prediction of performance with thousands of professionals. It has been demonstrated to have high reliability and to be a valid predictor of job tenure, sales performance, and managerial performance in a range of organizations. The EBI meets equal employment opportunity guidelines for both women and racial minorities. In addition, the procedures followed in the development and refinement of the EBI have resulted in a highly interpretable instrument. More information about London House inventories is available from London House, Inc., 1550 North Northwest Highway, Park Ridge, Illinois 60068 (1-800-323-5923).

Three biodata inventories are available from Richardson, Bellows, Henry, & Co. (RBH), intended for use with managers, first-line supervisors, and clerical personnel, respectively. Each of these has been heavily researched and has yielded very good prediction of job performance. Again for brevity, only the Manager Profile Record (MPR) is discussed.

The MPR is a multidimensional questionnaire that addresses an individual's early and more recent background as well as behavior in certain types of work settings. Responses are made on an answer sheet that is scored by computer to provide both a total score and subscore profile. Ongoing use of the instrument entails mailing answer sheets from management candidates to RBH, which then provides scoring and results for the candidates. The MPR can be used in a low-cost validity research trial provided by RBH, which gives an organization the opportunity to evaluate the inventory's effectiveness before making a decision regarding its use.

In previous research, the MPR has been used with thousands of managers and management candidates in numerous organizations ranging from manufacturing to financial. Validities obtained with the MPR are very high in predicting various measures of management success and management potential. RBH reports that these validities hold for all groups studied, including women and racial minorities, and the MPR meets all equal employment guidelines. Further information about the RBH biodata inventories is available from RBH at 1140 Connecticut Avenue, Washington, D.C. 20036 (202-659-3755).

DEVELOPING A BIODATA INVENTORY

For many organizations, it may be preferable to have a customized biodata inventory that has been developed specifically to fit that company's unique needs. Constructing a biodata inventory is not extremely difficult, and the advantages of a customized form may greatly outweigh the costs, especially if the form will be used widely.

The majority of the cost associated with a customized form is incurred during development and depends in part on whether development can be done in-house. England (1971) suggests that approximately 100 hours will be needed to produce a valid biographical inventory, but this figure will vary a great deal depending on decisions made during development. If the inventory is used by a large number of people over a period of time, however, this money will be returned quickly.

A second consideration, content control, is often a very important advantage of the customized biodata inventory. A company can decide the length, the diversity, and the format of the inventory it wishes to use and develop its form according to those specifications. For example, an organization may choose to construct a biodata form with a large number of items that deal with prior leadership behavior. Alternatively, the organization could construct an inventory that asked a few questions about many diverse aspects of an applicant's past behavior. This type of flexibility in content and length is usually possible only when the inventory is developed specifically for one organization or job.

Even more important than cost and content control, however, is the question of the validity of the form to be used. Will a company obtain better results with an inventory developed specifically for that company and its job(s), or can an existing commercial instrument provide equivalent validity? This question cannot be answered without information about the particular setting in which the inventory will be used. Based on the validity results currently available, it seems that a well-developed commercial inventory is likely to obtain acceptable validities in any application similar to that for which it was developed. A customized inventory may yield higher validities, but how much higher depends on a number of factors, such as the job(s) and criteria involved and the quality of the commercial and customized inventories.

An organization that is unsure whether to develop its own biodata form will need to weigh each of these issues in more detail before making a decision. It is fairly easy to come up with reasonable estimates for cost and validity once more is known about the situation in which the form will be used. Each factor (and perhaps others not mentioned here) can then be weighed in making the decision.

If it is decided to develop a customized inventory, the procedures to be followed are fairly simple and clear-cut. Decisions will need to be made along the way, as is true for any other task, but references are available that provide instructions for each step. A pamphlet by England (1971) provides an excellent guide to the empirical strategy of development, which historically has been the most frequently used procedure. This procedure is described briefly here. Comments are added where appropriate to suggest alternative procedures when they may increase the usefulness of the resulting inventory.

Step 1—Choosing the Criterion

This first step appears to be extremely simple since it merely involves choosing what the organization wishes to predict (e.g., job performance or turnover). The step is of critical importance, however, because the value of the entire development process is dependent on the adequacy and accuracy of the criterion chosen. The most the biodata inventory can do is predict the criterion used in its development. If the criterion is not a good measure of what the organization wants to predict, then predictions from the biodata instrument will necessarily be inaccurate.

The main problem in choosing the criterion is not in deciding that you wish to predict job performance; it is in finding a measure of job performance that accurately and adequately reflects the levels of job performance that employees display. For example, an organization may have information about the output from each of its manager's divisions, and this output could be used as the criterion measure of manager performance. It is possible, however, for someone to be an excellent manager and have a division with low output or be a poor manager and have a division with high output. Factors such as length of time on the job or economic conditions could affect division output and produce misleading information about the manager's performance.

No criterion chosen is going to be perfect. Performance ratings, for example, can avoid some of the problems of production information, but ratings may be subject to other biases from the person doing the ratings. The important point is to choose a criterion that (1) measures what it is that the organization wants to predict, (2) can be obtained for all the persons performing the job in question, and (3) is as objective, complete, and accurate as possible. Information from two different sources can also be combined if this produces higher-quality criteria.

Step 2—Identifying Criterion Groups

In this step, data for the criterion chosen in step 1 are used to identify two criterion groups—a high group and a low group. If the criterion is job tenure, for example, the members of the high group would be those with fairly lengthy company employment, while those in the low group would have been employed a short time. Each group should contain as many persons as possible; at least 125 persons are needed in each group to ensure the results are statistically reliable.

The high group might be made up of the top 50 percent of employees in the study, and the low group might contain the bottom 30 percent. If the criterion is job tenure, the high group might be employees with two years or more of service, while the low group might be employees who were employed for six months or less. When identifying distinct criterion groups is not feasible, criterion information can also be used by including the range of criterion scores for all employees in one distribution. The procedures that are associated with this approach will be discussed in more detail later and may represent a useful alternative in certain situations.

Step 3—Choosing Biodata Items

Performing this important step depends somewhat on whether the organization wants to include only information that is currently available for all employees (such as that on the application form or personnel record) or whether it wishes to measure additional aspects of an applicant's background. If existing information is to be used, this step simply includes collecting all available background information for employees and setting the information up in item format. For example, "amount of education" might be an item that is currently available that could be used with response categories of "high school

graduate," "vocational school graduate," and so on. Response categories should be chosen carefully in order to show the differences among respondents as clearly as possible.

A potential problem with the use of only existing information is that it may not be available for all current employees, and, more important, it may not be the information that would be most useful for selecting new applicants. Many times existing information has been collected without any consistent rationale and may not relate well to the behavior required in the current job or organization.

A better approach, therefore, for at least part of the inventory is to develop past behavior items that parallel behavior currently required on the job. In a sales job, for example, items might ask about the applicant's previous experience and success in various types of activities related to sales. Items can be written based on many sources of job and organization information such as job descriptions, surveys, or interviews with persons who perform successfully in the job.

There are several advantages to this type of item writing. First, the items are more likely to be valid because they incorporate a very close correspondence between specific past behavior and future behavior required on the job. Second, because they are job based, they are more acceptable to applicants and more defensible legally. Third, responses to these type items are more interpretable than responses to an item that has no obvious relationship to job requirements.

Regardless of whether new items are written or existing information is converted into items, it is important to have many more items available initially than will ultimately be needed (perhaps two or three times as many). This is because only a portion of the items will predict the criterion and be included in the final inventory. Next, for each employee with criterion information available, the new items must be administered or existing information must be recorded in item form. The items can then be compared with criterion information so that the best items can be selected and weighted for use in the final inventory.

Step 4—Selecting and Weighting Items

The first step to be taken in analyzing the item and criterion data is the identification of items that predict the criterion at a significant level. Responses to some items will be highly predictive of the criterion, while other items will show almost no relationship to it. The predictive, or valid, items are the ones retained for use in the final inventory.

In order to understand this process more thoroughly, assume that for the job of salesperson, there is a high-criterion group and a low-criterion group, with the groups based on performance over the last year. Information is available for all salespersons on all biodata items, and responses to the items are compared between the high and low groups. Those items that are answered significantly differently by each group are retained for use in the final inventory. For example, an item asking for educational background might show that salespersons with some post–high school education were members of the high-criterion group significantly more often than salespersons who had not pursued education after high school.

Once the items have been identified that are significantly related to the criterion, these items may be weighted according to their predictive ability. England (1971) provides tables that can be used to determine the item weights, but a statistical procedure, multiple regression, is much easier and more accurate for deriving a large number of item weights. To assist in these more technical areas of the development and validation process, it may be necessary to work with a consultant experienced in questionnaire construction.

It is very important that the selection and weighting of items be both accurate and representative for the range of persons who perform the job in question. In order to ensure that this occurs, two procedures must be followed. First, the size of the sample must be large enough so that results are not biased by a small number of atypical employees. Second, the sample needs to be subdivided into development and holdout groups, so that the holdout group can be used to verify results from the development group.

Step 5—Applying Weights to the Holdout Group

To form the holdout group, information for approximately one-third of all study participants should not be considered in the initial selection and weighting process. For example, if there are 150 employees in each of the criterion groups, 50 from each group should be randomly assigned to the holdout group (table 26–1). Item selection and weighting is done with the 200 persons (100 from each group) who are not assigned to the holdout group. The items and

weights are then used with the independent holdout group in order to produce an unbiased estimate of the questionnaire's validity. This process of verifying the predictive power of the items and their weights is known as cross-validation.

Results from the cross-validation can be considered in several ways. Total scores can be computed for each employee in the holdout group, and scores for those in the high-criterion group can be compared with those in the low-criterion group. If the multiple regression approach is used, a cross-validated correlation can be computed from scores within the holdout group. This correlation can then be tested statistically to see if the level of criterion prediction obtained (validity) is significant.

Step 6—Setting Selection Cutoff Scores

The final step in preparing the biodata inventory for use requires establishing a cutoff score to be used in decisions about future job candidates. Candidates who score below the cutoff will not be given further consideration for the job, while those scoring above the cutoff might be selected or might receive further evaluation, such as a test or interview. The best cutoff score is one that results in the highest number of correct decisions about persons completing the inventory. It is therefore the score that does the best job of differentiating persons with high-criterion scores from those with low-criterion scores.

As described by England (1971) and Cascio (1982), cutoff scores can be chosen by inspecting the distribution of scores and choosing the score that produces the best differentiation. Expectancy charts can also be constructed to show the likelihood of successful criterion performance at different score levels on the biodata inventory. Many factors can be considered in the development of cutoff scores, such as the number of applicants versus the number of openings, the cost of hiring a poor employee, the gain expected from

Table 26–1
Sample Organization for Cross-Validation

	Development Group	Holdout Group
High-criterion group	100 employees	50 employees
Low-criterion group	100 employees	50 employees

an outstanding employee, and the risk of not hiring an applicant who could have become a successful employee. By entering this and other information into what is known as a utility formula, it is also possible to estimate the dollar value of increased productivity produced by the use of the biodata inventory.

SUMMARY

This chapter has provided an overview of biodata—their advantages and how they can be used. Many topics have been discussed only briefly; for a more complete understanding, it may be necessary to consult the references or a researcher with experience in biodata. In a sense, however, we are all experienced users of biodata, since we use past behavior to predict future behavior every day. The information provided in this chapter is intended to help use the power of biodata in a more systematic way in order to produce better personnel decisions. Summarized below are the major points of the chapter related to that goal:

1. Biographical data are very effective predictors of future behavior because they measure how people behaved in the past. Biodata are able to predict criteria such as job performance, job tenure, and job satisfaction as well as or better than cognitive ability tests, personality inventories, or interviews and are therefore valuable in selecting and classifying an organization's employees.

2. Biodata have other advantages in addition to their validity as a predictor of employee performance. They meet legal and equal employment opportunity criteria effectively, are easy and inexpensive to collect, and are often verifiable.

3. Biodata information can be collected using published, commercially available inventories or with an inventory especially developed to meet a particular organization's needs. Information available in this chapter can be used to evaluate and obtain existing inventories or to develop a customized inventory for a given job or company.

REFERENCES

Albemarle Paper Company v. Moody (1975). 10 F. Supp. 1181.

Asher, J.J. (1972). The biographical item: Can it be improved? *Personnel Psychology, 25,* 251–269.

Barge, B.N., & Hough, L.M. (1983). *Biographical data.* Minneapolis: Personnel Decisions Research Institute.

Booth, R.F., McNally, M.S., & Berry, N.H. (1978). Predicting performance in paramedical occupations. *Personnel Psychology, 31,* 581–593.

Brush, D.H., & Owens, W.A. (1979). Implementation and evaluation of an assessment-classification model for manpower utilization. *Personnel Psychology, 32,* 369–383.

Cascio, W.F. (1982). *Applied psychology in personnel management.* Reston, VA: Reston Publishing.

England, G.W. (1971). *Development and use of weighted application blanks* (Bulletin 55). Minneapolis: Industrial Relations Center, University of Minnesota.

Equal Employment Opportunity Commission (1978). Uniform guidelines on employee selection procedures. *Federal Register,* August 25.

Haymaker, J.C., & Erwin, F.W. (1980). *Investigation of applicant responses and falsification detection procedures for the Military Aptitude Predictor* (TR 1-80). Washington, DC: Richardson, Bellows, & Henry, Inc.

Ghiselli, E.E. (1973). *The measurement of occupational aptitude.* Berkeley: University of California Press.

Harrell, T.W., & Harrell, M.S. (1976). *Predictors of business managers' success at 10 years out of MBA* (Technical Report N00014-76-C-0009). Arlington, VA: Office of Naval Research.

Owens, W.A. (1976). Biographical data. In M.D. Dunnette (Ed.), *Handbook of industrial and organizational psychology.* New York: Wiley-Interscience.

Reilly, R.R., & Chao, G.T. (1982). Validity and fairness of some alternative employee selection procedures. *Personnel Psychology, 35* (1), 1–62.

27 STRUCTURED INTERVIEWING TECHNIQUES FOR PERSONNEL SELECTION

Michael A. Campion, Elliott D. Pursell, Barbara K. Brown

PROBLEMS WITH TRADITIONAL EMPLOYMENT INTERVIEWS

Traditional employment interviews have been the primary means of making selection decisions for most of this century. However, the reliability (similarity between the judgments of different interviewers) and validity (accuracy in predicting future job performance) of the traditional interview have always been in question (e.g., Arvey & Campion, 1982; Eder & Ferris, 1989; Harris, in press; Hollingworth, 1922; Mayfield, 1964; Wagner, 1949).

Traditional interviews are usually very unstructured, with no predetermined questions or criteria to evaluate candidates. Questions are not based on a job analysis, different questions may be asked of different candidates, and different interviewers may evaluate the same candidate's answers differently. As such, the traditional interview has many disadvantages:

1. It is highly susceptible to distortion and bias.

2. It is highly susceptible to legal attack.
3. It is usually indefensible if legally contested.
4. It usually has very low validity.
5. It is usually not totally job related.
6. It may incorporate personal items that invade privacy.
7. It lacks consistency due to its unstructured nature.
8. It allows interviewers to use different criteria.
9. It encourages hiring decisions to be made early in the interview without gathering adequate job-related information.
10. It allows interviewers to look for qualities that they prefer and then to justify the hiring decision based on these qualities.

STRUCTURED INTERVIEWING—AN IMPROVED ALTERNATIVE

Given the questionable effectiveness of traditional interviews and the desire of managers to continue to use interviews for employee selection, an improved interviewing technique is necessary. Research recommends the use of a structured interview format because it reduces subjectivity and inconsistency. A structured interview is a series of job-related questions with predetermined answers that are consistently applied by a panel of interviewers across all interviews for a particular job.

When compared to the traditional employment interview, the structured interview offers many advantages:

1. Bias is reduced because candidates are evaluated on job-related questions, which are based on an analysis of job duties and requirements. Subjective and irrelevant questions are not asked.

2. All candidates are asked the same questions so everyone has the same opportunity to display qualifications.

3. Anchored rating scales to evaluate answers to interview questions are determined in advance. This reduces disagreements among interviewers and increases accuracy of judgments.

4. A panel of interviewers is used to record and evaluate answers in order to minimize idiosyncratic biases.

5. Research has demonstrated that properly developed structured interviews can have high reliability among interviewers and predictive validity for future job performance.

6. Job-related procedures used to develop structured interviews increase content validity (validity appears justified based on the content of the interview).

7. Procedures used to develop structured interviews are consistent with the advice of professional and governmental testing guidelines. As such, they may be more legally defensible.

8. Structured interviews allow managers to take part in the selection process in a role in which they are familiar (that is, as interviewers).

9. Job relatedness and consistency of the process may increase the perception of fairness among candidates. The job relatedness may also help candidates get a realistic perspective of the job, which can aid self-selection.

DEVELOPING A STRUCTURED INTERVIEW

The procedures used to develop structured interviews were designed to be consistent with testing guidelines published by professional organizations (Principles for the Validation and Use of Personnel Selection Procedures; Society of Industrial and Organizational Psychology, Inc., 1987) and governmental organizations (Uniform Guidelines on Employee Selection Procedures; Equal Employment Opportunity Commission, Civil Service Commission, Department of Labor & Department of Justice, 1978).

Structured interviews can be developed and used by following eight steps.

Step 1: Conduct a Job Analysis

The objective of a job analysis is to determine the job duties and tasks and the required knowledge, skills, abilities, and other worker characteristics (KSAOs). Both professional and governmental guidelines require some form of job analysis for test development, and there is evidence of the importance of job analysis to avoid bias against minorities (Kesselman & Lopez, 1979) and to win court decisions (Kleiman & Faley, 1985). The actual method used to collect job information depends on the specific job and the selection situation.

One easy method is to conduct a job analysis meeting with a group of supervisors and incumbents who are knowledgeable about the job. Duties and requirements of the job are generated through discussion and brainstorming. Care should be taken to list specific job duties and tasks because information that is too general is of little use. Also, identify the KSAOs that are needed to perform each specific job duty. This is necessary to ensure that interview questions are based on KSAOs that are needed to perform critical work.

Another method of job analysis is the critical incident technique. Here a group of supervisors or other job experts generates lists of behaviors on the job that contribute to particularly effective and ineffective

performance (or distinguish between particularly effective and ineffective employees).

Regardless of the job analysis method employed, the testing guidelines require that KSAOs assessed in a selection procedure be necessary prerequisites to perform critical work. Criticality can be determined by evaluating the importance and amount of time spent on each duty or task. These evaluations could be collected in a variety of ways, including rating scales, percentage estimates, or rankings. Several supervisors and incumbents should provide these evaluations in order to obtain assessments from different perspectives. Results can then be placed into four categories:

1. Duties that are important and consume a large amount of time.

2. Duties that are important but do not consume a large amount of time.

3. Duties that are less important but consume a large amount of time.

4. Duties that are less important and do not consume a large amount of time.

These categories are ordered from most to least critical. Generally questions are based on KSAOs that are needed to perform duties in categories 1 and 2.

Step 2: Develop Questions Based on the Job Analysis

It is usually desirable to have the same people who were involved in the job analysis help develop the interview questions because of their familiarity with the job. Although there is much overlap, it is useful to think of four different types of questions. Each type is described below, and examples are provided in Appendix 27–A.

1. *Situational Questions.* These are questions that pose a hypothetical job situation to the candi-

date. The candidate must respond with what he or she would do in the situation. The critical incident job analysis technique lends itself to the development of this type of question.

2. *Job Knowledge Questions.* These questions often deal with the technical aspects of the job or basic knowledge that is essential to learn the job. Depending on the level of the job and its requirements, these questions may merely assess basic educational skills such as reading, writing, and math, or they may assess very complex technical or management skills.

3. *Job Sample and Simulation Questions.* When possible, it is useful to have questions that approximate the content of the job. Sometimes the candidate can actually perform a sample task from the job. When a job sample is not possible, a simulation of a job task may be an alternative. Simulation questions range from mock-ups of job tasks to simply phrasing questions in terminology and examples from the job. Job samples and simulations may increase content validity and realism for the candidates.

4. *Worker Requirements Questions.* These usually include questions on background (e.g., education, experience) or "willingness" questions (e.g., shift work, travel, relocation). These questions are frequently placed at the beginning of the interview because they can act as good warm-up questions to put the candidate at ease. Furthermore, because they refer to the duties of the job, they may serve as a realistic job preview for the candidate and aid self-selection.

In question development, the following criteria should be followed to ensure question quality and to increase content validity:

1. Questions must be complete and unambiguous. Having to clarify questions during the interview reduces standardization and may introduce bias.

2. Questions should not be leading or be overly influenced by the verbosity of the candidate.

3. Questions must be strictly and clearly job related. "Nice-to-know" questions are not permitted.

4. Questions must not assess KSAOs that employees will learn with brief training or experience on the job. For example, in selecting an entry-level salesperson, one should not assess the candidate's knowledge of the product line because this will be taught on the job. Instead, it would be preferable to assess oral and persuasion skills because they are much more difficult to learn.

5. Questions should be geared to the appropriate complexity level of the job. For example, if the job requires math skills at the level of whole numbers, it would be inappropriate to develop questions involving decimals and fractions. The questions should assess the KSAOs at the same level as the KSAOs that are needed on the job.

6. Questions must be reviewed to eliminate any bias that might make them discriminatory. If possible, this review should be conducted by independent job experts who are members of protected groups (e.g., minorities and females).

7. Questions should be included in proportion to the importance of the KSAOs they assess. That is, more questions should be included on KSAOs needed for important duties and fewer on KSAOs needed for less important duties. This is usually better than weighting the questions differently on importance.

8. Questions should be explicitly linked to the KSAOs or duties they are intended to measure. A matrix chart of KSAOs or duties across the top and interview questions down the side, with all links indicated, is ideal for this purpose. This linking process ensures the questions are all job related, and it provides content validity documentation, which may be needed if the procedure is legally challenged.

Step 3: Anchor the Rating Scales for Scoring Answers with Examples and Definitions

A scoring system is developed for each question by generating a rating scale with examples or definitions of good (5), marginal (3), and poor (1) answers. One approach is to ask job experts for example candidate answers they have actually heard that subsequently distinguished different levels of performers on the job. A simpler approach is to brainstorm potential answers with experts and personnel representatives familiar with the job and with interviewing comparable candidates. Regardless of the approach chosen, each question should have a five-point answer rating scale constructed using the following guidelines:

5—What would one expect or want a well-qualified candidate to give as a good answer? What answer would one expect the top third of all candidates to give?

4—

3—What is a marginal answer that would tell one the candidate is somewhat knowledgeable or skillful on the requirement or that would constitute a partial answer? What answer would one expect the middle third of all candidates to give?

2—

1—What would one expect as a poor answer from a candidate who has little knowledge or skill on this job requirement? What answer would one expect the bottom third of all candidates to give?

It is important to note that in some circumstances there will be single best 5, 3, and 1 answers, while in other situations there may be many answers of similar quality. In the latter case, the anchors are simply examples or illustrations of answers of that score level.

Generally it is not essential to describe 4 or 2 answers, because the 5, 3, and 1 answers give adequate anchor points for making a rating decision of 5, 4, 3, 2, or 1. After the interview questions have been administered several times, however, it may be possible to develop answers for 4 and 2. In developing the answers, it is normally advisable to describe a 5 answer first and then a 1 answer. The 3 answer should be developed last because it is typically the most difficult answer to develop.

It is important that the levels of the actual job requirements be considered in the development of anchor points. For example, business school (or equivalent training or experience) may be a necessary requirement for an executive secretary position. Listing a college education as a 5 answer and a business school education as a 3 answer would be altering the job requirement. Example answers should be scaled to the requirements of the job so that 5 answers do not far exceed the requirements, and 1 answers are not so low that they do not help distinguish between candidates.

One should also avoid the tendency to have the 5 answer be a reworded (e.g., more sophisticated) version of the 3 answer. Terms or expressions used only within the organization, as well as acronyms and slang, should also be avoided. It is useful to generate synonyms and equivalent alternatives for each answer developed.

The development of the answers is an evaluative measure of the question. If there is great difficulty in determining the answers, then the question should be reviewed for possible refining, restructuring, or eliminating.

Preparing rating scales for scoring the answers prior to conducting the interviews has several distinct advantages:

1. They give credibility to the interview by the obvi-

ous fairness of having predetermined scoring schemes.

2. They serve as an assessment of the questions.

3. They increase the consistency of interviewer evaluations by increasing objectivity and reducing potential for bias.

4. They minimize the postinterview disagreement that may arise among interviewers.

Step 4: Have an Interview Panel Record and Rate Answers

Having an interview panel reduces the impact of idiosyncratic biases that single interviewers might introduce. Normally, the panel should consist of a subset of the job experts who helped analyze the job and develop the interview questions because of their familiarity with the job and questions. Three members are typically used, including supervisors of the job to be filled and a personnel representative. It is also advisable to use the same members for all interviews to increase consistency. However, an excessively large number of interviews or other constraints (e.g., turnover) may make this infeasible.

The interview panel should be assembled well in advance of the first interview to review job duties and requirements, questions and answers, and the interview process. Panel members should also be precautioned about potential rating errors (e.g., leniency, severity, central tendency, first impression, contrast, similarity, halo, and stereotypes). Ideally, the interview panel should not review application forms, resumes, or other materials prior to the interviews. This may cause them to form impressions that could bias their subsequent evaluations of the candidates.

All panel members record and rate the candidate's answers during the actual interview. This recording should be exactly as the candidate responded. If that is not possible, special care should be taken to provide clear paraphrases and abbreviations. These recorded answers become a critical part of the documentation. Candidate responses must be able to be reconstructed accurately in case a particular hiring decision or the entire process is ever challenged.

Step 5: Consistently Administer the Process to All Candidates

All candidates are asked the same questions. There is no prompting or follow-up questioning because this decreases standardization of the interview. Questions may be repeated if necessary.

The interview is administered in a quiet, comfortable room. All panel members should be present before the candidate enters the room. Every attempt should be made to administer the interview in as nonstressful a manner as possible. Panel members are introduced to the candidate. Then one selected member of the panel asks all the questions for all the candidates to ensure consistency.

Between successive candidates, the panel members should not discuss the questions, the answers, or the candidates in order to avoid potential bias from changing standards or comparisons among candidates. After all the interviews are completed for a given job, any large discrepancies between interviewers are discussed.

Candidates are allowed to ask questions in a subsequent nonevaluation interview with a personnel representative.

Step 6: Decide Who to Hire

Hiring decisions are based in whole or in part on the total score of the interview, which is calculated as the average across all questions and all interviewers. There are at least three possible decision methods. First, one can rank the candidates and choose those with the highest scores. This method yields the highest expected future job performance, thus giving the highest expected utility (i.e., value) from the selection procedure. This system has the drawback of potentially creating the most adverse impact against protected groups (minorities and females), but this problem can be circumvented by selecting the highest-ranked candidates within each of the groups.

Second, one can determine a cutting score above which all candidates are qualified. This method has the advantage of being consistent with promotion stipulations in many union contracts that require that the "most senior qualified" be accepted. The determination of "qualified" on a selection instrument ultimately translates into a cutting score. Also, in intermittent hiring situations, a cutting score is efficient in that interviews need to be conducted only until an adequate number of qualified candidates are found. However, if cutting scores are set too low, they can have the disadvantage of reducing selection utility. Furthermore, there are no universally acceptable ways of setting cutting scores, and substantial judgment is always necessary. At a minimum, cutting scores should be set with consideration of the following factors: number of hirees needed, likely adverse impact, expected job performance of those selected, and the judgement of job experts as to the level of

performance on the interview that might be expected of minimally qualified employees on the job.

Third, the interview score can be used as one piece of information that is considered along with other relevant information on the candidate in order to make an overall assessment. Although this approach sounds intuitively appealing, it may be the least acceptable of the three. The subjective and potentially inconsistent weighting of qualifications can result in a decrease in the selection utility of the entire decision process, as well as possible discrimination against protected groups (minorities and females). Recall that these are the very problems with the traditional interview that one is attempting to avoid.

Step 7: Conduct a Performance Appraisal

Performance appraisal is an essential follow-up to any selection decision. It gives an evaluation of the accuracy of the selection procedures, it provides information for employee counseling, it provides input to performance-based pay decisions, and it generates documentation for corrective action when selection mistakes are made.

A detailed examination of performance appraisal techniques is beyond the scope of this chapter. However, the job analysis information collected to develop the structured interview gives an ideal base to build a performance appraisal instrument. For example, anchored rating scales much like those developed for the interview could be generated for each job duty. The anchors could distinguish good, marginal, and poor performance on the job. Such an appraisal instrument would enjoy many of the same advantages as the structured interview (e.g., job relatedness, objectivity, consistency).

Step 8: Give Special Attention to Job Relatedness, Fairness, and Documentation in Accordance with Testing Guidelines

Consideration of professional and governmental guidelines is important throughout the process. The structured interviewing approach described in this chapter was designed to be consistent with these guidelines. Components needing written documentation include the job analysis and interview development procedure, candidate responses and scores, validity evidence, adverse impact analysis, and other aspects as appropriate.

These guidelines should be consulted for more specific procedural and documentation requirements. Expert advice and assistance may also be necessary in some situations.

Conclusions

The traditional interview is commonly used to make employment decisions, but a long history of research has not supported its reliability or validity for predicting future job performance. Structuring the interview is proposed as an improved alternative. The procedures to develop a structured interview are grounded in the professional and governmental testing guidelines, and research is accumulating to support its reliability and validity. A structured interview is defined as a series of job-related questions with predetermined answers that are consistently applied by a panel of interviewers across all interviews for a particular job. This section laid out eight steps that can be easily followed to develop and use a structured interview for personnel selection.

RESEARCH SUPPORTING STRUCTURED INTERVIEWING

Research has provided empirical evidence regarding the reliability and validity of structured interviews. Discussed here is a sampling of recent studies in the published literature and in technical reports of which we are aware.

The approach to structured interviewing described in this chapter was originally presented by Pursell and Gaylord (1976) and by Pursell, Campion, and Gaylord (1980). In a study using this approach, Campion, Pursell, and Brown (1988) found high reliability, predictive validity, utility, and test fairness for a structured interview used to select 149 entry-level production employees in a pulp and paper mill. Campion and Pursell (1981) reported detailed content validity evidence for the same interview. In another extensive study, Pursell, Campion, et al. (1980) demonstrated the content validity of this approach for selecting employees for thirty-one skilled and semiskilled jobs in a pulp and paper mill. Finally, Wright, Lichtenfels, and Pursell (in press) reported additional favorable validity evidence for four of six samples of mostly production employees in a forest products company.

A highly similar approach to structured interviewing is the situational interview, which, as the name implies, uses only situational questions. Latham, Saari, Pursell, and M. Campion (1980) found reliability and validity for situational interviews in separate samples of first-line foremen, hourly workers, minorities, and females in a forest products company. More recently, Weekly and Gier (1987) found similar results for a situational interview designed for selecting salespersons in a chain of retail stores, and Maurer and Fay (1988) found that agreement among raters regarding job applicants was higher with situational interviews than with past experience—based interviews.

Another similar approach is the patterned behavior description interview. It is comparable in many regards to the approach described in this chapter, with the exception that the interviewer does not have to ask the same questions of each candidate but instead selects from an array (or pattern) of questions. Janz (1982) found reliability and validity for this technique in a study of teaching assistants, and Orpen (1985) found similar results for selecting life insurance salespersons.

The validities discovered for these structured interviews are far superior to those for traditional unstructured interviews (Wiesner & Cronshaw, 1988), comparable to those of paper-and-pencil tests, and superior to those of most other alternative selection procedures (for a review of selection procedure validity, see Hunter & Hunter, 1984). Structured interviews have the advantage over tests of allowing managers to participate in the selection process. Also, the obvious job relatedness of structured interviews may be perceived as fairer by candidates. In addition, the developmental procedures may make structured interviews easier to content validate, which can be appealing to small employers who cannot conduct empirical validations.

More research is needed on structured interviews. We are looking for research sites to evaluate and refine the structured interviewing process.

APPENDIX 27–A: EXAMPLE STRUCTURED INTERVIEW QUESTIONS

Situational Questions

1. Question assessing awareness of meeting attendance protocol, which is necessary for most managerial and professional jobs:

Suppose you were going to miss an important business meeting due to unforeseen circumstances (e.g., illness, family emergency). What would you do?

(5) I would contact the person in charge of the meeting to forewarn of my absence, and I would arrange for a responsible person to attend in my place.

(3) I would send someone in my place.

(1) Afterwards, I would try to find out what went on in the meeting.

2. Question assessing communication skills at a level needed by many jobs:

Suppose you had many important projects with rigid deadlines, but your manager kept requesting various types of paperwork, which you felt were totally unnecessary. Furthermore, this paperwork was going to cause you to miss your deadlines. What would you do?

(5) Present conflict to your manager. Suggest and discuss alternatives. Establish mutually agreeable plan of action. Communicate frequently with manager.

(3) Tell your manager about the problem.

(5) Do the best you can.

Job Knowledge Questions

1. Question assessing low-level mechanical knowledge such as that needed for many entry-level factory jobs:

Several of these questions were adopted from Campion, Pursell & Brown (1988, pp. 25–42).

When putting a piece of machinery back together after repairing it, why would you clean all the parts first?

(5) Particles of dust and dirt can cause wear on moving parts. Need to have parts clean to inspect for wear and damage.

(3) Parts will go together easier. Equipment will run better.

(1) So it will all be clean. I don't know.

2. Question assessing specialized electronics knowledge needed for some process control technician jobs:

What is the difference between a thermocouple and a resistance temperature detector?

(5) A thermocouple will produce a millivolt signal itself. A resistance temperature detector is usually connected to a balanced wheatstone bridge. When the resistance changes due to temperature changes, an unbalanced voltage is produced on the bridge.

(3) Defines one correctly.

(1) Incorrect answer.

Job Sample or Simulation Questions

1. Question simulating a task and assessing low-level reading ability for a forklift operator job:

Many of the jobs require the operation of a forklift. Please read this (90-word) forklift checkout procedure aloud.

(5) Reads fluently pronouncing all words accurately.

(3) Can read most words but hesitates.

(1) Reads with great difficulty.

2. Question simulating a task and assessing selling skills for a sales job:

Please sell me this product using basic selling techniques.

(5) Candidate simulates selling the item to the interview panel by incorporating the following selling techniques: (a) identifies and presents the product, the customer needs, and the benefits of the product; (b) demonstrates the product; (c) handles resistance; and (d) closes the sale by asking for an order.

(3) Candidate uses only three of the techniques or performs one poorly.

(1) Candidate uses only two of the techniques or performs them very poorly.

Worker Requirements Questions

1. Question assessing willingness to work at heights as may be required by many construction or factory jobs:

Some jobs require climbing ladders to a height of a five-story building and going out on a catwalk to work. Give us your feeling about performing a task such as this.

(5) Heights do not bother me. I have done similar work at heights in the past [and gives examples].

(3) I do not think I am afraid of heights. I know that this would have to be done as part of the job:

(1) I am afraid of heights. I would do it if absolutely necessary.

2. Question assessing willingness to travel as may be required by many professional and managerial jobs:

This job requires traveling out of town at least three times a month. Usually each trip will involve flying on a commercial airliner and staying overnight. Would this pose any difficulties for you?

(5) No, this would not be a problem. I have traveled in previous jobs (gives examples). I enjoy traveling and flying.

(3) I am willing to travel as part of the job.

(1) I do not like to travel, but would do it if necessary.

REFERENCES

Arvey, R.D., & Campion, J.E. (1982). The employment interview: A summary and review of recent research. *Personnel Psychology, 35,* 281–322.

Campion, M.A., & Pursell, E.D. (1981). *Plymouth fiber extraboard validation report: Content and criterion-related validation of a structured interview and written test battery for an entry-level production job family.* Plymouth, NC: Weyerhaeuser Company.

Campion, M.A., Pursell, E.D., & Brown, B.K. (1988). Structured interviewing: Raising the psychometric properties of the employment interview. *Personnel Psychology, 41,* 25–42.

Eder, R.W., & Ferris, G.R. (Eds.). (1989). *The employment interview: Theory, research, and practice.* Newbury Park, CA: Sage.

Equal Employment Opportunity Commission, Civil Service Commission, Department of Labor, & Department of Justice (1978). Adoption by four agencies of Uniform Guidelines on Employee Selection Procedures. *Federal Register, 43,* 38290–38315.

Harris, M.M. (in press). Reconsidering the employment interview: A review of recent literature and suggestions for future research. *Personnel Psychology.*

Hollingworth, H.L. (1922). *Judging human character.* New York: Appleton. Hunter, J.E., & Hunter, R.F. (1984). The validity and utility of alternative predictors of job performance. *Psychological Bulletin, 96,* 72–98.

Janz, T. (1982). Initial comparisons of patterned behavior description interviews versus unstructured interviews. *Journal of Applied Psychology, 67,* 577–580.

Kesselman, G.A., & Lopez, F.E. (1979). The impact of job analysis on employment test validation for minority and nonminority accounting personnel. *Personnel Psychology, 32,* 91–108.

Kleiman, L.S., & Faley, R.H. (1985). The implications of professional and legal guidelines for court decisions involving criterion-related validity: A review and analysis. *Personnel Psychology, 38,* 803–833.

Latham, G.P., Saari, L.M., Pursell, E.D., & Campion, M.A. (1980). The situational interview. *Journal of Applied Psychology, 65,* 422–427.

Maurer, S.D., & Fay, C. (1988). Effect of situational interviews, conventional structured interviews, and training on interview rating agreement: An experimental analysis. *Personnel Psychology, 41,* 329–344.

Mayfield, E.C. (1964). The selection interview—A re-evaluation of published research. *Personnel Psychology, 17,* 239–260.

Orpen, C. (1985). Patterned behavior description interviews versus unstructured interviews: A comparative validity study. *Journal of Applied Psychology, 70,* 774–776.

Pursell, E.D., Campion, M.A., et al. (1980). *Plymouth fiber complex expansion projects validation report: Content validation of structured interviews for 31 skilled and semi-skilled jobs in the pulp and paper industry.* Plymouth, NC: Weyerhaeuser Company.

Pursell, E.D., Campion, M.A., & Gaylord, S.R. (1980). Structured interviewing: Avoiding selection problems. *Personnel Journal, 59,* 907–912.

Pursell, E.D., & Gaylord, S.R. (1976). *Structured interviewing.* Tacoma, WA: Weyerhaeuser Company.

Society of Industrial and Organizational Psychology, Inc.

(1987). *Principles for the validation and use of personnel selection procedures* (3d ed.). College Park, MD: Author.

Wagner, R. (1949). The employment interview: A critical summary. *Personnel Psychology, 2,* 17–46.

Weekley, J.A., & Gier, J.A. (1987). Reliability and validity of the situational interview for a sales position. *Journal of Applied Psychology, 72,* 484–487.

Wiesner, W.H., & Cronshaw, S.F. (1988). A meta-analytic investigation of the impact of interview format and degree of structure on the validity of the employment interview. *Journal of Occupational Psychology, 61,* 275–290.

Wright, P.M., Lichtenfels, P.A., & Pursell, E.D. (in press). The structured interview: Additional studies and a meta-analysis. *Journal of Occupational Psychology.*

28 CRITICAL ISSUES IN DRUG TESTING

Deborah F. Crown, Joseph G. Rosse

Substance abuse in the workplace promises to become one of the most significant issues for human resource managers in the 1990s. While recent data suggest that the number of individuals using drugs has begun to level off, there is increasing evidence that substance abuse in the workplace occurs at a level to justify concern. Of the various forms of response to this problem, drug testing seems to be the most visible and controversial.

As recently as seven years ago only 3 percent of organizations tested either employees or job applicants for drug use (Bureau of National Affairs, 1986). More recent estimates suggest that as many as 36 percent of employees and 50 percent of applicants are being tested (American Management Association, 1987). Nor does a change in this trend seem likely, as recent surveys indicate that 50 percent of firms without testing programs are considering implementing one ("One quarter of firms," 1987).

The recent growth in drug testing has been accompanied by significant emotion on the part of many policymakers. In response to such personal tragedies as the deaths of athletes Len Bias and Don Rogers,[1] there has been an increased national awareness of the consequences of drug use and abuse. The government, employers, and citizens are naturally concerned with finding means to reduce such tragedies, and drug testing seems to offer the necessary technology. Additional impetus has been provided by calls from both the Reagan and Bush administrations to use drug testing as a major weapon in the war on drugs. Drug testing has been mandated in federal agencies, and private sector employers have been strongly encouraged to implement testing procedures as well.

However, opponents of drug testing have raised legitimate concerns about the appropriateness of drug screening. Those concerned with social liberties wonder if the benefits warrant the threats to constitutional protections. Social scientists question the empirical basis for many of the assumed social costs of drug use and ponder whether routine acceptance of such invasive procedures dangerously increases governmental control of society. Industrial-organizational psychologists similarly question the assumed relationship between drug testing and employees' attitudes and performance. Among other questions they raise is the effect of such programs on applicants' and employees' attitude toward the firm and how these attitudes may affect the ability to recruit and retain employees.

To date, few of these questions have received the serious attention they deserve. Instead, the bulk of the debate has addressed the issues of accuracy and legality. While important, we feel that these questions have been answered for the most part and that it is now time to move on to other critical issues affecting drug testing.

In this chapter, we will address five major assumptions that seem to underlie, explicitly or implicitly, the use of drug testing in employment settings. After describing various forms of drug tests, we will discuss the fairly extensive literature addressing the assumption that current testing methods can accurately identify drug users. We will then shift our attention to three assumptions that are generally less well articulated and for which there is less evidence: that drug use adversely affects employers and society, that drug testing can reduce such drug use, and that drug testing is cost-effective.

We will then complete our review by discussing the assumption that drug testing is legal, drawing on the latest Supreme Court rulings at the time of this writing (October 1989). Finally, after having explored the logical and empirical bases for each of the assumptions, we will provide recommendations for organizations interested in drug testing.

WHAT IS MEANT BY DRUG TESTING?

The simple term *drug testing* belies the complexity of issues involved in screening people for evidence of drug use. Drug testing programs vary according to what drugs are being targeted (most typically marijuana, cocaine, opiates, phencyclidine, and amphetamines); who is tested (applicants versus employees; safety-sensitive jobs versus all jobs); impetus for testing (preemployment screening, postincident or accident investigation, as a follow-up to rehabilitation, or random); frequency (one time versus periodic testing of current employees); the extent to which those being tested are informed prior to the testing; the actual testing methods used (type of testing procedure; degree of security in obtaining urine sample and maintaining its integrity through the analysis and reporting process); the extent of feedback offered (ranging from none at all, to simple announcement of results, to announcement of results with opportunity for rebuttal); and the consequences of positive findings (rejection or discipline versus rehabilitative assistance). These subtle differences may have major implications for the effectiveness, legality, and morality of drug testing efforts.

In evaluating drug testing procedures, it may be useful to distinguish between tests with a physiological basis (e.g., urine or blood tests) and paper-and-pencil "psychological inventories." Physiological tests are intended to determine whether a person has used a targeted substance, generally by detecting the presence of the substance (or its metabolites) in a sample of urine, blood, or hair. Urinalysis, in one form or another, is the most common type of drug test, and it forms the primary basis for most of our remarks.

The self-report inventories seek to determine an individual's likelihood of using drugs either by asking about past drug use or by assessing attitudes and personality. Unlike most physiological methods, paper-and-pencil tests often allow for detection of abusers of alcohol, as well as illegal drugs. (See appendix 28–A for more information about types of tests.)

Urinalysis and Other Physiological Measures

There are three major methods of urinalysis: thin-layer chromatography, enzyme immunoassay/radioimmunoassay, and gas chromatography/mass spectrometry (GC/MS) (Miners, Nykodym & Samerdyke-Traband, 1987). Thin-layer chromatography is the least expensive method ($8 to $15) but also the least sensitive. Enzyme immunoassay/radioimmunoassay tests (e.g., EMIT, Abuscreen) are the most widely used form of urinalysis. They cost a bit more than TLC methods ($11 to $20) and are more sensitive but are especially prone to detecting incorrectly over-the-counter drugs as illegal substances. The premier form of urinalysis is the gas chromatography/

mass spectrometry test, which is also the most expensive (from $30 to more than $100, depending on volume).

The newest urinalysis method on the market—the KDI QUIK TEST—is a simple procedure in which a drop of urine is placed on the QUIK TEST paper. Ironically, the major criticism of the QUIK TEST is its ease in nonlaboratory settings. The kit, which sells for $6.50, includes warnings that the test will produce positive results for a variety of over-the-counter and prescription medications and that it should be used only to eliminate negatives, not as a determination of positives. But Ben Jackson, director of the American Drug Use Testing Association, fears that despite these warnings, this on-site procedure has the potential for great misuse ("New on the Spot Drug Test," 1986).

Blood samples can also be used to detect the use of drugs, but they suffer from the limitation that most drugs are quickly removed from the bloodstream. Because of this, blood tests are rarely used except to detect very recent use or impairment (e.g., with alcohol). Two additional but infrequently used techniques involve analysis of hair samples (Psychemedics, 1987) and electrical patterns in the brain (the Veritas 100).

Paper-and-Pencil Measures of Substance Use

Much as concerns over the validity and fairness of the polygraph led to development of paper-and-pencil measures of honesty, concerns about privacy have generated interest in nonphysiological measures of drug use. In their review of this type of test, Rosse and Miller (1989) describe two types of self-report measures. *Overt measures* directly ask about current and past drug use. These are typically part of integrity tests (e.g., the Personnel Selection Inventory, Phase II Profile, Reid Report, and Wilkerson Pre-Employment Audit) that depend on systematic differences in self-reported behavior between dishonest (or drug-using) and honest (or non-drug-using) populations. Although most typically used for preemployment screening, overt tests are also available in a form suitable for current employees (see appendix 28–A for more information).

Indirect measures attempt to determine a person's predisposition to use drugs by measuring either attitudes toward drug use (e.g., the Milby Total Personnel Selection System or the Employee Reliability Inventory) or personality profiles that are empirically related to drug use patterns. For reasons that will be described more completely in the next section, these tests are probably more suitable for preemployment screening than for "cause" testing.

IS DRUG TESTING ACCURATE?

Regardless of type, when used as a selection device or in a manner that otherwise affects one's employment status, drug testing should meet professional and legal standards for employment testing procedures. Primary among these standards are reliability (consistency of results across samples, time periods, and laboratories) and validity. In employment selection contexts, two aspects of validity are typically considered: *validity of measurement* (whether the test measures what it is supposed to measure, i.e., do the tests accurately indicate use of drugs) and *validity of prediction* (i.e., whether the test results are predictive of job performance). Most of the research to date has been concerned with reliability and validity of measurement; only a few studies have attempted to confront the question of validity of prediction.

Measurement Validity of Urinalysis Methods

The measurement validity of urinalysis is typically determined by sending samples with known concentrations of targeted substances to test laboratories. Accuracy is generally defined in terms of the number of true positive (detection of substances) and true negatives (correct reporting of no substances) relative to false positives (incorrectly identifying specimens as containing the tested-for substance) and false negatives (failure to identify specimens containing the tested-for substance).

The research on urinalysis screening methods suggests that their reliability and measurement validity depend on the type of test used, the adequacy of sample collection procedures, and the proficiency of the laboratory. The primary determinant of accuracy is the type of test. Research has consistently shown that thin-layer chromatography, enzyme immunoassay, and radioimmunoassay techniques are vulnerable to high levels of errors, particularly false negative errors (Boone, Hansen, Hearn, Lewis & Dudley, 1982; Dakis, Pottash, Annitto & Gold, 1983; Gottheil, Caddy & Austin, 1976; Hansen, Caudill & Boone, 1985). These tests are also known to be cross-reactive with common over-the-counter and prescription medications. For example, Bloch (1986) reported that the EMIT test may provide positive readings for marijuana when traces of Advil or Nuprin exist in a urine sample and to test positive for amphetamines when a subject had taken Contac or Sudafed.

Gas chromatography/mass spectrometry methods, on the other hand, are virtually error proof if performed in laboratories using well-trained personnel and proper chain-of-custody procedures. Two recent studies conducted by the American Association for Clinical Chemistry used laboratories that met these conditions. The mean accuracy rates were 99.2 percent and 97 percent, respectively (Frings, White & Battaglia, 1987; Frings, Battaglia & White, 1989).

For that reason, it is a standard recommendation that all positive results from less accurate screening methods be verified with the GC/MS procedure. Only five years ago it was rare for a laboratory to confirm initial positives with GC/MS because of the specialized and expensive equipment that is required for the latter (American Management Association, 1987). Today, an estimated 68 percent of laboratories are utilizing the GC/MS test as one means of confirmation (Davis, Hawks & Blanke, 1988; Frings, Battaglia & White, 1989).

While the increased use of GC/MS has had a dramatic effect in increasing the measurement validity of urinalysis, two cautionary notes are in order. The first is that many firms continue to make personnel decisions on unconfirmed immunoassay-type results. Until GC/MS confirmation becomes universal, our optimistic portrayal of accuracy needs to be interpreted cautiously. The second point is that it is typical in employment settings to confirm only initial positives. While this protects the applicant or employee from false accusations, it does nothing to protect the organization from the far more common false negative error.

Much of the credit for the increased use of the GC/MS test goes to the National Institute on Drug Abuse's efforts to standardize laboratory procedures through a national certification program. In order to qualify for NIDA certification, a laboratory must (1) have the capability to test for five classes of drugs, (2) employ qualified personnel, (3) provide quality control and quality assurance programs, (4) utilize strict security and chain-of-custody requirements, and (5) store confirmed positive test results for at least one year and maintain meticulous documentation that is available for at least two years. The laboratory must also pass three test cycles that evaluate error rates. The overall accuracy rate must be maintained at 90 percent or higher, and a single false positive will immediately disqualify a laboratory. Upon certification the laboratory is subject to six challenges per year with similar standards required. Because of these high standards, we recommend that firms use only NIDA-certified laboratories; a current list of certified laboratories is published regularly in the *Federal Register,* and is also available directly from NIDA.

NIDA also provides a useful set of guidelines for collecting urine samples, maintaining chain of custody, and eliminating false positives that are due to use of medications. A recent development in this area is the establishment of medical review officers (MRO). The MRO is a licensed physician whose function is to analyze positive test results in the light of the tested employee's medical history. The MRO serves as an intermediary between the laboratory that reports results to the MRO and the organization that receives the MRO's final report. In addition to medical expertise, the MRO can offer increased confidentiality in the reporting of urinalysis results.

Measurement Validity of Paper-and-Pencil Methods

Self-report methods of testing for drugs provide a different set of challenges to validity of measurement, since they generally do not purport to assess directly recent use of a controlled substance. Rather they seek to measure some set of characteristics—not always well defined—that serve to predict future use of drugs.

One subcategory of pencil-and-paper tests identified by Rosse and Miller (1989) consists of personality tests. If validity is defined as the accuracy with which these tests measure basic personality traits, measurement validity varies from poor to good (with better evidence generally available for more traditional measures such as the California Psychological Inventory, Minnesota Multiphasic Inventory, or 16PF). On the other hand, one could argue that the real issue is their ability to measure some construct like "substance use potential." (In fact, many of the more recently developed measures focus on a broader construct usually labeled "dependability" or "deviance.") Far less evidence of measurement validity is available for these more specific purposes.

The second category of paper-and-pencil test consists of "overt" measures that more directly inquire into employees' past use of drugs or their attitudes toward drug use. Generally, the measurement validity of such measures is more assumed than tested. For example, it is common for publishers of such tests to contend that the "validity" of an admission of drug use is obvious. However, as Rosse and Miller (1989) note, the validity of claiming never to

have used drugs is not so obvious. Nevertheless, the primary emphasis of most paper-and-pencil tests is validity of prediction rather than measurement.

Validity of Prediction

As previously noted, validity of prediction concerns the ability of tests to predict how well examinees will perform on the job (job relatedness). Two approaches are possible, depending on what one assumes a positive test result implies. One assumption is that a positive test result implies impairment of ability to perform one's job safely and effectively. This approach, similar to a roadside sobriety check, requires evidence of a direct correlation between test results and job performance. Unfortunately, for a variety of reasons, this approach and its underlying assumptions are difficult to validate.

One very basic problem is the necessity to document current, rather than past, use. This implies that testing must be done on a regular basis, for example, prior to every work shift, or when there is reason to suspect a person is working under the influence. Since one would expect few job applicants to show up for an preemployment drug test while high, this approach would seem to rule out preemployment screening.

A second limitation is that even highly accurate urinalysis methods are generally incapable of indicating precisely when a substance was last used. Marijuana metabolites, for example, can remain in the blood for as long as twenty-eight days (depending on the length of time and the frequency which with the person has been using the drug). Thus, it is possible that a person receiving a positive test result may have used the drug in question only once, days or even weeks prior to the test. Or it may be that the individual is a regular user who last partook only hours before. Such evidence is insufficient to show current impairment and leads to the criticism that drug testing is an invasion of workers' right to privacy during their nonworking hours.

A third concern with this approach is that most drug tests do not provide the quantitative results necessary to document an effect on performance. Rather, most simply indicate whether drugs were detectable at any level above the minimum threshold. Blood tests are generally considered better than urine tests for determining impairment because the chemical is circulating in the bloodstream, where it potentially can affect performance, rather than in the urine, where it is waste material. But not even blood tests are completely valid indicators of impairment because a blood-drug level of a specified percent may cause impairment in one individual and not in another (Hansen, Caudill & Boone, 1985). Moreover, no generally accepted standards for impairment currently exist except for alcohol (Rosen, 1987).

A possible solution to this problem is provided by the Veritas 100. Unlike typical blood or urine tests, the Veritas 100 monitors the electrical activity in a person's brain to detect current impairment due to a number of drugs. Although Richard Hawks, the director of the National Institute for Drug Abuse, expresses skepticism about its validity (personal communication, February 2, 1988), it is touted as the most conclusive test for drug impairment (Bureau of National Affairs Special Report, 1986).

Despite the problems inherent in using drug tests to assess impairment directly, this approach does have its advocates. Following the *Exxon Valdez* oil spill, Exxon was reported to be requiring tanker captains and pilots to undergo Breathalyzer tests when reporting for duty. Others have suggested that safety-sensitive personnel such as air traffic controllers and railroad engineers demonstrate proficiency on a complex psychomotor test (similar to a video game) prior to beginning a work shift. While such procedures would create logistical challenges, they would probably generate fewer complaints and be much easier to defend than typical uses of drug tests.

The second, and more typical, approach to demonstrating validity of prediction is to show that people identified as drug users (with either physiological or paper-and-pencil methods) are more likely to demonstrate poor job performance in general. Rather than emphasizing impairment while under the influence of a drug, this type of evidence seeks to demonstrate that drug users typically produce less or poorer quality work, are absent more often, are more likely to quit (or be fired), and are more likely to be involved in such counterproductive behaviors as on-the-job intoxication, hangovers, theft, or violence.

Due to the heavy emphasis that has been placed on their measurement validity, very little evidence of validity of prediction has been collected for physiological drug tests. Paper-and-pencil measures, on the other hand, have placed primary emphasis on this type of evidence. For that reason, Rosse and Miller (1989) argue that, as a class, paper-and-pencil measures may be more suitable for "suspicionless" (pre-employment and random) types of testing. (However, they also note that there is a scarcity of this type of evidence even for most paper-and-pencil tests. They also conclude that physiological measures' greater evidence of measurement validity makes them preferable for "cause" testing, especially when there is reason to believe that the person's behavior may be impaired at the time of testing.)

Because much of the evidence of validity of prediction is inferred from more general data dealing with the effects of drugs, further discussion of this issue will be deferred to the next section, dealing with the effects of drugs on employers and society.

DRUG USE AND JOB PERFORMANCE

On the face of it, the relationship between use of drugs and job performance may seem obvious. Drug use can adversely affect work performance and may result in safety hazards to employees and the public. The recent attention to the possible role of drug use in aircraft and train accidents demonstrates the potential costs (Yesavage, Leirer, Denari & Hollister, 1985). Moreover, addictive and expensive drugs may increase the likelihood of a worker's engaging in criminal activity on the job (Milbourne, 1984).

However, it also seems reasonable to argue that the consequences of drug use are likely to be a function of the type of drug, the manner in which it is used (e.g., frequency, dosage, whether it is used during work or nonwork hours), and the type of work (Rogers & Colbert, 1975). Most of us have known individuals whose regular use of a drug (especially alcohol) had little effect on their job performance. We have also known supervisors who were unwilling to discipline users of substances (e.g., amphetamines) that increased short-term performance. Indeed, the U.S. military is reported to have regularly prescribed such medications for flight crews making long transatlantic flights. Therefore, the job relatedness of even reliable tests is not ensured in all situations.

One approach to proving job relatedness involves studies in a controlled setting of simulated performance while under the influence of drugs. For example, Yesavage and his colleagues (1985) studied the effect of marijuana on pilots' performance in a flight simulator. Their most surprising result was not that the pilots' performance was impaired 1 and 4 hours after smoking but that impairment was also detected 24 hours later (even though the subjects reported no subjective awareness of being intoxicated or impaired). This finding provides a basis for concerns that off-the-job drug use may affect later performance on the job.

Additional laboratory research reporting positive correlations between drug use and job impairment can be found for both alcohol and other substances (Heishman & Henningfield, 1989; Janowsky, Meacham, Blaine, Schoor & Bozzetti, 1976; Jobs, 1989; Kandel & Yamaguchi, 1987). While limited, these data provide the best evidence of direct impairment effects.

Other studies have attempted to validate the hypothesis that drug users will demonstrate poorer performance in general. While lacking the ability to show direct evidence of impairment, these studies generally have the advantage of using more realistic work settings.

A number of these studies have used turnover as a measure of performance and have generally shown that those who test positive for drug use are more likely to quit or be terminated (Blank & Fenton, 1989; Lewy, 1983; McDaniel, 1989; Normand & Mahoney, 1989; Parish, 1989). Winkler and Sheridan (1989) have also shown that substance abusers use more medical benefits and are involved in more accidents. Unfortunately, a number of these studies are flawed by findings that were not statistically significant or practically useful or by research designs that make it difficult to determine if the terminations were due to supervisors' awareness of the test results rather than the subordinate's poor performance.

One of the most methodologically sophisticated studies was conducted with 4,375 applicants to the U.S. Postal Service (Normand & Mahoney, 1989). Because the Postal Service kept the results confidential rather than using them for decision making, they were able to reduce many of the biases possibly operating in other studies. They found that the absen-teeism rate for applicants who tested positive was 41 percent higher than for those who tested negative; they also reported a 38.5 percent higher rate of involuntary separation for the positive group.

A major limitation of these studies is the use of attendance or turnover as the primary measure of performance. While these are obviously important outcomes, it is difficult to determine whether they are due to drug use or other factors that might be correlated with use of drugs (such as education, gender, or ethnicity). We could be more confident in the tests' validity with evidence that is more directly related to drug use, such as being caught intoxicated or in possession of drugs, being hung over on the job, or displaying behavior indicative of intoxication. At this time, the few studies that document such relationships tend to be in the paper-and-pencil category (see Rosse & Miller, 1989).

In sum, much of the evidence showing detrimental effects of drug use on job performance is anecdotal. In reality, the very dramatic and widely cited estimates of the costs of drug use (cf. "Taking Drugs," 1983; Hosty, 1985) are based on little more than speculation. Moreover, much of the anecdotal evidence is based on fairly extreme cases of chronic users; whether this generalizes to more casual users is unclear. Fortunately, there seems to be a trend toward development of more credible evidence of the effects of drugs on performance. We hope that future research will provide more attention to the moderating effects of type of drug, type of job, and manner of use.

WILL DRUG TESTING REDUCE DRUG USE?

A crucial assumption is that instituting drug testing programs will reduce the "drug problem," but the mechanism through which this will occur is not always clear. It is generally implied that such an effect could occur through screening drug users out the work force, deterring those who are in the work force from using drugs, and/or rehabilitating those employees who are found to be using drugs.

Selection Effects

At first blush, the most obvious effect of drug testing should be to remove drug users from an organization's applicant pool. Given accurate testing procedures, this effect would appear to be straightforward. However, three caveats should be noted. The first is the implicit assumption that employers can afford to reject those who are identified as drug users. While the cost-effectiveness of drug testing will be discussed further in a subsequent section of the chapter, suffice it to say that the combined effects of true and false positives, plus any reduction in the applicant pool due to unwillingness to apply to a company that conducts drug testing, could result in a pool of candidates that is insufficient to meet labor demand.

A second caveat is that while a selection effect may reduce the organization's problem, it alone would have little effect on the societal problem of drug use. Detected users may simply move from one potential employer to another, until they find one that does not test for drugs. Indeed, many firms have instituted testing programs primarily to avoid being the only employer in a labor market that is not testing.

While some employers may feel that such societal effects are outside their control (and perhaps responsibility), these macroeffects cannot be so readily dismissed. The drug user who fails to find a job presumably becomes part of an unemployed drug user underclass, which must rely either on crime or welfare to subsist. While some argue that drug abusers have to hit rock bottom before they can be helped, surveys of drug users show nearly twice as many chronic users among the unemployed (Kopstein & Gfroerer, 1989; Maranda, Frank, Marel & Schmeidler, 1989). As we will describe in the next section, there is also reason to believe that rehabilitation is more likely among drug users who are holding a job. Thus, while preemployment screening (or other testing that results in termination) may reduce an organization's internal drug problem, it may actually exacerbate the problem at a societal level.

It should also be noted that a selection effect assumes that workers bring their drug problem with them to a job. It seems equally plausible that many workers will begin to abuse drugs (particularly alcohol) sometime after being on a job. Indeed, some drug use is likely to be caused, at least in part, by one's job.

Deterrence Effect

Another possibility is that the mere presence of a screening program will deter use of drugs. Presumably, this could be true whether or not the tests are valid, as long as they are perceived to be valid and employees are concerned about the consequences of detection. In fact, the Supreme Court in its *Railway Labor Executives* decision (1980) concluded that urinalyses do not necessarily need to show impairment because one of their functions is to deter drug use.

However, one problem with the hypothesized deterrent effect is the presumption that drug use is wholly voluntary (is not based on addiction). It seems likely that drug users (particularly those with a chemical dependency) would react to the threat of detection by subterfuge, especially if testing is not carefully controlled (e.g., by determining through the grapevine when testing will occur and then abstaining during the critical period or by enlisting others to provide phony urine samples). We have also heard stories of drug users switching from their drug of first preference to one that cannot be as readily detected in anticipation of being tested.

There are few data that address this question with sufficient rigor to rule out alternative explanations. Allen (1989) reported that a Department of Transportation study conducted between September 1987 and March 1989 found a reduction in positive test results following the full implementation of random testing. Similarly, the U.S. Navy reported that 47 percent of seamen under age twenty-six reported using illegal drugs prior to their testing program; within a month after testing began, only 4 percent reported using illegal drugs (Bureau of National Affairs Special Report, 1986).

Unfortunately, it is impossible to determine whether these results reflect reduced drug use among employees or a selection effect due to screening out drug users. Moreover, if the effect was due to reduced use among the same employee group, the lack of a control group makes it impossible to say if the reduction was due to testing or other effects, such as the general decline in drug use among the U.S. population. Thus, while it seems likely that drug testing may deter drug use among occasional users, the extent of this effect is difficult to estimate.

Rehabilitation Effect

Another way that drug testing could reduce drug use would be to detect drug users among current employees and encourage them to "shape up or ship out." While discipline (and often termination) has historically been a common response to drug use, a nationwide survey conducted by the American Management Association found that rehabilitation now appears to be the response of choice.

Rehabilitation obviously has much in its favor. At a societal level, it is the only approach that really solves the problem of current drug users. It is also generally argued to be preferable for the employer, who stands to recapture the often large capital investment made in the abusing employee. It is further assumed that a commitment to rehabilitation will improve the stature of the employer in the eyes of other employees, who will not only become more committed to the firm but who will also become more likely to come forward voluntarily with their own substance abuse problems.

Although rehabilitation of detected users is a more desirable outcome, it is not yet one that appears to command a lot of optimism. Despite the pervasive view that employee rehabilitation programs are successful and cost-effective, the reality is that very little rigorous evaluation data actually exist (Luthans & Waldersee, 1989; Myers, 1984; Weiss, 1987). Employee assistance programs (EAP) have received a good deal of attention and support, yet much of this literature is more descriptive than evaluative. Moreover, most research has focused on alcohol rehabilitation. The situation for other drugs may be even less encouraging, according to a NIDA study that found little evidence of effective methods for dealing with drug problems in industrial settings (Madonia, 1984).

However, as Rosse, Crown, and Feldman (in press) note, there is some emerging evidence that drug rehabilitation can be successful. Biase and Sullivan (1989) and Trice and Sonnestuhl (see Bureau of National Affairs, 1986) both reported a 55 percent recovery rate for drug users who attended an EAP. United Airlines reported a 77 percent decline in absenteeism as well as an improvement in performance for both alcohol and other drug users who had participated in their EAP (Wrich, 1988). And an unusually well-designed study by Hazelden, a company providing EAPs and inpatient rehabilitation

programs, reported that 72 percent of their sample were drug free twelve months after leaving the treatment facility.

As encouraging as these data are, it is difficult to overlook some continuing problems with EAP research. Most continues to be conducted in-house and published without the benefit of peer review. Research designs are often inadequate, and the obvious potential for inflation of positive results (as well as nonpublication of negative results) is always present. There is also a pressing need for research that compares the effectiveness of alternative rehabilitation strategies (and with different drugs).

IS DRUG TESTING COST EFFECTIVE?

Little research has addressed the issue of the cost-effectiveness of drug testing (see Normand & Mahoney, 1989, for a very recent exception). Determining the direct cost of the testing program itself (the personnel, material, and laboratory costs involved in collecting, testing, and retesting specimens and reporting results) should be relatively straightforward. Indirect costs as well as benefits are more difficult to estimate.

In addition to cost estimates that could be inferred from the Normand and Mahoney (1989), Blank and Fenton (1989), Parish (1989), and Lewy (1983) studies reported earlier, the Georgia Power Company conducted a retrospective study to determine costs directly (Hunt & Winkler, 1989; Winkler & Sheridan, 1989). Through matched group comparisons, the researchers determined that employees identified as either drug users or problem drinkers cost the organization significantly more than nonusers. Specifically, drug users who were detected through the for-cause testing program had higher absenteeism rates (165 hours versus 47 hours annually), more vehicular accidents (.23 versus .109 per person) and lost time due to accidents (.008 versus .000 per person) and also used more medical benefits ($1,377 versus $163 per person annually). The drug users who took advantage of the EAP also produced higher costs than matched controls who entered the EAP for other reasons (annual absenteeism rates, 91 hours versus 60 hours; annual medical benefits usage, $1,347 versus $678).

There are obviously additional costs that are not measured in these studies. One example is recruitment costs, which could increase both as a function of applicants who are rejected and because of job seekers who do not apply either out of fear of being

rejected or because of philosophical objections. Other potential costs include development of drug treatment programs and the direct and indirect costs of lawsuits challenging testing programs.

Recent court decisions exemplify the damages an employer may be required to pay as a result of misusing tests. In *Evans v. Casey* the Philadelphia Division of the U.S. Postal Service agreed to pay $5,000 in damages to each of eleven persons who tested positive and were subsequently rejected for employment. Seven of the eleven were later hired after passing a second test, and an additional applicant was hired after determination that his positive result was triggered by prescription medication. The Postal Service was also liable for $12,000 for the plaintiff's attorney's fees. In *Houston Belt & Terminal Railway Co. v. Wherry,* the company was ordered to pay $150,000 in compensatory damages and $50,000 in punitive damages to the plaintiff for defamation of character. As a result of a positive drug test, the employee was fired, and his supervisor wrote a letter to the Department of Labor that stated that methadone had been found in his urine sample. The plaintiff had his urine independently tested by another lab that reported that a substance similar to methadone was found.

An interesting perspective on the issue of cost-effectiveness was provided in a recent survey of 190 organizations from a variety of industries. Gomez-Mejia and Balkin (1987) found that firms that were currently using drug tests were neutral about the need for a cost-benefit analysis of the drug testing program (3.3 on a five-point Likert scale). Most of the firms did not believe turnover had increased, that supervisor-employee relations had deteriorated, or that it had become more difficult to hire people because of the tests. However, since these results appear to be based on personnel managers' beliefs, it remains to be seen whether they are corroborated by empirical trends.

There is clearly a need for further research investigating the cost-effectiveness of drug testing programs. Moreover, such research needs to consider not only different forms of drug testing programs (e.g., for applicants versus employees; with and without rehabilitation options) but also alternatives to testing. Some have argued that the focus should not be on drug use per se but on job performance. From this perspective, management's responsibility is to monitor workers' behavior and counsel those whose performance is deficient, regardless of the cause (Muczyk & Heshizer, 1986; Rosen, 1987). In situations in which the only options are to improve or be disciplined, this approach may be the least costly (although not necessarily most cost-effective). Muczyk and Heshizer (1986) argue that it is almost certainly easier to defend in court. Other alternatives to drug testing include drug education and/or drug treatment programs (see Rosse, Crown & Feldman, in press). Although some utility estimates for EAPs exist (McGaffey, 1978; Ray, 1972), an attempt to consider the total cost-benefit of alternative drug reduction programs simply or in combination is problematic.

IS DRUG TESTING LEGAL?

Perhaps the most widely debated aspect of drug testing is its legality. In response to mandated testing in the military, government agencies, and such government-regulated industries as transportation and utilities, at least fifty lawsuits are currently working their way through the federal courts. While many of these cases are still in various stages of appeal, the legal status of testing is beginning to become apparent.

Constitutional Law

Interestingly, the most widely cited "legal" objection to drug testing is that it represents an invasion of privacy. Many people erroneously believe that the U.S. Constitution guarantees a "right to privacy." There are specific "privacy rights" such as freedom from unwarranted search and seizure of property, as well as the right to protection against self-incrimination. But constitutionally these offer protection only if the employer is a governmental institution or agency (Lehr & Middlebrooks, 1985). Therefore, the most publicized defense, and the one most often cited by drug testing opponents, applies directly only to a minority of employees. Whether such protections will be extended to private sector employers remains to be seen.[2]

Within the public sector, challenges to drug testing programs have generally described urine tests—particularly those that are not based on any "particularized suspicion"—as violations of the Fourth Amendment's restriction on unwarranted searches. The government has typically argued that such procedures are justified for jobs in which the safety of coworkers or the public outweighs the individual's right to privacy.

This issue was partly determined on March 21, 1989, when the U.S. Supreme Court handed down its first, landmark rulings on two cases dealing with drug testing. In *National Treasury Employees Union et al. v. Von Raab,* the federal employees' union alleged that the drug-testing requirement for employees seeking positions requiring the employee to carry a gun or be directly involved in drug interdiction violated the Fourth Amendment. The Supreme Court decided that the "extraordinary safety and national security hazards that would attend the promotion of drug users to the sensitive positions in question" justified the use of drug testing in this situation. Specifically, they found that drug screens "are searches that must meet the reasonableness requirement of the Fourth Amendment" but that neither a warrant nor probable cause is required. The requirement for probable cause was waived in this instance because of the compelling government interests of national safety that outweigh the privacy interests of employees seeking promotion.

The second Supreme Court ruling on that date involved railway workers employed by private railroads but regulated by a federal agency. (Although private sector employees are not generally protected by the Fourth Amendment, when regulations are enforced by order of government officials the affected employees' Fourth Amendment rights become relevant.) In *Skinner, Secretary of Transportation, v. Railway Labor Executives' Association,* the labor organization sought to enjoin the 1985 Federal Railroad Administration's regulations that require train crews involved in accidents resulting in death, injury, or property damage to submit to drug and alcohol tests. The regulations also authorize, but do not require, railroads to test employees who violate certain safety rules.

Similar to the *Von Raab* decision, the Supreme Court held that these tests constituted searches protected by the Fourth Amendment, but because of the "special needs" of this case, the warrant requirement and the need for probable cause were waived. The justices waived the warrant requirement in part because of the need for timeliness and also because the testing procedures were well known to covered employees. The probable cause requirement was waived for a variety of reasons. First, the justices decided that

> the testing procedures contemplated by the regulations pose only limited threats to covered employees' justifiable privacy expectations, particularly since they participate in an industry subject to pervasive safety regulation by the Federal and State Governments.

Second, by conducting the drug tests in a medical environment without direct observation, the intrusiveness of the test was reduced. Finally, the government interest in detecting drug-impaired employees was judged to be compelling. The justices stated that

> a substance-impaired railroad employee in a safety sensitive job can cause great human loss before any signs of the impairment become noticeable, and the regulations supply an effective means of deterring such employees from using drugs or alcohol by putting them on notice that they are likely to be discovered if an accident occurs.

These decisions seem to provide greater latitude for employers wishing to use drug testing. However, two important limitations of these decisions need to be noted. The first is that both decisions did recognize the relevance of Fourth Amendment protections against unreasonable search in the context of urinalysis. The Court was willing to waive the normal requirements of reasonable suspicion due to the safety-sensitive nature of the jobs in question but seemed to indicate that such a waiver would not be automatic. This is most clearly seen in *Von Raab*, where the Court was unable to ascertain whether positions involving the handling of classified information were sufficiently "safety sensitive" to justify testing for drugs in the absence of reasonable suspicion.

A second important caveat has to do with the legal status of random testing. The two Supreme Court decisions dealt with testing of candidates for promotion (*Von Raab*) or employees who had been involved in accidents (*Railway Labor Executives*); neither related directly to the controversial issue of testing all employees on a random basis. This issue

has taken on particular importance since the Department of Transportation's publication of guidelines that mandate random testing of a variety of safety-sensitive positions in the transportation industry. These guidelines, due to take effect December 21, 1989, were put on hold by a Northern California District Court's injunction in January 1989 (*Owner-Operators Independent Drivers Association of America v. Skinner*). This case is currently being appealed, but a companion case has been decided in the Eleventh Circuit Court of Appeals.

In this case, *American Federation of Government Employees, AFL-CIO, et al., v. Skinner, Secretary Department of Transportation,* the court found that "the privacy interests of employees occupying the three specifically challenged positions were outweighed by the Department's compelling interests in preventing drug use among such personnel." It is important to note that each of these positions was classified as safety sensitive by the Department of Transportation and then reaffirmed as such by the circuit court. (The positions included motor vehicle operators, hazardous material inspectors, and Federal Aviation Administration aircraft mechanics.) The court's determination that these jobs were safety sensitive led the way to their conclusion that the department's plan to test randomly these employees went beyond the normal needs of law enforcement and indeed served special government needs. However, the likelihood that this case will be appealed to the Supreme Court (especially if the similar case currently being heard by the Ninth Circuit Court is decided differently) means that the final word on the issue of random testing may still be some time in the future.

Statutory Law

Although the bulk of attention has dealt with constitutional cases that affect primarily public sector employers, there are additional statutory requirements that may affect either public- or private-sector employers. The Vocational Rehabilitation Act (as amended in 1973) prohibits employment discrimination against handicapped individuals by the federal government, government contractors, and recipients of federal funding. The act clearly protects former drug users, but its protection of active users is more controversial. The act states that the term *handicapped*

> does not include any individual who is an alcoholic or drug abuser whose current use of alcohol or drugs prevents such individual from performing the duties of the job in question or whose

employment, by reason of such current alcohol or drug abuse, would constitute a direct threat to property or the safety of others.

The issue of drug use being a covered disability was raised in *AFL-CIO v. Skinner*, but the court ruled that this statutory claim was "nonsignificant" because they did not agree with the theory that "every potential employee testing positive for drug use is an otherwise qualified handicapped person."

Title VII of the Civil Rights Act has also been cited as a protection against drug testing programs. Title VII prohibits discrimination in employment on the basis of race, sex, religion, color, or national origin. If a company's drug testing policy shows disparate impact, it becomes the employer's duty to prove that the tests are job related or that the policy was of business necessity and that no alternative procedures with less adverse effect are available. Since there is evidence that minorities are more likely to test positive for drug use (Normand & Mahoney, 1989; Kopstein & Gfoerer, 1989; Maranda et al., 1989), a lack of evidence that all drug use affects job performance or that drug testing accurately identifies drug users could make this difficult.

On the other hand, evidence of job relatedness does not seem to have played a major role in court decisions to date. The issue of whether drug test results are related to performance impairment was raised by the circuit court in *Railway Labor Executives*. However, when the case was decided by the Supreme Court, the question was relegated to a footnote in which the Court indicated that it was unwilling to "second-guess the reasonable conclusions drawn by the [defendant] after years of investigation and study" into alternatives to urinalysis.

Collective Bargaining Agreements

Collective bargaining agreements represent one of the most significant obstacles to drug testing programs in unionized firms. Because drug testing is considered a working condition and as such is subject to collective bargaining, employers generally cannot implement drug testing without consulting with the union (Johnson-Bateman Co., 295 NLRB No. 26, 6/15/89). In *Consolidated Rail Corporation v. Railway Labor Executives Association*, the Supreme Court ruled that unilateral imposition of drug screening is also subject to compulsory and binding arbitration under the Railway Labor Act.

Even when drug testing is accepted by both parties, disciplinary measures triggered by testing are frequently subject to arbitration. Because of the social stigma concerned, arbitrators have typically applied much more stringent evidentiary requirements for cases concerning controlled substances; Geidt (1985) reports that arbitrators have overturned more of these discharges than they have sustained.

The manner in which tests are conducted seems to have a great influence on arbitrators' decisions. The Washington Metropolitan Area Transit Authority's decision to discharge a bus driver after he tested positive on both blood and urine tests following an accident was upheld by an arbitrator because the samples were double checked (Bureau of National Affairs Special Report, 1986). Arbitrators often require the employer to prove not only a test's accuracy and chain of custody but also that the employee had notice of the rules of the drug policy, that the rules were applied fairly, that management gave the employee a reasonable chance to refute the charges, and that the punishment fit the crime (Wollett, 1983/1984). Arbitrators also frequently require evidence that the use of drugs affected job performance, safety, or customer relations (Wynn, 1979). Employers dealing with unions would be prudent to consider these factors when implementing and enforcing drug testing programs, especially if discharge is their primary disciplinary measure.

Other Legal Considerations

Further complicating the legal environment is the evolving case law concerning wrongful discharge, employment at will, and employers' responsibilities for maintaining a safe working environment.

Traditionally, management has had nearly complete discretion in terminating employees for any (nondiscriminatory) reason, but recent cases have stated that employers may be bound by implicit contracts formed by verbal agreements, employee manuals, or past precedents. Firms must now consider whether testing and/or termination may violate an implied duty of "good faith and fair dealing" or of public policy. If testing and disciplinary procedures fail to meet the standards previously described in our discussion of arbitration, employers may have difficulty defending themselves against a wrongful discharge suit.

Employers also have basic rights and responsibilities that influence their decision to implement drug testing programs. These include the right to investigate violations of legitimate rules as well as their right to maintain discipline, protect their property, and protect the safety of other employees and clientele.

The Occupational Safety and Health Act and

state safety laws impose specific requirements on employers to maintain the safety of their employees and clients. An intoxicated employee represents a liability because of the higher risk of accidents to self, other employees, or clients. An even more inclusive obligation on the part of the employer was upheld in *Otis Engineering Corp. v. Clark*. In this case an intoxicated employee was sent home because of the hazard he posed to himself and others at work. On the drive home the employee was involved in an accident, resulting in his own death and the deaths of several occupants of the other vehicle. The other victims' family sued the company because it allowed the employee to drive home. This is an unusual case, but it demonstrates the importance of not only detecting the presence of workers under the influence but also a continuing responsibility to manage the consequences of drug use.

This continuing responsibility may extend to liability for workers compensation benefits attributable to drug use (Geidt, 1985). In California, an employee was awarded benefits from the Workers' Compensation Appeals Board because they agreed that his nervous tension, which was attributed to work overload, caused his drinking problem. It is also possible that employees undergoing rehabilitation will seek protection from discharge because their absence is due to an "industrial injury" (Geidt, 1985). As such, the advantages of early detection and treatment are clearly evident.

IMPLICATIONS

We began this chapter by noting that drug testing rests on a number of assumptions. Two of these— that drug testing is accurate and legal—are addressed by an increasingly substantial base of knowledge. Three additional assumptions—that drug use is an important problem and that drug testing represents an effective and efficient solution—are less well addressed by verifiable evidence.

In addressing the issue of the accuracy of drug testing procedures, we drew an important distinction between validity of measurement and validity of prediction. For physiological measures, principally urinalysis, there is ample evidence that validity of measurement is not a concern if a laboratory meeting NIDA certification requirements is used and all initial positive results are confirmed using the gas chromatography/mass spectrometry technique. There is an increasing body of evidence showing the validity of prediction, although there are still significant gaps. Paper-and-pencil measures may represent a reasonable alternative to urinalysis for selection purposes, particularly if there is an interest in predicting a wider range of "deviant" behavior than just drug use. For both types of measures, however, we feel that more validation research is needed.

The legal status of drug testing seems to be fairly clear at present. With few exceptions, private sector employers appear to have few constraints on their decision to test employees for drug use. (The exceptions involve a few state laws that provide an expanded definition of privacy rights, some uncertainties about the applicability of the Civil Rights Act of 1964, and certain confidentiality requirements.) The legal status of testing has been most controversial in the public sector, but two recent Supreme Court decisions seem to make it clear that Fourth Amendment protections will not impede testing for positions that are safety sensitive. The remaining legal questions appear to involve random testing and the definition of safety-sensitive jobs.

We are less confident that conclusions can be drawn about the assumptions that drug testing will reduce the drug problem at work in a cost-effective manner. There are significant gaps in our understanding of how drug use affects behavior on the job, and we are greatly concerned that drug testing may be far too narrow an approach. There is little evidence that drug testing will reduce the drug problem at the societal level and good reason to suspect that it could even increase it in the short run. There is a near-complete absence of knowledge about the unintended consequences of drug testing, at either an organizational or societal level. Particularly in the absence of a rehabilitation program for detected users, we are reluctant to conclude that drug testing will necessarily be cost-effective.

To a substantial extent the controversy over drug testing is one of value preferences. Issues of public safety, individual rights versus the common good, and privacy are both critical and complex. Public sector organizations, and private sector firms falling under the jurisdiction of the Drug Free Workplace Act and other federal regulations, have little choice in deciding whether to test. Other firms will have to weigh these factors in coming to their decision. We hope that firms opting to test will incorporate our recommendations concerning appropriate testing procedures.

We would also like to emphasize that a drug testing program should be only one part of a comprehensive substance abuse program. The other components should include drug awareness, education, and employee assistance. Research investigating the over-

all cost-effectiveness of each of these programs should be conducted in order to determine the amount of emphasis each should receive.

APPENDIX 28–A: SOURCES FOR TESTS DESCRIBED

Physiological Measures

Urinalyses. EMIT. Enzyme Multiplied Immunoassay Technique, Syva Corporation/Syntex Corporation, 900 Arastradero Road, Palo Alto, CA 94304.

Abuscreen. Roche Diagnostics, Division of Hoffman LaRoche, Kingsland Street, Nutley, NJ 07110.

KDI QUIK Test. Keystone Diagnostics, Inc., Division of Keystone Medical Corporation, Columbia, MD.

Other. Veritas 100. Electroencephalographic analysis. National Patent Analytical Systems, Inc., Washington, D.C.

RIAH. Radioimmunoassay of hair. Psychemedics Corporation, 1807 Wilshire Boulevard, Santa Monica, CA 90403.

Paper-and-Pencil Inventories

Personality Inventories. California Psychological Inventory. Consulting Psychologists Press, 577 College Avenue, Palo Alto, CA 94306.

Employment Inventory. Personnel Decisions, Inc., 2000 Plaza VII Tower, 45 South Seventh Street, Minneapolis, MN 55402.

Hogan Personnel Selection Series. National Computer Sys-

tems, P.O. Box 1416, Minneapolis, MN 55440.

Minnesota Report: Personnel Selection System. National Computer Systems, P.O. Box 1416, Minneapolis, MN 55440.

Personnel Reaction Blank. Consulting Psychologists Press, 577 College Avenue, Palo Alto, CA 94306.

16 PF (Sixteen Personality Factor Questionnaire). National Computer Systems, P.O. Box 1416, Minneapolis, MN 55440.

Overt Measures–Admissions. ADendum. Phase II Profile, 3740 South Royal Crest Street, Las Vegas, NV 89119.

Reid Report/Survey. Reid Psychological Systems, 200 South Michigan, Suite 900, Chicago, IL 60604.

Overt Measures—Attitudes. Employee Reliability Inventory. Bay States Psychological Associates, 225 Friend Street, Boston, MA 02114.

Total Personnel Selection Series. Milby Systems, 8040 Cedar Avenue South, Minneapolis, MN 55420.

Overt Measures—Combination. Peronnel Selection Inventory. London House, Inc., 1550 Northwest Highway, Park Ridge, IL 60068.

Wilkerson Pre-Employment Audit. Team Building Systems, 15710 Drummet Boulevard, Suite 150, Houston, TX 77032.

NOTES

1. Len Bias, a first-round draft choice of the Boston Celtics, died of a cocaine overdose the night of the 1986 National Basketball Association draft. Don Rogers, a defensive back for the Cleveland Browns, died of a cocaine overdose shortly before he was to be married.

2. However, there seems to be a trend toward privacy rights being included in state laws and in common-law theories (Geidt, 1985). For example, a recent superior court ruling in California struck down a drug testing program, holding that it violated an inalienable right to privacy guaranteed by a 1974 amendment to the state constitution. However, even in this case, the judge stated that he might have favored the testing program had the company shown that it increased worker safety or "reduced a major drug problem" (Judge Allen Steele, personal communication, January 14, 1987). Montana also has a state law that forbids blood or urine tests except for cause or when hiring for safety-sensitive positions.

REFERENCES

Allen, M.J. (1989). *The Department of Transportation's random drug testing program: Analysis and findings.* Presented at the NIDA Drugs in the Workplace Conference at Bethesda, Maryland, September.

Amalgamated Transit Union v. Southern California Rapid Transit District (1986). Los Angeles Super. CT., No. C628562.

American Management Association (1987). *Drug abuse: The workplace issues.* New York: Author.

Biase, D.V., & Sullivan, A.P. (1989). *Outcome of drug abuse treatment for mass transportation workers.* Presented at the NIDA Drugs in the Workplace Conference at Bethesda, Maryland, September.

Blank, D.L., & Fenton, J.W. (1989). Early employment testing for marijuana: Demographic and employee retention patterns. In S. Gust and J. Walsh (Eds.), *Drugs in the workplace: Research and evaluation data* (NIDA Research Monograph 91). Rockville, MD: U.S. Department of Health and Human Services.

Bloch, J. (1986). So what? Everybody's doing it. *Forbes,* August, 102.

Boone, J., Hansen, H., Hearn, T., Lewis, S., & Dudley, D. (1982). Laboratory evaluation and assistance efforts: Mailed, on-site and blind proficiency testing surveys conducted by the Centers for Disease Control. *American Journal of Public Health, 72,* 1364–1368.

Brotherhood of Locomotive Engineers v. Burlington Northern Railroad Co. (1984). 117 LRRM 2739 (D. Montana).

Bureau of National Affairs Special Report (1986). *Alcohol and drugs in the workplace.* Rockville, MD: Bureau of National Affairs.

Consolidated Rail Corporation v. Railway Labor Executives Association (1989). U.S. Supreme Court, No. 88-1, June 19.

Dakis, C., Pottash, A., Annitto, W., & Gold, M. (1983). Urine testing for detection of marijuana: An advisory. *Morbidity and Mortality Weekly Report, 32.*

Davis, K.H., Hawks, R.L., & Blanke, R.V. (1988). Assessment of laboratory quality in urine drug testing. *Journal of the American Medicial Association, 260* (12), 1749–1754.

Evans v. Casey (1986). USDC EPa, No. 86–1217 (Penn.).

Frings, C.S., Battaglia, D.J., & White, R.M. (1989). Status of drugs-of-abuse testing in urine under blind conditions: An AACC study. *Clinical Chemistry, 35*(5), 891–894.

Frings, C.S., White, R.M., & Battaglia, D.J. (1987). Status of drugs-of-abuse testing in urine under blind conditions: An AACC study. *Clinical Chemistry, 33,* 1683–1686.

Geidt, T. (1985). Drug and alcohol abuse in the work place: Balancing employer and employee rights. *Employee Relations Law Journal, 11*(2), 181–205.

Gomez-Mejia, L., & Balkin, D. (1987). Dimensions and characteristics of effective drug testing programs. *Personnel Psychology, 40,* 745–763.

Gottheil, E., Caddy, G., & Austin, D. (1976). Fallibility of urine drug screens in monitoring methadone programs. *Journal of the American Medical Association 236,* 1035–1038.

Hansen, H., Caudill, S., & Boone, J. (1985). Crisis in drug testing. *Journal of the American Medical Association, 252,* 2382.

Heishman, S.J., & Henningfield, J.E. (1989). *Application of human laboratory data for the assessment of performance in workplace settings: Practical and theoretical considerations.* Presented at the NIDA Drugs in the Workplace Conference at Bethesda, Maryland, September.

Hosty, R. (1985). Drug abuse in industry: What does it cost and what can be done? *Security Management,* October, 53–58.

Houston Belt & Terminal Railway Co. v. Wherry (1977). 548 S.W. 2d 743 (Ct. Civ. App. Texas).

Hunt, L., & Winkler, H. (1989). *A cost-benefit analysis of Georgia Power Company's cause-related drug testing program.* Presented at the NIDA Drugs in the Workplace Conference at Bethesda, Maryland, September.

Janowsky, D.S., Meacham, M.P., Blaine, J.D., Schoor, M. & Bozzetti, L.P. (1976). Marijuana effects on simulated flying ability. *American Journal of Psychiatry, 133* (4), 384–388.

Jobs, S. (1989). *Impact of moderate alcohol consumption on business decision making.* Presented at the NIDA Drugs in the Workplace Conference at Bethesda, Maryland, September.

Kandel, D.B., & Yamaguchi, K. (1987). Job mobility and drug use: An event history analysis. *American Journal of Sociology, 92*(4), 836–878.

Kopstein, A., & Gfoerer, J. (1989). *Drug use patterns and demographics of employed drug users: Data from the 1988 NIDA Household Survey.* Presented at the NIDA Drugs in the Workplace Conference at Bethesda, Maryland, September.

Lehr, R., & Middlebrooks, D. (1985). Work-place privacy issues and employer screening policies. *Employee Relations Law Journal,* Winter, 407–421.

Lewy, R. (1983). Preemployment qualitative urine toxicology screening. *Journal of Occupational Medicine, 25*(8), 579–580.

Lovvorn v. City of Chattanooga (1986). No. CIV-1-86-389 (Tenn.).

Luthans, F., & Waldersee, R. (1989). *Employee assistance programs: A critical analysis.* Presented at the annual meetings of the Academy of Management at Washington, DC, August.

Madonia, J. (1984). Managerial responses to alcohol and drug abuse among employees. *Personnel Administrator, 29*(6), 134–139.

Maranda, M. Frank, B., Marel, R., & Schmeidler, J. (1989). *Drugs in the workplace: Survey findings for New York State's labor force.* Presented at the NIDA Drugs in the Workplace Conference at Bethesda, Maryland, September.

McDaniel, M. (1989). Does pre-employment drug use predict on-the job suitability? In S. Gust and J. Walsh (Eds.), *Drugs in the workplace: Research and evaluation data* (NIDA Research Monograph 91). Rockville, MD: U.S. Department of Health and Human Services.

McDonnel v. Hunter (1985). USDC No. 84-71-B (Iowa).

McGaffey, T. (1978). New horizons in organizational stress prevention approaches. *Personnel Administrator, 23,* 26–32.

Milbourne, G. (1984). Alcoholism, drug abuse, and job stress: What small businesses can do. *American Journal of Small Business,* Spring, 36–48.

Miners, I.A., Nykodym, N., & Samerdyke-Traband, D.M. (1987). Put drug detection to the test. *Personnel Journal, 66,* 91–97.

Muczyk, J., & Heshizer, B. (1986). Managing in an era of substance abuse. *Personnel Administrator, 31,* 91–105.

Myers, D.W. (1984). Measuring cost effectiveness of EAPs. *Risk management,* November, 56–61.

National Treasury Employees Union v. Von Raab (1986). 649 F. Supp 380 (E.D.La.). New on the spot drug test gets plaudits, skepticism (1986). *National Report on Substance Abuse, 1,*(5), 3.

Normand, J., & Mahoney, J. (1989). *The validity and utility of preemployment drug testing.* Presented at the NIDA Drugs in the Workplace Conference at Bethesda, Maryland, September.

One-quarter of firms said to screen employees (1986). *The National Report on Substance Abuse, 1* (1), 4–5.

Parish, D. (1989). Relation of the pre-employment drug-testing result to employment status: A one-year follow up. *Journal of General Internal Medicine, 4,* 44–47.

Penny v. Kennedy (1986). No. CIV-1-86-417, USDC (E.Tenn.).

Psychemedics (1987). *A very sensitive test for a very sensitive issue.* Santa Monica, CA: Author.

Railway Labor Executives Association et al. v. Long Island Railroad Co. (1980). USDC CV-86-2330 (ENY).

Ray, J. (1972). Drug abuse in business: Part of a larger problem. *Personnel, 49,* 15–21.

Rogers, R., & Colbert, J. (1975) Drug abuse and organizational response: A review and evaluation. *Personnel Journal, 54,* 266–271.

Rosen, T. (1987). *Using physiological measures in job selection: The role of the I/O psychologist.* Paper presented at the Second Annual Conference of the Society for Industrial and Organizational Psychology, Atlanta, April.

Rosse, J., Crown, D., & Feldman, H. (in press). Alternative solutions to the workplace drug problem: Results of a survey of personnel managers. *Journal of Employment Counseling.*

Rosse, J. & Miller, H. (1989). *Psychological screening for drug use among employees.* Presented at the annual meetings of the Academy of Management at Washington, DC, August.

Taking drugs on the job (1983). *Newsweek,* August 22, 55.

Turner v. Fraternal Order of Police (1985). No. 83-1213 (CA DC).

Weiss, R. (1987). Writing under the influence: Science versus fiction in the analysis of corporate alcoholism programs. *Personnel Psychology, 40,* 341–356.

Winkler, H., & Sheridan, J. (1989). *An analysis of workplace behaviors of substance users.* Presented at the NIDA Drugs in the Workplace Conference at Bethesda, Maryland, September.

Wollett, D. (1983/1984). What an arbitrator looks for in management discharge cases. *Employee Relations Law Journal, 525.*

Wrich, J.T. (1988). Beyond testing: Coping with drugs at work. *Harvard Business Review,* January–February, 120–127, 130.

Wynn, P. (1979). Arbitration standards in drug discharge cases. *Arbitration Journal, 34,* 19.

Yesavage, J.A., Leirer, V.O., Denari, M., & Hollister, L.E. (1985). Carry-over effects of marijuana intoxication on aircraft pilot performance: A preliminary report. *American Journal of Psychiatry, 142* (11), 1325–1329.

PART V

ASSESSMENT, ADVANCEMENT, AND REWARD

29 DETERMINING PROMOTABILITY: AN OVERVIEW

Herbert H. Meyer

The purpose of this chapter is to provide an overview of the issues and problems involved in determining the promotability of employees in work organizations. It will focus especially on determining promotability to positions at professional and administrative levels.

Determining promotability is essentially a selection problem. The process of identifying promotable people in an organization culminates in promotional decisions. The subsequent chapters in this part will focus on specific procedures or techniques used in making these critical selection decisions.

PROMOTION DECISIONS IMPORTANT

Among the most important decisions made in any organization are those that involve promotions of individuals to positions of greater responsibility. The success of organizations of all types will depend in the long run on the skills and abilities of the people who comprise them. The greater the responsibility is of the person, which usually means the higher the level of the person in the organization, the greater is that person's contribution to the success or failure of the organization. Therefore, decisions that are made as to whom to promote to those positions of greater responsibility must be made with great care. The long-term success, and in the private sector, even the survival, of the organization will depend on the capabilities of the people who are promoted to positions where decisions are made that are critical to organizational performance.

To make promotion decisions on the basis of the wrong criteria or to make such decisions in an unsystematic and haphazard manner will often prove to be disastrous. In the past, for example, it was customary in many organizations to rely on seniority as the dominant criterion for promotion. In the private sector, this practice often seemed to contribute to the demise of such organizations. Some of the country's former largest railroads would seem to provide a case in point.

PROMOTION DECISIONS DIFFICULT

Unfortunately, promotion decisions are not only critical, but they are also among the most difficult of the decisions that administrators must make. It is also unfortunate that this fact is frequently unrecognized. The best performers at any one level are automatically considered the best candidates for promotion to the next higher level, even though the higher-level job may require completely different abilities, skills, and other personal characteristics. The old cliché is manifested again and again: we promote our best engineer and thereby lose an outstanding engineer and gain a very poor engineering manager.

In making promotion decisions we are too often dealing with the unknown. The open position may require skills that few candidates for the position have had an opportunity exhibit. Moreover, all too frequently the administrators making the promotion decision may not be fully aware of the critical requirements of the open job. Selections that are not targeted to the demand characteristics of the jobs to be filled can be far off the mark. The effects on organizational performance can be destructive to say the least.

ANALYZING JOB REQUIREMENTS

The systematic and thorough analysis of job requirements is probably the most overlooked aspect of the promotion decision process. Without identifying clearly the target you are shooting for, the results are likely to be unpredictable. Analyzing the critical requirements of positions at the higher levels in an organization is often complex. Most positions at higher levels are managerial in nature. There are likely to be relatively few high-level positions in any organization that could be defined as essentially "individual contributor" jobs. Even in cases where the position title connotes individual contributor responsibilities, such as secretary, legal counsel, treasurer, or senior engineer, the position will usually involve managing a staff.

Managerial skills are often difficult to identify and define because of their nebulous characteristics. The role of the leader has probably been the focus of more research by psychologists and management scientists than any other topic in organizational science. Yet the results of that research have been largely inconclusive. We know little more about what makes a good leader than we did fifty years ago. About fifteen years ago, Stogdill (1974) undertook an exhaustive search of the literature on leadership. He found over 3,000 articles and books that reported reasonably respectable research studies of leadership or supervisory behavior. Stogdill concluded after this monumental survey of the research literature, "Four decades of research on leadership have produced a bewildering mass of findings. . . . It is difficult to know what, if anything, has been convincingly demonstrated by replicated research. The endless accumulation of empirical data has not produced an integrated understanding of leadership." (p. vii).

To make the problem even more complex, managerial jobs are likely to be dynamic in character. Texas Instruments, for example, found that as a product moves through different phases of its life cycle, different kinds of management skills become dominant (*Business Week,* February 25, 1980). General Electric and Corning Glass companies reported similar observations. In the rapidly changing technology that most industries are facing today, such changes in the critical requirements of managerial positions are accelerating.

In determining the personal characteristics needed for a replacement in a higher-level opening, it is also important to project future organizational changes. How is the job likely to change in the future? This is especially important in a dynamic business or in a growing company. One company that I worked with as a consultant several years ago had promoted their senior and most effective sales representative to the job of sales manager when the company was small. This man was fairly effective when the staff was small and he could work with sales representatives individually. However, as the company grew and the sales staff became large, he was less and less effective. The company then needed a marketing manager to head the staff, not a technical supervisor. After suffering great losses in momentum for this growing business, the president finally had to face up to the fact that the man had to be removed and a more capable executive found. The change was actually welcomed by the sales manager. He had suffered personally from the stress of being over his head in the job.

IDENTIFYING NEEDED COMPETENCIES

Sometimes the characteristics that are required for success in performing a particular job are not easy to identify. The job description, or even a very detailed list of tasks performed, may not reveal the skills needed to carry out the job effectively. David McClelland and his colleagues have discovered this many times in applying "competency analysis" to the study of key jobs (Goleman, 1981). They studied in great detail through observations and interviews the differences between the way average performers and superior performers actually carried out a particular job. The essential "competencies" revealed in this type of analysis are often subtle and very different from the personal characteristics typically sought in candidates for the respective jobs.

Often in filling a particular opening, it is wise to take into account situational factors that are very important as the position stands today. In selecting a plant manager, for example, it may be important to appoint someone who can not only manage the plant effectively but also remedy deteriorated community relations. In replacing a very effective retiring manager, it may be important to consider the type of leadership style his or her people have been experiencing. To make a radical change in this aspect of the position could have a deleterious effect on productive morale. When any replacement is contemplated, it is also wise to consider whether the job should be restructured. Would the organization as a whole be more effective if certain responsibilities that have traditionally characterized this position were deleted or others added?

THE PROMOTION PROCESS

The procedure used in making promotion decisions should not be a static process of filling key jobs in the organization one by one as vacancies occur. It should be part of an ongoing, long-range human resources planning activity. Mahoney and Weitzel (1969) in an analysis of data from many studies of organizational effectiveness identified five factors related to organizational success. One of the most important of these five factors was the development and utilization of human resources effectively. An essential component of this factor was the analysis of individual employee potential and promotion planning.

Formal procedures for identifying potential are most likely to be found in large, highly structured organizations, such as large multinational companies and the federal government. Such organizations will almost always have staff groups whose primary responsibility is human resources planning. However, it is important even in small organizations that someone assume primary responsibility for succession planning. This person might be the owner of the business, the president, the plant manager, or the personnel director of a company large enough to have such a position. All too often a successful organization flounders or even fails after a very able chief executive officer dies or retires because no one had been groomed systematically and effectively to take over that role. This can happen, of course, in positions at any level.

Every promotion made should be from a long-range, organization-wide perspective. The candidate who would be best qualified to carry out the position now may not always be the best choice when the final selection is made. The position may offer an excellent development opportunity for someone with top management potential who could carry out the job satisfactorily.

Another important consideration is where the position can lead for the selected candidate. Would it probably be a dead end in the career progress of the individual? This possibility may be acceptable in some cases, both from the individual's and the organization's standpoint. In other cases, it may not be in the best interest of either the individual or the organization. What valuable experience will it provide for the person with considerable potential? How long will it take to gain that experience? Are there ways in which the high-potential person could gain comparable experience more efficiently?

IMPORTANT TO MONITOR THE PROCESS

Because of long-range, organization-wide considerations, all promotions should be monitored by some person or persons with an organization-wide perspective. This might be the chief executive officer, the personnel director, the manager of human resources planning and development, or one or more management committees. Some companies use committees of managers to monitor all promotion decisions. For promotions to first- or second-level supervision, the committee might be composed of higher-level managers within the respective department. For promotions to positions at a middle-management level, managers at positions at least two levels above the target positions, who also represent different departments, might serve on such a committee. For selections at executive levels, the chief executive officer and his or her reporting staff might serve as the selection committee.

In a large company, the manager of human resources planning and development, or someone on his or her staff, would usually serve as an adviser to each such committee. That person might also provide detailed information gathered in advance for the committee about the open position and the respective candidates for the opening. This person would also draw on materials filed on employees, such as from a human resources inventory or information relating to a career planning program.

EQUAL EMPLOYMENT OPPORTUNITY

Another very compelling reason for ensuring that the promotion process is monitored on an organization-wide basis is the need to comply with civil rights laws. In many organizations, it is incumbent on management to compensate for past discrimination by promoting disproportionate numbers from the protected groups under the laws, such as minorities and females. Individual managers, acting alone, are not likely to demonstrate sensitivity to company-wide equal opportunity goals for promoting such persons. The company-wide monitoring agent, whether the chief executive officer, the manager of human resources planning, the equal employment opportunity coordinator, or selection committees, must often bring to the attention of each promoting manager the need to consider the organization's equal opportunity objectives as each promotion decision is made. The civil rights laws also make it essential that management is able to defend each promotion decision made with objective criteria. As the landmark case of Rowe v. General Motors demonstrated, supervisor judgments alone are not likely to be accepted as sufficient evidence on which to base promotion decisions (Lubben, Thompson & Klasson, 1980).

TAP ORGANIZATION-WIDE SOURCES OF CANDIDATES

Any systematic procedure for determining promotions should provide for organization-wide opportunity for employees and organization-wide surveillance in identifying candidates for specific job openings. Often very capable people with considerable potential to advance may have very limited opportunities to advance within their own departments. Moreover, utilizing organization-wide sources can often tap talent for a specific opening that is superior to the talent available within the department where the opening occurs. Providing organization-wide opportunity also helps to protect against hoarding of talent by managers who have become accustomed to depending upon certain very capable people on their staffs to make their own jobs easier.

It is highly desirable that the system for determining promotions provide for two-way participation.

Employees should have the opportunity to express their own desires or preferences with regard to career progress. Many organizations provide for employee participation through a formal career planning program. The career planning program can also provide information to employees about the nature of jobs in the different parts of the organization and the qualifications needed to fill such jobs.

The promotion decision process should also be explained very clearly to employees. The desire to advance is strong in most employees. A study of factors contributing to turnover and to productive morale of professional employees in a very large company revealed that perceived future opportunity was more important to overall satisfaction with one's lot in the organization than satisfaction with the immediate job itself (Meyer & Scalia 1970).

JOB POSTING

Many companies use an open system for determining promotions. Under such a system, all job openings are posted, and any employee with the specified minimum qualifications can bid on the job. The qualifications of each bidder are considered carefully, and feedback is provided to each. This process, of course, puts a tremendous burden on management, since it is not uncommon to find that very large numbers of employee may bid for a particular opening. The open system is designed to ensure that no potential talent is overlooked and to boost morale by providing unlimited opportunity for all employees. Whether it actually does have a positive effect on morale has not been determined definitively. With unrestricted bidding, the rejection rate among interested candidates is likely to be very high. Repeated rejection would be expected to have a negative effect on motivation.

Some evidence for the expected negative effect on motivation was found in a large company that practiced job posting (Canger, 1987). The company has consistently found in biannual attitude surveys that attitudes expressed toward the promotion system are more negative than attitudes dealing with any other aspect of organizational life covered in the surveys. In their 1986 survey, for example, only 23 percent of the respondents answered in a favorable direction to a question that read, "All employees who bid for jobs are evaluated fairly by managers with the vacancies."

Levine (1984) surveyed a large sample of companies regarding their employee promotion practices and found that many (71 percent) reported using job posting for at least some types of jobs. Only about one-third of these companies said that job posting seemed to result in "improved morale." However, in most cases these same companies admitted that they had not actually measured the results of their programs in any systematic way. Several said that the fact that many unqualified applicants bid on jobs caused problems, and some reported that employees reacted negatively to the job posting program because they felt that their bidding was futile—that the heir apparent will get the job regardless of who bids for it.

USE MULTIPLE APPRAISAL SOURCES

Promotability in an employee should not be determined by that employee's supervisor acting alone. This is especially true for professional employees, an increasingly larger share of the working population each year. Each employee should have other ties to the organization—others who are cognizant of his or her performance and potential. An increasingly popular practice in large organizations in both the public and private sectors is to conduct annual human resources reviews to appraise the performance and potential of each employee in the organization—at least all of those at professional and administrative levels. In such a review, the peer-level managers or professionals meet as a team with their manager to discuss the performance and potential of all employees at the next level down in their units.

Using a team of people to evaluate individual potential helps to provide a broader frame of reference than is the case where each employee's potential is appraised only by his or her own supervisor. Even though some of the participants in this appraisal process may have had little or no exposure to some of the employees being appraised, they can contribute to the validity of the appraisal process by insisting that judgments being expressed are backed by objective or behavioral evidence. The effects of individual biases and other rating errors thus tend to be minimized.

Some organizations have used peer ratings in appraising the potential of individual employees. The military services, for example, have found that peer appraisals of the future effectiveness and promotional potential of officers had more predictive validity than did ratings made by superiors (Bass & Barrett, 1981). The RCA Corporation also found that multiple assessments, which included appraisals by peers and others in the organization at any level with whom the individual had contacts in his or her work, provided more reliable predictors of performance over time than did appraisals made only by the individuals' supervisors. They found that appraisers at different levels in the organization often had significantly different views of the individual's performance and potential than did the employee's immediate supervisor (Lazer & Wikstrom, 1977).

Where the annual human resources review approach is not used, supervisors should at least review with their own managers the performance, progress, and potential of each of their direct reports. In addition, the manager of human resources planning and development will often maintain an inventory of the talents and career plans of each employee. This inventory can be referenced when promotion decisions are impending. Without such safeguards there is considerable danger that essential talent will be hidden or lost to the organization. Supervisors are not all seeing and all knowing. They are likely to be influenced in making their appraisals by their personal biases, their own working styles, or how they think the work should be done.

SUMMARY AND CONCLUSIONS

Determining promotability is an extremely important activity in an organization of any size. It is essential that it be conducted with great care. As many sources of data as possible should be tapped in making such determinations. In addition to supervisor judgments, many other sources of evidence can be utilized, such as selection tests, assessment centers, interviews with candidates, field review interviews with supervisors and others with whom the respective candidate works inside or outside the organization, peer appraisals, and possibly even subordinate appraisals. Some of these kinds of informational sources will be described in the subsequent chapters in this part of the *Handbook*.

REFERENCES

Bass, B.M., & Barrett, G.V. (1981). *People, work and organizations*. Boston: Allyn & Bacon.

Business Week, 1980. Wanted: A manager to fill each strategy. February 25.

Canger, J. (1987). Personal correspondence.

Goleman, D. (1981). The new competency tests: Matching the right people to the right jobs. *Psychology Today,* January, 1981, 35–46.

Lazer, R.I., & Wikstrom, W.S. (1977). *Appraising managerial performance: Current practices and future directions* (Report No. 723) New York: The Conference Board.

Levine, H.Z. (1984). Job posting practices. *Personnel, 61*(6), 48–52.

Lubben, G., Thompson, D., & Klasson, C. (1980). Performance appraisal: The legal implications of Title VII. *Personnel, 57*(3), 11–21.

Mahoney, T.A., & Weitzel, W. (1969). Managerial models of organizational effectiveness. *Administrative Science Quarterly, 14,* 357–365.

Meyer, H.H., & Scalia, F.A. (1970). *Determining causes of turnover among exempt personnel.* A study report of the Personnel Research Unit of Corporate Employee Relations' General Electric Company, Charlottesville, Virginia.

Stogdill, R.M. (1974). *Handbook of leadership.* New York: Free Press.

30 ASSESSMENT FROM NONTRADITIONAL POINTS OF VIEW

Richard Klimoski

It is clear that performance appraisal is a prominent and important feature of organizational life. It is relevant to recruiting, selection, training, and most aspects of performance management. Indeed, some have argued that it represents the central feature of an integrated human resource management system (Latham & Wexley, 1981). Because it is so important,

it is perhaps no coincidence that there exists a great deal of research and practical experience dealing with this topic. This in turn, has generated a wide variety of options to guide the design and implementation of appraisal programs. This chapter addresses one area of choice often overlooked: who should provide appraisal information.

TYPICAL SOURCE OF APPRAISAL INFORMATION

"The ideal rater who observes and evaluates what is important and reports his judgment without bias or appreciable error does not exist, or if he does, we don't know how to separate him from his less effective colleagues" (Barrett, 1966, p. 7). While this may be true, we usually rely on an employee's immediate supervisor to provide assessments of performance and potential. Thus, it is probably safe to say that the bulk of the writing on appraisals in organizations deals with the supervisor and the factors affecting (for better or for worse) the quality of his or her judgments (see Bernardin & Beatty, 1984; Carroll & Schneier, 1982).

The choice of the supervisor is neither arbitrary nor unreasonable. In terms of organizational structure, the supervisor is administratively in a position to understand the nature of the work to be done by subordinates and how this work fits into the larger scheme of corporate goals and work flow. In terms of legitimate authority, it is the supervisor who is expected to manage the performance of others. It is part of his or her job description. In fact, the super-

visor is usually given a variety of rewards and sanctions with which to do this. Moreover, the supervisor is the one most likely to be able to observe a subordinate's work-relevant behavior on a regular basis so that an appraisal can be an informed one. Finally, for a variety of reasons, the supervisor is often felt to have personal qualities that would seem to serve well in conducting appraisals. For example, he or she is likely to have skill and experience in the subordinate's jobs and have had experience in other personnel decisions.

The point of this chapter is to highlight the possibility of using alternative, less traditional agents for appraisal purposes, specifically, the job incumbent and coworkers or peers of the incumbent. But in doing this, it will not attempt to refute or reject the immediate supervisor as possessing an important and valid perspective on performance. In fact, to anticipate a theme stressed later, it seems clear that for many purposes, the desirable and prudent thing to do when conducting appraisals is to assess effectiveness from multiple points of view.

LOGIC OF QUALITY APPRAISALS

Wexley and Klimoski (1984) stress that when it comes to the selection of who is to be conducting performance appraisals, four factors should be considered.

In order to ensure quality, the person must (1) be in a position to observe the performance and the behavior of the employee, (2) be knowledgeable about what constitutes effective performance, (3) have an understanding of the instrument or the scales to be used, and (4) be motivated to be accurate. Some of these have been touched upon already. But because they are important to the issue of when and where to use alternative agents of appraisal, they deserve some elaboration. This will be done with reference to the perspective of the supervisor, the job incumbent and the incumbent's coworkers.

Observing Behavior and Performance

It has already been asserted that the supervisor is in an excellent position to observe the work being performed. This is indeed the general case. But there are numerous instances where this might not hold. Supervisors who are physically removed from the subordinate's workstation would have to make special efforts to monitor behavior. Those with a large span of control may have difficulty keeping up with what each direct report is doing. The work load directly assigned to the supervisor may be such that regular contact and observation become problematic. There is only so much time available. And often the degree of work interdependence among subordinates serves to frustrate accurate observation. Even with opportunity, it may be difficult to discern just who is responsible for work products or outcomes.

On the face of it, one would think that the incumbent might be in the best position to "observe" behavior and performance. After all, he or she is usually present when it occurs. Moreover, the incumbent knows not only what occurred but what was intended and why. That is, he or she has access to the behavior options that were considered but not chosen, the factors involved in the decision, and the amount of effort expended on the choices actually made. Once again, in most cases this is a reasonable assumption.

Yet recent research in psychology has identified numerous tendencies on the part of individuals that call into question their capacity to observe and interpret their own behavior or effectiveness. While some of these will be related to motivational forces that will be addressed shortly, others appear to stem from dynamics of perspective and information processing.

It has been discovered, for example, that when describing and interpreting behavior (the essence of most appraisals) it makes a difference whether you are the one performing or the one observing what is going on. As the "actor" there appears to be a predisposition for the employee to consider and interpret his or her behavior in terms of forces in the situation that could constrain our effectiveness. A person would notice and take into account such things as the degree of helpfulness of peers and supervisor, the availability of needed information or resources, or task difficulty. These factors would be entered into self-assessments. This seems to be especially true if performance is not what it should be or what is expected. To put it another way, there is a tendency for other job incumbents' observations to be selective and self-serving, even though he or she might be quite unaware that this is what is going on (Weary, 1979). Thus, while it is true that the incumbent would be in a good position to observe, it is wrong to assert that this is a point of view without difficulties in this regard (DeVader, Bateson & Lord, 1986).

There seems to be no doubt however, that coworkers would be high on this aspect of quality appraisals. Indeed, the opportunity to observe the employee on a daily basis has been offered as a major advantage of the coworker's point of view (DeNisi & Mitchell, 1978; Kane & Lawler, 1978). In most work settings, there is extensive interaction among coworkers. Moreover, they often perform parallel duties and share common space or equipment. In short they spend a lot of time together. Thus if the goal is to base performance assessments on a large and representative sample of instances, in most settings the use of coworkers would seem appropriate.

Knowledge of the Nature of Effectiveness

For most jobs, effectiveness is likely to be complex and multifaceted. It is likely to involve aspects of personal qualities, behavior, and behavior outcomes. In measuring and indexing effectiveness, we must sort through all of the information we have about an incumbent and make use of only that which is relevant (Blum & Naylor, 1968). We want assessments that are neither deficient nor contaminated. This takes experience with the job, a capacity for analytic thinking, and skill in applying all of this.

As one might guess, it would be hard to assert unequivocally that any one of the three points of view under discussion will meet these standards. However, in most contexts, we would hope that the supervisor, by virtue of selection, training, and/or experience, would be strong in this capacity to understand what constitutes an effective job.

There is some evidence that training can indeed increase the capacity of the rater to identify and focus on the appropriate dimensions of effectiveness (Hedge & Kavanaugh, 1988; Smith, 1986). However, other research has also made it clear that supervisors, incumbents and peers do approach and interpret effectiveness in rather different ways. For example, Klimoski and London (1984) found that ratings produced by these three groups reflected different factor structures. This was interpreted to mean that judgments were based on different aspects of job-related behavior (different capacities), all of which, incidentally, might still be valid.

Understanding the Specific Scales to Be Used

It seems almost self-evident that high-quality performance appraisals can be obtained only if those responsible for them are skilled in the use of the scales involved. However, it is worth stressing this because it is problematic in many organizations. It is all too often the case that individuals who are asked to conduct appraisals do so without a lot of training. In any event, when considering the use of the incumbent or peers, it should be a major consideration. These alternative agents must be systematically exposed to scale format and features prior to their participation.

The particular type of instrument involved would certainly make a difference as to how extensive any training would have to be. For instance, behavior checklists, employee pair comparisons, and ranking are more straightforward to use than management by objectives (MBO) systems. However, in most cases, there is no getting around the need for training designed to create a clear understanding of how to interpret particular scale points and what standards to be used.

Differing standards might be especially problematic if alternative appraisal agents are to be used. It would be quite confusing if, when evaluating employee effectiveness, one party were to use job relevant (more absolute) standards, while another were to consider performance relative to other employees (i.e., comparative standards). In this regard, Farh and Dobbins (1989) found that the quality of self-assessments could be improved by sharing with employees the same comparative information available to supervisors.

Motivation to Be Accurate

Of the four factors thought to contribute to quality appraisals, this may well be the most important. In any case, it is extremely relevant to consider when discussing the potential of assessing effectiveness from nontraditional points of view.

The activities of forming impressions and documenting these for purposes of appraisals are known to be affected by the motivational forces operating in that situation. But the exact nature of these forces and their net impact on appraisal quality is hard to predict. Predicted consequences really must be considered on a case-by-case basis. However, we know enough that a few generalizations can be made. First, in the context of human interaction, most people will be motivated to form some kind of an evaluative impression about themselves and others. When it comes to our life's work or our work effectiveness, this tendency is accelerated. Just how good are we? How do we compare to others? What is our potential? These are issues we want to resolve as they relate to our self-definition and self-efficacy (Bandura, 1978). And research has indicated that generally, we tend to settle on (are motivated toward) a more rather than a less favorable self-image (Mabe & West, 1982).

As individuals, we seem to be similarly motivated to observe and evaluate others. There are strong personal incentives for evaluating coworkers in the light of task-relevant competencies and abilities. For the most part, we depend upon and must pork with others. Getting a "fix" on what they are like, what they can or can not (will or will not) do is important. Moreover, given the hierarchical nature of work systems (and the usual limits to available promotions), we become in some ways competitors with our coworkers. This too motivates regular and continuous evaluations (Mumford, 1983).

When it comes to the motivation of the supervisor, there are similar forces influencing impression formation. Work flow interdependencies clearly exist. The supervisor often depends on the employee for his or her own success in the work place. Thus, exchange dynamics occur that foster the need for accurate impressions as the relationship is based on give and take (Graen, 1976). Moreover, as a supervisor, one is held responsible for accomplishing objectives. This too implies monitoring and managing the performance of subordinates. All this suggests that supervisors should be motivated to form an assessment of those who report directly to them.

These arguments notwithstanding, for the supervisor, job incumbent, or the coworkers, it appears that a major cause of appraisals of poor quality is the lack of willingness to report these assessments. That is one might truly believe one thing with regard to an individual's effectiveness but report something else. This point has been repeatedly made with regard to supervisors (Barrett, 1966; Larson, 1984; Wherry & Bartlett, 1982). Especially in the case of poor or marginal performers, supervisors are reluctant to be candid or forthright (Blumberg, 1972; Fisher, 1979; Tesser & Rosen, 1975). The fact is, while none of us like to receive negative evaluations or criticism, few of us like to give it to others. Besides, in many cases, a negative evaluation is not really likely to have a favorable impact. Instead, it may actually produce negative consequences for working relationships and work group morale. For these and numerous other reasons, the motivation to be accurate is weak. Lenient or inflated assessments become recorded.

The story is similar when it comes to self and peer appraisals. There are a large number of forces operating to motivate distortion, usually in the direction of more favorable or more positive evaluations than are warranted (Mabe & West, 1982; Kane & Lawler, 1978). This is especially the case when friendship dynamics exist in peer groups (Kingstrom & Mainstrone, 1985).

To summarize, theory of appraisal behavior postulates four factors that are thought to affect the quality of recorded assessments. These are relevant to describing and understanding the potential value of self, peers, and supervisors as agents of appraisal.

EVIDENCE ON THE USE OF SELF AND PEER ASSESSMENT

Comparative Studies

A number of studies have examined self- and peer assessments, usually in contrast to supervisor judgments. In most cases they have focused on their relative psychometric properties. The findings of these studies will be reviewed briefly.

Leniency. This term refers to distortion in assessments in a favorable direction. In comparative studies, it is inferred to exist when evaluations from different sources on the same ratee group are significantly different (Holzbach, 1978). The research evidence would lead us to conclude that self-ratings are indeed more lenient than either supervisor or peer ratings (Klimoski & London, 1974; Holzbach, 1978; Mount, 1984; Thornton, 1968). Harris and Schanbroeck (1988), in a review of studies in this area, found that, on average, self-ratings were over half a standard deviation higher than supervisory ratings and about one-quarter of a standard deviation higher than peer ratings. Although there have been some exceptions (Heneman, 1974). For example, McEvoy and Butler (1987) reported restriction in range of scores and leniency for both self- and peer assessments: only half of the six-point scale was used. And in field settings at least, this is true for females as well as males (Shore & Thornton, 1986). While the evidence is not as extensive, it appears that supervisor and peer ratings do not differ appreciably (Harris & Schanbroeck 1988; Holzbach, 1978; Klimoski & London, 1974), although here, too, exceptions can be found (Schneier, 1977).

Halo. Halo is inferred when assessments are not differentiated among distinct items or dimensions. Instead, evaluations tend to be global or reflect some overall judgment. In comparative studies, halo is typically indexed by the magnitude of the intercor-relations among items from ratings obtained from different sources. Supervisor ratings usually reveal greater halo than self-ratings (Heneman, 1974; Holzbach, 1978; Klimoski & London, 1974). Peer ratings tend to show halo comparable to that of supervisors (Dickenson & Tice, 1973; Holzbach, 1978), once again with exceptions (Klimoski & London, 1984). Holzbach (1978) did find that he could statistically adjust supervisor ratings to a greater extent than peer and self-ratings by using an overall assessment rating gathered at the same time. From this he infers that the bases of halo for these three points of view might be different.

Dimensionality. A few studies have empirically examined the dimensionality or complexity of assessments. Despite efforts to develop instruments to measure multiple aspects of effectiveness and models of performance calling for complexity, the results have been consistent and disappointing. In most cases, researchers have failed to find independent dimensions in ratings built around homogeneous items, regardless of whether the data come from supervisors, peers, or the incumbent. Instead, rating sources seem to determine the type of dimensions obtained. That is, the judgments of different sources appear to reflect differing points of view and to show up as different factors. Further, the complexity and specific nature of these factors will depend upon just which agent of appraisal is supplying the data (Dickenson & Tice, 1973; Holzbach, 1978; Klimoski & London, 1974).

Convergence. Given the results reported above, it is not surprising that there is limited evidence of agreement on scores on specific dimensions across the three points of view for a particular sample (e.g., Holzbach, 1978). This is not to say however, that one can not find convergence in terms of global assessments.

Klimoski and London (1974), Lawler (1967), and Holzbach (1978) found supervisor and peer ratings significantly and positively correlated with one another. In some studies, self-ratings frequently show little agreement with other sources (Thornton, 1968).

A recent metaanalysis by Harris and Schanbroeck (1988) was somewhat more reassuring on convergence, however. After correcting for measurement error and range restriction (something that other studies did not do), they found moderate agreement between self-peer ($r = .36$) and self-supervisor ($r = .35$) ratings. But there was a much higher agreement between peers and supervisors ($r = .62$). They argue that despite this, all three positive and significant correlations do imply that the various points of view have at least some things in common.

In this review the authors also found that job type made a difference. There was greater convergence across points of view for ratings of blue-collar and service employees while little or none for managerial and professional workers. The authors speculate that point-of-view bias (hence lack of convergence) is more likely to occur in ambiguous contexts where job duties and responsibilities are less clear and where different styles and approaches to performance are possible. It is also interesting to note that rating scale or format (e.g., rankings verses ratings) did not have significant effects on convergence. Finally, the authors stressed the importance of the opportunity to observe job performance as an explanation for lack of convergence between the three points of view.

Accuracy or Validity. These terms are being used somewhat interchangeably here, although a case can be made that they are not exactly the same. The essence of accuracy is the extent to which subjective assessments (e.g., ratings) do in fact reflect what has occurred with regard to behavior or performance. In studies involving simulations, this may be established when the researcher compares subject ratings to scripted or contrived (acted-out) performance. In field settings, subjective ratings might be related to more objective indicators (e.g., test performance or production data) for similar insights. In contrast, validity is reflected in the ability of assessments to predict some future event. This may be future performance. But validity may be demonstrated in a rater's capacity to anticipate any aspect of individual achievement (e.g., promotions) as well (Smither, Barry & Reilly, 1989; Sulsky & Balzer, 1988).

It seems curious (to me at least) that no comparative studies could be found involving two or more of the agents of appraisal under discussion where the focus was on accuracy or validity. This is not to say that these factors have not been examined; it has just not been done in a comparative analysis. More will be said about this in the next sections.

In summary, this brief review of comparative studies is only moderately encouraging. The best we might say at this point is that peer and self-assessments are no worse than those supplied by supervisors. They may be just different. However, it is important to note that in none of the studies referred to were conditions created or described to be appropriate for obtaining evaluations of maximum quality. Data were gathered without regard to ensuring an equal and optimum opportunity to observe, the amount of training in the use of scales provided, or creating motivation to be accurate. As will be seen, these factors do make a difference, especially when self and peer assessments are involved.

Studies of Peer Assessment

There exists a fairly large amount of research involving peer assessments. Fortunately, there are also some fairly good reviews on the topic available (Kane & Lawler, 1978; Mumford, 1983). Rather than replicate these efforts, this section will focus on what the literature implies for using peer assessments in applied settings.

What is a peer? When asking this question for purposes of peer assessments, members of work groups or teams come to mind. Alternatively, coworkers might be envisioned. In fact, much of the work published in this area has involved individuals in training classes (e.g., Amir, Kovarsky & Sharon, 1970). But it is important to realize that for purposes of appraisal, the term *peer* implies (or should imply) certain critical features with regard to the individuals providing assessments. Foremost is the notion of opportunity to observe and interact with those to be evaluated. Current thinking is that the actual period of time need not be long (only a few days), but behavior observed must be characteristic of the person being evaluated and relevant to the goals of the appraisal.

A peer should be one who has a fair amount of knowledge regarding the work to be done or the Masks to be performed. He or she can empathize with the demands placed on the person to be evaluated. More to the point, a peer has to have some clear idea of what constitutes effectiveness in a current or in likely future assignments.

In most work settings, being a peer connotes some kind of interdependence. This can be task interdependence, where the nature of the work flow brings people together, or it might take the form of outcome interdependence where policy or practice dictates that rewards or punishments are to be administered in a shared manner. In either case, how one functions on the job has direct implications for the individual who will be providing assessments.

Thus, peers in the context of appraisal, are members of what Katz and Kahn (1978) call a person's "role set." While they may not be in the same work group, because of organizational realities, they are closely tied to the person to be evaluated. And although they may differ in status in the work organization, they are officially at the same level of authority as the person to be assessed.

The Format for Peer Assessments. The terms *peer appraisals* and *peer assessments* have been used often and somewhat interchangeably up to this point. However, it is important to note that the process of obtaining evaluations from peers can vary considerably. Specifically, Kane and Lawler (1978) distinguish three common methods: Peer nominations, peer ratings, and peer rankings.

In the peer nomination technique, each person providing data is asked to designate a specified number of group members as being the highest or the best on a particular aspect of effectiveness. This also might be done with regard to those who would be considered lowest in the same domain. Sometimes those nominated as the best (or the worst) are also to be placed in rank order. An individual's score thus becomes the frequency with which he or she gets nominated to either category (best or worst) and/or the average rank earned in either category. It should be noted that the nomination technique is designed to identify people at the extremes of the effectiveness continuum. Consequently, some individuals may never be given a "score" using this technique. Usually, the group members are required to exclude themselves from those being nominated.

In contrast, peer rating consists of having each person in the work or training group assess one another using any of a number of types of scales (behaviorally anchored scales, adjective checklists, etc.). A hallmark of peer ratings is that any number of dimensions of effectiveness may be used. Another is that one typically gets data on all group members, including the respondent. A person's score is the average rating received by dimension or across dimensions. As with ratings of any other type, it is quite possible for several individuals to receive the same or similar score.

Finally, peer ranking involves having each respondent place his or her colleagues on a list in order of their effectiveness. While it is feasible to have this done on any number of dimensions, it is common to obtain rankings for overall effectiveness. With several peers providing this information, a person's score becomes the average rank obtained. Kane and Lawler (1978) argue that peer ranking is likely to provide data that are most discriminating among individuals in terms of effectiveness inasmuch as the ranking task forces systematic consideration of all workers and requires that no two individuals occupy the same position on the effectiveness continuum.

According to Kane and Lawler (1978) the research data on all three methods are quite "encouraging with respect to the reliability, validity, and freedom from biases" (p. 583). However they do point out that the different methods appear to be more or less appropriate depending on your purpose. specifically:

1. Peer nominations are best when the goal is limited to identifying individuals at the extremes of effectiveness, such as required for making promotion or assignment decisions or when considering a reduction in force.

2. Peer ratings may be applied to any number of contexts. But for reasons that will be made clear shortly, they might be best suited for purposes of performance feedback in the service of employee development.

3. Peer rankings should be used when it is important to achieve discrimination throughout the effectiveness continuum. For example, Siegel (1982) reports the successful use of peer-produced pair comparison judgments in the context of classification and promotion decisions in a bank.

The Issue of Peer Motivation. A major concern with regard to the potential use of peer assessments relates to the nature of the motivational forces affecting those involved. Early research couched this issue in terms of the possibility of a friendship bias operating. That is, given an opportunity to provide peer judgments, friendship bias would imply that coworkers would be motivated to distort their ratings, rankings, and so forth in order to reward their friends (and presumably punish their enemies). But current research indicates that this should not be viewed as a major problem. While indexes of friendship and favorable peer evaluations may covary, Kane and Lawler (1978) suggest this may be a case of "performance causing friendship rather than the independent influence of friendship on judgments or performance" (p. 583). Indeed, one study has found little or no biasing effects of race on peer assessments in an industrial training context (Schmidt & Johnson, 1973).

However, the purpose for which peer assessments are to be used *will* have a major impact on the motivation to be accurate and hence the quality of the information obtained. In general, the limited evidence on this important parameter is that employees dislike and resist the use of peer assessments for administrative purposes. For example, Medland, Yates, and Downey (1974) found that the majority of their military sample rejected the regular use of peer assessments for promotion purposes. Similarly, Cederbloom and Lounsbury (1980) found a great deal of resistance among the faculty of a university who regularly received signed evaluation forms from their colleagues in a program that had been in operation for over six years. DeNisi and Mitchell (1978) point out that the problems with peer ratings seem to be magnified as the stakes increase.

The basis for this resistance to the administrative use of peer assessments is not clear. In some cases, it may be a function of the perceived illegitimacy of using this source for information. The question might be raised by employees as to what right peers have to be making these important decisions. Aren't they more appropriately the job of the supervisor? Alternatively, Cederbloom and Lounsbury (1980) report in their study that it was the "perceived friendship bias" and "perceived value for feedback" that were the major correlates of the acceptance of peer assessments.

Still others have noted in the literature that the use of peer assessments is divisive and promotes distrust. Peer assessments are thought to be based on what might be considered privileged information. To use them for administrative purposes would disrupt working relations. Finally, Kane and Lawler (1978) imply that not being asked to participate in the design of a peer assessment program will also create resistance.

And yet there are some examples of the acceptance of peer assessments in an administrative context. Siegel (1982) reports an instance of the successful application of peer judgments to promotion decisions in a bank. While no reactions data were explicitly obtained, participation rates in the program were high, and the quality of the data appeared excellent. However, a close reading of this study suggests that senior managers asked to provide data viewed this not as a chore but as an opportunity to have input in key staffing decisions where in the past they had none. Thus, despite the potential for embarrassment (e.g., being evaluated negatively), it was viewed as a favorable experience. And, indeed, the top management group did take peer assessments into con-

sideration and modified their promotion decisions accordingly.

Similarly, in a more recent study, McEvoy and Buller (1987) found that for over 200 industrial employees who had used a peer evaluation system for over a year, there was a fair amount of user acceptance. But even here there was significantly more support for peer appraisals when they were used for developmental rather than administrative purposes. As a side note, those who were with the company only a short time and those who perceived few elements of friendship affecting the peer assessments also reported more favorable attitudes.

McEvoy and Buller (1987) feel that the particular rating process used in the organization that they studied may account for the relatively positive feelings toward peer appraisals obtained. For example, in contrast to Cederbloom and Lounsbury (1980), who used individual signed forms, the rating system in the more recent study made use of anonymous, averaged peer ratings given to employees. In fact, most employees felt that the confidentially of the peer ratings was very important. And, in this regard, the company was doing a good job at maintaining this confidentially.

All of this implies that the conditions surrounding and obtaining the use of peer assessments are extremely important, especially as they affect motivation to evaluate accurately. In most cases where assessments are to be generated for feedback and development purposes, one can usually presume a willingness to be candid and accurate. Thus, the motivational forces operating are to likely actually promote valid assessments. However, when the purpose is administrative, resistance should be anticipated. Under these conditions, the only way to ensure quality is to appeal to or make use of other, potentially stronger forces (e.g., the desire for procedural justice or to have input over important decisions) to ensure good information.

Based on the available research, we can assert with some confidence that peer assessments *can* provide unique and valid insights with regard to employee effectiveness. A peer's perspective is an important one. However, one needs to create the right conditions in order to realize the potential of peer appraisals.

The Ubiquity of Peer Assessments. There is a natural and spontaneous tendency for people to be evaluative. This is especially true in work settings where interdependencies and competition exist simultaneously. This implies that regardless of the existence of any formal program of peer appraisals, such judgments will abound. Thus, arguments can be made that it would be wise for decision makers to have access to such "intelligence."

The recognition and use of widely shared opinions regarding effectiveness would seem to have their greatest impact on employee reactions to decisions that have a large "fairness" component. Decisions regarding promotions, reprimands, or termination create what could be called "metamessages" with regard to the values and priorities of the organization (Peters, 1978). These types of decisions will almost always be second guessed by employees. Was the promotion justified? Was the person to be terminated really that poor a worker? The point is that inconsistencies between perceptions of what coworkers feel is fair and decisions actually made will cause, at best, feelings of ambiguity. At worst, these can produce resentment and disillusionment. If the goal is to create a climate where procedural justice prevails (Folger & Greenberg, 1985), an awareness of and use of peer assessment information would seem especially useful.

Self-Appraisals

The logic for self-appraisals as outlined earlier emphasized the potential for using this point of view. The research in this area clearly points out that important limitations or boundary conditions exist and must be considered by anyone contemplating their operational use. However, with some effort it appears that self-appraisals can indeed contribute effective human resource management.

Types of Self-Appraisals. The nature and dynamics of self-appraisals are such that it will make a difference what kind of an assessment is being called for. Specifically, it appears that distinguishing among assessments of abilities (or skills), performance, and potential is worthwhile.

The bulk of the research on self-appraisals has focused on abilities. Such assessments might be sought in the context of selection or placement, where a match on abilities would be important. Alternatively, they are also warranted in the diagnosis of performance. It would be reasonable for the supervisor to attempt to index or infer lack of ability as a proximal cause when performance is poor or below standards.

To illustrate some findings, DeNisi & Shaw (1977) had subjects rate themselves on ten ability areas. They were then given a battery of tests designed to assess these same areas. Correlations between self-rated and tested abilities, although statistically signif-

icant, were too low to have practical value (median $r = .29$). Using a similar paradigm, Ash (1980) found that self-assessments of straight copy typing ability were the best predictor of tested typing ability ($r = .40$). Minority group members were significantly less accurate in the estimates that they provided. While self-assessments from all subjects were somewhat inflated.

In a major review of the literature on the self-evaluation of abilities, Mabe and West (1982) were able to locate fifty-five studies in which self-evaluations of ability were compared to measured ability. Their analysis revealed a mean validity of $r = .29$ but a high degree of variability (s.d. = .25). They observed that over twenty categories of ability (or performance potential) were examined against a variety of criterion measures. In the twenty-one studies that presented data relevant to the tendency for self-enhancement, fifteen reported data supporting the notion that people tend to overestimate their ability. However, the contrary evidence from other studies caused the authors to believe that certain conditions can be created to minimize this tendency.

In contrast, self-appraisals of performance are usually studied in relationship to ratings provided by an immediate supervisor. In his review, Thornton (1980) concluded that the most that can be said is that research findings on this relationship have been inconsistent. Even in cases where there is a significant correlation between supervisor and self-appraisals of performance, the amount of common variance is typically small, For example Heneman (1974) found the correlation to be positive and significant at .26. And, as noted, Harris and Schaubroeck (1988) found a corrected average correlation of .35. This too was statistically significant.

Once again in the area of performance assessments the problem seems to be one of inflation of self-ratings and resultant lack of variability. For example, Meyer (1975) reported that across four samples, 70 percent to 80 percent of employees rated themselves in the top 25 percent. This serves to reduce the possibility of obtaining a large correlation with any other variable.

There is surprisingly little research on the self-assessment of potential. This would involve obtaining self-estimates of level of functioning in some future and somewhat different setting and following up on actual achievement or success. Even in the area of assessment centers, which are ostensibly designed to get at potential, the self-assessments that are obtained pertain more to current performance on assessment exercises than likely functioning in higher levels of the organization (Finkle, 1976).

Possible Explanations for Distortion. A number of writers have speculated about the reasons for lack of consistency between self-assessments and other criteria, whether they are test scores, supervisor ratings, or productivity data. One interpretation is that self-ratings reflect a self-serving bias: individuals are predisposed to want to look good. Thus, when given an opportunity, individuals will distort their ratings in an upward direction. Another explanation is that self-assessments are based on different factors from those provided by others. Klimoski and London (1974) report that the dimensionality of self-ratings was distinctly different from those of supervisors or peers. Steel and Ovalle (1984) suggest that self-raters place greater emphasis on personal skill and technical competence, while supervisors might emphasize output or results.

Still a third perspective is that individuals who provide self-assessments are using different standards. That is, even if there is some motivation to be candid and particular dimensions are used in common, what constitutes acceptable levels of effectiveness may be interpreted in unique ways. Self-raters may have a different frame of reference. For example, is the self-evaluation with regard to absolute or relative (to others') levels of performance? If a relative judgment, what is the reference group? In this regard, Farh and Dobbins (1989) found that agreement between self- and supervisor ratings was greater when self-raters were presented with the same comparative information available to supervisor. Thus all raters were working from the same standards.

It is likely that all these explanations are potentially valid under certain circumstances. But it is also important to note that the factors cited reflect a mixture of ability and motivational forces, not dissimilar to those reviewed in other sections.

Conditions for Quality Self-Appraisals. It does appear that self-assessments can be of high quality under the right conditions. An important consideration relates to the motivational forces operating at the time self-assessments are to be obtained. In most contexts we can assume that the employee will be disposed to augment self-esteem and to distort assessments in a favorable direction. This would be especially true if the assessments were to be used in selection (Thornton, 1980). But even under these extreme conditions, there is evidence that this tendency can be curtailed. Specifically, Mabe and West (1982) discovered that when subjects in the studies they reviewed believed that their self-assessments would be validated in some way, there were significantly smaller amounts of leniency. For example,

Anderson, Warner, and Spencer (1984) asked applicants to list names and telephone numbers of individuals who could verify their past training and experience at the time that they got self-ratings in these domains. The authors felt that this increased the quality of the ratings received.

Alternatively, valid self-appraisals are more likely under conditions of high trust. Rather than use the fear of being caught to induce accuracy, those seeking self-relevant information should attempt to reduce the possibility that there will be any negative consequences for being candid. Managers or researchers would instead highlight the potential benefits that would follow. Mabe and West (1982) report that instructions of anonymity consistently produced better self-appraisals in the studies they reviewed. More practically, self-appraisals might be used in the context of personal development or counseling. Under these circumstances, the employee can only gain by being honest.

It has been argued that producing quality self-appraisals also involves certain skills that have to be developed over time in most people. In fact, previous experience with self-evaluations has been found to be a correlate of the accuracy of self-appraisals. The improvement in self-evaluation accuracy through experience may come from increased awareness of one's post performance (as a result of feedback) as well the skill that comes with practice (Mabe & West, 1982). It might be that this skill is somewhat specific so that increased accuracy would only be with reference to the particular ability or performance domain where practice has occurred. This is one implication of the study by Farh and Dobbins (1987) where clear performance standards and comparative performance information improved self-supervisor agreement.

A final set of conditions for producing quality self-assessments relate to what might be called specificity of measurement (Mabe & West, 1982). As obvious as it seems, there is a fair amount of evidence that clear and operational instructions to employees can improve results—for example:

Obtain self-assessments on the same measures that will be used as the criterion (e.g., supervisor ratings) for maximum convergence. Be certain that employees are familiar with whatever scales are involved. Moreover, there is some evidence that one pill typically get greater convergence among differing agents of assessment if the focus is on ability rather than performance. This seems to be due to the fact that the determination of responsibility for a given performance level is often difficult in settings of high work-flow interdependency.

Be clear about what standards to use. Should assessments be relative to the ability or performance of others? relative to past ability or performance? relative to supervisor's expectations? To illustrate, Steel and Ovalle (1984) obtained high levels of correspondence between self- and supervisor-provided performance appraisals when employees were asked to reflect on and use the supervisor's standards. And when employees have comparative information, they too seem to rate themselves more realistically. In general, however, for a variety of reasons, self-evaluations made relative to other workers (or at least relative to a clear and well known reference group) are easier to conduct and thus more likely to be accurate. They are expected to correlate more highly with criterion measures as well (Mabe & West, 1982).

In summary, self-assessments can provide useful insights. But they must be obtained under conditions that will insure their quality. Fortunately, research evidence has made it clear as to what some of these are.

The Ubiquity of Self-Appraisals. As in the case of peer assessments, it is almost inconceivable that individuals do not spontaneously develop (and over time modify) a work-relevant self-image, particularly in the light of the central role that work plays in our society (Korman, 1970). Given this, it is also reasonable to assume that a great deal of behavior in the work setting is likely to be influenced by a person's self-concept. In the context of performance assessment, self-appraisals would seem to have a great impact on a given employee's reaction to feedback, whether it is provided on an ad hoc basis (Larson, 1984) or as part of a formal annual review. This point is important and deserves elaboration.

Ostensibly, performance feedback is given with the goal of changing behavior in the service of higher performance. Thus, to be effective, the conditions for modifying behavior must exist. Specifically, the employee must clearly understand what aspects of performance are deficient, must accept the critical feedback as valid and appropriate, and know what needs to be done differently in the future.

An employee's private impressions of his or her effectiveness and its causes (e.g., ability, effort, luck) are likely to have a major impact on feedback acceptance (Fisher, 1979; Taylor, Fisher & Ilgen, 1984). At the most basic level, how you feel about yourself affects the perceptions of your work and the work of others. This, in turn, will influence what you attend

to and remember. It also shapes expectations. In discussions associated with performance feedback, these perceptions, recollections, and expectations will confront reality, as seen by the feedback giver (usually the supervisor). These will affect what gets heard and the employee's subsequent reactions. To the extent that there is congruence between self-assessments and those of the supervisor, a relatively easy session would be anticipated. However, as in most other cases, disagreement regarding the level of performance and/or the causes of that performance is going to produce tension. Even worse, the dynamics of the feedback session may serve only to build up resistance on the part of the employee even to constructive suggestions.

It would thus seem to be in everyone's best interest if the inevitability and impact of self-assessments were to be formally acknowledged. These could then be taken into consideration in the performance management and performance assessment context. At a minimum, this would imply that a supervisor would become aware of each of his or her subordinate's performance-related self-image. This insight would allow for an appropriate structuring of feedback sessions in a manner so as to reduce defensiveness (e.g., Stone, Gueutal & McIntosh, 1984). Indeed, some organizations require employees to self-assess using the formal appraisal form prior to the appraisal feedback session. The meeting starts with a sharing of this self-assessment, giving the supervisor an opportunity to anticipate areas of discordance (Bassett & Meyer, 1968).

A more ambitious approach to the use of self-assessments relates to the notion of employee self-management. Any number of authors have come out in favor of general (verses close) supervision and the frequent use of delegation (Yukl, 1981). And yet it would seem that the effective use of these practices can operate only under certain conditions. Most important, employees can operate autonomously only if they can be counted on to regulate their own behavior appropriately. And a prerequisite for this to occur, it would seem, is the capacity to recognize accurately in performance what is correct and what needs to be modified (Taylor et al, 1984).

Training and skill in self-assessment thus would facilitate self-management. The goal of the supervisor would not be to shape and direct behavior but to transmit the right attitude and the capacity to subordinates for defining, recognizing, and documenting instances of effective behavior. In some sense, by doing this the supervisor is creating a substitute for the traditional controlling function of management (Kerr & Jermier, 1978), transferring external control to self-control. In doing so, he or she could free up time to do potentially more valuable activities (e.g., planning). At the same time, a work environment is created which encourages personal growth and development.

A CASE EXAMPLE: MAKING USE OF NONTRADITIONAL VIEWPOINTS

Personal or individual development activities need to be guided by an assessment of the employee's weaknesses and strengths relative to current job responsibilities or some likely future assignment. This assessment is usually carried out by the employee in conjunction with his or her supervisor or manager. Further, the diagnosis and planning associated with development activities may be carried out informally (usually at the request of the employee), or it can be made part of the organization's human resource management system. In the latter instance, development efforts are usually based on the results of a performance appraisal. And they might be initiated by the supervisor (Wexley and Latham, 1980).

However, based on the arguments put forth earlier, in a recently conducted project, it was felt that there are others in the employee's role network who are in a position to assess performance deficiencies and provide insight into areas needing improvement. Specifically, it was felt that the opinions of an employee's peers could supplement self-assessments as a source of training needs information. This case will describe the use of self and peer evaluations in a personalized development program for managers in city government agency.

The Participating Agency

The agency sought to create a management development program that would be truly sensitive to the particular needs of a given individual. It is also wanted developmental activities to be based on something more systematic than the opinions of a single supervisor. And it needed something that would be potentially applicable to a pool of over 250 managers in as many as twenty-five job categories. Thus, the program had to be flexible but with sufficient specificity to be informative and useful in developing and monitoring developmental experiences for a particular manager.

The Program

The Options II program is an individualized management development program. Participation is volun-

tary. Unlike many other developmental efforts, this program is designed to provide tailor-made remedial experiences for those involved. There is close personal attention to the needs and desires of a given manager. The goal is to solve on-the-job problems so as to increase long-term potential.

The heart of the program is a systematic needs assessment, an action plan, individualized training, and a support group for personal development. The last feature is reflected in the fact that the program involves people who become familiar with the focal manager's plans and are personally committed to assist in his or her efforts. They are also in a position to see the manager's day-to-day behaviors. This includes work group peers and a "buddy," the latter nominated by the focal manager to help formulate the developmental action plan, monitor progress, and provide encouragement, reinforcement, and critical feedback.

The program consists of several phases. The first is a diagnosis of the focal manager's strengths and weaknesses. To do this, a self-assessment is conducted and integrated with data produced from a survey of peers. Developmental needs information is used in a second phase where an action plan is devised to strengthen a selected number of areas for improvement. The third phase involves implementation of the action plan and monitoring the manager's progress. This third phase is highly variable in length, inasmuch as it is dependent on the specific goals set and strategies (plans) designed to achieve them. In general, however, the program staff encouraged the setting of objectives that could be accomplished in a relatively short period (e.g., three months) in order to provide participants with the possibility of early success.

A survey of peers was used, in part, to determine training needs. In the case of peers, the quality of assessments is clearly related to the opportunity to observe the participating manager as well as the willingness to be candid. Thus, the selection of peers was done with care. In this regard the focal manager was asked to nominate at least two individuals who were thought to meet these criteria. They were not restricted to members of their work group and, in fact, were encouraged to include people who would have a valid perspective but who might be in a different functional area. In all cases, however, it was a staff member who was responsible for briefing the nominees about the program and their potential role in it, soliciting cooperation, and finally, coordinating the peer assessments. Most individuals nominated as peer assessors were willing to participate.

The Assessment Tool

The dimensions of the assessment tool were selected to cover the general areas of management functioning. In fact they were derived from the writings on managerial assessment centers. This literature has consistently identified a set of capacities or capabilities important to management success and career advancement. When necessary, these were relabeled to have meaning in the context of a city agency. The dimensions used are presented in table 30–1.

While all dimensions *could* have had relevance to a participating manager's job, it was recognized that this may not actually be the case. Thus, as a preliminary step, the supervisors of each of the Options II participants were asked to indicate which dimensions were appropriate for each specific manager. Thus, the dimensions in table 10–1 constituted a pool from which to select. A sample page of the survey is presented in figure 30–1.

The focal manager and his or her peers were asked to complete the assessment form to the best of their ability. They were told to attend to only those dimensions deemed relevant. Descriptive comments were encouraged, especially where deficiencies were indicated. After this was done, the manager and his or her peers were asked to designate, in rank order, three areas most needing improvement. This was done to give guidance in those instances where the manager was thought to be weak in several areas (where should we start?) or, more likely, when some-

one might be rated as effective across the board (a halo or leniency bias). Rankings would ensure some discrimination.

Using the Peer and Self-Assessments

Twelve managers (eleven men) from five divisions of the city agency from different levels of responsibility participated in the initial offering of the Options II program. A staff person was responsible for distributing, retrieving, and summarizing the assessments for each manager.

At the outset it was decided to hold two sessions with each participating manager: a feedback session and an action planning session. For the feedback session a staff person was responsible for summarizing the data on a form specifically designed for the purpose. The goal was to identify those dimensions on which there was some consensus that a deficiency existed.

The tone of the discussion in the feedback session was a developmental one. The fact that only the focal manager (and of course the staff person) would see the summaries facilitated this. The bulk of the meeting was devoted to identifying two or three areas that could be the basis for remedial effort. The assessments become a means toward that end. While managers varied considerably in their needs for development, all had at least one area requiring attention.

The feedback session was designed to share and interpret the assessment data. It emphasized diagnosis and getting at possible causes for the perceived deficiencies. It was especially important to isolate those areas where the problem really was lack of knowledge or skill. These could be remediated through developmental experiences.

The second session with the focal manager was devoted to action plan formation. In addition to the staff person and the participating manager, the buddy was at this session. The focus of the session was the two or three areas identified for development. The task of the group was to outline steps and activities to be carried out by the focal manager that would improve his or her functioning. Whenever possible the staff person would stress activities that would be performed on a day-to-day basis. The idea was to encourage the view that remedial experiences can be carried out in the job context. One did not have to go to a training program to become more effective.

The various activities thought to be helpful were discussed in the planning session, and behavioral contracting was carried out. The participating managers

Table 30–1
Areas Assessed by Self and Peers

1. Impact	14. Listening Skills
2. Energy	15. Flexibility
3. Oral Communication Skills	16. Tenacity
	17. Risk Taking
4. Written Communication Skills	18. Initiative
	19. Independence
5. Creativity	20. Planning and Organization
6. Range of Interests	
7. Stress Tolerance	21. Management Control
8. Motivation	22. Use of Delegation
9. Work Standards	23. Problem Analysis
10. Career Ambition	24. Judgment
11. Leadership	25. Decisiveness
12. Salesmanship	26. Effective Supervision
13. Sensitivity	27. Technical Ability

Figure 30–1. Format of the Peer Needs Assessment Survey

Options II Program Peer Feedback Form

Date _____   Manager being assessed _____
                                      Division _____

The manager whose name is noted above is involved in the Options II program. He or she is participating in Options II as a way to strengthen skills needed for effective management. This is a voluntary program. In order to identify areas in which improvement is needed, your help is required. Specifically, we would like you to provide feedback to the manager by using this form. Please rate the manager in each of the areas listed on the scales provided. Your assessment, along with those of others, will form the basis for a development action plan.

Since the Peer Feedback Form is designed to be used by managers at different levels of responsibility and in different divisions, it is possible that not all of the areas listed would be appropriate or relevant. Therefore, the participating manager has indicated those areas that he/she would like you to consider. Only rate (provide feedback in) those areas checked off by the manager.

The form is being used to gather feedback information in a systematic way. However, do not be constrained by it. Offer whatever comments you wish in the spaces provided.

Rate only those areas checked here	Area of management	Your Rating
✔	1. IMPACT: ability to create a good first impression, to command attention and respect, to show an air of confidence, and to achieve personal recognition. COMMENT:	_____ Very Effective _____ Adequate _____ Needs Improvement _____ Cannot Judge
✔	2. ENERGY: ability to achieve a high activity level. COMMENT:	_____ Very Effective _____ Adequate _____ Needs Improvement _____ Cannot Judge
✔	3. ORAL COMMUNICATION SKILLS: effectiveness of expression in individual or group situations (includes gestures and nonverbal communication). COMMENT:	_____ Very Effective _____ Adequate _____ Needs Improvement _____ Cannot Judge
✔	4. WRITTEN COMMUNICATION SKILLS: ability to express ideas clearly in writing in good grammatical form. COMMENTS:	_____ Very Effective _____ Adequate _____ Needs Improvement _____ Cannot Judge

were required to write down what they were to do, how they would index progress toward their goal, and what time frame was envisioned. The buddy agreed to monitor progress and serve as a resource when necessary. In some cases the buddy took a more active role in promoting development. For example, in seeking to improve his writing skills, one manager arranged to submit drafts of reports to the buddy for critical comment. In all cases the manager was expected to keep a diary of the activities actually completed.

The Role of the Supervisor

The manager's supervisor played only a peripheral role in this program. This was a result of a conscious decision and based on several considerations. Most important, the program administrator wanted to ensure that the focus was truly going to be on development. Even in the best of conditions, for example, where the supervisor is highly motivated toward helping subordinates improve (which did not always exist here), the supervisor's multiple administrative obligations can deflect this thrust. In a similar vein, it was felt that the focal manager would be more likely to self-disclose and acknowledge his or her weaknesses when a boss would not become aware of this information. Peers, too, would be more forthcoming with their opinions and assertions with the boss not there.

All this is not to say that supervisors were prohibited from getting involved. Quite the contrary. Focal managers were encouraged to discuss their plans with their manager, to focus their developmental efforts in a particular area. Moreover, if this were done, the latter could then arrange for work assignments that would actually reinforce skill or knowledge development. The main point is, however, the focal manager controlled the timing and amount of involvement of his or her boss. After all, it was their program.

THE OBJECT LESSONS

Object Lesson 1

Peer and self-assessments will be valid and useful under certain circumstances. Some of these have been detailed in earlier sections. However, in general, these involve ensuring that the participants have both the capability and the motivation to rate accurately. In the case illustration the managers and their peers were given a careful orientation to the Lating dimensions and the rating forms. They were shown how to relate these to observed behavior. This contributed to their capability to making valid judgments. All participants in the program were volunteers. They knew what was expected of them and were motivated to do a good job. Moreover, because the context for the program was development, it encouraged open and accurate communications. Finally, a staff person was involved at all points. He was able to ensure confidentiality of the ratings. Moreover, his regular presence in the workplace served to remind people of the need for care in their assessments. As a result of all this, the program worked. Peer and self-assessments served as the basis of useful and appropriate remedial efforts.

Object Lesson 2

The nature of the assessments produced as part of this program reaffirmed that there is "safety in numbers." That is, consistent with the research findings reviewed in this chapter, both peer and self-assessments appeared to produce somewhat differing and unique insights regarding the manager's strengths and weaknesses.

The staff person was responsible for arraying and discussing the ratings. While he was told to emphasize what appeared to be the common threads among three or four sets of assessments, points of disagreement were carefully considered as well. This in itself appeared to generate additional information for the manager as he or she could now clearly see how others perceived and interpreted behavior. This type of metaperspective (Smircich and Chesser, 1981) has been found to have positive consequences for more authentic and effective interactions. It was likely to occur in this context as well.

Object Lesson 3

Obtaining assessments from nontraditional sources takes effort. Even under the supportive conditions that existed in the city agency, the program was sufficiently different from prevailing practices so that there were numerous opportunities for distraction. It is uncommon to provide written candid feedback to others. Participants had to be frequently reminded of the need for honesty and the potential usefulness of the information to the focal manager. Under most circumstances, then, one should expect to commit resources to keep peer and self-assessment programs going.

REFERENCES

Amir, Y., Kovarsky, Y., & Sharon, S. (1970). Peer nominations as a predictor of multistage promotions in a ramified organization. *Journal of Applied Psychology, 54,* 462–469.

Anderson, C.D., Warner, J.L. & Spencer, C.C. (1984). Inflation bias in self-assessment examinations: Implications for valid employee selection. *Journal of Applied Psychology, 69* (4), 574–580.

Ash, R.A. (1980). Self-assessments of five types of typing ability. *Personnel Psychology, 33,* 273–282.

Bandura, A. (1978). The self system in reciprocal determinism. *American Psychologist, 33,* 344–358.

Barrett, C.J. (1966). *Performance rating.* Chicago: Science Research Associates.

Bassett, G.A., & Meyer, H.H. (1968). Performance appraisal based on self-review. Personnel Psychology, 21, 421–430.

Bernardin, H.J., & Beatty, R. (1984). *Performance appraisal: Assessing human behavior at work.* Boston: Kent Publishing.

Blum, M.L., & Naylor, J.C. (1968). *Industrial psychology: Its theoretical and social foundations.* New York: Harper & Row.

Blumberg, H.H. (1972). Communication of interpersonal evaluations. *Journal of Personality and Social Psychology, 23,* 157–162.

Carroll, S.J. & Schneier (1982). *Performance appraisal and review system.* Glenview, IL: Scott Foresman.

Cederbloom, D., & Lounsbury, J.W. (1980). An investigation of user acceptance of peer evaluation. *Personnel Psychology, 33,* 567–579.

DeNisi A.S., & Shaw, J.B. (1977). Investigation of the abuses of self-reports of abilities. *Journal of Applied Psychology, 62,* 641–644.

DeNisi, A.S., & Mitchell, J.L. (1978). An analysis of peer ratings as predictors and criterion measures and a proposed new application. *Academy of Management Review, 3* (2), 369–373.

DeVader, C.L., Bateson, A.G., & Lord, R. G. (1986). Attribution theory: A meta-analysis of attributional hypotheses. In E. Locke (Ed.), *Generalizing from laboratory to field settings* (63–81). Lexington, MA: Lexington Books.

Farh, J.L., and Dobbins, G.H. (1989). The effects of comparative information on the accuracy of self-ratings and agreement between self and superior ratings. *Journal of Applied Psychology, 79.*

Dickenson, T.I., & Tice, T.E. (1973). A multitrait-multimethod analysis of scales developed by retranslation. *Organizational Behavior and Human Performance, 9,* 421–438.

Finkle, R.B. (1976). *Managerial Assessment Centers.* In M.D. Dunnette (Ed.), *Handbook of industrial/organization psychology.* Chicago: Rand McNally.

Fisher, C.C. (1979). Transmission of positive and negative feedback to subordinates: A laboratory investigation. *Journal of Applied Psychology, 64,* 533–540.

Folger, R., & Greenberg, J. (1985). Procedural justice: An interpretive analysis of personnel systems. In K. Rowland & G. Ferns (Eds)., *Research in personnel and human resource management* (vol. 3, 141–183). Greenwich, CT: JAI Press.

Graen, G. (1976). *Rule making processes within complex organizations.* In M.D. Dunnette (Ed.), *Handbook of industrial and organizational psychology.* Chicago: Rand McNally.

Harris, M.M., & Schanbroeck, J. (1988). A meta-analysis of self-supervisor, self-peer and peer-supervisor ratings. *Personnel Psychology, 41,* 43–62.

Hedge, J.W., & Kavanaugh, M.J. (1988). Improving the accuracy of performance evaluations: Comparison of three methods of performance approval training. *Journal of Applied Psychology, 73* (1), 68–73.

Heneman, H.G. III (1974). Comparisons of self and superior ratings of managerial performance. *Journal of Applied Psychology, 59,* 638–642.

Holzbach, R.L. (1978). Rater bias in performance ratings: Superior, self, and peer ratings. *Journal of Applied Psychology, 63, 579–588.*

Kane, J.S., & Lawler, E.E. (1978). Methods of peer assessment. *Psychological Bulletin, 85* (a), 555–586.

Katz, D., & Kahn, R.L. (1978). *The social psychology of organization* (vol. 2). New York: John Wiley and Sons.

Kerr, S., & Jermier, J.M. (1978). Substitutes for leadership: Their meaning and measurement. *Organizational Behavior and Human Performance, 22,* 375–403.

Kingstrom, P.O., & Mainstrone, L.R. (1985). An investigation of the rater-ratee acquaintance and rater bias. *Academy of Management Journal, 28* (3), 641.

Klimoski, R.J., & London, M. (1974). The role of the rater in performance appraisal. *Journal of Applied Psychology, 59,* 445–451.

Korman, A.K. (1970). Toward an hypothesis of work behavior. *Journal of Applied Psychology, 54,* 31–41.

Larson, J.R. (1984). The performance feedback process: A preliminary model. *Organizational Behavior and Human Performance, 33,* 42–76.

Latham, G.P., & Wexley, K.N. (1981). *Increasing productivity through performance appraisal.* Reading, MA: Addison-Wesley.

Lawler, E.E. (1967). The multitrait-multirater approach to measuring managerial job performance. *Journal of Applied Psychology, 51,* 369–381.

Mabe, P.A., & West, S.G. (1982). Validity of self-evaluation of ability: A review and meta-analysis. *Journal of Applied Psychology, 67,* 280–296.

McEvoy, G.M., & Butler, P.F. (1987). User acceptance of peer appraisals in an industrial setting. *Personnel Psychology, 40,* 785–797.

Medland, P.F., Yates, L.G., & Downey, R.G. (1974). Associate ratings of senior office potential. *Research Problem Review, 74–2* (U.S. Army Research Institute for the Behavior and Social Sciences).

Meyer, H.H. (1975). The pay for performance dilemma. *Organizational Dynamics, 3,* 39–50.

Mount, M.K. (1984). Psychometric properties of subordinate ratings of managerial performance. *Personnel Psychology, 37,* 687–702.

Mumford, M.D. (1983). Social comparison theory and the evaluation of peer evaluations: A review and some applied implications. *Personnel Psychology, 36,* 867–881.

Peters, T.J. (1978). Symbols, patterns, and settings: An optimistic case for getting things done. *Organizational Dynamics, 7,* 7–21.

Schmidt, F.L., & Johnson, R.H. (1973). Effect of race on peer ratings in an industrial situation. *Journal of Applied Psychology, 57,* 237–241.

Schneier, C.E. (1977). Multiple rater groups and performance appraisal. *Public Personnel Management, 6,* 13–20.

Shore, L.M., & Thornton, G.C. III (1986). Effects of gender on self and supervisory ratings. *Academy of Management Journal, 29,* 115–129.

Siegel, L. (1982). Paired comparison evaluations of managerial effectiveness by peers and supervisors. *Personnel Psychology, 35,* 843–852.

Smircich, L., & Chesser, R.J. (1981). Superiors' and subordinates' perceptions of performance: Beyond disagreement. *Academy of Management Journal, 24*(1), 195–205.

Smith, D.E. (1986). Training programs for performance appraisal: A review. *Academy of Management Review, 11*(1), 22–40.

Smither, J.W., Barry, S.R., & Reilly, R.R. (1989). An investigation of the validity of expert time score estimates in appraisal research. *Journal of Applied Psychology, 74*(1), 143–151.

Steel, P., & Ovalle, N.K. (1984). Self-appraisal based upon supervisory feedback. *Personnel Psychology, 37,* 667–685.

Stone, D., Gueutal, H., & McIntosh, B. (1984). The effects of feedback sequence and expertise of the rater on perceived feedback accuracy. *Personnel Psychology, 37,* 487–506.

Sulsky, L.M., & Balzer, W.K. (1988). Meaning and measurement of performance appraisal rating accuracy: Some methodological and theoretical concerns. *Journal of Applied Psychology, 73*(3), 497–506.

Taylor, M.S., Fisher, C.D., & Ilgen, D.R. (1984). Individuals' reactions to performance feedback in organizations: A control theory perspective. In K. Rowland and G. Ferris (Eds.), *Research in personnel and human resources management* (vol. 8, pp. 81–124). Greenwich, CT: JAI Press.

Tesser, A., & Rosen, S. (1975). The reluctance to transmit bad news. In L. Berkowitz (Ed.), *Advances in experimental Social Psychology* (vol. 8) New York: Academic Press.

Thornton, G.C. (1968). The relationship between supervisory and self-appraisal of executive performance. *Personnel Psychology, 21,* 441–456.

Thornton, G.C. (1980). Psychometric properties of self-appraisals of job performance. *Personnel Psychology, 33,* 263–271.

Weary, G. (1979). Self-serving attributional biases: Perceptual or response distortions? *Journal of Personality and Social Psychology, 37*(8), 1418–1420.

Wexley, K.N., & Klimoski, R.J. (1984). Performance appraisal: An update. In K.M. Rowland & G.R. Ferris (Eds.), *Research in personnel and human resources management* (vol. 2, 35–79). Greenwich, CT: JAI Press.

Wexley, K.N., and Latham, G.P. (1980). *Developing and training human resources in an organization.* Pacific Palisades, CA: Goodyear Publishing.

Wherry, R.J. & Bartlett, C.J. (1982). The control of bias ratings: A theory of rating. *Personnel Psychology, 35,* 521–551.

Yukl, G. (1981). *Leadership in organizations.* Englewood Cliffs, NJ: Prentice-Hall.

31 ESTABLISHING AN ASSESSMENT CENTER FOR PERSONNEL DECISIONS AND DEVELOPMENT

William C. Byham

High turnover, extensive time required for training and development, poor performance, equal employment opportunity problems: all of these may be symptoms of poor selection or development decisions. If the "wrong" person is placed in the "wrong" job, he or she at the very least will be unhappy. Ultimately, this will result in poor morale or lack of motivation and, most likely, poor performance. If the wrong people are sent to a training program, the training expense is wasted, and a person who might benefit from the experience is deprived of the opportunity.

To help make better selection and personnel development decisions, an increasing number of organizations are using assessment centers. Assessment centers provide a comprehensive, standardized evaluation of behavior based on multiple inputs. Multiple assessment techniques are used to evaluate individuals for various purposes. A number of trained evaluators conduct the assessment and make recommendations regarding the participant's management potential and development needs.

The assessment center method has been applied most frequently to individuals being considered for selection, promotion, placement, or special training and development in management. The original industrial centers developed by American Telephone and Telegraph (AT&T) involved line personnel being considered for promotion to first-level supervisory positions. Since then, organizations have applied the assessment center method to select the most qualified individuals for many positions (middle managers, top executives, salespeople, management trainees, and employees to fill high-involvement positions). Assessment centers are most valuable when the participant is aspiring to a job significantly different from the position he or she currently holds. Simulating job requirements for the new position provides an opportunity to evaluate skills that are not observable through normal performance on the current job.

DESCRIPTION OF AN ASSESSMENT CENTER

Assessment centers are built around dimensional competencies. Some typical dimensions are:

- Individual Leadership—Using appropriate interpersonal styles and methods in guiding individuals (subordinates, peers, superiors) toward goal achievement; modifying behavior according to tasks and individuals involved.

- Group Leadership—Using appropriate interpersonal styles and methods in guiding a group toward meeting its objectives; modifying behavior according to tasks and individuals present; keeping meetings on course.

- Planning and Organizing—Establishing a course of action for self and/or others to accomplish a specific goal; planning proper assignments of personnel and appropriate allocation of resources.

- Oral Presentation—Effectively presenting ideas or tasks to individuals or groups when given time to prepare (including gestures, nonverbal communication, and visual aids).

- Analysis—Relating and comparing data from different sources; securing relevant information and identifying key issues and relationships from a base of information.

- Judgment—Developing alternative courses of action and making decisions that are based on logical assumptions and factual information.

- Initiative—Making active attempts to influence events to achieve goals; self-starting rather than

299

accepting passively; taking action to achieve goals beyond what is required.

Dimensions are identified through a professional job analysis. Because all facets of the assessment center method are designed to assess the dimensions, accurate identification is critical to the validity of the process.

The number of dimensions that an assessor can mentally process in an assessment center is an important research topic. Some researchers feel that only two to five dimensions can be rated effectively (Russell, 1985; Sackett & Hakel, 1979), while others believe that a larger number can be targeted (Thornton & Byham, 1982). The quality and quantity of assessor training provided is an important consideration in deciding the appropriate number of dimensions in a given situation.

As many as twelve individuals can be assessed effectively in one center. The most common arrangement is six assessees, three assessors, and one program administrator.

Assessors may include trained management personnel, professional psychologists, or a combination of both. The low ratio of assessees to assessors (typically 2:1) is important because it allows close observation of participants. It also lets several assessors evaluate each assessee during a center, a factor in the methodology's validity and fairness. Assessors are assigned different participants for each exercise. Management personnel who serve as assessors usually are at least two levels above the participant in the organizational hierarchy, trained for the assessment task, and not in a direct supervisory capacity over the participants.

Observing, recording, and evaluating behavior in an assessment center are complex tasks; most assessment centers require extensive training for management and professional assessors.

Industrial assessment centers employ a number of performance simulations to ensure complete coverage of management abilities: management games, leaderless group discussions, and role-playing exercises. The simulations allow participants to engage in job-like situations and to display job-relevant behaviors around the target dimensions. Some organizations also use background interviews and tests as part of their assessment centers.

The process of integrating assessment information and making predictions is quite systematic. Assessors share their behavioral observations and then reach a consensus rating for each target dimension assessed. Then, after reviewing the behavior pattern shown by the dimensional ratings, the assessors reach an overall decision. Some organizations replace assessor discussion of an overall assessment rating with statistical methodology. The accuracy of this methodology is debated, but research seems to indicate that statistical data integration is equally as or more accurate than judgmental integration (Wingrove, Jones & Heriot, 1985; Heriot, Chalmers & Wingrove, 1985; Huck, 1974; Moses, 1973; Wollowick & McNamara, 1969; Mitchel, 1975).

Assessment center feedback, in the form of oral and written reports, describes the participant's performance in the center and identifies immediate supervisor strengths and developmental needs.

Although most assessment centers are designed to predict supervisory and management capabilities, centers also can be used to select first-level employees and diagnose individual training needs at all organizational levels. Recently, the largest area of application has been the use of assessment center methodology to hire personnel in "high employee involvement" organizations. Companies such as Nissan, Toyota, Suzuki, GenCorp, American Motors, Colgate, Goodyear, and Budd have used the assessment center method to select nonmanagement individuals with the skills and motivation necessary to work in settings requiring high degrees of independence, responsibility, decision-making skills, and so forth.

VALIDITY FOR SELECTION AND PROMOTION DECISIONS

The assessment center method is unique in that extensive research established its validity before it came into popular use. The assessment center method came into existence as a result of the ATQT Management Progress Study (Bray, Campbell & Grant, 1974). In this study, which began in the mid-1950s, individuals entering management positions in Bell Telephone operating companies were assessed, and from then on their careers were followed. The study was unusual because neither the individuals assessed, nor their bosses, were given information about their performance in the center, nor was this information allowed to affect participants' careers.

Not only did the researchers follow participant advancement over the ensuing years, a second assessment was conducted eight years later (Howard & Bray, 1987). Figure 31–1 shows the validity of both assessment predictions. The criterion used was

Figure 31–1. Ratings at Original Assessment and Eight Years Later and Management Level Attained at Year 20

	N	Attained Fourth Level
Original Assessment Rating of Potential		
Predicted to Achieve Fourth Level or Higher	25	60%
Predicted to Achieve Third Level	23	25%
Predicted to Remain Below Third Level	89	21%
	137	

	N	Attained Fourth Level
Eighth Year Assessment Rating of Potential		
Predicted to Achieve Fourth Level or Higher	30	73%
Predicted to Achieve Third Level	29	38%
Predicted to Remain Below Third Level	76	12%
	135	

advancement within twenty years to the fourth level of management in a seven-level hierarchy. The eight-year prediction is more valid—an expected finding since most individuals would have started consolidating their skills after eight years in management. Yet the original assessment ratings were still valid—even after twenty years.

Thornton and Byham (1982) reviewed twenty-nine studies of the validity of the assessment center method. They found more support for the assessment center method than for other selection methodologies, while still lamenting the fact that most of the studies were conducted by a few large organizations (AT&T, GE, IBM, SOHIO, Sears).

Some writers have asserted that the assessment center method is better at predicting subjective ratings of job performance than actual job performance (Klimoski & Strickland, 1977; Russell, 1985; Sackett & Hakel, 1979). They argue that assessors are making the same global subjective judgments about assessees that future managers make in developing the job performance criterion.

In 1985 Thornton and his associates at Colorado State University processed 220 validity coefficients from fifty studies using a statistical approach called metaanalysis. They estimated the method's validity at .37 (Gaugler, Rosenthal, Thornton & Bentson,

1987). Working independently of Thornton, Wayne Cascio of the University of Colorado arrived at the same figure (.37) in studying the validity of first-level assessment centers in an operating company of the Bell System. Cascio's main interest, however, was to measure the bottom-line impact of promotion decisions based on assessment center information and decisions based on criteria extracted from other methods (Cascio & Ramos, 1986).

To determine the financial impact of assessment centers, Cascio needed cost data (fully loaded costs of the assessment process) plus job performance data expressed in dollars. Over a four-year period he developed a methodology for expressing in dollar terms the job performance levels of managers. Using information provided by more than 700 line managers, Cascio combined data on the validity and cost of the assessment center with the dollar-valued job performance of first-level managers. With these data, he estimated the organization's net gain in dollars resulting from the use of assessment center information in the promotion process. Over a four-year period, the company's gain in terms of improved job performance of new managers was estimated at $13.4 million, or approximately $2,700 per year for each of the 1,100 people promoted to first-level management positions.

ADVERSE IMPACT

Compared to most other selection methodologies, the assessment center method is affected less by gender and race. The only area in which substantial assessment center research has shown significant differen-

tial mean performance by gender or race is in selecting first-level supervisors; in about half of the reported studies, whites performed better than blacks. However, the differential performance in many of these studies can be explained by other factors—especially differential applicant populations necessary for evaluating a large number of blacks to meet affirmative action goals. Most important, there is consistent research showing that assessment centers are unbiased in predicting future performance. These studies have considered candidates' age, race, and gender. They have found that predictions by the assessment center method are equally valid for all candidates. (See Thornton & Byham, 1982, for a complete discussion of these issues.)

Federal courts have viewed assessment centers as valid and fair. Indeed, the courts often have mandated using assessment centers to overcome selection problems stemming from the use of paper-and-pencil tests and other selection instruments. A case in point involved a valve company whose use of paper-and-

pencil tests to select supervisors was struck down by a federal appeals court. As part of the settlement, the judge allowed the company to substitute the assessment center method as the principal means of selecting supervisors—even though slightly more whites than blacks succeeded in the centers. The judge based the ruling on the finding that a sufficient number of black candidates had acceptable potential for management to meet the company's affirmative action goals.

One final bit of evidence suggesting the acceptance of the assessment center method comes from the use of the method by the Equal Employment Opportunity Commission (EEOC) in 1977 and 1978. The EEOC used the method to evaluate executives from both inside and outside the government to fill high-level positions that resulted from a reorganization.

USING ASSESSMENT CENTERS FOR PERSONNEL DEVELOPMENT

The assessment center method aids personnel development in a number of ways. It can be used to:

- Identify individuals with potential for development early in their careers—to "fast track" people and optimize their development opportunities.
- Diagnose individual training or development needs—to guide an individual's development, to motivate the individual, to guide the organization's training efforts and get the right people in the right training program at the right time, and to guide the organization in making developmental assignments (task forces, product start-up).
- Determine a group's common development needs—to concentrate organizational efforts on programs that will help the most people.
- Evaluate the effectiveness of training programs.

Early Identification

It is important for organizations to identify a candidate's management potential at an early stage so they can take appropriate administrative actions. For example, many organizations use assessment center programs to identify the management potential of individuals early in their employment; this helps in planning training and development activities that are designed to advance the development of individuals with high potential.

Diagnosing Individual Training and Development Needs

The assessment center method is an excellent diagnostic tool because it provides specific examples of effective and ineffective behavior within job-related dimensions. This helps the assessee and his or her boss determine more precisely what training and development activities are required. For example, an assessment center might determine that an individual is poor in decision making and then find that the poor performance is caused by poor fact-finding skills (gathering information to make the decision). In addition, the assessment center might find that the individual's fact-finding skills are adequate when dealing with statistical information but poor when obtaining information verbally. The precision of this assessment would aid greatly in determining appropriate development actions.

Most organizations that use assessment centers for selection or promotion purposes also use the information obtained to diagnose their training needs. However, a major shift in focus has become more prevalent in recent years. Many firms now use assessment centers solely to diagnose training needs. An article describing the use of assessment centers as a diagnostic tool was first published in *Training and Development Journal* in 1971 and updated in 1980 (Byham, 1980).

Figure 31–2 shows a profile of two individuals who were assessed in a training-needs diagnostic pro-

Figure 31–2. Dimensional Profiles of Two Middle Managers

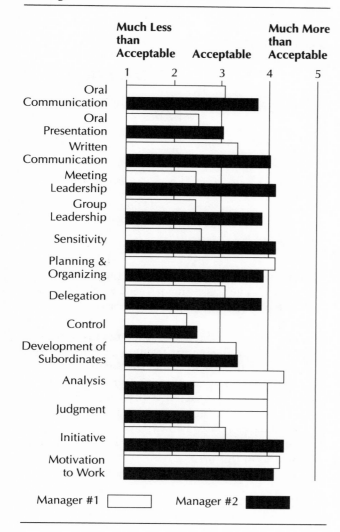

	Much Less than Acceptable	Acceptable	Much More than Acceptable
	1 2 3 4 5		

Oral Communication
Oral Presentation
Written Communication
Meeting Leadership
Group Leadership
Sensitivity
Planning & Organizing
Delegation
Control
Development of Subordinates
Analysis
Judgment
Initiative
Motivation to Work

Manager #1 ☐   Manager #2 ■

gram. One has extensive needs in interpersonal skills, the other in decision-making skills. These profiles produced very different training prescriptions. By determining the right training program for each person, these data saved the individuals and their organizations a great deal of time and effort.

Most assessment centers provide feedback on participants' performance. The amount of feedback varies greatly and is related to organizational level. Higher-level participants receive much more information than those at lower levels. Career counseling and planning discussions often are combined with feedback for higher-level participants.

In addition to providing insights to guide individual and organizational training efforts, assessment center results can be a powerful motivator for the individual receiving feedback. People often do not believe they need training and are not receptive when it is provided. Assessment center reports are very persuasive because of their behavioral documentation; when people see the written evidence, they usually become convinced that a need exists. To expand the insights that an assessment center report provides, some organizations combine assessment center feedback with specially collected data from bosses, subordinates, and, sometimes, customers or peers. Ratings on the same dimensions (using the same rating scales) are collected and then processed by a computer to form a diagnostic profile. Thus, the individual gets multiple views of his or her behavior. Comparing and contrasting these views give the individual unique perceptions of his or her performance and tend to motivate him or her to take action.

Diagnosing Common Group Development Needs

After an organization processes several candidates, it can use the data as an aid in allocating training and development expenses and planning new development programs. Information from multiple assessments also helps design new programs. For example, if some people have greater difficulty leading groups than leading individuals, the organization can implement more group leadership skills training into leadership programs.

Evaluating the Effectiveness of Training Programs

The American Society for Training and Development (ASTD) estimates that U.S. companies spend $212 billion yearly on training (Carnevale & Goldstein, 1983). The fastest growing portion of this amount is for sales, supervisory, and management training. Yet by not properly evaluating the effectiveness of their training programs, most companies fail to see if they are getting a return on their investment.

Assessment center methodology provides an excellent tool for establishing the validity and effectiveness of training programs involving interpersonal or managerial skills. Figure 31–3 shows three common research designs. In the first design, a group of individuals is trained, while another matched group is not. Then both groups go through an assessment center. The second and third designs have a group of individuals assessed, trained, and then assessed again. Figure 31–4 shows the results of the first method. This is an evaluation of the interaction management

Figure 31–3. Research Designs for Training Evaluation

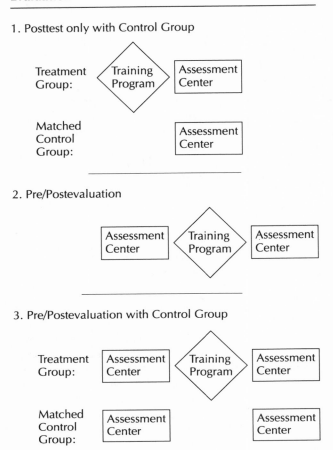

1. Posttest only with Control Group

2. Pre/Postevaluation

3. Pre/Postevaluation with Control Group

Figure 31–4. Overall Ratings of Performance in Three Assessment Center Simulations by Trained and Nontrained Supervisors

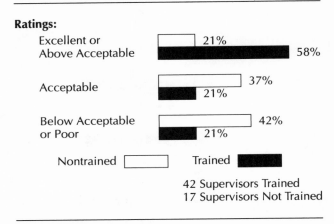

42 Supervisors Trained
17 Supervisors Not Trained

supervisory training program at the Lukens Steel Company. The assessment center results show marked changes in individuals' performance after training.

In addition to Lukens Steel, organizations such as SOHIO, AT&T, Central Telephone Utilities Corporation, and the New York Metropolitan Transit Authority have used assessment center technology to evaluate training programs (Byham, 1982). The advent of video technology, which allows individuals to be evaluated relatively inexpensively, has dramatically increased the application of the assessment center method in this area.

NEW METHODOLOGY

The biggest concern with the ongoing use of assessment centers is the amount of managerial time required. In a typical assessment center a manager leaves his or her job for two to three days to observe participants' performance in simulations and then spends an additional day or two meeting with other members of the assessment team to make final evaluations. Although managers recognize the importance of selection and promotion decisions, they still are often reluctant to commit this much time to assessment.

A related problem is the formality of the traditional assessment center, which tends to make the center an "event." This may build expectations and focus on who is assessed and who was not asked to participate. The traditional assessment center also requires organizations to put people through in groups; this method is useless when there are only two candidates for a position.

These constraints force some organizations to limit assessment center applications to only a few selection or promotion decisions. As a result, many important and effective selection and promotion applications along with the use of assessment centers to define training needs are ignored. As in many other fields, technology is helping to overcome the problems that are limiting the use of the assessment center method. Assessment centers now can be conducted with less time and effort, especially for developmental purposes.

Deformalizing the Method

A number of organizations in the United States and overseas have overcome the management time problem by making their assessment centers more informal and flexible while still retaining their validity. Organizations do this by incorporating the assessment center method into their day-to-day activities rather than having their managers go off to a special place or center.

The individual being assessed is responsible for scheduling a series of meetings with managers who will be doing the assessing. The assessee makes his or her own appointments over a period of several weeks, according to the schedules of all parties. The participating managers fit the time for the exercises into their normal activities.

During these meetings the managers put the assessee through the same job simulations used in traditional assessment centers. For example, one manager might interview the assessee about why he or she took certain actions in the in-basket exercise; another might have the assessee present findings from an analysis or planning exercise; and another might observe the assessee in a one-to-one interaction with another manager who role-plays a subordinate.

At an appointed time the managers (assessors) hold an assessor discussion, which works exactly like traditional assessment center discussions. The assessors give examples of the participant's behavior to support their dimensional ratings. After sharing their observations, the assessors reach a consensus on the participant's strengths and weaknesses in each dimension. If the objective of the assessment center is to provide the basis for selection or promotion decisions, the assessors then make an overall evaluation. If the objective is to diagnose training needs, the assessors' final step is to develop a profile of the participant's developmental strengths and needs.

All key components of the assessment center method are present: conducting multiple job simulations, using behavior observed in simulations to predict future behavior in the target job, organizing observed behavior around job-related dimensions, and holding a systematic data integration session with several assessors who have observed the participant independently in the simulations. Only the rigid-

ity is removed. This allows even the smallest organization to apply the assessment center method when making selection and promotion or development decisions.

Using Videotape to Record Behavior

The use of videotape is becoming increasingly popular in observing and preserving assessee behavior. The technology saves time and money because it eliminates the need for managers to observe individuals directly in simulations. By recording participants' behavior, assessors can view and evaluate simulations at their convenience. After each assessor has observed and evaluated the assigned simulation, a typical data integration session can be held, or the data can be integrated mathematically.

To date, the largest application of this technology occurred when Development Dimensions International, a Pittsburgh-based human resources consulting firm, evaluated more than 600 business school graduates as part of a project sponsored by the American Assembly of Collegiate Schools of Business (AACSB). Students from six representative universities worked through four assessment center exercises administered by the staff of each institution. Participants' written outputs and their videotaped performances were then sent to DDI, which evaluated and mathematically integrated the data to arrive at dimensional ratings. DDI used a computer to process the data and produce a report describing each participant's developmental strengths and needs.

In addition to AACSB, several other organizations in the United States are using the videotape approach. They include SOHIO, Ingersoll Milling Machine Company, National Semiconductor, Central Telephone of Illinois, Massachusetts Mutual Life Insurance Company, U.S. Department of Agriculture, and the Sperry Corporation.

CONCLUSION

The assessment center method is not a perfect predictor of managerial success, but it is a significant aid in making promotion decisions (Guion & Gibson, 1988). Its validity is increased when coupled with such methodologies as behavioral interviews and appropriate paper-and-pencil tests.

Traditional assessment center applications have been better suited to situations where a large number

of positions had to be filled. New methods that have taken the "center" out of the assessment center and use videotape technology have made the method appropriate for a much larger number of hiring or promotion situations.

While the validity of the assessment center method is widely accepted, there is considerable debate about how and why it works (Russell, 1985).

Ongoing research into how assessors make their evaluations should lead to efficiencies in assessment center exercises, the number of dimensions assessed, and assessor training.

REFERENCES

Bray, D.W., Campbell, R.J., & Grant, D.L. (1974). *Formative years in business: A long-term AT&T study of managerial lives.* Malabar, FL: Robert E. Krieger Publishing Company.

Byham, W.C. (1980, June). The assessment center as an aid in management development. *Training and Development Journal, 34*(6), 24–36.

Byham, W.C. (1982). How assessment centers are used to evaluate training's effectiveness. *Training, 19*(2) (February), 32–38.

Carnevale, A.P., & Goldstein, H. (1983). *Employee training.* Washington, DC: ASTD Press.

Cascio, W.F., & Ramos, R.A. (1986). Development and application of a new method for assessing job performance in behavior/ economic terms. *Journal of Applied Psychology, 71*(1), 20–28.

Gaugler, B., Rosenthal, D.B., Thornton, G.C. III, a Bentson, C. (1987). Meta-analysis of assessment center validity. *Journal of Applied Psychology, 72,* 493–511.

Guion, R.M., & Gibson, W.M. (1988). Personnel selection and placement. *Annual Review of Psychology, 39,* 349–74.

Heriot, P., Chalmers, C., & Wingrove, J. (1985). Group decision making in an assessment center. *Journal of Occupational Psychology, 58,* 309–12.

Howard, A., & Bray, D.W. (1987). *Managerial lives in transition: Advancing age and changing times.* New York: Guilford Press.

Huck, J.R. (1974). *Determinants of assessment center ratings for white and black females and the relationship of these dimensions to subsequent performance effectiveness.* Ph.D. dissertation, Wayne State University.

Klimoski, R.J., & Strickland, W.J. (1977). Assessment centers: Valid or merely prescient. *Personnel Psychology, 30,* 353–363.

Mitchel, J.O. (1975). Assessment center validity: A longitudinal study. *Journal of Applied Psychology, 60,* 573–579.

Moses, J.L. (1973). The development of an assessment center for the early identification of supervisory potential. *Personnel Psychology, 26,* 569–580.

Russell, C.J. (1985). Individual decision processes in an assessment center. *Journal of Applied Psychology, 70*(4), 737–746.

Sackett, P.R., & Hakel, M.D. (1979). Temporal stability and individual differences in using assessment information to form overall ratings. *Organizational Behavior and Human Performance, 23,* 120–137.

Thornton, G.C. III, & Byham, W.C. (1982). *Assessment centers and managerial performance.* New York: Academic Press.

Wingrove, J., Jones, A., & Heriot, P. (1985). The predictive validity of pre- and post-discussion assessment center ratings. *Journal of Occupational Psychology, 58,* 189–92.

Wollowick, H.B., & McNamara, W.J. (1969). Relationship of the components of an assessment center to management success. *Journal of Applied Psychology, 53,* 348–352.

32 BEHAVIORAL PERFORMANCE MEASURES

Elaine D. Pulakos

Rewarding and promoting effective performers as well as identifying less effective performers for training or other personnel actions is imperative to the successful management of personnel in organizations. Although there are various types of measures that can be used to evaluate employee performance, the focus of this chapter will be on the development of behaviorally based performance appraisal instruments. Prior to discussing behaviorally based measures, however, a general introduction to performance measures is presented.

PERFORMANCE MEASURES

Performance measures can be classified into two general categories: objective measures and subjective measures. Objective performance measures include such things as dollar volume of sales, number of words typed per minute, number of pieces produced, number of errors made, days absent from work, number of accidents, and tardiness. Unfortunately, there are several problems associated with the use of objective measures that preclude their use in many jobs. Consider the job of salesperson as an example. Although dollar volume of sales could be used as an objective measure of performance, sales volume is only one aspect of a salesperson's job. There are other important factors of the job, such as maintaining good customer relations, for which there are no objective measures of performance effectiveness. If one were to focus on only the objective dollar volume criterion, these other aspects of the job would be neglected, leaving an incomplete picture of the employee's job performance. Thus, dollar volume of sales would be a *deficient* criterion measure.

A second major problem with objective measures of performance is that they are often affected by factors outside the employee's control. Using the dollar volume of sales example, it is likely that this measure will only be partly a function of the effectiveness with which a salesperson performs on the job. Other factors outside the salesperson's control (e.g., territory

location, number of accounts, distances between accounts, quality of the product) can also have an impact on the total dollar volume of sales. Such *unequal opportunities* to make sales create difficulties in comparing effectiveness levels of different salespersons using a dollar volume criterion.

The problems associated with the use of objective measures have led researchers and managers to place more emphasis on *subjective* measures of job performance. In fact, performance appraisal ratings are the most frequently used measure for obtaining estimates of employees' job performance levels. One advantage of using ratings as job performance measures is that essentially all of the performance requirements of a job can be defined on a rating form (Borman, 1987). Thus, subjective measures need not be plagued by the types of criterion deficiency problems referred to in the discussion of objective performance measures. This is not to suggest, however, that subjective measures are not without problems of their own. In fact, because they rely on human judgment, subjective measures are prone to certain kinds of errors associated with the rating process (see chapter 34 for a further discussion of these). Nonetheless, it is definitely possible to define job performance comprehensively using rating scales. The issue, then, is one of deciding what type of rating format should be utilized.

GRAPHIC RATING SCALES

One of the more widely used rating scale formats is the graphic rating scale. On a graphic rating scale, the scale points are defined on a continuum, usually using numerical and/or verbal anchors. Examples of this type of scale appear in figure 32–1.

The first graphic rating scale in figure 32–1 (type a) contains qualitative end anchors only, while scale type b in the figure includes both numerical and verbal anchors. A major problem with this type of rating scale is that the scale points are *not* well defined. It is thus quite likely that raters will have difficulty understanding what is meant by the different rating scale points or levels of effectiveness. Further, raters may not agree about what types of performance constitute the different effectiveness levels. For example, assume that raters are using a seven-point scale. A 5 rating for one rater might be the same exact performance as a 4 rating or a 6 rating for other raters. The main problem is that graphic rating scales do not adequately define the meaning of different performance levels, making difficult the rater's job of distinguishing between effectiveness levels on the rating scale.

Figure 32–1. A Graphic Rating Scale

(a) Quality of Work

Low ⌊___|___|___|___⌋ High

(b) Quality of Work: Neatness and accuracy as well as volume and consistency in completing work.

1	2	3	4	5
Needs Work		Competent		Commendable

The remainder of this chapter will be devoted to describing the development of behaviorally based rating scales, rating formats that address the lack of specificity inherent in graphic rating scales. The following sections will focus on three types of behaviorally based scales: behaviorally anchored rating scales (BARS; Smith & Kendall, 1963), behavioral summary scales (BSS; Borman, Hough, & Dunnette, 1976), and behavioral observation scales (BOS; Latham & Wexley, 1981).

BEHAVIORALLY BASED RATING FORMATS

Behaviorally Anchored Rating Scales

BARS use actual examples of incumbent job performance to anchor different levels of performance effectiveness on each rating dimension. Raters are thus able to match actual observations of ratee behavior to appropriate effectiveness levels on the rating scale dimensions. An example BARS developed for evaluating Navy recruiter performance is shown in figure 32–2.

The development of BARS relies heavily on input from job incumbents and/or their supervisors. In particular, these "subject matter experts" provide the raw material necessary to construct the rating scales (the rating dimensions and behaviors that will be used to define the different levels of effectiveness within each dimension). The steps often used to develop BARS can be summarized as follows:

Step 1: At an initial workshop, a group of incumbents and/or supervisors attempt to identify and define all important dimensions of performance for a target job.

Step 2: A second group knowledgeable about the job then generates behavioral incidents describing effective, average, and ineffective job performance for each rating dimension. In particular, workshop participants are asked to think back over the entire time they have been on the job and to relate actual behaviors that they themselves have exhibited or they have observed others exhibit. Participants are asked to record the circumstances leading up to the incident, what behavior occurred, and any consequences of the behavior. Although the number of incidents written by each subject matter expert will vary, it is probably reasonable to expect that an average of fifteen to twenty behavioral examples can be generated by each person in a half-day (4-hour) time period. This estimate includes approximately 30 minutes that would be devoted to training participants how to write good behavioral incidents. In most cases, 200 to 300 incidents should be sufficient for describing a job's performance requirements.

Step 3: The behavioral incidents obtained from step 2 are edited to a common format.

Figure 32–2. Example BARS

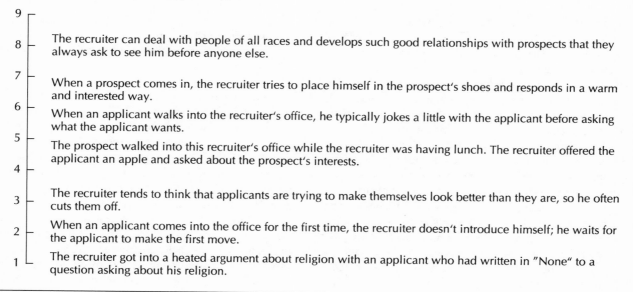

Gaining and Maintaining Rapport

Being hospitable to prospects in the office; gaining the trust and respect of prospects; adjusting to applicant's styles and acting appropriately with different types of applicants.

9 —

8 — The recruiter can deal with people of all races and develops such good relationships with prospects that they always ask to see him before anyone else.

7 —

6 — When a prospect comes in, the recruiter tries to place himself in the prospect's shoes and responds in a warm and interested way.

When an applicant walks into the recruiter's office, he typically jokes a little with the applicant before asking what the applicant wants.

5 —

The prospect walked into this recruiter's office while the recruiter was having lunch. The recruiter offered the applicant an apple and asked about the prospect's interests.

4 —

3 — The recruiter tends to think that applicants are trying to make themselves look better than they are, so he often cuts them off.

2 — When an applicant comes into the office for the first time, the recruiter doesn't introduce himself; he waits for the applicant to make the first move.

1 — The recruiter got into a heated argument about religion with an applicant who had written in "None" to a question asking about his religion.

Source: Borman, Hough & Dunnette (1976).

Step 4: Each member of a third group (known as the retranslation group) of incumbents and/or supervisors is presented with a list of the dimensions (generated in step 1) and their definitions as well as a randomized list of the edited behavioral incidents (generated in step 2). Each respondent's task is to sort each critical incident into one dimension based on its content and then rate the effectiveness level of that incident. A seven-point scale is often used for these ratings, where 1 = extremely ineffective and 7 = extremely effective.

Step 5: Data from the retranslation group are analyzed by calculating the mean and standard deviation of the effectiveness ratings given to each behavioral incident. Also calculated for each incident is the percentage of respondents who agreed that the incident belonged in a particular performance dimension (how many respondents placed each incident into the *same* performance dimension).

Step 6: The scale developer decides which incidents will be used as anchors within each performance dimension. The criteria for selecting incidents to anchor the scales are (1) that each incident used has a low standard deviation for the effectiveness rating (indicating good agreement between

raters) and (2) that a high percentage of the raters agreed that a given incident belonged in a particular performance dimension. If a seven-point scale is used to make the effectiveness ratings, a standard deviation of 1.5 can be used as a cutoff for retaining behavioral incidents (any incident with a standard deviation greater than 1.5 would be eliminated). A cutoff of 60–70 percent for the percentage of raters agreeing that a given incident belongs in a particular dimension is reasonable. Behavioral incidents that meet these criteria are used to anchor the rating scale points.

To evaluate performance using BARS, raters are first asked to record behavioral observations of a ratee's performance related to each rating dimension. Because these observations typically occur over the course of a six-month or year-long rating period, raters are often encouraged to keep notebooks in which they record relevant performance examples as they occur. Then, at the end of the rating period, raters compare the effectiveness of observed ratee performance with the effectiveness reflected in the scaled behavioral examples. A rating is assigned based on this comparison process. Thus, in using BARS, raters are encouraged to attend to and record actual behaviors rather than rely on general impressions as the basis for making their ratings. Further, the scaled behavioral anchors serve as comparison points against which a ratee's observed performance can be matched.

Behavioral Summary Scales

The BARS rating format was an important step in the development of well-defined performance rating scales. However, a potential problem surrounding the use of BARS is that raters can have trouble matching a ratee's actual performance to the behavioral examples that are used to anchor the rating scales (Borman, 1979). Using the example BARS shown in figure 32–2, imagine the difficulty a rater might encounter comparing a ratee's performance to those very specific scale anchors. Even though a ratee is performing at an effectiveness level represented by one of the anchors, it is unlikely that he or she will have exhibited the exact behavior shown on the scale. This puts the rater in a position of having to decide which scaled behavior is the most similar to the ratee's actual performance. Such judgments can be very difficult to make, leaving raters unsure about how a ratee's behavior compares to the scaled effectiveness levels.

In response to the above problem with BARS, the behavioral summary scale (BSS) format was developed (Borman, Hough & Dunnette, 1976). BSS are very similar to BARS, except for the fact that BSS are anchored with more general or abstract behavioral statements. To develop these general behavioral statements, the highly specific incidents representing a given performance category and effectiveness level are examined for similar underlying content. Statements are then written to represent a wider range of behaviors that are characteristic of several of the specific incidents scaled at each effectiveness level. Forming broader scale anchors that encompass several behavioral incidents enables the scale developer to include more performance relevant information on the rating scales.

To develop BSS, one would first complete steps 1 through 4 of the BARS development process outlined above. Then the goal would be to develop BSS rating scale anchors that reflect as much content as possible of *all* of the reliably retranslated behavioral incidents. Specifically, BSS development would proceed as follows:

Step 5: Assume for the example that during retranslation, ratings for several hundred critical incidents were made using a seven-point scale (1 = extremely effective to 7 = extremely effective).

The incidents within each dimension would be grouped into three levels according to their mean effectiveness rating. The following levels could be used for this grouping: low (1.00–2.49), average (2.50–5.49), and high (5.50–7.00).

Step 6: Behaviorally oriented statements would be written describing the content of all of the behavioral incidents grouped into each category and effectiveness level.

Shown in figure 32–3 is an example Navy recruiter BSS dimension containing summary statements like those described above. As shown in the figure, BSS statements cover more of the behavioral domain of the performance dimension than do the specific behavioral incidents used to anchor the BARS (see figure 32–3). By providing a more comprehensive description of the various behaviors that constitute different effectiveness levels, it is more likely that one of the anchors will describe a ratee's observed performance on each dimension. Accordingly, the rater's task of matching actual observations of job performance to the scaled behavioral anchors should be facilitated.

Only one empirical study has been conducted comparing ratings made using BARS with ratings made using BSS. The results of this study showed no consistent differences between the two formats with respect to psychometric rating error or accuracy. Thus, the potential advantages that BSS would seem to have over BARS may not be realized in practice.

Behavioral Observation Scales

Behavioral observation scales (BOS; Latham & Wexley, 1981) present raters with a number of specific effective and ineffective critical incidents; no average behaviors are included on these scales. For each critical incident, raters are asked to evaluate employees on a five-point scale ranging from 1 = Almost Never (performs the behavior) to five = Almost Always (performs the behavior). Hence, rather than making an evaluative rating of performance effectiveness on each dimension (as was the case with BARS and BSS), BOS require raters to record the frequency with which they have observed a number of specific critical behaviors. Example BOS items are presented in figure 32–4.

BOS performance dimensions and critical incidents are obtained from workshops like those conducted to develop BARS or BSS. However, rather than using only selected behavioral incidents as anchors (as with BARS) or summarizing the content of many

Figure 32–3. Example BSS

Gaining and Maintaining Rapport

Being hospitable to prospects in the office; gaining the trust and respect of prospects; adjusting to applicants' styles and acting appropriately with different types of applicants.

9 or 10

Extremely Effective Performance

Deals very effectively with persons of all races; greets all prospects appropriately; is adept at setting them at ease and getting them to talk, regardless of their background, race, or personality.	Is adaptable, but not phony in interacting with all types of prospects; maintains a sincere, courteous, and friendly atmosphere in the office.	Answers prospects' questions politely and patiently, no matter how unimportant they seem.

6, 7, or 8

Effective Performance

Is almost always able to put prospects at ease when they first enter the office.	Expresses concern toward recruits and shows interest in their recruitment activities; for example, warmly wishes a recruit good luck in boot camp.	Shows interest in most persons who enter the office and interacts with them in a warm and friendly way.

3, 4, or 5

Marginal Performance

Has a standard approach with all persons which, at times, is inappropriate, such as a manner of greeting, speech, or telling sea stories.	Occasionally appears disinterested when with a prospect; sometimes forgets an applicant's name.	Is discourteous at times; for example, will sometimes interrupt an applicant while he/she is speaking.

1 or 2

Ineffective Performance

Ignores or is rude to applicants who do not seem, at first sight, to be "good Navy recruits."	Will interrupt an ongoing interview to interview another person or will perform other duties during an interview and give an impression of being disinterested in the person.	Is cold and impolite upon initial meeting and answers questions in a disinterested, nonpersonable way.

Source: Borman, Hough and Dunnette (1976).

Figure 32–4. Example BOS Items

1. Stops talking to a fellow employee as soon as a customer approaches the counter.

   Almost Never   1   2   3   4   5   Almost Always

2. Serves customers within five minutes of receiving their order.

   Almost Never   1   2   3   4   5   Almost Always

Source: Latham & Wexley, (1981).

specific examples into more general anchors (as with BSS), the BOS procedure retains all of the specific behavioral statements generated for use on the scales.

These statements are placed into a format like that shown in figure 32–4 and used as a basis for evaluating employee performance. Ratees can be scored on each performance dimension by first summing the ratings across all of the items contained in a dimension and then dividing this total by the number of items in the dimension.

Latham and Wexley (1981) have argued that an important feature of the BOS is that raters are required to focus on relatively specific ratee behaviors and then simply record the frequency with which they have observed those behaviors. Thus, raters are not required to make complex evaluative judgments about performance effectiveness. Research has shown that raters often have difficulty integrating information to make complicated evaluative judgments (Cooper, 1981; Feldman, 1980); hence, performance appraisal systems like BOS can be advantageous. However, some research has shown that BOS might measure traitlike judgments rather than simple observations of performance frequency (Murphy, Martin & Garcia, 1982). Thus, the apparent advantages of the BOS format may not be realized in practice.

ADVANTAGES AND DISADVANTAGES OF BEHAVIORALLY BASED RATING SCALES

One advantage of behavioral approaches for developing rating scales is that the performance domain for a target job is exhausted (Borman, 1987). This is because participants in behavioral incident workshops are asked to generate performance examples by drawing on their experience observing every aspect of job-relevant behavior. Thus, a comprehensive sampling of job content should be obtained.

A second related advantage of behaviorally based scales is that they are based on actual job *behavior* as opposed to vaguely defined personal traits, characteristics, or other rating factors. Further, the performance dimensions and behavioral anchors are rigorously defined and can be easily distinguished from one another.

A third advantage is attributable to the behaviorally based rating scale development process itself. That is, there are high levels of rater and ratee participation throughout all phases of the scale development process. This participation is advantageous because it better ensures acceptability of the resultant rating scales, as well as commitment to making them work. High levels of rater and ratee participation also better guarantee that the scales will be relevant to the job in question. Moreover, since job incumbents and/or their supervisors generate the behavioral examples used to develop the anchors, the scales are phrased in the jargon of the user rather than the jargon of the scale developer.

A final advantage of behavioral rating scales is that they can facilitate giving specific job-relevant feedback to employees. That is, a supervisor can focus on specific behaviors in need of improvement and then use the scale anchors to convey to employees what they need to do behaviorally to perform more effectively on the various dimensions. This advantage is important; the facilitative effect of specific feedback on future performance has been well documented (Ilgen, Fisher & Taylor, 1979).

One potential disadvantage of behavioral rating scales is that their development involves a relatively costly and sometimes long process that requires the input of many job incumbents and their supervisors. In addition, separate scales must be developed for dissimilar jobs. Consequently, this approach may not be the most practical in some organizations. However, it is also true that behaviorally based rating scales have been developed for a wide variety of jobs. Thus, it is sometimes possible simply to revise existing scales for use in similar jobs or organizations.

One important issue regarding the advantages and disadvantages of behavioral performance appraisal instruments is whether ratings that are made using these formats are more accurate and of higher quality than ratings that are made using other types of rating formats. Some studies have shown that behavioral rating instruments yield ratings with less psychometric error (e.g., halo, leniency/severity) than do other kinds of rating scales (Campbell, Dunnette, Arvey & Hellervick, 1973; Keaveny & McGann, 1975). However, in many cases, only small improvements in rating quality have resulted with behavioral scales versus other rating instruments. Other studies have indicated no psychometric superiority for behavior-based scales over other rating formats (Bernardin, 1977; Borman, 1979; DeCotiis, 1977).

In all, the net result of research investigating differences in rating formats indicates that no consistent differences in rating quality exist between different types of behavior-based rating scales or between behavior-based scales and other rating formats. However, other research (Pulakos, 1984, 1986) has shown that when appropriate rater training is provided in conjunction with using behaviorally based rating instruments, rating quality can be improved. The topic of rater training is discussed in detail in chapter 34 of this *Handbook* and thus will not be elaborated on here. Nevertheless, the mere use of any rating format is probably not enough to ensure high-quality ratings without also providing appropriate training on how those scales should be employed to evaluate ratee performance.

SUMMARY

This chapter has provided an overview of various types of rating instruments, with a focus on behaviorally oriented approaches to rating scale development. Specifically, procedures used to develop three different types of behaviorally based formats were explained. These were behaviorally anchored rating scales, behavioral summary scales, and behavioral observation scales. Although there are distinct conceptual differences among BARS, BSS, and BOS in terms of the formats themselves and what judgments raters are required to make in using these scales, they share similar format development steps as well as similar advantages and disadvantages.

Even though behavioral formats have not been shown to be appreciably superior in terms of yielding ratings with reduced psychometric error or increased accuracy, they have other advantages that warrant recommendation of their use. First, behavioral formats can be used as a guide for providing specific job-relevant feedback to employees. Giving this type of feedback has been shown to be important for improving performance effectiveness. Second, behavioral approaches to scale development provide a comprehensive picture of a job's performance requirements and also focus on precisely the performance criterion of interest, that is, what job behaviors differentiate between effective and ineffective performers. Finally, it has been shown that the use of behaviorally oriented rating scales in conjunction with proper rater training can yield high-quality performance information.

As a final point, it should be noted that irrespective of what type of rating scale is used to evaluate performance, it is extremely important that care be taken to ensure that the rating scales are properly developed. Performance appraisal researchers generally agree that differences in rating formats will probably not be very important, provided that care is taken to develop a comprehensive job-relevant rating instrument (Bernardin, 1977; Landy & Farr, 1980). Doing this probably is critical for generating high-quality ratings and also for ensuring that the performance appraisal instrument will be legally defensible.

REFERENCES

Bernardin, H.J. (1977). Behavioral expectation scales versus summated scales: A fairer comparison. *Journal of Applied Psychology, 62,* 422–428.

Borman, W.C. (1979). Format and training effects on rating accuracy and rating errors. *Journal of Applied Psychology, 64,* 410–421.

Borman, W.C. (1987). Behavior-based rating scales. In R.A. Berk (Ed.), *Performance assessment: Methods and application.* Baltimore, MD: Johns Hopkins University Press.

Borman, W.C., Hough, L.M., & Dunnette, M.D. (1976). *Development of behaviorally-based rating scales for evaluating the performance of U.S. Navy recruiters* (Technical Report TR-76-31). San Diego, CA: Navy Personnel Research and Development Center.

Campbell, J.P., Dunnette, M.D., Arvey, R.D., & Hellervick, L.V. (1973). The development and evaluation of behaviorally based rating scale formats. *Journal of Applied Psychology, 57,* 15–22.

Cooper, W.H. (1981). Ubiquitous halo. *Psychological Bulletin, 90,* 218–244.

DeCotiis, T.A. (1977). An analysis of the external validity and applied relevance of three rating formats. *Organizational Behavior and Human Performance, 19,* 247–266.

Feldman, J.M. (1981). Beyond attribution theory: Cognitive processes in performance appraisal. *Journal of Applied Psychology, 66,* 127–148.

Ilgen, D.R., Fisher, C.D., & Taylor, M.S. (1979). Consequences of individual feedback on behavior in organizations. *Journal of Applied Psychology, 64,* 349–371.

Keaveny, T.J., & McGann, A.F. (1975). A comparison of behavioral expectation scales. *Journal of Applied Psychology, 60,* 695–703.

Landy, F.J., & Farr, J. (1980). Performance rating. *Psychological Bulletin, 87,* 72–107.

Latham, G.P., & Wexley, K.N. (1981). *Increasing productivity through performance appraisal.* Reading, MA: Addison-Wesley.

Murphy, K.R., Martin, C., & Garcia, M. (1982). Do behavioral observation scales measure observation? *Journal of Applied Psychology, 67,* 562–567.

Pulakos, E.D. (1984). A comparison of rater training programs: Error training and accuracy training. *Journal of Applied Psychology, 69,* 581–588.

Pulakos, E.D. (1986). The development of training programs to increase accuracy with different rating tasks. *Organizational Behavior and Human Decision Processes, 38,* 76–91.

Smith, P., & Kendall, L.M. (1963). Retranslation of expectations: An approach to the construction of unambiguous anchors for rating scales. *Journal of Applied Psychology, 47,* 149–155.

MANAGING PERFORMANCE WITH A BEHAVIORALLY BASED APPRAISAL SYSTEM

Douglas G. Shaw, Craig Eric Schneier, Richard W. Beatty

Communications Inc. (CI), a group of related high-technology and telecommunications businesses owned by one of the largest companies in the United States, had just completed one of their first business strategy planning cycles. The cycle culminated with not only an articulation of the group's mission and specific competitive strategies for each of their businesses but also statements of the values they needed to emphasize as an organization. Top management wanted to hold executives accountable for implementing the strategy. As a part of the action planning process, CI management hence committed to developing a management by objective (MBO) process within each of their businesses. Objectives were determined from the action plans, based on each executive's opportunity to affect key organizational results. Performance against objectives would be tied to the executives' compensation.

After working with the MBO process for a year, CI management became dissatisfied with it for three reasons. First, CI's top management found that while some of their managers delivered the results identified through the objectives, they "didn't like the way the results were achieved." For example, managers seemed to propose only the safest new projects, those that had been only modestly successful in the past. Few risks were taken because managers were not willing to gamble on not meeting their objectives. Second, in the businesses that included all salaried employees in the MBO process, developing the objectives became more a required exercise than a useful management tool for implementing their business plans. Considerable time was spent arguing over the objectives, which were not well integrated into the strategy and action planning processes. Third, the values that were agreed

to by the management team were not being reinforced by the MBO system.

After considerable discussion, CI's top management agreed that their MBO process had to be replaced, or at least augmented, by a process that better captured how and what performance should be measured. The process should be one that would hold people accountable for reinforcing CI's key values and would be a useful tool to track and measure performance accurately.

The values discussed in CI's first business planning cycle were narrowed to five most important values agreed upon by the top management team. CI management then developed a process for better integrating the organizational values into the management and appraisal process. First, each of the five values (Do what it takes to get the job done, make timely decisions, take calculated risks, revise plans and adapt to change, serve clients' interests) was defined. Second, the values were communicated to all employees, along with the introduction of a process for linking the values to the responsibilities of all positions previously included in the MBO process. Third, small groups met to discuss the values and how they are (or could be) manifested in their jobs. For each value they also developed examples of what exceeds, meets, and does not meet expectations would constitute for their jobs. After these examples were drafted, they were refined and consolidated to be used in the process of planning and appraising performance.

CI management preserved the objective-setting process for its executives, augmented by the process just described.

By measuring its executives on what was achieved and how it was achieved, the chief executive officer (CEO) had a performance planning and appraisal process that more accurately captured the performance he needed from his executives to grow and meet CI's competitive challenges. According to the CEO, the process was the key means of integrating the espoused values throughout the organization, which he believed was necessary to gain competitive advantage through each of the divisions' strategies. The values chosen to be reinforced were consistent with CI's rapidly changing, highly competitive marketplace. CI management overcame some of its earlier problems, such as taking a very narrow view of responsibilities, slow decision making, overanalyzing issues, and taking an overall management approach that was too conservative.

This case is a good illustration of why companies look for an alternative to objective setting for planning and appraising performance of executives, other managers, and nonmanagerial employees. In this case, the company chose a technique commonly referred to as behaviorally anchored rating scales (BARS) (see Schneier & Beatty, 1979; Beatty & Schneier, 1981) to assess performance, a process used to appraise individuals' performance in difficult-to-quantify job dimensions or factors. (These were CI's values in the case.)

WHY BARS

In many cases, solely meeting objectives defined through an action planning process of a business's strategy does not adequately capture an executive's or manager's performance. (CI's predicament was similar.) Often the achievement of such objectives is not sufficient as a criterion for pay and promotion decisions, either because of the objective-setting process itself (e.g., were manager A's objectives as challenging as manager B's?) or because the achievement of results could have been accomplished in a counterproductive manner.

For example, a manager could achieve a given financial objective by working a small group of people too hard, later resulting in unwanted turnover. But the manager might be promoted or rewarded through the pay program because he or she met objectives, hence sending the wrong message about desired behavior. To capture such nonquantitative aspects of performance, managers often use a nebulous criterion such as "Overall job Performance," or a scale for "Managing Effectively" or "Interpersonal Relations" will be included, with adjectives (Outstanding, Average) at each scale value. Both allow evaluators to consider important aspects other than achieving objectives in appraising performance. While these scales may provide an evaluator with the needed latitude to appraise an individual's total contribution, they provide too vague a means of communicating expectations and providing feedback. In addition, such scales can be inaccurate, leading to inflated ratings (see e.g., Landy & Farr, 1983).

Also illustrated in the introductory CI case is another predicament of many managers using MBO: stretching the objective-setting process too far down in an organization. This can be an exercise in futility because of a position's distance from, or lack of control over, the results that are measured in an objective-setting process. In such cases, the objective-setting process itself becomes the goal rather than a tool to achieving the organization's goals. The consequences are a lot of wasted time and energy (see Bernardin & Beatty, 1984).

To address these issues with a practical technique, this discussion (1) defines BARS terminology, (2) reviews the process for developing BARS, (3) contrasts BARS to other means of appraising performance, (4) describes how BARS can be used, and (5) provides guidelines for effective development and implementation of a BARS process.

TERMINOLOGY

Three terms should be defined to understand BARS. *Dimensions* are broad categories of duties and responsibilities that comprise a job or number of jobs. A *scale* is a continuum of performance, ranging from the lowest to the highest level of performance. BARS use scales containing from as few as three levels of performance to as many as nine. *Anchors* are specific descriptors of behavior attached to each level of performance used on a behaviorally anchored scale.

Figure 33–1 provides an example of a BARS scale for the planning, organizing, and scheduling dimension of a manager position. Note that the scale uses

Figure 33–1. Example of a Behaviorally Anchored Rating Scale: Planning, Organizing, and Scheduling Project Assignments and Due Dates

7 [ ] Excellent — Develops a comprehensive project plan, documents it well, obtains required approval, and distributes the plan to all concerned.

6 [ ] Very Good — Plans, communicates, and observes milestones; states week by week where the project stands relative to plans. Maintains up-to-date charts of project accomplishments and backlogs and uses these to optimize any schedule modifications required.

Experiences occasional minor operational problems but communicates effectively.

5 [ ] Good — Lays out all the parts of a job and schedules each part; seeks to beat schedule and will allow for slack.

Satisfies customers' time constraints; time and cost overruns occur infrequently.

4 [ ] Average — Makes a list of due dates and revises them as the project progresses, usually adding unforeseen events; investigates frequent customer complaints.

May have a sound plan but does not keep track of milestones; does not report slippages in schedule or other problems as they occur.

3 [ ] Below Average — Plans are poorly defined; unrealistic time schedules are common.

Cannot plan more than a day or two ahead; has no concept of a realistic project due date.

2 [ ] Very Poor — Has no plan or schedule of work segments to be performed

Does little or no planning for project assignments.

1 [ ] Unacceptable — Seldom, if ever, completes project because of lack of planning and does not seem to care.

Fails consistently due to lack of planning and does not inquire about how to improve.

Figure 33–2. Example of a Behaviorally Anchored Rating Scale: People Development

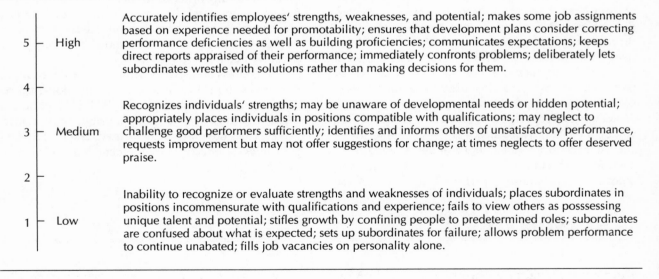

5 — High — Accurately identifies employees' strengths, weaknesses, and potential; makes some job assignments based on experience needed for promotability; ensures that development plans consider correcting performance deficiencies as well as building proficiencies; communicates expectations; keeps direct reports appraised of their performance; immediately confronts problems; deliberately lets subordinates wrestle with solutions rather than making decisions for them.

4 —

3 — Medium — Recognizes individuals' strengths; may be unaware of developmental needs or hidden potential; appropriately places individuals in positions compatible with qualifications; may neglect to challenge good performers sufficiently; identifies and informs others of unsatisfactory performance, requests improvement but may not offer suggestions for change; at times neglects to offer deserved praise.

2 —

1 — Low — Inability to recognize or evaluate strengths and weaknesses of individuals; places subordinates in positions incommensurate with qualifications and experience; fails to view others as posssessing unique talent and potential; stifles growth by confining people to predetermined roles; subordinates are confused about what is expected; sets up subordinates for failure; allows problem performance to continue unabated; fills job vacancies on personality alone.

seven points, each accompanied by an anchor that describes different types of behavior. Figure 33–2 provides an example for the people development dimension of an executive's job.

Although two or more positions may share a job dimension (most managers could be rated on planning, organizing, and scheduling), the anchors on the scale may vary from position to position, given different roles and responsibilities. In other words, a job dimension can be exhibited differently for differ-

ent jobs, leading to different anchors for the same dimension.

DEVELOPING BARS

Involving Raters and Ratees— The Systems Users

Although there are different approaches to developing BARS, involving incumbents of those positions for which BARS are being developed is critical to the success of the program. One of the advantages of the BARS performance appraisal process is the degree of specificity of relevant performance factors or dimensions. If incumbents are not involved in BARS development, the anchors could become too general and lose their meaning to job incumbents, therefore lessening the utility of the BARS.

A second advantage to involving job incumbents in the development of BARS is that there is likely to be more credibility in the appraisal process itself and its applicability if one has either been involved in its development or knows that one's peers have been. In the introductory case, CI management expected to achieve a greater "buy-in" and understanding of the organization's values by having them examined as closely as they were in the development of BARS by the job incumbents.

Emphasizing Job Behaviors

Most people think of their jobs or their subordinates' jobs in terms of responsibilities or results rather than behaviors. For example, when describing a financial analyst's job, people will often think of responsibilities (e.g., data gathering) or outputs (e.g., monthly budget variance report). Rarely do people think of the financial analyst in terms of what the financial analyst actually does (e.g., soliciting input from the target audience regarding a report's utility). Behaviors can be used as descriptors or anchors describing various levels of performance. Nevertheless, when a financial analyst's performance falls short of expectations because reports lack needed data or analyses, a performance planning and appraisal process that concentrates on how the report is done (behaviors), rather than on the untimeliness of reports (results), can be more useful in improving the analyst's reports.

Once the intended uses of the appraisal system are determined (e.g., compensation, promotion), BARS can be developed by following the eight steps outlined below:

1. Determine the job or jobs for which BARS are to be developed. BARS can be developed for a single job (e.g., marketing managers) or for a group of similar jobs (e.g., managerial, executive, computer analyst). Then provide an orientation to BARS to all those participating in the process. The agenda should include why BARS are to be developed, definitions and illustrations of key terminology, an overview of the process, and a description of how the BARS will be used.

2. Job incumbents and their managers meet to identify the most relevant dimensions of the job under discussion. It is helpful to provide a list of possible job dimensions as a basis for identifying the most relevant dimensions of a particular job. Lists of dimensions previously developed by others in the same job group can also be used as a starting point. However, the process should ensure that the dimensions decided upon for a particular job are truly the most relevant. Following are some examples of dimensions (Bray, 1976):

Oral communication

Leadership

Personal impact

Sensitivity

Flexibility

Independence

Work standards

Career ambition

Work involvement

Resistance to stress

Energy

Decisiveness

Planning and organization

Tenacity

3. Participants write anchors for each job dimension defined for a given job. Participants should be given guidelines and examples before they begin drafting anchors. (Figure 33–3 provides a useful set of guidelines for writing anchors.) Anchors should

Figure 33–3. Suggestions for Writing Useful Behaviors

1. Use specific examples of behavior, not conclusions about the "goodness" or "badness" of behavior.

   Use This: This supervisor tells a secretary when the work was to be completed, the degree of perfection required, the amount of space it must be typed within, and the kind of paper necessary.

   Not This: This supervisor could be expected to give very good instructions to a secretary. Instructions would be clear and concise.

2. Avoid using adjective qualifiers in the anchor statements; use descriptions of actual behavior.

   Use This: This supervisor understands employees such that the supervisor can repeat both the employee's communication and the intent of the message. They also make certain to talk in private when necessary and do not repeat the conversation to others.

   Not This: When supervising associates, this supervisor does a good job of understanding their problems. This supervisor is kind and friendly.

3. Avoid using anchors that make assumptions about employee knowledge about the job; use descriptions of behavior.

   Use This: This employee performs the disassembly procedure for rebuilding a carburetor by first removing the cap and then proceeding with the internal components, gaskets, etc. If in doubt about the procedure, the mechanic will refer to the appropriate manual.

   Not This: This mechanic knows how to disassemble a carburetor and will do so in an efficient and effective manner.

4. Avoid using frequencies in anchor statements; use descriptions of behavior.

   Use This: This officer performs the search procedure by first informing those arrested of their rights, asks them to assume the search position, and then proceeds to conduct the search by touching the arrested in the prescribed places. When the search is complete, the officer informs the arrested and proceeds to the next step in the arrest procedure.

   Not This: This officer always does a good job in performing in search procedure.

5. Avoid using quantitative values (numbers) within anchors.

   Use This: This accountant submits reports on time that contain no misinformation or mistakes. If discrepancies occur on reports from the last period, this accountant identifies the cause.

   Not This: This accountant could be expected to meet 90 percent of deadlines with 95 percent accuracy.

---

not contain words such as *feel, think, know,* or other descriptors that cannot be observed. A useful process for developing anchors is to have each participant write two or more behavioral anchors for each point on the scale (write two anchors for each of the five performance levels on a five-point scale) for each dimension. These can be written on index cards. This step can be completed in a group, provided a reasonably sized pool of anchors (five to eight for each scale value) is developed by the group.

4. The participants reach a consensus on which specific job dimension each anchor best illustrates, regardless of the dimension for which it was originally written. By distributing the deck of index cards containing the anchors to all participants and having each person identify each anchor's relevant dimension, the process identifies ambiguous anchors. If there is considerable disagreement as to which job dimension an anchor best illustrates (e.g., if more than 25 percent of participants disagree on the relevant dimension), the anchor is probably too ambiguous to be a useful behavior descriptor. A worksheet such as the one illustrated in figure 33–4 can be used to link anchors and job dimensions. (The second half

of the worksheet is used for step 5 in the development process.)

5. Participants determine scale values for all remaining anchors. In other words, each behavioral anchor is placed somewhere on a dimension's scale (1–5 on a five-point scale, 1–7 on a seven-point scale, etc.) by each member of the group. Group members hence individually determine the level of performance an anchor represents, regardless of the level for which it was originally written (see figure 33–4 for a worksheet).

6. The final scale value is determined according to the mean scale value given to an anchor by the group. (The mean could be rounded to the nearest whole number.) Each participant's scale rating is averaged for each anchor, dimension by dimension. This can be done outside the group meeting.

It is important to look at the variance around the mean value given to an anchor by a group. If the variance is large, the group disagreed as to the anchor's placement. For example, a calculated mean of 4 on a seven-point scale could be derived from half of the participants rating the anchor as a 1 (lowest performance) and half rating the anchor as a 7 (higher

Figure 33–4. BARS Anchor Reassignment and Scale Value Worksheet

Instructions: Randomly order all anchors below in the left-hand column. Then put all of the job dimensions in the middle column. Ask participants to decide which job dimension each anchor most clearly illustrates by placing an "X" in one and only one job dimension column. Then participants note the degree the performance they feel is illustrated by each anchor by placing an "X" in one of the columns numbered 1 through 7.

Behavioral Anchors	Job Dimensions								Scale Values						
	1	2	3	4	5	6	etc.		Excellent 7	Very Good 6	Good 5	Average 4	Below Average 3	Very Poor 2	Unacceptable 1
1.															
2.															
3.															
4.															
5.															
6.															
7.															
8.															
9.															
10.															
11.															
12.															
13.															
14.															
15.															
etc.															

performance), thus placing the anchor at the fourth point on the scale, indicating average performance. Yet the anchor was not rated as illustrative of average performance by anyone; hence it should be discarded. (A variation of this step is to conduct a group session to discuss each anchor's scale value and reach consensus.)

7. All anchors are arranged according to their calculated (or agreed-upon) scale value for each dimension to prepare for the final step.

8. The group and then management review all the scales carefully to ensure that proper terminology is used. The group should also determine whether additional anchors should be used to clarify a performance level. (BARS are not meant to be exhaustive but rather illustrative. They cannot describe all possible behaviors for each job dimension and scale value.)

Since jobs and expectations frequently change, as do job incumbents, job dimensions and anchors should be reviewed by incumbents and their managers at least annually to ensure the relevance of the BARS. The annual review need not involve large numbers of people unless significant restructuring of

jobs and expectations occurred. A critique soon after the completion of a performance review should be sufficient to modify any anchors or dimensions.

Legal Issues and BARS

Those involved in the development of a BARS system, or any other performance appraisal approach, should be aware of specific legal issues. Based on Title VII of the Civil Rights Act, guidelines for federal employees (*Uniform Guidelines on Employee Selection Procedures*), the Civil Service Reform Act of 1978 (especially section 430), and case law, those involved in designing a BARS appraisal process should ensure that it:

1. Uses specific performance criteria that are relevant to a job (critical work behaviors and outcomes determined through appropriate job analysis).

2. Communicates the performance appraisal standards to employees.

3. Relies on ratings that are not biased based on race, color, religion, national origin, sex, or age.

4. Draws on multiple ratings from different raters with direct knowledge of ratee job performance to reduce potential biases associated with a single rater.

For a more complete discussion of performance appraisal legal issues, see Schneier and Beatty (1984) and Burchett and DeMeuse (1985).

HOW BARS DIFFER FROM OTHER APPRAISAL SYSTEMS

The principal difference between most objective-setting processes and BARS is that while objectives focus on *what* people *achieve*, BARS provides a way to assess *how* results are achieved or *what people do* to achieve specified results. In the CI case, *how* results were achieved were at least as important as the results themselves because of CI's need to change certain managerial work processes and behaviors, such as decision making, risk taking, and teamwork. BARS can be a powerful tool for focusing individuals on what the organization believes are key behaviors or for changing certain aspects of an organization's culture, especially when linked to pay and selection decisions (see Beatty & Schneier, 1984).

An appraisal system must do more, however, than assess how work is performed or objectives are met. They do take time to develop, and it is sometimes difficult for job incumbents to write good behavioral anchors. BARS anchors are not completely observable and are open to interpretation, even if they do describe behavior. BARS are far from perfect. How do BARS stack up against a few commonly used appraisal systems in meeting other human resource management needs?

Table 33–1 compares how well BARS and three other common appraisal approaches meet different

performance appraisal objectives. The three additional performance appraisal approaches are:

1. *Management by objectives,* in which specific, often quantifiable, objectives are set and individuals are rated whether they meet their objectives (see Odiorne, 1979; Locke & Latham, 1984).

2. *Forced distribution ranking*, in which individuals are ranked against others in the same department or job class, typically on a global measure of overall job performance; a specific distribution of scores is mandated, often to conform to a "normal" distribution (see Carroll & Schneier, 1982; Bernardin & Beatty, 1984).

3. *Personal trait scales*, in which individuals are rated for specified traits, such as energy, assertiveness, and ambition, but each scale is defined only with adjectives, such as *Excellent, Outstanding,* or *Average* (see Carroll & Schneier, 1982; Bernardin & Beatty, 1984).

It is obvious from table 33–1 that forced distribution ranking and personal trait scales have severe limits when considering such uses for appraisal systems as providing performance feedback and identifying training needs.

Table 33–1
Relative Ability of Performance Appraisal Methods to Attain Appraisal System Objectives

Performance Appraisal Objectives	Behaviorally Anchored Rating Scales (BARS)	Management by Objectives (MBO)	Forced Distribution Ranking	Personal Trait Scales
Feedback and development requires: Specific, behavioral terminology on the format Setting behavioral targets for ratees to work toward; participation of raters and ratees In development; job relatedness; problem-solving performance review, which ends with a plan for performance improvement Reduction of ambiguity/anxiety of ratees regarding job performance required and expected by raters/organizations	Very good to excellent	Fair to good	Poor	Poor

continued on next page

Table 33–1 *continued*

Measuring performance accurately requires: 　Lessening of rater response set errors (e.g., leniency, halo) 　Agreement with other performance measures not on the format (e.g., direct indexes, such as salary, sales volume) 　Reliability across multiple raters 　Flexibility to reflect changes in job environment; job-related criteria 　Commitment of raters to observe ratee performance frequently and complete format seriously 　The use of the same standards across raters	Good	Good to excellent	Poor to fair	Fair to poor
Rewards allocation requires: 　Ability to rank-order ratees or results in quantifiable performance score 　Facilitating a variance or spread of scores to discriminate among good, bad, fair, etc., ratees 　Measuring contributions to organizational/departmental objectives 　Perception of accuracy and credibility by employees	Very good to excellent	Good to excellent	Good to very good	Fair
Assessing training needs requires: 　Specifying deficiencies in behavioral terms 　Incorporating all relevant job dimensions 　Eliminating motivation/attitude and environmental conditions as causes of inadequate performance	Very good	Fair to good	Poor	Poor to fair
A rationale for personnel decision making (e.g., identifying promotion potential, job assignments, demotions and termination, etc.) requires: 　Job-related criteria 　Job dimensions dealing with ability to assume increasingly difficult assignments built into form 　Ability to rank ratees comparatively 　Measurement of contribution to organization/department objectives 　Assessment of ratee's career aspirations and long-range goals	Good (varies)	Fair to good	Fair to good (varies)	Poor to fair
Validation of selection techniques requires: 　Job relatedness, comprehensive list of dimensions tapping behavioral domain of the job 　Systematic job analysis to derive criteria 　Assessment of interrater reliability 　Professional, objective administration of format 　Continual observation or ratee performance by raters	Very good to excellent	Fair to good	Poor	Poor

Source: Beatty and Schneier (1981).
Note: Each method's ability to attain the objectives would, of course, depend on several issues particular to each rating situation, such as rater biases, number of raters available, care taken to develop the format, or reward structure in the organization.

USING BARS

Compatibility of Bars and Objectives

Although BARS have many uses (see Carroll & Schneier, 1982), their primary applications are in planning and appraising performance. BARS can be used as the only performance tool or as a complement to an objectives-based system. In the introductory case, CI used BARS *and* objectives for its top executives and only BARS for its lower-level employees (see Odiorne, 1979; Locke & Latham, 1984 for further discussions of objectives-based systems). Determining whether to use BARS in conjunction with objectives depends on several factors:

1. The degree to which business plans have been articulated and detailed in order to provide a basis for individual objectives.
2. The degree of control a person may have over meaningful objectives by virtue of his or her position responsibilities.
3. The degree to which results and objectives are a sufficient guide for planning and guiding performance.
4. The need to measure both results and the process by which results are achieved.

For Selection, Promotion, Development, and Compensation

Selection and Promotion. BARS can be used as a selection tool in a company's succession planning process (Burnett & Waters, 1984). Once critical job dimensions are identified for key positions included in the succession planning process, BARS can serve to identify those who perform well on the identified dimensions. Promotion or external selection decisions can be made more effectively once a position's critical dimensions have been defined. Candidates can be assessed against relevant dimensions in a number of ways (see Bray, 1976; Byham, 1980).

Training and Development. BARS can be used as a training and development tool for current positions and potential future positions identified through a formal or informal career planning process. BARS help identify the principal ways people can improve performance in their current position. Significant weaknesses identified by behaviors on the lower end of a behaviorally anchored scale can be addressed through relevant training and development programs. If a person is aspiring to a specific higher-level position, he or she can work toward developing the behaviors required to succeed at that position, as identified through the higher-level position's job dimensions and relevant BARS. Assignments, either permanent or part time, can be made to develop the needed skills.

Compensation. Results of BARS appraisals can also be used in making pay decisions. The specificity of BARS standards increases the directness and consistency of the performance-pay linkage (see Cumming, 1987, and McLaughlin, 1987, for discussions of linking pay to performance).

Ratings from BARS-based appraisals can be especially useful in determining appropriate salary levels. Most salary administration systems determine increases according to an individual's performance rating in combination with his or her current positioning in the salary range (in the lower, middle, or top third of the range). With uniform BARS for the same position being applied to all position incumbents, managers have a higher probability of giving consistent performance ratings and the appropriate salary treatment. Some appraisal systems, such as objectives-based systems, may not apply the consistent measurement standards that a BARS system provides. Often the level of rigor of objectives varies across incumbents in the same position and salary grade or level. These systems therefore may be more likely to result in uneven salary increase treatments.

Some incentive programs have an individual component, sometimes in addition to a company and/or division component, used to determine an award. The results of a BARS appraisal can, of course, be used as a determinant of individual incentive award adjustments (as can the achievement of individual objectives). Some managers have difficulty paying similar individual incentive awards to top people who both achieve their objectives yet do not have as equally good performance in their overall job responsibilities (as in the case at the beginning of this chapter). Tying BARS ratings, either alone or in conjunction with performance on a set of objectives, to the determination of individual incentive awards is an effective way of linking overall job performance to individual incentive awards.

GUIDELINES FOR EFFECTIVE DEVELOPMENT AND IMPLEMENTATION OF BARS

One concern with BARS is the amount of time needed to identify relevant job dimensions and develop appropriate behavioral anchors. A second concern is the difficulty people have in developing useful behaviors. BARS development can, however, be efficient. Using such aids as a list of possible job dimensions and useful examples of behavioral anchors can both facilitate and expedite BARS development. The key issue, however, is that time spent with design and development process of an appraisal system pays great dividends in its use. Once performance expectations are defined, behavioral performance feedback and performance problem solving are improved significantly because both raters and ratees know what is required to attain each rating level.

A third concern is having a large enough group of incumbents in a job to develop the number of anchors needed to develop a set of BARS. One supervisor and a single or a few subordinates could use BARS effectively. They do not need to use index cards, develop a pool of anchors, and calculate mean scale values. They simply need to discuss what different levels of performance would look like and come to an understanding as to what is expected.

Managers should remember that the real benefit of BARS (and any other performance appraisal process) lies in its developmental process and its use, not in its paperwork. No appraisal system, however well designed, solves problems of unwilling performance coaches, unskilled performance problem solvers, and/or biased performance raters (see Murphy & Constans, 1987; Landy & Farr, 1983).

To manage performance effectively, managers and their subordinates should determine what is important to measure. Forms serve as a guide to the communication required to manage performance. In the end, the degree of detail required should match the comfort level of the participants.

A final concern that should be addressed is the degree of commitment and accountability necessary to develop and use BARS effectively. There must be commitment to the process from a company's or division's influential managers. The commitment of the users of the system can be built through participation in the development of the BARS. In CI, the managers changed from resisting further use of the objective-setting process to enthusiastically using BARS as a useful management tool when they saw it meet their needs.

Accountability for managing performance is also required. One practical way to develop accountability is to rate each manager on his or her performance management competence. Once accountability is built, people will have a need to develop the requisite skills.

To make appraisal systems work, manage performance all year; don't just appraise it once a year. Appraisal systems fail all too frequently. Sometimes, as was the case with CI, the design was deficient—it did not provide a mechanism to measure *how* the objectives were accomplished and corporate values were reinforced by managers. BARS can help here. Often, however, the appraisal system is seen as a once-a-year *rating* of performance, not an ongoing process of *managing* it. The key to effective systems lies in their ability to measure what counts and their users' ability (and willingness) to operate them effectively (see Schneier, Beatty, & Baird, 1986; Schneier & Beatty, 1986).

Regardless of whether BARS are used alone or with objectives, there are certain fundamentals to ensure the effective use of any appraisal system. *Managers*, not staff professionals, must:

1. *Define the overall purpose or mission* of the relevant work group, department, or division and job. Why does this unit exist? Who are its "customers" (internal or external), and how does it serve them? How does this unit's work help meet organization-wide objectives? Why does each job exist? How does each job help accomplish the mission?
   The mission should be reviewed at least annually, based on new directions or emphases of the organization, as well as performance actually achieved in the prescribed time period. Overall unit goals or objectives can be derived from the mission (see Beatty & Schneier, 1984).

2. *Determine roles and responsibilities* of the unit members once their job's mission is determined. What roles and responsibilities are required to achieve the job's mission? How does each person help achieve the mission as he or she performs their job?

3. *Set performance expectations* by identifying a set of job dimensions (and relevant, illustrative behavioral anchors, to the extent necessary). These are the aspects of the job on which people should be rated. If outcomes or results should be

evaluated (see the criteria for use of objectives cited above), specific, individual objectives must be set. Define a limited number of clear, measurable objectives. BARS can be used in conjunction with objectives.

4. *Monitor performance, solve performance problems, and provide performance feedback* during the performance period. Coaching, counseling, and solving performance problems are required throughout the year, not just at year end. The goal is to eliminate surprises at the assessment step, for both managers and subordinates.

5. *Evaluate performance* based on data collected on performance against expectations (both process and results), and communicate it to ratees with clear examples that support the evaluation. Ask "customers," peers, and even subordinates, who have relevant data.

6. *Define performance development action plans* to address improvement opportunities identified in the previous step. Both ratees and their managers should be held accountable for meeting these targets. Training, self-development, job rotation, closer supervision, and expanded responsibilities are all options here.

7. *Link performance to specific consequences* (e.g., salary increases, incentive awards, and promotion opportunities). Most companies talk about merit pay and pay for performance, yet very few have effective systems (see McLaughlin, 1987). A prerequisite to paying for performance is a viable mechanism for identifying, defining, and measuring performance, as well as a committed and skilled group of managers.

Figure 33–5. A Performance Management Model: An Ongoing, Management-Driven, Participative Process

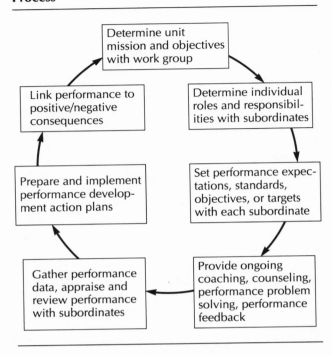

Figure 33–6 illustrates a performance management cycle (see also Schneier. Beatty, & Baird, 1987). Managers who follow these seven steps are likely to develop a performance management *process*, not merely an appraisal *form*, that effectively improves the performance of individuals, and therefore departments, units, divisions and the company as a whole.

COMPELLING BUSINESS NEED: A NECESSARY PRERESQUISITE

Having a compelling business need for managing performance is, above all other factors, the principal driver for having a performance management system that works (Peters, 1987). In the introductory case, CI's compelling need was to turn the *modus operandi* of management into a more action-oriented, risk-taking mode in order to increase the company's competitive advantage. There are many examples of companies turning to an active performance management process to help it achieve important goals. GE's emphasis on customer service (Trachtenberg, 1986) and American Express's measurement of departments' impact on customers (Uttal, 1987) are two examples.

In addition to having a strong business need, other factors, noted above, are necessary to ensure the effectiveness of a performance management system. However, these factors (identified below) are more likely to be addressed once the compelling business need is clear. The key factors are:

1. *Management commitment* to the performance management process (summarized in figure 33–5).

2. *Accountability* for managing performance, reinforced through pay and promotion decisions.

3. Addressing performance management *skill development*, made easier once the needs are recog-

nized through management accountability for the process.

Unless a performance appraisal approach such as BARS is linked to specific business needs and ad-dresses them, the process will have limited utility and appeal and will fall into disuse. After all, the ultimate purpose of any appraisal system is to improve organizational performance via effective individual appraisal, development, and rewards.

REFERENCES

Beatty, R.W., & Schneier, C.E. (1981). *Personnel Administration: An experiential skill-building approach.* Reading, MA: Addison-Wesley Publishing Company.

Beatty, R.W., & Schneier, C.E. (1984). Strategic performance appraisal issues. In R.S. Schuler & S.A. Youngblood (Eds.), *Readings in personnel and human resource management.* St. Paul; MI: West Publishing Co.

Bernardin, H.J., & Beatty, R.W. (1984). *Performance appraisal,* Boston: Kent Publishing.

Bray, D.W. (1576). The assessment centers method. In *Training and development handbook.* New York: McGraw-Hill.

Burchett, S.R., & DeMeuse, K.P. (1985). *Performance appraisal and the law. Personnel,* 62 (7), 29–37.

Burnett, R.S., & Waters, J.A. (1984). The action profile: A practical aid to career development and succession planning. *Business Horizons,* 27 (3), 15–21.

Byham, W.C. (1980). Starting an assessment center the correct way. *Personnel Administrator,* 27–32.

Carroll S.J., & Schneier, C.E. (1982). *Performance appraisal: A systems Approach.* Glenview, IL: Scott, Foresman & Company.

Cumming, C.S. (1987). New directions in salary administration. *Personnel,* 64 (1), 68–69.

Landy, F.J., & Farr, J.F. (1983). *Measurement of work performance: Methods, theory & applications.* San Diego: Academic Press.

Locke, E.A., Latham, G.P. (1984). *Goal-setting: A motivational technique that* Englewood Cliffs, NJ: *works!* Prentice-Hall.

McLaughlin, D.J. (1987). Pay for performance: A perspective. *Compensation and Benefits Management.* 3 (2), 37–41.

Murphy, K.R., & Constans, J.I. (1987). Behavioral anchors as a source of bias in Ratings. *Journal of applied psychology,* 72 (4), 573–577.

Odiorne, G.S. (1979). *MBO II: A system of managerial leadership for the 80's.* Belmont, CA: D.S. Lake Publishers.

Peters, T. (1987). *Thriving on chaos: A revolutionary agenda for today's manager.* New York: Alfred A. Knopf.

Schneier, C.E., & Beatty, R.W. (1979). Developing behaviorally-anchored rating scales. *Personnel Administrator,* 24, 59–68.

Schneier, C.E., & Beatty, R.W. (1984). Designing a legally defensible performance appraisal system. In M. Cohen & M. Golembiewski (Eds.), *Public personnel update.* New York: Marcel Dekker.

Schneier, C.E., & Beatty, R.W. (1986). How to construct a performance appraisal system. *Training and Development Journal,* 40 (4), 38–42.

Schneier, C.E., & Beatty, R.W., & Baird, L.S. (1986). Creating a performance management system. *Training and Development Journal,* 40 (5), 74–79.

Schneier, C.E., & Beatty, R.W., & Baird, L.S. (1987). *The Performance Management sourcebook.* Amherst, MA: Human Resource Development Press. Inc.

Trachtenberg, J.A. (1986). Shake, rattle and clonk. *Forbes,* 138 (1), 71–74.

Uttal, Bro (1987). Companies that serve you best. *Fortune,* 116 (13), 98–116.

34 RATER TRAINING FOR PERFORMANCE APPRAISAL

Elaine D. Pulakos

The most widely used instrument for obtaining performance measures is the rating scale, and many personnel decisions rely on supervisory ratings. For example, ratings are often the only criteria available for validating selection procedures, promoting employees, and selecting individuals for training programs. Given the central role that performance appraisals occupy in a variety of personnel decisions, it is important to strive for the highest-quality ratings possible.

A major problem with performance appraisals, however, is that they are often contaminated by various rating errors or effects that are faults in judgment that occur in a systematic manner when one individual evaluates another. Rating errors are problematic because they render performance appraisals of questionable reliability, accuracy, and, consequently, usefulness. The problems imposed by rating errors have led to the development of rater or observer training programs to improve the quality of performance evaluations. The majority of this chapter will be devoted to describing various types of rater training programs that have been developed. However, prior to discussing specific training techniques, some of the more common rating errors are reviewed.

COMMON RATING ERRORS

Halo Error

Perhaps the most pervasive error made in appraising performance is halo error. It occurs when a rater assigns ratings based on a global, overall impression of a ratee rather than distinguishing among levels of performance on different rating dimensions. An individual ratee is thus evaluated either high or low on several performance factors because the rater believes the individual is high or lot on some specific factor. For example, a supervisor may be rating a nurse on a number of, dimensions including ability to keep accurate records, ability to dispense medications properly, and ability to respond effectively to emergency situations. If the supervisor observed the nurse performing exceptionally in an emergency situation, he or she would be committing halo error if he or she similarly assumed that the nurse was also highly effective in keeping medical records and dispensing medications properly. The overall result of halo error is that ratings on different job performance dimensions tend to be at approximately the same level of effectiveness and consequently, fail to portray accurately an individual ratee's relative strengths and weaknesses in the different performance areas.

Leniency and Severity Errors

Leniency and severity errors occur when raters are inordinately easy or inordinately difficult evaluators of performance. The overall result of these errors is that ratees are given either relatively high ratings on all performance dimensions (leniency) or relatively low ratings on all dimensions (severity). There are numerous assumptions that raters may be operating under that lead to leniency or severity effects. For example, lenient ratings can result if raters believe that unfavorable ratings will reflect poorly on their own effectiveness as supervisors or if they fear that their relationships with subordinates will be jeopardized as a consequence of subordinates, learning about their lot performance ratings. Alternatively, some raters may believe that no individual performs at exceptional levels of effectiveness and may thus rate all subordinates too severely. The unfortunate consequence of leniency and severity errors is, again, that individual strengths and weaknesses are not accurately depicted, and much of the value of systematic performance appraisal is lost.

Central Tendency

Central tendency error occurs when raters assign all of their subordinates ratings that are neither too good nor too bad. In other words, raters avoid using the high and lot extremes of the rating scales and tend to cluster all of their ratings in the center of the scale.

Ratings plagued by central tendency error fail to discriminate among ratees who are performing effectively and those who are performing ineffectively. Consequently, the ratings become virtually useless as decision aids for selection, promotion, and training, as tell as for giving feedback to subordinates that will facilitate their performance improvement.

CHARACTERISTICS OF EFFECTIVE RATER TRAINING PROGRAMS

The remainder of this chapter will focus on different training approaches that have been developed to facilitate error-free and, importantly, accurate performance evaluations. First, the general characteristics of effective rater training programs will be described. This will be followed by a discussion of two general types of rater training programs: rater error training and rater accuracy training. Error training programs are concerned with teaching raters how to avoid one or more of the common ratings errors when they evaluate performance. Rater accuracy training, on the other hand, focuses on teaching raters particular rating skills that should enable them to make more accurate evaluations of ratee performance.

Rater training programs that apply the basic principles of learning arelikely to be more effective than training that does not incorporate these principles. In particular, successful rater training programs have been characterized by four key learning components:

1. Lecture. Trainees should receive instruction on such matters as basic rating concepts, how to use the rating scales, how to avoid rating errors, or any other content related to the desired training objectives.
2. Practice. Trainees should be provided with an opportunity to practice evaluating ratee performance. A popular mechanism for providing such practice i s to show trainees videotapes of ratees performing the target job or task. Then trainees are asked to evaluate the videotaped ratees on several job-relevant performance dimensions.

3. Group Discussion. Trainees should be given an opportunity to discuss and provide rationales for their practice ratings. Discussing personal examples of rating problems and generating solutions to these can also be incorporated into the group discussion component of training.
4. Feedback. Trainees should be given feedback on their practice ratings. Feedback should be given close as possible to the time the practice ratings are completed, with opportunities for more practice and feedback. The content of the feedback should be specific and reflect the desired objective of training.

In summary, rater training programs should be designed to teach basic rating concepts, elicit active trainee participation, and provide trainees with practice and feedback on their judgments. A training program consisting, for example, of lecture or group discussion alone will typically not be as effective as training that incorporates all four of the learning components discussed. In the absence of resources to conduct such training, however, research has suggested that some positive effects can be gleaned from less intensive rater training efforts. Thus, although lecture alone, for instance, is not the advocated or preferred approach to rater training, it is probably better at least to provide some instruction on how to make ratings than to provide no training whatsoever.

RATER TRAINING APPROACHES

Rater Error Training

Traditionally, rater training has focused on teaching raters hot to eliminate systematic rating errors such as halo, leniency-severity, and central tendency. This has generally been accomplished by providing definitions and examples of the various rating errors and then teaching trainees hot they can avoid these errors in their ratings. For example, to avoid halo error, trainees are taught *not* to rate individuals at the same level of effectiveness across multiple performance dimensions. Instead, they are instructed to spread out their effectiveness ratings (use different rating scale points) when they are evaluating a ratee on different performance dimensions. To avoid central tendency error, trainees are taught *not* to use only the middle points of the rating scale. In essence, then, error training focuses on "how to" and "how not to" rate performance in order to avoid the different rating errors.

Although various types of rater error training programs have been developed, the most consistently successful program to date is a workshop training approach developed by Latham, Wexley, and Pursell (1975). This workshop, which provides participants with an opportunity to practice observing and rating videotaped ratees, was shown to reduce sharply several rating errors. The components of the workshop are as follows:

1. A videotape of a job being performed is shown to trainees.

2. Trainees evaluate the target ratee on a set of rating scales.

3. Ratings made by trainees are placed on a flip-chart.

4. Differences in the ratings and reasons for these are discussed by the group.

5. The trainer provides the correct ratings that illustrate avoidance of the error(s) being studied and also points out why those ratings are correct.

6. The trainer discusses the specific error(s) being studied.

7. Trainees are asked to think of and relay actual examples of the error(s) as it has occurred in their own judgments or as they have observed it occur in others' judgments.

8. The group discusses ways of avoiding the error(s) being studied.

Although error training programs have been quite successful in reducing common rating errors, recent research has shown that these programs have not been particularly effective in increasing rating accuracy or validity, which is the crucial criterion in judging the quality of performance appraisals. Accuracy is the extent to which a rater's ratings reflect a ratee's true level of job performance.

A likely reason that error training approaches have not been successful for increasing accuracy is that they teach raters particular rating response sets (e.g., to avoid halo, raters are taught to spread out

their ratings across the different rating dimensions; to avoid central tendency, raters are taught to use all of the rating scale points, not just those in the middle of the scale). Unfortunately, response sets such as these may or may not reflect a particular ratee's actual performance. For example, a given ratee may actually perform at approximately the same level of effectiveness in several performance areas. Under such circumstances, training to avoid halo error would likely result in an inaccurate appraisal of the ratee's performance. This is because the trained rater's ratings would probably be more variable across the rating dimensions than the employee's actual job performance. Such problems with error training approaches led to the development of other training techniques that focus more directly on improving a rater's ability to evaluate performance accurately. These accuracy training approaches are described below.

Rater Accuracy Training

Rather than focus on the elimination of common rating errors, accuracy training approaches have focused on such things as improving raters' observational skills and teaching raters the proper use of the rating scales being used to evaluate performance.

Accuracy Training Based on the Rating Task Demands. Research has shown that no one rating scale type is appreciably superior to another in terms of yielding higher-quality ratings. However, different rating scale formats do place different demands on raters. For example, some rating scale formats require raters to make evaluative judgments of performance effectiveness, while others ask raters to record the frequency with which they have observed particular behaviors. Alternatively, some rating scales require raters to evaluate a ratee's job-relevant knowledge, skills, and abilities, while others involve assessing ratees on several behavioral performance dimensions.

Industrial psychologists (DiNisi, Cafferty & Meglino, 1984; Feldman,1986) have recently argued that the particular demands placed on raters by different rating tasks have important implications for how raters should be trained to perform those tasks. It has thus been suggested that the development of training to increase rating accuracy should start with the rating task itself. Training should then be specifically tailored to teaching raters how to make the particular types of judgments required by the given rating task.

As an example of the type of training outlined above, a program developed by Pulakos (1986) for increasing accuracy with Behaviorally Anchored Rating Scales (BARS; Smith & Kendall, 1963) will be discussed. BARS contain several performance dimensions, each anchored by scaled behavioral examples describing different effectiveness levels within the dimension.

The rater's task in using BARS is to select a level of effectiveness for each ratee on each rating dimension by matching actual observations of the ratee's job behavior to the most similar scaled behavioral anchor. In order to perform the BARS rating task accurately, raters need to have a thorough knowledge of the rating dimension content as tell as of the types of behavior that constitute the different effectiveness levels within each dimension. Accordingly, a rater accuracy training program was developed that focused on these objectives. The training content was as follows:

1. Trainees were first lectured on the multidimensionality of jobs and the need to pay close attention to ratee performance in terms of those job dimensions.

2. The actual BARS that would be used to evaluate performance were distributed to trainees.

3. One by one, the trainer reviewed each dimension definition along with the types of behaviors associated with each effectiveness level within the dimension. For example, the trainer discussed what types of behavior would be expected of a ratee who should be rated a 7 versus a 4 versus a 2.

4. A videotape of a trainee performing the target job was shown to the trainees.

5. Trainees evaluated the videotaped ratee using the BARS that were provided.

6. Trainees' ratings were placed on a flipchart.

7. Differences in the ratings and reasons for these were discussed among the group of trainees.

8. The trainer provided feedback to the trainees by telling them the correct rating for each dimension and by discussing how the ratee's behaviors should have been matched to the behavioral examples anchoring the different effectiveness levels on the rating scales.

9. Steps 4 through 8 were repeated, providing trainees with additional practice evaluating performance and receiving feedback on their accuracy.

Through providing an understanding of the rating dimensions themselves as well as the effectiveness of various behaviors that attend upon them, the accuracy training strategy described promoted accuracy by facilitating the match between observed behaviors

and levels of evaluation as depicted on the rating scales. In fact, this training was shown to be more effective for increasing rating accuracy than error training or no training (McIntyre, Smith & Hassett, 1984; Pulakos, 1984). However, this general approach to training was effective only it was used in conjunction with the rating format (BARS) for which it was developed (Pulakos, 1986). Use of this general training strategy with other rating scales had no effect whatsoever on accuracy.

Pulakos (1986) also developed an accuracy training program to be used in conjunction with Behavioral Observation Scales (BOS; Latham & Wexley, 1981), which take a different approach to making ratings than do BARS. Specifically, rather than requiring raters to select a level of effectiveness on several performance dimensions (as is the case with BARS), BOS present raters with a number of specific, observable behaviors and then ask raters to report the frequency with which they have observed each of these behaviors.

Given the particular demands placed on raters by the BOS, training that focused on matching observations of ratee behavior to effectiveness levels on various dimensions did not seem the optimal form of training to increase accuracy. Instead, it seemed that accuracy would be better facilitated by sharpening raters' observational skills and by ensuring that the target BOS behaviors were recognized quickly and recorded efficiently. Thus, a training program was developed that focused on these objectives (see Pulakos, 1986, for the details of training). This training, which included the four key learning components discussed earlier, was shown to be the most effective strategy for increasing accuracy with a BOS format. In summary, then, the training research discussed above shows that rating accuracy can be increased, provided that training is developed in accordance with the demands placed on raters by the particular rating format.

Other Forms of Accuracy Training. Unlike error training programs, which have been in existence for many years and researched extensively, rater accuracy training is only in its early stages of development. Thus, researchers are just beginning to explore which training approaches might be optimally effective for increasing performance rating accuracy. With this in mind, we will now turn to examining a few alternative approaches to rater accuracy training that hold promise as effective training techniques but have not yet received extensive research attention.

One accuracy training approach, proposed by Banks and Roberson (1985), is called assessment skills training. Banks and Roberson pointed out that raters must often know how behaviors indicative of performance are manifested in situations in which they do not have an opportunity to observe ratee performance directly. For example, a rater may be asked to evaluate a ratee's interpersonal skills with clients. However, the rater may not have actually observed managers interacting with clients, but only subordinates. Banks and Roberson thus proposed assessment skill training, which teaches raters how different performance dimensions might be manifested in numerous situations and how to identify common characteristics between situations in which performance-relevant behavior can be observed versus situations in which it cannot be observed.

Two other accuracy training approaches have been proposed by Hedge and Kavanagh (1988). The first, observational training, is concerned with training raters to recognize and avoid several systematic errors of observation, contamination from prior information, and overreliance on a single source of information. The second, decision training, focuses on the processes by which judgments are made rather than on observational strategies. Specifically, decision training involves introducing trainees to decision-making strategies as well as judgment errors that can occur when various inferential errors (e.g., insensitivity to biased data, inappropriate causal inference, inappropriate weighting of observed behaviors) are made.

The three training programs described in this section (assessment skills training, observational training, and decision-making Training) have a potential advantage over the accuracy training programs described earlier. That is, training focused on a particular set of rating scales (the BARS and BOS training) is concerned with teaching raters how to observe accurately and evaluate specific types of behaviors contained in the scales. Unfortunately, behaviors that comprise a given set of rating scales often do not match exactly with the behaviors exhibited by ratees. As such, training raters to use appropriate observation, decision making, and/or assessment strategies instead of (or possibly in addition to) training them how to use a particular set of rating scales accurately may be a more important determinant of rating accuracy.

ERROR TRAINING OR ACCURACY TRAINING?

Thus far, the focus of this chapter has been on describing the general characteristics and content of various error and accuracy training approaches. Now we will turn our attention to the advantages and disadvantages of each general type of training program.

A major advantage of training raters using an error training approach is that such programs are relatively easy to develop and administer. Further, because the elimination of rating errors is the focus of training, one generic training program can be used across multiple jobs, rating scale formats, and even organizations. In addition, error training programs are generally well received, and research has shown them to be fairly effective in decreasing rating errors.

The net effect of error training, however is that trainees are taught particular rating response sets that may or may not accurately reflect a ratee's true performance levels. Thus, rater error training might have the unintended consequence of yielding inaccurate ratings. One possible approach for preventing this problem might be to temper the error training such that trainees are encouraged to avoid rating errors only to the extent that doing so will not compromise accuracy. For example, in addition to training raters how to avoid various common rating errors, Pulakos and Borman (1986) encouraged trainees to "call the ratings the way they saw them." Thus, if a rater truly believed that a given subordinate was performing at approximately the same effectiveness level in several performance areas, then he or she was instructed to rate the individual accordingly.

Regarding accuracy training approaches, one obvious advantage is that the training is specifically focused on increasing accuracy, which is the crucial criterion in judging the quality of performance appraisals. However, a potential disadvantage is that accuracy training is often bound to a particular set of rating scales. Thus, if a given organization has fifty jobs with fifty different sets of rating scales, a slightly different accuracy training program would likely need to be developed for each. A second potential disadvantage has to do with the fact that accuracy training approaches are relatively new. Thus, research on their effectiveness is somewhat limited. On the positive side, however, research is continuing on various training methods, and in fact, several more generic accuracy training approaches (assessment skills training, decision making training) are in the process of being developed and evaluated. It is thus quite likely that improved approaches to rater accuracy training will be forthcoming in the near future.

THE WIDER CONTEXT OF PERFORMANCE APPRAISAL

The final issue that will be explored in this chapter is the circumstances under which rater training (error or accuracy) is likely to have the most profound effects. The major impetus for developing rater training was to improve the quality of performance appraisal ratings. This was deemed important because of the central role that performance appraisal s play in many personnel decisions. However, in all of the job-relevant assessment situations in which it is desirable to provide raters with training (e.g., employment interviewing, assessment centers), the situation in which training may well have the least potential impact is ongoing performance appraisal. This is because in ongoing performance appraisal situations, there are often extraneous factors that have a greater influence on ratings than a rater's sheer ability to evaluate performance accurately. Thus, although it may be possible to teach raters how to appraise performance accurately, various situational factors impede their ability and/or motivation to do so.

Some of the organizational factors that can have substantial effects on ratings include rater-ratee interpersonal relationships, the purpose of the appraisal (e.g., whether it will be used for personnel decisions, to validate a selection system, or simply to provide feedback for performance improvement), time constraints, the opportunities raters actually have to observe performance, political and union pressures on raters, and the extent to which raters are responsible for and/or made to justify their ratings. The main point is that performance appraisal does not occur in a vacuum; it occurs in the wider context of an organization. Thus, in order to reap the maximum benefits of training or a particularly well-developed set of scales, broader organizational issues must also be addressed since appraisal outcomes are likely to be a function of organizational contextual variables and rater motivation as well as a function of a rater's ability to rate accurately.

As examples of what might be done to deal with various organizational factors, the following ideas are offered. First, support from upper management and other relevant parties (e.g., unions) for the performance appraisal system and process is crucial for its effective implementation. Also, the purpose for which performance appraisals will be utilized as well as the consequences of ineffective ratings should be made clear to raters and ratees. In addition, it is important to identify raters who have adequate opportunities to observe ratee performance. Sufficient time for completing appraisals should also be given to raters—in other words, performance appraisal should be made a formal part of supervisors' jobs. As a final suggestion, to the extent that raters can be made accountable for providing fair, accurate ratings, performance appraisals are likely to be of higher quality. One possibility toward this end might be to make appraising subordinates' performance a formal rating dimension for any supervisory job in which incumbents are required to do this. Or alternatively, raters might be required to provide particular types of supporting materials, hence justification, for their ratings.

SUMMARY

This chapter has provided an overview of the characteristics of effective rater training programs as well as presenting several specific rater training techniques, along with some of their advantages and disadvantages. This has, by necessity, been only a brief introduction to the area of rater training. For more detailed descriptions of the specific training techniques and/or the research supporting them, the reader is referred to the References or may want to consult a researcher with more experience in the rater training area. Summarized below are the major points of this chapter:

1. Effective rater training programs have been shown to be characterized by four key learning components: (1) lecture (trainees should be instructed on the desired training content), (2) practice (trainees should be provided with an opportunity to practice evaluating ratees), (3) discussion (trainees should discuss and provide rationales for their practice ratings), and (4) feedback (trainees should receive feedback reflecting the desired training objectives.

2. Rater training programs focused on reducing common rating errors have been quite successful. To the extent that they teach raters response sets that do not match ratees' actual performance, error training might have the unintended consequence of leading to inaccurate ratings. However, given that appropriate precautions are included

in training, this potential problem can probably be minimized. Finally, error training programs are relatively easy to develop and administer, and they can also be used across a variety of jobs, rating scale formats, and even organizations.

3. Rater accuracy training programs have the advantage of being specifically focused on increasing accuracy, which is the crucial criterion in evaluating performance rating quality. At present, most approaches to accuracy training require that training be developed for particular sets of rating scales. Thus, these programs are not so versatile in the sense that they cannot be used across various jobs and rating formats. However, the devel-

opment and evaluation of accuracy training is only in its early stages, and it is quite possible that more efficient approaches to training will be forthcoming.

4. It is important to remember that performance appraisal does not occur in a vacuum. Thus, in order for training or any other performance appraisal intervention to be maximally beneficial, consideration must also be given to the broader organizational issues that have an impact on appraisals. That is, rater training might be thought of as a necessary but not sufficient condition for ensuring high quality performance evaluations in organizations.

REFERENCES

Banks, C.G., & Roberson, L. (1985). Performance appraisers as test developers. *Academy of Management Review, 10,* 128–142.

DiNisi, A.S., Cafferty, T.P., & Meglino, B.M. (1984). A cognitive view of the performance appraisal process: A model and research propositions. *Organizational Behavior and Human Performance, 33,* 360–369.

Feldman, J.M. (1986). Instrumentation and training for performance appraisal: A perceptual-cognitive viewpoint. In K.M. Rowland & J.R. Ferris (Eds.), *Research in personnel and human resource management* (vol 4) Greenwich, CT: JAI.

Hedge, J.W., & Kavanagh M.J. (1988). Improving the accuracy of performance evaluations: Comparison of three methods of performance appraiser training. *Journal of Applied Psychology, 73,* 68–73.

Latham, G.P., & Wexley, K.N. (1981). *Increasing productivity through performance appraisal.* Reading, MA: Addison-Wesley.

Latham, G.P., Wexley, K.N., & Pursell, E.D. (1975). Training managers to minimize rating errors in the observa-

tion of behavior. *Journal of Applied Psychology, 60,* 550–555.

McIntyre, R. M., Smith, D., & Hassett, C. (1984). Accuracy of performance ratings as affected by rater training and perceived purpose of rating. *Journal of Applied Psychology, 69,* 147–156.

Pulakos, E.D. (1984). A comparison of a rater training programs: Error training and accuracy training. *Journal of Applied Psychology, 69,* 581–588.

Pulakos, E.D. (1986). The development of training programs to increase accuracy with different rating tasks. *Organizational Behavior and Human Decision Processes, 38,* 76–91.

Pulakos, E.D., & Borman, W.C. (1985). *Development and field test of Army–wide rating scales and the rater orientation and training program* (ARI Technical Report 716). Alexandria, VA: U.S. Army Research Institute.

Smith, P., & Kendall, L.M. (1963). Retranslation of expectations: An approach to the construction of unambiguous anchors for rating scales. *Journal of Applied Psychology, 47,* 149–155.

35 TACIT KNOWLEDGE: ITS USES IN IDENTIFYING, ASSESSING, AND DEVELOPING MANAGERIAL TALENT

Richard K. Wagner, Robert J. Sternberg

Jim Hurley had been a standout all his life. He ranked third in his high school class in a large school in Cincinnati. His academic success continued during his undergraduate studies at Yale and through completion of his M.B.A. at Harvard.

When he joined the company five years ago, he was the golden-haired boy who had it all. He was highly motivated, often being one of the first to arrive in the morning and the last to leave at night. His oversized briefcase usually was filled with work to be done on weekends. Jim could be counted on to have read just about any book on how to manage and how to succeed in business. Describe to him a situation, and Jim could analyze it in terms of Theory Y, Theory Z, or Theory H (Hurley's theory about managing).

There was only one problem: for all of his promise and effort, Jim simply had not done all that well in his five years with the company. There were no glaring weaknesses, and to be sure, his performance was no worse than average, but it was far shy of what had been expected of Jim when he was hired.

Jim's story is a common one, judging from interviews we carried out with highly successful executives in a number of different industries. Our informants disagreed about many particulars, but what was notable was their agreement with two key points that may help to explain Jim's failure to meet what was expected of him.

First, IQ and scores from other ability and achievement tests make little difference to managerial success. Most of the executives knew colleagues who obviously had very high raw general intelligence but who were ineffective as executives; similarly, these executives knew of less "intelligent" colleagues who nonetheless were extraordinarily successful.

Our review of the research literature confirmed these views. IQ and performance on traditional employment tests are only weakly related to managerial performance (Ghiselli, 1966; Wigdor & Garner, 1982). Beyond a given level of intelligence—estimated to be in the range of 115 to 125—IQ makes no difference at all. Furthermore, an extraordinarily high IQ may even be a detriment to managerial success. Highly intelligent individuals may lack patience with their less able peers, subordinates, and even their superiors. They also may tend to rely too heavily on their considerable analytical powers, thereby neglecting important sources of information and advice around them.

The second key point of agreement was that formal training in business school, or comparable academic settings, also makes little difference to managerial success. Our informants indicated that such schooling could be useful up to a point but that much of the learning that really matters to managerial performance happens after completion of one's formal schooling. What counts, according to our informants, is the ability to acquire knowledge informally on a day-to-day basis in the absence of explicit instruction.

There are a number of common phrases that describe this kind of learning, including "learning the ropes," "getting one's feet wet," and understanding "what goes without saying." Experienced managers who are not skilled at this kind of learning are sometimes said to have had one year of experience ten times as opposed to ten years of experience.

We call what managers learn informally from their on-the-job experience *tacit knowledge,* which we define as work-related practical know-how that is acquired in the absence of direct instruction (Wagner

Preparation of this chapter was supported by contract MDA90385K0305 from the Army Research Institute. Helpful comments were provided by Kelly Hartley, Deborah Perkins, and Carol Rashotte.

& Sternberg, 1985). Because tacit knowledge is rarely articulated, we refer to it as an unspoken key to managerial success.

If we had stopped our investigation at this point, we would have done nothing but apply a fancy label (tacit knowledge) to a phenomenon that most managers already know exists (something that we academic psychologists are prone to do). What we have done over the past five years is to follow the lead given to us by our original informants with a series of empirical studies that addressed the nature of tacit knowledge and its acquisition and use by successful managers (Wagner & Sternberg, 1985, in press a).

Our purpose in writing this chapter is to discuss implications of our research for identifying, assessing, and developing managerial talent.

Our chapter is divided into three major parts. In the first part we describe our model of tacit knowledge and the research we have carried out that supports it. This part provides necessary background for the rest of the chapter. In the second part, we consider practical implications of our research for identifying and assessing managerial talent. In the third and final part, we consider practical implications of our research for developing managerial talent.

A MODEL OF TACIT KNOWLEDGE

We have identified a number of different kinds of tacit knowledge that we have found to be related to managerial performance. We have classified the different kinds of tacit knowledge according to (1) its content, that is, whether the knowledge is primarily about the management of oneself, the management of others, or the management of one's tasks; (2) its context, that is, whether the knowledge concerns short-term or long-term aspects of accomplishment; and (3) its orientation, that is, whether the knowledge concerns the ideal quality of work-related judgments and decisions, or their practicality. This tacit knowledge framework is presented in figure 35–1.

Content, Context, and Orientation

Three kinds of content. Tacit knowledge about *managing self* refers to knowledge about self-motivational and self-organizational aspects of managerial performance. An example of tacit knowledge about managing self is knowing how to deal with the problem of procrastination.

Tacit knowledge about *managing others* refers to knowledge about managing one's subordinates, peers, and superiors. An example of tacit knowledge about managing others is knowing how best to reward a given subordinate so as to maximize productivity as well as job satisfaction.

Tacit knowledge about *managing tasks* refers to knowledge about how to do specific managerial tasks well. An example of tacit knowledge about managing tasks is knowing how to get a point across when making a presentation.

Although there are situations that primarily involve only one of the three kinds of tacit knowledge

Figure 35–1. The Tacit Knowledge Framework

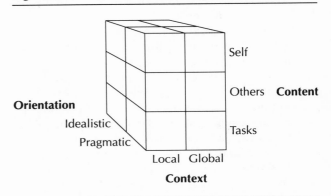

(the problem of procrastination, for example), many situations require each of the three kinds of tacit knowledge to lesser or greater degree. For example, chairing a group assigned to write a policy manual for awarding contracts to outside bidders is a task that requires considerable tacit knowledge about the management of self, others, and one's tasks.

Two contexts. A *local* context refers to a concern with short-term accomplishment. The focus is on the task at hand. A *global* context refers to a concern with long-term accomplishment. The focus is on how the situation fits into the bigger picture.

Successful managerial performance requires practical knowledge that can be applied in both local and global contexts. It is not enough to have global knowledge such as how to select tasks that will pay off in the longterm if one lack the local knowledge required to accomplish the tasks one has selected. Conversely, having local knowledge about how to do specific tasks well but lacking global knowledge about the long-term significance and the interrelations among one's tasks can result in doing well at what may turn out, in the long run, to be the wrong tasks or in missing a connection between a problem faced today and one faced last month, thereby missing an opportunity to discover their root cause.

Two orientations. One way to judge ideas and products is in terms of their *idealistic* or absolute quality, without regard to their practicality. A second way to judge ideas and products is in *pragmatic* terms, that is, in terms of how workable they are.

Of course, the best ideas or products are ones that are high on both ideal quality and practicality, but it makes sense to consider ideas and products from idealistic and pragmatic orientations separately. Consider the task of maintaining morale in the face of changes in policy that employees in your division of the company will find threatening. Writing a memo to employees in your division stating that you expect their morale to remain positive is a very practical idea but one that happens to be not very good ideally. Conversely, taking one's employees out to dinner individually for the purpose of convincing them that the policy changes will be to everyone's benefit in the long run may be a good idea in terms of ideal quality but a highly impractical one if there are a large number of employees in one's division. It would be a mistake to consider ideas and products only from a strictly pragmatic or a strictly idealistic orientation.

How Tacit Knowledge Is Acquired

Three cognitive processes are believed to be critical to the acquisition of tacit knowledge: selective encoding, selective combination, and selective comparison (Sternberg, 1985).

Selective Encoding. Selective encoding involves separating, in an array of inputs, information that is relevant for your purposes from information that is irrelevant for these purposes. The manager will inevitably be presented with an overload of stimulus inputs. He or she will have to filter this information, extracting what is needed and discarding what is not. It will simply not be possible to absorb everything in the voluminous reports one typically has to read or to remember everything said in the numerous meetings one attends. An effective manager has to use selective encoding to decide with what degree of care to attend to the various inputs that confront him or her.

Selective Combination. Selective combination involves putting together the information selectively encoded in just the way that is relevant for one's

purposes so as to form an integrated and coherent cognitive structure. The manager cannot stop with selective encoding. Having decided what information is relevant for his or her purposes, a decision must now be made as to how that information fits together. Usually, a given stream of information can fit together in many different ways, some of which may have drastically different implications from others. Many poor decisions are made not because tie wrong information is encoded but because it is put together in the wrong way. Selective combination is used by effective managers to piece together things in just the right way.

Selective Comparison. Selective comparison involves properly relating the new information and cognitive structure to old information and cognitive structures so as to integrate the new information fully with the old. Is is not enough to encode and combine new information. The information has to be fit into some preexisting set of procedures, values, needs, and so on. It would be impossible to determine the implications of new information for individual or organizational action unless there were some way of relating that new information to the needs that drove acquisition of the new information in the first place. An effective manager is able to bring the new information to bear upon his or her preexisting needs for that information.

Research Support for the Tacit Knowledge Framework

We have carried out three studies of managerial tacit knowledge. The results of these studies are reported in detail elsewhere (Wagner & Sternberg, 1985, in press a), so we will only summarize the results here.

We measured tacit knowledge with a paper-and-pencil test that presented individuals with descriptions of common work-related situations that required practical know-how. Respondents demonstrated their tacit knowledge by rating the quality of alternative responses to the situations. Performance was scored by comparing an individual's responses to those of an expert group of highly successful and experienced executives from around the country.

We administered our tacit knowledge measure to nationwide samples of managers and executives, totaling over one hundred individuals in all. We also gave our measure to M.B.A. students and to Yale undergraduates with no business experience. The purpose of including these samples was to compare the results of experienced managers to those with less or no management experience. There were five major results:

1. Individuals with more managerial experience have more tacit knowledge than individuals with less managerial experience. There are, however, some highly experienced managers who lack tacit knowledge, leading us to conclude that it is not experience per se that matters but one's ability to learn from it.

2. When one compares individuals who have equivalent amounts of managerial experience, those with more tacit knowledge also are higher performers than those with less tacit knowledge on a variety of criterion measures of managerial performance. In fact, tacit knowledge is a much better predictor of managerial performance than IQ or traditional employment tests typically are.

3. Tacit knowledge is unrelated to IQ, at least for groups of relatively high-scoring (IQs of 110 or over) individuals, as managers tend to be. Thus, our measure is not just an IQ test in disguise.

4. Individuals who are highly knowledgeable about one kind of tacit knowledge tend to be highly knowledgeable about the other kinds as well. Conversely, individuals who lack tacit knowledge about one kind of tacit knowledge tend to lack tacit knowledge about the other kinds as well.

5. With increasing levels of experience and accomplishment, there is closer correspondence between what one considers to be ideally good and what one considers to be practical. In other words, experienced managers value what works.

Having described our tacit knowledge framework and our research results, we are ready to consider their practical implications for identifying and assessing managerial talent and their practical implications for developing managerial talent in the final section of our chapter.

IDENTIFYING AND ASSESSING MANAGERIAL TALENT

There are a number of information sources available that are used in identifying and assessing managerial talent. We will briefly review the more common ones before considering how to use tacit knowledge to identify and assess managerial talent.

Methods of Identifying and Assessing Managerial Talent

Traditional Tests. Managers represent a highly selected sample of individuals in terms of performance on IQ and IQ-related employment tests. Even if such tests are not routinely used by a manager's employer, the tests will have served as gateways for admission to undergraduate school and to graduate programs. Contributing to this selection process is the fact that academic performance (e.g., grade point average, class rank), which is in part a reflection of the same abilities measured by the traditional tests, also is used in deciding whom to admit to college, to M.B.A. programs, and ultimately to the management track.

Advantages of using traditional tests for identifying and assessing managerial talent include that the tests are easy to administer, require relatively little time to take and to score, and have well-established psychometric properties. Additionally, the tests represent a common standard with which to evaluate individuals. A common standard is useful because it can be difficult to compare the academic performance or managerial performance of two individuals whose schools or jobs differ in important ways.

The major disadvantage of such tests is that they are not very predictive of managerial success. Part of the problem of poor predictability may be that the individuals to whom the tests are given already represent a highly selected sample in terms of the kind of abilities measured by the tests. But it is likely that another part of the problem is that the tests sample only a subset of the competencies required by managers.

Interviews. Structured interviews by skilled interviewers can be informative in identifying and assessing managerial talent. Because of their widespread use, there is a great wealth of data on the issue of the validity of interviews. The results have been only partially supportive of the validity of interviews, but some useful guidelines have emerged for minimizing the liabilities of this approach.

An advantage of the interview is the flexibility in subject matter that can be covered. Interviews can be tailored to questions of specific interest with relative ease. Another advantage of the interview is that, if nothing else, it does elicit a sample of the interviewees' interpersonal behaviors, albeit an admittedly brief and perhaps contrived one.

Disadvantages of the interview include difficulty in deciding what questions to ask and the standards for judging answers, concerns about reliability and bias, and the problem of faking good. A nontrivial determinant of how well individuals come across in interviews is their (probably tacit) knowledge about how to do well in interviews, as opposed to more basic aspects of their experience, knowledge, or character.

Simulations. One reaction to the limitations of traditional methods for identifying and assessing managerial talent has been the development of simulation exercises that require a candidate to engage in work-related behavior under as realistic conditions as can be created. A well-publicized example of this approach is the assessment center concept, a program of evaluation that includes one or more days of simulation exercises along with other more traditional assessment methods (Thorton & Byham, 1982).

An advantage of the simulation approach is that the tests are very similar to the criterion to be predicted—managerial performance. It usually is true that the more a test resembles a criterion, the more predictive the test will be. Another advantage of simulations is that they assess what an individual actually can do, as opposed to assessing only what an individual knows to do. Finally, simulations permit a degree of control that cannot be attained by merely observing individuals on the job.

There are a number of disadvantages associated with this approach. Simulations are costly, not only in terms of dollars but in time and in training requirements for examiners. It can be difficult to decide just what to simulate, and because the inefficiency of the approach allows one to simulate only a few situations, deciding what to simulate is a critical decision. It also can be difficult to decide on criteria to use in judging performance. Last, because examinees are aware that the simulation is a test that may affect their careers, simulations measure what individuals are capable of doing under test conditions, not necessarily what they actually will do when they are not being tested.

Performance Appraisal. In many ways, the best predictor of future success as a manager is an individual's record of past managerial performance, usually generated by a performance appraisal system. Performance appraisal systems vary considerably from one company to the next, and many are not at all informative about managerial competence. However, a well-designed performance appraisal system can be an invaluable tool for assessing managerial talent.

The major advantage of performance appraisal is that the test is identical to the criterion, thus maximizing the validity of the measure. As was the case for simulation, performance appraisal taps an individual's ability to do what he or she knows how to do.

But performance appraisal goes one step further by assessing what an individual does on a daily basis rather than just what is done under test conditions.

There are a number of important limitations of performance appraisal. First, it can be applied only to individuals who already hold management positions; thus it cannot be used with management recruits. Second, it can be difficult to compare individuals who have had different managerial positions. Different jobs present different opportunities as well as challenges. Third, performance appraisal is very difficult to do well, judging from the quality of extant performance appraisal systems.

Using Tacit Knowledge to Identify and Assess Managerial Talent

Perhaps the most obvious implication of our research for identifying and assessing managerial talent is that measures of tacit knowledge should be employed in addition to other assessment tools.

There are a number of possible approaches that might be used to assess an individual's tacit knowledge, ranging from relatively brief interviews to simulations of managerial performance lasting several days. Our approach to the assessment of tacit knowledge has been to use a paper-and-pencil test. We present descriptions of a number of common work-related managerial situations that require tacit knowledge. For some of the situations we use a rating format. We ask respondents to rate the quality of a variety of responses that we provide them. Our interest here is in measuring tacit knowledge that can be used to assess the quality of ideas put forth by others, such as by members of one's working group. For other situations we use a free-response format. We ask respondents to describe what they would do without providing them with any alternative responses, and, because we believe that with experience, one learns not only what to do but what not to do, we ask respondents to describe what an inexperienced manager might do mistakenly. Our interest here is in measuring tacit knowledge that can be used when one is required to generate one's own ideas. Successful managers are those individuals who can both come up with good ideas of their own and recognize the good ideas of others.

An example of the kind of work-related situation we present on our tacit knowledge test follows:

> You have been notified that because of a recently installed computer-based accounting system, employees in your department will be required to

begin filling out cumbersome weekly reports. Neither you nor your employees have had input into this decision, and you are sure that the weekly reports will be resisted by your employees.

You have called a meeting to inform the employees of the new procedures.

Recall that we present work-related situations such as these in two response formats. If presented in the free-response format, the respondent would be asked to describe how he or she would introduce the new procedure at the scheduled meeting, and then to describe common mistakes an inexperienced manager might make in such a meeting. An example of a good response might be to promise to make the concerns of your employees known to those responsible for the decision but only after they have made a good-faith effort by trying the new system for six weeks. An example of a mistake inexperienced managers could make is to agree with the employees that the new procedures are ridiculous but to say that their hands are tied because the decision was made from higher up. This strategy could have the short-term benefit of taking the heat off the manager in the meeting but may also have the long-term consequence of eroding the employees' positive regard for the company and their jobs.

If presented in the rating format, respondents would be asked to rate the quality of a number of strategies for handling the meeting, including the ones above.

Our particular test—the Tacit Knowledge Inventory for Managers (Wagner & Sternberg, in press b)—is undergoing final revision at the Center for Creative Leadership before publication, so we do not have final results to report. However, preliminary results are encouraging.

For example, we gave a preliminary version of our test to a group of bank branch managers for whom annual performance evaluations were available. The degree to which a test predicts a criterion variable is usually reported in terms of a correlation coefficient. Correlation coefficients are measured on a -1 to 1 scale. A correlation of 0 indicates no (linear) relationship between the test and the criterion variable. A correlation of 1 indicates a perfect relation

and a correlation of -1 a perfect inverse relation. The typical correlation found between IQ or traditional employment tests and criterion measures such as salary or performance ratings is .2, which indicates a small positive relationship between test performance and criterion performance. The correlation we obtained between scores on our tacit knowledge test and the criterion of percentage of merit salary increase was 48, and, of most interest to the bank, the correlation between tacit knowledge scores and amount of new business generated by a branch manager was .56.

Summary

We recommend including an assessment of tacit knowledge in procedures for identifying and assessing managerial talent. Tacit knowledge appears to be more strongly related to managerial performance than traditional tests. Moreover, because there appears to be little relation between tacit knowledge and performance on traditional tests, it is likely that using both a tacit knowledge measure and traditional methods will be more effective than using either alone.

One potentially valuable use of a tacit knowledge measure for identifying and assessing managerial talent, which arises from its relatively weak relations with IQ and performance on other traditional assessment procedures, is to identify managerial recruits from minority populations whose success in a managerial role may be underpredicted by their performance on traditional tests.

There is an important limitation of measures such as ours. We measure whether an individual knows what to do, not the ability or willingness to act on what he or she knows to do, especially back on the job where motivation to perform at maximum levels is likely to be less than under testing conditions. Because there are limitations associated with any one approach, we recommend using a tacit knowledge measure to supplement rather than to replace existing identification and assessment procedures.

DEVELOPING MANAGERIAL TALENT

Successful managers are those individuals who continue to improve their skills over the course of their careers. In this section we consider practical implications of our research for promoting managerial development.

Two approaches to training are suggested by our research. The focus of the first approach is on the *application* of one's existing tacit knowledge to managerial tasks. The focus of the second approach is on the *acquisition* of new tacit knowledge.

Developing Better Application of Tacit Knowledge

We have found that managers who are highly knowledgeable about one kind of tacit knowledge, say managing others, also tend on average to be relatively knowledgeable about managing themselves, their tasks, and the other kinds of tacit knowledge we described earlier. Furthermore, amount of tacit knowledge is related to criterion measures of managerial performance. However, there are a few individuals who appear to be knowledgeable about say managing their tasks but whose daily performance suggests a limitation is their knowledge about say, managing others. How do we explain this apparent paradox?

Consider the example of a mutual acquaintance of ours, a manager who has been passed over for promotion in his department. He appears to be highly knowledgeable about how to approach the tasks before him and to have considerable insight into himself and his colleagues. In our framework, we would describe him as having considerable tacit knowledge that can be applied to the local or short-term context. His problem appears to be that he lacks major accomplishment after a number of years at work. It appears as though he has spent quite a bit of time working on the wrong tasks, and his work on the right tasks has been fragmentary rather than cumulative. He is the kind of individual who is busy when you see him, yet when one steps back to look at the bigger picture, surprisingly little of value has been produced.

One might be tempted to describe this individual as someone who has local tacit knowledge but lacks global tacit knowledge about how to select and relate tasks on the basis of their long-term importance. But upon closer inspection, based on a number of conversations with the individual, it is obvious that he has at least some global tacit knowledge too. He is aware of his predicament, its causes, and what he should have done to avoid it. He even is able to state with some sophistication what he needs to accomplish in the very near future if there is any hope to salvage the situation. But chances are, consistent with his past performance, he will not do what he knows and, in all probability, is able to do.

Discrepancies between what one is able to do and what one actually does such as those exhibited by our acquaintance are common to many areas of human performance. In fact, it is so common that the term *competence-performance distinction* was coined to describe it.

There are two common reasons for doing less well than one is able to do. The first is motivational: individuals either do not value doing their best, or their real interests lie elsewhere. We suspect there is little that can be done in such a situation.

The second reason better describes our acquaintance and can potentially be remedied: individuals develop suboptimal styles of thinking and behaving that fail to capitalize on all of their tacit knowledge. Our acquaintance is the kind of individual who gets caught up with any task he finds in front of him. He does not take time to consider the long-range consequences of his task selection, even though he is capable of doing so.

Effective application of one's tacit knowledge is analogous to effective application of one's knowledge of the game of tennis during a match: both require practice to maintain high levels of proficiency.

How might we train managers so as to reduce discrepancies between what they know how to do and what they actually do? Based on our research, we recommend that managers learn to ask questions on a regular basis that promote effective application of their tacit knowledge. The regularity we recommend provides the practice required to become proficient at applying one's tacit knowledge and to maintain one's proficiency. One set of such questions, labeled as to the kind of tacit knowledge for which they are designed to promote application, follows. We assume that only a subset of these questions would be used at any one time.

Managing Self, Local Context

1. *Is it necessary or desirable that I become involved in this problem or task? If so, what manner of involvement is the most desirable?* One of the first questions a successful manager asks when confronting a task or problem is who really should be doing it. You should not only consider the issue of delegation but also the possibility that it would be to your benefit to handle a task or problem even though there is someone else who could do it. For example, as a special favor to a valued client or friend, you might elect to handle a situation personally that normally you would delegate to another.

2. *What priority should I give this problem or task in relation to my other immediate assignments and responsibilities, and how specifically will I (1) handle the problem or task in a way that reflects its priority and (2) monitor myself so that I continue giving the problem or task no more or no less of my*

time and effort than it deserves? How to set priorities has been dealt with by hundreds of popular books and articles, but coming up with a list of priorities is the easy part. The hard part is in using your list not simply for deciding what to do first but for making decisions about how, and how well, to handle your problems or tasks. Perhaps an even harder part is sticking to your priorities because it is very easy to end up spending more time and effort than you planned on trivially important problems.

Consider, for example, how to handle routine reports and memos. Provided they are accurate and the writing is adequately clear, it would be a mistake to spend the same amount of time revising and rewriting that would be appropriate, say, for an important presentation to be made to a group of one's superiors.

Yet it is easy to get carried away and, without thinking, get bogged down in such routine tasks.

3. *How can I combine this problem or task with another I am already dealing with to maximize my efficiency?* If the new problem or task can be handled by combining it with another problem or task you already are dealing with, the new item may require less effort. For example, suppose you are asked to provide suggestions for promoting better communication among divisions in your organization. Rather than deal with this task separately, it may be desirable to get it on the agenda of a group you are a member of that is made up of vice-presidents from each division and whose purpose is to chart the future direction of the organization.

Managing Self, Global Context

1. *What are the implications, if any, of my performance on this task for my long-term value to my part of the organization, to other parts of the organization, and to other organizations?* Some tasks and problems are of special importance in that they potentially can affect your value to the organization and to other organizations, whereas others are not. However, some tasks that are important to your part of the organization may not be considered important to other parts of your organization or to other organizations, and increases in responsibility and professional development may require moving to another division or another company. For example, obtaining further professional training may not pay off in your department, yet such training may dramatically increase your marketability in terms of offers from other divisions or other companies. On the other hand, spending a lot of time and effort to solve a troublesome personnel-related problem in one's department may not enhance your value outside your department yet may pay off in your department. Which you do should reflect the stage of your career you are in (e.g., beginning, middle, or end) and your ambitions.

2. *How can I structure my involvement in this situation so as to maximize my learning and development as a manager?* If approached in the correct way, many tasks and problems represent opportunities for growth. For example, you may elect to take responsibility for finding out about legal aspects of a new hiring policy not because you are knowledgeable in such matters but rather because you desire to become knowledgeable.

Managing Others, Local

1. *How shall I assign tasks and responsibilities so as to maximize accomplishment?* The productivity of a group of individuals is greatest when the assignments reflect the strengths, weaknesses, and interests of individual members of the group. For example, tasks that involve a high degree of accuracy and careful checking are best assigned to individuals who can tolerate such tasks.

2. *What are realistic expectations for each of the individuals I am working with on this task or problem, and how can I maximize the contribution that each individual will make?* Explicitly considering what you expect from others helps in planning for task completion and also provides a more salient baseline from which to evaluate others (see question 2 for Managing Others, Global Context). Also, there are differences in the optimal mix of praise, responsibility, and perhaps tangible rewards that work best for different individuals.

3. *Who is the target audience who will judge and perhaps use the outcome from my work on this task or problem, and how can I convince the target audience of the worth of the outcome from my work on this task or problem?* It helps to keep in mind who the audience is when working on a task or problem, especially because a common difficulty for many projects is that there are multiple, diverse audiences. For example, when writing reports for superiors, less experienced managers commonly assume mistakenly, that their report is as important to their superior as it is to them, and that their superior will spend almost as much time reading and studying it as it took them

to write it. In many cases, a superior is only interested in the gist of a report, and it should be written in such a way that the main message can be gotten quickly.

Also, it usually is not enough to do good work and to know who your audience is unless you also are able to convince them of the worth of your ideas or products. For example, when your plan for reorganizing a department is one of two plans being considered, there may not be objective grounds for choosing one plan over the other. Your ability to sell your plan can be as important as how sound the plan is.

Managing Others, Global

1. *How shall I assign tasks and responsibilities so as to maximize the long-term development of others working on this task or problem?* Assignment of tasks and responsibilities represents an opportunity to foster the professional development of others. For example, there may be little or no loss of efficiency in assigning an individual to handle the financial aspects of a report because he or she will learn something valuable by doing so, or you may decide that some loss of efficiency may be an acceptable trade-off for a gain in professional growth.

2. *Am I fostering the best balance between short-term and long-term productivity?* The pressures of the moment can result in "riding" others to an extent that working relationships are impaired and future cooperation from others nay be harder to obtain. On the other hand, it usually is important to complete the task at hand in as efficient a manner as is possible. Consideration of the trade-off between immediate and more distal productivity is necessary for a balanced approach.

Managing Tasks, Local

1. *Is there a problem or task to be done, and if so, what is its true nature?* Sometimes there is little doubt about whether there exists a problem or task to be accomplished, as when your immediate superior assigns you one. But sometimes there is doubt. For example, you may have noticed that your working group seems to be less effective in handling recent assignments. Are the recent assignments more difficult, or has a problem developed, and if so, what is it? Even when you are convinced that you have a problem, it is important to consider whether what you see as the problem may not be the real problem at all but merely a symptom of another more serious problem.

2. *Having identified the problem or task, how can I conceptualize it in the most manageable way?* There usually are multiple ways to formulate a given problem, some of which may render the problem soluble, others of which may render the problem insoluble. For example, an acquaintance of one of us related a serious work-related problem he solved only after reformulating his problem. Two years ago he ran afoul of his superior. He tried to patch things up but was unsuccessful, and their relationship worsened. His problem, as he conceptualized it then, was that he knew he should leave, but a move would present a real hardship to his family and they were against it. Try as he might, he could not solve his problem until he got the idea to give his superior's name to a friend in an executive placement service. A year later his superior left to take a better job (there is some question about whether that happened directly as a result of providing the superior's name to the placement service), but the important point is that what appeared to be an insoluble problem became a soluble one after reformulating the problem.

3. *What are reasonable expectations regarding a time line for my progress in this situation?* In addition to determining a deadline for completing a task or solving a problem, it can be helpful to establish a time line for completing parts of the task or problem. There now exist computer programs called project managers that can be used to devise time lines.

Managing Tasks, Global

1. *How is this task or problem related, if at all, to previous tasks and problems I have faced?* There are at least two reasons to consider this question. First, observing a relation between a previous problem and a present problem may result in discovering their underlying origin. For example, making the connection that none of the last three individuals who attempted to manage the quality control department could do the job can lead to the realization that the problem is not with the particular individuals but with the job or the department. A second reason to relate a present problem or task to other problems or tasks is that a good strategy for thinking about tasks and problems is by analogy to other ones.

2. What is called for: solving the root problem or a temporary fix? Problems have a way of coming back unless the root of the problem is taken care of. Consider the example of a subordinate who manages to ruffle the feathers of someone regularly. You might try simply "putting out the fires" as they occur by smoothing things out with those whom your subordinate has upset, but it probably is better to deal with the problem directly with your subordinate. On the other hand, sometimes it is better to be satisfied with a temporary solution. For example, if the individual described who managed to upset others regularly was a member of a temporary committee you headed rather than a permanent subordinate, it might be easier just to put out the occasional fire.

We do not wish to suggest that these questions all are novel ones or that managers never consider at least some of them occasionally. What we do suggest is that frequent consideration of questions associated with each of the kinds of tacit knowledge will reduce the discrepancy between what managers know to do and what they actually do.

We next consider another problem that prevents a substantial portion of managers from doing what they know to do that concerns idealistic and pragmatic viewpoints.

Balancing Idealistic and Pragmatic Orientations

Problems and tasks are not equally important. For example, it is not a good use of one's time to revise again and again routine reports and memos, provided they are clearly written in the first place.

This is not news to most managers, who can tell you which of their tasks are key and which are relatively trivial. Yet many managers routinely spend too much time and effort on their less important tasks.

One source of this inability to spend just as much time and effort on a task as it merits is an overly perfectionistic or idealistic orientation. Managers have been reinforced throughout their formal schooling for doing their best, and it has paid off for them. But once they face the managerial firing line, the strategy of always doing one's best can lead to failure and high stress.

An obvious and commonly recommended solution to this source of inefficiency is to train managers how to match their standards for performance to the importance of their tasks. We do not recommend such a training strategy, however, because in our experience, perfectionistic individuals are not easily able to lower their standard of performance. Their need to do the best possible job no matter what the task appears to be is deeply rooted in their personalities and values.

What we do recommend is training in time allocation. We encourage perfectionistic managers to continue to do their absolute best on each of their tasks but to limit the *total amount of time* they permit themselves to work at a task. Instead of asking managers to do less than their best—something that goes against their competitive nature—we ask them to strive for the best possible product or solution that they can complete by a specific deadline. Specifically, we recommend that managers decide how many minutes, hours, days, or months of their time a particular task is worth. Based on this information and when they intend to begin working at the task, a deadline can be established.

Individuals who begin to use this system often are amazed by how far off the mark they are in allocating time on the basis of task importance, which raises an important point. There is a need for flexibility in the system because it is easy to underestimate the amount of time a task will require, and thus it is easy to miss deadlines. When this happens, you simply continue on with the task until it is complete before beginning the next task. Even if you consistently miss your deadlines, you should find that your time allocation and your productivity will be better than if you had not set deadlines in accord with the importance of your tasks.

The strategies we have outlined deal with application of tacit knowledge a manager already possesses. We turn now to the issue of how to enhance the acquisition of new tacit knowledge.

Developing Better Acquisition of Tacit Knowledge

Our recommendations for improving the acquisition of tacit knowledge are tentative ones because we still are in the process of studying how tacit knowledge is acquired. However, we believe we have learned enough about its acquisition to begin to consider how to facilitate this process.

We make a distinction between direct and indirect methods of improving the acquisition of tacit knowledge, which we will consider separately.

Direct Methods for Increasing Tacit Knowledge. One method for attempting to increase tacit knowledge is through direct instruction, either formal or informal in nature. Formal tacit knowledge instruction entails instructional methods similar to those used in academic settings to convey academic knowledge. Informal tacit knowledge instruction is the kind of instruction a mentor provides when he or she tells you the inside story about how to get the cooperation you need from another department.

An advantage of direct instruction is that it is a relatively efficient way of acquiring needed tacit knowledge. When a manager is faced with a new problem, the best strategy often is to seek out someone who has faced that problem or a similar one in the past. It is much less efficient to rely on learning from one's own mistakes.

Unfortunately, there is an important limitation of direct instruction of tacit knowledge: the knowledge must be available and in a form suitable for direct instruction. Direct instruction of tacit knowledge requires having a knowledgeable individual available to learn from, something that will not always be the case, especially if the problem or situation is a novel one. Also, much tacit knowledge appears to be disorganized and informal, making it ill suited for direct instruction.

Another difficulty of direct instruction is that whereas there does appear to be general tacit knowledge that can be used in the management of oneself, others, and one's tasks, a nontrivial portion of tacit knowledge may be specific not only to one's company but to one's immediate coworkers and perhaps even to oneself as well.

Indirect Instruction. The goal of indirect methods of training is not to teach tacit knowledge directly but rather to train individuals in strategies they can use to accelerate their rate of acquisition of tacit knowledge.

This type of training avoids some of the limitations of the direct instruction approach. For example, acquisition strategies can be used by individuals to acquire tacit knowledge that is too specific to be suitable for direct instruction, and there need not be a knowledgeable individual available.

There are a number of acquisition strategies that could be trained. Consider a few examples:

1. *After completing an important task or problem, consider the question, "What, if anything, have I learned about my strengths, weaknesses, values and ambitions from my performance on this assignment?"* A review of one's performance can yield valuable insights about one's strengths, one's weaknesses, and what one values and desires. For example, the experience of having to work every weekend for the past month to meet a deadline may teach you that you

may not want to be on the "fast track" as much as you thought previously.

2. *After completing an important task or problem, consider the question, "What, if anything, have I learned about the strengths, weaknesses, values and ambitions of others (subordinates, peers, and superiors) I have worked with on this assignment?"* One of the best ways to learn about others is to observe them in action. We routinely form impressions based upon our observations of others, but by explicitly considering this question, one may reach more valid conclusions about others and be less likely to forget them.

3. *After completing an important task or problem, consider the question, "What, if anything, have I learned about this task or problem that will help me deal with similar tasks or problems in the future?* The focus of this question is what you have learned that will be helpful should you face identical or similar problems or tasks in the future. For example, having supervised a contractor's refurbishing of a wing of offices, you may have learned something about what to watch out for that will apply to other kinds of contractor's jobs you may be asked to supervise in the future.

4. *Ask individuals who have reputations for being highly skilled at managing themselves, others, or their tasks for their observations about how they do what they are good at.* It has been our experience that most individuals are flattered by such requests and are generous in providing helpful advice, especially to individuals who are new to the organization or at least are much less experienced than themselves.

5. *Consider who are the most valued members of your organization and why they are so highly valued and who are the least valued members of your organization and why they are not valued highly.* On the surface, organizations purport to value each of their members. However, on closer inspection, there will be large differences in the value of individuals to the organization, even for individuals at the same level of the organization's hierarchy. This information can be helpful in determining what really counts in the organization.

6. *Find out as much as you can about your value to your organization, and your value to other comparable organizations, by obtaining feedback from individuals whose opinions you value.* Whereas organizations routinely provide some feedback, typically it is rudimentary. One often can obtain much more valuable feedback simply by asking others to provide it.

CONCLUSIONS

A key that differentiates highly successful from less successful managers is their ability to acquire tacit knowledge—the practical know-how that must be learned informally if it is to be learned at all. The ability to acquire tacit knowledge does not appear to be closely related to either IQ or performance on traditional employment tests, at least for individuals who perform as well on these tests as managers generally do.

Perhaps the most important practical recommendation we make concerning the identification and assessment of managerial talent is to consider an individual's level of tacit knowledge along with his or her other attributes. Individual differences in tacit knowledge can be measured reliably and validly. For example, performance on a preliminary version of our Tacit Knowledge Inventory for Managers is more highly predictive of managerial performance than performance on IQ or employment tests usually is.

The practical recommendations we make regarding the development of managerial talent are twofold. First, we think it is important to train individuals how to apply what tacit knowledge they have, thereby lessening the gap between what they know to do and what they actually do. Second, we think it is important to train individuals in strategies for increasing the rate of their acquisition of tacit knowledge. We are exploring both methods of training tacit knowledge.

We do not mean to suggest that tacit knowledge is in any way a panacea for identifying, assessing, and developing managerial talent. We suspect that much of what makes for highly successful management will always remain a mystery. Nevertheless, our research suggests that it is time to apply in a more formal way an observation that managers have informally acted on in the past: namely, that it is important to consider practical know-how in deciding who should manage and how their managerial talent might fully be developed.

REFERENCES

Ghiselli, E. (1966). *The validity of occupational aptitude tests.* New York: Wiley.

Sternberg, R.J. (1985). *Beyond IQ: A triarchic theory of human intelligence.* New York: Cambridge University Press.

Thorton, G.C., & Byham, W.C. (1982). *Assessment centers and managerial performance.* New York: Academic Press.

Wagner, R.K., & Sternberg, R.J. (in press a). Tacit knowledge and intelligence in the everyday world. In R. Sternberg & R. Wagner (Eds.), *Practical intelligence: Nature and origins of competence in the everyday world.* New York: Cambridge University Press.

Wagner, R.K., & Sternberg, R.J. (in press b). *The tacit knowledge inventory for managers.* San Antonio: Psychological Corporation.

Wagner, R.K., & Sternberg, R.J. (1985). Practical intelligence in real-world pursuits: The role of tacit knowledge. *Journal of Personality and Social Psychology, 49,* 436–458.

Wigdor, A.K., & Garner, W.R. (Eds). (1982). *Ability testing: Uses, consequences, and controversies.* Washington, DC: National Academy Press.

36 IDENTIFYING HIGH-POTENTIAL EXECUTIVE AND PROFESSIONAL PERSONNEL THROUGH PSYCHOLOGICAL ASSESSMENT

Melany E. Baehr

The study of Individual differences has been a dominant theme in psychological research. In the Industrial-organizational context, the application of this research has often been directed toward the measurement of the individual's potential for successful performance in any given position. The ultimate objective is appropriate placement of personnel in the organization, followed by the development of high-potential employees and their orderly deployment through the organizational structure. The expected outcome is the full utilization and adjustment of the individual and the strengthening of the organization. Today, many resource executives see systematic resource assessment and planning and its incorpora-tion in the broader, strategic plans of the organization as vital to determining whether the organization gains the competitive edge (Panel Discussion, 1985)

While industrial-organizational psychologists are in general agreement on the objectives to be achieved through assessment, there is much less unanimity of opinion on the means for achieving them. The major issues surroundlng the measurement of higher-level potential are the particular abilities, skills, or attributes (traits) that should be measured, the method that would most effectively measure them, and, in organizational settings, the legal defensibility and the time and cost-effectiveness of the procedure.

HUMAN ABILITIES AND BEHAVIOR ATTRIBUTES

A brief description is given below of the history of the measurement of cognitive abilities and behavior attributes. This is followed by a more detailed description of a particular system for testing and evaluation of potential of professionals and executives, which has been developed for large-scale application in organizations. Finally, a description of the identified characteristics of high-potential executives and nonmanagement professional specialists is presented.

Cognitive Measures

The first research on cognitive measures (as opposed to measures of sensory and motor skills) in describing differences in human behavior is generally attributed to Alfred Binet in his study of the learning problems of French school children (Binet, 1903). The first Binet test was published in 1905. The translated and greatly revised American version, developed by Lewis Terman of Stanford University, was published in 1915, with revisions in 1937 and 1950. All of the Binet tests involve tasks or items of increasing difficulty, and, while there are differences in the way they are calculated, all of the Binet tests produce a single score. As a result of studies of the Binet test, researchers typically conclude that Binet regarded the single score merely as an average of a number of different abilities (Dunnette, 1975). Spearman (1927) first formulated the theory of a single general factor of Intelligence.

Thurstone (1938, 1947) pioneered multiple factor analysis and identified a number of specific primary mental abilities, which have survived pretty much unchanged to the present day. Thurstone also defined the correlational relationship between tests that would produce a general factor, as defined by Spearman, in either a first-order (analysis of correlations between test scores) or second-order (analysis of correlations between correlated primary abilities) analysis.

Definitions of specific mental abilities proliferated in the many years of research undertaken by Guilford (1959, 1957), some of which, such as the concept of divergent thinking, have survived and been unique contributions to theories of intelligence. Later thinking and research, as exemplified by Ekstrom (1973), has analyzed, refined, and tended to reduce the number of specific mental abilities deemed worthy of further study.

One of the more valuable recently developed research techniques, metaanalysis and validity generalization, introduced by John E. Hunter and Frank L. Schmidt, has been applied predominantly to cognitive measures and has been associated with a return to an emphasis on a single general factor of cognitive ability as the most effective predictor of performance (Hunter, 1986; Schmidt, 1988). This view has been contested by other investigators (Goldsteln & Patterson, 1986; Seymour, 1986).

In a recent research study involving higher-level personnel, Baehr and Orban (in press) have shown that measures of cognitive ability and personality each contribute variance over and above that which is explained by the other in the prediction of performance, as measured by earnings, and that the best prediction is obtained by a combination of cognitive ability and personality measures.

Background Data

Personal background data, in a variety of forms, have been used for over three decades in the selection process and for the prediction of a large spectrum of behavior, including work performance. Its widespread and continuing use probably owes much to the belief first suggested by Galton(1902) at the turn of the century and later expressly stated by Owens that"what a man *will do* in the future is best predicted from what he *has done* in the past" (Owens, 1976, p. 612). This measurement axiom is supported by extensive validity evidence listed in Owens's (1976) comprehensive review of the development and application of biographical data.

The most usual form in which biodata have been used is in personal interviews, application blanks, and personal history questionnaires. The history of their usage in the industrial context has been largely one of increasing standardization and objectivity of the procedures to produce data that lends themselves to conventional psychometric evaluations. As early as the 1930s Hovland and Wonderlic (1939) developed a standardized interviewer's guide containing questions of work, social and personal history, and reported validities for a tenure dismissal criterion.

After the standardization of questions on the application form, the next logical development was to test the predictive efficiency of the individual questions or groups of items. Later, item scores from the application form were weighted through the application of psychometric procedures such as multiple regression against the performance criterion (Manson, 1925; England, 1961).

The items in standardized biographical questionnaires occur in a number of formats, the most usual of which are a dichotomous or yes-no response, multiple choice, or, for the attitudinal items, a scaled response. One approach to the validation of these items was to validate each item separately with respect to some criterion, such as performance, and to use the high-validity items to produce either an unweighted or weighted sum as an overall score on the questionnaire. This approach produces high primary (initial) validity but suffers from two serious defects: significant shrinkage in cross-validation (Scollay, 1957; Berkely, 1953) and "dust bowl" empiricism, which precludes psychological interpretation of results (Dunnette, 1962). The grouping of biodata items by psychometric clustering or by factorial procedures, which produces interpretable dimensions with high reliability, is now widespread and regarded as a more desirable approach to validation (Frye, 1967).

The use of background data for prediction in organizational settings has become a sensitive and legal issue in connection with the successive federal guidelines that prohibit discrimination against minority and other protected groups. Contrary to expectations, however, there has been empirical evidence that background data have less discriminatory impact against minority groups than conventional cognitive tests (Sparks, 1965; Baehr, Furcon & Froemel, 1968). Baehr and Froemel (1980) have recently published a unisex background inventory, which is the one used in the statistical analyses described later.

Personality Measures

While there is overlap, personality measures may be roughly divided into those used predominantly in clinical practice (e.g., projective tests) and those used to assess the relatively permanent behavior tendencies and traits that span the normal range of behavior. Some of the more structured clinical tests, such as the well-known *Minnesota Multiphasic Personality Inventory* (Hathaway & McKinley, 1943), have been used quite extensively in industrial settings and often show validity for selection into stressful occupations (Hargrave, 1985). A more recently developed test of emotional stability and health will be discussed later.

Measures of temperament traits and personality in the normal range of behavior have had mixed results as predictors in occupational environments. Early reviews (Ghiselli & Barthol, 1953; Guion & Gottier, 1965) have indicated that personality measures are not particularly useful as predictors of job performance. Indeed, personality measures as predictors were so out of favor that an attempt to update the Guion and Gottier review of personality test validation for selection was abandoned because of the low level of reported use of those measures during the mid-1960s.

It seems highly likely that a major cause of the poor performance of personality measures was inadequately developed tests of constructs, which are more complex than the mental ability dimensions. The construction of most of the tests reviewed probably preceded the computerization of item and multivariate analysis procedures. Refinements in test construction may be responsible for what Guion (1987) sees as some changing views of the role of personality assessment in the employment process. Guion cites successful efforts in the recent quarter century to measure work-oriented personality characteristics in assessment centers. Among these, he mentions Gough's (1985) measure of "work orientation" and a measure of "service orientation" reported by Hogan, Hogan, and Busch (1984).

As in the case of the use of background data, the more recently developed tests tend to use factorially developed dimensions of personality as a basis for measurement. A good example of this approach is described in the *Handbook for the Sixteen Personality Factor Questionnaire—16PF* (Cattell, Eber & Tatsuoka, 1970) with measurement dimensions based on first— and second-order analyses of source traits of temperament. An illustration of one method of using specific tests of mental ability and aptitude and factorially determined dimensions of background data and personality is given below. The assessment system that incorporates these different types of tests, questionnaires, and inventories is used to predict higher-level performance in the work settings.

THE SYSTEM FOR TESTING AND EVALUATION OF POTENTIAL (STEP)

The STEP program has been successfully used by a wide variety of organizations (Baehr, 1984). It is based on two interlocking measurement systems: one for measuring the demands of the job and the other for measuring the abilities, skills, and attributes of individuals. Dunnette (1976) has emphasized the importance of establishing the link between categories of human work performance and categories of human attributes as an important research objective. In a similar vein, Eberhardt and Muchinsky (1982) and Neiner and Owens (1985) have attempted to relate human characteristics measured on the dimensions of Owen's *Biographical Questionnaire* (BQ) to Holland's model of vocational typology (Holland, 1966). In addition, job requirements established through use of the *Position Analysis Questionnaire* (PAQ) (McCormick, Jeanneret and Mecham, 1959) have been related to scores on the nine aptitude tests of the *General Aptitude Test Battery (GATB)* (Dvorak, 1956) in a study by Mecham and McCormick (1969). In later studies, the *PAQ* job dimension requirements were related to commercially used tests (McCormick, DeNisi & Shaw, 1979).

The relationships among the measures of work performance and human ability used in the STEP program have been extensively studied as one approach to the validity of the system (Baehr, In press). On the basis of these relationships, "potential" has been defined as the empirically derived estimate of the degree of fit between the requirements of the functions to be performed in the position and the abilities, skills, and attributes that the individual has at his or her command for high-level performance on the job. It follows that one cannot speak of high-potential individuals in a vacuum. Potential is specific to a particular position and level of organizational functioning. An individual may have different potential for different positions or for the same type of position at different levels of organizational functioning.

THE STEP MEASUREMENT SYSTEMS

Before implementing a system like the STEP, the demands of the job are measured through the use of a standardized and quantified job analysis instrument like the *Managerial and Professional Job Functions Inventory (MP-JFI)* (Baehr, Lonergan, & Hunt, 1978). For example, for any given position, the *MP-JFI* provides a profile of the relative importance for overall successful performance of sixteen factorially determined job functions. The technical details of its construction, the definition of its dimensions, and their reliabilities are given in the *MP-JFI Interpretation and Research Manual* (Baehr, 1988).

A managerial and professional test battery was constructed, specifically for the higher-level employees, that could accurately and consistently predict the various job functions assessed by the MP-JFI (Baehr, 1987). The test battery consisted of eleven pencil-and-paper tests, 75 percent of which were self-report questionnaires. The details of the construction of each test and the reliability and validity of the measurement dimensions are given in the test's *Interpretation and Research Manual.* References for the tests and their accompanying *Manuals,* together with definitions of the most predictive measurement dimensions that each test provides, are given below. The following tests and assessment instruments are accurate predictors of higher-level potential.

Definitions of the Most Predictive STEP Dimensions

1. Experience and background

   Experience and Background Inventory (Baehr & Froemel, 1980)

   School Achievement: Adjustment and achievement in school and other academic environments.

   Drive: Drive for upward movement within the organization or through changes of organizations.

   Leadership and Group Participation: Active participation and demonstration of leadership skills in social, work, or professional organizations.

   Professional Work/Vocational Satisfaction: Satisfaction with a vocation that is consistent with professional or technical training and past experience.

   Financial Responsibility: Good management of personal finances—the ability to earn, save, and invest.

   General Family Responsibility: Family-oriented life-style with successful assumption of financial and family responsibility.

   Job and Personal Stability: Established stability indicated by long-term employment and relative permanency in personal residence.

   Active Relaxation Pursuits: History of enjoyment of physical activity and active sports.

2. Cognitive measures

   Nonverbal Reasoning (Corsini, 1957) Capacity for deductive and analytical reasoning measured nonverbally.

   Word Fluency (Human Resources Center, 1961) Facility and fluency in extemporaneous speaking.

   Bruce Vocabulary Inventory (Bruce, 1974) Breadth of English Vocabulary.

   Closure Flexibility (Thurstone & Jeffrey, 1984) Ability to hold a visual configuration (or concept) in mind despite distractions.

3. Special aptitude

   Cree Questionnaire (Thurstone & Mellinger, 1957) Overall creative potential as reflected by the extent to which the individual's behavior resembles that of identified creative individuals.

   Sales Potential Attitudes endorsed by successful sales professionals.

4. Personality attributes

   Press Test (Baehr & Corsini, 1957)

   Reaction Time to Verbal Stimuli: Reaction time to verbal stimuli under normal conditions.

   Reaction Time to Color Stimuli: Reaction time to color stimuli under normal conditions.

   Ability to Work under Pressure: Reaction time to color stimuli under the pressure of distracting stimuli.

   Temperament Comparator (Baehr, 1957)

   Extroversion: Demonstrative, expressive, and sometimes impulsive behavior.

   Emotional Responsiveness: Emotionally responsive and enthusiastic behavior.

   Self-Reliance: individually goal-oriented and self-confident behavior.

   Socially Orientated: A liking for company, social ease, and self-confidence.

Personal Insight: Demonstrated consistency in self-ratings of behavior.

5. Emotional health and stability

EMO Questionnaire (Baehr & Baehr, 1958)

KI-Internal Adjustment: Freedom from generalized, unfocused tension and over preoccupation with self.

KE-External Adjustment: Seif-acceptance and the objective interpretation of the motives and behavior of others.

KS-Somatic Adjustment: Feelings of well-being and absence of physical complaints.

KG-General Adjustment: General buoyancy and healthy feelings of pleasure concerning everyday experiences.

Level of Response: The number of acknowledged emotional responses to items which represent stressful experiences.

The ability of the different types of predictors and of the STEP battery as a whole to predict performance was investigated over a fifteen-year span through a series of traditional performance criterion validations based on multiple regression analysis (Baehr, 1984) and, more recently (Baehr, 1987), through more generalized approaches to validation. The STEP battery exhibits useful levels of validity, and is presently based on a national norm group of more than 5,000 higher-level employees (e.g., managers, executives, sales and technical professionals).

CHARACTERISTICS OF EXECUTIVES AND NONMANAGEMENT PROFESSIONAL PERSONNEL

In order to Identify the psychological profiles of different types of higher-level employees, the total norm group of employees was classified by level of organization functioning and occupational speciality (hierarchy). This resuited in the 4 x 3 matrix described in table 36–1.

A detailed analysis of the significant differences among STEP test scores at the three levels in each of the hierarchies was undertaken by Baehr (in press) to identify the particular abilities, skills, and attributes characteristic of executive and nonmanagement professional personnel. The major trends from this analysis are reported below. A more technical and statistical interpretation of these trends is reported

elsewhere (Baehr, 1987). Parenthetically, the scores of all test dimensions are given on a normalized standard score scale of 0 to 100 with a mean of 50 and a standard deviation of 10.

Experience and Background

A common pattern in all hierarchies is significantly increasing scores on the Drive, Financial Responsibility, General Family Responsibility, and Job and Personal Stability test dimensions, with executives being the highest-scoring groups. The general picture for top executives is of individuals who successfully

Table 36–1
Managerial Hierarchies

Occupational Level	Line	Professional	Sales	Technical
I	Executives Vice-presidents General managers	Executives Vice-presidents General managers	Executives Vice-presidents General managers	Executives Vice-presidents General managers
II	Middle managers of line personnel	Middle managers of professional personnel	Middle managers of sales personnel	Middle managers of technical specialist personnel
III	Supervisors (1st and 2nd line)	Nonmanagement professionals (engineers, scientists, lawyers, architects)	Sales representatives (professional sales of products or services)	Technical specialists (actuaries, accountants, analysts, programmers)

assume personal family responsibility at an early age, are the principal providers for the family, handle their personal finances effectively, and move steadily up their hierarchical ladder, with or without moves to other organizations. The significant differences on the Job and Personal Stability dimension are largely an artifact of higher age and tenure in the Level 1 group (refer to figure 36–1). Hence, age norms are available for the interpretation of the experience and background scores.

The items that define the Drive dimension come closest to what McClelland (1961) has defined as the "power drive." The rewards sought by high scorers on this dimensions are power and tangible benefits. While all executives enjoy these rewards of high-level management positions, they differ markedly in the degree of intrinsic satisfaction obtained from doing a good job. This is apparent from their scores on the Professional Work and Vocational Satisfaction test dimension. In contrast to the high-scoring employees in the Professional and Technical hierarchies, no occupational group at any level in the Line and Sales hierarchies has scores that exceed the midpoint (50) on this dimension, with sales personnel generally being the lowest-scoring groups.

Sales personnel at all levels have the highest scores (at least a half standard deviation above the mean) for Active Relaxation Pursuits. It has been hypothesized that sales personnel enjoy social interactions and possibly the competitive aspects of sporting activities. It may be that success and achievement in athletic arenas is a compensation for lack of intrinsic job satisfaction, or it may be a means of draining off the tensions caused by an admittedly stressful occupation.

Cognitive Measures

The managerial and professional test battery contains four tests of specific mental abilities. An average mental ability score is also calculated for each individual, which is the closest approximation to a single measure of general intelligence or IQ in the test battery.

There are significantly rising levels of scores on the two tests of language facility in all hierarchies, with executives being the highest– scoring groups. The next highest score for executives is reasoning ability measured nonverbally, and their lowest score is on a test of visual perceptual skills. The last measures the ability to identify and maintain a complex diagramatic representation or concept that is embedded in a larger, distracting visual field. These results indicate that, for an executive with a good level of general reasoning ability, the essential characteristic

for success is language facility, covering both succinctness and ease of extemporaneous speech, and breadth of vocabulary, which facilitates precision and subtlety in written or spoken language. A generally similar pattern is evident in the Sales hierarchy.

By contrast, an obverse pattern of abilities is evident for Professional and Technical Specialist personnel. These groups have only moderate language facility, with a greater emphasis on breadth of vocabulary than verbal fluency. Their intellectual strengths are deductive and analytical reasoning and the visual perceptual skills. In fact, the last test provides the only instance in which the Level III groups significantly outscore their respective executive groups.

The average mental ability scores for the twelve occupational groups cluster fairly closely around 55 on the 0 to 100 scale and thus, would, not have been predictive for these personnel. However, the averaging has merely disguised the important differences on the specific skills. One of the lowest average mental ability scores (which is still 50 and at the mean of the higher-level population) is obtained by the group of sales representatives. It has been suggested that, given a reasonable level of general mental functioning, the behavior characteristics carry more weight than the cognitive abilities for success in selling.

Special Aptitudes

The two special aptitudes assessed in the battery are sales potential, which has reference only to the Sales hierarchy, and creative potential, which has reference to all the hierarchies. The measure of creativity is obtained from a behavior questionnaire that yields scores on thirteen factorially determined behavioral dimensions and an overall score based on all the items in the questionnaire. The latter represents the extent to which the individual's responses to the behavior items in the questionnaire are similar to those of an identified group of creative individuals.

There are significant increases in the overall scores of creativity across the three levels in all hierarchies, with executives being the highest-scoring groups. This indicates that the potential for creative and innovative behavior is a requirement for successful performance in all top management positions. However, it is of differential importance in the hierarchies. For example, in the Sales hierarchy creative potential is a characteristic at all levels, since the scores for all three groups fall above the mean.

By contrast, in the Technical hierarchy only the executive group falls above the mean. This is not surprising when one considers that the type of creativity measured here is characterized by subliminal reasoning and intuitive leaps to a solution rather than by the application of deductive reasoning and systematic analysis in problem solution. Following this reasoning, it is not surprising, either, that highly qualified hard science professionals also score below the mean for creativity, since their discipline is geared toward accurate measurement, systematic experimentation, and replication of results.

Contrary to widely held opinion, therefore, creative potential is not a uniformly desirable or necessary characteristic for success in all occupations and can, indeed, even be a hindrance. The underlying dimensions of the creative personality portray an individual who is socially dominant and indifferent to mores of group behavior, demands autonomy in the work environment and dislikes close supervision, dislikes repetitive work that requires accuracy and concentration, has a fast reaction time, and is capable of sustained and intense effort when interest is aroused but is otherwise a sporadic worker. Parenthetically, it is of interest to note that given a certain level of intelligence, there is no linear relationship between facility in intuitive thinking, which is represented by the creativity score, and the mental abilities.

Personality Characteristics

The *Temperament Comparator* provides measures on eighteen personality traits, which, in turn, contribute to five factorially determined behavioral dimensions. The behavioral dimensions behave differentially for the occupational groups. The Line and Professional hierarchies show rising levels of extroversive and emotionally responsive behavior. In the Sales hierarchy, these two behavior characteristics are common to the occupational groups at all three levels, since they all score well above the mean. By contrast, the occupational groups in the Technical hierarchy shot much more cautious, considered, and emotionally controlled behavior, especially at Level III. Indeed, except for the Sales hierarchy, all Level III groups score lowest in the Extroversion and Emotional Responsiveness factors. Unlike most other areas of the test battery, such as mental abilities, where a higher score is always a better score, a low score may be a desirable score in the behavioral area. The indications are that cautious and controlled behavior, which represents, respectively, the opposite ends of the Extroversion and Emotional Responsiveness continua, is desirable behavior in controlling and regulatory positions such as line supervisor, and in nonmanagement professional and technical positions that require methodical work and exacting attention to detail.

One characteristic common to all hierarchies is significantly rising levels of self-reliance with executives being the highest-scoring groups. The traits that contribute to this behavioral dimension indicate that successful executives are confident about their abilities, individualistic and not dependent on group support, decisive, and, when necessary, capable of making decisions based on incomplete information.

Another general requirement for all executives is a fast reaction time and an ability to maintain productivity under pressure. The Press Test (Baehr & Corsini, 1957) is used to assess this trait. Fast reaction time is particularly important in the Professional hierarchy, where all occupational groups score well above the mean.

Personal Emotional Adjustment

The final area in the test battery deals with emotional health status. Executives seem to have a greater tolerance for stress. This interpretation is in accordance with the results obtained from the objective test of pressure tolerance.

Although some Individuals scored poorly on the measure of emotional health, the occupational group means in all hierarchies exceed the screening standard on the four key adjustment factors. The only exception is the group of sales executives, which is borderline on the External Adjustment factor. This factor measures freedom from distorted perceptions of the external world and from tendencies to rationalize, to project, and to withdraw from difficult situations. It should be noted that executives in the Sales hierarchy seem to feel the effects of stress more than their counterparts in other hierarchies since they are the lowest-scoring executive group on three of the four adjustment factors.

The emotional health scores are important predictors of occupational success in stressful occupations (Baehr, 1976; Baehr, Penny & Foremel, 1980; Frost & Joy, 1987). In the industrial context, emotional health scores make an important contribution when gauging promotability. Increased pressure and stress is the inevitable accompaniment to a move to a position of greater responsibility, especially when relocation is involved. If the individual is generally subject to undesirably high levels of stress, the achievement of an efficient level of operation in the new position will be more difficult and take more time.

ESTIMATING POTENTIAL FOR SUCCESSFUL PERFORMANCE

Regardless of any other information one may have about the individual (e.g., academic qualifications, related work experience, performance in the present position), the critical information sought in making most human resource decisions is an overall estimate of potential for successful performance in the present and in possible future positions the individual may hold. In an attempt to derive such an estimate, the information from a number of approaches to the validation of the test battery scores, including regression analyses and the results of the analyses of variance described here, was combined, analyzed, and reanalyzed to identify those test dimensions that were most often predictive of successful performance. In order to avoid the pitfalls of mindless empiricism, the selected test dimensions had also to be interpretable and logical in the light of management and leadership theory. While the derivation of a potential score may sound complicated, it is a fairly straightforward procedure. For example, the overall requirements of an executive in the Line hierarchy are as described below.

In the area of experience and background, there should be high scores on the Drive, Financial Responsibility, and General Family Responsibility test dimensions. As discussed earlier in the background data section, a hypothesized explanation of the high validity of these scores is that individuals who have assumed responsibility and have been successful in one environment are more likely to be successful in another environment.

In the area of specific mental abilities and aptitudes, the individual should have an above-average score on deductive and analytical reasoning and high scores for word fluency and vocabulary. In other words, given an acceptable level of general mental functioning, the emphasis is on the ability to communicate. These intellectual assets should be reinforced by a high level of potential for intuitive thinking and creative and innovative behavior.

In the behavioral area, the individual should have at least a passing level of consistency of response in self-ratings of behavior (cf. Kipper & Baehr, 1988). This ensures that the responses are not merely random ratings which would produce meaningless behavior dimension scores. Given acceptable quality of response, the requirements are a moderate degree of extroversive and emotionally responsive behavior combined with a high degree of self-reliance. These characteristics, in combination with high creativity and an ability to work tell under pressure, describe the stereotypic entrepreneurial personality.

Finally, in the area of emotional adjustment, the individual should first pass on the built-in lie scale, which is designed to measure conscious or unconscious tendencies to repress, deceive, or otherwise fail to acknowledge the effects of stressful experiences. Thereafter, the individual should reach a minimum standard in the four key adjustment factors because, in contrast to the popular conception of executives who have made it to the top of the ladder at the expense of stomach ulcers and other symptoms of prolonged stress and pressure, successful executives maintain a good emotional health status. They are relatively free from undue feelings of insufficiency and anxiety, are realistic in the perception of themselves in relation to the external world, and maintain a buoyant attitude toward life.

Once the essential characteristics have been identified, the relevant estimate of Potential for Successful Performance (PSP) used in the STEP program is the weighted sum of the individual's scores on the relevant test dimensions. Parenthetically, since the scores for all occupational groups are obtained from the same test battery, a single administration of the battery will provide the individual's PSPs for the present position and for the vertically and horizontally linked positions in the organizational structure. A sample test report of a high-potential executive in the Line hierarchy is presented in figure 36–1.

It should be noted that the PSPs are based on mental abilities, aptitudes, and relatively permanent behavior characteristics, which are established by the time the individual is an adult. The PSPs are therefore, not affected by age or previous work experience. For full utilization in human resource decision making, the PSPs should be used in combination with other relevant information of past history or experience. One application of the *Managerial and Professional Job Functions Inventory* (Baehr, Lonergan & Hunt, 1978) is to provide standardized and quantified assessments of the level of acquired skill in the important functions to be performed in the position.

The widespread acceptance of the applications of traditional psychological research in American institutions has been a powerful factor in establishing modern Industrial-organizational psychology. Applications directed toward the development of the individual and the strengthening of the organization have utilized various combinations of measures of human abilities and attributes. The particular system described here uses a combination of factorially developed dimensions of background data, intellectual skills, personality attributes, and dimensions of

Figure 36–1. Sample Report for a High-Potential Executive in the Line Hierarchy

STEP PROGRAM INTERPRETATION
CONFIDENTIAL REPORT

The information in this report is confidential and must not be made known to anyone other than qualified individuals employed by this employer, unless released by the express written permission of the candidate. STEP scores should be considered in the context of the candidate's total job qualifications.

This report presents the evaluation of Potential in the
LINE HIERARCHY

John Henry
June 13, 1989
Battery No. 008900

SUMMARY OF RESULTS
POTENTIAL ESTIMATES

Level	Score	Percent	Potential
Executive	57	76%	Very Desirable
Middle Mgr.	54	66%	Desirable
Supervisor	51	54%	Good

INTERPRETATION

Score Range	Percentile Range (exceeds)	Qualitative Description
39 or less	14% or less	Questionable
40 — 43	16% — 24%	Marginal
44 — 47	27% — 38%	Fair
48 — 52	42% — 58%	Good
53 — 56	62% — 73%	Desirable
57 — 60	76% — 84%	Very Desirable
61 or more	86% or more	Outstanding

Test Date: 06/13/89
Name: John Henry

Step Predictor Profile in the Line Hierarchy

Battery #: 00890000

	SS		CS	
	Scale	25 30 35 40 45 50 55 60 65 70 75	Exceeds	
Background *1. Drive/Career Progress* Intrinsic satisfaction with the job itself.	60	ccccccccccccccccccccccccccccccccccc LM E	84%	Drive for upward movement in the organization.
2. Leadership Little or no interest in establishing interpersonal contacts through group activities or society memberships.	58	ccccccccccccccccccccccccccccccccc L M E	79%	Active participation and possible leadership in personal contact situations in work and/ or social environments.
3. Financial Responsibility Unsystematic management of personal finances.	61	ccccccccccccccccccccccccccccccccccccc L M E	86%	Good financial management — the ability to earn, save, and invest.
4. General Family Responsibility Has assumed no or little personal family responsibility.	57	ccccccccccccccccccccccccccccccccc L M E	76%	Family-oriented life-style with successful assumption of financial and family responsibility.
Mental Abilities *5. Non Verbal Reasoning* Little facility for deductive and analytical reasoning measured by solutions to pictoral problems.	53	ccccccccccccccccccccccccccccc L M E	62%	Good capacity for deductive and analytical reasoning measured nonverbally.

continued on next page

Figure 36–1 *continued*

	Score	Profile	%	Description
6. Word Fluency Preference for prepared presentations or scripts.	60	`cccccccccccccccccccccccccccccccccc` L M E	84%	Facility and fluency in extemporaneous speaking.
7. Vocabulary Narrow range of English vocabulary.	58	`cccccccccccccccccccccccccccccccc` L ME	79%	Breadth of English vocabulary.
Aptitudes *8. Creative Potential* Systematic and analytic approach to problems solving.	55	`cccccccccccccccccccccccccccccc` L M E	69%	Intuitive thinking and potential for creative behavior.
Temperament *9. Personal Insight* Inconsistency in self-ratings of behavior.	55	`cccccccccccccccccccccccccccccc` L M E	69%	Demonstrated consistency in self-ratings of behavior.
10. Extroversion Serious, persevering and consistent behavior.	53	`cccccccccccccccccccccccccccc` L ME	62%	Demonstrative, expressive and sometimes impulsive behavior.
11. Emotional Responsiveness Even-tempered, relaxed, undemonstrative behavior.	55	`cccccccccccccccccccccccccccccc` L M E	69%	Emotionally responsive and enthusiastic behavior.
12. Self-Reliance Group-oriented behavior with emphasis on teamwork and group support.	60	`cccccccccccccccccccccccccccccccccc` L ME	84%	Individually goal-oriented and self-confident behavior.
13. Ability to Work Under Pressure Deterioration of productivity under pressure.	60	`cccccccccccccccccccccccccccccccccc` L M E	84%	Ability to maintain or even increase productivity under pressure.
Emotional Adjustment *14. Level of Stress Response* Undesirably high level of stressful experiences.	54	`ccccccccccccccccccccccccccccc` L M E	66%	Relatively low level of stressful experiences.
15. Internal Adjustment Feelings of personal inadequacy accompanied by internal tensions and fear and anxiety.	47	`ccccccccccccccccccccccc` ME L	38%	Freedom from generalized, unfocused tensions and self-doubts.
16. External Adjustment Distorted interpretations of the motives and behavior of others.	45	`cccccccccccccccccccccc` L EM	31%	Objective interpretation of the motives and behavior of others.
17. General Adjustment Apathy and general lack of enjoyment concerning everyday experiences.	43	`ccccccccccccccccccccc` E M L	24%	General buoyancy and healthy feelings of pleasure concerning everyday experiences.

1% 2% 7% 16% 31% 50% 69% 84% 93% 98% 99%

C – Candidate's score

E – Executive
M – Middle Manager
L – Line Supervisor

* – Significant difference

emotional health. Whatever system is used, it should be shown to be valid, either through validations specifically implemented for key positions in the organization or through the use of professionally accepted job analysis procedures to demonstrate the transportability of validation results obtained for organization-specific or national samples of employees.

REFERENCES

Baehr, G.O., & Baehr, M.E. (1978). *EMO Questionnaire.* Park Ridge, IL: London House, Inc.

Baehr, M.E. (1961). *The Temperament Comparator.* Park Ridge, IL: London House, Inc.

Baehr, M.E. (1976). *National validation of a selection test battery for male transit bus operators.* (Report No. UMTA-MA-06-0011-77-1.) Springfield, VA: National Technical Information Service.

Baehr, M.E. (1984). *The development and validation of the estimates of potential for successful performance (PSP) of higher-level personnel.* Chicago: University of Chicago, Office of Continuing Education.

Baehr, M. (1987. A review of employee evaluation procedures and a description of "high potential" executives and professionals.*Journal of Business and Psychology, 1,* 172–202.

Baehr, M.E. (1988). *Managerial and Professional Job Functions Inventory: Interpretation and research manual.* Park Ridge, IL: London House, Inc.

Baehr, M.E. (In press). *A human resource management system for testing and the evaluation of potential: The STEP program.* Park Ridge, IL: London House, Inc.

Baehr, M.E.,& Corsini, R.J. (1965). *The Press Test.* Park Ridge, IL: London House, Inc.

Baehr, M.E., & Froemel, E.C. (1980). *Experience and Background Inventory.* Park Ridge, IL: London House, Inc.

Baehr, M.E., Furcon, J.E., & Froemel, E.C. (1968). *Psychological assessment of patrolman qualifications in relation to field performance.* Washington, DC: U.S. Government Printing Office.

Baehr, M.E., Lonergan, W.G., & Hunt, B. A. (1978). *Managerial and Professional Job Functions Inventory.* Rark Ridge, IL: London House, Inc.

Baehr, M.E., & Orban, J.A. (In press). The role of intellectual abilities and personality characteristics in determining success in higher-level positions. *Journal of Vocational Behavior.*

Baehr, M.E., Penny III, R.E., & Froemel, E.C. (1980). *A validation and analysis of selection procedures for male and female bus operators* (Report No. UMTA-MA-06-0011-77-1). Springfield, Va: National Technical Information Service.

Berkley, M.H. (1953). A comparison between empirical and rational approaches for keying a heterogeneous test. *USAF Human Resources* Research Center Bulletin, 53–54.

Binet, A. (1903). *Experimental studies in intelligence.* Paris: Schleicher.

Bruce, M.M. (1974). *Bruce Vocabulary Inventory.* New Rochelle, NY: Author.

Cattell, R.B., Eber, H.W., & Tatsuoka, M.M. (1970). *Handbook for the Sixteen Personality Factor Questionnaire (16 PF).* Champaign, IL: Institute for Personality and Ability Testing, Inc.

Corsini, R.J. (1985). *Non-Verbal Reasoning.* Park Ridge, IL: London House, Inc.

Dunnette, M.D. (1975) Aptitudes abilities and skills. In M.D. Dunnette (Ed.), *Handbook of Industrial-organizational psychology.* Chicago: Rand McNally.

Dunnette, M.D. (1962). Personnel management. *Annual Review of Psychology, 13,* 285–314.

Dvorak, B.J. (1956). The general aptitude test battery. *Personnel and Guidance Journal, 35,* 145–154.

Eberhardt, B.J., & Muchinsky, P.M. (19B2). Biodata determinants of vocational typology: An integration of two paradigms. *Journal of Applied Psychology, 56,* 714–727.

Ekstrom, R.B. (1973). *Cognitive factors: Some recent literature.* (Technical Report No. 2). Princeton, NJ: Educational Testing Service.

England, G.W. (1961). *Development and use of weighted application blanks.* Dubuque, IA: William C. Brown

Frost, A.G., & Joy, D.S. (1987). *The use of the Personnel Selection Inventory and the EMO Questionnaire in the selection of child care workers.* (Technical Report No. 52). Park Ridge, IL: London House, Inc.

Frye, R. (1967). *Analysis of patterns of life history antecedents of executives from different countries.* Greensboro, NC: Creativity Research Institute, Richardson Foundation.

Galton, F. (1902). *Life history album* (2d ed.). New York: Macmillan.

Ghiselli, E.E., & Barthol, R.P. (1953). The validity of personality inventories in the selection of employees. *Journal of Applied Psychology, 38,* 18–20.

Goldstein, B.L., & Patterson, P.O. (1986). Can we count on muddling through the *g* crisis in employment? *Journal of Vocational Behavior, 33* 452–456.

Gough, H.G. (1985). A work orientation scale for the California Psychological Inventory. *Journal of Applied Psychology,70,* 505-513.

Guilford, J.P. (1967). *The nature of human intelligence,* New York: McGraw-Hill.

Guilford, J.P. (1959). *Personality.* New York: McGraw-Hill.Guion, R.M. (1987). Changing views for personnel selection research. *Personnel Psychology, 40,* 199–213.

Guion, R.M., & Gottier, R.F. (1965). Validity of personality measures in personnel selection. *Personnel Psychology, 18*, 135–164.

Hargrave, G.E. (1985). Using the MMPI and CPI to screen law enforcement applicants: A study of reliability and validity of clinicians' decisions. *Journal of Police Science and Administration, 13*, 221–223.

Hathaway, S.R., & McKinley, J.C. (1943). *Minnesota Multiphasic Personality Inventory*. New York: Psychological Corporation.

Hogan J., Hogan, R., & Busch, C.M. (1984). How to measure service orientation. *Journal of Applied Psychology, 59*, 167–173.

Holland, J.L. (1966). *The psychology of vocational choice*. Waltham, MA: Blaisdell.

Hovland, C.I., & Wonderlic, E.F. (1939). Prediction of industrial success from standardized interviews. *Journal of Applied Psychology, 23*, 537–546.

Human Resources Center, University of Chicago (1961). *Word fluency*. Park Ridge, IL: London House, Inc.

Hunter, J.E. (1986). Cognitive ability, cognitive aptitude, job knowledge, and job performance. *Journal of Vocational Behavior, 29*, 340–362.

Kipper, D.A., & Baehr, M.E. (1988). Consistency as a moderating factor in self and observational assessments of personality. *Perceptual and Motor Skills, 66*, 559–568.

McClelland, D.C. (1961). *The achieving society*. New York: Van Nostrand Reinhold.

NcCormick, E.J., DeNisi, A.S., & Shaw, J.B. (1979). Use of the Position Analysis Questionnaire for establishing the job component validity of tests. *Journal of Applied Psychology, 64*, 51–56.

McCormick, E.J., Jeanneret, P.R., & Mecham R.C. (1969). *Position Analysis Questionnaire*. West Lafayette, IN: Purdue University.

Manson, G.E. (1925). What can the application blank tell? *Journal of Personnel Research, 4*, 73–99.

Mecham, R.C., & McCormick, E.J. (1969). *The use of data based on the Position Analysis Questionnaire in developing synthetically derived attribute requirements of jobs*. Lafayette, IN: Purdue University, Occupational Research Center.

Neiner, A.G., & Owens, W.A. (1985). Using biodata to predict job choice among college graduates. *Journal of Applied Psychology, 70,* 127–136.

Owens, W.A. (1976). Background data. In M.D. Dunnette (Ed.), *Handbook of Industrial-organizational psychology*. Chicago: Rand McNally.

Panel discussion on the changing role of the human resources executive (1985). *Personnel*, pp. 22-28.

Schmidt, F.L. (1988). The problem of group differences in ability test scores in employment selection. *Journal of Vocational Behavior, 33*, 272–292.

Scollay, R.W. (1957). Personal history data as a predictor of success. *Personal Psychology, 10, 23–26.*

Seymour, R.T. (1986). Why plaintiffs' counsel challenge tests, and how they can successfully challenge the theory of "validity generalization." *Journal of Vocational Behavior, 33*, 331–364.

Sparks, C.P. (1965). *Prediction of cognitive test scores by life history items: Comparison across two different ethnic groups*. Houston: Author.

Spearman, C. (1927). *The abilities of man*. New York: Macmillan.

Thurstone, L.L. (1938). *Primary mental abilities* (Psychometric Monograph No. 1). Chicago: University of Chicago Press.

Thurstone, L.L. (1947). *Multiple factor analysis*. Chicago: University of Chicago Press.

Thurstone, L.L., & Jeffrey, T.E. (1984). *Closure Flexibility (Concealed Figures)*. Park Ridge, IL: London House, Inc.

Thurstone, T.G., & Mellinger, J.J. (1986). *Cree Questionnaire*. Park Ridge, IL: London House, Inc.

37 CORPORATE WAGE AND BENEFIT POLICY: EMPLOYEE BEHAVIOR AND PRODUCTIVITY

William A. Schiemann

The compensation field has never been more controversial and lively than today. Consultants, managers, and students of compensation are rapidly digesting recent tax legislation, trying to project family trends, debating about changes in values, and questioning U.S. corporations' approach to managing such policies in the light of declining U.S. productivity. Furthermore, compensation policies can have a profound and often dramatic impact on individual attitudes and behaviors and, as a consequence, on corporate productivity and profitability. This chapter will:

1. Examine the impact of compensation policy on employee attitudes and behaviors, such as turnover, absenteeism, work performance, and decision to join an organization.

2. Identify factors that have reduced the effectiveness of many compensation plans.

3. Present a model that explains how compensation plans affect employee behaviors and organizational productivity.

4. Offer specific steps for evaluating and improving the effectiveness of benefit and compensation systems.

5. Discuss future trends in compensation.

In many ways, compensation policies, as major components of the organizational reward system, create,

define, and reflect an organizational culture. (In this chapter, compensation will refer to both wages and fringe benefits.) They communicate and reinforce what is valued in the organization (what will be rewarded), who shares in organizational wealth (financial success or failure), and how employees' needs will be met both now and in the future. Employees place great value on their pay and benefits (Lawler, 1971; Schiemann, 1983); thus, these tools can be powerful motivators, *if used effectively*.

Because of its important role, the compensation system should be a leading function in developing a culture that is aligned with strategic direction. And yet, in far too many organizations, the compensation system is incongruent with corporate goals and strategy and inconsistent in practice. Many plans have been too completely shaped by legislation and tax codes; they are overly complex, poorly understood, and therefore only partially effective in achieving major organizational objectives.

Much of this stems from a failure to realign corporate compensation objectives with corporate strategy periodically. New rules and procedures, amended policies, and a plethora of exceptions often exacerbate a once purposeful system. The sad truth, unfortunately, is that these overgrown, often inappropriate systems have a large effect on corporate profitability through work force productivity.

A TIME FOR CHANGE

In order to understand the dramatic changes that are taking place and the impact these changes have on productivity and profitability, it is important to understand the factors that affect employees' attitudes and behaviors. Figure 37–1 displays a model showing the forces that affect compensation and benefit design, and the subsequent impact on employee

and employer goals. The remainder of this chapter will discuss the relationships depicted in figure 37–1, followed by specific steps for evaluating an existing plan, and recommendations for compensation policy in the future. First, it is useful to examine the ultimate objectives of the organization (beginning with the right side of figure 37–1).

Figure 37–1. Compensation and Benefits Model

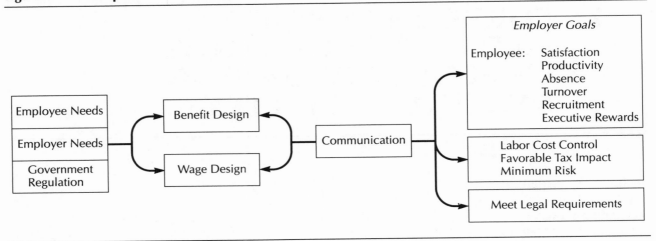

EMPLOYER COMPENSATION GOALS

Employers obviously have myriad goals that vary from one organization to another. However, there are a number of common goals that transcend most organizational boundaries: profitability (except in non-profit organizations), longevity, growth, and mission. For most organizations, this implies an effective use of labor. The cost of labor continues to be a major variable in the overall expense equation of most firms. The major labor costs come from direct and indirect forms of compensation, usually wages and fringe benefits. Moreover, there are other costs that must be considered as well: recruitment, selection, training, occupancy, and separation costs, for example.

To maximize organizational goal attainment and productivity, it is crucial for employers to evaluate carefully both labor costs and output in all forms. That is, most employers wish to increase output (individual performance levels; quality of products and services) more rapidly than they increase their costs to deliver the output. This implies the use of compensation and benefit policies that improve output yields while controlling costs.

Practically, this means increasing employee motivation, attitudes, and performance at costs that are less than the gains from increasing labor output. For example, if increases in compensation reduce unwanted employee turnover at a cost that is less than the labor replacement cost, then the investment might prove valuable.

Another example might be in recruitment. If a certain employer sponsors a child care program as part of the fringe benefit package, then presumably some employees would be more likely to work for this organization instead of its competitors (which do not have this benefit). If this benefit were to reduce recruitment costs (by increasing recruitment rates), increase employee commitment, and reduce turnover, the program might improve overall productivity. In this case, if the increased costs of sponsoring a child care program are surpassed by the savings in greater tenure, lower recruiting expense, and so forth, then the employer would improve the bottom line, other things being equal.

COMPENSATION PRACTICES AND EMPLOYEE BEHAVIORS

The human resource objectives that are often discussed as desired outcomes of compensation policy are strong attendance, longer tenure, higher commitment and performance, and improved recruitment and selection success.

Attendance

There have been few studies demonstrating any strong relationship between absence and fringe benefits. Numerous writers have postulated that child care programs or wellness programs should reduce employee absenteeism (Hernandez, 1986; Levine, 1984), but the number of studies is few, and the evidence is mixed at best (Friedman, 1986; Miller, 1984).

However, it is clear that certain pay policies have a positive impact on attendance (Allen, 1981; Chelius, 1981). Piece rate payments, for example, have the effect of increasing employee attendance, and organizations that pay above the scale tend to have lower absenteeism. Also, positive incentive systems that reinforce attendance have been shown to reduce absenteeism (Schmitz and Heneman, 1980; Chelius, 1981).

Employee Turnover

A number of studies have documented the positive impact of wages and benefits on employee voluntary turnover (Merrilees, 1981; Bartel, 1982; Mitchell, 1982). For example, Merrilees found that firms with a 10 percent higher compensation package have work forces with greater tenure (one year greater). Moreover, Merrilees and others have concluded that certain fringe benefits—most notably pensions—are the major contributors to greater employee tenure.

Both Bartel (1982) and Mitchell (1982) found that fringe benefits have a stronger effect on turnover than wages. A 10 percent increase in fringes was shown by Bartel to decrease turnover by approximately 10 percent. Mitchell found that the existence of a pension plan reduced the probability of turnover by as much as 20 percent. Other fringes, with the exception of stock plans and health coverage, showed only small effects on turnover.

Recruitment

There have been a number of studies describing the importance of compensation in recruiting new employees (e.g., Sutton, 1986). In general, most organizations keep an eye on what competitors are offering in an effort to keep pace. For most employers, there are particular job groups that are more difficult to recruit (e.g., technical specialists). Higher wages also enable an employer to be more selective in hiring.

With respect to fringes, it is unclear how much impact they have on recruiting and hiring success. The extent to which they are different or substantially more attractive than those offered by competitors may have a modest effect. Moreover, certain types of benefits may be more likely than others to have an impact. For example, an in-house child care program

may be quite attractive to potential employees who are parents in a difficult-to-recruit profession. Unusually rich time-off benefits may bring a similar response. On the other hand, pension benefits may be of marginal value to a job applicant who is forty years from retirement.

Another factor that must be weighed is the likelihood of attracting less desirable employees with rich benefits. For example, a liberal time-off or sick leave policy may invite those expecting to make heavy use of such benefits.

Individual Performance

There has been little demonstrated relationship between fringes and individual job performance. This is not surprising in that most fringes are not contingent on performance. The most notable exceptions to this are profit sharing and performance-based stock options (bonus pay is considered under wages). In most cases, profit sharing is based on profit center or total corporate profitability. The connection between this type of profitability and individual performance is usually so remote for most employees (except senior executives or principals) that it has little direct impact on individual motivation (Schroeder et al., 1987) unless strongly accompanied by a major communication effort and frequent payouts. The same holds for stock payouts based on similar criteria.

Bonus and financial incentive programs have become very popular tools to motivate certain employees (O'Dell and McAdams, 1987). A recent Conference Board study indicated that 92 percent of manufacturing companies in the United States have annual incentive plans for their managers (Tharp, 1985). The size of the incentive varied among organizations, ranging from an average of 57 percent for chief executive officers to 20–25 percent for lower managers.

Bonuses are typically paid out based on some criteria of success or goal attainment. However, corporate profitability often increases or reduces the pool of funds available for distribution. Incentives of various types (e.g., cash, prizes, awards) are usually paid out on some preestablished formula. Most frequently used for managers, sales, and certain professionals, there are myriad research and case studies documenting increases in individual performance, attendance, profitability, and other positive behaviors associated with incentives (Dierks & McNally, 1987; Ellig, 1982; Freedman, 1985; Lawler, 1983; Locke et al., 1980; Schuster & Zingheim, 1986; Teas, 1982; Tharp, 1985), although several disagree (e.g., Lovrich, 1987; Pearce et al., 1985).

In a review of numerous research studies on the impact of incentives on group performance, Guzzo, Jette, and Katzell (1985) found that incentives on average have a positive effect on group performance, although they can have a negative impact when inappropriately designed or applied. Incentive systems can fail for a number of reasons: rewards of low importance are used, the size of the incentive is too large (creating dysfunctional behavior) or too small (why bother?), they are tied to the wrong behaviors or activities, they create inequities leading to net decreases in overall performance, or they are overly tied to measurable outcomes and miss key activities that are less measurable.

Impact of Benefits

It is clear from the research that has been conducted that benefits and compensation practices can have an impact on labor productivity. What is even more apparent from the literature is the limited impact that compensation programs have on employee behaviors because the plans do not function as reward systems. Compensation systems have the potential to be powerful motivators of employee behavior and must be carefully designed to produce intended behaviors. An effective compensation system is powerful because it has the potential to fulfill important employee needs.

There are numerous theories of work motivation (e.g., need, goal, reinforcement, expectancy, or equity theories) that support the contention that compensation should play an integral role in motivating and directing employee behavior. For example, from expectancy theory, we know that employees value pay and benefits as desired outcomes. If an organization can demonstrate a clear relationship between desired performance and the important compensation outcomes, employees will exert more effort toward intended goals. Or, from a reinforcement model, pay and benefits can serve as important reinforcers (because of their importance in attaining basic needs) of desired behaviors, *if the compensation is tied closely and directly to the performance of these desired behaviors.* Without belaboring all of the theories, suffice it to say that compensation can be a powerful performance tool when:

1. Pay and benefits fulfill important individual needs and goals (e.g., security, short– and long-term financial objectives).

2. Employees see a clear relationship between certain behaviors (e.g., improved quality, higher output) and compensation.

3. Rewards are distributed equitably relative to past performance and objective criteria and across employees both inside and outside the organization.

EMPLOYEE ATTITUDES TOWARD COMPENSATION AND BENEFITS

How do employees perceive their compensation? Following is an overview of some recent findings.

Attitudes toward Pay

Recent data on employee attitudes toward pay show decreases in favorable pay ratings among managers, exempt, and nonexempt employees (Morgan & Schiemann, 1986). These downturns are attributed to (1) diminishing pay increases due to lower inflation and lower merit increases (since the late 1970s), (2) poor pay-for-performance relationships, and (3) poor employee understanding of how pay is determined. An important link with these factors is the process through which pay issues are frequently communicated—the performance appraisal process.

Most organizations have great difficulty with their performance appraisal systems. Many employees do not believe they are administered fairly. Morgan and Schiemann (1984) show data indicating that 31 percent of managers, 34 percent of professionals, and 39 percent of hourly employees rate their performance appraisal process as either "not too" or "not at all" effective.

Another problem is the lack of good communication regarding the relationship between the appraisal and subsequent pay. Furthermore, annual appraisals without continual supervisory feedback are unlikely to be effective in establishing accurate feedback regarding a subordinate's location in the performance distribution.

Still another cause of low pay-for-performance ratings is the relatively small spread in merit increases. Recent reviews of such practices suggest that most organizations give more than two-thirds of their employees increases spread over a 2 percent pay differential. That is, an organization with an average pay increase of 5 percent generally gives over 66 percent of the employees an increase between 4-6 percent (Teel, 1986). Such differences are barely perceptible to most employees.

Finally, in focus groups on pay I have conducted and research conducted by others (Kerr, 1988), it is quite common to find that a strong majority of employees do not understand how their pay is determined or how it can be affected, and most do not know where to obtain this information. Many express cynicism regarding the likelihood of obtaining this information from their immediate supervisor.

Attitudes toward Benefits

In theory, increasing levels of benefits should be satisfying to most employees. However, recent findings indicate that improvements in employee attitudes toward benefits have not kept pace with increases in employer contributions to benefit plans (Schiemann, 1986).

Attitudes toward various benefits differ substantially, as shown in figure 37–2 (Schiemann, 1987). The most favorably rated benefits are profit sharing, savings plans, and stock purchase plans. The least favorably rated benefits are pensions, disability (short and long term), and sick leave (for some job groups). Although 84 percent of employees rate medical benefits as the most important benefit they receive (White & Becker, 1980), only 67 percent rate health insurance favorably. Moreover, 60 percent or fewer rate dental, sick leave, and disability insurance favorably. Furthermore, some of the most expensive benefits (pensions and health-related benefits) are not rated most favorably; in fact, pension plans are rated favorably by only half of the employees with retirement programs.

Pension Benefits. Employees today (regardless of age) are rating their pension plans quite low. Many younger employees expect never to reap the rewards, middle-aged employees appear uncertain about funding and pension realization, and older employees are not sure that the benefit will maintain value with inflation over time. Moreover, with the recent wave of downsizing and early retirement offerings, many employees believe that they will never realize the full value of their plans. Despite reductions in vesting schedules for many organizations, which increase the portability of pension value, most employees still understand very little about this benefit and do not rate it highly compared to other benefits. Employees do, however, say it is one of the most important benefits (Olian et al., 1985).

Figure 37–2. Employee Ratings of Specific Benefits

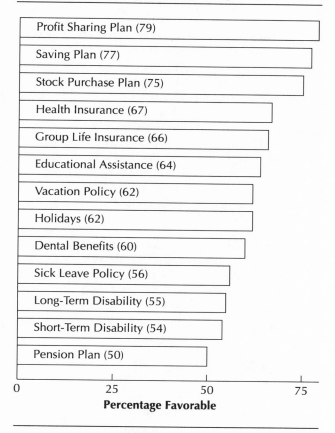

Profit Sharing Plan (79)
Saving Plan (77)
Stock Purchase Plan (75)
Health Insurance (67)
Group Life Insurance (66)
Educational Assistance (64)
Vacation Policy (62)
Holidays (62)
Dental Benefits (60)
Sick Leave Policy (56)
Long-Term Disability (55)
Short-Term Disability (54)
Pension Plan (50)

0   25   50   75
Percentage Favorable

Note: Based on 108,000 employees in the U.S., 1983–1986

Health Benefits. Attitudes toward various health benefits, another high cost item for employers, are also depressed. The reasons vary. Causes include recent employer efforts to share these costs with employees by increasing deductible levels or copayment levels, the bureaucracy involved in claims administration, and more limited employee control over medical delivery. In an effort to control health care costs, many organizations have implemented mandatory second surgical opinions, created disincentives for hospital usage, and instituted other practices that employees view with disfavor.

On the other hand, employees in organizations that have a strong communications program regarding benefits seem to have a better understanding of the importance of controlling health care costs. In numerous focus groups I have conducted, employees have expressed deep concern about rising health care costs and anger toward their employers for not using their influence to help curtail such costs. Few employees seem to understand how the health care delivery system works and the role that their employers play in the process. Hence, employee education is a major gap that remains to be filled in most organizations.

Investment and Savings Benefits. Employees rate savings and investment benefits quite favorably. In part, this may be due to perceptions of greater financial control. Having had recent experiences with Individual Retirement Accounts (IRAs), 401Ks, and matched savings plans, employees have a greater sense of control over "their" money. With these benefits, they receive frequent feedback (from financial statements, for example) regarding their benefits and have a heightened sense of cash equivalence. Most employees I have interviewed believe this money is somehow safer than that held in traditional vehicles (e.g., pension plans).

Time-off Benefits. With the increasing value of leisure, time-off benefits have retained high ratings. Time-off benefits represent the one category where females rate benefits less favorably than their male counterparts. Most of our recent interviews suggest that women still take primary responsibility for child

care. When the child is sick, it is more often the mother who stays home to care for the child. These ratings, therefore, may reflect greater needs by women of sick leave and vacation time to care for young children.

Thus, it appears that employers are not receiving the value in employee satisfaction with benefits that current expenditures might warrant. Some of the most expensive benefits are the least favorably rated. In surveys I recently conducted across organizations in various industries, pensions and health coverage are the two benefits that employees most want to see improved. Clearly something is wrong given that these two benefits represent the largest and fastest-growing expenditure for most employers (Hefferan, 1985).

Part of the problem stems from compensation systems that fail to address employee needs. Regardless of the design features of a compensation program, if it fails to meet work force needs, then it will fail to serve as a powerful motivator.

CHANGING NEEDS

Never before has there been such a dramatic period of change in employee and employer needs. These changing needs are a result of numerous forces at play.

Changing Employee Needs

Figure 37–3 displays some of the major forces influencing employee needs today. A multitude of factors affecting employees have created a work force that is quite different from that of ten to twenty-one years ago.

Demographic Change. The work force is aging as baby boomers continue to move through it. Life expectancies continue to increase, creating employees who are willing and able to work longer. The number and percentage of women in the work force has grown so that women now represent close to 45 percent of American workers. The percentage of two full-time wage earner families reached 50 percent in 1987. And when part-time work is considered, in nearly 75 percent of marriages, both spouses work. (U.S. Department of Commerce, 1980). These changes and others have created some rather dramatic shifts in family structure in the United States over the last three decades.

Family Composition. The traditional family of a male breadwinner, a nonemployed spouse, and 2.6 children is no longer the norm. In fact, this type of family is almost extinct (less than 10 percent of families today). Instead, there has been rapid growth in the number of singles of all types: single parents, never marrieds, divorced without children, and singles sharing households with other singles. In total, these groups represent over 41 percent of the work force today (U.S. Department of Commerce, 1980). Furthermore, there are many childless couples, two-earner families, and families with adult dependents that have unique family needs. Thus, the traditional

Figure 37–3. Factors Influencing Employee Needs

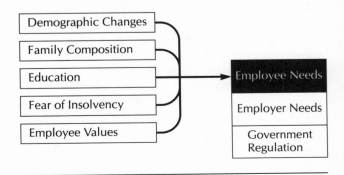

benefit and compensation needs of our model 1950s family have changed because family heterogeneity has increased.

Values. Employees today are sporting some different values from their 1950 or 1960 counterparts. They voice their opinions more openly, are willing to challenge authority to a greater extent, are more independent, desire more participation in organizational decision making, and want more control over their careers and personal finances. However, it appears that the importance they attach to pay and benefits remains quite high (Schiemann, 1986).

Education. Some of the changes above may be due to increasing education levels in the United States. In contrast to 1950, when one-third of the work force completed four or more years of high school, the percentage of four-year completions has doubled to over 68 percent today (U.S. Department of Commerce, 1980). This has created employees who are better consumers of information about business, their organizations, benefits, and personal finance. Good consumers will question policies and evaluate them more carefully.

Fear. Employees today express many concerns about their future: concerns about social security insolvency, pension plan fraud, and tax law uncertainty. With increasing education and more options for investment and personal control of assets (e.g., IRAs, lower vesting periods for pensions), employees are questioning the value of long-term benefits and in some cases asking for cash because it is more tangible (despite the tax bite).

In summary, numerous forces have combined to create more sophisticated consumers of benefits and compensation policies—employees who are better educated, more independent, more skeptical, and more heterogeneous than their 1960s counterparts. Moreover, this new breed of employees expects to participate more in compensation and benefit decisions, and they desire greater choice among a wider array of benefit options now available. This may range from choice regarding levels of traditional benefits (e.g., life insurance, health insurance) to options regarding the purchase of new benefits such as child care (Friedman, 1986) or prepaid legal coverage (Burger, 1986; Rader & Sharenow, 1986).

Changing Employer Needs

Not only have employee needs changed dramatically, but a number of factors have converged to create

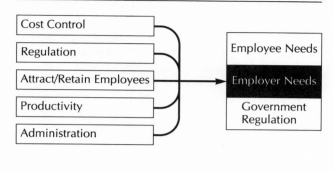

Figure 37–4. Factors Influencing Benefit Policy

serious forces affecting employers as well (figure 37–4). These forces have created a new climate in which to evaluate the effectiveness and appropriateness of historical compensation policies and practices.

Declining U.S. Productivity. U.S. productivity has been declining due to increasing foreign competition, unfavorable exchange rates, and cheaper labor costs abroad, which have put pressure on American business to reduce costs or increase productive output (Hayes & Abernathy, 1980). Even at home, competition has increased due to deregulation in certain industries, scarce resources, and the threat of corporate takeovers. It appears that competition over labor costs may become the primary basis for battle in an environment where market and financial consolidations have matured, materials costs have diminished in importance (relative to labor costs) in many industries, and service industries continue to grow.

Rising Benefit Costs. Employers have also been stunned by the rising costs of fringe benefits. As a percentage of total payroll costs, nonwage compensation costs have risen dramatically over the past three decades (Wilson et al., 1985); fringes in 1985 represented approximately 38 percent of payroll ($8,166 per employee) compared to 24 percent in 1959 (U.S. Chamber of Commerce, 1985). The largest components of benefit costs come from mandated taxes and from voluntary employer contributions to pension and health benefits. Both mandated and voluntary costs have risen substantially over the past three decades. For example, as a percentage of total fringe benefits, health insurance has risen from 7 percent in 1951 to 18 percent in 1984. Moreover, this increase is not simply due to inflation. As a percentage of gross national product (GNP), health care expenditures have risen from 4.4 percent of GNP in 1950 to over 10 percent in 1985 (with projections of 14 percent by 1990) (U.S. Department of Health & Human Services, 1985).

Wage and Benefit Administration. New advances in computer software and hardware have made it possible to calculate the costs of various components of wages and benefits administration and utilization that have been heretofore cost prohibitive. For example, it is now feasible for employers to offer multiple benefit packages or flexible benefit designs at reasonable costs. Or it is possible to track benefit utilization rates so that benefit programs can be fine tuned and costed to reflect usage.

Government Regulation. Pension and tax laws continue to play an important role in shaping employer policy with respect to compensation and benefits. These laws have allowed more flexibility in plan offerings, have mandated better communication, have encouraged greater savings, and have changed the marginal (and effective) tax rates for both employers and employees. A number of economists have discussed the impact of taxation on employees' choices among wages and fringe benefits (e.g., Adamache & Sloan, 1985; Long & Scott, 1982; Woodbury, 1983).

Because of these major changes, it is no wonder that employers are having a difficult time deciding what to do with their compensation systems. From a reward and productivity standpoint, it is unfortunate that many employers have their compensation systems frozen in place, waiting for the changes to stop. Given the causes of the changes discussed in this chapter and in other articles (Schiemann, 1987), it is unlikely that such a period of stability will reappear soon. Therefore, it is important for employers to begin addressing outdated compensation systems so that they can achieve potential productivity gains.

KEY STEPS TO AN IMPROVED COMPENSATION SYSTEM

There are no quick fixes in changing a compensation system. In fact, too many current systems show the signs of numerous quick fixes that have created an archaic monster. Real improvement requires solid commitment to continual change to meet new organizational goals. There are five primary phases involved in the evaluation and redesign of a compensation system: assessment, design, pretesting and fine tuning, implementation, and evaluation.

Assessment

Before fixing a system that may not be broken, four key assessments are needed to determine the effectiveness of the existing compensation system:

1. *Policy Assessment*. An assessment of current compensation policy relative to strategic goals.
2. *Employee Needs Assessment*. An assessment of the operational impact of the compensation plan on the work force.
3. *Practice Assessment*. An examination of actual procedures, communications, and operating practices relative to policy goals.
4. *Design Assessment*. An evaluation of the structure of the compensation plan.

Policy Assessment. This evaluation requires a review of the *total* benefit and compensation policy to determine if existing policy matches the current strategic goals of the firm. Does it match long -ange objectives?

Does the system support the corporate culture desired? The view here should be to the present and the future with an eye toward the adequacy of the compensation policy in relation to planned strategic direction.

Senior managers should devote adequate time to their "ideal" reward structure. What values should be encouraged in the organization? What behaviors should be rewarded? Should different functions or job types receive different rewards? How important is status? Will risk taking be rewarded or punished? How important is the encouragement of innovation? This stage lays the groundwork for the overall goals of the compensation system *within the context of the broader organizational objectives*. It is important to conduct this assessment without imposing current operational problems and legal or tax constraints on the evaluation.

Employee Needs Assessment. This step is critical to the success of any compensation evaluation and one that is often forgotten in the haste to design a new plan. Without knowing the impact of existing practices on employees and the current and projected needs of the work force, it is almost impossible to design a system that will have maximum impact. For example, a firm that wants to encourage long-term commitment may design a much stronger pension and deferred compensation plan at the expense of current salary growth. After a discovery that employees leave in droves, a tardy employee assessment might uncover a work force with high short-term needs and serious perceived problems with the pension plan (stemming from the communication associated with the earlier plan and not the level of funding).

At this stage, therefore, it is important to answer a number of important questions:

- What are the current values and needs of the work force? Are they heterogeneous or homogeneous across job groups?

- How satisfied are employees with the current benefits and compensation? What relationships do they see between various elements of compensation and their behaviors (e.g., absence, sickness, performance)? What are the causes of dissatisfaction?

- How informed are employees about the elements of the compensation plan? Even the best designed plan, when poorly communicated, will fail to have an impact. What components of the plan are best and least understood?

A number of techniques are available to accomplish this assessment. An employee survey (featuring values, benefits, compensation, and job related issues) is often the best tool to assess work force values, needs, attitudes, and behaviors. In addition, in-depth interviews and focus groups can be a source of detailed information on how these needs are being met through the current compensation system. "What-if" analyses can be conducted, allowing the evaluation team to identify strategies that are likely to be successful in the design phase.

Furthermore, today there are a number of sophisticated multivariate techniques available (e.g., trade-off analysis) that enable an employer to determine the value or utility that employees place on specific components of the benefit or compensation package. This analysis can be conducted for specific locations or subgroups of the work force (e.g., exempt, nonexempt). Moreover, a ratio of utility or satisfaction per dollar spent can be calculated for each benefit or compensation feature. This analysis then enables the employer to modify benefits, for example, to maximize the return on investment for specific subgroups and the work force as a whole. Finally, because of the approach used, this type of trade-off analysis does not raise employee expectations about new or different levels of benefits.

Practice Assessment. The next step is to evaluate existing practices to determine if they are consistent with the intended design. In many organizations, existing practice is so far removed from intended practice that it is not surprising that employees do not understand or value the current system.

A major cause of this gap is inconsistent application of policies and procedures. Often department heads or supervisors follow different practices from what is called for in the plan. This inconsistency is one of the most frequent causes of employee perceptions of inequity and favoritism. In one focus group after another I conducted, blatant examples of discrepancies and violations surfaced. From our research, it appears that the better managed organizations execute more uniform practices and thereby communicate an unambiguous message to employees.

It should be noted, however, that many deviations from plan may indicate that the plan is inadequate and should be reevaluated. Good managers will not allow a poor plan to deter them from motivating and directing their employees. Thus, in a number of organizations, the plan in practice is far better than the plan in design (with the exception of the usual discrepancies in implementation across managers that create perceptions of inequity).

Much of the information for this assessment can be collected through the same vehicles as the employee needs assessment. Focus groups and survey methods can provide most of the information required. It is important to identify how the "real" organization works.

- What do managers do to facilitate their compensation objectives and reduce red tape? How timely is feedback? Are there frequent and serious violations of standard practices? What are major obstacles to successful implementation?

- How are current practices carried out? Do employees see a discrepancy between plan and action? How and why have employees learned to "beat the system"? Are there major gaps between the intended effect of the plan and current outcomes?

Design Assessment. This component of the assessment phase entails the reexamination of the plan structure in relation to corporate compensation policies. For example, if the firm has a policy aimed at rewarding outstanding contributors, can the current structure accommodate this goal without creating other incongruities? This analysis entails an evaluation of such issues as:

- Is the balance between short- and long-term rewards appropriate?

- Are rewards being used that match policy goals?

- Is the distribution between wages and benefits appropriate?

- Is there enough flexibility in the system to meet individual needs? For example, can we accommodate the needs of different demographic or job groups?

- Is the distribution of individual, group, and profit-center rewards appropriate?
- Should the system reward performance differenes to attain policy objectives?
- Do compensation system rewards match (in priority) the organizational goals? For example, one might design a compensation system that rewards service speed but is incongruent with higher-priority goals of customer service, which may not be totally dependent on service speed.

This assessment is best conducted by both internal and external evaluators. Internal consultants—particularly those who designed the current system—may have too much at stake in the existing system to be objective. An objective third party who can discuss policy and design objectives with senior management and evaluate the current plan can often offer a fresh perspective before rebuilding a new compensation system. Caution should be exercised in working with external consultants who have only single plans to sell.

Design

Following the assessment phase, the design of a new plan or the modification of the prior plan will flow naturally. Most important, the plan will be driven by current and future organizational goals, by a thorough understanding of current and past practices, and by direct knowledge of work force needs, behaviors, and understanding. Without any of these components, the plan will have limited value and in all likelihood will need to be revamped shortly.

The design phase entails the structuring of wages and benefits that truly meet both individual and organizational needs. In this phase, cost-benefit trade-offs must be made for elements of the compensation plan. Elements must be selected that will have maximum impact on the work force. Furthermore, at this point, legal and tax constraints should be considered. Finally, such issues as ease of communication and administration need to be evaluated.

Pretesting and Fine Tuning

Preliminary Evaluation. Next, the newly designed plan should be subjected to evaluation before implementation. What the experts think may not be what employees perceive. Focus groups can be conducted to assess features of the new plan, including administration, practical barriers to implementation and communication, likely impact on motivation and behavior, and resistance to change. It is also important to obtain senior management feedback to confirm the support that will be needed to carry the new plan to fruition.

Plan Modification. Based on the input from the preceding step, the plan may need modification in design or in planned implementation. Key information that should determine the modification includes the likelihood that major elements of the plan will drive behaviors toward desired organizational goals, the acceptance and support of senior management, and the difficulties involved in implementation or communication.

Implementation

The implementation phase will typically include the following elements:

- A clear step-by-step task timetable.
- A well-developed communication plan, including an initial announcement of the new plan (describing the purpose and goals of the new plan), resource materials explaining the new plan, resource individuals (along with a hot line) who will be available to discuss the plan, clear communication (usually both written and oral) on the major differences between the old and new plan (including both advantages and disadvantages and the reasons behind the new choice), and strong management training on the key elements and "spirit" of the new plan.

    Communication shortfalls often contribute to high failure rates of both new and existing plans. Many implementors fail to see this because they do not conduct the necessary follow-up evaluations to assess the impact of the new plan. Shortfalls occur more often in employee perceptions that are likely to detract from expected behavior rather than in the physical implementation of the plan.

- The administrative structure to execute the new plan. One of the most frequent blunders I have observed is a premature announcement of the new plan (usually for tax or financial reasons) before the administrative structure has been put in place. Typically, this leads to chaos, a rampant rumor mill of negative information, and a serious loss of credibility for the new program at its most vulnerable stage.

- Finally, tracking mechanisms must be implemented to provide regular feedback on benefit utilization, performance-wage relationships, incentive and bonus utilization, employee behaviors (e.g., absence, turnover, performance indicators), and related factors. These tracking vehicles provide essential feedback on plan effectiveness and early data on developing problems.

Evaluation

Finally, it is crucial to implement a regular evaluation program to assess whether plan goals are being realized. A regular evaluation might include:

- An employee assessment (e.g., focus groups and employee survey on plan usage, understanding, satisfaction, perceived relationship to performance factors, and barriers to effectiveness).
- A review of key indicators of plan goal attainment.
- A review of utilization rates, salary distribution, employee behaviors, job evaluation data, external compensation survey data, and other relevant information.

A thorough periodic review can prevent plan deterioration and signal the appropriate time period for reevaluation of the entire plan.

THE FUTURE OF COMPENSATION AND BENEFIT POLICY

Given the dramatic changes taking place, it is certain that the policy of tomorrow will need to be more flexible and modified more frequently to meet changing needs. It is also clear that several trends will continue and become more salient in the design of compensation plans.

Compensation for Performance

Employees at all job levels are questioning historical pay policies that provide little incentive to perform better. There are strong norms in a free enterprise society that support expectations of higher rewards for better value or contribution. A distinction must be made between "better" relative to others and "better" in an absolute sense (e.g., relative to the past or a fixed yardstick). Neither of these expectations is well supported in large corporate settings.

Most policies *in vivo* entail rewards for "better" relative to others within the organization. Therefore, even among firms that do differentiate rewards for performance across employees, many still lack a substantive incentive for all employees to improve (in an absolute sense or relative to the past). Even performers who cannot (or do not wish to) compete with the "stars" can improve their effectiveness over time. They are more likely to do so, however, if *there is an incentive* for such growth. For example, corporate education benefits are well received by those who wish to improve themselves and are seldom resented by those who do not use them. Organizations employing gain sharing, for example, also capitalize on this type of incentive.

Another cause of employee disillusionment is a result of poor performers being tolerated and paid similarly to average or high-performers. Higher-performing employees want to see compensation that varies with their performance. The problem here does not stem from an intolerance of average performers but rather from the organizational tolerance of clearly bad performance. Both high and average performers become frustrated and cynical regarding their management when such blatant performance is accepted in the long run. It sends a mixed message regarding the importance of performance, organizational waste, and the allocation of corporate wealth. It sends a clear message regarding the extent to which management is in touch with the operation and the extent to which others will have to subsidize this deficiency.

A note of caution is in order, however. There are few data on the impact of lower wages and/or fringes on average or marginal performers. Presumably high increases to top performers will come at the expense of average and poorer performers. If the organization has purged its poorest performers, then many essentially satisfactory performers would receive small increases, and this may conflict with their personal perceptions of performance or value to the organization and possibly lead to lower self-esteem, higher turnover, or poorer performance. After all, in any performance curve based on comparisons to peers, some employees will be rated lower than others. If differences across performance are small or average performers are truly satisfactory, then caution must be exercised in both the use of this system and how it is communicated.

Equity

We do know from a great deal of research that perceptions of equity or fairness are quite strong in this society. There are many different types of equity, but two are called into play in the preceding discussion. One form of equity is receiving higher rewards associated with higher individual (or absolute) performance levels. The second form is equity relative to others based on comparisons of individual input and output.

The first form is less difficult to satisfy and involves only the individual or group relative to certain performance levels. If the individual or group puts in more effort, achieves higher performance levels, and receives higher rewards, then equity can be reached without serious complications. On the other hand, the second form of equity involves a more extensive assessment of the merits of each person's inputs and outputs to achieve equity. And for a number of reasons (e.g., self-esteem), perceptions of individual inputs and outputs vary substantially across individuals and raters—a serious dilemma for most organizations.

Flexible Compensation

Changing employee needs and values give impetus to more flexible compensation systems. Because of the greater heterogeneity of individual needs, a more rapidly changing organizational milieu, and future tax law uncertainty, compensation systems will need to be more flexible if they are to achieve the desired objectives discussed throughout this chapter. For example, because of unique financial needs and lower tax incentives for indirect compensation, more individuals will find greater satisfaction in wage rather than fringe benefit payouts.

It is unlikely that this will satisfy all types of employees, however; many will still value the group purchase and administrative advantages of buying through their employer. Moreover, many employers will most likely want to provide protection against catastrophic losses and encourage wellness programs to promote continued health and productive behavior.

Restructuring of Benefit Packages

In order to meet cost constraints and changing employee needs, most benefit plans will need to be redesigned to improve effectiveness. The return on benefit dollars invested should become an important criterion of fringe benefit effectiveness. In order to achieve higher returns, most benefit packages will need to become more diversified, more flexible, and administratively more efficient. Employee attitudes toward benefits will remain strong only if the fringes offered meet real needs.

Achieving an optimal return on benefit dollars invested is unlikely without careful scrutiny of work force trends in specific employment locations, an analysis of employee needs, and informed projections about likely changes in the work force over the next five to ten years. Furthermore, single employee surveys of global satisfaction with benefits will not be sufficient to estimate return on investment, likely enrollment rates in alternative plans, and trade-offs that employees will make across benefits. More sophisticated trade-off techniques (discussed earlier in this chapter) must be employed to make accurate decisions in benefit design.

Profit Sharing

Because of many of the shortcomings of individual pay-for-performance strategies discussed above and in order to promote cooperative behaviors, many organizations will adopt more sophisticated forms of profit sharing that reward employees for team performance in addition to individual performance. In return for greater commitment to corporate goals and higher levels of productivity, more organizations will be willing to share increases in profitability that are employee driven.

In simple economics, if employees are willing to increase their efforts in systematic ways that improve productivity (e.g., waste reduction, quality improvement, more volume, or faster service), employers can afford to provide additional incentives from the increased profit resulting from such activity. Moreover, this is likely to be market driven; employers who do not provide these types of incentives will in all likelihood fall behind their competitors who do.

Incentive Periods Based on Goal Periods

Too often in the past, compensation incentives were ineffective because the payouts were only remotely associated with objectives accomplished. For example, line workers are given feedback on performance that is attainable in very short periods, while senior executives are often rewarded based on quarterly results while we keep telling them how important long-term strategic objectives are. New compensation systems will offer incentives based on actual goal periods: longer-term incentives for senior executives, variable-period incentives for professionals, sales personnel, and middle managers, and short-term incentives for lower managers, clerks, operatives, and service workers. Incentive systems work far better when rewards are distributed *in close proximity* to goal attainment and as frequently as feasible.

Multitiered Incentive Systems

Many group- or organization-wide incentive systems have been introduced. Gain sharing, Scanlon plans, Improshare, and Rucker plans are all based on providing additional incentives to employees for specified increases in productivity. Although the formulas differ, the conceptual framework is similar. Much has been written about each of these systems and the opportunities for real productivity gains (Dulworth & Usilaner, 1987; Goggin, 1986; Jewell & Jewell, 1987; Lawler, 1984; Miller & Schuster, 1987; O'Dell, n.d.; Swinehart, 1986; Werther et al., 1986). A major weakness in these systems is the difficulty of measuring *all* types of performance.

The system of tomorrow is likely to contain tiers of incentives or rewards for performance or productivity gains. For example, it is conceivable that an individual will receive a pay increase, bonus, or incentive payout based on individual performance, a group or team level of goal attainment, and some overall level of profit center success. Obviously, all kinds of combinations are possible. The advantages of such a

system are that it recognizes both individual and team contribution and creates high awareness of organizational mission and success—something that is sorely missing in most compensation systems today.

Risks in Using Incentives

There are some risks associated with incentive pay. One concern is putting too much focus on the behaviors that are reinforced at the expense of other less important, but nevertheless needed, behaviors. There are many examples of this in organizations: bank managers with lending and depository goals that are incompatible; product managers competing for the same market share; or maintenance and production managers who must limit their specific tasks for the organization to maximize its effectiveness.

To solve this problem, incentives should be focused on broader organizational objectives and must recognize potential dysfunctional levels of performance. Furthermore, cooperative behavior can be rewarded, thereby reducing some incentive for dysfunctional competition.

Another risk of incentive pay is a tendency to develop incentives for those activities that are more measurable, potentially reducing some activities that are important but almost impossible to measure. Still another caution is to control expectations that employees will be given incentives for every responsibility, thereby creating an expectation that individuals must be rewarded financially for every act they perform. This risk can be reduced by carefully balancing individual, group, and organizational incentives.

SUMMARY

It is becoming clear that compensation and benefits policy plays a crucial role in productivity through its impact on individual and organizational goals. This can best be attained by structuring these rewards in a way in which individual needs are met through accomplishment of organizationally important objectives. Rewards used effectively can have a positive impact on absenteeism, turnover, accidents, recruitment, and individual and group performance. It is also clear that many current pay and benefit practices are far from optimal in creating effective reward systems.

Because of changing employee and employer needs today, new approaches to pay and benefit design are needed. A five-step approach for improving a compensation system was presented along with seven major issues facing compensation managers in the next decade. Although today's system is far from optimal, it is an exciting period of opportunity to create new systems that will better link individual and organizational goals.

REFERENCES

Adamache, K.W., & Sloan, F.A. (1985). Fringe benefits: To tax or not to tax? *National Tax Journal, 38* (1), 47–64.

Allen, S.G. (1981). Compensation, safety, and absenteeism: Evidence from the paper industry. *Industrial and Labor Relations Review, 34* (2), 207–218.

Bartel, A.P. (1982). Wages, nonwage job characteristics, and labor mobility. *Industrial and Labor Relations Review, 35* (4), 578–589.

Burger, L.S. (1986). Group legal service plans: A benefit whose time has come. *Compensation and Benefits Review, 18* (4), 28–34.

Chelius, J.R. (1981). Understanding absenteeism: The potential contribution of economic theory. *Journal of Business Research, 9* (4), 409–418.

Dierks, W., & McNally, K. (1987). Incentives you can bank on. *Personnel Administrator, 32* (3), 60–65.

Dulworth, M.R., & Usilaner, B.L. (1987). Federal government gainsharing systems in an environment of retrenchment. *National Productivity Review, 6* (2), 144–152.

Ellig, B.R. (1982). *Executive compensation: A total pay perspective*. New York: McGraw-Hill.

Freedman, S.C. (1985). Performance-based pay: A convenience store case study. *Personnel Journal, 64* (7).

Friedman, D.E. (1986). Child care for employees' kids. *Harvard Business Review, 64* (2), 28–34.

Goggin, Z. (1986). Two sides of gain sharing. *Management Accounting, 68* (4), 47–51.

Guzzo, R.A., Jette, A.D., & Katzell, R.A. (1985). The effects of psychologically based intervention programs in worker productivity; A meta-analysis. *Personnel Psychology, 38*, 275–291.

Hayes, R.H., & Abernathy, W.J. (1980). Managing our way to economic decline. *Harvard Business Review* (July–August), 67–77.

Hefferan, C. (1985). Employee benefits. *Family Economics Review*, (1), 6–14.

Hernandez, J.P. (1986). *Child-care and corporate productivity: Resolving family/work conflicts*. Lexington, MA: Lexington Books.

Jewell, D.O., & Jewell, S.F. (1987). An example of economic gainsharing in the restaurant industry. *National Productivity Review, 6* (2), 134–143.

Kerr, S.K. (1988). Some characteristics and consequences of organizational rewards. In E.D. Schoorman and B. Schneider (Eds.), *Facilitating work effectiveness* (43–76). Lexington, MA: Lexington Books.

Lawler, E.E. III (1971). *Pay and Organizational Effectiveness: A psychological approach*. New York: McGraw-Hill.

Lawler, E.E. III (1983). Merit pay: An obsolete policy? In J.R. Hackman, E.E. Lawler III, & L.W. Porter (Eds.), *Perspectives on behavior in organizations* (2d ed.): (305–309). New York: McGraw-Hill.

Lawler, E.E. III (1984). Whatever happened to incentive pay? *New Management, 1* (4), 37–41.

Levine, J.Z. (1984). Child-care policies. *Personnel, 61* (2), 4–10.

Locke, E.A., Feren, D.B., McCaleb, V.M., Shaw, K.N. (1980). The relative effectiveness of four methods of motivating employee performance. In K.D. Duncan, M.M. Gruenberg, & D. Wallis (eds.), *Changes in Working Life*. London: Wiley.

Long, J.E., & Scott, F.A. (1982). The income tax and non-wage compensation. *Review of Economics & Statistics, 64* (2), 211–219.

Lovrich, Jr., N.P. (1987). Merit pay and motivation in the public workforce: Beyond technical concerns to more basic considerations. *Review of Public Personnel Administration, 7* (2), 54–71.

Merrilees, W. (1981). Interindustry variations in job tenure. *Industrial Relations, 20* (2), 200–204.

Miller, C.S., & Schuster, M.H. (1987). Gainsharing plans: A comparative analysis. *Organizational Dynamics, 16* (1), 44–67.

Miller, T.I. (1984). The effects of employer-sponsored child care on employee absenteeism, turnover, productivity, recruitment, or job satisfaction. *Personnel Psychology, 37* (2), 277–289.

Mitchell, O.S. (1982). Fringe benefits and labor mobility. *Journal of Human Resources, 17* (2), 286–298.

Morgan, B.S., & Schiemann, W.A. (1986). Employee attitudes: Then and now. *Personnel Journal, 65* (10), 100–106.

Morgan, B.S., & Schiemann, W.A. (1984). *Supervision in the 80s: Trends in corporate America*. Princeton, NJ: Opinion Research Corporation.

O'Dell, C. (n.d.). Sharing the productivity payoff: A gain-sharing primer. *Productivity Brief*, 24. Houston, TX: American Productivity Center.

O'Dell, C., & McAdams, J. (1987). The revolution in employee rewards. *Management Review, 76* (3), 30–33.

Olian, J.D., Carroll, S.J., & Schneider, C.E. (1985). It's time to start using your pension system to improve the bottom line. *Personnel Administrator, 30*, 77–83, 152.

Pearce, J.L., Stevenson, W.B. & Perry, J.L. (1985). Managerial compensation based on organizational performance: A time series analysis of the effects of merit pay. *Academy of Management Journal, 28* (2), 261–278.

Rader, J., & Sharenow, I.L. (1986). Picking prepaid legal plans. *Personnel, 63* (10), 17–19.

Schiemann, W.A. (1983). Major trends in employee attitudes toward compensation. In W.A. Schiemann (Ed.), *Managing human resources: 1983 and beyond* (pp 1–69). Princeton,NJ: Opinion Research Corporation.

Schiemann, W.A. (1986). Major trends in employee attitudes toward benefits. In J.J. Parkington & W.A. Schiemann (Eds.), *Employee benefits: Regaining control* (1–35). Princeton, NJ: Opinion Research Corporation, 1–35.

Schiemann, W.A. (1987). The impact of corporate compensation and benefit policy on employee attitudes and behavior and corporate profitability. *Journal of Business and Psychology, 2* (1), 8–26.

Schmitz, L., & Heneman, H. (1980). *The effectiveness of positive reinforcement programs in reducing employee absenteeism: A review of the evidence.* Academy of Management Meeting, Boston, Mass.

Schroeder, E.A. IV, Sherman, J.D., & Elmore, R.C. (1987). A long-term profit-sharing plan to stimulate motivation and innovation among personnel. *Personnel Review, 16* (3), 34–38.

Schuster, J.R., & Zingheim, P.K. (1986). Designing incentives for top financial performance. *Compensation and Benefits Review, 18* (3), 39–48.

Sutton, N.A. (1986). Are employers meeting their benefit objectives? *Benefits Quarterly, 2* (3), 14–20.

Swinehart, D.P. (1986). A guide to more productive team incentive programs. *Personnel Journal, 65* (7), 112–117.

Teas, R.K. (19B2). Performance-reward instrumentalities and motivation in retail salespersons. *Journal of Retailing, 58,* 4–26.

Teel, K.S. (1986). Are merit raises really based on merit? *Personnel Journal, 65* (3), 88–95.

Tharp, C.G. (1985). Linking annual incentive awards to individual performance. *Compensation and Benefits Review, 7* (6), 38–43.

U.S. Chamber of Commerce Survey Research Section. (1985). *Employee benefits 1985.* Washington, DC: Government Printing Office.

U.S. Department of Commerce (1980), Bureau of Census, Washington, DC: Government Printing Office.

U.S. Department of Health and Human Services (1985). Washington, DC: Government Printing Office.

Werther, W.B., Jr., Ruch, W.A., & McClure, L. (1986). *Productivity* through people. St. Paul, MN: West Publishing Co.

White, W.L., & Becker, J.W. (1980). Increasing the motivational impact of employee benefits. *Personnel, 57* (1), 32–37.

Wilson, M., Northcraft, G.B., & Neale, M.A. (1985). The perceived value of fringe benefits. *Personnel Psychology, 38,* 309–320.

Woodbury, S.A. (1983). Substitution between wage and nonwage benefits. *The American Economic Review, 73* (1), 166–182.

38 DEFINING THE ORGANIZATION'S PAY SYSTEM USING WAGE SURVEYS AND JOB EVALUATIONS

Brian D. Steffy

The design and administration of compensation systems is not a traditional focus of psychologists. Instead, we tend to think that compensation activities should be relegated to those with an expertise in labor economics and wage surveys. The traditional view of compensation specialists is that they are primarily interested in measuring and identifying "going rates" of their organization's labor market. If, for example, a hospital is interested in how much to pay an entry-level psychiatric nurse, the hospital's compensation specialist determines, through wage surveys, what the competition is paying, and then the compensation specialist assigns a price, or value, to the job according to the "prevailing wage." Given this stereotype of what compensation practice entails, it is no wonder that psychologists view themselves as having only a peripheral role in designing and administering compensation systems (i.e., motivational aspects of pay).

The chapter nevertheless argues that a fusion of labor economics and industrial psychology is essential to the design and administration of an effective compensation program. A fusion is essential because compensation practice, in order to deal with complexities of organization life, entails more than conducting wage surveys to uncover that mythical going rate. A number of factors explain the complexity of compensation practice. First, it is simplistic to assume that a single going rate exists for a job. Wage survey data should show a range of going rates, and the compensation specialist must choose among the range of wage rates that is best suited to the job being priced and that meets the goals and strategy of the organization. Second, many jobs are either partially or totally unique to the organization, meaning that either a particular job has no comparison group in the general labor market or, even if comparison jobs do exist for which wage survey data can be collected, the job's technology and required skills, knowledge, abilities, and characteristics (SKACs) may be dissimilar enough from those in the comparison group that wage survey data must be adjusted and interpreted with caution. As will be discussed, while port-of-entry jobs, or key jobs, in a job class are typically uniform to content and stable in price across organizations, jobs further up the nonmanagerial and managerial job ladders may be more specialized and custom tailored to the unique needs of the organization. In these latter jobs, wage survey information will need to be complemented by job evaluation information in order to price jobs accurately and equitably. Fourth, when wages are determined through collective bargaining or when other interested parties are concerned about the fairness of a job's price due to suspected market imperfections and employee discrimination, the union and other employee groups may want to assess the "worth" of a job independent of the prevailing market rate. Here, interested parties may want to conduct a point-factor job evaluation to assess job worth independent of the market's valuation of the job. Once both measurement systems are used, the price of the job is then negotiated.

In this chapter I will examine two basic measurement systems employed in pricing the organization's job structure: wage surveys and job evaluation. I provide an overview of alternative measurement methodologies and techniques and discuss how decision makers can use this information. I cannot review many measurement techniques, but I will emphasize procedures that organizations can build in-house.

EQUITY CONCERNS IN DESIGNING AND ADMINISTRATING A COMPENSATION SYSTEM

Organizations use wage surveys and job evaluation to design and administrate their internal wage structure. An organization's internal wage structure consists of a job system in which similar jobs are grouped into job classes, where they are hierarchically arranged so that employees enter a job class at a port-of-entry position(s) and move up a job ladder(s) extending upward from the entry position according to internal selection rules (merit, seniority). There is also a pricing component to this job structure, whereby a new employee enters a rate range and progresses up a rate range according to performance and seniority. Figure 38–1 depicts an internal wage structure for a small service organization. It consists of four job classes (maintenance, clerical/secretarial, professional, managerial), which are juxtaposed along an x and a y axis, where the vertical y axis represents wages and the x axis defines discrete job classes. The internal wage structure is organized so that when an individual moves up the job structure, either by moving up a job ladder or across job classes (A to B, B to C, C to D), wages also rise. Figure 38–1 also depicts the components and important parameters of a typical job class. A job class has a floor and ceiling that defines the range of wage rates paid in that job class. The floor is the minimum rate typically paid to entry-level employees when they first join the organization. As employees move up the job ladder and up the rate range, their salary progresses. A maximum, or ceiling, rate is also defined. Organizations have a limit to the amount of pay labor is worth. They do not want employees to exceed this ceiling (red circle rate) but want to construct the rate range and distribute employees across the rate range such that, over the employees who stay in the job class, their pay steadily increases from floor to ceiling. As will be discussed later, the compensation specialist wants to define the width of the rate range so that is leads to desired results. If, for instance, the organization wants to conserve wages and encourage turnover after five years, the range can be defined narrowly where progression up the rate range is in small increments. If, however, an organization is interested in retaining employees in a job class for ten to twenty years, then the range must be wide enough to provide continual incentives and room for progression.

Figure 38–1 also shows the midpoint of the rate range. I will be referring to the midpoint frequently in discussing how to design the internal wage structure. When I link the internal wage structure to the market using wage surveys, I typically do so using midpoints.

The compensation specialist is perhaps most an artist when she or he actually constructs the structure, as is depicted in figure 38–1. Here we combine wage survey job evaluation information to (1) identify the jobs that fall in a job class; (2) identify the midpoint, maximum, and minimum points of each rate range; (3) juxtapose the rate ranges so that pay is equitable among different job classes; and (4) decide what the parameters of our internal wage structure will be relative to our competitors who are competing for the same labor.

If the design of the internal wage structure is very much an art, what theoretical framework can the compensation specialist use to make subjective decisions? Most compensation theory is based upon "equity theory" (Milkovich & Newman, 1984; Wallace & Fay, 1983). Equity theory is a theory of social justice, a theory explaining equitable and fair distribution of scarce resources, in this case a firm's compensation budget. If employees *perceive* an equitable payment for their work, then the system is fair. The theory assumes that individuals have no conception of the absolute or "true" worth of their work. We gauge whether we are being paid fairly by comparing our pay to the pay of some relevant reference group.

Compensation specialists must therefore appreciate that they want to design and implement compensation systems that foster perceptions of equity. This, however, is not easy, for individuals consider numerous factors in their equity perceptions. Three equity perspectives must be considered in designing a compensation decision: external, internal, and employee equity (Wallace & Fay, 1983). External equity is the judgment of whether the pay an individual receives in

Figure 38–1. Internal Wage Structure

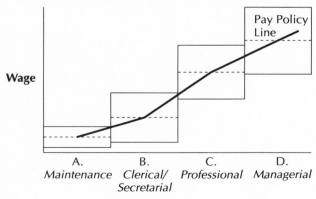

their job is competitive with the pay offered for similar jobs in other organizations. A professional nurse may continually scout the labor market to determine whether his or her pay is higher, competitive with, or lower than that paid by other hospitals in the region. If many nurses find that their wages lag the market, there may be, as a consequence of pay policy, an incentive to leave or a tendency to withdraw and retard performance. The compensation specialist must continuously audit the external labor market using wage surveys and other sources to determine the company's position in the market, as well as understand the consequences of that position.

Until recently, organizations and even the general public have not entertained the internal equity perspective. The comparable worth issue, a type of internal equity problem, has brought this perspective to the surface. The internal equity perspective forces the compensation specialist to focus on pay differences between dissimilar jobs in the same organization. The perspective asks the question: Is the job I am working in equitably priced relative to dissimilar jobs in the same organization? If, for example, a job requires a high degree of responsibility and learning and the working conditions are poor, then we would expect that job to be priced higher than one where responsibility and learning requirements are minimal and working conditions are comfortable. If, however, the market demands that his latter position be paid more than the former, then a condition of internal inequity may exist. For example, if I am a director of nursing in a large hospital making $40,000 annually, is this salary fair, given that male-dominated middle-management hospital administrators are making, on average, $75,000? Or is it fair that a law professor makes $50,000 while a history professor makes $25,000? These two examples may be overly dramatic, though in most cases we can ask ourselves whether the valuation of various jobs in our organization is equitable according to our assessment of the job's worth, independent of the market.

Of course, the standard answer is that the wages for a job are determined in the general labor market and not by the firm. In our society a wage is assumed to be defined as the function of the demand for labor and its supply. Yet even though the market is the final arbiter, the internal equity perception cannot be ignored. True, the market carries the greatest weight in determining the juxtaposition of the job classes as depicted in figure 38–1. Compensation specialists nevertheless need to consider the internal equity perception for other practical and "political" reasons. At a practical level, the internal equity perception may guide the pricing of a job that is totally or partially unique to the organization, meaning there is no similar job in the external labor market. Second, organizations should be sensitive to internal inequity perceptions, particularly among women congregated into female-dominated potentially undervalued job classes, since these women in the next decade may decide that organizing and collective bargaining is the only means of circumventing and literally adjusting the market. The market is an imperfect instrument of valuation, so the organization should conduct job evaluations to be aware of anomalies in the internal wage structure. Finally, and related to this second point, some states (e.g., Minnesota, Washington) have passed pay equity laws that mandate that state employers adjust pay levels to counter market inequity. Here, state employers are required to conduct job evaluations to assess the value of a job, independent of wage survey information. If internal equity exists, the undervalued job's wages will be increased over time. It will be both interesting and instructive to evaluate the organizational and market consequences of this legislation.

Employee equity concerns revolve around the question of whether employees in the same job or job class feel that the organization has distributed the pay such that better performers and more senior employees make more than less senior and poorer performers. This perspective is most consistent with the traditional notion of equity theory. That is, employees in a job compare their pay with others in their job relative to their assessment of the quantity and quality of their work efforts as compared to that of others in the job. Inequity perceptions may lead to withdrawal and retarded performance or a downward adjustment in work input to compensate for the perception that their pay is consistent with or less than individuals who put forth less quality and quantity of effort. (We will not concern ourselves with this perception in this chapter. Other chapters in this *Handbook* deal with problems of measuring performance.)

JOB EVALUATION

The theoretical principles underlying job evaluation extend back to Adam Smith's labor theory of value. Smith attempted to explain the relationship between labor's input into the production process and the price of the product or service consumed by the public. According to Smith, the price of a unit of product produced varies with the quantity and quality of labor's input required to produce a unit of the product; the greater all the quantity and quality of labor, the greater is the price. The relationship between the quantity of labor and the price of the product is obvious. When much labor is required to produce a unit of some product, that product will cost more than when less labor is required, holding all other factors constant. More interesting is Smith's proposition that the price of a commodity will increase according to the quality of labor input of the characteristics of the job in which labor is employed. Job characteristics that lead to greater commodity price include high risk, difficulty learning the job, harsh physical and mental demands, and high expected responsibility. These job characteristics are, in essence, "compensable factors" used in many job evaluation procedures that claim to assist management in assessing the worth of a job to the organization. Given rational employers and job candidates, the compensation paid to an employee should equal that labor's marginal contribution to the value of the firm defined in terms of these job characteristics or the contribution of that labor to the price of the product consumed. It is curious that Smith's job characteristics, or compensable factors, resemble the factors outlined in the Equal Pay Act of 1963, which states that individuals in a job should be paid equal wages if it is determined that the work done by different individuals is substantially equal in effort, responsibility, skills required, and working conditions.

Formal job evaluation procedures, used to rank jobs hierarchically according to their worth to the organization, have been in existence for a century. Some of the earliest examples of their use can be found in the work of Frederick Taylor, the father of scientific management. The U.S. Civil Service Commission also employed job evaluation in the early 1900s. However, it was not until the National War Labor Board sanctioned its use for establishing wage policy and controls during World War II that job evaluation began to be widely used in the private sector. Subsequent to World War II, job evaluation use was most extensive in unionized firms, where it was used as an instrument to bargain over wages. By the latter 1980s, most private and public sector organizations have used some form of job evaluation.

Job evaluation has become prevalent for a number of reasons. Job evaluation information, for instance, is used to supplement wage survey data collected to determine what labor market competitors are paying for various types of labor. In many cases, organizations have jobs that are partially or totally unique to their business. In such cases, wage survey information does not exist, or it may be deficient, since the surveyed jobs do not closely resemble the jobs being priced. Here job evaluation data are employed to price the jobs according to some rationale of what the organization values. Second, firms may conduct job evaluations because they want an assessment of a job's worth independent of the market, for example, to audit internal equity problems. Third, organizations conduct job evaluations so that they understand what dimensions of the job they are compensatings for. Those dimensions that are valuated greater may receive greater scrutiny at performance appraisal time.

Basic Concepts

Job evaluation is a subjective estimation system for establishing mutually acceptable criteria of equitable payment, usually defined by compensable factors and a system for measuring job differences according to those compensable factors. Job evaluation procedures may be divided into two types: those that consider only the inherent worth of the job, independent of labor market data, and those that explicitly include market data (wage survey) in defining the worth of jobs. In the latter case, job evaluation procedures directly suggest the wages that should be paid. However, when job evaluation is conducted without using wage survey data, the pricing of the internal wage structure is determined by juggling both job evaluation and wage survey data.

Job evaluation techniques can be divided into one of a number of categories: classification methods, broad-based classification methods, factor comparison, techniques employing large multiple regression models, and point-factor methods. There are numerous job evaluation products sold by vendors and consultants. Some are briefly described in table 38–1. This chapter will focus solely on a point-factor job evaluation procedure that any compensation specialist should be able to design and administrate in-house.

Point-Factor Job Evaluation

The advantage of point-factor job evaluation is its flexibility. It is a procedure of choice for most firms that want to design and custom-tailor their own job evaluation system. Some compensation specialists suggest that 80 percent of all employers who do job evaluation employ some variant of the point-factor method (Milkovich & Newman, 1984). Below, I briefly outline the steps of conducting a point-factor program.

Table 38–1
Sampling of Job Evaluation Techniques

Technique	Description
Classification Broad Based Arthur Young International's Decision banding	Decision-making style is a single compensable factor used to classify jobs
Maturity curves	Used for professional and R&D jobs Years since degree assumed to measure worth
General service classification (old system)	Discrete grades predefined according to agreed-upon criteria Jobs within each job class are slotted into these hierarchically arranged grades
Point-Factor In-house	Discussed in chapter
Hay Plan	Uses three or four universal compensable factors with two or three subfactors Points defined a priori Employs guide charts to measure job on know-how, problem solving, accountability, and working conditions
Factor comparison	Implicitly uses current market data on key jobs Involves first vertically ranking jobs under five or six compensable factors Next, wages are horizontally ranked across the compensable factors A measurement scale is developed that derives a wage for a job
Regression-based procedures TPCF method	Uses many firm-level, industry, and market data to predict pay for a job Uses quantitative proxies for subjectively defined compensable factors As many as 100 predictor variables may be used
MULTICOMP	Uses eleven quantitative variables and twenty-two compensable factors to predict wages Uses computer program to evaluate all jobs based upon model built for predicting pay of key jobs

Conduct a Job Analysis. The need to conduct a job analysis should not even have to be mentioned. I emphasize, however, that any job evaluation program that uses a committee or selected individuals to estimate job worth is going to be reliable and accurate if the jobs evaluated are thoroughly analyzed. Job descriptions communicate to estimators the characteristics of a job. If job descriptions are vague, lack detail, or are erroneous, job evaluation results will be erroneous. I caution personnel specialists to stay away from tidy prefabricated job analysis techniques for job evaluation purposes. A structured interview is more likely to provide the rich and detailed data that are required for passing judgment on a job's worth. If the organization has neither the time nor ability to pay for structured interviewing, the organization should employ job analysis techniques that lead to detailed and information-rich essays of job characteristics and employee requirements.

Select the Committee. The selection of the job evaluation committee is very important. As will become apparent, the committee must make numerous judgments that may ultimately affect the price of a job. Judgments on job worth can be biased according to the prejudices, values, and self-interests of the evaluators. Job evaluation is as much an art of consensus building as it is a scientifically based measurement system. Given this, job evaluation results could vary according to the sex composition of the committee (men and women may valuate male- and female-dominated jobs differently), whether job incumbents are allowed to represent themselves (if not, job evaluation scores for nonmanagerial jobs could be undervalued by the management-dominated committee; if incumbents or on the committee, especially if represented by a union, there may exist enough pressure to bias results upwardly). It is difficult to predict the types of bias that may be injected in the committee.

Nevertheless, it is necessary that the committee be chaired by someone who appears neutral and is able to evaluate critically and hold off any bias that may occur. This is not easy, for each of the following steps is highly subjective. Most organizations prefer to hire a consultant to chair the committee.

Choose Job to Evaluate. Most of evaluation plans are designed by first evaluating key, or benchmark, jobs. Key jobs are typically the bottom-rung job of the job ladder. These jobs are most important in designing the internal wage structure since they link together the external and internal labor markets; it is through the key jobs that people are recruited from the general labor market. Key jobs are common to many organizations, and the job's contents and characteristics are similar across organization. This is in contrast to "unique" jobs, where contents and characteristics are unique to the organization. it is also fair to say that the market is most "robust" with key jobs. For this reason the going rate for these jobs in the market tends to be stable and certain. Wage survey information is therefore prevalent for these jobs.

The compensation specialist should evaluate at least one or two key jobs for each job class or cluster of jobs grouped together on the basis of similar job content, functional responsibilities, and so on. Wage survey information should be available for these jobs and, once job evaluation information is obtained, the organization can begin to define the parameters of the internal wage structure. Once the system is set up, then all the other jobs can be evaluated and assigned a price based upon the information obtained on key jobs.

Choose the Compensable Factors. The compensable factors suggested by Adam Smith and the Equal Pay Act are "universal" compensable factors. These are general, abstract compensable factors that allow one to evaluate a wide range of jobs. Table 38–2 lists commonly used universal compensable factors. Many job evaluation procedures, including point-factor methods, include subfactors that define more specifically and concretely what the universal factors mean. Some organizations find it useful to use universal compensable factors but custom tailor subfactors for each job class. By doing this, the organization can employ the same universal factors across all job classes but, in effect, also use a "multiple" job evaluation system since subfactors can be written to capture the unique characteristics of each job class.

In choosing your compensable factors, it is important to bear in mind a number of issues. First, whether using a single set of compensable factors

Table 38–2
Common Compensable Factors

Universal	
Knowledge required by position	Skill requirements
Discretion	Know-how
Complexity	Problem solving
Scope and effect	Accountability
Physical demand	Mental stress
Work environment	Hazards
Skill	
Effort	
Responsibility	
Mental requirements	

Example of Subfactors	
Universal factor:	Responsibility
Subfactors:	Responsibility for materials
	Responsibility for tools and equipment
	Responsibility for operations
	Responsibility for safety of others
	Responsibility for budget

across all job classes or whether varying subfactors for each job classes, you need to check that the compensable factors chosen apply to all the jobs that are evaluated with those factors. For example, working conditions should not be narrowly defined to indicate only physical hardship. This might not do justice to clerical-secretary jobs that have aversive conditions but not in terms of physical danger, sweat, and brawn. In this case, define working conditions to measure physical stress, mental stress, video display terminal strain, and so on characteristic of clerical-secretarial work. Second, you should employ enough compensable factors so that no important aspect of a particular job or job class is not evaluated. For example, if you used only know-how, problem solving, and accountability to measure both exempt and nonexempt jobs in a manufacturing firm, characteristics such as hazard and physical working conditions may not be adequately evaluated, possibly leading to a downwardly biased pricing of some nonexempt positions. Third, committee members should be conscious of implicitly defining compensable factors so that they are sex biased. Using the example of working conditions again, if this compensable factor is defined solely in terms of strength, sweat, and brawn, clerical-secretarial jobs will be devalued, even though there exist hazards with this work (lower back pain, for example).

Weight the Compensable Factors. Point-factor job evaluation allows management to weight the relative importance of compensable factors by differentially allocating points across them. This is done by arbitrarily deciding upon some number of points, say 1,000 (if many factors, use more points), and then distributing the 1,000 points across the compensable factors. For instance, we may allocate the 1,000 points across five compensable factors as follows:

Factor	Points
Accountability	300
Responsibility	250
Education	150
Working conditions	100
Number supervised	200
Total points	1,000

In this example we have decided to valuate accountability the most and working conditions the least. But this decision is not without controversy, for different interest groups may wish to weight the compensable factors differentially. A union, for instance, would more than likely push to weight working conditions more. Such a move would probably substantiate greater wages for its members. Professionals, on the other hand, could substantiate higher wages if education received more points. Management will be able to justify receiving the greatest pay, as compared to other job classes, if accountability and responsibility are more heavily weighted.

Define Degrees and Build Scale. Once the compensable factors have been chosen and the weights assigned, you are ready to complete your measurement system. At this time you choose the number of degrees for the compensable factors, define the degrees, and develop an equidistant scale using the points allocated in the previous step. Table 38–3 depicts a complete scale for the compensable factor accountability. Notice that each compensable factor is first defined. In this example, five degrees were used, and each of the five degrees was defined. An equidistant scale was built by (1) allocating the 300 points to the highest degree, (2) establishing some much lower number for the lowest degree, and (3) assigning points to the second, third, and fourth degrees so that the difference in the number of points between each adjacent degree is equal.

Evaluate Jobs. At this point you are ready to evaluate your key jobs. Once the key jobs are evaluated, determine how consistent the ranking of a job's worth using the job evaluation is with the ranking of worth using market wages. Once you feel satisfied that results are rationale, then evaluate all of the other jobs.

Table 38–3
Point-Factor Scale for Accountability

Accountability
 Defined as the impact of the job on end results. The more critical the decisions made, the greater the assets responsible for, and the greater the budget responsible for, the greater the job's accountability.

Degree	Points
5. Decisions have impact on total firm—its success and efficiency; budget exceeds $10,000,000	300
4. Decisions affect policy-making and operational levels; budget exceeds $5,000,000	238
3. Decisions affect plant operations; budget exceeds $1,000,000	175
2. Decisions influence behaviors of nonmanagerial employees; not really responsible for budget	113
1. Little discretion, but behavior is prescribed; not responsible for budget	50

Other Considerations

Thus far we have been assuming that a single job evaluation system is being employed to measure worth across all job classes. Such an approach allows us to evaluate internal equity issues in which we assess the worth of dissimilar jobs from different job classes, independent of the market's valuation. In many cases, however, a single system will be too general and broad to detect specific differences among the worth of jobs within a job class. Many organizations find it necessary to employ multiple job evaluation systems. For example, it is common to find a separate evaluation system for exempt and nonexempt jobs. Professional and technical jobs may be evaluated using maturity curves. There exist job evaluation procedures that measure the worth of only clerical-secretarial jobs.

Whether to use a single or multiple system, or both, is an important decision. There are consequences to each procedure. If multiple systems are used, we will probably be better able to measure differences in worth within job classes, but if we compare dissimilar jobs, each valuated using a different system, it may be like comparing apples and oranges. If the organization has the resources, it might be best advised to measure each job twice—one time with a single system and another time with the system built of purchased specifically for that job class.

A second issue is whether to use multiple regression procedures to weight compensable factors. Here the dependent measure is the current salary for each job and the independent predictors the job's score on each compensable factor. Pay is regressed on the compensable factors, and the estimated beta weights are assumed to determine the importance, or weight, of each compensable factor. Although this procedure defers the weighing procedure to a seemingly objective statistical model, this technique is not without its problems. First, in most cases, the statistical assumptions underlying regression analysis will not be met. Since many of the compensable factors are often highly correlated, extreme multicollinearity may exist. But the most critical problem is not statistical. By using market data as the dependent measure to derive the weights, the user is not able to use job evaluation to assess a job's worth independent of the market. If it is true that the legacy of discrimination is embedded in the market, then this seemingly objective procedure will merely reflect that discrimination.

The potential for high correlations among compensable factors points out a third issue: how many compensable factors we should use. Since so many are redundant, some compensation specialists suggest that we use only two or three nonredundant factors. Still, to build consensus, practitioners seem to feel more comfortable using anywhere between five and fifteen (and even more) factors.

WAGE SURVEYS

We do not typically think of the wage survey as a complex and issue-ridden measurement tool. Yet it is somewhat incorrect to assume that, in assessing the external equity perspective, data procured through wage surveys all reliable and accurate. Therefore, it is necessary that we discuss the measurement problems associated with surveys. While it is not possible to discuss all of the wage survey techniques, products, and services that exist, I will provide a brief outline of commonly used data sources and focus most attention on designing and implementing a self-tailored, in-house survey. If a person understands how best to use a particular survey instrument, it may assist him or her in critically evaluating the products and services sold by vendors. In many cases an in-house survey may be complemented by information purchased from vendors or obtained free from trade or government documents. Also some vendor products integrate wage survey and job evaluation processes such that valuation independent of the market is not obtained. Here I treat wage surveys and job evaluation as if they are two mutually exclusive measurement systems.

By definition, a wage survey involves the systematic collection of external wage information and making judgments about the organization's pay policy (lead, lag, be competitive) (Milkovich & Newman, 1984). What I emphasize here is the kind of information that should be collected. While I acknowledge that there are constraints on an organization's ability to obtain all desired information, we will assume that employers can meet their wish list. Ideally, we want enough information to identify the "average" internal wage structure among the organizations in the relevant labor market. This means that we would like to reconstruct the pay parameters of job classes and jobs for those who compete for the same types of labor. Table 38−4 provides a wish list of information. Essentially, we want to identify our competitor's current position and the wage changes they anticipate in the next budget year(s). Important information includes the current midpoint, maximum point, and minimum point of rate ranges, as well as forecasted future changes. In addition, since base wages may constitute only 65−85 percent of the total compensation package, the surveying firm should identify the

Table 38−4
Information Desired Using Wage Surveys

Organizational characteristics
    Organization chart
    Size and location
    Union representation
    Products and services
Rate range characteristics
    Minimum, maximum, and midpoints
    Mean salary in range
    Distribution in range
Job characteristics
    Job description and specification
    Number in job
    Turnover
    Place in job ladder
    Bonus and incentive plans
Benefits
    Time without pay
    Insurance and health
    Pension
    Perks and other nonpecuniary benefits
Practices
    Job Evaluation practices
    Cost of living adjustments: Intentions

types and levels of benefits offered by the comparison group. Anticipated cost of living adjustments and anticipated changes in benefits would be informative.

Survey information widely varies in its capacity to provide the information outlined in table 38–4. Published sources available for free, for example, will provide less information, and the information presented may be inaccurate. Even surveys that are purchased through trade associations and consultants will not provide the detail and accuracy desired. For this reason, I will discuss how an organization can conduct its own in-house survey. While the detail and accuracy of information may still be far from perfect, at least when it is done in-house, the compensation specialist will have greater knowledge of the source of the data, the sources that are missing, and the specific limits of the data.

Three basic surveys are publicly available at no charge from the Bureau of Labor Statistics: area wage surveys, National Survey of Professional, Administrative, Technical, and Clerical Pay, and industry wage surveys. Area wage surveys are published for major metropolitan areas and provide data on selected occupations, such as white collar, skilled maintenance trades, and other nonproduction manual jobs common to a wide variety of jobs. The jobs surveyed tend to be key jobs. Midpoint levels are reported. The National Survey of Professional, Administrative, Technical, and Clerical Pay provides broad-based information on salary levels and distributions in private employment and is best used to compare the pay of salaried federal civil service administrative, technical, and clerical employees with those in private industry. Here we get information on specific service-sector jobs, but little regional background is provided. Industry wage surveys provide industry-specific data for a sample of jobs common across industries. This again is a generic survey that provides little regional data or data on occupations not common in the public sector.

Wage surveys prepared by consultants and trade and other types of associations can be specific or generic. Typically there is a direct trade-off between the detail and quality of data and the cost of obtaining the data. I will not describe these products and services, but it is important to develop a critical eye in judging the effectiveness of survey products and services.

Issues to Consider in Using External Survey Information

Recently, compensation specialists well informed on psychometric principles have developed schemes to evaluate wage surveys critically (Rynes & Milkovich, 1985; Wallace & Fay, 1983). Issues that should be considered are as follows.

Source of Data and Sampling. One of the most basic concerns is whether the organization has data on its "relevant labor market" or those organizations that compete for the same labor. Things to consider here are whether the data come from organizations in the same industry and geographical region and whether the surveyed organizations are similar in size, technology, mission, level of unionization, and composition of occupations. Organizations that resort to publicly available and vendor surveys should be cautious in interpreting these surveys, since the data source or the sampling procedures employed are unknown. That is, the organization does not know whether the information reflects the wage profile of its relevant labor market. This problem suggests that organizations should supplement externally acquired survey information with information obtained in-house where the company samples a number of organizations that are in its relevant labor market.

Another problem that may confront organizations is how to integrate survey information derived from different surveys (hence sources). In combining data you may be really comparing apples and oranges in that one survey develops its data base using its definition of the relevant labor market, while another survey's data source is built upon a different sampling of firms.

Are the Jobs Being Compared Similar? A basic concern is whether you feel certain that the jobs for which you have information are truly similar to the jobs that you are pricing. If you do not have access to the job descriptions for the jobs in other organizations that are surveyed, you can never be sure. This further substantiates that organizations employ in-house surveys in which they request the job descriptions from jobs surveyed in their relevant labor market.

How Did They Calculate Those Summary Statistics? A problem that arises when public and vendor surveys are used is that of not knowing how the summary statistics were calculated. We already acknowledge that externally derived surveys often lack the requisite detail, but uncertainty may also be introduced because each survey source may calculate its data differently (Rynes & Milkovich, 1986). For example, is it means or midpoints that I am looking at? Did one survey disregard "outliers" but another survey include them in their calculations? Do the data mean total pay (benefits, bonus, etc.) or base pay? How did the survey makers handle bonuses and other incentive pay schemes?

The In-House Survey

At this point assume that the information that we want to obtain from other organizations is that outlined in table 38–4. Now the question is, From whom do we obtain information, and how do we best obtain it?

It is recommended that ten to thirty organizations be surveyed to determine the parameters of their internal wage structure. The criteria for choosing which organizations to survey will vary from place to place, but, essentially, you want to survey those that compete with you for labor. The answer to this question may vary from job class to job class, suggesting that you will need to develop a number surveys. More specific criteria for deciding which organizations to survey are as follows:

1. Organizations that are in the same product or service markets.

2. Organizations that are similar in size (pay tends to increase with firm size).

3. When a job class is represented by a union, include organizations that are also unionized.

4. Give priority to local and regional employers, though if the recruiting market for the job in question is national, also sample firms outside you region.

Information can be produced through mailed survey forms, telephone conversations, or face-to-face meetings—sometimes even groups representing similar types of organizations. Some legal experts are now suggesting that surveys be conducted only through

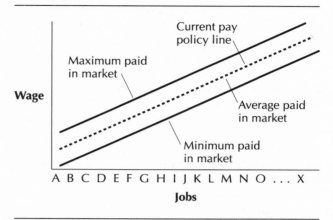

Figure 38–2. Pay Rates for Jobs in the Relevant Labor Market

the mail, since by meeting face to face, companies are running the risk of being accused of collusion. To prevent collusion, these same experts also suggest that the survey be conducted by a disinterested third party.

Assuming that the information outlined in table 38–4 is obtained from one's relevant labor market, the next task is to construct a scatterplot to identify the range of pay rates for jobs in the market (figure 38–2). In this example we see clearly that our organization is currently competitive in that the prices paid in our organization fall on a line at the midpoint of this range. We might call this our current pay policy line. If we want to move to a lead position in the market, we can tell from this plot the magnitude of pay increase that will be required.

DESIGNING THE INTERNAL WAGE STRUCTURE

At this point we are ready to employ our job evaluation and wage survey data to build the internal wage structure. The following must be determined: (1) the number of job classes, or rate ranges, that will be used; (2) the midpoints of each rate range; (3) the width of each rate range, defined by the distance between the minimum and maximum points; (4) the extend of overlap between juxtaposed rate ranges; and (5) the amount that the structure will be shifted upward to account for pay policy decisions and cost of living adjustments.

It is here that compensation becomes as much an art as a scientifically based practice. Choices will not be self-evident, and a trial-and-error attitude may work the best. It is not possible to speak to all the

issues and problems that might present themselves in designing the internal wage structure. I will outline only the basic steps in constructing the job and wage structure.

Group Jobs According to Similar Job Evaluation Score

While we expect that jobs of similar content (e.g., occupation) should naturally fall into self-contained job classes, we also want to check whether these jobs also cluster according to similar worth, as evidenced by their job evaluation scores. At this point we want to define pay grades based on job evaluation results. The decision at this point is how many pay grades should be used. Two options present themselves. You can elect to use few pay grades and construct wide rate ranges with ample room for movement through the job class. The other option is to create narrow rate ranges with few jobs but establish ample mobility opportunities between pay grades. One way of determining the number of pay grades is to plot jobs horizontally according to their job evaluation score, placing jobs with approximately the same value in the same grade. Jobs that have dissimilar evaluation scores should be put into separate grades. Problems arise when a job's evaluation score suggests that it should fall in a job class that is inconsistent with job content. In such cases a decision must be made as to whether to position the job with jobs with similar content and pay a price above the ceiling or below the floor for that job class or ignore job content and place the job in the pay grade that includes jobs with similar job evaluation scores. Using many grades allows greater flexibility in dealing with these exceptional cases.

Many times organizations not only look for natural clusters but define grades "a priori" according to an equidistant or progressive scale. For example, you might decide on having ten pay grades, dividing them by job evaluation scores as follows: Grade A, 200–300 points; Grade B, 301–400 points; Grade C, 401–500 points; and so on. When a progressive scale is used, you are assuming that as we move from lower-level to upper-level grades, the range of job values increases; therefore you allow for an increasing range of job evaluation scores as we move from Grade A to Grade J.

Once jobs are grouped along the horizontal scale according to job evaluation score, jobs within each job class, or rate range, are distributed along a vertical axis, a continuous scale from lower to higher wages (figure 30–3). We vertically rank positions using wage survey and job evaluation information. For each pay grade, we should have wage survey information to assist us in roughly defining the parameters of the rate range. We supplement this information with job evaluation scores to define the maximum and minimum points of the rate range and define loosely or rigidly structured job ladders within the range. This is an oversimplified account of how this is done, but it provides some direction in how to build an integrated job structure and pricing system. For those jobs in which no survey information is available, we have to rely on the job evaluation score to suggest an appropriate price. Using the wage survey and job evaluation information on key jobs in the pay grade, we compare the unique job's job evaluation score with that of key jobs and infer an appropriate wage using this base information.

There are additional considerations in constructing your internal wage structure. First, what is the appropriate width of your rate range? Should it be narrow (minimum and maximum points are less than 15 percent of the midpoint) or wide (minimum and maximum points are greater than 30 percent of the midpoint)? In determining the width of rate ranges it is important to bear in mind these questions: (1) What is the average length of stay in the job class? (2) Do I have a merit system requiring broad wage differentials among employees? (3) Do I want to dissuade employees from staying in a job too long? and (4) Are there opportunities for promotion out of the

Figure 38–3. Outcome of Horizontal and Vertical Ranking

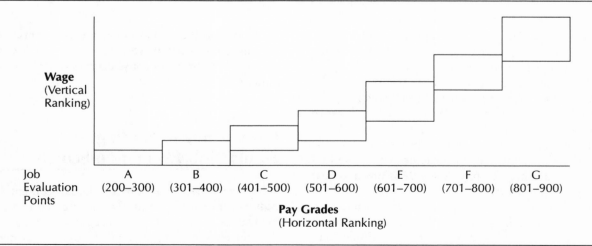

Wage (Vertical Ranking)						
Job Evaluation Points	A (200–300)	B (301–400)	C (401–500)	D (501–600)	E (601–700)	F (701–800)	G (801–900)

Pay Grades (Horizontal Ranking)

grade, or is it a grade that employees will remain in throughout their organizational career? If you have an incentive program and want to hold on to your employees for some time in the same pay grade, you must provide a rate range wide enough to allow steady upward movement during employees' expected tenure in the grade. On the other hand, labor costs can be held down if, for a job class where labor is easily acquired and replacement costs are low, you construct a narrow rate range that actually frustrates employees and motivates them to leave after a short tenure in the grade.

Once we have defined with width of our rate ranges, we want to observe the degree of overlap between rate ranges. Some compensation specialists suggest that less than 15 percent overlap is too little and greater than 50 percent overlap is too great. Some overlap between adjacent rate ranges is assumed, since entry-level employees in Grade B may be thought of as equal to or less in value than high tenured employees in Grade A. We are all aware, however, of problems in equity perceptions when a lower-level job class shifts upward such that the wage differential between adjacent job classes is negligible. We define this as wage compression. The causes of such compression are many, and sometimes the economic forces causing compression cannot be controlled by management. Still, the compensation specialist should identify these problems and attempt to minimize the damage.

OTHER CONSIDERATIONS

Thus far, I have provided a brief sketch of how to design a compensation system using an in-house point-factor job evaluation and wage survey. The examples have been simple, but the steps outlined here should provide a framework for understanding compensation practices. Space does not allow me to discuss all the complexities and issues encountered in designing compensation systems. For example, I have not discussed how to plan and budget a compensation system. Ability to pay can constrain the best intentions and prevent one from designing an equitable pay structure. Economic realities (high demand, low supply) may dictate that some job classes be priced higher than job evaluation results suggest. Other issues and considerations are as follows:

1. Does the organization have one internal wage structure, or does it have two or more structures? For example, the organization might consist of two distinct internal labor markets: exempt and nonexempt. If this is the case, separate job evaluation procedures might be employed for each sub-structure. Pay policy might also differ for each sub-structure.

2. Different organizations weight the external and internal equity perspectives differently. For example, some firms to not seek an evaluation of job's worth independent of the market. Their job evaluation procedures implicitly employ wage data and compensable factors to define directly wage levels (e.g., factor-comparison, MULTI-COMP, TPFC job evaluation).

3. Some job classes have more rigidly defined job ladders than others. For example, maintenance and clerical-secretarial job classes have more patterned and rigidly defined port-of-entry positions and job ladders than professional and managerial job classes. This has implications on how easy it is to define job grades and rate range parameters.

REFERENCES

Milkovich, G.T., & Newman, J.M. (1984). *Compensation.* Plano, TX: Business Publications.

Rynes, S.L., & Milkovich, G.T. (1986). Wage surveys: Dispelling some myths about the market wage. *Personnel Psychology,* 71–90.

Wallace, M., & Fay, C. (1983). *Compensation theory and practice.* New York: Kent.

39 APPLYING EQUITY THEORY TO COMPENSATION

Michael Duane

The notion that people should receive just or fair treatment for their efforts dates back to the beginning of civilization. Aristotle (Ross, 1966), for example, noted that rewards should be allocated according to qualifications: "The problem. . . . is to divide the distributive honor or reward into parts which are to one another as the merits of the persons who are to participate" (p. 1131). Today, there is a general agreement among scholars and compensation practitioners that a key, if not the key, to work motivation, with its subsequent effects on performance, is whether employees believe that they are being adequately compensated for their jobs. While there are a number of modern theories that incorporate this equity criterion in describing and making predictions about the relationship between pay and motivation (Greenberg, 1982; Leventhal, 1976) Milkovich and Newman (1987) argue that Adams's equity theory plays a particularly important role in the management of pay programs. In this chapter, the basic tenets of equity theory as proposed by Adams (1963) are examined, followed by a discussion of their practical applications to compensation systems.

At the heart of equity theory is the ratio of outcomes to inputs. In an industrial relations system, outcomes are anything of value that employees perceive as returns for performing their jobs, such as pay, fringe benefits, status symbols, recognition, and opportunity for achievement. Inputs, on the other hand, are anything of value that employees perceive as relevant contributions to job performance; examples include education, intelligence, experience, effort, or, as will be noted later, even race or sex of employees. When making judgments as to whether they are being fairly treated by management, employees compare their own outcomes to inputs ratios with those of one or more referent others. A referent other, in this case, may be someone in the same organization, someone in a different organization holding a similar position, a neighbor, or even the comparer in a previous job. The important point here is that as with the selection of relevant input; and outcomes, the choice of the referent other is a personal action exercised by each employee.

Inequity exists whenever individual employees perceive their ratios to be unequal to the ratios of their respective referent others. As a consequence, the comparers experience a sense of uneasiness or tension, which, when sufficiently severe, motivates them to seek an equitable state either through perceptual or actual adjustments of inputs and/or outcomes (Adams, 1963, 1965). According to Adams (1963), there are two basic states of inequity: underpayment inequity and overpayment inequity. With the underpayment condition, the employees feel that they contributed more to their jobs than they receive from them. Overpayment inequity, on the other hand, occurs when they feel overly compensated for their work-related inputs. In either case, however, the employees will attempt to achieve equity in order to reduce the anger or frustration generated by the underpayment condition or the quilt produced by the overpayment state.

According to Adams (1963), there are a number of equity–restoration devices. They included the following:

1. *Alter inputs.* In opting for this adjustment mechanism, employees attempt to achieve an equitable condition by actually increasing (overpayment inequity) or decreasing (underpayment inequity) input levels. An obvious example of such action occurs when employees reduce effort expended or time spent on their jobs as a means of adjusting to perceived underpayment inequity.

2. *Alter outcomes.* Employees may also act to restore equity by attempting to increase (underpayment inequity) or decrease (overpayment inequity) their outcome levels. Thus, for example, employees who feel underpaid and who are well monitored by their supervisors, making effort reduction more difficult, may simply ask for a raise. Indeed in responding to perceived pay

I am grateful to Ross Azevedo and Nancy Blades for their help in preparing this chapter.

inequities of their members, unions resort to this mechanism through contact negotiations with management.

3. *Distortion of one's inputs or outcomes.* Rather than seeking to change actual inputs or outcomes, employees may perceptually distort them. In an over reward situation, for instance, an employee may initially experience guilt from the perceived inequity but, after further consideration, accept the salary or wage level as deserved for a job that is now celebrated as more difficult, (involving more effort or skill,) than previously believed.

4. *Leave the field or organization.* When employees are not able to adjust inputs or outcomes to inequities actually or perceptually, they may attempt to remedy their condition by searching for an organization that does adequately compensate them for performing identical or similar jobs, or they may choose to enter an entirely new profession. This perhaps explains why many K–12 teachers, who generally enjoy their profession, leave it due to inadequate pay.

5. *Act on the referent other.* Another way equity can be achieved is to alter the referent other's inputs or outcomes actually or perceptually. Consider the case in which those women who enter a previously male— dominated profession are harassed by some individuals who view "femaleness" to be a less valuable input than "maleness." Obviously, the intention is to eliminate the reference source from the comparer's environment, thereby regaining equity.

6. *Change the referent other.* A final method of adjusting to an inequitable situation is for the person to change the referent other. Thus, instead of comparing input-outcomes ratios with a co-worker(s), the person may, for example, achieve a state of equity by drawing a comparison with a neighbor. Although Adams (1965) does not specify the conditions under which a particular adjustment mechanism will be employed, it can be argued that change of referent other would probably be used as a last resort when actual or perceptual methods of varying outcomes or inputs have failed to result in an equitable assessment.

PRACTICAL APPLICATIONS OF EQUITY THEORY TO COMPENSATION SYSTEMS

Pay has significance for equity theory in that it is among the many outcomes used in assessing the exchange relationship. Moreover, as Milkovich and Newman (1987) note, since "money is one of the most visible components and frequently one of the easiest to modify of the variables in the (equity) model, it becomes extremely important." (p. 283). In the remainder of this chapter, several applications of the equity criterion are discussed: internal and external pay, hourly versus piece-rate pay plans, two-tier compensation plans, pay-secrecy policies, time considerations in equity adjustment, comparable worth, and merit-pay plans.

Internal and External Pay

A major objective of a compensation program is to assign salary and wage rates in line with the value of jobs to an organization. The challenge, of course, is to accomplish this in a fashion so that pay levels are acceptable to employers and employees alike. According to equity theory, employees are prune to compare wage rates within their organizations in determining their acceptability. In an effort to ensure pay consistency and it is hoped, acceptability, most organizations use some form of job evaluation method in making compensation decisions.

Several job evaluations devices are available, including simple management judgment, ranking method, classification method, point method, and factor comparison method. Although separate treatment of each of these techniques is beyond the scope of this chapter, a discussion of the point method, the most widely used job evaluation device, is in order. Briefly, it begins by conducting an analysis of those jobs under consideration and selecting compensable factors common to them. These factors are then assigned points or weights and are broken into degrees on separate scales. For the typical organization, the point method is recommended for several reasons. First, it takes into consideration the components of a job rather than the total job. Moreover, current pay levels are not considered; rather, compensable factors and total points are evaluated prior to establishing the current wage structure. "In this way, a realistic assessment of relative worth can be made instead of just relying on past patterns of worth" (Mathis & Jackson, 1985, p. 389). Finally, the point method is easily understood by managers and employees.

While use of a job evaluation method may promote internal equity comparisons of job hierarchies and pay structures, they do not generally address an organization's environment. Since current and potential employees are likely to engage in external comparisons as well, considerations of the external labor market will be necessary in establishing equitable pay systems. But as Pinder (1987) notes, there is often "a trade-off between internal and external equity considerations, which can make it very difficult to maintain perceptions of equity inside the organization while permitting it effectively to recruit new employees from the labor market" (p. 125).

An important step in linking the internal and external criteria is to tie job evaluation results closely to the externalmarket.In most cases this is done by gathering pay information through wage and salary surveys. There are a variety of different sources of such surveys. Indeed, employers may choose to conduct their own surveys. This method of collecting pay data, however, is not only time-consuming and expensive but may in fact be impossible in that the employer is attempting to survey organizations with similar jobs and, thus, fellow competitors in the labor market.As a result, most employers rely on other agencies to perform wage and salary surveys, where participants can remain anonymous.Some of the organizations that perform national studies of wages and salaries for a wide variety of jobs and industries include the American Compensation Association, American Management Association, American Society for Personnel Administration, U.S. Bureau of Labor statistics, Administrative Management society, and federal reserve system.

On the regional or local level, employers may participate in and receive pay information from wage surveys sponsored by the chamber of commerce. Regardless of the survey mode, it is important from an external equity standpoint "that the jobs covered by the survey are comparable to those being priced; that data are current; and that data are collected, analyzed, and interpreted accurately" (Heneman, Schwab, Fossum & Dyer, 1986, p. 445).

Hourly versus Piece-Rate Pay Plans

Equity theory makes different predications about how employees will react to inequities depending on the nature of the pay plan, in particular whether it is an hourly based plan or a piece-rate plan, where employees are paid on the basis of what they produce or sell. According to equity theory, hourly paid employees who are experiencing underpayment inequity may adjust by decreasing quantity and/or quality of production, depending on which action is the least noticeable to supervisory personnel. Conversely, employees working under a piece-rate plan, who feel unfairly treated, are expected to produce more with lower quality, in an effort to maximize the net level of overall pay.

Hourly paid employees who feel overly compensated for their efforts are predicted to increase quality and/or quantity, depending on which reduces the imbalance most efficiently. Responses by these same employees under an incentive plan would involve an increase in quality of production along with a decrease in quantity produced (Campbell & Pritchard, 1976).

Two-tier Compensation Plans

A rather recent development in compensation that poses interesting pay equity ramifications is the two-tier wage structure in which wage differentials are based solely on when an employee was hired. The two-tier plan is primarily a product of the collective bargaining process where management and labor negotiate lower pay rates for employees hired after a specific date than rates for their more senior peers. While admitting that such pay systems violate one of the labor movement's most cherished principles of equal pay for equal work, unions have reluctantly accepted them as alternatives to personnel cuts or wage freezes.

Initially management took a favorable position on the two-tier pay plan. American Airlines, for example, credited an estimated savings of $100 million in 1984 to its two-tier plan (Jacoby & Mitchell, 1985). Indeed, Milkovich and Newman (1987) observe that, at least in the short term, wage savings mount quickly as turnover permits substitution of lower-priced employees for their higher-paid predecessors.

Not surprisingly however, serious inequity perceptions have arisen among those employees in the lower-tier category, and these perceptions have produced some unforeseen consequences for unions and employers. To illustrate, Ross (1985) observed that two-tier structures have had negative effects on the attitudes of the lower-paid employees, as well as on their willingness to work toward the goals of a relevant organization. She found, for example, that differing wage rates led to considerable divisiveness among union workers. Moreover, Wessel (1985) notes that Hughes Aircraft recently experienced some major difficulties with its two-tier wages structures. Soon after they were implemented, the company began to suffer high turnover among the newer workers, as well as attitudinal and morale problems with the remaining workers. Such reactions, according to management, contributed to a deterioration in product quality, which eventually led to the suspension of federal government contracts.

There is also some concern that by participating in two-tier bargaining, unions are guilty of discriminating against their newer members and thus in violation of the Labor-Management Relations Act. Milkovich and Newman (1987) note that such concerns and problems have resulted in the belief on the part of many compensation experts that two-tier wage structures have peaked and will not be a significant item in future bargaining sessions.

Pay Secrecy Policies

Many organizations attempt to conceal pay information from employees in the hopes of creating equitable perceptions among employees, thereby avoiding discontent, petty complaining, and tension. secret or closed pay systems, however, have some major drawbacks. First, it is very difficult to enforce a policy of pay secrecy. Employees frequently talk among themselves about their pay or that of others; often their information is accurate, but sometimes it is not. Ironically, therefore, closed compensation systems may actually contribute to feelings of underpayment and, in turn, produce the effects they were intended to prevent.

There is also related evidence that employees, working under a closed pay system, overestimate the pay levels of their peers, triggering requests for raises and/or effort reductions, while at the same time they underestimate the salaries of supervisors, making promotion and advancement less attractive than they normally would have been (Lawler, 1965; Pinder, 1984). Consequently, Lawler (1972) has recommended that compensation levels should be disclosed despite the initial problems that the opening-up process is likely to create.

Time Considerations in Equity Adjustment

Azevedo, Duane, and Rhee (1987) and Cozier and Dalton (1982) have argued that a person's input-outcomes ratios are not static but rather constantly changing. Thus, in the event that a person seeks a raise in an attempt to adjust to an underpayment condition, management must take into account when, if at all, the raise will be granted. To illustrate, after receiving continued complaints of underpayment on the part of an employee, an employer may eventually raise the person's pay to a level equal to that of the referent other. Does this employee now perceive the condition to be equitable? Probably not. The employee may have become highly suspicious of management ("I know they could have given me the raise sooner") and no doubt still resents them for what he or she perceives as "lost" income ("Just think what I could have earned if they had been paying me what I am worth"). These inequity-causing agents must be compensated for through perceptually distorting inputs and outcomes or actually altering them before the person feels equitably treated.

Comparable Worth

Probably unbeknown to it, the U.S. Congress applied equity theory when it passed the Equal Pay Act of 1963, which asserts that persons performing equal work should receive equal pay, regardless of their sex. Surprisingly, there has been only a slight reduction in the pay gap between men and women since the law was implemented. Some have argued that the remaining differential is not due to sex discrimination but rather to several other factors: differences in seniority, differences in quality of performance, differences in quantity and quality of production, or some factor other than sex. Others, however, have argued that while the Equal Pay Act has made sex-based discrimination within jobs or occupations more difficult, such discrimination persists across them. Indeed, McDonald (1977) notes that almost half of the pay differential can be attributed to the fact that market rates for jobs dominated by women are lower than rates for jobs primarily held by men. It is contended, therefore, that to achieve pay equity for women, the concept of equal pay for equal work must be extended to include the notion of equal pay for comparable value to the organization.

There is no question that the comparable-worth issue is controversial. For example, while Eleanor Homes Norton, director of the Equal Employment Opportunities Commission (EEOC) under the Carter administration characterized comparable worth as the "EEO issue of the 1980s," Clarence M. Pendleton, Jr., chairman of the U.S. Commission on Civil Rights in the Reagan Administration referred to comparable worth as the "looniest idea since Looney Tunes." (Heneman et al., 1986). Moreover, while the

U.S. Supreme Court has decided that sex discrimination suits can be filed under Title VII of the Civil Rights Act of 1964, even when the jobs involved are not similar (*Gunther v. County of Washington,* 1981), it "emphasized that it was not defining what must be done to prove sex discrimination in compensation and that it was not ruling on the comparable worth issue" (Mathis & Jackson, 1985). But as a result of considerable political activity on the part of state and local organizations, fourteen state legislatures have incorporated the comparable-worth standard in their equal pay acts.

Aside from the legal and political concerns over comparable worth, evidence indicates that, at least from the perspective of women, it is a major consideration in achieving pay equity (Rosen, Rynes & Mahoney, 1983). In response to such evidence, Milkovich and Newman (1987) offer the following steps in implementing a comparable worth policy:

1. Use only one job evaluation system for all jobs within a facility. In most cases, the point method is recommended.

2. Calculate the gender representation (percentage male and female employees) of each job group. Any job group in which 70 percent or more of the incumbents are one gender is considered sex segregated.

3. Jobs with equal evaluation points and sex segregation should be paid equally (i.e., single policy line).

4. The wage-to-job evaluation point ratio should be based on the wages paid to male-dominated jobs.

Merit pay plans

Unlike seniority systems, which allot pay increases on the basis of experience or length of service, merit systems link raises to employee job performance. In terms of equity theory, the objective of merit systems is, of course, to tie outcomes (e.g., pay) directly to inputs (e.g., effort or performance). Cascio (1987) notes that linking pay to performance not only promotes employee motivation but also assists in attracting and maintaining good performers: "when performance is the basis for reward, high performers will tend to be the most satisfied and least likely to

quit. Low performers will tend to be least satisfied and most likely to quit" (p. 412)

Certainly there are potential barriers to an effective merit pay system. To be sure, merit systems will fail when employees are distrustful of management, when the incentive reward offered is too low, when merit pay decisions are based on biased or contaminated performance assessments, or when the link between pay and performance is too weak, which may occur, for example, when raises are automatically built into the compensation model.

Merit pay systems, however, can work if the following guidelines are adhered to:

1. *Establish appropriate standards of performance.* The expected standards of performance must be both difficult and acceptable to employees. Standards that are too low will bore employees, while overly difficult ones will frustrate them (Lock, 1968).

2. *Accurate performance appraisal systems should be used.* Performance appraisal systems that are viewed by. employees as fair and objective are an essential component of merit pay systems. An appeal mechanism should be available to employees in the event that they disagree with their supervisors' appraisals.

3. *Supervisors should be trained in the mechanics of evaluating employee performance.* Performance dimensions and standards should be well understood by those conducting the appraisals. The importance of constructive employee feedback should be emphasized to them.

4. Pay must be closely linked to performance. If performance is measured over a long period of time on a unidimensional scale, employees will be confused about what is being rewarded (Cascio, 1987). Common practice involves six-month reviews for new employees and once-a-year reviews for more senior ones (Heneman et al., 1986).

5. *Use a broad range of increases.* The merit increases should be meaningful and wide ranging in order to reflect variance in performance. Digital Equipment awards increases that range from 0 tu 30 percent; Westinghouse's raises vary from 0 to 19 percent (Cascio, 1987).

SUMMARY

Equity theory has considerable intuitive appeal to people in general; after all, most of us at some point in our work lives have felt inadequately compensated for our efforts when comparing ourselves with others. For managers, equity theory has a couple of basic messages. First, the theory points out the importance of comparison in the workplace. Identification of referent others, therefore, may have some potential value when developing compensation programs (Ivancevich & Matteson, 1987) The theory also stipulates that employees' reactions to inequity can take on different forms. Attempts to achieve an equitable condition may involve changes in inputs or outcomes or both, "with the level or direction depending on whether the inequity was perceived to be underpayment or overpayment" (Szilagyi & Wallace, 1983, p. 102).

While the research on equity theory has been somewhat limited in that pay has been the primary, if not the only, outcome used, its predictions have been generally supported, particularly those involving underpayment. As a result, there is little doubt that equity and the factors that contribute to it or subvert it should be of great concern to managers.

REFERENCES

Adams, J.S. (1963). Toward an understanding of inequity. *Journal of Abnormal and Social Psychology, 67,* 422–436.

Adams, J.S. (1965). Inequity in social exchange. In L. Berkowitz (Ed.), *Advances in experimental social psychology* (vol. 2, 267–299). New York: Academic Press.

Azevedo, R.E., Duane, M.J., & Rhee, Y.S. (1987). *Reactions to inequity: The time parameter.* Manuscript submitted for publication.

Campbell, J.P., & Pritchard, R.D. (1976). Motivation theory in industrial and organizational psychology. In M.D. Dunnette(Ed.), *Handbook of industrial and organizational psychology.* Chicago: Rand McNally.

Cascio, W.F. (1987). *Applied psychology in personnel management* (3d ed.). Englewood Cliffs, NJ: Prentice-Hall.

Cozier, R.A., & Dalton, D.R. (1982). Equity theory and time: A reformulation. *Academy of Management Review, 8,* 311–319.

Greenberg, J. (1982). Approaching equity and avoiding inequity in groups and organizations. In J. Greenberg & R.L Cohen (Eds.), *Equity and justice in social behavior* (389–435). New York: Academic Press.

Gunther v. County of Washington (1981). 451 U.S. 161.

Heneman, H.G., Schwab, D.P., Fossum, J.A., & Dyer, L.D.(1986). *Personnel/human resource management* (3d ed.). Homewood, IL: Irwin.

Ivancevich, J.M., & Matteson, M.T. (1987). *Organizational behavior and management.* Plano, TX: Business Publications.

Jacoby, S.M., & Mitchell, D.J.B. (1986) Management attitudes toward two-tier pay plans. *Journal of Labor Research, 7,* 221–237.

Lawler, E.E. (1965). Managers' perception of their subordinates' pay and of their superiors' pay. *Personnel Psychology, 18,* 413–422.

Lawler, E.E. (1972). Secrecy and the need to know. In H. Tosi, R.J. House, and M.D. Dunnette (Eds.), *Managerial motivation and compensation.* East Lansing, MI: MSU Business Studies.

Leventhal, G.S. (1976). What should be done with equity theory? In K.J. Gergen, M.S. Greenberg, & R.H. Willis (Eds.), *Social exchange: Advances in theory and research* (27– 55). New York: Plenum Press.

Locke, E.A. (1968). Toward a theory of task motivation and incentives. *Organizational Behavior and Human Performance, 3,* 157–189.

McDonald, L. (1977). Wages of work. In M. Stephenson (Ed.), *Women in Canada* (rev. ed.). Don Mills, Ontario: General Publishing.

Mathis, R.L. & Jackson, J.H. (1985). *Personnel: Human resource management* (4th ed.). St. Paul, MN: West Publishing.

Milkovich, G.T., & Newman, J.M. (1987). *Compensation* (2d ed.). Plano, TX: Business Publications.

Pinder, G.C. (1984). *Work motivation: Theory, issues, and application.* Glenview, IL: Scott, Foresman.

Rosen, B., Rynes, S., & Mahoney, T. (1983) Compensation, jobs, and gender. *Harvard Business Review,* 170–190.

Ross, I. (1985). Employers win big in the move to two-tier contracts. *Fortune, 111,* 82–92.

Ross, W.D. (Ed.). (1966). *The works of Aristotle* (vol. 9). London: Oxford University press.

Szilagyi, A.D., & Wallace, M.J. (1983). *Organizational behavior and performance.* Glenview, IL: Scott, Foresman.

Wessel, D. (1985). Split personality: Two-tier pay spreads, but the pioneer firms encounter problems. *Wall Street Journal,* (October 14), 1,9.

40 MERIT PAY: ROAD TO THE BOTTOM LINE OR BOTTOM OF THE BARREL?

Mo Cayer, Richard E. Kopelman, Janet L. Greenberg

> "Merit raises had become quasi-automatic," says one executive. "Almost all employees were rated as 'superior' or 'outstanding'.... This year ... a merit increase is something you have to earn," says Roy S. Roberts (GM's vice-president for corporate personnel). "To treat people fairly you have to treat people differently."
> —*Wall Street Journal*, January 26, 1988.

Pay-for-performance is one of the most frequently and loudly espoused values in American business organizations today. In fact, we have never heard of a chief executive officer say that his or her organization was *not* an aggressive pay-for-performance company or at least striving to be one.

Pay-for-performance reward systems come in many shapes and sizes. One way to classify these reward systems is in terms of the degree of subjectivity allowed in determining rewards. Simplifying matters somewhat, reward systems can be divided into two categories: those that employ relatively objective criteria (e.g., measured outputs, sales dollars, percentage defective) and those that rely on judgmental assessments of merit or performance (e.g., judged or rated skills, performance quality). The first category can be furthur subdivided into reward systems that are based on individual performance (e.g., piece-rate plans) and those that are based on group achievements (e.g., gain-sharing plans).

There is abundant evidence regarding the effects of objective, output-based reward systems on productivity. Across several controlled studies, individual output-based pay plans (e.g., piece rates, commissions) have been found to raise productivity by 20 to 30 percent; group plans have been found to increase productivity slightly less, by 15 to 20 percent (for an extensive review of the evidence see Kopelman, 1986).

But most organizations must rely on subjective appraisal-based merit pay programs to create a pay-for-performance linkage. For example, a survey of 557 industrial and service firms by the Conference Board (Peck, 1984) found 96 percent used some form of merit pay, usually relying on managers' and supervisors' judgments of employee performance to decide how much of an annual pay increase (the reward?) to give each employee. Even the federal government attempts to apply some degree of merit pay among its managers. In the mid-1980s President Reagan urged the nation to install merit pay for teachers, a large occupational group that historically grants pay increases based on tenure, level of education, and cost of living but not individual performance.

Despite widespread use, a study sponsored by the American Compensation Association reports organizations slightly reducing their reliance on traditional merit pay plans. Instead, a number of different pay and incentive-related activities are being tried by companies to improve their link between pay and performance. For example, about 30 percent of the firms say they now use one-time, lump sum bonuses (though many of these do not appear to be tied to individual performance). This is twice as many as five years ago (O'Dell & McAdams, 1987).

The concepts underlying merit pay seem straightforward:

- Create the belief among employees that better job performance will result in bigger (or faster) pay increases than lower performance levels and they'll be more motivated to do those things that lead to better performance.

- The flip side? Superior employees are likely to become more dissatisfied and lower their performance motivation when their supervisors don't give them greater merit increases and nonfinancial rewards than poorer performers. Even worse, those less than-superior performers— most of us—will become more satisfied and probably stay with the organization longer, though without any increase in effort.

While research findings on models of work motivation (e.g., reinforcement, goal setting, expectancy theory) provide some support for expecting better performance under merit pay (see Lawler 1973, 1981; Pinder, 1984; Locke & Henne, 1986), putting the concept into practice has been rocky.

Ed Lawler III, one of the most forceful and thoughtful champions of using pay-for-performance plans to increase work motivation, has apparently thrown in the towel on merit pay:

> In the case of merit increases, the approach itself is so flawed that it is hard to imagine a set of conditions that would make it effective.... Simply stated, they [merit pay plans] fail to create the perception that significant amounts of pay are tied to performance and thus they fail to motivate performance. (Lawler, 1987, p. 166)

He cites, for example, a 1983 study by the Public Agenda Foundation that revealed that only 22 percent of American workers say there is a direct link between how hard they work and how much they are paid. More recently the compensation consulting firm Wyatt Company found only 28 percent of the workers it surveyed nationally see a clear link between their work and the pay increases they get (*Wall Street Journal*, February 9, 1988, p. 1).

N.B. Winstanley (1981, 1982), then the compensation research manager for the Xerox Corporation, even recommended scrapping typical merit pay plans and giving 90 percent of the work force the same pay increase. He felt that managers do not accurately evaluate performance so they should not make distinctions between workers' performances, and self-esteem suffers so much when people get negative feedback that the net impact is too damaging. The result of his suggestions is to give across-the-board pay increases, meaning *not* paying for performance. Recently, American Cyanamid revamped its performance appraisal and merit pay processes to reduce dissatisfaction by drastically reducing pay-for-performance distinctions (Gellermann & Hodgson, 1988).

According to Pearce (1987), merit pay does not lead to more effective organizations because realities like uncertainty of performance requirements, task interdependence, and complexity of organizational work result in a need for employees to be flexible and cooperative. These behaviors, she suggests, do not happen with merit pay for individual performance plans.

Meyer (1987), former head of personnel research at General Electric, says that when managers using merit pay differentially award pay increases based on performance, "it is likely to create dissatisfaction and loss of self-esteem among the majority and cutthroat competition between employees.... There are relatively few situations where the conditions hold for making merit pay work" (pp. 179–180).

The purpose of this chapter is to challenge these and others (e.g., Cook, 1986; Hughes, 1986; Stankard, 1987) who advocate doing away with individual performance-based merit pay by (1) describing the major problems with traditional merit pay plans, (2) recapping research showing the effectiveness of merit pay, and (3) identifying how organizations can improve their pay-for-performance linkage with better merit pay design and implementation.

PROBLEMS

Why is there so much disappointment? There are several factors getting in the way of typical merit pay plan effectiveness.

Poor Measures of Performance

To have a strong perceived link between merit pay increases and individual performance, the latter needs to be measured. Most jobs do not have valid, easy-to-measure, objective productivity, output, or sales figures available, so organizations rely on supervisors' observations and subjective judgments.

A strength of merit pay plans is also its weakness: flexibility. Managers can take into account employee performance in several areas, including degree of collaborating and cooperation, not just the few easy-to-measure ones. The downside is that some managers will probably also fold in their evaluations of minor or irrelevant factors such as employee agreeableness, similarity of personality, age, or sex. The effect of such poor management appraisal judgments can cripple the power of the merit pay plan to motivate better work performance.

Even in the most mechanical, results-oriented versions of management by objectives, there is still considerable room for fallible judgments, such as in setting challenging and achievable goals and taking into account factors not under employee influence.

Overall research shows numerous, stubborn obstacles to supervisors observing and accurately rating their employees' performance (e.g., see Bernardin & Beatty, 1984, for a review). The result? "Because the performance measures are not trusted when pay is based on them, little is done to create the perception that pay is based on performance. . . . Indeed, in the eyes of many employees, merit pay is a fiction, a myth that managers try to perpetuate" (Lawler, 1984, p. 6).

Nonperformance Reasons for Raises

Most organizations try to achieve several objectives with their merit pay program in addition to "increasing performance motivation." These include providing a mechanism to (1) adjust salary ranges, and employees' position within them, along with increases in the labor market, competitive salaries, and inflation, (2) control payroll expenses by putting limits on raises, (3) reducing gross pay discrimination based on sex, race, and age by, at least on the surface, explicitly linking performance rating to pay increase decisions, and (4) keeping down dissatisfaction with pay to a mild roar. With so many different objectives, merit pay plans have become the compensation equivalent of the bulging Swiss Army knife—it does many things but none of them very well.

Factors other than performance also creep into managers' merit pay allocations. These include paying to restore equity among coworkers, keep morale up, and personal biases. For example, researchers found that while rated employee performance was the biggest factor in deciding on merit pay increases, many managers also gave a lot of weight to the employee's tenure in the organization (Sherer, Schwab & Heneman, 1987).

In a study of the correlates to managers' pay decisions, Heneman and Cohen (1988) found a negative rather than positive relationship between employee pay increases and their tenure in the organization. Other relationships between employee pay increases and characteristics of their supervisors were also shown.

Managers also allocate pay increases based on the degree to which they are dependent on their subordinates (Bartol & Martin, 1988). For example, managers are more likely to give larger pay increases to people who are hard to replace because of specialized skills (Fossum & Fitch, 1985).

With so many factors in addition to rated performance being used to allocate merit pay increases, it is no wonder people feel there is not much of a link.

Little Communication

Because most organizations do not publicize their merit pay practices, it is unlikely that employees know the merit payoff for different levels of performance. Employees are often left in the dark about the actual connection of performance, ratings, and merit pay. It is a lot to ask of employees to accept on faith that better performance leads to better merit pay rewards. They do not have the facts. And if anything, the usual rumors and second- or third-hand reports of "who got how much of a raise" probably do more damage than good in strengthening the pay-for-performance connection in employee minds. No wonder employees, both nonmanagement and management, complain, "It doesn't matter how much you bust your butt around here; it's the same dinky raise."

One way to clear up some of this murkiness might be to communicate to everyone the kinds of merit raises given at different levels of performance and the distribution of employees likely to receive each performance rating level. This probably results in people recognizing that a higher performance rating in fact means a higher pay raise. The downside? Most employees will also grasp how small the merit increase difference really is among performance levels characterized as "truly superior," "outstanding," or "exemplary" versus "satisfactory," "average," or "acceptable." And many managers would make less rather than more differentiation in ratings and corresponding raises. They would try to avoid having to explain different treatment (Cook, 1986a).

Poor Merit Pay Plan Design

Companies tend to put a cap on the motivational clout that can be produced from their merit pay plans. They are designed with several flaws from a motivational perspective.

Merit pay increases, usually an annual event, rarely are received immediately after performance or nonperformance since most merit pay adjustments occur long after employees have completed (or failed to complete) their many responsibilities. These distant pay increases often lack full power to reinforce, modify, and increase the frequency of those desired performance behaviors.

Perhaps most damaging is that too often only a few percentage points separate the raises given very good performers and those given to lower performers. The difference in pay from lots of hard, successful work rather than doing just enough to get by, seems unimportant, not worth it, or invisible to most people. The Wyatt Company, a national compensation consulting firm, reports as "typical" the 1987 merit pay increase percentages in figure 40–1 for employees at different rating levels and positions in their salary range. The difference in merit percentages for employee performance rated a 2 (usually defined as "better than average") from performance rated lower, a 3, is only .5 percent. The following list shows the tiny net pay impact of that performance difference:

Average workers earn in 1987: $26,800.

Average annual incremental increase (1/2 of 1 percent): $134.

Monthly increase: $11.

After-tax monthly increase: $9.

A similar analysis in a 1986 Hay compensation report indicates that the difference between an average and the top, excellent raise in 1986 was about 3 percent, or for a $30,000 per year employee, yielding about $17 per week before taxes (Bates, 1984). A similar 3.1 percent spread occurred in 1987 (*Hay Compensation Quarterly,* 1987).

At the JCPenney Company in 1985, merit guides allowed for a difference in merit pay increase of about 2 percent between "excellent" performers and those rated as "good" and a difference of about 1 percent between the latter and those rated as "satisfactory."

Teel (1986) studied the merit increase percentages given at sixteen organizations. He found that about three-quarters of exempt employees in most companies received a merit increase that was within plus or minus 2 percent of the average increase in their organization. Teel concludes that better performers do get larger raises (e.g., 8.5 percent for a 4 rating versus 6.7 percent for a lower 3 rating), although the difference does not seem sizable.

Actual decisions by managers make the payoff spread even smaller. In 1986, JCPenney managers gave merit increases of 8.4 percent to their "excellent" performers, 7.3 percent to those rated "good," and 6.8 percent to those whose performance was judged as satisfactory.

In sum, the differences in merit pay increases for different levels of performance are usually very small, both because of the constraints imposed by merit pay guides and managers' being reluctant to give different raises to employees with different performance levels.

Almost everyone who has pointed a finger at all the problems with merit pay has laid much of the

Figure 40–1. Typical 1987 Merit Pay Guide

		Percentage Increase in Base Salary			
5 (Highest)		7.0	6.5	6.0	5.5
4		6.5	6.0	5.5	5.0
Performance Ratings 3		6.0	5.5	5.0	4.5
2		5.5	5.0	4.5	4.0
1 (Lowest)		0.0	0.0	0.0	0.0

80% (Minimum)   100% (Midpoint)   120% (Maximum)

90%   110%

Pay Range

Source: Wyatt Company.

blame on pay increases that are not "meaningful." Just what is a "meaningful" pay increase?

Some research has studied this question. It appears "that the issue of meaningful pay increases is considerably more complex than a single percentage pay increase that devotes a universal threshold of meaning" (Krefting, Newman & Krzystofiak, 1987, p. 135).

Research shows people perceive at least two main categories of meanings. Merit pay increases can have meaning because of the impact they have on purchasing power and as a measure of organizational recognition, appreciation and nonfinancial feedback (Krefting & Mahoney, 1977).

Also people differ in which of these two categories of meaning dominates their interpretation of merit pay increases (Krefting, Newman & Krystofiak, 1987). Some workers who are more focused on the feedback and organizational recognition facet of their pay raise may put more value in even small pay differences. It still has motivational power, and some managers probably load up meaning of the increases they give to their employees by also telling them things that stress, based on performance, different degrees of recognition, appreciation for their efforts, and constructive feedback. Supervisors who do these can make the difference in boosting performance of at least some of their workers.

Also, when people feel that pay is earned or contingent on their performance, it tends to more positively valued and appreciated than when it is merely an entitlement of a position or membership in an organization—as in an across-the-board increase (e.g., Mahoney, Anderson Swan & Wyttenback, 1986). The importance of this is that even with the little pay differentiation in most merit pay plans, there is probably still some motivational value to them. But it is far from robust.

Another big design flaw is that since typical merit pay raises become forever built into an employee's base salary, they lose their motivational power. This is because the raise becomes a permanent part of the person's salary, normally not subject to removal if performance later drops. It is pay that is not at risk. As a result, base salary is perceived as an entitlement, received simply for occupying the job. In short, "pay raises tend to become annuities, forever paying dividends, with salaries reflecting the accumulation of performance ratings over a number of years. Thus the relationship of recent performance to base salary often remains quite foggy" (Whitney, 1988a, p. 38).

Researchers have found that people tend to put more effort at risk to reduce losses and take-aways—such as to keep from not receiving a pay increase or bonus that had been earned in the past—than they will risk at the prospect of an equivalent gain (Tversky & Kahneman, 1986). Specifically, losses loom larger than gains. Withholding money from those who no longer meet goals or higher performance standards goes against the grain of most employees and employers alike—there are always a lot of screams of unfairness. But based on the research evidence, pay plans that lead to the most gains in individual performance, (piece-rates and commissions) have both an upside *and* a downside risk, resting squarely on the employee:

> Research has shown that a very powerful motivational system is one that provides rewards for good performance, and that takes rewards away for poor performance. However, if good performance merely leads to token increases in rewards while poor performance is ignored, many people will conclude that it pays to do as little as possible; performance will fall to the lowest acceptable level. A more effective approach, therefore, is to employ both rewards and penalties. *The consequences of performance should be leveraged across all levels of performance, not just the highest levels.* (Kopelman, 1986, p. 46)

Distinctions in Rated Performance Less Than True Performance

It is frequently shown that managers do not make fine enough distinctions in rating their workers' performance unless they are forced to rank them (Bernardin & Villanova, 1986). Are finer distinctions justified?

How different is performance really across different employees in the same job? It is usually hard to show in a dollars and cents fashion; there are are many jobs with objective, countable indicators of performance and productivity, and where the performance opportunity is the same, not confounded by differences in technology, location, availability of customers and other factors.

But there are several studies of employee differences using hard, objective performance output measures across a range of occupations (except for hardest-to-measure executives) that show big performance differences between people (Schmidt & Hunter, 1983; Cascio & Ramos, 1986). For nonexecutive jobs, the typical top workers produce about twice as much as the bottom workers in the same assignment. For example, in a study comparing salespeople working in the same department of thirty-five JCPenney stores (a total of 320 departments sampled), there were big differences between sales people in their average personal sales per hour, even though they all had equal access to the same merchandise, same mix of heavy and slow customer traffic hours, and so forth. The typical top performer outsold the typical bottom performer by 115 percent more sales—better than two to one.

Differences in people can lead to substantial differences in performances. A combination of skills, aptitude, and motivation is thought to account for these big performance differences. When 85 to 100 percent of employees in most organizations are rated as performing in one or two categories, real performance distinctions are lost.

Managers' Emotions

Merit increases depend on performance appraisal ratings. Much of the literature on performance appraisals concludes that managers give ratings (and oral performance feedback) that are, on average, better and more lenient than truly deserved; they often "soft-pedal." Research confirms that many managers try to avoid giving honest ratings and feedback when they believe employees will react with disappointment, anger, resentment, or depression (e.g., Fisher, 1979; Cayer, DiMattia, & Wingrove, 1988). That results in managers' procrastinating and distorting, so performance feedback and ratings are sometimes not reflective of true performance. There are fewer low ratings and fewer raises being withheld than ought to be and more tiptoeing around discussions of improvement rather than direct, on-the-level talk.

Why so much emotion? Managers recognize

there is sometimes a low correlation between how they rate subordinates and how their subordinates rate themselves. Research confirms that employees *tend* to evaluate their own performance higher than do their supervisors or peers (Meyer, 1975), so many managers back down from facing up to what might be an uncomfortable discussion or conflict.

Managers and executives even admit to giving performance ratings that are deliberately influenced by political and policy factors. For example, in one study of sixty executives (Longenecker, Gioia & Sims, 1987) many said they manipulated appraisals to get higher raises for some of their people, to "keep them happy," and at other times followed a directive from higher management that there would be no "outstanding" ratings given out because of a tight merit budget.

In another case that one of us came across, a high-level executive refused to allow any of his 4,000 managers to be rated in the top performance category ("outstanding") because, as he said, "no one is perfect."

Adding to this complex situation is that managers fill several roles in trying to get their employees to work better, smarter, harder, and so forth. At times managers may offer support and counsel and advise their staff, and at other times they evaluate, judge, and hand out rewards and reprimands. Some feel these roles are in conflict and therefore too tough for one person to perform well, especially within the condensed time period of a performance appraisal review discussion (Meyer, Kay & French, 1965).

Because of this difficulty, Meyer (1987) recommends organizations put more of their efforts in a well-designed and -administered promotional process. This would allow "significant monetary rewards for performance . . . [and] yield greater returns in motivating employees to excel than efforts expended in trying to make merit pay work" (p. 185). We agree that the prospect of getting promoted can be a powerful motivation. But in our view, people's self-esteem may still be negatively affected when they do not receive the promotion they want, and promoting excellent salespeople, engineers, and the like into management or other jobs that they are not qualified for only creates more problems.

DOES MERIT PAY WORK?

It is especially hard to evaluate how well typical merit pay plans are actually causing people to perform better than they would without merit pay. The biggest reason for this is that most jobs that are covered by these plans do not have "hard," objective, and countable output measures—the kind that would allow easy comparison in performance results between merit pay workers and those in a control group performing similar work. Second, organizations resist conducting true experiments with random assignment to conditions. So the little evaluation that has been published has often used criterion measures that are proxies for the real thing and in nonequivalent settings.

Subjective performance appraisal judgments or ratings have been used in a few cases. In a study of three engineering firms, each claiming merit pay for performance, Kopelman (1976) found differences between them in how well they related merit pay to performance ratings (r's ranging from .30 to .70). The higher who a firm's pay-for-performance correlation, the more workers said they expended effort and the better they said they performed their jobs, on average.

Researchers studied the impact of replacing a university's merit-based pay plan with one giving equal percentage pay increases to all faculty (Keaveny & Allen, 1979). As predicted, those faculty members who felt more equitably rewarded by the new across-the-board pay plan were also lower performers. Better performers tended to feel underrewarded by the new plan.

In a comparison of two hospitals, one that reportedly gave rewards based on merit and the other on seniority, researchers found that employees in the merit hospital said they worked harder and valued rewards higher (Schneider & Olson, 1970).

After one of two very similar paper manufacturing plants dropped its merit pay plan, there was a significant decline in average rated performance, and high performers became also more dissatisfied (Greene & Podsakoff, 1978).

Kopelman and Reinharth (1982) studied the correlations between performance ratings and merit pay increases in ten branches of a large white-collar, financial institution. They found these pay-for-performance correlations varied widely (from .09 to .66) between branches even though they used the same performance appraisal and pay increase procedures. As predicted, employees in branches with higher pay-for-performance correlations tended to have higher average performance ratings.

In an attempt to improve work motivation among managers in the federal government, Congress enacted the Civil Service Reform Act (CSRA) in 1978. One feature of this legislation was to convert from an across-the-board pay increase system, where all managers received the same pay increase percentage, to a partial merit or performance-linked pay increase process; half of the allowable pay increase was to be awarded based on rated performance and the other half was automatic. Pearce, Stevenson, and Perry (1985) studied the impact of new merit pay practices across district offices of the Social Security Administration. The authors, using a complex longitudinal design, concluded that "the merit pay program had no effect on organizational performance, suggesting that merit pay may be an inappropriate method of improving organizational performance" (1985, p. 261). The authors did acknowledge that "implementation of the federal merit pay program was flawed in several ways" (p. 271). These included the very small amount of pay increase at risk (1–2 percent); controversy and widespread mistrust about the motives of government leaders, from the president on down, for pushing merit pay on them; and simultaneous and problem-riddened conversion from a trait-based appraisal rating process to a goals and objectives-setting approach.

These led an administrator at the U.S. Office of Personnel Management to conclude, "We could not have designed a system for the purpose of foiling any better than the way we implemented the CSRA" (Fiss, 1983).

Markham (1988) found a low correlation ($r = .19$, n.s.) between supervisors' ratings of their managerial and professional employees and resulting merit pay raise percentages. In this organization managers of supervisors (a level above the raters) decided how many merit pay dollars a supervisor's work group could receive. Those supervisors who had higher average appraisal ratings were able (or willing?) to give higher merit increases, but those supervisors who had groups with lower average ratings had fewer dollars to give their workers. This process resulted in a significant relationship between work groups' average performance ratings and their average raises:

> When a manager has to make decisions which affect his/her direct subordinates, then no systematic differentiations appear to be made. In other words, whether the superior rates a direct subordinate relatively low or high within the group makes little difference in the total amount of raise awarded. However, when making decisions about the pool of merit monies for those employees two levels below, it appears that managers are willing

to differentiate between groups based on the units' average performance ratings, (hence the inter-unit correlation of $r = .45^*$).

Hills, Scott, Markham, and Vest (1987) studied how well a "classic" merit pay plan worked in a public sector transportation agency. Among their findings were reported correlations between performance appraisal ratings and percentage pay increases ranging from $r = .32$ to $r = .73$, indicating low to high pay-for-performance linkages. Units varied in the strength of their reward system responsiveness. In addition, almost three-quarters of the over 800 employees who responded to an attitude survey disagreed to some extent that merit increases accurately reflected their job performance.

Still, we believe that dissatisfaction with a merit pay plan does not automatically mean it is not working well. If those who are most dissatisfied are also among the poorest performers and those who are most satisfied are also among the best performers, then the merit plan may be rewarding high performers, triggering higher work motivation, and giving low performers relatively correct feedback.

Organizations can use several different reward methods, at varying degrees of risk and reward and for different groups of its employees. There is a lot of variety. Some seem to respond vigorously versus negligibly to differences in the performance of its members. A handful of studies have looked to see if companies that offer or withhold significant performance-based pay (bonuses) for their executives also do better on hard financial measures than companies offering fewer or less robust executive incentives. These are usually not traditional judgment-based merit pay plans but the studies are relevant.

Redling (1981) correlated a measure of corporate performance (five-year making on combined earnings growth and return on shareholders' equity) with growth in executives' base salary plus bonus pay. He found only a tiny relationship ($r = .09$) between pay increases and improvements in corporate performance.

Others find different results. Crystal (1984) reports that "when company size is held constant, [CEO] pay does vary—and significantly—depending on a company's performance [return on equity, E.P.S.]."

In an article titled "Executives' Pay: Is It Too High?" (*New York Times*, April 27, 1988, p. D2), results of a study of 1,300 companies over thirteen years are reported: "For every $1,000 gained in market value and dividends ... chief executives were rewarded with an extra 2 cents. Thus for a company in the middle of the Fortune 500 with a market value around $1 billion, a doubling of the share value would typically net the chief executive a mere $20,000 in extra pay." That contrasts with a study of CEO incentive pay plans in sixty-seven firms after they were restructured in a leveraged buyout (LBO). With these tightly held companies, CEOs could expect, on average, $64 in extra pay for an extra $1,000 in total return to stockholders, a whoppingly more meaningful pay incentive than received by the biggest group of companies, which are publicly held.

In two separate but similar studies, Shuster and Zingheim (1985, 1986) classified seventy-five sales organizations and fifty financial service firms (in the second study) into "the best" and "the rest" groups according to their financial performance. In both cases the researchers also examined descriptions of each company's pay plans and judged their pay-for-performance incentive opportunity. On average, better-performing companies allowed for bigger gains and reductions in pay and bonus incentives based on performance.

However, no objective data were presented on actual merit pay practices, and many other differences that relate to pay practices (marketing strategies, technology, leadership) could have accounted for differences in financial performance rather than pay plan responsibilities.

For example, organizations differ in the extent to which they are controlled by owners and large shareholders versus those with no dominant shareholder or family, resulting in a high degree of control by lesser-owning top management. In firms where one owner, owning family, or other dominant shareholder exists,

top managers tend to receive pay and bonuses that are more closely linked to their firm's performance than firms in which top management is primarily in control (Tosi, Gomez-Mejia & Hinkin, 1987).

Apparently, many executives pursue increases in personal earnings by increasing sales volume and size of their firm rather than maximizing profit unless challenged and held accountable by significantly powerful owners or shareholders.

What does all of this research mean? Overall, the research that has actually computed merit pay-for-performance correlations shows mixed results. In some organizations or their branches, there is no relationship between individual performance ratings and the size of merit pay increases, while in others it is moderately high. Most correlation coefficients are in the low range—.20 to .40—but all merit pay plans are not equally well designed or executed. Apparently some places are more responsive to performance than others.

Should organizations work to strengthen their merit pay-for-performance relationship? Theoretically, the answer ought to be "yes." Will the effort actually lead to better performance? Despite the problems, the research we covered also suggests "yes." But the research does not directly focus on both profitability and how well merit pay is actually linked to performance. Do units with a stronger merit pay-for-performance linkage have higher profits? To answer this bottom-line question with the most direct evidence to date, we were able to see if differences in merit pay-for-performance practices corresponded to differences in unit profitability.

JCPENNEY STORES CASE STUDY

We collected archival data on management-level merit pay increases and appraisal ratings for years 1981 and 1982 and store profitability for 1982 and 1983.

Merit Plan

The basic merit pay procedures of this nationwide retailer have been in place for many years. Like most other merit pay plans, they rested on the use of a guide chart to help managers determine pay percentage increases. The size and the timing of the increases were driven by both their performance ratings and the position of their employee's base salary within their salary range or grade level. Table 40–1 shows the guide used in 1982. Typical of merit guides, managers

still used some discretion in deciding on the exact merit pay percentage and timing within a narrow range.

Appraisal

Each management employee's performance was formally evaluated annually by his or her manager and then reviewed and approved by that manager's boss. At the time, the appraisal focused on performance results, strengths, weaknesses, ratings of management characteristics (e.g., traits), and potential for advancement. The performance of these managers is often partially reflected in objective figures like sales gains, profit margin percentages, and salary costs. An overall performance appraisal rating was subjectively

Table 40–1
1982 Merit Increase Guidelines

Performance Rating	Normal Percentage of Associates Qualifying	Relation to Total Earnings Range					
		Below Minimum	First Quartile	Second Quartile	Third Quartile	Fourth Quartile	Over Maximum
1	5–10	13–15% 6–8 Mos.	12–15% 10–12 Mos.	11–14% 11–13 Mos.	10–13% 12–14 Mos.	9–12% 13–15 Mos.	6–10% 15–Mos. +
2	30–40	9–13% 7–9 Mos.	9–12% 10–13 Mos.	8–11% 11–13 Mos.	7–10% 12–14 Mos.	6–8% 13–15 Mos.	5–8% 15–Mos. +
3	40–60	8–10% 8–10 Mos.	7–10% 11–13 Mos.	7–9% 11–14 Mos.	6–8% 13–15 Mos.	5–7% 14–16 Mos.	No Increase
4	4–10	Follow-up performance review 3–6 months				No increase	
5	0–2	No increase; termination required					

Notes: Total earnings for the purpose of determining relationship to range is the associate's actual salary plus incentive compensation units @ $1.00.
    The store's actual unit value should be considered when determining the mix of increase (only units or a combination of both).
    The table suggests approximate time and percentages of increases based on the associate's performance and position in the total earnings range.

decided on by the manager according to the following scale (since modified):

1 = Outstanding

2 = Good performance, exceeds requirements

3 = Satisfactory performance, meets requirements

4 = Fair performance, improvement needed to meet requirements

5 = Unsatisfactory, problem list performance

6 = Too new to rate in this assignment

Among this sample, 93.4 percent of management employees were rated either a 2 or 3, indicating limited performance differentiation between employees.

Sample

Our sample initially consisted of 5,802 management employees working in 475 larger department stores. Cases were eliminated for such reasons as a mismatch between reported pay increases and calculated pay increases, managers who transferred to other stores, missing data, or having fewer than five managers in a store. The final sample totaled 5,097 managers in 398 stores.

Reward System Responsiveness

The extent to which each store's merit reward practices were responsive to performance (RSR) was assessed by calculating the correlation between employees' performance ratings (averaged for 1981 and 1982) and their merit pay increases, within each of the 398 stores.

The lower was the RSR correlation for a store, the weaker was the responsiveness of merit pay to performance, and presumably, the lower was the store's performance; the higher was the RSR, presumably the higher was a store's performance. Store performance was operationalized as store operating profit as a percentage of store sales volume.

We chose to use merit dollar increase rather than percentage increase as our measure of merit pay increase because the merit guide allowed for smaller percentages the higher a manager's base salary increased in the pay range. That contaminated the pay percentage size since it could be small or large depending on the size on the person's base salary alone, regardless of his or her performance.

Even though they all had the same merit guide and performance appraisal process, stores differed in how well they linked pay for performance. But what is more interesting is those differences related to store profitability. Lots of factors affect store profits, such as location, competition, and store size. We still found a statistically significant relationship between RSR and store profits, though the magnitude was small: $r = .18$ ($p < .001$). Even with such a low relationship, we found substantial practical impact or utility. We divided the stores into three RSR categories. Those stores where the RSR correlation was negative were classified as the low RSR group; stores where the correlation was positive but less than .30 were categorized as the middle RSR group; and stores where the relationship equaled or exceeded +.30 were designated as the high RSR group. The results of an analysis of variance with store profitability as the criterion show a statistically significant difference between the RSR groups (table 40–2).

Utility

What does this all mean to the organization? After further subtracting noncontrollable expenses—approximately 9 percent for things like rent, utilities, and corporate charges—the difference in 1982 net store profitability between the high-RSR group (8.32 percent) and the low-RSR group (7.22 percent) is about 15 percent. That is, stores with stronger pay for performance are 15 percent more profitable (net store profits) than stores in the lowest pay-for-performance group, a yield averaging about $200,000 per store. If one-quarter of the 600 large stores in the total company increased their pay for performance, or RSR, from the level of the lowest group to the highest, the impact on pretax company profits would be a hefty gain of about $30 million. Of course, this assumes a causal connection between RSR and profits—something not testable in this study.

The results were obtained despite a number of practical impediments. First, more than 90 percent of all performance scores were one of two values. Second, rated performance was often geared (unofficially) to time in rank, the norm being the requirement that at least two years pass before raising a manager's rating. Third, as a consequence of the first two and other factors, the average within-store performance pay increase correlation was only $r = .26$. Fourth, because salary increases and performance appraisals did not usually occur at the same time, this likely capped the potential motivational clout of the merit reward plan. With management attention to these problems, the potential profit payoff of merit pay might be considerably greater.

A few factors in JCPenney probably helped the merit pay plan work to some extent. In comparison to the weak merit pay situation found in some settings described earlier (e.g., federal government, transit authority), merit pay at JCPenney has had a better implementation. First, many managers are held accountable for performance that is more easily measured—sales, profits, salary expenses—though there are still major performance areas not easily measured, like customer service, attractiveness of displays, and employee development. Second, performance appraisals are done annually and have been for many years.

Third, the attitudes of store management employees toward merit pay are fairly positive. Figure 40–2 shows they feel motivated to perform because of it; about half think merit increases have been fair and that their performance is perceived to have had at least a moderate influence on their merit increases.

We believe there is some motivational value even with the small pay increase differentials applied in JCPenney stores. As reported by Krefting et al. (1987), pay increases for employees who put primary value on their work role and pursue feedback about

Table 40–2
Impact of RSR on Store Profitability

RSR Categories	N	Mean Operating Profitability in 1982	Mean Operating Profitability in 1983
Low RSR ($r < .00$)	105	16.22%	16.59%
Middle RSR ($r = .00–.29$)	95	16.79%	17.40%
High RSR ($r > .30$	198	17.32%	17.65%
		$F_{(2,395)} = 5.86$ ($p = .003$)	$F_{(2,395)} = 5.23$ ($p = .004$)

Note: Performance scores were reversed in computing RSR such that a high level of performance was associated with a high score.

Figure 40–2. Management Attitudes toward Merit Pay

In comparison to the quality of my performance, my base salary is:

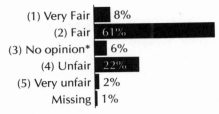

(1) Very Fair — 8%
(2) Fair — 61%
(3) No opinion* — 6%
(4) Unfair — 22%
(5) Very unfair — 2%
Missing — 1%

Average Rating = 3.04
Standard Deviation = 1.22

In comparison to the quality of my performance, the merit increases I have received are:

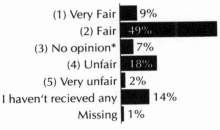

(1) Very Fair — 9%
(2) Fair — 49%
(3) No opinion* — 7%
(4) Unfair — 18%
(5) Very unfair — 2%
I haven't recieved any — 14%
Missing — 1%

Average Rating = 2.40
Standard Deviation = 1.02

In comparison to the quality of my performance, my total earnings are:

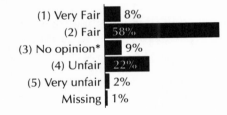

(1) Very Fair — 8%
(2) Fair — 58%
(3) No opinion* — 9%
(4) Unfair — 22%
(5) Very unfair — 2%
Missing — 1%

Average Rating = 2.81
Standard Deviation = 0.96

How much has your performance influenced the amount of your merit increases?

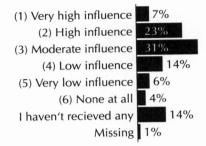

(1) Very high influence — 7%
(2) High influence — 23%
(3) Moderate influence — 31%
(4) Low influence — 14%
(5) Very low influence — 6%
(6) None at all — 4%
I haven't recieved any — 14%
Missing — 1%

Average Rating = 3.04
Standard Deviation = 1.22

How much does the chance to get an early merit increase motivate you to perform your best?

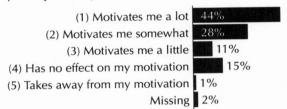

(1) Motivates me a lot — 44%
(2) Motivates me somewhat — 28%
(3) Motivates me a little — 11%
(4) Has no effect on my motivation — 15%
(5) Takes away from my motivation — 1%
Missing — 2%

Average Rating = 2.01
Standard Deviation = 1.14

How much does the chance to get a large merit increase motivate you to perform your best?

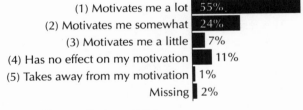

(1) Motivates me a lot — 55%
(2) Motivates me somewhat — 24%
(3) Motivates me a little — 7%
(4) Has no effect on my motivation — 11%
(5) Takes away from my motivation — 1%
Missing — 2%

Average Rating = 1.78
Standard Deviation = 1.04

Note: N = 4,000 JC Penney managers surveyed in 1984.

their abilities and performance (recognition oriented) are still likely to direct effort toward goals that lead to even tiny differences in raises between different performance ratings. With the help of their managers, some people will attribute enough positive meaning to the prospect of an above-average raise that it fuels motivation—effort toward goals that are important in deciding on performance ratings.

Other employees who place primary value on economic utility—and marginal gains–probably will decide that the extra effort required to earn a 1 percent larger pay raise is too much to contribute. The payoff is not worth the extra effort. The combined effect is a limp, but still useful, pay-for-performance process.

Last, some of the JCPenney managers do a better

job monitoring their employees' performance—they stay on top of what is happening, comparing it to expectations. Some coach and give feedback and differentiate between employees based on performance results—even if done imperfectly—so that differ-ences in ratings and merit pay increases correspond somewhat. Various internal and external surveys show that managers differ in these key behaviors (e.g., Hinkin, Podsakoff & Schreisheim, 1987).

RECOMMENDATIONS FOR ORGANIZATIONS

Most merit pay plans are hurting. If they were race horses, they would probably be put out of their misery. But as flawed as they are, we believe the positives outweigh the negatives and that they can be made better. Though they are difficult and uncomfortable, we do not think most organizations should give up trying to influence motivation through responsive individual-based reward practices. Managers need all the tools they can use to get their employees to care about the same thing they care about (or ought to)—better job performance. And when managers frequently monitor the performance of their staff (Komaki, 1986), give rewards like pay increases and bonuses for good work, and alternatively, omit rewards and/or deliver undesirable consequences for less than good work, research confirms they are more likely to get results (e.g., Mount, 1987; Hinkin, Podsakoff & Schriesheim, 1987; Luthans, Hodgetts & Rosenkrantz, 1988). Without a well-designed merit pay plan, most managers will have less leverage influencing employee commitment to goals and boosting motivation.

What should organizations do? There are no simple, painless solutions, but several actions ought to help establish management's credibility that the organization truly pays for performance.

1. Different compensation strategies should be applied where they fit best; one size *does not* usually fit all. In some extreme, problem-ridden situations (very low trust; no agreement on what is good performance) or in settings where individual performance does not matter much, it may be necessary to abandon individual merit pay for across-the-board, time—or skill—or group-based incentives (see Lawler, 1983, and Newman, 1987, for specifics). But in our view, these are the exceptions. Most organizations ought to work to improve individual-based merit and incentive or bonus pay *before* adding on other incentives. These other schemes can be valuable (Bullock & Lawler, 1984; Pritchard et al., 1988) and better fit total business strategy, but holding individuals accountable for their performance, even within interdependent groups, tends to lead to higher perfor-mance and less loafing (e.g., Tetlock, 1985; Weldon & Gargano, 1986).

2. Clarify the objectives of the merit pay increase program. Accept that there will be several objectives, but return increasing "performance motivation" to the top of the list. Build consensus among management that, although it is sometimes uncomfortable to deal with, it is the right objective. Show them some of the research cited here. Conduct research on pay-for-performance effectiveness in your own organizations. Compute correlations between raises and ratings, show distributions of each, and survey managers and employees about their views.

3. Make better performance more rewarding. Restructure merit guides for people below midpoint in the salary range to receive larger-than-usual pay increases to superior or outstanding performers, and smaller (or no) raises for average or satisfactory performers: increase the frequency and differential from around a slim 2 per cent, to at least 5 to 6 per cent between satisfactory and superior workers. That means many workers will get smaller increases than they are used to. Also separate out general increases to keep competitive from *merit*.

Compensation directors need to lead their organizations by creating a pay-for-performance vision and not just rely on competitive surveys. Top management needs to buy in to this approach and accept that there may be some disgruntlement and dissatisfaction. Several resources describe how more meaningful differences in pay increases can be built into merit guidelines (Hildebrandt, 1978; Bates, 1984; Smith, O'Dowd & Christ, 1987; Wagel, 1988; Sullivan, 1988).

A one-time, lump-sum bonus rather than a permanent increase to base salary ought to be used to reward employers for their performance after they reach the midpoint of their salary range. Bonuses can immediately follow major accomplishments. They must be earned anew. This removes the fixed, annuity feature of traditional merit pay plans, and the size of the lump sum may be perceived as more meaningful and attractive (Lawler, 1981; Gluckman, 1983; Whitney, 1988a). Employees like them but there is no direct research on how well they motivate better performance.

It still requires an effective performance appraisal process and managers must have the courage to allocate (grant and withhold) bonuses based on their evaluation of that performance, workers who do not get bonuses they expect are still likely to experience dissatisfaction.

4. There is some confusion among researchers, personnel practitioners and, executives on what "pay" means in pay-for-performance processes. Is it the total compensation received—base salary plus any bonuses, pay increases, and benefits? Is it the salary increase percentage or the dollar amount of increase received? Is it short-term pay (one year) or cumulative over the long term (several years or even over an entire career)? Does it include pay increases associated with promotions? Does "pay" also include nonfinancial status symbols—corner office, bigger desk, title, exclusive secretary? Chances are workers vary in what is the focus of their attention and energy.

Whitney (1988a) recommends that organizations shift their espoused policy from "the better you do, the bigger the raise" to "the better you do, the more you make." The change in emphasis is from focusing on the size and frequency of a pay raise to making *total* compensation equal for equal levels of performance. This can happen by lots of communication (Bookbinder & Seraphin, 1987) and leadership so that, as a result, employees perceive a stronger link between their overall performance contributions and their *total* earnings.

5. Upgrade performance appraisal and management processes (see books such as Bernardin & Beatty, 1984; Patton, 1982; Latham & Wexley, 1981). Make them flexible and goal oriented—using objective indicators of results and outcomes where appropriate. Offer managers forms that are user friendly and that prompt them to give their employees more job-specific behavioral feedback and coaching. Throw away generic forms that only vaguely describe traits. The end product ought to be a clear, concrete agreement about what results and behaviors are expected from the employee, with flexibility to change them as conditions do.

6. Train managers to appraise. A recent report on findings from a survey of human resource and compensation managers from more than 800 companies shows only 31 percent of responding companies rate their present programs "successful" in linking pay to performance. The barrier most often cited (by 55 percent of respondents) was "inadequate training of managers," according to the Wyatt Communicator (cited in *Compensation and Benefits Review*, May–June 1988).

Ask most people what they felt when they received a less than favorable performance feedback or a lowered appraisal rating. Their answers are often emotional reactions like being dissatisfied, angry, depressed, shocked, defensive, anxious, demoralized, demotivated, and withdrawn; they are "downers."

These and other employee emotional reactions fall under the umbrella of "damaging to self-esteem" in the pay-for-performance literature. Managers frequently worry that their staff will become demotivated as a result of hearing unfavorable feedback or receiving a lower than-expected-raise. Does giving negative feedback to improve performance make things worse?

In many cases it does harm. At the root of employee emotional reactions like demotivation is the tendency for humans to rate mistakenly their *total* self, their worthiness as a person, based on some perceived shortcoming, problem area, or imperfections (Ellis & Harper, 1975) and to make excessively internal attributions about their causes (Snyder & Higgins, 1988). Of course some employees may not hold these irrational beliefs, so giving them constructive but unfavorable feedback is relatively painless; they are resilient. And some managers are especially good at delivering on-the-level, corrective feedback without making people feel small.

Unfortunately, many more people exaggerate the meaning of their managers' feedback, performance ratings and less-than average raises, making it hard for them to hear what is really being said and objectively decide if it fits. Some get defensive. Some will be left with self-doubts that they can meet the challenge of improved performance. Those who perceive their self-efficacy to be low (uncertain or low belief in their capability to achieve success) may become discouraged and lower their goals and, in the end, performance motivation (Bandura & Cervone, 1986). This issue should be tackled directly.

Feedback that is harsh, blaming, vague, and not prompt tends to backfire, leaving recipients resentful and with lowered motivations. Some managers are not naturally good at giving less-than-favorable feedback (including lower-than-expected raises). Training programs exist that are especially good at improving those managers' skills in active listening, giving specific, behavioral (not traits) performance feedback—favorable as well as improvement opportunities—and ratings so as to maintain and boost the recipient's self-esteem and self-efficacy in the process (Larson, 1986; Baron, 1988).

For example, *Interaction Management* is used by JCPenney and hundreds of other companies to train their managers and supervisors (available from Development Dimensions International, Pittsburgh,

PA). Other resources are available to structure effective training experiences (for either or both givers and recipients) that transfer to performance problems faced on the job (e.g., Gordon, 1977; McLagan & Krembs, 1988; Drury, 1984; *Mind over Myths*). Training employees in how to receive and constructively respond to feedback seems especially promising (Wilson & Linville, 1985; Ellis, 1972).

Most managers can benefit from practical training in setting and communicating goals and objectives that have traction and in how and when to change them (Patton, 1982). Observing and rating performance accurately is also tough for many managers to do well but can be improved with training (Hedge & Kavanagh, 1988).

Even in organizations with very responsive reward systems, lots of managers we have come across admit to doing a sloppy job in deciding on the exact pay increase. Further, they fumble so much in communicating the raise (or withholding it) that it punctures what could be a powerfully motivating event. Training managers in specific areas could go a long way to bolster pay for performance in organizations—but almost no one does it. Practice with realistic cases in making and communicating pay increases is sorely needed. For example, these are the questions managers frequently ask:

How do I give someone a raise that's less than I think they he or she deserves?

How do I give someone a raise that's right for performance but less than the person thinks he or she deserves?

How do I keep my people motivated when the merit guide doesn't allow for meaningful pay increases?

How do I get a 3 (satisfactory) rated person motivated to improve performance while giving him or her a smaller-than-average raise?

What should I say when my employee challenges me on the rating I've given him?

How do I drop someone from a "satisfactory" to "needs improvement rating without his or her reacting as if it were the "kiss of death"?

How much should results and accomplishments count in the appraisal rating in comparison to management behaviors or characteristics?

What's the best way to motivate someone who's got a lot of potential but is not producing strong results?

How do I reduce someone's defensiveness so I can give constructive feedback?

How do I keep a young, good performer motivated when there's little room for advancement?

What do I say to someone who asks, "What do I have to do to get a bigger raise?"

Probably the biggest developmental opportunity is in emotional management. Managers avoid, distort, and procrastinate in dealing with employees with performance problems. It is uncomfortable, so they often delay and delay until they blow up or rationalize that it is not really important. Research by Cayer, DiMattia, and Wingrove (1988) shows that managers frequently step around improvement discussions, on-the-level ratings, and responsive pay for performance because of their own exaggerated beliefs (e.g., "He'll get defensive and angry at me for giving him such a small raise and that would be too uncomfortable. I guess I'll give him the average increase to keep the peace"). Cayer et al. describe training experiences to help managers overcome these common, troublesome emotions and beliefs and become more assertive (not aggressive) and constructive supervisors.

Training will not fix everything, but some research has shown these kinds of supervisory experiences to have a big payback in terms of more productive employees (e.g. Decker & Nathan, 1985; Mathieu & Leonard, 1987). Still, these experiences are not likely to change managers from tiptoeing, nondifferentiating supervisors to assertive performance-responsive rewarders overnight. Training experiences are not that powerful, so compensation directors need to lobby for making sure that assertive supervisory skills are a major criterion in promotion decisions.

Another roadblock in the way of upgrading managers' skills and behaviors in these areas is that most middle and senior managers who could benefit from it probably will not attend the training. That will put a significant crimp in the consistent application of merit pay to boost employee performance, and spark griping about unfairness. But that will not be any worse than what happens today.

7. Use higher-level managers regularly to review and challenge evaluations, raises, and coaching practices of lower- and middle-level managers. They should press for making valid distinctions in performance ratings and corresponding pay increases or bonuses and hold management accountable. As Kopelman points out:

> Certainly, it is not realistic to expect lower-level managers to uphold performance standards and to make sizable distinctions in merit rewards if higher-level managers do not lend their support to

such efforts. Top management must make a vigorous and enduring commitment to the merit reward concept, and its imprimatur must be clearly communicated by actions—not just words—throughout all levels of the organization. In this vein, consider the comments of Andrep Grove, president of Intel Corporation: "In spite of the criticisms [of performance appraisal and merit pay], I remain steadfast in my conviction that if we want performance in the workplace, somebody has to have the courage and confidence to determine whether we are getting it or not. We must also find ways to enhance what we are getting. . . . We are paid to manage our organizations. To manage means to elicit better performance from members of our organization. We managers need to stop rationalizing, and to stiffen our resolve and do what we are paid to do. (Kopelman, 1986, pp. 46 to 47)

8. A powerful individual incentive can lead some people to sacrifice group goals. But just like other aspects of performance, cooperative behavior can be emphasized and observed to reduce the frequency of counterproductive behaviors. For example, where tasks are interdependently linked among employees, managers can specify what cooperation means, why it is important, and how they will be observed and evaluated.

At JCPenney managers are evaluated and given feedback on many observable team-work behaviors, including these:

- Contributes good ideas that are accepted and used by the team.
- Listens to and cooperates with others.
- Sensitive to needs of other areas or functions.
- Maintains appropriate balance between regular duties and teamwork.

Building these into everyone's vision of good performance, and following through with both rewards and enforcement sanctions, as appropriate, ought to be enough to control significant problems (Podsakoff and Todor, 1985). Group incentive pay (e.g., gain-sharing) can also be used in addition to individual merit pay.

CONCLUSION

These kinds of actions will probably strengthen the pay-for-performance relationship. Are the costs involved in taking them worth the benefits? The time and expense involved in mustering top management support for a more responsive merit pay guide, creation of a lump-sum bonus plan, training managers, continuous attention to the evaluation and coaching process, and other costly steps may not be worth an average gain of, say, 15 per cent in profitability in every organization. But we believe these actions can make the difference between just giving lip-service to being a pay-for-performance company and truly delivering it. Do not fall victim to this temptation: "When all is said and done, more is said than done." (Lou Holtz, Coach, Notre Dame University).

REFERENCES

Bandura A., & Cervone D. (1986). Differential engagement of self-reactive influences in cognitive motivation. *Organizational Behavior and Human Decision Processes* 38, 92–113.

Balkin, D.B., & Gomez-Mejia, I.R. (1987). *New Perspectives on Compensation.* Englewood Cliffs, NJ: Prentice-Hall.

Baron, R.A. (1988). Negative effects of destructive criticism: Impact on conflict, self-efficacy, and task performance. *Journal of Applied Psychology*, 73, (2), 199–207.

Bartol, K.M., & Martin, D.C. (1988). Influences on managerial pay allocations: A dependency perspective. *Personnel Psychology*, 41, 361–378.

Bates, M.W. (1984). Administering Salaries in an inflation-prone economy. In M.L. Rock (Ed.), *Handbook of wage & salary administration* (2d ed.) New York: McGraw-Hill Book Co.

Bernardin, J.H. and Beatty, R. (1984). *Performance appraisal: Assessing human behavior at work.* Boston: Kent.

Bernardin, J.H., and Villanova, P. (1986). Performance appraisal. In E.A. Locke (Ed.) *Generalizing from laboratory to field settings: research findings for industrial-organizational psychology, organizational behavior, and human resource management.* Lexington, MA: Lexington Books.

Bookbinder, S.M., and Seraphin, R.M. (198?). Making pay for performance work. *Personnel,* (September), 66–69.

Brennan, E.J. (1985). Merit pay: Balance the old rich and the new poor. *Personnel Journal,* (May), pp. 82–85.

Bullock, R.J., & Lawler, E.E. (1984). Grainsharing: A few questions and fewer answers. *Human Resources Management,* 23, 1, 23–40.

Cascio, W.F., & Ramos, R.A. (1986). Development and application of a new method for assessing job performance in behavioral/ economic terms. *Journal of Applied Psychology,* 71, 20–28.

Cayer, M., DiMattia, D.J., & Wingrove, J. (1988). Conquering evaluation fear. *Personnel Administration,* (June) pp. 97–107.

Cook, F.W. (1986a). Contaminants of pay for performance. *Personnel,* (July), 8–10.

Cook, Frederic W., & Co., Inc., (1986b). *Rethinking compensation practices in light of a strong economy; stable prices, and lower tax rates.* New Yorky, June 10.

Crystal, G.S. (1984). Pay for performance: It's not dead after all. *Compensation Review,* (Third Quarter), 24–25.

Crystal, G.S. (1985). To the rescue of pay for performance. *Personnel,* (January) 8–11.

Dansereau, F., & Markham, S.E. (1987). Levels of analysis in personnel and human resources management. In K.M. Rowland, and G.R. Ferris (Eds.) *Research in personnel and human resources management,* (vol. 5, 1–50) Greenwich, CT: JAI Press.

Decker, P.J, & Nathan, B.R. (1985). *Behavior modeling training: Principles and Applications.* New York: Praeger Publishers.

Doyel, H.W., & Johnson, J.L. (1985). Pay increase guidelines with merit. *Personnel Journal,* (June), 46–50.

Drury, S.S. (1984). *Assertive supervision: Building involved teamwork.* Champaign, IL.: Research Press.

Early, P.C. (1988). Computer-generated performance feedback in the magazine-subscription industry. *Organizational Behavior and Human Decision Processes,* 41, 50–64.

Ellis, A. (1972). *Executive leadership: A rational approach.* New York: Institute for Rational Living.

Ellis, A., & Harper, R.A. (1975). *A new guide to rational living.* North Hollywood, CA: Hal Leighton Printing Co.

Fisher, C.D. (1979). Transmission of positive and negative feedback to subordinates, *Journal of Applied Psychology,* 64 (5), 533–540.

Fiss, B. (1983). Comments at the conference, Risk-Taking and Earning Rewards in Federal Employment, Harper's Ferry, West Virginia.

Fossum, J.A., & Fitch, M.K. (1985). The effects of individual and contextual attributes on the sizes of recommended salary increases. *Personnel Psychology,* 38, 587–602.

Gellermann, S.W., & Hodgson, W.G. (1988). Cyanamid's new take on performance appraisal. *Havard Business Review* (May-June), p. 367–41.

Gluckman, D.M. (1983). Lump sum merit increases. *Compensation Review,* (First Quarter), 66–72.

Goldberg, M.H. (1977). Another look at merit pay programs. *Compensation Review* (Third Quarter), 20–28.

Gordon, T. (1977). *Leader effectiveness training (L.E.T.): The foundation for participative management and employee involvement.* New York: G.P. Putnam's Sons.

Greene, C.N., & Podsakoff, P. M. (1978). Effects of removal of a pay incentive: A field experiment. *Proceedings of the Academy of Management,* 206–210.

Harris, M.M., & Schaukroeck, J. (1988). A meta-analysis of self-supervisor, self-peer, and peer-supervisor ratings. *Personnel Psychology,* 41, 43–62.

Hathaway, J.W., (1986). How do merit bonuses fare? *Compensation and Benefit Review,* (September–October), 50–55.

Hedge, J.W., & Kavanagh, M.J. (1988). Improving the accuracy of performance evaluations: Comparisons of three methods of performance appraiser training. *Journal of Applied Psychology,* 73, 68–73.

Heneman, R.L., & Cohen, D.J. (1988). Supervisory and employee characteristics as correlates of employee salary increases. *Personnel Psychology,* 41, 345-360.

Hildebrandt, F.D. (1978). Individual performance in incentive compensation. *Compensation Review,* (Third Quarter).

Hills, F.S. (1979). The pay for performance dilemma. *Personnel,* 56 (5), 23–31.

Hills, F.S., Madigan, R.M., Scott, K.D., and Markham, S.E. (1987). Tracking the merit of merit pay. *Personnel Administrator* (March), 50–57.

Hills, F.S., Scott, K.D., Markham, S.E., & Vest, M.J. (1987). Merit pay: Just or unjust desserts. *Personnel Administrator* (September), 53–59.

Hinkin, T.R., Podsskoff, P.M., & Schriesheim, C.A. (1987). The mediation of performance-contingent "compensation" by supervisors in work organizations: A reinforcement perspective. In D.B. Balkin and L.R. Gomez-Mejia, *New perspectives on compensation.* Englewood Cliffs, NJ: Prentice-Hall.

Hughes, C.C. (1986). The demerit of merit. *Personnel Administrator,* (June), 40.

Jenkins, G.D., Jr. (1986). Financial incentives. In E.A. Locke (Ed.) *Generalizing from laboratory to field settings* (pp. 167–180), Lexington: Lexington Books.

Keaveny, T.J., & Allen, R.E. (1979). The implications of an across-the-board salary increase, (Working Paper No. 279). University of Wyoming, Laramie.

Komaki, J.L. &1986). Toward effective supervision: An operant analysis and comparison of managers at work. *Journal of Applied Psychology,* 71, 270–279.

Kopelman, R.E. (1976). Organizational control system responsiveness, expectancy theory constructs, and work motivation: Some interrelations and casual connections. *Personnel Psychology* 29, 205–220.

Kopelman, R.E. (1986). *Managing productivity in organizations: A practical, people-oriented perspective.* New York: McGraw-Hill.

Kopelman, R.E., & Reinharth, L. (1982). Research results: The effect of merit-pay practices on white collar performance. *Compensation Review,* 14, 30–40.

Krefting, L.A., and Mahoney, T.A. (1977). Determining the size of a meaningful pay increase. *Industrial Relations,* 16, 83–93.

Krefting, L.A., Newman, J.M., & Krzystofiak, F. (1987). What is a meaningful pay increase? In D.B. Balkin and L.R. Gomez-Mejia, *Perspectives on Compensation*. Englewood Cliffs, NJ: Prentice-Hall.

Larson, J.R. (1986). Supervisors' performance feedback to subordinates: the impact of subordinate performance valence and outcome dependence. *Organizational Behavior and Human Decision Processes*, 37, 391–408.

Latham, G.P., & Wexley, K.N. (1981). *Increasing productivity through performance appraisal*. Reading, MA: Addison-Wesley Publishing Co.

Lawler, E.E. (1987). Paying for performance: Future directions. In D.B. Balkin and L.R. Gomez-Mejia, *New perspectives on compensation*. Englewood Cliffs, NJ: Prentice-Hall.

Lawler, E.E. (1984). *Pay for performance: A motivational analysis*. Paper presented at New York University Conference on Pay for Performance.

Lawler, E.E. (1983). Merit pay: An obsolete policy? In J.R. Hackman, E.E. Lawler, & L.W. Porter. (Eds.), *Perspectives on Behavior in Organizations*, (2d ed.). New York McGraw-Hill Book Co.

Lawler, E.E. (1981a). *Pay and organization development*. Reading, MA: Addison-Wesley.

Lawler, E.E. III (1981b). Merit pay: Fact or fiction? *Management Review*, 70 (4), 50–53.

Lawler, E.E. III (1973). *Motivation in work organizations*. Monterey, CA: Brooks/Cole.

Locke, E.A., & Henne, D. (1986). Work motivation theories. In G.L. Cooper and I.T. Robertson (Eds.) *International review of industrial and organizational psychology*. New York: John Wiley & Sons.

Longenecker, C.O., Gioia, D.A., & Sims, H.P. Jr. (1987). Behind the mask: The politics of employee appraisal. *Academy of Management Executive*, 1, 183–193.

Luthans, F., Hodgetts, R.M., & Rosenkrantz, S.A. (1988). *Real managers*. Cambridge, MA: Ballinger Pub. Co.

McLagan, P., & Krembs, P. (1988). *On-the-level: Performance communication that works*. (2d ed.), St. Paul, MN; McLagan International, Inc.

Mahoney, T.A., Anderson, L., Swan, M., & Wyttenback, D. (1986). *The meaning of compensation and source of payment*. Paper presented at 1986 Academy of Management Convention, Chicago.

Markham, S.E. (1988). The pay-for-performance dilemma revisited: An empirical example of the importance of group effects. *Journal of Applied Psychology*, 73, (2), 172–180.

Mathieu, J.E., & Leonard, R.L. (1987). Applying utility concepts to a training program in supervisory skills: A time-based approach. *Academy of Management Journal*, 30 (2), 316–335.

Meyer, H.H. (1975). The pay-for-performance dilemma. *Organizational Dynamics*, 3 (3), 39–50.

Meyer, H.H. (1987). How can we implement a pay-for-performance policy successfully? In D.B. Balkin and L.R. Gomez-Mejia, *New perspectives on compensation*. Englewood Cliffs, NJ: Prentice-Hall.

Meyer, H.H., Kay, E., & French, J.R.P. (1965). Split roles in performance appraisal. *Harvard Business Review*, 43 (1), 123–129.

Mind over myths: Managing difficult situations in the workplace (1987). New York: Rational Effectiveness Training Systems.

Mount, M.K. (1987). Coordinating salary action and performance appraisal. In D.B. Balkin, and L.R. Gomez-Mejia, *New perspectives on compensation*. Englewood Cliffs, NJ: Prentice-Hall.

Newman, J.H. (1987). Selecting incentive plans to complement organizational strategy. In D.B. Balkin & L.R. Gomez-Mejia, (Eds.), *New perspectives on compensation* (214–224). Englewood Cliffs, NJ: Prentice-Hall, Inc.

O'Dell, C., and McAdams, J. (1987). *People, performance, and pay*. Houston, TX: American Productivity Center.

Patton, T.H. (1982). *A manager's guide to performance appraisal: Pride, prejudice, and the law of Equal opportunity*. New York: Free Press.

Pearce, J.C. (1987) Why merit pay doesn't work: Implications from organization theory. In D.B. Balking and L.R. Gomez-Mejia. *New perspectives on compensation*. Englewood Cliffs, NJ:Prentice-Hall.

Pearce, J.L., Stevenson, W. B., & Perry, J.L. (1985). Managerial compensation based on organizational performance: A time series analysis of the effects of merit pay. *Academy of Management Journal*, 28, 261–278.

Peck, C. (1984). *Pay and performance: The interaction of compensation & performance appraisal*. Research Bulletin No. 155. New York: Conference Board.

Perry, J.L., & Pearse, J.L. (1983). Initial reactions to federal merit pay. *Personnel Journal*, 62 (3), 230–237.

Pinder, C.C. (1984). *Work motivation: theory, issues, and applications*. Glenview, IL: Scott, Foresman and Co.

Podsakoff, P.M., and Todor, W.D. (1985). Relationships between leader behavior and group processes and productivity. *Journal of Management*, 11 (1), 55–73.

Prince, J.B., and Lawler III, E.E. (1986). Does salary discussion hurt the developmental performance appraisal? *Organizational Behavior and Human Decision Processes*, 37 357–375.

Printz, R.A., & Waldman, D.A. (1985). The merit of merit pay. *Personnel Administrator*, 84–90.

Pritchard, R.D., Jones, S.D., Roth, k.L., Stuebing, K.K., & Ekeberg, S.E. (1938). Effects of group feedback, goal setting, and incentives organizational productivity. *Journal of Applied Psychology*, 73 (2), 337-358.

Redling, E.T. (1981). Myth vs. reality: the relationship between top executive pay and corporate performance' *Compensation* Review, (Fourth Quarter), 16–24.

Rock, R.H. (1984). Performance management: chasing the right bottom line. In M.L. Rock (Ed.), *The handbook of wage and salary administration*. New York: McGraw-Hill Book Co.

Rogers, B. (1987). *Getting the best out of yourself and others*. New York: Harper & Row. Rollins, T. (1987). Pay for performance: The pros and cons. *Personnel Journal*, (June), pp. 104–111. Schmidt, F.L., & Hunter, J.E. (1983). Individual differences in productivity: An empirical test of estimates derived from studies of selection procedure utility. *Journal of Applied Psychology, 68,* 407–414.

Schneider, B., & Olson, L.K. (1970). Effort as a correlate of organizational reward system and individual values. *Personnel Psychology, 23,* 313–326.

Schuster, J.R., & Zingheim, P.K. (1985). Sales compensation strategies at the most successful companies. *Personnel Journal, 65* (6), 112, 115–116.

Schuster, J.R., & Zingheim, P.K. (1986). Designing incentives for top financial performance. *Compensation and Benefits Review, 18* (3), 39–48.

Scott, K.D., Hills, F.S., Markham, S.E., & Vest, M.J. (1987). *Evaluating a pay-for-performance program at a transit authority.* Paper presented at the 47th Annual Meeting of the Academy of Management New Orleans.

Sherer, P.D., Schwab, D.P., and Heneman, H.G. (1987). Managerial salary-raise decisions: A policy-capturing approach. *Personnel Psychology, 40,* 27–38.

Smith, M.L., O'Dowd, E.J., & Christ, G.M. (1987). Pay for performance—one company's experience. *Compensation and Benefits Review, 3* (May–June), 19–27.

Snyder, C.R., & Higgins, R.L. (1988). Excuses: Their effective role in the negotiation of reality. *Psychological Bulletin, 104,* 23–35.

Stankard, M.F. (1987). Pay for productivity: a concept revisited. *Compensation and Benefits Management, 3* (4), 187–191.

Stokes, D.M. (1981). A new mathematical approach to merit-based compensation systems. *Compensation Review* (Fourth Quarter), 43–55. Sullivan, J.F. (1988) The future of merit pay programs. *Compensation and Benefits Review,* (May–June), 22-30.

Teel, K.S. (1986). Are merit raises really based on merit? *Personnel Journal* (March), 88–95.

Tetlock, P.E. (1985). Accountability: The neglected social context of judgment and choice. In L.L. Cummings & B. Staw (Eds.), *Research in Organizational Behavior,* (Vol. 7). Greenwich, CT: JAI Press.

Tosi, H., Gomez-Mejia, L.R', & Hinkin, T.R. (1987). When the cat is away the mice will play: Managerial control, performance, and executive compensation. In D.B. Balkin and L.R. Gomez-Mejia. *New perspectives on compensation.* Englewood Cliffs, NJ: Prentice-Hall.

Tversky, A., & Kahneman, D. (1986). Rational choice and the framing of decisions, *Journal of Business, 59,* pt. 2, S251–S278.

Wagel, W.H. (1988). A software link between performance appraisals and merit increases. *Personnel* (March), 10–14.

Weldon, E. & Gargano, G.M. (1986). *Accountability discourages cognitive loafing: The effects of accountability and shared responsibility on cognitive effort.* Paper presented at the Academy of Management Convention, Chicago.

Wilson, T.D. & Linville, P.W. (1985). Improving the performance of college freshman with attributional techniques. *Journal of Personality and Social Psychology, 49,* 287–293.

Winstanley, N. (1981). *Are merit pay plans really effective? Current practice vs. future direction.* Paper presented at Challenges to Compensation Practice—Motivation, EEOC and Inflation, Executive Study Conference, Inc., New York.

Winstanley, N.B. (1982). Are merit increases really effective? *Personnel Administrator,* (April), 37–41.

Whitney, J.L. (1988a). Pay concepts for the 1990s; part 1. *Compensation and Benefits Review,* (March-April), 33–44

Whitney, J.L. (1988b). Pay concepts for the 1990s part 2. *Compensation and Benefits Review* (May-June), 45–50.

41 EMPLOYMENT AT WILL: A LEGAL REVIEW AND IMPLICATIONS FOR PERSONNEL PRACTICES

Raymond A. Noe, Eric Simmerman

Employees in the United States enjoy dramatically dissimilar levels of protection against the risk of wrongful discharge by employers. Public sector employees and employees covered by collective bargaining agreements can only be discharged for just cause. However, it is estimated that 75 million employees are unprotected by either statutory or contractual just cause provisions (BNA, 1982). These employees who are unprotected are considered at-will employees. The common law rule of employment at will (EAW) means that at any time and without notice, employees may change employers. Similarly, employers can discharge at will employees with or without cause. Currently, forty-eight states, plus the District of Columbia, have adopted the EAW doctrine (Lorber, Kirk, Kirschner & Handorf, 1984). Based on estimates of the size of the unionized labor force, Youngblood and Bierman (1985) estimate that approximately 65 percent of all U.S. workers are at-will employees.

The EAW doctrine can have detrimental consequences for employers as well as employees. The loss of a job produces physical and emotional stress from embarrassment and loss of status. Heavy costs are incurred by the discharged employee resulting from job search activities and moving expenses. For the employer, an arbitrary discharge may mean loss of training investments, as well as the expertise of the employees.

Due to labor market conditions and the nature of the employment relationship, employees have become increasingly dependent on the employer. Employees can no longer easily move from job to job because modern technology and specialization have narrowed the range of alternative employment. Seniority policies have also contributed to the decreasing mobility of employees (Calvey, 1982).

The dependence on the employer is based on both psychological and economic factors. Studies have indicated that much of an employee's self-esteem is based upon a stable employment relationship (Drucker, 1950; Aiken, 1968; Kahn, Campbell & Converse, 1973). Interest in job security is often based on financial considerations such as participation in profit-sharing plans and pension rights. The termination of employment may sever the employee's right to collect these benefits.

Youngblood and Bierman (1985) provide an excellent overview of the legal and historical basis for EAW. Youngblood and Tidewell (1981) suggest that discharge of at-will employees may be found to be invalid if (1) the employee was discharged for complying with a statutory duty, (2) the court determined that the discharge was motivated by malice or retaliation that is contrary to public policy, (3) the employee had an implied contractual right to employment, (4) the employee was deprived of due process rights guaranteed under the Fourteenth Amendment to the U.S. Constitution, or (5) the employee was discharged for reasons specifically prohibited by a state or federal statute. However, the types of exceptions granted to EAW doctrine and recent litigation have not been analyzed. Such an analysis is necessary in order to identify the human resource practices that may protect an organization against unfair discharge claims. The purpose of this chapter is to review the types of exceptions granted to EAW doctrine and representative litigation in order to understand the conditions under which such discharges are legally unacceptable. Also, recommendations are presented regarding personnel practices that can limit the employer's risk of wrongful discharge litigation.

In order to uncover cases dealing with the EAW issue, a number of law and personnel journals were reviewed: *Employee Relations Law Journal, Marquette Law Review, Journal of Law Reform, Harvard Law Review, Industrial Relations Law Journal, American Business Law Journal, Labor Relations Journal, New Mexico Law Review, Labor Law Jour-*

This chapter is based on Raymond Noe's master's thesis completed under the direction of Eric Simmerman.

nal, Academy of Management Journal, Personnel Psychology, Personnel Journal, and *Personnel.* Although these journals are not the only available sources for EAW cases, they are likely to cite cases with important implications for personnel practices. (Because of space limitations, complete citations of the cases exemplifying the exceptions to EAW doctrine, presented in the tables, are notincluded. A complete list of case citations is available from the first author.)

It is important to note that employment-at-will doctrine varies from state to state. The interested reader should refer to Koys, Briggs, and Grenig (1987) for an excellent review of specific state appellate court decisions. Although exceptions to the employment-at-will doctrine vary across states, the conclusions drawn from this review may help managers decide upon a socially responsible employment policy, regardless of the particular state in which they are employed.

FEDERAL LEGISLATION

Federal legislation limits the authority of employers to terminate employees. However, there is currently no federal law protecting employees from unjust discharge. Protection for employees is available for selected reasons. Table 41–1 presents the major federal and civil rights statutes that provide the most common prohibited basis for terminations of at-will employees. In general,these statutory exceptions to

the common law of EAW seek to prevent terminations of employees in retaliation for behavior deemed worthy of public protection or employees who are members of protected classes who have been victims of employment discrimination. Many of these statutes prohibit employers from retaliating against an employee for exercising a right presented by Law (e.g., file complaints, give testimony).

Table 41–1
Federal Labor Laws and Civil Rights Statutes Prohibiting Illegal Discharge of Employees

Labor Statute	Protected Activity
National Labor Relations Act (1935)	Union activity
Fair Labor Standard Act (1938)	Exercise of rights regarding wage and overtime provisions
Railway Labor Act (1962)	Union activity of railroad employees
Judiciary and Judicial Procedure Act (1982)	Service on grand jury
Consumer Credit Protection Act (1968)	Indebtedness resulting in wage garnishment
Federal Water Pollution Control Act (1948)	Testify against employer violation
Railroad Safety Act (1975)	Testify against employer violation of safety laws or work conditions
Federal Mine Health & Safety Act (1977)	Activity in support of health and safety laws
Air Pollution Prevention Control Act (1977)	Activity to enforce pollution control requirement
Employee Retirement Income Security Act (1974)	Right of employees to obtain vested pension rights
Civil Rights Act of 1964 Title VII	Right of employment regardless of race, sex, color, religion or national origin except where bona fide occupational qualification
Age Discrimination in Employment Act (1967)	Right of employment for employees forty years or older
Equal Pay Act (1963)	Activity resulting from employer violation
Rehabilitation Act (1973)	Right of employment of handicapped
Vietnam Era Veterans Readjustment Assistance Act (1974)	Discharge resulting from military status

CASE LAW

The types of exceptions to the EAW doctrine and developments in case law will be discussed below. It is important to note that case law has not been unani-

mous in abrogating EAW where the employer has not violated a clear and compelling public policy.

Tort Theory Exceptions

Tort law mediates relationships between parties who may have no contracts or agreement. Tort law is founded on rules obtained from community values that may be viewed as a social contract. Frequently, courts have used tort theory to create exceptions to EAW doctrine when it is believed that the employer has violated a public duty owed to the employee.

Public policy theory holds that a discharge is wrongful if the discharge is motivated by an employee action that public policy encourages or if the employee refuses to perform an act that public policy condemns. Public policy exceptions under tort theory include (1) discharge for refusal to commit a crime or unlawful act, (2) discharge for performance of an important public obligation or upholding the law, (3) discharge for exercising a statutory right or privilege, and (4) discharges that contravene a more general idea of public interest.

Discharge for Refusal to Commit a Crime or Unlawful Act. In table 41–2, cases dealing with employee discharge due to refusal to commit a crime or unlaw-

ful act are presented. The trend appears fairly clear: the courts will grant relief to at-will employees who are terminated for refusing to engage in activities that are expressly prohibited by state or federal statute. Examples of these activities include refusal to manipulate reports to benefit the employer (*Trombetta v. Detroit, Toledo, & Ironton Railroad*), refusal to violate public policies (*Sabine's Pilot Service, Inc. v. Hauk*), and refusal to commit perjury in testimony (*Petermann v. International Brotherhood of Teamsters*).

Discharge for Performance of an Important Public Obligation or Upholding the Law. In table 41–3, cases involving employee discharge for upholding the law or performance of an important public obligation are presented. For example in *Bowman v. State Bank of Keysville*, employees' discharge was overturned by the courts because termination was due to failure to vote for a merger proposal. The employees were stockholders in the bank that employed them. This is an EAW when a discharge did not contravene an expressed legislative statute but was contrary to a less well-defined notion of the public interest (e.g., jury

Table 41–2
Cases Involving Discharge for Refusal to Commit a Crime or Unlawful Act

Case (Action)	Year	Discharge Decision
Petermann v. Int'l Bro. Team., Lo. 396 (ee refused to commit perjury)	1959	ot
Tombetta v. Detroit, Toledo, and Ironton R.R. (ee refused to manipulate reports)	1978	ot
Tameny v. Atlantic Richfield Co. (ee refused to commit illegal act)	1980	ot
Pierce v. Ortho Pharmaceutical Corp. (ee refused to perform unethical research)	1980	ot
Gil v. Metal Service Corp. (ee refused to participate in deceptive practice)	1982	up
Embry v. Pacific Stationary and Printing Co. (ee refused to exhaust grievance procedures)	1983	up
Wagenseller v. Scottsdale Memorial Hospital (ee refused to expose herself indecently)	1985	ot
Hansrote v. American Indep. Tech. Corp. (ee refused to influence other firm)	1985	ot
Sabine's Pilot Service, Inc. v. Hauk (ee refused to violate federal clean water law)	1985	ot
Williams v. Tennessee In-Home Health Ser. Inc. (ee refused to falsify reports)	1985	ot
Knieriem v. ARA Services, Inc. (ee refused to violate antitrust laws)	1985	up
Crossen v. Foremost-McKesson, Inc. (ee refused to violate foreign law)	1982	ot

Note: er: employer; ee: employee; dc: discharged, ot: overturned; up: upheld. All employees were terminated in these cases. In cases upheld, the court ruled in favor of the employer; in cases overturned, the court ruled in favor of the employee(s).

Table 41–3

Cases Involving Discharge for Performance of an Important Obligation of Upholding the Law

Case (Action)	Year	Discharge Decision
Nees v. Hocks (ee dc for serving on jury duty)	1975	ot
Contra Bender Ship Repair, Inc. v. Stevens (ee dc for serving on jury duty)	1980	up
Palmateer v. International Harvester Co. (ee dc for disclosing employer wrongdoing)	1981	ot
Adler v. American Standard Corp. (ee dc for disclosing improper employer conduct)	1981	up
Pavolini v. Bard Air Corporation (ee dc for disclosing safety violations to FAA)	1982	up
Burke v. Georgia Power Company (ee dc for filing action against employer)	1983	up
Bowman v. State Bank of Keysville (ee dc for exercising vote at stockholders' meeting)	1985	ot

Note: er: employer; ee: employee; dc: discharged; ot: overturned; up: upheld. All employees were terminated in these cases. In cases upheld, the court ruled in favor of the employer; in cases overturned, the court ruled in favor of the employee(s).

duty or disclosure of alleged illegal employer conduct to internal or external authorities or agencies). Although the courts are generally willing to recognize the good intentions of terminated employees, they are not willing to create exceptions to EAW in the absence of a clear and compelling public policy. This is clearly illustrated by *Pavolini v. Bard-Air*. In this case, the employee claimed that he had been discharged for reporting violations of air safety regulations to federal authorities. However, the court ruled in favor of the employer because the Federal Aviation Act of 1958, which established air safety regulations, does not prohibit employers from terminating employees who report safety violations.

Discharge for Exercising a Statutory Right or Privilege. Table 41–4 presents cases dealing with employees who were dismissed for exercising a statutory right or privilege. Employees who have been able to cite an established public policy as the basis for their action have been able to invalidate a dismissal. There appears to be a trend in case decisions suggesting that employees may not be discharged for filing worker's compensation claims under state statutes granting this right (e.g., *Frampton v. Central Indiana Gas, Murphy v. City of Topeka*). In addition, employees have been granted relief when they have been discharged by the organization to prevent pension vesting or because of a wage garnishment (e.g., *Savodnik v. Korvettes*).

A controversial issue has been the dismissal of employees who refuse to submit to polygraph or drug testing. Thirty states now have laws regulating the use of polygraph tests in the employment context (BNA,

1985). For example, in *Perks v. Firestone Tire & Rubber*, the court ruled that employee discharge was a violation of public policy because of a state statute prohibiting polygraph tests. Also, polygraph testing may be viewed by the courts as an invasion of employees' privacy rights (e.g., *Cordle v. General Hugh Mercer*).

The exact number of firms using drug screening is unknown, but a survey of 180 *Fortune 500* companies revealed that 18 percent of the companies used drug tests to screen applicants or employees; an additional 20 percent were expected to begin drug testing within two years (BNA, 1986). If employees are represented by a union, discharge on the basis of the results of drug testing would have to be part of the collective bargaining agreement because it is a condition of employment. For nonunion employees, discharge decisions for refusal to submit to drug tests as creating an exception to EAW doctrine are sparse. Bakal and Grossman (1985) suggest that employees who refuse to comply with drug testing programs may be legally terminated because the employer has the discretion to determine the conditions of employment, (drug-free employees), and employees have the obligation to carry out employer directives (requests for drug testing). For example, in *Allen v. City of Marietta,* the court ruled that the city had a right to administer urinalysis tests to employees for the purpose of determining drug use that would affect ability to perform their job duties properly and safely. In making future rulings regarding drug testing and at-will employees, the courts may weigh the costs of invasion of privacy of drug tests against the safety risks posed by employees who are substance abusers.

Table 41–4
Cases Involving Discharge for Exercising a Statutory Right or Privilege

Case (Action)	Year	Discharge Decision
Frampton v. Central Indiana Gas Co. (ee dc for filing a worker's compensation claim)	1973	ot
Scott v. Union Tank Car (ee dc for filing a worker's compensation claim)	1980	ot
Green v. Amerada Hess Corporation (ee dc for filing a worker's compensation claim)	1980	up
Murphy v. City of Topeka (ee dc for filing a worker's compensation claim)	1981	ot
Firestone Textile Co. v. Meadows (ee dc for filing a worker's compensation claim)	1982	ot
Perks v. Firestone Tire and Rubber Co. (ee dc for refusing polygraph test)	1979	ot
Savodnik v. Korvettes, Inc. (ee dc to prevent pension vesting)	1980	ot
Smith v. Cotton Bros. Baking Co., Inc. (ee dc due to wage garnishment)	1980	ot
Glen v. Glearman's Golden Cock Inn, Inc. (ee dc for signing union organizing card)	1961	ot
Cuerton v. Abbott Labs, Inc. (ee dc for failure to prove work-related illness)	1982	up
Hack v. Oxford Health Care, Inc. (ee dc for testimony at state legislature)	1983	up
Khanna v. Microdata Corp. (ee dc for filing suit that interfered with performance)	1985	ot
Warthen v. Toms River Community Memorial Hospital (ee able to cite established public policy)	1985	ot
Ducote v. J.A. Jones Construction Co. (ee dc for filing a worker's compensation claim)	1985	ot
Savage v. Holiday Inn Corp., Inc. (ee dc prompted by state discrimination laws)	1985	up
Allen v. City of Marietta (ee refused urinalysis testing for drug use)	1985	up
Burgess v. Chicago Sun Times (ee refused to work for fear of health threat)	1985	up
Luck v. Southern Pacific (ee refused to take random drug test)	1985	?
Cordle v. General Hugh Mercer Corporation (ee refused to take polygraph test)	1984	ot
Whistleblowing Cases		
Geary v. U.S. Steel Corporation (ee alleged firm's products unsafe)	1982	up
Sheets v. Teddy's Frosted Foods, Inc. (ee wanted er to comply with labeling law)	1980	ot
Murphy v. American Home Products Corp. (ee revealed illegal accounting practices)	1982	ot
Maus v. National Living Centers, Inc. (ee stated abuse of nursing home patients)	1982	up
Campbell v. Eli Lilly Co. (ee stated violations of Food, Drug & Cosmetic Act)	1980	up
Martin v. Platt (ee stated supervisor's solicitation of kickbacks)	1979	up
Suchodolski v. Michigan Consolidated Gas Co. (ee complained about interim accounting practices)	1982	up

continued on next page

Table 41–4 *continued*

Kalman v. Grand Union Co. (ee asked for pharmacy licensing and regulation)	1982	ot
Goodroe v. Georgia Power Co. (ee dc before finding criminal behavior of ee)	1978	up
Petrick v. Monarch Printing (ee reported embezzlement by chief operating officer)	1982	ot
Parnar v. American Hotels, Inc. (ee refused to join price-sharing action)	1982	ot
Witt v. Forest Hospital, Inc. (ee reported illegal threat to commit patient)	1983	up
Donovan v. R.D. Anderson Construction Co. (ee reported safety concern to newspaper protected by OSHA)	1982	ot
Hentzel v. Singer Co. (reasonable and good-faith protest protected by Title VII)	1982	ot
Covell v. Spengler (Whistleblower's Protection Act cited as cause)	1985	ot
Rossi v. Pennsylvania State University (ee complained about department management and use of resources)	1985	up
Schmidt v. Yardney Electric Corp. (ee disclosed fraud to outside auditors)	1985	ot

Note: er: employer; ee: employee; dc: discharged; ot: overturned; up: upheld. All employees were terminated in these cases. In cases upheld, the court ruled in favor of the employer; in cases overturned, the court ruled in favor of the employee(s).

Discharges That Contravene a More General Idea of Public Interest. These types of discharges involve whistleblowers, employees who disclose employers' illegal, immoral, or illegitimate practices under the control of the employer (Miceli & Near, 1984). The encouragement and protection of whistleblowers is currently a controversial and contested area of case law. Whistleblowers can help the organization avoid adverse consequences by revealing unsafe products or fraudulent or wasteful operating practices (Miceli & Near 1985). However, whistleblowers may threaten the organization power structure by ignoring established procedures and communications networks used to inform management of unsafe or illegal practices (Weinstein, 1979).

The second half of table 41–4 presents cases involving discharges for whistleblowing. Two types of whistleblowing cases have been litigated: protective and active. In protective cases, employees are asked to commit a crime in order to benefit or protect the employer (e.g., *Parnar v. American Hotels, Inc.*). In active cases, the employee reports alleged illegal conduct of the employer to others (e.g., *Maus v. National Living Center, Inc.*).

According to Malin (1983), the courts have taken three different positions regarding under what circumstances discharging whistleblowers violates public policy. The least protected position requires a demonstration of a clearly expressed public policy before a cause of action is recognized. Because employees cannot generally cite a statutory right or obligation to support disclosure of their employer's

illegal conduct, the whistleblower is left without redress. A more protected position finds that certain statutes embody such statements of public policy (e.g., *Sheets v. Teddy's Frosted Foods*). The most protected position on wrongful discharge allows the court to go beyond the legislation and apply its own notion of public policy.

Recent research has focused on identifying organizational and individual characteristics related to whistleblowing (e.g., Miceli & Near, 1984; Near & Miceli, 1985). Miceli and Near (1985) suggest that organizations can reduce the probability of undesirable litigation by (1) generating alternatives to activities that could be viewed as wrongful, (2) reducing the threat of retaliation from management for employees reporting illegal activities, (3) establishing "inspector" roles and supporting employees in these roles, and (4) increasing employee awareness of internal reporting channels.

Contract Theory Exceptions

Contract law regulates the manner in which agreements between the employer and employee are interpreted and enforced. Based on contract theory, courts have created exceptions to EAW when evidence indicates the true intention of the parties was protection of the employee's right to employment or the employment agreement created an implied duty of fairness owed by the employer to the employee. Because in many cases at-will employees do not have employment agreements of definite duration, the courts have considered the totality of the events surrounding an employment relationship when deciding if an employment agreement in unexpressed terms was implied as part of the the events surrounding an employment relationship when deciding if an employment agreement in unexpressed terms was implied as part of the employment contract. Calvey (1982) has identified several factors in the employment relationship that lend support for implied rights to job security: (1) special consideration given to the employee for the position on the basis of benefits gained by the employer such as technical expertise or special demands placed on the employee (e.g., changing jobs, relocation), (2) the common law and nature of job within the industry as well as consideration of the policy of the firm, and (3) longevity of the employee in the job, including deferred compensation and recognition of satisfactory performance through promotions and salary increases.

Under contract theory, discharge for cause could be used as the standard, or the court could suggest that a covenant of good faith and fair dealing be established whereby a discharge motivated by bad faith or malice would constitute a breach of the employment contract. In table 41–5, cases are presented that involved discharges under good faith and

fair dealing and implied contractual rights. Expressed promises of job security is one exception to EAW doctrine. For example, in *Martin v. Federal Life Insurance* an employee was offered a job with one of the employer's competitors. In order to retain the employee, the company agreed that discharge without good cause would not occur. Due to this agreement, Martin was no longer an at-will employee. As a result, Martin's subsequent discharge was found to be illegal by the courts.

Courts have also ruled on whether it is wrongful for an employer to discharge an employee based on bad faith or a malicious reason. Using this exception to EAW, employee discharges were overturned in *Monge v. Beebe Rubber Co., Fortune v. National Cash Register Co.,* and *Clearly v. American Airlines.* For example, in *Cleary v. American Airlines,* the court determined that termination after eighteen years of employment without legal cause violated the implied employment contract. However, as table 41–6 illustrates, courts in many jurisdictions still refuse to judge whether employers have acted in bad faith or maliciously when discharging at-will employees. The majority of court decisions have ruled that the presence of a bad faith motive on the part of the employer does not mean the discharge of at-will employees is wrongful (e.g., *Cloutier v. Great Atlantic and Pacific*

Table 41–5
Cases Involving Discharges Actionable under Good Faith and Fair Dealing and Implied Contractual Rights

Case (Action)	Year	Discharge Decision
Monge v. Beebe Rubber Co. (ee refused to socialize with supervisor)	1974	ot
Cloutier v. Great A&P Co. (dc must have malice and violate public policy)	1981	up
Fortune v. National Cash Register Co. (ee dc to avoid big commission payment due him)	1977	ot
Gram v. Liberty Mutual Insurance Co. (ee dc in bad faith for sending notes to customers)	1981	up
Cleary v. American Airlines, Inc. (tenured ee dc for alleged work rule violations)	1980	ot
Pugh v. See's Candies, Inc. (long-term ee dc for no reason)	1981	ot
Chamberlain v. Bissel, Inc. (ee dc for alleged performance deficiencies)	1982	ot
Cook v. Alexander & Alexander of Connecticut (ee dc to avoid bonus pay and pension vesting)	1985	ot
Melley v. The Gillette Corporation (ee cited for age discrimination)	1985	up
Novosel v. Sears, Roebuck, and Company (ee who signed EAW application cannot expect just-cause protection)	1980	up
Rynar v. Ciba Geigy Corporation (personnel policy on dc and severance pay not a contract)	1983	up

continued on next page

Table 41–5 *continued*

Pine River Bank v. Mettile (ee handbook detailing dc constitutes unilateral contract)	1983	ot
Muller v. Stromberg Carlson Corporation (oral contracts of indefinite deviation terminable according to clause)	1983	up
Eales v. Tanana Valley Medical (er told ee dc only for just cause if work properly performed)	1983	ot
Phillips v. Flowing Wells Unified School District (contract of definite duration terminable at will according to clause)	1983	up
C.J. Brockmeyer v. Dun and Bradstreet (good faith not considered part of unjust dc)	1983	up
Martin v. Federal Life Insurance (consideration of er offer, if proved, creates enforceable contract)	1982	up
Gordon v. Matthew Bender and Company (ee bought equipment in reliance on er letter of employment not consideration)	1983	up
Tenedios v. Wm. Filene's Sons Co. (ee cited damage to future employment opportunities)	1985	up
Hudson v. Moore Business Forms, Inc. (er received damages for ee disloyalty under GFFD)	1985	up
Santa Monica Hospital v. Superior Court (management memo re warnings prior dc not contract)	1985	up
Graves v. Anchor Wire Corp. (if ee handbook implied contract, still terminable at will)	1985	up
Wooley v. Hoffman-La Roche, Inc. (without disclaimer job security may exist)	1985	ot
Ferraro v. Keolsch (handbook setting terms and conditions of work modifies at will)	1985	up
Fleming v. Kids and Kin Head Start (er evidence regarding dc conclusive)	1985	up
French v. Dillard Department Stores, Inc. (profit sharing and stock plans do not modify at will)	1985	up
Gianaculas v. T.W.A., Inc. (disclaimer in ee manual regarding employment contract)	1985	up
Sivell v. Conwed Corp. (employment contract may include ee manual terms)	1985	ot
Sorosky v. Burroughs Corporation (ee failed to show breach of implied contract)	1985	up
Staggs v. Blue Cross of Maryland, Inc. (ee handbook rules may bind, not general policies)	1985	up
Tobias v. Montgomery & Co., Inc. (HR policies not sufficiently communicated, not implied contract)	1985	up
Trembath v. St. Regis Paper Co., Inc. (in age discrimination claim ee's cannot cite nonstatutory remedy)	1985	up
Weaver v. Gross (tort of wrongful dc not recognized in DC)	1985	up
Birizianis v. U.S. Air Inc. (guidelines setting steps before dc not binding)	1985	up
Johnson v. Ford Motor Company, Inc. (oral promises to contract terms implied job security)	1985	ot
Allen v. Safeway Stores, Inc. (subjective assurances about job does not create contract)	1985	up
Martin v. Federal Life Insurance Company (ee dc although er promised job security) (employment interview and handbook expressed job security)	1982	ot
Weiner v. McGraw-Hill, Inc.	1982	ot
Toussaint, v. Blue Cross and Blue Shield	1980	ot

Note: er: employer; ee: employee; dc: discharged; ot: overturned; up: upheld. All employees were terminated in these cases. In cases upheld, the court ruled in favor of the employer; in cases overturned, the court ruled in favor of the employee(s).

Table 41–6

Cases Involving Discharges Actionable under Other Theories Creating Exceptions to EAW

Case (Action)	Year	Discharge Decision
Chin v. American Telephone and Telegraph Co. (ee dc for political beliefs unrelated to job)	1978	up
Boniuk v. New York Medical College (ee dc based on tort of abusive dc)	1982	up
Yaindl v. Ingersoll-Rand Co. (ee dc for criticizing product safety standards)	1980	up
Borseen v. Rohm and Haas, Inc. (dc in violation of public policy without tort interference)	1981	ot
Erb v. Federal Reserve Bank of Kansas City (ee dc for interference with contract in bad faith)	1982	ot
Agis v. Howard Johnson Co. (ees dc alphabetically to coerce information)	1976	ot
Novasel v. Sears, Roebuck, and Co. (no intentional infliction, emotional distress unless outrageous)	1980	up
Milton v. Illinois Bell Telephone (ee not dc, sued for intentional infliction of emotional distress)	1981	--
Shaitelman v. Phoenix Mutual Life Insurance Co. (ee failed to establish special damages for prima facie tort)	1980	up
Balancis v. American Optical Corp. (ee dc after years of exemplary service)	1981	ot
Kovalesky v. A.M.C. (dc based on public policy and malicious motivation)	1982	ot
Grouse v. Group Health Plan, Inc. (ee quit job for er, er revoked job offer)	1981	ot
Pepsi-Cola General Bottlers v. Woods (ee quit two jobs for third, er dc ee prior to start)	1982	ot
Chamberlain v. Bissel, Inc. (er didn't tell ee steps to improve performance before dc)	1982	ot

Note: er: employer; ee: employee; dc: discharged; ot: overturned; up: upheld. All employees were terminated in these cases. In cases upheld, the court ruled in favor of the employer; in cases overturned, the court ruled in favor of the employee(s).

Tea Company, Gram v. Liberty Mutual Insurance Co., Melley v. Gillette Co. and *Tenedios v. Wm. Filene's Sons Co.*).

Most courts appear to be unwilling to accept the theory of good faith and fair dealing and to identify implied contract terms in the employment agreement. As Lorber et al. (1984) state: "Courts are without external standards by which to decide whether a particular discharge was motivated by bad faith and they are unwilling to make up their own standards by which to judge what is proper employment relations" (p. 10).

Additional Theories Creating Exceptions to EAW

Other theories cited by the courts to grant exceptions to EAW are intentional infliction of emotional distress

(e.g., *Agis v. Howard Johnson, Co.*), employer failure to exercise reasonable care in performing an obligation owed to the employee (e.g., *Chamberlin v. Bissel*), and federal preemption theory. In *Chamberlin v. Bissel*, the employer held regular performance reviews (a contractual obligation) but did not inform the employee at the performance review that discharge was being considered. The court ruled that the evaluations detailed only some performance inadequacies and did not provide the employee with an opportunity to improve performance. The preemption issue concerns whether an unjust discharge is prohibited because it violates employees' rights to engage in union organizing activities, which are protected by the National Labor Relations Act. In table 41–6, cases involving discharges actionable under the emotional distress, employer negligence, and federal preemption theory are presented.

LIMITING EMPLOYER RISK OF WRONGFUL DISCHARGE LITIGATION THROUGH THE APPLICATION OF EMPLOYMENT PRACTICES EMPHASIZED BY PERSONNEL PSYCHOLOGISTS

Employers can take preventative actions to lessen the risk of wrongful discharge litigation based on the breach of an implied employment contract. The review of the litigation regarding EAW indicated that organizations can ensure the legality and fairness of employee discharges by developing effective personnel practices. Specific personnel practices that may reduce employer liability for employee discharge *and* increase employee satisfaction and productivity include (1) establishing appropriate work rules, (2) conducting periodic employee evaluations, (3) providing employees with appraisal feedback, (4) training managers in the mechanics of employee termination, (5) developing uniform discipline procedures, and (6) ensuring that recruitment practices do not portray unintended employment contracts. Personnel psychologists have identified the characteristics of recruiting and performance appraisal systems that are related to positive employee attitudes, attendance behavior, and job performance. Recruiting and performance appraisal systems that would be considered effective by personnel psychologists would also help protect the organization against wrongful discharge litigation.

Problems can arise for employers defending against unfair discharge suits when the discharged employee claims no knowledge of organization work rules. In evaluating whether an employment contract is violated, the courts may scrutinize internal work rules. Therefore, it is imperative that appropriate work rules are established and communicated. Brown (1982) suggests that work rules should be reasonably related to the satisfactory operation of the business. In addition, requiring employees to sign an authorization signifying they have read and received a copy of the work rules may discourage employees from claiming ignorance of the basis for their termination.

Employers who conduct regular employee evaluations are best prepared to defend against claims of arbitrary treatment. In order to meet legal requirements, the performance appraisal system should be based on job analysis information, performance standards and appraisal results should be communicated to employees, performance dimensions should be behaviorally based, and a mechanism should be provided for appeal (Cascio & Bernardin, 1981). Timely evaluations benefit the organization by providing the organization with documented evidence for employee

discharge. Similarly, the employee benefits by gaining an awareness of perceived performance problems and having an opportunity to take corrective action in order to reduce the possibility of discharge.

Managers are responsible for both the feedback of appraisal results to employees and planning developmental actions to overcome performance deficiencies. The *Chamberlin v. Bissel* decision emphasizes the need for managers to inform employees of performance problems and attempt to help the employee to correct performance deficiencies before a discharge decision is reached. Research by personnel psychologists suggests that successful performance appraisal feedback sessions include discussion of both satisfactory and unsatisfactory elements of the employee's job performance and possible situational constraints such as obsolete equipment, insufficient training, or burdensome time demands (Burke, Weitzel & Weir, 1978). Daily informal discussion between managers and employees about performance problems, successes, and factors that impair job performance will likely improve productivity and employee satisfaction.

Managers must be aware of the company's termination policies and new statutes and rules regarding employee relations and discharge. Lorber et al. (1984) suggest that manager training regarding employee discipline and termination should focus on three areas. First, managers should understand the process of providing employees with information concerning organization policies and work rules, as well as performance appraisal results. Second, managers need to understand the procedures for documenting efforts to correct employee misconduct and work performance. Last, the importance of consistent and equitable evaluation and discipline of all employees should be made salient to managers.

A progressive discipline procedure can also help reduce the potential for an unjust discharge suit. In a progressive discipline system, the severity of punishment varies depending on the type and duration of a performance problem. For example, a verbal warning may be given for any minor violation of work rules. A written warning or suspension would be given for a more serious or repeated violation of work rules. Such a discipline system ensures that employees will be notified of work rule violations and of probable consequences should misconduct continue. Also, many systems include mechanisms for employee appeal. Documented use of progressive discipline system demonstrates that the employer has followed in good faith a discipline system that informs employees of misconduct and the ramifications of continued violations or failure to improve performance.

Termination should result from employee failure to heed warnings and corrective feedback about performance or work rule violations. Burke (1980) provides guidelines for employers to consider if dismissal is warranted. These guidelines stress that employers can protect themselves from court challenges of discharge if (1) employees are aware of the possible disciplinary consequences of conduct, (2) the relationship of the work rule or standard to the efficient and safe operation of the company's business is clearly established, (3) rules are consistently applied to all employees, and (4) the severity of disciplinary actions is related to the seriousness of the employee's offense and previous work record.

In order to ensure that employees do not enter into an employment relationship with unrealistic expectations concerning work assignments, the work environment, promotion practices, and termination policies, employers should utilize realistic job preteen

views (see Wanous, 1980). Basically, a realistic job preview (RJP) involves using booklets, films, and conversations alone or in combination to provide potential job candidates with realistic information about the job and the organization prior to the time a job offer is made. For the job candidate an RJP may result in more realistic expectations about the job and the organization. For the organization, the benefits of an RJP may include increased employee retention, commitment, and protection from lawsuits based on claims of continued employment contracts. Employment notices should be free from language that could imply an employment period of definite duration (Lorber et al., 1984). All ambiguous or misleading statements concerning job security or permanent employment should be deleted from application forms and employee handbooks. Employment interviewers should be careful to refrain from making oral assurances regarding career opportunities, longevity, or continuation of employment. These assurances may later be viewed by the court as evidence of both parties' mutual interest and agreement upon an employment relationship of a specified duration (e.g., *Walker v. Northern San Diego Hospital District, Weiner v. McGraw-Hill*).

CONCLUSION

Despite the fact that twenty-five states now recognize public policy exceptions to EAW and fourteen states recognize implied contractual terms in the employment relationship, results of case law in this area are inconclusive. In many jurisdictions courts may not be sufficiently qualified or knowledgeable of industry standards to impose protection for either employees or employers. In order to avoid costly litigation and establish a work environment perceived by employees to be fair and equitable, organization performance appraisal systems and discipline policies should emphasize discussion of standards and performance information between manager and employee. A mechanism for employee appeal of appraisal results and discipline decisions is also necessary.

One promising development is the use of grievance resolution systems for the settlement of EAW disputes. Although arbitration is traditionally available only for unionized employees, more than two-thirds of nonunion employers have grievance resolution mechanisms (Conference Board, 1979). These systems range from informal open-door policies, in which the employee reports the problem directly to the immediate supervisor, to arbitration. Typically, arbitration involves presenting the case to

an impartial third-party, who issues a ruling (Bakaly & Grossman, 1985). Arbitration is likely perceived to be fairer by employees than an open-door system because the immediate supervisor, who may be a party in the dispute, does not have the authority to make a decision regarding the dispute. The arbitrator should have expertise and an awareness of issues concerning the occupational group involved in the discharge case. This is critical for determining the fairness of the discharge, considering acceptable industry practices (Aram & Salipante, 1981).

Arbitration may benefit both the employer and the employee. Arbitration may result in a quicker decision regarding discharge than court proceedings, which may last several years. The adverse financial consequences of discharge for the employee may be lessened because settlements are reached sooner. Even if the decision is not for reinstatement, the employee is certain of his or her employment status much sooner than if the dispute was contested in court. From the employer's standpoint, arbitration may help reduce the time investment and costs for legal representation because such a system helps ensure no employee is terminated without justifiable cause.

Youngblood and Bierman (1985) describe a successful arbitration program for nonunionized employees in South Carolina. In this system, employees are required to register a formal complaint with a state agency. The employer is asked to review the complaint and the precipitating circumstances and is requested to make a formal statement of the results of this investigation. Each case is assigned to a conciliator who decides on the basis of the compliant whether to pursue the case. The most frequent remedy in cases pursued is employee reinstatement. Other remedies include employer assistance in helping the discharged employee find a new job, modification of the reasons for the discharge in the employee's personnel record, and monetary relief.

REFERENCES

Aiken, M. (1968). *Economic failure, alienation, and extremism*, Ann Arbor, Michigan: *The* University of Michigan Press.

Aram, J.D., & Salipante, P.F. Jr. (1981). An evaluation of organizational due process in the resolution of employer/employee conflict. *Academy of* Management Review, 6, 197–204.

Bakaly, C.G., & Grossman, J.M. (1985). *Modern law of employment contracts:* Formation, operation, and remedies for breach. New York: Harcourt Brace Jovanovich.

Brown, F. (1982). Limiting your risk in the new Russian roulette—Discharging your employees. *Employee Relations Law Journal, 8,* 380–406.

Bureau of National Affairs (1982). The employment-at-will issue: A BNA special report. *Labor Relations Reporter, 3,* 1–57.

Bureau of National Affairs (1985). State fair employment practices findings list. *Labor Relations Reporter, 120,* (3), 206.

Burke, M.J. (1980). *Discharge: Current issues and trends,* Eau Claire, WI: Mulcahy and Wherry.

Burke, R.J., Weitzel, W., & Weir, T. (1978). Characteristics of effective employee performance review and development interviews: Replication and extension. *Personnel Psychology, 31,* 903–919.

Calvey, F.L. (1982). Termination of *the at will employee: The general rule and* the Wisconsin rule. *Marquette Law Review, 65,* 637–659.

Cascio, W.F., & Bernardin, H.J. (1981). Implications of performance appraisal litigation for personnel decisions. *Personnel Psychology, 34,* 211–226.

Conference Board (1979). *Managing Labor Relations* (Report No. 765). New York: ?.

Drucker, P. (1950). *The anatomy of the industrial order.* In *The New Society* (p. 47–48). New York: Harper.

Kahn, A.C., & Converse, P. (Eds.) The meaning of work: Interpretation and proposal for measurement. In Campbell, J., (1973) *The human meaning of social change* (4–10). Special task force to the Secretary of HEW, Work in America. Cambridge, MA: MIT Press.

Koys, D.J., Briggs, S., & Grenig, J. (1987) State court disparity on employment at-will. *Personnel Psychology, 40, 565–577.*

Lorber, Z., Kirk, J., Kirschner, H., & Handorf, R. (1984) *Fear of firing: A legal analysis of employment-at-will.* Alexandria, VA: ASPA Foundation.

Malin, M.H. (1983). Protecting the whistleblower from retaliatory discharge. *Journal of Law Reform, 16,* 277–318.

Miceli, M., & Near; J. (1984). The relationship among beliefs, organizational position, and whistle blowing status: A discriminant analysis. *Academy of* Management Journal, 27, 687–705.

Miceli, M., & Near, J. (1985). Characteristics of organizational climate and perceived wrongdoing associated with whistleblowing decisions. *Personnel* Psychology, 38, 525–544.

Near, J., & Miceli, M. (1985). Organizational dissidence: The case of whistleblowing. *Journal of Business Ethics, 4,* 1–16.

Wanous, J.P. (1980). *Organizational entry: Recruitment, selection and socialization of newcomers.* Reading, MA: Addison-Wesley.

Weinstein, D. (1979). *Bureaucratic opposition.* New York: Pergamon Press.

Youngblood, S.A., & Bierman, L. (1985). Due process and employment-at-will: A legal and behavioral analysis. In K.M. Rowland & G.R. Ferris (Eds.), *Research in Personnel and Human Resources Management* (vol. 3, 185–230). Greenwich, CT: JAI Press

Youngblood, S.H., & Tidewell, G.L. (1981). Termination at will: Some changes in the wind. *Personnel, 58,* 22–33.

PART **VI**

CAREER PLANNING AND TRAINING

MANAGING EMPLOYEE CAREER TRANSITIONS

Frank J. Minor and L. Allen Slade

When an organization adopts new technologies and operating methods, restructures, or engages in downsizing actions, a common result is that some employees must change jobs or in some way accept a career transition. A career transition can be a job transfer and geographic relocation, promotion, demotion, or expedited retirement. Managers need to understand the problems that career transitions impose upon employees and how the organization's human resource management programs and practices can be drawn upon to help employees adapt to transitions.

Career transitions disrupt employees' established work behavior patterns and decrease their ability to predict and control their work environment. The consequences can be manifested at the behavioral level by reduced performance or increased absenteeism, at the psychological level by increased stress and anxiety, and at the physiological level by an increase in the occurrence of illnesses. Employees seek ways to cope with the ambiguities created by a career transition by sense-making activities (Louis, 1980) and by reorganizing their job activities so as to reduce the uncertainties of their new role (Katz, 1984). Sense making involves several kinds of activities: resolving the differences in duties, responsibilities, performance criteria, power structures, and peer relationships between one's old job and the new one, clarifying the paths and goals to which this job can lead, and developing skills and behaviors to master the new role. During the sense-making process employees draw upon their personal resources, attributes, and social networks. The organization, however, also provides supportive resources in the form of personnel programs and practices, which can be drawn upon to help employees adapt to their new roles. These include the organization's career development programs, job skills training courses, mentoring programs, job fairs, relocation assistance programs, and educational support programs. Schein (1971, 1978) referred to the employees' transition adaptation process as a socialization process during which they learn new skills and develop new attitudes and values toward their work and the organization.

EMPLOYEE PERFORMANCE AT THE TIME OF A CAREER TRANSITION

Innovative job performance by employees may be temporarily depressed by a career transition. In its broadest sense, innovation can be defined as any form of job behaviors exhibited by the new role incumbent that were not engaged in by the previous incumbent (Brett, 1984). It can be as diverse as a new salesperson's attention to a different set of customers, a new executive's redesign of the organizational structure, or a laboratory technician's automation of a manual testing process. Managers can be very instrumental in assisting their subordinates through the socialization and sense-making processes and consequently can improve the job climate needed for innovative job performance. Immediately following a job or career change, employees typically prefer less autonomy than before the change and need structure and guidance from their immediate manager (Katz, 1984). Given the manager's close interpersonal contact with the employee, his or her control over the employee's new assignment, and organizational resources, the manager is in an ideal position to facilitate the subordinate's career transition. A close relationship with the manager is far superior to impersonal lectures or printed and videotaped organizational orientation materials (Katz, 1984).

EMPLOYEE DEVELOPMENT ASSIGNMENTS

Developmental assignments intended to enhance the skills, experiences, or knowledge of an individual obviously lead to career transitions. Line managers may be rotated into staff positions such as in the headquarters personnel function to learn about the organization's human resource management philosophy and programs (Hall, 1976) or into a variety of other functions to increase their multipotentiality or reduce the chances of stagnation (Odiorne, 1984). The length of an assignment affects the quality of the development experience. Rotations lasting only a few months or weeks are often counterproductive. Often these short rotational assignments provide little opportunity to learn new skills and a minimum of job challenge and consequently generate a low level of motivation (Hall, 1976). Therefore, managers should ensure that developmental assignments have meaningful objectives, which preferably last a minimum of one year. They can be shorter if they produce important results or recommendations that will be used by management (e.g., a problem-oriented task force).

Career transitions can also take place in support of the development of the organization. Organizational-role development transitions occur when an organization fills a position with a person who is expected to engage in innovative behaviors for the good of the organization. One form of organizational role development is the use of a "strategic misfit" (Hall, 1984). For example, an experienced production manager could be put in charge of a dynamic research and development unit to provide more stability to its operations. Another form of organizational role development could be the staffing of positions with employees who have completely different skills from those of previous incumbents. For example, a microcomputer retailer might hire salespeople with teaching experience in order to tap the educational market more effectively.

Managers who wish to maximize employees' developmental experiences from career transitions should understand the conditions necessary for this development to occur (see Brett, 1982, 1984). Personal development is maximized when the individuals learn new skills from the job and receive in-depth feedback concerning their performance in assigned job goals. In contrast, organizational role development is maximized when the individual is expected to make changes in the job, uses previously acquired skills and knowledge, and is not dependent upon feedback from superiors. Given the disparity between the criteria for personal and organizational role development, the assignment of employees to these two types of role should be based on the employees' career state. Managers should offer career transitions that promote personal development experiences to employees during their early career stages. This investment in personal development will pay off for the organization when these same employees, later in their careers, successfully take on assignments that promote organizational role development (Brett, 1984).

MANAGING DIFFERENT TYPES OF CAREER TRANSITIONS

Different types of career transitions present unique problems to the employee. These special problems often require different forms of organizational support systems and management practices. We will describe the problems associated with common forms of career transitions along with management actions that have the potential to reduce the severity of the problems.

Geographic Relocation

A job transfer that involves a geographic relocation is one of the most disruptive types of transitions because it entails an abrupt environmental change for the employee's family as well as a work role change for the employee. Yet this form of career transition is quite common. Approximately 800,000 heads of households are annually relocated by their employers (Sell, 1983).

Employees either accept or refuse job offers that require relocation based on the career opportunities associated with the move, the employee's current career status, and family or spouse career factors (Brett, 1981; Minor, 1981). In general, employees who accept relocation offers do so because they perceive the job offer to be a challenging, positive career step. Younger employees and those in marketing or sales are more likely to accept a relocation offer (Brett, 1981; Minor, 1981). Reasons for accepting or refusing a relocation vary significantly as a function of the employee's present career status. Managers are most influenced by career growth, advancement, and salary factors, while nonmanagerial employees are influenced by a wider range of factors, which in addition to career and salary factors also include their spouse's career, perceptions about quality of life in the present versus the proposed location, financial risks (such as the cost of living and mortgage rates), and social ties (Minor, 1981).

When making a relocation offer, managers should:

- Be certain that the transfer supports the employee's career plans.
- Clearly define the new job in terms of content, challenge, and developmental experiences.
- Involve the employee's spouse through trips to the proposed location to investigate community characteristics and job opportunities.
- Provide financial information about the move by means of a cash flow analysis of income, taxes, mortgage payments, and other major expenses.

When deciding upon candidates for a relocation offer, managers should not assume that certain individuals would automatically accept or reject a relocation offer because of age, family status, or sex. Such assumptions are often incorrect because of the diversity of factors that make up an actual relocation decision. Therefore, management should make the offer to the most qualified person rather than using stereotypes about an employee's relocation mobility.

Once the relocation takes place, a number of activities contribute to the personal, home environment adjustment of the individual and the family. The time required for personal adjustment is affected by the spouse's success in securing a new job, selling and buying of a house, moving expense reimbursement, establishing ties in the new community, the children's adjustment to school and peers, and the attractiveness of the new location (Brett & Werbel, 1980; Minor, 1981, Pinder, 1977, 1978).

The time required for on-the-job adjustment depends on the degree of correspondence between the actual job duties and the job preview given to the transferee (Minor, 1981). Relocations that are anticipated in advance and involve only a moderate change in level or function are the easiest because of the carry-over from the old job (Brett & Werbel, 1980). After relocation, a short, demanding orientation may result in more rapid job adjustment than a leisurely orientation, at least when job content and level are the same (Bateman, Karwan & Kazee, 1983).

For employees who decide to relocate, the organization can take several steps to facilitate family adjustment and job adjustment:

- For dual career households, provide spouse job counseling and placement services (Trippel, 1985).
- Provide a voluntary host (an employee who is familiar with the new community) to help the family adjust to the new location.
- Provide early and clear definition of performance objectives followed by feedback and coaching.

Promotion

There are a number of advantages for promoting from within rather than hiring experienced outsiders: motivation is increased when promotions are used to recognize good performance, performance effectiveness data on internal candidates' become more comprehensive and reliable, and internal promotion candidates require less orientation (Sonnenfeld, 1984).

A strategy of promotion from within requires a pool of individuals willing to accept promotions, but this willingness may not always be present. Individuals rate advancement opportunities as the second most important factor in evaluating a job during good times, but it drops to sixth place during bad times (Yankelovich, Skelly & White, 1980). The current generation of new managers is less motivated for upward mobility than were the new managers in the 1950s (Howard & Bray, 1980b). The adjustment process associated with frequent career transitions often required for hierarchical advancement probably contributes to this reduced desire for promotions (Sonnenfeld, 1984).

This declining desire for promotion could adversely affect an organization's ability to promote from within. Organizations can increase the acceptance of promotion offers that involve geographic relocations by following the suggestions in the previous section. If a promotion offer is turned down by an individual, this does not necessarily signal a lack of desire for advancement. Managers should carefully explore an individual's reasons for rejecting a promotion offer rather than automatically categorizing the individual as "plateaued because of lack of career motivation." A later promotion offer might be accepted because of differences in the individual's household composition or the geographic location of the new job. Organizational practices supportive of promotion transitions include developmental on-the-job assignments and work experiences, management coaching, and active career development planning.

Demotion

Demotion can be part of an effective human resources strategy that combines employment security with the uncertainty of position security (Goldner, 1965). With this strategy, employees who perform inadequately are demoted rather than dismissed from the organization. The possibility of demotion motivates employees to pursue excellence, while employment security gives a sense of stability needed to take appropriate business risks. In contrast, if the organization fires employees for reason of failure, employees will avoid risky decisions. Similarly, if failure has no adverse impact on the individual's career (the person is neither fired nor demoted), employees may take inappropriate risks. A policy of demotions with employment security can discourage both risk avoidance and excessive risk taking.

There are several ways an organization can make demotion less traumatic for the employee. One method is by cloaking the demotion (Goldner, 1965). For example, geographic relocation can make a demotion more acceptable by providing the individual with a new set of coworkers. Similarly, the use of special job or training assignments can cloak a demotion.

Another way an organization can ease the adjustment to a demotion is by fostering zig-zag mobility so that demoted employees can later be promoted if their job performance warrants it (Goldner, 1965). If there is no possibility of future advancement, demotions will severely demotivate upwardly mobile employees. Zig-zag mobility holds open the possibility of future promotions after a demotion, making it a viable human resource strategy for organizations that use demotions.

Demotions may not be as negative as sometimes assumed. Managers have shown surprising acceptance of the possibility of a demotion sometime in their careers (Goldner, 1965). Nondemoted managers may improve their performance when they observe that other executives with mediocre performance are demoted (Organization & Performance, 1983). Two-way communication has been unexpectedly improved after demotions, apparently because demoted individuals acted as communication links between managers at their previous level of the organization and their new peers (Hall, 1976).

To make downward moves less traumatic for the employee and the organization, organizations should (1) encourage input from the employee about the new job, (2) not reduce salary, (3) place the employee in a new physical and social setting, (4) select a job that demands that new skills be learned that broaden the employees' skill base and increases their flexibility, and (5) counsel the employee about future options, possibly through life and career planning workshops (Hall & Isabella, 1986).

Plateauing

Like geographic relocation, promotion, or demotion, plateauing leads to a period of personal adaptation to new expectations. Yet plateauing is a unique form of career transition. There is no change in tasks to cause task-related ambiguity. Also, while most career transitions have a very distinct point of transition, plateauing usually involves a gradual change in mobility expectations. Plateauing is a career transition that is often triggered by a "nonevent" such as an expected promotion that does not occur (Schlossberg, 1981). This leads to an ambiguous boundary for the plateau transition. As a result, it is difficult for managers to know when a specific employee is experiencing a transition to a career plateau.

Despite the difficulty of knowing when employees experience plateauing, managers should be concerned with this career transition because some form of plateauing is ultimately faced by all employees. Plateauing is important because of potential consequences to motivation and performance. Plateaued employees have been characterized as "shelf-sitters" (Connor & Fielden, 1973), suggesting that they become relatively inactive after becoming plateaued. Reductions in the mobility expectations of employees can have an adverse effect on their work behavior (Goldner, 1965); therefore the plateauing process should be managed so that effective job performance is sustained.

There are several types of plateauing. One distinction can be made based on the impact of plateauing on the type of expectations employees have about future job changes. *Structural plateauing* occurs if there is no expectation of future promotion. *Content plateauing* occurs when there is no expectation of new job challenges or variability in job duties. Because of the pyramidal structure of most organizations, structural plateauing is virtually inevitable (Bardwick, 1984). Yet a person who is structurally plateaued does not have to be content plateaued. Lateral transfers or changes in specific job duties can provide continuing challenge and new skills for those who do not expect further promotions (Spruell, 1985).

A second distinction can be made based upon the performance of the plateaued employees. *Deadwood* workers are low-performing plateaued employees. In contrast, *solid citizens* are plateaued but maintain a high level of performance. Solid citizens are central to the organization's effective functioning, since they often compose a large part of the experienced management group, and they provide stability to the organization (Ference, Stoner & Warren, 1977).

Several studies have investigated employee individual reactions to structural plateauing. In a study of the careers of AT&T managers, Howard and Bray (1980a) found that "most managers had accepted their career plateaus and adjusted to them" (p. 5). Only 10 percent of another group of managers were concerned about career plateauing in their career planning, and this percentage decreased with age (Tausky & Dubin, 1965). The research evidence suggests that structural plateauing is reasonably well accepted by most individuals.

Several management practices can minimize the negative effects of plateauing. First, individuals should be prepared for plateauing. Structural plateauing should be clearly communicated in order to maintain acceptance by organizational members (Kelly, 1985). As part of the hiring process, a realistic job preview (Wanous, 1975) should include an appraisal of the opportunities for promotion and highlight the eventuality of structural plateauing. Career development planning sessions should communicate that plateauing is an expected stage of the employee's career (Christianson, 1983) and should emphasize the need for broadening the range of one's skills and increasing flexibility in preparation for future opportunities and alternative career paths.

Second, plateaued employees should be managed according to their level of performance (Odiorne, 1984). Deadwood employees should be managed as poor performers. The manager should review behavioral deficiencies with poor-performing employees, plan remedial activities to address the deficiencies, and set performance goals within the context of a measurable assignment. If performance does not improve, the manager should consider demotion, retraining, or separation of the individual from the organization.

Solid citizens require a different type of management attention. Management tends to ignore solid citizens (Ference et al., 1977) because their sustained good performance causes no crisis. This tendency increases the likelihood that solid citizens will ulti-

mately become deadwood. To avoid this, solid citizens should be provided with career development planning services, special job assignments, and skills training, all of which will provide opportunities for ongoing career revitalization (Ference et al., 1977).

Retirement

Retirement is a transition to a role that provides for more leisure or for the initiation of a new career. Managers should help subordinates ease into retirement transition in order to maintain the performance of late-career-stage employees. A large proportion of employees are choosing to accept early retirement with the objective of starting a new career rather than withdrawing from the workplace (Manning, 1979). Many early retirees, however, are disappointed with their new career because of inadequate planning to achieve their objectives (Holt, 1979). A successful transition to a postretirement career can be thwarted by insufficient knowledge about how to enter a new organization, deficient skills or experience, or a drop in the number of positions available. Early retirement programs should include counseling designed to address these problems.

Managers of employees eligible for retirement should be aware of the employee's retirement strategy and encourage the use of the organization's retirement planning programs at the appropriate time. Preparation for retirement should begin at a minimum of one to two years in advance (Collins, 1971; Dunning & Biderman, 1973). Although all retirees experience some degree of stress, the level of stress is related to the level of postretirement plans (Kilpatrick & Kilpatrick, 1979). While most retirement planning programs focus on improving attitudes toward retirement, the usual result is an improvement in knowledge about retirement issues with no change in attitudes (Kasschau, 1974). However, this improvement in knowledge may lessen postretirement dissatisfaction (Holt, 1979).

While some organizations focus their efforts on preretirement planning, others are turning their attention to increased utilization of specialized skills of their retirement-age employees (Hergenrather, 1985). Some companies are offering part-time employment to their retirees rather than using temporary employment agencies. This practice allows the organization to draw upon an experienced pool of employees who possess specialized, hard-to-acquire skills (Sonnenfeld, 1984).

CONCLUSIONS

Over the next decade, business forces and societal trends will require that employees become more career flexible and accepting of career transitions. Changing technology, operating methods, and organization restructuring result in shifts in an organization's skills demands, job duties, and the numbers of employees needed in different kinds of jobs, the consequence of which is rebalancing of the work force and employee career transitioning. The increased occurrence of career transitions will be further reinforced by societal trends such as affirmative action programs, which expect women and minorities to move through a variety of developmental positions, and by the need for immobile dual-career family workers, single parents, and plateaued baby boomers to discover and plan for new and challenging developmental job assignments.

Organizations that anticipate the need for employee job transfer and career change because of changing business demands should place emphasis on employee use of their career development planning programs. Career planning programs can help employees cope with an organization's unstable job

and career environment by improving their career insight (their ability to relate their personal attributes to the organization's career development avenues) and by improving their career resilience (the extent to which they are able to self-manage and build flexibility into their careers in response to changing business conditions) (London and Stumpf, 1986). For such programs to be effective, however, management must put into place job design, job linkage, and training programs that enable employees to acquire the skills needed to implement their plans.

In this chapter we have suggested a number of practices management can apply to help their subordinates through the career transition process. We recognize that such practices cut across a wide range of an organization's human resource management programs, and therefore it would be impractical to package a unique human resource management program for career transitioning. It would be useful, however, for an organization to communicate to its management an inventory of managerial actions that can help employees adapt to their career transitions.

REFERENCES

Bardwick, J.M. (1984). When ambition is no asset. *New Management, 1*(4), 22–28.

Bateman, J.S., Karwan, K.R., & Kazee, T.A. (1983). Getting a fresh start: A natural quasi-experimental test of the performance effects of moving to a new job. *Journal of Applied Psychology, 68,* 517–524.

Brett, J.M. (1981). *Employee transfers: The effects of job transfers on employees and their families.* Paper presented at the annual meeting of the Academy of Management, San Diego, August.

Brett, J.M. (1982). *Job transitions and personal and organizational development.* Paper presented at the American Psychological Association Convention, Washington, DC, August.

Brett, J.M. (1984). Job transitions and personal and role development. In K.M. Rowland & G. Ferris (Eds.), *Research in personnel and human resources management:* (vol. 2, pp. 155–185). Greenwich, CT: JAI Press.

Brett, J.M., & Werbel, J.D. (1980). *The Effect of job transfer on employees and their families.* Research Report. Washington, DC: Employee Relocation Council.

Christianson, B.K. (1983). *Case study of a career management system.* Paper presented at the annual meeting of the American Psychological Association, Anaheim, California, August.

Collins, K. (1971). *The second time around.* Cranston, RI: Carroll Press.

Connor, S.R., & Fielden, J.S. (1973, November–December). Rx for managerial "shelf-sitters." *Harvard Business Review,* 113–120.

Dunning, D.D., & Biderman, A.A. (1973). The case of military retirement. *Journal of Industrial Gerontology, 17,* 18–37.

Ference, T.P., Stoner, J.A.F., & Warren, E.K. (1977). Managing the career plateau. *Academy of Management Review, 2,* 602–612.

Goldner, F.H. (1965). Demotion in industrial management. *American Sociological Review, 30,* 714–724.

Hall, D.T. (1976). *Careers in organizations.* Dallas: Scott, Foresman.

Hall, D.T. (1984). Human resource development and organizational effectiveness. In C. Fombrun, N.M. Tiche, & M.A. Devanna (Eds.), *Strategic human resource management.* New York: Free Press.

Hall, D.T., & Isabella, L.A. (1986). Downward moves: Alternative career development. *Career Center Bulletin, 5,* 6–7.

Hergenrather, E.R. (1985). The older worker: A golden asset. *Personnel, 62,* 56–60.

Holt, L.J. (1979). Retirement: A time to enjoy or endure? *Personnel Administrator, 24,* 69–73.

Howard, A., & Bray, D.W. (1980a). *Career motivation in mid-life managers*. Presented at the meeting of American Psychological Association, Montreal, September.

Howard, A., & Bray, D.W. (1980b). *Continuities and discontinuities between two generations of Bell System managers*. Presented at the meeting of American Psychological Association, Montreal, September.

Kasschau, P. (1978). Re-evaluating the need for retirement preparation programs. *Industrial Gerontology, 1,* 42–59.

Katz, R. (1978). Job longevity as a situational factor in job satisfaction. *Administrative Science Quarterly, 23* (June), 204–223.

Katz, R. (1984). Organizational stress and early socialization experiences. In T. Beehr & R. Bhagat (Eds.), *Human stress and cognitions in organization: An integrative perspective.* New York: Wiley Press.

Kelly, J.F. (1985). Coping with the career plateau. *Personnel Administrator, 30,* 65–76.

Kilpatrick, A.C., & Kilpatrick, E.C., Jr. (1979). Retirement from the military: Problems of adjustment. *Journal of contemporary Social Work, 60,* 282–288.

London, M., & Stumpf, S.A. (1986). Individual and organizational career development in changing times. In D.T. Hall (Ed.), *Career development.* San Francisco: Jossey-Bass.

Louis, M.R. (1980). Career transitions: Varieties and commonalities. *Academy of Management Review,* 329–340.

Manning, B.A. (1979). *Study of preretirement planning and factors related to second-career job satisfaction and retirement satisfaction of military personnel.* Ph.D. dissertation, Auburn University.

Minor, F.J. (1981). *Employee Relocation Mobility Study.* Paper presented at the 41st annual meeting of the Academy of Management, San Diego, August.

Odiorne, G.S. (1984). *Strategic management of human resources.* San Francisco: Jossey-Bass.

Organization & performance (1983). *Rydge's* (August), 82–85.

Pinder, C.C. (1977). Multiple predictors of post-transfer satisfaction: The role of urban factors. *Personnel Psychology, 30,* 543–556.

Pinder, C.C. (1978). Corporate transfer policy: Comparative reactions of managers and their spouses. *Relations Industrielles, 33,* 654–665.

Reichers, A.E. (1987). An interactionist perspective on newcomer socialization rates. *Academy of Management Review, 12,* 278–287.

Schein, E.H. (1971). The individual, the organization, and the career: A conceptual scheme. *Journal of Applied Behavioral Science, 4,* 401–426.

Schein, E.H. (1978). *Career dynamics: Matching individual and organizational needs.* Reading, MA: Addison-Wesley.

Schlossberg, N.K. (1981). A model for analyzing human adaptation to transition. *Counseling Psychologist, 9* (2), 2–18.

Sell, R.R. (1983). Transferred jobs: A neglected aspect of migration and occupational change. *Work and Occupations, 10,* 179–206.

Sonnenfeld, J.A. (1984). *Managing career systems: Channeling the flow of executive careers.* Homewood, IL: Richard D. Irwin.

Spruell, G. (1985). Say so long to promotions. *Training and Development Journal, 39,* 70–75.

Tausky, C.T., & Dubin, R. (1965). Career anchorage: Managerial mobility motivations. *American Sociological Review, 30,* 725–735.

Trippel, A. (1985). Spouse assistance programs: Relocating dual career families. *Personnel Journal, 64,* 76–78.

Veiga, John F. (1981). Plateaued versus nonplateaued managers: Career patterns, attitudes, and path potential. *Academy of Management Journal, 24,* 566–578.

Wanous, J.P. (1975). Tell it like it is at realistic job previews. *Personnel, 52,* 50–60.

Yankelovich, Skelly and White, Inc. (1980). *A continuing study of changing work values and employee motivations: Signal 1980 overall findings.* New York: Author.

Manuel London

Organizational processes affecting career development are often a matter of policy. This chapter reviews a number of issues organizations face in designing employee development programs. Firms need to understand these issues and their implications because employees' career development should be strategically linked to the goals of the business.

DEFINING CAREER DEVELOPMENT

Career development is preparing employees to make a contribution to the organization in the future. In times of organizational growth, career development was synonymous with preparing people for advancement. However, in times of organizational change—which often means downsizing and reorganization—advancement opportunities are usually constrained. Some firms in this situation seem to limit career development opportunities to those few individuals who have been identified as having high potential for advancement and who need to be groomed for promotion. Other firms recognize that the continued viability of the organization depends on having the human resources to meet changing skill requirements. In this context, career development applies to all employees.

Given that organizations vary in their approach to career development, managers and psychologists charged with developing or revising career planning and development programs should recognize that this entails making a number of policy decisions. This chapter reviews some of these choices. These include deciding on the appropriate degree of integration of career and personnel programs, establishing the degree of centralized control over these programs, determining the extent to which employees are treated as a resource for the future as well as a resource for today, deciding how to assess and react to organizational circumstances (such as downsizing), determining the extent to which today's personnel decisions should be linked to tomorrow's business objectives and environmental changes (e.g., how changing labor force demographics should be taken into account in human resource forecasting and planning), and deciding on the criteria for evaluating the success of a career program and designing an appropriate evaluation of the program.

CAREER SYSTEMS

One organizational choice is the degree to which career-related policies and programs fit together as an integrated system. Career-related policies and programs cover many important human resource functions, including analyzing skill needs and job requirements, recruiting and selecting new employees, socializing these newcomers into the organization (e.g., with orientation sessions, new supervisor training), establishing career paths, supporting employee efforts at career planning, facilitating job moves (both lateral transfers and promotions), providing technical and managerial training, outplacing people whom the company wants to leave, and helping employees plan for their retirement. Other personnel programs are related to career development, such as performance appraisal, feedback, and reward and recognition systems.

Figure 43–1 outlines the ties between factors that contribute to career policies and programs and a broad array of human resource programs. Organizational objectives along with environmental trends and local department needs are input to selecting appro-

Figure 43–1. Components of an Integrated Career System

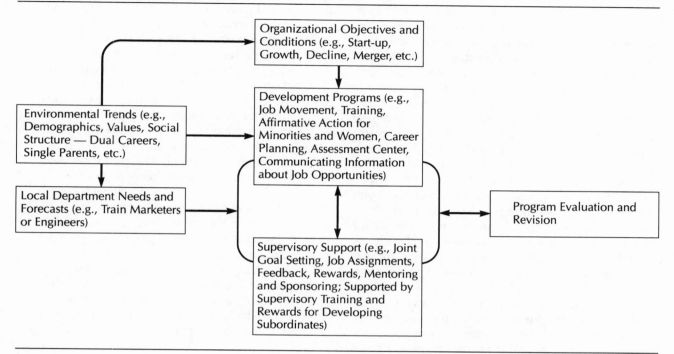

priate development programs. The diagram recognizes the supervisor's role in supporting these programs and, in general, contributing to the development of subordinates. Evaluations of current programs in meeting the organization's needs provide feedback for program improvement.

An integrated career system will use common formats and common language across the various programs and policies. For instance, the skill dimensions used to describe job requirements will also be used on employee profiles that describe skills and knowledge levels. The performance appraisal form may use similar language in describing dimensions for evaluating employees. Management training courses will cover the same skills. This consistency is important because it clarifies behavior and output expectations. Employees learn what the different skills mean in terms of behaviors, and supervisors learn how to evaluate and reward these skills.

CENTRALIZATION OF CAREER PROGRAMS

Organizations decide about how much commonality there should be in career policies and programs across department in the organization. One option is strong central control with uniform systems for performance appraisal, performance feedback, position vacancy announcements, internal job application and staffing procedures, compensation policies, promotion criteria, and so forth. One reason for standard procedures is to ensure equal employment opportunity, required by good business practice and law. Another is to make it easier to move people between departments within the organization in that managers will have a common understanding of performance criteria and promotion standards. Common procedures provide a framework for raising these standards over time by, for example, controlling definitions of excellent and good performance, the percentage of people who can be placed in different performance categories, and the rewards and recognition available.

Organizational career policies and programs may be decentralized, with each major department determining its own performance and promotion standards, career paths, training curricula (possibly delivered by a central corporate training organization), counseling programs, and other efforts that reflect the specialized functions in the department. Of course, an organization could have some programs that are centrally developed and uniformly administered throughout the organization and other programs that are tailor made by a department to meet that department's specific needs. For instance, career interest inventories, training for supervisors on how to work with subordinates on their career development, and staffing procedures that monitor consideration of minorities for jobs may be centrally controlled by the firm's corporate headquarters. Mentorship programs, career paths, and technical skill development may be controlled by departments and will take on a different form in each department.

An alternative to decentralization is tailoring corporate-wide programs to meet the needs of individual departments. Major business units may tailor corporate programs to reflect their part of the business. For instance, forms may use the name of the business unit. Skill and job analysis methods may ask employees about behaviors and skills that are specific to the department's function as well as skills that are more generally applicable. The extent of such "branding" and customization will depend on the uniqueness of the business unit or department on the one hand, and, on the other, the desire of the corporation to be viewed by its employees as a single enterprise.

One large firm established an interdepartmental work group to outline a career development strategy. Representatives from each major department met with corporate headquarters representatives to discuss issues related to employee career development, share ideas, describe programs that were already running or being developed by each department, and agree on areas for generic programs that they could all share or could easily be tailored to reflect the special needs of a given department. The group members agreed that corporate headquarters should develop a "manager as developer" course that would train supervisors on their role in supporting the career development of their subordinates. The work group also agreed to participate jointly in writing a document describing highly populated jobs in the company and regularly publicizing the availability of job openings. This information would be available to all employees to help them with their career plans.

EMPLOYEES AS CORPORATE RESOURCES

Corporate philosophy also plays a major role in the purpose and extent of development supported by the company. Companies that view their employees as meeting an immediate business need are likely to provide them with training and experiences that improve their current job performance. Companies that view employees as corporate resources for today and the future are likely to value development even if it does not meet a current business objective. For example, such a firm is likely to transfer people solely to give them broader experiences, even if the transfer causes some disruption in work operations in the short run. In these companies, supervisors are likely to be rewarded for contributing to their subordinates' development, and supervisors develop a reputation as good bosses partly based on their support for employee development. Such supervisors are willing to transfer their best people to other departments and in turn are likely to attract the best people to them (London, 1985).

ASSESSING THE ORGANIZATIONAL CONDITIONS

As figure 43–1 suggests, the organization needs to match its objectives to environmental circumstances in order to design career development programs.

Career Development in a Downsizing Environment

Consider what happens when there is a downturn in the economy and a consequent decline in the size of the organization. In a downsizing environment, organizations seek ways to foster employee growth without opportunities for advancement. One way is through certification programs and mastery paths that specify selection criteria, performance expectations at different points of learning the job, training courses, and supervisory evaluation procedures to determine when mastery has been attained. Mastery paths increase the professionalism of the organization and provide goals for employee development (London & Mone, 1987).

Another way to foster career development in a downsizing environment is retraining in new fields needed by the organization or needed outside the organization (as a way to make leaving easier). Movement into a new job or a new functional area—possibly at a lower level—is another way to increase learning and development opportunities (Hall, 1985).

Career Programs as an Extension of Business Plans

Supporting employees' career development is easier under positive business conditions (growth and start-up) than under negative business conditions (decline). Organizational redirection, mergers, and acquisitions pose a challenge to managers to encourage and support employees and provide them with information about changing business conditions. Periods of stability also pose a challenge to managers to encourage professional development and growth in subordinates rather than be content with the status quo.

Companies may be tempted to create career programs in a vacuum apart from the needs of the business. Career programs can be fads that take on a life of their own apart from the needs of the organization. Human resource professionals may ignore the specific business they are in and apply their tools and techniques irrespective of setting. Consequently, a human resource program may be laden with personnel jargon that does not obviously tie back to the needs and direction of the corporation. Human resource managers and consultants should learn their employer's or client's businesses and be able to write materials that reflect the language and processes of the organization. Customization and involving employees in program development go a long way toward increasing user acceptance (London, 1988).

LINKING CAREER DEVELOPMENT TO HUMAN RESOURCE FORECASTS

Human resource professionals in an organization need to decide the extent to which they are focused on current needs versus forward thinking. This is related to the above point about treating people as meeting immediate business needs versus resources for the future. It is hoped they are doing both. Envisioning and planning for the future is critical in changing organizations (e.g., organizations that are growing, declining, or anticipating a merger, acquisition, or divestiture). Of course, these changes cannot always be anticipated well beforehand. However, it is possible to develop scenarios of the future that suggest likely changes and alternative courses of action (Manzini & Gridley, 1986).

Critical Skills for the Future

Human resource planning requires analyzing employees' current skills, the skill levels needed by the business in the future, and the availability of those needed skills in the internal and external labor force. The gap between current skills and future skill requirements suggests the need for hiring different people or retraining current employees. Whether selection or training is an appropriate strategy will depend on the availability of people with the right skills in the external labor market and the feasibility of retraining current employees. This type of analysis may suggest the importance of supporting educational programs for college and high school students, and perhaps even grade school children, to increase their capabilities. Information about skill requirements for the future should be communicated to employees so they can plan their development and pursue a career path that will lead to career opportunities rather than a dead end.

One high-technology organization conducted a study of changing job requirements in critical positions (jobs that were highly populated in the company or that were highly influential in making business decisions). The results reflected the changing nature of the business and technology. Salespeople were increasingly being required to be systems design consultants to their customers. The goal was to have the company's products used in the customer's products, and customers were more likely to be systems designers than purchasing agents. This implied that effective selling required demonstrated expertise and professionalism as "value added" to the customer. Managers of branch sales offices needed to be entrepreneurial executives with knowledge of finance and other elements of running a business in addition to knowing the product and marketing techniques. The firm's technicians were moving from subject matter experts who worked alone to install a product for a customer to project team members who developed a long-term relationship with the customer as a trusted member of the customer's team and the employees's project team. This increased the importance of interpersonal skills as well as knowledge about new technology. The company used this information about changing critical jobs to design professional development programs for current employees and to establish new selection criteria for new hires.

Environmental Trends

Analysis of environmental trends is just as important as analysis of internal conditions. Environmental scans should be conducted of labor force and population demographics, social trends, economic conditions, and government regulatory and legislative actions (e.g., federal funds available for training)—all of which may influence the type and quality of people who are available to the corporation. These trends also influence what competitors are likely to do to attract the people they need. This has implications for the career opportunities available to current and prospective employees and the ability of the corporation to have the right people available at the right time.

Consider the impact of several key demographic trends based on statistics from the U.S. Bureau of the Census (1986) and the U.S. Department of Labor (1985). The work force is growing older. The median age of the work force will increase from thirty-two in 1987 to thirty-six in 2000. The thirty-five to fifty-four age group will increase from 38 percent of the work force in 1985 to 51 percent of the work force in 2000. (This aging work force trend is even more dramatic in Japan and European countries.) Another trend is the "baby bust"—the declining birthrate beginning in 1964 after the post–World War II baby boom. The sixteen to thirty-four age group will decrease from 50 percent of the work force in 1985 to 38 percent in 2000. Overall, the work force will grow at a slower rate, while new jobs will grow at an increasing rate. These data suggest a major gap between available people and jobs. Evidence that companies are already feeling the pinch can be seen in daily employment ads and commercials showing senior citizens in a growing number of low-paying service jobs. The gap is worse for firms seeking highly skilled people because of a growing illiteracy rate. One-third of the adults in the United States in 1987 have not finished high school.

Demographics also influence social and political trends. For example, 85 percent of the new entrants to the work force between 1985 and 2000 will be women, minorities, and immigrants (Hudson Institute, 1987). The white population in the work force will decline from 82.6 percent in 1985 to 76.3 percent in 2000, whereas the proportions of Hispanics and blacks will increase. Women are a growing share of the work force, shifting from 42.5 percent in 1980 to 47 percent in 2000. Fifty-four percent of all women were employed in 1985, while 61.1 percent will be employed in 2000. The percentage of single parents and dual career couples is also increasing. In 1987, only 3.7 percent of all married couples were the traditional nuclear family with the husband working and the wife at home with two children.

This change in family patterns suggests that more people will be seeking different career patterns to match their life-styles. Corporate loyalty may decline for people in a two-income family. Single parents are likely to want more flexible work hours and perhaps work-at-home alternatives. To remain competitive for the most talented people, corporations will have to offer alternative work structures (such as part-time employment), flexible schedules (e.g., flex-time), and new benefits (including child care and elder care). In addition, managers will have to have a mind-set that treats family as a valuable part of the worker's life that needs to be balanced with work demands. These changing life patterns also affect the career paths and opportunities that people seek. Career planning needs to be done jointly with one's spouse and children, taking into account organizational opportunities, individual interests and abilities, and family desires.

Companies will have to build a track record that causes minorities to want to work in those companies. Equal employment opportunity and affirmative action become business necessities directly related to meeting the company's human resource needs. Organizations will have to be supportive of minority development and advancement and make these activities known to prospective candidates. Firms will need to identify and develop more high-potential minority employees. These individuals should then be involved in recruiting other minorities. In addition, companies should support minority education from grade school through college. Firms should sponsor community programs (e.g., tutoring), scholarships, loaned managers as teachers and professors, internship programs, and site visits to company facilities.

The director of a department of about 3,000 people wanted to assess the need for employee career development in the unit during the next five years. This would be tied to the needs of the business in terms of educating employees in changing technology and changing ways of doing business in a more competitive environment. The director, with the help of the firm's human resource staff, collected data on current employee skill levels. They developed a profile of the number of employees in different job functions. They projected the numbers of people who were likely to retire during the five-year planning period (based on age profiles and past data on retirement rates among those who were eligible to retire). They examined the characteristics of recently promoted managers (e.g., skill levels and prior job experiences) to determine whether the criteria for advancement needed to be revised. And they studied the number and type of transfers between jobs within the department and to and from other departments to determine whether employees were obtaining job experiences that increased their value to the firm and prepared them for promotion. The result was a staffing and development plan that provided employees with clear information about development possibilities and began to meet the department's future human resource needs.

EVALUATING CAREER PROGRAMS

Managers who implement career programs can choose the extent to which they evaluate the success of the program, which includes the option of no evaluation at all. Program evaluation is important for several reasons. It provides an indication of the return on the corporation's investment in the career program. It also provides a basis for improving the program.

Evaluating career programs requires establishing criteria for success. Stated another way, the manager has to answer the question, "How will I know if the program is a success or failure?" There are many possible criteria—some objective and some subjective. Objective criteria include improvement in performance (e.g., quantity and/or quality of output). Subjective criteria include improvements in supervisory ratings of employees' performance and advancement potential and employees' feelings of professional growth and career satisfaction.

An action research approach to evaluation focuses on developing goals, identifying and trying different processes or applications of a program, and observing the incremental change. This suggests the need for evaluation while the program is being implemented (Blacker & Brown, 1985). One role of the human resource professional is to educate managers in the value of different research designs and assist in conducting the evaluation and feeding back the results. Human resource professionals not skilled in research can obtain evaluation support from university faculty and graduate students, for instance in industrial and organizational psychology and organizational behavior programs.

A one-week career sensitivity program helped employees to understand their career interests, identify career opportunities in the company, and establish goals and action strategies for achieving them. The evaluation was an attitude survey of participants several months after attending the program. The survey asked participants about their motivation for taking the course, their perceived development needs, potential career outcomes, actual career outcomes since taking the course, and feelings about the components of the course (e.g., whether they found the module on resume writing useful). The results were used by the trainers to revise the course and by management to justify continuing the program.

Another more general tracking approach used in many companies is to include items on the company-wide attitude survey about perceived career opportunities, promotion criteria (e.g., "Are the best people promoted?"), and satisfaction with career growth. The results in one firm highlighted to top management the importance employees placed on career development and the perceived weakness of staffing processes and supervisor support for development.

The reader should not conclude that simple approaches to evaluation are necessarily the best. Indeed, less rigorous research designs are likely to yield misleading results. However, managers should be encouraged to evaluate the success of a career program using practical methods that recognize the multiple factors that may affect the data collected. (See London, 1988, and Cascio, 1982, for descriptions of alternative evaluation methods and further examples of human resource program evaluations.) Just as other management decisions are based on collecting information and making reasoned judgment, program evaluation provides a guide for improvement, not sure-fire answers or solutions. Given that many factors affect career development, managers need to take a holistic approach to understanding which factors (i.e., career policies and strategies such as those reviewed above) are levers for improvement. Manipulating these levers is often a matter of trial and error and a willingness to experiment.

CONCLUSION

This chapter has reviewed a series of organizational choice points and activities for supporting employee development. These involve defining career development in terms of preparing for promotion or preparing to do better on one's current job and preparing to maintain one's contribution to the organization, designing common career programs across a company, integrating career programs into a comprehensive system, treating employees as corporate resources, tying career programs to the firm's business objectives, and exploring future corporate directions and human resource needs in the light of environmental trends. (See London, 1985, for a discussion of other issues, such as the degree to which the organization promotes from within, whether the organization develops generalists and/or specialists, and the application of high-potential-employee development programs and standard career tracks.)

Career programs both support employees' development and further the objectives of the corporation. Organizations must decide which policies and programs best match their business needs (e.g., degree of central control, consistency of practices across the organization). Moreover, managers, guided by human resource professionals, should evaluate the success of career development policies and programs using practical yet meaningful research methods.

RECOMMENDATIONS

The chapter concludes with several recommendations for human resource practitioners and managers involved in designing and implementing career programs:

1. The organization should establish career programs that make sense for the organization today and in the future. That is, managers should take a future perspective, forecasting the future needs of the business and the strategies that will allow the firm to attract the people they need.

2. Employees should be given a chance to understand the needs of the business in the future and what they need to do to prepare themselves to maintain their contribution to the organization (increase their employment security) and further their professional development. This implies the need for open communications about likely corporate directions and skill requirements.

3. Training to improve current skills and retraining to learn new skills and new functions should be available to help employees further their careers in line with corporate goals.

4. Supervisors should be trained in their role as developer of people and rewarded for carrying out this role well.

5. Individuals should realize that they play a critical role in their own development. The corporation, in the form of programs and supervisor actions, provides the resources to support employee development. Organizations need to communicate this to employees and highlight people who are successful at furthering their own careers. Corporate programs, then, can be voluntary and often self-administered. (These include self-reflection guides, which help individuals think about their skills, abilities, and interests and guide them in scoring and interpreting the results. Holland's Self-Directed Search, 1985, is an example.)

6. Many different personnel practices have implications for employee development. These implications should be recognized and exploited. These include the use of assessment centers, performance appraisals, and job assignments for development, career paths, career counseling, and training programs.

7. Managers should understand how personnel programs fit together to affect employees' career development. Integrated career systems, as outlined in figure 43–1, may be developed using similar language and formats. However, what is more important is that the users of the programs comprehend how the different techniques and tools contribute to each other in furthering the employee's growth. For instance, performance appraisal feedback should contribute to helping subordinates set development goals in line with information about advancement opportu-

nities, and training curricula should be offered in skill and knowledge areas needed by the company.

8. In line with the importance of having a future perspective, organizations should consider the effects of environmental trends on being able to meet future human resource needs. The baby bust, the aging work force, and the growing number of new jobs indicate stiff competition among companies for the most talented people. Corporations that provide opportunities for career growth and development will have a competitive edge in being able to attract, retain, and motivate the best people. Also, changing social structures (e.g., more dual career couples, single parents, and women in the work force) suggest the need for alternative work structures, schedules, and benefits to meet the career needs of people in the labor force. Recognizing the growing number of minorities in the work force, companies will have to be a place that educates, develops, and advances minorities. Finally, corporations need to realize that their career development resources must extend beyond their employees to affect people in the community—especially children in the educational system. Joint corporate-educational system efforts are needed to communicate and support the development of skills likely to be needed by the corporation in the future.

9. The meaning of career development needs to be defined and redefined to reflect the realities of the current and future environment. For instance, the changing economic environment led many firms to redefine career development from promotion to doing better on one's present job and preparing to make a contribution to the company in the future. Another trend that will affect the meaning of career development is the globalization of the economy. Global companies deal with people in diverse cultures. These cultures differ not only in how business is conducted but also in the values and expectations of employees in different countries for work and career (Derr, 1986). Global businesses will have to understand these differences and design flexible programs, or multiple programs, to meet the needs of different employee bodies (e.g., differences in how rapidly people want to advance, the importance of job security, which may be dictated by local law, and willingness to relocate for a new assignment). Competitive firms will value these differences and offer programs to match the values and desires of immigrants to the United States and local citizens in operations abroad.

10. Plans for program evaluation should be part of plans for program design and implementation. Evaluation should be unbiased (e.g., conducted by impartial evaluators) and as clear as possible in identifying causal relationships. Practical research designs that lead to improvements in the program are important and should be encouraged.

REFERENCES

Blacker F., and Brown, C. (1985). Evaluation and the impact of information technologies on people in organizations. *Human Relations, 38*, 213–231.

Cascio, W.F. (1982). *Costing human resources.* New York: D. Van Nostrand.

Derr, C.B. (1986). *Managing the new careerists.* San Francisco: Jossey-Bass.

Hall, D.T. (1985). Project work as an antidote to career plateauing. *Human Resource Management, 24,* 271–292.

Holland, J.L. (1985). *Making vocational choices: A theory of vocational personalities and work environments.* Englewood Cliffs, NJ: Prentice-Hall.

Hudson Institute (1987). *Workforce 2000: Work and workers for the 21st century.* Indianapolis: Hudson Institute Inc.

London M. (1988). *Change agents: New roles and innovation strategies for human resource professionals.* San Francisco: Jossey-Bass.

London, M. (1985). *Developing managers.* San Francisco: Jossey-Bass.

London, M., and Mone, E.M. (1987). *Career management and survival in the workplace.* San Francisco: Jossey-Bass.

Manzini, A.O., and Gridley, J.D. (1986) *Integrating human resources and strategic business planning.* New York: AMACOM.

U.S. Bureau of the Census (1986). *Household and family characteristics: March 1985.* Current Population Reports, Series P-20, No. 411. Washington, DC: U.S. Government Printing Office.

U.S. Department of Labor. Bureau of Labor (1985). *Handbook of labor statistics, June 1985.* Washington, DC: U.S. Government Printing Office.

44 USING PERSONALITY DATA IN CAREER DEVELOPMENT PROGRAMS

Gary Behrens, Marilyn Johnson

Organizational career development programs are designed to aid employees in analyzing their own potential for advancement and identifying opportunities for reaching that potential within the company (Moses, 1987). The intended benefit to the company is a stable and productive work force of increasing skill and competence.

The successful organizational career planning program communicates information that is clear, concise, relevant, and purposeful, according to Mirabile (1987). However, as Moses points out, it is also vital that employees actively participate in the program. Super (1983) explains that career development works best when individuals believe that significant personal control over the process is attainable. In other words, employees are motivated to get involved in planning their careers by seeing how personal effort can directly affect the end result. And yet the desire to take control is rooted in one's personality (Super, 1983).

THE LINK BETWEEN PERSONALITY AND CAREER DEVELOPMENT

A typical organizational career development program consists of three distinct components: (1) assessment, (2) goal setting, and (3) action planning (Moses, 1987). The assessment component usually conforms to the traditional model of matching individuals with an optimal set of career fields on the basis of their aptitudes and similarity to people in those fields (Super, 1969).

The underlying assumption of this model is the belief that individuals are more likely to adjust successfully to the demands of work pursuits that others like themselves have found suitable and therefore are more likely to perform effectively. In this likeness approach to career development, the focus of assessment is usually on determining an employee's vocational interests and job-related skills and abilities to build a foundation for informed goal setting and action planning.

Another aspect of the matching approach to career development that has gained increased attention since the 1960s concerns the role of personal values, attitudes, and behavior patterns, which are elements of individual personality. By extension, the chances for adjusting successfully to a career in a given occupation are improved to the degree that a person thinks, acts, and feels much the same way as others in that line of work. Of course, there is a certain amount of socialization into the value system of any occupation that results from training and experience. But according to the model's assumptions, there must also be predisposing personality traits that would be more similar to some occupational groups than others.

If, as this matching model implies, members of specific career fields are so much alike in interests and personality as to allow comparisons of an individual's compatibility, it is reasonable to ask how people with such similar natures were drawn into their respective careers in the first place. In answer to this question, Holland (1985a) has proposed that career choice reflects a stable pattern of personality characteristics. Thus, individuals tend to select a given occupational endeavor over other alternatives because their personality traits are more adaptive to the various task activities and working conditions of the chosen occupation, enabling greater fulfillment of personal potential.

The authors wish to acknowledge the contributions of the following human resource professionals to our thinking in the development of this chapter: Larry Axline, Management Action Planning; Thomas McGaffey, McGaffey & Associates; Bob Gentile; Linda Oxman; Judy Quest; Mary Russell; and Nancy Yugo.

Holland has defined six broad personality patterns, called occupational types, that are adaptive for different kinds of work. The occupational types and work interests typically associated with them are: (1) Realistic—skilled crafts and mechanical; (2) Investigative—scientific and analytical; (3) Artistic—creative and self-expression; (4) Social—supportive and interactive; (5) Enterprising—directive and influential; and (6) Conventional—practical and systematic. The six types are conceived as a framework for a hexagonal model that places compatible types adjacent to one another and incompatible types opposite one another. By reference to trait descriptions in the Labor Department's *Dictionary of Occupational Titles* (1977), every job can be categorized into a combination of a dominant type and two adjacent occupational types (Gottfredson & Holland, 1989).

Holland's model of occupational personality types has received support from research with personality instruments such as the Sixteen Personality Factor Questionnaire (16PF) (Cattell, Eber & Tatsuoka, 1970). Studies by Bolton (1985) and by Turner and Horn (1977) have shown that personality can distinguish between people on the basis of occupation with a much better accuracy than would be expected by chance. In fact, these studies and another by Johns (1985) found that, on average, about 80 percent of the personality differences among groups of employed individuals were related to their vocational choices. This agrees with an average 80 percent correspondence between personality and stated vocational preferences of college students in studies using the 16PF and vocational interest surveys (Costa, Fozard & McCrae, 1977; Ward, Cunningham & Wakefield, 1976; Zak, Meir & Kraemer, 1979). Such findings support the notion that personality traits have an influence on career choices. Table 44–1 shows the personality features that seem to be characteristic of each occupational type, as measured by the 16PF (adapted from Walter, 1985).

Table 44–1
Personality Traits Associated with Occupational Types

16PF Personality Traits[a]	Holland Types[b]					
	R	I	A	S	E	C
Reserved versus warm-hearted			−	+	+	+
Concrete versus conceptual		+	+	+	+	+
Upset versus realistic	+	−				
Accommodating versus assertive					+	−
Serious versus enthusiastic	−	−		−	+	−
Expedient versus conscientious	+	+				+
Cautious versus bold	−		+		+	
Tough versus tender-minded	−		+	+		−
Trusting versus suspecting				+		
Practical versus imaginative	−		+		−	
Forthright versus shrewd				−	−	+
Assured versus worrying				−	−	
Traditional versus experimentive		+				
Group oriented versus self-reliant		+	+	−		
Undisciplined versus controlled	+	+				
Calm versus tense	+				−	−

[a]The 16PF traits are presented in opposing pairs, where + designates the right-side trait, and − designates the left-side trait.
[b]The Holland types are designated by the first letter: R: Realistic; I: Investigative; A: Artistic; S: Social; E: Enterprising; C: Conventional

TRANSLATING PERSONALITY RESEARCH INTO PRACTICE

Holland's model of occupational personality types has been adapted to several career interest inventories that are available for use in corporate career development programs. For example, the hand-scored Vocational Preference Inventory (Holland, 1985b) translates individual choices among 160 sets of occupations into eleven personality dimensions, including Holland's six occupational types.

Perhaps the most popular instrument for career planning needs assessment is the Strong Campbell Interest Inventory (Campbell & Hansen, 1981), a program that has evolved over more than sixty years of research and development. In this 325-item computer-scored survey, respondents indicate personal preferences for a wide variety of occupations, vocational and recreational activities, and different kinds of people. Respondents also have a chance to describe their personal characteristics in a few of the items. Their answers yield several kinds of information, including the occupational personality types, which are presented as organizing themes for comparison of individual career interests to those of people in specific occupational categories.

Another approach to measuring occupational types has been taken in the Kuder Occupational Interest Survey (Kuder & Diamond, 1979). Reasoning that people are often unfamiliar with the actual nature of different jobs and may have stereotyped impressions that give inaccurate readings of vocational interest, Kuder (1977) designed his instrument to assess interest in activities that are typical of everyday life. In addition, the activities are grouped into 100 sets of three—usually reflecting skills with people, data, or things—from which a person chooses a most preferred and a least preferred one. The choices are then translated into estimates of relative interest in ten general vocational areas and into direct comparisons with other people in specific occupational groups. Holland's occupational type patterns may also be determined from the vocational results using a conversion table.

By using individual interests in vocations and related activities to identify broader personality patterns, the range of potential matches can be projected beyond the scope of the immediate occupational groups for which data are available. This is, without doubt, an important advantage of using interest inventories for the assessment component in an organizational career development setting where there are unique positions that do not fit typical job categories.

There is, however, also a limitation in relying too heavily on assessment of individual interests. Although it helps concentrate the career development activity on optimal job categories, it does not usually provide much guidance on preparing oneself to assume more responsibility. Moreover, it gives no indication as to whether an individual is even ready or willing to undertake the process of goal setting and action planning. The fact that a person matches up well with some occupational group can in no way ensure that effective follow-through will occur. An individual employee may not be sufficiently experienced, sophisticated (self-aware), or motivated to begin exploring his or her own personal characteristics and potential, which is a necessary first step as one begins the career development process.

Super (1983) has suggested that certain attitudinal qualities, or personality characteristics, play a key role in effective career goal setting and action planning. These pivotal qualities include one's sense of identity and self-esteem, decision-making style, and degree of autonomy. In addition, personal acceptance of responsibility for actively pursuing realistic career goals depends upon gaining a self-awareness of one's own attitudes, values, and potential.

Providing insight into the individual's temperament, then, becomes a major part of the assessment process in career development. Exploring personality characteristics and values allows the employee to gain greater insight into his or her own attitudes, beliefs, and behaviors. With this knowledge of self to supplement the details of specific occupational direction obtained from interest measurement, the transfer of personal skills into new organizational roles can be more easily mapped out.

ASSESSING PERSONALITY IN A CAREER READINESS FRAMEWORK

An objective approach to the task of assessing employee personality has been carefully constructed in the Personal Career Development Profile (PCDP) (Walter, 1985), a career-oriented assessment derived from the 16PF. Based on computer analysis of a person's answers to the 16PF, the PCDP is a narrative report four to six pages in length. The purpose of the report is to provide insights about work styles, career values, and personal needs that can influence a person's adjustment to specific job demands and other general working conditions. It is written in nontechnical, nonthreatening language, and is designed for sharing with the employee. Table 44–2 lists the personality domains assessed by the PCDP. Acceptable levels of validity and reliability have been reported (Walter, 1985).

The PCDP is used as an integrating mechanism in the career development planning sequence. It offers an ideal way to measure the personality characteristics described by Super as indicators of readiness for career development and to look at how an employee's personal qualities may relate to a given work setting. The employee can draw conclusions about preferred work settings and individual suitability based on self-understanding of strengths and weaknesses. That, in turn, leads to goal setting and action planning that puts career interests in perspective and is oriented toward preparing oneself for career growth.

The PCDP report itself begins with a brief statement as to how realistically the person sees himself or herself. It then explores how the person problem solves and copes with stress. Next it examines the person's typical interaction styles and describes the individual's behavior in an organizational setting. The report then shifts toward considering the types of occupational areas, following Holland's model, to which the person might be suited best. The report narrative concludes with a summary section, suggest-

Table 44–2
**Personality Domains Addressed by the
Personal Career Development Profile**

Problem-solving patterns
    Concrete versus conceptual
    Practical versus imaginative
    Traditional versus experimentive
    Objective reasoning versus subjective feeling
    Ability to learn from experience
    Susceptibility to accidents or errors
    Creative potential
    Achievement motivation

Stress-coping patterns
    Easily upset versus realistic
    Self-assured versus worrying
    Undisciplined versus self-controlled
    Calm versus tense
    Nonanxious versus anxious
    Reaction to conflict

Interpersonal interaction patterns
    Reserved versus warm-hearted
    Accommodating versus assertive
    Serious versus enthusiastic
    Cautious versus socially bold
    Trusting versus suspecting
    Forthright versus shrewd
    Group-oriented versus self-reliant
    Introverted versus extraverted

Organizational role and work-setting patterns
    Expedient versus conscientious
    Tough-minded versus tender-minded
    Group oriented versus self-reliant
    Subdued versus independent
    Leadership style
    Need for structure

ing ways in which the person can improve his or her overall effectiveness. A brief example of the narrative format from the sections of the report on problem-solving and organizational role patterns is presented below.

> *Problem-Solving Patterns:* Ms. Sample's approach to tasks is usually balanced between getting things done efficiently and having an awareness of the hidden steps that are part of the process. However, she may sometimes get caught off guard when it's important to watch her actions and to be careful. She can, therefore, easily act without thinking first. She likes to experiment with and test new ideas and approaches. She is usually open to new ways of doing things and welcomes changes. She generally likes to put her own ideas into action. However, she may at times be cautious about accepting changes suggested by others.

> Organizational Role and Work-Setting Patterns: Ms. Sample may prefer a role of leadership in organizational settings, and she is likely to accept such a role with a group of friends or coworkers if provided the opportunity. She may not always be strongly interested, though, in pushing for appointment to such a role. If she were to take on a leadership role, she would probably strive to administer duties by focusing attention on the conditions which foster or hinder the performance of subordinates rather than on personnel problems which may be present. Being more solution-seeking than blame-oriented, she strives to remove personality and power struggles from the work situation.

The PCDP helps clarify for employees how their personality characteristics, beliefs, and behaviors are related to career success. It also helps individuals understand what career activities are satisfying based on their own personality characteristics. This information, linked with direction from the corporation concerning its own objectives and career options, is vital in determining various career paths to pursue and how to pursue them.

Finally, the summary and growth suggestions on the PCDP can help an individual begin to see a framework for action planning by looking at strengths and the areas in which growth is encouraged. The report therefore can round out the corporate career development process as it provides credible and supportive feedback, pinpoints career-related activities, and offers suggestions for increasing personal effectiveness. To illustrate how the PCDP might be used for individual planning purposes, an actual case is described.

IMPROVING EMPLOYEE CAREER PLANNING WITH PERSONALITY DATA

Since its introduction in 1977, the PCDP has been used successfully with employees across many levels and functions to prepare them for seeking viable career opportunities within their own companies. A case in point was the proved administrative assistant at a national insurance company's headquarters who wanted to be considered for advancement into a supervisory position that was opening soon. To get a better idea of her chances for success and to find out how best to pursue her objective, she went to see the company's career planning counselor.

The counselor suggested she begin the exploration process by reviewing her own PCDP. The administrative assistant learned that she already possessed certain desirable supervisory qualities. These included a good appreciation for practical issues and commonsense solutions, a strongly directive and decisive nature, a warmly enthusiastic outlook, and a cooperative orientation. Her authoritative style and team spirit were promising signs of her future potential as a supervisor.

At the same time, she became more aware of a tendency to get easily distracted, an often hasty action response, and a somewhat casual attitude toward accepted procedures. Such characteristics are not altogether unknown among supervisors and managers; however, their combined effect might well detract from her performance as a supervisor, as reflected in poor planning and execution that could lead to a crisis management mentality.

As a result of this joint review of the PCDP, the administrative assistant and the counselor agreed on a series of steps the assistant could take to prepare herself for a supervisory role. These included developmental tasks aimed at improving her skills in the area of self-management, such as enrollment in a time management training course and independent study of resource materials about setting personal and professional standards.

The administrative assistant's experience illustrates how personality assessment can provide useful information to facilitate the career planning process. The PCDP report describes individual qualities in a nonthreatening style and occupational activities for which an employee is well suited. It provides supportive feedback as to what is achievable and what needs to be done to get there. It can activate employees to pursue realistic career opportunities. Most important, the report is based on a reliable and valid assessment instrument (Cattell et al., 1970).

ORGANIZATIONAL APPLICATIONS OF PERSONALITY TO CAREER DEVELOPMENT

Beyond giving employees a greater stake in the process, inclusion of a personality assessment component can also serve the larger organizational purposes of career planning. Often a program is designed in response to a specific human resource concern. A personality-based approach to career development can extend the capability of the overall effort, as shown by the following case studies involving the PCDP.

Career Paths

The company where the administrative assistant worked, whose case was described above, had about 1,500 job titles. This created confusion for employees who wished to pursue a long-term career growth strategy within the company. They either were unaware of opportunities in other parts of the company than their own or were unable to evaluate them realistically in terms of self-potential.

To resolve this obstacle, the coordinator of the career development program classified each job title using the categories from Holland's occupational model. These were arranged in a pamphlet for use by employees in career planning. By reference to the model's definitions of occupational personality, employees could get an idea of the kinds of characteristics that would be suitable for a given position.

The next step was to help employees discover how well their own traits, styles, and values matched the ideal type for a desired position. The PCDP was chosen for this purpose because it was not limited to a mechanical restating of preferences but instead gave a dynamic picture of the employee's capabilities along with specific goals for growth. In reality, other assessment systems such as the Kuder, Vocational Preference, or Strong-Campbell could have been used too. To facilitate action planning by employees, the PCDP was supplemented by a series of insight and analysis exercises contained in other career planning materials (e.g., Walter & Wallace, 1984).

Employees had a chance to formulate and refine their plans for seeking out career opportunities within the company. Participants were encouraged to identify positions that potentially fit their objectives and to follow up with informational interviews. Personal discussion with the career counselor about optimal ways to reach career goals was available upon request. The program attracted mainly support personnel who, like the administrative assistant, wanted to explore their potential to move up into supervisory and managerial ranks.

Reorganization

The large U.S. subsidiary of a major international firm was undergoing massive reorganization, primarily because of financial containment. The corporate selection and employment manager and his staff of about twenty-five human resource professionals were charged with managing the employment aspect of the changes.

Restructuring at the firm produced predictable insecurity among employees, the human resource staff itself, and upper-level management. Employees saw positions to which they aspired being filled by newly hired individuals. The human resource staff felt pressure from all sides; they wanted to satisfy the objectives of upper management, to maintain and increase their own credibility throughout the company, and to help individual employees make the best possible choices.

The objective of the human resource staff became, then, to set up an effective structure that would assist them in finding the best possible employees for the given positions, including identifying those individuals who were most likely to fit in with upper management objectives. The corporate selection and employment manager also genuinely cared about those individuals who were outplaced or disappointed in advancements and was determined to work with them at least minimally.

The company began using the PCDP, predominantly for newly hired persons and at various stages in the hiring process. The report was also utilized in outplacement. The nonthreatening, easy-to-read, and positively stated format of the personality assessment approach aided in the human resource efforts. The results, generated in report form by computer, were easy to digest. The human resource staff was relieved of the time-consuming job of integrating scores into an understandable report. Upper managers, not all of whom were knowledgeable about testing, felt secure with the report, recognizing it was not subject to interpretation errors on the part of the human resource personnel.

The human resource staff developed a cohesive and shared-value attitude during their group training process with the use and interpretation of the PCDP. Individual pressures to make the "right" decisions were alleviated due to this group support. The human resource staff gained credibility and respect with employees and management alike because of the accuracy of the report. Because of the objectivity and computer-generated nature of the report, vital decisions were removed from the possibility of fallible judgment on the part of the human resource staff, in the eyes of management.

Succession Planning

At another national insurance company, a need for management succession planning was the impetus for a comprehensive career development program. Human resource planners had forecast a requirement to replace 50 percent of senior management positions due to retirement over a five-year period. Age curves in the administrative and underwriting departments were especially top-heavy, but all departments would soon face a personnel crisis.

There was a wealth of talent within the organization upon which to draw. About 6,000 employees were eligible to be considered for advancement. However, upper management worried that the uncertainty over future roles might cause many junior managers and staff members to seek career opportunities elsewhere.

To establish a clear commitment to looking for internal candidates, the human resource department initiated an assessment center process. Employees were given a trial exposure to realistic management responsibilities in groups of up to twelve persons. Individual potential was judged by senior management observers, and recommendations for areas in need of further attention were made.

At the same time, employees were also provided with the PCDP to help them identify their own talents and channel these effectively toward desired goals. During a four-day seminar, emphasis was given to creating individual action plans and taking responsibility for making things happen.

In support of this effort, information about developmental resources available within the company, the community, or through professional outlets was communicated by the human resources team. In addition, program counselors worked with individual employees, monitoring progress toward goals, advising of possible opportunities, and generally stimulating ideas on ways to move productively in new career path directions. The response was very positive, and many employees were encouraged to participate in the program once they saw the experiences of others producing results. By the end of the five-year period, the immediate challenge of management succession had been successfully met, as shown by minimal disruptions in business and a lowered turnover rate among junior personnel.

Employee Development

The PCDP has been an integral part of career planning and management development at one regional division of a large telecommunications firm for the last few years. Over that time, several thousand employees have participated in growth-oriented workshops, with the assistance of an external consultant.

The initial momentum for the program came from a perception by the top executive that people in the organization were languishing in their careers. As a result, the organization had become stagnant and lacked a sense of individual excitement or commitment. A major restructuring of the company was about to unfold, and this provided the ideal chance to get employees involved again in planning for their own futures, as well as that of the company.

At the outset, the focus of activity was pointed on dealing with organizational problems at the department level. Employee task forces were charged with looking at all facets of each situation, including personality issues, to come up with action plans for improvement.

As many as fifty people at once worked together on these projects, with emphasis placed on team-building, conflict-resolution, and problem-solving processes during intensive seminars of two or three days. Part of each seminar was spent on the personality dynamics elicited by the PCDP. Individual employees discovered how their personal styles affected coworkers and considered making changes in themselves that might support the overall effort.

Since that time, the focus has shifted more toward individual effectiveness in the context of leadership development. Now groups of district managers, who have direct lines of supervision that include up to 200 employees, use the PCDP to explore ways of becoming more fulfilled in their positions.

Participants try to validate the data by reviewing their own experiences and through informal discussions with colleagues. Next they develop a personal vision of success as a leader and what it will take to accomplish that. This requires a step-by-step action plan for specific refinements of individual behavior styles.

The program continues to receive a positive response and has achieved some dramatic results besides improving the climate for career growth. In one case, a manager who had a reputation for being a very unpleasant person in the work setting was able to turn his career around through a series of gradual self-improvements. Former associates have expressed astonishment at the extent of personal transformation when meeting him again after several years. Current associates express disbelief that he could have been viewed so negatively.

SUMMARY

Personality data can serve a beneficial function in career development programs within companies. The growth needs of the individual employee and the human resource objectives of the company can be fulfilled more effectively when the personality-related aspects of career planning are directly addressed.

Personality assessment systems that are designed for use in career development programs, such as the PCDP offer a convenient and efficient way to introduce personality data as a focal point of employee planning activities. Providing individual feedback in an objective, easy-to-read format backed by well-documented research can add greater credibility to the organizational career development process.

Although their versatility has been demonstrated in a wide variety of applications, perhaps the greatest strength of these systems lies in their impact as action planning tools. By going beyond simple impressions to give specific recommendations for increasing personal effectiveness, these personality assessment systems form a basis for stimulating individual growth motivation. Goal-oriented behavior among participating employees is the key to success of any career development program.

REFERENCES

Bolton, B. (1985). Discriminant analysis of Holland's occupational types using the Sixteen Personality Factor Questionnaire. *Journal of Vocational Behavior, 27,* 210–217.

Campbell, D.P., & Hansen, J.C. (1981). *Manual for the Strong-Campbell Interest Inventory* (3d ed.). Stanford, CA: Stanford University Press.

Cattell, R.B., Eber, H.W., & Tatsuoka, M.M. (1970). *Handbook for the 16PF.* Champaign, IL: Institute for Personality and Ability Testing, Inc.

Costa, P.T., Fozard, J.L., & McCrae, R.R. (1977). Personological interpretation of factors from the Strong Vocational Interest Blank scales. *Journal of Vocational Behavior, 10,* 231–243.

Gottfredson, G.D., & Holland, J.L. (1989). *Dictionary of Holland Occupation Codes* (2d ed.). Odessa, FL: Psychological Assessment Resources.

Holland, J.L. (1985a). *Making vocational choices: A theory of vocational possibilities and work environments* (2d ed.). Englewood Cliffs, NJ: Prentice-Hall.

Holland, J.L. (1985b). *Manual for the Vocational Preference Inventory*. Odessa, FL: Psychological Assessment Resources.

Johns, E.F. (1985). *Holland's occupational taxonomy in terms of personality traits and discriminant functions.* Master's thesis, Cleveland State University.

Kuder, F. (1977). *Activity interests and occupational choice.* Chicago: Science Research Associates.

Kuder, F., & Diamond, E.E. (1979). *General manual: Kuder DD Occupational Interest Survey* (2d ed.). Chicago: Science Research Associates.

Mirabile, R.J. (1987). New directions for career development. *Training and Development Journal* (December), 30–33.

Moses, B. (1987). Giving employees a future. *Training and Development Journal* (December), 25–28.

Super, D.E. (1983). Assessment in career guidance: Toward truly developmental counseling. *Personnel and Guidance Journal, 61* (9), 555–562.

Turner, R.G., & Horn, J.M. (1977). Personality, husband-wife similarity, and Holland's occupational types. *Journal of Vocational Behavior, 10,* 111–120.

U.S. Department of Labor. (1977). *Dictionary of occupational titles* (4th ed.). Washington, DC: U.S. Government Printing Office.

Walter, V. (1985). *Personal Career Development Profile manual* (rev. ed.). Champaign, IL: Institute for Personality and Ability Testing, Inc.

Walter, V., & Wallace, M. (1984). *A guide to self-motivated career planning* (rev. ed.). Champaign, IL: Institute for Personality and Ability Testing, Inc.

Ward, G.R., Cunningham, C.H., & Wakefield, J.A. (1976). Relationships between Holland's VPI and Cattell's 16PF. *Journal of Vocational Behavior, 8,* 307–312.

Zak, I., Meir, E.I., & Kraemer, R. (1979). The common space of personality traits and vocational interests. *Journal of Personality Assessment, 43* (4), 424–428.

Mark Michaels

Tellabs, Inc., a leading-edge developer of digital telecommunications equipment, was changing fast. To stay ahead in its highly competitive market, the fourteen-year-old company decided in 1986 to change from traditional manufacturing methods to a highly participatory manufacturing system stressing quality management. The change would require extensive development activities for its 1,050 employees. And the new management philosophy required developing an ability to identify quickly key organizational problems that inhibited its quest for quality.

The human resource department would play a major role in integrating the philosophy and new operating procedures into the organization. But it also had to be able to apply the new philosophy to its own operations.

At the start of the new program, Tellabs's methods for managing human resource information were typical. Payroll information and its associated reports were contracted out to a payroll processing firm. Otherwise personnel transactions were handled manually, with data stored in individual employee files. Compilation of data that could be used to support the

Figure 45–1. An Information Processing System

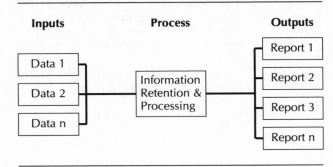

new program, such as available skills, turnover, absenteeism, rates, and employment costs, was next to impossible to obtain.

The problem is typical for many human resources departments, which are mired down with paper record-keeping systems that cannot serve the multiple masters who make demands on the understaffed departments.

HUMAN RESOURCES AS AN INFORMATION PROCESSING SYSTEM

The problem is easily understood when studying the human resource function as an information processing system. Figure 45–1 describes a typical information processing system in which inputs, in the form of data, are fed into the system for processing. The organization, acting like a brain, stores the data and, later, formats the data into meaningful information, the system's output.

The human resource function in organizations evolved from two directions. Although both the social service foundation and the payroll processing foundation fit the same information processing model, the development of the model is best under-

stood from the development of personnel as a payroll function.

Most personnel departments were originally established to process payroll. These departments were specifically structured to keep records of individual employees. As an information processing system, this meant designing the system to provide information that would describe individual employees. Employee data, such as hours worked, attendance, benefits, and performance evaluations, were the primary form of information coming into the department. The individual employee personnel file was the system output.

Two developments in personnel management

changed the type of data coming into personnel. The first was the growth of government regulation of the human resource function. Requirements ranging from labor-management compliance to equal employment opportunity (EEO) and safety management were fed into the personnel department. And outputs that compiled data across employee files were required for reporting purposes.

The new regulations caused an outcry from the personnel management profession. There was no complaint about the goals of the programs, but the output requirements appeared exhaustive. Cross-tabulating information from individual employee files were expected to require an excessive amount of additional manpower. In short, the existing system could not serve two masters.

The second change was the growth of the human relations approach to management. The goal of human relations practitioners was to match organizational and employee needs to improve productivity. To achieve this goal required new information coming into the personnel department—information about the organization itself such as organizational goals and manpower planning needs. Calculation of the degree to which employee and organizational goals were combined required new system outputs, including historical statistics such as turnover, absenteeism, and safety rates, and predictive statistics for developmental and manpower planning.

Now the system was required to serve three masters. There quickly developed a system overload. As shown in figure 45–2, the individual personnel file remained the depository of the data, with no effective method of retrieval for meeting regulatory and organizational needs.

The demands of the human resource function now require a new perspective on the input sources and output needs of the function as it processes information. As the result of the growth of human resource management, the three activities—payroll, legal compliance, and organizational requirements—translate into three main sources for data input—employee data, organizational data, and environmental data. Just managing the voluminous incoming data provides justification for computerization.

But the real problem is how to get away from the employee file as the sole mode of system output. As was described, the system now must serve at least three masters: individual employee information, productivity and problem identification information, and regulatory information (figure 45–3).

The only effective way to achieve the requirements of this system is through implementation of a computer-based human resource information system (HRIS).

Figure 45–2. Traditional HR Information Systems

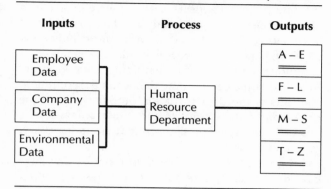

Figure 45–3. The New HR Information System

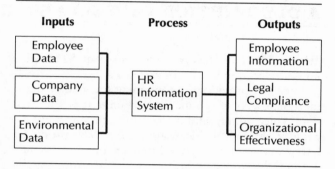

An HRIS is a data base, just like the filing cabinet. It can store and process large volumes of data in individual fields, like the pieces of paper in that cabinet. The difference is that a good HRIS is "relational"; it enables the user to develop outputs in any relational format desired.

For instance, a very simple traditional personnel file might be a sheet of paper for each employee with name, address, telephone number, title, starting date, salary, race, and sex. Any request for information will require reviewing all the bits of information. If a person wants to develop a report of salaries paid according to race and sex, he or she will have to review each sheet a number of times before the report is made. The data will always be accessed by name first.

The situation is exactly like a telephone book. It is possible to find out someone's telephone number only if the person's name is known. To find out who lives on Mulberry Street is virtually impossible.

The traditional solution is to develop a second filing cabinet with a sheet of paper for each race, listing the salaries received by each employee of that race. The idea, which is similar to special telephone directories that list people by address, is not outlandish. Many companies have managers develop separate staffing reports by other than name basis for report compliance with affirmative action plans.

A relational data base can effortlessly rearrange the data pieces to appear as if they were in a second filing cabinet. In a relational data base, each bit of information is saved as if it were on an individual piece of paper. The general heading—name—is a temporary definition for identifying data location. Any field name can become the heading, resulting in rearranging the data to fit the output needs. If the EEO report request is made, the data base ignores the "name" and organizes the information under salary, race, and/or sex.

A good HRIS is composed of modules that have built-in data compilation and formatting, or output instructions, to serve a group of needs. For instance, there may be one or more modules addressing the legal compliance report needs. That module rearranges the data to be like the second filing cabinet, following instructions developed from the environmental data and inputted into the system.

Obviously, it would be just as difficult to develop a report on employees' salaries by departments from this second module, as it would to find John Smith's telephone number if only the street directory is available. But the programming of the HRIS makes it a simple task to rearrange the filing system back to the individual employee-file-based system.

Implementation of a microcomputer-based HRIS became the obvious solution for Tellabs.

A DESCRIPTION OF TELLABS, INC.

Tellabs, Inc. manufactures and sells over $115 million of telecommunications systems a year. Its broad product line provides the equipment for sending digital signals over telephone lines, making it possible to send voice, data, and video information simultaneously through a telephone system. The products have a major impact on the future of communications around the world, which is why the company is involved in a very competitive market.

The company has production facilities in Illinois, Texas, and Puerto Rico and other facilities in Canada and the U.S. Virgin Islands. The company currently employs about 1,050 people, with manufacturing being the largest employer group. Production workers build electronic components, which are the products of the company.

In 1986, in response to the need to increase margins, the company changed its management philosophy to what it calls Total Quality Commitment (TQC). The philosophy is based on work done by W. Edward Deming and others in developing the management systems in Japan after World War II. Similar management systems are found at Hewlett-Packard and Ford Motor Company.

The company defines TQC as "a commitment to excellence in which all functions focus on continuous process improvement, resulting in increased customer satisfaction." By "all functions" the company means every employee. And "process improvement" means the methods by which work is accomplished.

The key indicator of performance in TQC is the achievement of a zero defect rate in the product and in each process of the organization. Achieving a zero defect rate requires the ability to reduce these quality costs to zero. Achieving the goal requires tracking performance over time and tracking variables relating to performance concurrently.

The primary method for achieving zero defect rates is through TQC teams—quality task forces that review quality problems and design and implement solutions. The TQC teams are taught techniques in data gathering, data analysis, and planning and in applying those techniques.

The management of the TQC program is done by the Corporate Quality Council, a team of the company's top managers. The human resources department is charged with the training and much of the organization-wide data management needs relating to human resources necessary to support the new work environment. Obviously, the traditional employee file-oriented information system would no longer meet the company's needs.

IMPLEMENTING THE HRIS AT TELLABS

In 1985, before the TQC program had started, the President's Committee (the Quality Council predecessor) recognized the need to improve the data management systems in human resources. Up to that time, all payroll records were being handled by an outside payroll agency, and most other records were filled in the traditional manner.

William Keating, Tellabs's human resource director, company president Michael Birk, and finance director David Sneider were assigned to evaluate and select a system to meet company needs.

The team began with a needs analysis, which identified the system parameters. As part of TQC, the company often uses the Pareto Principle as an analysis tool (which states that when there are many sources for a common effect, a relative few sources account for the bulk of the effect). They needed to design reports that could identify the vital few issues affecting the company's management of human resources.

To meet developmental needs, the team wanted a system that included a skills bank—a data base of employee skills that facilitates manpower planning, helps identify training needs, and facilitates selection based on skills for participation in special task forces. The company also wanted to be able to track skills development through training.

The cost of the system was defined by the company's current costs using the outside payroll company, based on that company's bid to combine the HRIS needs with payroll.

The team decided on purchasing a microcomputer-based system, HR 1. The cost for the system was approximately $50,000; $18,000 of the cost was for hardware (an IBM AT system with multiple input terminals), $25,000 for the proprietary software, and the remaining funds for training. The cost was equivalent to two years of HRIS service from the payroll company.

HR 1 was installed in early 1987. By October, the basic system was in place. All personnel transactions from the point of implementation on are now being tracked by the system.

However, many of the historical data remain to be installed. In particular, the company still needs to install the skills bank and training modules. Because these modules have not been established, the system is not yet meeting the full needs of the company.

Installing an HRIS is always problematic. First, with most systems, the system itself must be customized to meet the company's needs. This will involve instructing the software program of the company's personnel policies in a form understandable by the computer. For instance, the computer needs to know which types of employees may receive what types of benefits and how exceptions are made. The costs for the various transactions must also be identified. Then codes are assigned to this information to standardize it for easy data manipulation.

For Tellabs, this process was critical and extremely developmental because it forced the company to make policy decisions on such issues as compensation management, since those polices had been handled haphazardly up to that time.

Once the policies are inputted, an extensive amount of paper records must be manually formatted to match the new codes. Some HRIS installation programs include formatting sheets, which can be completed directly by managers and employees, reducing the efforts necessary for compiling the data directly from existing personnel files.

But the most time-consuming process is inputting all this information into the computer. Many companies use temporary staff for the project. At Tellabs, the work was first done with existing staff. The extensive time necessary for the process was a major factor in the slow implementation of the system. Eventually, temporary employees were brought in to help.

USING THE INFORMATION

Although system implementation is not complete, Tellabs has already begun benefiting from its use. The results appear to show that the implementation of the system solves the problem of responding to the three major output areas in the information processing system model.

Individual personnel information is used for the traditional payroll through a link with the payroll processing company's computer, benefits management, and employee management purposes. The system is used for routinely reporting information required by the Equal Employment Opportunity Commission, Occupational Safety and Health Administration, and immiration agencies.

The system is also being used for organizational performance information. Traditional reports, such as employee master lists, hiring, and termination, turnover, and absenteeism reports, are used by the President's Committee to help assess overall company performance.

Tellabs has also integrated the information into its TQC program. The human resource and quality assurance directors were originally assigned as a team to identify what would be measured by the system and tracked for the TQC program. Since the TQC program was developed after the selection of the HRIS, the team had to develop a sense of what could be measured. They took a three-step approach.

First, the team looked at information coming from the system to identify what the top quality issues were. Tellabs has defined the cost of quality as the "failure cost"—the direct costs associated with mistake correction—the "audit cost"—the costs necessary to discover a mistake—and the "prevention cost"—the cost necessary to avoid the mistake in the future.

Four areas within the human resource function were targeted for tracking quality costs in human resource management: turnover, absenteeism, performance appraisal, and safety. Of these high-cost quality areas, turnover was identified as the first issue to be addressed using a TQC team.

The TQC team's first task in attacking turnover was to understand where it was occurring. Applying the Pareto Principle to the turnover reports, the team identified Electronics Associates as the major employee group experiencing turnover. The computer was also able to generate data on the stated reason for terminations in this group, which showed resigna-tions to accept other employment as the primary cause. This led the committee to question why this classification was leaving for supposedly greener pastures. Through a survey of the former employees, the team learned that the new employees were being better compensated in their new positions.

Again the HRIS was able to help. The team gathered industry salary data for the position and inputted it into the HRIS. The system conducted a regression analysis comparing time in grade (in the position) against terminations and salary levels. The report showed that an adjustment was needed in the base pay rate for the position.

Tellabs estimates that the cost of the salary increases, plus TQC team time, for the solution will be about $150,000 if annualized. But the turnover cost (cost of employment and training of replacements) was about $200,000 per year. The net savings would be $50,000. Based on the implementation times, it would take only one year to pay back the costs of the solution.

THE FUTURE FOR AUTOMATING HUMAN RESOURCE MANAGEMENT AT TELLABS

Tellabs is looking forward to the complete installation of the HRIS and other microcomputer applications to increase the effectiveness of its human resource management program.

According to Keating, in addition to providing valuable data for future TQC team projects affecting the function, the HRIS will be particularly helpful for tracking TQC training and skills development in the employees. But Keating expects to go beyond the HRIS. He looks forward to the eventual development of an electronic notebook system where employees can share information on what is happening within their TQC teams and management can track the emerging issues and solutions. Other applications will include on-line attitude surveys, employment testing, and computer-based training.

CONCLUSION

The Tellabs case demonstrates the importance of an integrated solution to what is really a systems problems. Tellabs is now able to receive, manage, and process data received from multiple sources and effectively supply meaningful information from those data to multiple clients.

Other companies have taken a more haphazard approach. There is microcomputer software available for specific applications such as affirmative action planning, compensation planning, and strategic human resource planning, but maintaining separate systems by function just recreates the multiple filing cabinets on the computer system. In reviewing some of these packages, most are designed to be incompat-ible with each other. Companies buying the special applications have not experienced any real increase in their effective management of human resource data.

Alternatives to large, expensive HRIS programs should be considered. HR 1 cost Tellabs $50,000, including $25,000 in software. Other good HRIS software programs cost as little as $700. One non-profit organization in Illinois took a generic data base program, DBase II, and created its own HRIS, saving a lot of cash in the process.

As Tellabs discovered, the issue of selection must first be based on the organization's needs. The needs assessment must begin by defining the outputs needed by the organization: what information is needed in what kinds of reports to help the organization achieve its mission.

Some reports, such as regulatory reports, are needed in most organizations. Other reports, or the ability to produce them, will be specific to an individual company. At Tellabs, for instance, the company needed reports that could either be directly developed to be analyzed with the Pareto Principle or could be integrated into a spreadsheet program for such analysis.

As specialization and specificity for reports increase, the need for flexibility increases. This will generally result in selection of a more expensive HRIS.

The needs assessment should also identify what data are available to determine the potential imple-

mentation costs and time schedule. An organization that has kept incomplete records will find it very difficult to convert to a complex HRIS. The company may need to develop basic personnel policies and get into the habit of good record keeping first.

Outside of traditional business applications like word processing, the HRIS was the first computer application to become widely used in the human resource function. Numerous other specific applications are now being developed, some of which Keating hinted at. These include computer-assisted selection, computer-based training, and meeting management programs. Each new application is adding to human resource management's ability to serve its various clients more effectively in ways that respond directly to those client needs.

Ann Howard

How would you describe your career? With what aspects of your career are you most preoccupied? What produces the most excitement and arouses your greatest concern? Would your answers be the same when you began your career? Will they be the same as you approach retirement?

As these questions imply, a full description of your career would include not only the sequence of jobs and work experiences that comprise your occupational life but your own subjective reactions to those job sequences as well (Hall, 1976). But chances are good that those subjective reactions would differ markedly at various points in time across the span of your work life.

This chapter attempts to document some of the interests, concerns, and salient issues for workers at various career stages. Because this book is directed toward managers, advice is offered on how to help meet the needs of subordinates in various career stages.

RESEARCH DATA BASE AND CAREER MODEL

Various researchers have suggested that the career can be broken into stages with unique sets of physical and psychological tasks to be mastered (e.g., Hall & Nougaim, 1968; Super, 1959). Often a match is attempted between career stages and what have been theorized as stages of adult life (e.g., Erikson, 1963; Levinson et al., 1978). Yet adult life stage theories, including the notion of a midlife crisis, have not fared well in terms of gathering empirical support. This is especially true for those theories that try to relate stages to specific ages or that insist that one must pass through one stage before confronting the next. On the other hand, data are accumulating that suggest the existence of various career stages, especially where it is realized that they are not necessarily tied to specific ages (cf. Cron & Slocum, 1986).

For the purpose of this chapter, empirical data on key concerns at various career stages will be provided by perhaps the most comprehensive longitudinal study of managers ever undertaken, the Management Progress Study. Since the managers in the study, all white males, were employed for most of their careers in the stable bureaucratic environment of the Bell System, their career stages followed a fairly regular progression. Their career patterns would not show the vicissitudes of, say, today's young manager who is likely to begin new career sequences in several organizations over the life span, or a woman whose childbearing and family responsibilities result in an interrupted career. Even within this rather homogeneous sample, it is clear that managers and their careers come in many different sizes and shapes. Nevertheless there were many similarities of response to different career stages, from which conclusions can be drawn.

THE MANAGEMENT PROGRESS STUDY

The Management Progress Study (MPS) was begun by Douglas W. Bray at AT&T in 1956 and continued there until 1987. A complete description of the study and its major findings over the first twenty years can be found in Howard and Bray (1988). As shown in table 46–1 the study began with a three-day assessment center in which assessees in groups of twelve were brought together for a variety of exercises, including interviews, group and individual simulations of managerial work, projective tests, and paper-and-pencil measures of aptitudes, motivation, personality, and attitudes. While undergoing many of their assessment tasks, they were observed by groups of assessors who wrote reports describing their performance. Later, the assessors met in group sessions to read their reports aloud, to hear all other information gathered about the assessees, and to rate them on twenty-six dimensions, or variables considered important to managerial work.

The initial assessment centers occurred during the summers of 1956 through 1960, all shown as year 0 in table 46–1 (MPS:0). For each of the first seven years following the original assessment, interviews were conducted both with the participants and, independently, with someone in the company about them (initially a personnel department representative; later an ex-boss or boss). In addition, the participants were asked to fill out two questionnaires that indicated their expectations about their careers and their attitudes toward their work experiences. The assessment center was repeated in year 8 of the study (MPS:8), following which interviews were continued triannually. A third assessment center was conducted in year 20 (MPS:20), which repeated some of the previous exercises but added many new measures of midlife and midcareer concerns. The last interviews were conducted in year 25. Also interviewed, when appropriate, were those who terminated from the company in the early years and retirees in the later years.

There were two types of participants in MPS. A group of 274 college graduates had been brought into the telephone companies while in their twenties (their average age was twenty-four). Many had been recruited directly from the college campus. The recruits were assigned to jobs in the lowest rung of management with the expectation that they would learn and develop and eventually be promoted at least into middle management (the third of a seven-level telephone company hierarchy). In addition, another group of 148 men without college degrees had joined the telephone company in craft positions. They had risen through the ranks and had been promoted into management by the age of thirty-two. By the time they joined MPS, they had on the average nine years of experience with the company and were twenty-nine to thirty years of age.

Because the noncollege men already had a substantial time commitment to the company by the time of the assessment center and because their opportunities for management jobs elsewhere were more limited than those of the college graduates, there was very little attrition from this group over the first twenty years of the study. However, many took an early retirement in their fifties, so that by 1987 less than half of the original group remained. Many of the college men left the company in the early years; 40 percent had left by the assessment in the eighth year (MPS:8) and 50 percent by year 20. Only a handful had retired by 1987.

The noncollege men did not fare as well as the college graduates in terms of later advancement in management, partly because of lesser ability and motivation and partly because the company did not have as high expectations for them. Table 46–2 gives the distribution of both groups of men by management level at year 25, including the retirees at their last level attained. The typical noncollege man progressed to the second level, one shy of middle management. One-third of this group did attain a middle management position, although none advanced into the executive ranks. Among the college men, the entry into middle management (third level) was the most typical level attained. One-third of this group also went higher than their modal level, with fifteen pushing into the executive ranks (fifth level or higher) and one man going beyond the telephone company presidency into the holding company of a divested regional operating company.

Table 46–1
Management Progress Study Design

Year	Activity	Population
0	Assessment	Participants
1–7	Interviews (annual)	Participants, company personnel, bosses, terminators
8	Assessment	Participants
10–20	Interviews (3-year interval)	Participants, bosses, terminators
20	Assessment	Participants
25	Interview	Participants, bosses, terminators
20–30	Interviews (upon retirement)	Retirees

Table 46–2
MPS Management Levels at Year 25

Level	College		Noncollege	
	(N)	(%)	(N)	(%)
7+	1	1		
6	4	3		
5	10	7		
4	32	23	5	4
3	61	45	40	29
2	24	18	61	45
1	5	4	31	23
Total	137	100	137	100

Note: Includes retirees.

When the college and noncollege participants are considered together, the MPS provides a comprehensive look at managers in all career stages. These range from entry into the company, to disenchantment and termination by some, through promotions well into the executive ranks or plateauing at the bottom, and into retirement.

The question could be raised as to whether the MPS results are particular to one time period in history or to one organization. To help answer this question, comparison data have been collected from other samples. The Management Continuity Study (MCS) is a study parallel to that of MPS (for a complete description, see Howard & Bray, 1988). It was also comprised of telephone company managers in the Bell System, with the original assessments conducted between 1977 and 1982.

In the Inter-Organizational Testing Study, paper-and-pencil test data were collected for middle-aged and young managers in ten different organizations (eight industry, two government). These results indicated that the differences between the middle-aged MPS managers and the young MCS managers were typical of managers in other organizations and suggested that the findings of the longitudinal studies have much generalizability.

Career Stages

To illustrate the progression of the MPS men's careers, the four stages described by Cron and Slocum (1986) are used as a compatible scheme:

Exploration: People are typically concerned with finding an appropriate occupation in this stage, and they may flounder as they attempt to match their skills and interests with opportunities offered by employing organizations.

Establishment: A commitment to an occupational field is made at this stage, and the worker strives to establish roots. With the initial learning stages over, the emphasis is on bettering one's performance to attain financial and personal success.

Maintenance: Advancements may slow or cease in this stage, which is devoted to maintaining what one has already achieved.

Disengagement: In this stage, workers are planning for retirement and adjusting to the transition from work to retirement.

When this scheme was used in a study of salespeople, Cron and Slocum (1986) found that the average age for those in the Exploration stage was 27.9, for those in the Establishment stage 34.4, for those in the Maintenance stage 40.4, and for those in the Disengagement stage 55.1. In MPS, these stages would roughly translate into using the original assessment (MPS:O) as an indicator of the Exploration stage, the MPS:8 assessment as an indicator of the Establishment stage, MPS:20 as an indicator of the Maintenance stage, and the late career experiences of the early retirees as indicators of the Disengagement stage. A great deal of age heterogeneity for each stage was noted by Cron and Slocum, however, which is also evident in MPS when the data are considered by time of plateauing.

CAREER ISSUES IN DIFFERENT CAREER STAGES

The longitudinal nature of MPS makes it possible to compare the same participants in terms of their abilities, motivations, personalities, and attitudes at different points in their careers. From these series of snapshots over time can be pieced together a moving picture of the career development process.

Exploration

The Exploration stage of a career is a time of abundant enthusiasm but also of considerable vulnerability. Hopes and expectations run high, but this means that disappointments can be profound. The desire to prove oneself is urgent, but new workers generally need the support of others to learn the ropes.

At the original assessments of both the MPS and

MCS groups, participants were asked to fill in a fifty-six-item questionnaire that measured their expectations for a management career. The items focused on a variety of areas, including anticipated salary and advancement, intellectual stimulation of peers, availability of needed resources, and the desirability of the work community as a place to live. Participants were to indicate the likelihood that each outcome on the questionnaire would or would not occur five years hence. The questionnaire was also administered with each follow-up interview in the early years of the MPS and MCS studies. The instructions were changed so that in the first four years, participants always described anticipated conditions in MPS:5 while in year 5 and those following, they were simply asked to describe current conditions.

For both samples it was evident that expectations

Figure 46–1. Expectations Inventory over Time: MPS and MCS College Graduate Groups

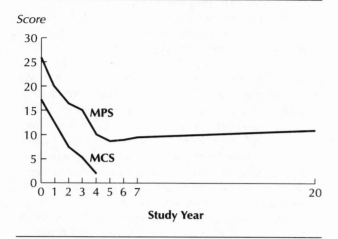

Score

p < .005 time effect.

Figure 46–2. Edwards Affiliation and Intraception Scales: MPS over Time

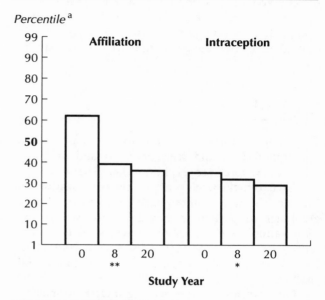

Percentile [a]

[a] 1958 Bell System Norms
*p < .05, **p < .005 time effects.*

were highest at the beginning of the career. Results are shown in figure 46–1 for the college graduate samples of MPS and MCS. The MCS group scored significantly lower than the MPS group in all administrations; this was a function of a general change in American culture between the 1950s and the 1970s, which introduced a streak of pessimism and cynicism into the general populace (Howard & Wilson, 1982; Howard & Bray, 1988). However, the same general trend was found of lessening expectations with each of the succeeding years of the early career. Thus the Exploration stage of a career may include unrealistic expectations, which are soon tempered by organizational realities.

In the Exploration stage, high ambitions are concomitant with high expectations about what a management career can offer. A number of college graduates in MPS stated at the original assessment that they had their eyes on becoming a telephone company president. As the years wore on, the participants gradually lowered their aspirations until most were content to be in middle management.

Another characteristic of managers in the Exploration stage was greater dependence on others. A scale from the Edwards Personal Preference Schedule called Affiliation, which measures enjoyment of and attraction to friends, showed that at the time of the MPS:0 assessment, the MPS college graduates scored higher than they would at any later time in their careers (figure 46–2). The MCS managers scored similarly to the MPS managers at their original assessment. Another scale from the same questionnaire (Intraception; also shown in figure 46–2) showed that the new college recruits were most interested in

analyzing the motives and feelings of others but that this too declined in later career stages of MPS.

About half of the MPS and MCS college graduates were unmarried at the time of the initial assessment, and friends were still an important aspect of their personal lives. Moreover, the recruits were often fresh from college campus social activities (as well as the military life for MPS) and were used to mixing with others. (The MPS noncollege managers, five years older, mostly married, and more settled at the original assessment, were less involved with others.)

In addition to needing friends and colleagues at work, new managers often need both technical and emotional support. The MPS men's Resistance to Stress (an assessment center dimension) was lower at MPS:0 than later. They were also most inclined when new to the organization to take the blame when things went wrong (higher early scores on a scale of Abasement from the Edwards).

Because those in the Exploration stage are both unrealistic in their expectations and vulnerable to failure and its emotional consequences, they may be more likely to become disillusioned with the company and leave. Among those in MPS who left the company within the first eight years, about half were forced or encouraged to leave because of poor performance, but the remainder left voluntarily. When asked in interviews for their reasons for leaving, most frequently mentioned were uninteresting or unchallenging work and lack of opportunity. However, the interviewers often felt that the reasons given were socially acceptable responses and that the managers often did not really know why they had left (Bray, Campbell & Grant, 1974). They were apparently unfulfilled in the company and decided to explore elsewhere.

Establishment

Once a new employee has accepted his or her role in the organization and feels accepted and at home there, a new force propels him or her. That is a surging drive to make one's mark on the organization, to prove one's merit. Although the lives of new college graduates in particular may be unfocused in the Exploration stage, the Establishment stage is characterized by an increasing interest in the content of one's work and a will to mastery of problems and challenges.

One indicator of the swelling interest in mastering tasks in the Establishment stage comes from the Edwards Achievement scale, which measures the motivation to accomplish difficult tasks, to solve tough problems and puzzles, and to perform well on tasks requiring skill and effort. As shown in figure 46–3, the MPS men rose significantly on this scale between MPS:0 and MPS:8. This was true regardless of educa-

Figure 46–3. Edwards Achievement Scale over Time: MPS College and Noncollege Groups

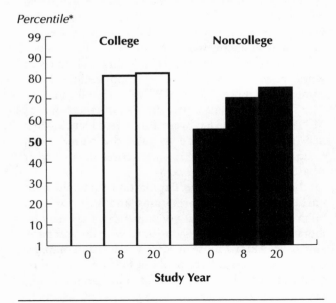

Percentile*

*1958 Bell System Norms
p < .005 time effect.

tional status or management level attained, although the increase in achievement drive was more dramatic for those who later became executives.

When the men were asked at the MPS:20 assessment to explain why their drive to achieve accelerated over time, many pointed to positive job-related factors as responsible for the change. Their jobs were perceived as tough but satisfying, providing both challenge and interest. There were other indications that those with the greatest amount of job stimulation early in their careers were more successful later. Research with men in two of the six MPS companies showed that those with the most job challenge in their first year with the company were rated more successful in terms of salary progress and performance ratings six and seven years later (Berlew & Hall, 1966).

There is no guarantee, however, that experience alone, even in challenging assignments, will result in an improvement in managerial skills. Although job knowledge and organizational know-how will certainly accumulate to the benefit of the experienced manager, the skills the manager needs to lead and direct others are quite another matter. In fact, the average MPS manager declined in both administrative and interpersonal skills between the MPS:0 and MPS:8 assessments. Only cognitive abilities showed a true increase with age.

The decline in managerial skills was much more characteristic of those who remained at the lower levels of management than of those who progressed further upward. In fact, the executives showed a significant increase in overall managerial competence between the MPS:0 and MPS:8 assessments. Figure 46–4 illustrates this phenomenon with the General Effectiveness factor, a composite score of ratings on the important assessment dimensions. The pattern of results, showing the greatest decrements among the men at the lowest level at MPS:20 in the face of increases by the highest-level men, seem to illustrate the saying, "The rich get richer and the poor get poorer."

Why should managerial abilities deteriorate in the Establishment stage? At first glance it seems inconceivable that an individual could retrogress in, for example, the ability to relate interpersonally. The most plausible explanation emerges from the realm of motivation. As was illustrated in figure 46–2, the interest in maintaining friendships and understanding others waned after the Exploration stage. Moreover, as shown in figure 46–1, expectations subsided as managers became less idealistic about the company and their role in its functioning.

The noncollege men, who primarily remained in the lower rungs of management, were more likely to decline in managerial skills than the college men. This

Figure 46–4. General Effectiveness Factor over Time by MPS: 20 level

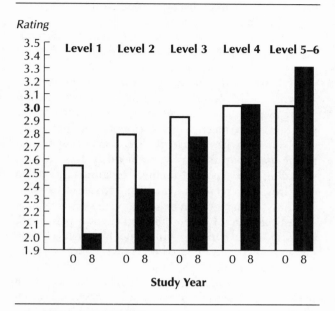

Rating

p < .005 group × time effect.

suggests another explanation for their lower performance in the MPS:8 assessment (see Howard, 1986). It has been suggested that individuals adopt characteristics appropriate to the roles assigned them by their educational status. The noncollege men were quite aware of the better prospects for advancement encountered by their college-educated peers; they may have focused on the qualities characterizing those in lower- rather than higher-level positions because they assumed that would be their place.

Maintenance

At some point, often five or six years after the last promotion, an individual realizes that no more promotions may be forthcoming, that he or she has plateaued. Although writers portraying the midlife crisis have often painted a picture of this realization as a sudden trauma, the MPS data suggest that the realization dawns more gradually and gracefully (Howard & Bray, 1980). Ambition declined significantly even during the Establishment stage, but by the time the men had reached the Maintenance stage, it had nearly faded from sight. Figure 46–5 illustrates this with the Advancement scale from the questionnaire Survey of Attitudes Toward Life. The noncollege men had not been as ambitious as the college men from the start, but by the twentieth year of the study, both groups had declined to only the seventh or

eighth percentile of the original norms. The higher the man's level was, the more interested in further advancements he was at year 20, inasmuch as promotions were in the more recent past for higher-level groups. Yet even the highest-level men had to some degree banked the fire to strive for high places.

When queried about their loss of drive for advancement at the MPS:20 assessment, many mentioned being resigned to a lack of advancement in the future. But nearly as many also commented on the rejection of advancement as a goal. They expressed contentment with their current work status and situations, noted changes in priorities, and expressed concern about work demands and life-style changes that would likely accompany further advancement. Thus the reality of decreasing opportunities was reconciled with entry into a new career stage that emphasized satisfaction with what one had rather than striving for what one did not have. Concern for job security mounted during this stage while the investment in advancement receded.

Loss of ambition did not imply a lessening interest in the challenge of present job assignments. As figure 46–3 showed, the motivation for Achievement, which rose in the Establishment stage, remained at the higher level during the Maintenance stage. But as the men gained experience, a new motivation colored their achievement style—they wanted to do it on

Figure 46–5. Sarnoff Motivation for Advancement Scale over Time: MPS College and Noncollege Groups

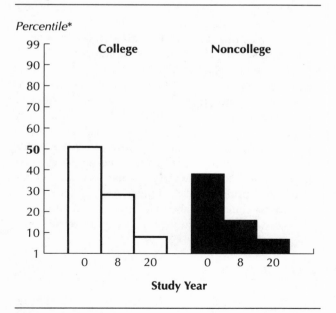

Percentile*

*1956 – 60 MPS Norms
p < .005 time effect.

Figure 46–6. Edwards Autonomy and Aggression Scales: MPS over Time

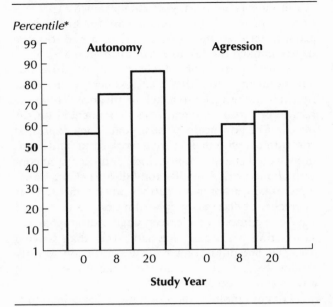

Percentile*

*Bell System Norms
p < .005 time effect, both scales.

their own. This is illustrated in figure 46–6 with the Edwards Autonomy scale, which measures the desire for independence and doing things without regard for what others might think. All groups of managers, regardless of educational status or level of management attained, showed this surge in Autonomy, which continued throughout the first and second decades of the career until the average manager stood at the eighty-sixth percentile of the Bell college hiring norms.

The MPS men also showed an increase in aggressive impulses by the time they reached the Maintenance stage, also shown in figure 46–6. The Aggression scale of the Edwards measures not mere assertiveness but the inclination to attack, criticize, and openly express hostility. Many MPS men explained their augmented scores on both the Autonomy and Aggression scales by citing increased self-confidence with age that made it easier to express aggression and to handle tasks in their own way. Guidance and support were no longer sought; they knew how to do their jobs and wanted to go about their business with a minimum of hassle and interference.

Disengagement

Eventually one comes to a point in a career when the end is in sight. The importance of work begins to diminish as thoughts turn to retirement and the enjoy-

ment of other activities. Although this seems a natural progression in the work cycle, it may come as a surprise that for some, disengagement from work actually begins at a very young age.

This was well illustrated in MPS with the occupational life theme, which was coded from thirteen interviews with the men that took place between years 0 to 25 of the study. Codes for this theme, shown by MPS:20 level in figure 46–7, were a composite of ratings on current involvement, current satisfaction, retrospective involvement, and projective involvement with the work life. The occupational theme was contrasted with eight other areas of life, including the marital-family, religious-humanism concerns, and recreational-social activities (Howard and Bray, 1988). As can be seen, the lowest-level men decreased in involvement and satisfaction with work early in their careers, while the higher-level men increased early and leveled out much later.

Although some psychological detachment was taking place among the lower-level managers early in their careers, actual disengagement occurred when they retired. This happened sooner than expected for many in MPS because early retirements were encouraged by the reorganization and downsizing efforts that followed the 1984 divestiture of the telephone companies by AT&T. The noncollege men in MPS were most susceptible to these offers, not only because they were already psychologically closer to disengagement but because they were on the average more than five years older than the college men and more likely to be pension eligible. In 1987, eighty-five noncollege men who had taken early retirement were compared to fifty-two who remained on the payroll (Howard, in press).

Those who would retire early could be spotted

Figure 46–7. Occupational Life Theme over Time by MPS: 20 Level

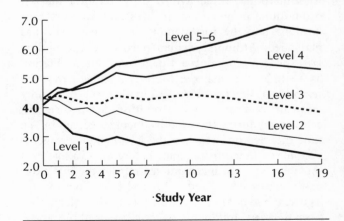

p < .005 × time effect.

well in advance of the event, in fact, even before the divestiture was contemplated. Although the jobs of the stayers and retirees did not differ in challenge, stress, or type of supervision, the retirees had developed more negative attitudes toward the company, their jobs, and their supervisors by year 20. The MPS:20 assessment also found the retirees less invested in work as a primary source of pleasure in life, less identified with the company, and more realistic about their prospects for future advancement than those who remained with the company. Other factors that differentiated the retirees were greater financial security, more interested in recreational activities, and less religious involvement. Thus while those who stayed were motivated to do their moral duty and continue to earn a salary, those ready to disengage from work were psychologically and financially prepared to shed their responsibilities and have a good time.

A readministration of the Edwards Personal Preference Schedule to the retirees revealed an additional motivational change that occurred after retirement. As shown in figure 46–8, the early retirees had shown the typical rise in Achievement desires during the Establishment stage, and the scale remained there during the Maintenance stage. But after disengagement, scores had fallen to their original level in the Exploration stage. The tough problems and chal-

lenges of work had receded into the past; the men had come full cycle.

Figure 46–8. Edwards Achievement Scale over Time: MPS Noncollege Early Retirees

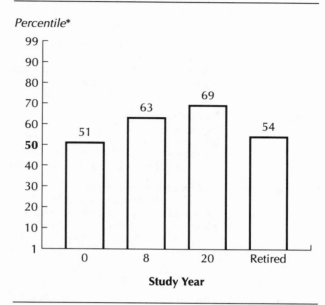

*Percentile**

* 1958 Bell System Norms
p < .05 time effect.

HOW MANAGERS CAN HELP

Career development is often conceptualized as running along a continuum from career planning, where the individual plays a leading role, to career management, where the institution has primary responsibility (Gutteridge, 1986; Hall, 1986). Other chapters in this *Handbook* provide perspectives on various of these processes. The focus here is confined to the role of the supervisor in managing employees in the various career stages. Because different motivations and concerns become salient at different points in the career, the supervisor needs to adapt his or her behavior accordingly to maximize employee motivation and satisfaction. A summary of the various career issues and the concomitant appropriate supervisory behavior is presented in table 46–3; a more complete discussion follows.

Exploration

During the Exploration stage, the primary role for the supervisor is one of being a *mentor*. The new

employee has high expectations and ambitions, probably the highest they will ever be, although he or she may still be uncertain that the chosen career will best meet his or her needs. It is important that the supervisor provide information about the company, the job, and the prospects for the employee's career. But this should be done in an objective way, so that the employee's hopes are not raised, only to come crashing back to a disappointing reality.

The organization can, of course, provide valuable assistance to the supervisor in this early informative role. New manager orientation programs can lay out the terrain of the organization and point the way to potential career achievements. Alternative early career tracks may also be helpful to distinguish those more comfortable with technical or nontechnical specialties and those better suited to general management roles.

Because new employees, especially young college graduates, have strong needs for emotional support during the initial career stage, this is the time for supervisors to be nurturant and helpful. Once again

Table 46–3
Career Issues and Supervisory Role in Each Career Stage

Stage	Career Issues	Supervisory Role
Exploration	High expectations and ambition Uncertain in career choice Strong need for emotional support	Mentor Provide realistic information Provide guidance and help Be nurturant Be a good role model
Establishment	Increased achievement motivation More realistic expectations Lessened interest in friendly relationships Rich get richer, poor get poorer	Sponsor Provide job challenge Provide visibility Sponsor high performers for promotion Develop and reward managerial skills
Maintenance	Decline in ambition Continued achievement needs Increased need for job security Heightened motivation for autonomy Increased likelihood of aggressive responses	Trust Maintain job challenge Entrust subordinates with responsibility Offer free reins
Disengagement	Reduced primacy of work Less identification with company Increased interest in outside activities More negative attitudes to company, work, and supervisors by early retirees	Respect Express appreciation for years of service Support withdrawal from work without rejection Make voluntary retirement offers truly voluntary

the company can assist by providing fast-track management development programs, such as those developed in the Bell telephone companies as an outgrowth of the MPS. Such programs were geared to provide early job challenge but also to support the new manager with a middle management mentor and role model.

An unfortunate mistake often made with new managers is to have them report directly to uninspiring second-level managers, often up-from-the-ranks types who not only are poor role models but are ill inclined to provide the emotional support the new manager needs. This may be because they are often middle-aged managers who have grown far beyond needing emotional bridges for themselves. It also occurs when a less-well-educated supervisor carries a resentment toward a privileged junior expected to be eased up the corporate ladder.

Establishment

Once a new manager or employee has taken root, the supervisor should shift into the role of a *sponsor*. By this time, the employee will long to make his or her mark in the company by mastering the problems and complexities of work. The supervisor must make sure that the job has sufficient challenge to inspire the employee's growing achievement motivation. The need for emotional support will decline as the employee becomes established in the company, but the

need for political support will become paramount. Supervisors should place their high-performing subordinates into positions with visibility and should sponsor them for deserving promotions.

A risk during the Establishment stage is that employees will become established in the wrong frame of mind. As the MPS data showed, experience alone does not guarantee the development of managerial skills, particularly if the motivation to impress and persuade others declines. Supervisors will need to reinforce the importance of sound managerial skills, such as leadership, oral and written communications, behavior flexibility, planning, organizing, and decision making. External training programs can help here as well.

Particular attention should be paid to the average or somewhat above-average employee. Following the "rich get richer, poor get poorer" paradigm, the best employees may respond well on their own to the challenge inherent in their work and develop their own skills, while the poorest employees may not be good bets for expenditures of time, money, and energy. Yet the average or somewhat above-average employee might benefit greatly from extra attention and be inclined to slip if left alone.

Maintenance

When employees reach the Maintenance stage, their ambitions for further promotions have often receded into the past. This is not necessarily to be mourned, for they have often achieved quite responsible positions and may be unwilling to make the sacrifices required by further movement up the corporate hierarchy. At the same time, challenge is still quite important for employees in this stage. Supervisors should be alert to the need for refreshment and stimulation among this group, lest employees fall into a tiresome routine and their attitudes begin to sour. Because further promotions are probably unlikely, supervisors should look for other ways for Maintenance stage employees to find visibility and recognition.

There is a great advantage in supervising employees in the Maintenance stage, for they require little of the emotional, technical, or political support of those in the other career stages. In fact, freedom is a primary motivation for them. The primary theme for supervisors of employees in this stage, then, is *trust*. Controlling such employees is likely to be difficult, for they are little inclined to tolerate it and can react with hostility if threatened or annoyed. Rather, this is the time when supervisors should let go of the reins, be tolerant of subordinates' urge to do their own thing, and relax in the knowledge that they will probably do it capably and responsibly.

Disengagement

Employees who are ready to disengage from the company are likely to give signals of their impending departure. While not necessarily lowering their performance levels, they may become less identified with the company and turn their thoughts more and more toward outside activities. The supervisor can support this natural process but should do so without making the employee feel rejected or unappreciated.

Negative situations surrounding the Disengagement stage are most likely to appear when the retirement is inspired by the company's wish to downsize. The least acrimonious way to downsize is for the company to offer a financial incentive for employees to terminate voluntarily. This may be particularly palatable for those in the Disengagement stage who are financially and psychologically prepared to leave the company. Yet many employees are still made to suffer through their departure because of the way the exodus is handled.

Some of the MPS men's experiences drive home the point that voluntary retirement offers should be truly voluntary. If in addition to the "carrot" of a retirement bonus is added a "stick" of reduced benefits for staying with the company, the offer is less voluntary than coercive. Supervisors, too, may be tempted to help less attractive employees make a "voluntary" decision to retire early. Yet this often leaves a bad taste in the mouths of both the retirees and their peers who stay with the company. If an employee is not producing up to par, the supervisor should deal with that as it happens, not at the time of an early retirement offer. Similarly, sudden lowering of performance appraisals leads to feelings of betrayal on the part of those being pushed into early retirement.

The key theme for supervisors of employees in the Disengagement stage is *respect*. Even if it is clear that an employee will not fit into a new and changing environment, he or she should be respected and appreciated for past contributions to the company. A disengaging employee should leave the company with positive memories and self-esteem intact.

The career stages of Exploration, Establishment, Maintenance, and Disengagement all bring their unique blend of pleasures, challenges, and frustrations. With greater insight and understanding about these stages, supervisors can help their subordinates brave the inexorable winds of time that reshape and redefine careers.

REFERENCES

Berlew, D.E., & Hall, D.T. (1966). The socialization of managers: Effects of expectations on performance. *Administrative Science Quarterly, 11,* 207–223.

Bray, D.W., Campbell, R.J., & Grant, D.L. (1974). *Formative years in business.* New York: Wiley.

Cron, W.L., & Slocum, J.W., Jr. (1986). The influence of career stages on salespeople's job attitudes, work perceptions, and performance. *Journal of Marketing Research, 23,* 119–129.

Erikson, E.H. (1963). *Childhood and society* (2d ed.). New York: Norton.

Gutteridge, T.G. (1986). Organizational career development systems: The state of the practice. In D.T. Hall et al. (Eds.), *Career development in organizations* (50–94). San Francisco: Jossey-Bass.

Hall, D.T. (1976). *Careers in organizations.* Pacific Palisades, CA: Goodyear.

Hall, D.T. (1986). An overview of current career development theory, research, and practice. In D.T. Hall et al. (Eds.), *Career development in organizations* (1–20). San Francisco: Jossey-Bass.

Hall, D.T., & Nougaim, K. (1968). An examination of

Maslow's need hierarchy in an organizational setting. *Organizational Behavior and Human Performance, 3,* 12–35.

Howard, A. (in press). Who reaches for the golden handshake? *Academy of Management Executive.*

Howard, A. (1986). College experiences and managerial performance. *Journal of Applied Psychology, 71,* 530–552.

Howard, A., & Bray, D.W. (1980). *Career motivation in mid-life managers.* Paper presented at the meeting of the American Psychological Association, Montreal, Canada. (ERIC/CAPS Clearinghouse document ED 195894)

Howard, A., & Bray, D.W. (1988). *Managerial lives in transition: Advancing age and changing times.* New York: Guilford.

Howard, A., & Wilson, J.A. (1982). Leadership in a declining work ethic. *California Management Review, 23* (4), 33–46.

Levinson, D.J., with Darrow, C.N., Klein, E.B., Levinson, M.H., & McKee, B. (1978). *The seasons of a man's life.* New York: Knopf.

Super, D.E. (1959). *The psychology of careers.* New York: Harper.

47 A METHOD FOR CAREER PATHING

Brian D. Steffy

In recent years a new construct, intraorganizational career mobility, has emerged in the organizational literature. Broad reviews and conceptual models of relevant components and causal structures of intraorganizational career mobility (ICM) have been presented. Both Vardi (1980), for example, and Anderson, Milkovich, and Tsui (1981) have outlined comprehensive integrative models of behavioral, organizational, and environmental determinants of ICM. Other conceptual presentations have analyzed the decision-making processes implicit in ICM (Stumpf & London, 1981) and the motivational antecedents and consequences of ICM (Latack, 1984).

For purposes here, intraorganizational career mobility is narrowly defined as a logical and pattern-like sequence of jobs in an organization within which employees typically move over time. This analysis departs from previous studies in that the focus is not on behavioral variables but on developing a comprehensive vocabulary and theoretically based measurement system for operationalizing and analyzing structural properties of ICM. As suggested by past research, the mobility of personnel through sequences of job roles can be viewed as systematic, bureaucratized, pattern-like, and amenable to analysis (Rosenbaum, 1984; Anderson, Milkovich & Tsui, 1981; Vardi, 1980; & Martin & Strauss, 1965). Analytical investigation of actual structural properties of ICM networks, however, can best be described as barely adequate. As pointed out by Anderson et al. (1981), investigation into ICM is "noncumulative and atheoretical.... Methods, measures, and samples have varied to such a great extent from study to study that comparison and theoretical development are difficult" (p. 536). Though the careers literature has employed a number of indexes, or hard structural measures of ICM, these studies, when examined as a whole, do not employ an integrated methodology based upon a common language and methodology (Vardi, 1980). In this study "empirical network analysis" or "network theory" is presented as an integrative paradigm for describing and measuring structural properties of ICM networks. By an "empirical network" is meant the structure of relationships linking a set of objects, actors, or events (Harary, 1959; Knoke & Koklinski, 1982; Fombrum, 1982; Tichy, Tushman & Fombrum, 1979). As defined by Berkowitz (1982), an empirical network constitutes a regular and persistent pattern in the behavior of components of a social system. The network paradigm as applied to ICM facilitates the systematic representation of jobs (objects) and the mobility linkages between them. Once these relationships are defined, indexes can be developed to describe and measure the identified structure.

PREVIOUS STRUCTURAL MEASURES EMPLOYED IN THE CAREERS LITERATURE

For clarity of discussion, four basic measurement categories are identified: (1) measures of overall network structure; (2) career path measures; (3) transition, or population flow measures; and (4) measures of job-career properties (how a single job relates to a career path or the whole network structure). Measures employed in previous research are summarized using these four categories in table 47–1. This analysis suggests that most of the measures, or indexes, employed in the literature fit within the general network paradigm. Table 47–1 also provides a descriptive summary of the measures proposed in this study.

Overall Network Properties

Measures of overall network structure define the properties of the ICM structure as a single unit. Properties measured might include a network's density, compactness, or diameter. In a research context, such

Table 47–1
Sample of Indexes Suggested by Network Analysis

Measures	Definition	Operationalization[a]	Similar Previously Employed Measures[b]
Job properties			
1. Inradius	1. Distance (shortest or longest) from floor to focal job	1. Number of linkages from floor to focal job	1. Circumferential Radial Degree (Schein, 1971)
2. Outradius	2. Distance (shortest or longest) from the focal job to ceiling	2. Number of linkages from focal job to ceiling	2. Vertical Degree (Milkovich et al., 1976; Schein, 1971)
3. Indegree	3. Activity level, or traffic, moving toward focal job	3. The number of adjacent, or adjacent and nonadjacent, linkages in which the focal job is the source of mobility	3. Advancement Opportunities (London, 1983; Veiga, 1983; Rosenbaum, 1984)
4. Outdegree	4. Activity level, or traffic, moving from the focal job to higher-level jobs	4. The number of adjacent, or adjacent and nonadjacent, linkages in which the focal job is the source of mobility to higher-level jobs	
5. Total Degree	5. Activity level, or traffic, moving from and to the focal job	5. Sum of indegree and outdegree	
6. Relative Degree	6. A job's activity level taking into consideration the number of linkages possible	6. The number of direct and/or indirect linkages divided by the number of total linkages possible	
7. Inprominence	7. Efficiency of access that lower-level jobs have to the focal (object) job	7. The number of direct and indirect indegrees divided by the product of the mean distance of the indegree jobs and the number of other jobs in the network	
8. Outprominence	8. Efficiency of access that the focal job (source) has to upper-level jobs	8. The number of direct and indirect outdegrees divided by the product of the mean distance of the outdegree jobs and the number of other jobs in the network	
9. Total Prominence	9. Job's overall prominence in the network defined in terms of efficient mobility to and from the job	9. Sum of inprominence and outprominence	
10. Status	10. Hierarchical placement of a job within the network	10. The number of jobs that have the focal job as their object plus twice the number of their subordinate jobs plus three times the number of their subordinates, and so on	
11. Relative Status	11. A job's status relative to the hierarchical status of the total job system	11. Job status divided by gross status (sum of all status scores)	
12. Mobility-Ability Signal (Rosenbaum, 1984)	12. A measure of future mobility potential as a function of past and current ICM	12. Job status divided by organizational tenure	

Measures	Definition	Operationalization[a]	Similar Previously Employed Measures[b]
Flow properties			
1. Transition Probability	1. Probability of moving from a source to object job during some specified discrete interval of time	1. The proportion of employees in the source job who move to the object job during some specified interval of time	1. Rates (Milkovich et al., 1976; Rosenbaum, 1984)
2. Probability of Staying In Job	2. Probability of remaining in the job during a discrete interval of time	2. The sum of a source job's transition probabilities (assuming wastage but no demotions) subtracted from IO	2. Expected Job Tenure (Scholl, 1983)
3. Expected Job Tenure	3. The expected number of periods (years) we might count the average employee in a specific job	3. Finding the inverse of the fundamental matrix, which consists of a hierarchical arrangement of transition probabilities	3. Position Ratio (Scholl, 1983)
4. Expected Organization Tenure	4. The expected number of periods (years) we might count the average employee in the organization	4. The sum of the expected job tenures in each job along a career path	4. Predecessor's Stay Time (Veiga, 1983)
Career path properties			
1. Length	1. The distance of a career path between two jobs, or the length of the job ladder from floor to ceiling	1. The number of linkages between two adjacent or nonadjacent jobs	1. Direction, Pattern, Length, Ceiling, Floor (Scholl, 1983; Milkovich et al., 1982, 1976)
2. Length of Vacancy Chain	2. Given a position vacancy at the top of the organization, what is the expected length of the chain of position openings in lower-level jobs created by the upper-level vacancy	2. The number of linkages that a position opening "flows" once created at an upper level of the network; this flow is downward	
3. Gravity-Attraction	3. Strength of attraction between two jobs on a career path	3. The ratio of the "attractiveness" of an object job (e.g., percentage increase in compensation) to the distance (length between the two jobs)	
Overall network properties			
1. Diameter	1. The distance (shortest or longest) from floor to ceiling	1. The number of linkages from the floor to ceiling	
2. Gross Status	2. The degree of vertical-horizontal hierarchy of the network	2. The sum of the status of each job for each job in the network	
3. Density	3. The capacity of the network for a wide range of mobility through diverse paths	3. The total number of direct linkages in the network divided by the number of all possible ties	

[a]More detailed formulas are provided in the chapter or referred to by citation.
[b]These measures are not ordered so as to correspond to any specific measure drawn from network analysis.

measures would facilitate the comparison of different ICM networks. For example, we might be interested in comparing the ICM networks of a number of organizations, or we could compare distinct subnetworks in a single organization. No measure of overall network structure has emerged in the literature. In later sections such measures are presented.

Career Path Properties

Career path measures facilitate the analysis of specific components of the ICM network, for example, properties of mobility paths or job ladders, that individuals transverse over their organizational tenure. These measures are structural and independent of time. The typical ICM network will consist of numerous career paths, and any job in the network may be a point on a number of paths. A few measures of this type have appeared in the literature, for example, a career path's direction and pattern (Milkovich & Anderson, 1982; Milkovich, Anderson & Greenhalgh, 1976; Veiga, 1981), as well as its length, or distance (Milkovich et al., 1976; Scholl, 1983). The identification of the starting point (port or entry) and ceiling (uppermost level) of a path have also been of interest to researchers (Milkovich et al., 1976; Scholl, 1983). These measures are limited, however, because they are nominal and there is no indication that a theoretically based method was in mind in constructing them.

Another class of career path measures is derived from job vacancy models drawn from the human resource planning literature. These measures analyze the flow of job openings created as upper-level vacancies are filled by employees in lower-level positions. In other words, as employees are promoted to fill vacancies, a chain of openings is created moving from the top to the bottom of the organization (Stewman, 1975; Bartholomew & Forbes, 1979).

Flow Properties

Perhaps the best-represented measure in the literature is that of personnel flows through sequences of job states. Unlike the above measures, these measures are time dependent in that transition flows between job states are measured according to discrete time intervals, for example, the proportional flow of personnel from one state to another during the course of a year. The majority of these measures are based on transition probabilities that are fundamental to Markov analysis. Markov analysis has been used primarily to forecast and plan for future stocks and flows of human resources. In this analysis, however, we are more interested in descriptive measures of the pattern of flows between job states, and it is in this sense that Markovian measures will be used. As will be discussed later, Markov analysis is actually a theoretical subset (or drawn from) general network, or structural analysis (Berkowitz, 1982).

Flow measures previously employed include the probability of promotion to and demotion from a job (Rosenbaum, 1984) and the amount of time a person can be expected to remain in a job (Milkovich & Anderson, 1982; Veiga, 1981; Scholl, 1983) or organization (Grinold & Marshall, 1977; Bartholomew & Forbes, 1979). Another measure, unrelated to transition probabilities, includes the predecessor's duration time in a job (Veiga, 1983).

Job Properties

The last group of measures focuses on jobs as they relate to the ICM network as a whole. Measures of interest here might include the advancement opportunity afforded by holding a particular job. For example, some jobs have a broader range of upward-mobility linkages than other jobs (e.g., dead-end jobs). Similarly, some jobs may be the object of many mobility flows, meaning something akin to the phrase "all roads lead to Rome." A number of different measures fall into this category, for example, the circumferential, radial, and vertical degree of a job (Schein, 1971), its advancement opportunities (London, 1983; Veiga, 1983), or its upward mobility opportunity (Scholl, 1983). Again, these measures have all been constructed by their authors to meet their immediate research needs. No theoretically based methodology seemed to be in mind.

THE GENERAL PARADIGM

Two methodological approaches to the analysis of ICM networks are possible: (1) graph-theoretic methods, which are valuable in descriptively mapping ICM networks (Peay, 1982), and (2) network-matrix methods, which go beyond graph theory by allowing mathematical manipulation of binary-coded network matrices. Network-matrix methods are somewhat advantageous in that they can handle large and complex structures (graphic approaches can become cumbersome), and they facilitate the development of indexes that measure structural characteristics of ICM. My purpose in this chapter is the discussion of the operationalization of the structural properties of ICM networks. Such a discussion is most easily pursued by limiting itself to graph-theoretic analysis. Network matrices are simply algebraic translations of graphs; a more detailed account can be found in Harary and Cartwright (1965), Burt and Minor (1983), Knoke and Kuklinski (1982), Peay (1977, 1982), and Steffy and Fay (1984).

Graph Theory

A simple "graph" of an ICM network is illustrated in figure 47–1. It consists of 25 points, A, B, . . . , Y, or jobs, and the lines linking pairs of points indicate the presence of a mobility relationship. For example, mobility linkages exist between jobs AC, BD, and EF but not between jobs AB and CD. These mobility linkages are direct (adjacent pairs) and ordered, meaning, in this case, that mobility is one-directional (upward mobility only). Reciprocal linkages (with both promotions and demotions represented) are possible, but in this analysis, only recursive, upward-directed linkages exist. Jobs within the mobility network are referred to as either source or object jobs. If we are discussing a job in terms of its capacity to act as a stepping-stone for other jobs (e.g., upward mobility potential), then we are speaking of that job as a source of mobility. If we are discussing a job in terms of the mobility flows moving toward it, then that focal job is an object of mobility.

The visual mapping of mobility linkages also facilitates the observation of ICM lines, or career paths, between nonadjacent points. The indirect mobility linkages permit the analysis of career path distance, or length, giving the number of sequential moves required in taking a specific career path. When a path exists between two adjacent or nonadjacent jobs, then we say that an object job is reachable from the source job. Limited reachability describes the situation in which a job is reachable from another job within a specified length. For example, J (object) is reachable from A (source), but it is not reachable within a length of 3. Given that more than one path may exist between two nonadjacent jobs, the geodosic is the path of minimum length (Harary & Cartwright, 1965).

The distance from the floor, the lowest-level job (probably the port-of-entry) in the network (or career path), to the ceiling, or the highest-level job, is the diameter of the ICM network. Assuming an individ-

Figure 47–1. Career Network

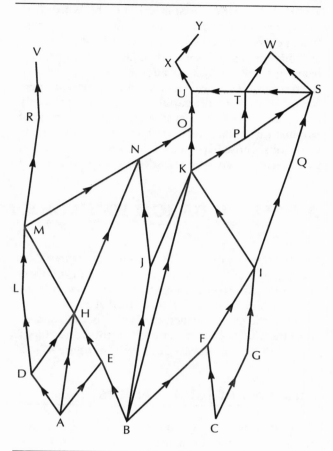

ual is in a job at the present time, the distance from the floor job on the career path(s) of which the job is a member is defined as the inradius. The distance to the ceiling job of the career path is its outradius. If a number of career paths transverse a job, then either the shortest or longest inradius/outradius can be used.

A job can also be defined according to its range, or the number of its direct and indirect linkages. Range can be defined in three ways: (1), as the number of linkages in which the focal job is the object of flows, (2) as the number of linkages in which the focal job is the source of flows, and (3) as the number of jobs in which the focal job is both the source and object of mobility flows. These three measures provide a sense of the "activity level" of a job or the level of "traffic" within which it is immersed (Burt, 1983). A high level of traffic would suggest that the job is important in terms of ICM.

Another characteristic of the ICM network in figure 47–1 is that it is completely connected, meaning that each job is adjacent to at least one other job. If, however, job M was hypothetically eliminated, the graph would be disconnected, meaning that at least one job is not adjacent to another. Similarly, if we assume a number of disconnected graphs, which constitute a number of distinct ICM subnetworks within a single organization, we can hypothetically locate mobility linkages that would act as a mobility bridge from one subnetwork to another. This may be of interest for a few reasons. First, one subnetwork may consist of clerical-secretarial jobs occupied primarily by women. A higher-level subnetwork may consist of administrative jobs dominated by men. By identifying those jobs whose hypothetical linkage would connect two disconnected subnetworks, management could find where they might start training higher-level clerical employees to move them into lower-level administrative positions, thus facilitating the upward mobility potential of women. Those jobs that form the bridge are referred to as key jobs. Key jobs also include those jobs that, if they were eliminated, would result in a disconnected network. The identification of these jobs is important because they are critical linking pins that hold the ICM structure together. Harary (1959) outlines a procedure for identifying key jobs on a graph.

A SAMPLE OF ICM NETWORK MEASURES

So far, four types of ICM network measures have been identified: (1) measures of overall network structure; (2) career path measures; (3) flow, or transition measures; and (4) measures of jobs as they relate to the overall structure. At this point a sample of indexes is illustrated for each of these four types. These indexes are drawn directly from figure 47–1.

Measures of Job Properties

Operations are introduced for measuring the properties of jobs within the structure of an ICM network. These include (1) the "degree" or activity level of a job and (2) the "prestige" or status of a job.

Degree of a Job. The most basic job measure is its degree, by which is meant the number of other jobs with which a job has direct and adjacent contact, though it is also possible to measure "degree" as the number of both direct and indirect contacts. Burt (1983) refers to these degree measures as measures of the range of a job, "an index of the extent to which the [job] is involved in many [mobility] relationships" (p. 177). Following the theoretical work of Knoke and Kuklinski (1982), three simple measures of a job's degree are adapted here: the outdegree, indegree, and total degree of a job. All three measures can be made using direct linkages only or using both direct and indirect linkages. The measure of total degree probably offers a more dynamic and long-term analysis of a job's mobility activity.

A job's outdegree specifies the number of linkages from the focal job to upwardly mobile object jobs. The measure is simply obtained by counting how many direct or indirect and reachable jobs an individual in the source job can move to. A job's indegree is the number of jobs that have as their mobility object the focal job. Total degree is simply the sum of indegree and outdegree. While these measures quantify the activity level or traffic of a job, they are limited in that the level of activity will also be a function of the number of jobs in the network. That is, the number of direct and indirect linkages should rise in direct proportion to the size of the network. Berkowitz (1982) points out that it may be more appropriate to divide these three degree measures by the total number of possible linkages in the network, $N-1$, where N is the number of jobs in the network. The result is what Berkowitz (1982) calls a measure of relative degree, and it takes on a value between .00 and 1.0, where the mobility value of a job increases as relative degree approaches 1.0. Of course, we would expect higher values when measuring indirect linkages as opposed to direct linkages only. As a rule, if jobs of different organizational networks are compared according to their ICM activity level, it is necessary to use the relative degree index (Freeman, 1979).

Prominence of a Job. Whereas the degree index measures the activity level, or the volume of traffic through a job, prominence indicates which jobs in the ICM network are the object of most of the mobility flows. Though prominence measures the volume of inflows into (or out of) a job, it differs from degree measures in three respects. First, both direct and indirect mobility linkages are always accounted for. Second, prominence measures capture the closeness of mobility relationships, where the distance between job pairs is of interest (Freeman, 1979). For example, when a job is connected with numerous jobs of close distance, then that job is thought to have greater prominence because numerous career lines have efficient access to that job. Third, not only does the prominence index measure the volume and closeness of relationships, but it can also be expanded to incorporate the prominence strength of each job with which the focal job has direct or indirect contact. Therefore, the status of a job within the network structure is measured as more than the volume of its connections. A job can have a few connections (e.g., the chief executive officer's job) but still have high prominence if those few jobs with which it is connected have high prominence.

A basic measure of prominence is suggested by Knoke and Burt (1983). As adapted here, the prominence of a job is measured as the number of direct and indirect indegrees (those jobs that have the focal job as their object) divided by the product of the mean distance of the indegree jobs and the number of other jobs in the network ($N-1$). Alternatively stated, a job's prominence can be calculated:

$$\frac{\text{(number of direct and indirect indegrees to a job)}}{\text{(mean distance of indegree jobs) } (N-1)}$$

The mean distance of the indegree jobs from the focal jobs is simply derived by summing the total distance (path length) of direct and indirect indegree linkages by the volume of indegree linkages. This index can be further refined by weighting each source job by its own prominence value. By doing this, prominence is measured not only by the strength, or closeness, of its numerous direct and indirect contacts but by the prominence level of each source job with which the focal job has contact. Prominence is then measured by summing the prominence values of those jobs, direct and indirect, that have the focal job as an object.

The above prominence measures can be expanded so that the outprominence of a job is measured. While the inprominence of a job measures the extent to which it receives mobility flows, a job's outprominence measures the job's capacity to provide efficient outflows to other parts of the ICM network, that is, its upward mobility potential. Further, by summing inprominence and out-prominence, it is possible to define a job's total prominence. A job has a high total prominence when it is both the object of numerous and prominent flows and also the source of many efficient upward flows. In sum, these three indexes offer a fairly sophisticated measure of a job's structural position within the mobility network.

Status of a Job. The status of a job is a measure of its hierarchical placement within the ICM network. The measure is introduced in the communication's literature where an attempt is made to evaluate the flow of information through superior-subordinate chains (Harary & Cartwright, 1965). In this context, an individual with high status has many subordinates who also have numerous subordinates, and so on. In the context of ICM, the ceiling job would have the highest status, and the floor jobs would have status = .00. In a hierarchical network where only upward mobility is possible, the status of a job is defined as the number of jobs that have the focal job as their object plus twice the number of their "subordinate" jobs that have these source jobs as their object plus three times the number of jobs that have these source jobs as their object, and so on. While arbitrary, these multipliers give emphasis to the hierarchical level of the job in determining status. Early and current job status, as measured according to hierarchical level, has been shown to be a strong indicator of future status (Rosenbaum, 1984).

The gross status of the ICM network is the sum of the status measures of the constituent jobs. This number should equal the summed distances of all adjacent and nonadjacent job pairs. The gross status of a network is highest when a single vertical path exists from floor to ceiling. Given the same number of jobs, gross status decreases as horizontal differentiation in ICM is introduced. In other words, we might expect tall, hierarchical organizations to have higher gross status than flat, differentiated ones. Once gross status is obtained, then the relative status of a job can be found as the ratio of the job's status to the gross status of the ICM network. Relative status defines a job's status relative to the vertical hierarchy of the overall ICM network. It becomes valuable if comparing the status of the same job type across a sample of organizations.

Rosenbaum (1984) suggests that we might conceive of the future motivation for mobility as a function of current job status and career history, as reflected by organizational or occupational tenure. His mobility ability signal is defined by how high an individual rises in the career hierarchy in a given space of time. He vaguely defines this indicator as the ratio of job status to organization tenure, though no formal measure is suggested. Given the job status measure provided here, we can define mobility ability as the ratio of job status to organizational tenure. According to this simple measure, an employee's indicator increases when a high-status position is attained in a short period of time. A higher indicator score might suggest high future job status and be strongly related to behavioral and attitudinal variables such as need for achievement and organizational commitment.

In general, status measures differ from indegree and inprominence in a subtle way. A job's indegree is a measure of the upward-flowing volume of traffic through the focal job. A job's inprominence captures both the volume and the efficiency of these inflows. A job's status reflects more its structural position within the ICM network and the vertical-horizontal shape of that network.

Transition or Flow Measures

A number of transition measures are suggested in the human resource planning literature. As a whole, these measures are distinguished by the fact that they focus not so much on the structural properties of ICM as they do the mobility flows of personnel over time. Thus, the measures are time dependent. Though transition measures analyze population flows and not actual structures, indexes still provide job-specific information of the type we are interested in here. Stochastic flow models such as Markov analysis can suggest properties about the underlying structure of ICM. For example, we can measure expected job tenure, expected organization tenure, and the probability of moving from the source job to some designated object job. These measures are briefly discussed.

Transition Probability. Most of the measures are a direct extension of the transition probability between two adjacent jobs. Taking any two adjacent jobs in figure 47–1, the probability of moving from a source job, i, to an object job, j, is defined p_{ij}. Formally, p_{ij} can be found by calculating the proportion of employees in the source job who move to the object job during some specified interval of time, say, one year. Better estimates are found by examining proportional moves over two or three previous years and finding the mean value (Bartholomew, 1982). Every adjacent job pair in figure 47–1 can be assigned a transition probability. The measure, in essence, gives the mobility "strength" or "intensity" between two adjacent jobs (Harary & Cartwright, 1965).

Assuming that all directly linked jobs are assigned a transition probability, then by partitioning the hierarchically arranged network into mutually exclusive and exhaustive job classes, a square matrix is formed. The upper triangle of the matrix constitutes promotions, the lower matrix demotions (p_{ij}), and the diagonal is the probability of staying in the job (p_{ij}) over some discrete period of time (usually one year). Organizational exits are expressed as P_{io}. As Bartholomew (1982) and Rapoport (1983) have noted, if P_{ii}, the diagonal elements of the matrix, is the probability that an employee will stay in a job for one year, the probability of moving to another job or leaving the organization is $(1 - P_{ii})$. Further, the probability of staying in the present job i for k years and then moving is $[(P_{ii})^k (1-P_{ii})]$.

Transition probabilities can also be used to determine expected job tenure and expected organizational tenure (see Bartholomew, 1982; Grinold & Marshall, 1977). Expected job tenure, or length of stay, in a job is found by taking the inverse of the probability of moving $(1-P_{ii})$, or $(1-P_{ii})^{-1}$. Expected organizational tenure is then found by summing the expected job tenures for each job along the career path of interest. It follows that because a focal job may be connected to more than one career path, alternative career paths will lead to different expected organizational tenures.

Other measures are also suggested by the human resource planning literature. For example, transition probabilities can be partitioned to account for heterogeneity or "individual histories" (Rapoport, 1983). Two rules of partition have been suggested: by years of seniority and by demographic attributes such as race and sex (Schinnar & Stewman, 1978). Each of these measures assumes that either the probability of upward mobility should increase as duration of stay increases (e.g., job tenure), or it should vary because of inherent inequalities in the system due to race, sex, or age discrimination.

Career Path Measures

Of the measures discussed so far, career path measures seem to have the least utility for research. While previous research has measured path lengths from source jobs (e.g., distance to ceiling job), career paths themselves have not been investigated. The majority of these measures are developed for human resource planning purposes, specifically the development of job vacancy measures. The job vacancy model analyzes the downward flow of position vacancies as opposed to the flow of persons. Its primary purpose is to analyze the underlying causal structure of job vacancy mobility, which leads to a clearer understanding of personnel mobility. For example, assuming only internal selection, when a position opens at the top of the organizational hierarchy due to turnover or expansion, that position may be filled by promoting an individual from a lower level. The vacated position of that promoted individual then needs to be filled from below, and so on. Therefore, it is possible to conceive of a chain of vacancies. It follows that it should be possible to analyze the length of such a chain (how far down the organization the chain will extend), as well as the length of time it takes for the chain to stop once initiated. For a further discussion of such models, see Stewman (1975) and Bartholomew and Forbes (1979).

The gravity model is another interesting measure deserving attention. This model, originally employed in urban planning for measuring the flow of retail trade between regional areas (Foot, 1981), can be adapted to define the strength of attractiveness of two nonadjacent jobs as a function of the attractiveness of the object job (e.g., percentage increase in compensation) and the distance between the source and object job. It seems intuitive, for example, that as attractiveness increases and distance decreases, employees in the source job will feel more strongly pulled (gravitate) to the object job. Formally, the model is defined, $G = A/d_{ij}$, where G is the gravitational force of mobility motivation, A is the degree of attractiveness of the source job, i, for the object job, j, and d_{ij} is the number of linkages (career path length) between job i and j. For example, if the distance between jobs A and G is 3, with a corresponding salary increase of 20 percent, the gravitational pull is equal to .066. If the distance was increased to 4, then G would be .050. If the percentage increase in salary was 50 percent and the distance was 5, the G would be .10. Of course, research needs to be conducted to verify whether G measures the strength of gravitational pull, or mobility motivation. Like Rosenbaum's (1984) mobility ability indicator, the construct, if shown to be valid, may prove useful in linking mobility intensity with behavioral variables such as intent to leave and organizational commitment.

Measures of Overall ICM Network Structure

Overall ICM network structure measures facilitate the comparison between different organizations or between distinct internal labor markets within a single organization (Rosenbaum, 1984). For example, a researcher may be interested in measuring whether ICM in a sample of organizations is confined to few noninteractive and strongly hierarchical career paths or whether employees move freely among numerous career paths, suggesting greater ICM flexibility. Previously we defined the gross status and diameter of an ICM network. The former analyzes the extent of vertical hierarchy of ICM, while the diameter gives a gross assessment of the distance from the floor to the ceiling. An additional structural measure useful for comparative studies is an index of career network density.

The connectedness of an ICM network is defined as the extent to which the jobs within the network are linked. In other words, a network that is strongly connected is one whose ratio of actual linkages to the potential number of linkages is large (Knoke & Kulinski, 1982). A lower ratio indicates low network density, hence little range of career mobility. Career network density is a simple ratio that defines this index. It is defined as the total number of direct linkages in the network divided by the number of all possible ties, given the number of jobs. The density of the ICM network in figure 47–1 is therefore defined as the number of adjacent linkages divided by the number of possible linkages, or $L/N^2 - N$, where L is the number of linkages, defined as the number of adjacent job pairs, and N is the number of jobs in the network. As density approaches a value of 1.0, the network is characterized as possessing a wider range, flexibility, and capacity for mobility. Lower values suggest that there is little opportunity to move "geographically" within the ICM network.

SUMMARY AND EXAMPLE

Empirical research in career mobility has been hampered by the lack of a measurement system for quantifying structural properties of ICM. Previous research employs measures on a piecemeal or ad hoc basis. This chapter represents a step toward identifying a descriptive language and system of measurement for measuring structural properties of ICM. As was pointed out, most of the previously employed measures summarized in table 47–1 fit within the paradigm presented here.

A number of questions come to mind with respect to the differences between measures. For example, how exactly do degree, prominence, and status measures of job properties differ? We might expect degree, prominence, and status values for a sample of jobs in an organization to be highly correlated, yet they may be different enough in conceptualization that they lead to significantly different results. Of course, high-status jobs should possess low outdegree and low outprominence. Also of interest is the correlation between time-dependent transition measures and time-independent structural measures. Little relationship may exist. This is because regardless of whether a job is characterized as low or high on volume, efficiency, or status, the expected job (or organizational) tenure or the probability of promotion may be relatively independent of structure. On the other hand, it seems plausible that high volume and efficiency of flow are related to high transition probabilities. Efficiency will probably be related to high transition probabilities. The human resource planning literature has ascertained that high transition probabilities are associated with lower expected job tenure (see Grinold & Marshall, 1977). We also might expect that volume and efficiency of mobility will be positively associated with high network density and centrality. As suggested earlier, assuming a sample of networks with the same number of jobs, high gross status should be associated with low density and centrality. Organizations having high gross status and low density are most likely characterized as allowing high vertical mobility but little horizontal mobility. Such an organization should also possess specific and rigid career paths.

Some of the measures were derived for the contrived example in figure 47–1. The results are summarized in table 47–2. Of course, this example may be simplistic. In an actual research context, a graph

would probably be larger and more complex. Findings generally support the expectations mentioned above. Indegree (indirect), inprominence, and status results are generally consistent. Likewise, outdegree (indirect) and outprominence lead to similar results. Overall network measures were also derived. For the network in figure 47–1, the longest diameter is 8 (starting at job C) and the shortest is 5 (starting from B, to K, to O, to U, to X, to Y). Gross status is 175, and density is 0.063. Transition measures were not obtained. The overall network measures do not mean much in this example. They take on greater meaning when a sample of networks is compared with one another.

Table 47–2
Measures of Job Properties

Job	Degree Measured by Direct Linkages			Degree Measured by Indirect Linkages			In-prominence	Out-prominence	Total Prominence	Job Status
	In	Out	Relative Degree	In	Out	Relative Degree				
a	0	3	.125	0	18	.792	.000	1.758	1.758	0
b	0	4	.167	0	19	.750	.000	1.901	1.901	0
c	0	2	.083	0	12	.500	.000	1.060	1.060	0
d	1	2	.125	1	10	.458	.041	.621	.662	1
e	2	2	.467	2	15	.708	.083	1.086	1.169	2
f	2	1	.125	2	9	.458	.083	.810	.893	2
g	1	1	.083	1	10	.458	.041	.622	.663	1
h	2	2	.167	4	8	.500	.257	.414	.671	9
i	2	2	.167	4	9	.542	.285	.616	.901	8
j	2	3	.208	3	10	.542	.176	.643	.819	6
k	3	1	.167	8	7	.583	.411	.597	1.008	31
l	2	1	.125	2	8	.417	.096	.543	.639	3
m	2	2	.167	6	7	.542	.541	.388	.929	19
n	2	1	.125	8	4	.500	.691	.161	.852	29
o	2	1	.125	9	3	.500	.898	.161	1.059	74
p	1	2	.125	9	6	.625	.729	.402	1.131	39
q	1	1	.083	5	6	.417	.323	.375	.698	14
r	1	1	.083	7	1	.333	.582	.047	.629	33
s	2	2	.167	11	5	.667	.981	.192	1.173	41
t	2	2	.167	12	4	.667	1.145	.193	1.338	61
u	2	1	.125	18	2	.833	2.087	.098	2.185	122
v	1	0	.042	9	0	.375	.739	.000	.739	40
w	2	0	.083	13	0	.583	1.351	.000	1.351	73
x	1	1	.083	20	1	.833	2.289	.042	2.331	153
y	1	0	.042	21	0	.833	2.517	.000	2.517	184

DIRECTIONS FOR RESEARCH

Given a descriptive language, system of measurement, and the indexes presented here, three directions for research are suggested. First, the indexes should be used in actual settings and evaluated as to what each differentially measures. This need was discussed above. Second, the career-related aspects of organiza-

tional, behavioral, and affective variables could be better examined in the light of these structural measures. Third, following the advice of Rosenbaum (1984), much can be learned by comparing actual ICM structures with employees' perception of ICM. Rosenbaum points out that more than likely, organizations sponsor misperceptions about the opportunities of ICM.

It should also be pointed out that the sample of measures introduced here may only skim the surface of what is possible. For example, the discussion has been confined to operations involving single-type linkages, that is, mobility. Network analysis, however, is not confined to uniplex linkages but can also be used to analyze multiple, or multiplex, relationships (see Peay, 1977, 1982). Thus career paths can be analyzed not only in terms of historical movement but also in terms of job specifications such as skill levels, education, ability, and training. Such an analysis can be used prescriptively to point out what kinds of career development efforts employees must make if they are to be qualified to follow one or more career paths. While such analysis is complicated, computer programs have been developed that can conduct both uniplex and multiplex network analysis (see Fombrum, 1982; Peay, 1982).

REFERENCES

Anderson, J.C., Milkovich, G.T., & Tsui, A. (1981). A model of intra-organizational mobility. *Academy of Management Review, 6*, 529–538.

Bartholomew, D. (1982). *Stochastic models for social processes.* New York: John Wiley & Sons.

Bartholomew, D.J., & Forbes, A.F. (1979). *Statistical techniques for manpower planning.* Chichester, England: Wiley.

Berkowitz, S.D. (1982). *An introduction to structural analysis.* Toronto: Butterworth.

Burt, R.S. (1983). Range. In R.S. Burt, and M.J. Minor, *Applied network analysis.* Beverly Hills: Sage.

Burt, R.S., & Minor, M.J. (1983). *Applied network analysis.* Beverly Hills: Sage.

Fombrum, C.J. (1982). Strategies for network research in organizations. *Academy of Management Review. 7*, 280–291.

Foot, D. (1981). *Operational urban models.* London: Methuen & Co.

Freeman, L. (1979). Centrality in social networks: Conceptual clarification. *Social Networks, 1*, 215–239.

Grinold, R.C., & Marshall, K.T. (1977). *Manpower planning models.* New York: Elsevier North-Holland.

Harary, F. (1959). Graph theoretic methods in the management sciences. *Management Science, 5*, 387–403.

Harary, F. (1965). *Graph theory.* Reading, MA: Addison-Wesley.

Harary, F., & Cartwright, D. (1965). *Structural models: An introduction to the theory of directed graphs.* New York: Wiley.

Knoke, D., & Burt, R.S. (1983). Prominence. In R.S. Burt and M.J. Minor, *Applied network analysis.* Beverly Hills: Sage.

Knoke, D., & Kuklinski, J.H. (1982). *Network analysis.* Beverly Hills: Sage.

Latack, J.C. (1984). Career transitions within organizations: An exploratory study of work, nonwork, and coping strategies. *Organizational Behavior and Human Performance, 34*, 296–322.

London, M. (1982). Toward a theory of career motivation. *Academy of Management Review, 8*, 620–630.

London, M., & Stumpf, S.A. (1982). *Managing careers.* Reading, MA: Addison-Wesley.

Martin, N., & Strauss, A. (1956). Patterns of mobility within industrial organizations. *Journal of Business, 29*, 101–110.

Milkovich, G.T., & Anderson, J.C. (1982). Career planning and development systems. In K.M. Rowland and G.R. Ferris (Eds.), *Personnel management* (364–389). Boston: Allyn and Bacon, Inc.

Milkovich, G.T., Anderson, J.C., & Greenhalgh, L. (1976). Organizational careers: Environmental, organizational, and individual determinants. In L. Dyer (Ed.), *Careers in organizations: Individual planning and organizational development* (17–30). Ithaca, NY: New York State School of Industrial and Labor Relations.

Peay, E.R. (1977). Matrix operations and the properties of networks and directed graphs. *Journal of Mathematical Sociology, 15*, 89–101.

Peay, E.R. (1982). Structural models with qualitative values. *Journal of Mathematical Sociology, 8*, 161–192.

Rapoport, A. (1983). *Mathematical models in the social and behavioral sciences.* New York: John Wiley & Sons.

Roberts, F. (1978). *Graph theory and its applications to problems of society.* Philadelphia: Society for Industrial and Applied Mathematics.

Rosenbaum, J.E. (1984). *Career mobility in a corporate hierarchy.* New York: Academic Press, Inc.

Ross, I.C., & Harary, F. (1957). Identification of the liaison persons of an organization using the structure matrix. *Management Science, 2*, 251–258.

Schein, E.H. (1971). The individual, the organization, and the career: A conceptual scheme. *Journal of Applied Behavioral Science, 7*, 401–426.

Schinnar, A., & Stewman, R. (1978). A class of Markov models of social mobility with duration memory patterns. *Journal of Mathematical Sociology, 6*, 61–86.

Scholl, R.W. (1983). Career lines and employment stability. *Academy of Management Journal, 26*, 86–103.

Steffy, B.D., & Fay, C. (1984). The application of network-matrix methods of the analysis of intraorganizational career mobility. In *Academy of Management Proceedings.* Boston: AMA.

Stewman, S. (1975). An application of the job vacancy chain model to a civil service internal labor market. *Journal of Mathematical Sociology, 4*, 37–39.

Stumpf, S.A., & London, M. (1981). Management promotions: Individual and organizational factors influencing the decision process. *Academy of Management Review, 6,* 539–549.

Tichy, H., Tushman, M., & Fombrum, C. (1979). Social network analysis for organizations. *Academy of Management Review, 4,* 507–519.

Vardi, Y. (1980). Organizational career mobility: An integrative model. *Academy of Management Review, 5,* 341–355.

Veiga, J.F. (1981). Plateaued versus nonplateaued managers: Career patterns, attitudes, and path potential. *Academy of Management Journal, 24,* 566–578.

Veiga, J.F. (1983). Mobility influences during managerial career stages. *Academy of Management Journal, 26,* 64–85.

White, H. (1976). Stayers and movers. *American Journal of Sociology, 76,* 307–324.

48 MENTORING RELATIONSHIPS FOR EMPLOYEE DEVELOPMENT

Raymond A. Noe

One of the major trends in the employee development area has been the use of behavior modeling training programs for work-related interpersonal skill development (see Decker & Nathan, 1985). Behavior modeling training is based on Bandura's (1977) social learning theory, which emphasizes observational learning by exposure to a model, opportunity for skill practice, reinforcement for correct skill usage, and the setting of target behaviors, which are the desired outcomes of the training process. The success of behavior modeling training has stimulated organizations to focus on other modeling-based methods for facilitating employee skill development and socialization. As a result, many organizations and consulting firms have begun to use mentoring relationships as part of their employee development strategy (see Leibowitz, Farren, & Kaye, 1986; Zey, 1984). Walker and Gutteridge (1979) found mentoring activities to be the most frequently used career assistance strategy in organizations.

The purpose of this chapter is to acquaint the reader with the potential uses of mentoring relationships, individual and organizational gains from mentoring relationships, the characteristics that influence the success of mentoring relationships, and the potential problem with using mentoring for employee development.

WHAT IS A MENTORING RELATIONSHIP?

According to Kram (1985), a mentor is an experienced, productive, senior employee who facilitates the personal and professional development of a less-experienced employee (the protégé). The mentor is usually not the protégé's immediate manager because of fear that the formal reporting relationship may stifle development of a supportive atmosphere and willingness of the protégé to try new behaviors and career strategies. The mentor usually is eight to fifteen years older than the protégé, who frequently is a young professional with high career aspirations (Hunt & Michael, 1983). The relationship may be initiated by either party. Often, the protégé attracts the attention of the mentor through outstanding job performance or similarity in interests or hobbies. Also, the protégé may seek out a more experienced organizational member to help answer work-related questions and to explain formal and informal organizational norms.

The majority of mentoring relationships are informal; the two persons establish the relationship without any pressure to do so by the organization (Phillips-Jones, 1983). However, formal mentoring programs in which the organization assigns or matches mentors and protégés are increasing in popularity in both the public and private sector (Klauss, 1981; Roche, 1979). Formal mentoring programs have been used for employees in a wide range of positions, including managers, nurses, lawyers, police officers, and educators. Successful formal mentoring programs are characterized by top management support, careful selection of mentors and protégés, an extensive orientation program emphasizing the development of realistic expectations concerning the relationship, clearly stated responsibilities for both the mentor and protégé, and established minimums for amount and frequency of contact between mentor and protégé (Lean, 1983; Phillips-Jones, 1983; Zey, 1985).

PURPOSES OF FORMAL MENTORING PROGRAMS

Typically, mentoring programs are used for employee socialization, to facilitate transfer of training, to provide opportunities for women and minorities to gain exposure to managers, and to assist in the personal and professional development of protégés. For example, a large consumer-goods producer uses a formal mentoring program for socialization of new engineers and helping them gain an understanding of administrative and technical processes used in manufacturing. In the first year of the two-year program, protégés are located at headquarters, where they are paired with a mentor who assists them in understanding the different engineering specialties in the organization and the role engineers play in product development. The mentor also provides information to the protégé regarding the historical background of the organization and the prevailing corporate culture. After the one-year headquarters appointment, engineers are assigned to a plant location. At the plant, engineers are assigned to a new mentor who is responsible for helping the neophyte engineer acquire specific technical skills and knowledge related to the plant objectives. Protégés and mentors are required to complete a variety of job-related tasks such as review of project procedures, purchasing functions, and technical reference materials and experts available throughout the organization. Many of the mentors and protégés continue to interact after the formal plant and headquarters assignments are completed, suggesting that the relationship may have beneficial interpersonal outcomes for both parties. The mentors are competent senior engineers who participate voluntarily in the program. Task checklists and workbook and project assignments are used as vehicles to facilitate mentor and protégé interactions.

Mentoring relationships can also be used to increase the likelihood of skill transfer from the training environment to the work setting. A key problem in training is how to motivate employees to use skills acquired in training on the job. A professional education organization utilizes mentors to facilitate transfer of training. Aspiring school administrators attend a two-day behavior modeling–based simulation designed to improve their interpersonal and administrative skills. Protégés are matched with mentors who observe the behavior of the protégés in the simulation. The mentor and protégé meet to discuss the protégé's skill development goals, the mentor provides feedback regarding the skill strengths and weaknesses she or he observed in the protégé, and a discussion as to how to develop the target skills back

on the job occurs. A plan of action is agreed upon by both parties, which includes specific steps the protégé will take to try and improve skills in the current job (e.g., involvement in projects, agreement to try to use skills in daily interactions). The mentor and protégé meet three months following the simulation to discuss achievements and problems related to skill development and reformulate and refine the original skill development goals. Although the focus of the relationship is on skill development, issues related to the personal and career development needs of the protégé are often discussed.

The number of women and minorities seeking management positions is increasing as a function of their greater participation in the labor force, expanded access to educational and employment opportunities, and affirmative action programs. Without a mentor, women and minorities often are unable to understand the reality of business culture and fail to obtain the sponsorship needed to identify them as highly talented and to direct them in their career advancement (George & Kummerow, 1981; Solomon, Bishop & Bresser, 1986; Stewart & Gudykunst, 1982). Without a formal mentoring program, women and minorities may be unable to find a mentor due to a lack of access to the "old boy network," a preference for interacting with others of similar status in the organization, or intentional exclusion by managers resulting from negative stereotypes regarding minorities' abilities to manage (Noe, 1988a). Additionally, organizations may use affirmative action plans that give women and minorities preferential treatment for jobs that are prerequisites for managerial positions. Potential mentors may view minorities as a threat to their job security and therefore may be reluctant to initiate a developmental relationship with them. In order to ensure that minorities and women with managerial ability gain visibility and exposure to organizational decision makers, many organizations have decided to develop formal mentoring programs for all employees with managerial potential (as identified by assessment centers, past performance history, or psychological assessment). In these programs, individuals with managerial talent are paired with an upper-level manager who provides detailed exposure to a functional area and assigns the protégé to special projects and task forces where he or she has the opportunity to interact with managers who have substantial input into promotion decisions.

Zey (1988) suggests several innovative uses of mentoring relationships that deserve comment. For example, when corporate mergers occur, one of the keys to overcoming productivity disruptions is how quickly the parent company can make managers comfortable operating in a new corporate culture. Mentors from the parent company could be assigned to managers of the acquired company to advise them of procedures, business practices, and expectations of the parent company. Awareness of corporate and social culture is a major determinant of success of U.S. managers working in foreign corporations. Although managers may participate in cross-cultural training prior to their assignment in a foreign country, additional support from managers in the host country who serve as mentors may help overcome culture shock and provide a more in-depth understanding of how businesses operate in the host country. Finally, a mentoring program may be a useful intervention for new product development. Senior scientists in research and development functions can serve as mentors for newly hired scientists. The mentor can support the protégé's efforts at trying out new ideas and processes. Also, the combination of the establishment talents of the senior scientists and the newly trained Ph.D. will likely result in information and idea exchange that helps facilitate innovation.

BENEFITS INDIVIDUALS GAIN FROM PARTICIPATING IN MENTORING PROGRAMS

Protégé Benefits

The majority of research studies regarding mentoring have focused on identifying the outcomes protégés receive from participating in the relationship. A number of testimonials, case studies, and descriptive research studies suggest that mentors can facilitate personal development and advancement of their protégés in the organization by providing challenging assignments, guidance and counseling, increased exposure and visibility to top management, and serving as role models (Burke, 1984; Fagan & Ayers, 1985; Jennings, 1976; Phillips-Jones, 1982, 1983; Roche, 1979). The most systematic and detailed work regarding the mentoring process has been conducted by Kram and her associates (Kram, 1983, Kram, 1985; Kram & Isabella, 1985). Kram (1983) conducted detailed biographical interviews with eighteen managers in a public sector organization in order to identify the functions provided by mentors. Content analysis of the interviews revealed that mentors provided career and psychosocial functions. *Career functions* included those aspects of the mentoring relationship that prepared the protégé for career advancement. These functions included nominating the protégé for desirable projects, lateral moves and promotions (Sponsorship); providing the protégé with assignments that increased visibility to organizational decision makers and exposure to future opportunities (Exposure and Visibility); sharing ideas, providing feedback, suggesting strategies for accomplishing work objectives (Coaching); reducing unnecessary risks that may threaten the protégé's reputation (Protection); and providing challenging work assignments (Challenging Assignments). *Psychosocial functions* increase the protégé's sense of competence, identity, and work role effectiveness. These functions included serving as a role model of appropriate attitudes, values, and behaviors for the protégé (Role Model); conveying unconditional positive regard (Acceptance and Confirmation); providing a forum in which the protégé is encouraged to talk openly about anxieties and fears (Counseling); and interacting informally with the protégé at work (Friendship). Kram (1985) suggests that the greater the number of functions provided by the mentor, the more beneficial the relationship is to the protégé.

Wilbur (1987) investigated the influence of mentoring and achievement motivation on the career success of corporate managers. Career success was measured by six factors: career wage level, rate of position change, rate of wage growth, career position attained, speed of career success, and range of career success. All career success factors were significantly predicted by at least one mentoring variable (number of mentors, functions received, number of protégés, functions provided to protégés). Utilizing a quasi-experimental design, Shelton (1982) found that lower-level managers who were mentored received higher promotability ratings than managers who did not participate in a formal mentoring program.

Unfortunately, what we know about the types of benefits protégés gain from participating in mentoring relationships has failed to advance beyond Kram's initial work. No published studies have focused on the effectiveness of mentoring for transfer of training, movement of minorities into management ranks, or other outcomes related to organizational effectiveness. In an unpublished study, Kozlowski and Ostroff (1987) found that new employees with mentors more completely utilized available resources to learn about the organization than those employees without mentors.

The lack of research regarding the effectiveness of mentoring programs may be due to the lack of attention devoted to operationalizing the mentoring functions. Recently, three studies have attempted to develop a measure of mentoring functions. Olian, Carroll, and Giannantonio (1988) found that mentors were perceived as providing two roles that were similar to those identified by Kram (1983): an instrumental role, which included the mentor's behavior that influenced the protégé's visibility in the organization, and an intrinsic role, which included the mentor's behavior that provided psychological support to the protégé. Alleman (1986) developed a questionnaire of 123 items assessing different types of mentor behavior, perceived career benefit, and a measure of career satisfaction. Noe (1988b) developed 30-item measure based on Kram's (1983) work in an attempt to verify previous qualitative results regarding mentoring outcomes (see table 48–1). Factor analysis results revealed that the items were best explained by two factors remarkably similar to the career and psychosocial functions identified in previous work.

Mentor Benefits

The types of benefits that mentors received from participating in mentoring relationships have yet to be formally investigated. However, a number of outcomes are likely to be obtained by mentors. Employees who serve as mentors may realize an increase in self-esteem and feelings of worth to the organization. For example, Fagan and Ayers (1985) found that veteran police officers who served as mentors reported higher levels of job satisfaction than officers who were not mentors. Also, mentors may have the opportunity to develop their interpersonal and delegation skills. Individuals in technical fields such as engineering or the health services who serve as mentors may be motivated to engage in professional updating activities (and therefore avoid becoming technically obsolete) because of the responsibility for nurturing a new engineer. Clearly, we need to know more about the benefits that mentors obtain from participating in the mentoring relationship.

Table 48–1
Measure of Mentoring Functions
Items Measuring Psychosocial Functions

1. The mentor has shared history of her or her career with you. (Coaching)
2. Mentor has encouraged you to prepare for advancement. (Coaching)
3. Mentor has encouraged me to try new ways of behaving in my job. (Acceptance & Confirmation)
4. I try to imitate the work behavior of my mentor. (Role Model)
5. I agree with my mentor's attitudes and values regarding education. (Role Model)
6. I respect and admire my mentor. (Role Model)
7. I will try to be like my mentor when I reach a similar position in my career. (Role Model)
8. My mentor has demonstrated good listening skills in our conversations. (Counseling)
9. My mentor has discussed by questions or concerns regarding feelings of competence, commitment to advancement, relationships with peers and supervisors, or work/family conflicts. (Counseling)
10. My mentor has shared personal experiences as an alternative perspective to my problems. (Counseling)
11. My mentor has encouraged me to talk openly about anxiety and fears that detract from my work. (Counseling)
12. My mentor has conveyed empathy for the concerns and feelings I have discussed with him/her. (Counseling)
13. My mentor has kept feelings and doubts I shared with him/her in strict confidence. (Counseling)
14. My mentor has conveyed feelings of respect for me as an individual. (Acceptance & Confirmation)
15. Mentor reduced unnecessary risks that could threaten the possibility of becoming a school principal or receiving a promotion. (Protection)
16. Mentor helped you finish assignments/tasks or meet deadlines that otherwise would have been difficult to complete. (Protection)
17. Mentor helped you meet new colleagues. (Exposure and Visibility)
18. Mentor gave you assignments that increased written and personal contact with school administrators. (Exposure & Visibility)
19. Mentor assigned responsibilities to you that have increased your contact with people in the district who may judge your potential for future advancement. (Exposure & Visibility)
20. Mentor gave you assignments or tasks in your work that prepare you for an administrative position. (Sponsorship)
21. Mentor gave you assignments that present opportunities to learn new skills. (Challenging Assignments)

Note: The specific type of mentor behavior that the item was written to assess is listed in parentheses. A five-point Likert-type response scale is used with 5 – To a very large extent to 1 – to a very small extent.

CHARACTERISTICS INFLUENCING THE SUCCESS OF MENTORING RELATIONSHIPS

Individual Characteristics

A number of recent research studies have attempted to identify the influence of personal characteristics, work, and career attitudes of mentors and protégés on the success of mentoring relationships. For example, due to jealousy, gossip, or fear of sexual innuendos, same-gender mentoring relationships are believed to be more effective than cross-gender relationships. Also, protégés who are more involved in their work and have an active interest in improving their skill weaknesses will likely benefit more from participation in formal mentoring programs.

Olian and her colleagues have conducted two studies investigating the determinants of establishing a mentoring relationships from both the mentor's and protégé's perspective. Olian, Carroll, Giannantonio, and Feren (1988) found that mentors' interpersonal competence was a key determinant of protégé attraction to the relationship. Older protégé were less attractive to mentors. There was no consistent evidence of preference for same-gender mentors. In an experimental study, Carroll, Olian, and Giannantonio (1988) had banking managers respond to stimuli materials in which performance, sex, and marital status of the protégé were manipulated. They found no evidence to support the hypothesis that mentors prefer to have a mentoring relationship with protégés of the same gender. Mentors reported it was more likely they would develop a relationship with a protégé who had a past record of good performance, believed they would receive more intrinsic and extrinsic benefits in a relationship with a well-performing protégé, and reported they would be more likely to engage in friendship behavior and career-enhancing behavior for protégés with a good performance record. Noe (1988) examined the influence of protégé career and job attitudes, gender similarity of the mentoring relationship, the quality of the relationship, and the amount of time the protégé spent with the mentor on the career and psychosocial benefits gained by protégé. Women reported receiving more psychosocial outcomes than men. The gender similarity of the mentoring dyad had no relationship to time spent with the mentor. However, mentors reported that different-gender protégés more effectively utilized the relationship. Additionally, protégés' level of job involvement and career planning was related to perceived benefits obtained from the relationship.

Protégés with high levels of job involvement and career planning activity reported they received more psychosocial outcomes from the mentor. The mentor and protégés included in the study were participants in a formal mentoring program in which mentors and protégés were matched. Comments to open-ended questions regarding barriers to the mentoring relationship revealed that physical distance and time were major reasons that mentors and protégés did not meet more frequently. The positive outcomes that protégés reported receiving from the relationship suggest that concerns regarding the negative consequences of formal mentoring programs may be unwarranted. Campion and Goldfinch (1983) studied the effects of having had a mentor, willingness to share knowledge and understanding with less experienced employees, belief in career planning for less experienced employees, and tenure on hospital administrators' involvement and interest in mentoring. Experience with mentors, willingness to share knowledge and understanding, and belief in career planning were positively related to interest in becoming a mentor. Also, individuals who had a mentor were more interested in becoming a mentor.

Organizational Characteristics

According to Schneider (1975), the climate of the organization affects the behavior of employees because they will want to behave in ways that are consistent with their perceptions of norms, values, and "correct" practices and procedures in the organization. Kram (1985) suggests that for mentoring relationships to be successful, the organization has to encourage employees to be self-disclosing about personal and professional problems, encourage interpersonal interactions across hierarchical and department boundaries, reinforce managers for development of subordinates, and value managers who have interpersonal skills necessary to engage in a mentoring relationship. These notions are encompassed in the construct of prosocial behavior (Brief & Motowidlo, 1986). Prosocial behavior is behavior performed by an organization member with the intention of promoting the welfare of the individual, group, or organization toward which it is directed. This includes such behavior as assisting coworkers with job-related and personal matters, providing exemplary customer service, representing the organization favorably to outsiders, and volunteering for extra job assignments. Formal mentoring programs are likely to be most successful in organizations or functional areas characterized by a warm, friendly, supportive climate that facilitates prosocial behavior. No empirical research has specifically investigated the impact of the organizational climate on the success of mentoring relationships, but studies in the training area indicate the importance of work group attitudes for use of trained skills in the work environment (e.g., Hand, Richards, & Slocum, 1973).

POTENTIAL NEGATIVE IMPACT OF MENTORING RELATIONSHIPS

It has been suggested by numerous authors that finding a mentor is necessary for advancement within the organization, and mentoring programs are a key component of a successful employee development system. However, it is important to consider some of the limitations and potential negative effects of mentoring programs.

One of the potential limitations of formal mentoring programs is that it may not be possible for mentors to provide career and psychosocial guidance to protégés in these artificially created relationships. According to Kram (1983), it may take two to five years before the mentor is comfortable with and willing to engage in such activities as counseling or provide indicators of acceptance and confirmation to the protégé. Formal mentoring programs, in which the mentor is directed to provide psychosocial functions, may fail because the relationship between the mentor and protégé is underdeveloped. Mentors and protégés may also react negatively to programs that limit personal interaction and interpersonal development and restrict the purpose of the relationship to specific task accomplishment (e.g., socialization or skill learning).

Mentoring relationships may cause the protégé to become too dependent on the mentor for help, encouragement, and direction in regard to career development. This overdependence may result in the protégé's failing to develop important interpersonal relationships with peers, managers, and other valuable personal resources in the organization. For example, Kram and Isabella (1985) emphasize that peer relationships provide individuals with a unique opportunity to both give and receive help concerning problems, empathy, and counseling. The lack of hierarchical separation between peers might make it easier to communicate and learn about organization norms and values than with a mentor. Because of the dependent nature of the mentoring relationships, mentors may use the protégé for their own personal and political gains within the organization. This may be especially the case for mentors who are motivated to develop their own sense of accomplishment or further their own advancement in the organization. The mentor may give the protégé routine, mundane tasks that do little for the protégé's development but free up time for the mentor to gain visibility within the organization.

Another potential problem with mentoring relationships is that they may circumvent the traditional manager-subordinate relationship. Managers may be reluctant to assist the subordinate with career development activities because the organization has formally assigned a mentor to assist in that process. Managers may also feel that the mentor takes away some of the power they need to stimulate subordinate performance. That is, managers may use career discussions, friendship, and extended visibility in the organization as rewards for good performance. By introducing a third party to provide these functions, the manager has lost incentives to motivate good performance.

The protégé may be looked on unfavorably by coworkers if the relationship is perceived by others as developing out of favoritism. This may be the case where participating in mentoring programs is limited to certain individuals (e.g., programs arising from affirmative action concerns, needs to develop employees with managerial potential). Sabotage, dissatisfaction, and lack of group cohesion can be unfortunate consequences. Participation in a mentoring relationship can also be a negative experience for protégés if the mentor engages in unethical behavior, makes poor decisions, or decides to leave the organization after personal problems with influential people in the organization. Because of their close association, the protégé may be perceived to be "guilty" simply because of his or her association with the mentor. Organization decision makers may retaliate against the protégé (e.g., give poor performance ratings, less desirable job assignments) because of previous actions of their mentor.

STEPS TO ENSURE THE SUCCESS OF MENTORING PROGRAMS

Academic research and organizational experience with mentoring programs indicate the protégés can gain beneficial outcomes from participating in mentoring relationships. Although they may not be considered to be true mentoring relationships because the full range of career and psychosocial functions is not provided, mentoring relationships established as a result of organizational initiatives have and will continue to be used for employee socialization, training, and the development of special populations. However, the lack of research studies regarding the benefits that mentors can obtain from the relationship, the effectiveness of mentoring programs for the attainment of organizational outcomes (e.g., socialization or transfer of training), and the individual and organizational characteristics necessary for mentoring relationships to be successful suggests that organizations should use caution in utilizing mentoring programs for employee development. Kram (1986) and Zey (1985) emphasize the importance of educating program participants and senior management before implementing a mentor program. Workshops focusing on program goals and their relationship to organizational objectives and communicating an understanding of the range of mentoring functions and the potential benefits and costs are needed. Program developers need to be concerned with the mentor selection process, the mentor-protégé matching process, creating realistic expectations of the program for participants, and how to facilitate and maintain interactions between the mentor and protégé.

In order to maximize the chances of a successful mentoring program the following suggestions should be considered:

1. Program participation should be voluntary. Mentors and protégés should be allowed to terminate the relationship at any time without fear of punishment.

2. The mentor-protégé matching process should not limit the autonomy of the participants. Do not force mentors and protégés to participate in a relationship if they do not feel they can work together. For example, a mentor pool could be established allowing the protégé to choose from a variety of qualified mentors.

3. Criteria for choosing mentors should include examination of their past record for developing employees, a willingness to serve as a mentor, and evidence of positive coaching, communication, and listening skills. All mentors should attend training activities, which include opportunities to participate in role plays and receive feedback regarding how to initiate, cultivate, and terminate a mentoring relationship.

4. The purpose of the mentoring program should be clearly understood by participants. Projects and activities that the mentor and protégé are expected to complete should be specified. Checklists or other means to direct the completion of these activities should be provided.

5. The length of the program should be clearly specified, but mentors and protégés should be encouraged to pursue the relationship beyond the official program period.

6. A minimum contact level between the mentor and protégé should be established. Without an established contact level, work demands, projects, and other activities will grow to fill the time devoted to the relationship.

7. Protégés should be encouraged to contact each other, to serve as sounding boards for problems and concerns, and to share successes.

8. The mentoring program should be assessed as it develops. Interviews with mentors and protégés can provide immediate feedback regarding specific areas of satisfaction and dissatisfaction. Surveys can be used to gather more detailed information regarding the benefits that mentors and protégés received from program participation.

9. In order to encourage managers to get involved in the development of their employees, including participation in formal and informal mentoring relationships, employee development needs to be recognized and rewarded by the organization's formal appraisal system. Rewarding employee development sends a signal to managers that mentoring, career discussions, coaching, and other activities are worth their time and effort.

REFERENCES

Alleman, E. (1986). Measuring mentoring: Frequency, quality, impact. In W.A. Gray & M.M. Gray (Eds.), *Mentoring: Aid to excellence in career development, business, and the professions.* Proceedings of First International Conference on Mentoring. Vancouver, BC, Canada: International Association for Mentoring.

Bandura, A. (1977). *Social learning theory.* Englewood Cliffs, NJ: Prentice-Hall.

Brief, A.P., & Motowidlo, S.J. (1986). Prosocial organizational behaviors. *Academy of Management Review, 11,* 710–725.

Burke, R.J. (1984). Mentors in organizations. *Group and Organizational Studies, 9,* 353–472.

Campion, M.A., & Goldfinch (1983). Mentoring among hospital administrators. *Hospital & Health Sciences Administration* (November–December), 77–93.

Carroll, S.J., Jr., Olian, J.D., & Giannantonio, C.M. (1988). Mentor reactions to protégés: An experiment with managers. Unpublished manuscript.

Decker, P.J., & Nathan, B.R. (1985). *Behavior modeling training.* New York: Praeger.

Fagan, M.M., & Ayers, K., Jr. (1985). Police mentors. *FBI Law Enforcement Bulletin* (January), 8–13.

George, P., & Kummerow, J. (1981). Mentoring for career women. *Training, 18,* 44–49.

Hand, H.H., Richards, M.D., & Slocum, J.M., Jr. (1973). Organizational climate and the effectiveness of a human relation program. *Academy of Management Journal, 16,* 185–195.

Hunt, D.M., & Michael, C. (1983). Mentorship: A career training and development tool. *Academy of Management Review, 8,* 475–485.

Jennings, E. (1976). *Routes to the executive suite.* New York: McGraw-Hill.

Klauss, R. (1981). Formalized mentor relationships for management and development programs in the federal government. *Public Administration Review* (July–August), 489–496.

Kozlowski, S.W., & Ostroff, C. (1987). *The role of mentoring in early socializations experiences of organizational members.* Paper presented in symposium at 2d Annual Conference of the Society for Industrial and Organizational Psychology, Atlanta.

Kram, K.E. (1983). Phases of the mentoring relationship. *Academy of Management Journal, 26,* 608–625.

Kram, K.E. (1985). *Mentoring at work: Development relationships in organizational life.* Glenview, IL: Scott-Foresman.

Kram, K.E. (1986). Mentoring in the workplace. In D.T. Hall & Associates, *Career development in organizations* (160–201) San Francisco: Jossey-Bass.

Kram, K.E., & Isabella, L.A. (1985). Mentoring alternatives: The role of peer relationships in career development. *Academy of Management Journal, 28,* 110–132.

Lean, E. (1983). Cross-gender mentoring—Downright upright and good for productivity. *Training and Development Journal, 5,* 60–65.

Leibowitz, Z.B., Farren, C., & Kaye, B.L. (1986). *Designing career development systems.* San Francisco: Jossey-Bass.

Noe, R.A. (1988a). Women and mentoring: A review and research agenda. *Academy of Management Review, 13,* 65–78.

Noe, R.A. (1988b). An investigation of the determinants of successful mentoring relationships. Unpublished manuscript.

Olian, J.D., Carroll, S.J., Giannantonio, C.M., & Feren, B. (1988). What do protégés look for in a mentor? Results of three experimental studies. *Journal of Vocational Behavior, 33,* 15–37.

Phillips-Jones, L.L. (1982). *Mentors and protégés.* New York: Arbor House.

Phillips-Jones, L.L. (1983). Establishing a formalized mentoring program. *Training and Development Journal, 2,* 38–42.

Roche, G.R. (1979). Much ado about mentors. *Harvard Business Review, 57*(1), 14–31.

Schneider, B. (1975). Organizational climates: An essay. *Personnel Psychology, 28,* 447–479.

Shelton, C. (1982). Mentoring programs: Do they make a difference? *National Association of Bank Women Journal, 58*(5), 22–24.

Soloman, E.E., Bishop, R.C., & Bresser, R.K. (1986). Organizational moderators of gender differences in career development: A facet classification. *Journal of Vocational Behavior, 29,* 27–41.

Stewart, L.P., & Gudykunst, W.B. (1982). Differential factors influencing the hierarchical level and number of promotions of males and females within an organization. *Academy of Management Journal, 25,* 586–597.

Walker, J.W., & Gutteridge, T.G. (1979). *Career planning practices.* New York: AMACOM.

Wilbur, J.L. (1987). Does mentoring breed success? *Training and Development Journal, 41*(11), 38–41.

Zey, M.G. (1984). *The mentor connection.* Homewood, IL: Dow-Jones-Irwin.

Zey, M.G. (1985). Mentor programs: Making the right moves. *Personnel Journal* (February), 53–57.

Zey, M.G. (1988). A mentor for all reasons. *Personnel Journal* (January), 46–51.

49 UNDERSTANDING EXECUTIVE DERAILMENT: A FIRST STEP IN PREVENTION

Cynthia D. McCauley, Marian N. Ruderman

Organizations invest a great deal in the individuals occupying their upper-level management positions. They may spend large amounts of money, time, and energy identifying the high-potential managers in their organizations and grooming them for more responsible positions. Or they may invest their resources in selecting and recruiting more experienced managers to fill these positions.

Not everyone expected to be a top corporate executive makes it. A significant number of people who are very successful in their careers do not live up to their full potential in the eyes of the organization. When individuals do not live up to the organization's expectations and derail (e.g., are fired, demoted, forced into early retirement, or plateaued), the organization has wasted a portion of its time, money, and human resources. Derailments also cause personal loss for the individual who derails and can affect the morale of the people whom the individual was managing.

Failure rates in upper-level management positions vary from organization to organization. Tung (1982) reports that over half of the eighty corporations she surveyed reported failure rates of 10 to 20 percent for expatriate management assignments. *Business Week* (1983) reported a 9.8 percent involuntary turnover rate in top positions across 100 large corporations, while Sorcher (1985) reported estimates of failure rates as high as 33 percent for senior executives.

Organizations do not expect to eliminate derailment completely. They do, however, want to keep it to a minimum level. When failure rates begin to reach an uncomfortable level, the organization begins to look for ways to remedy the situation. The first information they seek is why the derailments are occurring.

For the organization experiencing high derailment rates in upper-level management positions, there is little systematically researched information available to answer the question "why?" Few studies have dealt specifically with derailment in high level management positions.

McCall and Lombardo (1983), in the first study to look at this issue, explained derailment in terms of the characteristics of individual executives. They contrasted descriptions of successful and derailed executives provided retrospectively by savvy corporate insiders. They found that reasons given for derailment may be related to the individual's managerial skills (e.g., poor staffing), personal qualities (e.g., insensitivity, overly ambitious), or ability to lead others (e.g., overmanaging). In addition they noted four dynamics of the derailment process: (1) an early strength became a weakness; (2) a deficiency, such as an inability to work with peers, overlooked at lower levels of the hierarchy eventually mattered; (3) bad luck (e.g., some executives were caught in an economic downturn or were tainted by a series of events that were out of their control); and (4) success went to their heads (they lost their humility).

Bentz (1985) also found that many executive-level failures lacked one or more of the managerial skills needed at the upper levels (e.g., ability to deal with a large-scale organization). His study was also based on retrospective interviews and focused on executives who were judged to be failures, although none was fired. Bentz observed that in many cases a single overriding weakness stalled otherwise successful careers.

Gabarro (1987) observed that successions at the general management level often failed when the manager had a lack of relevant background and troubled relationships with key people. A second pattern associated with failure was having ineffective relationships with two of the following groups of people: peers, subordinates, and superiors.

In contrast to the previous studies that looked at derailment in executive men, Morrison, White, and Van Velsor (1987) used the McCall and Lombardo

The research from which this chapter was drawn was originally published in Lombardo, M. M., Ruderman, M. N., & McCauley, C. D. (1988). Explanations of success and derailment in upper-level management positions. *Journal of Business and Psychology.*

methodology to examine derailment in a population of executive women. For the most part, women derailed for the same reasons as the men. Only three differences stand out: (1) women were more likely to be described as having a poor physical image, (2) women were more likely to have too narrow a range of business experience to reach the top, and (3) men who derailed were more likely to have had poor work relationships than derailed women.

Additional research on male executives across eight corporations (Lombardo & McCauley, 1988) suggests that reasons for derailment are perceived to vary in importance across organizations. For example, personality flaws are more strongly associated with derailment potential in some companies, moderately associated in other companies, and not associated at all in others. These variations are likely due to differences in organizational cultures and reward systems. Thus, although these general studies of derailment provide useful information to the organization facing a derailment problem, it is important for the organization to examine its own situation more carefully.

For multinational corporations experiencing derailment problems among managers in overseas assignments, another source of information comes from studies of failure among expatriate managers (Hays, 1971; Tung, 1982). In addition to personality factors and management skills, failure among these managers is also attributed to more situational factors: the inability to adapt to a different culture, family-related issues, and lack of motivation to work overseas. Since expatriate managers are subjected to different pressures and challenges than are managers in domestic businesses, they may be more vulnerable to derailment.

The case presented below represents an organization that was concerned about the large number of upper-level manager derailments that it was experiencing in its international division. Each failure was estimated to have cost the organization a minimum of $500,000. The organization was particularly concerned because these individuals were managing important operations far from corporate headquarters; they had to make decisions more autonomously and had few opportunities to receive coaching. The organization's first step in attacking their derailment problem was to examine why their managers had failed in the past.

THE CASE STUDY

To look at possible reasons for derailment, the organization identified two groups of upper-level managers: one set of eighty-three derailed managers who had been involuntarily terminated between 1983 and 1985 and a set of eighty-six managers who were currently successful in their positions in the organization and were expected to be promoted. The groups were made up entirely of male managers and were representative of the international division's fifteen regions around the world.

Each manager in the study was rated on an inventory by a boss or peer who had worked with the manager for at least one year. The majority of the survey items were taken from the Executive Development Profile, a questionnaire assessing managerial behaviors. The items in the instrument were developed from the results of several qualitative studies involving over 400 executives across several different companies (Lindsey, Homes & McCall, 1987; McCall, Lombardo & Morrison, 1988), which generated data on the skills, attitudes, and values that successful executives develop over their careers and on factors related to derailment. The items in the Executive Development Profile were developed to measure these characteristics of success and derailment factors.

A statistical technique called factor analysis was used to group these items into eight different dimensions. Table 49–1 provides samples of the items comprising these dimensions. One of the most valuable insights provided by this part of the inventory is this categorization of the perceived factors differentiating derailed from successful executives.

In addition to the items from the Executive Development Profile, each manager was also rated on three items that reflected potential reasons for derailment particular to an overseas assignment: spouse adjustment, ability to work with different languages or cultures, and motivation for an international career.

Table 49–1

Sample Items for Each Dimension Used to Study Derailment

Handling business complexity
Can handle a job requiring the formulation of complex organizational strategies.
Is an astute business person.
Is versatile (can handle new ventures *and* turnaround situation *and* big leaps in responsibility)

Directing, motivating, and developing subordinates
Understands the art of directing and motivating his or her employees or building a team with the skills and motivation to get things done.
Helps subordinates learn from their mistakes; doesn't beat on them for their foul-ups.
Sets clear performance standards for subordinates.

Honor
Promotes the company's and businesses's interest rather than his or her own.
Doesn't blame others or the situation for his or her mistakes.
Knows that he or she had personal limits or blind spots

Drive for excellence
Has a good track record
Demands excellence of subordinates
Is ambitious; personal career goals are important

Organizational savvy
Knows that most important management situations are characterized by ambiguity, uncertainty, and stress and that you have to learn to be comfortable with it and act in spite of it
Understands how higher management operates, how they see things, agrees with overall strategy

Composure
Is emotionally stable and predictable
Stays cool and composed in crisis situations
Can adapt to bosses with different management styles

Sensitivity
Is sensitive, tactful, and positive when interacting with others
Can get along with all kinds of people

Staffing
Chooses a broad subordinate group
Recruits and hires good people

DIFFERENCES BETWEEN THE SUCCESSFUL AND DERAILED EXECUTIVES

Differences between the ratings of the derailed managers and those of the successful managers were examined to understand explanations for the disappointing ends to the derailed managers' careers. Comparison of the successful and derailed executives suggests that these two groups are viewed very differently. Each of the effect sizes presented in table 49–2

represents important differences between the two groups. The bosses' perceptions suggest that expatriate derailment occurs for a variety of reasons:

1. Derailment and managerial skills. Scores on the Handling Business Complexity and Organizational Savvy dimensions are different for success-

Table 49–2

Comparison of Mean Differences between Derailed and Successful Executives

| Executive Profile Scales | Group | | | | Effect Size[a] |
| | Derailed | | Successful | | |
	M	SD	M	SD	
Handling Business Complexity	3.12	.56	2.29	.47	1.26
Directing, Motivating, and Developing Subordinates	3.21	.48	2.45	.41	1.29
Honor	3.00	.55	2.27	.44	1.20
Drive for Excellence	2.86	.53	2.11	.44	1.21
Organizational Savvy	3.03	.65	2.36	.48	1.02
Composure	3.06	.80	2.25	.54	1.03
Sensitivity	2.96	.78	2.21	.57	.71
Staffing	3.30	.59	2.60	.47	1.09
Spouse Adjustment	4.27	1.73	3.36	1.92	.48
Language and Culture Differences	3.10	1.40	2.65	1.53	.30
Motivation to Go Overseas	3.52	1.62	2.78	1.25	.79

Note: Higher scale scores indicate lower performance. N = derailed: 83; successful: 86.
[a]Effect size is a measure of the magnitude of the difference between the two groups. It equals the mean difference divided by the total group standard deviation.

ful and derailed managers. Derailed individuals were much more likely to be seen as lacking the cognitive capabilities or skills to handle complex business ventures, think strategically, make high-quality decisions in ambiguous circumstances, and demonstrate needed political skills than were the successful.

2. Derailment and personality factors. The ratings of the two groups were also different on the Honor, Composure, Drive, and Sensitivity dimensions. These factors seem to indicate that personal flaws led to derailment. Derailed individuals were much more likely to be seen as unstable, abrasive, untrustworthy, or lacking drive than were the successful.

3. Derailment and the leadership of others. Scores on the Directing, Motivating, and Developing Subordinates and Staffing dimensions were different for successful and derailed managers. Failure to direct, motivate, teach, develop, and select wisely were seen as associated with derailment.

4. Derailment and situational factors. The scores of derailed and successful executives on the three items assessing situational factors were quite different. Bosses perceived that derailed executives were more likely to have spouses with adjustment problems, difficulty with the language, or less motivation to go overseas than their successful counterparts.

DISCUSSION

This study helped provide the client with an understanding of the reasons that executives in their international operations derail. They learned about the types of managerial, personality, leadership, and situational factors that their executives believe distinguished derailed from successful executives. This list of factors overlaps with that from the original McCall and Lombardo study (1983) of derailment but is not identical to it.

Also, many of the managerial, personal, and leadership skills that differentiated derailed and successful managers in this study have been cited as important factors in studies that focused on assessments of successful managers. However, the inventory used in this study suggests characteristics for assessment that often are overlooked in assessments of executive style based solely on successful executives. The factors that result from including items derived from studies of derailed individuals as well as the successful add to our understanding of success.

For example, consider the Handling Business Complexity scale. It is obvious, as well as an established research finding, that intellectual ability is related to career progress (e.g., Bray & Howard, 1983). The Handling Business Complexity dimension, however, suggests that something more than

intelligence distinguishes the derailed from the successful executives. This dimension reflects astuteness in business matters, versatility, and the ability to handle many different kinds of job assignments in addition to intelligence. To rise to the executive level, both the successful and derailed executives were probably very bright. The comparison of derailed to successful executives reveals that successful executives are better at applying their intelligence and business knowledge quickly in a variety of specific situations than those that derailed. The study suggests it is application of intellect that is critical in distinguishing successful from derailed executives.

Another example is the Honor scale. Although successful executives describe themselves as having integrity (Korn/Ferry International, 1986), being honorable is not often cited in studies examining predictors of executives success. The Honor scale used in this study elucidates the way integrity plays out in the business context. Not blaming others, admitting personal mistakes, putting company over self, and admitting personal limits are elements of honorable behavior that distinguished ratings of the derailed executives from those of the successful executives. Considering reasons that people fail illuminates the role honor and integrity play in career success.

WHAT CAN BE DONE TO PREVENT DERAILMENT

Understanding the Causes

As we have illustrated with this one organization, the first step in the prevention of derailment is under-

standing the predominant reasons for derailment in your own organization. Although lack of management skills, personality flaws, inability to lead, and situational factors have contributed to derailment in various organizations, the specific factors that are most related to derailment in a single organization can vary considerably depending on that organization's culture.

The method to look at derailment chosen by the company in our case fit well with their immediate needs. Derailment had already reached uncomfortable levels; thus they needed some quick insights into the problem. Since their managers were spread around the world, the company felt that a boss in the managers' immediate work location would be the best judge of their strengths and weaknesses. A retrospective survey met these needs.

However, other options are available to the organization trying to understand derailment factors. One could conduct interviews like those used in the McCall and Lombardo (1983) study in which "savvy insiders" (people at the top of an organization who had observed many executives' careers) described an individual who had derailed in the organization and one who had not. Although also a retrospective method, the savvy insiders may have a broader perspective than an immediate boss on a manager's career and the factors contributing to his or her success or derailment. It may be the preferred method when decision making about managers' careers is highly centralized in the organization.

Retrospective reports can be subject to bias; thus the organization that does not feel it is in a crisis situation with respect to derailment may opt for a method that would avoid some of these biases. One option would be to study each derailment case when it has occurred, interviewing the significant actors about what happened and why. The most predictive design would be to assess managers regularly on a wide range of skills and qualities and then see which of these are most predictive over time of who derails in the organization.

Early Warning System

An organization can incorporate the derailment factors they uncover into an early warning system as did the organization that requested this study. As part of this system, managers begin systematically receiving feedback early in their careers as to how they are perceived on the derailment factors. The feedback comes from various sources, including peers and subordinates, who are often the first to notice personality flaws or difficulties in leading others. In a typical organization, managers are measured and rewarded on reaching goals and objectives and on their technical expertise. Unless a systematic effort is put in place, receiving feedback on the derailment factors is rare.

Feedback is followed by recommended developmental steps—coaching, developmental assignments, behavioral change efforts, coursework, and placement with exceptional role models—that are targeted toward improving a weakness. These efforts are most effective when the organization takes learning, not just results, seriously. Managers need to understand why they are involved in certain developmental activities and how they are expected to improve. Managers may need help in structuring their learning and making the most of their experiences. Bosses have to be supportive of the development efforts, and the reward system has to provide incentives for improvements.

Support during Transitions

Derailment is perhaps more likely to occur at critical transition points in a manager's career (e.g., promotions, losing a supportive boss, becoming a general manager). A blind spot that was minimized in the old situation may cause greater problems in the new one. For example, insensitivity may be tolerated in a technical manager who was seen as brilliant by the professionals he or she managed. But as this manager moves into a position directing several people who do not know or care about his technical brilliance, the insensitive behavior may do him or her in. A new job may also require skills a manager has never tested or require mental transitions he or she was never aware of.

Organizations can help prevent derailment by better preparing managers and giving them assistance through transitions. They can point out what challenges are inherent in a particular transition and what adjustments and learning will be necessary for success in the new situation. Opportunities to interact with and learn from previous incumbents and from peers experiencing similar transitions are needed.

This type of advance preparation becomes particularly important when the assignment is an overseas one. Executives need to be prepared for the different business and cultural challenges they will face. Tung (1982) found that 68 percent of the American expatriates she queried did not receive any formal type of orientation for the cultural changes awaiting them. Preparation could help these executives in both learning from and dealing with the overseas assignment.

Advance preparation may be helpful to the families of overseas managers as well. Vivan (1968) observed that the families of expatriates are perhaps even more susceptible to culture shock than the executives. Orienting them to the local customs, language, and social environment before transferring them abroad may help reduce the number of expatriate derailments due to family adjustment problems.

Varied Leadership Experiences

Compared to the derailed executives, McCall and Lombardo (1983) found that the successful ones in their study had more diversity in the kinds of leadership challenges they had faced. Thus, an additional strategy for reducing derailment is to expose managers early in their careers to varied leadership challenges before the stakes get too high (see McCall, Lombardo & Morrison, 1988). (By this we mean turning around a small unit in trouble, having to persuade those over whom one has no authority, or starting something—a small unit, a procedure or process—from scratch.) Exposure to a variety of small challenges is the key; the different types of job challenges develop very different strengths while the cost of failure is reduced. For example, some of the executives in the McCall and Lombardo derailment study confronted their first turnaround situation when the stakes were staggering and they failed. Exposure to miniversions of some of the challenges in a turnaround job at an early age allows time for learning and a strategy of small wins, small losses.

For a number of managers, derailment will come regardless. They will inherently lack the sensitivity or the ability to inspire or simply will not be good strategists. But many others, we believe, do not have to derail. Derailment may be prevented by feedback, developmental interventions, preparation and support for critical transitions, and early varied leadership challenges.

The organization that commissioned this study is taking an active role in trying to reduce the number of future derailments. They have used their understanding of the differences between the derailed and successful managers described here to advise current managers of their own potential for derailing. They are optimistic that this type of feedback combined with the appropriate developmental steps will reduce derailments in the years to come.

REFERENCES

Bentz, V.J. (1985). *A view of the top: A thirty year perspective of research devoted to the discovery, description and prediction of executive behavior.* Paper presented at the annual convention of the American Psychological Association, Los Angeles.

Bray, D.W., & Howard, A. (1983). The AT&T longitudinal studies of managers. In K.W. Shaie (Ed.), *Longitudinal studies of adult psychological development.* New York: Guilford Press.

Hays, R.D. (1971). Ascribed behavioral determinants of success-failure among U.S. expatriate managers. *Journal of International Business Studies, 2,* 40–46.

Korn/Ferry International (1986). *Korn/Ferry International's executive profile: A survey of corporate leaders in the eighties.* New York: Author.

Lindsey, E.T., Homes, V.B., & McCall, M.W. (1987). *Key events in executives' lives* (Technical Report No. 32). Greensboro, NC: Center for Creative Leadership.

Lombardo, M.M., & McCauley, C.D. (1988). *The dynamics of management derailment* (Technical Report No. 34). Greensboro NC: Center for Creative Leadership.

McCall, M.W., & Lombardo, M.M (1983). What makes a top executive? *Psychology Today, 17*(2), 26–31.

McCall, M.W., Lombardo, M.M., & Morrison, A.M. (1988). *The lessons of experience.* Lexington, MA: Lexington Books.

Morrison, A.M., White, R.P., & Van Velsor, E. (1987). *Breaking the glass ceiling.* Reading, MA: Addison-Wesley.

Sorcher, M. (1985). *Predicting executives success: What it takes to make it into senior management.* New York: Wiley and Sons.

Staff (1983). Turnover at the top. *Business Week,* December 19, 104–106.

Tung, R.L. (1982). Selection and training procedures of U.S., European, and Japanese multinationals. *California Management Review, 25,* 57–71.

Vivan, J. (1968). Expatriate executives: Overpaid but undercompensated. *Columbia Journal of World Business, 3,* 29–40.

50 OUTPLACEMENT COUNSELING FOR THE TERMINATED MANAGER

Robert J. Lee

WHAT IS OUTPLACEMENT?

Outplacement is the process by which an individual whose employment has been terminated makes the transition from an organizational employer to another work situation with the assistance of reemployment professionals and appropriate support services, provided by the former employer.

Within this straightforward definition are a great many subtle issues and a lot of corporate and social history. Even as these words are being written, a significant percentage of executives do not know much about outplacement, and some have never heard of it. Ten years ago this statement could have been made about human resources managers too.

The outplacement profession began perhaps twenty-five years ago and has been growing rapidly since about 1975. It is not exactly clear why this growth and corporate acceptance have occurred, but certain facts are easy to identify:

1. An enormous amount of pressure has been put on companies in America and elsewhere to keep pace with rapid change. Ultimately all the abstract discussions about technology, imports, deregulation, and Wall Street's myopia come to rest on the question, "Who should we have working in our company?" People are terminated as companies reorganize, reposition, and relocate. The swinging pendulum of mergers and acquisitions and then divestitures, consolidations, and leveraged buy-outs (LBO) is also part of this pattern.

2. There have been important changes in the laws applicable to employment. Affirmative action and equal employment opportunity laws have some effect, but the Age Discrimination in Employment Act (ADEA) and the erosion of the employment-at-will doctrine have had considerable impact on how companies think when they talk about terminations.

3. The psychological contract between employee and employer has been shifting. Companies do not promise lifetime careers, and professionals look forward to managing their own lives, which may include a lot of mobility, no mobility, or even two or three career paths. These attitudes lead to a new openness about who should stay with the company, when they should leave, and for what reasons.

4. The rapidly increasing acceptance of outplacement is also due to satisfaction by the corporate users and the individuals involved. Although a hard-to-evaluate service, it seems to meet the needs of people, and it seems to help the companies as well. About 90 percent of all major companies now use outplacement, as do a great many smaller organizations.

Components

Let us take a closer look at the components of an outplacement program for a terminated executive. (While reading this section, as well as the rest of this chapter, please keep in mind that no two outplacement situations are identical; we are dealing here with the more frequently occurring patterns.)

1. Departure assistance: Helping the company implement smoothly what could be a distasteful, threatening, and unnecessarily hurtful event.

2. Personal support: Helping the individual deal with the fact that suddenly he or she is out of a job. This is true whether or not lots of others are also being let go, and whether or not he or she saw it coming or feels in any way partly responsible.

3. Career assessment and counsel: What kind of career path has been created by this person's series

of jobs, assignments, and earnings? What does it all add up to, and what are the options now?

4. Personal assessment and counsel: What are the strengths, limitations, preferences, resources, and styles of this person? Which kinds of environments would be most compatible? Where are the traps to avoid?

5. Career plan and job search campaign: Getting agreement on what the future probably will hold for this person, based on a coherent presentation of the facts, insight into the candidate, and a sense of realism about the job market. A well-prepared campaign is consistent with the facts and furthers the life goals of the person.

6. Marketing counsel: Coaching and supporting the person as she or he goes through the competitive steps of using the formal job market, networking, interviewing, and negotiating.

7. Administrative services: Providing the space, telephones, word processing, reference materials, secretarial support, and general office services needed by the person for what will typically be four or five months but can range from one to eighteen or more.

Key Participants

Terminology has not been standardized in the outplacement field. The only real agreement seems to be on the word *outplacement* itself, though sometimes one hears such terms as *career continuation*.

The person who is being outplaced should be called the *client*. This usage underscores the point about the whole service, which is to help the person who has the immediate need. The client is sometimes called the *candidate* because he or she is in fact a candidate for a job somewhere. Another term used for the client is *counselee*, although this term is losing popularity because of its psychological overtones.

The former employer is best referred to as the *sponsor* or as the *sponsoring company*. The term *client company* is also heard, which points out the double-client nature of the outplacement service. The person who was most recently the client's boss is known as the *terminating manager*.

The person providing the professional services is generally called the *consultant*. He or she may be known as the *counselor*, but that phrasing has psychological overtones and is a protected title in some states (as is *dentist* or *lawyer*), which means its use is restricted to people who hold a certain license.

In some outplacement firms, the delivery of professional services is formally divided among staff specialists, which may include people expert in oral and written communications, data base research, or some other area, and there may be a *psychologist* who performs the personal assessment.

Types of Outplacement

Outplacement programs may be designed differently on the basis of the level of the client: senior executives, middle managers and professionals, first-level supervisors, and group outplacement.

Programs for nonexempt and hourly employees usually are designed around a group format. A typical program will be two or three days in length and may or may not provide follow-up counseling. Since group outplacement is not usually offered to managers, it is not directly discussed in this chapter.

Professional outplacement may be provided by outplacement consulting firms or may be offered internally by a company's own staff.

What Is Not Outplacement

Outplacement is related to but not the same as the larger events that often lead to the need for outplacement: unemployment, downsizing, termination, work force reduction, and so on. These are much bigger issues with economic, social, and legal dimensions to them. Outplacement is specifically concerned with helping someone find a new job or a new career after having lost the old one—regardless of the reasons why the old one was lost.

Similarly, there are familiar terms that may be part of an individual's outplacement experience but are by no means the whole of it: vocational guidance, career planning, resume writing, and interview skills training.

Outplacement does not include job finding. Outplacement firms may help in this area, but it is usually not an important part of the service. Organizations such as executive recruiters and personnel placement agencies do this kind of work. During outplacement, the client remains fully responsible for finding his or her own new job.

Outplacement is not therapy. The borderlines between the two services may be hard to define, since a good outplacement firm will try to help the client through the emotional rollercoaster of termination and job hunting, but there clearly are limits to what the outplacement firm should be doing in this area. The topics of symptom recognition and clinical referral will be taken up later.

Finally, for purposes of this discussion, we

exclude the field of retail outplacement, in which similar services are sold directly to the terminated person. The economics and marketing involved in a retail-oriented firm are quite different than in a corporate-oriented one, creating some inevitable and unfortunate differences in service delivery.

ORGANIZATIONAL CONSIDERATIONS

Reasons for Offering Outplacement

Certain of the benefits of outplacement counseling accrue directly to the sponsoring company, and others apply directly to the client individuals. Ultimately the company benefits on all counts, but it will be easier to discuss the reasons for offering outplacement by looking at these two rationales separately.

The sponsoring company realizes the following benefits:

1. The company receives professional consulting advice on proper pretermination planning. This advice may touch on the severance package, the performance-related documentation, the logistics of the termination meeting, or on the kinds of things that should be written down, said to the individual, or not mentioned at all.

2. Managers who are enlightened about outplacement services tend to act confidently on decisions to release employees who no longer respond to the needs of the organization.

3. Outplacement appears to reduce the time needed by the client to find new employment, thereby reducing the costs for salary continuation, benefits, or unemployment compensation.

4. It is generally assumed that a terminated employee whose energies are focused on the future is less likely to dwell on the unfairness of life and seek legal means for "getting even."

5. The fact that a company is helping the people who had to be let go is a mark in its favor among the people who were not let go. The morale of the surviving work force may, in fact, be a company's primary concern.

6. The sponsor does not have to provide the space for the client to use during his or her outplacement. This may be a matter of simple logistics: the office may be occupied by someone else, or the space may have been shut down. Alternately, the benefit may be that the client no longer has access to proprietary or secret information, such as marketing plans. Some sponsors are eager to have the client away from the premises because of fears that he or she will be a depressing influence on the remaining staff.

7. The human resources (HR) staff is relieved of most of the time-consuming work if consulting firms are used. In some situations, the client is not eager to be counseled by the HR staff because of their continuing relationship to management.

8. A formal outplacement program provides tracking of the individual's progress. Although the sponsor may not get all the details, they will know if the client is actively pursuing a job search and generally how well it is going. A vehicle is in place for monitoring without intruding and for providing additional help if needed.

The client realizes the following benefits:

1. Professional, experienced, and objective support is available whenever needed as the client goes through the unfamiliar experience of looking for work while unemployed. In its simplest form, there is someone to talk to. Beyond that basic fact, the consultant should know how to help the client with the ups and downs of the search and provide solid reality testing at each stage of the process.

2. The client develops an understanding of what went wrong at the former employer. The consultant is in a position to tell the truth in a way the former management may not have felt comfortable doing. Since the usual reasons for performance-based terminations are stylistic rather than intellectual, the style problems become evident in the way the client goes about job hunting and thereby they become topics for conversation between consultant and client. These data can be used not only to refocus the techniques of the job search but also can affect the choice of career, the choice of next employer, and the on-the-job behavior of the person when he or she gets that next job.

3. Most managers and professionals never really learn how to manage their careers or find new jobs. The usual pattern has been a passive one: the company took care of it, or a recruiter found me, or things "just happened." The client may

not even want to learn the skills to self-manage a career. The outplacement consultant can provide these skills and can teach them if the person does wish to learn them.

4. Even with greater confidence, crystallized goals, and better insights into one's self, the job hunt process can be threatening to the strongest ego. The consultant will be there to slow down the flailers, energize the procrastinators, lift up the depressives, and redirect the many people who get stuck in a rut. This leads to a smoother, more comfortable, and generally more effective job search.

5. Outplacement provides a base of operations for someone who has just lost the use of his or her usual base. For those who do not retain their offices at the former employer, there is a place to go, to leave things and get things, to be with people. For the more fortunate who do retain their former office, there is a place where it is "safe" to talk about being unemployed and where messages and correspondence can be handled without awkwardness.

6. Resources will be available to help with the job search. Among these resources are data bases, reference libraries, videotape equipment for interview training, word processing systems, and some amount of referral help for networking.

7. Spouse counseling can be a central issue for perhaps 15 percent of clients. The situations that tend to call for this service are those involving geographic relocations, two-career families, radical career path shifts, and clients with prolonged, difficult job searches leading to a heavy stress burden.

8. Some clients continue their discussions with their consultants in the first few weeks or months on the new job. The issues brought up during the search now take on new meaning. What had been material for the employment interview now becomes relevant to making the most of the new job. (In some situations, if the new job does not work out, the client returns to the outplacement firm to continue the search.)

Costs and Risks

As with any other consulting service, there are costs and risks to consider. The obvious cost is the fee charged by the consulting firm. The industry standard is 15 percent of the client's total annual compensa-

tion, which may include the client's bonus, and there may be an administration charge in the $500 to $1,000 range. Most firms have minimum and/or maximum fees. For large projects there may be some downward adjustment in the fee. Some firms absorb and others charge to the sponsor the costs of long distance telephone calls made by the client.

These fees are billed to the sponsor shortly after the work with the client begins. In effect, there is a one-time fixed price for a service that may prove to be very easy, typically difficult, or impossibly draining on the consultant. The risk, in this sense, remains with the consulting firm.

From the sponsor's point of view, there are risks at both ends of the difficulty continuum. If the case proves to be rather easy—the client gets a new job in a few weeks—then the sponsor may feel that the consultant did not really earn the fee. There may even be difficulty explaining to higher management why a fee of perhaps $8,000 or so was paid for only a few weeks work involving four or five counseling sessions.

At the other end of the continuum, if a client's job search extends toward or even beyond twelve months, which is not all that rare, the sponsor may wonder what good the consultant is doing. The risk here is that the money will have been paid and no result appears forthcoming.

The answer is that some risks are inherent—no one knows on day 1 how long the search will take, or how much effort will be required from the consultant—and the responsibility for finding the job truly rests with the client, not the consultant. When it is all over, the client is supposed to feel "I did it myself."

From the consultant's point of view, the hard cases and the easy cases average out over time. Explaining this to managers and HR directors who are unfamiliar with outplacement is not always easy.

There are several risks that should be monitored closely. One is the risk of drifting. Consultants get busy with whatever is crying for attention and find it hard to give time to cases that are quiet. But a case that remains quiet for too long can mean real trouble—a client who is not putting energy into his or her search. An experienced sponsoring company stays on top of its vendor firms to make sure they do not let clients drift.

Inappropriate job search campaigns represent another type of risk. For example a thirty-six-year-old accounts payable manager decides he wants to be a chief financial officer and convinces the outplacement consultant to support such a campaign. Five months later, there is no tangible progress despite enormous effort networking, mailing, and researching.

Company Policies

In theory, every organization should have an explicit policy regarding its use of outplacement services. In practice, most companies do not. Their use of outplacement is governed by the needs of the moment, the precedents of their own prior use of outplacement, or the practices of other companies. This approach gives a company a lot more flexibility, of course, but may get it into trouble if its practices are not equitable and explainable.

The key issue here is: Which employees are eligible for which types of outplacement, under which circumstances? Is there to be full outplacement for officers only? for people over age forty? for people with ten or more years tenure? Should outplacement be given to people who are released for poor performance or just to those who are caught in downsizings and reorganizations? Should some people get group outplacement programs, while others get the individualized version? These and similar questions can be answered in advance with policy statements, there may be general guidelines, or each case can be decided when it comes up, perhaps with help from the outplacement consultant.

A second topic that deserves some policy-level thought is the matter of who within the company has the authority to decide about outplacement matters. Some corporations keep this option at the headquarters level for reasons of professional control, cost control, or other purposes. Increasingly, authority for outplacement decisions has been pushed down to lower levels, such as local personnel managers. Each company should find its own answer to this question; there is no one right answer.

A related topic is the selection of outplacement firms as vendors to the company. How many should there be? How do we evaluate them? Are they all alike? Discussion of these questions will be picked up later. The relevant point here is that this is an issue that each sponsor should think about as a matter of policy.

A matter of policy consideration is the connection between outplacement and the larger set of arrangements involved in a termination. For example, some companies will not offer outplacement until the employee signs a release agreement agreeing to the termination and the entire severance package. Some companies will offer outplacement in conjunction with voluntary termination, early retirements, returns from disability leave, and so on.

A practice that is particularly distasteful to outplacement firms is offering the departing employee a reduced amount of severance if he or she also elects to use the outplacement services. This is essentially the same as asking the employee to pay for the outplacement. Most professional outplacement firms will not accept an assignment under these conditions.

Some sponsors allow a client to visit two or more firms to make a decision on their own, based on comfort and fit. The HR directors who work with this policy claim that it is better than assigning a client to a firm because it leads to a better match and a sense of buying in. Outplacement firms do not like this practice usually, since it places a decision burden on an unsophisticated buyer at a time when he or she is very vulnerable to sales pitches and overpromising.

TERMINATION GUIDELINES

Most bosses enter a termination meeting with a great deal of apprehension. While it may not be possible to eliminate the trauma connected with a termination, it can be held to a minimum by avoiding major mistakes through adequate preparation and proper communication with the person being terminated. The following guidelines may be helpful to an executive who needs to terminate an employee:

1. *Planning.* Whenever possible, HR is involved in the pretermination phase. Obvious advantages accrue, ranging from an audit of the separation reasoning to policy application, a review of options, alerting the outplacement firm if appropriate, and preparation of the severance and benefit entitlement.

The exit statement should be prepared if the departure is to be made public, and the logistics of the termination day should be reviewed, including communication with the appropriate remaining employees, and availability of the HR director to clarify the severance terms, if necessary.

2. *Timing.* Terminations should not take place on Friday afternoon, very late on any day, or just before a holiday. Early in the week is preferred in order to provide the individual with several days of immediate outplacement counseling support and/or dialogue with corporate HR. Without this precaution, the weekend can produce emotional reactions that can be overwhelming and a "support system" that can be misguided.

3. *Place.* Although there are many options in this area, the most usual practice is in the employee's office. This allows the boss to leave when appropriate and the terminated person a quiet place to be for a while. A bar or restaurant is not an option. At certain times, it may be advisable for a third person, perhaps from HR, to be present during the termination meeting. This can be helpful in explaining the severance and outplacement package. In sensitive cases when a severe reaction is expected or where third-party testimony will likely be needed, a third person is essential.

4. *Length.* Almost all termination meetings should be short and to the point, ideally no longer than 10 minutes. The termination itself should occur within the first minute or two. The remainder of the time should be used to explain briefly the separation benefits and to allow the individual to express his or her feelings. The terminating manager should listen to whatever the individual wants to say and should try to answer any questions raised at that time. It is often appropriate for the boss and employee to set another time, perhaps the next day, to continue the conversation.

5. *Approach.* The best approach is a straightforward explanation, stating the reasons for termination. The reasons should not be debated, argued, or discussed in a manner that gives the individual hope for a reversal of the decision. The statement should indicate that the decision to terminate was made by the immediate boss, supported by management, and is irrevocable. No effort should be made to persuade the person that the action is justified. Naturally, this is no time for a detailed performance appraisal.

Above all, avoid statements like, "I know how you feel" or "You will find this a blessing in disguise." Termination is never a positive experience and cannot be made so. Of equal importance, avoid statements such as, "I don't want to do this, but . . ." The decision to terminate was made with your concurrence, so you need to take this action and the affected employee must know that.

If possible, emphasize the job rather than the person. "Due to budget cuts, your position is being eliminated" is better than "Due to budget cuts, we have to let you go." This is a business event more than a personal event. If the decision is really due to poor performance, the termination discussion will be a short one following many long hours of earlier counseling discussions.

6. *Benefits.* The written statement of salary continuation, benefits continuation, and other terms and conditions should be handed to the individual after the highlights are verbally described. Even the clearest communication will not fully penetrate at this time, so the written memo can be reviewed by the terminee later. It may even include such details as office arrangements, secretarial support, credit cards, company cars, club membership, benefits, and outplacement support.

7. *Other issues:*

- Never terminate an employee over the telephone.

- Have telephone numbers available for medical or security emergencies.

- Do not tell the individual how to spend the rest of the day. Allow the flexibility for reactions and emotions, yet maintain a business atmosphere.

- Be sure the individual understands early in the discussion that he or she has been terminated and that no other options are possible. Be firm. However, there is no need to be so abrupt or harsh that the individual is unnecessarily jolted.

- Termination is a challenging management act. The key word is *management,* which requires planning and keeping things relatively simple. It is not a time to change your management style or personality. Follow your instincts, being mindful of the basic guidelines and rules.

- However difficult this meeting may be for you, it is tougher for him or her. Do not get onto the topic of your needs, feelings, or problems. You can always get together again later to discuss your friendship or other issues.

PROVIDING INDIVIDUAL OUTPLACEMENT SERVICES

Facilities, Resources, and Services

What should you expect an outplacement firm (or an internal outplacement unit) to make available to terminated executives? The primary service is very good counsel from very good consultants. Backing that up

there should be a facility with resources and services appropriate to the tasks at hand.

The offices themselves should be comfortable, functional, and well appointed. In practice, this means that the offices should appear to be a reasonable continuation of the kind of offices that the company provides to its employees. The big difference is that usually the client will not be given a dedicated private office at the outplacement firm. There may be a private office that can be used as needed. If you wish the client to have a private or semiprivate office, you may need to select an outplacement firm that offers an upgraded senior executive service.

Most clients find that they can operate quite effectively from a library-type carrel or from desk space in whichever office is available when they happen to come in. Initially some clients resist working out of anything except a private office. Much of the resistance really has more to do with being uncomfortable with their unemployed status than it does with functional work arrangements.

The location of the facility can be important. Most clients want their outplacement firm to be near their home, their former office, or their primary job hunt area. Wherever the location, commuter access and/or parking are important.

Telephones are central to job searches. The firm should have lots of them and enough trunk lines to avoid busy signals. Message services are always required. The one variable in regard to telephones has to do with who pays for the long distance calls. Some firms will absorb this charge, while others expect the client to use a credit card or the firm will bill the sponsor. Telex and/or FAX equipment is not generally needed but can be helpful.

Job searches generate a great deal of paper. The firm should be prepared to provide printed resumes, personalized stationery, and the cover letters and correspondence that go with a search. It is true that very few executives will get new jobs through mass mailings, but it is also true that no one wants to have problems getting out whatever mailings seem appropriate.

Reference materials, data bases, and mailing lists are important resources. They are never large enough and certainly never current or detailed enough, but they help. Some firms rely heavily on this resource, while others have them available. Information overload does not help, but neither does a shortage.

Every outplacement firm is also in the hospitality business, whether it knows it or not. Creating an "at-home" feeling can make all the difference in the world to the spirit, attitude, and energy level of the clients. This includes a warm decor, refreshments, a lounge area, newspapers, office supplies and services, and, most important, a friendly "Good morning!"

Planning the Reemployment Campaign

For some people, the intelligent reemployment campaign is perfectly obvious. These are the people who want to recreate the position, career, life-style, and work environment they have just lost. The work of the consultant during this stage is merely to help such clients confirm that this is really what they want and then move directly to the implementation phase.

If all outplacement clients wanted to recreate their former worlds, the consultant would have very little counseling to do. The real world of outplacement practice is very different, however, especially for executives, professionals, and managers (and even among clerical and blue-collar workers, to a surprisingly large degree).

The more typical situation involves a person who wants to or really needs to renavigate the course of his or her life. The reasons for this may be:

1. The termination was caused, at least partly, by a degree of misfit between the person and the work or working situation, and there is a need to avoid repeating this problem.

2. There is essentially no chance for the person to find similar employment.

3. The client has never done any intensive career planning or self-assessment and wants to use this opportunity to do so.

4. The client is tired of the former kind of work, or feels plateaued, or is curious if he or she would be hired into another career area.

5. If the outplacement occurs when the client is fifty-five or older, considerations having to do with the retirement years become relevant.

6. The client's family situation may be rather different than it was the last time any career planning was done; there may be a working spouse, an empty nest, or even a divorce or second marriage.

These are very real possibilities. Because they happen so often, the consultant cannot automatically assume that the only need is for the client to recreate the former situation. The initial discussions explore these needs and give the consultant information on which to base a reemployment campaign.

The skills and experiences needed by the consultant at this point are a catalog of all the things someone needs in order to help someone else. A partial list would include understanding of adult life stages, corporate career paths, organizational politics, depression, burnout, anxiety reactions, marital dynamics, entrepreneurial options, and methods for surfacing the values, interests, and personality characteristics of a wide variety of clients. Since a discussion of all this would require a library of books, the following is a very brief outline of the kinds of activities that go on before a client enters the market.

1. An evaluation is made of the impact of the termination on the client. Some are relieved and optimistic, others are sad but ready to move on, and still others—and these are the ones who need the greatest amount of help—are confused, frightened, emotionally in turmoil, and in no shape to look for a job until they work through these feelings.

2. Areas of special concern to the client need to be clarified and dealt with. For example, has he told his family and friends? Is there a health problem? Has the client started talking with a lawyer? Did the termination coincide with a family problem or major financial decision?

3. Does the client feel that he or she knows what to do next? Is there some familiarity with the career planning and job search processes, or are we dealing with the more typical "I've never gone through this before" reactions?

4. Does the client want a job, a position, a career, a life-style, or a "deal"? The client will not be able to answer a direct question on this topic, but it is an important one. The client who needs a job because of financial pressures will have to be counseled very differently from the one who wants to make his fortune through an LBO or some other equity deal.

5. Unemployed job searchers have an understandable tendency to want to keep their options open, sometimes so wide open that they appear to be looking for whatever might be available. Some clients want to spend the first month or two just finding out what jobs are out there. These strategies tend to be counterproductive. They need to be replaced with a more focused strategy, which will allow the client to be in control of his or her actions and will allow him or her to take the initiative.

6. An integrated story needs to be developed. The reasons that the person left the last job need to be logically related to why he or she wants this next job. The resume, cover letters, employer references, career goals, and self-assessment all need to point in the same direction. This story has to be realistic, true, and believable. It has to add up to something that the client can feel good about, something that is supported by the facts and references. Getting this complex equation to balance is sometimes very difficult.

7. Materials need to be prepared, based on the discussion of a desired next job. Writing the resume is done jointly by consultant and client. There is also a need for at least one version of a cover letter and clearly understood statements as to why the person left the last job, what he or she is looking for, what kind of person he or she is, and all the other questions likely to be asked by an interviewer.

8. In a sense, all the previous steps described are summarized in the client's "plans." These plans will have timetables, contingency plans, criteria for making decisions about alternative career objectives, and checkpoints for evaluation of progress. For the person with limited severance and few financial resources, the plan will have to allow for new sources of income and reduced expenses and will have fewer opportunities for implementing lifetime dreams. The more fortunate people will have plenty of time to look for their next step in life, but plans still have to be prepared because nonfinancial reasons will come into play such as frustration, dead ends, and a concern that a long period between positions will hurt their reputation.

This list is not comprehensive, but it is representative of what could happen with a typical assignment. Not included in the list are the mechanical steps such as assigning a backup consultant, showing the person around the outplacement firm's offices, explaining how to use the firm's workbooks, ordering personalized stationery, and so on.

Total time for this premarket phase can vary from a week to several months, usually averaging two or three weeks. Often a preliminary resume will be prepared, perhaps within the first day or two, so that no momentum will be lost. Many clients are eager to get going on day 1 with real interviews, and they perhaps should not be totally dissuaded from doing so, but in almost every situation the client is better served by a thorough preparation for these meetings. There is much damage that can be done by allowing the client to blow his or her best contacts with disorganized interviews that could have waited a week or two.

Implementing the Reemployment Campaign

Implementing a job search campaign is primarily a process of working your way from who you know to who you would like to know. It is not a process of letting your availability be known and then waiting for someone with a job opening to find you. The higher your level in the organizational world, the truer this becomes.

The process begins with the results of the preparation phase, perhaps in the form of a list of probable next employers and the rationale for why the client should be working for them. A second step is to make a list of all the potentially relevant people the client knows. Then the task is to figure out how to get to the people on the target list through a network that begins with the list of contacts.

As obvious as this seems, a great many clients resist doing the networking. They will hide, have things to do at home or for the former employer, go on vacation, or find other excuses rather than pick up the phone and call an acquaintance to ask for some help. A significant part of the consultant's work is in helping the client to overcome these resistances.

There is a legion of books on how to find a new job. Some of them are directed to particular age groups, genders, industries, or geographies. Some of them are good books. Consultants may ask a client to read parts of one or another because of a good list of suggestions, sources, or techniques. But they are books, and they cannot do what a well-trained consultant can do. Specifically, they cannot see what the client is doing wrong, or not doing, and confront the person on that issue.

As the search campaign progresses, the client gets feedback from the people he or she is dealing with. The most obvious kind of feedback is the degree of success in getting the interviews required to meet the job search plan. If the targeted companies are not interested or will not grant second interviews, then something is wrong either with the plan or with the techniques being used. This is important feedback, and analyzing it can consume a lot of time.

The client must remain primarily responsible for the letter writing, telephoning, interviewing, and negotiating. The consultant is responsible for evaluating, supporting, monitoring, advising, and giving encouragement when needed. Even when the consultant and client disagree on strategy or on tactics, the consultant must remember that it is the client's life that is at stake and the client has to remain responsible for it and for the job search.

The issue of responsibility is a slippery one for some clients. Many of them have never been asked to be so responsible for their lives; the corporation did it for them, in return for their loyalty and effort. Dependency needs frequently surface and intrude into the relationship.

As a source of reality, the consultant takes two routes. One is to give opinions to the client as to what kind of job search is likely to be successful. The other is to help the client review the results of his or her search efforts from time to time. The choice between these routes is based on the amount of data available from the job search and on the clarity of the consultant's views. Clients who bring a great deal of dependency to the relationship will expect more from their "expert" consultant, while clients with greater initiative will look more directly at the results of their own efforts.

As a source of support, some clients will need a good deal more from their consultant than will others. Most clients, however, will need a time to talk things over, several times a week at first and then less often as the search progresses. There will be times for venting, for celebrating, for brainstorming, and for replanning. These needs will wax and wane during the course of the search.

The average search lasts about five months. The factors that determine this length of time are almost too numerous to list but include age, industry, time of year, skill at interviewing, reputation, salary level, energy level, general appearance, size of network, and flexibility. People who are looking to get a promotion have a harder search than those who wish to replace their lost jobs. People who want to or need to leave their industries also have a longer search. The familiar myth about one-month-per-$10,000 simply does not work very well in reality.

The range for a job search will be from a couple of weeks up to eighteen months or more. The people who take more than six months require additional care, if only to make sure they are not doing something counterproductive.

An outplacement consultant cannot change any of the realities about a person. The consultant's role is to help the client make the most of whatever he or she has, not to create out of thin air what the client would like to have. Life is often not fair, rational, or legal, especially in the job market.

Traditionally, most outplacement clients have come from larger corporations. About 60 percent also find jobs in such organizations. The other clients either do not want to or find that they cannot get jobs in big companies, so they seek out the smaller ones or enter into entrepreneurial ventures. This trend reflects the fact that almost all of the growth in America's labor market occurs in the small companies; big ones seem designed more for efficiency than for growth in head count, at least during recent years.

A comment is in order regarding search firms, newspaper ads, and cold letter direct mail campaigns to corporations. These techniques are part of most searches, but represent perhaps 15 to 20 percent of the success stories. The vast majority of managers, executives, and professionals find their jobs through networking. (The value of networking is less for clerical and blue-collar clients but still is a very significant factor at that level too.)

The daily routine of consultant and client during the implementation phase consists of reviewing the tactics of approaching a particular person or company, rehearsing what will be said, debriefing on what was said, and brainstorming ways to develop additional leads. Periodically there will be reviews of trends, reality checks, and possibly an adjustment in the search campaign.

Points for Crisis Intervention

The most likely time for a crisis situation is right at or just after the client has been terminated. Perhaps 20 percent of the clients have a visibly difficult time with the termination. The reaction can be one of anger or depression, or it can be more severe and appear as rage, total withdrawal, or massive denial.

Of those who have strong reactions, most will recover within 1 to 3 hours, at least to the point where they can deal somewhat productively with the real world. Relatively few will need medical or psychiatric attention on an emergency basis, although it is not a bad idea for the terminating manager to have access to such help if needed.

During this critical period, the client should not be pressed to hear things or do things that he or she does not seem ready to deal with. It may take some time for the person to adjust to this new fact of life before going on to deal with other matters. He or she should not be left alone unless that is his or her strong preference.

Dealing with a sense of failure is also a potential crisis time for clients. Even in large downsizings, some clients will come away with a feeling of failure—failure to survive, failure to perform well enough on the job, or failure to establish personal loyalties. (The bald fact is that companies do use the opportunity of large downsizings to terminate the poorer performers, less likable people, or employees with less promotion potential.) People who have clearly been asked to leave a company because of performance problems should be wrestling with the failure issue.

The human mind has great powers of defense. It is a matter of consultant judgment as to whether to support or challenge the client's rationalizations and denials. The client who truly was caught in a bad situation can become immobile over needless guilt, and this person should be helped to appreciate the true situation. On the other hand, the client who refuses to see obvious data, and is likely to repeat inappropriate behavior, should be challenged when he or she defends against the facts.

A related type of emotional crisis can occur as the client gets well into the search campaign: dealing with the failure of the marketplace to encourage and accept his or her efforts. Job hunting is a process of self-exposure and rejection; it is usually ego devaluing. Fifty contacts may be needed to get ten leads, which generate three interviews, which result in maybe only one second interview. That is a rough dose of rejection even for the strongest egos. Those among us who are less robust can find it overwhelming. At best, job hunting at middle age is something we are all glad to have out of the way and do not want to do again.

Finally, the stress of termination and job search may be combined with an already shaky life space to create a crisis. Among outplacement clients will be a fair share of the alcoholics, other substance abusers, rape victims, asthmatics, epileptics, cancer victims, auto accident victims, and others already suffering from a disability or trauma. Also, terminations may coincide with divorces, deaths in the family, financial reverses, or even major financial investments, combining to cause undue levels of stress.

The symptoms and management of stress reactions are quite another topic. It will be sufficient at this point to note that the outplacement consultant should be alert to the typical symptoms (digestive and sleep disturbances, body aches, irritability, mild depression, free floating anxiety) and also watchful for the more severe ones (suicidal thoughts, cardiovascular difficulty, ulcers, impotence, intense withdrawal patterns). Referral agencies and professionals should be known and used when appropriate.

Psychological Assessment

Outplacement counseling is a disciplined art form; it is neither a science nor a lockstep regimen. Psychological tests are an aid to the consultant as he or she practices that art form. They are tools and can make a real contribution when used for good reason by someone who knows how to use them well. They can be useless or even disruptive when used mechanically or inappropriately.

Generally testing is indicated for these clients:

1. Clients who must change career directions because of adverse labor market conditions.

2. Clients who were terminated from their previous positions because of difficulties in the areas of management style, interpersonal competence or personal motivation.

3. Clients who are experiencing serious stress due to either the manner and/or circumstances of the termination or the stresses of the job search itself.

4. Clients who request testing because they want to use this opportunity to learn as much as possible about themselves.

5. Clients who appear to have long-standing emo-

tional adjustment difficulties, if the consultant needs this information in order to make a decision about a clinical referral.

Situations where testing is not generally recommended are:

1. Older clients—seldom with people over age forty-five, almost never with people over age fifty-five, since these people are not as likely to consider seriously changes in career direction or interpersonal style.
2. Clients who do not want to take tests.
3. Clients with histories of mental health problems or extensive therapy.
4. Clients for whom English is a second language.

The primary purposes for testing are to get to know the client better and to provide a means for feedback to the client to improve his or her self-knowledge. This means that in every case the consultant provides feedback and explanation of the test scores to the client. There may or may not be a written report; if so, it would be given only to the client.

Some firms make regular use of one or a few instruments with virtually every client. Commonly used tests are a vocational interest inventory and a Jungian styles survey. The main advantage of this practice is that every consultant in the firm becomes familiar with the tests.

Other firms have psychologists who administer and interpret a battery of tests. The psychologist may be a full-time employee, on retainer, or an outside service. Few firms go to the trouble of training all of their consultants to interpret a full battery of tests.

In situations where a battery of tests is available, it is important that discretion be used as to which tests to include. Administering a 6-hour battery to every client is certainly not called for.

As in any other setting where testing is employed, the tests should be selected and used to help answer questions that are relevant to the consulting task. Further, tests should not be used unless by people who are trained to use them. For these reasons, "clinical" testing is not part of the process; tests such as the Minnesota Multiphasic Personality Inventory (MMPI), Thematic Apperception Test, or other projectives are seldom involved, with the exception of a sentence completion instrument. The data developed by these tests are not generally part of the outplacement discussion, and the consultants are not usually trained in their use.

Ability tests are sometimes included, such as verbal and quantitative skills, or critical thinking. Practical experience suggests that they are useful in about 10 percent of counseling situations, usually with younger clients. For the most part, clients have track records and academic records that adequately testify to their intellectual skills, making the use of cognitive power tests rather redundant. (In a very few instances, it can be helpful to show someone that his or her extremely high scores on these tests are part of a problem of boredom or of a pattern of intellectual domineering over subordinates and peers.)

Interest inventories can be very helpful for a client who is considering a career shift or is trying to understand why he or she has not been getting much satisfaction from working life. The Strong-Campbell and Holland tests seem to be most popular for this purpose, and the 16PF is sometimes used in this way. Clients with concerns in this area seem eager for the feedback and value the computer-generated reports.

"Personality" testing is more difficult and more likely to engage the client in sensitive discussions. There are hundreds of tests available for this purpose, without counting the clinically oriented projective tests or the tests specifically intended to diagnose pathology. The challenge here is to identify and use tests that will be effective for the purposes at hand, in the hands of the people on the outplacement firm's staff. The risk of parlor-game psychologizing exists, even when the testing is done by a psychologist or under the general supervision of one.

Frequently used tests for assessing personality are the 16PF, California Psychological Inventory, Guildford-Zimmerman Temperament Survey, Edwards Personal Preference Survey, and the Shostrom Personal Orientation Inventory.

A fourth category of instruments is in the interpersonal style and skills area. Included here are the various tests of supervisory skill and style, such as the Leadership Opinion Questionnaire, and tests of salesmanship. Also in this category are the styles tests, such as the Myers-Briggs Type Indicator, which tap into global behavior patterns.

There is no simple answer to the question about the level of competence required to administer and effectively use these tests. Some firms limit their use to licensed psychologists, but that person seldom has much more to do with the client after the feedback session. Firms that have the consultants do the interpretations run the risk of having either untrained people making incorrect statements or of limiting their tests to the one to three instruments that are used with every client.

Assuming that reliable tests are being used and that administration conditions are satisfactory, the question of validity arises. The answer here is that the validity of the tests is limited primarily by the skill, insight, and experience of the person interpreting them and applying them to the ongoing consulting process. The validity is in the tester, not in the tests. Not a single one of these tests has a published norm for people going through the outplacement process.

When used skillfully, the tests can bring out data that can have a great deal of impact. This tends to be much truer when the consultant has narrowed the questions to be asked of the data. When used as part of a fishing expedition, just to see what might surface out of the testing, the psychometrics tend to be a curiosity at best and an intrusion or waste of time.

Because of the expense and time associated with testing, some firms are moving toward using only computer-generated reports.

Marital Issues

About 15 percent of the male clients will want to bring their wives in to the outplacement firm for one or more meetings. This option is open to all clients, of course, but is not of interest to many of them.

Wives can have a major influence on the course of events during outplacement. It is not uncommon for them to feel (and to express) considerably more anger than their husbands at the former employer because of the termination. This is especially true for the wives of long-tenure managers and for those who have relocated or otherwise incurred sacrifices on behalf of the former employer. It is true that while he was working there, the wife was considered a member of the company family; it is equally true that virtually no company will consider including her in the termination discussions. She is simply told by her husband when he comes home after the termination meeting. These problems are heightened if her social network consists largely of other company wives, a group from which she is now largely excluded.

During the months of outplacement the husband will be almost totally preoccupied by the job search. He will usually want his wife to listen to his thoughts, worries, and frustrations, perhaps to the point of a discussion every evening. This pattern can become extremely burdensome for a wife, no matter how interested she may be in the result.

A supportive wife will seek ways to help, without much success. There really are not many tangible things she can do to help; she does not have any job leads for him, nor can she make calls for him. A useful discussion with the wife can be around the issue of how she can be emotionally helpful.

Wives can feel threatened in a number of ways.

Some are concerned that the family's larger interests will be traded off in favor of the husband's career (e.g., a move to an undesirable location). Some are concerned that the family's standard of living will be seriously affected. The dynamics in a two-career family are especially complex.

The importance of job loss to a traditional husband can be quite great. Without his job is he still really a "man"? Can he ask his wife to cut costs because of his inability to earn a living? How will he react to the possibility of his wife having to get a job? If she has a good job, how will he react to the role of being a secondary wage earner or actually being supported by his wife?

Given the likelihood of these problems, it is not surprising that a prolonged job search may lead to withdrawal and distancing between husband and wife exactly at the time when they need to be closest. He does not know how to ask for her help, she does not know how to help, and both feel vulnerable. The opportunity for the consultant to work at least somewhat with the wife should be exploited to the fullest in these situations. The most serious problems should be considered for referral.

Female clients almost never bring in their husbands, although the same option is offered to them. Increasingly, a large number of these women are single. Among the married ones, most are secondary wage earners.

Women in Outplacement

The topic of women in outplacement needs a great deal of research and a book-length treatment in its own right. The points listed below are a sampling of anecdotal findings.

The number of women in outplacement has been growing steadily as women represent a greater factor in the managerial and professional work force. In the New York area they represent about 25 percent of the clients, but this number is smaller elsewhere (in Australia, they are hardly represented at all yet, for example). They tend to be younger than the men by about five years, and they more often are single.

Counseling with women often involves a wider range of topics than with the men. Women are frequently dealing with more of their total life space as they consider what to do next with their careers. Specifically, women who are in their thirties may need to give serious consideration to family planning or to the resources available for help in caring for their children.

A particularly knotty problem for many women is networking. Despite major advances in the "old girl network," most of the power in this society still rests within the old *boy* network. Many women are unskilled or uncomfortable calling on men for help, especially men they do not know well or at all.

Men in business generally dress in a rather standard fashion. Women, however, have a greater degree of flexibility, and much greater attention needs to be given to this matter by them. Unfortunately, how a woman looks is of much greater importance during the employment process than how a man looks, to the point that some women are effectively blocked from certain opportunities strictly on the basis of their appearance.

Most outplacement consultants are men, which means that a large number of women clients will receive their consulting from a man. The ability of a male consultant to work effectively with women cannot be accurately gauged from his ability to work with male clients. By virtue of their professional training and their life experiences, some men are better able to bond with women clients than are others. Two aspects of the consulting relationship seem to serve as benchmarks for a male consultant's skill with women clients: emotional support during the "down" phases and the ability to help her with the male networking process.

Financial Issues

Frank discussion of financial issues is necessary during the preparation phase to determine staying power and the priority given to the financial aspects of the desired next job. Most executives, managers, and professionals have a fairly good idea of their status and needs in this area, and most have access to accountants if needed.

The financial side of outplacement arises as an important topic for clients whose searches significantly exceed their severance arrangements, and for clients seeking an entrepreneurial career.

The outplacement consultant is well advised to avoid becoming the client's major source of guidance on finances. The consultant needs to be aware of the client's circumstances and how the money issue affects the job search but should not get into complex budget or tax discussions.

The client who is running out of money before obtaining a new job should have a contingency plan for bringing some money in. This may take the form of consulting, part-time work, sale of assets, a working spouse, or a full-time but temporary job. These options need to be discussed well in advance.

The client who is looking to go into consulting as a career or to start or buy a small business will need

detailed budget planning. This is more legitimately the domain of the outplacement consultant or a specialist on that topic within the consulting firm. The client also must have a relationship with a lawyer or accountant who will stay with him or her once the outplacement is finished.

All clients should have had thorough discussions with the benefits or employee relations representative from their former employer. This cannot happen in the first day or two following termination but should happen within the first week or so. Matters such as insurance conversion, savings plans, stock options, lump sum payouts, tax-deferred retirement plans, company car, and use of credit cards need to be discussed when they can be understood.

Potentially the most emotional financial issue is applying for and collecting unemployment compensation. For many managers, this means having hit the bottom of the dignity pit. Some people simply will not go through the steps required by the state.

Legal Issues

Legal issues arise in the outplacement relationship primarily around the departure of the client from the sponsoring company. The frequency of these situations is not great—perhaps one person in twenty or twenty-five—partly because some of the litigation-prone people do not want anything to do with the outplacement firm since it is legally an agent of the company.

It is every American's right to sue a former employer if he or she feels a wrong has been committed. It is also well known that many people institute suits as much out of anger as out of legal merit; it is their way of getting even, so to speak. Terminations have often been described as analogous to divorces, and there is some truth to that when it comes to how the anger is expressed.

Outplacement is in part designed to redirect the feelings of the client away from the past and toward the future, and this really does happen. Along the way, however, some clients will talk about suing the company and seek the consultant's advice. The standard answer to this question has two components: "yes, you can sue," and "please be very sure it is what you want to do because there are real costs in terms of dollars, time, energy, and risk to references."

In the event a suit does begin, the client's lawyer will probably tell the client to stop seeing the outplacement firm. If that does not happen, there is no reason to stop or modify the outplacement program.

Any and all records, notes, and files held by the outplacement firm may be subpoenaed. I am not not aware of any state that provides a defense against producing the files based on professional confidentiality or other reasons.

The difficult ethical question is whether the outplacement firm should tell the sponsoring company about the client's plans. The client clearly expects confidentiality, and the sponsor expects a little cooperation on this critically important matter. The firm can get caught between them. When asked what they would do in such situations, firms usually say they will hold confidence with the client.

Suits brought under the ADEA, EEO, or termination-at-will laws seldom actually go to court. Nonetheless, an outplacement firm can find itself involved with lawyers and depositions and time-consuming, awkward meetings as the two sides jockey for position before settling out of court. The plaintiff's lawyer may want to know what the company "really" said was the reason for the termination. The defense lawyer wants to document the significant amount of help given to the client by the company and the limited degree to which the client made efforts to find new employment and thereby contain the damage done to him or her. The whole thing becomes as sensible as a messy divorce, at least from the outplacement firm's perspective.

A reasonable practice for an outplacement firm is to strip the files on completed assignments about a year following the end of work with the client.

At the other end of the outplacement process, a few clients at the higher organizational levels may find a discussion of employment contracts useful. Referral to an independent lawyer is the only reasonable alternative for the consultant.

Apart from the legal matters that would be connected with any kind of small service business, the only important legal issue not included in this discussion is professional liability. This topic is raised among outplacement firm owners from time to time, and a few in fact buy insurance for this risk. I am not aware of any outplacement firm that has been sued by a client, however.

Medical and Psychotherapy Issues

In the previous discussion on crisis intervention, there is a short listing of the kinds of personal problems a client may have to deal with during the outplacement. Some are caused by the termination or job search, and some are chronic or at least continuing problems for the person, which may be intensified by the stresses of being out of work.

What has not been discussed is what the consultant is supposed to do about these problems or even if the consultant is supposed to do anything at all. To make that decision we need a criterion or at least a rule-of-thumb guideline.

One criterion that has proved reasonably workable is whether the personal problem interferes significantly with the process of getting a new job. A second criterion is whether the job search stresses will be so great as to be damaging to the client. If the answers to these questions are "no," then we proceed with the outplacement. Our thinking is that no matter what the person's problems are, they are worse if he or she does not have a job, an income, insurance, and a place in the community of employed professionals. Therefore, if at all possible, we should try to help the person find new employment first and then let him or her get help for the other problems afterward.

Certain illnesses must be given attention prior to continuing with outplacement. Prominent among these is active substance abuse. Clients with addictions represent high risks during the outplacement in that they frequently undo the best efforts of the consultant and of themselves by not being in control of their actions, especially at times of stress, such as the night before a big interview.

Very severely depressed and acutely anxious clients also display behavior that is counterproductive for the purposes of outplacement. Weeks of work can be for naught if the client cannot relax and smile, at least a little, in front of a prospective employer. These clients can be helped by didactic and/or pharmacological means and should stay in treatment (in most cases) through the course of the outplacement.

People with cardiac and pulmonary difficulties should be under treatment as well, for reasons of their own health and to give them the best chances for reemployment.

Some states have laws protecting the disabled or handicapped from employment discrimination unless there is a job-related reason for not employing them. Even where this is the law, questions frequently come up from clients about whether to tell a prospective employer about a nonvisible disability, such as diabetes or epilepsy, or about medical problems with family dependents.

Mental health considerations are the most difficult to manage for the consultant. We like to think of outplacement as a process that not only helps heal the wounds of the termination but also positions the client for a happier, more constructive future life. Does this sound like therapy? No one knows quite where the line should be drawn. The two criteria mentioned above help make the distinction.

Outplacement consultants do not want to be

therapists, if for no other reason than it takes too much time. Also, we are not licensed to be therapists, we were not hired to do therapy, and—the most telling point—we do not know how.

In practice, the cross-section of America that we see does include many who are severely troubled or ill. In a few cases, we must have outside professional help before and while we do our kind of helping. In a larger number of cases, we strongly recommend that clients get outside help during the outplacement program. In some situations, we suggest to a person that he or she consider working on personal problems after getting another job.

It is wise for an outplacement firm to keep handy a list of medical emergency numbers, perhaps even an ambulance service, as well as the numbers for psychotherapists, social workers, cardiologists, and physicians and facilities that treat substance abuse.

UNDERSTANDING OUTPLACEMENT FIRMS

Outplacement is most frequently obtained from consulting firms. It will serve the buyer's interests to have some understanding of where these firms came from, the kinds of pressures they feel, and what to look for when selecting one. Outplacement had a beginning after World War II when the government attempted to help the large number of military officers it no longer needed to find jobs in the private sector. The notion of corporate-sponsored outplacement began about twenty-five years ago in New York and Chicago. By 1975 there were five or six firms in New York offering this service on a regular basis, with trained staff and relevant facilities, and a few more firms elsewhere in the country, including the West Coast. In 1987 there were, at best guess, about 300 outplacement firms in the United States sharing a $350 million revenue flow. (There also are firms in Canada, Europe and elsewhere.)

Many of these firms are quite small, as is common in the consulting world generally. Especially in cities other than the ten largest, firms of two to four professionals are often found.

The largest firm has billings in the $65 million range, and there are about a dozen firms with billings in excess of $7 million. These firms have offices in at least four or five locations and as many as forty or more in the cases of the larger firms.

The largest number of professionals in these firms are people with personnel backgrounds, either as recruiters or as human resources managers. A significant number of the professionals come from business backgrounds, especially marketing. A third cluster have behavioral science training, usually psychology but sometimes social work or other allied fields. Also counted among the professionals in the outplacement firms are ministers, teachers, trainers, and entrepreneurs.

There are no credentialing agencies for outplacement firms or professionals. The Association of Outplacement Consulting Firms, founded in the early 1980s, maintains a code of ethics, has certain membership requirements, and is developing measurable standards of competence and quality. (For further information, contact Jeanne O'Donnell, AOCF, 364 Parsippany Road, Parsippany, N.J. 07054, (201) 887-6667).

The best form of credential is the satisfied client. In this regard, it is easier to obtain the names of satisfied sponsoring companies from a firm since the names of individual clients are not likely to be given out.

The economics of an outplacement firm are important for a sophisticated buyer to understand. An outplacement firm has a relatively high and fixed overhead relative to other kinds of consultants, and at the same time it has less advance notice of revenue than other kinds of firms. Its services are hard to distinguish from those of competitors. The sponsoring companies have a rapidly increasing variety of vendors from which to choose. By the time a layoff or termination is public knowledge, the outplacement vendor has already been determined. Many companies regularly use multiple vendors. The key contact person in the human resources department in many companies seems to change every couple of years.

These facts lead to considerable marketing anxieties and a temptation to pay more attention to next week's new business than to the clients who started the process last week. Competent firms have found ways to manage this kind of anxiety. Signals that it is not being managed well are:

- Drifting on the part of clients who have been in the process a while but nobody at the firm quite knows what they are really doing.

- Consultants who get paid a commission on new business representing a major portion of their income.

- Deep discounts on fees.

- Promises being made by the firm that they clearly should not be making and probably cannot keep.

In the light of the above, how should a company select an outplacement vendor? Reputation, location, facilities, background of consultants, and quality and quantity of experience should play a part. The firm should be making a real effort to do the outplacement work in a professional way and not just be a commercial success. Is there staff development? Is there a peer review process within the firm? Does the firm provide timely, informative feedback to the sponsor? Does the firm modify its program to meet the needs of the clients? Are the consultants' caseloads kept within reasonable bounds?

People have been getting fired since God fired Adam from the Garden of Eden, and until the mid-twentieth century these people have been surviving without outplacement. Today corporations provide this service to departing employees because they know it does really help. But the fact remains that many people will get their next jobs in about the same way and in about the same time whether or not they have help from an outplacement consultant—many people, but not all. Some of the people—maybe 20 percent, maybe 50 percent—will find that their outplacement experience made all the difference in the world to them. There is no good way to tell which departing employees fit into which category. One useful way to select an outplacement firm, then, is to use the one that can reach the full range of the needs of its clients.

ROLE OF THE HUMAN RESOURCES DIRECTOR

The primary responsibility for implementing a smooth termination rests with the boss, the terminating manager. The primary responsibility for helping him or her do that rests with the HR director. The outplacement consultant is a resource available as needed.

Firing people is probably the most hated task managers ever face. They do it seldom; have little skill, training, or practice at it; and usually do it too quickly, too slowly, too late or just badly. If done badly enough, they can get the company in real trouble. Even if done only somewhat badly, they can create unnecessary pain and conflict.

The HR director must monitor the process starting from an early point to ensure that approved, legal, and humane methods are being used. The terminating manager has to know what to say, what to have in writing, what to demand and what to offer, and how to direct the terminated person toward the next steps in the process.

Once the decision has been made to release the employee, the HR director must also put together the package of services the company will make available. The outplacement service is one of these, as are severance, salary continuance, notice period, office space, and insurance coverage. The HR director will have brought all of these decisions together, including the selection of the outplacement firm and preliminary discussions with the consultant.

An immediate decision has to be made as to whether the consultant should be on site at the time of termination. Some sponsors always want it that way, others never do, and some make a decision in each situation.

During the course of outplacement, the HR director serves as the primary contact point for follow-up reports. These may be frequent at first and then perhaps once or twice a month, by telephone or in writing, as the director wishes.

The HR director plays a key role in several other aspects of the consultant's work:

1. Clarifying the company's version of the cause of the termination.
2. Coordinating the exit statement (what the public will learn) and the reference statement (what people will learn if they ask).
3. Facilitating a graceful exit from the company, which may mean anything from a glorious farewell party to helping to arrange for shipping of the client's personal possessions.
4. Making a decision, if available and if appropriate, to extend the severance period.
5. Arranging for the closing out of the benefits package, including insurance conversion, buying the company car, and return of company property.
6. Paying the outplacement firm's bill.

A sophisticated, organized, and compassionate HR director can make an enormous difference in how well a client starts on the job search. This task should be seen as one of the more important ones on the director's agenda, not as a nasty chore. There is some tendency recently, as companies become more familiar with outplacement, to push the liaison role down to lower levels within the HR department. This tendency often does not serve the interests of the company in the long run.

There are times when the HR director can be the direct provider of the outplacement service. The internal outplacement option has one very major benefit and several additional ones:

1. The major benefit is cost. Even if a full-time, professional staff is hired to do the work, the cost to the company will be no more than half what it would cost on the outside. If the HR director and staff do the outplacement work as an additional duty, there will be little out-of-pocket cost.

2. The client continues to go to the same building and can be reached at the same telephone number.

3. The internal people know the whole story behind the person and behind the termination.

There are quite a number of drawbacks to the use of internal outplacement: confidentiality, lack of specialized skills and facilities, not enough time to devote, limited knowledge of other industries, unprepared to handle the anger and other emotions, and others. A decision to create an internal outplacement capability must be made on many dimensions, not just cost.

Professional internal capabilities now exist within a few of the larger corporations. At times of significant layoffs, many other companies have built temporary capabilities. These programs tend to work best with employees at lower levels, such as associates in accounting firms. In many of these organizations, outside firms are used in conjunction with the internal capabilities.

EVALUATION

Evaluating the success of an outplacement assignment or of an outplacement firm is not easily done. With greater understanding of the process, however, it is possible to set reasonable expectations and define appropriate measures. This section presents some suggestions on these topics.

The Wrong Questions

The most frequently asked question by newcomers to the field of outplacement is: "How many of the people who use your firm's services get new jobs?" The answer is: virtually 100 percent, the exceptions being the few people who leave the labor market for retirement, school, or full-time parenting. This answer will be true for any outplacement firm and would be true even if those same people had not received outplacement help, so we must search for a better question.

Part of the evaluation problem is that it is close to impossible to find a control group. Theoretically, the only pure control group would be the same people leaving those same companies at the same time. A reasonable approximation would be for a company to offer outplacement to only a percentage, maybe half, of a large group of terminees, but that never happens either. Comparing the job hunt success of people from company X, which did offer outplacement, to the success of people from company Y, which did not provide the service, would be an interesting study, but the results would be tainted by the difference between the two companies and the differing characteristics of the terminating populations—assuming they entered the same job market at the same time.

Somewhat more useful measures of success are (1) how long it takes for the average client to find a job and (2) how the salary on the new job compares to the former salary? When averaged across many firms, cities, time periods, and types of clients, the answers to these questions are roughly (1) five months, and (2) about 50–60 percent obtain increases, about 30 percent hold even, and the balance take a cut, excluding those who do not return to work full time. These measures can serve as a basis for comparing two outplacement firms competing in the same city, if that is the purpose for the evaluation. But even these measures leave a lot out.

The Right Questions

Better questions will be phrased by going back to the stated objectives for the outplacement service.

As a consultative management service, the bottom line is whether the buyers are satisfied. How do the hr Directors feel about the service? Do they complain a lot and switch from vendor to vendor in a ceaseless search for need satisfaction? When they are satisfied, what is it about the firm's services that they look for and like? The items listed below seem to be the important ones, not necessarily in order of priority:

1. Flexibility and responsiveness to the unpredictable demands that emerge when terminations are implemented—delays, preferences for one kind of consultant or another, and others.

2. Ability to bond with the various kinds of people who are terminated, ranging from senior line

executives to sensitive artists to frightened salesmen to tough career women to backroom accountants.

3. An adequate understanding and appreciation of the industries, probable employers, and career paths that are important to the people leaving the company.

4. Sensitivity to the HR director's needs for information about the progress being made in terms of timeliness, confidentiality, and insight into the client's situation.

5. Competence in the less ordinary aspects of job searches, such as entrepreneurial ventures and consulting careers.

6. Competence in handling the range of personal problems and emotional reactions presented by the clients.

As a service intended to help individuals, the questions become focused on what the outplacement firm did that was helpful, important, or critical for a person that he or she could not have done without the service. The answers will vary widely if the outplacement firm did its work in a customized, tailored fashion. The administrative services (e.g., message taking, personalized stationery) are done for almost everyone but surely are not the pivotal forms of help. It is the counseling service that make the difference—the reality checks, the support, the ideas for where to look for jobs leads, the networking techniques, the time spent with a spouse, the rehearsals before interviews, the revisions to cover letters and resumes, the late-night telephone calls—and these are never the same for any two clients.

The bottom line on this aspect of the outplacement service also tends to be qualitative: when it was all over, did the client feel it was a waste of time, worthwhile, or essential? Did he or she pick up the telephone and call the HR director to say "thanks for making outplacement available"?

There is no real way to measure the number of problems avoided, a major concern as the client and consultant go through the process. There is no way to know how long each client would be in the job market if there were no consultant offering suggestions and building the client's confidence. There is no count of the lawsuits not filed.

On the positive side, there are many dozens of small gifts given to consultants by grateful clients. There are files of letters expressing appreciation to the firms. There are the referrals made to the outplacement firm by "alumni" when others are terminated from their new employers. There are the invitations to "feel free to use my name" if future clients need help in networking. And there are telephone calls a year or two later when the alumnus needs to hire someone at his or her new company and wants to know if there is an appropriate candidate among the current group of clients.

The research currently available on the success of outplacement has not generally gone beyond measures of satisfaction. Some analyses support the conclusion that outplacement shortens the job search period. From a commercial point of view, that is all that is needed. From a professional point of view, there is much room for progress.

OPEN ISSUES

This section briefly presents sixteen areas in which the field of outplacement consulting will hopefully make progress in the coming years.

Professional

1. Selecting, training, and certifying consultants. The range of styles and skills among consultants is quite impressive. As in any other new field, it would be wrong to fix on a particular model until data are available to show what works and what does not. It is hoped we will soon agree as to what does work and then apply that knowledge to building a corps of uniformly qualified consultants.

2. Certifying outplacement firms. The overall management of quality service delivery is the firm's responsibility. There is a need for agreed-upon minimum standards and desired optimums.

3. Providing full service to minorities and women. There is reason to believe that the nonwhite male clients have somewhat different needs during outplacement from white males. Exactly what these needs are is not clear. There almost certainly are skills and sensitivities lacking among some consultants for consulting effectively with these client populations. (A related issue is that only about 10 to 15 percent of outplacement consultants are women, although this number seems to be growing, and there are only a handful of minority consultants.)

4. Defining the therapy-consulting border. A definitive distinction probably is neither needed nor obtainable, but there would be benefits from clearer guidelines. The well-being of the clients is involved here, as are liability issues. Immediate applications would be in regard to the most effective use of psychometrics and to the handling of crises.

Consulting

1. Managing anxiety over cash flow. Perhaps this is only a temporary problem due to the rapid growth of the number of firms, but nonetheless it is a real factor in the daily life of outplacement firms. The problem may resolve if and when some form of certification is available or perhaps after some kind of shake-out occurs within the industry. Some firms and companies are experimenting with retainer relationships, without clear conclusions thus far. Countercyclic lines of service, such as recruiting, also may play a part if conflict of interest issues do not materialize. Ownership by very large parent companies is also a possibility.

2. Working with a double client. Although not unique to the outplacement field, this issue of having both an individual and an organization as clients does create ethical quandaries from time to time. As yet there is no standard industry-wide response to these questions.

3. Mechanization of procedures. Efforts are being made by a number of organizations to reduce the outplacement process to its core of necessary steps and actions and then arrange for these to be delivered by computers, videotapes, audiotapes, workbooks, and paraprofessionals. There has been some acceptance of this approach among clerical, blue-collar, and younger clients but not without criticism as well. Sponsoring companies are tempted to explore these possibilities because of the great cost savings. If they can be shown to be effective, they could represent a breakthrough in service delivery.

4. Job lead development. Outplacement firms come under pressure at times from either the sponsoring companies or the individual clients to do a lot more in the area of identifying job openings. Some firms have been developing lists of job openings from corporations and/or from recruiters, although it is not yet clear whether these projects have much more than excellent

public relations value. This issue takes on very real importance when economically depressed communities or industries are involved—situations in which "everyone knows" that personalized counseling is not going to be helpful because there just are not any jobs to be had. Proposed solutions to this problem tend to blur the lines that distinguish the outplacement profession from that of recruiter.

Managerial

1. Outplacement as an effective management tool. The best way to use outplacement in various corporate situations is not fully understood. Some companies are heavy users, while others use it only sporadically. There is much to be learned about how and when to offer outplacement, how to have it available at the right time and in the proper form and place, and how to have it viewed as a legitimate business alternative. (These are the same growing pains experienced by other new management tools and services, such as systems analysis, management training and development, industrial engineering, and so on, at earlier times.)

2. Outplacement policy management. Related to the above point is the issue of how best to formulate company-wide policies about the use of outplacement. Which aspects of the service are in need of control via policies, if any?

3. Budgeting. The costs for outplacement are almost never included in the annual operating budgets of most companies. The key exceptions occur when there is a planned major layoff in connection with a plant or office closing, downsizing, or acquisition, in which case funds will be reserved for this purpose. The costs for outplacements needed during a normal operating year tend not to be budgeted, yet the need for them inevitably occurs. How much money should a prudent management put aside for this purpose? How can the level of need be projected when the budgets are drawn up twelve to eighteen months in advance?

4. Integration with other HR services. Outplacement does not stand by itself within the scope of the human resources department's services. It is connected in one way or another with transfers, (lack of) promotions, career planning, retirement counseling and early retirement programs, performance counseling, and, most directly, with manpower planning. Clarifying and publicizing these connections have yet to be done in most organizations.

Theory and Research

1. Measurement methods. As discussed at length in the previous section, there is room for great strides to be made regarding how to measure the results of outplacement. Criteria need to be generated, and models have to be developed for adequately controlled field research.

2. Crisis intervention models. The fields of clinical and marital counseling have made some real progress in providing models for understanding crises among healthy adult populations. Those of us working with adults who have lost jobs should now develop models of what happens to them psychologically and what should be done to help them. Practical experience has already been accumulated, but there is no cooperative effort under way to build coherent, generalized models from this experience.

3. Longitudinal studies. The outplacement experience may have significant value for the client in the years following the end of the relationship with the consultant. No one knows which of the learnings stay with the clients, how they use them, whether they facilitate better performance and/or greater likelihood of surviving future lay-offs. Anecdotal evidence suggests that the clients take away a lot of learning from their outplacement experiences, but there have been no professionally directed studies of this possibility. Other observers suggest that the learnings are not what they might appear to be in amount or type because of the extremely high levels of anxiety that exist during the outplacement period.

4. Theory of midlife employment search. The ideal, ultimate contribution from the behavioral science community would be a comprehensive theory describing how adults at midlife go about seeking reemployment. There are theories describing the earlier tasks having to do with career selection and entry among people in the fifteen- to twenty-five-year-old age range. There is need for theories explaining how adults seek new jobs, new careers, new organizational affiliations, and new life-styles. How do they collect and process the relevant data? How do values, interests, and energy levels affect their decisions? How do they use the resources available to them? What kinds of decision-making operations go on in their heads? Is there an optimally rational model that becomes polluted by anxiety and depression? How does the severity of the termination affect the course of the job search?

A FINAL COMMENT

There are dozens of other questions to be asked and answered. Behavioral science professionals have just barely noticed the existence of outplacement services and have given little attention to the reemployment process. There are no courses taught in psychology departments or in business schools, nor are there any professionally oriented texts.

Productive, financially rewarding, and psychologically healthy adult lives are not easy to achieve, especially without interruptions. Understanding the adult reemployment process becomes increasingly important as our society tries to balance our traditional individual liberties and responsibilities with rapid social and technological change. We cannot guarantee lifetime employment, and we cannot afford to have competent unemployed people. Outplacement is the helping service between these two facts. It deserves to be understood, improved, delivered well, and used wisely.

51 TRAINEE CHARACTERISTICS AND TRAINING EFFECTIVENESS

Raymond A. Noe

Training can be defined as a planned learning experience designed to bring about permanent change in an individual's knowledge, attitudes, or skills (Campbell, Dunnette, Lawler & Weick, 1970). Training and management development activities are currently receiving increased attention in industry. This emphasis is illustrated by recent figures, which report that organizations spend upwards of $30 billion annually for training programs involving 15 billion work hours (Huber, 1985).

Although the "bottom line" for most training programs is effectiveness, little attention has been devoted to studying why training programs are effective for some individuals and ineffective for others. In a recent review of the training and development literature, Latham (1988) suggests that individual characteristics are an important determinant of learning and training effectiveness. Training effectiveness is usually determined by assessing some combination of the criteria presented in Kirkpatrick's (1967) model of training outcomes. This model is composed of four levels of training outcomes: trainees' reactions to the program content and training process (reaction), knowledge or skill acquisition (learning), behavior change (behavior), and improvements in tangible individual or organizational outcomes such as turnover, accidents, or productivity (results). Each training outcome provides different information about the effectiveness of the program. Satisfaction and learning deal with the administration and content of the program. Behavior change and performance improvement indicate that knowledge and skills acquired in training have had an effect on trainees' behavior in the work setting.

Positive trainee reactions, learning, behavior change, and improvements in job-related outcomes are expected from well-designed and administered training programs. However, trainee attitudes, interests, values, and expectations may attenuate or increase training effectiveness. Determining the specific individual characteristics that influence the effectiveness of training is of utmost importance in order to understand how to increase the likelihood that behavior change and performance improvement will result from participation in training program.

TRAINABILITY

One of the first models of managerial performance was developed by Porter and Lawler (1968). They proposed that performance was a function of abilities and traits, effort, and role perceptions. The basic notions of this model may be useful for understanding why learning, behavior change, and performance improvement differ among training program participants. Trainability is hypothesized to be a function of three factors: ability, motivation, and perceptions of the work environment (Trainability = f[Ability, Motivation, Work Environment Perceptions]). The cognitive and psychomotor skills that trainees possess directly influence whether they will be able to understand and master the content of the training program. The ability component of trainability has received the most attention; most studies addressing the trainability issue have focused on the relationship between the trainees' prerequisite ability levels and mastery of the training program content (e.g., Gordon & Cohen, 1973; Siegal and Ruh, 1973). However, as Maier (1973) indicates, even if trainees possess the prerequisite skills needed to learn the training program content, performance in the program will be poor if motivation is low or absent.

This chapter is based on "Trainees' attributes and attitudes: Neglected influences on training effectiveness," *Academy of Management Review, 11,* 736–749.

Steers and Porter (1975) suggest that motivation is composed of energizing, directing, and maintenance components. In a training situation, motivation can be seen as a force that influences enthusiasm about the program (energizer), a stimulus that directs participants to learn and attempt to master the content of the program (director), and a force that influences the use of newly acquired knowledge and skills even in the presence of criticism and lack of reinforcement for use of the training content (maintenance). The influence of the work environment on trainability is another factor that should not be ignored. Of particular importance is the climate of the organization concerning change and the extent to which the social context (supervisors, coworkers) of the work setting provides reinforcement and feedback. A supportive work climate in which reinforcement and feedback from coworkers are obtained is more likely to result in transfer of skills from the training environment to the work environment; trainees are more likely to use the skills acquired in the training pro-

gram on the job (Bahn, 1973; Marx, 1982; Salinger, 1973). In addition, work by Peters and his associates (e.g., O'Connor, Peters, Pooyan, Weekley, Frank & Erenkranz, 1984; Peters, Fisher & O'Connor, 1982; Peters, O'Connor & Rudolf, 1980) suggests that trainees' perceptions of task constraints such as lack of equipment or financial resources may indirectly influence behavior change and learning by reducing motivation to learn new skills or apply skills acquired in training to job tasks.

The purpose of this chapter is to identify and integrate relevant concepts, theory, and research in organizational behavior into a model describing the influences of trainee attributes and attitudes on training effectiveness. The chapter provides an overview of the individual characteristics that may influence training effectiveness. In order to maximize training effectiveness, training and development professionals should consider the influence of the factors discussed in this chapter prior to the development of training activities.

A MODEL OF THE MOTIVATIONAL INFLUENCES OF TRAINING EFFECTIVENESS

A conceptualization of the motivational influences of training program effectiveness is shown in figure 51–1. The variables on the right side of the model

include the multiple measures of training effectiveness described by Kirkpatrick (1967). The model describes the possible influences of trainees' attitudes concern-

Figure 51–1. Motivational Influences on Training Effectiveness

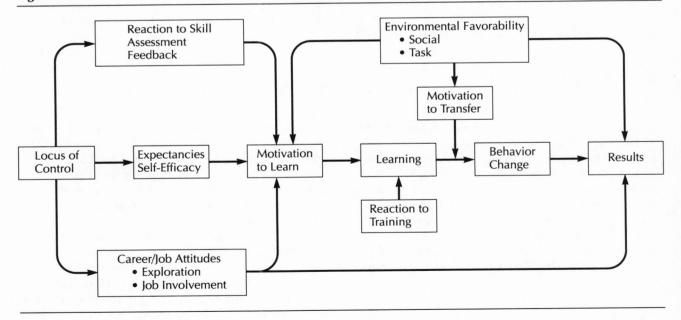

ing their behavior, job, career, and work environment on learning, behavior change, and attainment of desirable organizational outcomes. The variables included in the model were chosen on the basis of a review of the organizational behavior and training and development literature. The purpose of this review was to identify attitudes and attributes that likely have an influence on trainees' motivation to learn, motivation to apply newly acquired skills in the work setting, or training effectiveness criteria. Modification of the model will likely be necessary as more academic and industrial studies on this topic are conducted.

MODEL OVERVIEW

The extent to which the individual is likely to make internal or external attributions regarding work outcomes (locus of control) directly influences his or her reaction to skill assessment feedback, expectancies concerning the link between effort and mastery of training program content (Expectancy I) and rewards resulting from successful completion of the program (Expectancy II), and career and job attitudes. Internals are more likely to identify psychologically with their work and career (Thornton, 1978), to perceive effort-performance and performance-outcome linkages (Broedling, 1975), and to accept assessment of their skills, strengths, and weaknesses than Externals (Phares, 1976).

Reaction to skill assessment feedback, expectancies, and career and job attitudes directly influences motivation to learn. Three conditions are necessary for maximal motivation to learn. First, trainees should feel that the assessment of their skill strengths and weaknesses that resulted in their training assignment or opportunity to participate in the training program is accurate. Second, it is essential that trainees believe they can master the content of the training program with a reasonable amount of effort. Also, it is important that trainees believe that program participation and mastery of content are related to the attainment of desired outcomes such as prestige, promotion, interesting work assignments, greater self-confidence, or salary increases. Third, motivation to learn is influenced by the extent to which trainees value good job performance, identify psychologically with their job, and engage in career exploration behavior, including self-assessment of interests, skill strengths and weaknesses, and career planning. Fourth, trainees who perceive the work setting as providing the necessary resources to perform job tasks and have supportive interpersonal relationships with peers and supervisors characterized by open communications and opportunities to receive feed-

back and reinforcement are likely highly motivated to learn.

A direct link between career and job attitudes and the results criterion is hypothesized. Cues in the work environment that can improve work behavior are likely more salient to highly job-involved individuals because performance gains result in self-image improvement, which are reinforcing to these persons. As a result, improvements beyond those directly related to training program participation in product quality, accident rates, and other results criteria are more probable for highly job-involved trainees.

Motivation to learn is a direct antecedent of learning (i.e., acquisition of knowledge and skills presented in the training program). Trainees' satisfaction with the trainers and content of training program (reaction criteria) also likely influences subsequent learning.

The relationship between learning and behavior change is likely moderated by trainees' motivation to use learned skills and knowledge in the work setting. Maximum behavior change is likely to result when trainees have mastered the program content and are highly motivated to use newly acquired skills on the job. Trainees' perceptions regarding work group support for the use of new skills and task constraints (environmental favorability) are hypothesized to influence motivation to transfer. It is likely that trainees will be motivated to use acquired skills in their daily work activities when supervisors and coworkers can be expected to support behavior change by providing reinforcement and feedback. Also, if trainees do not perceive that the necessary equipment, monetary support, or information necessary to meet job demands will be provided, learned skills may not be demonstrated on the job, and consequently, no improvements in cost-related outcomes will be realized.

MOTIVATIONAL COMPONENTS

Locus of Control

Locus of control is a stable personality trait that is likely to affect individual motivation and ability to learn. Based on Rotter's (1966) definition, individuals who are *Internals* believe that job performance and events that occur in the work setting are contingent on their own behavior and are therefore under personal control. Because Internals feel they can control their environment, opportunities at work that may increase the probability of receiving rewards such as promotion, pay increases, or recognition are particularly salient to these individuals. *Externals* believe that work outcomes are beyond personal control and therefore attribute the cause for work outcomes to luck, fate, or the actions of others. Rotter (1966) developed the Internal-External Control of Reinforcement Scale to assess locus of control. Andrisani and Nestle (1976) have developed a more work-oriented version of this scale, using eleven of the items from the original Rotter scale.

In a recent review of the effects of locus of control on organizational behavior, Spector (1982) suggested that because locus of control is a personality characteristic that influences belief about the ability to improve skills, it should be an important determinant of individual trainability. Internals may exert greater effort toward collecting relevant information in a training situation than Externals. As the model indicates, locus of control is hypothesized to have a direct influence on trainees' expectations regarding the training program, career and job attitudes, and reactions to skill assessment information. A study by Broedling (1975) supports the link between locus of control and effort-performance expectancies (Expectancy I). Internals were more likely to believe that performance was contingent on their personal effort than Externals. Applied to a training situation, the results of this study suggest that Internals may exert greater effort toward collecting relevant knowledge and skills in a training situation than Externals because mastery of program content is believed to be under their personal control.

The influence of locus of control on career and job attitudes has also received attention. A number of studies have demonstrated that Internals have higher levels of job involvement than Externals (Dailey & Morgan, 1978; Reitz & Jewell, 1979; Runyon, 1973, Wood, 1974). Thornton (1978) found that Internals reported more career planning activities and career information–seeking behavior following a career planning workshop than Externals. These studies suggest that because Internals are more likely to seek control over their own fate, they are expected to become more involved in their work and career.

Trainees with an internal locus of control are more likely to act upon feedback regarding their skill strengths and weaknesses than Externals; that is, Internals are more likely to exhibit high levels of motivation to learn in a training program. Internals may doubt the accuracy of negative feedback (Stone, Gueuthal & McIntosh, 1984). However, research findings indicate that in comparison to Externals, Internals are more likely to accept feedback and take overt action to correct personal shortcomings (Weiss & Sherman, 1973).

Expectancies

Vroom's (1964) notions concerning effort-performance and performance-outcome perceptions as causes of behavior have particular relevance in training situations. Trainees have preferences among the various outcomes (e.g., promotion, recognition) resulting from participation in the program (valences). Trainees may also have expectations regarding the likelihood that effort invested in the training program (i.e. participation in group exercises, answering questions, and practicing skills), will result in mastery of the training content (Expectancy I). Finally, trainees differ in the extent to which they believe that good performance in the training program will lead to desirable outcomes (Expectancy II). Two studies have found that individual expectancies concerning training programs are related to performance and behavior change (Moitra, 1976; Froman, 1977).

Measures of effort-performance expectancies should assess trainees' perceptions regarding the relationship between different levels of effort and different levels of mastery of program content. In order to assess performance-outcome expectancies, items regarding trainees' beliefs concerning training performance levels and the attainment of both intrinsic and extrinsic outcomes (e.g., increased self-image, greater promotion possibilities, recognition from peers) should be included. The interested reader should refer to Mitchell (1974) and Ilgen, Nebeker, and Pritchard (1981) for reviews of the methodological and conceptual problems involved in trying to operationalize expectancy theory constructs.

Effort-performance perceptions are related to

personal efficacy expectations. According to Bandura (1977), self-efficacy is the belief that one can successfully execute the behavior required to cope with potentially threatening situations. Individuals with a high level of self-efficacy will exert considerable effort in order to cope with situations that may demand new behavior patterns or higher performance levels. In a training situation, assessment of trainees' self-efficacy should focus on affective responses to learning and change (e.g., confidence in learning situations, ease of comprehension of new material, difficulty in adjusting to new work situations).

Studies in clinical psychology have shown that various phobias can be overcome by increasing self-efficacy perceptions (e.g., Bandura, Adams & Beyer, 1977; Bandura, Jeffery & Wright, 1974). In a training situation individuals with a high degree of self-efficacy are likely to exert considerable effort to master program content and achieve organizational goals. Decker and Nathan (1985) suggest that the success of behavior modeling training is attributable to an increase in trainees' self-efficacy. Behavior modeling programs incorporate a number of the strategies outlined by Bandura (1977) for increasing self-efficacy (the use of verbal persuasion to present the key behaviors, vicarious learning through presence of a model, and performance accomplishment during skills practice).

Recent research demonstrates the powerful effect of self-efficacy on training outcomes. Frayne and Latham (1987) used training consisting of goal setting, a behavioral contract, self-monitoring, and the selection and self-administration of rewards and punishment as a strategy to increase government employees' attendance at work. Compared to a group who received no training, training in self-regulation skills taught employees how to manage personal and social obstacles to job attendance and raised their self-efficacy. The higher was the perceived self-efficacy, the better was the subsequent job attendance.

The expectancy theory and self-efficacy literature suggests that trainees' beliefs that they can learn the material presented in the program and desirable outcomes such as promotion, salary increases, or prestige will result from skill and knowledge acquisition may influence motivation to learn the behavior, knowledge, or skills presented in the training program.

Career and Job Attitudes

Exploratory Behavior. Hall (1976) defined a career as the "individual's perceived sequence of attitudes and behaviors associated with work-related experi-

ences and activities over the span of the person's life" (p. 4). Super's (1957a, 1957b) theory of adult career development defines four work-relevant life stages: exploration, establishment, maintenance, and decline. According to Super, a person strives to implement self-concept by choosing to enter the occupation most likely to permit self-expression. One of the key assumptions of Super's theory is that any given person possesses the potential for success and satisfaction in a variety of occupational settings (Osipow, 1968).

Jordaan (1963) emphasized exploratory behavior as a key determinant of occupational success and satisfaction. Exploratory behavior refers to mental or physical activities undertaken with the purpose of eliciting information about oneself or one's environment or forming decisions regarding occupational adjustment, progression, or choice. Exploratory behavior includes self-assessment of skill strengths and weaknesses, career values, interests, goals, or plans, as well as the search for job-related information from family friends, counselors, and other career information outlets (Stumpf, Colarelli & Hartman, 1983; Mihal, Sorce & Compte, 1984). Stumpf et al. (1983) developed the Career Exploration Survey, which measures several aspects of exploratory behavior (Environment Exploration, Self-Exploration, Intended-Systematic Exploration, Focus), as well as reaction to exploratory behavior (stress, satisfaction) and beliefs about opportunities (labor market conditions, importance of obtaining a preferred position).

Exploratory behavior has been found to be related to occupational satisfaction and interview performance (Greenhaus & Sklarew, 1981; Stumpf & Colarelli, 1980; Stumpf et al., 1983). Additionally, the extent to which individuals engage in career planning, a type of exploratory behavior, has been demonstrated to be related to the likelihood of participation in self-development activities, salary level, and advancement (Gould, 1979). Gould's (1979) career planning scale assesses the extent to which career plans exist, how frequently career plans are changed, how clear career plans are, and whether a strategy exists for achieving career goals.

The relationship between exploratory behavior and training effectiveness is unknown. One possible hypothesis is that trainees who frequently engage in cognitive or environmental search activities are likely to have a better understanding of their strengths, weaknesses, and interests. This results in a high level of motivation to learn in training programs that are congruent with their career goals. These individuals are likely highly motivated to learn because of the self-realization of skill weaknesses resulting from their investments and interests in career growth and progression as evidenced by the frequency and intensity of exploratory type behaviors.

Job Involvement. Trainees' motivation to improve work-related skills may be influenced by the extent to which they are job involved (i.e., the degree to which the individual identifies psychologically with the work, or the importance of the work for the person's total self-image) (Lodahl & Kejner, 1965). The original job involvement measure was developed by Lodahl and Kejner (1965). Several studies have demonstrated that this measure is multidimensional (e.g., Gorn & Kanungo, 1980; Wood, 1980). As a result, Kanungo (1979) has criticized the measure because job involvement is believed to be a unidimensional construct. He presents an "uncontaminated" three-item scale believed to assess specifically an individual's identification with work.

Highly job involved individuals are more likely to be motivated to learn new skills because participation in training activities can increase skill levels, improve job performance, and elevate feelings of self-worth. Positive changes in the criteria used to evaluate training effectiveness, independent of motivation to learn, are also probable. Regardless of motivation to learn, cues in the work environment, such as coworkers' suggestions that can facilitate behavior change and performance improvement, are likely more salient to high- than low-job-involved individuals. These cues are more salient because the self-image of high-job-involved individuals is directly tied to their success or failure at work—cues that can increase job performance are more likely to be focused on.

Reaction to Skill Assessment Feedback

Positive or negative reactions to the information individuals receive regarding their strengths and weaknesses are likely determinants of motivation to improve skills in a training program and subsequent learning and behavior change resulting from training program participation. Credibility of the source, usefulness of the message, belief in the accuracy of the information presented, and level of detail of the information provided are important determinants of whether feedback is perceived as positive or negative, is accepted, and motivates the individual to change behavior.

Currently, no measures of trainees' reaction to skill assessment feedback are available. However, the work by Ilgen et al. (1979) suggests that such measures should include items addressing trainees' beliefs concerning the accuracy of the needs assessment information and overall satisfaction with the needs

assessment method. Also, the extent to which the needs assessment procedure results in an improvement in trainees' understanding of their skill strengths and weaknesses and provides skill information at the appropriate level of specificity should be determined.

One of the important steps in designing a training program is to conduct a person analysis: Who needs training? What skills need to be trained? Person analysis usually involves evaluation of employees' current performance levels through traditional performance appraisal techniques, self-assessment, and/or diagnostic achievement tests. If trainees perceive the needs assessment as credible and providing useful information regarding skill strengths and weaknesses, they will react favorably to the information received. As a result, trainees will likely be motivated to improve skill weaknesses through participation in a training program specifically designed on the basis of the needs assessment information.

Motivation to Learn

Trainee attitudes and attributes are hypothesized to have an impact on motivation to learn. Motivation to learn can be described as a specific desire of the trainee to learn the content of the training program. Measures of motivation to learn include items assessing trainees' enthusiasm for learning and persistence when program material is difficult (e.g., Hicks, 1984). Most of the research regarding motivation to learn has been conducted in educational settings in which academic achievement and knowledge acquisition are of primary concern (e.g., Chapman, Cullen, Boersma & Maguire, 1981; Kahn, 1969; Marjoribanks, 1976). A limited number of studies have investigated the relationship between motivation to learn and training effectiveness.

For example, Hicks (1984) analyzed how the realism of preliminary training information and the amount of discretion employees were given to select participation in training influenced motivation to learn, amount of learning, and program attendance. Motivation to learn explained significant variance in a self-report learning measure ($r^2 = .38$). Similarly, Ryman and Biesner (1975) found that motivation to learn was useful for predicting success ($r^2 = .05$) and class dropout rates ($r^2 = .09$) of U.S. Marine recruits in three Navy diving training classes. Cohen's (1977) definition of small, medium, and large effect sizes corresponds to coefficients of determination (r^2) of .01, .09, and .25, respectively. According to this criterion, the results of these two studies suggest that motivation to learn may have a substantial impact on training effectiveness.

Trainees' motivation to learn may be influenced

by beliefs concerning effort-performance and performance-outcome relationships, career-job attitudes, and reactions to skill needs assessment. Assuming similar ability levels, it is hypothesized that trainees who are enthusiastic about attending the program and desire to learn the content of the training program are likely to acquire more knowledge and skills and demonstrate greater behavior change and performance improvement than trainees not motivated to learn.

Motivation to Transfer

Traditionally, research and practical applications of the concept of transfer of training have emphasized the importance of ensuring the congruence between the tasks in the training environment and the work setting (Wexley & Latham, 1981). Additionally, trainees' attitudes concerning the use of the new skills in the work setting may have an important influence on behavior change in the work situation. Motivation to transfer can be described as the trainees' desire to use knowledge and skills mastered in the training program on the job. Trainees are likely motivated to transfer new skills to the work situation when they feel confident in using the skills, are aware of work situations in which demonstration of the new skills is appropriate, perceive that job performance improvements may likely occur as a result of use of the new skills, and believe that the knowledge and skills emphasized in the training program will be helpful in solving work-related problems and frequent job demands. Any measure of motivation to transfer should include items designed to assess trainee confidence in the use of new skills and perceived applicability of trained skills to the job. To my knowledge, motivation to transfer remains an unexplored area.

As the model indicates (see figure 51–1), motivation to transfer is believed to moderate the relationship between learning and behavior change. Behavior change will likely be greatest for trainees who learn the material presented in the training and desire to apply the acquired knowledge and skills to the work situation.

Perceptions Concerning the Work Environment: Environmental Favorability

Trainees' perceptions of the favorability of the work environment influence the transfer of skills from the training situation to the work setting, motivation to learn, and results criteria. Environmental favorability

is conceptualized as consisting of a task component and a social component. First, the extent to which technological necessities such as proper tools and equipment, materials and supplies, and monetary support are perceived to be available determines the extent to which knowledge and skills acquired in training will be used or constrained in the work setting. Initial work by Peters and O'Connor (1980) identified eight categories of constraints believed to restrict the use of abilities and hinder the influence of individual motivation on effective task performance: lack of skills to perform job tasks, lack of needed services from coworkers, insufficient job-related information, improper tools and equipment, inadequate budgetary support, unfamiliarity with the task, insufficient time to meet deadlines, and poor physical working conditions. O'Connor et al. (1980) and Peters and O'Connor (1980) found that frustration, task dissatisfaction, and turnover where possible consequences of constraining work situations.

Peters, O'Connor, and Eulberg (1985) have summarized the literature relevant to the taxonomic structure of work constraints. They describe the various methods that have been used to identify constraints. Also, they caution that perceptual measures of constraints may be confounded because employee responses reflect justification for work failures. As a result, it may be necessary to verify trainees' perceptions of work constraints collected from questionnaires using more objective methods such as observations from trained observers.

Trainees' perceptions regarding the social context of the work situation are proposed as the second component of environmental favorability. Trainees' beliefs regarding opportunities to practice skills or use knowledge acquired in the training program and receive reinforcement and feedback from supervisors and peers are of particular importance (Bahn, 1973; Byham, Adams & Kiggins, 1976; Eddy, Glad, & Wilkins, 1967; Ehrenberg, 1983; Michalak, 1981; Salinger, 1973). The more opportunities trainees have to use and practice the skills emphasized in training on the job, the greater is the probability these skills will be maintained, behavior change will result, and positive increments in job performance will be realized. The importance of reinforcement from members of the social network in the work setting, including recognition and feedback from supervisors, coworkers, and subordinates, cannot be overemphasized. House (1968) suggests that the degree to which social influences (i.e., peers or supervisors) reward or punish trainees for adapting attitudes or behavior prescribed in training is a major determinant of whether trainees will demonstrate learned attitudes or behaviors. Feedback maintains behavior by providing information to the trainee concerning the appropriateness of demonstrating new skills in the work setting and indicating what modifications in behavior are necessary to meet standards of successful performance. Studies by Fleishman (1955) and Hand, Richards, and Slocum (1973) demonstrated the influence of work group attitudes on use of leadership skills emphasized in human relations training programs. The extent to which newly trained attitudes were evident in trainees' job behavior depended on supervisors' and subordinates' expectations.

Trainees' perceptions regarding peer and supervisor support for training activities may be considered one indicator of the organizational climate for employee development. In their work on organizational climate, Schneider (1972) and Jones and James (1979) describe measures of work group friendliness and cooperation, managerial support, and organizational concern for employees. These measures are applicable to any assessment of the supportiveness of the social environment for training activities. Also, such an assessment should include items concerning peer and supervisor attitudes toward training and supervisor-subordinate communications.

As depicted in the model, environmental favorability is suggested to have a direct influence on motivation to learn, motivation to transfer, and results criteria. Prior to participating in the training program, trainees may be cognizant of task constraints and/or a nonsupportive social network present in the work setting that will likely inhibit use of knowledge and skills acquired in training. As a result, motivation to learn is likely to be low and learning, behavior change, and performance improvement less likely to occur. Trainees may be motivated to learn the content of the training program for personal development but lack motivation to use newly acquired skills and knowledge in the work setting because of perceptions of an unfavorable work environment. Finally, trainees may master the content of the training program and modify their behavior, but perceptions of constraints inhibit application of knowledge, skills, and behaviors to job tasks. As a result, quality and productivity improvements expected as a result of employee participation in the training program will not be realized.

IMPLICATIONS FOR TRAINING PRACTICE

The model presented in this chapter suggests that training funds may be wasted by forcing those employees with low job involvement and a lack of career interest to attend skill improvement programs. Self-assessment measures completed prior to training concerning career goals, interests, and skills may help to increase training effectiveness. Employees may self-select themselves out of programs they feel are inappropriate considering their career goals and skills.

From a developmental perspective, providing employees with information concerning the needs assessment technique may reduce suspicion, fear, and animosity toward the training program. Training can be conceived as a change intervention designed to influence learning and behavior change (Huse, 1975). If employees do not understand why and how their strengths and weaknesses were identified and doubt the accuracy of the information, they will likely be resistant to change. As a result, motivation to learn in the training program will be low, less learning will occur, and evaluation of the training will find fewer effects than expected.

Career workshops provided by the organization may provide employees with a clearer picture regarding career paths and the prerequisite skills for promotions and lateral moves throughout the organization. These sessions are likely to stimulate exploratory-type behaviors and improve employees' "readiness" for training by increasing motivation to learn. Programs offered in advance of participation in training provide trainees with the opportunity to complete a more detailed self-assessment of their skills and career interests, which may maximize motivation to learn.

Finally, trainers need to recognize the importance of work group support and reinforcement and situational resources for facilitating or inhibiting behavior change and performance improvement. Perhaps training programs will be more effective if attention is given to ensuring that the work group climate is supportive and encourages change and personal development. The development of this type of climate may be stimulated by providing organizational rewards for managers and coworkers who provide feedback and encouragement for trainees' use of new skills. The commitment of managers to making the training program work may be increased by having them actually participate in the program before the trainees. Trainers should ensure that materials, tools, job-related information, and budgetary support necessary for task completion are provided in the work setting prior to employees' participation in the training program. Employees' perceptions of the availability of situational resources prior to program participation likely influence motivation to learn.

In most work situations, interruptions are frequent, time pressures and deadlines are part of the daily work routine, services and help from others are needed to complete job assignments, and supervisors are reluctant or unavailable to provide feedback and reinforcement for use of new skills trainees need to be prepared to deal with. Trainees will lapse into ineffective habits and behaviors if they are not prepared to deal with the environment they will encounter when they try to use new behavior or skills. In order to maximize the potentially powerful effects of trainee self-efficacy, trainers should consider teaching trainees strategies for making the environment responsive or ways to cope in a hostile environment. Such strategies should include goal setting, self-monitoring, and self-administration of rewards. Marx (1982) suggests that it is necessary to (1) make trainees aware of possible obstacles to effective use of new skills and encourage self-monitoring of these obstacles, (2) identify specific situations that constrain use of new skills, (3) provide coping responses that enable trainees to overcome unfavorable environmental influences, and (4) teach trainees to experience a sense of accomplishment at attempting to use coping skills in problematic situations. Training in time management, assertiveness, and how to rely on peers for support and feedback may also help to overcome the negative influence of task constraints on training effectiveness.

REFERENCES

Andrisani, P.J., & Nestle, G.L. (1976). Internal-external control as contributor to and outcome of work experiences. *Journal of Applied Psychology, 61,* 156–165.

Bahn, C. (1973). The countertraining problem. *Personnel Journal, 28,* 1068–1072.

Bandura, A. (1977). Self-efficacy: Toward a unifying theory of behavioral change. *Psychological Review, 84,* 191–215.

Bandura, A., Adams, N.E., & Beyer, J. (1977). Cognitive processes mediating behavioral change. *Journal of Personality and Social Psychology, 35,* 125–139.

Bandura, A., Jeffery, R.W., & Wright, C.L. (1974). Efficacy of participant modeling as a function of response induction aids. *Journal of Abnormal Psychology, 83,* 56–64.

Broedling, L.A. (1975). Relationship of internal-external control to work motivation and performance in an expectancy model. *Journal of Applied Psychology, 60,* 65–70.

Byham, W.C., Adams, D., & Kiggins, A. (1976). Transfer of modeling training to the job. *Personnel Psychology, 29,* 345–349.

Campbell, J.P. (1971). Personnel development and training. In P.M. Mussen & M.R. Rosenzweig (Eds.), *Annual Review of Psychology* (vol. 22). Palo Alto: Annual Reviews, Inc.

Campbell, J.P., Dunnette, M.D., Lawler, E.E., III, & Weick, K.R., Jr. (1970). *Managerial behavior, performance, and effectiveness.* New York: McGraw-Hill.

Chapman, J.W., Cullen, J.L., Boersma, F.J., & Maguire, T.O. (1981). Affective variables and school achievement: A study of possible causal influences. *Canadian Journal of Behavior Science, 13,* 181–192.

Clement, R.W. (1978). *An empirical test of the hierarchy theory of training evaluation.* Ph.D dissertation, Michigan State University.

Cohen, J. (1977). *Statistical power analysis for the behavioral sciences.* New York: Academic Press.

Dailey, R.C., & Morgan, C.P. (1978). Personal characteristics and job involvement as antecedents of boundary spanning behavior: A path analysis. *Journal of Management Studies, 15,* 330–339.

Decker, P.J., & Nathan, B.R. (1985). *Behavior modeling training: Principles and applications.* New York: Praeger.

Eddy, W.B., Glad, D.D., & Wilkins, D.D. (1967). Organizational effects on training. *Training and Development Journal, 22,* 36–43.

Ehrenberg, L.M. (1983). How to ensure better transfer of learning. *Training and Development Journal, 37,* 81–83.

Fleishman, E.A. (1955). Leadership climate, human relations training, and supervisory behavior. *Personnel Psychology, 6,* 205–222.

Frayne, C.A., & Latham, G.P. (1987). The application of social learning theory to employee self-management of attendance. *Journal of Applied Psychology, 72,* 387–392.

Froman, L. (1977). Some motivational determinants of trainee effort and performance: An investigation of expectancy theory. *Dissertation Abstracts, 45,* 2411–5 (University Microfilms No. 77-23975).

Fromkin, H.L., Brandt, J., King, D.C., Sherwood, J.J., & Fisher, J. (1975). An evaluation of human relations training for police. *Catalog of Selected Documents in Psychology, 5,* 206–207.

Gordon, M.E., & Cohen, S.L. (1973). Training behavior as a predictor of trainability. *Personnel Psychology, 26,* 261–272.

Gorn, G.J., & Kanungo, R.N. (1980). Job involvement and motivation: Are intrinsically motivated managers more job involved? *Organizational Behavior and Human Performance, 26,* 265–277.

Gould, S. (1979). Characteristics of career planners in upwardly mobile occupations. *Academy of Management Journal, 22,* 539–550.

Greenhaus, J.G., & Sklarew, N.D. (1981). Some sources and consequences of career exploration. *Journal of Vocational Behavior, 18,* 1–12.

Hall, D.T. (1976). *Careers in organizations.* Santa Monica, CA: Goodyear Publishing

Hand, H.H., Richards, M.D., & Slocum, J.W. Jr. (1973). Organizational climate and the effectiveness of a human relations program. *Academy of Management Journal, 16,* 185–195.

Hicks, W.D. (1984). The process of entering training programs and its effects on training outcomes. *Dissertation Abstracts, 44,* 3564B (University Microfilms No. DA8403528).

House, R. (1968). Leadership training: Some dysfunctional consequences. *Administrative Science Quarterly, 12,* 556–571.

Huber, V.L. (1985). Training and development: Not always the best medicine. *Personnel, 62,* 12–15.

Huse, E.F. (1975). *Organization development and change.* St. Paul, MN: West Publishing

Ilgen, D.R., Nebeker, D.M., & Pritchard, R.D. (1981). Expectancy theory measures: An empirical comparison in an experimental simulation. *Organizational Behavior and Human Performance, 28,* 189–223.

Jones, A.P., & James, L.R. (1979). Psychological climate: Dimensions and relationships of individual and aggregated work environment perceptions. *Organizational Behavior and Human Performance, 23,* 201–250.

Jordaan, J.P. (1963). Exploratory behavior: The formation of self and occupational concepts. In D.E. Super, R. Steratishersky, N. Mattin, & J.P. Jordaan (Eds.), *Career development self-concept theory.* New York: College Examination Board.

Kahn, S.B. (1969). Affective correlates of academic achievement. *Journal of Educational Psychology, 60,* 216–221.

Kanungo, R.N. (1979). The concepts of alienation and involvement revisited. *Psychological Bulletin, 86,* 119–138.

Kirkpatrick, D.L. (1967). Evaluation of training. In R.L. Craig, & L.R. Bittel (Eds.), *Training and development handbook* (87–112). New York: McGraw-Hill.

Latham, G.P. (1988). Human resource training and development. *Annual Review of Psychology, 39,* 545–82.

Latham, G.P., Wexley, K.N., & Purcell, E.D. (1975). Training managers to minimize rating errors in the observation of behavior. *Journal of Applied Psychology, 60,* 550–555.

Lodahl, T.M., & Kejner, M. (1965). The definition and measurement of job involvement. *Journal of Applied Psychology, 49,* 24–33.

Maier, N.R.F. (1973). *Psychology in industrial organizations.* Boston: Houghton Mifflin.

Marjoribanks, K. (1976). School attitudes, cognitive ability, and academic achievement. *Journal of Educational Psychology, 68,* 653–660.

Marx, R.D. (1982). Relapse prevention for managerial training: A model for maintenance of behavior change. *Academy of Management Review, 7,* 433–441.

Michalak, D.F. (1981). The neglected half of training. *Training and Development Journal, 35,* 22–28.

Mihal, W.L., Sorce, P.A., & Compte, T.E. (1984). A process model of individual career decision making. *Academy of Management Review, 9,* 95–103.

Mitchell, T.R. (1974). Expectancy models of job satisfaction, occupational preference, and effort: A theoretical, methodological, and empirical appraisal. *Psychological Bulletin, 81,* 1053–1077.

Mitra, S. (1976). A prel-program evaluation model determining training effectiveness based on expectancy theory of work motivation. *Dissertation Abstracts, 42,* 1455B (University Microfilms No. 77-18, 182).

O'Connor, E.J., Peters, L.H., Pooyan, A., Weekley, J., Frank, B., & Erenkranz, B. (1984). Situational constraints effects on performance, affective reactions, and turnover: A field replication and extension. *Journal of Applied Psychology, 69,* 663–672.

Osipow, S.H. (1968). *Theories of career development.* New York: Appleton-Century-Crofts.

Peters, L.H., Fisher, C.D., & O'Connor, E.J. (1982). The moderating effect of situational control of performance variance on the relationship between individual differences and performance. *Personnel Psychology, 35,* 609–621.

Peters, L.H., & O'Connor, E.J. (1980). Situational constraints and work outcomes: The influence of a frequently overlooked construct. *Academy of Management Review, 5,* 391–397.

Peters, L.H., O'Connor, E.J., & Eulberg, J.R. (1985). Situational constraints: Sources, consequences, and future considerations. In K.M. Rowland & G.R. Ferris (Eds.), *Research in personnel and human resource management* (vol. 3, 791–814).

Peters, L.H., O'Connor, E.J., & Rudolf, C.J. (1980). The behavioral and affective consequences of performance-relevant situational variables. *Organizational Behavior and Human Performance, 25,* 79–96.

Phares, E.J. (1976). *Locus of control in personality.* Morristown, NJ: General Learning Press.

Porter, L.W., & Lawler, E.E. III (1968). *Managerial attitudes and performance,* Homewood, IL: Irwin.

Reitz, H.J., & Jewell, L.N. (1979). Sex, locus of control, and job involvement: A six-country investigation. *Academy of Management Journal, 22,* 72–80.

Robertson, I., & Downs, S. (1979). Learning and the prediction of performance: Development of trainability testing in the United Kingdom. *Journal of Applied Psychology, 64,* 42–50.

Rotter, J.B. (1966). Generalized expectancies for internal vs. external control of reinforcement. *Psychological Monographs, 80* (1, Whole No. 609).

Runyon, K.E. (1973). Some interactions between personality variables and management styles. *Journal of Applied Psychology, 57,* 288–294.

Ryman, D.H., & Biesner, R.J. (1975). Attitudes predictive of giving training success. *Personnel Psychology, 28,* 181–188.

Salinger, R. (1973). *Disincentives to effective employee training and development.* U.S. Civil Service Commission. Washington, DC: U.S. Government Printing Office.

Schneider, B. (1972). Organizational climate: Individual preferences and organizational realities. *Journal of Applied Psychology, 56,* 211–217.

Siegel, A.L., & Ruh, R.A. (1973). Job involvement, participation in decision making, personal background, and job behavior. *Organizational Behavior and Human Performance, 9,* 318–327.

Spector, P.E. (1982). Behavior in organizations as a function of employee's locus of control. *Psychological Bulletin, 91,* 482–497.

Steers, R.M., & Porter, L.W. (Eds.) (1975). *Motivation and work behavior.* New York: McGraw-Hill.

Stone, D.L., Gueutal, H.G., & McIntosh, B. (1984). Effects of feedback sequences and expertise of the rater on perceived feedback accuracy. *Personnel Psychology, 37,* 486–506.

Stumpf, S.A., & Colarelli, S.M. (1980). Career exploration: Development of dimensions and some preliminary findings. *Psychological Reports, 47,* 979–988.

Stumpf, S.A., Colarelli, S.M., & Hartman, K. (1983). Development of the career exploration survey (CES). *Journal of Vocational Behavior, 22,* 191–226.

Super, D.E. (1957). *The psychology of careers.* New York: Harper & Row.

Super, D.E., Crites, J., Hummel, R., Moser, H., Overstreet, P., & Warnath, C. (1957). *Vocational development: A framework for research.* New York: Bureau of Research, Teachers College, Columbia University.

Thornton, G.C. III (1978). Differential effects of career planning on internals and externals. *Personnel Psychology, 31,* 471–476.

Vroom, V.H. (1964). *Work and motivation.* New York: John Wiley & Sons.

Weiss, H., & Sherman, J. (1973). Internal-external locus of control as a predictor of task effort and satisfaction subsequent to failure. *Journal of Applied Psychology, 57,* 132–136.

Wexley, K.N., & Latham, G.P. (1981). *Developing and training human resources in organizations.* Glenview, IL: Scott, Foresman, & Company.

Wood, D.A. (1974). Effect of worker orientation differences on job correlates. *Journal of Applied Psychology, 59,* 54–60.

Wood, D.A. (1980). Investigation of possible sex differences in the prediction of job performance in an industrial setting. *Educational and Psychological Measurement, 40,* 1153–1158.

52 PROGRAM EVALUATION FOR TRAINING

Ross E. Azevedo

Organizations engage in a wide variety of programs as part of their routine operations. Such programs may include the design of a new product or service, the development of a new fringe benefit program, the marketing of a new sales effort, or entrance into a new and different service or product market. Each of these programs has something unique about it but also has a great deal in common with the others. Thus, while each program is a set of activities intended to achieve a specified set of objectives, the objectives, the techniques used to attain them, and the measures of success employed typically are program specific.

The issue of program evaluation is new to most managers in the private sector. The concept or idea of program evaluation arose out of questions raised primarily in the public sector; subjects like the evaluation of education programs, the effectiveness of social casework, and the assessment of pilot programs for social services come to mind (Cook & Shadish, 1986). Yet the orientation of program evaluation, which involves statistical measurement of program processes and outcomes, on assessing the economic effectiveness of any of a host or programmatic efforts carries important implications for the private sector.

Complicating the difficulties associated with program evaluation is its duality of purpose (Rutman & Mowbray, 1983). That is, while its purpose for senior management is to answer questions of purpose (i.e., intention), contribution to organizational goals, and financial viability, its role or purpose for those actually conducting the program(s) is to assess effectiveness, isolate weaknesses, and identify routes for possible improvement. Obviously, a tool with so many possible tasks (and their associated outcomes) creates significant opportunities for conflict and disagreements over its use.

The purpose of what follows is to look at the question of program evaluation through an analysis of a training program. While training programs have their own very specific goals and purposes, they are excellent examples of what program evaluation is about and illustrate many of the problems and diffi-

culties that management runs into when engaged in program evaluation. This is a general analysis of the purposes of program evaluation, particularly as it applies to training; for a statistical treatment of training assessment see chapter 47 in this *Handbook*.

At the outset, it may be worth noting that the application of the ideas of program evaluation to training is consistent with the evolution of the way training has been defined. Thus, while Goldstein (1974, p. 3) defined training as "the systematic acquisition of skills, rules, concepts, or attitudes that result in improved performance," Wexley and Latham (1981, p. 3) have termed it "a planned effort by an organization to facilitate the learning of job-related behavior on the part of its employees," and Laird (1985, p. 11) has described it as "the acquisition of the technology which permits employees to perform to standard," Good (1982, p. 11) has more recently brought these ideas together and described training as a total system involving "analyzing . . . , designing . . . , developing . . . , conducting . . . , and . . . evaluating." It is this last approach that is most closely associated with the program evaluation strategies outlined here.

The reader should note that the tone of what follows may, at first, appear somewhat negative as the text details a litany of problems that may plague any training program. The intent, however, is to sound a note of caution so that the manager involved in deciding whether to implement a training effort will be aware of the possible pitfalls such a program may encounter. By being aware of potential difficulties in advance, the manager will be better equipped to deal with what may appear to be unfavorable results from training and have a more complete understanding of the steps necessary to determine where the problems actually lie.

The basic issue when considering the decision to embark upon any program is whether—in some fashion—that program will pay its own way (Rutman, 1980). Thus, the organization considering a decision to begin a new research program must ask whether there are expectations that the program will yield marketable ideas. Similarly, the organization considering whether to have employees participate in a training exercise, either in-house or at public programs, is concerned with whether it is going to get its "money's worth." The rising costs of training—as well as all costs of operation—have made this issue even more acute, as decisions on training expenditures affect the entire range of resource expenditures. But the question arises: "How do you evaluate such a training program?"

The notion of program evaluation is more complicated, however, than what is termed a cost-benefit analysis. Often a program will have many factors to it that cannot be translated directly into pure costs and benefits, which then are assessed in dollars-and-cents terms (Thurow, 1970). Thus, the evaluation of a new sales program that generates new clients, a product refinement that improves it at no additional cost, or a training program that upgrades supervisory skills cannot measure particular uncosted outputs or the "what might have beens." In each of these cases, and many more like them, there must be a somewhat subjective determination of at least a portion of the program's impact.

To put this in context, Kirkpatrick (1976) has defined multiple levels of training outcome: reaction, learning, behavior, and results. Reaction might be termed the overall feelings the trainee receives from his or her learning experience. "I enjoyed it," "It was terrible," and "What a teacher!" are possible reactions to training. Obviously, these do not indicate whether any learning took place. Learning involves the transmission and reception of information. But it is more complicated than this in that, as Hilgard and Bower (1966) have pointed out, "learning is the process by which an activity originates or is changed through reacting to an encountered situation" (p. 2). In the training context, tests, questionnaires, and interviews might determine whether a trainee has

assimilated what has been taught in class if the level of knowledge before the training is known. A serious difficulty in this situation, pointed out by Cook and Shadish (1986), is the anticipation of great change when "large" effects should not be expected.

The crucial outcome for the manager is whether there has been, or will be, a behavioral change that will produce results in the expected and correct direction. That is, in the terms of this chapter, has there been a positive transfer of the training to the behavior of those who received it? The issue of positive transfer (Fleishman, Harris & Burtt, 1955; Mosel, 1957; Royer, 1979; Michalak, 1981; Newstrom, 1984), which really involves learning and the correct application of that learning in the work environment, is the crucial element in the process. It is what we will be focusing our attention on through what follows. Suffice it to say at this point that there is a wide variety of behaviors, some costable and some that must be measured through other means, that are subject to assessment in the evaluation of the outcomes of a training program.

In what follows, a multistage discussion is presented. The first stage outlines the very basic issue of needs assessment. This is followed by a discussion of training design. The third stage covers what might be termed a "pure" strategy for assessing the value of a program through the training example. The attempt here is to offer what might be the best way to evaluate the results of a program (i.e., training), albeit with both strengths and weaknesses considered.

Following this "pure" strategy, a set of alternative approaches is set forth. The purpose of these alternative methods is to provide guidance as to what forms of assessment are available together with their strong and weak points. Obviously, any organization deciding to employ such techniques must do so with the foreknowledge as to what they will and will not provide.

AN OPENING CAVEAT

Notwithstanding the subjective elements discussed above, any attempt to assess the value of any program also must pay its own way (Rutman, 1980). Such an evaluation involves short-run and long-run considerations for effective decision making. Thus, if it costs $150,000 to evaluate that effectiveness of a $100,000 piece of machinery, the machinery may not be worth purchasing in the first place. Or we may just have to assume that the machinery is effective because it is not worthwhile to conduct the inquiry. The evaluation

may pay off, however, if it is an analysis that considers the rate of return on the piece of machinery over some appropriate period of time. Similarly, if training costs $1,000 and the organization spends $2,000 evaluating it, serious questions arise as to the justifiability of the expenditure. On the other hand, if training costs are $1,000 annually, a once-and-for-all $2,000 evaluation expenditure could be justified with a master proviso: training needs, pretraining capabilities of the trainees, and posttraining trainee tasks are

Figure 52–1. The Training Evaluation Decision

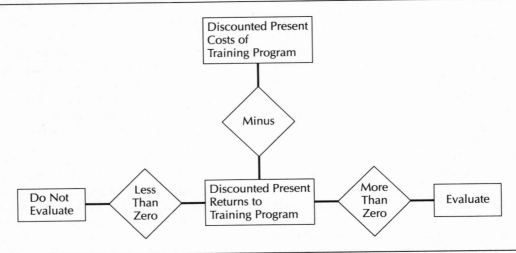

unchanged through the period of the training effort and into all the foreseeable future. This may be a heroic assumption with respect to many organizations given the dynamics of growth and change they typically experience.

The generalized form of the training program evaluation decision that explicitly accounts for time, characterized in figure 52–1, allows consideration of both single-period and multiple-period training programs and their results. What this means is that the organization must consider and compare the discounted present value of all of the costs (both finan-

cial and noncosted) of the training program and the discounted present value of all of the returns (both financial and noncosted) to the training program (Becker, 1964). If the discounted present value of the returns exceed the discounted value of the costs, the training program is cost-effective from a strictly economic basis, although it may fail by other standards. This approach, derived from economics, is being integrated into the personnel literature and practice (see, for example, Flamholtz, 1974; Boudreau, 1983; and Cronshaw & Alexander, 1983).

THE IDEA OF NEEDS ASSESSMENT

The true first step, and one that is often missed, in the evaluation of any program is the determination of what type of program the organization needs. Is it a sales incentive program that will improve market position? Or should it be a redesign of the product or service offered? In other words, what will the program deliver? This is illustrated in the most common shortcoming of any training program: the lack of a needs assessment. The organization must define what it is doing and what it will be doing over the foreseeable future and then utilize this information to identify what training needs exist. In this sense, training (needs) must be linked to organization strategy (Latham, 1988). The next step involves deciding who then should receive the training when it is offered. This leads to the question of trainability (Noe, 1986): are the workers who need the training ready to learn and apply that training to their jobs?

Trainability is a function of readiness, ability, motivation, and work environment perceptions. Readiness is crucial; a worker who is not ready for training will gain little from sitting in on a session that presents facts, techniques, and/or applications that he or she is not yet capable of absorbing. Similarly, if a worker does not have the ability (or the cognitive and psychomotor skills) to apply the lessons of training in the workplace, it is falling on deaf ears. It is the issue of ability that is perhaps most often studied in assessing the effectiveness of training and typically explains the largest portion of any improvements in performance (Robertson & Downs, 1979; Noe, 1986).

This leads us to a common mistake managers make when deciding who will receive training. Many times training is given as a reward for past performance. The boss feels one or more workers are doing an excellent job and, as a way to reward that performance, sends them to training to let them have "a few days off" the job. Since the training really has little or nothing to do with these workers' abilities or readiness—at least when it is received—they are not expecting or expected to get much from it, and the dollars and time spent on it are wasted.

Motivation and perceptions of workplace environment tie things together (Goldstein, 1974). The worker must be motivated to learn from training, or it will have little impact. Often this motivation results from the employee's perceptions about what training leads to in the organization. If the worker perceives that there is little or no gain associated with training or simply does not want training for whatever reason, there will be limited motivation to participate or little incentive to learn if the training is forced upon him or her. But motivation involves more than the desire to learn; there must be the desire to apply that learning to the job (Noe, 1986). All of have heard of the "perpetual student," the one who takes class after class but never does anything with the knowledge gained. The motivation to transfer the learned material to the job is as crucial as is the motivation to learn the material in the first place.

To put all of this in context, the organizational environment must provide an adequate set of rewards for training (and its transfer to the job) if it is to be well received by employees. This is a concept management often misses because it perceives training as something it can gain from and ignores the possible rewards to the "trainee," an issue Becker (1964) has addressed. Something as basic as continued employment may be sufficient, particularly if the labor market is very loose. However, to train a hundred workers for supervisory positions where only ten are to be promoted may be very counterproductive. Similarly, to reward trained employees with a 6 percent wage increase while giving nontrained workers "only" 5 percent may yield dissatisfaction for those

who have been trained. One potential risk from these situations is that the workers may move into rivalry with each other, further subverting the ends of the training program.

The remaining issue in needs assessment is the determination of the performance standards to which trainees will be subjected when the training program is completed. While it is possible to stop after assessing the organization's needs and identifying who will be receiving training to meet those needs, one must go the extra step and decide what the ultimate performance levels of the trained workers should be to complete this step. It is these standards that will shape the remainder of the training effort, and to fail to establish them at this point means that the training program will be designed without sufficient direction to meet the organizational objectives.

In sum, the organization must be very careful at this stage of the process. It is faced with the task of merging the needs it has identified, the talents and skills of those workers most able to meet those needs, and the assessment strategy it will ultimately employ to determine if the training has been successful. There is a foundation to be laid at this point, and many organizations pass over it because of the felt need to press on with designing and implementing the program. A measure of caution at this point will do far more for the implementation of an effective program than a headlong rush into getting the program "on and off the drawing board."

A further difficulty should be noted here. The idea of a needs assessment is predicated upon there being a need for training that can be met. It should be obvious that motivational problems, ability limitations, and inappropriate selection mechanisms (for new hirees or promotions) may be at fault and that no training program (at least for the workers in question) will produce satisfactory results for the organization.

THE ISSUE OF PROGRAM DESIGN

The next issue to consider is the design of the training program. It is designed to meet the organization's needs? It is often too easy to purchase a canned training program rather than create a new one. This canning may be both internal and external. Thus, an internal training unit may design what it feels is necessary for the organization and deliver the program without a thorough assessment of the program's ability to meet organizational needs. This typically happens when an organization hires so-called subject

matter experts to handle its training. They often decide what is needed based on their expertise rather than upon the organization's true needs and fail to conduct an adequate needs analysis.

The problem may be made more difficult when dealing with external suppliers of training services. Most such vendors have canned offerings they provide publicly or to a variety of employers on long—or short—notice. The real difficulty with such programs is whether they are specifically applicable to your organization. Obviously, this is generally less likely with publicly offered programs, and it may be a problem even if they are presented in-house.

Too often an outside vendor will spend a few hours, or at most a few days, gaining familiarity with an organization—possibly even reviewing an internal needs analysis—and claim to be able to provide training to meet the organization's needs. By and large, the idiosyncratic nature of most organizations prevents such a brief analysis from providing an accurate picture of all the characteristics that affect the training requirements. However, such a needs analysis is better than no analysis at all if it is used by the consultant.

IMPLEMENTING THE TRAINING

Given the training design meets the organization's needs and those appropriate for taking the training have been selected, the next question is whether the training is implemented in a fashion consistent with that design. Too often shortcomings interfere with adequate delivery. A crucial problem that faces many training programs at this initial point is the failure of the organization to communicate to the trainees what they are expected to gain from the training program. It is common for potential trainees to be told to show up at a certain time and place and be ready for a training program on this or that subject. This is particularly crucial when employees are sent to an outside training program; the organization should carefully instruct them as to precisely what they are to gain from their seminar or conference so that they know what to expect and what to ask the instructor for at the beginning so that he or she can act to include it in the material presented.

There are further problems with the implementation process. Trainers with the best of intentions may deviate from the intended topics. The environment may be inappropriate for the training process (e.g., room too cold, too hot, too noisy), the time allocated may be too short to provide adequate coverage or too long to ensure the continued attention of the trainees, or, in a problem particular to on-site training, situations can lead to employees' returning to their workstations because of telephone calls, emergencies, production problems, or other interruptions, thereby short-circuiting the training process.

PROMOTING TRANSFER

When a training program has been completed—or even when it is still under way—the organization may want to act to ensure its effectiveness by working to promote transfer. Traditionally, attempts to promote transfer have included overlearning, identical elements or tasks in training and work, and the teaching of underlying theoretical principles to allow generalization to other aspects of work (McGehee & Thayer, 1961), but researchers have found that these approaches are not effective in bringing about significant positive transfer of training in many, if not most, situations (Leifer & Newstrom, 1980; Michalak, 1981).

More recent approaches investigated focus on employer-assigned goal setting, self-assigned goal setting, and behavioral self-management schemes. This last methodology involves management of available environmental stimuli (Marx, 1982) whereby individual workers establish self-generated systems of incentives, rewards, and punishments in an effort to maintain desirable performance. Marx (1982) went a step further and defined relapse prevention (a strategy derived from the treatment of addictive behavior), where the worker is taught to deal with the possibility of relapse, as another form of behavioral self-management.

While a complete empirical review of the effectiveness of these strategies is not available currently, there is a suggestion that assigned goal setting appears to be more effective in transfer of learning than participative goal setting or relapse prevention, which appear to be fairly similar in effectiveness (Wexley & Baldwin, 1986). Obviously, while more needs to be done to answer this question completely, the manager should be aware of the issues involved and work to ensure the greatest level of transfer possible.

ASSESSMENT OF A TRAINING PROGRAM

Provided that the incentive for training is established, that the training program is designed and implemented, and that positive transfer is promoted, the organization moves to the testing or evaluating phase. This necessarily involves a before-and-after comparison in the case of a training program based on the training of all workers.

The assessment of performance change brings together the substantial array of factors discussed above. The needs analysis should set the standards. That is, the specific performance behaviors the organization wishes to have improved should be identified, and standards of performance for these behaviors should be established so that assessment of

results and transfer is possible. Ideally, the communication of the standards has or will occur before, during, and after the training (Leifer & Newstrom, 1980). Workers about to enter a training program should have been led to understand the specific purposes of the training—what it is supposed to do for them. During the training program, the expected standards of performance must be combined with the transmission of information. At the conclusion of the training and in an ongoing fashion thereafter, employees must be reminded of the expected changes in performance associated with the training they have received.

A "PURE" TEST OF A PROGRAM

Certainly the best way to assess any program effort is to utilize what is termed a controlled experiment. A very traditional approach, this design involves comparing one group or process that is treated or changed to another, a control group, that is not treated or changed (Goldstein, 1974). For a new sales promotion, this might involve making the effort in one region and utilizing the traditional sales program in another region. In a training program, this would involve assigning workers on a random basis to two groups. One group goes through a training program; one does not. After the training is completed, the performance of the two groups is compared.

Another major caveat is in order here. For many organizations it is not possible to engage in a program only partially (e.g., to enter only a portion of the market or to train only half the work force). Thus, it may not be possible to launch a marketing campaign in only one or a few markets. It often is very difficult to redesign only part of a service or product; interrelationships may require an entire revision of what came before. In turn, a manufacturer must be certain that all workers on the production line can perform their jobs at an acceptable level; to train only half would be counterproductive. Similarly, it would not be possible to operate a nuclear power generating plant or an airliner with only half the staff trained in emergency procedures. In these circumstances, the training of every worker is imperative.

This pure design involves the selection of the performance criteria upon which the results of the two groups will be assessed. The possibilities are exten-

sive, ranging from absenteeism and accuracy through productivity and quality to readiness to work and zealousness. Note again that the set of criteria that is to be assessed should be determined and communicated before the training begins lest one shape them after seeing what has happened during training (Rutman & Mowbray, 1983). Then for each of the criteria chosen, a procedure must be established to compare whether the trained group performs better than the untrained one. If it does, the training may be a good investment for the organization.

The use of the word *may* is deliberate. Even if the training works, it is appropriate to ask, "How well?" A very well-designed and expensive training program may produce gains that, while measurable, are not of sufficient size to be cost justifiable (Cook & Shadish, 1986). When this happens, the training is described as "statistically significant" but not "practically significant." In this situation the organization may be better off not providing the training in dollars-and-cents terms.

Another issue is important here: on what proportion of the measures must the trained group be better performers than the untrained to justify the training? Is one-half sufficient? a majority? or must it be nearly all? Again it may be a case where the nature of the business is likely to be the determining factor, with a virtually perfect transfer of knowledge needed in some cases and a much less stringent requirement in others.

An assessment of any such change in performance must consider other aspects of the training. One very crucial possibility is unintended results, what might be termed side effects in medicine (Goldstein, 1974). The training may make workers very unhappy with their jobs because they now know what possibilities are available to them but are as yet unattainable. The stress of the training program may degrade performance in the present position. Obviously, it is the employer's responsibility to determine the nature and extent of these changes if they occur, as it is to assess the beneficial results of the training program.

Another aspect that must be considered is durability of the transfer. Does the training provide an ongoing improvement in performance, or does decay follow? If the training program provides a boost in performance that lasts a few weeks or months and then disappears, again it must be called into question. Perhaps it is the training program that is deficient; then it must be changed to provide continuing improvement. Perhaps regular "booster" efforts must be made to ensure the maintenance of the better performance levels. Alternately, there may be serious organizational impediments to making the training effective in the long term, impediments that neutralize the effects or worth of the training.

ORGANIZATIONAL IMPEDIMENTS TO PROGRAM EVALUATION

One of the most common organizational impediments is a manager who "knows better," who feels he or she has a better way of doing things. This may be a sales manager who knows the "best" way to market the product in his or her district despite the new, centrally managed marketing effort. Or it may be a supervisor greeting the trainee who returns from a training session with a new and better way to do something and sets up a stone wall of resistance to the employee's new ways of doing things. Managers, supervisors, or others higher up in the organization know how things have been done for many years, and "they're still going to be done that way." It does not take much of an imagination to know what the evaluation of any program facing this type of opposition will show.

Other organizational mistakes can lead to equally disastrous training evaluation. The newly trained employee who is assigned to a job where that training cannot be utilized will bias any evaluation. The freshly trained supervisor who is put in charge of so many workers that proper supervision is impossible is unlikely to produce favorable evidence on a training program. A neophyte supervisor who is assigned a task he or she is not familiar with will perform poorly. The list could go on, but the point should be clear.

A further problem or impediment facing the organization attempting a pure test of any program is the difficulty of making only half an effort. Thus, an organization's pure test of its training programs generates the risk associated with leaving one-half of its work force untrained. Assuming that the training is effective, the trained group should have better performance appraisal results or other measure of change in behavior and will, in turn, be more likely to receive larger performance-based wage or salary increases and more opportunities for promotion, transfer, or other forms of advancement. Put differently, the organization has created a permanently undertrained group among its workers. That is, even if the control group workers ultimately are trained, there is the likelihood they will remain behind those already given training in terms of performance, transfer, and promotion.

The existence of such a group is likely to generate a host of problems for the organization. Those who are left behind are unlikely to be motivated to perform well, feeling their chances have been curtailed. This might even lead to substantial legal problems if protected class workers are among this group and they decide to sue based on the belief they have been discriminated against. Even those who have received training and, in turn, the benefits associated with it may be dismayed if friends and associates are left behind because of their failure to be included in the trained group. In essence, this situation raises the ethical question of who receives and who does not receive training, and any such decision must be weighed very carefully.

Two possible cures suggest themselves, however; one will be considered here and one will be discussed in the section on partial methods of measurement. The first alternative involves establishing a uniform policy with respect to both the trained and control groups, regardless of the training they have received. Thus, for example, if the intention is to raise six rank-and-file workers to supervisor, promote the best three from the trained and the best three from the untrained—based on performance appraisal results, supervisor ratings, or whatever other objective criteria the organization employs in such decisions.

Here again there are substantial risks to the organization. How can it justify promoting individuals with poorer performance ratings (the untrained) than those with better ratings (the trained)? The risk of lawsuit is obvious, and the impact to morale of the trained workers should be clear.

The conclusions one comes to at this point are that a true "best" test of training is difficult, time-consuming, risky from legal and ethical perspectives, and likely to lead to motivational problems among both the trained and the untrained. Moreover, it is difficult to predict what the implementation side effects may be (Cook & Shadish, 1986). This is not meant to imply that such a "best" test cannot be run, only that the organization must be extremely careful in the design, application, and subsequent follow-up of the procedure. Moreover, it is clear that the organization should do something to evaluate training, for to do otherwise is to leave the organization with no guides as to how it should tinker with the program in order to be able to improve it.

PARTIAL TESTS OF A PROGRAM

This leads to a consideration of the possibility of one of a variety of "partial" tests or assessments of a program. The first approach, alluded to above, is to alternate the application of the program to different targets or groups at different times. This might involve implementing the new marketing effort in various regions during different quarters of the fiscal year. For the trainer, this would entail a system with first one group being trained and then another and so on, thereby ensuring that all workers receive the opportunity. While in principle this should work, the timing of training, performance appraisal, or other assessment and subsequent personnel decision (if the organization is going to be fair) becomes incredibly complex, and most organizations are unwilling to establish the tracking system necessary to ensure this type of design is implemented properly on an ongoing basis.

A second approach would involve, for example, monitoring the implementation of a new program as a totality at all possible stages from design through to postmortem. A new sales effort could be tracked from the initial marketing campaign through to its impact on the bottom line. In the context of training, the organization trains all workers within the groups designated for training and then assesses its impact. This is a "before," "during," and "after" form of analysis, which entails repeated assessment of the trained workers or, to put it more precisely, the measurement of worker performance prior to training, during the course of training, and upon its completion. Again, this is not a simple task, and many organizations are reluctant to pursue it because of the record-keeping requirements.

A further alternative would be to train only on an as-needed basis where people are selected, perhaps after being promoted or put into a new job, and given the training necessary to perform in the new position. This has obvious limitations in that the worker may not succeed in the new position, the training program may not be applied efficiently to only one or a few workers, or the immediate demands of the new job may limit the employee's ability to undertake training.

ASSESSMENT OF TRANSFER

The specific assessment of the transfer of training is the next issue to be considered in the process. This involves the measurement of the output criteria, consistent with the training objectives, which have been indicated before training as outputs to be assessed to quantify improvement. It is valuable to note here that the results of training involve both what the individual receives and the gains accruing to the organization, and, if the individual achieves personal gains from the training, his or her willingness to participate in additional development activities may be significantly increased.

Measures that might be used to assess the transfer of training include, but are not limited to, performance appraisal results, output changes, productivity improvements, loss reduction, reduced complaint levels, and increased sales. Note that some of these measures are capable of being costed, while some are not, a point made above, and that they link the economic and the psychological. We will consider each of these in turn.

Performance Appraisals

These are perhaps the most general of the measures possible, and their global nature may include any or all of the other possible measures. The risks associated with performance appraisal are several. Obviously, there may be halo or recency effects (Heneman, Schwab, Fossum & Dyer, 1986) as the supervisor, knowing that the subordinates have just been trained, may overstate their appraisal results because they *should* be doing better. If an appraisal system suffers from the ceiling effect—a very narrow range of employee evaluation scores (say 8, 9, and 10) on a much larger scale (say 0 to 10)—the results of training are not likely to indicate much improvement if before and after average scores are compared. Similarly, if an organization requires managers to distribute appraisals according to some formula (e.g., a normal curve), it is not likely that training will show improved average performance, although the location of individual workers within the distribution may change.

Output Changes

Training may lead to higher levels of output on the part of employees. They may be able to produce more because greater knowledge of the production process will facilitate their work. However, the real issue is how much of a gain can be expected. Is 10 percent likely? 5 percent? 1 percent? The gain may be small but significant and well worth the training effort. The risk is that small output increase may be looked upon as not worthwhile, although in reality it is significant and important.

Productivity Improvements

One possible result of training is increased productivity, with workers being able to do their jobs more efficiently although output may not be increased due to the limits of the market. Here the risk is that the employer does not really measure productivity because of the complications involved in doing it accurately (Greenberg, 1973). Workers may fear the loss of jobs if they become too efficient and hold back on their performance potential. Another risk here involves changes in the production process. If the employer introduces new technology in combination with (or subsequent to) the training, the workers' efficiency will rise to the new production level associated with that technology, and there is no longer

likely to be a measurable effect due to the training under the earlier technology. The employees work with the new technology with the training already embodied in their performance, and any gains already have been accounted for. Any assessment at this point is unlikely to show any impact of the training effort.

Loss Reduction

This is a criterion that often is ignored when considering the impact of training. It is just as important for an organization to gain through reductions on the loss side as it is to profit from increases on the output side. Fewer defective parts, less waste, and fewer mistakes are all valuable gains for the organization. Here the issue may involve either new techniques or improvements in existing waste measurement systems, changes that many organizations fail to associate with training, causing an inappropriate measurement bias.

Reduced Complaint Levels

This is a crucial issue for all organizations that deal with the public. Given the competitive nature of many goods and service markets and competition among social service and other public and private agencies, it is imperative that customers or clients be treated honestly, fairly, and courteously. Training can be crucial in ensuring that all of these criteria of service deliverers can be met. The risk, however, is that complaints can arise from sources beyond the cause of those being assessed. Two examples would be production delays and problems caused by the delivery company, both of which could lead to complaints about the "sales" staff. Obviously, to blame the sales staff, or the training program, in this type of situation is a mistake.

Increased Sales

Many organizations offer training to their sales force with an expectation of improved sales levels. Indeed, this is a legitimate expectation, although serious evaluation mistakes can be made. The performance of trainees starting out in a market that is on an upswing (or downturn) can lead to an overstatement (or underestimation) of the effectiveness of training. Moving trainees into new markets or initiating new products or services in the market can affect the measured results of training without allowing a clear assessment of the training on its own terms.

Here again a serious caveat is in order. Given that the organization has evaluated the trained employees on any one or more of the factors listed above, how does the organization deal with poor performance or total failure on the job? The typical approach is to discipline the employee through a small pay increase, lack of promotion, discharge, reassignment, or another similar action. It should be apparent at this time that the real problem may have nothing to do with the individual employee but may be associated with the needs assessment, trainee selection process, design of the training program itself, its implementation, or the evaluation procedure. Unless there is certainty as to where the problem lies, it makes no sense to discipline the employee in such a situation.

It is quite clear at this point that the assessment stage is a crucial one and potentially subject to many errors of omission and commission. But it is truly the capstone of the program evaluation effort and therefore requires the utmost care. Any breakdown in the system at this point leaves the organization in the position of wasting what has come before. This only leads to wasted time and money and may significantly shortchange the training effort.

STAYING ON TRACK

At this point, the circle needs to be completed. Any organization is a dynamic entity, with change being the order of the day. It is not acceptable to leave things as they are for very long. The results of the training program evaluation, which include all of the available information from the process itself, as well as the evaluation results for the participants, are combined with the planned future of the organization, to be used as inputs to design the next round of training. It is a never-ending process that must constantly be kept on track. Like almost everything else in the operation of an organization, the only constant is that nothing is constant.

SUMMARY AND CONCLUSIONS

My purpose here has been to consider and explore the complications associated with a program evaluation effort aimed at assessing a training program. Such an assessment is, as should be obvious, a complicated job, which must be undertaken with great care. I have detailed what is admittedly a long litany of problems that can befall any training program. It must be noted, however, that identifying their well-recognized existence is not the same as being able to specify with precision their particular impact upon the evaluation of any such program. Indeed, the effect of any of these "imperfections" is likely to vary for each program and within every organization in which it is operationalized.

The objective at this point is to summarize these potential pitfalls and reemphasize the iterative nature of the program evaluation process when applied to training. As is evident in figure 52–2, needs assessment is the foundation to any training effort. The first step in the needs assessment process is crucial: determine the organization's objectives. Given the needs or objectives are identified, the assessment of the trainability of the appropriate members of the current work force is the next step in the needs determination process. The final task at this juncture is to combine the organizational objectives with the trainability considerations in the establishment of performance standards, that is, what performance changes the training program should yield. Note that a failure at any step in this process causes the organization's training foundation to be weakened and requires the redoing of these steps so that future progress can be made in the construction of the overall training program.

Given that the needs are adequately assessed, the organization must move to the design of a training program to meet them. The needs assessment defines the organization's objectives, and, in turn, those objectives are the inputs to the selection of delivery strategies. If the objectives cannot be identified and/or a delivery strategy specified, it is again necessary to backtrack on the steps that led to this stage of the process. The process is captured in the intersection of the first and second layers of our training structure in figure 52–2. As noted, the needs analysis is key, for it sets the parameters for the design of the program and makes its power felt early in the developmental stages of the process. Without it the training program design is on a shaky foundation and cannot be supported.

If the needs analysis has led to an effective design of the training program, the next step is an appro-

Figure 52–2. Program Evaluation for Training

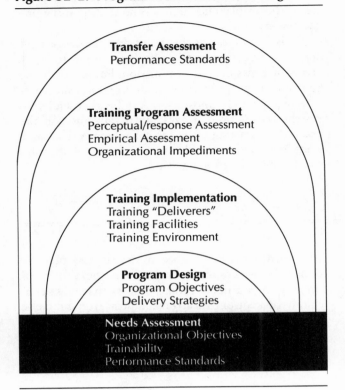

priate implementation of the training effort. As is indicated in figure 52–2, this involves selecting those who will deliver the program, procuring the appropriate facilities for conducting the training, and establishing an environment that is conducive to the effective delivery of the training material. Here again the existence of a difficulty in implementing the training program calls for an iterative approach to the previous stages of the program evaluation process, testing and identifying where the causes of the unsuccessful implementation lie. While the difficulties at this point may appear to be due to implementation problems, it may be necessary to re-review the needs assessment and design stages for identification of those difficulties that inhibit the organization's ability to implement the training effort, for it is these stages that provide the joint foundation for the implementation process to follow.

Training program assessment is an ultimate testing time for the organization, for it is here that the rubber meets the road in one sense. The organization initially must decide what approach to take, with perceptual and response assessment being perhaps the most common types of assessment. However, that form of assessment usually does nothing to measure the impact of the training on knowledge and/or skills.

This leads to a variety of empirical assessment strategies where the organization measures as precisely as is possible the effects that training has had on individual ability to perform on the job. The crucial aspect of this assessment is to ensure that the evaluation procedure adequately differentiates between the performance potential of those who complete training and those who did not.

The crucial caveat here is the removal of organizational impediments to the effective implementation of the training. Too often an organization will introduce a training program, all the while having guaranteed that it cannot work because of personality, structural, policy, or other rigidities that limit or totally restrict the transfer of the training to on the job performance.

The top level of figure 52–2 ties the idea of program evaluation together, for it brings us to the measurement of transfer through the comparison of actual job performance with the performance standards, which were set forth in the needs assessment. This is the point where the worker's relative success at performing the job is compared to the expectations that have been set out at the earliest stages of the development of the training program, a link to the foundations established by the needs analysis. Success is hoped for and expected, but at times it does not occur.

Note that failure to achieve successful indication of transfer at this stage may suggest a rather complex review process is in order. It is not enough to assume that the workers are at fault; the organization must investigate all steps in the training program to determine where the system breaks down, a fact highlighted by positioning the transfer assessment portion of figure 52–2 on top of each of the stages preceding it in the program evaluation process. A thorough assessment is crucial at this point, for to blame the employee(s) who fail without a complete understanding of the cause of that failure is likely to lead to further difficulties as the untrained may become resistant to participating in future training if they see it as a risk to their success with the organization. Any of the layers below the transfer assessment level may be at fault.

The message of this summary is that any organization proposing a training program must be aware of a wide range of potential problems and take some steps to account for them in its analysis of the results of that program. Such an analysis, if it is to be truly scientific and accurate, should adjust or compensate to the extent possible for all of the limitations identified above, as well as those elsewhere in the organization that are beyond the scope of this chapter. Barring such a compensation, the awareness of them is a necessary ingredient in deciding the actions an organization will take following the completion of a training program to improve the performance of its workers.

REFERENCES

Becker, Gary S. (1964). *Human Capital.* New York: Columbia University Press.

Boudreau, John W. (1983). Economic considerations in estimating the utility of human resource productivity improvement programs. *Personnel Psychology, 36* (3) (Autumn), 551–576.

Cook, Thomas D., & Shadish, William R., Jr. (1986). Program evaluation: The worldly science. In Mark R. Rosenzweig & Lyman W. Porter (Eds.), *Annual review of psychology* (vol. 37). Palo Alto, CA: Annual Reviews.

Cronshaw, Steven F., & Alexander Ralph A. (1983). The selection utility model as an investment decision. *Academy of Management Proceedings,* 297–300.

Flamholtz, Eric (1974). *Human resource accounting.* Encino, CA: Dickenson Press.

Fleishman, Edwin A., Harris, Edwin F., & Burtt, Harold E. (1955). *Leadership and supervision in industry.* Columbus, OH: Personnel Research Board, Ohio State University.

Goldstein, Irwin (1974). *Training: Program development and evaluation.* Monterey, CA: Brooks/Cole Publishing Co.

Goldstein, Irwin I. (1986). *Training in organizations: Needs assessment, development, and evaluation.* Monterey, CA: Brooks/Cole Publishing Co.

Good, Tom W. (1982). *Delivering effective training.* San Diego, CA: University Associates.

Greenberg, Leon (1973). *A practical guide to productivity measurement.* Washington, DC: Bureau of National Affairs.

Heneman III, Herbert G., Schwab, Donald P., Fossum, John A., Dyer, Lee D. (1986). *Personnel/human resource management* (3d ed.). Homewood, IL: Richard D. Irwin.

Hilgard, Ernest R., Bower, Gorden H. (1966). *Theories of learning* (3d ed.). New York: Appleton-Century-Crofts.

Kirkpatrick, Donald L. (1976). Evaluation of training. In R.L. Craig (Ed.), *Training and development handbook.* New York: McGraw-Hill.

Laird, Dugan (1985). *Approaches to training and development* Reading, MA: Addison-Wesley.

Latham, Gary P. (1988). Human resource training and development. In Mark R. Rosenzweig & Lyman W. Porter (Eds.), *Annual Review of Psychology* (vol. 39). Palo Alto, CA: Annual Reviews.

Leifer, Melissa S., & Newstrom, John W. (1980). Solving the transfer of training problem. *Training and Development Journal, 34* (August), 42–46.

McGehee, W., & Thayer, P.W. (1961). *Training in business and industry.* New York: John Wiley & Sons.

Marx, Robert D. (1982). Relapse prevention of managerial training: A model for maintenance of behavioral change. *Academy of Management Review 7* (3) (July), 433–441.

Michalak, Donald F. (1981). The neglected half of training. *Training and Development Journal, 35* (5) (May), 22–28.

Mosel, James N. (1957). Why training programs fail to carry over. *Personnel, 34* (3) (November–December), 56–64.

Newstrom, John W. (1984). *A role-taker/time differentiated integration of transfer strategies.* Paper presented to the Annual Convention, American Psychological Association, Toronto, Canada.

Noe, Raymond A. (1986). Trainees' attributes and attitudes: Neglected influences on training effectiveness. *Academy of Management Review, 11* (4) (October), 736–749.

Robertson, Ivan, & Downs, Sylvia (1979). Learning and the prediction of performance: Development of trainability testing in the united kingdom. *Journal of Applied Psychology, 64* (1) (February), 402–405.

Royer, James M. (1979). Theories of the transfer of learning. *Educational Psychologist 14* (1), 53–69.

Rutman, Leonard (1980). *Planning useful evaluations: Evaluability assessment.* Beverly Hills, CA: Sage Publications.

Rutman, Leonard, & Mowbray, George (1983). *Understanding program evaluation.* Beverly Hills, CA: Sage Publications.

Thurow, Lester C. (1970). Comment on Yoram Ben-Porath, The production of human capital over time. In W. Lee Hanson (Ed.), *Education, income and human capital.* New York: National Bureau of Economic Research.

Wexley, Kenneth N., & Latham, Gary P. (1981). *Developing and training human resources in organizations.* Glenview, IL: Scott, Foresman.

Wexley, Kenneth N., & Baldwin, Timothy T. (1986). Post-training strategies for facilitating positive transfer. *Academy of Management Journal, 29* (3) (September), 503–520.

PART VII

OPTIMIZING THE ORGANIZATION

53 A PSYCHOLOGICAL THEORY OF WORK ADJUSTMENT

René V. Dawis

"There is nothing so practical as a good theory," said Kurt Lewin. This chapter is about the Minnesota Theory of Work Adjustment, a psychological description of how the individual adjusts to the work environment (Dawis & Lofquist, 1984; Lofquist & Dawis, 1969). It is hoped that the theory described here can be of some practical use to business managers.

To "adjust," according to the dictionary, means "to alter so as to make fit or correspondent." Adjustment, therefore, can be defined as the process by which an individual achieves and maintains correspondence with an environment. There are many environments to which an individual adjusts—home, school, work, social, marital, to name the major ones. The Minnesota theory limits its scope to the work environment, acknowledging that there are influences from other environments and from adjustment to these other environments that can affect adjustment to the work environment. Furthermore, the work environment is not just the physical environment but, more important, includes the people with whom the individual comes in contact in the course of work.

Work adjustment, then, is the process by which an individual achieves and maintains correspondence with the work environment. This definition involves three key terms: *individual, work environment,* and *correspondence.* The Minnesota theory focuses on selected aspects of the individual and the work environment and defines "correspondence" in a particular way—and these are what is distinctive about the theory.

The individual, in the theory's view, has certain requirements for survival and well-being. (These requirements are also called needs.) There are requirements for physical survival and well-being (biological needs), as well as requirements for psychological survival and well-being (psychological needs). Psychological needs develop from, and are influenced by, biological needs. The Minnesota theory limits its scope to psychological needs but recognizes that work adjustment can also be influenced by biological needs.

It is a basic premise of the Minnesota theory that *individuals behave in order to satisfy their require-ments.* That is, all human behavior—work, play, rest, even sleep—occurs in order to satisfy some human need. Individuals differ in their needs, both in terms of kind (need pattern) and degree (need level). In psychology, the entities and events that satisfy needs—and therefore maintain behavior—are technically called *reinforcers.* Accordingly, we can define needs as requirements for reinforcers.

Reinforcers are found in the environment. Environments differ in the kinds and amounts of reinforcers they can provide. We might say that environments differ in reinforcement capability. We can therefore describe environments in terms of their respective reinforcement capabilities. For work environments, we are, of course, interested in work reinforcers and in the work environments' capabilities for the reinforcement (maintenance) of work behavior.

The environment itself has its requirements. The Minnesota theory focuses on the work environment's requirements for behavior by the individual. It is hard to visualize the physical environment (by and large, passive) as having requirements. But the work environment (which, in the main, is the work organization) is active, not passive, and does have requirements for behavior. Briefly, the work organization has goals; achieving these goals requires that certain tasks be done. These work tasks are the behavior requirements for individual employees.

Individuals are able to do some work tasks but not others. Individuals do some tasks better than other tasks. In other words, individuals differ in their behavior capability.

To summarize, a given individual has reinforcer requirements that different work environments can fill to varying degrees, depending on their reinforcement capabilities. A given work environment has behavior requirements that different individuals can fill to varying degrees, depending on their behavior capabilities. When a given individual and a given work environment get together, it is with the expectation that the other party will meet (at least minimally) each party's requirements. In more common terms, an individual takes a job, and is selected for a job, because the individual believes the job will meet his or her needs, and the employer believes the individual will meet its needs, at least to an extent that is acceptable to both. Because each party is able to respond to the other's requirements, we call this condition of mutual responsiveness *correspondence* (figure 53–1). That is, correspondence is the condition in which the individual responds to the work environment's requirements and the work environment responds to the individual's requirements. To the extent that not all requirements can be responded to, there are degrees of correspondence, or conversely, degrees of discorrespondence.

How do we know that correspondence has occurred? One basic indicator of correspondence is the satisfaction of individual and work environment. Satisfaction is defined as the evaluation of correspondence in cognitive and affective terms. To differentiate individual satisfaction from environmental satisfaction, and because a psychological theory focuses on the individual, the Minnesota theory calls the work environment's satisfaction the *satisfactoriness* of the individual. That is, when the work environment is satisfied with the individual, this is equivalent to saying that the individual is satisfactory to the work environment. The Minnesota theory reserves the term *satisfaction* to refer to the individual's satisfaction. Correspondence, therefore, is indicated by the individual's satisfaction and satisfactoriness. Conversely, discorrespondence is indicated by the individual's dissatisfaction and unsatisfactoriness.

Correspondence, when it occurs, has a final consequence that can be forecast from the individual's satisfaction and satisfactoriness. The satisfied individual will tend to stay in the work environment; the dissatisfied individual will tend to leave. The satisfactory individual will be retained in the work environment; the unsatisfactory individual will be encouraged to leave. That is, *tenure,* the individual's staying in the environment as the consequence of correspondence, is predictable from the individual's levels of satisfaction and satisfactoriness (figure 53–2).

Requirements change, and because they do, adjustment has to occur. From the individual's point of view, a certain amount of discorrespondence can be tolerated, but beyond that the individual does something about the situation. Tolerance for discorrespondence defines the individual's flexibility; the more tolerant of discorrespondence, the more flexible the individual is.

When the individual can no longer tolerate the discorrespondence, two modes of adjustment are possible: (1) the *active* adjustment mode, in which the individual tries to change the environment, and (2) the *reactive* adjustment mode, in which the individual makes changes in self. The objective of either

Figure 53–1. Correspondence (Coresponsiveness) between Individual and Work Environment

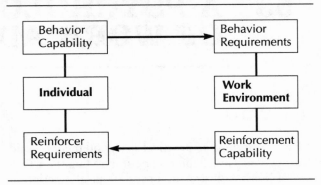

Figure 53–2. The Consequences of Correspondence

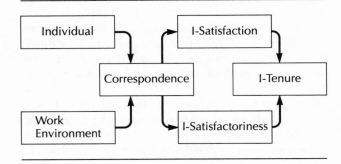

change is, of course, to reduce discorrespondence (or conversely, to improve correspondence). The active mode meets this objective by effecting change in the environment's reinforcements or in its behavior requirements. The reactive mode effects change in the individual's reinforcer requirements or behavior capabilities (figure 53–3). Adjustment can occur in either mode, or in both modes at the same time, or the individual may not even try to adjust. The last route can lead to serious, pathological consequences for the individual.

If attempts at adjustment do not succeed, the individual may persist up to a point. Beyond that point, the individual will seek to separate self from the work environment. How long the individual persists in attempts at adjustment defines the individual's *perseverance.*

All that has been said about the individual, from the individual's point of view, can be said about the work environment, from its point of view. That is, the work environment can be described in terms of its flexibility (tolerance for discorrespondence) and perseverance (persistence in adjustment) and its use of active or reactive modes of adjustment.

These, then, are the main ideas of the Minnesota theory: satisfaction, satisfactoriness, and tenure can

Figure 53–3. Work Adjustment

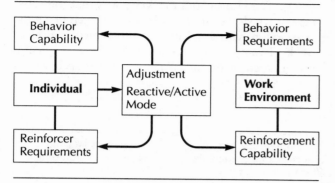

predicted from individual-environment correspondence. In turn, correspondence can be inferred from knowledge of the individual's reinforcement requirements and behavior capabilities and the work environment's behavior requirements and reinforcement capabilities. Also, correspondence can be improved (or discorrespondence reduced) by effecting changes in the individual (reinforcement requirements, behavior capabilities) or in the work environment (behavior requirements, reinforcement capabilities). Finally, the total system can be monitored by readings of the individual's satisfaction and satisfactoriness.

To make use of the theory requires that data be obtained on the reinforcement requirements and behavior capabilities of workers and on the behavior requirements and reinforcement capabilities of jobs. Furthermore, the data have to be in such a form as to allow the evaluation of correspondence between behavior capabilities and behavior requirements and between reinforcement requirements and reinforcement capabilities. Ideally, the data should be parallel or commensurate; that is, the data on the worker should have their counterpart for the job, or vice versa. For example, if the job's requirements are described in terms of skills, the worker should be described in terms of those same skills. If the worker is described in terms of abilities, the job requirements should be described in terms of those same abilities.

Behavior requirements are usually written down as job descriptions and job specifications, typically in terms of tasks required and conditions under which the tasks are to be performed. Behavior capabilities are usually assessed directly, by using ability tests, skill tests, and work sample tests, or indirectly, from work histories, certificates of training, and reference letters from previous employers. Ordinarily, then, data on behavior requirements and behavior capabilities are not commensurate.

An example of commensurate capability-requirement data at the ability level of measurement is to be

found in the system employed by the U.S. Employment Service (USES). To describe behavior capabilities, the USES developed the General Aptitude Test Battery (GATB; U.S. Department of Labor, 1970). The GATB measures the following nine abilities that are most frequently involved in work performance:

General ability (G)

Verbal ability (V)

Numerical ability (N)

Spatial perception ability (S)

Form perception ability (P)

Detail perception ability (Q)

Eye-hand coordination (K)

Finger dexterity (F)

Manual dexterity (M)

The first three abilities (G, V, N) are "central processing" or cognitive abilities, the next three (S, P, Q) are "input" or perceptual abilities, and the last three (K, F, M) are "output" or motor abilities.

To describe behavior requirements in ability terms, the USES developed the Occupational Aptitude Pattern (OAP; U.S. Department of Labor, 1979). An OAP describes a job in terms of the one to four abilities most essential to performing the job, as well as the minimum level of such ability(-ies) required for satisfactory job performance. For example, jobs in engineering technology would require minimum scores of 105 on G, 100 on N, and 100 on S. By comparing the individual's GATB scores on G, N, and S with this OAP, one can evaluate whether the individual has the behavior capability to respond to the behavior requirements of engineering technology jobs. Extensive studies by the USES have documented the utility of this commensurate-data correspondence system in the selection and placement of workers in literally hundreds of occupations (U.S. Department of Labor, 1970, 1979).

With the exception of data on pay and benefits, data on reinforcement requirements and reinforcement capabilities are not routinely collected in organizational settings. Since the 1950s, job satisfaction surveys have been used to infer both the worker's reinforcement requirements and the work environment's reinforcement capabilities. Much better precision (and therefore a better guide for action) can be attained if reinforcement requirements and reinforcement capabilities could be measured directly and separately.

The Work Adjustment Project at the University of

Minnesota has devoted much research to the problem of measuring the reinforcement requirements of workers and the reinforcement capabilities of work environments. In this research, the project's first step was to develop a multiaspect rating scale measure of job satisfaction, the Minnesota Satisfaction Questionnaire (MSQ; Weiss, Dawis, England & Lofquist, 1967). The idea behind the MSQ was that job satisfaction consists of many satisfactions, each being the satisfaction with a separate reinforcement aspect of work. Twenty of the satisfactions most frequently encountered in studies of many diverse occupations

Table 53–1
Scale Titles and Sample Items

Scale	Minnesota Satisfaction Questionnaire (How satisfied am I with . . .)	Minnesota Importance Questionnaire (Which is more important?)	Minnesoata Job Description Questionnaire (Workers on this job . . .)
1. Ability Utilization	The chance to make use of my best abilities	I could do something that makes use of my abilities	Make use of their individual abilities
2. Achievement	The feeling of accomplishment I get from the job	The job would give me a feeling of accomplishment	Get a feeling of accomplishment
3. Activity	Being able to stay busy	I could be busy all the time	Are busy all the time
4. Advancement	The chances of advancement in this job	The job would provide an opportunity for advancement	Have opportunities for advancement
5. Authority	The chance to tell people what to do	I could tell people what to do	Tell other workers what to do
6. Company Policies & Practices	Company policies and the way they are administered	The company would administer its policies fairly	Have a company that administers its policies fairly
7. Compensation	How my pay compares with that of other workers	My pay would compare well with that of other workers	Are paid well in comparison with other workers
8. Co-Workers	The friendliness of my co-workers	My co-workers would be easy to make friends with	Have co-workers who are easy to make friends with
9. Creativity	The chance to try out some of my own ideas	I could try out my own ideas	Try out their own ideas
10. Independence	The chance to be alone on the job	I could work alone on the job	Do their work alone
11. Moral Values	Being able to do the job without feeling it is morally wrong	I could do the work without feeling it is morally wrong	Do work without feeling that it is morally wrong
12. Recognition	The recognition I get for the work I do	I could get recognition for the work I do	Receive recognition for the work they do
13. Responsibility	The chance to make decisions on my own	I could make decisions on my own	Make decisions on their own
14. Security	The way my job provides for steady employment	The job would provide for steady employment	Have steady employment
15. Social Service	The chance to do things for other people	I could do things for other people	Have work where they do things for other people
16. Social Status	The chance to be "somebody" in the community	I could be "somebody" in the community	Have a position of "somebody" in the community
17. Supervision— Human Relations	The way my boss backs up his/her employees (with top management)	My boss would back up the workers (with top management)	Have bosses who back up their workers (with top management)
18. Supervision— Technical	The way my boss trains his/her employees	My boss would train the workers well	Have bosses who train the workers well
19. Variety	The chance to do something different every day	I could do something different every day	Have something different to do every day
20. Working Conditions	The working conditions	The job would have good working conditions	Have good working conditions

were incorporated in the MSQ. These satisfactions are shown in table 53–1.

Because the twenty MSQ scales identified distinct reinforcement aspects, the next step was to develop a rating scale measure of reinforcement capability, the Minnesota Job Description Questionnaire (MJDQ; Borgen, Weiss, Tinsley, Dawis & Lofquist, 1968). Reinforcement capability was described as an Occupational Reinforcer Pattern (ORP; Borgen at al., 1968) that shows the level of reinforcement for each aspect as rated by incumbents or their supervisors. ORPs have been developed for 185 occupations (Stewart, Greenstein, Holt, Henly, Engdahl, Dawis, Lofquist & Weiss, 1986). Figure 53–4 shows the ORP for an electrical engineer. The ORP statements describing the reinforcers are also shown in table 53–1.

To complete the instrumentation, a measure of reinforcement requirements was also developed, the Minnesota Importance Questionnaire (MIQ; Gay, Weiss, Hendel, Dawis & Lofquist, 1971), which asks respondents to rank reinforcers according to their importance to the individual. Studies of the MIQ have shown that the twenty reinforcer requirements group into six clusters. Each cluster of reinforcer requirements reflects an underlying theme that represents a work value. The six work values reflected in the MIQ are:

1. Achievement—the importance of conditions that encourage accomplishment.

2. Comfort—the importance of conditions that promote comfort and reduce stress.

Figure 53–4. ORP for Electrical Engineer

	Scale Value
Achievement	**1.20**
Ability Utilization: make use of their individual abilities	1.39
Achievement: get a feeling of accomplishment	1.01
Comfort	**.55**
Activity: are busy all the time	.70
Independence: do their work alone	.33
Variety: have something different to do every day	.30
Compensation: are paid well in comparison with other workers	.30
Security: have steady employment	.97
Working Conditions: have good working conditions	.72
Status	**.31**
Advancement: have opportunities for advancement	.60
Recognition: receive recognition for the work they do	.63
Authority: tell other workers what to do	.29
Social Status: have the position of "somebody" in the community	-.27
Altruism	**.46**
Coworkers: have coworkers who are easy to make friends with	.65
Social Service: have work doing things for other people	.23
Moral Values: do work without feeling it is morally wrong	.49
Safety	**.08**
Company Policies: company administers its policies fairly	.10
Supervision — Human Relations: bosses back up their workers	.18
Supervision — Technical: bosses train their workers well	-.04
Autonomy	**1.01**
Creativity: try out their own ideas	.96
Responsibility: make decisions on their own	1.10
Autonomy: plan their work with little supervision	.97

Scale: -1.0   0.0   +1.0   +2.0   +3.0

3. Status—the importance of conditions that provide recognition and prestige.

4. Altruism—the importance of conditions that foster harmony with and service to others.

5. Safety—the importance of conditions that establish predictability and stability.

6. Autonomy—the importance of conditions that increase personal control and stimulate initiative.

Each of these conditions represents a distinct group of reinforcers. Achievement and Autonomy encompass internal or self reinforcers, Status and Altruism involve social reinforcers, and Comfort and Safety pertain to external environment reinforcers. Achievement and Comfort are opposing values, as are Status versus Altruism and Safety versus Autonomy.

The MIQ has been used extensively in vocational rehabilitation, vocational counseling, and career planning. Because the MIQ and the ORPs are commensurate, an individual's MIQ can be compared with the 185 ORPs, and MIQ-ORP correspondence can be used in career planning and career choice. Several studies following up on counseled clients have verified that MIQ-ORP correspondence predicts subsequent career and job satisfaction (Dawis & Lofquist, 1984).

To complement the MSQ, which measures the individual's satisfaction, the Minnesota Satisfactoriness Scales (MSS; Gibson, Weiss, Dawis & Lofquist, 1970) were developed. The objective was a measure of satisfactoriness that could be applied to all occupations. Three basic aspects of generic satisfactoriness were identified by research: *performance,* or how well the worker did the tasks of the job; *conformance,* or how well the worker conformed to the rules of the workplace; and *adjustment,* or how well the worker adjusted emotionally to work and the work environment. All three aspects were incorporated in the MSS. Later research showed that MSS scores could be predicted from GATB-OAP correspondence, and the combination of MSS and MSQ scores could predict tenure and turnover.

Whether the instruments described above are used or whether other, equivalent instruments are preferred, the instrumented Minnesota theory can be applied in three basic ways: First, it can be applied in a straightforward manner toward the prediction or the evaluation of work adjustment status, that is,

toward the prediction or evaluation of satisfaction, satisfactoriness, and tenure or turnover.

Second, given more detailed measurement, areas of correspondence can be distinguished from areas of discorrespondence on both behavior capability-requirement and reinforcement requirement-capability aspects. Areas of correspondence can then be maintained and strengthened, whereas areas of discorrespondence can be addressed and alleviated. The results of such intervention can be tracked and evaluated on the satisfaction and satisfactoriness indicators.

Third, assuming that the theory is an adequate representation of reality, certain inferences and deductions can be made from incomplete information—for example:

- From behavior capability and behavior requirement data, satisfactoriness can be inferred.
- From behavior capability and satisfactoriness data, behavior requirements can be inferred.
- From behavior requirement and satisfactoriness data, behavior capability can be inferred.
- From reinforcement requirement and reinforcement capability data, satisfaction can be inferred.
- From reinforcement requirement and satisfaction data, reinforcement capability can be inferred.
- From reinforcement capability and satisfaction data, reinforcement requirements can be inferred.
- From satisfactoriness and satisfaction data, tenure or turnover can be inferred.
- From predicted satisfactoriness and actual satisfactoriness, when actual is much higher than predicted, overachievement can be inferred.
- From predicted satisfaction and actual satisfaction, when actual is much higher than predicted, flexibility can be inferred.
- From predicted tenure and actual tenure, when actual is much higher than predicted, perseverance can be inferred.

These three basic applications give an idea of the potential use value of the Minnesota theory. Although the jury is still out, in the end—as Kurt Lewin's aphorism implies—the verdict on the Minnesota Theory of Work Adjustment (or any other theory, for that matter) will be rendered on the basis of its usefulness.

REFERENCES

Borgen, F.H., Weiss, D.J., Tinsley, H.E.A., Dawis, R.V., & Lofquist, L.H. (1968). The measurement of occupational reinforcer patterns. *Minnesota Studies in Vocational Rehabilitation*, no. 25.

Dawis, R.V., & Lofquist, L.H. (1984). *A psychological theory of work adjustment*. Minneapolis: University of Minnesota Press.

Gay, E.G., Weiss, D.J., Hendel, D.D., Dawis, R.V., & Lofquist, L.H. (1971). Manual for the Minnesota Importance Questionnaire. *Minnesota Studies in Vocational Rehabilitation*, no. 28.

Gibson, D.L., Weiss, D.J., Dawis, R.V. & Lofquist, L.H. (1970). Manual for the Minnesota Satisfactoriness Scales. *Minnesota Studies in Vocational Rehabilitation*, no. 27.

Lofquist, L.H., & Dawis, R.V. (1969). *Adjustment to work*. New York: Appleton-Century-Crofts.

Stewart, E.S., Greenstein, S.M., Holt, N.L., Henly, G.A., Engdahl, B.E., Dawis, R.V., Lofquist, L.H., & Weiss, D.J. (1986). *Occupational reinforcer patterns*. Minneapolis: Vocational Psychology Research, Department of Psychology, University of Minnesota.

U.S. Department of Labor (1970). *Manual for the USES General Aptitude Test Battery*. Washington, DC: U.S. Government Printing Office.

U.S. Department of Labor (1979). *Manual for the USES General Aptitude Test Battery, Section II: Occupational aptitude pattern structure*. Washington, DC: U.S. Government Printing Office.

Weiss, D.J., Dawis, R.V., England, G.W., & Lofquist, L.H. (1967). Manual for the Minnesota Satisfaction Questionnaire. *Minnesota Studies in Vocational Rehabilitation*, no. 22.

54 ORGANIZATIONAL CLIMATE AND CULTURE: THE PSYCHOLOGY OF THE WORKPLACE

Benjamin Schneider, Sarah Gunnarson

A manager in a construction company reviews his safety records and finds that employee accidents have doubled in the past five years. What could account for this increase? A bank manager reports to the bank's stockholders that their company is the industry leader in financial services innovation. How can she ensure that this lead will be maintained? The manager of a retail store has received numerous customer complaints about service and resolves to improve the store's customer service. What can this manager do to foster good service?

Psychologists think the answer to these questions lies in the concepts of climate and culture. Climate and culture can explain why well-intentioned managers can have their efforts go awry and can also explain why making changes in an organization can feel like "turning the *Queen Elizabeth* around while going downstream under a full head a steam." AT&T is an extreme example of an organization that had to make a monumental shift from being a regulated utility company to a deregulated marketing company in order to survive. To make these changes, AT&T had to change its entire orientation and identity, or as psychologists would call it, its climate and culture.

Climate and culture, while interrelated concepts, are distinct in one basic way: climate refers to the visible practices, procedures, and rewarded behaviors that characterize an organization. Climate tells the "what" that happens in an organization. Culture, on the other hand, is the underlying or latent assumptions, values, and philosophies that help explain "why" things happen the way they do in an organization. In fact, a particular organizational climate is usually a manifestation or outgrowth of an organization's culture (Schneider & Rentsch, 1988).

In this chapter, we will define and explain the concepts of climate and culture and then explore three specific climates and cultures an organization might want to establish or maintain: a climate and culture for safety, innovation, and service. Our intent is to illustrate how the concepts of climate and culture can facilitate an understanding for achieving organizational effectiveness.

ORGANIZATIONAL CLIMATE

Organizational climate refers to the themes or imperatives that employees believe describe their organization. These themes are based on and consist of the practices, procedures, and rewarded behaviors (collectively referred to as activities) that employees see happening to them and around them. The activities develop into themes because they tend to occur repeatedly, and employees have a shared perception that these activities are the "way things are done around here." For example, some of the practices,

procedures, and rewarded behaviors that might characterize an organization are:

- Employees always leave their office door open, unless there is a serious meeting going on inside.
- Employees acknowledge and celebrate each others' birthdays at work.
- When employees have financial difficulties, the organization's policy to is provide low-interest loans.

This particular set of practices and procedures might be indicative of a supportive social climate. In

The authors are grateful to Joan Rentsch, Katherine Klein, Michele Laliberte, and Jill Wheeler for their helpful comments and suggestions on earlier versions of this chapter.

this example, only three practices and procedures have been mentioned. However, a particular climate or theme can consist of hundreds of practices, procedures, and rewarded behaviors. A climate is a summary perception of clusters of activities that together connote a particular goal or orientation of an organization. A climate evolves in an organization when employees learn what behaviors are acceptable or unacceptable and what behaviors get rewarded. In one organization, arriving 10 minutes late for work may be inconsequential, while in another organization, the same behavior might be grounds for probation. Employees quickly learn what practices and procedures are characteristic of and acceptable or unacceptable in an organization and which behaviors are likely to be rewarded. They use this information to guide their current and future actions.

In trying to create a new climate, managers can make the mistake of thinking that simply proclaiming what the "new climate" should be is adequate for change to occur. Speeches by the chief executive officer (CEO), newsletters, or catchy slogans promoting a new service orientation ("customer service is number 1") will fail if the practices, procedures, and rewards do not support it. For example, attempts to improve customer service will be ineffective if companies fail to provide employees proper customer service training, if the equipment needed to provide service breaks down repeatedly, or if employees do not see changes in the behaviors that get rewarded. If a rude and discourteous bank teller is promoted before another bank teller who is always courteous with customers, employees learn quickly that the new service slogan is just management's latest "kick."

As another example, consider a company that requires employees to take a safety training course prior to using new machinery, even when workers are needed on the line due to production schedule demands. The practice of training first communicates to employees that the organization takes safety very

seriously. This is not to say that speeches and catchy slogans are not useful; they are just inadequate in and of themselves to maintain or establish a particular climate. In other words, a climate is created by following the old adage that actions speak louder than words (Kilman, 1985).

An organization can possess many climates because practices, procedures, and rewards can be focused on numerous goals. Some of the most commonly studied climates by psychologists are climates of autonomy or closeness of supervision (the degree to which employees are expected to work on their own), decision centralization (the degree to which decisions are made by a few people or many and at what level), and work group cooperation, friendliness, and warmth (James, Joyce & Slocum, 1988). Even different units in the same organization can have different climates. For example, a high-tech firm might have a climate for innovation in the R&D department, a climate for safety in manufacturing, and a climate for service in the sales and customer service units. In addition, all three departments might share an overall climate for service: the R&D department considers only products that would be user friendly, the manufacturing department emphasizes quality to ensure customer satisfaction with product reliability, and the sales and service department consider that customers have higher priority than the completion of paperwork.

In summary, organizational climate refers to the themes that emerge from practices, procedures, and rewarded behaviors that characterize a work setting. The themes evolve from the activities people see happening to them and around them, especially those activities that are rewarded both formally (pay and incentive systems) and informally (peer and supervisory rewards and recognition). Finally, organizations can have different climates in different parts of the organization and/or certain climates may characterize entire workplaces.

ORGANIZATIONAL CULTURE

While climate summarizes the kinds of practices, procedures, and rewarded behaviors that happen in an organization, culture focuses on the assumptions, values, and philosophies that give meaning or interpretation to what happens. Employees in one company, for example, may interpret a new cafeteria-style benefit plan as a sign that management wants to be more sensitive to their needs by offering more options, while in another company, employees may interpret the new benefit plan as management's latest money-

saving scheme for reducing employees' benefits. This latter interpretation would be more likely in an organization where there is a history of a lack of trust between management and employees.

The assumptions, values, and philosophies that constitute an organization's culture tend to be broadly focused and concern wide-ranging issues such as the nature of human beings and the role of work in life. For example, an implicitly shared assumption in an organization might be that work should be the central focus of a person's life. This shared philosophy of life would probably result in a climate where employees regularly work overtime and take work home with them on the weekends; the organization might be said to have a climate for long hours. Those employees who do not share this value about the role of work in life will be more likely to leave, while those who stay may learn to live with it or even come to agree with it.

As another example, consider an organization that operates under the shared assumption that human beings are basically lazy and dislike working. As a result, a tightly controlled climate might be the result—a climate characterized by the practices of employees' punching time clocks when they arrive and leave work and documenting how they spend every hour of their time. As previously mentioned, a climate is generally an outgrowth of an organization's culture.

Culture, then, consists of the assumptions, values, and philosophies that give meaning or interpretation to the practices, procedures, and rewarded behaviors of organizations. Culture is mainly communicated through employees' either sharing their interpretations of why they think things happen the way they do ("They are bringing in computers so that they can get rid of us peons") or through storytelling ("One day there was a blizzard, and the manager drove a customer home because she was afraid to drive in the snow"). In fact, it can be difficult for an entire organization to develop a strong, shared culture if employees have little opportunity to interact with each other or if different divisions of a company have little contact with each other.

Organizations vary on the degree of intensity and integration of their culture (Rousseau, in press). *Intensity* refers to the extent to which employees agree and share similar assumptions, values, and philosophies. *Integration* refers to whether employees at the various levels of the hierarchy and in different functional areas share a common culture. Companies that have a great deal of turnover, particularly among top-level leaders, can have a difficult time establishing a culture and, consequently, climates. Also, a particular climate and culture can exist in one part of a company and not in another. This, however, is not necessarily bad. It may be desirable, as we noted ear-

lier, for an R&D unit to have a culture for innovation where issues of safety are irrelevant, while the opposite might be true for the production unit where reliability and quality control, rather than creativity, may be the theme of utmost importance.

Psychologists think that an organization's culture evolves over a period of time as members of a group confront specific problems posed by everyday situations. As employees devise solutions that enable the organization to survive despite hardships and obstacles, the solutions and assumptions about how the business world works become taken for granted. When an organization is first established, the culture is usually determined by the founding leader or leaders who project their assumptions, values, and philosophies onto the procedures and practices used to achieve organizational goals (Schein, 1985). Since there are often multiple strategies to approach any business endeavor, it is common to encounter businesses in the same industry that act, look, and behave quite differently from each other; they have different cultures and climates. Also, organizations tend to attract and select newcomers who agree with its assumptions and ways of going about work. Furthermore, employees tend to leave organizations that are not a good fit for their own personal values and philosophies (Schneider, 1987).

If an organization is successful, then the implicit assumptions held by leaders, and the strategies promoted by leaders, are reinforced, and, over time, these assumptions and strategies are taken for granted by employees. As a result, it can be difficult to articulate and identify the precise nature and etiology of a particular culture. We find in our research on climate and culture, then, that employees can fairly easily describe and agree on the practices and procedures and the kinds of behavior that get rewarded as reflections of their organization's climate. In contrast, employees have a much harder time describing why they believe the practices and procedures are there in the first place. For example, a typical response to the question, "Why does everyone document how they spend their time?" would be, "I don't know. I guess it's always been done that way." Culture is so fundamental to the way an organization goes about its business that it is often difficult to articulate the assumptions, values, and philosophies that make up the culture.

CHANGING CLIMATE AND CULTURE

Can organizational climate and culture be changed? Climates and cultures are always in some state of flux

as new employees join the organization with new ideas or existing employees try different approaches to solving problems. However, climates and cultures generally do not change much on their own unless the organization is faced with a crisis that threatens its existence. When an organization is in the mature stage of its life cycle, it can be especially difficult to change its climate and culture.

The most important guideline in changing or creating a new climate or culture is consistency across all facets of an organization's practices, procedures, and rewarded behaviors. Research shows that having only one or two people or elements of the organization supporting a new climate or culture will not be effective in creating a change. All facets of the organization must be examined for their support or inhibition of a new climate or culture (Bolman & Deal, 1985).

The difficulty of changing a climate and culture is painfully experienced by anyone who has been through a merger or acquisition. Unless the climates and cultures of the companies involved are very similar, it is difficult for employees to change "the way things have always been done around here." Unfortunately, decisions to merge are often based only on financial information or the feasibility of incorporating the particular technology involved rather than the cultural or climate aspects of a merger (Mirvis, 1985). The similarity of the combined cultures can often mean the difference between a smooth or a rough transition in a merger. In extreme cases, companies fire everyone in top management in the acquired company to extinguish "culture clash."

Climate and culture issues also explain why some of the Japanese management techniques have had only a modest degree of success when used in American companies. Organizational researcher Eugene Koprowski (1983) has identified some of the fundamental ways in which the Oriental worldview and the Western, or Occidental worldview, differ drastically. The Oriental worldview stresses the unity of all people in contrast to the Occidental worldview of the importance of the individual. Americans value rapid promotions because there is an underlying belief that there is a beginning and end to life. In contrast, the Oriental culture assumes that life is an endless cycle, so that time takes on a different meaning. Koprowski argues that "it may be necessary to modify certain promising Japanese practices to make them compatible with our American cowboy mentality" (p. 47).

To demonstrate the point that most, if not all, of the systems in an organization must consistently support a climate and culture in order for it to be a reality for the employees, we present next the kinds of research that reveal how consistency in practices, procedures, and rewarded behaviors can lead to a climate and culture for safety, innovation, and service.

THE CLIMATE AND CULTURE FOR SAFETY

Zohar (1980), an Israeli psychologist concerned with differential accident rates in Israeli factories, asked the following question: Why do organizations, including organizations producing essentially the same items, have significantly different safety records? Based on his understanding of climate, Zohar reasoned that a good safety record was probably not due to just one or two organizational practices and procedures but many. Zohar conducted a research project where he had safety inspectors rate twenty different factories representing four product categories: metal fabrication, food processing, chemical industry, and textile industry. Zohar wanted to test whether an organization's "climate for safety" could accurately predict which organizations would be considered safe by safety inspectors. Based on questionnaires filled out by employees, Zohar concluded that the following organizational practices, procedures, and rewarded behaviors accurately predicted a company's safety level:

1. Safety training programs are taken seriously by employees and are viewed as important prerequisites for successful performance on the job.

2. Safety is considered when establishing a required work pace. A higher work pace is viewed as potentially hazardous.

3. The safety committee is accorded high status by the high level of committee participants and actual implementation of committee recommendations by upper management.

4. The safety officer is given high status as evidenced by the executive authority relegated to him (e.g., authority to remove workers from production or to stop production processes when safety regulations are not being followed).

5. Safe conduct is used in promotion decisions.

6. Safe conduct has a positive impact on social status.

It is clear in reviewing these organizational practices and procedures that an effective climate for safety permeates all aspects of an organization: training, job design, production scheduling, and so on. In fact, Zohar concluded from his study that the key to a lower accident rate is for people in the organization to view safety needs as an integral part of the production system.

Of the practices and procedures listed the first two, importance of safety training and effects of required work pace on safety, were the practices and procedures most critical to a higher level of safety ratings. These two critical factors as well as the other four suggest that management's commitment to safety through its actions and the setting of priorities is what largely creates and maintains a climate for safety. In addition, coworkers, in the way that they treat each other and relegate status, also create and maintain a climate for safety. Zohar's research on the climate for safety shows how many features of a workplace can influence employee perceptions and how these perceptions are, in turn, related to organizational outcomes like low accident rates and safe behavior in general.

In terms of a culture for safety, Zohar suggested that a management philosophy that is not strictly production oriented but is also people oriented is part of a culture for safety. Other values and assumptions that we can speculate would be part of a culture for safety concern broad issues, such as the best way to solve problems, the best way to manage people, and human beings' relationship with the environment:

- The best way to solve problems is to anticipate them and prevent them from happening in the first place; it is better to be proactive rather than reactive in solving problems. A long-term strategy is better than a short-term strategy.

- Employees' well-being should be given higher priority than production. While meeting a production deadline is important, keeping workers safe and unharmed is even more important.

- It is more important to be cautious physically than to be "macho" and take risks. Dominate and control the physical environment rather than let the environment control you.

These three assumptions are examples of the basic assumptions, values, and philosophies that could support a climate for safety. Other cultural assumptions that might be just as effective in establishing a climate for safety would be defensive: a "let's not get sued" philosophy or a philosophy that says "let's keep ourselves out of the press at all costs." In order to know the "why" behind a company's safety record, it is necessary to know about its history, the past and present leaders' philosophies on safety, and significant events concerning safety that are part of the organization's history.

THE CLIMATE AND CULTURE FOR INNOVATION

Andre Delbecq and Peter Mills (1985) of the University of Santa Clara in California were interested in identifying the climates and cultures that lead to successful innovation in organizations. Their findings, which distinguish highly innovative companies from companies less successful at innovation, are based on studies of several hundred managers in high-technology and health service organizations. They defined innovation as the capacity for organizational readjustment, as well as the actual development and effective marketing of innovations. Delbecq and Mills discovered that the practices and procedures shown in table 54–1 were the major ways in which the highly innovative organizations differed from less innovative organizations. Some of the highlights of table 54–1 are:

Degree of commitment from top management and sponsorship. In organizations with low innovation, top management does not commit resources of emotional support or money to get the innovation project started. In contrast, organizations high on innovation commit many resources to the innovation project, such as special funds for innovations, assigning employees to the job of finding and promoting innovations, and making sure that each innovation has an assigned advocate or sponsor.

Emphasis on market analysis and sensitivity to the customer. The low innovators were characterized by relying on poor or nonexistent feasibility studies that resulted in an overestimation of demand for the innovation, implementing an overly complex design, and giving little attention to the support required for success (e.g., training, marketing). High innovators, on the other hand, were characterized as being "close to" and "in touch with" the average potential user so that market demand could be accurately assessed.

Table 54–1
Climate for Innovation: Practices, Procedures, and Rewarded Behaviors

Issue	Low Innovators	High Innovators
Commitment from the employee	Sponsorship sought from line managers who have other responsibilities Underresourced Feelings rather than the facts dominate decision to commit resources Poor integration of new idea with existing plans/priorities	Special committees/task forces who have resources to allocate and who review proposals for funds are responsible for innovations Feasibility studies, not personalities, are used to make decisions A sponsor, in addition to the original advocate, is assigned to champion the idea
Market analysis and customer sensitivity	Advocate overestimates demand in the market Only engineers, not users, design the innovation Little consideration is given to the support required for success (e.g., training)	Innovations are client focused Flexibility in design of the innovation Feasibility study includes design, production, marketing, and human resources
Adoption	Power, not data, determines adoption decision Lack of a formal commitment and lack of resources Excessive time delays	Firm, formal, commitments are made to the innovation and the needed resources Organization, not only advocate, commits so get diffusion of commitment and responsibility
Implementation	Underresourced Delusions of success/grandeur lead to premature full roll-out	Careful, critically evaluated, small steps for roll-out Fully resourced Plans made for complete roll-out include production, marketing, and human resources

Source: Adapted from Delbecq and Mills (1985).

Adoption procedures. The low innovators lacked formal commitment from the organization as well as the resources for implementation. High innovators, in contrast, received firm commitments from people throughout the organization. As a result, the innovation's advocate felt supported rather than alone and isolated.

Implementation. Low innovators were not only underresourced (as noted above), but they have delusions of grandeur, leading to premature implementations without adequate testing along the way. The high innovation organizations took small steps, evaluated each step as they went, and made the necessary adjustments for acceptance in the market. In addition, the gradual roll-out allowed for a realistic determination of the resources required to sustain the innovation.

The lessons to be learned from contrasting high and low innovation organizations can be summarized by speculating about the kinds of implicit assumptions, values, and philosophies that might differentiate a successful innovator's culture from an unsuccessful one:

- Success in the marketplace comes from complete knowledge of, and input from, the end user. Customer acceptance, not engineering sophistication, is what ultimately leads to a successful innovation.

- The quality of the idea itself is what is important, not the authority and power of the person behind the innovation. Decisions about the innovation should be based on information and data rather than on politics and power.

- Creative people need nurturance, support, and organizational commitment to succeed. No matter how creative an individual is, he or she cannot sustain the effort it takes to produce a successful innovation if left alone and unsupported.

- Decisions should be made one step at a time (i.e., one must walk before one can run).

THE CLIMATE AND CULTURE FOR SERVICE

Before discussing what climates and cultures lead to providing good service, it is important first to review some of the unique characteristics of service organizations. In fact, in the past five to ten years, it has become clear that service organizations need to be managed differently from goods-producing organizations. This is true because of the ways in which services differ from goods. In the extreme, services differ from goods in the following three ways (Bowen & Schneider, 1988):

1. Services are more *intangible* than goods; goods yield "things" while services yield "experiences." The experiential nature of services makes relationships between the consumer and the service deliverer more significant in the evaluation of a service than the evaluation of a product. The intangibility of a service is exemplified by air travel or the theater where once a flight or a play is over, the participant is left with only the experience.

2. Services tend to be *produced and consumed simultaneously.* Due to intangibility, services are usually produced and consumed in the presence of both an employee and a consumer. Thus, a cabin attendant in an airplane cannot deliver a service in the absence of a passenger. In contrast, a product is manufactured apart from the consumer, and the product is consumed or used by the customer apart from the production of the item.

3. *Services often require participation of the consumer in the production of the service.* Most services require at least information and usually other behaviors on the part of consumers for the delivery of a quality experience. Passengers provide information about where they want to go, what they want to eat, or where they want to sit, and, if they fail to arrive for departure, the service cannot be delivered.

The ways in which services differ from goods are not meant to be dichotomies; many goods have accompanying services (a computer with a service contract), and many services have accompanying goods (auto repair services yield a hopefully driveable car). Our reason for presenting the extremes is to acknowledge that these attributes of service have implications for designing organizations that will have service-oriented climates and cultures.

Along these lines, Benjamin Schneider of the University of Maryland (College Park) and his colleagues

Table 54–2
Climate for Service: Practices, Procedures, and Rewarded Behaviors

Emphasis on human resources
  Career planning and career counseling
  Supportive, considerate management and supervision
  Importance attached to work group as family/community

Management is a service enthusiast, not service bureaucrat
  Following rules and policies is less critical than meeting customer needs
  Rules and policies facilitate service delivery rather than facilitate internal efficiency standards

Participative or consultative decision making
  Employees are consulted about the design and implementation of new services, changes in service delivery, and the design of new internal procedures and equipment for service delivery
  Employee knowledge and information is acknowledged and rewarded

Active retention of consumers
  All customers are treated equally (e.g., in a bank, regardless of balance) and as nonexpendable
  Retention of accounts is facilitated and encouraged through personal attention, cross-selling, and free flow of information between organization and consumer

Attention to details
  Staff is well trained and sufficient in number
  Equipment and facilities are appropriate and well maintained
  The resources required for excellence (e.g., supplies, systems, information) are available

Source: Adapted from Schneider and Bowen (1985).

(cf. Schneider & Bowen, 1985) have produced a series of studies and papers that reveal the kinds of practices and procedures that characterize a climate for service. These findings are summarized in table 54–2. The table shows that the three attributes of service yield the following requirements for a climate for service to be created in an organization:

Human resources practices are a key to service quality. Employees deliver the kind of service to consumers that fits with the way they are treated as employees. When employees are treated well and have a sense of community at work, they will create a similar positive experience for consumers. It might be said that how an organization treats its employees is directly reflected in how employees treat consumers.

Management needs to adopt a service enthusiast style versus a service bureaucrat style. The enthusiast style of management puts a higher priority on customers' having a positive experience than on meeting internal efficiency standards.

Participative or consultative decision making with respect to service delivery practices is appropriate. Because employees interact with consumers all day, they are valuable sources of information about consumer wants and needs. In fact, Schneider and his colleagues have demonstrated that employee descriptions of the quality of service they deliver fit consumer descriptions of the quality of the service they receive.

The active retention of current consumers characterizes high-quality service delivery organizations. Effective service organizations are equally as concerned with retention of current consumers as they are with the attraction of new consumers.

Attention to details regarding the quality of staff, equipment, and supplies is a key to service quality. In an organization that delivers good service, staff are well trained, and equipment and supplies are up to date and well serviced. In general, the logistics of service excellence are very carefully monitored.

The major insight from these results is that organizations need to create a positive work experience, on many dimensions, for their service employees if they want to deliver good service. Because services are produced and consumed simultaneously, the organization cannot directly control the interaction between the service deliverer and the consumer at the time of delivery. An organization can only indirectly control the interaction by providing a foundation that facilitates the service employee. This foundation consists of the way employees feel about their jobs based on their training and skills, the staffing and equipment resources they have, and the rules and policies by which they are expected to behave. In sum, these practices and procedures create a climate for service.

Organizations that create and maintain a culture that supports an excellent climate for service might hold the following four kinds of assumptions:

1. People come first—even before production demands. Both customers and employees are valuable resources and should be considered long-term investments rather than expendable objects. Service employees are a valuable source of information about customers and should be included in decisions concerning customers.

2. It is human nature to treat others as you have been treated. Customer-contact employees who are treated as valuable persons by the organization will treat the organization's customers similarly.

3. It is the little things that count. Good service consists of many well-executed details.

4. Work should offer employees a sense of community and belongingness where employees treat each other like family.

Some might say that these issues sound like motherhood, apple pie, and the Golden Rule. The fact is that service organizations that subscribe to the ingredients required for motherhood, apple pie, and the Golden Rule are also organizations that have higher profitability, lower consumer and employee turnover rates, and greater long-term increases in the value of their stock.

SUMMARY AND CONCLUSION

Our hope is that this chapter has demonstrated the following:

1. Climates are summary perceptions employees have about their organization that develop from the practices and procedures employees observe happening to them and around them. These practices and procedures occur in all facets of a setting, forming a consistent system and a consistent set of messages.

2. The culture of an organization is the set of fundamental assumptions about human nature, the best way to solve problems, the role of work in life, and so on. Climates tend to be outgrowths of the culture of an organization.

A review of the tables reveals that climates are indeed a function of a consistent set of themes and messages. Further, the tables show that a wide variety of issues require attention if a particular climate is to be created and maintained. These issues requiring attention extend from an emphasis placed on training to attention placed on knowing client needs, as well as attention to details that may affect performance.

The following is a list of the areas decision makers need to review in their organization to see if the practices, procedures, and rewarded behaviors in their organization are consistent with the climate and culture they are trying to achieve:

1. Selection—the type of people being hired. For example, there are procedures now that can validly identify service-oriented people.
2. Training—new employee orientations; ongoing training programs being offered; follow-up programs for training.
3. Formal reward systems: pay (financial rewards available for people who exhibit desired behavior), promotion (promotion opportunities for people who exhibit desired behavior), and recognition (informal rewards, e.g., verbal praise or letters of appreciation for employees who exhibit desired behavior).
4. Equipment resources—how well the equipment supports or inhibits the desired behaviors.
5. Power delegation—who gets to make decisions; who is consulted in decision making.
6. Human resources practices—benefits and leave policies, for example.
7. Resource delegation—how money and time are prioritized.

The purpose of this list is to encourage managers to scrutinize every facet of their organization's prac-

tices, procedures, and rewards and look for inconsistencies between what is actually happening and what needs to happen to create or maintain particular climates and cultures (Kerr, 1988). All aspects of an organization must be considered for their facilitation or inhibition of the desired climate. Obviously, it would be too simplistic as well as impractical to say that every organization needs to have great human resources practices, good equipment and resources, expensive selection techniques, and so on. The fact is that managers have to make choices about what receives highest priority and what gets the greatest commitment of resources (Katz & Kahn, 1978). Our hope is that this chapter has provided managers with some guidelines regarding which facets might be particularly important for which climates. As illustrated, human resource practices are particularly crucial for service organizations; training seems to be important for establishing a good safety record; and resource delegation and support should be emphasized for high innovation.

Even more essential for managers than scrutinizing every facet of their organization is to identify the key assumptions, values, and philosophies they hold about the nature of people and the way the world works. Managers need to identify their assumptions because it is inevitable that their decisions will reflect those assumptions. Table 54–3 summarizes some examples of cultural assumptions that could underlie the three climates that were the focus of this chapter.

Table 54–3
Some Examples of Cultural Assumptions Underlying the Climates

Issue	Climate		
	Safety	**Innovation**	**Service**
The best way to solve problems	Anticipate and prevent problems from happening in the first place; be proactive in solving problems; a long-term strategy is preferable to a short-run view	Take one small step at a time; test, gather more data, and reevaluate; be proactive first but then be reactive and respond to the users' needs	Establish good human resources practices; be proactive when it comes to logistics (equipment, procedures)
Best way to manage people	Employees' well-being should be given higher priority than production deadlines; an organization has the obligation to take care of its employees; power resides at the top with people who ensure employees' safety	Nuture innovative employees and give them total organizational support; delegate power; power should reside where skill and information reside	Treat employees like family; power should be shared through participation in decision making when decisions concern customers; employees and customers should be viewed as long-term investments and non-expendable
Relationship with environment	Dominate and control nature to avoid catastrophes; it does not pay to be "macho"	Adapt to customer environment; innovations are successful only if the user is satisfied	Harmonize with others and the environment; please customers and employees

Given the fundamental nature of the assumptions and values in table 54–3, it is clear why it can be so difficult to change an organization. Our experience in working with a large number of organizations on climate and culture issues leads us to conclude that many managers are unaware of the kinds of assumptions they hold and that they want certain outcomes that are inconsistent with their underlying assumptions. Obviously, every service organization espouses good service, but how many managers hold the kinds of assumptions that lead to the promotion of the kind of environment necessary for their employees to deliver good service? Just as obviously, every organization would rather be a successful innovator than a failed innovator, but how many organizations hold the values and philosophies one needs for successful innovation? According to Delbecq and Mills, most of the organizations they studied were failures at innovation. We hypothesize that this is true because most decision makers hold assumptions about people and how to run a business that are inconsistent with high innovation.

Our view of the relationship between culture and climate is best shown pictorially, as in figure 54–1. Figure 54–1 shows that assumptions about human beings and the nature of the world yield decisions about how the organization will function. These deci-

Figure 54–1. Relationship between Culture and Climate

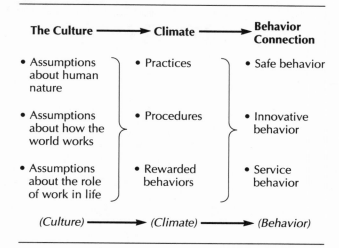

(Culture) ⟶ *(Climate)* ⟶ *(Behavior)*

sions result in particular patterns of practices, procedures, and rewards that dictate particular kinds of behaviors on the part of organizational members. The combination of assumptions, practices, procedures, and behaviors makes one organization look and feel different from another. That look and feel is the culture and climate of the organization.

REFERENCES

Bolman, L.G., & Deal, T.E. (1985). *Modern approaches to understanding and managing organizations.* San Francisco: Jossey-Bass.

Bowen, D.E., & Schneider, B. (1988). Services marketing and management: Implications for organizational behavior. In B.M. Staw and L.L. Cummings (Eds.), *Research in organizational behavior* (vol. 10). Grennwich, CT: JAI Press.

Delbecq, A.L., & Mills, P.K. (1985). Managerial practices that enhance innovation. *Organizational Dynamics, 14*, 24–34.

James, L.R., Joyce, W.F., & Slocum, J.W. (1988). Comment: Organizations do not cognize. *Academy of Management Review, 13*, 129–131.

Katz, D., & Kahn, R. (1978). *The social psychology of organizations* (2d ed.). New York: Wiley.

Kerr, S. (1988). Some characteristics and consequences of organizational reward. In F.D. Schoorman and B. Schneider (Eds.), *Facilitating work effectiveness.* Lexington, MA: Lexington Books.

Kilman, R.H. (1985). *Beyond the quick fix.* San Francisco: Jossey-Bass.

Koprowski, E. (1983). Cultural myths: Clues to effective management. *Organizational Dynamics* (Autumn), 39–51.

Mirvis, P.H. (1985). Negotiations after the sale: The roots and ramifications after conflict in an acquisition. *Journal of Occupational Behavior, 6*, 65–84.

Rousseau, D.M. (in press). Assessing organizational culture through quantitative methods. In B. Schneider (Ed.), *Organizational climate and culture.* San Francisco: Jossey-Bass.

Schein, E.H. (1985). *Organizational culture and leadership.* San Francisco: Jossey-Bass.

Schneider, B. (1987). The people make the place. *Personnel Psychology, 40*, 437–453.

Schneider, B., & Bowen, D. (1985). Employee and customer perceptions of service in banks: Replication and extension. *Journal of Applied Psychology, 70*, 423–433.

Schneider, B., & Rentsch, J. (1988). Managing climates and cultures: A futures perspective. In J. Hage (Ed.), *Futures of organizations.* Lexington, MA: Lexington Books.

Zohar, D. (1980). Safety climates in industrial organizations: Theoretical and applied implications. *Journal of Applied Psychology, 65*, 96–102.

55 UNDERSTANDING AND IMPROVING WORK CLIMATES

Rudolf H. Moos, Andrew G. Billings

Executives and managers have a vital stake in the work climate in their organizations. Consider these examples:

> The vice-president of marketing is puzzled. His department has been highly productive and has helped to move the company into new markets. Now, the creative spark has diminished, the level of energy in the department has slipped, and some valued staff have left. The VP senses low morale and lack of teamwork. How can he better understand the situation?

> A large commercial bank with many retail branches implemented a program to improve customer services. When the regional manager follows up with a customer service audit, she finds that the program is effective in many branches but has no impact in others. Success or failure seems to be related more to the branches' "style" or work environment than to the experience or competence of individual employees. The regional manager suspects that staff morale and sense of involvement influence how the staff deal with customers. How can she evaluate and change the situation?

In both cases, the social climate of the workplace plays a major role in the effectiveness of the organization and its ability to adapt to change. Most managers recognize the importance of the work environment, but they may not know how to understand, evaluate, and change it. In this chapter, we provide guidelines and tools for managers who seek to assess and improve their work climates.

WHAT IS A WORK ENVIRONMENT? WHY IS IT IMPORTANT?

Work environment, also labeled work climate, refers to the social-psychological characteristics of a work setting. The work environment includes the attitudes of employees toward the work tasks and their communication with each other and with their supervisors. Each work setting develops a "style" or a work climate, which influences how decisions are made and defines typical patterns of interactions at work.

As shown in figure 55–1 the work environment is determined by many factors, including the physical features and organizational policies in a work setting and the characteristic behaviors of people at work. The arrows reflect the mutual interaction between the work climate and these key aspects of an organization. (For a more conceptual understanding of work climates, see Moos, 1986a.)

People who experience a wide variety of organizations can best observe the power of the work climate. Researchers, management consultants, and the itinerant manager understand that each work setting develops its own image and distinctive work climate. They see how the work environment has a profound impact on the individual's productivity and the work group's effectiveness. Some work settings boost employee morale and productivity; the jobs provide structure for the employees' lives, a sense of satisfaction and achievement, and a basis for self-esteem and personal identity. Other work settings lead to dissatisfaction and despair; the rigidity and lack of compelling direction and participation leave employees feeling isolated, pressured, and frustrated.

Many of the human problems that confront managers are directly related to the work environment. For instance, work stress and low morale are closely associated with the pace and pressure of constant

Preparation of this chapter was supported by NIAAA Grants AA02863 and AA06699 and by Veterans Administration Medical and Health Services Research and Development Service research funds. Ann Margulies made helpful suggestions in editing the manuscript.

Figure 55–1. Relationship between Work Environment and Key Aspects of Organizational Functioning

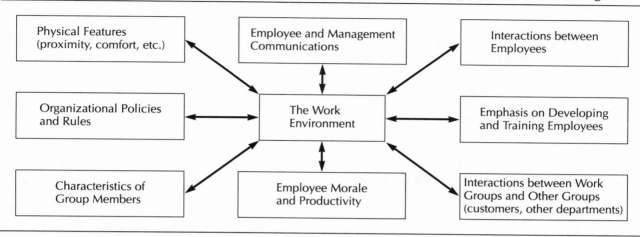

interaction with other people, such as customers, vendors, litigants, students, and clients. Employees and unions expect management to foster a psychologically positive work environment. Employees also expect to find opportunities for professional growth and development in their work. Managers face increasing demands to attract good new employees, maintain the morale of existing employees, and keep employee turnover low while creating a climate that promotes innovation and productivity. An understanding of work climate can help managers meet these varied demands.

WHAT ARE THE KEY DIMENSIONS OF THE WORK ENVIRONMENT?

To be of value, an assessment of a work environment must touch on the key elements of work climate and be practical, focused, and brief. The key elements of work climate can be prioritized and organized into three major categories:

1. *Relationship dimensions*—how employees relate to each other and how managers relate to employees.
2. *Personal growth dimensions*—how the work environment encourages or stifles personal growth.
3. *System maintenance and change dimensions*—the amount of structure and openness to change in the workplace.

These key aspects of work climate affect important outcomes for both organizations and their employees (Moos, 1986a). For example, in work settings where coworkers and supervisors have support-ive relationships, employees tend to be more satisfied with their jobs, to have better morale, and to be more motivated. Strong goal orientation tends to promote job performance and commitment; when it is combined with cohesive relationships at work, it helps to counter the negative impact of highly demanding, constrained work settings.

Moderation is the key to optimal system maintenance and change dimensions, which regulate and structure a work setting. Clear expectations about job tasks and policies, adequate performance feedback, and moderate organization and structure contribute to job satisfaction and effectiveness. Ambiguous job roles, sparse feedback, and lax organizational policies lead to increased health and behavioral problems. An overemphasis on control can restrict employees' opportunities for personal development and create tension and rigidity in the workplace. To use information about a work climate, managers need to understand all three sets of dimensions and how they interact.

WHEN IS AN ASSESSMENT USEFUL?

Work climate assessments are most useful when a work setting is encountering change or needs to change. They can also help managers learn how changes in their leadership behavior affect the climate in their work group. Here are some examples of useful times to conduct an assessment:

Diagnosing problems —An assessment helps to analyze and understand possible problems in a work group.

Before change —An assessment prior to a planned organizational change (such as a merger, restructuring, or technological change) sets a benchmark for measuring the impact of the change.

As a contributor to change —Assessment information can contribute to the process of change. Just as biofeedback can alleviate headaches, feedback of information about the work climate is a powerful way to promote change.

After change —An assessment evaluates how an experimental, planned, or unexpected change has affected the work group.

To appraise and improve leadership —A manager obtains information about his or her effectiveness in shaping the desired work climate in his or her area of the organization.

In team building —As a group seeks to increase its effectiveness, information about the work climate raises relevant issues for discussion and action.

To identify risks —An assessment identifies work groups with poor work climates that place them at risk for individual or organizational dysfunction, such as high absenteeism, high turnover, or poor work quality.

Having decided to conduct an assessment, a manger needs to enlist the support of both management and employees. First, key managers and executives should agree to receive feedback and to take necessary action. As assessments of work climates can reveal, superficial change programs may be ineffective; accordingly, management should be willing to invest time and resources in careful planning and implementation of modifications to the work climate.

Second, the manager needs to provide employees with a suitable rationale for participating in the assessment; he or she can explain the potential value of the assessment and should ensure the confidentiality of individual responses.

THE WORK ENVIRONMENT SCALE

The Work Environment Scale (WES) can be used to measure the work environment and to monitor and improve work settings. The WES is composed of ten subscales that measure the three sets of work climate dimensions (see table 55–1).

Development of the WES

The WES is based on a comprehensive program of research. The items were developed from interviews of employees and managers and naturalistic observations of actual work settings. The items are easy to understand and have high face validity. For example, coworker cohesion is assessed by the following kinds of items: "People go out of their way to help a new employee feel comfortable" and "People take a personal interest in each other." Two of the items that measure autonomy at work are "Employees have a great deal of freedom to do as they like" and "Employees are encouraged to make their own decisions." The WES taps clarity with such items as "Activities are well planned" and "The details of assigned jobs are generally explained to employees."

The *WES Manual* (Moos, 1986b) provides technical information about the development of the WES. In brief, the WES subscales are internally consistent and reliable; they are both stable over time and sensitive to change in work climates. The subscales reflect distinct but somewhat related aspects of work climate. Comparative data are available on over 3,000 employees in representative sets of business and health care work situations. The WES is easy to administer, requires only about 15 minutes to complete, and can quickly be scored by hand or by computer. The costs for materials and scoring are very low. The *User's Guide* (Moos, 1987) includes specific instructions for administering and scoring the WES and profiling the results.

Table 55–1
WES Subscales and Dimensions Descriptions

Relationship Dimensions

1. Involvement	The extent to which employees are concerned about and committed to their jobs
2. Peer Cohesion	The extent to which employees are friendly and supportive of one another
3. Supervisor Support	The extent to which management is supportive of employees and encourages employees to be supportive of one another

Personal Growth Dimensions

4. Autonomy	The extent to which employees are encouraged to be self-sufficient and to make their own decisions
5. Task Orientation	The degree of emphasis on good planning, efficiency, and getting the job done
6. Work Pressure	The degree to which the press of work and time urgency dominate the job milieu

System Maintenance and Change Dimensions

7. Clarity	The extent to which employees know what to expect in their daily routine and how explicitly rules and policies are communicated
8. Control	The extent to which management uses rules and pressures to keep employees under control
9. Innovation	The degree of emphasis on variety, change, and new approaches
10. Physical Comfort	The extent to which the physical surroundings contribute to a pleasant work environment

The Three Forms of the WES

The WES has three forms:

1. The Real Form (Form R) measures employees' and managers' perceptions of their current work environment.
2. The Ideal Form (Form I) measures employees' and managers' conceptions of an ideal work environment.
3. The Expectations Form (Form E) measures prospective employees' expectations about work settings.

The Real Form. The Real Form (Form R) allows employees and managers to describe their work setting as it is. Managers and consultants use this form to describe and compare actual work climates, to contrast employee and management perceptions, and to assess and facilitate change in work settings.

The Ideal Form. The Ideal Form (Form I) allows people to describe the type of work setting they prefer. This form was developed to measure employees' and managers' goals and value orientations about their workplace. Some managers and consultants use Form I to assess people's value orientations and how they change over time, such as before and after an employees' planning conference or retreat. Others use Form I with Form R to identify areas in which employees and managers want to change their workplace. Information about the discrepancies between the actual and an ideal work setting can guide attempts to change work groups to match employees' and managers' preferences more closely.

The Expectations Form. The Expectations Form (Form E) allows people to describe their expectations of what a work milieu will be like. In employment counseling, Form E clarifies prospective employees' or managers' expectations of a new work situation. Comparing a person's expectations of a work setting with the actual work climate helps identify expectations that might lead to difficulties in adjusting to the job. Form E can also identify the expectation of employees who have been seriously ill (such as an employee who has suffered a heart attack) so that, if needed, counseling can be started before they return to work.

EVALUATING WORK ENVIRONMENTS

The WES can be used to describe and improve the work environment. Managers and consultants use the WES both to determine where work groups are successful and where improvements are needed. To illustrate the use of the WES to describe work climates, we present WES profiles of three work settings. In each profile, WES scores are expressed as standard scores with a mean of 50 and a standard deviation of 10. A score of 60 is high; 70 is very high.

Manufacturing Management Team

The vice-president of operations had a productive manufacturing unit, but his management team was dissatisfied. The VP, in his mid-thirties, was bright, energetic, and proud of his hands-on leadership style. He thought he was a highly effective leader. He had five direct-report subordinates: director of engineering, director of production, materials manager, quality assurance manager, and distribution manager. In separate interviews, these subordinates reported that their individual departments functioned effectively but that there was considerable friction between departments. Production supervisors were frustrated by the engineers, who did not involve them in important production-line modifications. The distribution manager pointed out that delivery schedules were delayed because of the product-testing schedule of the quality assurance staff. Even the senior managers did not communicate regularly with each other. Some felt frustrated because the VP obtained input from each of them individually and then made all the key decisions himself.

Two WES Form R profiles are shown in figure 55–2: the profile for the VP and the average profile for the five senior managers. The VP and his subordinates have strikingly different perceptions of the environment. The VP describes a positive work climate in which managers know their roles, operating decisions

are carefully controlled, and new ideas are well received. In contrast, his managers see much less involvement and cohesion. They do not have the sense of being a team that works together. They agree with the VP that their individual responsibilities are clearly defined, and they report a higher degree of control over their actions. However, these potentially positive attributes come at the expense of a sense of autonomy and innovation.

These results provided the basis for change. The VP began to look more closely at his leadership style and how it helped and limited the effectiveness of his managers. To promote more involvement and teamwork, the VP delegated a number of decisions about production scheduling, new product rollouts, and cost containment to a manufacturing committee composed of his subordinate managers. Now the VP participates in these meetings, but the group makes the decisions. The managers also assume responsibility for getting their departments to work together to ensure that the company meets the manufacturing objectives set by the group.

Microcomputer Production Line

To keep production "on shore," microcomputer manufacturers must have highly productive employees so the companies can be competitive with foreign pro-

Figure 55–2. WES Profiles for a Vice-President of Operations and His Management Team

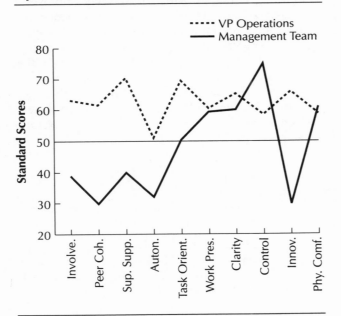

Figure 55–3. WES Profiles for High-Tech Production Workers and County Firefighters

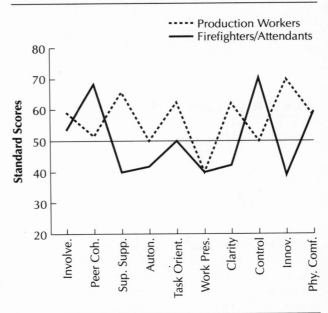

ducers who have lower labor costs. A particular manufacturer periodically evaluates work climate because of its important contribution to productivity.

Figure 55–3 shows the WES Form R profile for a production unit ($N=36$ employees) in this plant. These employees are involved in their jobs and see their supervisors as supportive. The work setting is task oriented and emphasizes good planning and efficiency. The employees know what is expected of them; there is variety in their work and little work pressure.

The WES profile is consistent with other information about the workplace. The plant is well known for its congenial work environment. The employees' jobs are individually paced, and although they work relatively independently, they talk with each other about their jobs and share common work breaks and an employee cafeteria. The employee turnover rate is low compared with local industry averages; about two-thirds of the employees have worked in the plant for a year or more.

Government

A county government has been having labor problems. Union agreements and contracts have become more difficult and time-consuming to negotiate. Inter-nal problems in some work groups have increased tensions during contract negotiations and membership ratifications. Therefore, county management wanted to improve the work climate of its employees and to reduce the dissatisfactions line employees felt with their supervisors and management.

Figure 55–3 shows the WES Form R profile for one county fire department ($N=30$ firefighters and station attendants). Employees in this work group are friendly and supportive, but their relationships with their supervisors are suspicious and mistrustful. Employees are not committed to their jobs. They feel little autonomy and no emphasis on variety or innovation. Moreover, the employees report that the supervisors want to keep them under control. However, supervisors have not communicated explicit rules and policies about acceptable work procedures.

Other information indicates that the employees spend a considerable amount of time interacting with one another in duties around the fire station, but the supervisors do not participate in these activities. The supervisors use a rigid timekeeping system and strict job requirements to keep employees under control. Although there has been little employee turnover in the prior year, the rates of absenteeism and of minor accidents are quite high. Together with the WES profile, these facts identify serious problems and show a clear need for organizational change.

IMPROVING WORK ENVIRONMENTS

Steps in Assessing and Changing Work Environments

Before trying to change the climate in a work setting, it is important to understand the organization, to plan the change process, and to anticipate the necessary steps and potential problems. Managers often collaborate with organizational consultants in these activities. Here, we provide a brief outline of eight steps involved in the process of assessing and changing work climates:

1. Develop an overview of the change program.
   What are its objectives?
   How can the changes be accomplished?
   Who needs to be involved in the planning?
2. Establish an assessment plan.
   What elements in the workplace need to be evaluated?

What is the anticipated time frame?
How will communications with the participants be handled?

3. Introduce the assessment to participants.
   Give the reasons for the assessment.
   Outline the possible uses of the work climate information.
4. Conduct the assessment.
   Include relevant groups.
   Administer the WES.
   Consider providing individuals the option to respond anonymously.
   Consider using interviews and other forms of data collection.
5. Analyze and interpret the assessment results.
   Compare different groups of employees.
   Identify the nature and causes of any problems.
   Develop objectives and procedures for an intervention, if necessary.

6. Give feedback to participants.

Provide feedback in a form that participants can understand.

Consider giving participants opportunities to discuss the results.

7. Plan and implement the change program.

8. Reassess the work climate.

Allow adequate time for changes to occur prior to reassessment.

Give feedback of new results to participants.

Fine-tune change programs as needed.

Improving the Work Environment in an Intensive Care Unit

In health care settings, work stress is sharply increasing. The quality of the work setting can erode as staff face growing numbers of acutely ill patients, endure pressure to conform to rigorous standards of cost-containment and quality assurance programs, and try to provide services superior to their competitors' at a lower cost (Moos & Schaefer, 1987). Here we present a case study, showing how the WES helped assess and improve a health care setting.

Assessment. We conducted an intervention to assess and improve the work climate in an intensive care unit (ICU) in a large general hospital (Koran, Moos, Moos & Zasslow, 1983). As is often done, an organizational consultant collaborated with the managers of the unit in the assessment and change process. Staff were unhappy with their work and the unit. Many were showing dysfunctional reactions, such as low morale, mild depression, and withdrawal from patients. These reactions seemed to be caused by high work demands, role ambiguity, lack of autonomy, and inadequate supervisor support. To help understand the problems and identify areas that needed to be changed, the ICU staff completed the WES Form R (Real) to describe their current work climate and Form I (Ideal) to describe their preferred work setting.

The Form R profile (figure 55–4) shows that the quality of relationships among coworkers and between coworkers and supervisors is average or below average. The staff have some autonomy in their work but experience relatively little involvement or innovation. The supervisors exert little control and do not make their expectations clear. Supervisors do not provide clear direction for the unit.

The Form I profile (figure 55–4), in comparison with Form R, reveals the problems with the ICU work setting by pinpointing the areas and extent of staff dissatisfaction. Staff members wanted substantial changes in all but one area (control). They wanted to be much more involved with their work and to have better relationships with coworkers and supervisors. They wanted more independence and task orientation and less work pressure. According to the staff, supervisors should state rules and policies much more clearly and even exert more control. Staff also wanted more variety in their work and much more physical comfort.

Intervention. After using WES Forms R and I to assess the work environment, the consultant met with the unit nursing director and the medical director to discuss the situation, set objectives, and develop a general plan. A program of team building was the primary focus of the intervention. The consultant then met with staff to clarify problem areas and guide staff in developing solutions.

The problems that the staff listed corroborated the WES findings. Staff members reported that they did not communicate with one another about how to cooperate in managing difficult patients. This lack of cooperation made staff angry and belligerent. Nurses felt that they were unable to deal with important patient care problems because they could not confront each other directly. These problems are examples of the specific issues underlying the relative lack of involvement, peer cohesion, and supervisor support shown by the WES profile.

Figure 55–4. Preintervention WES Profiles for Intensive Care Unit Staff

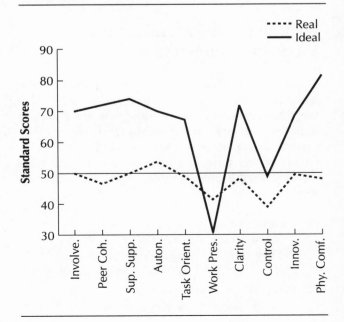

Staff members also expressed the need to increase autonomy and clarity by defining the roles and expectations for each shift and for specific staff members. Several staff members were angry because of criticism of their work, frustrated in dealing with patients' and families' anger and hostility, and annoyed with physicians who were often unavailable when decisions had to be made about patient care. Staff felt that they needed new and flexible approaches to these problems.

When the consultant showed the WES profiles to the staff, they felt that the discrepancies between their actual and preferred workplace clarified their subjective impressions. The consultant used WES profiles of work settings outside the hospital to provide some perspective. During several subsequent meetings, the consultant used the WES profiles to focus discussion and to guide staff in developing solutions to the problems in the work environment that affected their morale and patient care.

The consultant directed the group into a problem-solving orientation. Staff members ventilated their feelings about individual patient problems, staff communication gaps, and conflicts among staff and between staff and physicians. The consultant guided the group process and tried to increase staff cohesion by constructively examining and resolving disagreements. To increase autonomy and clarity, he helped the staff develop clearer definitions of their individual responsibilities. Finally, he continued to meet with the unit's head nurse and medical director to address their communication problems.

As with most other intervention programs, the group process did not always proceed smoothly. Sometimes meetings were canceled, and attendance varied from one meeting to another. In the overall course of the intervention, however, nursing staff developed a stronger sense of teamwork, better techniques for coping with work stressors, more acceptance of the inevitability of mistakes, and reasonable solutions to many administrative problems (such as arranging regular times to meet with staff physicians and changing the content of the nursing report). The staff successfully managed their anger toward an antisocial patient and their grief when a favorite patient on the unit died unexpectedly.

Postintervention Assessment. At the end of the intervention period, the consultant, the head nurse, and the medical director all felt that morale on the unit had improved substantially. The quality of patient care seemed better: the staff gave more systematic attention to the psychosocial aspects of patients' problems, nursing and medical staff communicated more openly about these problems and the feelings

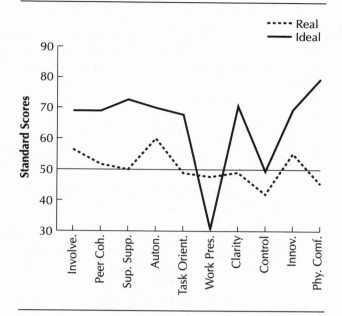

Figure 55–5. Postintervention WES Profiles for Intensive Care Unit Staff

they evoked, and staff showed more skill in dealing with patients' pain and psychological disorders.

As shown in figure 55–5, the staff also saw these improvements and reported subtle yet significant and credible changes. The changes are consonant with the problems resolved through the group meetings and consultations with the unit's head nurse and medical director. Because of the staff's success in airing and resolving disruptive interpersonal and administrative issues, involvement and peer cohesion increased. Because the group meetings clarified role expectations and responsibilities, staff autonomy and innovation increased.

Of the eight WES dimensions on which staff perceptions changed, all but physical comfort changed in the direction of the staff's preferred work setting. The changes reported are moderate in size, which is appropriate considering the limited magnitude of the intervention and the relative stability of the social system. There is still room for additional improvement.

Improving Work Environments in Other Settings

As the preceding case shows, the WES can be used to assess and change the work environment. Giving WES feedback to employees and managers guides them to focus on stressful or undesirable aspects of the workplace. It helps them to plan practical changes and to understand that the work environment can be altered. The WES also is an appropriate instrument for assessing changes in the work climate after an intervention.

The WES profile provides a comfortable and nonthreatening way to begin group discussions. It helps employees and managers to understand group norms and conflicts and to realize that they can change specific aspects of their work climate. Consistency between the WES and other information about the workplace boosts confidence in an appropriate intervention plan; a discrepancy between the WES and other information generates a search for new ideas and explanations.

Using the measurement-feedback-planning process, managers and consultants can:

- Encourage employees to think about their work setting along the ten dimensions of the WES instead of in a unidimensional way such as "good-bad" or "stressful-nonstressful."

- Highlight important but often overlooked characteristics of the workplace, such as the clarity of expectations and the degree of employee autonomy.

- Focus employees' change efforts on a few selected and well-defined areas; this reduces confusion and conflicting behavior and increases the likelihood of orderly change.

- Increase participants' involvement because managers and employees work together to improve their work setting.

- Provide an opportunity for managers and employees to consider the impact of the workplace on their morale and productivity.

Managers and consultants can use information about work climate to monitor and track the process of planned organizational changes. Wilderman and Mezzelo (1984) examined the effects on work climate of changing a community mental health center from a consultation model to a direct-service model in which staff spent much more time with clients and less with their colleagues. As regularity and structure increased, job clarity and supervisor control increased as well. However, staff cohesion declined, probably because staff members spent much less time with each other.

Quality assurance (QA) programs are being widely instituted in health care settings, but little is known about how they affect staff morale. To examine this issue, Sinclair and Frankel (1982) compared two outpatient treatment programs. They randomly selected one unit of each program to participate in QA activities, and they designated the other unit as a control. Contrary to their concern that QA activities might lower morale, the researchers found no significant negative changes in staff perceptions of the work environment. In fact, staff in the QA group reported increased supervisor support and decreased control. Moreover, staff members who provided higher-quality services saw the work climate as more cohesive and independent and less pressured.

Organizational development theorists believe that increased employee participation in decision making will reduce role conflict and ambiguity and promote job satisfaction and well-being. Jackson (1983) randomly assigned nursing and clerical employees in a hospital outpatient unit to work situations in which they enjoyed increased participation and control. Employees in the increased participation condition reported having more autonomy at work and more job satisfaction and less role conflict and ambiguity. Overall, employee involvement in decision making may lessen role strains and increase valued outcomes for both the individual and the organization.

OTHER APPLICATIONS

Counseling and Career Planning

Information about work climates can be applied in counseling with employees. Consider the employee or manager who is experiencing performance problems. Difficulties in work performance are often related to the employee's expectations and perceptions of the work setting, particularly when the employee has adequate technical competence but limited motivation. For instance, a person who feels uninvolved and excluded from participation in work decisions often lacks motivation or commitment to the work setting. The WES Forms R and I can help to clarify these issues. Employee counseling can focus on the WES profile as the basis for establishing action plans.

Career planning and professional development may also benefit from climate assessments. Comparison of an individual's ideal work environment (WES

Form I) with the current situation (WES Form R) provides information about compatible and incompatible work settings. For example, a person seeking a transfer may want to work in a highly cohesive, friendly, and interactive situation; information about other work environments in the company can help to identify a compatible setting. The Expectations Form (Form E) of the WES can help managers as they select and orient new members. When a person's expectations do not match the actual work environment, he or she is less likely to fit in well in the setting. During the orientation, a manager can address potential problems revealed by Form E and minimize potential misunderstanding and mutual disappointment.

Risk Management

The work environment has a powerful effect on behaviors that may increase the risk of injury to employees and to physical facilities. Work environments that have high work pressure and lack cohesion and clear expectations are especially stressful and may increase the likelihood of accidents. In some situations, the cost of mistakes is very high. For example, results can be catastrophic when the work behavior of nuclear reactor operators, air traffic controllers, pesticide manufacturing workers, and police officers is inaccurate or unreliable. In addition, workers' compensation claims have rapidly increased, especially for injuries and disability traced to work stressors.

Accordingly, many organizations now employ a professional risk manager to minimize such problems.

Risk management typically emphasizes the physical and operating competencies of individual employees. Thus, employers carefully screen nuclear reactor operators and air traffic controllers. Managers also need to evaluate the work climate in other high-risk situations. In this respect, the WES can be used to screen multiple work settings and identify specific groups that may be at increased risk. For example, all manufacturing units in a plant might be sampled to find out whether any units need special attention. Because health care providers, such as nurses and aides, now file more workers' compensation claims for stress and related conditions, health care facilities would benefit from periodic screening for risk indicators in their work environments.

The work environment can also influence the development and course of psychological and physical symptoms (Billings & Moos, 1982) and the process of recovery and relapse of disorders such as alcohol abuse. The relationship between alcoholism and work climate is complex. Alcohol misuse is related to role conflict and ambiguity, high work demands, and a lack of job challenge. Such work climates can cause boredom and frustration, erode self-confidence, and leave people feeling powerless. People experiencing these job stressors and work-related problems may find it easier to justify consuming more alcohol (for an extended discussion, see Moos, Finney & Cronkite, in press).

DEVELOPING NEW WORK ENVIRONMENTS

We have focused on assessments of existing work climates and how they may be improved. Yet another challenge for those concerned with work environments is nurturing desired climates in new or future work settings. As the rate of organizational restructuring increases, with corporate takeovers and mergers eliminating some work groups and creating new ones, managers have increasing opportunities to plan and develop new organizational climates. Entrepreneurial organizations provide additional challenges as two out of every three new jobs in the United States are created in either start-up or small organizations.

We now understand enough about work environments to plan and structure work situations with the desired climate. We have seen that work groups vary widely in the quality of interpersonal relationships, the emphasis on task orientation and work demands, and the level of clarity and organization. This raises

an intriguing question: Why do work climates develop in such different ways; that is, what leads to an emphasis on supervisor support or task orientation or work demands?

A growing body of research suggests that work climates are influenced by three major sets of factors in the workplace: physical and architectural features, organizational structure and policies, and characteristics of employees and the tasks they perform (Moos, 1986a). For example, open-plan offices may not provide enough privacy to support the formation of close friendships or to permit supervisors to offer candid evaluations to subordinates. In fact, employees in open-plan offices tend to report less coworker and supervisor feedback and a reduction in job autonomy. In terms of organizational factors, employees in larger and more centralized organizations tend to report less cohesion and autonomy and more manager control. An understanding of work climates can help managers and consultants to regulate and alter the potential influences of physical, organizational, and task factors.

At all levels of an organization, leadership and management methods influence each of these three sets of factors and in turn shape work climate.

Because the work climate can help or hinder an organization's success in adapting to change and retaining its effectiveness, work climate assessments are another tool to help organizational leaders direct their organizations in their chosen missions. Insight into work climate helps anticipate problems and provide solutions to today's organizational challenges.

REFERENCES

Billings, A., & Moos, R. (1982). Work stress and the stress-buffering roles of work and family resources. *Journal of Occupational Behaviour, 3,* 215–232.

Jackson, S. (1983). Participation in decision-making as a strategy for reducing job-related strain. *Journal of Applied Psychology, 68,* 3–19.

Koran, L., Moos, R., Moos, B., & Zasslow, M. (1983). Changing hospital work environments: An example of a burn unit. *General Hospital Psychiatry, 5,* 7–13.

Moos, R. (1986a). Work as a human context. In M.S. Pallack & R.O. Perloff (Eds.), *Psychology and work: Productivity, change, and employment,* vol. 5: *Master lecture series* (9–52). Washington, DC: American Psychological Association.

Moos, R. (1986b). *Work Environment Scale manual* (2d ed.). Palo Alto, CA: Consulting Psychologists Press.

Moos, R. (1987). *The Social Climate Scales: A user's guide.* Palo Alto, CA: Consulting Psychologists Press.

Moos, R., Finney, J., & Cronkite, R. (in press). *Alcoholism treatment: Context, process, and outcome.* New York: Oxford University Press.

Moos, R., & Schaefer, J. (1987). Evaluating health care work settings: A holistic conceptual framework. *Psychology and Health: An International Journal, 1,* 217–240.

Sinclair, C., & Frankel, M. (1982). The effect of quality assurance activities on the quality of mental health services. *Quality Review Bulletin, 8,* 7–15.

Wilderman, R., & Mezzelo, J. (1984). Paving the road to financial security: The direct service model. *Administration in Mental Health, 2,* 184–194.

56 AN INTEGRATING TAXONOMY OF MANAGERIAL BEHAVIOR: IMPLICATIONS FOR IMPROVING MANAGERIAL EFFECTIVENESS

Gary Yukl, Rick Lepsinger

A flood of recent books on managing for excellence, transforming leaders, excellent corporations, and one-minute managers are testimony to the continuing interest in finding the secrets of effective management. Researchers have tried for over a quarter of a century to discover the patterns of behavior that differentiate between effective and ineffective managers. This chapter describes a comprehensive taxonomy of effective managerial behavior. The taxonomy is based on a decade of original research by the first author, as well as on hundreds of earlier studies of managerial effectiveness by researchers in a variety of disciplines. The chapter describes applications of the behavior taxonomy to management development in three companies.

BACKGROUND

During the 1950s, the early research on managerial behavior identified two broad categories: task-oriented behavior and relationship-oriented behavior. A number of studies indicated that both types of behavior are necessary for effective management. However, the research failed to provide much insight into the nature of this behavior. It was not clear what managers actually do to accomplish task objectives or to build effective interpersonal relationships with subordinates and peers. A behavior taxonomy with less abstract managerial practices was needed to make further progress in understanding why some managers are more effective than others.

By the 1960s it was evident that aspects of the managerial situation determine what behavior is appropriate. The situation presents a manager with certain demands, constraints, and opportunities. The importance of different kinds of behavior varies from one type of manager to another. Even for the same manager, some aspects of behavior that are essential in one situation may be irrelevant or even detrimental in a different situation. A number of situational theories of managerial effectiveness were proposed, but progress was limited by the lack of an adequate behavior taxonomy on which to build situational theories.

During the same period, observational research showed that a manager's typical day is filled with many short, fragmented, hectic activities, most of which involve oral communication with subordinates, superiors, managers in other work units, and outsiders such as clients and suppliers. Once again, without an adequate taxonomy for classifying behavior, it is difficult to make much sense out of the confusing picture of managerial behavior provided by observational research.

A suitable taxonomy must be comprehensive enough to span the complete range of behavior relevant for managerial effectiveness, while at the same time distinguishing between forms of behavior with different consequences. During the 1960s and 1970s, several behavior taxonomies were proposed (e.g., Mintzberg, 1973; Stogdill, 1974), but none satisfied these requirements. Finally, after ten years of developmental research using a variety of research methods and involving over two thousand managers in a variety of organizations, Yukl (1983) identified a comprehensive set of managerial practices that could serve as an integrating taxonomy. Concurrent with the development of the taxonomy, research has been carried out to develop a questionnaire measuring the managerial practices. The questionnaire was initially called the Managerial Behavior Survey, and it is now called the Managerial Practices Survey. A detailed description of the validation research on the questionnaire can be found in Yukl, Wall, and Lepsinger (1990).

EXPLANATION OF THE MANAGERIAL PRACTICES

Managerial practices are categories of behavior used by managers in dealing with subordinates and peers. The new taxonomy encompasses behaviors found relevant to managerial effectiveness in research on leadership and management. The primary basis for forming categories was the common purpose and similarity of the component behaviors. However, in order to maintain some continuity with earlier literature, categories were defined in a way reasonably consistent with prior taxonomies and major lines of behavior research, such as research on participative leadership and positive reward behavior.

The current version of the taxonomy has eleven behavior categories. The categories were defined at a middle level of generality in order to ensure parsimony and avoid proliferation of categories. The categories are widely applicable to different kinds of managers. Every category in the new taxonomy has aspects of behavior that are relevant to every type of manager, even though the relative importance of the categories (and category components) will obviously vary from one type of manager to another. The generic nature of the categories makes them useful for describing managerial behavior with peers and outsiders as well as with subordinates. Thus, the taxonomy is applicable to matrix managers (e.g., product managers, project managers) as well as to functional managers with direct authority over subordinates. Each managerial practice will be described briefly. A more detailed description of the research literature supporting the relevance of each behavior category can be found in a book by Yukl (1989).

Planning and Organizing

This managerial practice includes decision making about objectives, priorities, strategies, formal structure, allocation of resources, assignment of responsibilities, and scheduling of activities. In other words, planning and organizing means deciding what to do, how to do it, who will do it, and when it will be done. There are many varieties of planning, ranging from the determination of strategic objectives and broad policies for the organizational unit ("strategic planning") to the development of detailed action steps and schedules for implementing a change or policy ("operational planning"). Planning includes both the design of the formal structure of the organizational unit ("organizing") and the design of individual jobs within the organizational unit ("job design"). Planning also includes the allocation of resources among different activities according to their relative importance. Finally, planning includes the development of procedures for avoiding potential problems or disasters ("potential problem analysis"), as well as the development of procedures for reacting in a quick and effective manner to unavoidable problems and crises ("contingency planning").

The purpose of planning and organizing is to ensure efficiency and effectiveness for the work unit, coordination with other parts of the organization, and adaptation to changes in the external environment. The importance of this managerial practice for managerial effectiveness has long been recognized in the management literature.

Problem Solving and Disturbance Handling

Like planning, problem solving involves processing information, analyzing, and deciding. However, there are some important differences between the two managerial practices. The primary purpose of problem solving is to maintain orderly, stable operations at the current level of efficiency and effectiveness. Problem solving occurs in response to some immediate disturbance of normal operations, such as an equipment breakdown, a shortage of necessary materials, a customer with a complaint, a mistake in the work, an accident, or an unusual request by higher management. In contrast, planning is more likely to be stimulated by the discovery of an opportunity to be exploited or by the anticipation of a future problem to be avoided. It is as much a difference in time perspective as in purpose. Planning is a proactive behavior with a long-term perspective, whereas problem solving is a reactive behavior with a short-term perspective. Under the pressure of time, problem solving typically occurs more quickly than planning. Some information seeking, analysis, and consultation with others may be involved in problem solving, but there is much less than with planning.

Observational research shows that most managers face relentless pressures for dealing with problems and responding to requests for immediate assistance, authorization, or direction (Mintzberg, 1973). Effective managers are able to recognize problems that need attention, diagnose the cause, and develop appropriate solutions (see Yukl, 1989).

Monitoring

The behavior in this category involves gathering information about the operations of the manager's work unit, the progress of the work, the performance of subordinates, and threats or opportunities in the external environment. Monitoring can take many forms, and some examples include the following: walking around to observe how the work is going, reading written performance reports or computer printouts, holding progress review meetings, inspecting the work, using a computer terminal to review information about current operations or the status of a particular project, and evaluating a project by getting reactions from clients or customers. The primary purpose of monitoring is to maintain stability of operations and facilitate adjustment to changes in the environment. This process of sensing and adjusting is sometimes referred to in the management literature as "controlling." Other terms describing this behavior include *tracking, checking, evaluating,* and *assessing.* External monitoring is sometimes called *environmental scanning.*

Monitoring is conceptually distinct from planning and problem solving, but it is closely related to them. Monitoring provides much of the information needed for planning and problem solving, and this is the reason that it is so important for managerial effectiveness. Monitoring, in turn, is facilitated by the development of detailed action plans and schedules, with checkpoints, intermediate targets, and concrete indicators of performance.

Motivating

Motivating behaviors involve the use of influence techniques to generate enthusiasm for the work, commitment to task objectives, and compliance with orders and requests. The influence attempts include making appeals based on logic, making inspirational

appeals, and leading by example ("role modeling"). The flavor of motivating is captured best by common action verbs such as *encouraging, inspiring, appealing,* and *persuading.* In addition to influencing subordinates, motivating includes influence attempts to obtain necessary cooperation and assistance from peers and outsiders and lobbying with superiors to obtain necessary resources, budget allocations, approvals, assistance, and authorization of changes.

The leadership literature, including recent research on transformational leaders, provides evidence that the influence behaviors included in motivating are relevant for organizational effectiveness (e.g., Bennis & Nanus, 1985). Motivating behavior involves the use of a manager's "personal power," and research strongly suggests that effective managers rely more upon personal power as the basis for influence attempts with subordinates and peers (see Yukl, 1989). For example, instead of merely ordering a subordinate to do a task, an effective manager may draw upon his or her personal expertise to explain why the task is important or why it needs to be done a particular way. The manager may articulate a compelling vision that appeals to the values and ideals of people and generates enthusiasm and commitment for a project or activity.

Recognizing and Rewarding

This managerial practice includes giving tangible or intangible rewards for effective performance, valuable contributions, and unusual efforts to accomplish the work. Tangible rewards for subordinates include such things as a pay increase, promotion, better work schedule, or better assignments; for peers, tangible rewards include doing a special favor or sharing resources. Intangible rewards include such things as giving praise, expressing personal appreciation, giving public recognition, holding a special ceremony to honor a person's achievements or contributions, and giving awards such as a special pin or certificate. Common action verbs for this behavior include *praising, commending, complimenting,* and *crediting.* Recognizing and rewarding is a managerial practice with the dual purpose of shaping behavior and improving relationships.

Recognizing and rewarding differs from motivating with respect to both the purpose and form of the behavior. Giving praise and rewards are reactive forms of behavior that occur after a person demonstrates competence or desirable behavior, whereas motivating involves proactive attempts to influence someone's attitudes and behavior. The purpose of motivating is clearly task oriented, even though it is based on personal power, whereas recognizing and rewarding has a dual purpose, and in some cases the objective is more relationship oriented than task oriented. For example, recognition and rewards may be used to strengthen a person's job satisfaction and ties to the organization, without any explicit intention to influence the person's immediate task behavior. Several decades of psychological research on positive reinforcement and recent leadership research on positive reward behavior demonstrate that recognition and rewards can be used to influence behavior and satisfaction under appropriate conditions (e.g., Hamner & Hamner, 1976; Peters & Waterman, 1982).

Informing

This managerial practice involves the communication of relevant information needed by people to perform their jobs. Informing behavior may take many forms, such as making an explanation in a group meeting, calling someone on the telephone to give information, writing memos and reports, sending electronic messages, holding private briefings, distributing technical documents, putting messages on the bulletin board, and distributing a newsletter. Some commonly used action verbs for Informing include *notifying, alerting, briefing, reporting,* and *interpreting.*

The major purpose of Informing is to facilitate the work of others who depend upon the manager as a source of important information. A secondary purpose is to increase job satisfaction and to facilitate the use of consultation and delegation. Dissemination of information to peers, superiors, and outsiders facilitates external coordination. The importance of Informing was noted by Rensis Likert (1967) in his early conception of the manager as a "linking pin," and more recently by Henry Mintzberg (1973) in his conception of the manager as a "nerve center" in the organizational communication network.

Clarifying Roles and Objectives

This category involves the communication of role expectations. In contrast to motivating, which seeks to energize behavior, clarifying seeks to orient and guide it. Clarifying can take a wide variety of forms, including requesting that a particular task be carried out, explaining procedures for doing a task, explaining someone's duties and responsibilities, providing coaching or instruction, explaining priorities, setting standards, setting performance goals, and meeting with a subordinate or peer to agree on action plans for attaining task goals.

Clarifying, like informing, involves communication of information. However, clarifying is an attempt to guide behavior, whereas informing seeks only to facilitate someone's work. This distinction does not imply that the two forms of behavior are unrelated. Sometimes the behaviors occur independently, but in many cases where clarifying is represented in a managerial behavior incident, informing will be represented also. For example, in giving a new assignment to a subordinate, a manager is likely to communicate specific task information needed by the subordinate to carry out the assignment.

The importance of clarifying for managerial effectiveness is suggested by the fact that it is a key behavior in most situational theories of leadership (see Yukl, 1989). These theories hypothesize, in approximate terms, that clarifying behavior by the leader will improve subordinate satisfaction and performance in situations where there would otherwise be role ambiguity and skill deficiencies. Additional evidence for the relevance of clarifying is provided by extensive research showing the importance of clear, specific, and realistic goals for effective performance by individuals and groups (Locke & Latham, 1984).

Supporting

Supporting includes a wide range of behaviors by which a manager shows consideration, acceptance, and concern for the welfare of other people. Examples of supporting include listening carefully to complaints and problems, showing sympathy when someone is upset, making a special effort to help someone with a problem, greeting someone in a cheerful manner, backing up a subordinate in a conflict with outsiders or superiors, and reacting to mistakes in a calm and helpful manner instead of blowing up. Supporting also includes mentoring activities such as providing career advice, encouraging a talented person to set higher career aspirations, and helping someone with high potential get more visibility (e.g., giving special assignments, mentioning the person's achievements and potential to influential people).

Supporting behaviors are intended to build and maintain effective interpersonal relationships. A manager who is considerate and friendly toward people is more likely to win their friendship and loyalty. The emotional ties that are formed make it easier to gain cooperation and support from persons upon whom the manager must rely to get the work done. A secondary objective of supporting behavior is to increase the job satisfaction of subordinates or coworkers.

Being supportive in times of stress helps others get over the rough spots in the job. The positive benefits for the organization are likely to include lower absenteeism and turnover, less alcoholism, and less drug abuse.

Supporting behavior has been the subject of more research than any other managerial behavior. The extensive research demonstrates that supporting influences subordinate attitudes and performance, although not to an equal extent in all situations (see Yukl, 1989).

Consulting and Delegating

The managerial practice called consulting and delegating involves encouragement of participation by others in making decisions for which the manager is responsible. Different degrees of participation are possible, from revising a tentative decision after receiving protests, to consulting with others before making a decision, to asking an individual or group to make the decision within specified guidelines. The last form of participation provides the maximum amount of power sharing for a decision. When used with an individual subordinate, it is usually called delegation. Consulting and delegating are intended to improve the quality of decisions and commitment to the decisions by others who must implement them. A secondary purpose is to enrich the job of subordinates and make it more interesting and challenging.

Some specific examples of consulting behavior include the following: asking for suggestions, encouraging critical evaluation of proposals, inviting people to attend planning meetings, holding special meetings or hearings to get reactions from people who will be affected by a decision, asking a group to solve a problem with you instead of solving it alone, and seeking group consensus for a decision. Like supporting, participative leadership has been the subject of hundreds of studies, and these studies find that it has important implications for managerial effectiveness (see Yukl, 1989). Encouraging subordinate participation is more likely to increase satisfaction than performance, but both may improve under some conditions.

Conflict Management and Team Building

This managerial practice includes a wide variety of behaviors involving development of teamwork, cooperation, and identification with the organizational unit or team. Examples include such things as mediating conflicts between others, smoothing over disagreements, guiding the resolution of conflict in constructive ways, stressing the importance of cooperation, encouraging sharing of information and ideas, using ceremonies and symbols to develop identification with the organizational unit, and facilitating social interaction among work unit members. The common purpose of these behaviors is to maintain effective working relationships among subordinates and between the manager and subordinates or co-workers. A secondary purpose is to build a cohesive work unit with strong member identification.

The importance of cooperation, identification with the work unit, and constructive resolution of conflict are central themes in the literature on organizations. This concern is reflected in the research on group cohesiveness and teamwork, in the organization development research on team building, in the organization design research on "integrators," in the conflict management literature, and in the recent literature on effective management (Bradford & Cohen, 1984; Yukl, 1989).

Networking

This category includes a wide variety of behaviors intended to develop and maintain contacts and cooperative working relationships with people who are important sources of information and assistance both inside and outside the organization. Some types of behavior within this category are used to help maintain good relationships with subordinates, particularly socializing and informal discussion of subjects not related to the work (e.g., sports, vacations, families, hobbies). However, most networking involves developing cooperative relationships with people other than subordinates, such as peers, superiors, and outside clients, customers, and suppliers. Examples of networking include attending social and ceremonial events, sendings cards and correspondence, participating in recreational and leisure activities (e.g., golf, handball), joining professional associations and social clubs, visiting clients and customers, meeting people for lunch, calling someone on the telephone to congratulate him or her on an achievement, and doing a favor requested by someone. As the examples show, behavior incidents involving networking may also involve other behaviors as well. Research by Kotter (1982) and Kaplan (1984) found that it is important for managers to develop an extensive network of contacts with persons in other subunits of the organization, and with important outsiders.

EXAMPLES OF APPLICATIONS OF THE MPS

Organizations are currently using the Managerial Practices Survey in a variety of ways to improve managerial effectiveness. Three examples will be described briefly.

Individual Training Needs Analysis

In a large health insurance company, managers in the data processing department were primarily technical wizards who needed to develop better interpersonal and project management skills. The director of the department wanted to assess individual training needs and increase each manager's awareness of strengths and weaknesses. A one-day workshop was developed by consultants to provide the managers with feedback about how their managerial behavior is perceived by subordinates and peers. The MPS was distributed to subordinates and peers of each manager, who used it to describe how they perceive the manager's behavior. A related importance questionnaire (self-report version and boss/report version) was filled out by each manager and the manager's boss. Questionnaires were scored by optical scanning equipment, and the results were analyzed by a computer software program that prepares individual feedback reports.

The workshop began with the presentation of a leadership model and explanation of the managerial practices. Under the guidance of a trained facilitator, participating managers worked first alone, and then in small groups, to interpret their feedback results. The first type of feedback involved the rated importance of each managerial practice. Importance ratings by a manager and corresponding ratings by the manager's boss were compared to identify differences in the way each party perceives the manager's job requirements. The feedback report also showed the four managerial practices selected as "most essential" by the manager and by the manager's boss. Figure 56–1 provides an example of the feedback for one manager.

In this example, ratings by the boss differed somewhat from those by the manager, and only two of the four "most essential" behaviors selected by the boss were the same as those selected by the manager. The manager was relatively new to his position, and he attributed the discrepancy to his failure to recognize some differences between his current and former managerial positions. He decided to sit down with his

Figure 56–1. Importance Scores

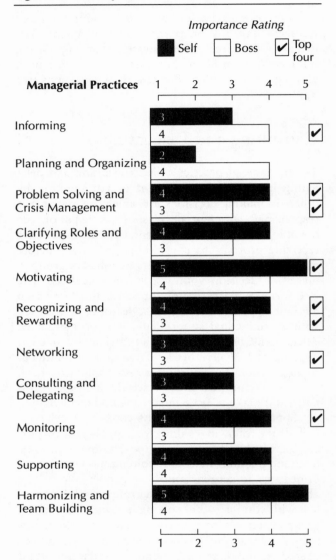

boss to talk about the differences in their perceptions of job requirements and reach a consensus about the relative importance of different managerial practices for effective performance of his job.

In the next part of the workshop, managers received feedback about their use of each managerial practice. The feedback report presented the scale score based on the manager's self-description, the average score provided by subordinates and peers, and the discrepancy between self-ratings and ratings by other people. The feedback report also showed norms based on average scores received by all managers who have used the MPS, although this average is not necessarily relevant for a particular manager in a unique situation. Figure 56–2 shows an example of the feedback for one manager.

The manager in the example noticed that his self-description agreed with the description of his behavior provided by other people for two managerial practices: recognizing/rewarding and motivating. He noticed that both informing and planning were below the norm. One managerial practice he thought he used extensively (consulting/delegating) was perceived by others to be used infrequently. Other discrepancies occurred also, although they were not as sharp. The individual diagnosis and group discussion of results helped the manager clarify the reasons for the discrepancies. The manager realized that because of his extensive technical competence, he tends to make decisions alone without consulting subordinates, and he involves himself too much in the details of his subordinates' day-to-day work. The manager considered whether all of his subordinates need so much supervision or whether some would perform just as well and be more satisfied with more autonomy and discretion. He also considered the possibility that subordinates would prefer more participation in making important task decisions.

In the next part of the workshop, participants received feedback on specific behaviors in each of the eleven middle-range categories. This item feedback is especially helpful, since some aspects of a managerial

Figure 56–2. Scale Scores

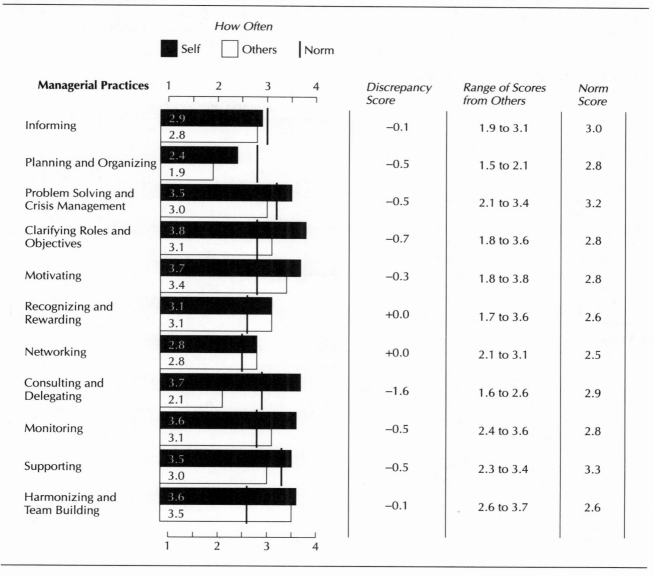

practice are more relevant for a manager than others. The feedback shows how a manager described his or her own behavior on each item in the questionnaire, and it shows the distribution of responses from other people who described the manager. The feedback report also shows the mean item score based on the responses of people who described the manager, but the frequency feedback is more informative than the item means. An example of the item feedback is provided in figure 56–3.

There are some important reasons that we provide frequency feedback for all items in the MPS. Scale scores are based on averaging across both items and respondents. This averaging process loses much useful information and occasionally causes some distortions in the results. Feedback programs that provide only scale scores implicitly make some dubious assumptions: that all examples of a behavior category are equally relevant, that data on all items are equally valid, and that managers treat all subordinates alike. Use of item means avoids some of the problems of scale means, but it also obscures important information, such as the extent of agreement among people describing the manager and whether anyone answered "don't know" or "not applicable" to an item. Instead of item means or frequencies, some feedback programs merely list behavior examples from any scales for which a manager received low scores in relation to general norms. In these programs, the manager is usually advised to make more use of the highlighted behaviors. Such programs reflect the rather arrogant assumption that program developers have a monopoly on knowledge about what behavior is appropriate and effective for a manager. In contrast, our program is based on the assumption that managers are able to evaluate detailed information and interpret it in a meaningful way. A manager can use the leadership model to help interpret the feedback, and assistance is available from the workshop facilitator and other participants,

Figure 56–3. Feedback on Specific Behaviors

Behavior Examples	Avg. Rating	Distribution of Responses — Planning and Organizing						
		don't know	not applicable	never	seldom	sometimes	usually
9. Plans in detail to accomplish a major task or project.	1.5			5	2	★ 1	
10. Plans in advance what resources are needed to carry out a task or project.	1.2			6	★ 2		
11. Plans how to organize the work so that personnel, equipment and facilities are utilized efficiently.	1.6			4	3	★ 1	
12. Plans how to eliminate unnecessary activities and procedures.	1.7	2	1	1	★ 2	2	
13. Determines priorities for different activities and plans an appropriate allocation of resources.	1.1	1		6	★ 1		
14. Plans in advance how to avoid potential problems that could disrupt operations or jeopardize an important project.	3.2					6	★ 2
15. Develops long-range plans indicating the objectives and strategies to be pursued in coming years.	1.7			3	★ 4	1	
16. Initiates improvements in policies, procedures or the organization of the work.	2.7			1	1	★ 5	1

★ Your resonse

but it is up to the manager to determine the relevance of any particular aspect of the feedback.

In the final part of the feedback workshop, managers determined how to capitalize on their strong points and remedy any deficiencies in patterns of behavior. With the aid of a workbook showing three general approaches to improve managerial practices, participants developed specific action plans for capitalizing on their strong points and remedying any weaknesses. Information was provided about workshops and courses sponsored or recommended by the company, and participants were helped to identify developmental opportunities relevant to their improvement goals. Finally, possibilities for more on-the-job coaching were discussed.

Development of Leadership Skills in Executive Teams

The MPS was used as part of a team building intervention conducted in a large corporation that manufacturers industrial and consumer products. The company had recently undergone a change in strategic direction under new ownership. The company president believed that a common strategic focus was especially important during the transition period. The team building intervention was designed to build executive skills in strategic thinking and planning. The intervention included a realistic, two-day management simulation in which executives acted as the management team of a fictitious organization facing numerous strategic and operational issues. Participants received feedback from observers regarding their management skills and behavior in the simulation. Participants also received feedback about their behavior toward subordinates back on the job from the MPS, which was administered to the subordinates of the managers. Each manager was given a feedback report based on the MPS, along with a brief explanation of the feedback and the leadership model. Feedback about management practices, feedback from the management simulation, and scores on standardized personality measures such as the Meyers-Briggs Type Indicator provided three different perspectives on the strategic behavior of the managers. The combination of these different types of information presented a comprehensive picture of each manager's strategic leadership skills and individual effectiveness.

After individual managers examined their feedback, the results were discussed by the team, and they identified several areas of deficiency. One problem was a lack of cooperation between different divisions in the company and a lack of effective conflict management between executives in charge of the different divisions. Another problem was role ambiguity among many subordinates of the executives. The recent sale of the company had created uncertainty and a lack of understanding about common goals. The executive team discussed the problems and determined how to deal with them.

Organization Development

A division of a large corporation that manufactures chemicals and industrial products had instituted an "Excellence Through Quality" effort based on J.M. Juran's quality approach. Top management wanted to extend the approach beyond manufacturing operations to develop a quality emphasis in human resources management and strategic planning. The MPS was used as a diagnostic tool to evaluate general patterns of managerial behavior in the organization, beginning with the top management team and extending to middle and lower-level management. In contrast to the earlier examples, the focus of the initial intervention was on aggregate data for each level and subunit of the organization rather than on feedback for individual managers. Patterns of managerial behavior were analyzed by the top management team with the assistance of the consultant to identify aspects of behavior in need of improvement. Developmental activities were planned to address these deficiencies, including appraisal and counseling sessions, skill training workshops, experiential learning opportunities (e.g., special assignments), and on-the-job coaching. Top management decided to administer the MPS on a yearly basis. Results will be used to provide individual feedback to managers, as well as to evaluate aggregate behavior patterns. Baseline results and subsequent progress are being charted in a manner similar to that used in the company's quality control program.

SUMMARY

The three examples demonstrate the adaptibilty of the MPS and the related importance questionnaire as tools for management and organizational develop-ment. The questionnaires can be used as part of a feedback workshop for individual managers, as part of a team building intervention, or as part of a more comprehensive organizational development program. Information from the questionnaires is useful for diagnosis of management problems at different levels of aggregation, including individual managers, management teams, and the overall management of the organization. The taxonomy of managerial behaviors serves as a conceptual tool to aid managers in diagnosing their behavior and interpreting it in meaningful ways. Managers who have used the questionnaire consistently report that the behavior categories are easy to understand and apply to their situation. The feedback workshop encourages managers to think in terms of overall patterns of behavior in relation to the requirements of different situations, and the emphasis is on flexibility and adaptability. Behavior is treated not as a set of discrete actions that are performed in mechanical "one-minute manager" episodes but rather as a set of interwoven strategies for discovering and coping with problems and opportunities determined by dynamic events within the organization and in its external environment. We are continuing to develop additional applications, and whenever possible, data are being collected to evaluate the validity of the questionnaire and the impact of interventions using it.

REFERENCES

Bennis, W., & Nanus, B. (1985). *Leaders: The strategies for taking charge.* New York: Harper & Row.

Bradford, D.L., & Cohen, A.R. (1984). *Managing for excellence: The guide to developing high performance in contemporary organizations.* New York: John Wiley & Sons.

Hamner, W.C., & Hamner, E.P. (1976). Behavior modification on the bottom line. *Organizational Dynamics, 4* (4), 2–21.

Kaplan, R.E. (1984). Trade routes: The manager's network of relationships. *Organizational Dynamics* (Spring), 37–52.

Kotter, J.P. (1982). *The general managers.* New York: Free Press.

Likert, R. (1967). *The human organization: Its management and value.* New York: McGraw-Hill.

Locke, E.A., & Latham, G.P. (1984). *Goal setting: A motivational technique that works.* Englewood Cliffs, NJ: Prentice-Hall.

Mintzberg, H. (1973). *The nature of managerial work.* New York: Harper & Row.

Peters, T.J., & Waterman, R.H. Jr. (1982). *In search of excellence: Lessons from America's best-run companies.* New York: Harper & Row.

Stogdill, R.M. (1974). *Handbook of leadership: Survey of theory and research.* New York: Free Press.

Yukl, G.A. (1983). *Development of a taxonomy of managerial behavior.* Paper presented at the Society for Organizational Behavior Annual Meeting, Minneapolis, Minnesota.

Yukl, G.A. (1989) *Leadership in organizations* (2d ed.). Englewood Cliffs, NJ: Prentice-Hall.

Yukl, G.A., Wall, S., & Lepsinger, R. (1990) Preliminary report on validation of the Managerial Practices Survey. In K.E. Clark (Ed.), *Measures of leadership* (223–228). West Orange, NJ: Leadership Library of America.

57 LEADERSHIP AND PROJECT MANAGEMENT

Deborah S. Kezsbom

A project's success is, in part, contingent upon effectively managing the constraints of time, money, and performance specifications. A basic ingredient, however, of schedule, cost, and quality efficiency is the degree of influence and leadership a project manager has over the people who make it all happen.

Effective project implementation relies on the integration of plans, schedules, and control mechanisms across contributing functions. A project manager's success therefore is contingent on influencing the diversity of personnel who are responsible for outlining and implementing project components. In fact, more than in any other form of organizational or managerial work, projects, because of their multidisciplined and highly interdependent nature, demand a leader with skills to build a strong sense of commitment and motivate a project team.

Leadership is more complicated in project organizations than it is in other forms. Project managers are usually faced with the responsibility for project integration and implementation and the accountability for success as well as failure. Yet because of their position within the structure of the organization, they possess minimum legal authority. Project managers working within a complex, multidisciplined organizational matrix must often cross departmental as well as divisional lines to attain the input and support necessary for project activities. Project leadership therefore involves not only understanding and working within the physical and political boundaries of a complicated organization but entails a firm appreciation of the diverse needs of the professionals who are part of the project team.

This chapter examines leadership within a project matrix environment and explores a variety of techniques and mechanisms by which a project manager achieves success.

SKILLS OF THE PROJECT MANAGER: HELP OR HINDRANCE?

Often one is promoted to project manager not so much because of one's excellence in managing people or even in projects but because of one's superior ability to meet technical demands. Excellent design engineers, masters of circuitry, or top-notch developers frequently are given their first opportunity in management through the promotion to a project manager's position. In many instances, the newly appointed project manager must struggle against tough odds. Faced with little authority and a lack of management skills, the newly appointed project manager finds himself or herself in what may well be considered a sink-or-swim situation.

Table 57–1
Project Manager Skills

Technical expertise/general knowledge
Forecasting/planning/scheduling/estimating
Problem identification/solving
Ability to establish project objectives/performance criteria/
  standards
Big picture orientation
Task organization
Flexibility/adaptability
Resource allocation
Team building/management/leadership
Accounting/budgeting/financial control
Training/development/delegation
Communications/interpersonal/written/oral
Conflict resolution/negotiation
Group dynamics/organizational development
Creativity/conceptual thinking
Systems/project management
Walk on water

From D.S. Kezsbom, D.L. Schilling, & K.A. Edward. *Dynamic Project Management: A Practical Guide for Managers and Engineers* (New York: John Wiley and Sons, 1989).

How can project managers make it through what appears, at times, to be an overwhelming professional challenge? They must first recognize that how well project work is accomplished depends upon their skills in fostering project integration and managing team performance. As table 57–1 indicates, the characteristics and skills needed for working with and through people seem to predominate. A project man-ager must possess the desire to get things accomplished with and through other people rather than in spite of them. Concern for project team members, an ability to integrate the personal objectives and needs of project personnel into project goals, and the ability to create enthusiasm for the work itself creates a project climate that is high in motivation and performance.

AUTHORITY AND INFLUENCE: THE KEYS TO EFFECTIVE PROJECT LEADERSHIP

Working with and through others to accomplish organizational objectives is the cornerstone of any management position. A major difference, however, between the more contemporary project manager's role and the more traditional functional manager's position is the degree of authority each possesses, or fails to possess.

Project managers often operate in a complex, multidisciplined environment and possess little command or control over contributing functional specialists. Lacking the traditional boss-subordinate relationship, project managers must frequently rely on developing the perception of authority as well as on influence strategies that are derived from a variety of interpersonal and political sources. The first step in influencing others is for project managers to become aware of the sources of power and influence that are available to them as they operate across the multiproject, multidisciplined, and multichaotic organization.

To deal effectively with the multiple chains of command as well as the conflicting priorities that are characteristic of most project-matrix organizations, project managers must be able to communicate a number of things. The first is their respect for the concerns and perspectives of others. Second, they must indicate their desire to encourage views different from their own. Above all they need to demonstrate that they can be trusted. Since they lack direct control or authority over the people performing the work, project managers must give and request support by using not only logic but a variety of interpersonal influence bases.

TRUST AND INFORMAL CONTACTS

It is common for project team members to tell project managers only what they believe the project manager wants to hear. Many organizations reinforce the fear of sharing problems by often "killing the bearer of bad news." Project team members will share their problems with the project manager only if a sense of trust has truly been established, that is, if they believe that the project manager understands their problems and the difficulties they face.

To be effective, a project manager must know the people involved—who they are and what their problems might be. Project managers must develop and use techniques that dig beyond surface indicators (e.g., reports and forms, schedules and budgets) and find out just how the team is working together, what their technical as well as organizational problems are, and what issues or conflicts are preventing the realization of project objectives.

By getting to the heart of the issues and talking about what is really going on, project managers demonstrate that they not only possess knowledge of the big picture but that they have taken the time to educate themselves sufficiently to be in a better position to help solve team problems. Such actions demonstrate a caring position and foster the development of trust in relationships.

DEVELOPING PROJECT AUTHORITY AND INFLUENCE

While position or "legal" authority may be regarded as an important basis of influence, it must be used judiciously and in accordance with the demands and characteristics of the particular project situation.

Although perceived to be an extremely important source of influence by project and functional managers alike, research indicates that project managers who are perceived to rely a great deal on position or legal authority are rated by peers as well as followers to be less effective in their ability to resolve project problems and conflict, and are rated lower in overall project performance.[1]

One cannot deny the importance of delegating as much organizationally derived authority to the project manager as the environment permits; however, once legal authority is available, a project manager will best be served by developing his or her expertise and interpersonal skills and providing work challenge.[2] Moreover, although technical expertise is still widely recognized as a potential basis of influence and as an important source of power, this expertise can be an effective source of influence only if it is recognized and actively sought after by project team members and colleagues. Technical expertise, therefore, can serve as a potential influence base only if it is associated with effective lateral communication and the development of a wide spectrum of organizational contacts and interpersonal relationships.

UNDERSTANDING THE BASIS OF PROJECT LEADERSHIP

Project managers, especially those who find themselves in a matrix environment, are in a very challenging leadership position. The better they understand the nature of leadership and how it relates to project efforts, the better they will be able to accomplish project objectives.

Effective leadership occurs when a symbiotic relationship is created between a leader and followers; that is, the leader attempts to achieve or accomplish certain organizational goals or even personal objectives through the activities of his or her followers. In turn, followers grant or bestow the right to lead to an individual who offers them the fulfillment of their own objectives, which may include professional growth, job challenge, respect, or a sense of integrity. The specific leadership style practiced by the project manager may indeed vary according to the demands of the task or the timing of the situation but must always consider the needs of the followers and provide opportunities for follower growth and development.

Project management is one of the most participative management strategies in today's corporate environment. To be successful, projects must be integrated across corporate divisional lines through consensus-seeking activities that produce a sense of buying in and team commitment. This is accomplished through the contribution of all project-related disciplines to the project planning, scheduling, and controlling processes. However, let us not confuse a participative management philosophy with a participative leadership style.

Project management techniques should be built on a general foundation of cross-functional, organizational participation. Specific project leadership style, however, is contingent upon the combination of a number of complex elements. To be participative (or democratic) at all times certainly would be ridiculous.

In the case of a crisis or safety hazard, for example, only the weak and ineffective project manager would turn to his or her peers or followers for a vote. Project managers must develop a variety of leadership styles that permit them to respond appropriately to the changing and complex challenges of a dynamic life cycle. In other words, project managers need to recognize that no one leadership style will work for all project conditions or situations. Project managers must be able to diagnose a variety of situations and adapt their behavior or leadership style to fit not only the changing life cycle demands of the project but the requirements and style of the customer, as well as the professional needs of project team members.

To accomplish project tasks effectively, a project manager must not only be aware of the characteristics of the task and the needs and goals of followers but must vary his or her leadership style to provide opportunities for follower growth, development, and "maturation."[3]

Appropriate leadership style therefore can be regarded as changing over the life cycle of the project. As the level of follower experience and independence continues to increase, a leader must reduce his or her control and task-directive behavior by delegating more decision-making authority to project specialists.

Project and functional managers alike must realize that to manage a project successfully, they will lead a variety of followers, including project team specialists, as well as the customer and top management. Project managers therefore must assess their followers in terms of each person's need for feedback, autonomy, and their understanding of specific technical, administrative, or monetary requirements and then adjust their leadership approach accordingly. Customers, for example, may well believe that they fully understand the requirements of the system they wish to have built but may need to be sold on realistic cost and scheduling requirements. The chief executive officers of a leading R&D firm may possess advanced technical degrees and broad-based administrative experience but require greater "clarification" (and therefore direction) regarding the success and feasibility of new project technologies.

A key to effective project leadership, therefore, is to develop the ability to assess the needs of followers, whoever they may be, and behave accordingly. Project and functional managers involved in the accomplishment of state-of-the-art projects, for example, will find that their engineers and technical specialists may vary greatly in their need for specific leadership behaviors not only over the duration of the project but in terms of the specific task at hand. An experienced design engineer may master the technology well enough to require minimum input and direction (for example, when determining specifications or estimating resource requirements) but may not have demonstrated the same capabilities in documenting specifications or reporting progress to management. It may thus be quite appropriate for a project manager to offer little technical direction over design activities yet provide a great deal of supervision over or the process of reporting to management.

POWER: THE LEADERSHIP POTENTIAL

It is generally agreed that leadership is the ability to influence others toward the accomplishment of organizational goals or objectives. Power may be conceived of as a leader's "influence potential." It is the means by which influence is accomplished. Indeed, it is difficult to separate the concepts of leadership and power. It would be impossible to influence another without utilizing some degree of power. Power is a feature of most organizational interactions and, at some time or another, is used by all employees to control resources, negotiate agreements, and establish or attain professional and organizational goals.

Individuals may possess substantial power even though they hold no formal leadership position. Legal authority is conceived of as the right to make final decisions that others are required to follow. Authority, therefore, is a formally sanctioned privilege that may or may not be available to employees. Power, on the other hand, implies an ability to get results independent of legal authority. As illustrated in figure 57–1, one may conceivably possess authority yet demonstrate no power, possess no authority and demonstrate power, or, ideally, possess both authority and power.

Especially in an R&D matrix environment, project managers' perceived power is highly related to their technical know-how and skills of persuasion and negotiation. In the extremely demanding project environment, project managers who rely primarily on their formal authority, formal rewards, or whatever coercive power they possess will be less effective than those who influence the course of events through their ability to deal with each situation as it occurs by practicing integrative planning and organizational interfacing.[4]

Project managers must find ways to increase their authority and power by establishing contacts and relationships both inside and outside the organization. This includes such entities as staff groups, functional departments, supervisors, the customer, subcontractors, consultants, and, at times, government officials and public interest groups.

The typical project liaison role involves maintaining a variety of communication contacts. Social relationships through which information is transmitted must be developed and maintained. Project managers must attend meetings, lunch with team members and arrange to talk with influential experts and scientists on a regular basis. These contacts provide the project

Figure 57–1. The Relationship between Authority and Power

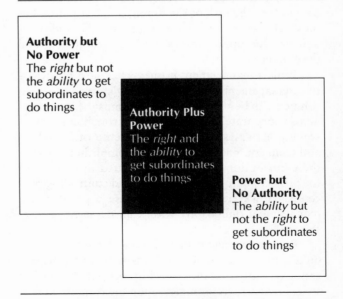

Source: Robert Keitner, *Management* (Boston: Houghton Mifflin, 1983).

manager with access to information unavailable to team members, thus strengthening his or her power and potential influence bases.

The project manager would be wise to develop as many sources of information as possible concerning the project's internal and external environmental influences. Verbal and written sources of information (such as reports, correspondence, journal articles, newsletters, etc.) place the project manager in a powerful central information processing position.

Research suggests that while traditional rewards, such as salary and promotion, are important to many technical professionals, of equal importance is work challenge and recognition.[5] The ability to provide these factors to project team members creates a significant source of power. Project managers must go to great lengths to ensure that the work of team members is recognized and communicated through their influence network.

CONCLUSION

Simply appointing a professional with technical expertise to a project manager role is insufficient. Achieving a unity of effort within the complicated matrix project structure requires a firm appreciation of the problem and diverse needs facing a project

team and an ability to create enthusiasm and commitment for the work itself. This ability evolves from a clear understanding of the nature of project leadership and the identification and development of a variety of influence and power bases.

NOTES

1. R.M. Hodgettes, Leadership techniques in the project organization, *Academy of Management Journal 11* (1968), 211–219; H.J. Thamhain & G.R. Gemmill, Influence styles of project managers: Some performance correlates," *Academy of Management Journal, 17* (June 1974), 216–224; G. Gemmill & H. Thamhain, The effectiveness of different power styles of project management in gaining support, *IEEE Transactions on Engineering Management,* EM-20. 38–44 (May 1973); G.H. Gemmill, J. Thamhain, & D.L. Wileman, The power spectrum in project management," *Sloan Management Review* (Fall 1970), 15–25.

2. Gemmill, Thamhain, & Wileman, Power spectrum, 16.
3. P. Hersey & K. Blanchard, *Management of organizational behavior utilizing group resources* (3d ed.) (Englewood Cliffs, NJ: Prentice-Hall, 1981).
4. Thamhain and Gemmill, Influence styles.
5. Gemmill and Thamhain, "Effectiveness of different power styles"; J.R.P. French and B. Raven, "The Bases of Social Power," in Dorwin Caerthwright (Ed.), *Studies in social power* (Ann Arbor, MI: Institute for Social Research, University of Michigan, 1959), 150–167.

58 PARTICIPATIVE MANAGEMENT STRATEGIES

Edward E. Lawler III

The most prevalent approach to designing work organizations calls for such features as hierarchical decision making, simple repetitive jobs at the lower levels, and rewards based on carefully measured individual job performance. This "control approach" separates the controlling and planning features of work from the production of the product or service. The result is that individuals end up in jobs that require little thinking and that do not allow them to participate in the management of the organization for which they work.

Numerous articles and books have recently argued that work organizations need to move toward a more participative or involvement-oriented approach to the design and management of work organizations (see e.g., Lawler, 1986; Walton, 1985). The advantages of the involvement approach are said to include higher-quality products and services, less absenteeism, less turnover, better decision making, and better problem solving, in short, greater organizational effectiveness. A number of large corporations have adopted one or more employee involvement programs. Ford, Xerox, TRW, and Motorola are prime examples of companies that are implementing involvement on a company-wide basis. The idea of participative management is not a new one—McGregor, Likert, and Argyris all wrote persuasively about its advantages in the 1950s—what is new is the adoption of it by major corporations.

Examination of the suggested approaches to involvement reveals that there is not a single approach but at least three different approaches to managing organizations in a participative way. These three different approaches have different histories, advocates, advantages, and disadvantages. An organization interested in adopting involvement needs to be aware of the differences among these approaches and strategically choose the approach that is best for it. It then needs to develop an implementation strategy that will lead to successful adoption of participative management.

APPROACHES TO INVOLVEMENT

The three approaches to involvement are parallel suggestion involvement, job involvement, and high involvement. They differ in the degree to which they argue that four key features of an organization should be moved to the lowest level. Briefly the features are:

1. Information about the performance of the organization.
2. Rewards that are based on the performance of the organization.
3. Knowledge that enables employees to understand and contribute to organizational performance.
4. Power to make decisions that influence organizational direction and performance.

Information, rewards, knowledge, and power are central issues in all organizations (Galbraith, 1973). How they are positioned in an organization determines the core management style of the organization. When they are concentrated at the top, traditional control-oriented management exists; when they are moved downward, some form of involvement or participative management is being practiced.

The parallel suggestion approach does the least to move power, knowledge, information, and rewards downward, while the high involvement approach does the most. Because they have different strategies for positioning power, information, knowledge, and rewards, these approaches tend to fit different situations and to produce different results. Let us consider how each of these three approaches operates and the results they produce. Once we have reviewed them, we can discuss when and how they are best utilized.

Parallel Suggestion Involvement

Probably the oldest and most common approach to employee involvement is suggestion involvement. Formal suggestion programs are the original approach to establishing a problem-solving relationship between lower-level employees and their work. In suggestion involvement, employees are asked—often for the first time—to problem solve and produce ideas that will influence how the organization operates. Traditional suggestion programs often include a reward system change as well, rewarding individuals based on the estimated value of the suggestions they produce. Much more extensive reward system change is involved in gain-sharing plans.

The oldest and best-known gain-sharing plan is the Scanlon Plan. Herman Miller and Donnelly Mirrors are well known for their early adoption of this approach; more recently, Motorola and Dana have adopted it on a company-wide basis (Graham-Moore and Ross, 1983). In gain sharing, employees are asked to suggest improvements, and they share in any overall performance improvement the organization makes. Some gain-sharing plans also move new information downward because they focus on organizational performance. In gain-sharing plans, unlike traditional suggestion programs, employees share in gains for as long as they are realized by the organization.

Suggestion involvement has recently become extremely popular because of the widespread adoption of quality circles. Thousands of companies have adopted them, some such as Westinghouse virtually on a company-wide basis. At this point, quite a bit is known about the effectiveness of quality circles and how they operate (Lawler & Mohrman, 1985). Like written suggestion programs and Scanlon Plan suggestion programs, they ask employees to recommend ways in which the operations of the organization can be improved. In the traditional quality circle approach, this is done through a group, or quality circle, rather than through an individual written suggestion. According to quality circle advocates, the group process typically leads to better suggestions and better-developed suggestions. In addition, in quality circles, considerable training is done to enable the group to function effectively and to help individuals become efficient problem solvers. In the more advanced programs, employees are trained in problem analysis and statistical quality control.

Quality circles have only recommendation power; they do not have the power to implement and decide on the installation of their suggestions. In this sense, they are a parallel structure to the ongoing organization. They are also parallel structures because they take people out of their regular organizations and put them in a separate new structure that operates differently from the traditional organization. Quality circles and other parallel structures are often easy to install and start quickly. However, they do not change the existing organization structure, and they affect only a small percentage of the work force. The groups often are small and can easily be installed in a single plant or department of a larger organization.

Closely related to the quality circle approach are the quality of work life programs that have been adopted by many companies and their unions. Ford and General Motors, in combination with the United Auto Workers (UAW), have adopted this approach in most of their plants. In addition to problem-solving groups, it creates a joint union-management steering committee structure to guide the program and to help ensure that suggestions are acted upon (Lawler & Ozley, 1979).

Suggestion involvement approaches do not represent a major shift in the way control-oriented organizations deal with most issues. Instead they rely on a special parallel structure to change the relationship between individuals and their work. This structure gives people the chance to influence things that they would not normally influence and in some cases to share in the financial results of this new role. It also usually leads to some additional information being communicated and individuals' acquiring greater knowledge. However, this change in knowledge, information, and rewards is limited to a part of the work force. In addition, it is encapsulated because individuals are asked to use it only when they are operating in special suggestion-type activities. During their regular work activities, it is very much work as usual.

Research on the parallel structure or suggestion involvement approach suggests that this approach can lead to improvement in organizational performance (Frost, Wakley & Ruh, 1974; Lawler, 1986). Case after case shows that individuals and groups often come up with suggestions that save a considerable amount of money (Schuster, 1984). There also seems to be no question that employees enjoy the opportunity to participate in problem solving. As a result, they are often more satisfied with their work situation, are absent less, and are less likely to leave.

There are a number of well-documented limitations of the parallel suggestion involvement approach. They tend to have a "program character" about them that leads to their being temporary systems in an organization. Parallel structures are expensive and difficult to maintain. In some situations, they run out of suggestions because individuals do not have enough expertise to solve the more complex problems. They also often are resisted by the middle levels of management because parallel structures threaten their power and put them in the position of having to do extra work. Conflict can develop between those who are in parallel structures and those who are not. Nonparticipants can come to resent being left out. Finally, over time, suggestion involvement approaches often lose their momentum and disappear. This comes about because of the fundamental limitation that they do not systematically change an organization's way of operating or the way the total work force relates to the organization and its performance.

Job Involvement Approaches

Job involvement approaches focus on enriching individual work in order to motivate better job performance. One strategy, originally called "job enlargement" and later "job enrichment," focuses on creating individual tasks that give people feedback, requires them to use a variety of skills, and gives them a whole piece of work (Hackman & Lawler, 1971). This approach has an extensive research history going back to the 1950s, when behavioral scientists tried to design alternatives to traditional standardized simplified work (Hackman & Oldham, 1980). It was widely adopted by AT&T as well as other major corporations.

A second approach to job involvement creates work groups or teams. This approach, too, has an extensive research history going back to the 1940s (Cummings, 1978). It differs from individual enrichment in that it takes the work group as the primary unit of involvement. It tries to create group goals, tasks, and motivation such that all group members feel responsible for the group's performance. Groups designed according to this approach are often called autonomous work groups, self-managing groups, or work teams.

The job involvement approach has significant implications for how an organization is structured and managed. In essence, individuals are given new skills and knowledge, new feedback, and an additional set of decisions to make and may be rewarded with skill-based pay (Lawler & Ledford, 1985). Both the individual and the team approach affect power, rewards, information, and skills, although the team approach carried to its fullest probably affects them to a greater degree. With the team approach, it is important to add interpersonal skills and group decision-making skills to those that are needed for individual enrichment. The reward system also is changed more with groups or teams, since skill-based pay is often added. Finally, teams can make certain decisions that individuals usually cannot. Both individuals and teams can control the way the work is done. They can do quality management, inventory, and other task-related activities, but teams can also make personnel management decisions. Teams, for example, can make decisions about hiring and firing and may select their own supervisors (Lawler, 1978).

Overall, job involvement represents a significant change in the fundamental operations of an organization. Individuals at the lowest levels get new information, power, and skills and may be rewarded differently. The new information, power, knowledge, and rewards relate to their particular work tasks; it typically does not have to do with structuring and operating the whole organization or the development of its strategic direction. Unlike parallel suggestion approaches, the day-to-day work activities of all individuals are affected. Involvement is not an occasional thing; it is the standard way in which business is done.

Theoretically, the choice between teams and individual job enrichment should be based upon the technology of the workplace (Hackman & Oldham, 1980). Teams are more complicated to build and to maintain but may be necessary if the work is such that no one individual can do all of it and get feedback about it. Teams are often appropriate, for example, in process production facilities such as chemical plants and oil refineries and in complex service organizations such as banks and airlines. Procter and Gamble, for example, has been a large installer of teams because most of its products (e.g., food, paper) are made in automated process production facilities. Where the technology allows for an individual to do a whole task or offer a whole service, often individual designs are preferred because they are simpler to install and give the individual more direct feedback.

Studies of the job involvement approaches show that they lead to improvements in productivity, quality, absenteeism, and turnover (Hackman & Oldham, 1980). Unlike suggestion programs, job involvement structures seem to have reasonably good stability, particularly in the case of teams, since they represent cohesive organizational units that are difficult to dissolve.

The limitations of the job involvement approach are primarily those of lost opportunities. Because they limit employee involvement to immediate work decisions, they often fail to capture the contributions that individuals can make to strategic decisions and to higher-level management work. This can also lead to a tendency for individuals in work teams to optimize their own performance without paying a great deal of attention to overall organization performance. This can be a problem because what is good for the team is not always good for the organization.

Work involvement efforts do have some significant start-up costs associated with them because they require considerable training. Often overlooked is the need for training the supervisor and for dramatically changing the supervisor's job (Walton & Schlesinger, 1979). Some evidence exists that many supervisors have difficulty changing from traditional management to job involvement. Also, they are often resisted by middle managers because they feel threatened by the new power that others have, and they feel they have lost some of their power.

In some cases, job involvement efforts call for an expensive physical reconfiguration of the workplace in order to allow for team interaction or for individuals controlling a whole piece of work. Volvo's Kalmar, Sweden, plant shows just how extensively an auto plant needs to be designed to fit teams. There the assembly line has been eliminated, and cars are moved around on motorized pallets.

Finally, job involvement approaches may be subject to cancellation because they do not influence higher-level strategic decisions concerned with organization structure, power, and the allocation of rewards. This is particularly true with individual job enrichment. Unless major restructuring is done to support it, supervisors are often in the position of being able to change jobs unilaterally in ways that take away the decision-making power that is critical to their being enriched. Job involvement efforts are particularly likely to be cancelled when they affect small parts of an organization. Like parallel structures, they can be installed only on a limited basis and, as a result, create friction between participants and nonparticipants. This friction can, in turn, lead to pressures to eliminate the job involvement program.

High Involvement Approach

The high involvement approach, which has also been called the "commitment approach," or perhaps more descriptively, the "business involvement approach," is relatively new. In many respects, it builds upon what has been learned from the suggestion involvement and job involvement approaches. It tends to structure an organization so that people at the lowest level will have a sense of involvement, not just in how they do their jobs or how effectively their group performs but in the performance of the total organization. It goes considerably further than either of the other two approaches toward moving power, information, knowledge, and rewards to the lowest level. It basically argues that if individuals are going to care about the performance of the organization, they need to know about it, be able to influence it, be rewarded for it, and have the knowledge and skills to contribute to it.

In order to have high involvement management, virtually every major feature of the organization needs to be designed differently from the control approach (Lawler, 1986). The high involvement approach builds upon what is done in the job involvement and the suggestion involvement approaches.

Parallel structures are used for certain kinds of problem solving and policy development, and work is designed according to the principles of individual job enrichment and work teams. High involvement is very different, however, in the kind of information it argues should be shared and in the decision power and reward systems areas. In the case of decision power, employees are not only asked to make decisions about their work activities, they are asked to play a role in organizational-level decisions having to do with strategy, investment, and other major organization decisions. Rewards are based upon the performance of the organization; hence, profit sharing, gain sharing, and some type of employee ownership are appropriate.

Creating a high involvement organization is a much different and more complex task than is implementing job involvement or suggestion involvement. Virtually every feature of a control-oriented organization has to be redesigned, and in some cases, innovation in design is necessary. Many of the methodologies and approaches for such practices as pay, selection, and training are readily available and well developed for control-oriented management. Installing them is simply a matter of taking established systems off the shelf and making them operational. On the other hand, there is a relative paucity of technology to support the development of high involvement organizations. This is largely due to the fact that this approach to management is new, and the technology has not had time to develop. Therefore, those organizations that adopt it are forced into somewhat of a research and development mode with respect to the technology of high involvement management.

There are relatively few data on the effectiveness of high involvement organizations. Indeed, there are few examples to study. The closest organizations to this approach would appear to be the many new plants that have been started around the world during the last twenty years (Lawler, 1978). It is hardly surprising that the best examples of high involvement organizations are new start-ups. The high involvement approach represents such an extensive change from the control approach to management that the difficulties in making a conversion are enormous. It is much easier to start with a clean sheet of paper and design the organization from the ground up (Perkins, Nieva & Lawler, 1983). This is in notable contrast to job involvement and suggestion involvement approaches, which are often put in place in existing organizations.

The limited evidence that exists on the performance of high involvement organizations generally shows they achieve superior operating results. For example, Procter and Gamble has close to thirty new high involvement plants and has made statements at conferences that they are at least 30 percent more effective than traditional plants. A good guess is that, in general, high involvement organizations are low cost, relatively flexible, adaptive organizations that are very quality and customer oriented (Lawler, 1986). They are not cheap to start, since they require a large investment in selection, training, and system development. In addition, as will be discussed next, they do not fit every person, situation, or business.

THE STRATEGIC CHOICE

Decisions about which approach an organization should adopt ought to be guided by a number of factors. The different approaches to participation fit different types of businesses, situations, and individuals. The key to effective utilization of any of them is installing them in conditions where they are congruent. Three major factors need to be examined in deciding which approach to pick: (1) nature of the work and technology, (2) values of the key participants, and (3) present management approach of the organization.

Work and Technology

Perhaps the overriding determinant of how an organization should approach participation is the kind of work it does and the technology it uses. Managers' values and attitudes can be changed over time, and older control-oriented organizations can evolve their practices from traditional to high involvement, but organizations cannot necessarily change the kind of technology they use or the kind of jobs that the technology dictates.

Admittedly, technology is only partly driven by the products and services the organization offers (Galbraith, 1973). There is some flexibility in the technology an organization chooses to use, as is shown by Volvo's Kalmar plant. In addition, the technology does not completely dictate the nature of the jobs an organization has. Some technologies can be modified to produce the types of jobs that are congruent with the desired form of involvement, but in many cases the control of a single organization is limited. There is, for example, little flexibility when it comes to refining oil and generating electricity. As a result, there are some situations in which the technology is not amenable to any of the involvement approaches, with the possible exception of suggestion involvement.

There are two aspects of technology that are particularly critical in influencing the appropriateness of different involvement approaches: (1) degree of interdependence and (2) the degree of complexity. Interdependence refers to how much individuals need to coordinate, cooperate, and relate to others in order to produce the product or service the organization offers. Organizations vary on this dimension from very high interdependence to low interdependence. For example, university professors and insurance salespersons are typically in a low interdependence situation, while chemical plant operators and computer design engineers are in high interdependence situations.

High interdependence argues for teams and against individual approaches to work design. Low interdependence favors maximizing individual performance through job enrichment or well-structured repetitive individual tasks with large amounts of incentive pay. A crucial issue in determining which way to go with low interdependent jobs is the complexity of the work involved.

Technology, to a substantial degree, determines the, complexity of the work. Complexity can vary all the way from the highly repetitive jobs associated with assembly lines to the highly complex knowledge work represented by professional jobs and state-of-the-art manufacturing. Where the work is simple and repetitive by necessity, it is hard to put in place a high involvement or even a job involvement approach unless the technology can be changed. These situations are often limited to parallel suggestion involvement approaches because they can operate with most approaches to work design and most types of technology.

With complex knowledge work, the clear choice is one of the participative approaches. At the very least, job involvement is called for—job enrichment in the case of independent work and teams in the case of interdependent work. If other conditions are right, high involvement would seem to be the best choice. High involvement flourishes where complex knowledge work exists because individuals who do this kind of work possess the ability to participate in a wide range of decisions and often expect and want this approach to management.

Values and Beliefs

The values and beliefs the key participants in an organization need to have vary widely among involvement approaches. If the values do not match the chosen approach, the approach is unlikely to be fully implemented and operated effectively (McGregor, 1960).

In the case of the suggestion approach, key managers do not have to have a profound belief that employees can and will exercise self-control, manage themselves, and be able to contribute to major organizational decisions. They simply need to believe that employees have useful ideas about how things can be improved.

The high involvement approach, on the other hand, requires that managers believe in the capabilities, sense of responsibility, and commitment of people throughout the organization (Lawler, 1986). In short, they need to believe that people not only are a key organizational resource but that people can and will behave responsibly if given the opportunity.

The values of the employees are also important to consider. For any form of involvement to work, most employees have to want to learn, grow, develop, contribute, and take on new responsibilities. Most researchers have argued that the vast majority of the American work force does want to be involved in their work, but no one argues that this view is universally true. Particularly where there has been a long history of autocratic management, the majority of the work force may not want to be more involved. They may have become conditioned to the control-oriented approach and appreciate the fact that they can just put in their eight hours and not have to take the job home with them. In addition, self-selection may have taken place so that those who most value participation quit long ago, leaving behind those who are less attracted to it.

Societal values can also come into play in determining the appropriate approach to involvement. Democratic societies provide much more supportive environments for the high involvement approach than do traditional autocratic societies. The United States, with its long democratic tradition and commitment to individual rights, appears to provide the ideal setting for participative management. Historically, the society has exempted the workplace from the societal commitment to democracy and individual rights. There are many signs of this breaking down in the area of individual rights, and it seems inevitable that it will also disappear as far as participation and involvement are concerned (Ewing, 1977).

Organizational Starting Point

In considering participative strategies, organizations need to assess their current operating approach. As was noted earlier, it is hardly surprising that most high involvement organizations start as new operations. Without question, it is easiest to install high involvement management where no management system currently exists. Not only is it possible to select managers who have philosophies supportive of high involvement, it is not necessary to overcome all the traditions, practices, and policies that are incongruent with it. This is not to say that it is impossible for an organization to evolve toward high involvement. If it seems to be called for because of the kind of work and technology the organization has and if the values of managers support it, it certainly is possible. However, it may not be feasible to start immediately with a high involvement approach.

In starting a change process toward high involvement, it is critical to see where the organization is and then map out a long-term strategy that will lead it to high involvement management. If an organization is very traditional in the way it operates and managers are very hesitant to give up decision-making power, then often the only place to start involvement is with a parallel suggestion approach. Xerox has used this approach extensively in dealing with its traditional unionized locations. Quality circles or Scanlon written suggestion programs are particularly good since they present a minimal threat to existing management prerogatives and power. Sometimes their success can convince management to move ahead to other forms of involvement (Lawler & Mohrman, 1987). As was pointed out earlier, however, they are limited in what they can accomplish because they do little to share power, knowledge, rewards, and information. If an organization is already relatively participative in its personnel policies, work structures, and managerial behaviors, it may not be necessary to start with a suggestion involvement program. The organization can immediately start with the job involvement approach.

The presence of a union organization can make a difference in which approach to involvement is most appropriate. Many unions have been willing jointly to create parallel structure approaches to involvement. Scanlon Plans, for example, have been widely used in unionized work places as have quality of work life programs. The latter, which usually create a hierarchical structure of joint union-management committees, have been adopted throughout the steel, auto, and rubber industries in the United States (Lawler & Ozley, 1979). These committees are involvement devices in their own right and they typically sponsor problem-solving groups and other participative activities for rank-and-file union members. In a few instances, this type of parallel structure involvement has led to the creation of high involvement efforts. The best example of this is the General Motors Saturn project. General Motors had quality of work life projects for years before they decided to ask the UAW to create jointly a new company called

Saturn, which is being developed to run in a high involvement manner.

Conclusion

The argument so far suggests that there is no one right approach to involvement. It needs to be dictated by a number of situational factors. At the extreme, an organization may only be able to move from control to suggestion involvement. If all an organization's systems are traditional, well developed, and firmly in place and its technology leads to relatively independent, simple, repetitive tasks, then suggestion involvement is appropriate. However, if the organization is new and has complex knowledge work, interdependent tasks, and managers who value employee involvement, it is possible to move to high involvement management and reap the rewards it has to offer.

Because participation is not a universal good for all organizations, it is important to take a differentiated view toward it. If organizations carefully analyze where they are and where they want to be, they can lay out a series of steps that will lead to the type of involvement that fits their situation. In the absence of this kind of process, they run the risk of managing in a way that suboptimizes the potential effectiveness of the organization.

CHANGE STRATEGY

Organizations that wish to adopt participative management approaches face a number of critical strategy decisions. Experience in organizations that have tried to move toward participative management suggests some general guidelines that should be followed (Lawler, 1986).

Business Strategy

For major organizational change to occur, there needs to be a reason for the change. Organizations that have successfully installed involvement have commonly stressed business strategy reasons for introducing participative management. In most cases, they have stressed that the very survival of the organization depends upon the use of employee involvement. Prime examples here are Ford, Motorola, and Xerox. In all three cases, they faced strong competitive threats that meant they needed cost reductions and quality improvements in order to stay in business. Their answer, among other things, was participative management. The reason for the change was clearly articulated as stemming from the need to remain competitive. In the case of Xerox, change was combined with a considerable amount of benchmarking work to illustrate just how much Xerox needed to improve in the copier business in order to be competitive. The combination proved particularly effective in mobilizing energy for a change.

Vision Guided

Change is often resisted in organizations when individuals lack a clear positive vision of where the organization is going. Particularly where substantial organizational change is involved, it is important to articulate a vision of the kind of organization that is being sought. A positive vision, like a business reason for change, can help overcome resistance to abandoning a well-understood, if not particularly effective, approach to management. Organizations that have emphasized a positive vision have talked about the opportunities for people to get involved, to experience personal growth and development, and to influence decisions that have previously been beyond their reach (Lawler, 1986; Ouchi, 1982).

Typically, visions need to be stated by top management, which also needs to provide considerable leadership during the change process. Leadership in this case means spending time reviewing results of participative management programs, supporting those individuals who introduce participative methods, and modeling participative behavior. Adoption of participative management can also be aided by leadership who appeals to the values and basic beliefs of the work force. As was noted earlier, this is often easy to do with participative management because it fits the basic American values of democracy and individual rights.

Long-term Orientation

Change from traditional management to participative management is not a short-term project. Precisely because so much needs to be changed, it can often take years to produce a major change in the way an organization is operating. In addition, as was noted earlier, an organization may need to move through several stages of employee involvement in order to reach the one that best fits its situation. It is often necessary to start with problem-solving involvement in order to implement other kinds of employee involvement. As a result, it may take five to ten years for an organization to reach the kind of employee involvement that best fits its technology and business strategy. It is critical that during this period, an organization not be overly concerned with its short-term operating performance and that it continue to make investments that will allow it ultimately to obtain the kind of management approach that best fits its situation. Again, the behavior of top management is critical here because it needs to continue to support the idea of involvement and the change process, even though the large payoffs may be a considerable distance in the future.

Total Organization Orientation

It is easiest to change the management style of an organization when the effort is targeted at the total organization. Experiments and other limited efforts can be useful at the beginning to acquaint people with the new management approach; however, ultimately, there is a certain economy of scale involved in changing the entire organization. Statements from the top can be made that apply to the total organization; communication and other corporate-wide systems can be consistently aligned to support the new management style. When only subparts of an organization are changed, it is difficult to avoid conflicts between that part of the organization and other parts. Different management styles almost always lead to conflicts because they have different ways of handling communication, problem solving, and relating to other organizations.

Ford provides a good example of the impetus that can be put behind a corporate-wide change program. Because the program is corporate wide, Ford was able to use product advertising, focusing on quality and involvement, to reinforce its internal management style. If only a small part of Ford had been involved in the change effort, it would not have had a consistently positive impact within the company to talk about the importance of involvement and quality improvement. Similarly because the change effort was corporate wide, it was possible to build involvement training into all training programs and into management development and selection programs. Volvo has in some respects gone further; it has built employee involvement into its car designs. It now designs cars so they can be built by teams.

Conclusion

Overall, changing a large organization from a traditional approach to a more participative approach is a major undertaking. It clearly can be accomplished, as is shown by Motorola and a number of other U.S. corporations. The accomplishment, however, takes careful planning and significant investments in training, communication, and perhaps, new technologies and physical plants. It is not likely to yield dramatic short-term results, but the evidence indicates that if participative management fits the business strategy and technology of an organization, it can produce significant long-term improvements in organizational effectiveness.

REFERENCES

Cummings, T.G. (1978). Self-regulating work groups: A socio-technical synthesis, *Academy of Management Review, 3,* 625–633.

Ewing, D.E. (1977). *Freedom inside the organization.* New York: Dutton.

Frost, Carl F., John H. Wakeley, & Robert A. Ruh (1974). *The Scanlon Plan for organization development: Identity, participation, and equity.* East Lansing: Michigan State University Press.

Galbraith, J. (1973). *Designing complex organizations.* Reading, MA: Addison-Wesley.

Graham-Moore, B., & T. Ross (1983). *Productivity gainsharing.* Englewood Cliffs, NJ: Prentice-Hall.

Hackman, J.R., & E.E. Lawler (1971). Employee reactions to job characteristics. *Journal of Applied Psychology, 55,* 259–286.

Hackman, J.R., and G.R. Oldham (1980). *Work redesign.* Reading, MA.: Addison-Wesley.

Lawler, E.E. (1978). The new plant revolution. *Organizational Dynamics,* 6(3), 2–12.

Lawler, E.E. (1986). *High involvement management.* San Francisco: Jossey-Bass.

Lawler, E.E., and G.E. Ledford (1985). Skill-based pay. *Personnel,* 62 (9), 30–37.

Lawler, E.E., and S.A. Mohrman (1985). Quality circles after the fad. *Harvard Business Review,* 85 (1), 64–71.

Lawler, E.E., and S.A. Mohrman (1987). Quality circles: After the honeymoon. *Organizational Dynamics.*

Lawler, E.E., and L. Ozley (1979). Winning union-management cooperation on quality of work life projects. *Management Review,* 68 (3), 19–24.

McGregor, D. (1960). *The human side of enterprise.* New York: McGraw-Hill.

Ouchi, W. (1981). *Theory Z.* Reading, MA: Addison-Wesley.

Perkins, D., V. Nieva, and E.E. Lawler (1983). *Managing*

creation: The challenge of building a new organization. New York: Wiley.

Schuster, M.H. (1984). *Union-management cooperation.* Kalamazoo, MI: W.E. Upjohn Institute.

Walton, R.E. (1985). From control to commitment in the workplace. *Harvard Business Review, 63* (2), 76–84.

Walton, R.E., and L.A. Schlesinger (1979). Do supervisors thrive in participative work systems? *Organizational Dynamics, 8* (3), 25–38.

Carol A. Paradise

THE ROLE OF TEAMS IN ORGANIZATIONS

The United States has always been a society that praised the rugged individualist. Most of our models of performance, achievement, and leadership, whether internal or external to organizations, have focused on the individual. This philosophy has been pervasive in how we structure our institutions and in the styles of interpersonal interaction we have used to manage them. However, the increasing complexity of the problems and the priorities that need to be managed in today's organizations have resulted in greater dependence on team performance. Teams of varying shapes, sizes, and configurations are taking on the challenges of addressing increased interdependencies among specialists and across functional area. Teams are involved in identifying and solving problems, implementing solutions, and bringing about change in organizations.

The increasing emphasis on team performance is also consistent with changing work force expectations for involvement in decision making and a heightened awareness of the motivational as well as task benefits of team performance. However, the manager who has been enculturated as a rugged individualist often finds himself or herself at a loss when trying to generate dynamic and synergistic team performance. Difficulties may arise from the manager's lack of experience, training, and skills in building and managing effective teams. The complex dynamics of group process and the interpersonal styles and differences of team members greatly complicate the management process. Roles and responsibilities must be clarified, goals agreed to, and effective communications and trust established. Interdependencies among team members must be recognized and dealt with, and the emotional, psychological, and behavioral implications of being a team explored. To build an effective team, both the process and the content of the team's performance must be addressed. Critical process factors include how decisions are made, openness of communication, influence and inclusion of team members, and the leadership style of the team leader.

WHAT IS A TEAM?

Not all work groups constitute a team. W. Warner Burke and other noted Organizational Development (OD) specialists, offer these distinguishing characteristics of a team (1982):

- A team has at least one goal common to all members.

- Accomplishment of that goal requires interdependent effort among the group members.

- The members recognize and acknowledge their membership in the team and see themselves as a team.

- The members share common operating norms.

- The skills, knowledge, and ability required to get the task done are held collectively by the group members.

According to this set of characteristics, the LA Lakers and the Pittsburgh Steelers are teams. Both (1) share a common goal (to win), which requires (2) interdependent activity (blocking, passing), and (3) the collective skills and abilities of individual team members (running, throwing, shooting baskets). Each group sees itself as a team with a common goal, and the team members tend to conform to a set of norms when they are together as a group.

The U.S. Olympic diving team, on the other hand, is, by this definition, less of a team. Each individual diver performs his or her task independently of the others, and each member's only interdependency is with the coach.

This distinction between groups and teams is an important one for the manager interested in using team building as a tool to improve group effectiveness. The interdependence of effort and results, central to the concept of team, provides a motivating force for the difficult task of looking at relationships and group dynamics within the team. When true interdependencies exist, these factors can greatly enhance or inhibit the ultimate performance of the team.

In a group where interdependencies do not exist, the group's performance can be defined as the sum total of each individual's performance (2 + 2 = 4). Strategies that improve the performance of each individual (e.g., practice or training) will provide the greatest increment in overall group performance. In ineffective teams, group performance is often impeded by poor communication, lack of coopera-

tion and creativity, inefficient decision-making processes, and resistance to the influence of group members and/or the leader. These factors cause a decrement in overall performance (2 + 2 < 4).

Improving the process of team interaction (i.e., team building) increases overall group performance. Obstacles to open communication, cooperation, decision making, and the building of effective working relationships are surfaced and resolved. As a result, the team is free to focus on creative solutions and alternatives for the task. The synergy (or synergistic energy) of effective team process leads to overall performance that can be greater than what team members could have accomplished individually (2 + 2 > 4).

CHARACTERISTICS OF AN EFFECTIVE TEAM

What is an effective team? Several definitions of effective teams have been offered (McGregor, 1967; Likert, 1961; Burke, 1982; Hackman & Walton, 1986). These definitions are based on the authors' studies and observations of effective teams. Among the common characteristics that emerge as aspects of effective teams are:

1. Clear, engaging direction. Team members understand and mutually agree with the goals and primary tasks of the team. In addition, they are engaged by the task. That is, they personally find it meaningful, important, and consistent with their own goals and values.

2. Open communication and mutual trust. Team members are candid about their ideas, opinions, and feelings regarding the task and its accomplishment. No serious obstacles to team performance are taboo. Openness is supported by mutual trust and respect, and members are allowed to influence each other, including the team leader.

3. Supportive team environment. The team provides a supportive environment, where concerns are aired and respected and assistance is offered to fellow team members as needed. Differences among group members are not only allowed, they are encouraged to help bring new perspec-

tives to the issues and problems faced by the group.

4. Supportive organizational environment. The organization recognizes and rewards excellence in team performance. It also makes the necessary resources and information available to the team.

5. Appropriate team mix. Collectively, the team members possess the required skills, knowledge, and abilities to achieve their goal, with minimum redundancy in talent.

6. Leadership. In effective teams, the leader ensures that the characteristics required for effectiveness are identified and integrated into the norms and dynamics of the team. (This may be accomplished with the help of a trained OD consultant.) The ongoing maintenance and compliance of these group norms is the responsibility of all group members.

7. High energy level. Team members appear motivated, committed, and supportive of the team's goals and of each other. There is a high degree of creativity and enjoyment in working together.

8. Availability of process support. Expert task and process support are available if needed to help members maximize team potential and minimize decrements due to team process variables.

WHEN IS TEAM BUILDING APPROPRIATE?

Team building may be appropriate whenever the process requirements of effective team performance are not being satisfactorily met in the opinion of the team leader or one or more members. Aspects of teams that may become dysfunctional and interfere with effective functioning of the team include:

- Communications and interpersonal relationships, especially issues involving power, influence, cohesion, and inclusion.
- Lack of clarity regarding the goals, objectives, mission, or vision of the group.
- Lack of clarity or disagreement with roles and responsibilities of group members.
- Ineffective use of team resources.

Dyer (1977) developed a brief checklist for managers to use to determine if there is a problem with the team, if the team is ready for a team-building intervention, and if an external OD consultant should be used. Dyer considers these as "signals" that team building may be required:

1. Loss of production, performance, or output.
2. Increase of grievances or complaints by team members.
3. Evidence of conflicts or hostility among team members.
4. Confusion about assignments, missed signals, and unclear relationships.
5. Decisions misunderstood or not carried through properly.
6. Apathy and general lack of interest or involvement of team members.
7. Lack of initiative, imagination, innovation—routine actions taken for solving complex problems.
8. Ineffective team meetings, low participation, minimal effective decisions.
9. Start-up of a new group that needs to develop quickly into a working team.
10. High dependency or negative reactions to the manager-leader.
11. Complaints from users or customers about quality of service.
12. Continued unaccounted increase of costs. (pp. 34–35).

Dyer provides some general guidelines for how to score his checklist and interpret the results. (Dyer's book is a useful reference for managers interested in learning more about team-building alternatives.) Dyer's checklist can help managers make an initial assessment of the need for team building. Additional situations when team building or team process consulting may be appropriate include:

- A reorganization has led to a reconfiguration of the team or a need to assimilate a new leader or manager.
- The team has completed its primary goals and is to be disbanded.
- The team is experiencing some conflict or change that cannot be effectively dealt with by the team's existing skills and/or norms.

WHAT IS TEAM BUILDING?

Francis and Young (1979) define team building simply as "the process of deliberately creating a team." They go on to say that team building implies the construction of something that requires effort, commitment, and time and involves the deliberate working through of the obstacles to effective team functioning.

Beckhard (1972) identified four purposes of team building:

1. To clarify the mission, vision, goals, and priorities of the team.

2. To facilitate the effective distribution of work among team members (i.e., roles and responsibilities).

3. To analyze and improve team process (norms, decision making, communications, problem solving).

4. To analyze and improve interpersonal relationships among the team members.

Burke defines team building as "an activity whereby members of a work group (1) begin to understand more thoroughly the nature of group dynamics and effective teamwork, particularly the interrelationships between process and content, and (2) learn to apply certain principles and skills of group process toward greater team effectiveness" (1982, p. 282).

In most cases, team building rests on the assumption that the talent, knowledge, energy, and commitment to resolve process-related issues reside within the team. The team must have or develop (1) a commitment to work on team performance, (2) a common language or frame of reference for discussing team performance issues, (3) valid data on the current level of team performance, and (4) time to work on team performance issues. The challenge in team building is to get the real team performance issues surfaced and to help the team to deal with them in a way that facilitates achieving the task and meeting the goals of the team.

There are many different approaches that an OD consultant or manager might pursue when team building is needed. In most cases, team building includes the following stages:

1. Information gathering. The consultant or manager will want to know why team building is being requested, the issues of primary concern to the group and how the team members view the issues, a brief history of the team, and the stated goals and objectives of the team, if they have been articulated. Any information relevant to the resolution of the issues should also be shared with the consultant or manager. In short, the consultant or manager must be brought into the confidence of the group.

2. Team-building design. The manager or consultant will design a team-building process based upon the nature of the team and the issues that need to be addressed. This stage can be more art than science, as a multitude of options are available from the highly analytic to the highly creative. The style of intervention should be consistent with the personal style of the consultant or manager, amenable to team members, and, obviously, appropriate to surfacing and addressing the issues of the team. Some sample designs are given in the next section of this chapter.

3. Intervention. The consultant or manager intervenes in the team by initiating the team-building process. The intervention will consist of introducing the team-building effort to the team, identifying the key issues surfaced in the information-gathering phase, setting objectives for the team building, and implementing the team-building design. The initial team-building meeting may take the form of an introduction or may comprise the entire design depending on the nature and extent of the issues to be dealt with.

4. Ending. The team building itself may have no formal ending to the extent that the team internalizes and continues to use the new process skills and insights gained through implementation of the team-building design. However, the consultant may discontinue his or her work with the group, or the manager may shift focus away from team building per se and back to the task goals of the team. This is not likely to occur until the team feels that significant progress has been made in addressing the issues and that they now have the skills needed to deal with the issues if they should arise again.

SAMPLE TEAM-BUILDING DESIGNS

There are many different strategies and types of designs that will have an impact on the process elements of team performance. Reference manuals are available that provide sample team-building designs matched to the nature of the issues to be addressed. These manuals are helpful in providing a starting point for managers in developing their own designs or to familiarize managers with the kinds of interventions that an OD consultant may use.

In general, there are two categories of team-building design strategies. *Analytical designs* place a heavy emphasis on the impact of data and information on group process. Analytical team-building techniques include the use of surveys or other instruments to gather and feed data back to the group on perceived issues and their importance. Ratings may be used to quantify opinions and add greater "objectivity" to the team-building process. Training or other didactic forms of information sharing with team members are also more analytic types of interventions, as are "role negotiation" (Harrison, 1972) and "responsibility charting" (Beckhard & Harris, 1977) techniques.

Experiential designs tend to utilize less structured, creative experiences to help the team to discover information about itself. These techniques include visioning exercises, story writing, drawings, collages, "brain maps" (Buzan, 1983), or other exercises that cause team members to view issues from a novel perspective. These exercises have the effect of "unfreezing" the existing group process and opening up alternative, creative approaches to group problem solving. Many trained OD consultants will use a combination of analytic, data-based techniques and more creative, "right brain" activities.

The following case studies are designed to demonstrate some sample team-building designs and how they were used. Where possible, the outcomes of the team-building intervention are also given. The case studies reveal both the art and the science of team-building techniques.

Case Study 1: The Function Merger

The Situation. A decision was made to merge two human resource (HR) groups within a large, 10,000-employee organization. Key functions and personnel from a large division HR group were merged with an existing corporate HR staff, causing numerous displacement (layoffs) including that of the former corporate HR head. In several cases, the division HR function heads replaced the corporate function heads. All HR functions experienced either a change in leadership or the addition of new members to their respective teams. The changes were announced (with little warning) at the end of a business year. There was a great deal of disruption to work in progress, and productivity took a serious turn for the worse. The new corporate HR head recognized that the department needed a good dose of its own medicine. He approached the internal team-building consultant with the following questions:

- How do we help everyone deal with this change?
- How do we build new working relationships within and between the new teams?
- What do the staff need from me as their new leader?
- How do we get down to business again?

The Team-Building Intervention. The consultant recognized that disruptions had occurred on several levels and that the relationships, leadership, tasks, goals, and mission of the department were all affected. She set the following priorities for the team building:

1. Help the HR staff deal more effectively with the transitions and changes they were experiencing as individuals.
2. Get the newly reconfigured teams to begin working effectively together and to define a unifying mission and goals for the upcoming year.
3. Surface transition and work issues that needed to be addressed at the individual, team, or department levels.
4. Facilitate communication between the staff and their new leader.

Here is the team-building design that was implemented. First, the consultant designed a brief presentation and discussion piece on the stages of transitions and the psychological process of change (Bridges, 1980). She also identified the following list of questions designed to help surface key issues and to assist the department to transition through the changes:

To move forward on planning:
   What are the key issues facing the corporate HR department?
   What are the key issues facing your functional area?
   What important decisions does the new leader need to make?
   What is most clear and least clear about our relationships with our internal customers?
   What is most clear and least clear about the relationships among the HR functional teams?
   What are you concerned will get lost or slowed down as a result of the consolidation?

To deal with feelings about the change:
   What do you most appreciate about the changes that have occurred?
   What do you most resent about the changes that have occurred?
   What do you most regret about the changes that have occurred?

To surface issues and concerns about the new leader:
   What would you like to see him do more of?
   What would you like to see him do less of?
   What would you like to see him do differently?
   What one thing would you most like to know about his leadership or management style?

Half-day team meetings were held for each functional area, facilitated by the OD consultant. In addition to responding to the above questions, each team worked collaboratively on the development of a mission statement and set of objectives for the upcoming year.

The results of the team meetings were consolidated and communicated upward to the HR department head. An all-day meeting with the full department was then scheduled to share some of the results and to provide the department head an opportunity to respond to some of the input he had received. Also, each function head presented his or her mission and objectives to the larger group, and an overall department mission was drafted.

Impact of the Team Building. Team members were given a framework and an opportunity to talk about their frustrations, fears, and concerns. This initiated a healthy recovery process, helping them to move through the changes more quickly and return to more normal levels of productivity. Team cohesion was increased as members learned more about themselves and each other by processing their views of the changes and developing a common mission and objectives.

Issues for the new leader were surfaced, giving him an opportunity to anticipate needs and concerns, and react accordingly. A transition he initially believed would take two to three years, he now believes will be accomplished in twelve to eighteen months. Each functional area moved toward a focus on the challenges that lay ahead rather than holding on to the past.

Case 2: An Issue of Inclusion

The Situation. The leader of a newly formed technical task team in a large computer company came to the internal consultant with the following concern: the six members of his handpicked product design team were not congealing as a group. The three meetings that had occurred were polite but not productive. One member, a minority with particularly important technical experience, was especially standoffish in the group. She would challenge the team with provocative design questions and then retreat when asked for her own opinion. This parrying left her feeling alienated. She had told the manager that she feared there were some biases in the team that accounted for her being left out. However, other members also felt the team was not working well together and were beginning to question the purpose of the meetings and the feasibility of accomplishing the task.

The Team-Building Intervention. After questioning the manager further and speaking individually with several of the team members, the consultant set the following priorities for the team building:

1. Get the team to identify the obstacles they saw to the effective functioning of the team.

2. Help the team begin to build a more open and trusting team environment.

3. Address the issues around inclusion, bias, and clarity of team goals.

A two-hour team building meeting was scheduled to be led by the consultant. Team members were informed about the purpose of the meeting, and all were asked to attend. At the meeting, each team member was asked to complete a brief "Team Development Scale" (Dyer, 1977). The seven-item scale measures feelings of inclusion and trust, openness of communications, effective use of team member input, understanding of, and commitment to, team goals, and perceptions of team effectiveness and planning. The results of the scale were summarized on a flipchart showing the ratings given by each team member for each scale. The team was given 5 to 10 minutes to look at the ratings. The team was then given 30 minutes for discussion of the results. Some questions were posed by the consultant to stimulate discussion:

- What's your initial reaction to the ratings? Are you more or less cohesive as a team than you thought?
- Who is feeling in or out? Why? In what ways do you feel part of the team? in what ways not?
- What are some specific issues involving open communications and trust in the team? What are some ways of building trust?

Following the discussion, the team was asked to identify the two or three most important issues for them to address to become a more effective team. They were then given 15 minutes to brainstorm strategies for addressing these issues. They came up with the following items:

Issue	Possible Action
Inclusion of team members	Be sure that everyone has an opportunity to contribute at team meetings
	Share information that other team members need
	Get to know each other better (have lunch)
	Find ways of benefiting from differences
	Begin next team meeting by having everyone say what strengths they bring to solving the task and process goals of the team
Understanding of and commitment to goals	Have a separate meeting to review team goals, surface issues and "hold out" opinions
	Team to write up goal statement, review, and reevaluate it periodically
	Ground rule that clarifying goals is *always* an open topic for team discussion
	Get personal, task-related goals out in the open; How can they be integrated into team goals?

Although other issues had been identified, the team felt that these were the most important given their stage of development as a team. The manager took responsibility for documenting the results of the team-building session and ensuring that the team finalized action items at its next meeting. The consultant was asked to help the manager to design a meeting to clarify the goals of the team and to be available to facilitate future discussions of team process issues.

Impact of the Team Building. The first team-building meeting had the following impact:

- The team members initiated a new level of com-

munication during the team building that carried over into subsequent team meetings.

- The team gained insight into process factors that were inhibiting their performance as a team and began to see ways of overcoming them.

- The team building contributed to building a sense of team identity because it engaged the team in joint exploration and problem solving. Again, this sense of having common objectives carried over into subsequent meetings.

- The manager felt supported by the internal consultant and saw his value as a resource in bringing the team to a higher level of effectiveness.

SUMMARY

In this chapter, I have explored the role of teams in today's organizations and defined the purpose of team building as action deliberately taken to improve team effectiveness. Some of the process factors that can impede or foster the performance of teams have been identified, and some general strategies for conducting team process have been provided. These strategies show team building to be both a science (based on research and understanding of group process, use of data-gathering, analysis) and an art (relying on the manager's or consultant's ability to diagnose team process issues and design effective team building interventions). The potential impact of team building is to increase team performance beyond what could be achieved by the same individuals working independently. The challenge of team

building is to capture the energy and commitment of team members and channel them toward overcoming personal and/or interpersonal obstacles to building effective working relationships. This challenge can be great. In addition, team building is not a panacea for all organizational or team problems. Some team problems cannot be improved with team building. For example, unwillingness to address issues of interpersonal style or leadership, lack of commitment or unyielding opposition to group goals, lack of resources, or lack of organization support for the team or its products are not problems amenable to team building. However, an experienced team-building consultant or manager will be able at least to help the team identify and surface such obstacles.

REFERENCES

Beckhard, R. (1972). Optimizing team building efforts. *Journal of Contemporary Business 1*, 3, 23–32.

Beckhard, R., and Harris, R.T. (1977). *Organizational transitions: Managing complex change.* Reading, MA: Addison-Wesley.

Bridges, W. (1980). *Transitions: Making sense of life's changes.* Reading, MA: Addison-Wesley.

Burke, W.W. (1982). *Organizational development principles and practices.* Boston: Little, Brown.

Buzan, T. (1983). *Use both sides of your brain* (rev. ed.). New York: E.P. Dutton.

Dyer, W.G. (1977). *Team building: issues and alternatives.* Reading, MA: Addison-Wesley.

Francis, D., and Young, D. (1979). *Improving work groups: A practical manual for team building.* San Diego, CA: University Associates.

Glaser, R., and Glaser, C. (1980, 1986). *Building a winning management team.* Bryn Mawr, PA: Organization Design and Development, Inc.

Hackman, J.R., and Walton, R.E. (1986). Leading groups in organizations. In P.S. Goodman, *Designing effective work groups.* San Francisco: Jossey-Bass.

Harrison, R. (1972). Role negotiation:a tough-minded approach to team development. In *The social technology of organization development,* ed. W.W. Burke and H.A. Hornstein. LaJolla, CA: University Associates.

Likert, R. (1961). *New patterns of management.* New York: McGraw-Hill.

McGregor, D. (1967). *The professional manager.* New York: McGraw-Hill.

Tjosrold, D. (1986). *Working together to get things done.* Lexington, MA: Lexington Books.

ADDITIONAL RESOURCES

Hill, M., and Petrella, T. (1974). *A mini-handbook for team building*. Plainfield, NJ: Block Petrella Associates.

Pfeiffer, J.W., and Jones, J.E. (Eds.) (1974–1985). *A handbook of structured experiences for human rela-* *tions training*, vols. 1–10. San Diego, CA: University Associates.

Petrella, T. (1974). *Managing with teams*. Plainfield, NJ: Block Petrella Associates.

60 ACHIEVING PRODUCTIVE SYNERGY BY INTEGRATING DEPARTMENTAL EFFORTS

Dean Tjosvold

Departments, divisions, units, and other groups within a company often misunderstand and fight each other. Managing these conflicts frustrates many corporate managers. Some theorists propose that competitive, negative dynamics are built into organizations (Blake & Mouton, 1983; Pfeffer, 1981). Divisions and other groups are inevitably suspicious, quick to blame but slow to assist. Decisions are made not on the basis of reason and the pursuit of the common good but on who has the power to push his or her interests. From this perspective, developing a single-purpose, united company is unrealistic, and calls to do so are naive.

Yet some successful companies have apparently established a high degree of cohesion and common purpose (Kanter, 1983; Ouchi, 1981; Peters & Waterman, 1982). They have a work force bound by shared values, personal relationships, and commitment to make the company the industry leader. Many business leaders have tried to emulate these "excellent" companies. Optimistic and hopeful that large companies in North America can be cohesive and innovative, companies are experimenting with ways to develop corporate synergy (Kanter, 1983; Porter, 1985).

Can managers be confident that the practices used by these model companies will work for them? It may be that market position, monopolies, patent holdings, and corporate financing, not their corporate management practices, have made these model companies successful (Carroll, 1983). Even if these practices are effective, managers need to know why they work in order to adapt them to fit their situation. Given that competitive intergroup dynamics are common, establishing synergy is unlikely to be easy.

This chapter combines research on coordination devices and interdependence dynamics to suggest how organizations can achieve productive synergy. Coordination mechanisms such as project teams and matrix designs are increasingly being used to foster collaboration among organizational units (Galbraith, 1973; Lawrence & Lorsch, 1967; Mintzberg, 1979). However, coordination devices must be used appropriately and skillfully (Galbraith, 1973). Interdependence dynamics suggest what it takes for different groups to use these procedures to work together (Deutsch, 1973, 1980; Tjosvold, 1986c). I argue that *practical procedures, cooperative goals, and the skills to work together and manage conflict are the bases for productive synergy.*

The chapter begins with an overview of research on design and coordination procedures. It then describes interdependence dynamics and reviews research documenting the value of cooperative goals. Cases illustrate how coordination procedures and cooperative goals can be used to integrate groups into a company.

DESIGN AND COORDINATION DEVICES

To be successful in today's highly competitive marketplace, companies must combine all their information, knowledge, expertise, and energy (Kanter, 1983; Galbraith, 1973; Lawrence & Lorsch, 1967; Mintzberg, 1979). Then the organization can meet challenges because knowledgeable employees, who must implement solutions, are involved in making them. A great array of coordination devices and mechanisms have been identified.

Traditionally, divisions and departments have used rules to coordinate, with managers given the authority to decide exceptions. Liaison managers, task

The author thanks the Social Sciences and Humanities Research Council of Canada for its financial support.

teams, and matrix designs are more recent devices.

These devices require the proper conditions and considerable skill to make them work. Liaison managers, for example, must develop goodwill among the department members, be able to take different perspectives, and facilitate communication (Galbraith, 1973). Employees in task teams and matrix organizations must know how to communicate and handle conflict. Indeed, groups may use procedures to fight against each other.

INTERDEPENDENCE DYNAMICS

How individuals and groups believe their goals are related greatly affects how they work together (Deutsch, 1973, 1980; Tjosvold, 1986a). Many studies document that goal interdependence substantially affects expectations, actions, feelings, and productivity. The three types of interdependence are cooperation, competition, and independence. In cooperation, groups believe that their goals are positively related; one's goal attainment helps others reach their objectives. Success for one means success for all. In competition, groups believe their goals are related in such a way that success for one precludes success for others. If one "wins," the other "loses." The third situation is independence. People believe their goals are unrelated so that one's success has no impact on whether others succeed. For example, department representatives are in cooperation when they seek to make a decision that leaves all departments stronger. They are in competition when they want to make their own department stronger and more important than others.

The impact of cooperative and competitive goals is considerable. In cooperation, other managers are likely to appreciate and improve a colleague's useful idea about how the group can make its recommendation. This idea will help all of them be successful. However, when they are competing to see who is the most important, the bright idea threatens the success of others, and they are likely to focus on the idea's limitations to discredit it.

We will discuss "pure" types of mutual dependence. Most situations have more than one goal interdependence, but typically one type dominates and influences interaction. The practical issue for managers is to identify the interdependence that will facilitate their objectives and to structure it to be the dominate one.

RESEARCH ON INTERDEPENDENCE

Groups with cooperative goals want each other to be effective because that helps them be successful. The beauty of cooperation is that people jointly pursue their self-interests; there is no need to assume that people are generally altruistic or self-sacrificing. Groups with competitive goals, on the other hand, are threatened by each other's effectiveness. They pursue their self-interest at the expense of each other. These orientations create contrasting ways of working together.

Considerable research conducted in a wide variety of settings has found that cooperative goals very much affect intergroup dynamics (Deutsch, 1980; Johnson, Johnson & Maruyama, 1983; Johnson, Maruyama, Johnson, Nelson & Skon, 1981; Tjosvold, 1984, 1986a, 1986b, 1988). Some of the major research trends are listed below:

1. Groups are optimistic and trust that they will work effectively.

2. Expecting support, groups communicate and give assistance.

3. Power is not ignored but handled constructively. Persons recognize and become aware of each other's valuable resources and exchange them profitably (Tjosvold, 1981, 1985b).

4. Groups with cooperative goals will conflict over how to share their resources, the burden of their joint work, and the rewards of their success. However, they discuss their opposing views openly and are able to integrate their ideas and information to create high-quality, accepted solutions to problems (Blake & Mouton, 1983; Tjosvold, 1983, 1985a).

5. Cooperative goals encourage employees to assist and exchange resources to complete a great variety of organizational tasks. A recent analysis of over a hundred studies found that cooperative goals induce higher productivity than either com-

petitive or independent goals, especially for more complex tasks (Johnson et al., 1981).

6. Cooperative goals foster feelings of well-being, improve morale, and strengthen relationships. Groups are more confident about themselves and their work relationships (Johnson et al., 1983; Tjosvold, 1986b).

Competitive goals create much different dynamics. Groups are pessimistic that their interaction will be successful and suspect that their interests may be harmed. These expectations make people wary and cause them to communicate in misleading ways. Fearing that others will work against them, competitors are reluctant to exchange resources. They also try to avoid conflicts, for they anticipate that the conflicts will be unmanageable. When conflicts are discussed, they tend to escalate and provoke challenges and insults that further intensify conflict (Barker, Tjosvold & Andrews, 1986). These interactions are emotionally draining and leave people feeling frustrated and hostile. Contrary to much popular opinion, competitive goals between groups or individuals

do not generally motivate and improve productivity except on some simple tasks (Johnson et al., 1981).

Independent goals have their own dynamics. Groups have few incentives either to assist or block others. The conflicts that do occur tend to be avoided. Independence can be useful for getting simple tasks completed that do not benefit from combining the ideas, energy, and resources of more than one group (Johnson et al., 1981).

Cooperative goals have been demonstrated to facilitate the interaction that promotes organizational productivity. My argument is not that cooperative dependence should be used exclusively. At times, competitive and independent goals are desirable. Competition can stimulate and foster camaraderie within groups, heighten group motivation, and be appropriate when there is no need for the groups to interact and exchange resources (Peters & Waterman, 1982). Independent goals encourage groups to work alone without using the time and energy to coordinate with other groups. However, cooperative goals promote the coordination needed to reach a great many organizational objectives.

CREATING COORDINATION DEVICES

Managers must establish appropriate procedures and cooperative goals to facilitate coordination among units. These efforts require practice and diligence but in the long run will be more successful than the common cajoling, demanding, and firefighting that most managers go through in their efforts to get divisions to work together.

Research indicates that additional coordination devices are needed as the organizational units are increasingly interdependent (Lawrence & Lorsch, 1967). Galbraith (1973) identified these coordination mechanisms beginning with the simplest:

1. Direct contact between managers who share the problem: Department members informally discuss common concerns directly with other departments, circumventing channels of the authority hierarchy.

2. Liaison roles to link departments: An employee is given the responsibility to facilitate the flow of information between departments.

3. Temporary task forces to solve problems: Employees from the departments involved in a problem form a group with the specific task to develop a solution and oversee its implementation.

4. Permanent teams for recurring interdepartmental problems: A committee meets regularly to solve ongoing issues.

5. Integrating managers to facilitate mutual decision making: These managers have the role to help departments discuss problems and come to a mutually advantageous solution. Sometimes they are given power to influence the decision through control over budgets for interdepartmental tasks.

6. Matrix management with project teams: Employees are members of both a functional department and a project team.

There is no simple formula organizations can use to decide which of these procedures is right for them. More thorough, costly methods are justified when groups are highly interdependent, the task is complex, and people with different backgrounds, knowledge, perspective, and departmental membership must collaborate. Managers must also choose procedures that are practical and fit the situation. Face-to-face meetings are less desirable, for example, if the units are geographically dispersed.

CREATING COOPERATIVE GOALS

Groups that believe their goals are cooperative will make good use of coordination procedures. Groups must conclude that their interests and goals overlap and go in the same direction.

They must also have the skills to work together and manage their differences so that they continue to believe their goals are cooperative. Managers can structure cooperative goals through common tasks, shared rewards, supportive attitudes and values, and interaction skills. See Tjosvold (1986c, in press) for a detailed account of developing cooperation in organizations.

Common Tasks

Assigning common tasks is a straightforward way to develop cooperative goals. Informing the groups that they have a common task is only the first step. The groups must perceive that their goals are positively related. It is not the objective state of affairs or how managers believe the goals are related that counts; it is how the groups themselves see their goals are linked that determines how they work together.

These tasks should be motivating. The groups should understand how the tasks can facilitate their needs, interests, and personal aspirations. The groups should believe that they can accomplish the task, know how to achieve the task, and realize that the tangible and intangible rewards for completing the tasks are immediate rather than distant.

Project teams and task forces, for example, not only provide a forum for departments to work together but can give employees a common task that makes their cooperative goals concrete. Members from engineering, production, research, marketing, and consumer affairs departments form a team to develop and market a new product, devise a new accounting system, implement performance appraisal, or solve problems in how departments work together (Friedlander & Schott, 1981).

Problems and conflicts inevitably arise, and they should be discussed and solved so that the departments can continue to coordinate. Groups need encouragement and settings to confront their difficulties. Intergroup meetings in which departments identify problems and plan ways to resolve them are useful but unfortunately tend to be undertaken only after conflicts have escalated (Beckhard, 1969; Blake & Mouton, 1983).

Task forces composed of persons from affected departments can be appointed to analyze conflicts and propose solutions. The Ford Motor Company and United Automobile Workers and management and labor from other companies have adopted regularly scheduled joint problem-solving groups (Ephlin, 1983).

Shared Rewards

Rewards should be distributed to reinforce cooperative goals. The groups should share in the prestige, bonuses, praise, promotions, and other organizational rewards for completing common tasks and reaching a bonus, and all are praised. When a specific group is given a larger degree of credit or bonus without clear justification, groups can easily come to think that they should try to look better than others and outdo each other in their ways.

Profit-sharing plans make the cooperative dependence of divisions concrete. Employees are rewarded to the extent the company as a whole is profitable. They should realize that they will be rewarded on the performance of their own and other departments. They then have a positive stake in other groups' being successful. They help themselves and their group by assisting other departments.

Shared information about the company reinforces cooperative dependence. Groups get feedback about their progress toward their common goal of promoting the company. They are kept informed of the needs and resources of other groups.

Decentralizing through cost and profit centers often allows divisions more autonomy, feedback, and incentives. Many executives complain, though, that they spend a lot of time mediating conflicts and lament their inability to get the centers to exchange their resources and assist each other (Williams, 1987). However, traditional ways to structure profit centers create independence and competition. The centers and their managers are evaluated on maximizing their outcomes; they have no positive stake in other centers' performance. They may even compete when they believe top management will compare their financial performance. Performance criteria of centers should reflect cooperative goals. A center's performance could be judged in part on the profitability and costs of other centers in the organization.

Attitudes and Values

A sense of community, shared vision, and supportive feelings also develops cooperative goals. Perceptions that they are on the same team, share values of honesty, and have common experiences help groups believe that their interests overlap. American Express has created synergy in part by emphasizing that the business units are all part of "One Enterprise" (Williams, 1987).

Innovative companies have framed their goals as serving the important needs of customers, providing high-quality products and service, developing a company that deserves employee pride, and improving society. These goals engender more commitment than profits and market share. Having employees discuss company goals and philosophy can help them become committed and understand that these goals are cooperative (Ouchi, 1981; Peters & Waterman, 1982).

Many companies are experimenting with creating a "corporate family." Company values that all employees are important and that they should know and value each other as persons seem to encourage links. Job rotation can help employees from different departments understand and develop personal links (Ouchi, 1981).

Interaction

Successful interaction is needed to reinforce cooperative goals (Deutsch, 1973). If one group fails to reciprocate help or fulfill its obligations, then others are likely to doubt that goals are really cooperative. Groups should contribute to the common task, coordinate their efforts, and recognize that they all must combine their energy and resources if they are to be successful.

Employees must actually use coordination devices to exchange information and assist each other. Social, informal interaction among all employees can facilitate the use of coordination mechanisms, whereas impersonal relationships interfere with cooperative dynamics.

Having offices close together and norms of openness can increase communication. A campus-like setting may also help persons from all parts of the company know each other and talk informally. Company dinners, bowling leagues, softball games, fitness classes, picnics, and community projects provide opportunities for informal, personal talk. For example, 3M sponsors a great variety of clubs, common activities, and joint memberships to increase the chances of communication (Peters & Waterman, 1982).

People need skills to communicate and manage their conflicts. If they avoid discussing their conflicts or do so in a win-lose way, the groups are likely to doubt their cooperative dependence (Baker, Tjosvold & Andrews, 1986; Tjosvold, 1985a). Workshops and training programs help employees learn to comprehend others' messages, express ideas and feelings, manage conflict, and develop other skills to coordinate. When these skills are coupled with cooperative goals, people can better use procedures to collaborate.

This analysis of how to develop cooperative goals suggests why competition is so common. Cooperative, company-wide tasks of productivity and profits seem general and their rewards distant. Top management, although it wants coordination, often rewards departments competitively by noting which department is superior. Budget and promotion decisions are often made competitively. People from different groups have few opportunities to develop feelings that they are dependable, reliable allies. Conflicts are avoided or are handled through channels with decisions that are not well understood and accepted. There is the temptation to displace internal tensions against other groups and see them as the cause of frustrations. While the rewards of collaboration among divisions and units can be considerable, developing strong, motivating, cooperative goals requires substantial change in many companies.

CASE STUDIES

Two cases illustrate the importance of developing both the appropriate devices and cooperative dynamics to improve coordination across divisions. One case illustrates that promoting cooperative goals without coordination mechanisms is insufficient. In the second case, divisional managers formed a group to learn management skills and improve coordination among the divisions.

Profit Sharing without Coordination Devices

AC Packaging is a medium-sized company that has enjoyed reasonable profits and growth over the years. Its owner and chief officer, excited about glowing accounts of other companies, decided to institute a profit-sharing plan. He wanted his company to be a "family" and departments to work together to improve the long-term stability and profitability of the firm. The managers agreed and with the help of accountants developed a plan whereby once sales exceeded a standard based on previous years, all employees would share in the profits.

The profit-sharing plan did strengthen cooperative dependence of departments. Company goals, productivity, and sales were concretely related to employee rewards. However, management failed to create practical, useful ways for employees actually to work together. They had no practical forum to coordinate their efforts and never took the initiative to meet during lunch or after work at a pub. Management apparently thought that workers would develop productivity improvements alone or in spontaneous groups. People from marketing, engineering, and production had no set times to develop ways to improve sales and productivity.

Without a way to further their cooperative goals and without involvement in actually working toward them, the profit-sharing plan did not motivate. Enthusiasm soon gave way to passivity. Employees hoped that they would get a bonus but did not see what concrete steps they could do to earn it.

The owner was especially disillusioned that the profit-sharing plan did not motivate, improve coordination, or develop a family atmosphere. He became more suspicious of employees and felt they did not really care about his company. However, it was not so much that employees were lazy and uncaring but management's failure to develop adequate coordination devices that undermined profit sharing.

Management Development

The chief administrator of a diversified health care organization wanted to improve coordination across the divisions that provided services to different client groups. The divisions often confronted similar problems, and there was the potential that they could find ways to exchange expertise and personnel. The administrator also saw a need to develop management skills. Managers were typically health professionals with uneven management training and background.

The top two managers from each of three divisions formed a management development group. The group was expected to model and encourage coordination among other employees as well as to develop skills. These managers met periodically for half a year to study management ideas, become more aware of the strengths and weaknesses of their management style, discuss common problems, learn skills, give each other feedback, and in other ways help each other become more effective. They visited each other's division to provide another perspective on difficulties. In this way, they learned more about the overall company and were more prepared to replace each other if necessary.

In addition to learning, they discussed how they and others in their group might work together to improve their divisions. They found ways to share information and avoid duplication of efforts; managers with similar responsibilities met outside the meetings to discuss specific issues. Task forces of employees from the divisions were formed to recommend solutions to high-priority problems the group identified. The group gave the manager motivating, cooperative goals to strengthen their leadership skills and develop opportunities to assist each other. These experiences in turn increased direct contact and developed new coordination devices to improve company-wide coordination.

CONCLUDING COMMENTS

Appropriate coordination devices, cooperative goals, and skills integrate departments and achieve synergy. Groups should have multiple cues that their goals are cooperative and have opportunities to combine their ideas, information, and efforts. Common tasks, shared rewards, a shared vision, supportive attitudes, and skills are convincing evidence that units have

cooperative goals and should use procedures to work together productively.

Research documents the value of cooperative goals, but competitive and independent goals have a role as well. Many tasks are given to a single group to complete independent of other departments; coordination would only interfere. Competition is also used; departments compete over sales, new customers, and quality of service. Companies have set up competing groups to develop new products. Competition can be a stimulating and challenging time to test one's ability, and it can increase group camaraderie and pride—at least for the winners. However, executives cannot establish serious, competitive goals and then expect them to exchange resources and manage conflicts productively.

Departments and other organizational units depend upon each other. Pressures to use resources efficiently to develop new products, reduce costs, respond to changing market conditions, and take advantage of opportunities intensify their dependence and need to work together. Units become one company when they have appropriate coordination devices, believe their interests are cooperative, and can work together and manage conflict.

REFERENCES

Barker, J., D. Tjosvold, & I.R. Andrews (1986). Conflict approaches of effective and ineffective project managers: A field study in a matrix organization. Manuscript, Simon Fraser University.

Beckhard, R. (1969). *Organizational Development: Strategies and models*. Reading, MA: Addision-Wesley.

Blake, R.R., & J.S. Mouton (1983). Lateral conflict. In D. Tjosvold & D.W. Johnson (Eds.), *Productive conflict management: Perspectives for organizations* (83–134). New York: Irvington.

Carroll, D.T. (1983). A disappointing search for excellence. *Harvard Business Review* (November–December), 78–88.

Deutsch, M. (1973). *The resolution of conflict*. New Haven: Yale University Press.

Deutsch, M. (1980). Fifty years of conflict. In L. Festinger (Ed.) *Retrospections on social psychology* (46–77). New York: Oxford University Press.

Ephlin, D.F. (1983). The UAW-Ford agreement—joint problem solving. *Sloan Management Review*, 61–65.

Friedlander, F., & Schott, F. (1981). The use of task groups and task forces in organizational change. In R. Payne and C. Cooper (Eds.), *Groups at work* (191–217). London: John Wiley.

Galbraith, J. (1973). *Designing complex organizations*. Reading, MA: Addison-Wesley, 1973.

Johnson, D.W., Johnson, R.T., & Maruyama, G. (1983). Interdependence and interpersonal attraction among heterogeneous and homogeneous individuals: A theoretical formulation and a meta-analysis of the research. *Review of Educational Research, 53*, 5–54.

Johnson, D.W., Maruyama, G., Johnson, R.T.; Nelson, D.; & Skon, L. (1981). The effects of cooperative, competitive, and individualistic goal structures on achievement: A meta-analysis. *Psychological Bulletin, 89*, 47–62.

Kanter, R.M. (1983). *The change masters*. New York: Simon and Schuster.

Lawrence, P.R., & Lorsch, J.S. (1967). *Organization and environment*. Boston: Harvard Business School.

Mintzberg, H. (1979). *Structuring organizations*. Englewood Cliffs, NJ: Prentice-Hall.

Ouchi, W. (1981). *Theory Z*. Reading, MA: Addison-Wesley.

Peters, T.J., & Waterman, R.H. Jr. (1982). *In search of excellence*. New York: Harper & Row.

Porter, M.E. (1985). *Competitive advantage*. New York: Free Press.

Pfeffer, J. (1981). *Power in organizations*. Boston: Pittman.

Tjosvold, D. (1981). Unequal power relationships within a cooperative or competitive context. *Journal of Applied Social Psychology, 11*, 137–150.

Tjosvold, D. (1983). Social face in conflict: A critique. *International Journal of Group Tensions, 13*, 49–64.

Tjosvold, D. (1984). Cooperation theory and organizations. *Human Relations, 37*, 743–767.

Tjosvold, D. (1985a). Implications of controversy research for management. *Journal of Management, 11*, 221–238.

Tjosvold, D. (1985b). Power and social context in superior-subordinate interaction. *Organizational Behavior and Human Decision Processes, 35*, 281–293.

Tjosvold, D. (1986a). Dynamics of interdependence. *Human Relations, 39*, 517–540.

Tjosvold, D. (1986b). An organizational test of goal linkage theory. *Journal of Occupational Behavior, 7*, 77–88.

Tjosvold, D. (1986c). *Working together to get things done: Managing for organizational productivity*. Lexington, MA: Lexington Books.

Tjosvold, D. (1988). Goal interdependence between organizational groups: A critical incident study, *International Journal of Management, 5*, 201–208.

Tjosvold, D. (in press). *The team organization: Applying group research to the workplace*. New York: John Wiley & Sons.

Williams, M.J. (1987). Synergy works at American Express. *Fortune* (February 16), 79–80.

Michael A. Campion, Chi Sum Wong

It is the manager's responsibility to ensure that employees are performing and satisfied with their jobs. In many instances, job design may help achieve these goals.

Many people believe that the design of a job is fixed, dictated by the technology or the work that has to be done. This may be in error. In many cases jobs can be changed, with fairly predictable consequences for efficiency and satisfaction.

WHEN SHOULD JOB DESIGN BE CONSIDERED?

There are at least five situations where job design should be considered:

1. *During innovation or technological change.* Continual innovation and technological change are important for survival in most organizations. These changes in procedures and equipment mean there are also changes in jobs. This is not unique to manufacturing industries. The introduction of electronic equipment is changing many office jobs, and innovation frequently results in changes in the responsibilities of many employees. Techniques in job design may be helpful in ensuring that effectiveness is improved.

2. *During reorganization.* Reorganizations of management hierarchies and organizational units frequently mean changes in job assignments or responsibilities of many employees due to the creation and elimination of jobs. A successful reorganization must consider the implications of these changes in job design.

3. *When starting up or building a new plant or work unit.* Building a new organization requires many decisions about the division of labor. That is, who will do what? Consideration of proper job design may help make these decisions more effective.

4. *When jobs are needed for special positions or persons.* Even existing organizations create new positions from time to time. Also, new persons may be entering the organization who have different skills and capabilities. Both of these situations may create a need to reevaluate job design. For example, physically demanding jobs may need to be redesigned to accommodate female workers, and hiring handicapped workers may require that managers carefully redesign jobs for them. Frequently, special jobs are also designed for newcomers to the organization or for special administrative assistants or temporary assignments.

5. *When there are performance or satisfaction problems.* There is a common tendency to blame the worker rather than the job when performance is poor. For instance, human error was initially blamed in the nearly catastrophic nuclear power plant incident at Three Mile Island. Closer examination revealed that the operator's job created excessive mental demands during emergency situations such that the job was actually predisposed to error. If there are performance or satisfaction problems with many employees on the same job, this is evidence that the job may be the problem. For example, in a recent article the following situation was described for a group of technical report writers. They have to write reference manuals that describe complex electronic equipment, yet they are not technical experts themselves. The number of details they must remember is excessive. The lighting in their office is poor, and there is a glare on their computer screen. Their chairs are uncomfortable, and the keyboards are too high. The office is noisy and

either too hot or too cold. Clearly, job design may be part of the problem here.

As a final example, in a different study, a group of sawmill employees were described as lazy and apathetic. Examination of the jobs revealed that they lacked variety and any significant skill requirements. The jobs were unimportant, repetitive, and boring. Not surprisingly, the employees were not motivated or satisfied.

HOW SHOULD JOBS BE CHANGED? THE INTERDISCIPLINARY PERSPECTIVE

Research has discovered four approaches to job design. They come from many different scientific disciplines (e.g., psychology and engineering). Effectively utilizing these techniques can improve many important outcomes, from efficiency to job satisfaction. In the following paragraphs, the four approaches to job design are described along with the outcomes they influence.

Motivational Approach

This approach stems from the work on job enrichment and enlargement and from the major theories of work motivation and organizational behavior. Its basis is organizational psychology.

Recommendations. According to this approach, jobs should be designed to give the worker autonomy and the opportunity to make some decisions about how tasks are done. The worker should get feedback on job performance, be able to use a variety of skills, and have opportunities for growth and learning. In addition to taking into account these characteristics that make jobs meaningful from a task-oriented perspective, this approach also considers the social or people-interaction aspects of the job content (including the need for participation, communication, and recognition).

Outcomes. This job design approach is intended to increase satisfaction and motivation. In addition, job performance may be higher, and absenteeism may be lower. Customer service may even be improved. On the other hand, jobs that are too high on the motivational approach may have longer training times and be more difficult and expensive to staff because of their greater mental ability requirements. Higher mental ability requirements can also lead to higher compensation requirements. Further, the stimulating nature of overly motivating jobs could predispose workers to stress and errors.

Examples. Many managerial and professional jobs are naturally high on the motivational approach.

Craft and technical jobs may also be high because of their skill requirements. Jobs usually low on the motivational approach include many factory, service, and other semiskilled or unskilled jobs. There are many jobs in every occupational group, as well as aspects of almost every job, where motivational features are low. However, most jobs do not have to be poorly designed on the motivational approach. Managers can change most of these job design features by following the recommendations above. Knowledge of motivational job design is a powerful tool for increasing the satisfying and motivating outcomes from jobs.

Mechanistic Approach

This approach comes from scientific management, time and motion study, and work simplification. Its primary discipline basis is industrial engineering.

Recommendations. This approach suggests that jobs be closely studied to determine the most efficient work methods and techniques. In addition, work should be broken down into highly specialized jobs, tasks and skills should be simplified, there should be repetition to benefit from practice, and there should be little idle time.

Outcomes. This approach is intended to increase human resource efficiency. Jobs high in mechanistic features can be easily and inexpensively staffed, training time is typically short, and lower compensation may be required. Because mental demands are less, errors may be less common. On the other hand, too much of the mechanistic approach may result in less satisfied and motivated employees. Sometimes overly mechanistic work can lead to health complaints from the physical wear that can result from highly repetitive and machine-paced work.

Examples. Jobs high on the mechanistic approach are often the same ones that are low on the motivational approach: many factory, service, and semiskilled or unskilled jobs. Assembly line jobs are good examples of this approach. Obviously, most managerial and professional jobs are usually low on this approach. Sales and negotiating positions, which have a less than optimal probability of success, and jobs that are needed only in emergency situations (e.g., firefighter) are low on this approach because of their inefficient nature. Many office jobs are also poorly designed from a mechanistic point of view. However, managers can apply concepts like specialization and simplification of tasks and skill requirements to many jobs in order to reduce staffing difficulties and training requirements. In addition, often jobs are simply too complex or too large for the employees, and so performance is poor or overtime is excessive. Sometimes work load rises without corresponding increases in staffing levels. These are times to apply the mechanistic approach to increase efficiency.

Human Factors Approach

This approach comes from human factors engineering and from research on skills and how humans mentally process information. Its basis, with its emphasis on perceptual and motor abilities, is experimental psychology. This approach has received public attention through the Three Mile Island incident. Government regulations issued since that time require that nuclear power plants consider human factors in their design.

Recommendations. This approach tries to ensure that the attention and concentration requirements of the job do not exceed the abilities of the workers. The job is designed to limit the amount of information the worker must pay attention to, remember, and think about. In addition, this approach is also concerned with such features as appropriate lighting levels, safety, and user-friendly equipment (simpler and easier-to-use equipment).

Outcomes. This approach is intended to decrease the likelihood of errors and accidents, as well as mental stress and fatigue. Like the mechanistic approach, it may also increase human resource efficiency (e.g., reduced training and staffing costs) because it reduces the mental ability requirements of the job. On the other hand, too much of the human factors approach may result in less satisfaction, less motivation, and more boredom because the jobs provide inadequate mental stimulation.

Examples. The nuclear power plant operator's job is low on this approach. An air traffic controller's job is also low because of the amount of information to attend to and the stress from the consequences of an error. Jobs involving the operation of complex machinery, like aircraft or heavy construction vehicles, are also low in this approach. Other jobs that can tax attention and concentration capabilities include many product-inspection and equipment-monitoring jobs. Not only must much information be attended to in these jobs, but the vigilance requirements are also mentally demanding. Jobs in numerous other occupations may also impose excessive attention and concentration requirements. For example, many managerial, administrative, professional, and sales jobs can be excessively demanding on the information-processing capabilities of the incumbents, thus predisposing errors and stress. All jobs may have periods of overload. The human factors approach can be used to reduce these demands of jobs through the redesign of tasks, equipment, or environments.

Biological Approach

This approach stems from biomechanics (the study of body movements), work physiology, occupational medicine, and anthropometry (the study of body sizes). It is often called ergonomics.

Recommendations. This approach tries to ensure that people's physical capabilities and limitations are not exceeded by the design of their jobs. Recommendations include reducing strength and lifting requirements, modifying or replacing chairs so that postural support is provided, redesigning tasks and equipment so that wrist movement is reduced, eliminating excessive noise, maintaining comfortable temperatures, and other changes that reduce the physical demands of jobs.

Outcomes. Jobs high on the biological approach require less physical effort, result in less fatigue, and create fewer injuries and aches and pains than jobs low on this approach. The jobs may even be associated with lower absenteeism and higher job satisfaction because they are less physically arduous. A drawback of this approach may be the expense of changes in equipment or job environments needed to implement the recommendations. In addition, it is possible to design a job with so few physical demands that the workers become drowsy or lethargic, thus reducing their performance or leaving their workplace.

Examples. Jobs low on this approach obviously include those in traditionally heavy industries (e.g., coal, steel, oil, forest, and construction), which have substantial physical ability requirements. But this approach also applies to many other jobs that have some physical component (e.g., production, maintenance). Recommendations from the biological approach have been applied to the redesign of equipment and tasks in physically demanding jobs so that women can better perform them (e.g., lighter tools with smaller hand grips). This approach can also be applied to many lighter jobs. For example, seating, size differences, and posture are important to consider in the design of many office jobs, especially those with computer terminals. This approach can also apply to many light assembly positions that require excessive wrist movements that can eventually lead to a chronic wrist condition known as carpal tunnel syndrome. On the other hand, there may be jobs with too little physical activity (i.e., movement restricted due to single position or work station) or jobs that require excessive travel, which results in poor eating and sleeping patterns.

IMPLEMENTATION

Step 1: Measure the Design of the Job

A questionnaire was developed to assess whether a job is well designed in terms of each of the approaches. The questionnaire is called the Multimethod Job Design Questionnaire (MJDQ) and is contained in appendix 61–A. It can either be administered to employees, or managers can complete it by observing the job or discussing it with employees. The MJDQ can also be used in any of the situations described earlier. For example, during the start-up of a new organization, it can be used as a checklist to evaluate equipment and job descriptions, during a reorganization or technological innovation it can be used to evaluate and guide proposed changes, and when problems occur it can be used to determine whether the job design is part of the cause.

Step 2: Analyze Potential Job Design Problems

The average score across the items on a particular approach represents how well the job is designed based on that approach, with smaller scores indicating better design. A simple rule of thumb is that if the score for an approach is larger than 3, the job is poorly designed by that approach and it should be examined. Even if the average score on an approach is greater than 3, you should examine any individual item scores that are at 2 or 1. As noted in discussing the four approaches, some jobs naturally score lower in certain approaches, and this should be considered in interpreting the scores. However, the designs of most jobs can still be improved on one or more approaches.

Step 3: Determine Job Design Changes

The MJDQ items not only help determine design problems, but they offer redesign recommendations as well.

Conflicts. It would be ideal to have jobs designed well on all approaches. Unfortunately, the four approaches are not independent. Although there are some similarities, there are also some conflicts. No one approach can satisfy all outcomes. Table 61–1 summarizes the outcomes from each approach.

The greatest potential conflicts are between the motivational approach on the one hand and the mechanistic and human factors approaches on the other. They produce nearly opposite outcomes. This occurs because the mechanistic and human factors approaches strive to design jobs that are simple, easy to learn, safe, and reliable, with minimal mental demands on workers. The motivational approach encourages more complicated, challenging, and stimulating jobs, with greater mental demands.

Trade-offs. Because of these conflicts, trade-offs may be necessary. But trade-offs are not unavoidable in all situations. Jobs can often be improved on one approach and still maintain their good scores on other approaches. The independence of the biological approach provides such an opportunity. Managers can reduce physical demands without sacrificing the mental quality of a job's design. The cost of equipment may sometimes be a significant deterrent to implementation.

The major trade-offs will be in terms of the mental demands of jobs. Table 61–2 illustrates the trade-offs on this dimension. Making the job more mentally demanding increases the likelihood of achieving the

Table 61–1
Summary of Outcomes from the Job Design Approaches

Design Approach	Positive Outcomes	Negative Outcomes
Motivational	Higher satisfaction Higher motivation Higher job performance Lower absenteeism Higher customer service	Increased training time Decreased staffing ease Greater error and stress likelihood Increased compensation
Mechanistic	Decreased training time Increased staffing ease Lesser error and stress likelihood Decreased compensation	Lower satisfaction Lower motivation Potential for more physical wear
Human factors	Lesser error and accident likelihood Decreased stress Decreased training time Increased staffing ease	Lower satisfaction Increased boredom
Biological	Less physical effort and fatigue Fewer injuries and aches and pains Higher satisfaction and lower absenteeism	Financial costs of changes in equipment or job environment Too little physical activity

Table 61–2
Mental Demands Continuum

Motivational-Designed jobs	Mechanistic- and Human Factors–Designed jobs
High satisfaction High motivation Low absenteeism (Individual outcomes)	Low training times High staffing ease Low error likelihood (Organizational outcomes)

Source: Figure adopted from M.A. Campion and P.W. Thayer, Job design: Approaches, outcomes, and tradeoffs. *Organizational Dynamics,* 15 (3) (1987) : 66–79.

workers' goals of satisfaction and motivation. On the other hand, making the job less mentally demanding increases the chances of reaching the organization's goals of reduced training and staffing costs and errors. Which trade-offs will be made depends on which types of outcomes a manager wants to maximize.

These trade-offs may not be absolute. There may be times when a job's design can be changed to gain certain benefits without incurring every cost. In a recent study, the motivational approach was applied to a group of clerical jobs to improve employee satisfaction and customer service. The expected benefits occurred along with some expected costs (e.g., increased training and compensation requirements), but not all potential costs occurred (e.g., quality and efficiency did not decrease).

In addition, adverse effects of trade-offs can often be minimized by avoiding extremes or by specifying minimum acceptable levels on each approach. Knowing all the approaches to job design and their corresponding outcomes may help make more intelligent job design decisions and avoid unanticipated consequences.

Step 4: Make the Job Design Changes

Workers are experts on their jobs. Therefore, they can provide excellent job design and implementation recommendations, and they should always be consulted. Participation in the redesign can also increase employee acceptance.

It should be noted that workers can significantly influence the design of their jobs by seeking out different tasks, ignoring other tasks, changing the physical environment (e.g., through homemade padding or extra lighting), or developing a job aid (e.g., chart of frequently used information). Observing such changes might indicate that job redesign is needed.

When jobs are changed, the abilities needed to perform the jobs may also change. The levels of abilities needed may be increased or decreased; new abilities may be required and others no longer required. This could mean changes in various human resources practices. For example, training programs may need to be developed, revised, or eliminated. Hiring standards may need to be raised or lowered. Promotion, transfer, and other employee movement systems may be influenced. The compensation program may need to be revised subject to changed job demands. Existing performance appraisal systems may also need revision due to changed responsibilities. Thus, many human resource programs may need to be reconsidered following job redesign. In fact, greater savings and increased flexibility in human resources may be a goal of the redesign.

Step 5: Conduct a Follow-up Evaluation of the New Design

After the job has been designed or redesigned, a follow-up evaluation should be conducted to ensure that the design actually turned out as expected and that the proper outcomes are emerging. The MJDQ can be used to evaluate the design. Again, it can either be administered to employees, or the manager can complete it by observing the job or discussing it with

employees. Scores on the different approaches can be compared with previous scores or with planned changes to determine how successful the intervention has been.

The proper outcomes anticipated from job design should also be evaluated. For example, if motivational features of jobs were increased, the resulting levels of satisfaction, motivation, and performance should be evaluated. If the mechanistic and human factors features were strengthened, the impact on training times, staffing ease, error rates, and so on should be evaluated. If biological job design was improved, subsequent levels of physical stress and strain should be evaluated.

It is not unlikely that other changes or fine-tuning of the job design will be necessary based upon follow-up evaluation. Job design is often an iterative process.

CONCLUSION

Poorly designed jobs may be the cause of more performance and satisfaction problems than managers realize. The four-factor job design framework and questionnaire described in this chapter are intended

to raise awareness of alternative job designs and the outcomes they influence and to provide a means of analyzing and changing job designs to enhance individual and organizational goals.

APPENDIX 61–A: MULTIMETHOD JOB DESIGN QUESTIONNAIRE (MJDQ)

Motivational Approach

1. *Autonomy:* The job allows freedom, independence, or discretion in work scheduling, sequence, methods, procedures, quality control, or other decision making.

2. *Intrinsic job feedback:* The work activities themselves provide direct and clear information as to the effectiveness (e.g., quality and quantity) of job performance.

3. *Extrinsic job feedback:* Other people in the organization, such as managers and coworkers, provide information as to the effectiveness (e.g., quality and quantity) of job performance.

4. *Social interaction:* The job provides for positive social interaction such as teamwork or coworker assistance.

5. *Task/goal clarity:* The job duties, requirements, and goals are clear and specific.

6. *Task variety:* The job has a variety of duties, tasks, and activities.

7. *Task identity:* The job requires completion of a whole and identifiable piece of work. It gives you a chance to do an entire piece of work from beginning to end.

8. *Ability/skill level requirements:* The job requires a high level of knowledge, skills, and abilities.

9. *Ability/skill variety:* The job requires a variety of knowledge, skills, and abilities.

10. *Task significance:* The job is significant and important compared with other jobs in the organization.

11. *Growth/learning:* The job allows opportunities for learning and growth in competence and proficiency.

12. *Promotion:* There are opportunities for advancement to higher-level jobs.

Adopted from M.A. Campion (1989), *Journal of Applied Psychology, 73*, 467—481.

13. *Achievement:* The job provides for feelings of achievement and task accomplishment.

14. *Participation:* The job allows participation in work-related decision making.

15. *Communication:* The job has access to relevant communication channels and information flows.

16. *Pay adequacy:* The pay on this job is adequate compared with the job requirements and with the pay in similar jobs.

17. *Recognition:* The job provides acknowledgment and recognition from others.

18. *Job security:* People on this job have high job security.

Mechanistic Approach

19. *Job specialization:* The job is highly specialized in terms of purpose, tasks, or activities.

20. *Specialization of tools and procedures:* The tools, procedures, materials, and soon used on this job are highly specialized in terms of purpose.

21. *Task simplification:* The tasks are simple and uncomplicated.

22. *Single activities:* The job requires you to do only one task or activity at a time.

23. *Skill simplification:* The job requires relatively little skill and training time.

24. *Repetition:* The job requires performing the same activity(s) repeatedly.

25. *Spare time:* There is very little spare time between activities on this job.

26. *Automation:* Many of the activities of this job are automated or assisted by automation.

Human Factors Approach

27. *Lighting:* The lighting in the workplace is adequate and free from glare.

28. *Displays:* The displays, gauges, meters, and computerized equipment on this job are easy to read and understand.

29. *Programs:* The programs in the computerized equipment on this job are easy to learn and use.

30. *Other equipment:* The other equipment (all types) used on this job is easy to learn and use.

31. *Printed job materials:* The printed materials used on this job are easy to read and interpret.

32. *Workplace layout:* The workplace is laid out such that you can see and hear well to perform the job.

33. *Information input requirements:* The amount of information you must attend to in order to perform this job is fairly minimal.

34. *Information output requirements:* The amount of information you must output on this job, in terms of both action and communication, is fairly minimal.

35. *Information processing requirements:* The amount of information you must process, in terms of thinking and problem solving, is fairly minimal.

36. *Memory requirements:* The amount of information you must remember on this job is fairly minimal.

37. *Stress:* There is relatively little stress on this job.

Biological Approach

38. *Strength:* The job requires fairly little muscular strength.

39. *Lifting:* The job requires fairly little lifting, and/or the lifting is of very light weights.

40. *Endurance:* The job requires fairly little muscular endurance.

41. *Seating:* The seating arrangements on the job are adequate (e.g., ample opportunities to sit, comfortable chairs, good postural support, etc.).

42. *Size differences:* The workplace allows for all size differences between people in terms of clearance, reach, eye height, legroom, and other factors.

43. *Wrist movement:* The job allows the wrists to remain straight without excessive movement.

44. *Noise:* The workplace is free from excessive noise.

45. *Climate:* The climate at the workplace is comfortable in terms of temperature and humidity, and it is free of excessive dust and fumes.

46. *Work breaks:* There is adequate time for work breaks given the demands of the job.

47. *Shift work:* The job does not require shift work or excessive overtime.

For jobs with little physical activity due to single workstation add:

48. *Exercise opportunities:* During the day, I have enough opportunities to get up from my work station and walk around.

49. *Constraint:* While at my workstation, I am *not* constrained to a single position.

50. *Furniture:* In at my workstation, I can adjust or arrange the furniture to be comfortable (e.g., ade-

quate legroom, foot rests if needed, proper keyboard or work surface height, etc.).

Instructions: Indicate the extent to which each statement is descriptive of the job on a scale of:

(5) strongly agree, (4) agree, (3) neither agree nor disagree, (2) disagree, (1) strongly disagree, and (blank) don't know or not applicable. Scores for each approach are calculated by averaging applicable items.

APPENDIX 61–B: RESEARCH UNDERLYING THE INTERDISCIPLINARY PERSPECTIVE ON JOB DESIGN

Extensive research has been conducted on the interdisciplinary approaches to job design. This research began with an exhaustive search of all the literature on jobs and the extraction of specific "rules" as to how to design jobs. Rules were collected for everything: equipment, facilities, and environments, as well as for job content and methods. These rules were then analyzed and sorted into distinct groups based on similarity of underlying theoretical orientation. Four job design approaches resulted, forming the basis of the MJDQ.

Five major studies have been conducted. Industries have included the low-technology forest products industry, the high-technology electronics industry, and the service-oriented financial industry. Over 220 jobs have been studied, including all levels and types. Nearly 2,000 employees and managers have been interviewed or surveyed. Information was also collected on a broad spectrum of outcomes, including satisfaction, absenteeism, training time, staffing difficulty, physical effort required, injury rates, error rates, job stress, mental demands, a large number of job-related abilities, and many compensation and job evaluation indexes. Additional ongoing research is examining how people naturally go about designing jobs and how specific tasks should be combined or changed in order to improve job design. The practical consequences of these studies are discussed in this chapter, and the technical details are presented elsewhere (see Additional Resources).

More research is needed on the interdisciplinary approaches in order to improve our understanding of job design. We are looking for research sites where jobs are being developed or changed in order to further the study of job design and to determine whether jobs can be designed optimally on all approaches with minimal trade-offs.

ADDITIONAL RESOURCES

Six technical articles describe the research on interdisciplinary approaches to job design:

Campion, M.A. (1988). Interdisciplinary approaches to job design: A constructive replication with extensions. *Journal of Applied Psychology, 73,* 467–481.

Campion, M.A. (1989). Ability requirement implications of job design: An interdisciplinary perspective. *Personnel Psychology, 42,* 1–24.

Campion, M.A., & Berger, C.J. (1988). Conceptual and empirical integration of job design and job evaluation. In F. Hoy (Ed.), *Academy of Management Best Papers Proceedings* (268–272).

Campion, M.A., & McClelland, C.L. (in press). Interdisciplinary examination of the costs and benefits of enlarged jobs: A job redesign quasi-experiment. *Journal of Applied Psychology.*

Campion, M.A., & Stevens, M.J. (1989). A laboratory investigation of how people design jobs: Naive predispositions and the influence of training. In F. Hoy (Ed.), *Academy of Management Best Papers Proceedings* (261–264).

Campion, M.A., & Thayer, P.W. (1985). Development and field evaluation of an interdisciplinary measure of job design. *Journal of Applied Psychology, 70,* 29–43.

Two practitioner-oriented articles also describe the interdisciplinary approaches to job design:

Campion, M.A., & Thayer, P.W. (1987). Job design: Approaches, outcomes, and trade-offs. *Organizational Dynamics, 15* (3), 66–79.

Campion, M.A., & Thayer, P.W. (1989). How do you design a job? *Personnel Journal, 68* (1), 43–44, 46.

Two contemporary books that summarize the literature for each of the job design approaches are cited:

Motivational Approach

Griffin, R.W. (1982). *Task design: An integrative approach.* Glenview, IL: Scott-Foresman.

Hackman, J.R., & Oldham, G.R. (1980). *Work redesign.* Reading, MA: Addison-Wesley.

Mechanistic Approach

Barnes, R.M. (1980). *Motion and time study: Design and measurement of work* (7th ed.). New York: Wiley.
Konz, S. (1979). *Work design.* Columbus, OH: Grid.

Human Factors Approach

McCormick, E.J. (1976). *Human factors in engineering and design* (4th ed.). New York: McGraw-Hill.

Van Cott, H.P., & Kinkade, R.G. (Eds.) (1972). *Human engineering guide to equipment design* (Rev. ed.). Washington, DC: U.S. Government Printing Office.

Biological Approach

Grandjean, E. (1980). *Fitting the task to the man: An ergonomic approach* (3d ed.). London: Taylor & Francis.
Tichauer, E.R. (1978). *The biomechanical basis of ergonomics: Anatomy applied to the design of work situations.* New York: Wiley.

62 SOME ISSUES TO CONSIDER WHEN SURVEYING EMPLOYEE OPINIONS

Vida Scarpello, Robert J. Vandenberg

Nearly 70 percent of firms with 5,000 or more employees use opinion surveys as a tool for identifying problem areas. Despite the widespread use of opinion surveys, little has been written on the survey process itself. This is unfortunate since conducting an employee opinion survey is an expensive proposition.

For example, one industry association we have worked with charges $20 per person to administer, process, and provide survey feedback to company managers and employees. The survey it uses is a standardized 120-item questionnaire, and the feedback is descriptive. The break-even cost is $30 per person.

Using the association's break-even survey cost, a company would spend $15,000 to survey 500 employees and $150,000 to survey 5,000 employees. The cost of working time for employees participating in the survey process is even higher. For instance, assume that the average hourly pay for the employees taking the survey is $12.00 and the benefit cost per hour is $4.56 (38 percent of $12.00). Furthermore, the survey time requirement for each employee participant is 2 hours (1 hour for completing the survey and 1 hour for receiving survey feedback). Taking the above factors into consideration, the cost of employee participation in the survey process is $33.12 per person. If we add the break-even cost of the survey process to the time cost, then the total cost of surveying one employee is $63.12, the total cost of surveying 500 employees is $31,560, and the total cost of surveying 5,000 employees is $315,600. Further, the survey costs are not constant. As companies repeat the survey process every two or three years, the costs increase.

Some employers attempt to control survey process costs by contracting with consultants who provide their services at very low rates, such as $5.00 per person. At this price, the employer is wasting money. Besides the cost of employee time, the indirect costs associated with using a poor survey instrument may be higher than the direct costs. The major indirect cost is incorrect interpretation of survey results, which may lead to implementation of action plans that are unrelated to actual problems within the organization. We have also seen numerous cases where employees had lost trust in management after they had perceived the survey questions to be useless.

The high costs of surveying employee opinions, as well as the lack of written information about the survey process, motivated us to write this chapter. We hope that our combined fifteen-year experiences working with organizations on survey issues may be useful to managers who want to use survey information to help diagnose and deal with organizational problems. In this chapter we will discuss seven basic issues that managers should consider before implementing the survey process in their organizations:

1. Which job concerns to measure
2. Measuring the job concern of Interest:
   Evaluating established scales
   Writing and evaluating survey questions
3. Choosing survey response formats
4. Designing the survey instrument
   Introduction and instructions:
   Employee classification information
   Survey questions
   Space for employee comments
5. Administering the survey:
   How to introduce the survey into the organization
   Who should administer the survey
   When the survey should be administered
   How the survey should be introduced to survey participants
   What processes should be used to maintain survey response confidentiality
6. Giving survey feedback
7. Responding to employee concerns

WHICH JOB CONCERNS TO MEASURE

Opinion surveys can measure a variety of job-related concerns. However, measuring too many factors may lead to difficulties in interpreting the survey results. The following example will illustrate this point.

A major U.S. corporation had contracted the services of a well-known consultant to develop a survey that would help improve the labor relations climate within its plants. The survey was available to the plants upon request. At the time we became involved with this corporation's survey process, the survey had been used within the corporation for about five years. We were called to help management in one plant interpret the survey results. The plant was experiencing a poor labor-management relationship, and the plant's management had requested the corporation to conduct an employee opinion survey.

The survey consisted of thirty-two items that measured eighteen areas of worker concerns: the work itself, career process, training, pay, benefits, supervision, coworkers, performance feedback, company policies and practices, communication, efficiency of work processes, working conditions, job security, quality of tools, safety, general job satisfaction, turnover intentions, and a number of personal feelings toward work and toward the company.

The survey items seemed reasonable, but the results were difficult to interpret. Some of the items that posed the greatest problems of interpretation were the following:

1. "I get recognition when I do good work." Sixty-five percent of the employees responded with "agree." Yet the same employees had verbalized extreme discontent with not getting recognition for doing good work.

2. "My supervisor is interested in my ideas." Sixty-nine percent of the employees responded with "agree." Yet supervisors and subordinates complained that relations between them were extremely poor.

3. "My job allows me to improve my skills." Eighty-five percent of the employees responded with "disagree." Yet the plant had introduced new technology the previous year and all employees had to improve their skills in order to work with the new technology.

4. "I enjoy working with the people here." Seventy-two percent of the employees provided an "undecided" response. Yet management perceived the bargaining unit to be an extremely cohesive group.

Because the answers to the above and the other "reasonable" questions were difficult to interpret, the plant's management asked us to conduct survey feedback sessions to try to identify the true problems in the plant. After meeting with small groups of employees per shift, we found that employees perceived that supervisors recognized good work by stealing their ideas. Eighty-five percent of the employees perceived that they had to change their skills in order to maintain employment, but the change in skills was not an improvement. The employees liked their coworkers because the coworkers were friendly but did not perceive that coworkers helped each other to get the work done, and some coworkers did not do their fair share of the work. Finally, the employees thought that their managers did not really care about their concerns because they did not ask the right questions on the survey and the survey contained too few questions.

After content analyzing the data we gathered during the meetings, we concluded that the major problems within the plant were dissatisfaction with immediate supervision, career progress, and plant rules. These problem areas were not identified by the survey.

The major problem with the thirty-two-item survey was that it attempted to measure too many job-related concerns with too few questions. Although there are well-known company-developed surveys that measure many job-related concerns with relatively few questions, such surveys are derived from research with longer versions of the survey and from identification of relationships between survey answers and organizationally relevant employee behaviors. Herein lies the problem for companies that use another company's survey: the questions that are useful for one company may not be useful for another company. In the long run, organizations without a history of surveying employee opinions would be better off if they measured concerns relevant to their own work forces.

Research has shown that employees are concerned with supervision, coworkers, pay, benefits, career progress, work load, administrative rules and procedures, tools and major equipment, use of abilities and skills, control over work processes, the physical work environment, and job security. These job concerns can be used as a starting point for determining the concerns that may be relevant to the organization's work force. The importance of these and other job concerns to a company's work force can be determined before implementing the survey process by:

1. Conducting focus group meetings with managers who supervise employees to identify the job-related areas that managers believe are of concern to their employees.

2. Conducting focus group meetings with representative cross-sections of managerial and nonmanagerial employees to identify job-related areas that are of concern to the employees.

3. Conducting a meeting with the human resource staff to obtain their perceptions of employee behavioral problems such as turnover, low performance, and absenteeism and to ask their opinion about possible causes of those problems.

After gathering information about job-related concerns from managers, employees, and the human resource staff, the information can be categorized into major areas of employee concerns. A useful matrix for categorizing the job concerns discussed by the focus groups is shown in figure 62–1.

Figure 62–1 lists twelve job-related concerns. We have seen surveys that measure all twelve concerns and also surveys that measure only three concerns. The number of job-related concerns measured on a given survey is somewhat dependent on the number of questions that are needed to measure any one job

concern. Some concerns such as job security can be accurately measured by a single item, provided the item responses have been shown to be reproducible (reliable). Other job concerns may require the use of fifteen or more items to ensure that the items capture the relevant content of the concern.

A frequent question we encounter regarding which job concerns to measure on the survey is the following: "Should we measure areas of concern that we cannot change?" This question is typically asked after management learns about a company that has dropped measuring a job concern simply because it could not change the situation. For example, one major corporation quit measuring pay satisfaction when it became evident that employee groups across the corporation typically provided "dissatisfied" responses to the pay questions. Another corporation stopped measuring employee satisfaction with working conditions because it could not afford to remodel its plants to control the temperature.

Although the decisions to quit measuring uncontrollable events may seem reasonable, our experience suggests that the issue is not whether to measure or not measure uncontrollable events but whether management wishes to communicate its recognition of a problem area and its concern for employees.

For example, management may have been wise to

Figure 62–1. Matrix for Categorizing Job Concerns

Job Concerns	Respondent Category				
	Managers Focusing on Subordinate Concerns	Salaried Exempt Personnel	Salaried Exempt Personnel	Hourly Paid Personnel	Human Resource Staff
1. supervision					
2. pay					
3. benefits					
4. use of abilities and skills (nature of work)					
5. control over work processes					
6. career progress					
7. tools and equipment					
8. work load					
9. coworkers					
10. rules and procedures					
11. physical environment					
12. job security					

stop measuring pay satisfaction. The intent of the pay administration process is to provide fair pay with respect to the external labor market for occupational skills, with respect to the relative value of the employee's job, and with respect to contributions individual employees make to a given job. Employees are also concerned that they receive fair pay with respect to the above factors. Thus, management could have shown concern about the fairness of the pay administration process by measuring employee perceptions of pay fairness. When surveys focus on assessing the fairness of the pay administration process, useful information is obtained. Depending on employee responses, management can often pinpoint pay problems that can be corrected through job reevaluation and through proper implementation of the pay adjustment processes.

Similarly, measuring employee concerns about working conditions is useful even if management cannot implement the ideal solution to eliminate physical discomfort. Employees are usually aware of what management can or cannot change. If exposed to unsatisfactory working conditions, employees want management to recognize that they are working under abnormal conditions and to show concern by adapting management practices to compensate for the physical discomfort the employees experience or to implement other partial solutions. For example, employees would feel that management was concerned about their exposure to extreme temperatures if management installed fans to circulate air in the summer and required employees to close outside doors when passing through them in the winter.

Perhaps the most efficient way of choosing the job concerns to measure on the survey is to choose those concerns that the majority of focus group participants indicated as being a job concern. These job concerns can serve as the survey core. Additional concerns may be included as survey space permits.

MEASURING THE JOB CONCERNS OF INTEREST

The typical survey usually contains standard measurement scales for some job concerns, and some questions are written specifically for the survey. Thus, the potential survey user should be familiar with how to evaluate the usefulness of a scale and how to write and evaluate survey questions.

Evaluating Established Scales

Many employee concerns are so frequently encountered that sets of questions called "scales" have been developed to measure these concerns in a wide variety of employment settings. Several sources that describe relevant published scales are listed in Additional Resources. Additionally, information on available scales can be obtained from vendors and by conducting computerized library searches for published scales.

Published scales usually provide statistical information about the reproducibility of responses to the scale's items. Some scale developers also provide statistical evidence that their scale's items measure a large proportion of content relevant to the job concern of interest. Sometimes, however, statistical information about the scale is not available and the potential user of the scale has to either consult with a subject matter expert or conduct his or her own "logical" evaluation of the scale. The importance of subject matter expertise in evaluating a scale is illustrated by the following example of a pay scale that did not result in obtaining the desired information.

Management of a flour mill became concerned when its hourly paid employees suggested that unionization may be a way of increasing their pay. The mill's management decided to contract the services of a consultant to survey a variety of employee opinions, including opinions about pay. The survey participants were asked to indicate the fairness of their pay level when compared with:

1. "What I could earn in a similar job outside this mill in another mill just like this one."
2. "What I could earn in another job, in another part of the mill or in the office."
3. "The amount of work I'm expected to do."

On the surface, the items seem reasonable. The items appear to be representative of the content relevant to the pay administration process. Survey respondents are expected to compare the fairness of their pay level with respect to the external labor market (item 1), the relative value of their job (item 2), and the pay they receive for their contributions to their job (item 3). However, a compensation expert would probably say that answers to the first two items are of little practical value, and thus, the three items are not adequate for assessing the content that employees consider when assessing the fairness of their pay level.

A compensation expert would first note that the pay items are applied to an employee group whose pay is largely determined by conditions in the local labor market. In this market, employers across industries compete for labor, and the mill employees can leave the mill for similarly paid work in a variety of local industries. Thus, employee responses to the first item, "compared to what I could earn in a similar job outside this mill in another mill just like this one," are of little practical value to the company.

A compensation expert would also note that pay systems are typically designed for groups of jobs, called job families. Yet, item 2 asks employees to compare their jobs to jobs outside their job family (office jobs) and also to other jobs whose job family is not known. Moreover, the wording of the item is confusing, a condition that will likely result in nonreproducible (unreliable) responses. Item 3, on the other hand, appears adequately to capture employee perceptions of being fairly paid on a given job.

Logical evaluation of a scale and its items may be facilitated by knowing how to distinguish between good and poor survey items. Some guidelines for evaluating survey scales and items are discussed below.

Writing and Evaluating Survey Items

There is no generally recommended approach for writing or evaluating survey items. Nevertheless, the approach we will outline has proved to be an approach that results in reproducible responses and scales that measure what they are intended to measure.

Good survey items can result from a two-step process: (1) generating items that reflect the content of each job concern and (2) writing items that reflect the meaning the survey respondents are likely to attribute to the item's wording.

Generating Survey Items. The easiest way to generate questionnaire items is to use the focus group meetings as the primary sources for generating survey items. In these meetings, the focus group leader's role is to control the discussion process and record the words each focus group participant uses to refer to each job concern.

The focus group leader should prepare for the meetings by developing a list of possible job-related concerns that may be discussed during the meeting. Each meeting should start by informing the participants that the purpose of the meeting is to obtain information about job concerns that should be measured on an employee opinion survey. The focus group leader can then introduce each job concern with the following statement: "Please tell me about the kinds of things you think about when you think about [job concern]." As each group participant discusses the meaning of the job concern to him or her, the focus group leader should record the exact words each person uses to discuss the job concern. When the discussion on the job concern seems to be exhausted, the leader can ask the participants if they have anything more to add. If the group has nothing more to add, the leader should read the recorded statements to the group and ask if the statements accurately represent the issues they had discussed. This process of soliciting information should be continued until all job concerns of interest are discussed.

Writing Survey Items. Two kinds of questions should be written to measure each job concern of interest: global and specific. The global question is intended to assess the respondent's overall opinion about the job concern such as: "How do you feel about your supervisor, in general?" Specific questions about the supervisor's behavior should also be written to assess respondents' opinions about the supervisor's behavior with respect to the technical, administrative, and human relations components of the supervisor's job.

Global items provide an overall assessment of how employees think or feel about "something." When those responses are positive, no action is necessary. However, in many cases, the responses to global items may not be positive. When this happens, the set of specific items may be used to identify the areas of concern that should be addressed by management.

In writing global survey items, it is important not to include extraneous words in the written item because the inclusion of such words may lead to unreliable or nonreproducible responses. For example, if the item asks, "All things considered, how satisfied are you with your supervisor?" the responses will be unreliable. We have found that some people consider the supervisor's height, weight, and baldness when responding to the item. However, the item, "How satisfied are you with your supervisor in general?" is reliable.

Writing sets of more specific items for each job concern is more difficult than writing global items. The goal of the item writer is to make sure that the content of the job concern is clearly and adequately measured by the items. For illustrative purposes let us consider three job concerns: plant rules, coworkers, and career progress.

Plant Rules. Suppose that the list of issues discussed by the focus groups reveals that in discussing plant rules, the participants referred to two kinds of rules: performance and discipline. They also discussed those rules with respect to fairness of the rule and the consistency with which the rule was enforced. To assess the content of the plant rules concept, four items have to be written:

1. The fairness of the plant's performance rules.
2. The consistency with which the plant's performance rules are enforced.
3. The fairness of the plant's disciplinary rules.
4. The consistency with which the plant's disciplinary rules are enforced.

Notice that the four items capture the content of concerns relative to plant rules. Each rule is paired with either a fairness or an enforcement concern. Such pairing is essential for ensuring that the meaning of "plant rules" is covered by the items on the survey and that the responses to the plant rule concern are reproducible.

For example, suppose the item writer wrote the following item: "The fairness and consistency with which the plant rules are enforced." This item is not a good one. The responses would probably be unreliable and thus random. The item is poor because it is ambiguous and thus subject to different interpretations. Some respondents may focus on performance rules, and others may focus on the discipline rules. Some respondents may average what they think about both performance and discipline rules. Similarly, some respondents may focus on the fairness issue and others on the enforcement issue. Furthermore, if the identical item were randomly placed in the survey more than once, the same respondent would likely shift his or her focuses and give different responses to the item in different parts of the survey.

Coworkers. Suppose that analysis of the focus group discussions reveals that participants focused on the following three issues when they discussed their coworkers: getting along, helping others, and doing a fair share of the work. The written items would then be:

1. The way my coworkers get along with each other.
2. The way my coworkers help each other.
3. The way my coworkers do their fair share of the work.

Again, if the writer combined any two of these ideas into one item, the responses to the combined item would probably not be reproducible. Furthermore, if one of the items were omitted from the survey, the content of the coworker concept would not be adequately represented within the survey.

Career Progress. Writing good survey items to measure career progress opinions is more difficult than writing good items to measure opinions about plant rules or coworkers. There is no logical basis for assuming that the term *career progress* evokes the same meaning for all survey respondents. In addition, it is clear that even if the meaning were shared, employees across job classifications would probably not use the same words to define the components of career progress. A broadly scoped concept such as career progress tends to be perceived somewhat differently by different employee groups. A useful survey instrument measuring career progress should capture the content of career progress for the majority of survey respondents.

Suppose that analysis of the focus group data reveals that participants discussed three issues: promotion-from-within policies, skills training, and opportunities for promotion. To capture the content representative of the meaning of career progress requires careful examination of the words used to discuss career progress. Those words should be used to write survey items.

For example, our studies show that the following six items capture the contents of career progress for diverse employee groups:

1. Training to improve my skills on my present job.
2. Opportunity for training for better jobs.
3. The way job openings favor people already working here.
4. Opportunities for upgrading or promotion.
5. Training I received when I first started the job.
6. Chances to get new jobs within the plant.

Notice the use of words such as *chances, opportunities, upgrading,* and *promotion.* When multiple terms are commonly used to reflect the same job concern, it is wise to include items on the survey that use all of the common terms because there will be no one term that will be interpreted the same way by all survey respondents. Sometimes, as in item 4, it is possible to use two terms, *upgrading* and *promotion,* in one item. The word *or* alerts the respondent that the two terms are synonyms.

Finally, notice that the measurement of plant rules required the use of four items, the measurement of coworkers required the use of three items, and the measurement of career progress required the use of six items. There is no magic number of items that should be included under each job concern to be measured. The important consideration is to ensure that the content of the job concern is adequately measured. Sometimes the job concern is multifaceted so it requires measurement of a large number of items (such as an eighteen-item scale we have developed for measuring satisfaction with immediate supervision). Sometimes the content of the job concern can be captured with few items (such as the three-item coworker scale). Sometimes there is no commonly agreed upon meaning for terms used to define a concept so that more words and thus more items are required to capture adequately the content of the job concern for the respondents (such as the six-item career progress scale).

The following guidelines may be used to write clearly worded survey items:

- Each survey item should consist of words that are commonly used by employees when they voice their concerns about a job concern.
- The content of each job concern should be fully

represented by the items that focus on measuring the job concern.

- Each questionnaire item should contain only one idea or a pairing of ideas.
- When a number of terms are used to represent a concept, each term should be represented by a questionnaire item, or one item may include two terms if the item is worded in such a way that it is obvious that the two terms are synonyms (e.g., *upgrading* or *promotion*).
- Extraneous material should not be included in the written item.

Following these guidelines when writing survey items will help ensure that the responses to the items are reproducible and thus, not random. The guidelines can also be used to evaluate the quality of the items on surveys marketed by consulting firms.

CHOOSING SURVEY RESPONSE FORMATS

A number of different response formats are used on surveys. The typical format is a rating scale where the response options are arranged from low to high along equal intervals such as 1, 2, 3, 4, 5, or 1, 2, 3, 4, 5, 6, 7.

When choosing a rating response format three things should be considered: (1) range of response values, (2) midpoint for multiple response choices, and (3) definition of the response options.

In deciding the range of values to use for a response format, it is necessary to think about what kind of information is desired. The 1–5 rating format is appropriate and adequate for obtaining most kinds of desired information and thus is the most widely used response format. This format provides for a range of response choices without dividing the possible response choices too minutely, which sometimes happens with a 1–7 or 1–9 rating format.

Whenever a multiple response format is chosen, it is important to choose an odd number of response options such as 1–3 or 1–5 rather than an even number such as 1–4 or 1–6. Even-number response options do not possess a midpoint. Without a response scale midpoint, the average response cannot be calculated.

Defining the response options for the rating scale seems like a simple task. The response options should be described clearly along a continuum of values relevant to one concept (e.g., very satisfied to very dissatisfied; strongly agree to strongly disagree; very fair to

very unfair). However, we have encountered a number of surveys with very poorly defined response options.

For example, one consulting company's survey summary report we were asked to interpret stated, "The hourly employees are satisfied with their compensation." The response options to six pay items were given on a 1–5 rating format. The definitions of the response options, however, were the following: (1) more than fair, (2) fair, (3) about right, (4) too low, and (5) much too low.

Notice that the response options confuse perceptions of pay fairness (response options 1 and 2) with pay satisfaction (response options 3, 4, 5). Although our studies show that the majority of people who obtain their income from fixed salaries and wages tend to equate perceptions of pay fairness to pay satisfaction, a large minority of people will provide lower ratings for pay satisfaction than they will for pay fairness perceptions. By using response options that confuse pay satisfaction with perceptions of pay fairness, the responses to the pay items are not interpretable. If the intent was to measure perceptions of pay fairness, the response options should have been defined as (1) very unfair, (2) unfair, (3) neither fair or unfair, (4) fair, (5) very fair. Similarly, if the intent was to measure satisfaction with pay, the response options should have been defined as (1) very dissatisfied, (2) dissatisfied, (3) neither satisfied nor dissatisfied, (4) satisfied, and (5) very satisfied.

DESIGNING THE SURVEY INSTRUMENT

The survey is typically made up of the following components: introduction and instructions, employee classification information, survey questions, and space for employee comments.

Introduction and Instructions

The first page of the survey should contain several statements of introduction to the survey and instructions to complete the survey. The introductory statements should include the purpose of the survey and a promise to maintain the anonymity of survey respondents. One example of commonly used introductory statements follows:

> This survey will help us understand how you feel about our effectiveness in working with people. In addition, it will help us assess our progress toward improving the work situation since the last survey was taken two years ago.
>
> The questions asked in this survey provide for complete anonymity for your responses. However, you should know that although great care is taken to provide anonymity for any comments that you may write in longhand, your management may be able to identify your comments from the way you write them. People tend to write comments in ways that are similar to how they speak.

Anonymity of responses is a major concern for participants of an opinion survey. Managers and employees often fear that their survey responses will identify them and, consequently, they will somehow be punished for providing negative responses. Managers fear that upper management may use the opinions of their subordinates as an appraisal of managerial performance, and negative subordinate opinions will have serious consequences for their career progression. Employees fear negative treatment from their supervisors if their survey responses are known. Such fears are particularly prevalent in work settings that are using the survey for the first time and in work settings where respondent anonymity was violated in previous survey administrations. The anonymity issue is therefore a very sensitive issue. It should be addressed several times. First, a promise of anonymity should be written in the introductory section of the survey, and second, ways of protecting anonymity should be explained when the survey is administered.

The survey form should contain clear instructions regarding the response options used in the survey. One example follows:

> This survey is divided into five parts. Please note that for most questions, you are given five response choices. Also note that the response options may focus on different things (e.g., satisfaction, fairness, agreement) in different parts of the survey. Be sure to read the instructions that appear before each set of questions and please use the response options given on each page before you circle or check your answers.

Employee Classification Information

The first page of the survey is a good place to request information about the respondent's job classification (hourly paid, salaried-nonexempt, salaried-exempt), company location (division, facility, or plant), department, supervisor's name, and other pertinent data. This information is typically used to group employee responses into classification groups for data analysis and to provide survey feedback by the classification group of employees who completed the survey.

On numerous occasions, management has asked us to help design questions that will provide information about employee perceptions of the company's compliance to equal employment opportunity (EEO) regulation. In these cases, we suggest that specific questions about EEO practice should not be asked. Rather, employee perceptions of compliance to EEO regulation can be addressed more accurately by collecting relevant demographic information and analyzing employee responses to the survey by the EEO category of interest. This process allows management to compare statistically the survey responses of employees by major EEO categories: race, age, sex, national origin, and religion. If significant differences are found among employee category responses, these differences can serve as guidelines for developing action plans for eliminating perceptions of differential treatment.

Employees fear that their survey responses will identify them. Thus, they are extremely nervous about providing demographic information. One way of decreasing their fear of being identified through the demographic data they provide is to preface the survey section, which asks for demographic information, with a statement similar to that which follows:

To make you more comfortable in providing demographic information, we will explain to you why this information is needed, how it will be analyzed, and how it will be fed back.

Our locations vary in their work force compositions. By obtaining demographic information we can analyze the data more thoroughly and therefore provide better feedback to each location.

We are interested in how different demographic groups of employees respond to the survey questions. But we are not interested in how particular individuals within a department respond to survey questions. Demographic information will allow us to analyze the data by demographic category. For example, one question of interest is: "Do older workers respond to the survey differently from younger workers?" Another question is: "Do males respond differently to the survey questions from females?"

The location will receive survey feedback for the following categories of respondents:

A. Responses for the total population of the facility.
B. Responses by demographic groups for the total population of the facility.
C. Responses by department, supervisor, and shift groups.
D. Feedback will not be provided for groups of fewer than ten people.

It may also be useful to state in written form that group responses will only be summarized and fed back to the group's management if the group consists of ten or more people. Survey responses of groups with fewer than ten people will be included with the responses from the next highest group. For example, a work group may consist of nine people, and the department may consist of fourteen people. One survey feedback report would be provided for the fourteen member department.

Survey Questions

There are two issues to consider with respect to survey questions item placement on the survey and length of the survey.

Item Placement. Most surveys we have seen organize the items to be measured by the job concern being measured. The job concern is defined, and the questions related to the job concern follow. Our experience in survey research suggests that organizing questions by job concern tends to produce biased responses. For example, suppose the survey asks five sequential questions about plant rules (one global item and four specific items). If the respondent is particularly dissatisfied with one aspect of plant rules, the tendency is to respond negatively to all aspects of plant rules. However, if the five "plant rule" questions are randomly mixed with questions focused on other job concerns, the tendency is to respond specifically to each question asked rather than to a set of similar questions. By randomly mixing items belonging to a variety of job concerns on a survey, response biases decrease. The survey items belonging to the relevant job concern can be regrouped mechanically prior to data analysis.

Survey Length. In developing surveys for corporations, we have asked the question: "What did you think about the length of this survey?" The response choices we used were: (1) much too long, (2) somewhat too long, (3) just about right, (4) somewhat too short, (5) much too short. Our data indicate that most nonmanagerial employees prefer longer rather than shorter surveys. The longer surveys act as indicators that management is truly concerned with their problems. Perceptions of survey length, however, are more influenced by the number of survey pages than by the number of survey items. Thus, if the survey measures a number of job concerns, care should be taken to space the items closely rather than to add pages to the survey. The preferred number of survey pages varies between nonmanagerial and managerial employees. Nonmanagerial employees prefer a twelve-page survey. Managerial employees prefer short surveys (three to five pages).

Space for Providing Comments

Most surveys provide a blank page for respondent comments. Our experience suggests that the number of comments obtained on a survey is inversely related to the quality of the survey. When the survey incorporates relevant job concerns and asks enough questions about each job concern, the number of comments decreases. Normally, fewer than 10 percent of the respondents provide comments. When they do, negative comments typically outweigh positive comments. Moreover, the negative comments often do not correspond to the overall objective survey results. In our view, providing space for comments serves an important catharsis function, but the comments are not very useful for identifying problem areas.

ADMINISTERING THE SURVEY

The survey administration process should be carefully thought out and executed. The issues to consider are how to introduce the survey into the organization, who should administer the survey, when and where should the survey be completed, how the survey should be introduced to the survey participants, and what processes should be used to maintain survey response confidentiality.

How to Introduce the Survey into the Organization

Introducing the survey into the organization should be a relatively straightforward process. First-time survey users should communicate to all managers and employees that the survey process is a tool for identifying problem areas and either correcting those problems or explaining to employees why those problems cannot be corrected. Use of focus groups to identify the job concerns to be included in the survey is also a way of helping personnel understand the logic behind administering a written survey.

Who Should Administer the Survey

The best approach is to choose a survey administrator who is external to the location in which the survey is applied. In most cases, a corporate human resource staff person is appropriate for the task. However, in locations experiencing poor employee-management relations, it may be wise to hire the services of an external consultant who will be responsible for administration, analysis of data, and survey feedback. When hiring a consultant, two criteria should be used: the consultant's expertise in human resource management and the consultant's interpersonal skills. The consultant's knowledge of the field of human resource management is invaluable for analyzing data, interpreting the survey results, and obtaining clarification of the issues of concern to employees during the survey feedback sessions. Analysis of survey data by an external consultant also increases trust in the confidentiality of the responses. Finally, interpersonal skills are necessary for gaining employee and management trust that the information given to the consultant will be held confidential but the essence of

the information communicated effectively to the relevant managerial personnel.

When and Where the Survey Should Be Completed

In companies where the survey process is institutionalized, employees are sometimes given the survey to complete at their own leisure within specified time constrains. In most situations, however, a better response rate and more carefully executed responses will be obtained if the survey is administered during working hours to small groups of employees.

Sometimes it is not possible to relieve employees of their job responsibilities to complete the survey during working hours. In such cases, it is advantageous to schedule employees to complete the survey either before or after work hours and to pay them for the time they take to complete the survey. When scheduling surveying times before or after work, it is important to consider employee schedule preferences. Lack of concern for employee preferences may result in hostility toward management and the survey process.

For example, one company with which we worked scheduled a survey administration meeting after the completion of a 3:00 to 11:00 shift. This schedule was accepted by all employees except those who were scheduled for an 11:00 P.M. meeting on Friday. The 3:00 to 11:00 shift had a tradition of getting together for a few beers after the Friday night shift. The scheduled employees went to the meeting but did not complete the survey because they felt that management did not consider their feelings when it scheduled the meeting.

How to Introduce the Survey to the Participants

Survey administrators should take the time to go over the survey with the survey participants. When doing so, the administrators should explain how confidentiality of responses will be protected, how the survey will be analyzed, and how the collected data will be fed back to the organization. Time should also be allocated for employee questions and straightforward answers given to those questions.

How to Maintain Confidentiality for Survey Respondents

There are five basic ways that respondent confidentiality can be maintained. First, survey participants can be told that if they write comments, they should use different words than they typically use when speaking. Second, after collecting survey data from each group, the survey administrator can place the surveys in sealed envelopes and tell the employees that he or she will take the responsibility for the envelopes while in the facility and will take the envelopes personally when leaving the facility at the end of the survey administration process. Third, the administrator can explain that the original surveys will be destroyed after the information is coded on a computer. Fourth, the administrator can explain the way groups will be combined in survey feedback reports. Fifth, the administrator can explain that the written comments will be examined, and if the respondent is easily identified by the comments, then the comment will not be included in the survey feedback report but the feedback will be anonymously given to the person about whom the comment is made.

GIVING SURVEY FEEDBACK

The survey results are normally organized into group data and fed back to the organization in small group meetings. The typical feedback process uses the following steps:

1. Total location responses and data grouped by job classifications and employee demographics are feed back to the top management group within the location.

2. Each department manager receives the department's total responses and responses of the supervisory group that reports to him or her.

3. Each supervisor receives the department's total responses and responses of the subordinate group that reports to him or her.

4. Employee work groups receive the department's total responses and responses of the work group.

The feedback meetings serve two purposes: they provide summary information about the positive and negative aspects of the job concerns measured by the survey, and they allow clarification and further specification of the problems that have been identified by the survey. To facilitate open discussion about identified problems, it is usually best to limit the feedback group to the employee category receiving the feedback. Supervisors are sometimes present in the feedback meeting with their subordinates, but this practice tends to inhibit the employee discussion. It is therefore best to ask the supervisors not to participate in the feedback meeting. The survey feedback consultant can schedule a meeting with the supervisor after the discussion with the employee group. At this meeting, the consultant can inform the supervisor about the content discussed in the employee meeting and help the supervisor develop an effective response to the employee concerns.

RESPONDING TO EMPLOYEE CONCERNS

An effective managerial response to the identified employee concerns is based on one fundamental principle: "Treat the issue seriously." Employees are intelligent people and expect management to treat them as intelligent people. This principle is seldom violated by external consultants but is frequently violated by managers whose role is to address the identified employee concerns. Three examples will serve to illustrate how the principle of treating the issue seriously can be violated. As the reader will shortly surmise, the statements below make no sense. They make no sense to employees receiving the communication either.

1. The survey indicated that employees were dissatisfied with their direct pay. The company decided that the best person to address this concern was the corporate vice-president of human resources. The intent was to clarify the company's pay level policy. Instead of explaining that the company's policy was to pay competitive (average) market rates, the vice-president explained that the company's pay level policy allows the employees to eat chicken instead of steak.

2. Employees were dissatisfied that management was not concerned about the extreme heat that they were subjected to during the summer months. Prior to the survey, employees had complained about the heat and suggested that the solution was to install air-conditioning. Management could not modernize the plant to install air-conditioning. The survey results showed extreme dissatisfaction with management's lack of "concern" for the employee heat problems. In responding to the problem, the local manager told the employees, "There is no way you people will ever get air-conditioning in this plant so you might as well get used to the heat and stop complaining."

3. Faculty in a major business school had been complaining that incoming junior faculty were being paid more than the more senior faculty members, a problem called wage compression. The dean of the business school held a faculty meeting and informed the faculty that wage compression should not be viewed as a problem. Rather, the faculty should view wage compression as a positive opportunity because if the salaries of senior business school faculty were not compressed, the faculty would be stagnating as was the case in the College of Liberal Arts where salaries were not compressed.

In all three cases, the person responding to the employee concern was perceived by the recipients of the response as someone who did not treat the issue seriously. Employees who received the pay level explanation felt insulted and did not believe that the vice-president of human resources ate chicken. The heat problem was handled poorly. The employees should have been provided economic reasons explaining why the plant could not install air-conditioning, and alternative solutions to deal with the problem, such as placement of fans, could have been developed. The faculty of the business school were well aware of their wage compression problem. Most of them had accepted the problem because they were not motivated to leave the school just to obtain better salaries. However, they also wanted their dean to continue pushing the university's administration to adjust their salaries so that they would be closer to salaries paid in other major institutions. The dean's statement was perceived as a strong indicator that the dean had no intention of supporting the faculty's equity concerns with higher administration.

SUMMARY

Conducting employee opinion surveys is an expensive proposition. The effectiveness of the opinion survey in identifying problem areas, however, is partly related to the care with which management implements the survey process and responds to employee concerns. In this chapter, we discussed seven basic issues that managers should consider before implementing the survey process in their organization. The examples we used to make our points came primarily from our experiences with working with corporations and our attempts to interpret results of many opinion surveys we have seen being applied in various work settings. Some readers may have had different experiences and therefore may disagree with some of our points. However, few readers would disagree with the following: "If you're going to do something, try to do it as well as you can." We hope our suggestions may help some companies improve their survey process.

ADDITIONAL RESOURCES

Cook, J.D., Hepworth, S.J., Wall, T.D., & Warr, P.B. (1981). *The experience of work*. London: Academic Press.

Price, J.L., & Mueller, C.W. (1986). *Handbook of organizational measurement*. Marshfield, MA: Pitman.

Scarpello, V., & Vandenberg, R.J. (1987). The satisfaction with my supervisor scale: Its utility for research and practical applications. *Journal of Management, 13* (3), 447–466.

USING EMPLOYEE SURVEYS TO INCREASE ORGANIZATIONAL EFFECTIVENESS

William A. Schiemann

Surveys have had a long tradition in the United States. Paper-and-pencil measures have been a part of most peoples' lives from early childhood. Most adults today have taken achievement tests, vocational interest inventories, skills assessments, and work proficiency measures and completed questionnaires for scores of reasons (e.g., hotel or airline preference, insurance applications, satisfaction with services, work-related issues). And although work force surveys have been around for many years (e.g., Kornhauser & Sharp, 1932; Roethlisberger & Dickson, 1939), they have only recently come into the spotlight as a primary vehicle for increasing organizational effectiveness.

At first, employee surveys typically concentrated on measuring employee morale or satisfaction (e.g., Hoppock, 1935), employee reactions to programs or plans (e.g., training programs or fringe benefits), employee awareness (e.g., Do you need more information on . . . ?), or employee preferences (e.g., Would you prefer plan A or B?). Although all of these uses have been important, they were not integrated into a broader model of organizational effectiveness, which includes other measures as well.

Partly this has resulted from a narrow focus on singular measures for more focused uses. In the case of job satisfaction, the early use of this measure was associated with a belief that a happy worker was a more productive worker (Filley et al., 1976; Schwab & Cummings, 1970). And despite the debate over the years regarding this belief, job satisfaction has been shown to be an important predictor of turnover, absence, and other important economic outcomes to the organization (Cascio, 1987; Mirvis & Lawler, 1977; Mobley et al., 1979; Steers & Rhodes, 1978). However, job satisfaction alone, or for that matter, any of the other measures described above, falls short as a comprehensive tool for assessing organizational effectiveness. Only by integrating multiple measures can a broader understanding of effectiveness be achieved. In this chapter, a variety of uses for employee surveys will be discussed within an organizational effectiveness context.

POTENTIAL BENEFITS OF EMPLOYEE SURVEYS

Employee surveys can provide numerous benefits to an organization. In the most basic sense, surveys offer a sound method and precision tools to measure employee attitudes, values, expectations, needs, intentions, beliefs, awareness and understanding, and perceptions of individual and group behaviors (see table 63–1). Moreover, in practice, surveys can be a powerful vehicle to help organizations achieve their objectives. Some of the major benefits follow.

Identification of Organizational Strengths and Weaknesses

A well-designed survey can provide a balanced profile of major strengths and weaknesses on such dimensions as operating practices, image of the organization, products and services, customers, policy effectiveness, motivation and morale, safety, and

Table 63–1
Surveys as an Assessment Tool

Measures	Examples
Attitudes	Job and company satisfaction
Beliefs	Performance is related to rewards
Intentions	Turnover, absence
Awareness/understanding	Policies and procedures, goals
Values	Importance of job security, pay, work, advancement
Expectations	Company will provide protection for retirement
Needs	Benefit coverage, challenging work
Evaluations	Training programs, management
Perceptions of individual or group behaviors	Frequency of performance feedback, cooperation between groups

company commitment. Moreover, certain employee groups are far closer to operating problems (e.g., hourly production workers) or customer service (e.g., sales or service representatives) than management and therefore often have an important perspective on current and future opportunities for improvement.

Assess Culture

Employee surveys (especially in conjunction with customer surveys) can provide a concise snapshot of the organization's culture. That is, culture is largely represented by collective perceptions of values, attitudes, behaviors, and beliefs within the organization. What does the firm stand for? Under pressure, how will it act? What is valued and rewarded? Is the business goal directed? These types of questions can be answered because the organization does not act except through the collective activity of its members. It is the collective belief system, which is mapped in daily activities, that can be partially measured and understood through a survey. (To gain a truly comprehensive understanding of culture, additional information must be gathered through other methods, such as interviews.)

Key Measure in Strategic Planning and Assessment

The strategic plan should set the direction for the organization. The strategic plan announces the agreed-upon nature of the business and long-term objectives. What type of culture will support those objectives? What types of human resources and behaviors will be needed to support that culture?

In essence, the strategic plan maps the desired state along with a series of strategies and plans to reach that state. Operational plans support the strategic plan by defining yearly, monthly, and daily activities that must take place in order to achieve the desired objective. Without an adequate measurement system, including feedback mechanisms, the firm has no way to determine if objectives are being met. A survey that includes key dimensions of importance to the plan can provide continuous or intermittent feedback on the attainment of milestones or desired change. For example, if the organization wishes to create a strong performance-reward orientation, then employee feedback on their perceptions of the relationship between performance and various rewards (e.g., bonus, pay) is important.

Upward Communication

Another benefit of employee surveys is the upward communication opportunity that it affords employees. In most organizations, straightforward, open communication (particularly related to problems or negative information) is difficult to come by. An extensive research literature on status differences and supervisory-subordinate communication suggests that subordinates are more likely to pass positive information up the line while screening out potentially important negative news. Also, employees are less likely to disagree with their superiors, even when they have important information. Furthermore, in many organizations, there are few opportunities to communicate directly above one's own supervisor. Thus, an employee survey represents one of the few vehicles that will provide open, balanced communication to higher management.

An additional advantage is timeliness. Top management receives multilevel information on important themes collected in a common manner and time frame rather than the usual sporadic flow of information on a multitude of subjects over wide spans of time.

Feedback on Organizational Change

A regular survey tracking program, using a core set of items of key importance, can provide important feedback on changes in employee perceptions over time. Data that track intended change efforts (e.g., operational plans resulting from a new strategic direction) or unintended changes (e.g., changes in employee values resulting from changing work force hiring) can provide essential feedback to management to determine whether corporate objectives will be achieved. For example, a change in hiring practices that yields employees who value benefits less (e.g., part-time workers) may have a significant impact on the value associated with expenditures on employee benefits. Or an erosion in employee perceptions of customer service may portend a dismal future in the marketplace.

Catalyst to Action Planning and Problem Solving

Employee surveys have been used quite effectively as a catalyst to focus attention on key issues in need of attention. Combined with action planning and problem-solving training, relevant data from employees in a given work unit can be effectively used to stimulate discussion on key issues, help determine the severity of problems, and identify potential solutions. In fact, survey data can be quite effectively used in participative work teams as well as in structurally defined units. This subject will be addressed in more detail later in the chapter.

Predictor of Key Productivity Measures

Employee attitudinal data can be quite useful in predicting important organizational outcomes such as turnover (e.g., Kraut, 1975; Mobley et al., 1979; Price, 1977), absence (e.g., Goodman & Atkin, 1984; Rosse & Miller, 1984; Smith, 1977; Steers & Rhodes, 1978), individual performance and motivation (Iaffaldano & Muchinsky, 1985; Petty et al., 1984), accidents or safety behavior (Davids & Mahoney, 1957; Pestongee et al., 1977), alcohol abuse (Cook et al., 1976; Hawthorne, 1977–1978), and health disorders and stress (Rosse & Hulin, 1985). All of these outcomes have bottom-line significance to the organization. A regular attitude survey program can provide key scales that predict these

outcomes and a rapid feedback vehicle for important corporate productivity dimensions.

Measures of Employee Needs

Surveys of this type can also yield valuable information on work force needs and preferences. For example, in the fringe benefits area, it is becoming increasingly important to control costs. One way to do this is by more carefully shaping benefits or benefit options to maximize the utility or satisfaction per dollar spent. Without clearly understanding the needs of a given work force, it is difficult to make decisions on benefit reconfirmation. Are the needs homogeneous across work groups? What potential hardships might be created? To what extent is health coverage duplicated between employees and their spouses? These and other questions need to be answered before benefits redesign. Without this information, benefit satisfaction may be adversely affected, resulting in higher turnover (Bartel, 1982; Mitchell, 1982) and lower recruitment success.

Evaluating Differences across Job or Organizational Groups

Another use of survey data is the understanding of values, needs, attitudes, and reactions to policies across different job groups or organizational units. For example, managerial and production employees may have very different reactions to a new policy on advancement. Professionals and sales employees often have different value structures and therefore might be motivated to perform more effectively with different reward structures. Because operational demands vary dramatically and managerial skills have a strong impact on worker attitudes and behaviors, it is likely that different business units will have different profiles of strengths and weaknesses and, therefore, different problems to attack. Without understanding these differences, many firms launch shotgun approaches to more narrowly focused problems, wasting enormous resources in the process.

Although the above areas do not represent all of the benefits to be derived from the use of employee surveys, they certain represent many of the primary advantages to be found in survey usage.

TYPICAL USES OF EMPLOYEE SURVEYS

Employee surveys are used for a wide range of purposes—some narrow and some quite broad. The following list represents some of the more frequent uses.

Overall Assessment of Corporate Human Resource Effectiveness

Probably the fastest growing usage of employee surveys today is in organizational assessments of human resource effectiveness. This type of survey typically includes measures of:

- Employee attitudes (e.g., toward pay, benefits, working conditions, supervision, safety, advancement, job security, communications).
- Perceptions of company policies and practices (e.g., regarding performance appraisal and promotional systems, operating efficiency, waste, coordination and cooperation across work units).
- Perceptions of company products and services (quality, service, raw materials, customer responsiveness).
- Values (what is important to employees and the organization).
- Image (e.g., financial health of the firm, market orientation, environmental concern).
- Needs (e.g., security, financial, training, communication).
- Expectations (e.g., pay for performance, promotional rewards).
- Understanding and awareness (e.g., policies, fringe benefits, corporate goals).
- Intentions (e.g., absence, turnover).
- Beliefs (e.g., company will reward risk taking; firm will not stand behind my supervisor).

Program Evaluation

Many organizations use surveys to evaluate the success of experimental or established programs. Usually employee acceptance and support is an important part of successful implementation. Furthermore, employee feedback can be an important part of corrective action. Example areas of such use include new training programs, introduction of technological change (e.g., office automation, introduction of robots), trial work methods (e.g., flextime, job sharing, shorter work weeks), employee benefits, new incentive or compensation system and other programs (e.g., child care center, employee assistance programs, direct deposit checking).

Key Component of a Turnover and/or Absence Study

Although other data should be collected (turnover rates and costs, performance measures), surveys of both current and former employees can be extremely valuable in isolating causes of high turnover or absence across certain job groups or locations.

Key Component in a Safety or Accident Study

Safety attitudes and behaviors are key contributors to a low accident or lost-time record. A survey conducted in conjunction with a safety assessment can identify safety attitudes, behaviors (actual work practices), dimensions of safety training and reviews, management support for safety policies, safety documentation process, accuracy of accident reports, and hidden violations that may later cause severe consequences to the organization. This type of survey can also identify potential solutions to current safety problems.

Communications Audit

Surveys of employees (and other publics) can be a major source of information about formal communication vehicles (e.g., annual report, employee handbook, company newsletter), perceptions of communication style (e.g., open versus closed), and the informal communication climate. For example, the survey can address the flow of communication upward, downward, and horizontally across work units. Preferred and current sources of information can be compared. The quality and understandability of various vehicles (formal and informal) can be evaluated. The credibility and impact of communication messages can be ascertained. Specific communication gaps can be identified and addressed as a result of this information.

It should be noted that the very conduct of a

survey has communication implications. As mentioned before, the survey itself is a powerful form of upward communication—and in most organizations one of the few formal upward communication vehicles. Also, if the survey is followed by feedback and action planning, another powerful communication activity takes place: with management, the supervisor, and coworkers. Finally, the content of an employee survey conveys certain messages to employees. If the survey is about cutting costs, then management interest in cost cutting is conveyed.

Merger and Acquisition Analysis and Integration

Another more recent use of employee surveys is in the blending of corporate cultures after a merger or new acquisition. Organizations develop rather distinct, stable cultures. Changing these cultures does not come easily, but the blending of different cultures is essential when creating a new organization from two or more distinct firms. Unfortunately, the assessment as to how well the cultures can be blended is rarely undertaken in the analysis of whether a particular merger makes sense. More often, financial and market considerations dominate these decisions. Furthermore, the track record for successful mergers is dismal; part of this can be attributed to an incomplete analysis of the cultural fit before the merger and an inability to create the expected synergy after consummating the deal.

Quite often, a survey is used to assess the distinct cultures of the component organizations to ascertain the kinds of changes that are needed in order to function as a unified entity. Differences in values, reward structures, communications climate, levels of bureaucracy, customer orientation, operational efficiency, and employee commitment characterize the individual organizations. The extent of differences can be determined through a survey so that constructive action plan for integration can be developed and implemented.

Assessing Labor Relations Climate and Predicting Contract Ratification or Union Certification Vote

Whether the work force is represented by a union or not, a survey with key labor relations dimensions can provide regular feedback on the quality of relations between various employee groups (e.g., production, clerical, professional) and management. There is ample research suggesting that certain employee attitudes (e.g., attitudes toward company and job) are good predictors of future unionization success (e.g., Getman, Goldberg & Herman, 1976; Fiorito et al., 1986; Heneman & Sandver, 1983; Rosse et al., 1987) and contract ratification (e.g., Cappelli & Sterling, 1988; Schiemann, 1987) when a bargaining unit is already in place.

A number of organizations have used surveys to assess vulnerability to a union organizing campaign. This can be assessed by geographic location for each grade of employees by collecting attitudinal data on key dimensions of satisfaction. Other variables (e.g., attitudes toward unions) may also help in the prediction. However, it should be noted that the conduct of a survey of employees after the successful petitioning to the National Labor Relations Board (NLRB) for a certification election may be construed as an unfair labor practice if the firm has not regularly used this form of assessment. Thus, it is far better to track attitudes on a regular basis not only to avoid the potential unfair labor practice but to develop adequate feedback measures to assess potential deterioration of labor relations climate.

For unionized firms, an innovative use of surveys has been to develop a clear understanding of employee values, needs, issues, and satisfaction before entering into regular contract bargaining. Certain attitudinal dimensions (along with economic and organizational variables) have been used to predict contract ratification vote across individual locals (Schiemann, 1987). This information has afforded the opportunity to develop action plans to address key issues in locals where the outcome is likely to be negative.

Quality of Service and Products

Another innovative use of employee surveys is in the quality of service and product arena. One of the failures of historic approaches has been to look at employee issues independent of market or customer issues. For years, market and human resource researchers have worked on different sides of a conceptual fence. More recently, others and I have integrated customer and employee research using common instruments and core dimensions of product and service quality. These data enable the firm not only to uncover shortfalls in customer perceptions but to have readily available information from employees on the likely causes of such failures.

The data can identify discrepancies in perception between customers and key customer contact personnel. It can also highlight shortcomings in quality control leading to poor customer perceptions. Or the data might show that company policies or employee service delivery are above and beyond what customers desire for the price they are willing to pay. In any case, this information enables the firm to develop coordinated solutions across marketing, operations, and human resources.

KEY STEPS IN THE SURVEY PROCESS

There are three key phases and a number of steps within each phase that ensure a successful survey process. These are shown in table 63–2. Missing important steps or executing them poorly can result in problems yielding outcomes ranging from simple frustration to overall project failure. Major steps in each phase will be briefly discussed.

Planning for an Employee Survey

The first and one of the most important phases in the process is clearly defining the major purpose for conducting the survey.

Purpose and Goals. The survey should be conducted with a major purpose in mind. A number of benefits and uses have already been discussed in this chapter. Each organization considering the process should identify the primary goal that will drive the design and execution of the survey and prepare end users for the results they will receive. Secondary objectives should also be listed. What do you expect to learn as a result of the survey? What information is most important, of secondary importance, and so forth? How will this information be used? What benefits will accrue from either the conduct of the survey or the information it yields? What are the potential costs? Only with a clear set of objectives in mind will the survey deliver the type of information that is desired.

Selecting the Survey Team. Once a decision to conduct a survey has been made, one must next decide if the survey will be conducted internally, by an external consultant, or some combination of the two. The decision should be based on answers to the following questions:

- Are there adequate internal resources (skills, time available) to conduct the project?

- How important are perceptions of confidentiality? Can desired information be obtained without using an objective third party?

- Will an outside expert bring added credibility to management? Can the outside consultant deliver news that internal agents cannot?

- Can the organization handle all phases of the survey? If not, with which components is help most needed?

- How important is comparative experience? Are external norms or an external perspective needed?

For example, because of the sensitivity of many issues normally covered in an employee survey, an external firm is frequently used at least to process the data and conduct interviews when appropriate. Often, external consultants are used to develop the questionnaire, provide norms when available and appropriate, interpret the findings, and make recommendations based on their experience in other organizations. Unless an organization has in-house expertise, is relatively large, and expects to conduct frequent surveys, the costs probably do not justify internal staffing to handle periodic surveys.

Selecting an External Consultant External consultants should be selected on the basis of experience in conducting employee surveys. The buyer of such ser-

Table 63–2
Major Steps in the Survey Process

I. *Planning for an employee survey*
   1. Purpose and goals
   2. Selecting the survey team
   3. Selecting an external consultant
   4. Selecting the internal team

II. *Conducting the survey*
   1. Planning and orientation
   2. Developing the survey instruments
   3. Administering the questionnaire
   4. Processing the data
   5. Analyzing, interpreting, and reporting the findings

III. *Using the survey findings*
   1. Reviewing the findings with management
   2. Feedback to employees
   3. Setting priorities on issues
   4. Identifying causes and potential solutions
   5. Communicating decisions, assigning tasks, and setting timetable

vices should evaluate the potential consultant on a number of factors:

- Quality and experience of the specific individuals who will work with your firm (e.g., educational training, years as a consultant in this specialty, clients with whom they have worked).

- Information on other successful projects they have completed in this area and client references.

- Quality of the proposal, including completeness of a work plan to accomplish the buyer's objectives, their understanding of the buyer's issues, and a clear indication of their costs.

- The depth of the firm to deliver what is needed. A firm offering hundreds of consultants is probably not needed to deliver a small survey or interview study; on the other hand, a single consultant may not be able to deliver all that is needed for a large, complex survey program. Size is less relevant than having assurances about how various parts of the survey process will be delivered.

- Custom or standard product. Most times, a consultant will be wanted who can design a custom survey (e.g., custom questionnaire, interviews, report) rather than purchasing an off-the-shelf product. Largely this depends on company needs, but off-the-shelf products may miss key issues pertaining to a particular business unless the need is standard. On the other hand, one does not need to reinvent the wheel to have a custom product. For example, standard scales that have worked well before should be favored over untried items when they meet specific needs (e.g., measures of pay or job satisfaction).

If at all possible, a meeting should take place with the prospective consultants before asking for a proposal. This will allow an opportunity to evaluate the individuals with whom the internal team will be working before narrowing to those who will be asked to submit proposals. At this meeting, it is important to convey the purpose for conducting an employee survey and to supply background information that is important to an understanding of the business. This affords an in-person opportunity to see how the consultant reacts to the specific needs, the type of approach offered, the amount of similar experience with other firms, and so forth.

Selecting the Internal Team. It is also important to select carefully the internal team who will work with the consultant and management to ensure the process is completed successfully. Several criteria are essential:

- *Influence level in the company.* The team or individual must have the clout to execute various parts of the survey process (e.g., scheduling questionnaire administration or interviews that might require employee time away from work; pulling the management team together when needed)

- *Access to management.* The most senior individual responsible for the survey internally must have access to management to obtain questionnaire approval, schedule meetings and interviews with senior executives when appropriate, and be able to argue for or defend decisions on survey steps.

- *Administrative coordination.* A survey requires a substantial amount of administrative coordination. Interviews, meetings, and administration sessions must be scheduled. Questionnaires must be reviewed and may need to be printed. Tables must be designed in conjunction with the consultant. Data on employee demographics and sample will need to be generated.

Conducting the Survey

There are five major steps in conducting the actual survey; however, there are many smaller steps that may also be important, depending on the particular survey.

Planning and Orientation.

Planning Meeting. Once survey goals have been developed and the consulting team has been selected (internal and/or external), a planning and orientation meeting should be scheduled to introduce all key members of the survey team and discuss survey logistics (e.g., when the survey will be conducted, timetable for survey steps, how the survey will be communicated, what data collection method will be used).

Management Orientation. This is best conducted with the most senior level of management who will be responsible for making decisions based on the survey data collected and upon whose support success will depend. This early step is important in bringing about line management commitment to the process and specific goals of the survey. It is better to discover lack of support or disagreement on objectives before beginning the process.

Respondent Selection. Early in the process, the organization must decide whether a census or a sample of employees will be included. If a sample is agreed upon, will employees across the entire organization be sampled or only those within specific locations, business units, or particular job groups? Several factors must be weighed in making this decision:

- Is this survey envisioned as a trial? If so, a somewhat autonomous business unit might be selected.

- How important is total employee buy-in to the successful implementation of changes resulting from the survey?

- Will credibility be lessened if certain groups are not included?

- Is it practically or economically feasible to include larger numbers than those needed for statistical or practical significance?

- To what extent will it be important to break out data for specific segments of the work force?

In all cases, the sampling frame must match the goals of the survey. For example, in a broad-based effectiveness survey designed to provide total organization and unit feedback (including specific feedback to most work units with enough employees to protect confidentiality), it is almost impossible to achieve the desired results without a census of the work force. For example, if the firm decides to provide feedback to all units with at least ten completed questionnaires, and a 50 percent sample is selected with a completion rate of 80 percent, units with as many as twenty-five employees may not have enough completed questionnaires to provide confidential data. Thus, units of this size would either have to use broader divisional or organizational data or forgo the feedback and action planning process that was a key objective of the survey.

Another issue that is seldom evaluated is the impact of exclusion. In my previous example, which included 50 percent of the work force, every other employee in the firm might feel excluded. With a 50 percent sampling, this perception is likely to be even greater because the survey is far more visible than it would be with lower sampling rates (e.g., 10 percent).

Finally, when sampling is used, it is important to estimate the error rate that is acceptable. This should be done by carefully evaluating the number of employees that are likely to be obtained in the smallest cells of the design. Thus, for example, in the simple design in table 63–3, the expected number of managers with completed surveys is seventy-five. This means that each score (e.g., percentage answering favorably) will have an error rate of approximately ±7–11 percent and an error rate of approximately ±10–16 percent when comparing this group to another group of seventy-five employees (e.g., sales or

Table 63–3
Example of Employee Sample by Job Groups

Job Group	Total Employees	Sample Drawn	Expected Completes
Managers	500	100	75
Sales	500	100	75
Clerical	750	150	75
Total	1,750	350	225

clerical employees in table 63–3). These are careful considerations that should be addressed at the outset of the process. There are many other complexities in sampling design, such as proportional sampling and weighting, that are beyond the scope of this chapter. The internal or external consultants should be able to guide the firm easily through these decisions.

Developing the Survey Instruments.

Conducting Developmental Interviews. Not all employee surveys require this step, but many do. Developmental interviews usually consist of one-on-one interviews with key employees (often senior executives) and focus group interviews with a cross-section of the targeted population. In a broad survey of effectiveness, this might include focus groups with major job groups (e.g., clerical, professional, hourly employees) or with representative employees in major locations or business units (e.g., different plants, product lines, functions).

There are several major reasons for conducting exploratory interviews and focus groups. They:

- Provide rich qualitative information that will assist in developing a high-quality, comprehensive questionnaire.

- Provide details about the reasons behind particular problems or issues.

- Provide an important introduction to and understanding of the organization for external consultants.

- Begin to set the proper climate for the survey—that is, they help to promote the correct information into the grapevine regarding the purpose and conduct (e.g., confidentiality of the process) of the survey.

- Encourage employee participation in the process. Again, this helps buy-in at later stages.

Typical focus group interviews contain a random sample of six to ten employees in the job class desired. It is important that employees be selected such that matching supervisors and subordinates are not in the same session, status differences are minimal, key gate-keepers or perceived informants (e.g., president's secretary) are not included, and all gripers or yea-sayers are not picked. Usually random selection eliminates most of these problems and ensures representation across major demographic categories.

Questionnaire Development. Input for the questionnaire typically comes from a variety of sources: interviews and focus groups as described previously, the planned goals of the survey, the internal team responsible for the survey, the consultant's experience with the area of study (e.g., benefits or broad satisfaction dimensions), internal documents on the subject (e.g., dimensions specified in a mission statement or credo), and prior surveys of the subject.

Usually the consultant or survey team drafts a questionnaire that is reviewed, revised, and often pretested with a sample of employees. Pretesting is not essential when the items have been used before with success. The questionnaire often contains:

- Core items for which there are normative data (historical or comparative) or an interest in tracking over time.
- Special items that deal with current issues only and are unlikely to be used again.
- Demographic and job-related items (e.g., age, tenure, department, location).
- Open-ended items that allow employees an opportunity to write in an unstructured way about various issues.

It is important that all comparison information (different tenure groups or different business units) be included in the questionnaire, or it will be impossible to analyze them later.

Administering the Questionnaire. There are numerous ways to administer questionnaires to employees. They all have trade-offs that must be considered. Most of these trade-offs juggle scheduling ease, cost, and response rate. Table 63–4 highlights the major approaches. The preferred method is group administration on paid company time because it yields the highest response rates (often 80–95 percent with good scheduling), provides the most control over the conditions under which the survey is being completed (full attention, quiet environment, a coordinator who can answer questions), affords a personal opportunity by the survey administrator to reinforce importance, confidentiality, and how the data will be used, and demonstrates the organization's commitment to the process (on company time; personal versus impersonal mode).

The approach that yields the next highest response rate is usually a questionnaire mailed to the work location ("At-Work Mail" in table 63–4). This approach typically results in response rates of 60–75 percent, which vary across job groups. For example, completed questionnaires among hourly employees are usually lower, while those among outside sales personnel are frequently higher (sales personnel are often used to dealing with the corporate location by mail).

Finally, participation is lowest when "At-Home Mail" approaches are used (typically 30–50 percent, depending on job group). Obviously, the control over the home environment is the least, and there is no guarantee that the employee actually completed the questionnaire.

No mention of telephone interviews has been made to this point. There is good reason. Telephone interviews with employees can be very difficult to administer (not to mention dangerous to interpret) because of the sensitive nature of many of the ques-

Table 63–4
Alternative Survey Administration Methods

Method	Typical Response Rate	Employee Involvement Level	Employee Understanding	Control Over Process	Administrative Complexity
In-person at work on company time	80–95 percent	Highest	Highest	Highest	Most complex
At-work mail	60–75 percent	Moderate	Good	Some control over conditions	Moderate complexity
At-home mail	30–50 percent[a]	Lowest	Lowest	Minimal	Minimal
Telephone[b]					

Note: Administrative complexity increases as sampling complexity increases.
[a] Often lower with hourly employees.
[b] Not normally recommended with employee surveys.

tions in a typical employee questionnaire. For example, it is hard to establish enough trust during a telephone interview so that an employee feels comfortable, for example, telling a stranger the problems he is having with his boss. He may be hard pressed to criticize corporate policies openly without some better assurance that his answers will be confidential. Thus, employee surveys are rarely conducted by telephone unless the subject matter is nonthreatening.

For certain purposes, other methods may be adequate. For example, in collecting benefits information, it may be important to have spouse input to determine levels and types of duplicate coverage. Thus, a questionnaire mailed to the home may be totally appropriate. A telephone questionnaire may be appropriate, for example, for a brief poll of employee interest in direct-deposit handling of paychecks.

Regardless of method chosen, key pieces of communication should include information on the importance of the survey (how it will be used), how confidentiality will be protected (in the handling of the questionnaire and the reporting of data), and a promise of feedback.

Processing the Data. After questionnaires are completed, care should be taken to ensure that the data are adequately cleaned (elimination of nonsense responses and other noninterpretable responses), coded, and entered (including data entry accuracy checks). Tables should be created that are easily interpreted and understandable to managers who may need to use them. Typically, it is useful to have information categorized by favorable and unfavorable responses so that quick scans of the data across different classifications can be made.

Data should be broken out as finely as possible without compromising confidentiality. Identification of groups with fewer than ten or so employees should be done with care. Identifying groups with fewer than five employees should definitely be avoided; most employees I have interviewed seem to feel quite safe when they are grouped with ten or more peers and quite threatened when the number drops below five peers. Why break data out even this finely? In an effectiveness survey, when follow-up employee participation is desired, data must be relevant to specific units. In such a survey, managers will be expected to discuss data from their units with their subordinates. Without a fine breakout, this goal would be nearly impossible. *It should be noted that information needed to break the data out should be included in the questionnaire or it will be impossible to segment the employee population later.*

Analyzing, Interpreting, and Reporting the Findings.

Analysis and Interpretation. Data can be analyzed in a number of ways:

- *Absolute.* A criterion of dissatisfaction or unfavorable responses might be set (e.g., 25 percent) that will trigger a more detailed analysis. Typically, favorable scores (percentage responding to a particular item favorably) are used to interpret most items across job, demographic, or organizational groups.

- *Comparative.* Differences in scores below or above other groups or the business unit as a whole can provide insight into comparative performance. This should be done cautiously, however, to ensure that similar groups or units are being compared. For example, comparing a unit comprised almost entirely of hourly employees to another with a majority of professional employees may be misleading. Furthermore, differences across similar groups may be due to a number of factors. The purpose of the comparison is to begin the inquiry as to likely cause(s).

- *Normative.* Differences in scores above or below previous surveys can be a useful way to evaluate change. This type of comparison can also be used with external norms (e.g., industry, job groups).

The best way to sort the results from an effectiveness survey is to ascertain overall organizational strengths and weaknesses. These are content areas that are generally weak or strong across most job groups and organizational units. A matrix (see figure 63–1) can be created that maps content areas by job groups or organizational units. This type of matrix can be created at any level (firm as a whole, a business unit, or an individual manager) to help profile major themes.

After overall weaknesses are determined, specific items can be evaluated along with the qualitative data (developmental interviews) to develop a better understanding of the causes of the areas of concern. Dramatic conclusions should not result from negative performance on a single item; instead, conclusions should be drawn only when clear patterns of results are obtained across numerous items relative to the same group. For example, quality of supervision should not be a major area of concern if one item of supervision is rated low for a particular job group. However, if most employees across the company rate supervisor communication skills low (along with many other skills), then a more thorough evaluation of supervisory selection and training might be in order.

Figure 63–1. Analysis Matrix

Topics	Job Groups					Content Summary
	Mgr.	Sup.	Prof.	Cler.	Hour.	
Benefits	+	+	+	+	+	Clear Strength
Job Security	+	+		+	+	Strength for Most
Pay	+	–		–		
Communications		–	–	–		Concern for Some
Supervision	–	–	–		–	Area of Concern
Advancement	+	–				
Productivity	+	–	–	–	–	Area of Concern
Job Group Summary	Positive Group	Depressed Group				

Notes: (+/–): Indicates group is substantially above (+) or below (–) norm of comparison group.

Job group codes: MGR = managers; SUP = supervisors; PROF = professionals; CLER = clerical; HOUR = hourly employees.

Job groups should not normally be compared to each other. Norms for each group frequently differ. There is often a hierarchy of expected responses, with managers most favorable and hourly employees least favorable.

Reporting of Results. The reporting of results for employee surveys will vary considerably depending on purpose. As has been the case throughout this chapter, the more complicated case of an overall effectiveness survey will be addressed in more detail. For simple program evaluation or targeted surveys (e.g., safety or benefits), results should be reported back to the primary decision makers in the respective functional areas. Again, if the survey has been conducted as a direct result of information that was deemed important for planning or decision making, then the survey results should flow naturally into action plans.

With broad-based effectiveness or attitude surveys, corporate culture assessments, or strategic evaluations, senior management should be intensively involved in the feedback of results and action-planning process that follows. An in-person presentation of overall findings should be made to the management team. It often includes a reasonably detailed review of the findings from each major con-

tent area coupled with a summary of strengths and weaknesses. Management should be encouraged to participate in a discussion of the findings both during and immediately after the formal presentation. I have found the in-person presentation to be one of the best catalysts to follow-up strategy and action.

Using the Survey Findings

Guidelines for Successful Action Planning. The most important part of a successful survey is the action that follows the collection of information from employees: decisions that naturally follow from clear answers to critical questions, planning, implementation of policies and procedures, redesign of training programs, modification of benefits, and so forth. Without a clear process for survey follow-up, one can end up with little improvement, poor communication, management frustration, and disillusioned employees.

For a simple, more narrowly focused survey, some of these steps are not needed; however, for more complex surveys (e.g., broad-based effectiveness survey), careful attention to these steps can help ensure successful action. An experienced external consultant can be useful in two roles at this stage: as a facilitator who can guide management through the action planning process and as a sounding board regarding what other firms have done in response to similar issues.

Review of Findings with Management. Immediately following the presentation of results, it is useful for management to discuss their reactions and decide on next steps, including the feedback of the results to employees. Often it is useful for each manager to review the findings before meeting again as a group to set priorities.

Feedback to Employees. While management is reviewing the results, a summary of the findings for employees can be prepared. Often this takes the form of a news article in the company newspaper or newsletter, a special survey feedback report to all employees within the surveyed unit (not just those who participated in the survey), a letter or memo to all employees from senior management, or an in-person presentation by a senior executive or various senior managers. One of the best forms of feedback is face-to-face feedback within each work unit, presented by each level of management. Because issues may vary across units, however, it is important that some form of written communication documenting overall findings is distributed to all employees in the units that were surveyed.

Caution must be exercised to present a balanced summary of the findings. A "whitewash" of results will seriously undermine survey credibility and damage future survey efforts. It must be remembered that employees "know" the issues; if management does not send back consistent feedback, employees will be disillusioned with management and the usefulness of this vehicle. Also, survey feedback should occur within a reasonable period following the conduct of the survey (probably no longer than six months).

Setting Priorities on Issues. After management has had a brief opportunity to review the findings, another session should be scheduled (within a few weeks) to review the findings and to identify key issues that management wishes to address at a corporate level. This list should be manageable. Usually six to ten issues can be handled effectively.

Then management should discuss each issue in terms of its relative impact on the organization (e.g., fit with strategic goals, operational impact, potential cost) to determine the relative priority that each issue should receive. It is far better to tackle three issues well than to identify fifteen that will remain unsolved.

Identifying Causes and Potential Solutions. Once priorities have been set, the management team must now evaluate potential causes of problem areas identified, working through each priority area in turn. The search for causes may require additional information. If clarification of data is needed or secondary questions must be answered, additional focus groups with relevant employees are often useful. Frequently, the information needed is already available in the organization (e.g., benefits utilization data or safety records). After causes are clearly delineated, alternative solutions are generated, yielding various actions that will be taken to ameliorate issues identified as high priority.

Communicating Decisions, Assigning Tasks, and Setting a Timetable. After specific actions have been identified to address each issue, management should communicate the decisions to key individuals (or task forces) who will be responsible for implementation. Tasks should be assigned along with specific deadlines for completion.

Feedback on implementation status is essential at identified milestones. Furthermore, it is important to communicate to employees the steps that management is taking to address issues identified in the survey. This communication is important and, unfortunately, often ignored by many firms. The best approach is to keep employees informed throughout implementation, with a major announcement upon project completion that ties the actions to the survey findings ("Because of the poor ratings of our performance appraisal system identified in the survey last March, a new system is being introduced effective . . . ").

A Total Organizational Approach. This process need not, and should not, be confined to top management alone (the "top-down" approach). Instead, survey data that are relevant to each unit in the organization should be distributed to managers responsible for those units (marketing, the Des Plaines plant, the Park Ridge sales office, the word processing center in Kensington—that is, every functional or managerial unit if there are enough employees to break out the data confidentially). *This is a crucial step to improving organizational effectiveness that cannot be underscored enough.* That is, senior management can analyze, evaluate, and attack issues only at a total corporate level. But each manager responsible for an operational unit can act on *relevant* data pertaining to his or her unit. In order for this to be effective, there must be data available pertaining to each specific unit. This again goes back to adequate planning in designing the questionnaire, particularly the demographics, so that break-outs can be made for relevant organizational units.

Thus, if the data are available (and if there are enough subordinates to protect confidentiality), a given supervisor can be given survey data from his or her direct and/or indirect reports. With the proper training, each manager can use this information as feedback on managerial effectiveness, to improve the operating unit's effectiveness, and to make recommendations up the line on issues that need to be decided at higher levels of authority. By utilizing this process at all levels and within all functions of the surveyed population, solutions at all levels will be enacted.

In order for all managers to carry out this task effectively, they must be trained in how to interpret and use survey data. This is usually best accomplished through a brief workshop that covers survey feedback, data interpretation, and principles of conducting a feedback and action planning session with subordinates. Training is particularly effective if participants have a model to observe and emulate. Following such a session, managers should be capable of and motivated to analyze their own data, determine strengths and weaknesses, conduct a feedback and action planning session with their subordinates (or a larger group of indirect reports), formulate solutions within their own units, and make recommendations to their bosses regarding issues that transcend hierarchical levels or functional areas.

Thus, this process entails the flow of survey data down the organization through feedback sessions across each hierarchical level, action plans being formulated and implemented within each feedback unit, and recommendations for improvement flowing up the organization to appropriate levels where decisions can be made to address these issues. *This is a total organizational effectiveness approach.*

EMPLOYEE SURVEY MYTHS

Over the years, I have encountered many myths regarding employee surveys that have been detrimental to effective survey use and are in most cases incorrect.

Myth 1: "We will only raise employee expectations"

Probably the most frequently heard myth, the statement is only partially true. Yes, employee expectations can be increased beyond that which can reasonably be delivered. However, this is not solely a function of participation in a survey but of management communication regarding the program. Communication should be carefully crafted at the outset of any new program (not just an employee survey) to set correctly expectations regarding feedback, employee involvement, and expected use of the information. Employees, by and large, will develop expectations based on what they have been told unless communications credibility is dismally low.

Organizations get into trouble by overselling the benefits of survey participation (e.g., "it will improve your job; eliminate problems; change pay and benefits") and then fail to deliver. Again, much of this is eliminated if there is a clear purpose for conducting the survey to begin with. When its use is clear from the beginning, decisions will be made and solutions will result from the process.

A more appropriate message to employees is that the survey is an opportunity for them to participate by sharing their views on the issues included in the survey. If the firm plans to involve employees in the action planning process as described earlier, then they should be told. If not, the firm should not make promises that cannot be kept. Finally, if survey after survey is conducted with no visible action resulting, employees will become disenchanted with this process (as they would any other process), and future participation and involvement will decline.

Myth 2: "Employees won't be candid"

This belief seems to stem from a view that employees are manipulative or dishonest; I have found neither to be true. In fact, in-depth personal interviews or focus groups tend to confirm employees' sincere interest in improving their work situation. In most cases, this means open admission of problems, candor in describing the good and poor supervisors, and a balanced appraisal of organizational strengths and weaknesses. Furthermore, survey data are clearly not one-sided and tend to map reality quite well. Most managers in final presentations freely admit that the perceptions are indeed correct or understandable. Again, assessment from multiple viewpoints usually leads to the same conclusions.

Myth 3: "Only the complainers or yea-sayers will participate"

Obviously, the two views come from different people, often within the same organization. Fortunately, neither is true. If the survey is well designed, communicated, and administered, participation rates will be quite high (with group administration, often over 80 percent), eliminating this myth. This is clearly one advantage of a high participation rate. However, even when lower response rates are obtained, the data are seldom skewed either positively or negatively in such a way that this myth appears to be operating. In some surveys (e.g., survey of an issue that affects only certain employees or an issue that is not of high importance to most employees), a more bimodal distribution results, possibly indicating that those employees who had little to contribute or those who felt indifferent did not participate. This situation might overemphasize the stronger positive and negative views, but it seldom biases the overall results substantially.

Myth 4: "Employees will never sit through this"

Although a somewhat frequent comment, particularly with longer surveys (over 45 minutes), it seldom is a problem. The key issue here is how germane the subject matter is to employees. For most people, their jobs are an extremely important part of their lives, and they will take an active role in completing a survey that may have an impact on their job or company. From my experience in market versus employee research, it is usually easy to secure employee commitment to a survey that can take up to an hour to complete when it has relevance to the employee (e.g., his or her job or firm), whereas it is difficult to obtain even 15 minutes if the respondent is disinterested in the subject (e.g., more life insurance or flavor of toothpaste).

Myth 5: "Management won't listen. Nothing will result"

This myth is not always a myth, but it certainly is a red flag for the external consultant. This can mean that a well-intentioned middle manager or internal consultant is pushing a process that has fallen on deaf ears for a number of reasons. It is important to remember that this process should be driven by a committed management and viewed as important information for decision making. In this case, often management is not aware of the potential benefits to be gained by using this tool. Or the internal consultant or manager may lack the credibility that an external consultant might bring (i.e., external referents, familiarity with similar firms or competitors, the expert or specialist role, not part of the day-to-day politics, perceived neutrality).

In my experience, management commitment is not only possible but essential to successful follow-up. Thus, I use several approaches to secure management commitment and involvement in the survey process from the beginning. Without this commitment, the survey should probably not be conducted unless there are rather compelling reasons.

Myth 6: "Managers won't understand or use the survey results"

If the process is well orchestrated, including adequate training of managers in survey interpretation and action planning, supported by top management, and relevant (important information was gathered), then this statement is unfounded. More often, managers refuse to get involved later because they were not informed or involved earlier in the process. They are too often being asked to act on overly complex information that was collected in a vacuum, without their input and without senior management support. Why should they bother? They see little benefit to them.

On the other hand, if they participated in the development of the survey, had input to the questionnaire (either directly or through similar managers), are thoroughly informed about the findings and their implications, are trained in survey action planning, and see strong management commitment, then they will quickly participate.

Myth 7: "Data are too general; there is no specific information"

This is a myth when the survey has been well designed. Frequently, surveys have been criticized for lacking specificity. This is overcome in several ways. First, developmental interviews (discussed earlier) help to identify specific issues and causes so that items can be written with more specificity to test various hypotheses. Second, the interviews can provide additional information regarding causes and potential solutions during the interpretation of survey findings, *if the interviews are detailed, well documented, and designed to elicit information about specific problems and alternative solutions.* Third, the survey should provide open-ended comments on specific issues. Finally, this comment is often a cop-out by those who do not wish to take the required steps to generate solutions. The survey should not be viewed as the solution but only as a catalyst in the decision process.

Myth 8: "This is not a good time to conduct a survey"

A frequently heard myth, it always seems to be a "terrible" time to conduct a survey. This complaint often stems from hidden fears that the conditions will not be perfect to collect "neutral" data, the organization is not in a steady state (too much fluctuation now), it will be inconvenient at this time, or the survey will create embarrassment. The myth can also stem from a manipulative objective (at a later time, the survey will add credibility or support to a favored program or department).

Most of these fears stem from a lack of understanding of the potential benefits to be derived from the survey process, an assumption that the survey will be used punitively, and a false belief that change will stop within the organization so that "ideal" data can be collected (hardly ideal if the lack of change is the exception). The manipulative objective is usually to collect data at a time when particular programs will receive the highest marks. The subsequent section on timing will address this issue further. From my experience over hundreds of surveys, *it is rarely a bad time to conduct a survey if the survey is goal driven and carefully designed to minimize the impact of potentially adverse events.*

EMPLOYEE EXPECTATIONS

A nonmyth is the expectations that employees do have regarding surveys:

1. That they will receive feedback on the survey findings.
2. That management will take actions based on the results.

These two expectations seem to be present after conducting most employee surveys. This does not imply that each employee wishes to see data from every survey item—far from it. Most employees expect to see a summary of the overall findings—both strengths and weaknesses. This signals that management has heard their views.

Second, without action being taken on survey findings, employees will soon learn to ignore the process. Such a process is best left uninitiated. Far too often, management gets caught up in follow-up action that leads to a number of activities—some directly tied to the survey and others only indirectly—and fails to report on actions or changes that were survey related. This failure is in communication, not the efficacy of the survey.

WHEN TO USE EMPLOYEE SURVEYS

This section might be better labeled "when not to conduct an employee survey." Employee surveys should be used as part of a broader decision process, when some of the potential benefits described in the first section of the chapter are obtainable. Surveys can provide a wealth of precise data on work force attitudes, behaviors, beliefs, and intentions. In fact, one of the major advantages of surveys is the precision they bring to the decision-making process. Too often, organizations operate on rumors about how people feel about issues. Surveys can separate fiction from fact in this process and identify precisely how employees in various segments feel about the issues.

Surveys do not deliver decisions. That must come from managers or researchers who interpret the information in the light of key corporate objectives. Surveys do not usually provide all the answers either. They can frequently represent the starting point for a change in corporate culture or a comprehensive look at organizational effectiveness. Sometimes additional questions are raised that required follow-up data collection.

There are a few occasions where the use of surveys may not be warranted or desired. Sometimes delay is appropriate; other times the survey is simply inappropriate:

- Immediately before or during a strike.
- During a union election campaign when an NLRB election has been scheduled.
- During periods of great internal strife when the process cannot be managed effectively.
- When there is curiosity but no commitment to action.
- When the survey is to be used for a different purpose than that which has been communicated to employees.
- When you are seeking an intensive understanding of a phenomenon where little data are available. Here, in-depth interviews might be a better starting point.

CONCLUSIONS

An employee survey can be a powerful tool to improve organizations when used to obtain information that will enable decisions to be made or actions to be taken that improve employee and organizational outcomes. Most important, an employee survey provides precise data that enable management to understand better the attitudes, beliefs, intentions, and behaviors of various groups of employees that comprise the unique culture of an organization. It is these perceptions that drive the activities of the business daily and in a large part determine its ultimate success.

REFERENCES

Bartel, A.P. (1982). Wages, nonwage job characteristics, and labor mobility. *Industrial and Labor Relations Review, 35* (4), 578–589.

Cappelli, P., & Sterling, W.P. (1988). Union bargaining decisions and contract ratifications: The 1982 and 1984 auto agreements. *Industrial and Labor Relations Review, 41* (2), 195–209.

Cascio, W.F. (1987). *Costing human resources: Financial impact of behavior in organizations.* Boston: Kent Publishing.

Cook, R., Walizer, D., & Mace, D. (1976). Illicit drug use in the Army: A social-organizational analysis. *Journal of Applied Psychology, 61,* 262–272.

Davids, A., & Mahoney, J. (1957). Personality dynamics and accident proneness in an industrial setting. *Journal of Applied Psychology, 41,* 303–305.

Filley, A.C., House, R.J., & Kerr, S. (1976). *Managerial process and organizational behavior.* Glenview, IL: Scott, Foresman.

Fiorito, J. Gallagher, D.G., & Greer, C.R. (1986). Determinants of unionism: A review of the literature. In Kendrith M. Rowland and Gerald R. Ferris (Eds.), *Research in Personnel and Human Resources Management* (vol. 4, 269–306) Greenwich, CT: JAI Press.

Getman, J.G., Goldberg, S.B., & Herman, J.B. (1976). *Union representation elections: Law and reality.* New York: Russell Sage Foundation.

Goodman, P.S., & Atkin, R.S. (1984). *New approaches to understanding, measuring, and managing employee absence.* San Francisco: Jossey-Bass.

Hawthorne, B. (1977–1978). Job dissatisfaction: A drug related issue. *Drug Forum, 6,* 187–195.

Heneman III, H.G., & Sandver, M.H. (1983). Predicting the outcome of union certification elections: A review of the literature. *Industrial and Labor Relations Review, 36* (4), 537–559.

Hoppock, R. (1935). *Job satisfaction.* New York: Harper.

Iaffaldano, M., & Muchinsky, P.S. (1985). Job satisfaction and performance: A meta-analysis. *Psychological Bulletin, 97* (2), 712–721.

Kornhauser, A.W., & Sharp, A.A. (1932). Employee attitudes: Suggestions from a study in a factory. *Personnel Journal, 10,* 393–404.

Kraut, A. (1975). Predicting turnover of employees from measured job attitudes. *Organizational Behavior and Human Performance, 13,* 233–243.

Mirvis, P., & Lawler III, E.E. (1977). Measuring the financial impact of employee attitudes. *Journal of Applied Psychology, 62,* 1–8.

Mitchell, O.S. (1982). Fringe benefits and labor mobility. *Journal of Human Resources, 17* (2), 286–298.

Mobley, W., Griffeth, R., Hand, H., & Meglino, B. (1979). Review and conceptual analysis of the employee turnover process. *Psychological Bulletin, 86,* 493–522.

Petty, M.M., McGee, G.W., & Cavender, J.W. (1984). A meta-analysis of the relationship between individual job satisfaction and individual performance. *Academy of Management Review, 9* (4), 712–721.

Pestongee, D., Singh, A., & Ahmod, N. (1977). Job satisfaction and accidents. *Indian Journal of Industrial Relations, 13,* 65–71.

Price, J.L. (1977). *The study of turnover.* Ames: Iowa State University Press.

Rosse, J.G., & Hulin, C.L. (1985). Adaptation to work: An analysis of employee health, withdrawal, and change. *Organizational Behavior and Human Decision Processes, 36,* 324–347.

Rosse, J.G., Keaveny, T., & Fossum, J. (1987). Predicting union election outcomes: The role of job attitudes, union attitudes, and co-worker preferences. *Proceedings of the 40th Industrial Relations Research Association Annual Conference,* Chicago.

Rosse, J.G., & Miller, H.E. (1984) Relationship between absenteeism and other employee behaviors. In P.S. Goodman & R.S. Atkin (Eds.), *New approaches to understanding, measuring, and managing employee absence* (194–228). San Francisco: Jossey-Bass.

Roethlisberger, F., & Dickson, W. (1939). *Management and the worker.* Cambridge: Harvard University Press.

Schiemann, W.A. (1987). Proprietary client research.

Schwab, D.P., & Cummings, L.L. (1970) Theories of performance and satisfaction: A review. *Industrial Relations, 9,* 408–430.

Smith, F. (1977). Work attitudes as predictors of attendance on a specific day. *Journal of Applied Psychology, 62,* 16–19.

Steers, R.M., & Rhodes, S.R. (1978). Major influences on employee attendance: A process model. *Journal of Applied Psychology, 63* (4), 391–407.

Steers, R.M., & Rhodes, S.R. (1984). Knowledge and spec-ulation about absenteeism. In P.S. Goodman & R.S. Atkin (Eds.), *New approaches to understanding, measuring, and managing employee absence* (229–275). San Francisco: Jossey-Bass.

64 CUSTOMER SURVEY RESEARCH: EXTENDING THE PARTNERSHIP

Maynard A. Howe, Dee Gaeddert

Corporations throughout the world are experiencing the problems of marketing their products and services in an environment frustrated with accelerated technological advances, heightened competitive pressures, and customers whose loyalty is a fragile, if not elusive, commodity. Corporate decision makers cannot afford to develop positioning strategies in a vacuum. If they and their companies are to survive, they will have to develop innovative information strategies that will help them recognize and capitalize on new and existing market opportunities. These information strategies, properly implemented, will arm executives with relevant and accurate information—information that will significantly reduce the number of risks in the decision-making process and provide specific direction for the company.

Strategies for gathering information that measure and monitor the pulse of the marketplace have involved a variety of methods and philosophies. Traditional marketing approaches, for the most part, have not been able to provide management with the data or confidence to plan strategically (Peters, 1987; Holt, Horst & Giovanni, 1984; McKenna, 1987; Desatnick, 1987). Traditional market research and statistical methods are often inappropriate in an accelerating business environment. Information collected from these methods has often forced management to make assumptive interpretations and draw conclusions upon incorrect, insufficient, or inappropriate data. Recently, traditional methods were used by three of the largest, most respected research firms in the United States to predict the growth of the personal computer software industry. A review of their findings demonstrated the inconsistency and unreliability of the data, as well as the inappropriateness of this method. Their projections for 1987 ranged from $3.7 billion to $13.6 billion (McKenna, 1987). How valuable and cost-effective was this research? What conclusions and strategic recommendations would you have made if you were in the software business or considering entering it? What actions could have been

tied to these research results? The lack of a systematic approach to the assessment of market and customer needs and the practical application of the information gathered is one of the most vital concerns that corporations will face during the next decade (Holt et al., 1984; Waterman, 1987; Peters, 1987; Peters & Austin, 1985; Peters & Waterman, 1982; Desatnick, 1987; Lele & Sheth, 1987).

How can corporations measure and monitor existing customer needs, discover new markets, and plan initiatives based on sufficient, accurate, and reliable information? How will they be assured of customer loyalty and commitment? How will they know whether their research departments are focusing on developing the right products or services? And when and how should their products or services be released to the marketplace? Discovering the answers to these questions requires a future-oriented, proactive strategy built around a sound partnering philosophy of the customer-vendor relationship. Both the contemporary research of others and our own research confirms this approach and supports the premise that to be successful in developing strategic marketing plans, companies must begin to establish better relationships with their existing customers. In addition, we have found the most vital component for creating and maintaining customers and markets is to identify, analyze, and manage partnership relations consistently. It is not a coincidence that the few companies that practice this philosophy are consistently the market leaders.

Neither is it a coincidence that a failure to assess the needs of customers leads to a serious decline in the marketability of a company's products or services. A recent analysis of Japanese marketing techniques (Lazer, Murata & Kosaka, 1985) points out that it was neglect by established American companies and markets that presented a remarkable opportunity for Japanese companies to produce products that met the demands of American consumers. The average Japanese consumer products engineer spends six months each year in the field listening to customers (Peters, 1986). How does that compare to the contact American workers have with their constituents?

From large to small organizations, management is becoming more aware of the fact that their profits and the growth of their businesses are dependent on their ability to develop closer relationships with their customers (Bohl, 1987; Lele & Sheth, 1987; Waterman, 1987; Peters, 1986, 1987; Peters & Austin, 1985; Peters & Waterman, 1982; Jackson, 1985; Desatnick, 1987). While many of the executives we have surveyed have proclaimed that customer relations is the number one priority in their company, until recently few have been willing to make the commitment to put their words into action. The research of Tom Peters and Nancy Austin confirms that while executives talk a good game of "customer first," the majority are hesitant to initiate programs that reinforce this philosophy. Their survey of 172 executives, 134 of whom were presidents of companies, unanimously ranked long-term customer relations and satisfaction as the number one priority in their companies. Yet *all* 172 executives admitted that they had not assigned accountability for measuring and monitoring these relationships (Peters & Austin, 1985; Marr, 1986). Numerous other studies, including those conducted by the American Management Association (AMA), have shown conclusively that successful, high-growth companies and those organizations nominated by their peers as the optimal performers in customer relations integrate the information they collect into their strategic business plans (Bohl, 1987). The AMA study also revealed that these successful market leaders make customer relations a total corporate objective, "the business of the business" (Jackson, 1985), and their expenditures are evidence that their commitment is more than mere posters and slogans that pay only lip-service.

If this is the kind of "corporate intelligence" that executives are convinced is the formula for success, then why the apparent reluctance to initiate programs and systematic procedures for measuring and monitoring customer relations and market trends? If creating and maintaining a customer is the undisputed objective of every business, then why is there a hesitancy to "partner" with the most important assets a company will ever have: its customers? The answer is simple: corporations do not know how. There are no established guidelines. There are gaping holes in the coverage of establishing and maintaining customer relationships by marketing academics and by marketing practitioners. "The literature on marketing clearly acknowledges the importance of the customer, but it pays surprisingly scant attention to the dynamics of customer relationships over extended periods: to patterns of account relationships over time and to strategies and tactics for winning and keeping customers for the long term" (Cron, 1974).

The remainder of this chapter will address the needs of the marketing practitioner and those organizations that desire the methodology for measuring and monitoring customer relations. It is an endeavor to fill a void in the marketing literature and provide a strategic model for accomplishing what every organization must commit to if it is to grow and remain competitive.

STRATEGIC MODEL

There is a demand for a more professional approach to meeting information needs that measures and monitors customer-vendor relations. In response to this demand, we have developed from our empirical base a strategic model aimed at providing a new, interesting, and, most important, a practical approach to this neglected problem. This approach is based on extensive work with a variety of organizations surveying their customers, vendors, and employees. It addresses a failure in the literature to provide a suitable solution to this issue. The strategic model for improving customer-vendor relationships in figure 64–1 provides an attempt to demonstrate visually the interaction process between the two parties. While the model incorporates elements from perception, communications, systems, and interactional theories, it is more dynamic in providing solutions to the often distorted perceptions and communications that are detrimental to the building of effective partnerships.

The strategic model illustrates both traditional and contemporary approaches to customer-vendor relations. The traditional approach, represented by the broken arrows connecting the customer and vendor (the organization), describes a relationship impeded by perceptual distortions resulting from information that is often inaccurate, inadequate, insufficient, and inappropriate. The information is typically transmitted or collected in piecemeal fashion through informal channels such as point of purchase

Figure 64–1. Strategic Model for Improving Customer-Vendor Relations

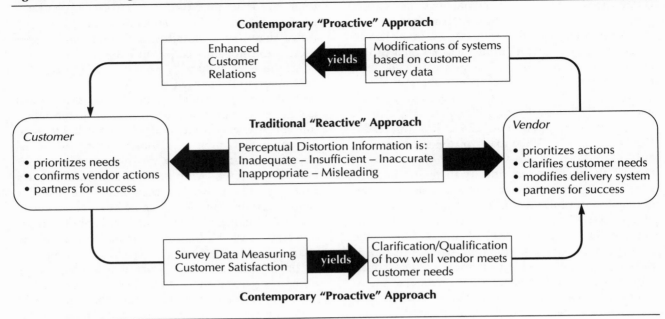

discussions, sales and customer service records, customer complaint records, the grapevine, and assumptions made about why customers terminate their relationships with vendors. While these may appear to be good sources for obtaining information that might be helpful in improving customer-vendor relations, our research and that of others described previously has demonstrated that few organizations systematically collect even this level of information. And when they do, the information collected is rarely meaningful and often unreliable. However, since these are the only data they have available to them, they are forced to make assumptions and draw conclusions that have not only cost their organizations substantial dollars but have done more to alienate customers than ally them.

What distinguishes the traditional methods of gathering customer information from the contemporary method we advocate? The traditional method waits for a customer to initiate the communication; it is reactive. The contemporary approach seeks the customer out; is proactive.

Reactive versus Proactive

A large Fortune 500 company that manufactures specialized graphics boards for computers was having a quality problem with three of its larger customers, which accounted for approximately 18 percent of its revenues. Two of the customers were threatening to terminate their relationship with the vendor, and the third was asking for financial remuneration for losses due to excessive delays in replacement of defective boards. The quality control department claimed that their defect rate was less than 0.1, and the manager had not been hesitant in telling the customers that it must be something in their system that was problematic; it certainly was not in his. After several months of finger pointing, substantial investments in quality control procedures, and the loss of one customer, the president asked for our assistance in solving the crisis. Within two days, by gathering information from customers, we were able to trace the problem to the shipping department, which had been marking these customer's boards with the wrong code. The problem was an administrative quality issue, not a defect issue. Shortly thereafter, we implemented a customer survey that included a section for assessing quality. Customers identified the mismanagement and mislabeling of product codes as their number one complaint. Changes were immediately made. Had this survey been implemented three months earlier as a proactive rather than reactive measure, a customer could have been saved and customer relations could have been improved instead of complicated.

Inundated with perceptual distortions and inaccurate, unreliable, and piecemeal information, the traditional approach to customer-vendor relations has distinct consequences. The interaction is both linear and reactive, resulting in an atmosphere of defensiveness: who is right versus who is wrong.

On the other hand, as the example suggests, the contemporary approach provides data that are quantitative, more reliable, and continuous and clarify how well the vendor is meeting the customer's needs in a variety of critical areas. Armed with this information, the vendor has the opportunity to implement actions that improve or modify delivery systems in those areas identified by the survey data as critical customer needs. This approach is then periodically repeated to ensure that the customer's pulse is continuously monitored.

The strategic model is an ongoing, dynamic process. It provides organizations with the ability to break from traditional approaches that are primarily reactive—waiting for a crisis to happen and reacting to it—to a more contemporary, proactive approach —anticipating, clarifying, and identifying customer needs as part of the planning process. Furthermore, as the model suggests, it is an interactive approach that keeps the channels of communication open and free from perceptual distortion, both key elements in creating strong customer-vendor partnerships. Strategies for achieving a contemporary proactive approach to customer relations implied by this model must be implemented with a keen attention to methodologically sound procedures.

SURVEY METHODOLOGY

Many methods can be used for building more effective customer relations. These include approaches such as mail and telephone surveys, focus groups, in-depth interviews, point-of-purchase surveys, 800 numbers for inbound customer comments, and others. The appropriateness and usefulness of each will vary depending on the type of industry and the size of organization. Our experience in organizational research nationally and internationally has resulted in a systematic procedure for conducting effective customer surveys. When this step-by-step approach is followed, it provides organizations with a methodologically sound data base that can be used for action planning, strategic positioning, and a periodic tracking mechanism for evaluating the effectiveness of actions implemented.

Step 1: Design of the Survey Instrument

The most important step of the entire survey process is the design of the instrument. This is the step that requires a clear definition of exactly what will be measured and, consequently, what will be learned. It is the step that determines how questions will be asked, in what format answers will be received, and consequently how the data can be analyzed. Finally, it is the step that makes it possible to increase the sense of ownership in the research project among various groups and levels within the organization, determining the level of acceptance the project will find. The survey design sets the agenda for the organization and its customers and in so doing communicates what is valued and what will hold priority.

To accomplish these tasks it is extremely important to involve key people within the organization in the survey design phase of the project. There are three ways to achieve this effectively. First, a focus group method can be used. This involves identifying and bringing together in one place those key individuals to discuss in a structured yet flexible format what is most important for the organization to know about its customers. Second, the same goal can be achieved by individually interviewing the key people identified, once again using a structured interview guide (see figure 64–2). The guide allows the flexibility to pursue topics of particular interest to those being interviewed. Third, the opinions of key individuals within your organization may be gathered by circulating a brief questionnaire asking them to indicate the topics that should be measured and the importance of each to the survey.

When designing a measurement tool, it is recommended to begin the process keeping in mind a hierarchy of topics that should be addressed. This hierarchy consists of examining topics at five levels: universal topics, topics unique to a particular industry, topics unique to a particular organization, topics that have surfaced through existing organizational listening channels, and topics that are required measurements of established programs.

1. Identify and include those universal topics proved through previous experience and research to be important in measuring customers' views. Our research has concluded that these topics include:

Advertising: Assess the impact of the advertising efforts through the eyes of customers.

Commitment: Go beyond customer satisfaction to evaluate the loyalty of your customers and your vulnerability to the competition.

Figure 64–2. Customer Survey Interview Guide

Quality

1. How do you, personally, define quality?
2. How do you think your customers perceive your product quality? Why?
3. Have you experienced any quality problems that you are aware of? [get specifics]
4. What specific steps have been taken to improve quality in the last year? Do you feel quality *has* improved?

Communication

5. What kinds of product information/training do you provide to your customers?
6. How do you keep them informed about new or improved products/services?

Advertising/Promotion

7. What types of advertising/promotion do you offer (print media, electronic media)?
8. Do you work *with* customers in any way regarding advertising or promotion? How (or should you)?
9. What kind of name recognition do you feel you have with your customers? Do you feel you need to work to improve it?
10. What feedback do you receive from your customers about your advertising/promotion?

Competition

11. Who are your biggest competitors?
12. How do you feel your company compares to the competition re: quality, price, service, reputation, delivery, administrative procedures (i.e., invoicing, scheduling)?
13. How do you think your customers perceive you compared to the competition in the above areas?

Customer Service

14. Do you have customer service personnel? [If not, who deals with customers?]
15. What are their specific job duties/responsibilities? (e.g., Are they responsible for on-time delivery? accurate, timely paperwork? problem solving? answering product/policy questions? taking orders? etc.)
16. How are these people selected/training?
17. Do you experience any turnover problems which might affect your customers?

General

18. What are the most positive aspects, in your opinion, of the XYZ Company – customer relationship right now?
19. What are the most negative aspects?
20. What do you think XYZ Company could be doing to help their customers that they are not doing now?

Communications: Evaluate efforts to disseminate information to customers.

Company image: Compare customer's perception of the company's image to the image desired.

Competition: Compare how well the organization stacks up against the competition.

Product: Establish how well the company's products or services are meeting the needs and wants of its customers.

Sales personnel: Find out if the company's personnel are coming across as problem solvers to their customers.

Service: Assess the company's service efforts as perceived by its customers.

Quality: Evaluate the customer's perception of quality as it relates to your products and services.

Excellence orientation: Determine if customers perceive excellence as your company's goal.

Driving force: What do customers perceive as the dynamics behind the company?

2. Identify and include those topics unique to the company's specific industry group. For example, service organizations will have different concerns about their customer relationships from organizations that manufacture a product. Or industries who sell through a distribution system will have a different focus from those who have a direct sales force.

3. Identify and include those topics unique to the specific organization—for example, specific programs (e.g., quality programs, customer service efforts, listening channels) that your organization has already implemented are prime topics for evaluation. In addition, actions being considered for the future present opportunities for measuring customer needs prior to implementation. For example, a company recently made plans to install a quality hot line at a cost of approximately $800,000. An assessment of customer needs was conducted prior to the implementation decision. The results of the assessment demonstrated that the quality hot line was not perceived as a quality improvement by customers but a potential detriment to their ability to communicate directly with technical service personnel. Any topic that affects an organization's customers is worthy of consideration for inclusion in the survey design.

4. Identify and include those topics that have surfaced through existing sales channels as topics of interest to customers. These channels may include feedback from the direct sales force, distributors, or customer service representatives. They may also

include comments or complaints that have been registered through the organization's listening channels. These customer comments or complaints are excellent targets for measurement through the survey process. Customer perceptions of problems, whether or not justified, are problems for the organization and should be assessed.

5. Identify and include topics that are required measurements for compliance with established programs. For example, if an organization is applying for the Malcolm Baldridge National Quality Award, it will be important to measure the organization's understanding of customer requirements and expectations in addition to how well those requirements and expectations are met.

When the topics to be included in the survey have been identified, they need to be translated into a viable survey instrument. While it is recommended that a survey design expert be consulted for this phase of the process, there are several general guidelines for survey design that should be followed:

1. Keep the length of the instrument to an administration time of 30 minutes or less. Remember that asking customers to complete a survey is asking them to do a favor for the organization.

2. Survey design is helped by simplicity. Straightforward, clearly worded items can be achieved by avoiding several common problems of item construction. For example, consider this double-barreled question: "Company XYZ's product warranties and product return policies compare favorably with those offered by other companies." If customers rated company XYZ negatively on this item, would one assume its warranty policy, its product return policy, or both warranty and return policies are problems? Or consider this item: "Please rate company XYZ on the accessibility of their staff." If respondents indicated room for improvement on this item, where would company XYZ take action to improve the accessibility of its personnel? More clarity is needed to specify which personnel are being rated (e.g., sales, customer service, order entry, receptionist).

3. Use response formats that lend themselves to the type of data analysis planned. This requires a consultation during the design phase with the person or group who will be responsible for analyzing the data. Various response formats are illustrated in figure 64–3.

4. Consider carefully the consequences of asking customers' their view of sensitive issues that can-

not or will not be changed. Asking questions about these topics may raise expectations that change will occur.

5. When designing a survey instrument for an international audience, determine the cultural and language nuances that may affect how the survey items will be interpreted. Consider, too, how the survey process itself will be received by the international respondents.

6. Be sure all items are behaviorally linked and action oriented. Ask this question of each item: "When the data are collected, will it be clear what actions can be taken to address the issue raised?"

7. Design items that measure both the areas assumed to be organizational strengths as well as those areas known to need improvement. It is very important to be able to identify what the organization is doing well in addition to those areas of concern. Employees need to hear both if they are to drive the solutions throughout the organization without defensiveness.

Step 2: Pilot Test

When the design of the instrument has been completed, conduct a pilot test of the survey with a small number of customers (fewer than twenty). Conduct the pilot test in a fashion that closely approximates the method planned for the full-scale survey project. Be sure to include a section for open-ended responses to a question such as, "In what other ways could company XYZ serve you better?" Examine the pilot test responses with the following in mind:

- Were questions interpreted by respondents as intended?

- Were all needed response options made available?

- Was the method of scaling adequate?

- Were technical or proprietary terms understood?

- Are additional items needed to address topics raised in the open-ended comment section?

When the responses have been collected and reviewed, debrief each of the pilot respondents for his or her reaction to the survey. This may be accomplished by preparing a questionnaire that accompanies the pilot survey or by interviewing respondents by telephone in follow-up. Ask them to address questions regarding the survey length, its clarity, its tone,

Figure 64–3. Sample Response Formats

Rating Scale

SD *refers to Strongly Disagree –* **SA** *refers to Strongly Agree.*

XYZ Company's advertising effort helps us meet the needs of our customers **SD** 1 2 3 4 5 6 7 **SA**

XYZ Company understands our business needs **SD** 1 2 3 4 5 6 7 **SA**

Please rate how important the following items are in your decision to purchase from a supplier.

Prompt Delivery **Low** 1 2 3 4 5 6 7 **High**

Prompt Availability **Low** 1 2 3 4 5 6 7 **High**

	Satisfaction	**Importance**
Access to sales representative when needed	1 2 3 4 5 6 7	1 2 3 4 5 6 7
Sales representatives providing effective solutions to problems	1 2 3 4 5 6 7	1 2 3 4 5 6 7

Product Grid

Please mark an (X) next to the product(s) ayou currently purchase from XYZ Company. Next to each product, mark (X) in the box which indicates the percentage of your total purchase you are not buying from XYZ Company.

XYZ Company Product % of Total Purchase

	(1) 0–10%	(2) 11–25%	(3) 26–50%	(4) 51–75%	(5) 76–100%
_____ Product A					
_____ Product B					
_____ Product C					

Open-Ended

What products or services do you feel companies like XYZ Company should provide in the next five years?

---

its completeness, and how they responded to the process itself. Evaluate the pilot test feedback for any revisions that might be included in the final draft of the instrument.

Step 3: Survey Administration

The administration of the survey instrument involves determining who will be surveyed, what method will be used to gather their responses, and how an adequate response rate will be ensured.

Choosing a sample of customers involves several major considerations. First, to what group will the survey results be generalized? For example, if the results will claim to reveal information about the views of distributors as well as end users, it will be important to select respondents from each group. Second, what will constitute a credible sample within the organization? While a statistical sampling method (e.g., Kish, 1987) may be selected to support the credibility of your sample, there may be an ethic within the organization (established on other projects, for example) that specifies a percentage of the customer base that must be sampled for the results to be acceptable. This "ethic" should not be the only consideration in choosing a sample; however, it must not be ignored. Third, the cost of the project will be affected by the size of the sample and will influence the sampling decision. For some companies, it is possible to survey the universe of their customer base. This is the ideal situation. Not only does it give each customer an opportunity to present his or her views, it also ensures the credibility of the "sampling" procedure.

When it is impossible to survey the entire customer base and a sample must be drawn, a stratified random sampling procedure is typically most appropriate. This is particularly true when the data analysis involves comparison of subgroups. Identify these subgroups in advance and sample accordingly. For example, subgroups may include customers representing different geographical regions, levels of sales volume, distributors versus end users, types of industry, types of product line purchased, and so forth.

When the sample has been selected, it is necessary to choose the method of administration. We recommend that surveys be administered by mail or by telephone or by a combination of these methods. While other methods can be used effectively, these present the most cost-effective options and result in the most defensible data.

Surveys administered via the mail have the following advantages: (1) more complex items can be included, for example, presenting a concept visually or in grid format; (2) respondents are afforded greater flexibility regarding when and where they complete the instrument; (3) the importance of the project to the sponsoring organization can be communicated by enclosing a cover letter with the survey (letters should be cosigned by the company president and the vice-president of sales); and (4) they are less expensive than other methods. To ensure a credible response rate with mailed surveys, the administration procedure should be designed to include a prequalifying contact or a follow-up contact. This contact may be a telephone call, a postcard, or a remailing of the survey and cover letter.

Surveys administered by the telephone have the following advantages: (1) the turnaround time for administration is quicker than for mailed surveys; (2) the personal contact provides an opportunity for customers to provide additional open-ended comments; (3) an interactive script can be used, allowing different questions to be asked of some respondents than of others (e.g., those who are dissatisfied with the technical knowledge of the sales personnel can be asked a different set of follow-up questions from those who are satisfied); and (4) a target completion rate can be achieved by calling until the desired number of completed surveys is accomplished.

These two methods can be combined very effectively as well. For example, customers can be contacted by telephone to ask for their participation in a survey that will be mailed to them. Or those who have been mailed a survey can be telephoned in follow-up to remind them to complete it.

Step 4: Data Processing

Two major data processing considerations are (1) how the processing should be accomplished and (2) who should be responsible for it. Data can be captured in one of three ways: using optical scanning sheets, key entry from paper-and-pencil surveys, and cathode ray tube (CRT) data entry during a telephone interview. The optical scanning method is most reliable because it reads responses as the customer marked them with no data transfer.

Processing may be accomplished by the sponsoring organization or by an independent firm. There are advantages to using an outside firm to provide the data processing service. The confidentiality of customers' responses will be ensured if their responses are collected by an independent firm. This method increases the probability of receiving candid responses from customers.

Step 5: Data Analysis

There is one important rule of thumb to follow when analyzing the survey data: the most clear and straightforward analysis is very often most useful to the organization. Descriptive statistics such as frequencies, percentages, means, and standard deviations can be reported very effectively in tables and through graphics and usually provide the best overview of the survey results.

More complex analyses may also be useful. Cross-tabulations comparing the responses of subgroups (e.g., regions, high versus low volume) may reveal significant differences between groups of interest. If these differences occur, subsequent analyses of the data should be performed separately for these groups. Sample reports are presented in figure 64–4 to illustrate various ways of presenting the data to the organization.

Regardless of the method of analysis chosen, it is imperative that the data presented allow for conclusions to be drawn and actions to be taken based on it. One way to ensure actionable data is to prioritize the results based on an importance measure. The importance dimension provides a means of weighting the results, thus allowing issues raised to be prioritized.

Figure 64–4. Sample Report Formats

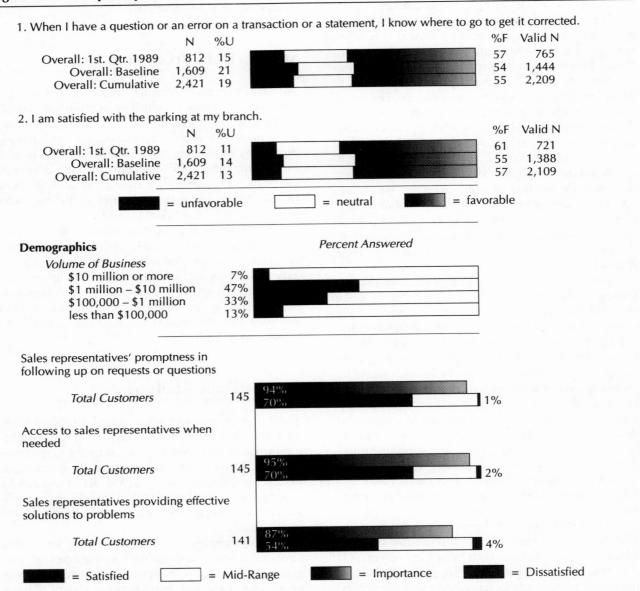

1. When I have a question or an error on a transaction or a statement, I know where to go to get it corrected.

	N	%U		%F	Valid N
Overall: 1st. Qtr. 1989	812	15		57	765
Overall: Baseline	1,609	21		54	1,444
Overall: Cumulative	2,421	19		55	2,209

2. I am satisfied with the parking at my branch.

	N	%U		%F	Valid N
Overall: 1st. Qtr. 1989	812	11		61	721
Overall: Baseline	1,609	14		55	1,388
Overall: Cumulative	2,421	13		57	2,109

■ = unfavorable   □ = neutral   ■ = favorable

Demographics   *Percent Answered*

Volume of Business

$10 million or more	7%
$1 million – $10 million	47%
$100,000 – $1 million	33%
less than $100,000	13%

Sales representatives' promptness in following up on requests or questions

Total Customers   145   94% / 70%   1%

Access to sales representatives when needed

Total Customers   145   95% / 70%   2%

Sales representatives providing effective solutions to problems

Total Customers   141   87% / 54%   4%

■ = Satisfied   □ = Mid-Range   ▨ = Importance   ■ = Dissatisfied

Step 6: Feedback to Management

The first audience to receive the results of the customer research should be the top management group of the organization. Make the results as clear and concise as possible. Draw conclusions and present data in support of those conclusions. When the information has been presented to the management group, they will be involved in deciding how the data will be used and what the next steps will be. There will likely be issues raised that can be addressed immediately. There will be other issues that may need more clarification and long-range planning.

Focus groups made up of a cross-section of survey respondents can be very useful in clarifying issues raised in the research. One-on-one interviews can also serve the same purpose. For example, the question may be raised, "What did our customers mean when they said we need to improve the quality of our products?" A clarification of this issue may reveal problems with the accuracy of the order-taking process; it

Figure 64–5. Sample Action Grid

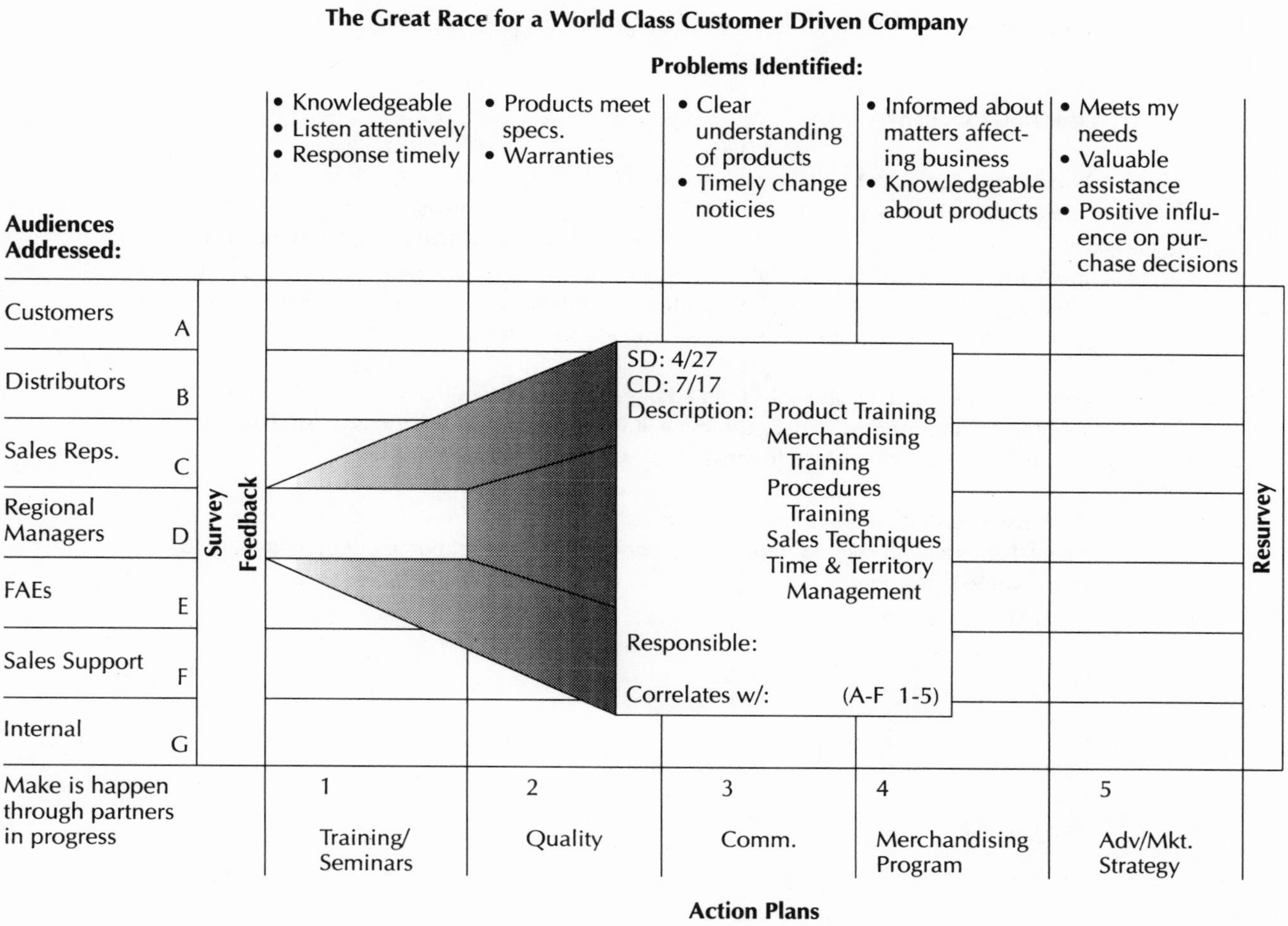
The Great Race for a World Class Customer Driven Company
Problems Identified:
• Knowledgeable
• Listen attentively
• Response timely
• Products meet specs.
• Warranties
• Clear understanding of products
• Timely change noticies
• Informed about matters affecting business
• Knowledgeable about products
• Meets my needs
• Valuable assistance
• Positive influence on purchase decisions
Audiences Addressed:
Customers A
Distributors B
Sales Reps. C
Regional Managers D
FAEs E
Sales Support F
Internal G
Survey Feedback
SD: 4/27
CD: 7/17
Description: Product Training
Merchandising Training
Procedures Training
Sales Techniques
Time & Territory Management
Responsible:
Correlates w/: (A-F 1-5)
Resurvey
Make is happen through partners in progress
1 Training/ Seminars
2 Quality
3 Comm.
4 Merchandising Program
5 Adv/Mkt. Strategy
Action Plans

may indicate product defect problems; it may call for a change in product packaging. Even the most carefully designed survey will likely require further clarification on several issues prior to taking action based on the results.

Step 7: Action Planning

Making plans to take action based on the survey results requires a system to carry out the actions. It then requires communication to the proper constituents about what actions have been taken or will be taken. Figure 64–5 illustrates one effective method for action planning. This method describes the steps to be taken and relates the steps to the group(s) that will be affected by the action. Within each cell, at the intersection of the action step and the description of the affected group, the grid contains a timetable and the person or group responsible for carrying out the plan and accountability. This grid can create the framework for identifying actions, involving key persons who will be responsible, and a mechanism for carrying out the plans. When establishing a method for action planning, include individuals from each functional area, key management employees, and a cross-section of employees from the nonmanagement ranks.

Step 8: Feedback to Customers

The survey process provides a means by which an organization's partnership with its customers can be strengthened. This occurs first by gathering information that allows organizations to be more responsive

Figure 64–6. Sample Letter to Customers

March, 19XX

Dear ABC Company,

A short time ago National Information Systems, an independent research firm, sent you a confidential survey requesting your comments about our products, service, and quality. The survey results have provided us with specific data that will be crucial in directing our efforts toward supplying you with the best products and services available in the industry. We would like to thank you for your participation in our survey and let you know that your satisfaction as a customer is of great importance to us at XYZ.

While there were many strengths pointed out in the responses that made us feel good about our relationship with our customers, it was not our intent to focus on strengths, but to direct our attention instead to those areas where we need to improve.

We have included, for your review, a summary of the survey results and the actions we have taken, and will take, to improve our performance and reinforce our commitment to you, a valued customer.

Sincerely,

John Doe
President
XYZ Company

---

to their customers. It happens next by communicating with them about what happened to the survey responses they provided. Think of this step as "closing the loop." By tying actions taken or changes made to the results of the customer survey, several objectives are accomplished. First, the credibility of the survey process is enhanced, and subsequent attempts to gather information from customers will be taken seriously. Second, the partnership bond is strengthened, and loyalty is increased when customers realize that their opinions are sought and are taken seriously. Finally, communicating with customers about the outcome of the survey process creates an open channel of give-and-take that sets the stage for ongoing communication.

Feedback to customers about survey results is best accomplished through a letter describing briefly the summary of results and planned actions (see figures 64–6 and 64–7). When issues have been raised that cannot be acted upon, it is important also to

mention these. Acknowledge that their message was heard and explain the reasons that the organization is unable to address those issues now.

Step 9: Feedback to Employees

Communicating to employees the results of the customer survey is also recommended. Where the survey results indicated that the organization has strengths, this information should be communicated to employees—particularly those employees who have been instrumental in creating that strength. When internal changes are implemented to address issues raised by the customer survey, it is recommended that employees be made aware of this link. To make changes because the customer has requested it places a greater importance on the action taken than if employees are left to believe the change had its origin only with management. This message can be sent to

Figure 64–7. Survey Results and Actions

Quality

Comments received can be summarized into how well products meet stated manufacturing specifications and level of accuracy in paperwork and physical distribution of finished goods.

Actions taken:
1. 5-year warranty implemented on products.

2. New equipment funded for field application use to help with local characterization and design-in support.

Actions to be implemented:
1. Quality Council chaired by the Division President and consisting of top-level management.

2. Quality Improvement System with a specific focus on improving control of all functions from definition of customer requirements to delivery of product.

Sales and Customer Service

Customers reported a need for increased product knowledge and problem-solving abilities; a desire for improved responsiveness; and the need for increased availability of personnel to customers.

Actions taken:
1. Appointed Marketing Management Information Systems manager.

2. Purchased and currently installing new state-of-the-art computer and order processing software.

Actions to be implemented:
1. Enhance sales and product knowledge of sales personnel through extensive sales and product training.

2. Enhance distributor and manufacturer representative knowledge by providing more frequent training seminars.

Customer Communications

Customers reported a desire to be kept more informed about XYZ decisions affecting their business, changes in products and actions taken as a result of customer suggestions.

Actions taken:
1. Study underway to enhance XYZ customer communications vehicles.

Actions to be implemented:
1. Development of program for responding to and tracking customer suggestions.

employees by internal memo or the company newsletter or directly through supervisory personnel. Include information about those employees involved in the development of action plans.

Step 10: Ongoing Communication

Just as it is important to communicate with customers and employees when the results of the customer survey have been analyzed, it is equally important to establish a pattern of ongoing communication with these groups regarding additional actions being taken. Not all issues will be addressed immediately. As actions related to survey results continue to be planned and implemented, they should be made known. This can be accomplished by preparing periodic memos, by newsletter, by direct communication through the sales force, or internally through managers and supervisors.

Step 11: Establishing a System for Ongoing Surveying

The first customer survey conducted by an organization serves, first and foremost, as a baseline of information against which comparisons can be made in subsequent periods. Conducting a full-scale survey of one's customers every six to nine months, as some have suggested (Peters, 1987), is perhaps a luxury few can afford. However, it is recommended that customer surveys be conducted yearly, with informal surveys conducted periodically during the year. These can be brief telephone surveys conducted to evaluate specific topics throughout the year, or they can be brief surveys enclosed with billing statements or other communications that go to customers regularly.

Collecting ongoing survey data provides the opportunity to establish a normative base by which the organization can measure itself from year to year. These data can serve as a basis for evaluating new programs, products, and services. They can also be used as a means by which departments and divisions are evaluated. Compensation bonuses for key customer-contact employees can also be determined in part by the results of the survey.

If designed, administered, and analyzed properly, any customer survey can be informative, actionable, and help establish a strong partnership with your customers.

SUMMARY

This chapter has provided a rationale for partnering philosophy between organizations and their customers. The tremendous advantages to be gained by adopting such a philosophy have been discussed, as well as the effects of not adopting this philosophy. A strategic model has been presented that illustrates the differences between a traditional reactive approach and a contemporary proactive approach to customer-vendor relations. In addition, step-by-step guidelines for adopting a proactive approach through a systematic survey research program are provided. These guidelines, coupled with the expertise of an internal or independent research staff, will help establish a data base that can serve as the baseline for the evaluation of current practices, for the planning of new strategies, and for the effective implementation of projects to address customer concerns.

Just as the assessment of organizational effectiveness through customers is essential, so it is also essential to work with other constituents of an organization both to evaluate and improve organizational effectiveness. Similar assessments must also be done with an organization's employees and an organization's vendors to assess the organization's position in the marketplace—its strengths and its areas for improvement. In this way the partnership established between an organization and its customers is extended to include all the vital links of an organization.

In those organizations that have adopted this partnership strategy, the benefits have been measurable: increased customer loyalty, increased employee commitment, and ultimately an increased revenue base.

REFERENCES

Bohl, D. (Ed.). (1987). *Close to the customer: An American Management Association research report on consumer affairs*. New York: AMA Membership Publications Division.

Cron, R.L. (1974). *Assuring customer satisfaction: A guide for business and industry*. New York: Van Nostrand Reinhold Company.

Desatnick, R.L. (1987). *Managing to keep the customer*. San Francisco: Jossey-Bass Publishers.

Holt, K., Horst, G., & Giovanni, P. (1984). *Needs assessment: A key to user-oriented product innovation*. New York: John Wiley & Sons.

Jackson, B.B. (1985). *Winning and keeping industrial customers: The dynamics of customer relationships*. Lexington, MA: Lexington Books.

Kish, L. (1987). *Statistical design for research*. New York: John Wiley & Sons.

Lazer, W., Murata, S., & Kosaka, H. (1985). Japanese marketing: Towards a better understanding. *Journal of Marketing, 49*(2), 69–81.

Lele, M.M., & Sheth, J.H. (1987). *The customer is key: Gaining an unbeatable advantage through customer satisfaction*. New York: John Wiley & Sons.

Marr, J.W. (1986). Letting the customer be the judge of quality. In *Quality Progress*. Milwuaki, WI: American Society of Quality Control Publishers.

McKenna, K. (1987). Playing for position. In *Marketing 1986/87*. Guilford, CT: Dushkin Publishing Group.

Peters, T. (1986). *Occasional Papers*. California: Excel.

Peters, T. (1987). *Thriving on chaos: Handbook for a management revolution*. New York: Alfred A. Knopf.

Peters, T., & Austin, N. (1985). *A passion for excellence: A leadership difference*. New York: Warner Books.

Peters, T.J., & Waterman, R.H., Jr. (1982). *In search of excellence: Lessons from America's best run companies*. New York: Harper & Row.

Waterman, R.H., Jr. (1987). *The renewal factor: How the best get and keep their competitive edge*. New York: Bantam Books.

65 UNDERSTANDING AND COPING WITH ORGANIZATIONAL EFFECTS OF COMPUTER-AUTOMATED TECHNOLOGY

Ann Majchrzak, Katherine J. Klein

Computerized automation of both the office and the factory began some twenty years ago, and, in the past two decades, it has proliferated with few bounds. So too has research on its impact—on employees, work groups, organizations, and even industries. The intention of this chapter is to summarize some of the findings from this research for its practical implications. In undertaking such a summary, it should be understood that this field of research is not a mature one, neatly organized or easily summarized. For example, different studies tend to focus on different effects at different levels of analysis. Some studies have used the individual level of analysis, focusing on the effects of technology on employees' perceived job characteristics and job satisfaction; other studies have examined work groups, focusing on the impact of new technology on work group productivity and group dynamics; while still others describe the impact of technology on the organization, examining changes in the organizational structure.

While this diversity will eventually help to clarify what generalizable statements can be made about technological effects, in the interim, the diversity makes it difficult to find replicated research results for comparison. Moreover, the target technology (e.g., word processors, robotics, computer-aided design) varies from study to study, as do the outcome variables of interest (satisfaction, structure, profitability) and the primary discipline of the individual doing the research (psychology, human factors, sociology, economics). This diversity then further limits the ability to identify results that have been found in more than one study.

A final limiting factor in summarizing research results to date is that much of the research is based on qualitative case studies of single plants or companies. The field is yet too new to have advanced far beyond this point. As such, experiment tests of true cause-and-effect relationships are virtually unknown in the field.

Despite these limitations of the research to date, conclusions about the effects of advanced computer-automated technological change that are shared by more than one study can be identified. In this chapter, it is those shared conclusions that will be described. In particular, we are concerned with identifying the practical consequences of the conclusions derived from research on the organizational effects of computer-automated technological change.

COMPUTER-AUTOMATED TECHNOLOGIES

The impacts of two types of computer-automated technologies are discussed in this chapter: programmable manufacturing automation and office automation.

Programmable manufacturing automation encompasses a variety of technologies varying in size, technical complexity, and impact, to include such equipment as:

- Robots (reprogrammable multifunctional ma-

Portions of this chapter have been reprinted from A. Majchrzak and K.J. Klein (1987) Things are always more complicated than you think: An open-systems approach to the organizational effects of computer-automated technology, *Journal of Business and Psychology*, 2(1), 27–47.

chines that manipulate material, parts, and tools through a programmed series of motions).

- Computerized numerical control (CNC) (devices that cut or form a piece of metal according to computer-programmed instructions).
- Computer-assisted design (CAD) (an electronic drawing board for draftsmen and design engineers that allows the programmer to analyze and test the performance of the computerized representation of the product).
- Computer-assisted manufacturing (CAM) (a battery of CNC equipment in which numerous CNC machine tools are controlled by a central computer).
- Manufacturing resource planning (MRP) (a software system that translates product orders into a listing of parts needed and then orders the parts from inventory or from suppliers).
- Computer-aided process planning (CAPP) (a software system that routes parts through the factory to maximize efficiency).
- Computer-integrated manufacturing (CIM) (fully integrated applications of most or all of the above technologies) (Gerwin, 1982; OTA, 1984).

Of these technologies, robots, CNC, and CAD are the most common in the United States today; for most plants, computer-integrated manufacturing remains a goal—in sight, but not yet in practice.

Office automation refers to the variety of computerized technologies now available to aid in the effective procurement, storage, analysis, retrieval, and communication of information. As a group, these technologies include:

- Mainframe computers.
- Microcomputers.
- Stand-alone or dedicated word processors and electronic typewriters.
- Optical character recognition (OCR) devices (devices that optically scan a page to read typed, printed, and in some cases, handwritten material).
- Facsimile technology (FAX) (devices to transmit images electronically from hard copy to hard copy).
- Software systems (e.g., word processing and spreadsheet packages).
- Telecommunication, electronic mail, and mobile phone systems.
- Printers.
- Copy systems (OTA, 1985b).

Microcomputers and their attendant components (printers, software systems) are by now standard office equipment. Indeed, the Office of Technology Assessment (OTA, 1985b) estimates that by the year 2000, computer terminals "are likely to be as ubiquitous as telephones on office desks" (p. 8).

OPEN-SYSTEMS THEORY

To help organize and convey the practical implications of research results on the effects of technological change, we have applied a basic open-systems model of organizational change. Open-systems theory is useful because it not only specifies key organizational processes that may change with technology but it also recognizes the interdependence of the different processes. That is, the impact of the computerized technology on any single organizational process must be considered within the context of all other organizational processes.

Originally developed by Von Bertalanffy (1956), the open-systems model is a metatheory designed to apply to all living systems that interact with their environments. As such, the open-systems framework has been applied to "systems" as diverse as the human body, the family, and the corporation. In a nutshell, open-systems theory states that every thriving system maintains a "dynamic equilibrium" between its subsystems and the larger environment.

Change in any subsystem or in the system's larger environment will reverberate through the system, causing changes throughout.

Katz and Kahn (1978), Nadler and Tushman (1980), and others have adopted Von Bertalanffy's basic model to the study of formal organizations. According to their models, formal organizations import energy (e.g., raw materials, clients) from their environment, transform these inputs (e.g., build bridges, repair cars, cut hair), and then export their products (e.g., new bridges, repaired cars, new hair styles) into their environment. The name of the game is congruence: fit among the organization's subsystems and fit between the organization and its larger environment. The organization that is not internally congruent and congruent with its larger environment will ultimately fail.

Figure 65–1 depicts an open-systems model of the impact of technological change. As indicated in the figure, organizations derive three types of inputs

Figure 65–1. An Open Systems Framework of Technological Change

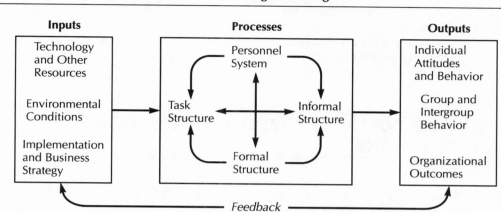

from the larger environment: (1) technology and other resources, (2) environmental conditions, and (3) strategies for technological implementation and business performance. *Technology and other resources* are intelligent and nonintelligent technologies, capital resources, raw materials, and people. (Computerized technologies are the resource of primary concern for this chapter.) *Environmental conditions* include the overall stability and homogeneity of the organization's marketplace, as well as the external entities with which the organization interacts (e.g., appliers, and competitors). Finally, *implementation and business strategies* refers to the organization's procedures in introducing the new technology as well as its plan of action to meet the constraints and opportunities the environment provides.

The effects of organizational inputs (including technological change) on organizational outputs are mediated by four organizational processes: task structure, personnel functions, formal organizational structure, and the informal organization. Thus, technology affects organizational outcomes only through its effects on these organizational processes. To clarify, *task structure* is the nature of jobs or tasks within the organization. *Personnel functions* are the means for selecting, training, and rewarding employees. *Formal organizational structure* refers to the structural mechanisms the company uses to organize and control employee behavior and organizational functions. Finally, *informal organization* is the informal social structure of the organization, including informal norms, goals, communication patterns, and power.

Within an open-systems framework, any organization has a variety of outputs, including individual attitudes and behavior (employee satisfaction, commitment, stress, performance, absenteeism, turn-

over), group and intergroup behavior (group productivity, cooperation, intergroup conflict), and organizational outcomes (sales, productivity, market share, return on investment).

There are several key points of this open-systems model for the purposes of studying the impact of technological change. First is that organizational inputs include technological changes as well as other organizational resources, market conditions, and strategies; thus, technological change is not the only input of concern. Second is that organization processes can be classified into at least four elements (task, personnel, structure, and informal organization) that are not only affected by the inputs but also affect one another. Third is that organizational outcomes are achieved only through interactive changes in organizational processes. Finally, the fourth is that congruence among organizational inputs and processes leads to successful organizational outcomes.

The third and fourth key points of the model deserve special attention here. Both underscore the importance of examining organizational processes, as well as outcome variables, in any discussion of technological change. These points suggest that conclusions about the direct impact of technological change on job satisfaction, organizational growth, and profits are misleading and inaccurate. Technological change enhances organizational outcomes only when organizational processes have been appropriately managed to yield those benefits. Furthermore, there is no single best way to manage these organizational processes. Rather, the organizational processes must be congruent with each other, as well as with the new technology, the external environmental conditions of the firm, and the firm's implementation strategies.

Below, we review research on the impact of computerized manufacturing and office automation for each of the four subsystems of the organizational processes. In the interest of presenting a comprehensive overview of the impact of computerized technologies, we have tended to emphasize the common effects of both manufacturing and office automation. We recognize that it is inappropriate to equate computerized technologies; CAD is not CIM; spreadsheets are not robots. Still, one somewhat surprising conclusion from our review is precisely the extent of common effects across very diverse technologies.

THE IMPACT OF COMPUTERIZED TECHNOLOGIES ON TASK STRUCTURE

Task structure refers to the job activities and skill requirements of workers directly and indirectly associated with the new technology. For office automation, changes in the jobs of secretaries, data clerks, and managers are of interest. For programmable manufacturing technology, changes in the jobs of semiskilled and unskilled machine operators, maintenance workers, manufacturing and R&D engineers, managers, and supervisors are key. Computerized technology affects seven dimensions of task structure: work pace, information, coordination, discretion, variety, flexibility, and physical intervention.

Work Pace

Without doubt, studies of the implementation of computerized technology conclude that the technology increases the speed of work of those directly involved (e.g., OTA, 1984, 1985a). With computerized technologies, it simply takes less time to edit a letter, balance the books, design a building, or build a car. Claims of substantially faster processing times in firms with office automation and programmable automation are legend (e.g., Kaplan, 1986). This increased speed means that those directly involved with the equipment must be able to keep up with the machine. For office automation, this may mean that a secretary who corrects one document every two hours now does one an hour, in addition to answering the telephone and ordering supplies. For programmable, automated manufacturing equipment, the machine operator may now feed the machine one part every 10 seconds instead of every 2 minutes, or inspect parts in shorter cycle times. Often, this increased speed is accompanied by stress symptoms because workers have difficulty adjusting to the new pace of their work (Argote, Goodman & Schkade, 1983; Brod, 1984; Majchrzak, Chang, Barfield, Eberts & Salvendy, 1987; OTA, 1985b; Sauter, Gottlieb, Jones, Dodson & Rohar, 1983; Smith, Cohen, Stammerjohn & Happ, 1981).

Information Needs

In addition to increases in speed, introducing computerized technologies typically creates an increase in the amount of information required by, or available to, workers using the new technology (e.g., OTA, 1985b; Shaiken, 1984). For example, with programmable manufacturing automation, equipment failures are often attributable to the complex interaction of electronic, electrical, hydraulic, and mechanical systems. Thus, a maintenance worker responsible only for the mechanical system is unlikely to be able to repair the equipment. He or she needs information about the other systems as well, information that would not have been needed to repair conventional manufacturing machinery.

Office automation dramatically increases the amount of information available to office personnel (OTA, 1985b). For example, before the advent of microcomputers in the office, upwardly communicated information was often screened by the natural reporting hierarchy of the organization; managers received information only from their immediate subordinates. With office automation, information on departmental performance, problems, and processing details is available at one's fingertips from a wider variety of sources.

The information requirements of computerized office and manufacturing technologies greatly increase the potential of operator information overload. There are ways to reduce the likelihood of information overload and still allow the technology to increase the amount of information being processed (e.g., Sheridan, 1981). Nevertheless, the dangers of extreme information overload must be recognized. Information overload has been blamed, for example, for the accident at Three Mile Island (Hirschhorn, 1984).

Coordination

A third impact of computer-based technologies is that workers using the technology must coordinate with others more frequently. Because computer-based technologies often tie together different technological subsystems (e.g., CAD and CAM, personnel data files and production records, electronic mail and text editing), individuals in different functional divisions or units often become more interdependent as well. For example, when CAD and CAM are linked, manufacturing and R&D engineers must work together more closely. Given electronic mail and text editing linkages, managers are often expected to share documents with other departments more frequently. Similarly, secretaries may coordinate with a central word processing unit, and machine operators often may coordinate with maintenance personnel to keep the computerized equipment running (e.g., OTA, 1984; Argote et al., 1983).

Worker Discretion

The impact of computer-based technology on the fourth task dimension, worker discretion, is open to debate. For programmable automation, cases of decreased discretion for machine operators (e.g., Wilkinson, 1983) are balanced by cases of increased autonomy (Manufacturing Studies Board, 1986). For office automation, evidence for both sides of the controversy is available as well (e.g., Bjorn-Andersen, Hedberg, Mercer, Mumford & Sole, 1979). These contradictory findings are best explained by the fact that of all the task dimensions discussed thus far, worker discretion is least affected by the technology per se and most affected by managerial decisions about job design. One company may, for example, increase CNC machine operators' discretion (by giving the operators responsibility for computer program debugging), while another company with the same equipment may decrease worker discretion (by forbidding operators to interrupt the production process) (Wilkinson, 1983). Thus, the effects of technological change on worker discretion are contingent upon managerial decisions. If managers truly value workers in decision making, the workers will have the right to make decisions about how to complete their tasks, regardless of their equipment.

Variety

The effects of computer-based technology on the fifth dimension, task variety, are very similar to the effects identified for worker discretion; evidence for both increased and reduced variety has been found (Bjorn-Andersen et al., 1979; Butera, 1984; Gutek, 1982; Manufacturing Studies Board, 1986). Once again, managerial decisions about job design explain the contradictory findings.

Because task variety is positively correlated with worker satisfaction and performance (e.g., Hackman & Oldham, 1975), managers should consider the importance of maintaining or increasing task variety when new technology is installed (Majchrzak & Cotton, 1988). For example, word processing clerks may assume responsibility for final reproduction and packaging documents as well as for editing changes.

Flexibility

Programmable manufacturing automation increases the need for flexibility in both job definitions and worker skills (e.g., OTA, 1984). The more broadly the job is defined and the more flexible are the job holders' skills, the greater is the ability of the manufacturing work force to adjust to both predictable and unpredictable change. Computerized manufacturing equipment often frees machine operators to take on new responsibilities (e.g., for maintenance and quality inspection), but they must be both allowed and trained to do so. Similarly, if equipment breaks down (as complex equipment often does), machine operators are best utilized if they can be switched to another machine or job. Finally, because companies typically upgrade their technologies slowly over time, the ability to shift the operators to new positions as they are created is most advantageous to the company. For all these reasons, then, flexibility assumes new importance in the computerized manufacturing workplace.

Office automation may also facilitate worker flexibility, if not necessarily require it. Electronic communication and networking capabilities allow certain workers to work at home, linked to their offices and/or clients by personal computer, telephone, and modem. This "home work" option may be viable—if not yet common—for a variety of workers, including professionals working alone in creative tasks (writing, programming) and clerical employees performing tasks that can be easily monitored and checked for errors by computer (OTA,

1985b). While there is considerable controversy over the merits and ethics of home-based work, its benefits include reduced costs for employers (e.g., for space, employee benefits, equipment, and possibly turnover and absenteeism as well) and greater employee freedom to manage time-consuming personal schedules for employees (Klein & Hall, 1988; Olson, 1983; OTA, 1985b; Pratt, 1984).

Physical Intervention

A final change in task structure is a reduction in the worker's physical intervention in the actual production process (OTA, 1984). The machine operator, for example, no longer physically holds and turns a part while it is cut; the equipment holds and turns it. This leaves the operator available for peripheral activities such as machine loading and unloading, monitoring, inspection, and clean-up. Unless the equipment is "sold properly" to the work force, the operators may feel they work for the machine, not vice versa. Moreover, workers may have difficulty feeling motivated to watch rather than do.

This reduction in the physical process of production is less obvious in the office setting, though it may still occur. For example, bank tellers may lose contact with bank customers as a result of customers' use of automated teller machines. Similarly, insurance claims clerks may miss the customer contact once a computer is brought on board to process most claims (Taylor, 1982). Drafters using CAD technology have reported experiencing less involvement in their work because they no longer put the "final, personal touches" on a layout; the computer does (Majchrzak, 1985). And home-based office workers, of course, experience less day-to-day contact with all aspects of the office (OTA, 1985b).

Conclusion

Both office and manufacturing automation appear to have quite similar effects on the five dimensions of task structure. They tend to increase work pace, information requirements, coordination, and flexibility and reduce physical intervention in the production process. (The last two effects are, however, most obvious and well documented in manufacturing settings.) Two dimensions of task structure—variety and discretion—are not predictable from technology but instead reflect managerial decisions about how the new technology is to be implemented.

THE IMPACT OF COMPUTERIZED TECHNOLOGY ON PERSONNEL SYSTEMS

The introduction of computerized technology requires changes in a variety of personnel functions, including staffing, selection, training, and compensation and reward systems.

Staffing Requirements

The possibility of layoffs because of the new technology is uppermost in most managers' and workers' minds. Indeed, computerized technology is often purchased in the hope of reducing direct labor costs (Ayres & Miller, 1983). Yet surveys and reviews of cases implementing computerized technology have found layoffs directly attributable to technology to be surprisingly rare (e.g., Gutek, Bikson, & Mankin, 1984). This low layoff rate is due to many factors, including the relatively slow diffusion of new equipment into the workplace, increased work volume offsetting workers' reduced roles in the production, labor contracts banning technology-induced layoffs,

and retraining of the displaced work force for newly created support positions (e.g., Majchrzak, 1988).

The last reason, worker retraining for new positions, often creates the greatest havoc for the staffing functions of personnel. Because of vendor marketing promises, the number of persons needed to operate computerized technology is often underestimated (Thompson & Scalpone, 1983). Simply because a robot does the direct labor work of four welders does not mean that those welders are no longer needed. Rather, the welders may be needed to maintain or program the robot. Thus, the staffing of the workplace becomes an exceptionally important and complicated issue in the implementation of new technology.

Selection

Because the impact of new technology on job discretion and variety differs greatly across companies, worker skills are neither universally upgraded nor downgraded with the advent of technological change. Nevertheless, a few key skills to consider in selecting workers for new computer-automated technologies can be identified. These skills include perceptual skills for monitoring the equipment, diagnostic skills for interpreting computerized information, and human relations skills for communicating, problem solving, and coordination (Majchrzak, 1988; Majchrzak & Paris, 1988).

For information systems, research on appropriate selection criteria is much scantier. This may well reflect the fact that office automation appears to require fewer specialized skills than does manufacturing automation. The successful applicant for a position as a word processor must, for example, know how to type, of course, but he or she does not necessarily need experience on the company's own computer equipment. Many computer systems are increasingly designed to be user friendly and thereby allow the operator to pursue a self-teaching program built into the standard software package (OTA, 1985b). If the office employee is likely to engage in home-based office work, however, selection may take on new and added importance. The organization must then attempt to assess applicants' abilities to work alone and unsupervised (Klein & Hall, 1988).

Training

Given the new skills, tasks, and staffing positions that come with technological change, it is not surprising that computerized technology makes dramatic demands on training (Majchrzak, 1986). Employees at all levels and occupations—even those only tangentially affected by the technology—must be trained to work in the new computerized environment.

Unfortunately, many existing in-house training programs for both office and manufacturing automation are woefully inadequate (Gutek et al., 1984; Jacobs, 1985; Majchrzak, 1988; Shaiken, 1984). Workers complain of their companies' heavy reliance on unstructured on-the-job training, their failure to provide sufficient opportunities to experiment, their failure to train all but those directly using the technology, their use of generic vendor training not geared to the particular needs of the users, and their inadequate documentation materials.

These complaints have implications far beyond the job satisfaction of users. Johnson et al. (1985) studied firms achieving effective use of office automation systems and found that providing system users with the time to experiment with the new systems as part of their daily activities was an important predic-

tor of success. Further, the provision of adequate in-house training programs to prepare the work force for computer-automated technology has been found to be directly related to the success of the implementation of these new technologies (e.g., Ettlie, 1986). Finally, the cost inefficiencies of reliance on unstructured on-the-job training are well known (Goldstein, 1986; Lusterman, 1977).

Compensation and Rewards

Computer-based technologies may alter both performance standards and the means to monitor them. As a result, the reward system must change as well to fit the computer-automated workplace. For programmable automation, an operator's mere physical presence is no longer as important or meaningful as how effective the operator is when at the machine. Similarly, with office automation, white-collar performance can often now be defined in terms of innovation as well as in the more traditional ways. For both manufacturing and office settings, then, performance may be redefined to include not only achieving quantity and quality objectives but also to include the innovative use of technology (Johnson et al. 1985; OTA, 1984, 1985b).

Computerization also often introduces the possibility of measuring performance in new—often surreptitious—ways (OTA, 1985). Many computers allow one to tabulate keystrokes, records completed, or telephone calls handled per hour, for example. Interestingly, research indicates that successful organizations tend not to make use of this method (Majchrzak et al., 1987); personal control is much more effective.

Finally, computer-based technologies change the focus of compensation. As described previously, computer-based technologies create an increased need to coordinate with others. To encourage this coordination, organizations with computerized technologies often introduce group-based incentives for work group output, quality circle innovations, or departmental profits (Majchrzak, 1988).

Conclusion

Clearly, the effects of computerized technology extend well beyond changes in task structure. Staffing requirements must change to consider not only the numbers of personnel needed to be directly involved in the computerized operations but the number needed in supporting functions as well. New skills must be considered in the selection process, particularly for programmable manufacturing technology. Training programs must be developed to provide broader skills to a broader audience for a broader range of purposes. Finally, compensation systems must provide rewards for a redefinition of perfor-

mance that includes quality, innovation, and teamwork. Thus, unlike the changes to job discretion and variety, these changes seem surprisingly uniform across many companies, managers, and computerized technologies.

THE IMPACT OF COMPUTERIZED TECHNOLOGY ON FORMAL STRUCTURE

Computer-based technology may influence three aspects of formal structure: integration, formalization of rules and procedures, and locus of decision-making authority.

Integration

As individuals need to coordinate more because of computerized automation, so too do organizational units and systems. Interdepartmental integration may be achieved through the creation of new reporting hierarchies. At one newly computerized plant, for example, engineering staff were reorganized to report to the director of marketing in an effort to encourage closer coordination between product development and customer needs (Roitman, Liker & Roskies, 1987). Similarly, maintenance workers may be asked to report both to their own maintenance department and to a work group of CAM operators (Majchrzak, 1988). Increased integration may also be achieved through the introduction of liaison devices such as task forces, committees, work teams, and even new departments. For example, CAD coordinating committees are often created to make sure that drafting, R&D, manufacturing engineering, and tooling departments use compatible software. Occasionally, the CAD committee may become a new organizational department in an effort to ensure that it has sufficient authority to facilitate the coordination process.

Formalization

One of the most frequently documented effects of computer-based technology is an increase in the extent to which rules and procedures are formalized (OTA, 1984). With office automation, for example, precise rules must govern the ways in which data are entered into the computer. Further, even workers not directly involved with the new technology may find that new rules are necessary for their work.

With CAD, for example, design engineers who use the CAD system only through their drafters often must formalize how they provide instructions to drafters. In this way, the formalization ensures that the drafters do not spend an inordinate amount of time translating the engineers' instructions into computer commands. For programmable manufacturing equipment, rules and procedures often become formalized in such areas as quality control (using statistical process control) and machining operations (through computer programming).

Increased formalization may create a dilemma for management, however. Formalization may reduce worker discretion and flexibility. Thus, only those procedures essential to efficient coordination and operations would be formalized.

Locus of Decision-Making Authority

A major controversy in research on the relationship of technology and structure is whether computer-based technologies decentralize or centralize decision-making authority. Markus (1984) concludes a recent review of the office automation literature with the finding that office automation facilitates decentralization in firms that choose to decentralize while facilitating centralization in firms hoping for increased centralization.

For programmable manufacturing automation, the unpredictability of the complex systems on the shop floor necessitates a certain degree of decentralization, such as the authority to stop production runs of bad parts. However, for the most part, Markus's findings hold here as well (Majchrzak, 1987).

Conclusion

The formal structure of an organization changes in two important and predictable ways with the adoption of computerized technology: both integration and formalization increase. However, changes in the locus of decision-making authority are not predictable from the technology. As with worker discre-tion and task variety, the effects of technological change on the centralization of decision-making authority reflect managerial choices rather than direct technological effects.

THE IMPACT OF COMPUTERIZED TECHNOLOGY ON THE INFORMAL ORGANIZATION

The informal organization includes the informal communication networks among employees, as well as the company's power distribution, culture, and future vision. The introduction of computerized technology affects all of these aspects of the informal organization.

Communication Networks

Informal patterns of communication change with the introduction of new technology. Simply put, some employees speak the language of bits, bytes, CIM, and MRP, and others do not. Those who do not may feel uninformed or inadequate. Furthermore, communication networks (who talks to whom, about what, and how often) may also change as a result of technological change. For example, Mosher and Majchrzak (1986) found that design engineers using CAD focused their informal conversations on new design opportunities, while design engineers not using CAD tended to converse about different subjects. Such changes in informal communication networks may significantly influence individual adjustment to the new technology. Information exchanged in informal conversations between peers may have a critical impact on employees' resistance to new technology (e.g., Leonard-Barton and Kraus, 1985).

Power

Often, those who are most experienced with and knowledgeable about the technology are not the managers or supervisors but their subordinates. Thus, supervisors and managers may well feel not only that they are missing out on important communication but that their power and influence has eroded while that of their subordinates has increased (Majchrzak, 1988). These shifts may make both subordinates and supervisors dissatisfied with the supervision and leadership that the supervisors can provide. For example, in a recent study of the implementation of CAD, Klein and Clemmer (1987) found that design supervisors and project managers complained that they were less "in touch" with the projects they supervised because they could no longer examine designs on the drafting board, and they lacked the expertise to understand the designs presented on the CAD computer terminal screen. For their part, designers questioned whether their work could be fairly evaluated by supervisors who did not understand the technology the designers used on a daily basis.

These shifts in power and expertise are evident in traditional office settings as well. A common finding is that office automation blurs the distinctions between professional and support staff (OTA, 1985b; Sokol, 1986). For example, the professional staff may write first drafts directly on the computer, leaving support staff to edit and finalize the drafts. On the other hand, some professionals may resist using a word processor or microcomputer because typing is "beneath them." In any case, the introduction of even minimal office automation may disturb established norms and expectations for employee behavior.

Company Culture

Many of the automation effects that we have already discussed suggest that automation may also bring about a significant change in the culture of the firm—its symbols, rituals, and shared philosophy (Majchrzak, 1988). For example, a set of symbols (e.g., recognition awards, prominently displayed graphs and posters, and company-sponsored competitions) that encourage high-speed work may be counterproductive if speed with the new computerized equipment then leads to poor-quality products. A company may then find it necessary to develop a new set of rituals (e.g., company-sponsored team sports and new awards) to foster teamwork, innovation, and long-term employee commitment to the job and company. Rewards and rituals commonly found in successfully automated companies include recognition for innovations; personal attention from managers; off-site activities such as retreats, picnics, seminars, and trips; periodic information-sharing meetings among employees and between employees and management; group incentives; and company-sponsored educational benefits. These rituals help to encourage employees to contribute to the organization in nontraditional ways—through innovative ideas, extra care, and personal involvement.

Future Vision

Finally, the adoption of computerized automation demands a vision of the future of the company—a vision shared by management and employees alike. This vision is necessary because employees harbor fears about present and future computerization: Will I have a job five years hence? Will I have the necessary skills? Will my job be boring? What will happen to my coworkers and boss? Does management know what it is doing?

These are very real fears that cannot be ignored. However, often management does not know the answers, particularly when the questions involve the long-term future of the company. Empty assurances are both unconvincing and inappropriate. Thus, managers need to develop a set of guiding principles that define the company's standards and goals for the future. Will the company provide job guarantees? Will the company provide retraining? Will the company allow worker input in decision making about new technology and new products? Will the company endeavor to maintain or increase worker discretion, variety, and challenge? A statement of principles, backed by formal mechanisms to ensure that the principles are followed, may create a positive vision of the company future, a vision that may begin to assuage worker concerns.

Conclusion

Just as change comes to tasks, personnel, and formal organizational structure, computerized technology also creates change in the informal organization. Informal communication patterns change as technology users find they talk with different colleagues about different subjects from before. Further, the distribution of power may be altered as those knowledgeable about the new technology gain more power and those who are less knowledgeable lose their power. Company symbols and rituals often change to reflect new company priorities. Finally, a clear vision of the company's future becomes an essential element of the informal organization. Without one, employees have difficulty appreciating or even perceiving the light at the end of the tunnel of adjustment.

OTHER FACTORS IN THE CHANGE PROCESS

We have examined technological change as if it exists within a vacuum, devoid of other organizational inputs, resources, and strategies. It does not. Rather, the impact of technological change is acutely influenced by the preexisting environmental conditions and resources of the firm, as well as the technology implementation strategy.

Environmental Conditions and Resources

The impetus for an organization to make technological improvements is often an environmental input—a competitor, supplier, or changing organizational environment. Many organizations, for example, adopt technological innovations when they discover that their competitors have adopted these changes and have turned them to a market advantage. Thus, for example, American automobile manufacturers are now scurrying to catch up with the Japanese in implementing robotics and other programmable manufacturing automation (Lynn, 1983). Similarly, a company may increase its use of computerized automation when it needs to cut costs to match the competition. Alternatively, the impetus for technological change may come not from the competitor but from the client or buyer, just as American automobile manufacturers are now demanding that their suppliers adopt new technologies that match their own (Flynn, 1985).

The inputs influencing the decision to adopt computerized technology dramatically shape the impact of technological change on organizational processes (Ettlie, 1984). When an organization's competitors are quickly and successfully bringing new products to market, the organization must encourage employee innovation to meet that competition. The organizational processes—task structure, personnel systems, formal structure, and informal organization—will reflect this fact. For example, the organization may strive to encourage innovation and loyalty by guaranteeing job security, providing retraining, increasing worker flexibility, and developing a supportive organizational culture.

If, however, an organization's competitors are successfully pushing low-cost products, efficiency becomes a key consideration. The company may then seek to use the technology to replace employees and may limit training programs, substantially increase the work pace, and limit worker discretion. These examples illustrate a key point: the effects of technological change on organizational processes are not due solely to the technological change per se but also to the interaction of technological change, environmental conditions, and resources.

Implementation Strategy

Researchers (e.g., Ettlie, 1973; Leonard-Barton & Kraus, 1985) have studied the determinants of effective implementation of technological innovations. This research suggests the importance of four facets of implementation for employee acceptance and support of new technology: top management support, employee education, user participation, and follow-through.

Common wisdom—widely known, if seldom practiced—suggests that top managerial support for a technological innovation is essential for its successful implementation. Recent research, however, sheds new light on this, suggesting just what form top management support should take. For example, top managers should know enough about the technology to establish clear strategic objectives for the new system and to know how to support it (e.g., where resources should go, to whom announcements should be directed) (Ettlie, 1973). However, top management should not put undue pressure on employees for a quick turnaround (e.g., Westcott & Eisenhardt, 1986). Finally, top management should not develop operational requirements for the system; that is the user's job (Hedberg, 1975; Mumford, 1979; Markus, 1984).

A second necessary part of the implementation process is employee education. Employees must understand the need for change in general and the need for this change in particular (Lewin, 1951). Moreover, they need to know that the change will not adversely affect them or their peers in the long run (Roitman et al., 1987). For computer-based technology, the educational need is particularly great because the technology is often poorly understood,

job security is of primary concern, and fears abound concerning skill degrading. The literature on the implementation of computer-based technology recommends that managers provide workers with convincing information about the current status and projected future of the company with and without new computerized automation and that they assure workers that there will be no layoffs due to the new technology (Majchrzak, 1988). In addition, because supervisors are primary sources of information for employees during the implementation process (Argote & Goodman, 1986), managers must remember that supervisors must also be convinced and knowledgeable of the benefits of new technology; if the supervisors do not believe the message, neither will the workers.

User participation in the change process is also critical for successful implementation of new technology. With computerized technologies, the organization must often be innovative in structuring user participation because of the number of workers affected and the technical sophistication of the equipment. Methods recommended by researchers include (1) involving users in "process" issues such as job redesign and training rather than technical issues (Johnson et al., 1985); (2) having users elect representatives to determine the operational requirements of the system (Mumford, 1979); (3) providing users prototypes of the new equipment to pilot (Markus, 1984); and (4) recognizing that system development should be a continuous reiterative process (Markus, 1984).

Finally, management follow-through is essential. Too often, management makes promises that it cannot keep, such as first assuring job security to the work force and then later discovering that the additional market capacity needed to avoid layoffs is not there (Roitman et al., 1987). Moreover, part of the follow-through on promises is to evaluate the implementation process as it occurs. Providing employees with early indicators of success and having a management that keeps its promises are exceptionally effective motivators for employees trying to adjust to new technology.

These implementation practices are important in and of themselves; in addition, they have important repercussions for the organizational processes of task structure, personnel systems, formal structure, and informal structure. For example, a company that follows the guidelines described above may prefer to involve employees not only in the implementation process but in other facets of company decision making as well. Thus, worker discretion, flexibility, and decentralization following the technological change are likely to be high. Furthermore, once involved, employees may push for job guarantees and retraining. Finally, the very act of involving workers in the implementation of the new technology may become a symbol or ritual of a new participative, team-oriented, and innovative company culture. In sum, the effects of technological change are due not only to the firm's technology, economic conditions, and resources but to the technology implementation strategy as well.

CONGRUENCE AMONG ORGANIZATIONAL PROCESSES

Thus far, we have discussed the effects of technological change on each input and process element identified in figure 65–1. The last remaining question, then, is how to combine these diverse elements into a successful whole. The answer, according to the open-systems model, is *congruence*. That is, the open-systems model suggests that an organization will be successful (high employee satisfaction, profits, etc.) if its organizational processes are congruent with each other and with the larger environment. Task designs must match personnel policies, personnel policies must match formal organizational structures, the formal and informal structures must match, and so on. Numerous alternative configurations of organizational processes can be successful as long as each consists of congruent processes. Below, we outline three successful organizational configurations in an effort to clarify how the effects of technology can be managed to ensure a successfully congruent set of organizational processes. We must emphasize, however, that these three represent a tiny fraction of the myriad of possibilities.

At company 1, our first example, scientific management is the guiding principle. Accordingly, managers have given workers little discretion in their work with the new technology (labeled TASK in the model). Furthermore, both decision-making authority and integration mechanisms are centralized at the highest level of the organization (FORMAL STRUCTURE). The company selects workers for the technology based on their ability to work within constrained rules, trains them for the desired knowledge—nothing more—and rewards them for following instructions and not for innovation (PERSONNEL). Finally, the company encourages upward informal communication, discourages informal lateral communication, and provides recognition rewards to those who closely follow instructions (INFORMAL STRUCTURE). This configuration is internally congruent. It will work for the company provided that neither the company's technology, market, nor implementation strategy requires significant worker innovation or input.

In our second example, things are very different at company 2. There, top management has long prided itself on its progressive management policies, its committed employees, and its innovative corporate culture. With the adoption of new technology, managers design the new jobs to maximize variety and discretion (TASK). Workers are selected based on their willingness to accept challenges, and they are trained to use their variety and discretionary responsibilities effectively (PERSONNEL). The formal organizational mechanisms encourage rather than inhibit worker variety and discretion (FORMAL STRUCTURE). For example, support staff are plentiful, and formal rules clearly delineate worker responsibilities. Finally, the company's rituals inspire employees to accept responsibility in their jobs (INFORMAL STRUCTURE). Company 2 is thus an internally congruent company. It is most likely to be successful given a technology, a business environment, and an implementation strategy that benefit from worker involvement and innovation but do not necessarily require coordinated group efforts.

At company 3, our final example, teamwork is the order of the day. The high degree of computer integration of its technology requires it. Thus, employees are organized in work teams where they work on large, varied, highly coordinated tasks (TASK). Furthermore, the company rewards group performance in addition to individual performance, selects workers based on their ability to collaborate, and trains workers in group process skills (PERSONNEL). In addition, the company uses many liaison devices such as committees of team leaders and technical specialists matricized to the team (FORMAL STRUCTURE). Finally, the company's rituals, future vision, power structure, and informal communication networks subordinate individual recognition and needs to the team and organization mission (INFORMAL STRUCTURE). The company will be successful if its technology implementation strategy also uses a team approach, which is congruent with the demands of the company's larger economic environment.

These cases illustrate that technological effects are neither singular nor independent. The new technology clearly necessitates certain predictable changes in organizational processes, but how those processes are translated into a configuration of matched processes is a managerial decision, not a technological imperative.

MANAGEMENT IMPLICATIONS

Computerized technologies create both opportunities and challenges for the company of the future. Organizational opportunities with computerized technologies include the ability to meet a broader range of customer needs much more quickly than ever before. Furthermore, technological change gives a company the opportunity to develop a work force that is highly skilled, flexibly trained, and committed to high quality. Finally, the company that meets these opportunities is likely to create in the process a shared company culture emphasizing quality, innovation, and teamwork.

These opportunities do not come without challenges, however. There is the challenge of constructing a reward system that promotes teamwork, yet because American workers pride themselves on individual performance, the reward system must incorporate individual rewards as well. There is the challenge of meeting the ever-increasing informational needs of computer-automated jobs, yet these needs must not become so overwhelming so as to create overload. There is the challenge of identifying new roles for managers and supervisors as workers accept more discretionary and traditionally supervisory responsibilities. There is the challenge of maintaining worker trust of management throughout the implementation process despite the unpredictabilities of organizational change, future economies, and equipment capabilities. There are also the structural challenges of determining how much formalization and centralization is too much or too little. And there is the ultimate challenge of new technology: creating a congruent configuration of organizational processes that can flexibly adjust to the dynamic effects of technological change as well as changing environmental conditions.

There are no simple solutions to these challenges; the wise practitioner knows that a list of "correct" strategies for coping with computer technologies would be presumptuous and inaccurate for many organizations and situations. Instead, what is provided here, with the open-systems approach, is a framework for systematically assessing what complexities apply to a particular organization and how to cope with these complexities. In particular, applying the open-systems framework leads to a list of dos and don'ts in making these assessments. This list includes the following recommendations:

Don't regard automation as a quick solution for basic manufacturing or human resource problems; look to the entire infrastructure as the solutions.

Don't assume that human resource problems can be resolved after the equipment is installed since some of the problems may have to do with the consequences of the type of equipment selected.

Do expect that different configurations of matches of technical and human infrastructure elements are equally effective as long as the organization can undergo all the needed changes.

Do expect to redesign jobs of operators, technical support, and supervisors.

Do involve marketing staff in equipment planning to ensure that equipment capacity can be fully utilized.

Don't look for broad-brushed deskilling or skill upgrading of the work force with computerized technologies; rather, some new skills are required, and others are no longer needed.

Don't make direct labor the prime economic target of computer automation since the displacement of direct labor is such a small part of the economic benefits.

Do begin facing the dilemma of changing the organizational structure to meet both coordination and differentiation needs.

Do expect resistance; begin convincing managers and the work force of the need for change before the equipment is selected.

Applying the open-systems framework, then, will help the practitioner to take the first step to managing the company in the age of computerized technologies.

REFERENCES

Argote, L., & Goodman, P.A. (1986). Investigating the implementation of robotics. In D.D. Davis (Ed.), *Managing technological innovation: Organizational strategies for implementing advanced technologies.* San Francisco: Jossey-Bass.

Argote, L., Goodman, P.S., & Schkade, D. (1983). The human side of robotics: How workers react to a robot. *Sloan Management Review, 24*(3), 31–41.

Ayres, R.U., & Miller, S.M. (1983). *Robotics: Application and social implications.* New York: Harper & Row.

Bjorn-Andersen, N., Hedberg, V., Mercer, D., Mumford, E., & Sole, A. (Eds.) (1979). *The impact of systems change in organizations.* Amsterdam: Sijthoff and Noordhoff.

Brod, C. (1984). *Technostress: The human costs of the computer revolution.* Reading, MA: Addison-Wesley.

Butera, F. (1984). Designing work in automated systems: A review of case studies. In F. Butera and J.E. Thurman (Eds.), *Automation and work design.* New York: Elsevier Science Publications.

Dickson, K. (1981). Pet foods by computer: A case study of automation. In T. Forester (Ed.), *The microelectronics revolution.* Cambridge: MIT Press.

Ettlie, J.E. (1973). Technology transfer—From innovators to users. *Industrial Engineering, 15,* 16–23.

Ettlie, J.E. (1984). Implementation strategy for manufacturing innovation. In M. Warner (Ed.), *Microprocessors, manpower, and society.* New York: St. Martin's Press.

Ettlie, J.E. (1986). Facing the factory of the future. In D.D. Davis (Ed.), *Managing technological innovation: Organizational strategies for implementing advanced technologies.* San Francisco: Jossey-Bass.

Flynn, M. (1985). *The Japanese challenge to U.S. suppliers.* Paper presented to the Annual Meeting of the Automotive Market Research Council. Atlantic City, New Jersey, September.

Goldstein, I.L. (1986). *Training in organizations* (2d ed.). Monterey, CA: Brooks/Cole Publishing.

Gutek, B.A. (1982). Effects of office of the future technology on users: Results of a longitudinal field study. In G. Menschand & J. Niehaus (Eds.), *Work, organizations, and technological change.* New York: Plenum Press.

Gutek, B.A., Bikson, T.K., & Mankin, D. (1984). Individual and organizational consequences of computer-based office information techniques. In S. Oskamp (Ed.), *Applied Social Psychology Annual, 5,* 231–254.

Hackman, J.R., & Oldham, G.R. (1975). Development of the job diagnostic survey. *Journal of Applied Psychology, 60,* 159–170.

Hedberg, B. (1975). Computer systems to support industrial democracy. In E. Mumford & H. Sackman (Eds.), *Human choice and computers.* New York: North-Holland Publishing.

Hirschhorn, L. (1984). *Beyond mechanization: Work and technology in a post-industrial age.* Cambridge: MIT Press.

Jacobs, J. (1985). *The training needs of Michigan automobile suppliers: Interim report.* Ann Arbor, MI: Industrial Technology Institute.

Johnson, B.M., & Associates (1985). *Innovation in office systems implementation.* NSF Report No. 8110791. Oklahoma City: University of Oklahoma.

Kaplan, R.S. (1986). Must CIM be justified by faith alone? *Harvard Business Review, 64*(2), 87–95.

Katz, D., & Kahn, R.L. (1978). *The social psychology or organizations* (2d ed.). New York: John Wiley.

Klein, K.J., and Clemmer, E. (1987). 3D CADD: The human side. Unpublished paper.

Klein, K.J., & Hall, R.J. (1988). Innovations in human resource management: Strategies for the future. In J. Hage (Ed.), *The future of organizations.* Lexington, MA: Lexington Books.

Leonard-Barton, D., & Kraus, W.A. (1985). Implementing new technology. *Harvard Business Review, 63*(6), 102–110.

Lewin, K. (1951). *Field theory in social science.* New York: Harper & Row.

Lusterman, S. (1977). *Education in industry.* New York: The Conference Board.

Lynn, L. (1983). Japanese robotics: Challenge and—limited—exemplar. *Annals of the American Academy of Political and Social Science, 470,* 16–27.

Majchrzak, A. (1985). *Changes to work resulting from CAD.* Paper presented to the American Institute of Industrial Engineers Conference. Chicago.

Majchrzak, A. (1986). A national probability survey on education and training for CAD/CAM. *IEEE Transactions on Engineering Management, 33*(4).

Majchrzak, A. (1988). *The human side of factory automation: Managerial and human resource strategies for making automation succeed.* San Francisco: Jossey-Bass.

Majchrzak, A., & Cotton, J. (1988). A longitudinal study of adjustment to technological change: The Case of job transfers from mass to computer-automated batch production. *Journal of Occupational Psychology* (January).

Majchrzak, A., & Paris, M. (1988). *Successful human resources practices for advanced manufacturing technology.* American Society of Manufacturing Engineers Conference, Atlanta, April.

Majchrzak, A., Chang, T.C., Barfield, W., Eberts, R., & Salvendy, G. (1987). *Human aspects of computer-aided design.* London: Taylor and Francis.

Manufacturing Studies Board (1986). *Human resource practices for implementing advanced manufacturing technology.* Washington, D.C: National Academy Press.

Markus, M.L. (1984). *Systems in organizations: Bugs and features*. Boston: Pitman.

Mosher, P., & Majchrzak, A. (1986). *Work place changes mediating effect of technology on individuals' attitudes and performance*. Paper presented at the Academy of Management Meetings, Chicago.

Mumford, E. (1979). Consensus systems design. In E. Frochla and N. Szyperski (Eds.), *Design and implementation of computer-based information systems*. Oslo, Norway: Sijthoff and Noordhoff.

Nadler, D.A., & Tushman, M.L. (1980). A congruence model for diagnosing organizational behavior. In D. Kolb, I. Rubin, & J. McIntyre (Eds.), *Organizational Psychology* (3d ed.). Englewood Cliffs, NJ: Prentice-Hall.

Office of Technology Assessment (OTA, 1984). *Computerized manufacturing automation* (84-601053). Washington, DC: U.S. Congress, Library of Congress.

Office of Technology Assessment (OTA, 1985a). *Automation of America's offices, summary* (OTA-CIT-288). Washington, DC: U.S. Congress.

Office of Technology Assessment (OTA, 1985b). *Automation of America's offices, 1985–2000* (85-600623). Washington, DC: U.S. Congress, Library of Congress.

Olson, M.H. (1983). Remote office work: Changing work patterns in time and space. *Communications of the ACM, 26*, 182–187.

Pratt, J.H. (1984). Home teleworking: A study of its pioneers. *Technological Forecasting and Social Change, 25*, 1–14.

Roitman, D.B., Liker, J.K., & Roskies, E. (1987). Birthing a factory of the future: When is "all at once" too much? In R.H. Kilmann and T.M. Covin (Eds.), *Corporate transformation: Revitalizing organizations for a competitive world*. San Francisco: Jossey-Bass.

Sauter, S.L., Gottlieb, M., Jones, K., Dodson, V., & Rohar, K. (1983). Job and health implications of VDT use: Initial results of the Wisconsin-Niosh study. *Communications of the ACM, 26*(4).

Shaiken, H. (1984). *Work transformed*. New York: Holt, Rinehart.

Sheridan, T.B. (1981). Understanding human error and aiding human diagnostic behavior in nuclear power plants. In J. Rasmussen and W.B. Rouse (Eds.), *Human detection and diagnosis of system failures*. New York: Plenum Press.

Smith, M.J., Cohen, B.G.F., Stammerjohn, L.W., & Happ, A. (1981). An investigation of health complaints and job stress in video display operators. *Human Factors, 23*, 387–400.

Sokol, M.B. (1986). *Innovation utilization: The implementation of personal computers in an organization*. Ph.D. dissertation, University of Maryland.

Taylor, J.C. (1982). Integrating computer systems in organizational design. *National Productivity Review, 1*(2), 218–227.

Thompson, H., & Scalpone, R. (1983). *Managing the human resource in the factory of the future*. Paper presented at the World Congress on the Human Aspects of Automation, Ann Arbor, Michigan.

Von Bertalanffy, L. (1956). General system theory. *General Systems, Yearbook of the Society for General Systems Theory, 1*, 1–10.

Walton, R.E. (1984). New work technology and its workforce implications. *Harvard Business Review*, Working Paper Number 84-13.

Westcott, B.J., & Eisenhardt, K.M. (1986). *The dynamics of process innovation in manufacturing*. Paper presented at the Academy of Management Meetings, Chicago.

Wilkinson, G. (1983). *The shopfloor politics of new technology*. London: Heinemann Educational Books.

Joseph G. Rosse

Absenteeism and turnover represent the dark side of organizational performance. According to the Bureau of National Affairs (1987), during 1988 absenteeism totaled 21.6 percent of scheduled work time, and 12 percent of workers quit their jobs. Absenteeism rates were even higher in large (more than 2,500 employees) companies (25.2 percent) and among health care employers (24 percent), while turnover rates were above average among employers in the financial and health care sectors (19.2 percent). Inspection of the historical data shown in figure 66–1 shows that these rates have been substantially higher in the recent past, probably due to differences in unemployment rates.

Moreover, recent research suggests that such behaviors as being absent or quitting represent only the tip of the iceberg; if one considered the total range of withdrawal or counterproductive employee behaviors, the problem would clearly be magnified substantially. It is little wonder that over 2,000 articles concerned with turnover and absenteeism have appeared in management and applied psychology journals.

Considering the wealth of studies concerning employee withdrawal, this chapter obviously cannot provide a comprehensive review of the literature. Rather, the intent is to provide a summary of what is known about these behaviors and then to describe some more contemporary—and exciting—perspectives on employee withdrawal from work. In particular, three themes underlie this chapter. First, employee withdrawal includes much more than just turnover and absence. In fact, our understanding of how workers cope with their jobs has probably been hindered by an overemphasis on these behaviors to the exclusion of others. A second theme is that withdrawal behaviors are fairly consistently related to

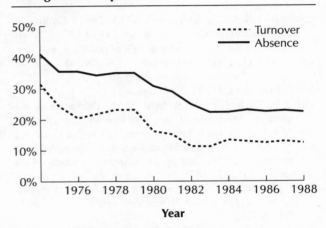

Figure 66–1. Annual Rates of Absence and Turnover among U.S. Companies

characteristics of work, many of which are at least partly under the control of management. Third, withdrawal behaviors may not really be all that bad. For too long, managers and researchers have focused only on the costs involved in absence and quitting (and usually from an exclusively management perspective). A more reasonable view may be that the cost (or benefit) of withdrawal depends very much on the relationship between withdrawal and performance. As long as the leavers are not excessive in number, are not the best performers, and/or are readily replaced, the benefits of hiring better-qualified replacements may exceed the costs of turnover. Similarly, if absence from a stressful work setting provides workers with an opportunity to "recharge" without unduly burdening others, traditional estimates may exaggerate the actual costs of absenteeism (Staw & Oldham, 1978).

WHAT IS EMPLOYEE WITHDRAWAL?

Managers have long been interested in absenteeism and turnover, primarily because both represent irritations, if not major expenses. Industrial-organizational

(I-O) psychologists have shared this interest due both to an interest in applied problems and because absence and turnover have appeared to represent "hard" criteria for evaluating the effects of various interventions (e.g., hiring strategies, leadership style, training programs). Only relatively recently has much attention been given to the theoretical significance of these variables in their own right.

A major theme of this chapter is that such single-minded attention to specific behaviors is counter-productive. There is a good argument that lateness, absence, and turnover have much in common and that it is inefficient to treat them as though each is unique. Not only is a general theory of employee withdrawal more parsimonious, but it also allows for consideration of complex interactions among the behaviors, such as when an employee who would like to quit but cannot decides to be absent more often instead.

The focus of this chapter, then, will be on a family of behaviors that I will initially label withdrawal. Consistent with the research literature, the primary emphasis will be directed toward the study of turnover and absence, although an effort will be made to consider a wider range of withdrawal behaviors. These include such strategies as coming to work late or leaving early, loafing and avoiding work while on the job, and daydreaming or using drugs to shut out the reality of work. Such behaviors have not been widely studied, particularly in the context of traditional withdrawal behaviors. Conceptually, our definition of withdrawal includes all behaviors that serve to increase the psychological or physical distance between employees and their work roles.

Before proceeding it bears noting that the term *withdrawal,* although common, is not without controversy. One concern is that it is inappropriate to treat lateness, absence, and turnover as being similar. Critics argue that each behavior is somewhat different and thus should be modeled individually. While there are undoubtedly differences among them, substantial evidence will be presented that lateness, absence, and turnover do have much in common. Not only do they tend to be correlated, but they also share many of the same causes and may even operate as partial substitutes for one another.

A second concern reflects the avoidance implication of the label *withdrawal.* Critics contend that while some lateness, absence, and turnover may reflect a desire to get away from work, other instances are better explained by the positive attraction of an alternative activity. The approach taken here is that withdrawal represents a motivated choice based on an evaluation of alternatives. That nonattendance is more attractive than attendance suggests relative dissatisfaction with the work role. Nevertheless, *withdrawal* may not be the ideal term. As will be described later, a more general term is *adaptation,* which includes a variety of strategies workers may use to

improve satisfaction with their work roles. In this framework, withdrawal is only one possible strategy.

The third concern also relates to the motivational assumptions of the withdrawal notion. Critics argue that much lateness and absence is explained by illness, emergencies, bad weather, and other factors outside the control of the individual. Similarly, the decision to quit may be based on a spouse's acceptance of a job that requires travel or on an unexpected pregnancy. Escape from an unpleasant job may not be an adequate explanation of such nonvolitional behavior. Again, we accept that some withdrawal is outside the worker's control and is thus not well explained by a rational model of motivated behavior. However, this does not mean that such models are inappropriate. The issue is how well withdrawal models can explain the total range of withdrawal behavior, both volitional and nonvolitional.

We believe that employee behavior is less situationally dependent than often assumed. If so, motivation to avoid dissatisfying work may in fact be a valid predictor of behavior. This point is well illustrated in a field experiment conducted in a major retail chain (Smith, 1976). Employee attendance was monitored on the day of an unusually severe blizzard; it was found that those who managed to make it to work were the same employees who had reported higher satisfaction with their work in an earlier survey. It was easy for those who did not want to come in to use the weather as an excuse, just as an unhappy employee can use spouse's career interests or pregnancy as a more acceptable explanation for the decision to quit.

Before discussing the causes of withdrawal, a final definitional point is in order. To the uninitiated, turnover, absence, and lateness often appear to be clear-cut behaviors—ideal "hard" criteria. People who are scheduled to work and do not show up at the appointed time are tardy; if they do not show up for the whole shift, they are absent; and if they continue to be absent without adequate explanation, they are typically considered to have terminated their employment relationship.

Although such informal definitions may be adequate for general understanding, they are inadequately specified for the purposes of managers who must make and defend compensation decisions, for arbitrators determining the legitimacy of grievances, and especially for researchers trying to untangle the causes of withdrawal.

These special needs have led to a plethora of definitions and measures; Gaudet (1963) describes forty-one different measures of absence that have been proposed. The most common distinction is between measures of absence frequency (the number of instances without regard for the duration of each) and time lost (total days absent without regard to the number of instances). Other less "objective" index attempt to attribute motives to absence; examples include excused versus unexcused, blue monday indexes (the number of absences on Mondays), or the simple assumption that frequency index represent attitudinal absence whereas time-lost measures better reflect involuntary absence due to illness or injury. In the turnover literature, analogous distinctions are drawn between voluntary or involuntary and, more recently, functional or dysfunctional turnover.

Unfortunately, these distinctions seem to have muddied the waters rather than provided greater clarity. Especially for absenteeism, different measures seem to be related to different variables, generally confusing the search for consistent predictors. These different findings are probably due to the fact that some measures are more reliable than others, although some suggest that they are indicative of differences in the meanings or functions of the different types of absence or turnover.

How then should one choose a measure? One possibility is to let one's theory or purpose determine which is more appropriate. For example, most turnover theories are individual choice models, which therefore imply that measures of voluntary quitting

should be used. Similarly, if the purpose of measurement is to develop an absence control program, the distinction between excused and nonexcused absence may be relevant. However, it is not clear that such distinctions can be made with reasonable accuracy. Designations such as voluntary or involuntary may tell us as much about social desirability or implicit theories of attribution as they do about a person's true motives for quitting or being absent.

Unfortunately, there does not seem to be any clear resolution to these issues. Researchers and practitioners are cautioned to be clear about their definitions, to use multiple measures where possible, and to do their best to determine their measures' reliabilities. For measuring absence, frequency indexes are generally recommended as the most reliable. In the absence of any generally accepted means of reliably distinguishing voluntary from involuntary turnover, we prefer to exclude only obvious terminations (preferably confirmed by interviews with those making the termination decision) from an overall measure of turnover. And, of course, firms need to expend considerable effort in developing and maintaining a reliable mechanism for recording behavior according to whatever standardized measures they decide to adopt.

CAUSES OF EMPLOYEE WITHDRAWAL

Two general points may serve as an introduction. The first is that nearly all research has been concerned with either absence or turnover; only a few researchers have studied lateness, and fewer still have concerned themselves with other examples of withdrawal. The second point concerns the intellectual heritage of withdrawal research. Historically, the study of turnover and absence has been multidisciplinary (although rarely interdisciplinary), with the primary traditions being economics, sociology, and psychology. Most recently, the field has been dominated by psychologists and other microoriented organizational scientists.

Economists have typically concerned themselves with the effects of labor markets and with economic models of choice. Unemployment levels, for example, have repeatedly been found to be extremely powerful predictors of both turnover and absence. Eagley (1965) reports a correlation of $r = -.84$ between unemployment levels and aggregate turnover. Similarly, Markham (1985) found the correlation between unemployment and absence at the national level to be $r = -.68$. Economic models of withdrawal processes have typically emphasized utility maximiza-

tion and such trade-offs as higher absence in occupations with greater risks and/or lower pay. As one would expect, turnover has generally been inversely related to level of pay.

Another trend in the literature, dominated by sociologists and organizational theorists, has explored work characteristics as precursors of withdrawal. At the more macrolevel, the strongest finding pertains to the effects of size. Work group size tends to be positively related to turnover and absence, whereas overall organization size seems to be inversely related to turnover (Muchinsky, 1977; Muchinsky & Morrow, 1980). Explanations for these findings usually invoke work attributes and group dynamics. Smaller groups often involve tasks with less repetition, greater autonomy and responsibility, less role ambiguity, and greater recognition and feedback, all factors related to reduced turnover (Muchinsky & Morrow, 1980) and, to a lesser extent, absence (Muchinsky, 1977). Group norms, recently the subject of a great deal of attention in explaining absence, are probably more salient and more readily transmitted in smaller work groups (Nicholson & Johns, 1985). At the same time, larger organizations may be more likely to offer higher pay and to have better systems for matching employees to jobs, both of which are also likely to reduce turnover (Muchinsky & Morrow, 1980).

Surprisingly, nonwork influences on withdrawal have not received a lot of attention, even by sociologists. They are mentioned—albeit rather secondarily—in two turnover models (Mobley, 1977; Steers & Mowday, 1981) but rarely assessed in empirical studies. One exception found that turnover was not well predicted by nonwork factors (Lee & Mowday, 1987). Absence theorists have placed greater emphasis on their role, and a number of studies have found evidence of their importance (Ferris & Rowland, 1987; Rousseau, 1978; Youngblood, 1984).

The third major research thrust, dominated by microoriented psychologists, has addressed the role of individual differences. In general, demographic factors do not seem very helpful in explaining either absence (Brooke, 1986; Muchinsky, 1977; Steers & Rhodes, 1978, 1984) or turnover (Mobley, Griffeth, Hand & Meglino, 1979; Muchinsky & Morrow, 1979). Turnover seems to be somewhat higher among younger, shorter-tenure employees and among those with fewer family responsibilities. Absenteeism is higher among women, employees with health problems (including alcohol use), and workers with greater family responsibilities. No consistent trends regarding personality are evident, although work ethic may play a role in explaining absenteeism (Steers & Rhodes, 1984). As will be discussed in a later section, the effect of job-relevant ability on turnover is mixed, although it appears that leavers are generally less competent than stayers (McEvoy & Cascio, 1987).

Without doubt, the largest body of literature pertains to individual differences in job attitudes. Recent metaanalyses of this literature show that turnover is consistently related to overall job satisfaction and satisfaction with work content (an average correlation in the mid-.20s) as well as organizational commitment (average correlation around .30) (Carsten & Spector, 1987; Knapp, 1984; Steel & Ovalle, 1984). Satisfaction with pay, promotion opportunities, and coworkers do not have much predictive power, while satisfaction with supervision appears to have a consistent but weak effect (correlations in the low teens). Turnover also seems to be related to leadership style, with more people-oriented styles being associated with lower turnover.

Metaanalyses of the absenteeism literature have been less consistent but generally suggest significant associations with overall satisfaction and work content satisfaction. Although the evidence is less consistent, absenteeism also seems to be negatively related to satisfaction with pay, coworkers, and possibly supervision (Scott & Taylor, 1985; Steers & Rhodes, 1984; Terborg, Lee, Smith, Davis & Turbin, 1982), as well as organization commitment and job involvement (Steers & Rhodes, 1984; Terborg et al., 1982).

Adler and Golan (1981) found significant associations between lateness and dissatisfaction with work content, supervision, pay, promotion opportunities, and coworkers, as well as overall job satisfaction. Rosse and Hulin (1985), on the other hand, reported nonsignificant relations for all of the same factors, and Farrell and Robb (1979) failed to obtain significant results with overall satisfaction. These nonsignificant findings may be due to the very low incidence of lateness and the small sample used by Rosse and Hulin (1985); more studies are needed before valid generalizations may be drawn for lateness.

These findings can be summarized by saying that withdrawal behavior is less likely among workers who (1) are satisfied with jobs that are relatively "enriched" yet match their abilities, (2) have effective and concerned leaders, (3) are equitably rewarded and (4) are experiencing a labor market that reduces their opportunities for finding alternative jobs.

Despite this optimistic summary, it could readily be argued that this body of research has contributed relatively little to our understanding of withdrawal. Through the 1970s, most studies were bivariate, atheoretical, and parochial. For example, correlational studies measuring only job satisfaction tell us nothing about how psychological attitudes interact with such macroeconomic conditions as unemployment rates. Thus it should not be surprising that reviewers lament that even such consistent predictors as job satisfaction explain only about 15 percent of the variance in turnover.

Models of Turnover

The solution seemed to be development of models that could incorporate variables from each of the research traditions and thus improve prediction (cf. Bluedorn, 1982; March & Simon, 1958; Mobley, 1977; Muchinsky & Morrow, 1980; Price, 1977; Steers & Mowday, 1981). These tend to be rational-cognitive models of individual choice; not surprisingly, they have a strong psychological flavor despite their inclusion of variables from the sociological and economic schools. All borrow a significant legacy from the participation model proposed by March and Simon in 1958.

As illustrated in figure 66–2, March and Simon suggested that turnover is the consequence of two variables: desirability of movement (which is in turn

Figure 66–2. March and Simon's (1958) Organizational Participation Model

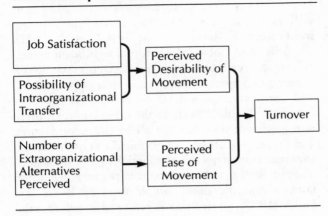

influenced by job satisfaction and the possibility of internal transfer) and ease of movement (a function of the level of business activity, the number of firms known to the individual, and the individual's marketability). Typical of most subsequent models, individual, task, group, and organizational characteristics are not emphasized per se; rather their importance lies in their effects (often of an interactive nature) on other, more proximal predictors of turnover. Macroeconomic conditions, on the other hand, are typically retained, usually in the form of perceptions of alternative employment opportunities.

Ironically, March and Simon's model had little apparent effect on turnover research until the advent of models proposed by Price (1977) and Mobley (1977). Mobley's model had a substantial effect on the field because of its great emphasis on the cognitive process that precedes a decision to quit. Briefly, Mobley proposed that the immediate precursor of turnover is an intention to quit, a proposal that is supported by substantial metaanalytic evidence (the average correlation across thirty-four studies is $r = .50$; Steel & Ovalle, 1984). The intention to stay or leave is in turn preceded by an elaborate decision process that includes thoughts of quitting, the expected utility of searching for an alternative job, the formation of an intention to search for alternatives, the actual search, and the evaluation of alternatives discovered. Job dissatisfaction is the precursor of thoughts of quitting. A number of studies have provided support for the model, although they typically suggest that a simplified model is adequate (cf. Miller, Katerberg & Hulin, 1979).

Steers and Mowday (1981) have proposed a framework that integrates much of the research on Mobley's and others' models (see figure 66–3). One advantage of their approach is a more complete treatment of the antecedents of job affect. Their model is also noteworthy for its consideration of alternative responses to job satisfaction, including attempts to change the situation rather than withdraw. Surprisingly, their model has received only one empirical test (Lee & Mowday, 1987), which provided mixed support.

Critics contend that the development of these models has produced few advances, as tests of the models typically account for only a modest proportion of the variance in turnover. On the other hand, considering the statistical problems in studying an infrequent behavior such as turnover, we believe that a more optimistic interpretation is warranted. In fact, even the estimates provided by metaanalytic reviews probably underestimate substantially the true relations of turnover with other variables (Hulin, in press). Moreover, these models represent a much more useful way of viewing the turnover process than do bivariate analyses of job satisfaction or demographic characteristics. They have demonstrated the key role of employees' intentions to quit and shown that job attitudes are a major factor in reaching this intention. Perhaps most important, they provide "road maps" to guide both managers and researchers in better understanding what leads a person to leave an organization.

If nothing else, these models have forced a more complex view of the antecedents of turnover. A particularly good example is the joint effects of job satisfaction and labor market conditions. As noted in the previous section, both variables have shown strong relations with turnover when studied alone. However, when used simultaneously in a model, their effects are less clear. Both seem to have an effect, but it remains unclear whether this effect is additive (e.g., dissatisfied people always quit but at an even higher rate when there are more job opportunities) or interactive (e.g., dissatisfied people quit only when there are alternative jobs). This ambiguity partially stems from the way in which opportunities are measured. If measured "objectively" by using unemployment rates, opportunities do seem to moderate the relationship between job satisfaction and turnover (Carsten & Spector, 1987). When converted to a psychological variable by asking respondents about their perceptions of alternative jobs, opportunities generally have no effect on turnover (Hulin, Roznowski & Hachiya, 1985).

How is it that a variable that is one of the most powerful predictors of turnover at the aggregate level has a weak and inconsistent effect when measured as a psychological variable? While the answer may be measurement error or the necessity of really dramatic economic conditions (Bluedorn, 1982), Hulin and his

Figure 66–3. Steers and Mowday's (1981) Model of Voluntary Employee Turnover

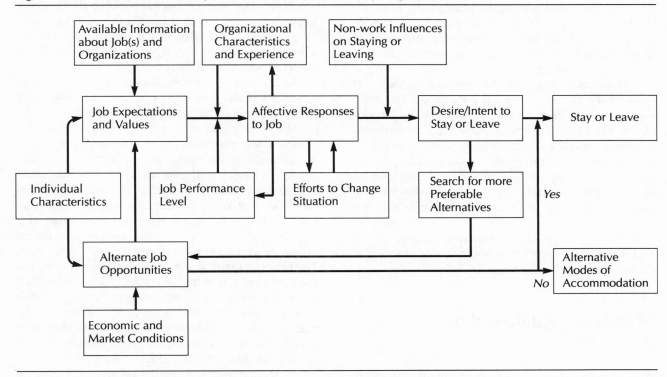

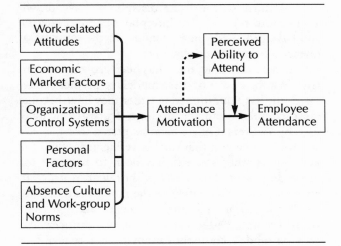

Figure 66–4. Steers and Rhodes's (1984) Attendance Model

colleagues (1985) suggest that economic conditions affect turnover primarily through their effect on job satisfaction (a link that is included only in Bluedorn's 1982 model). That is, rather than "blocking" dissatisfied workers' ability to quit, a lack of opportunities decreases the desire to quit by increasing job satisfaction. (Satisfaction typically increases during recessionary periods because of lowered frames of reference; simply put, any job looks better when the alternative is no job.) This distinction is important not only for its potential for improving predictions but also for its reminder to firms not to feel overly content with complacent employee attitudes during hard economic times.

Models of Absence

Although prior models had been proposed by Gibson (1966) and Nicholson (1977), the most influential model of absence has been that developed by Steers and Rhodes (1978). In a manner somewhat reminiscent of March and Simon's (1958) participation model, they propose that attendance is a joint function of motivation to attend and ability to attend. Motivation to attend is a function of job satisfaction and pressures to attend (e.g., work group norms, economic conditions, work ethic), while ability to attend

is affected by such things as illness, family responsibilities, and transportation problems.

Their model has been criticized as ambiguous and difficult to test, and indeed very few comprehensive tests have been attempted. As a result, Steers and Rhodes (1984) have offered a revised model (see figure 66–4) that they recommend using as a diagnostic checklist. Brooke (1986) has recently proposed a third-generation absence model that is also presented as being more readily testable. In addition, Brooke's model puts greater emphasis on the role of alcohol use and organizational permissiveness and offers a more detailed description of how various job attitudes affect absenteeism.

At present, none of the absence models has received the attention that has been devoted to models of turnover. Partial tests of the Steers and Rhodes (1978) model have offered general support, but none has tested enough components to allow generalizations about the overall model. No tests of the revised Steers and Rhodes model or the Brooke model have yet appeared. Overall, the safest conclusions are probably that both work and nonwork factors are important but that their relative influence is yet to be determined. It appears that relative to turnover, work attitudes are less important and nonwork factors of greater importance.

Models of Withdrawal or Adaptation

As has been noted, the development of integrative theoretical models of absence and turnover represents a major advance in the study of withdrawal behaviors. They have served to broaden perspectives beyond those of the basic disciplines, have drawn attention to the complex interplay of causal factors, and have provided valuable guides to the thinking of researchers and managers alike.

At the same time, there has been growing discontent with the power of these models to predict behavior. Some have questioned whether they have become more complex than the decision processes actually used by workers. Others have suggested that they are still too simple and that further refinements hold the key. Yet another strategy has been to improve the methodology used to study withdrawal in order to estimate better how effective the models can be.

While improved measurement and analytic strategies and better elaboration of turnover and absence models certainly cannot hurt, I believe that the key to improved understanding lies in the development of models that recognize a wider range of behaviors than simply absence or turnover. What is needed are frameworks that consider the complete range of behaviors a person may exhibit and that account for trade-offs among the behaviors.

One reason such frameworks are needed is that withdrawal behaviors are not independent of one another. Although some withdrawal is undoubtedly beyond the control of the individual, we contend that

most represents the outcome of a reasonably rational process of determining how to cope with dissatisfying work and/or life conditions. Howard Miller and I have previously described this as a model of employee adaptation (1984); a slightly amended version of this model is presented in figure 66–5.

In this coping process, dissatisfied workers may consider various strategies, possibly including being absent, coming in as late as possible, sleeping on the job, goofing off, or even quitting. In any particular situation we may observe one behavior, but it is important to realize that in another situation or time, another behavior might just as well have been exhibited. In other words, the various forms of withdrawal are to some extent substitutable, with the choice of one or another being dependent on such things as a lack of an alternative job, a stringent absence control policy, or social pressure from family or coworkers. The behaviors may also be a function of what one has done before; a number of studies have shown that prior absence is one of the best predictors of future absence (Breaugh, 1981; Keller, 1983; Rosse, 1988), and there is also evidence of a progression from lateness to absence and from absence to quitting (Gupta & Jenkins, 1982; Miller, 1982; Rosse, 1988).

A second problem with turnover and absence models is that they too narrowly define the behaviors of interest. Although the models of Mobley (1977) and Steers and Mowday (1981) mention the possibility of alternative forms of withdrawal, researchers' attention has been almost exclusively directed toward absence or turnover. These behaviors are better considered as two specific examples of a more fundamental behavioral family, that which I have previously labeled withdrawal. It seems intuitively obvious (and empirically verifiable) that the domain of withdrawal should include much more than simply absence and turnover. As one example, Beehr and Gupta (1978) have suggested that we think in terms of such categories of behavior as behavioral withdrawal (e.g., loitering in restrooms or near water fountains, arriving late or leaving early, wandering about trying to look busy) and psychological withdrawal (daydreaming, talking with coworkers, using alcohol and other drugs).

In the same vein, it is important to move beyond the idea of withdrawal. The primary reason people withdraw is to avoid undesirable aspects of a situation. However, it seems evident that avoidance is not the only means of coping with an undesirable situation; in fact, withdrawal may the option of last resort. Hirschman (1970) has suggested that employees have available to them three major classes of response: exit (essentially the same as withdrawal), voice (attempts to change rather than escape an undesirable situation,

Figure 66–5. A Model of Employee Adaptation

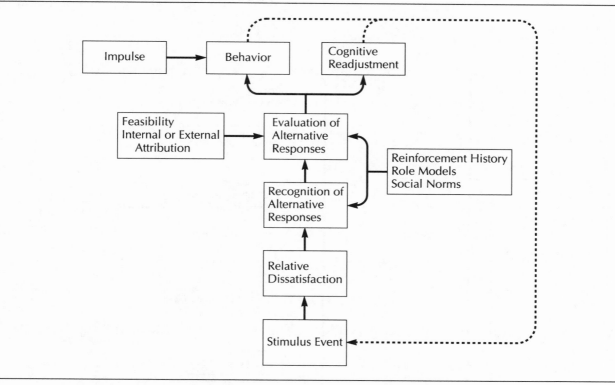

Source: Adapted from Rosse and Miller (1984).

including such strategies as changing the way work is done or grieving to a supervisor or union representative), and loyalty (waiting patiently for things to improve). Farrell (1983) has added a fourth response category he calls neglect, characterized by such "lax and disrespectful behavior" as lateness and increased errors.

It is for this reason that *adaptation* is suggested as a preferable summary term. Adaptation refers to the set of behavioral or cognitive strategies that a person may use to cope with dissatisfying working conditions. Under this umbrella term are multiple response families, each including a set of specific behaviors. Using these broader behavioral categories provides three major benefits: (1) behavioral families are likely to be more stable, and thus more predictable than individual behaviors; (2) multivariate models acknowledge the possibility that behaviors may substitute for one another; (3) thus they are more likely to represent actual behavior.

Hulin (in press) has built upon a variety of research traditions to offer the integrated model of adaptation and withdrawal described in figure 66–6. Consistent with past research and theory, job dissatisfaction is used as an indicator of a need to adapt. As described by Rosse and Miller (1984), the un-

happy worker begins a search for possible means of resolving his or her dissatisfaction. The success of strategies attempted in the past (either personally or the observed behavior of others), social norms, and perceptions of feasibility narrow the search for plausible strategies. Staw (1984) has implied that another factor influencing choice may be the person's beliefs about the cause of dissatisfaction. Internally directed blame may lead to either self-improvement or rationalization and cognitive readjustment, depending on the person's perceptions of the feasibility of improvement. Externally directed blame is more likely to produce efforts to change the situation; the feasibility of such change will determine whether the focus of such efforts will be constructive (e.g., grievances, lobbying, union activity) or destructive (e.g., sabotage and theft).

The development of these complex multibehavior models is still in its infancy, although initial tests have been encouraging. Farrell (1983) has presented evidence that people may in fact think in terms of exit, voice, loyalty, and neglect as dimensions of response. Rosse and Hulin (1985) and Roznowski, Miller, and Rosse (1989) have presented additional evidence of behavioral families and of their relationship to job attitudes.

Figure 66–6. Hulin's (in Press) Organizational Adaptation Withdrawal Model

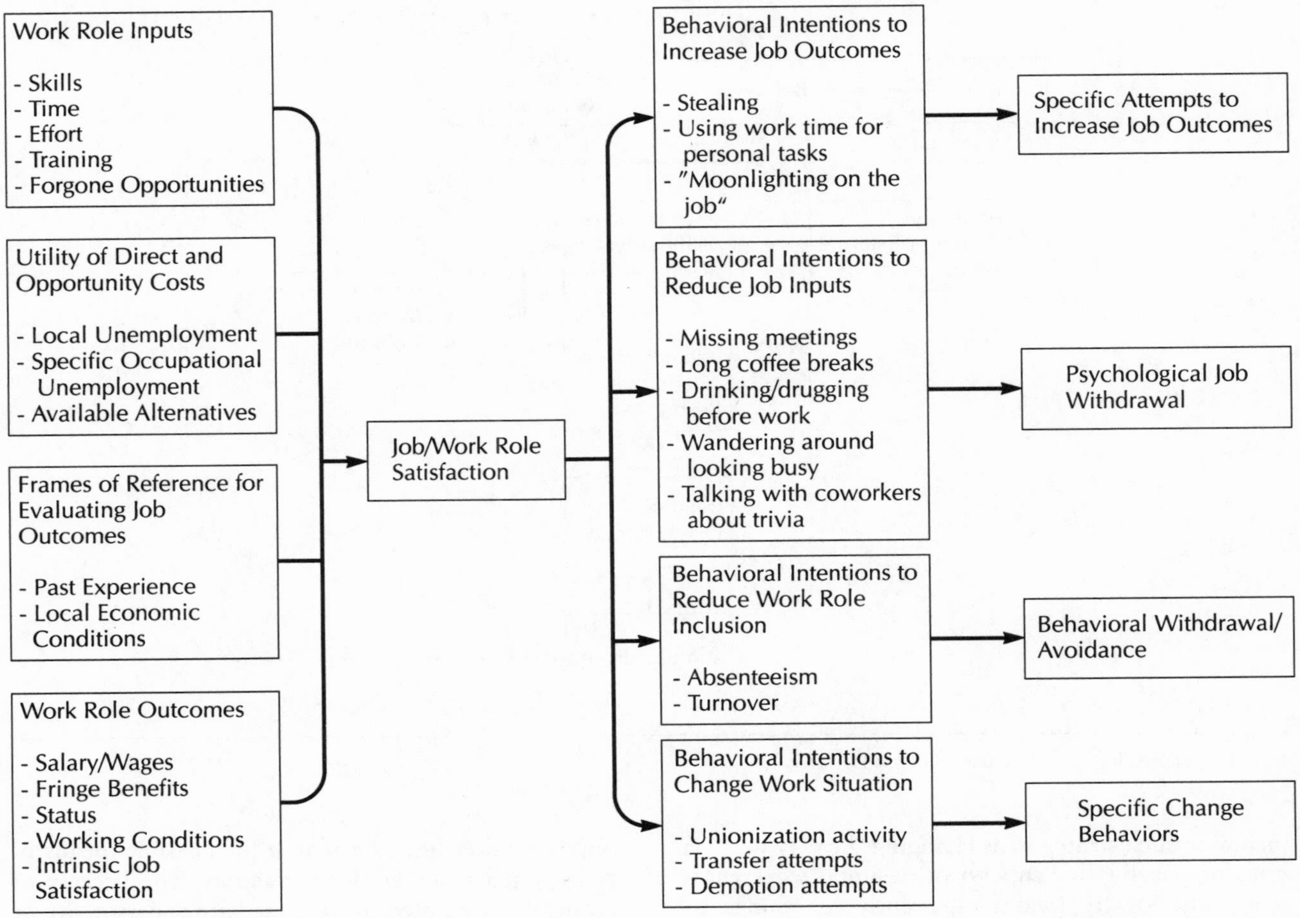

A particularly important aspect of this research is the emphasis on nonwithdrawal means of adapting to work. Although one recent study (Lee & Mowday, 1987) failed to find that people tried to change their jobs rather than quit, others have suggested that this may be a viable alternative. Spencer (1986), for example, found that turnover rates were lower when more opportunities for voicing complaints were present. Interestingly, Rosse and Hulin (1985) found that attempts to make changes were higher among more satisfied individuals, possibly because they were sufficiently committed to the firm to persist in trying to improve it rather than jump ship.

HOW SERIOUS A PROBLEM IS EMPLOYEE WITHDRAWAL?

As has repeatedly noted in this chapter, there has been a pervasive view that withdrawal is bad, due primarily to the costs associated with it. The obvious implication is that withdrawal should be reduced, and a variety of strategies for doing so have been suggested. Recently, however, a different perspective has evolved. According to this view, there is an optimal level of turnover, below which the costs of retention programs are likely to exceed their benefits. To evaluate this claim, we will briefly consider the costs and benefits of withdrawal. Since most of this research has concerned turnover, we will focus primarily on this behavior, although similar conclusions may be justified for other forms of withdrawal.

The Costs of Withdrawal

Conceptually it seems useful to appraise costs and benefits from the perspectives of the employee, the employing organization, and society, despite the fact that nearly all empirical research has adopted the organization's frame of reference.

From the individual's perspective, withdrawal (at least when it is voluntary) is typically assumed to be relatively beneficial. People presumably quit in order to accept better positions; they are absent in order to deal better with illnesses or to attend to errands; chatting with others around the water fountain may be more enjoyable than working. Nevertheless, quitting may involve some loss of accrued benefits, such transition costs as moving expenses, loss of friends, and disruption of children's and spouse's lives. Similarly, absenteeism may not always be covered under sick leave policies, and disciplinary procedures may be invoked for instances of tardiness, loafing, or theft. Thus, even for the individual engaging in them, acts of withdrawal may have detrimental consequences.

Costs to the organization of turnover generally take the form of (1) replacement costs, (2) lost production, (3) disruptions of social and communication structures, (4) decreased satisfaction among stayers, and (5) negative effects on public relations (Mobley, 1982). Less permanent forms of withdrawal also involve costs related to lost production, supervisors' time monitoring workers and arranging replacements, and added overtime (as well as increased stress and possibly even higher accident rates) for those who do show up for work (Goodman & Atkin, 1984). High levels of absenteeism may force the use of temporary labor services or even intentional overhiring in anticipation of absence. Ironically, a major problem in Italy (which has absenteeism rates approaching 14 percent) is how to handle the excess workers who show up on payday (Steers & Rhodes, 1984).

Most empirical assessments have focused on replacement costs. For nonsupervisory workers earning $10.90 per hour, Teel (1983) estimated that a company spends $2,042 for various separation costs, $1,449 for acquisition of a replacement, and $2,517 for training and lowered productivity, for a total cost of $6,008. His estimates range from $974 for hourly positions in the pharmaceutical industry to $39,502 (88 percent of annual pay) for a department manager in manufacturing. Gow (1985) estimated two months' pay for hourly employees, three months' pay for salaried workers, and six months' pay for managers. Although their figures are now obviously out of date, Mirvis and his associates estimated the cost of absence to be approximately $60 per incident for factory workers and bank tellers (Macy & Mirvis, 1976; Mirvis & Lawler, 1977).

Of course, replacement costs are likely to be somewhat different for every company, especially as a consequence of different labor markets. What is likely to be common to most firms is a tendency to underestimate (if not ignore) these costs. Thus, the development of a data base that allows managers to monitor not only the rates of turnover and absence but also their financial consequences, should be the first step in gaining top management's commitment to any programs designed to manage withdrawal. Wayne Cascio (1987) has authored an excellent guide for estimating the financial impact of turnover and absence (as well as many other human resource programs); it is highly recommended as a first step in analyzing the costs of withdrawal.

Before leaving the topic of costs, it should be noted that dysfunctional withdrawal has implications beyond the individual and his or her employer. Already mentioned is the effect on the morale of coworkers, who are presented with both a rejection, direct or indirect, and additional work. Training a replacement is likely to involve continued lower production, additional makeup work, and possibly additional risk of accidents for all involved. These factors also involve costs at the societal level; Steers and Rhodes (1984) estimated that the overall cost to society of absenteeism alone exceeds $30 billion.

The Benefits of Withdrawal

These cost estimates, while dramatic, represent only one side of the story. Under the proper set of circumstances many forms of withdrawal can provide distinct benefits to workers, their employers, and society. Indeed, the recognition of these benefits represents a dramatic and revolutionary change in the study of withdrawal.

As I have noted above, a person's decision to quit, be absent, or otherwise withdraw typically implies some expected benefits. People rarely quit their jobs without having a (presumably superior) alternative in mind (Matilla, 1974). That people respond to positive and negative incentive systems to reduce absenteeism suggests that when they are absent, they have decided that the benefits of absence exceed its costs. Aside from such direct benefits, researchers have shown that absence can play a safety valve function in helping workers cope with stressful jobs that might otherwise produce more permanent withdrawal or the development of stress disorders (Goodman & Atkin, 1984; Rosse & Miller, 1984.)

William Mobley (1982), among others, has noted that turnover may also be functional for an organization to the extent that it:

- Substitutes poor workers with more capable ones.
- Provides for infusion of new ideas (although Staw 1980 and Bluedorn 1982 have noted that this may be true primarily if newcomers are entering from outside the organization into relatively high-level positions).
- Increases opportunities for internal mobility.
- Results in a more satisfied group of remaining employees.
- Increases management flexibility to make structural or programmatic changes
- Results in a decrease in other withdrawal behaviors.

To this list, Dan Dalton and William Todor (1982) add savings due to lower salaries and reduced benefits with less senior employees, as well as possible recovery of unvested pension contributions. In their work with a public utility company, they calculated that these savings totaled $389,031 per year for a group of blue-collar workers experiencing a 15 percent turnover rate (note that this figure did not include the costs associated with the turnover).

Benefits of withdrawal to society are principally due to increased mobility. (Although one could probably suggest that any restriction of productivity also enlarges employment opportunities, the net effect to society of such "make-work" is arguably negative.) Because of the tendency of leavers to move quickly into a new job, turnover does not appear to increase unemployment (Bluedorn, 1982); rather this mobility is believed to allow for better person-job matches, to provide flexibility in migration patterns, and to allow upward mobility. As the baby boom generation has matured, promotions often become blocked, and external movement represents the only viable means of upward mobility. This increased mobility may be particularly important for increasing the representation of minorities and women in upper management positions.

Determining Acceptable Levels of Withdrawal

In sum, a more balanced view of withdrawal is that it involves both costs and benefits. The goal, then, should be to manage it in a cost-effective manner.

Dan Dalton and William Todor have made the point that when evaluating turnover rates, attention should be directed at that portion that is dysfunctional and avoidable. By dysfunctional, they mean the departure of workers that a firm would prefer not to lose (those above average in work performance or who would be difficult to replace). Avoidable turnover is essentially that which is voluntary. In a study of 190 branch banks they found that the overall turnover rate was 32 percent but that the rate of dysfunctional turnover was only 9 percent (using a replaceability criterion) to 18 percent (using a work performance criterion). Moreover, only 52 percent of turnover was judged to be avoidable. Combining the two criteria, only 4 to 10 percent of the turnover was both dysfunctional and avoidable (Dalton, Krackhardt & Porter, 1981). A recent metaanalysis showing that turnover is higher among poorer performers suggests that this finding is likely to apply to a majority of firms (McEvoy & Cascio, 1987).

Abelson and Baysinger (1984) have extended this argument to suggest that the loss of even good employees may be cost-effective. They contend that an analysis must include retention costs as well as separation costs. Retention costs include all measures taken to reduce attrition, as well as those costs associated with a longer-tenured work force (principally higher wage and benefit costs). They maintain that rather than focusing on individual cases of turnover, a firm should plot the separation and retention costs for different rates of turnover and then determine the optimal level (the point in figure 66–7 at which the two curves intersect). This point will probably be unique for every organization.

The advantage of Abelson and Baysinger's approach is simplicity. By focusing on an organization's total work force, they remove the difficulty of determining each individual's value to the firm. However, this simplicity is also the primary limitation of their model. Recent work by Frank Schmidt and Jack Hunter provides strong evidence that differences in ability can have substantial effects on a company's productivity (see part II of this *Handbook*). To assume that retention and separation costs are the same for all employees is unrealistic. Particularly disturbing is the assumption that the only difference between an experienced worker and a less experienced replacement is their relative wage and benefit costs.

As an example, Boudrea and Berger (1985) demonstrate that while a zero turnover rate for a ten-year period would result in zero acquisition and separation costs, such a strategy would be inferior to any situation (even random selection) in which a firm

Figure 66–7. Optimal Organizational Turnover Curve

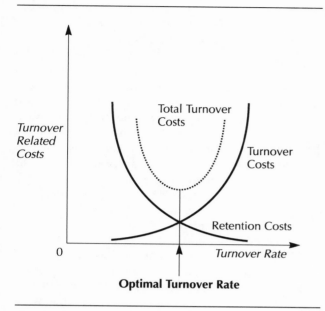

Source: Abelson & Baysinger (1984).

retains only the best performers or even to random retention when the selection system is highly valid.

The point is that the effective management of turnover requires the retention of experienced, high-performing workers and the replacement of "dead wood" with more capable (and also initially less expensive) newcomers who may also provide fresh insights. Boudreau and Berger (1985) provide an imposing but comprehensive set of equations for determining the cost-effectiveness of an organization's overall selection and retention processes; a less technical presentation is offered by Martin and Bartol (1985) in figure 66–8.

Reducing Withdrawal

If a cost-benefit analysis suggests a need to reduce withdrawal, the manager is faced with a number of options. As the reader can probably anticipate, there are no panaceas. I have emphasized throughout this chapter that withdrawal (or at least its volitional component) is primarily a matter of motivation—the desire to continue attending work rather than withdrawing. Thus, the best solutions are those that lead a person to decide to attend.

In determining what motivational factors to address, my advice is to use the various models of withdrawal as diagnostic guides to determine what factors are in need of attention in your particular

situation. Employee attitude surveys, custom designed to address the questions of interest, may be one of the most effective ways to obtain the necessary information. Hulin's (1968) field experiment provides an excellent example of how turnover can be reduced by an intervention that targets areas of employee dissatisfaction.

An honest and thorough diagnosis will probably highlight basic principles of effective human resource management rather than flashy quick solutions. In their cogent review of practical ways to increase attendance, Latham and Napier (1984) cite such fundamental strategies as matching people to jobs, measuring and publicly recording attendance, effective training, especially for supervisors, absence control programs using both positive and negative sanctions, redesigning jobs to make them more rewarding and to allow some discretionary time (e.g., flextime), stress management, and self-management training.

Figure 66–8. The Performance-Replaceability Strategy Matrix

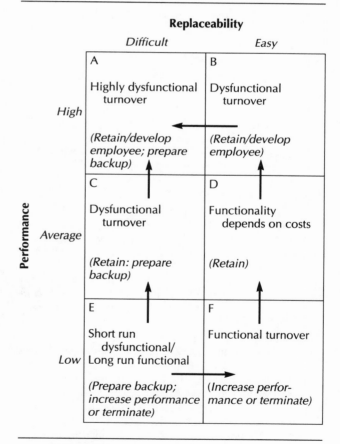

A similar conclusion emerges from McEvoy and Cascio's (1985) metaanalysis of strategies for controlling turnover. They concluded that two effective strategies include providing realistic job previews (an average 9 percent improvement in fifteen studies), and job enrichment (an average 17 percent improvement in five studies). Although not mentioned in their review, weighted application blanks (Breaugh & Dossett, 1989) have also proved to be an effective way to hire those least likely to quit.

Most of the empirical research on absence reduction has focused on the use of negative sanctions (Nicholson, 1976) on positive rewards (Pedalino & Gamboa, 1974), or combinations of them (Kopelman & Schneller, 1981). Schlotzhauer and Rosse (1985) demonstrated how a reward for attendance resulted in a 32 percent reduction in absence over a three-year period in a hospital setting. While some such programs have been criticized as not being cost-effective, Schlotzhauer and Rosse found that the program had an 11.7 percent return on investment.

I feel that such targeted programs, while impressive, should be treated only as stop-gap measures. The models of withdrawal and adaptation lead us to predict that such "Band-aid" solutions will likely produce other problems, such as increased use of medical leaves (Nicholson, 1976) or other forms of withdrawal that are not included in the program.

Consistent with Latham and Napier's suggestions, I would prefer to see a program that emphasizes hiring those who are well matched (in terms of both ability and motivation) to jobs that are both intrinsically and extrinsically rewarding. The match should then be bolstered by effective training, development, and career management programs throughout the employee's tenure. Positive forms of adaptation should be encouraged, and supervisors should be trained and rewarded for supporting such changes. Finally, the importance of attendance should be clearly expressed through policies and consistent measurement, and employees should be encouraged to manage their own behavior (see Frayne & Latham, 1987, for an excellent example of self-management training). As Latham and Napier note, a comprehensive program such as this should pay dividends in increasing performance, as well as reducing withdrawal tendencies.

REFERENCES

Abelson, M., & Baysinger, B. (1984). Optimal and dysfunctional turnover: Toward an organizational level model. *Academy of Management Review, 9,* 331–341.

Adler, S., & Golan, J. (1981). Lateness as a withdrawal behavior. *Journal of Applied Psychology, 66*(5), 544–554.

Beehr, T., & Gupta, N. (1978). A note on the structure of employee withdrawal. *Organizational Behavior and Human Performance, 21,* 73–79.

Bluedorn, A. (1982). The theories of turnover: Causes, effects, and meaning. *Research in the Sociology of Organizations, 1,* 75–128.

Boudreau, J., & Berger, C. (1985). Decision-theoretic utility analysis applied to employee separations and acquisitions. *Journal of Applied Psychology Monograph, 70*(3), 581–612.

Breaugh, J. (1981). Predicting absenteeism from prior absenteeism and work attitudes. *Journal of Applied Psychology, 66,* 555–560.

Breaugh, J., & Dossett, D. (1989). Rethinking the use of personal history information: The value of theory-based biodata for predicting turnover. *Journal of Business and Psychology, 3,* 371–385.

Brooke, P. (1986). Beyond the Steers and Rhodes model of employee attendance. *Academy of Management Review, 11*(2), 345–361.

Bureau of National Affairs (1987). Median job absence and turnover rates. *Policy and practice series: Personnel management, 267,* 49–68.

Carsten, J., & Spector, P. (1987). Unemployment, job satisfaction and employee turnover: A meta-analytic test of the Muchinsky model. *Journal of Applied Psychology, 72*(3), 374–381.

Cascio, W. (1987). *Costing human resources.* Boston: Kent Publishing.

Dalton, D., Krackhardt, D., & Porter, L. (1981). Functional turnover: An empirical assessment. *Journal of Applied Psychology, 66,* 716–721.

Dalton, D., & Todor, W. (1982). Turnover: A lucrative hard dollar phenomenon. *Academy of Management Review, 7,* 212–218.

Eagley, R. (1965). Market power as an intervening mechanism in Phillips Curve analysis. *Economics, 32,* 48–64.

Farrell, D. (1983). Exit, voice, loyalty and neglect as responses to job dissatisfaction: A multidimensional scaling study. *Academy of Management Journal, 26*(4), 596–607.

Farrell, D., & Robb, D. (1979). Lateness to work: A study of withdrawal from work. Unpublished manuscript, Department of Management, Western Michigan University.

Ferris, G., & Rowland, K. (1987). Tenure as a moderator of the absence–intent to leave relationship. *Human Relations, 40*(5), 255–266.

Frayne, C.A., & Latham, G.P. (1987). Application of social learning theory to employee self-management of attendance. *Journal of Applied Psychology, 72*, 387–392.

Gaudet, F. (1963). *Solving the problem of employee absence.* New York: American Management Association.

Gibson, R. (1966). Toward a reconceptualization of absence behavior of personnel in organizations. *Administrative Science Quarterly, 11*, 107–133.

Goodman, P., & Atkin, R. (1984). Effects of absenteeism on individuals and organizations. In P. Goodman et al., *Absenteeism.* San Francisco: Jossey-Bass.

Gow, J. (1985). Human resource managers must remember the bottom line. *Personnel Journal, 64*(4), 30–32.

Gupta, N., & Jenkins, G.D. (1982). Absenteeism and turnover: Is there a progression? *Journal of Management Studies, 19*(4), 395–412.

Hirschman, A. (1970). *Exit, voice and loyalty: Responses to decline in firms, organizations, and states.* Cambridge, MA: Harvard University Press.

Hulin. C. (1968). Effects of changes in job satisfaction levels on employee turnover. *Journal of Applied Psychology, 52*, 122–126.

Hulin, C. (in press). Adaptation, persistence and commitment in organizations. In M. Dunnette (Ed.), *Handbook of industrial/organizational psychology* (2d ed.). New York: Elbraum.

Hulin, C., Roznowski, M., & Hachiya, D. (1985). Alternative opportunities and withdrawal decisions: Empirical and theoretical discrepancies and an integration. *Psychological Bulletin, 97*(2), 233–250.

Keller, R. (1983). Predicting absenteeism from prior absenteeism, attitudinal factors, and nonattitudinal factors. *Journal of Applied Psychology, 68*, 536–540.

Knapp, D. (1984). Personal communication, December 13.

Kopelman, R.E., & Schneller, G.O. (1981). A mixed consequence system for reducing overtime and unscheduled absence. *Journal of Organizational Behavior Management, 3*, 17–28.

Latham, G., & Napier, N. (1984). Practical ways to increase employee attendance. In P. Goodman et al., *Absenteeism.* San Francisco: Jossey-Bass.

Lee, T., & Mowday, R. (1987). Voluntarily leaving an organization: An empirical investigation of Steers and Mowday's model of turnover. *Academy of Management Journal, 30*(4), 721–743.

McEvoy, G., & Cascio, W. (1985) Strategies for reducing employee turnover: A meta-analysis. *Journal of Applied Psychology, 70*, 342–353.

McEvoy, G., & Cascio, W. (1987). Do good or poor performers leave? A meta-analytic analysis of the relationship between performance and turnover. *Academy of Management Journal, 30*(4), 744–762.

Macy, B., & Mirvis, P. (1976). Measuring quality of work and organizational effectiveness in behavioral-economic terms. *Administrative Science Quarterly, 21*, 212–226.

March, J., & Simon, H. (1958). *Organizations.* New York: Wiley.

Markham, S. (1985). An investigation of the relationship between unemployment and absenteeism: A multilevel approach. *Academy of Management Journal, 28*(1), 228–234.

Martin, D., & Bartol, K. (1985). Managing turnover strategically. *Personnel Administrator, 30*(11), 63–73.

Matilla, J. (1974). Job quitting and frictional unemployment. *American Economic Review, 64*, 235–239.

Miller, H. (1982). *Some evidence concerning the progression of withdrawal hypothesis.* Paper presented at the 42d annual meeting of the Academy of Management, New York, August.

Miller, H., Katerberg, R., & Hulin, C. (1979). Evaluation of the Mobley, Horner and Hollingsworth model of employee turnover. *Journal of Applied Psychology, 64*(5), 509–517.

Mirvis, P., & Lawler, E. (1977). Measuring the financial impact of employee attitudes. *Journal of Applied Psychology, 62*(1), 1–8.

Mobley, W. (1977). Intermediate linkages in the relationship between job satisfaction and employee turnover. *Journal of Applied Psychology, 62*, 237–240.

Mobley, W. (1982). Some unanswered questions in turnover and withdrawal research. *Academy of Management Review, 7*(1), 111–116.

Mobley, W., Griffeth, R., Hand, H., & Meglino, B. (1979). Review and conceptual analysis of the employee turnover process. *Psychological Bulletin, 86*(3), 493–522.

Muchinsky, P. (1977). Employee absenteeism: A review of the literature. *Journal of Vocational Behavior, 10*, 316–340.

Muchinsky, P., & Morrow, P. (1980). A multidisciplinary model of voluntary employee turnover. *Journal of Vocational Behavior, 17*, 263–290.

Nicholson, N. (1976). Management sanctions and absence controls. *Human Relations, 29*, 139–151.

Nicholson, N. (1977). Absence behavior and attendance motivation: A conceptual synthesis. *Journal of Management Studies, 14*(3), 231–252.

Nicholson, N., & Johns, G. (1985). The absence culture and the psychological contract—Who's in control of absence? *Academy of Management Review, 10*(3), 397–407.

Pedalino, E., & Gamboa, V.U. (1974). Behavior modification and absenteeism: Intervention in one industrial setting. *Journal of Applied Psychology, 59*, 694–698.

Price, J. (1977). *The study of turnover.* Ames: Iowa State University Press.

Rosse, J. (1988). Relations among lateness, absence and turnover: Is there a progression of withdrawal? *Human Relations, 41*(7), 517–531.

Rosse, J., & Hulin, C. (1985). Adaptation to work: Analysis of employee health, withdrawal, and change. *Organizational Behavior and Human Decision Processes, 36*, 324–347.

Rosse, J., & Miller, H. (1984). Relationship between absenteeism and other employee behaviors. In P. Goodman et al., Associates, *Absenteeism.* San Francisco: Jossey-Bass.

Rousseau, D. (1978). Relationship of work to nonwork.

Journal of Applied Psychology, 63(4), 513–517.

Roznowski, M., Miller, H., & Rosse, J. (1989). Employee attitudes, withdrawal cognitions and adaptive behaviors. Unpublished manuscript, Department of Psychology, Ohio State University.

Schlotzhauer, D.L., & Rosse, J. (1985). A five-year study of a positive incentive absence control program. *Personnel Psychology, 38*, 575–585.

Scott, K., & Taylor, G. (1985). An examination of conflicting findings on the relationship between job satisfaction and absenteeism: A meta-analysis. *Academy of Management Journal, 28*(3), 599–612.

Smith, F. (1976). Work attitudes as predictors of specific day attendance. *Journal of Applied Psychology, 62*(1), 16–19.

Spencer, D. (1986). Employee voice and employee retention. *Academy of Management Journal, 29*(3), 488–502.

Staw, B. (1980). The consequences of turnover. *Journal of Occupational Behavior, 1*, 253–270.

Staw, B. (1984). Organizational behavior: A review and reformulation of the field's outcome variables. *Annual Review of Psychology, 35*, 627–666.

Staw, B., & Oldham, G. (1978). Reconsidering our dependent variables: A critique and empirical study. *Academy of Management Journal, 21*(4), 539–559.

Steel, R., & Ovalle, N. (1984) A review and meta-analysis of research on the relationship between behavioral intentions and employee turnover. *Journal of Applied Psychology, 69*(4), 673–686.

Steers, R., & Mowday, R. (1981). Employee turnover and post-decision accommodation process. *Research in Organizational Behavior, 3*, 235–281.

Steers, R., & Rhodes, S. (1978). Major influences on employee attendance: A process model. *Journal of Applied Psychology, 63*, 391–407.

Steers, R., & Rhodes, S. (1984). Knowledge and speculation about absenteeism. In P. Goodman et al., *Absenteeism.* San Francisco: Jossey-Bass.

Teel, K. (1983). Estimating employee replacement costs. *Personnel Journal, 62*(12), 956–960.

Terborg, J., Lee, T., Smith, F., Davis, G., & Turbin, M. (1982). Extension of the Schmidt and Hunter validity generalization procedure to the prediction of absenteeism behavior from knowledge of job satisfaction and organization commitment. *Journal of Applied Psychology, 67*(4), 440–449.

Youngblood, S. (1984). Work, nonwork, and withdrawal. *Journal of Applied Psychology, 69*, 106–117.

67 MANAGING YOUR ORGANIZATION'S USE OF TEMPORARY EMPLOYEES

Bruce N. Barge

Historically, the stereotype of a temporary employee has been that of a clerical or light industrial worker with limited skills who "fills in as best he or she can" for a permanent worker who is sick or on vacation. Temporary employees have been viewed as persons who lack the abilities or temperament to be able to hold a permanent job. Temporary assignments were traditionally composed of tasks that were too short-lived, boring, or unpleasant to be suitable for permanent employees. In short, the use of temporaries was a stop-gap measure employed in a limited number of jobs to meet emergency or undesirable organizational requirements.

Today, however, the status of temporary work is considerably different. Average annual employment in the temporary help industry nearly doubled between 1982 and 1986, rising to 786,000 employees nationwide (Dennis & Silverman, 1987). This was three times the rate of increase for the expanding service sector and more than eight times the rate for all nonagricultural workers (Carey & Hazelbaker, 1986). The U.S. Office of Personnel Management alone (which keeps separate statistics) reports filling 244,692 jobs with temporary employees in 1984 (Granrose & Appelbaum, 1986). Annual payroll for temporary employees topped $7.3 billion in 1986 (Dennis & Silverman, 1987), and many organizations include temporary work as a separate line item in their annual budgets (Macauley, 1986). The use of temporary workers is increasingly seen as a stable and important part of an organization's total work force strategy.

The range of jobs held by temporary employees has also increased dramatically. Only 43 percent of temporary employment today is in the administrative support and clerical area (Bureau of Labor Statistics; Howe, 1986). This area has also expanded to include large numbers of word processing and data entry assignments in addition to traditional clerical and accounting work. The remainder of temporary employment is largely in four occupational markets: light industrial, medical, sales and marketing, and technical (Carey & Hazelbaker, 1986). Light industrial includes precision and manual assembly, operation of machines, material handling, and janitorial assignments. Medical includes short-term health care by registered nurses and licensed practical nurses in hospitals, nursing homes, and, increasingly, private homes. Sales and marketing assignments involve telemarketing, retail, and convention and promotion activities. Finally, the technical area pertains to engineering, design, computer programming, and other technical work performed on a project basis.

PATTERNS OF INDUSTRY GROWTH

The growth experienced by the temporary industry has traditionally been cyclical, in response to broad economic trends. Temporary employment declines early in a recession and recovers quickly at the begin-

Figure 67–1. Comparison of Employment Growth Indexes in the Temporary Help, Services, and Nonagricultural Industries, 1978–1985

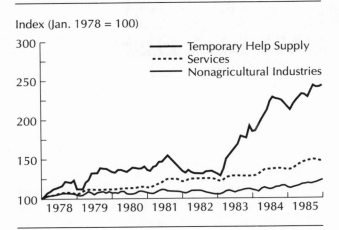

Index (Jan. 1978 = 100)

— Temporary Help Supply
···· Services
— Nonagricultural Industries

ning of an expansion. This pattern is illustrated in figure 67–1 for the period from 1978 to 1985. As shown, temporary employment varied with the cycles of the economy. The industry also recorded a steady increase in total employment that far exceeded the growth rate of the economy as a whole.

In projecting growth for the 1990s, economists expect this trend to continue. The Bureau of Labor Statistics predicts an annual growth rate of 5 percent through 1995 in the temporary help market if a scenario of moderate national economic growth is assumed. This rate compares favorably with the 4.2 percent projected for business services as a whole and the 1.3 percent projected for all industries. Similar ratios are estimated if scenarios of greater or lesser national growth are assumed (Carey & Hazelbaker, 1986).

FACTORS CONTRIBUTING TO GROWTH IN TEMPORARY EMPLOYMENT

A number of economic and societal changes have contributed to the continuing expansion of the temporary work force, and these changes have produced advantages in temporary work for both the employer and the employee. The underlying theme for nearly all of these advantages is the increased flexibility afforded. For the employer, short-notice access to qualified temporary personnel allows the organization to keep permanent staffing levels to a minimum. Temporary employees can be brought on board during peak periods and retained for only the interval needed. This allows the company to reduce labor costs overall and particularly during slack periods.

The strategy described above is sometimes referred to as a "core and ring" system. Permanent employees are the core, and temporary employees serve as a buffer for the economy. The organization's permanent employees are more secure from layoffs, and the company also reduces its costs for labor and especially for benefits. Even in industries that are not highly cyclical, the flexibility of temporary workers allows them to be used for one-time projects that are not well suited for the permanent work force. For example, a temporary with a library background might be brought in to develop an indexing system when no permanent employee had experience in that area. A temporary might also be enlisted for computer-assisted design (CAD) work that was short

term in nature but that required knowledge of CAD equipment. Temporary employees thus provide a flexible and less expensive way to augment the permanent work force.

The flexibility of temporary work can be an advantage for the employee as well. Many potential employees do not care to work in permanent jobs because of family, school, or personal commitments. Temporary employment allows them the ability to choose when they wish to work. Other potential advantages for the temporary worker include a higher cash wage (typically without benefits), the variety of differing assignments, and the chance to explore various jobs before choosing a permanent position.

In many ways, the growth of temporary work is a reflection of the changing nature of society. Mothers with small children are entering the work force earlier and at a higher rate, but they may wish to retain the option of not working during certain periods. Professionals with strong outside interests or persons who retire early may want to continue working but only on a limited, flexible basis. Even permanent employees are sometimes interested in reduced hours, job sharing, or other arrangements that might require use of a temporary. Thus, the higher premium placed on flexibility by today's work force has contributed to greater participation in temporary work.

STRATEGIC MANAGEMENT OF THE TEMPORARY WORK FORCE

Since temporary employment is likely to remain an important part of an organization's total staffing capability, it is important that the special demands and considerations associated with use of temporaries be understood. Temporary work is not just an abbreviated form of permanent work; it has its own unique set of requirements and potential problems. The temporary resource is also best utilized when employed in a proactive, strategic manner rather than a reactive, crisis-management mode. Organizations can plan their use of temporaries and can thereby minimize disruptions and unnecessary wage and benefit costs. Organizations can also plan the acquisition of new skills, perhaps experimenting with a temporary at a much lower cost than that available from a permanent employee.

The remainder of this chapter presents information designed to aid an organization in optimizing its use of temporary employees. First, characteristics of temporary work are discussed that differentiate it from permanent work. Knowledge of these characteristics is essential for working effectively with the employees and/or a temporary employee firm. Next, the question of procuring temporaries is explored. When is a temporary employee preferable to a permanent employee? Should procurement be handled internally or externally, and what does an employer need to know about the process? Finally, orientation and supervision of temporaries are addressed. Procedures are described to aid the integration of temporaries into the total work force.

UNIQUE CHARACTERISTICS OF TEMPORARY WORK

Temporary work differs from permanent jobs in a number of ways, yet many of these differences are not readily apparent. The differences are often very important, however, and understanding their significance can greatly improve communication and performance. For example, a permanent employee often has a job description, a training or initiation period that may last several days or weeks, and a chance to shape the job gradually to fit personal preferences and abilities. By contrast, a temporary is usually given verbal instructions, is expected to become oriented to the assignment within a much shorter period (often just a few minutes), and is asked to perform the assignment following a format that may or may not fit the employee's personal style. Thus, the short-term nature of temporary work may greatly change the way in which a person approaches a given job.

Another difference for temporary employees is the way in which they are treated by coworkers. Temporary employees are frequently ostracized by permanent employees, left out of conversations, and treated as "just a temp." This isolation makes the temporary feel uncomfortable and less likely to ask for help or to offer suggestions. Some of these experiences may be encountered by permanent employees when beginning a job, but they are faced by temporaries with each new assignment.

A third unique feature of temporary work is the lack of dependability and stability for the employee. An employee may not know his or her work schedule until shortly before the assignment begins and is sometimes unsure how long the assignment will last. One-week assignments sometimes extend to six months, and the reverse can also occur. One assignment might start work at 10 A.M. and the next at 7 A.M. The tasks and coworkers can also vary greatly from one assignment to another.

From a management perspective, temporary employment is similarly unique. Supervisors may feel that they are just beginning to be familiar with an employee when the assignment is ending. They may find it difficult to know how much trust to place in an employee or when the employee is being underutilized. A supervisor may also be unsure how much time to invest in training or orientation for a temporary employee. Thus, the unique nature of temporary work supplies special challenges for both the temporary and the supervisor.

PROCURING TEMPORARY EMPLOYEES

Forming an Employment Strategy

Perhaps the first question an organization faces in the area of temporary employment is when and where to use temporary employees. An organization's strategy can range from simple replacement of absent workers to an elaborate "core and ring" system as described earlier. Factors to consider in evaluating possible strategies include the type of organization, the nature of the labor market available, and the costs associated with use of either permanent or temporary workers. Specific considerations for each of these factors are shown in table 67–1.

The questions shown in table 67–1 serve as an informal checklist of the many issues that may affect an organization's strategic plan regarding temporary workers. If desired, these questions could serve as a starting point for a more formal analysis of the feasibility of various strategies. This type of analysis, whether formal or informal, can be of great value to an organization. The information provided allows the organization to position itself so that it can maximize the potential benefit of temporary employees and minimize any possible risk.

As an example, an organization may find that per-hour wage and benefit costs are approximately 10 percent higher for permanent workers than temporary workers (in the local labor market). This cost advantage for temporary workers might increase by another 20 percent if total employee hours were reduced by adjusting quickly to fluctuations in work load. The organization may find an adequate supply of temporary workers available but only in certain skill areas. Variability of work load and the need for employee continuity might also differ by department or type of job. Other factors addressed in table 67–1 could be an approximately equal trade-off between use of temporary and permanent workers.

In this situation, the organization would be well prepared for implementing an informed strategy regarding temporary employment. The organization could decide the levels of "core" permanent employees that were required on a long-term basis, as well as the areas in which temporary workers might serve as a buffer for work load and economic variability. The payoff in reduced labor costs for using temporary employees could also be calculated. Procedures could be established to anchor the new strategy into ongoing personnel decisions in areas such as the budget, staffing, and work force management. If warranted, the permanent work force could be reduced in certain departments or job types through attrition, transfers,

Table 67–1
Criteria for Developing a Temporary Employment Strategy

Type of Organization	
Cyclical nature of work	How stable is the work load over time?
Type and level of jobs	What skills would temporaries need to have?
Length of work activities	How important is employee continuity to performance?
Structural differences	Are temporaries more feasible for some departments?
Labor Issues	
Permanent work force	How adequate is the selection pool for permanent workers?
Temporary help agencies	Are local agencies able to meet employment needs?
Internal temporary pool	Is it feasible to maintain your own temporaries?
Union position	Are permanent workers opposed to temporary workers?
Demographics	Will using temporaries change the mix of workers?
Potential Costs	
Wages	How do temporary and permanent wages compare?
Benefits/pension/fringe	How much can use of temporaries save in this area?
Recruiting/selection	Are temporary employees cheaper to bring on board?
Administration	How much administrative cost is involved for each?
Training	Do temporaries receive less training overall?
Turnover	What does it cost to move temporaries in and out?
Performance differences	Will performance be lower among temporaries?
Legal	Are legal liabilities different for temporaries?
Organizational image	Will using more temporaries create an image problem?

and early retirement. Overall, the organization would possess the information to maximize flexibility and cost-effectiveness across the full range of employment options.

The Process of Obtaining Temporary Employees

Organizations obtain most temporary employees from external sources such as a temporary employee agency, but some organizations prefer to maintain their own temporary employee pool. Such an internal pool may be particularly well suited to an organization that employs large numbers of temporaries or that has specialized needs that are not easily met externally. To determine whether an internal pool is feasible for your organization, calculate the amount of money saved by avoiding external agency fees and contrast it with the costs of administering your own temporary agency. Factors to consider are similar for administering either an internal or external service, as is described below.

The central task of a temporary employment service is the same as for permanent employment: employees need to be recruited, screened, placed, and compensated in a fair and accurate manner. This process is not as straightforward in the temporary as in the permanent market, however, because of the brevity and variety of temporary assignments. For temporaries, recruitment and screening decisions may be based on many rather than one assignment. Placement and compensation decisions may vary from one assignment to another even for the same employee. A temporary agency must also make these decisions quickly and inexpensively in order to maintain profitability.

An agency's hiring process begins with recruiting, which is typically done through signs, newspaper and radio ads, and personal referrals. Most temporary employers are interested in a broad spectrum of skills and can therefore draw applicants from many sources. Unfortunately, employees with skills that are in shortest supply may be the least interested in temporary work. Additional advertising and incentives may therefore be necessary with this group. Overall, the goal of the recruiting effort is to obtain on file the names and qualifications of a large number of potential employees who are suited in differing ways to the relevant employee market. Temporary work and temporary workers tend to be transitory, so the larger and more diverse is the available talent pool, the better is the chance for an effective person-assignment match.

Screening these applicants represents an interesting challenge, since the applicant is not being screened with a particular job in mind. Applicants typically indicate broad areas of assignment in which they are interested (which may include a very wide range of knowledge, skills, and abilities), and the agency then administers some combination of the interview, application form, reference check, and tests. Screening needs to be broad in order to pertain to a range of assignments but must also be tailored to the individual applicant and his or her employment potential. Characteristics that may be addressed include a variety of specific knowledges and skills (e.g., word processing procedures, fine dexterity) as well as appearance, punctuality, honesty, and similar other characteristics. Since an applicant for temporary work is applying for a number of potential assignments, results from a single screening are often used as the basis for several possible placements. These placement decisions may also be made months and even years after initial screening. To avoid placing an employee who is over- or underqualified, screening results need to be augmented or updated periodically. Results also need to be compared carefully to the requirements of each potential assignment in order to ensure the best possible match between the employee and the assignment. Employers today have high expectations for temporary workers, and validity of the screening and placement process is absolutely necessary if an organization is to utilize these workers as a key part of the total staffing strategy. Validity is also necessary to meet the legal requirements set forth by the courts, the Equal Employment Opportunity Commission, and by professional guidelines.

Temporary employers must be able to demonstrate that their employee assessment process (1) is based upon the requirements of each assignment to be performed, (2) does not result in adverse impact against protected groups, and (3) can be shown to be job related if it does result in adverse impact. Employers that do not possess evidence regarding these points are liable for suit by applicants or employees who are dissatisfied with screening-based decisions. A satisfactory system for temporary employees may, however, be quite different from one for permanent employees because of the diversity and number of assignments a temporary might perform. The key here is to group the requirements of assignments into defensible categories and to establish direct linkages between components of the screening process and these assignment requirements.

Compensation of temporary employees is largely in wages, although a long-term temporary can obtain benefits from some agencies. Wages are typically based on skill and experience level (e.g. registered nurse versus licensed practical nurse versus health aide), as well as the prevailing wage in the local permanent market. In some cases, wage adjustments may be made based on the assignment. For example, a temporary may receive more money for an assign-ment with special requirements or may request a raise midway through a long-term assignment. Temporary work agencies try to pay at a level that will attract applicants but that is also sufficiently lower than the acceptable billing rate to allow a profit.

ORIENTING AND SUPERVISING TEMPORARY EMPLOYEES

Temporary employees are usually given a brief orientation by the employer when beginning an assignment. This orientation acquaints the employee with the resources and requirements involved and also helps the temporary feel more comfortable in the new work setting. Supervisors should tailor the length of the orientation according to the duration and complexity of the assignment as well as the skills of the individual employee. As a rule of thumb, the orientation should be long enough and detailed enough that the temporary can function effectively with only occasional supervision or help.

The orientation should be designed to accomplish four simple objectives. First, the temporary should understand the tasks required in the assignment and the procedures that need to be followed to accomplish these tasks. Second, the resources available to aid in the work should be explained. Third, the temporary should know who to contact if he or she has questions about the work. Finally, the orientation should make the temporary feel comfortable and welcome in the new work environment. These objectives are fairly obvious if the supervisor thinks about them, yet temporaries are often asked to function without one or more of these critical pieces of information. By spending the extra few minutes that may be required to cover each objective, the supervisor can greatly increase the productivity of the employee.

Following orientation, the temporary employee must be managed, which involves many of the issues that apply to permanent employees and also some unique requirements. The key throughout each of these requirements is the integration of temporaries into the total work force effort, as described below. First, the work performed by temporary employees must be seen as essential to the organization by both permanent employees and the temporaries themselves. This message can come from management in a number of ways, including both formal communications and the manner in which management works with temporaries. Second, cooperation and commu-nication must take place between both types of employees. The focus here should be on permanent employees since they may feel they have much to lose and nothing to gain from cooperating with temporary workers. Permanent employees also have the knowledge and network to be able to sabotage the working relationship if they are opposed to use of temporaries.

Third, the use of temporaries needs to be viewed as a planned activity that provides important flexibility and skills rather than an interruption or crisis-management effort. Again, this is in part an organizational perception that needs to be managed. In addition, it will require managers to use the organization's overall strategy to project ways in which temporaries can augment the permanent work force. Finally, the temporary employees need to be treated as valued resources who are deserving of attention and respect. This applies as well to permanent employees but is particularly important for temporaries because of the uncertainty they experience in the new work setting.

The overall focus for this integration of temporary employees into the total work force revolves around the organizational strategy that was described earlier. Managers need to be aware of the organization's position on temporary work and the way in which these employees will be utilized. They can then adapt this information to fit the needs and style of their department or work unit. Managers whose departments will use a lot of temporaries may choose to make structural or supervisory changes that would be more conducive to integrating temporary employee work. Another approach might be to provide training to permanent employees regarding the best way to cooperate with their temporary coworkers. A number of management strategies could be effective in recognizing the unique status of temporary employment and making corresponding adjustments. The objective of all of these strategies will be to create a work atmosphere that is conducive to cooperative effort and performance throughout the entire work force.

CONCLUSION

This chapter has presented evidence regarding the changing nature of temporary employment in organizations today. This type of employment is growing rapidly in size and is also expanding greatly in breadth and skill level. The organization of tomorrow is likely to make increasing use of the temporary resource as the economy continues to fluctuate and diversify and the labor force demands greater flexibility in working arrangements. Temporary work is here to stay, and the organizations that appreciate and incorporate this trend are likely to gain a significant advantage in total employee productivity.

In order to maximize the respective strengths of permanent and temporary employees, an organization needs to develop an explicit strategy of work force utilization. This strategy will then drive decisions regarding procurement, training, and management of all employees. Without such a strategy, an organization is doomed to function in a reactive mode that cannot fully access the considerable advantages of the temporary resource. By contrast, the organization that possesses a strategy can be proactive in obtaining the employee resources best suited to its immediate needs and utilizing them in an intelligent and integrated manner.

REFERENCES

Carey, M.L., & Hazelbaker, K.L. (1986). Employment growth in the temporary help industry. *Monthly Labor Review* (April), 37–44.

Dennis, S., & Silverman, L. (1987). The temporary help industry—An annual update. *Contemporary Times, 19* (6), 6–8.

Granrose, C.S., & Appelbaum, E. (1986). The efficiency of temporary help and part-time employment. *Personnel Administrator* (January), 71–83.

Howe, W.J. (1986). Temporary help workers: Who they are, what jobs they hold. *Monthly Labor Review* (November), 45–47.

Macauley, W.W. (1986). Developing trends in the temporary services industry. *Personnel Administrator* (January), 61–68.

68 PREVALENCE AND TYPES OF SEXUAL HARASSMENT IN THE WORKPLACE

Ann Fuehrer, Karen Maitland Schilling, Peggy Crull, Meg Bond, Ann D'Ercole, Pat O'Connor

According to Department of Labor statistics, women currently make up 44.3 percent of the employed labor force (Monthly Labor Review, 1987). Women's numerical representation in the workplace has been steadily increasing, creating a threat to men who believe that they will lose their jobs, or their influence in those jobs, to newly hired women. Although women's numbers have increased, it is still true that men are likely to be in positions to hire and fire female colleagues. And when men and women occupy the same job title, men are often more senior than women coworkers. Thus, the nature of the modern workplace is still determined by men's decisions.

This situation is a problematic one for many women because they have been socialized to have somewhat different expectations for work and relationships from their male counterparts. To the extent that women are unable to influence the nature of their work environment, they may feel as if they have to endure responses to the threat of their increasing numbers that are sexualized and, in some cases, harassing.

We believe that women's decreased productivity, experience of stressful relationships, and flight from many major corporations are, in part, a result of this harassment. This chapter provides clear definitions of sexual harassment, develops a number of theories of its causes, and provides a number of recommendations for its elimination. Prevention of harassment, education of employees about its costs, and investigation and resolution of all complaints of sexual harassment are the legal responsibility of all employers. Thus, employers need to understand the unacceptability of sexual harassment in the workplace and work toward its elimination.

DEFINITIONS OF SEXUAL HARASSMENT

Guidelines of the Equal Employment Opportunity Commission (EEOC) (1980) suggest that sexual harassment be defined as unwelcome sexual advances, requests for sexual favors, and other verbal or physical conduct of a sexual nature that occur under one of three conditions:

> 1) submission to such conduct is made either explicitly or implicitly a term or condition of an individual's employment; 2) submission to or rejection of such conduct by an individual is used as the basis for employment decisions affecting such individual; or 3) such conduct has the purpose or effect of unreasonably interfering with an individual's work performance or creating an intimidating, hostile or offensive working environment.

Recently, Crull (1987) has discussed the differences between two forms of harassment that have been identified in the literature and in court rulings: quid pro quo harassment—the requirement that a woman provide sexual favors in return for job security or benefits, such as a promotion or a raise—and atmosphere harassment—the existence of a hostile work environment in which women are subjected to stress or made to feel humiliated because of their sex (e.g., as a result of sexual jokes and taunts from male coworkers).

Examples of each type of harassment are readily observed in many organizations. Quid pro quo sexual harassment begins with subtle or forced pressure for sexual interactions, such as uninvited visits to women's hotel rooms during out-of-town trips or conferences or unwanted invitations for drinks, dinner, or dates. When the victim refuses, the perpetrator

We are grateful for the contributions of Irma Serrano-Garcia who was part of the symposium from which this chapter developed.

retaliates with other forms of work harassment, such as exerting pressure on her to quit, denying training or educational opportunities, providing inaccurate job evaluations, or ultimately firing her or laying her off. Sometimes this retaliation is very subtle, and it may not be clear to the victim if it is directly related to her refusal of sexual attention (e.g., being ignored by a supervisor) or experiencing delays in response to work requests.

Atmosphere harassment is often more subtle and, according to Renick (1980), it is so pervasive in some organizations that it becomes invisible because it is part of the accepted work environment. Atmosphere harassment takes the form of offensive graffiti; close physical contact initiated by men, such as unwanted touching or kissing; sending of lewd cartoons, cards, or presents; staring at women's breasts; and public sexual invitations or remarks. The effect of these behaviors is to create an embarrassing, unpleasant, or hostile working environment for all women, one that detracts from their ability to perform their work duties in comfort.

A number of signs of a harassing environment can alert the employer to a need for early intervention:[1]

Hostile attitudes toward women conveyed by jokes, comments, graffiti, or cartoons that put women down; identification of female employees as "girls" or "dear."

Refusal to take women's work seriously, with women being complimented more for their looks than for their achievements; refusal to assign women to "dangerous" or "complex" tasks.

The use of hugs, pats on the back, arms around shoulders, or sexually suggestive tones or body language to convey work-related approval.

Assignment of regulation uniforms that are not designed to fit women or that are too sexually revealing.

Questions directed to women about their social or personal lives; congratulation of men who are known for their "harmless flirtation" or "playboy reputation."

Other forms of sex discrimination, such as unequal hiring practices or unequal pay; lack of pregnancy and child-care benefits.

All of these are indicators of a workplace that is unnecessarily sexualized, reinforces sexual rather than professional behaviors, or does not treat men and women equitably. Such workplaces are also likely to be characterized by sexual harassment.

INCIDENCE OF SEXUAL HARASSMENT

A number of surveys have generated data on the prevalence of sexual harassment. In all of these studies, it is clear that sexual harassment has affected (and continues to affect) a significant portion of female employees. In a 1976 *Redbook* magazine survey of its readers, 88 percent of the 9,000 who responded had reported some form of unwanted sexual attention in their work lives (Safran, 1976). Since this early study relied on the accounts of self-identified victims, it was necessary to do systematic studies of large samples of workers to arrive at more reliable estimates of sexual harassment in the broader population. In 1980, a large-scale study of federal government employees revealed that 42 percent of the women had experienced sexual harassment within the previous two years of their federal service (U.S. Merit Systems Board, 1981). And from the results of a telephone survey of 1,257 working men and women in Los Angeles County, Gutek (1985) estimated that, depending on how sexual harassment is defined, between 21 and 53 percent of women have been sexually harassed by men at least once during their working lives.

In order to understand better the nature of harassing incidents, Working Women's Institute sent questionnaires to 325 women whose letters to the institute indicated that they had personally experienced sexual harassment on the job (Crull, 1980). Their results suggested that women of all ages are subject to sexual harassment, with respondents ranging in age from 16 to 65. The average age of the women at the time of the sexual harassment was thirty years. More than three-quarters of the women were single, divorced, or widowed, and over half of them provided the sole support for their families and/or themselves, so they had little economic leeway when the incident happened. Twenty-four percent of the women had been fired as a result of their noncompliance, while another 42 percent had been pressured into resigning.

It is likely that these surveys underreport the occurrence of harassment, since the most commonly accepted definitions of harassment are of the more extreme quid pro quo forms, which are the least common (Collins & Blodgett, 1981). In addition, many women are unaware of the legal definitions of harassment, so they may not label behaviors that cause stress at work as sexual harassment.

DESTROYING THE MYTHS ABOUT SEXUAL HARASSMENT

Sexual harassment occurs frequently, has serious consequences, and will not go away if ignored. It is neither caused nor welcomed by the victims, and when women protest by refusing to comply with sexual demands, their "no's" should not be interpreted as "yes, I am flattered." According to one survey, many (31 percent) women who are harassed experience some negative consequence (Bond, 1987).

In addition to threatened job security, the consequences of sexual harassment may range from psychological symptoms to long-term, internalized barriers to professional development. Many women respond with decreased motivation, loss of self-confidence, and doubts about their professional competence (Bond, 1987). Women who are harassed are of all ages and races. The consequences are serious for all women; however, because of minority women's greater economic vulnerability, the consequences for them may be even more severe than those for white women.

There seem to be differences in the types of harassment experienced by women in different types of occupations. According to Carothers and Crull (1984), women in traditionally female jobs (clerical, service profession) are more likely to be victims of quid pro quo harassment, while women in nontraditional occupations (blue collar, management) are more likely to be subjected to hostile environments. Silverman (1976) describes a similar dynamic, noting that working-class women are more likely to experience both physical and verbal abuse, while middle-class and professional women typically experience only verbal harassment. Blue-collar women may have an added dilemma in reporting harassment if they do not want to bring charges against fellow union members (Carothers & Crull, 1984).

Although some men do report being sexually harassed, the incidence is far less. In the study conducted by the U.S. Merit Systems Protection Board (1981), 15 percent of male federal employees reported being harassed during the previous two years. Gutek (1985) has noted that since the perpetrators in these situations are most often identified as younger coworkers or subordinates who have little power to deliver negative work consequences, many of these situations may not be accurately labeled as harassment.

THE IMPACT OF SEXUAL HARASSMENT

Eliminating sexual harassment will result in a more positive work environment, increasing women's satisfaction and productivity. In addition, employers can avoid the possibility of legal action, which often results in financial settlements against the employer. The legal definition of sexual harassment identifies such behaviors as a form of sex discrimination. Title VII of the 1964 Civil Rights Act prohibits sexual discrimination, and the 1985 guidelines of the Equal Employment Opportunity Commission define sexual harassment as a form of discrimination (Carothers & Crull, 1984). In addition, a recent Supreme Court decision (*Meritor Savings Bank v. Vinson*, 1986) upheld the opinion that a sexually hostile work environment may be seen as harassing, that it is not necessary to prove tangible economic cost to the victim, and that even if the victim acquiesced to the sexual advances, if the sexual behavior is unwanted, it is illegal. Several other court rulings have found that an employer may be held liable for the actions of an employee who is designated as his or her agent.

In addition to the legal sanctions that employers might face, the impact of sexual harassment on worker health, morale, and productivity demonstrates the need for employers to take a proactive stance against such discrimination. Renick (1980) notes that in a study conducted by the Illinois Task Force on Sexual Harassment and Sangamon State University, only 1.5 percent of 1,495 state female employees who responded to a survey reported that they were flattered by sexual harassment. Sexual harassment, rather than delivering promised benefits, deprives women of opportunities that are available to men without the need for sexual cooperation.

Severe effects of sexual harassment on women's physical and mental health have been documented. Researchers at the Working Women's Institute have reported that almost all women who are harassed experience at least one symptom of psychological stress, with 94 percent of one sample reporting excessive tension and 36 percent reporting physical ailments, such as nausea, tiredness caused by depression, and headaches. In another sample of victims of harassment, stress symptoms were so severe that 12 percent of the women sought therapeutic help to alleviate them (Crull, 1980).

Not all women, however, report negative consequences. There is a vocal subgroup of women who report no negative effect of sexual harassment, and in fact many of these women may make extraordinary efforts to be productive. Crull (1984) understands this response as a result of cultural attitudes, which encourage women to internalize their discomfort with sexual hostility and to make sure that they are in no way responsible for harassment directed toward them. Ultimately, though, such a response does not eliminate the harassment.

Decreases in emotional and physical health are likely to have an effect on work performance. In one study (Crull, 1980), 83 percent of women who had experienced sexual harassment recognized that the situation had in some way interfered with their job performance. The presence of a coworker or supervisor who repeatedly forced sexual attentions on them interfered with work concentration, as they spent valuable energy looking for ways to steer clear of the hostile situation. Decreased performance spiraled into decreased self- and professional esteem and led to decreased work motivation.

In a follow-up to an earlier study, the U.S. Merit Systems Protection Board (1988) concluded that the costs to employers of sexual harassment may be considerable. According to their calculations, a conservative estimate of the costs of the consequences of sexual harassment to the federal government over a two-year period ending in 1987 was $267 million. This figure took into account the personnel costs associated with identifying a replacement when an employee leaves or is fired, the cost of a background check on potential employees, and the cost of training a replacement. The total also included estimates of productivity lost during sick leaves, both in terms of individual and group productivity. These costs were, of course, in addition to psychological and physical consequences of harassment to individuals. Although it might be difficult for an individual employer to identify accurately the costs to his or her company of sexual harassment, the federal government has taken an important first step in identifying the nature of the monetary consequences.

Finally, sexual harassment affects not only the victim but also others who observe the situation. In a study of women with Ph.D.s, Bond (1987) found that awareness of harassment had a more consistently negative impact on the perception of the supportiveness of the environment for observers than for actual victims of harassment. This finding suggests that there are potentially many victims of any single incident of sexual harassment.

CAUSES OF SEXUAL HARASSMENT

Tangri, Burt, and Johnson (1982) suggest three possible views of the causes of sexual harassment; however, two of these views ignore the prevalence and relative acceptance of harassment. First, the suggestion that harassment is caused by seductive women or by "dirty old men" (individual level of analysis) creates an unrealistic image of organizations staffed by individuals pathologically obsessed with forming sexual relationships with coworkers. Second, suggesting that harassment is condoned by the climate, structure, and pattern of authority relations in only some organizations (institutional level of analysis) cannot explain why some sexual harassment may be observed in most organizations.

A sociocultural explanation is much more useful in explaining observed rates of harassment. Russell (1984) adopts such a position to suggest that sexual harassment is a form of social control by which women are kept in their subordinate roles. This limiting of women's status in the workplace is seen as a response on the part of men to women's attempts to gain more power by leaving their places in the home in order to achieve equality in the workplace. By sexualizing interactions with women in the workplace, men call attention to women's sexuality, thereby detracting from women's work. Sexual harassment is viewed as an appropriate behavior for men within the context of typical patterns of relationships between powerful men and powerless women. Ultimately women's ambitions are curtailed (Goodman, 1978).

Similarly, in Renick's (1980) sociocultural analysis, sexual harassment is seen as an extreme form of powerful men's legitimate use of influence over less powerful women, mirroring the relations between men and women outside the workplace. This carry-over of sex role stereotypic behavior between men and women into their professional relationships with each other is labeled by Gutek and Morasch (1982) as sex role spillover. Sex role spillover is a process, then, whereby men and women respond to each other in the workplace according to sex role stereotypes instead of norms for coworker interaction.

Sex role spillover can affect interactions among male and female employees in subtle and unconscious ways. Recently, Carothers and Crull (1984) have suggested that both quid pro quo and atmosphere harassment may be understood as caused by sex role spillover. Specifically, they find that quid pro quo harassment is more likely to occur when women are employed in traditionally female jobs, which are often supervised by men. In this situation, the male supervisor exercises his recognized power, which comes to him both as a male and as an authority, to remind the female subordinate that she is beholden to him for work privileges. The woman faces strong pressure to comply both because of her work role vulnerability and because of gender-related expectations of women. When she refuses his sexual demands or decides that she no longer wants to comply, he continues to use his power by causing tangible work penalties, such as demotion or firing.

When women are employed in nontraditional blue-collar or professional jobs, work role expectations do not overlap with sex role expectations; thus, the dynamic of harassment appears to be slightly different. The very presence of women in these settings brings into question the male domination of the occupation. The response of male coworkers may be to try to reestablish their domination of their profession by acting in subtle ways to create a sexual and hostile work environment, thus reminding women that they are intruding on male territory. Since coworkers often have no legitimate authority to penalize women's work behavior, they respond to the threat to their culturally sanctioned male dominance by trying to harass women enough so that they will leave the situation. In reference to both forms of sexual harassment, then, we see that sex role spillover increases the power that men have over women in the workplace; threats to a man's power by a woman increase the likelihood of sexual harassment.

The response of women to such behaviors can be explained by a lack of fit between the perspective with which women have been socialized and prevailing organizational norms (Fuehrer & Schilling, 1987). That relationships with coworkers are valued by women more than by men has been documented by a number of researchers (Dubin et al., 1976; Nieva & Gutek, 1981). Women see the development of close relationships as crucial to their work satisfaction. Men, on the other hand, appear to value different aspects of work than do women and do not see the formation of relationships as central. They might, however, see the formation of sexual relationships with women as appropriate role-relevant behaviors if organization socialization supported the formation of sex role stereotypic relationships among employees. As has been noted, such a dynamic exists in situations in which power relationships between men and women mirror the power differentials in larger society, that is, when powerful men control access to resources by less powerful women.

There are other crucial ways in which men's and women's perceptions of interactions in the workplace have been found to differ. Linenberger (1983) states: "Employers and employees are aware that two well-intentioned people could thoroughly misread each other's signals. What one person intends or views as a compliment might be classified by another as sexual harassment." Although Linenberger's comments may be taken as indicative of widespread disagreements on what constitutes harassment distributed in random fashion across the population, these differences break down in gender-based patterns. Gutek (1981) and other researchers have consistently noted differences between men and women in their evaluation of the propriety of sexual attention in the workplace. Gutek has noted that males are more likely than females to see women as flattered by sexual attention in the workplace. Tangri, Burt, and Johnson (1982) noted that for each kind of harassing behavior assessed in their survey, more women than men said that the behavior would bother them and that they would view it as harassing.

These differences in the perception of harassment appear consistent with more general differences in perceptions of social reality described by Gilligan (1982) and others. Two well-publicized cases of sexual harassment provide examples. In the first, the defendant suggested that "the tone of the conversation was not meant to be offensive" (*New York Times*, June 1, 1982); in the other, the defendant stated that "normal, affectionate pats on the shoulder were misinterpreted by the women" (*New York Times*, March 23, 1984). In response to appeals from women to right the injustice of sexual harassment may come claims of misunderstanding and exaggerated sensitivity.

Walker, Erickson, and Woolsey (1985) suggest that at least three sets of issues are raised by the lack of shared understanding between men and women about the definition of sexual harassment. First, unwanted sexual advances limit the victim's ability to choose when and with whom she will have a sexual relationship, an important aspect of control of her life. Second, the sexualization of a professional relationship interferes with the primary tasks of the workplace and compromises the trust placed in a supervisor or coworker. Finally, when a male supervisor or coworker's definition of what is appropriate prevails, he abuses his power in order to obtain personal gratification. Thus, the victim's right to full participation in the organization is prohibited both through denial of her definition of harassment and imposition of behaviors she finds objectionable.

Because there is a difference in perspectives between men and women about the meaning of a common set of behaviors and about the role of relationships in the work environment, conflict is likely to result. When conflict does result, the organization is likely to provide support for the professional role behaviors that are more consistent with the definitions of those in power. Harassment continues to remain a problem because organizations maintain the sanctity of individual rights of dominance. Women perpetuate harassment only insofar as they value the centrality of caring relationships with coworkers and supervisors at their own expense.

THE ROLE OF MANAGEMENT IN PREVENTION

Because managers and supervisors are responsible for the morale and productivity of their work units, it is incumbent on them to prevent sexual harassment and its consequences. Sometimes this is difficult because managers and supervisors may themselves be engaging in sexual harassment of their subordinates and so may be reluctant to give up the benefits they gain. In addition, to the extent that the definition of sexual harassment is not clearly understood, managers and supervisors may not always be aware of its occurrence. However, because managers and supervisors are agents of their employers, they are responsible for the education of employees about the illegality of sexual harassment, for the prevention of harassment, and for investigating any grievances filed by employees. Thus, it is important that managers are aware of the norms that exist in their work groups and that they play a major role in developing norms that encourage interactions among employees based on mutual respect and valuing of contributions to the work task.

The role of managers is especially crucial when a woman initially complains about harassing incidents. According to Crull (1980), the rejection of explicit demands for sexual favors is often followed by other forms of work harassment. In her study, 76 percent of the victims did ask their harassers or other authorities for relief from the sexual demands. However, the requests were met with negative reactions; in only 9 percent of the situations did the harassment stop, while in 17 percent of the cases it was reduced. But in 49 percent of the cases nothing changed, and in 26 percent of the situations the perpetrator engaged in some form of retaliation.

The most proactive stance on the part of management is to address directly, through discussions and workshops, the difference between mutually rewarding sexual relationships and harassing interactions. Zemke's (1981) research suggests that sexual relationships among employees are indeed prevalent. However, Quinn and Judge (1978) suggest that most of these relationships have some sort of negative impact, either through generating gossip or through some impact on the performance of those involved in the relationship.

Not all sexual relationships among employees have significant negative consequences, and not all relationships that negatively affect work performance fit the definition of sexual harassment. However, harassment may be ignored because managers do not want to "interfere in the personal lives" of their workers. Thus, they may choose not to comment on any sexual relationships among employees. As has been discussed, however, sexual harassment is very different from a mutually defined sexual relationship. In order for managers and supervisors to ensure that sexually harassing interactions are prevented, norms for sexual relationships among employees must be openly discussed.

THE NATURE OF EMPLOYERS' AND SUPERVISORS' RESPONSES

There are a variety of responses that can be made by employers and their managerial staff to try to prevent and to respond to incidents of harassment. There is a need for action on many fronts: development of an organizational policy; creation of a mechanism that makes that policy accessible to all employees; education about the definition, causes, and consequences of harassment; and prevention of its occurrence. The following recommendations build on strategies suggested by a number of authors (U.S. Merit Systems Protection Board, 1981; Gutek, 1985).

1. According to a survey conducted by the *Harvard Business Review* (Collins & Blodgett, 1981), small companies tend to rely on informal controls to regulate harassment. EEOC guidelines make it clear that such a strategy will not only be ineffective in eliminating sexual harassment but will also put a company in the position of being held liable for harassment. In reviewing harassment cases, courts may conduct four tests of company policy and process:

1. Does the employer have an unequivocal policy statement, made available to every employee, that condemns sexual harassment?

2. Does the employer review supervisory decisions to hire, fire, and promote employees so that patterns that relate to sexual harassment might be discovered?

3. Is the grievance procedure one that would make it likely that incidents of harassment would be reported to higher management?

4. Does the employer respond in a prompt manner to charges of sexual harassment by its employees?

Thus, it is recommended that employers have a clear policy, published in a handbook made available to all employees, that states that the employer will not tolerate sexual harassment. The purpose of such a policy is to create awareness among all employees that sexual harassment has a negative impact on the workplace and that it is illegal.

Policies should be specific to the needs of the individual employer. However, the following sample policy, taken from a handbook published by the American Federation of State, County and Municipal Employees (AFSCME, 1983), may provide a good model:

Title VII of the Civil Rights Act prohibits discrimination because of race, color, religion, sex or national origin in all employment practices including conditions of employment.

Employee conduct, whether intentional or unintentional, that results in harassment of other employees regarding race, color, religion, sex or national origin is illegal and will not be tolerated. Such conduct will result in disciplinary action, including possibility of discharge.

All employees have the right to expect their employer to maintain a place of employment that is free of conduct that can be considered harassing, abusive, disorderly or disruptive. Management fully intends to abide by the law and supervisors will, when required, take firm disciplinary action in accordance with the management policy and/or applicable labor agreement to assure that the management meets its responsibilities to employees.

Existence of such a policy does not guarantee that an employer will not be held liable for the actions of his or her employees, but it makes legal action less likely since employees will understand the need to avoid sexual harassment.

2. Discussion of the policy should occur during the orientation and training of all new employees and all new management personnel. A sample training module is available from the federal Office of Personnel Management (Renick, 1980), since training needs to involve more than a simple reading of company policy during orientation sessions. The employer needs to demonstrate a commitment to enforcing the policy, beginning with a discussion of the harm caused by sexual harassment, held during orientation sessions.

3. In investigating a complaint of sexual harassment, employers are responsible for protecting the legal rights of both the victim and the accused harasser and for conducting the investigation in such a way as to protect the company, as much as possible, from liability. The major goal of the employer is, ultimately, to make the harassment stop. A number of recommendations will assist in this process.

There needs to be a well-spelled-out grievance procedure that is followed until the victim is satisfied that the harassment has stopped. Initially, the victim should be encouraged to use informal means, confronting her harasser with her complaint and a request that the harassment cease. An ombudsman may be identified to support the use of such actions. If informal strategies are not successful, the victim should contact an affirmative action officer, who is respected by and accountable to top-level management and who has the responsibility for receiving and investigating all charges of sexual harassment. At this point, the complainant should be interviewed thoroughly, and careful documentation should be made of this interview (as well as of all subsequent steps in the process).

The victim should be assured of confidentiality in order to limit the occurrence of further work harassment. The officer should look at all of the victim's documentation; it is important that her complaint be taken seriously and that her entire account of all incidents be heard.

Once the complainant's version of the situation has been investigated, the alleged perpetrator should, with the victim's permission, be interviewed. All potential witnesses should be identified and interviewed. If the officer decides that harassment has occurred, the perpetrator should be told to change his behavior, with reference being made to company policy defining and prohibiting harassment. The officer must conduct a follow-up to ensure that the harassment has stopped and may institute sanctions if required. Ultimately, the primary responsibility of the company is to make sure that the harassment stops.

EEOC guidelines (1980) make a distinction in employer liability depending on whether the harasser is a supervisor or coworker. An employer will be held liable when the harasser is a supervisor, whether the victim has reported the incident to anyone within the company or not, since the supervisor, as an agent of the employer, represents all company policy. If the harasser is a coworker, however, the victim typically must inform someone else in the company so that there is a reasonable chance for agents of the employer to be aware of the harassment. The company policy should make this distinction clear.

4. Employers should be prepared to work with union representatives to reach a commonly agreed upon policy and process for responding to sexual harassment. Some unions have statements in their contracts that prohibit sexual harassment. The United Auto Workers was one of the first unions to include such a clause and has such clauses in several of its contracts (Carothers & Crull, 1984). The 1983 publication of AFSCME, *Sexual Harassment—On-the-Job Sexual Harassment: What the Union Can Do,* is an example of a number of handbooks published by unions to provide support to their members.

A number of women's support groups and unions have instituted task forces, workshops, and training programs in an effort to eliminate sexual harassment (Crull, 1984).

5. It is important that perpetrators be held accountable for their actions and that managers be evaluated according to their success in preventing and responding to incidents of sexual harassment in their work groups. To the extent that sexual harassment has a negative impact on the environment and performance in a work unit, managers must be held accountable, through formal performance appraisal criteria, for eliminating harassment.

6. By acting as role models for their subordinates, managers can play a major role in preventing sexual harassment. In order to show their disapproval of sexual harassment, managers must show respect for both male and female subordinates, evaluate their employees according to professional rather than personal criteria, and reward male and female employees equitably. Such actions will demonstrate their valuing of the contributions of both female and male employees and decrease the sexualization of the work environment. It will also provide support to female employees who are not privy to other informal sources of support readily available to male employees, such as lockerroom chats with male managers and executives.

Management actions should include open and frank discussions of the norms of the work setting around sexual interactions among employees. Just as other types of interactions among employees are open for examination and should be ones that increase morale and performance, sexual interactions should not create a negative work environment. Managers must be frank about their own attitudes toward sexual relationships among employees and foster a corporate culture that exposes the costs of sexual harassment.

7. The role of interpersonal relationships in general must be examined, and the expectations of all employees must be taken into consideration. A morality of caring and responsibility, in which relationships are evaluated not solely for their ability to deliver benefits to the powerful but also for their ability to improve the functioning of all men and women, should be adopted. Decisions regarding personnel actions and employee evaluation should be made on the basis of the maintenance of healthy employee relationships and the rights of all workers, not just those with a high level of social status.

CONCLUSION

Top-level management must become aware of the prevalence of sexual harassment and work to prevent it. In a survey conducted by the *Harvard Business Review,* it was revealed that top-level management in many companies is perceived as unaware of incidents of sexual harassment (Collins & Blodgett, 1981). According to women employees, even when male managers know that harassment is occurring, they are likely to do nothing in response. When such a perception reflects reality, managers must change their attitudes and practices and take a proactive stance in regard to the elimination of sexual harassment. Sexual harassment will be eliminated only when men and women obtain equal social power (Crull, 1984) and when organizations provide a better fit for the expectations of women regarding relationships among coworkers and between coworkers and supervisors (Fuehrer & Schilling, 1987). Until then, the costs of harassment in the workplace are too severe for managers to ignore.

NOTES

1. These descriptions have been generated by researchers at the Working Women's Institute, an organization that has provided training on the prevention of sexual harassment to employers, and counseling to the victims of sexual harassment.

REFERENCES

American Federation of State, County and Municipal Employees (1983). *Sexual harassment—On-the-job sexual harassment: What the union can do.* Washington, DC: AFSCME.

Bond, M. (1987). *Sexual harassment: A barrier to women's professional development in community psychology.* Paper presented at the American Psychological Association Convention, New York, August.

Carothers, S., & Crull, P. (1984). Contrasting sexual harassment in female- and male-dominated occupations. In K. Sacks & D. Remy (Eds.), *Troubles are going to have trouble with me: Everyday trials and triumphs of women workers,* (219–228). New Brunswick, NJ: Rutgers University Press.

Collins, E., & Blodgett, T. (1981). Sexual harassment . . . some see it . . . some won't. *Harvard Business Review, 59* (2), 76–95.

Crull, P. (1980). The impact of sexual harassment on the job: A Profile of the experiences of 92 women. In D. Neugarten & J. Shafritz (Eds.), *Sexuality in organizations: Romantic and coercive behaviors at work* (67–71). Oak Park, IL: Moore Publishing Company.

Crull, P. (1984). Sexual harassment and women's health. In W. Chavkin (Ed.), *Double exposure: Women's health hazards on the job and at home* (100–120). New York: Monthly Review Press.

Crull, P. (1987). Searching for the causes of sexual harassment: An examination of two prototypes. In C. Bose, R. Feldberg, & N. Sokoloff (Eds.), *Hidden aspects of women's work* (225–244). New York: Praeger.

Dubin, R., Hedley, R.A., & Taveggia, T.C. (1976). Attachment to work. In R. Dubin (Ed.), *Handbook of work, organization and society* (281–341). Chicago: Rand McNally College Publishing Co.

Fuehrer, A., & Schilling, K.M. (1987). *Sexual harassment of women graduate students: The impact of institutional factors.* Paper presented at the American Psychological Association Convention, New York, August.

Gilligan, C. (1982). *Marital dialogues.* Paper presented at the conference, Developing through Relationships, University of Kansas, Lawrence.

Goodman, J.L. (1978). Sexual demands on the job. *Civil Liberties Review, 4* (6), 55–58.

Gutek, B.A. (1985). *Sex and the workplace.* San Francisco: Jossey-Bass Publishers.

Gutek (1981). Experiences of sexual harassment: Results from a representative survey. In S. Tangri (Chair), *Sexual harassment at work: Evidence, remedies and implications.* Paper presented at the meeting of the American Psychological Association, Los Angeles.

Gutek, B.A., & Morasch, B. (1982). Sex ratios, sex role spillover and sexual harassment of women at work. *Journal of Social Issues, 38* (4), 55–74.

Linenberger, P. (1983). What behavior constitutes sexual harassment? *Labor Law Journal, 34,* 238–247.

Meritor Savings Bank v. Vinson (1986). Supreme Court of the United States. No. 84-1979.

Monthly Labor Review (1987). Current labor force statistics. *110* (10), p. 66.

New York Times (1982). Teacher to offer to leave his post. June 1, A, 18, 3.

New York Times (1984) Minnesota law school sued in a

sexual harassment case. March 23, B, 18, 5.

Nieva, V., & Gutek, B. (1981). *Women and work: A psychological perspective.* New York: Praeger.

Quinn, R., & Judge, N. (1978). The office romance: No bliss for the boss. *Management Review, 67* (July), 43–49.

Renick, J.C. (1980). Sexual harassment at work: Why it happens, what to do about it. *Personnel Journal, 59* (8), 658–662.

Russell, D. (1984). *Sexual exploitation: Rape, child sexual abuse and workplace harassment.* Beverly Hills, CA: Sage.

Safran, C. (1976). What men do to women on the job. *Redbook, 148,* (November), 149.

Silverman, D. (1976–1977). Sexual harassment: Working women's dilemma. *Quest: A Feminist Quarterly, 3* (3), 15–24.

Tangri, S., Burt, M., & Johnson, L. (1982). Sexual harassment at work: Three explanatory models. *Journal of Social Issues, 38* (4), 33–54.

U.S. Merit Systems Protection Board. Office of Merit Systems Review and Studies (1981). *Sexual harassment in the federal workplace: Is it a problem?.* Washington, DC: Government Printing Office.

U.S. Merit Systems Protection Board. Office of Merit Systems Review and Studies (1988). *Sexual harassment in the federal government: An update.* Washington, DC: Government Printing Office.

Walker, G., Erickson, L., & Woolsey, L. (1985). Sexual harassment: Ethical research and clinical implications in the academic setting. *International Journal of Women's Studies, 8,* 424–433.

Zemke, R. (1981). Sexual harassment: Is training the key? *Training Magazine,* February, 22.

69 CONTROLLING SEXUAL HARASSMENT IN THE WORKPLACE

Paula M. Popovich

Sexual harassment, particularly the harassment of women by men, is now recognized as a pervasive problem in many organizations. Although reports of incidence rates do vary, Gutek (1985) has estimated that "between one quarter and one half of all women have been sexually harassed sometime during their working lives" (p. 58). Recent court cases arising from complaints of sexual harassment have resulted in judgments of $100,000 or more from a single organization (Garvey, 1986). Along with the direct costs from litigation, sexual harassment also contributes indirectly to other costs for the organization through increases in absenteeism, turnover, and medical expenses, as well as reductions in job involvement,

job performance, and job satisfaction (Terpstra & Baker, 1986), all of which contribute to climate problems for the organization.

Despite the recognition of sexual harassment as a major concern in organizations, there is a great deal of confusion both in the research literature and in practice in trying to define sexual harassment and deciding how best to deal with this growing problem. The purpose of this chapter is to outline a way in which sexual harassment can be defined and controlled using a framework already familiar to many managers and trainers in organizations: role theory and role clarification techniques.

DEFINING SEXUAL HARASSMENT

There are many definitions of sexual harassment, but the most influential has been provided by the Equal Employment Opportunity Commission (EEOC). The first part of this definition describes the types of behaviors that may be considered to be sexual harassment: "Unwelcome sexual advances, requests for sexual favors, and other verbal or physical conduct of a sexual nature" (1980, p. 74677). The guidelines go on to describe the two types of situations in which these behaviors can be labeled as sexual harassment. The first situation occurs when employment decisions (such as hiring, firing, or promotion) are made contingent on a person's submitting to or rejecting these advances or requests. This is sometimes referred to as "economic injury" sexual harassment. The second situation that may be labeled as sexual harassment is when these behaviors hinder the person's work and/ or create an uncomfortable work atmosphere. This has been labeled the "hostile environment" form of sexual harassment.

Sexual harassment that results in economic injury has obvious consequences for the individuals involved as well as for the organization. Sexual

harassment that leads to a hostile environment is more difficult to deal with; it is subtle, pervasive, and hard to detect. Unfortunately, it also can be disruptive in its consequences. A recent *Wall Street Journal* article described several incidents that the courts have considered. One woman who filed suit described an office situation in which the men passed around pinup calendars and magazines that could be characterized as pornographic. She also complained that one male coworker had grabbed her breasts on more than one occasion. Although there did not appear to be any threat of economic injury, the woman complained that "the whole atmosphere was poisoning my system. . . . I would go home and cry every night" (Pereira, 1988, p. 21).

One difficulty with the descriptive approach taken by the EEOC is that it does not provide a framework for either understanding the causes of the harassment or for specifically suggesting how to control such behaviors. A more recent approach attempts to define sexual harassment in terms of role theory. In these terms, sexual harassment arises in situations where there is confusion about which role behaviors are appropriate. This role confusion has been described in one of the early reviews of sexual harassment (Farley, 1978) as occurring when a man "asserts a woman's sex-role over her function as a worker" (p. 33). Gutek and Morasch (1982) have more recently proposed that sexual harassment of women on the job is the result of "sex-role spillover," which they define as the "carryover into the workplace of gender-based expectations for behavior that are irrelevant or inappropriate to work" (p. 55).

Defining and describing sexual harassment in terms of roles helps to elucidate the process of sexual harassment and provides some insight into why these situations occur and how to control them. This perspective also allows both researchers and practitioners to access the large body of research literature on role theory and to utilize training techniques designed to control role problems in the organization (Popovich & Licata, 1987).

SEX ROLES AND SEXUAL HARASSMENT

A role may be defined as the set of behaviors that a person performs and that are expected of him or her by other organizational members (Kahn, Wolfe, Quinn, Snoek & Rosenthal, 1964). We all have multiple roles, reflecting the various groups that we are part of as we move through our daily lives. Each of us is, at various times and places, a member of a work group, a family, a social group, and a religious group.

It is obvious that a person's sex role, or the expectations that others have of a person based upon his or her sex, can become part of all other roles that he or she may have, including his or her work roles. Sex role stereotypes have been shown to affect selection decisions, performance appraisals, and even the actual performance of women on the job (e.g., Schein, 1978). What may not be so obvious are the subtle ways in which these roles are communicated and confused in organizational situations.

The communication of expectations occurs during a role episode. Kahn, Wolfe, Quinn, Snoek, and Rosenthal (1964) have developed a four-part model of the role episode process, which can also be used to describe the communication of expectations between a male role sender and a female focal person in a sexual harassment situation. The role episode process may be affected by three context factors: the characteristics or climate of the organization, the attributes of the persons involved, and the interpersonal relations between these persons (Katz & Kahn, 1978). These three factors may also contribute to labeling a particular role episode as an incident of sexual harassment.

In step 1 of the role episode model, role demands arise from the organizational situation. For example, a male member of the work group (supervisor or coworker) is working closely with a female focal person on a project. Certain organizational characteristics may operate to increase the likelihood that an incident of sexual harassment develops. According to the "sex-role spillover" hypothesis described earlier

(Gutek & Morasch, 1982), if the job is a traditionally female one, the role sender may be more likely to see the focal person in terms of her sex role because the job has become defined in terms of such characteristics (e.g., nurses are kind, caring, and nurturant). If the job is a nontraditionally female one, the male focal person may not be able to see the female focal person in terms of the job (e.g., engineers have certain skills that women do not possess) and, instead, will revert to seeing the focal person in a role that he is more familiar with, that is, her sex role. It may also be that the climate of the organization is one that allows a sexist atmosphere (or "hostile environment") to flourish, which could contribute to the likelihood that a role episode becomes a sexual harassment situation. Similarly if the personal characteristics of the role sender include a sexist attitude, this may also contribute to the episode's becoming an incident of sexual harassment.

In the second step, these role demands become expectations for a focal person in the role set (the two or more organizational members involved in the situation) for a focal person. As we have seen, the characteristics of the organization or the persons involved may have led to a situation in which the woman's sex role and her work role have become confused.

The third step involves the communication of the role expectations within the role set to the focal person. Unfortunately, the communication of these expectations is not always direct, clear, or appropriate for the situation. The message may be implied by a comment or tone of voice or even through a nonverbal cue such as body posture, gesture, or touch. The interpersonal relationships between the role sender and focal person may also affect the communication. Research has shown that certain behaviors exhibited by a supervisor are perceived to be more sexually harassing than when those same behaviors are exhibited by a coworker (e.g., Popovich, Licata, Nokovich, Martelli & Zoloty, 1986).

In the fourth step, the focal person has received and must then interpret these expectations and translate them into appropriate behaviors. Once again, organizational and personal characteristics may contribute to problems in this episode. For example, research by Terpstra and Cook (1985) has shown that women with higher levels of education tend to report a higher incidence of sexual harassment experiences. As these researchers point out, whether these women are actually more often the recipients of sexual harassment or whether they perceive themselves to be harassed more often has yet to be determined. However, such findings highlight the subjective, perceptual nature of the role episode and sexual harassment.

It is interesting to note that the role episode model can be used to describe both mutual sexual attraction as well as sexual harassment on the job depending upon the various factors in the episode. It has been pointed out by McGrath (1976) that the steps in the role episode may become a problem or "stress cycle" when something goes wrong in the episode. The possible problems can be categorized as role conflict or role ambiguity. The effects of these problems on the focal person can include reduced trust and respect for the role sender(s) and, especially in the case of role conflict, reduced communication. Additionally, the effects of these role problems may be seen in a variety of physical and emotional symptoms associated with stress, including tension, anxiety, and job dissatisfaction (Jackson & Schuler, 1985). The negative consequences of role problems in the organization are similar to the effects of sexual harassment on the job, which also lead to stress for the focal person or "victim" of harassment (Crull, 1982).

Role conflict can have several causes, but it refers primarily to conflicting expectations between members of the role set and the focal person (VanSell, Brief & Schuler, 1981), such as when there is a confusion between a female focal person's work role and her sex role. Conflict may also occur when there are inherent conflicts or contradictions in the expectation itself, such as when a woman is expected to concentrate on her work while being subjected to sexual comments (Crull, 1982).

Role ambiguity may result when there is a lack of clear and/or adequate communication between members of the role set and the focal person (Kahn et al., 1964), such as when a male role sender who is uncertain of how to deal with women on the job sends the female focal person unclear cues about her expected role behaviors (Driscoll, 1981). It is also possible that a woman who is not given clear cues or who is not sure of how to behave on the job may interpret the sent role as a sex-role cue or revert to sex role behaviors with which she is more comfortable (Popovich & Licata, 1987). Women who experience sexual harassment also report ambiguity in that they frequently did not know what to do or where to go to get help with their sexual harassment situations (Crull, 1982).

As can be seen from these examples, sexual harassment can be conceptualized as a role problem. Whether it is described as role conflict or role ambiguity, adding to the confusion that surrounds this problem is the subjective, perceptual nature of sexual harassment.

THE PERCEPTUAL NATURE OF SEXUAL HARASSMENT

Sexual harassment probably exists in some form in any organization. It is often confused with, and sometimes grows out of, the mutual sexual attraction that is inevitable when people work together. Research has shown that there are differences in the way the these incidences are perceived, not only by those who are involved but also by those who make judgments about the consequences of these situations. For example, several studies have shown that women tend to perceive certain behaviors as more sexually harassing than do men (Gutek, 1982; Popovich et al., 1986; Powell, 1983).

Because of the subjectivity of sexual harassment, it is important to be able to identify characteristics that distinguish a sexual harassment incident from other types of role episodes in the organization. As presented earlier, there are several context factors that may affect the role episode process, including the interpersonal relations between these persons. Two elements that characterize these interpersonal relations and may be used to help determine if a role episode is an incident of sexual harassment are nonmutuality and abuse of power (Popovich & Licata, 1987).

The following statements describe situations that may or may not be considered to be sexual harassment. Consider each statement in terms of nonmutuality and abuse of power between those involved in these incidents:

1. A man and a woman who are coworkers begin to date.

2. A woman who dresses provocatively hoping that one of her coworkers will notice and ask her out.

3. A man who asks a coworker on a date and after she refuses does not ask again.

4. A woman who offers to have sex with her supervisor in exchange for a promotion.

5. A foreman who tells sexual jokes to a employee in order to embarrass her.

6. A man who repeatedly asks a woman coworker on dates, even after she has refused him.

7. A supervisor who tells his subordinate that unless she has sex with him, she will never be promoted.

8. A man who will not hire a woman because he thinks that she will be out too many days of the month with "female problems."

The first example is a case of mutual sexual attraction that does not seem to involve any abuse of power because they are coworkers. Mutual sexual attraction is common on most jobs, and, although it can be distracting for those who are involved, it is not always a problem (Jamison, 1983). However, if at any time the relationship should become nonmutual (e.g., one of the parties wants to end it and the other does not) or one party moves into a position of authority over the other, what started out as mutual attraction may become sexual harassment. Cases of a superiors dating a subordinate involve a power differential and have a higher chance of becoming sexual harassment since there is always the question of whether the subordinate is really dating the superior of his or her own free will. A recent article surveying women who are clinical psychologists found that a number of these women had sexual contact with professors in graduate school. The authors noted that "evaluations at the time of contact were neutral but currently are notably more negative; many currently perceive the contact as extremely exploitative and harmful" (Glaser & Thorpe, 1986).

Examples 2 and 3 also describe situations that can be characterized as the result of sexual attraction. The second example is actually a description of a situation that some believe to be sexual harassment but is more correctly called "sexual hassle." This is a term coined by authors Dziech and Weiner (1984) to describe situations in which a female student flirts with a male faculty member (which is analogous to a subordinate flirting with a supervisor). Although this situation may be potentially troublesome for the faculty member, it is still the faculty member and not the student who has the power in the relationship (through grades, recommendations, etc.). This lack of power on the student's part should keep the incident from becoming a true harassment situation. However, if the faculty member (or superior) does respond to the student (or subordinate), it may escalate into sexual harassment.

In the fourth example, a woman offers to have sex with a superior in exchange for a promotion. This case does not involve sexual attraction, but there is an abuse of power, although it appears to be a mutual arrangement. This is an example of "sexual politics," and, once again, although this may not start out as a sexual harassment situation, it may eventually become one as the confusion between the woman's sex and work roles expands to areas beyond this agreement.

The fifth, sixth, and seventh examples are descriptions of sexual harassment, although they do vary in degree. They all involve a nonmutual situation with an abuse of power. Example 7 is of the economic injury type of harassment, and examples 5 and 6 can be categorized as hostile environment sexual harassment.

The final example is actually a description of sexism and sex discrimination. Sexism refers to the prejudicial attitudes that one may have about a particular sex, such as the idea presented in example 8. These attitudes may lead to the differential treatment of men and women that characterizes discrimination. Although sexist attitudes may lead to sexual harassment, the possession of these attitudes alone does not constitute sexual harassment. However, sexual harassment is considered to be a subset of sexual discrimination because it describes a particular type of discrimination behavior.

As can be seen from these definitions, it is difficult to pinpoint exactly what is considered to be sexual harassment because what may begin as, or appear to be, mutual sexual attraction may actually become sexual harassment. Although nonmutuality and abuse of power are useful guidelines in detemining whether a particular situation is sexual harassment, even these characteristics may be affected by the differential perceptions of those involved.

Discussions using such examples will provide different viewpoints, just as questionnaires listing such behaviors have shown perceptual differences in terms of variables such as sex of rater (e.g., Popovich et al., 1986). Such discussions play a useful part in determining organizational members' current ideas about sexual harassment and should also be part of any training to control this type of problem in the organization.

CONTROLLING SEXUAL HARASSMENT IN THE ORGANIZATION

Although absolute prevention of sexual harassment in the organization is an ideal, there are several reasons why this goal is not always possible. First, sex roles are attended to in organizations, and, as a result, sexual attraction is inevitable in the workplace. A second problem is that whether a particular incident is labeled as sexual harassment is strongly influenced by perceptual differences. Finally, because of its sensitive nature, sexual harassment is difficult to detect. Harassers often do not realize that what they are doing is harassment, and victims often feel confusion and guilt in such stressful situations. Because of these problems, control rather than prevention is often a more realistic goal.

Along with the definition provided earlier, the EEOC (1980) suggests that organizations should act by making an effort to raise the issue of sexual harassment and indicating that such behavior is not acceptable. It is further suggested that employees be made aware of how to make a sexual harassment complaint and that disciplinary sanctions be developed for those who are found guilty of harassment. Finally, organizations are encouraged to develop means by which all organizational members may be sensitized to this problem.

Along with the use of policy statements and grievance procedures, many organizations are working to sensitize organizational members to the problem of sexual harassment through training. A recent survey of 160 Fortune 500 companies conducted for *Working Woman* magazine found that almost 60 percent of the organizations surveyed did have sexual harassment training programs (Sandroff, 1988).

Traditionally, sexual harassment training has consisted primarily of programs designed to increase organizational members' awareness of the potential for sexual harassment, stressing its legal (and consequently financial) consequences for the organization (Popovich & Licata, 1987). These "awareness" programs, while providing participants with useful information about organizational policies and grievance and disciplinary procedures, still do not go far enough in helping organizational members to understand the possible causes of sexual harassment.

An alternative to these traditional awareness approaches is to add to such a program a more proactive element based upon the techniques used in role clarification (Licata & Popovich, 1987; Popovich & Licata, 1987). The proposed program emphasizes more than just making participants aware of sexual harassment. It allows them to explore their possible perceptual biases and to become involved in a more experiential approach to understanding what sexual harassment is and how to control it.

The initial phases of this proactive program are similar to the more traditional programs and involve making participants aware of the problem of sexual harassment. The EEOC definition described earlier is a useful starting point for a discussion of the characteristics of sexual harassment. The eight statements provided in this chapter are also useful in stimulating discussion among participants concerning their beliefs about sexual harassment. Another goal of this initial part of the training program is to make participants aware of the direct and indirect costs of sexual harassment to the organization, including the legal issues (cf. Faley, 1982). Participants should also be made aware of their responsibility to detect and control harassment.

It is useful to note that women in mixed-sex groups often feel inhibited about discussing their experiences and in sharing their views about sexual harassment. Because of this, some time may be devoted to having women, who are more often than men the "victims" of sexual harassment, meet together. However, it is also important that both men and women interact at some point in order to become aware of the possible differences in each others' perceptions. Therefore, much of the training should be conducted with both sexes present.

The major phase in the proposed training program is an application of role negotiation techniques (RNT) (Harrison, 1973) to resolving the problems that occur when work roles are confused with sex roles (Licata & Popovich, 1987). In role negotiation, members of the work group participate together in an attempt to clarify their roles by stating their own roles as well as their expectations of the roles of the other group members. The goal here is to provide lines of communication between group members, allowing them to clarify what is and what is not part of their job. It is hoped that by more clearly defining the expectations of a particular position (their work role), there will be less opportunity for other factors (their sex role) to interfere.

The first step in the RNT phase of the training program is a *warm-up* in which participants discuss their work and nonwork roles and how they handle the problems they face with balancing these roles. This step also involves establishing trust between group members and also with the trainer. The second step is *contract setting* in which the rules for negotiation are set. Because of the sensitive nature of sexual harassment, rules for providing feedback should be agreed upon, such as never referring to someone who exhibits a possible harassment behavior by name during the training sessions. In the *diagnosis* step, the participants define their work roles, and, it is hoped, "minimize the perceived relevance of their sex roles" (Licata & Popovich, 1987). During the *negotiation* step, the actual exchange of expectations takes place. Because this step has the potential of being very emotional and possibly hostile, it is important that changes be discussed in terms of specific behaviors (Licata & Popovich, 1987).

The final phase of the training program is evaluation. As in any other training program, reaction, learning, behavioral, and organizational results changes should be assessed (cf. Kirkpatrick, 1976). However, because of the sensitive nature of sexual harassment, it may be difficult to detect any changes in attitude or behavior in the organization since these incidents are often not reported or are dealt with informally. One possible way of detecting an effect is to assess the levels of role problems (such as conflict and ambiguity) in the organization (Popovich & Licata, 1987).

SUMMARY

Sexual harassment in organizations continues to be a problem that is difficult to control. The confusion surrounding its definition and the sensitive nature of these situations contribute to this difficulty. It is proposed that defining sexual harassment as a role problem will allow researchers and practitioners to be able to deal with this problem in a more well-established framework.

REFERENCES

Crull, P. (1982). Stress effects of sexual harassment on the job: Implications for counseling. *American Journal of Orthopsychiatry, 52,* 539–543.

Driscoll, J.B. (1981). Sexual attraction and harassment: Management's new problems. *Personnel Journal, 60* (1), 33–35.

Dziech, B.W., & Weiner, L. (1984). *The lecherous professor.* Boston: Beacon Press.

Equal Employment Opportunity Commission (1980). Interpretative guidelines on sexual harassment. *Federal Register, 45* (219), 74677.

Faley, R.H. (1982). Sexual harassment: Critical review of legal cases with general principles and preventative measures. *Personnel Psychology, 35,* 583–599.

Farley, L. (1978). *Sexual shakedown: The sexual harassment of women on the job.* New York: Warner Books.

Garvey, M.S. (1986). The high cost of sexual harassment suits. *Personnel Journal* (January), 75–79.

Glaser, R.D., & Thorpe, J.S. (1986). Unethical intimacy: A survey of sexual contact and advances between psychology educators and female graduate students. *American Psychologist, 41,* 43–51.

Gutek, B.A. (1982). A psychological examination of sexual harassment. In B.A. Gutek, (Ed.), *Sex role stereotyping and affirmative action policy* (p. 131–163). Los Angeles: University of California, Institute of Industrial Relations.

Gutek, B.A. (1985). *Sex and the workplace.* San Francisco: Jossey-Bass Publishers.

Gutek, B.A., & Morasch, B. (1982). Sex-ratios, sex-role spillover, and sexual harassment of women at work. *Journal of Social Issues, 38* (4), 55–74.

Harrison, R. (1973). Role negotiation: A tough minded approach to team development. In W.G. Bennis, D.E. Berlew, E.H. Schein, & F.I. Steck (Eds.), *Interpersonal dynamics.* Homewood, IL: Dorsey Press.

Jackson, S.J., & Schuler, R.S. (1985). A meta-analysis and conceptual critique of research on role ambiguity and role conflict in work settings. *Organizational Behavior and Human Decision Processes, 36,* 16–78.

Jamison, K. (1983). Managing sexual attraction in the workplace. *Personnel Administrator, 28* (8), 45–51.

Kahn, R.L., Wolfe, D.M., Quinn, R.P., Snoek, J.D., & Rosenthal, R.A. (1964). *Organizational stress: Studies in role conflict and ambiguity.* New York: John Wiley and Sons.

Katz, D., & Kahn, R.L. (1978). *The social psychology of organizations.* New York: John Wiley and Sons.

Kirkpatrick, D.L. (1976). Evaluation of training. In R.L. Craig (Ed.), *Training and development handbook.* New York, McGraw-Hill Book Co.

Licata, B.J., & Popovich, P.M. (1987). Preventing sexual harassment: A proactive approach. *Training and Development Journal, 41* (5), 34–38.

McGrath, J.E. (1976). Stress and behavior in organizations. In M. Dunnette (Ed.), *Handbook of industrial and organizational psychology.* Chicago: Rand McNally College Publishing Co.

Pereira, J. (1988). Women allege sexist atmosphere in offices constitutes harassment. *Wall Street Journal,* February 10, 21.

Popovich, P.M., & Licata, B.J. (1987). A role model approach to sexual harassment. *Journal of Management, 13* (1), 149–161.

Popovich, P.M., Licata, B.J., Nokovich, D., Martelli, T., & Zoloty, S. (1986). Assessing the incidence and perceptions of sexual harassment behaviors. *Journal of Psychology, 120,* 387–396.

Powell, G.N. (1983). *Sex-role identity and definition of sexual harassment: Are they related?* Paper presented at the national meeting of the Academy of Management, Dallas, Texas.

Sandroff, R. (1988). Sexual harassment in the Fortune 500. *Working Woman* (December), 69–73.

Schein, V.E. (1978). Sex role stereotyping, ability and performance: Prior research and new directions. *Personnel Psychology, 31,* 259–268.

Terpstra, D.E., & Baker, D.D. (1986). A framework for the study of sexual harassment. *Basic and Applied Social Psychology, 7* (1), 17–34.

Terpstra, D.A. & Cook, S.E. (1985). Complainant characteristics and reported behaviors and consequences associated with formal sexual harassment charges. *Personnel Psychology, 38,* 559–574.

Uniform Guidelines on Employee Selection (1980). *Federal Register, 43* (166).

VanSell, M., Brief, A.P., & Schuler, R.S. (1981). Role conflict and role ambiguity: Integration of the literature and directions for future research. *Human Relations, 34* (1), 43–71.

PART VIII

DEALING WITH WORKPLACE STRESS

70 STRESS IN THE WORKPLACE: AN OVERVIEW

Terry A. Beehr

Stress is a process in which some characteristics of the work or workplace lead to harmful consequences for the employees there. The information that has been learned about occupational stress in the last several years has multiplied dramatically. Partly because the knowledge about occupational stress has come from a wide variety of approaches to stress (e.g., medicine, engineering psychology, clinical psychology, and organizational psychology), one result has been a mass of confusion about what the term *stress* actually means (Beehr & Franz, 1985). The term usually means one of three things, however. Occupational stress is alternatively defined as (1) the characteristics of jobs or the workplace that cause the person some illness, discomfort, or strain, (2) the discomfort or illness itself that people experience due to the work situation, or (3) the process in which characteristics of a working situation cause people to feel discomfort or illness. The first two of these definitions use stress to mean a specific part of the stress process, while the third defines stress as the whole process (Beehr & Franz, 1985; Mason, 1975).

In addition to these three relatively technical definitions, the public at large has taken a liking for the word and has used it to mean an extremely wide variety of things. Therefore, taking all of this into consideration, the technical definition that is most general is probably the best one to use in order to communicate most clearly to the most people. That is the last of the three definitions offered above. Occupational stress is a process in which characteristics of the workplace or of the job itself cause employees to experience discomfort or ill health. The job characteristics that cause the problem are labeled *stressors,* and the individuals' ill health is labeled *strain.*

THE FACETS OF OCCUPATIONAL STRESS

Occupational stress as a process is composed of many parts. Reviewing the research literature on it has led to the conclusion that these parts can be grouped into seven categories, however (Beehr & Newman, 1978): (1) the characteristics of the person or employee himself or herself, (2) the characteristics of the individual's (organizational) environment, (3) some processes that occur within the person experiencing stress, (4) some consequences to the human being, (5) some consequences to the organization, (6) ways that people and organizations try to adapt to, cope with, or treat their stress, and (7) the time or duration for which the occupational stress lasts. Furthermore, most theories of stress as well as common sense propose that elements that make up these facets are related to each other in consistent ways. Figure 70–1 illustrates the relationships among the seven stress facets, and the next few paragraphs briefly describe the facets. Much more detail is available in the original article (Beehr & Newman, 1978).

The elements of the personal facet and the environmental facet are usually considered the causes of stress. Regarding the personal facet, different individuals may react more or less strongly to stressful situations. One example of the type of person who might react strongly to stressors is the well-known Type A person (Friedman & Rosenman, 1974). This hard-driving, always-pressed-for-time person is thought to be especially susceptible to one of the primary stress-related diseases, coronary heart disease. A second example of an element of the personal facet is the discovery of the individual difference characteristic called hardiness (Kobasa, 1979), a combination of personal characteristics that are reputed to make executives, and presumably people in other occupations, less susceptible to experiencing strains when they are in contact with stressors on the job.

Occupational stressors constitute the environmental facet. These are characteristics of the job that make the occupation stressful. The three sources of

709

Figure 70–1. The Beehr-Newman Facet Model of Job Stress

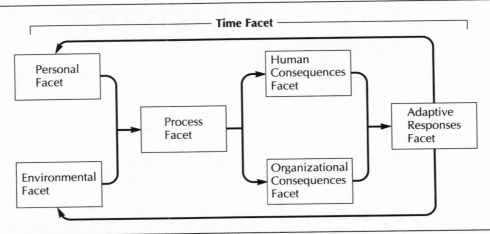

stressors in the workplace are the task and its characteristics, interpersonal relationships with others in the workplace, and the characteristics of the organization as a whole. If any part of these features of the workplace causes employee strains, that feature is a stressor for the employees.

Fortunately, other characteristics of the workplace may help the employee to combat stress in the same way that the personal characteristic of hardiness can help people to counter the negative effects of stress. One example is social support, probably consisting of the frequency and the way in which supervisors and coworkers talk to employees and treat them. This may help to reduce the negative effects of stress also (Beehr, 1985; Cohen & Wills, 1985).

Constituting the process facet are processes occurring within the employee, including both physical and psychological processes. The physical processes include initial changes in some of the body's systems such as secretions from the adrenal glands into the bloodstream. Psychological processes consist primarily of two types: perceptions and decision making. The way people perceive or appraise their situations in part makes the situation more or less stressful (e.g., Lazarus, 1966). While some people perceive or experience interactions with others as being full of role conflict, others experiencing the same interactions might experience very little conflict in the situation. In addition to employees' interpretations or perceptions of the situation, employees are required to make decisions in their work environment. The perceived conflict, for example, would not have any particular consequence if the employees were not required to take some sort of actions in their work roles. The decision making refers to how to do the work. Should the manager of the production

department mail a complaint letter to the manager of his or her company's major supplier or not? What should the letter say? Some action is required, but what action is best? Uncertainty is an important part of the process facet for occupational stress. When it is important to take some action at work, when important outcomes hinge on the actions, and when we are uncertain what the outcomes of our actions will be, the situation is stressful (Beehr & Bhagat, 1985).

The human consequences or strains resulting from stress are physical, psychological, and behavioral. They include physical illnesses such as coronary heart disease, psychological "illnesses" such as depression, and maladaptive behaviors such as smoking or failure to quit smoking. These consequences are a key part of identifying occupational stress because the definition of such stress is a situation in which work-related stressors cause individual strains. Without work-related stressors or without the existence of employee strains, a situation has no occupational stress. For example, efforts to ease employees' pains, discomforts, illnesses, and substance abuse through employee assistance programs are excellent benefits for employees, but they have no necessary relationship to occupational stress unless it is known that stressors are present in the workplace and that strains present in the employee are related to them.

The organizational consequences of occupational stress are those activities of employees that stressed employees are likely to do and have important consequences for organizational effectiveness. Examples of these are employees' being absent at high rates or quitting their jobs at high rates or changes in employees' job performance. Employees experiencing job-related stressors are more likely to be absent from work and to want to quit work than other employees are. It is not clear whether their typical job performance in stressful situations tends to get worse, better, or neither, however. Placing excessive pressure on employees to produce more (thereby eventually inducing role overload, a stressor) may actually result in more productivity in the short run, although it is not clear what will happen in the long run to productivity. In addition, one might consider the fairly direct costs of employee illnesses to the organization in the form of workers' compensation rates and medical insurance rates.

The adaptive consequences facet of figure 70–1 consists of attempts by employees, their employing organization, or third parties to treat, adapt to, or cope with the employees' occupational stress. The primary target of these adaptive strategies can be either the individual employee, the organization, or both (Newman & Beehr, 1979). Individually targeted treatments are those that attempt to alter some characteristic of the individual directly. Many such treatments, for example, attack the strains or human consequences directly. These include medication for reducing high blood pressure, psychological counseling for reducing depression, and relaxation training for reducing any physical symptom related to tension. These individually targeted adaptation strategies often treat the effects or symptoms of stress directly — they treat the individual's strains. In contrast, organizationally targeted adaptation strategies usually attempt to change the causal factors or stressors directly. Examples would include attempts to reduce the strength of any of the stressors that exist in the workplace. As noted earlier, the stressors are characteristics of the tasks, the interpersonal relationships, and the organization itself. Therefore, organizationally targeted treatments would attempt to change one or more of these parts of the organization directly.

Organizational approaches require two things that the individual approaches to stress treatment do not. First, the stressors in the organization need to be diagnosed, since they will be the targets of the treatment. Obviously, it is not very cost-effective to try to remove or reduce stressors that are not a problem in the organization. Second, the people in the organization, especially the managers, must believe that treatment of occupational stress is important enough for them to change some of their ways of working. For example, if role ambiguity is a stressor for some of the employees, managers (and nonmanagers also) may need to work on changing their typical ways of communicating with each other. Perhaps because of these two special requirements of organizationally targeted strategies, they are only rarely tried. That seems a shame, since they are the approach most clearly focusing on the actual cause of occupational stress. Much more often, treatment programs that focus on the strains or effects of stress are used.

The final facet of figure 70–1 is time. The duration or amount of time people are exposed to occupational stressors is thought to be related to the severity of the strains that will be caused. Role overload for a day, for example, might ordinarily be no problem at all for most people. If it lasts for days, weeks, months, and years, however, it will probably affect almost anyone. Time or duration of stress is considered one of the three key elements to the experience of occupational stress in a model developed by Beehr and Bhagat (1985). This approach to occupational stress proposes that the employee's experience of stress is a function of (1) the *importance* of the situation and the potential rewards or outcomes to the employee, (2) the *uncertainty* described earlier as part of the process facet, and (3) the *duration* or time during which the stress lasts.

MONITORING OCCUPATIONAL STRESS

Anything that is important enough for managers to want to control in their organization's first needs to be measured. Just as sales, production, and profits are monitored for control purposes, so can occupational stress be monitored — if management deems it important enough to control. Although there are seven facets to the stress process, it is probably not necessary to monitor all of them. As figure 70–2 indicates, there are three key indicators of occupational stress, and these are all that usually need to be measured. As the definition of the stress process would imply, two of the facets are the most important

keys to knowing whether occupational stress exists: stressors, or elements of the environmental facet, and strains, or elements of the human consequences facet. In addition, since organizational outcomes are traditionally important to the organization and its management, it makes sense to monitor them as well. Fortunately, because of their importance to employers, they usually are already monitored in most organizations. In many cases, therefore, the monitoring of occupational stress means only two new types of measures are needed. Figure 70–2 illustrates the key indicators of job stress that need to be monitored.

Figure 70–2. The Three Key Indicators of Job Stress

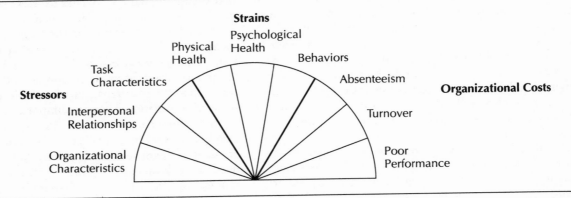

One likely location for this proposed stress-monitoring function is within the human resources or personnel unit(s) of the organization. In many organizations such units have two special strengths that would be helpful in performing this function: they have contact with many different parts of the organization, and they often employ people who already have some of the skills necessary for monitoring job stress.

Monitoring the Environmental Stressors

Organizational characteristics and practices, interpersonal relationships, and task characteristics are the three potential sources of job stress in most organizations. Several organizational characteristics are likely to be associated with job stress. Larger companies, long workdays (for example, frequent use of overtime work) or shift work, rapid sociotechnical changes (perhaps due to technological developments in the industry), the requirement for some employees to relocate geographically at frequent intervals in order to progress in their careers, organizational structures that are unduly rigid (especially if the organization's external environment, markets, and suppliers are rapidly changing), and a punitive, untrusting internal human relations climate are all warning signs for the potential of job stress. If many or most of these situations exist within an organization, serious stress management programs may be appropriate.

The interpersonal characteristics that can be stressors include the types of demands that supervisors and coworkers make of each other. For example, a supervisor may require an employee to do more work than can be done in the time available without also giving the employee additional resources (for

example, temporary assistants or special equipment). In addition to this role overload, other interpersonal characteristics that constitute stressors in the workplace include role conflict and role ambiguity. If the employee is demanded to do two or more things that are incompatible (that is, complying with one of the demands makes it more difficult to comply with the other), then role conflict exists. If it is unclear to the employee what he or she is expected to do on the job, then role ambiguity exists. These stressors are surprisingly widespread in the work force. Many American workers experience enough of these types of stressors to feel anxious about them (Kahn, Wolfe, Quinn, Snoek & Rosenthal, 1964).

Some of the task characteristics that are potential stressors include both over- and underutilization of the employee's skills (having a poor fit between the abilities of the worker and the skills required by the job), having a rapid pace of work, extensive travel as part of the job, and having responsibility for other people's welfare (either their immediate physical welfare, such as an air traffic controller may have, or their long-term welfare, such as any supervisor has who makes decisions regarding the future of employees' careers).

The stressors (organizational characteristics, interpersonal relationships, and task characteristics) can be monitored through direct observation, interviews of employees and their supervisors, or the use of questionnaires. In especially large organizations, however, questionnaires are probably the most cost-efficient means for monitoring many of these factors. Fortunately, some published surveys exist that have been used to study such job stressors. Alternatively, such questionnaires are not too difficult to construct for someone who has a strong background and training in survey methods.

Monitoring the Individual Strains

If the stressors are widespread in an organization, they will often result in several employee responses that are not immediately apparent unless someone in the organization looks for them. These reactions or strains are generally aversive to the employee, and as noted earlier they fall into three categories: physical strains, psychological strains, and behavioral strains. It is becoming apparent that many physical ailments can indeed be related to psychological causes. Examples include ulcers, various symptoms associated with heart disease such as high blood pressure and cholesterol levels in the bloodstream, respiratory problems, and skin disorders. Several psychological strains are also related to job stress experienced by employees, including low self-esteem, depression, dissatisfaction with the job and with life in general, tension, and feelings of fatigue.

Employees may also engage in some actions or behaviors that indicate potential job stress. If there is a high rate of dispensary visits, for example, or a good deal of drug or alcohol use and abuse by employees (both on and off the job), there may be excessive stress in the company. For other employees, actions such as over- or sometimes undereating, nervous gesturing and pacing, and poor interpersonal relations with coworkers, friends, and family are potential indicators.

The individual strains (physical, psychological, and behavioral) are more difficult than the organizational stressors are to monitor and are less obvious to observers. Visits to the company dispensary, if certain types of complaints occur frequently (especially the bodily complaints that are more susceptible to psychological causation), and if they occur primarily in employees in particular structural subunits of the organization, are potential signs. There are available some psychological tests or questionnaires that can measure some of these strains, but more sophistication is usually required to construct and use this type of questionnaire successfully.

Monitoring the Organizational Consequences or Costs

Some of the ultimate results of excessive job stress are quite noticeable in employees' behaviors that have long been of concern to managers: changes in employees' levels of absenteeism, turnover, and job performance (especially performance quality). Managers have long been attuned to notice these types of subordinate behaviors, but they have not been trained to see them as potential results of occupational stress. Compared to the organizational stressors and especially compared to the individual strains, the organizational costs are relatively easily monitored.

SUMMARY

In summary, stress is a process in which characteristics of the organization or the job lead to poor employee health and well-being. There has been a great deal of confusion about the various terms associated with occupational stress, but the term *stressor* commonly refers to the characteristics of the organization or job, and the term *strain* usually refers to the individual's health or well-being.

There are seven facets or parts of occupational stress, and they are thought to be arranged in a rough order of causation. Characteristics of the person and stressors in the work environment combine with each other to cause some stress processes to occur within the individual employee. These stress processes include the feeling of uncertainty about how to achieve desired results at work, and they in turn lead to the human consequences called strains and to some

important consequences for the employing organization such as absenteeism, turnover, and changes in job performance. Because of these human and organizational consequences, somebody usually attempts some adaptive treatments to alleviate the situation. To the extent that this takes place over a longer duration of time before the situation is resolved, the stress is likely to be worse than if it is only brief and fleeting.

These elements of the stress process can be monitored through the use of interviews, questionnaires, and already-existing company records. Managers can create a program to monitor them periodically, just as production, sales, and profits are monitored. This approach would allow comparisons over time so that the company would have timely warnings when the work situation is becoming stressful.

REFERENCES

Beehr, T.A. (1985). The role of social support in coping with occupational stress. In T.A. Beehr and R.S. Bhagat (Eds.), *Human stress and cognition in organizations: An integrated perspective* (375–398). New York: John Wiley and Sons.

Beehr, T.A., & Bhagat, R.S. (1985). Introduction to human stress and cognition in organizations. In T.A. Beehr and R. S. Bhagat (Eds.), *Human stress and cognition in organizations: An integrated perspective* (3–19). New York: John Wiley and Sons. 19.

Beehr, T.A., & Franz, T.M. (1985). The current debate about the meaning of job stress. *Journal of Organizational Behavior Management, 8*(2), 5–18.

Beehr, T.A., & Newman, J.E. (1978). Job stress, employee health, and organizational effectiveness: A facet analysis, model and literature review. *Personnel Psychology, 31,* 665–699.

Cohen, S., & Wills, T.A. (1985). Stress, social support, and the buffering hypotheses. *Psychological Bulletin, 98,* 310–357.

Friedman, M., & Rosenman, R.H. (1974). *Type A behavior and your heart.* New York: Knopf.

Kahn, R.L., Wolfe, D.M., Quinn, R.P., Snoek, J.D., & Rosenthal, R.A. (1964). *Organizational stress: Studies in role conflict and ambiguity.* New York: John Wiley and Sons.

Kobasa, S.C. (1979). Stressful life events, personality, and health: An inquiry into hardiness. *Journal of Personality and Social Psychology, 37,* 1–12.

Lazarus, R.S. (1966). *Psychological stress and the coping process.* New York: McGraw-Hill.

McGrath, J.E. (1976). Stress and behavior in organizations. In M. Dunnette (Ed.), *Handbook of industrial and organizational psychology* (1351–1395) Chicago: Rand-McNally.

Mason, J.W. (1975). A historical view of the stress field: Part I. *Journal of Human Stress, 1*(March), 6–12.

Newman, J.E., & Beehr, T.A. (1979). Personal and organizational strategies for handling job stress: A review of research and opinion. *Personnel Psychology, 32,* 1–43.

Lawrence R. Murphy

Occupational stress continues to be a topic of concern for employees and employers alike. The nature and complexity of the problem of occupational stress has been addressed in numerous published articles (e.g., Caplan et al., 1975; Cooper & Marshall, 1976; Ivancevich & Ganster, 1987) and in other chapters in this *Handbook*. It has become clear that (1) stress occurs in all aspects of life, including work, and can lead to ill health; (2) stress is a highly individual experience that is determined by personal appraisals of work environment factors (one person's meat is another person's poison); and (3) stress is costing companies increasingly large amounts of money in terms of health care, productivity losses, and worker compensation claims (DeCarlo, 1987; National Institute for Occupational Safety and Health, 1987; Rosch & Pelletier, 1987). This state of affairs has prompted more and more companies to seek ways to deal with occupational stress.

Three distinct approaches to the problem of occupational stress are evident in organizational settings, each reflecting a different perspective on the problem. The most common approach is to provide treatment services to "troubled" workers, usually in the form of employee assistance programs. This is a reactive approach (a problem already exists) that considers stress a personal problem. It typically does not involve efforts to identify stressful work factors. A second approach seeks to identify and change workplace factors that produce employee stress. This approach can be reactive or proactive (to prevent stress from becoming a problem). The approach acknowledges that work factors can contribute to employee stress and deals with the sources of stress, not employee distress. Unfortunately, scientific evaluations of this type of intervention are extremely rare in the published literature.

A third approach (and the topic of this chapter) is to offer health promotion or wellness programs to employees. Commonly labeled stress management, these programs have become popular in work settings and have been the subject of a growing number of scientific evaluation studies. By and large, these programs have been proactive; they are offered to all employees (not just those with evident problems), and the aim is stress prevention, not treatment. As a reactive measure to employee stress problems, these programs are clearly inappropriate.

STRESS MANAGEMENT TECHNIQUES

Many of the techniques commonly used in stress management were borrowed from clinical psychology where they have demonstrated success in the treatment of anxiety and psychosomatic disorders (Pomerleau & Brady, 1979). Examples include biofeedback, progressive muscle relaxation, meditation, and cognitive (appraisal) restructuring (Murphy, 1984a).

In *biofeedback,* the individual is provided with information or feedback about the status of a biological function and, over time, can learn to control that function. For example, the electrical activity produced when muscles contract (tense) can be recorded and transformed into a tone whose pitch rises as the muscle tenses and falls as the muscle relaxes. By "listening" to their muscle tension levels over a period of daily trials, individuals learn how to create a state of deep muscle relaxation. Through biofeedback, individuals have learned to control a range of biological functions, including heart rate, blood pressure, blood flow, stomach contractions, and muscle tension (Birk, 1973).

Progressive muscle relaxation (PMR) involves a series of tensing and relaxing exercises designed to foster awareness of muscle activity and heightened control over muscle activity (Jacobson, 1938). This is accomplished by first creating tension in a muscle group (e.g., making a tight fist), studying the feelings of tenseness, and then allowing the muscles to relax, noticing differences between the two states. By systematically moving through the major muscle groups of the body, individuals become proficient at recognizing tension in a muscle and relieving that tension. Exercises are continually abbreviated in length and scope to the point where a state of muscle relaxation can be self-induced in a matter of minutes. A number of audiocassette tapes containing PMR exercises are commercially available (e.g., Budzynski, 1974).

Various forms of *meditation* exist ranging from transcendental meditation (TM) to a nonreligious method developed by Benson (Benson, 1976). In Benson's method, one finds a quiet place and sits comfortably for 20 minutes twice a day. While main-taining a passive attitude toward intruding thoughts, the word *one* is repeated with each exhalation. Benson argues that such meditation invokes a relaxation response, the opposite of the stress response. With practice, individuals learn to invoke the relaxation response at will.

Finally, *cognitive strategies* focus on modifying perceptual or appraisal processes, which determine the stressfulness of situations. Such training involves examination of thinking patterns to modify irrational thoughts (e.g., "everybody must like me all the time," "everything I do must be perfect"), substitution of positive self-talk for the more common negative self-talk, and development of flexible problem-solving skills (Meichenbaum, 1977).

STRESS MANAGEMENT IN WORK SETTINGS

In clinical settings, these techniques are taught to patients over an extended period of time (at least 12 weeks), during individualized, weekly sessions in the therapists' office. This format was modified extensively for application in work settings as follows. Program emphasis was on prevention, not treatment, training was compressed into six consecutive days, sessions were conducted with small groups and using taped instructions, and sessions were held at the worksite. These modifications were deemed necessary because the intended participants (workers) were not clinical patients with evident stress problems and the program needed to be cost-effective for organizations to implement.

As applied in work settings, stress management is usually offered as a prevention activity designed to educate workers about the nature and sources of stress and to provide basic relaxation skills that are useful in everyday life. Programs typically contain brief training sessions and range from one-day programs to several-week-long programs. These programs are not designed for treatment of troubled workers or those with manifest clinical problems.

The research questions asked in the first two case studies were: Can "normal" workers learn stress management skills in a short period of time in small groups at the worksite? and Will the modified training format be effective in helping workers reduce tension levels and feelings of distress?

CASE STUDY 1: HOSPITAL SETTING

The first study (Murphy, 1983) was performed at a local hospital in Cincinnati, Ohio. Its purpose was to evaluate the feasibility and effectiveness of stress management as applied in a work setting. Since the program sought to foster well-being and not to treat stress problems, the assistance of the hospital training department (not medical department) was sought. The director of training at the hospital was contacted to explain the nature and intent of the study. The program included stress education and training in biofeedback, progressive muscle relaxation, or self-relaxation (comparison group).

Training was conducted on-site during normal working hours and involved daily 1-hour sessions over two consecutive workweeks. The hospital supplied a room to conduct training and allowed nurses to receive training without loss of pay. During the first two days of the program, participants were given information on the nature and sources of stress, with specific attention to stressors at work, and common reactions to stress. Training took place on days 3–8. During each session, participants were instructed to listen to taped muscle relaxation exercises or try to lower the biofeedback tone. On the last two days, participants were asked to apply what they had learned and become as relaxed as possible during the session.

Physiological recordings were taken of muscle

activity and hand temperature at the start and end of each session, and detailed questionnaires were administered at various times during the study. (The detailed data collection procedures were necessary given the experimental nature of the study; in practice, inexpensive instruments can be used to assess training effectiveness. See Stainbrook and Green, 1987).

The results indicated significant benefits for the trained groups compared to the comparison group: for the muscle relaxation group: lower muscle tension and reduced anxiety; for the biofeedback group: higher hand temperature (indicative of relaxation) and lower anxiety. Three months later, follow-up questionnaires were administered to all participants. Between the end of training and the follow-up period, nurses in both trained groups reported increases in stress coping. Nurses in the self-relaxation group, on the other hand, reported more job dissatisfac-

tion at follow-up relative to the trained groups. All groups reported improvements in sleep behavior at follow-up.

The study demonstrated that stress management was feasible in work settings and that nurses could learn relaxation skills in a matter of four or five days. It showed that relaxation training led to significant changes in subjective and physiological measures associated with stress. Finally, it showed that even nurses in the self-relaxation group felt that they benefited from the study, though they did not receive stress management training.

Some negative features of the program are also noteworthy. For example, physiological measures were not taken at the follow-up to corroborate the self-report results. Also, there was no mechanism developed to continue the program once the experiment was finished. These shortcomings were rectified in the second case study, described next.

CASE STUDY 2: HIGHWAY MAINTENANCE WORKERS

The second case study (Murphy, 1984b) was conducted in a municipal public works department and used the same experimental design as the first study. Its purpose was to replicate and extend the findings of the prior study using a blue-collar work group. Again, since the program focused on prevention, not treatment, the program was offered through the training department of one division (highway maintenance). The division agreed to provide a quiet room in which to conduct the study and permitted employees to participate during normal working hours without loss of pay.

Significant changes were made to the program based upon experience gained from the first case study. First, the stress education materials were expanded and group discussions were held with participants during the first two days of the program (baseline recording days). Second, on each training day (days 3–8) and each application practice day (days 9–10), participants were given feedback on their muscle tension and hand temperature levels after each session. This feedback was in the form of a graph showing daily pre- and postsession levels. Participants could thus track their progress at the end of each day. Third, physiological recordings were taken at the three-month follow-up in addition to questionnaire assessments. These were used to determine whether changes on physiological measures were durable over time. Finally, an attempt was made to involve an employee assistance program in the study. The director of the city's public employees

assistance program (PEAP) was invited to attend training sessions for the purpose of continuing the program after the experiment was completed. I also conducted seminars for PEAP staff on the use of biofeedback equipment.

The results indicated that biofeedback (but not muscle relaxation) training led to significant reductions in muscle tension levels. The lack of effects in the muscle relaxation group was thought to be due to providing too much learning material to participants. The cassette tape series used in this study (Budzynski, 1974) included instruction in differential relaxation, conditioned relaxation, and autogenics in addition to progressive muscle relaxation. The manual associated with the cassette tapes suggested that the listener master each relaxation exercise before attempting others. The abbreviated training format used in the study precluded this type of mastery. It was concluded that either fewer relaxation techniques be taught in a short training program or that the length of the program be extended to counter the negative effects of overtraining.

At the three-month follow-up, muscle tension levels increased in all groups compared to day 10 levels but were still significantly lower than day 1 levels for the two trained groups.

This case study had a second component: to assess program impact on organization variables of absenteeism, performance ratings, and worker accidents. Although these programs are not designed to influence such variables directly, indirect effects might be predicted. For example, Kohn (1979) has shown that workers trained in progressive muscle relaxation made fewer performance errors under conditions of high noise stress compared to controls. Thus, beyond health-related benefits, relaxation training may directly improve work performance under conditions of elevated stress.

To assess organizational effects of stress management, a quasi-experiment was designed in which data on employee absenteeism, performance ratings, equipment accidents, and work injuries for two and a half years before training were compared with those one and a half years after training (Murphy and Sorenson, 1988). A group of eighty workers who did not participate in the program were selected randomly from the division personnel roster to serve as a comparison group.

The results indicated that workers in the muscle

relaxation group had fewer absence periods in the year following training compared to controls. (An absence period was a consecutive period of absence regardless of the number of days absent.) The reductions were small, amounting to −1.23 absence periods per worker per year but statistically significant. Biofeedback-trained workers also had lower absenteeism after training and fewer work injuries, but the changes were not statistically significant. Neither trained group showed reductions on performance ratings or equipment accidents after training.

It was apparent from this study that the primary effects of stress management were on worker physiology and feelings of distress. The results confirmed other reports in the research literature supporting the feasibility and effectiveness of worksite stress management programs (Murphy, 1984a).

CASE STUDY 3: FEDERAL WORKERS

The preceding case studies evaluated stress management as a discrete health promotion offering in organizations without apparent stress problems. In organizations under stress, stress management has obvious limitations since it does not attempt to reduce or eliminate stressors at work. It has been suggested that stress management is appropriate as a supplement to organizational change interventions (Ganster, Mayes, Sime & Tharp, 1982), but no studies have described or evaluated such an application.

The final case study (Murphy & Hurrell, 1987) differed dramatically from the foregoing studies in that it was conducted in an organization with apparent stress problems. In this case, stress management represented but one step in what was conceptualized as a process of occupational stress reduction. Stress management was used to (1) legitimize stress as a topic for discussion, (2) educate workers about the nature, sources, and consequences of stress, and (3) provide workers with relaxation skills. After training, workers would seemingly be in a better position to provide input to both an assessment of work stress and the formulation of stressor reduction interventions.

The program was developed at the request of a department manager of a U.S. federal agency who felt that employees were dissatisfied with their work and that morale was low. Assistance was sought in the form of advice on how best to deal with these problems.

The program was conceptualized as an ongoing

process with five phases: (1) a stress management workshop, (2) an employee stress survey, (3) formulation of stressor reduction recommendations based upon survey findings, (4) implementation of organizational change interventions, and (5) program evaluations. (At the time of this writing, only the first three phases have been completed and are described here).

The stress management workshop was conducted by a local hospital that designs health promotion programs for community and work settings. The standard workshop offered by this hospital consisted of a single 6-hour training session. However, the department requested that the 6 hours of training be distributed over four sessions, each 1 1/2 hours in length. Two sessions would be held each week for two consecutive weeks. Additionally, the department requested that the workshop trainer solicit information from participants regarding job features felt to be stressful and that this information be tabulated and provided to the department at the end of the workshops. The hospital agreed to modify their program accordingly.

The workshop goals were to improve conceptual understanding of stress and its consequences, equip workers with the ability to diagnose personal and environmental stressors and attendant stress reactions, and foster the development of personalized action strategies for preventing negative stress effects. The program was 25 percent conceptual and 75 percent skill development. Each participant received a seventy-three-page workbook (Bethesda, 1983) containing the educational, assessment, and exercise information.

Employee feedback collected by the trainers indicated that most participants found the workshop to be informative and helpful. "Unrealistic time lines" was mentioned by over half of the participants who made comments. No other job factor was mentioned with such high frequency. The next most frequently mentioned stressors formed a cluster having supervisory-related factors as its core. Examples here included lack of clear directions, lack of recognition or respect, unrealistic work loads, and unresolved conflicts.

Two months after the stress management workshop, an employee committee was formed to make recommendations to management for reducing employee stress. The committee was composed of members from each of four work groups within the department. All members except one were nonsupervisory employees. The first action of the committee was to propose an employee stress survey be conducted to identify and quantify work stressors.

A short (fifty-two-item) questionnaire was assembled that solicited information on age, gender, work group, job type, supervisory status, organizational tenure, perceptions of job characteristics, and job satisfaction. Perceptions of job characteristics were assessed using Form S of the Work Environment Scale (WES) (Moos & Insel, 1974). The WES produces scores on ten subscales corresponding to Job Involvement, Peer Cohesion, Supervisory Support, Autonomy, Task Orientation, Work Pressure, Clarity of Expectations, Management Control Over Workers, Innovation, and Physical Comfort. Normative data for these scales are available for over 600 workers in 44 aggregate work groups representing white-, pink-, and blue-collar occupations (Moos & Insel, 1974). Job satisfaction was measured using four items from the Quality of Employment Surveys (Quinn & Staines, 1977).

Questionnaires were distributed to employees at their workstations by a representative of the Stress Reduction Committee. A cover letter described the intent of the survey, its voluntary and anonymous nature, steps that were taken to ensure respondent confidentiality, and a request for all employees to participate. Employees were granted work time to complete the questionnaire at their desks. Each employee placed the completed questionnaire into a blank envelope, which was collected 15–20 minutes after distribution by a committee member. A record was kept of each questionnaire distributed and collected. The response rate to the survey was 100 percent.

The results indicated that the sample did not differ significantly from WES norms on any scale ($p > .05$), though scores on all scales except Work Pressure were lower than norms. In particular, scores on Job Involvement (WES 1), Task Orientation (WES 5), and Clarity (WES 7) approached significance ($p < .10$). Sample data were also compared to specific occupational groups for which the National Institute for Occupational Safety and Health had comparable WES data (e.g., video display terminal [VDT] operators, machine-paced assembly line workers, and warehouse workers). The sample more closely resembled the VDT operators and warehouse workers (high-stress sample groups) in terms of their WES profile than the non-VDT worker group (a low-stress sample group). Only the group of machine-paced workers (high stress) had a WES profile indicative of higher stress than our sample.

Regression analyses revealed that Job Involvement and Supervisor Support were the variables associated with job dissatisfaction for these workers. The following recommendations for reducing stress and improving job satisfaction were prepared by the employee stress committee and offered to management:

- Employee participation in the work planning process should be increased. At the very least, employees should be informed, on a timely basis, of events that might disrupt normal work routines and/or work schedules.

- Work assignments need to be communicated clearly to reduce employee ambiguity and to clarify supervisor expectations. The scope of work, time frame for completion, and ultimate goal of the assignment need to be routinely included in such communications. When work assignments involve two or more employees, one should be given the lead role so as to reduce overlapping and redundant work.

- A mechanism is needed to inform the department director when "fast response" demands become excessive and create unrealistic deadlines. When the latter occur, requests for extension of deadlines need to be initiated by the director.

- Department managment needs to encourage employee initiative and freedom to make decisions within the scope of the job.

- Supervisor training should be ongoing and opportunities to take additional training in modern management practices (e.g., a course based upon *The One Minute Manager*) should be encouraged by the department.

This case study used stress management as one component of an organization's stressor reduction activities. The application described here is not being offered as the best or the only role that stress management can play in organizations. Rather, it illustrates the complementary role of stress management within a more comprehensive stressor reduction program.

DISCUSSION

The results of these case studies and other reports in the literature indicate that stress management programs are feasible in work settings and that many techniques can be effective in helping workers to recognize stressors and to reduce physiological arousal levels and psychological manifestations of stress. Such programs have potential for improving worker well-being and partially offsetting the costs of stress arising from productivity losses and stress-related disorders. In the light of the fact that excess stress can promote cigarette smoking and alcohol use, stress management also may be a useful adjunct to other worksite health promotion effects.

Rising worker compensation claims for stress-related disability and the knowledge that behavioral factors play a significant role in seven of the ten leading causes of death will likely prompt a significant growth in worksite stress management programs. Despite the benefits to workers, it is not recommended that such programs be established in a cavalier fashion. For example, stress management can be used to complement organizational change and job redesign efforts to deal with stressors that cannot be designed out of the job (Ganster, Mayes, Sime & Tharp, 1982). As a prevention activity, organizations could offer stress management to employees on a periodic basis much like other training programs (e.g., safety, materials handling) or on a continuous basis through employee assistance-type programs. In this way, training would emphasize health promotion and disease prevention goals and parallel the preventive focus employed in research studies.

There is a danger, however, of organizations' offering brief stress management workshops to workers while making no attempt to alter work factors that may be generating stress. The choice of a primary intervention strategy for reducing occupational stress should be based upon a careful evaluation of the sources of stress in the work environment (i.e., organizational, ergonomic, and psychosocial) and the most promising, realistic, and cost-effective strategies for reducing stress. While stressors cannot be designed out of some jobs, in many cases, work environment and organizational factors can be modified to improve worker health and well-being.

REFERENCES

Benson, H. (1976). *The relaxation response.* William Morrow & Co.

Bethesda Hospital (1983). *Stress management workshop.* Cincinnati, Ohio: Bethesda Health Management Services.

Birk, L. (1973). *Biofeedback: Behavioral medicine.* New York: Grune & Stratton.

Budzynski, T.H. (1974). *Progressive relaxation training.* New York: BMA Audio Cassette Programs.

Caplan, R.D., Cobb, S., French, J.R.P., Jr., Harrison, R.V., & Pinneau, S.R. (1975). *Job demands and worker health* (DHHS [NIOSH] Publication No. 75-160). Washington, DC: U.S. Government Printing Office.

Cooper, C.L., & Marshall, J. (1976). Occupational sources of stress: A review of the literature relating to coronary heart disease and mental ill health. *Journal of Occupational Psychology, 49,* 11–28.

DeCarlo, D.T. (1987). New legal rights related to emotional stress in the workplace. *Journal of Business and Psychology, 1,* 313–325.

Ganster, D.C., Mayes, B.T., Sime, W.E., & Tharp, G.D. (1982). Managing occupational stress: A field experiment. *Journal of Applied Psychology, 67,* 533–542.

Ivancevich, J.M., & Ganster, D.C. (1987). *Job stress: From theory to suggestion.* New York: Haworth Press.

Jacobson, E. (1938). *Progressive relaxation.* Chicago: University of Chicago Press.

Kohn, J.P. (1981). Stress modification using progressive muscle relaxation. *Professional Safety, 26,* 15–19.

Lazarus, R. (1966). *Psychological stress and the coping process.* New York: McGraw-Hill.

Meichenbaum, D. (1977). *Cognitive-behavior modification.* New York: Plenum Press.

Moos, R.H., & Insel, P.M. (1974). *The Work Environment Scale.* Palo Alto, CA: Consulting Psychologists Press.

Murphy, L.R. (1983). A comparison of relaxation methods

for reducing stress in nursing personnel. *Human Factors, 25*, 431–440.

Murphy, L.R. (1984a). Occupational stress management: A review and appraisal. *Journal of Occupational Psychology, 57*, 1–15.

Murphy, L.R. (1984b). Stress management in highway maintenance workers. *Journal of Occupational Medicine, 26*, 436–442.

Murphy, L.R., & Hurrell, J.J. (1987). Stress management in the process of occupational stress reduction. *Journal of Managerial Psychology, 2*, 18–23.

Murphy, L.R., & Sorenson, S. (1988). Employee behaviors after stress management training. *Journal of Occupational Behavior, 9*, 173–182.

National Institute for Occupational Safety and Health (1987). *National strategy for the prevention of work-related psychological disorders* Cincinnati, Ohio: Author.

Pomerleau, D.F., & Brady, J.P. (1979). *Behavioral medicine: Theory and practice*. Baltimore, MD: Williams & Wilkins Company.

Quinn, R.P., & Staines, G.L. (1977). *The 1977 Quality of Employment Survey*. Ann Arbor, MI: Institute of Social Research, University of Michigan.

Rosch, P., & Pelletier, K. (1987). Worksite stress management programs. In L.R. Murphy and T.F. Schoenborn (Eds.), *Stress management in work settings* (DHHS [NIOSH] Publication No. 87-111). Washington, DC: U.S. Government Printing Office.

Stainbrook, G., & Green, L.W. (1987). Evaluating stress management programs. In L.R. Murphy and T.F. Schoenborn (Eds.), *Stress Management in Work Settings* (DHHS [NIOSH] Publication No. 87-111). Washington, DC: U.S. Government Printing Office.

72 PHYSIOLOGICAL EFFECTS OF STRESS IN THE WORKPLACE

William H. Hendrix

A great deal of research suggests that occupational or worksite stress is a causative factor in a large variety of physical and mental health problems (Haw, 1982; House, 1974a, 1974b; House & Jackman, 1979; House, Strecher, Metzner & Robbins, 1986; Jenkins, 1971, 1976; Kahn, 1981). The evidence, however, is fragmentary and difficult to replicate (House et al., 1986), and generally the research has not been conducted within a comprehensive stress model framework (Hendrix, Ovalle & Troxler, 1985). The purpose of this chapter is to look at the physiological effects of stress in the worksite. In accomplishing this objective, not only will the physiological effects of stress be addressed but the relative contribution of stress to major illnesses and disease in comparison to other causative factors will be reviewed. While reviewing the effects of stress, emphasis will be placed on the link between stress and its relationship to the major causes of death in the United States. In particular, coronary heart disease (CHD) and diseases of the circulatory system (e.g., strokes) will be discussed as a separate topic. The emphasis on CHD is due to its prominence in causing premature death. In fact, heart attacks and strokes kill more people than all other diseases combined (Albrecht, 1979). Also heart disease, diseases of the circulatory system, and cancer (the second leading cause of death) account for over 70 percent of all deaths in the United States (U.S. Department of Health and Human Services, 1980). Since stress has been implicated in the development of cancer, it will be discussed as a result of stress-induced immune deficiency.

Medical science has made great strides in conquering infectious disease during this century. Today it appears that these infectious diseases, to a large extent, have been replaced by degenerative diseases or diseases due to stress. Of chief concern is coronary heart disease.

PHYSIOLOGY OF THE STRESS RESPONSE

The stress response, which is frequently called the fight-or-flight response, consists of a series of well-organized events. These events primarily involve two major systems working together within the body: the sympathetic nervous system (SNS) and the endocrine system. The effect of the combined actions of these two systems, in reaction to stress, is to direct increased blood flow to the brain and muscles while decreasing the blood flow to the skin, intestines, and extremities, and constricting smaller blood vessels, resulting in increased blood pressure. The stress reaction causes a mobilization of glucose or blood sugar, and the fatty acids stored in the body are dumped into the bloodstream for energy fuel. One's field of vision narrows, the heart rate increases, digestion is reduced, perspiration may occur underarms, breathing deepens, and the palms may sweat as a result of the stress reaction (Albrecht, 1979; Selye, 1976). These reactions were reasonable and necessary reactions for our ancestors to survive in the wild from challenges such as those posed by wild animals and warring tribes. These responses within the executive office or on the floor of a plant, however, can result in adverse health outcomes since the manager or worker generally cannot mobilize a response by fighting or through flight.

The general physiology associated with the stress reaction starts within the brain by activating the sympathetic nervous system, which causes a release of adrenal hormones called catecholamines into the bloodstream. The major catecholamines released are adrenaline (epinephrine) and noradrenaline (norepinephrine). The catecholamines released have an effect on the reticular activating system (RAS) within the brain, which leads to an increased alert state. At the same time the hormonal system is activated within the brain by stimulation of the hypothalamus by a message from the brain's cortex. This causes the hypothalamus to release a hormone called the corticotropin releasing factor (CRF), which causes the pituitary gland to release a second hormone called adenocorticotropic hormone (ATCH). In turn, ATCH stimulates the adrenal gland to secrete into the bloodstream the hormones of adrenaline and noradrenaline from its medulla or center and a series of adrenal cortex (outer cover) hormones called glucocorticoids. One of the most important of the glucocorticoids for the stress response is the hormone cortisol. The effect of cortisol is to increase the level of fatty acids and glucose (sugar) in the bloodstream. It accomplishes this by stimulating fat cells to release fatty acids and stimulates the liver to produce and to release into the bloodstream glucose. Cortisol can have some adversive effects however, such as breaking down protein (muscle) for energy, suppressing the immune system's ability to ward off disease, inhibiting the inflammatory response, and weakening bones. The adrenal cortex, when stimulated by ATCH, also releases aldosterone and a group of hormones called mineralcorticoids. These hormones cause increase in blood pressure. Some of the major physiological effects follow:

Reduced level and thickened siliva.

Bronchi of lungs relax and respiration increases.

Decreased blood flow to intestines and stomach, decreased digestive activity.

Liver releases glucose (blood sugar) into bloodstream.

Heart rate increases, volume of blood pumped increases, and force of pumping increases.

Pupils of eyes dilate.

Increased blood flow to muscles.

Fatty acids released into bloodstream by fat cells.

Blood vessels constrict in lungs, intestines, and skin, causing decreased blood flow to them.

Hair stands on end.

Sweating in selected areas (e.g., palms, brow, underarms).

Increased secretion of adrenaline and noradrenaline.

Muscle tension.

This brief description of the physiological response to stress paints a picture of individuals who are raised to the peak of their ability to fight or flee from the "tigers" in their lives. Their alertness, muscle strength, blood pressure, and pulse rate are up, while blood sugar (glucose) and fatty acids are dumped into their bloodstream as an emergency energy source. The problem is that within our society, we cannot release this energy directly by fighting or fleeing. Instead, we have to endure the stresses in our lives while controlling our natural stress response to take direct physical action toward stressful events and people. What is the cost to each of us and to the organization due to worksite or job stress? The cost of stress is extremely difficult to estimate accurately. It appears, however, that the cost is quite high. A rough estimate of the cost of stress by Ivancevich and Mattison (1980) based on a variety of sources, is in the $75 billion to $90 billion range annually. They note that their estimate was probably conservative and that that this cost was nearly 10 percent of the U.S. gross national production in 1980. There is little reason today to believe the cost has been reduced significantly. More likely, the financial cost due to stress has probably increased. In addition to financial cost, an attempt to show the cost due to stress in terms of physical and mental effects is included in descriptions below.

STRESS AND CORONARY HEART DISEASE

Stress is frequently cited as a risk factor in developing coronary heart disease (CHD) (Cooper & Marshall, 1976), which can lead to a heart attack. However, establishing the relative importance of stress compared to other risk factors has been plagued with difficulty. This, in part, is due to the variety of different concepts and measurement techniques of stress and because true experimental research in this area is very limited. Nevertheless, research has suggested a link between stress and coronary heart disease.

One of the best single laboratory predictors of coronary heart disease is the cholesterol ratio (Malaspina, Bussiere & LeCalve, 1981; Uhl, Troxler, Hickman & Clark, 1978). The cholesterol ratio is obtained by dividing total serum cholesterol by high-density lipoprotein (HDL) cholesterol. The cholesterol ratio has been found to be a better predictor of CHD than is total cholesterol or HDL cholesterol when used separately. Uhl et al. (1978) found the cholesterol ratio to be an excellent predictor of CHD based on an empirical study of 572 asymptomatic air crew members who were screened for CHD through the use of a electrocardiographic (ECG) treadmill test, which is usually called a stress test. Coronary angiography was then performed on those who had abnormal stress test results. Coronary angiography involves heart catheterization by inserting a tube into the coronary arteries of the heart and injecting a radio-opaque dye that when x-rayed will outline the arteries and the extent of CHD. The results of their research led them to conclude that the cholesterol ratio was a better predictor of CHD than all of the other traditional risk factors normally used. Malaspina et al. (1981) arrived at the same conclusion, but their conclusion was based on a review of literature on the cholesterol ratio's predictive power in studies conducted in the United Kingdom, France, and the United States. Not only is the cholesterol ratio a good predictor of CHD, but, as noted by Chadwick, Chesney, Black, Rosenman, and Sevelius (1979, p. H-4), it is more sensitive to changes due to stress than is total cholesterol.

Since the cholesterol ratio has been identified as a good predictor of CHD, it and total serum cholesterol have been used in stress research as a surrogate criterion for CHD (e.g., Hendrix, Ovalle & Troxler, 1985). Although the exact relationship of stress leading to cholesterol production is not clear, it appears to be an indirect relationship. What appears to occur is that there is a release of adrenocorticoids (e.g., cortisol), which causes a release of fatty acids and activates an enzyme HMG-CoA reductase, which results in an increase in cholesterol production. This increase in cholesterol production is not immediate. Selye (1950) found in the early phase of stress exposure that the relationship between stress and cholesterol level was negative. Only after extended exposure did the cholesterol level rise.

Of course, other factors can also increase the serum cholesterol level. Two of these major factors include dietary cholesterol and fat, particularly saturated fat. When evaluating the effects of stress on cholesterol levels, these dietary factors need to be considered. Troxler and Wetzler (1981) reported on a series of studies looking at cortisol and cholesterol as predictors of CHD using monkeys. They used four groups of monkeys that were free of CHD. Each group received diets with varying levels of cortisol and cholesterol. One group (control group) received a diet low in cholesterol and no cortisol. The second group had a low-cholesterol and high-cortisol diet. The third group had a high-cholesterol, no-cortisol diet. The last group had a diet high in both cholesterol and cortisol. Results indicated that the control group developed cholesterol deposits or plaque on only 5 percent of the coronary arterial walls. Group 2 (low cholesterol–high cortisol) developed deposits affecting 7 percent of the arterial wall. For group 3 (high cholesterol–low cortisol) approximately one-third of the wall developed plaque, while in the fourth group (high cholesterol and cortisol) over two-thirds of the arterial walls were diseased. The results suggest an interaction between cholesterol and cortisol. Individuals on high-cholesterol and high-saturated-fat diets are known to have higher serum cholesterol levels and higher cholesterol ratios. Stress would appear to increase significantly the risk of CHD for individuals who have high levels of serum cholesterol. As noted earlier, the release of cortisol and adrenaline during stress also results in the production of cholesterol by the body. Therefore, stress compounds the problem not only by interacting with existing cholesterol to produce CHD but also by increasing the overall level of cholesterol, and increasing blood pressure or hypertension, another risk factor of CHD.

If CHD progresses, a point of plaque buildup can be reached where blood flow through the coronary arteries is significantly reduced and a heart attack may occur. A heart attack occurs when the blood flow is blocked or severely decreased so that the muscle tissue of the heart becomes starved for oxygen. Frequently a blood clot forms in the restricted coronary artery due to significant blockage from plaque. Also, emotional stress has been found to precipitate the formation of a clot by platelet clumping. Platelets are the body's defense mechanisms against bleeding and clump or aggregate together to stop the blood flow when bleeding occurs. If clumping occurs within a coronary artery, a thrombosis or clot forms, which can reduce or stop the blood flow (Ornish, 1982, p. 39) and possibly cause a heart attack. Another source of heart attacks that is not necessarily related to CHD is coronary artery spasm. Emotional stress has been found to be a major factor causing arterial spasms (Ornish, 1982, pp. 11, 39–43). When a spasm occurs, the blood flow through the coronary artery can be shut down, resulting in a heart attack. The more blockage that has occurred due to CHD, the less spasm is required to close off the blood flow. Therefore, a heart attack can occur due to blockage from CHD (plaque buildup), platelet clumping, and coronary artery spasms or a combination of these. Emotional stress can be a factor associated with each of these three conditions.

To evaluate the contribution of stress to CHD and heart attacks, stress should be evaluated or compared to other risk factors. This will be accomplished later when discussing individual differences and the relative importance of stress.

DISEASES DUE TO STRESS-INDUCED IMMUNE DEFICIENCY

Numerous studies (e.g. Hendrix, 1985; McClelland, 1979; McClelland, Davidson, Floor & Saron, 1980) have found a relationship between stress and various types of illnesses and disease. These findings have led researchers to look at the possibility that stress suppresses the immune system's ability to fight disease and therefore increases the occurrence of disease in those experiencing chronic stress. The immune suppression process starts with the stress reaction described earlier with the release of ATCH, which causes the adrenal cortex to release adrenal glucocorticoids (e.g., cortisol), which, in turn, appears to have a destructive effect on portions of the immune system. Also the sympathetic nervous system, when activated by stress, causes the release of epinenephrine and norepinephrine. Combined, these appear to cause immune function suppression by decreasing the ability of the immune system to fight disease by effecting T-cells (thymus produced), serum white cell count, natural killer (NK) cells, and salivary immunoglobulin A (S-IgA) (Newberry & Gerstenberger, 1986; McClelland, Alexander & Marks, 1982; Trainin, Small & Gabizon, 1978). In particular glucocorticoids block the production of two of the more important immune system components, the lymphocyte activating factor (LAF) and T-cell growth factor (Gillis, Crabtree & Smith, 1979; Guyre, Bodwell & Munck, 1984). As noted by Crabtree, Gillis, Smith, and Munch (1980), this goes a long way in explaining why glucocorticoids in particular are so effective in suppressing the primary immune responses. It should be noted, however, that the stress-disease link is far from conclusive since although the stress reaction does suppress some of the more important components of the immune system, it has an enhancing effect on others (Newberry & Gerstenberger, 1986).

There has been a great deal of speculation concerning the possibility of a stress-cancer link (Bammer & Newberry, 1981; Stoll, 1979). Upon reviewing the research, it appears that it is too early to make a firm conclusion regarding the stress-cancer link. Research using animals, primarily mice, has found that tumors (cancer) can be influenced by stress. That is, cancer cells held in check by the immune system tend to grow when the animal is exposed to stressful conditions (Riley, 1978, p. 1770). However, when trying to establish the stress-cancer link in humans, the results are not clear. Human experiments cannot be controlled as easily as animal experiments; therefore, determining the effects of stress is much more difficult to establish. Also, development of cancer due to some causative agent may take up to twenty years before it can be diagnosed. This makes identification of causative factors even more difficult. However, based on our present knowledge, it appears that stress has the potential for increasing cancer cell growth; however, in humans the research to date does not suggest that it is a major contribution to causing the disease (Newberry & Gerstenberger, 1986).

There are a number of diseases, however, that seem to be related to stress-induced immune suppression. Infectious diseases such as streptococcal infections (Meyer & Haggerty, 1962) and upper respiratory infections (Jacobs, Spelkin, Norman & Anderson, 1970; McClelland et al., 1982) have been noted to increase after stressful events. In addition, recovery from illnesses such as pneumonia, flu, and mononucleosis seems to be impaired by experiencing stress (Greenfield, Roessler & Crosley, 1959: Hendrix et al., 1986; Imboden, Canter & Cluff, 1961). Rheumatoid arthritis has been found to be influenced by stress also (Selye, 1976). Those who are more stress prone (e.g., more rebellious and aggressive) and those who have experienced stress due to the loss of a loved one were at greater risk of developing arthritis or experiencing an arthritic attack (Bunney et al., 1982). Selye (1976, pp. 860–861) noted that stress could precipitate attacks of hay fever, asthma, atopic dermatitis, or lupus erythematosus (an autoimmune disease) and in general make individuals susceptible to a wide range of infectious diseases. Some of the clearest results linking stress to asthma have been from the research of Luparello and associates (1968). Luparello et al. found that severe bronchoconstriction (asthma) could be produced in individuals through stress by exposing asthmatics to harmless substances to which they thought they were allergic.

STRESS AND GASTROINTESTINAL DISEASES

The majority of research looking at the relationship between stress and gastrointestinal diseases has focused on ulcers. It has been clearly established through rather elegant studies that emotional stress can influence stomach acid secretions. Hostility and anger tend to increase the level of acidity, while depression tends to decrease it (Bunney et al., 1982). Individuals who have experienced catastrophic physical stress such as major burns, severe trauma, extensive surgery, and brain injury have a higher frequency of ulcers than people in general. Due to this phenomenon, research has looked at the possibility that emotional stress can lead to ulcers. Research to date, however, suggests that emotional stress plays a limited role in the development of ulcers (Bunney et al., 1982). Other factors seem to be much more highly related to ulcer development than is emotional stress.

Some of these factors that are related to ulcer development are one's sex, blood type, hypertension, chronic obstructive pulmonary disease, smoking cigarettes, and drinking coffee and carbonated beverages (Sturdevant, 1976).

Although not conclusive, it appears probable that emotional stress does play a part in other gastrointestinal disorders, including colitis, esophageal spasm, spastic colon, and various diarrheal conditions (Bunney et al., 1982).

STRESS AND ENDOCRINE DISEASE

Some of the most comprehensive research on stress has been on endocrine system diseases (Bunney et al., 1982). Diabetes mellitus, in particular, has been singled out for extensive research. Although the condition of diabetes is a genetically inherited trait, stress can precipitate its development. Both physical and emotional stress appear to aggravate the diabetic condition and can cause considerable fluctuations in blood sugar levels (Selye, 1976). This can result in a need for increased dosage level of insulin or oral antidiabetic drugs.

Another condition that appears to be affected by stress is hyperthyroidism. Studies (Bennett & Cambor, 1961; Weiner, 1978) have indicated that stressful events can precipitate hyperthyroidism. Stressful events that have been related to hyperthyroidism include loss of a loved one, demand to provide care beyond one's ability, job loss, and illness. Also, anecdotal evidence has linked frightening and other stressful events to the onset of hyperthyroidism (Bunney et al., 1982). It has been suggested that increased cortisol production is the factor causing this condition (Selye, 1976, p. 858).

Last, the female reproductive system seems to be affected by stress. The evidence comes from both anecdotal data and a limited number of research studies. The evidence suggests that stress can produce menstrual dysfunction, with the most common condition being cessation of the menstrual cycle. It has been found to be a factor in premenstrual tension and pelvic congestion, which causes pain. These occurrences are found in women who otherwise have no endocrine abnormalities.

STRESS AND OTHER DISEASES

Stress has also been implicated in the development of numerous other conditions, including oral-dental diseases, skin disease, backaches, and headaches. Each of these will be briefly discussed.

One of the most common effects of stress related to the oral-dental area is the occurrence of bruxism—the gnashing, grinding, or clenching of the teeth. Emotional stress appears to be a primary factor in the development of bruxism (Morse, 1982). It can take three forms: acute bruxism which is situational specific and of a short duration; noctural bruxism, which is a grinding type; and diurnal bruxism, the silent clenching type.

Emotional stress has also been implicated in a wide variety of skin disorders (Seyle, 1976). These include "prickly heat," psoriasis, acne, contact dermatitis, and eczema. Skin disease is probably the most visible physical consequence of stress and can be a major source of anguish due to its unsightliness. Stress research has found individuals prone to developing eczema, a condition involving itching, swelling, redness, and scaling and fluid discharge, when subjected to stressful events. It has also been shown that people who develop hives often do so when under stress (Quick & Quick, 1984, pp. 62–63).

Backache is a major cause of lost time from work and one of the most frequent complaints seen by physicians. Stress seems to be a major factor associated with chronic backaches, especially those not associated with physical trauma. Much of the problem of chronic backaches appears to be due to muscle spasms induced by stress and to decreased flexibility and strength from a lack of exercise (Quick & Quick, 1984, p. 60). Muscle spasms due to stress can cause other musculoskeletal complaints, including chronic neck and jaw pain. A universal symptom of stress is the tension headache that seems to result from spasms of the facial and scalp muscles. On the other hand, migraine headaches are caused by spasms of blood vessels supplying blood to the brain. Migraines can also be precipitated by stress, but they are frequently a result of a variety of other nonstress-related causes.

INDIVIDUAL DIFFERENCES

If we could identify groups of individuals similar in all major aspects such as genetics, race, sex, and exposure to disease-causing organisms, we would still note differences in the development of diseases among them. Why is it that some people seem to develop backaches, headaches, and colds when subjected to stressful events and others do not? Research is starting to isolate factors that help explain these individual differences to stress and the resulting physiological reactions.

Type A Behavior

Type A behavior is a behavioral pattern characterized by a sense of time urgency, impatience, feeling of anger and hostility, competitiveness, and aggressiveness (Friedman & Rosenman, 1974). Chesney and Rosenman (1980) found that the Type A behavioral pattern is related to higher occupational status, higher education, and higher income for males and females. Also those classified as Type A describe their jobs as having more responsibility, longer hours, and heavier work loads than do Type B.

There is evidence that Type A behavior is associated with an increased risk of developing coronary heart disease (Roseman et al., 1975). The psychological process leading to Type A behavior and the development of CHD is poorly understood. The need for control has been suggested as a primary component of Type A behavior (Glass, 1977). Williams et al. (1980), however, suggested that a Type A person's hostility may be the major component affecting CHD. More recently, research (Hendrix et al., 1986) has indicated that individuals who exhibit Type A behavior, when compared to the more laid-back Type B individuals, tend to experience more life stress and job stress. This was true even when the effects of other job-related, nonjob-related, and personal characteristics were controlled. Therefore, the data suggest that Type A behavior results in a more exaggerated reaction to stress, which might place the individual at higher risk of ill health than individuals exhibiting Type B behavior.

Locus of Control

Locus of control is a concept describing an individual's perception of control over any given situation. Furthermore, the concept is broken down into two subgroups: internally oriented (or internal locus of control) and externally oriented (or external locus of control) individuals. Internal locus of control individuals preceive that their decisions and actions will influence what happens to them. That is they, to a large extent, control their furure. External locus of control individuals, on the other hand, believe that their future is dependent on fate or luck, not on their decisions and actions. Research indicates that internals, perceiving they have more control, tend to be less threatened by stressful events and therefore experience less adverse reactions (Quick & Quick, 1984, p. 66). A study by Anderson (1977) found that internal and external locus of control small business owner-managers who had extensive damage due to flooding had different reactions. The internals following the flood became task oriented in taking actions to recover from the damage, while the externals responded with greater anger, anxiety, and hostility. Hendrix et al. (1986) looked at the relationship between locus of control and stress for 370 Department of Defense employees. They found that externals tended to exhibit higher life stress than internals when job, nonjob, and other personal characteristics were controlled.

Self-Esteem

Higher levels of self-esteem are associated with more confidence in one's ability to cope with the environment. Therefore, those high in self-esteem tend to experience lower or less negative effects due to stress than do those who have lower self-esteem. A classic example of this is given by Bettelheim's studies (1958) on wartime concentration and forced labor camps. He found that those with high self-esteem who escaped death from their captors were able to cope much better than those with low esteem. The latter were more likely to succumb to insanity and suicide. In addition, Mueller (1965) found that those with high self-esteem perceived less work overload than those who had low self-esteem. This suggests that self-esteem serves as a buffer against job and life stressors. In addition, individual differences have been demonstrated where self-esteem has acted as a buffer against the development of coronary heart disease risk factors (House, 1972; Kasl, & Cobb, 1970). Therefore, it appears that self-esteem is an important factor that buffers the adverse effects of stress.

Tolerance for Ambiguity

Tolerance for ambiguity is a concept related to how well one's work environment requirements are defined. This includes what tasks are to be done, how they are to be done, and in what order they are to be accomplished. Individuals who have a strong need for

everything to be defined are said to score low on tolerance for ambiguity. What is generally found by research is that those scoring low on tolerance for ambiguity, when in a job that does not provide clear goals and structure, experience higher anxiety and stress when compared to those who have higher tolerance for ambiguity (Ivancevich & Matteson, 1980).

Assertiveness

Assertiveness is a characteristic of an individual where one stands up for one's rights while protecting or being concerned for the rights of others. What research indicates is that those who are more assertive, given stressful situations, tend to experience less stress than those who are less assertive. For example, Hendrix et al. (1985) found that the more an individual was assertive, the less stress he or she experienced in life.

RELATIVE CONTRIBUTION OF STRESS TO DISEASE

The physiological effects of stress have been reviewed separately in the previous discussion. The relative contribution of stress compared to other possible causative factors is, however, an issue of equal importance to the previous discussion. When developing health promotion and wellness programs within industry, the relative effect of various factors on health are necessary so that specific and appropriate actions can be taken. In order to understand better the relative contribution of stress to illness and disease, a series of case studies based on research will be presented.

Case of Stress Effects on Performance, Absenteeism, and Health

Two organizations were concerned about the effect stress had on the health of their employees and if stress affected their employees' absenteeism and productivity rates. In attempting to find an answer to this problem, a study was conducted in these two organizations using 225 of their employees (Hendrix, 1985). The organizations were a large accounting and finance organization and a large health care organization. The data used to help solve the problem were collected as part of an employee health promotion

program. The factors measured and evaluated during the research study included job stress, number of cold and flu episodes during the last year, somatic symptoms (the extent one had headaches, restless sleep, and fatigue), job satisfaction, organizational commitment, absenteeism (sick leave taken during last six months), and performance (last merit performance appraisal rating).

Path analysis was used to establish the relationship of stress, health, absenteeism, and productivity. The results of this analysis are provided in figure 72-1. The presence of an arrow indicates a direct link between two variables. The number on the arrow is the partial regression weight and indicates the magnitude of the relationship.

The results indicate that as job stress increased, there was an increase in the number of cold and flu episodes and the extent that individuals had somatic symptoms. Also high stress was associated with job dissatisfaction. Stress also had an effect on absenteeism and performance; however, the effects were indirect. That is, job stress affected cold or flu and somatic symptom levels and job satisfaction, which in turn influenced absenteeism rate. In the case of job satisfaction, it affected organizational commitment before affecting absenteeism. Similarly, job stress influenced performance indirectly through its effects on job satisfaction and organizational commitment.

The companies therefore were able to determine

Figure 72–1. Path Model

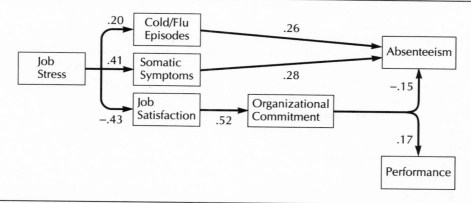

Source: Reprinted with permission from *Aviation, Space, and Environmental Medicine, 56* (1985) , p.657.

not only that stress had an effect on absenteeism and productivity but also affected the employees' general health, job satisfaction, and commitment to the organization.

Case of Stress Effects on Coronary Heart Disease Potential, General Health, and Performance

A more comprehensive study involving organizations in Colorado, Texas, and Florida attempted to establish if job and life stress affected their employees' potential for developing coronary heart disease, general health, absenteeism rates, and performance (Hendrix, Leap & Steel, 1986). A single indicator of coronary heart disease potential was used, specifically the cholesterol ratio. Using a survey, a series of job, nonjob, and individual characteristic factors, hypothesized to be related to stress and health, were measured. The survey also measured satisfaction and health-related factors. Absenteeism, which was measured as number of sick leave days taken in the past six months, and productivity (last merit performance rating) were obtained from employee records.

The results based on path analysis indicated that neither job nor life stress was related to the cholesterol ratio. Instead, more traditional risk factors were the major predictors when controlling for other job, nonjob, and individual characteristics. The results indicated that the cholesterol ratio tended to be higher (at higher risk of CHD) if the person was a male, was overweight, was older, and smoked

cigarettes. On the other hand, the ratio was lower if the person jogged and consumed alcohol moderately. None of these factors related to other health factors. First, life stress tended to increase or add to one's perception of stress on the job. Both life and job stress were significantly related to increasing feelings of anxiety, anger, and depression. In turn, this led to increased emotional exhaustion or burn-out, higher somatic symptoms, and more cold and flu episodes. Finally, the effects of stress, through its impact on the above factors, led to higher sick leave rates or absenteeism. In addition to the above influences, as emotional exhaustion increased, there was a significant decrease in performance ratings of the employees, and as job stress increased, job satisfaction and organizational commitment decreased. It might be of interest to note that the major job-related stressors isolated during the research included supervision, job enhancement, role conflict, quantitative work load, job boredom, coworker relations, and physical stressors (e.g., adversive temperature and noise).

The results provided the organization with some answers that were helpful in deciding what actions would be useful in improving employee health and effectiveness. If reducing CHD risk is the major goal for an organization, then programs in diet and nutrition, smoking cessation, exercise, and weight control appear to be more appropriate than management of stress. However, if improving general health in the form of reducing cold and flu episodes, feelings of anxiety, depression, anger, and emotional exhaustion is the primary goal, then effective management of stress is appropriate. This should have an additional payoff in reducing absenteeism and slightly improving performance.

RECOMMENDATIONS

If management is concerned about stress in the organization, it would be worthwhile for them first to examine the basis of their concern. Is it because they are concerned for their employees and want the quality of their worklife to improve? This in itself is a worthwhile and desirable goal, and managing stress more effectively would be appropriate and desirable. However, if the basis is that one believes that reducing stress will reduce the overall incidence of coronary heart disease and cancer, then their beliefs are not supported by research, and there is likely to be little improvement. This conclusion is noted in the previous discussion and by Chadwick et al. (1979, p. H-3) who found little support for job stress being a major component in CHD development.

On the other hand, there is support that job stress is related to respiratory problems (e.g., cold and flu episodes, allergies, and asthma) and emotional exhaustion (or burn-out), anxiety, and depression. In turn these have been found to lead to higher illness, which is reflected in higher sick leave rates. Therefore, managing stress could have a positive effect on employees' general health and reducing their absenteeism due to illness.

In attempting to deal with job stress, a manager might consider the following recommendations:

1. *Diagnose the basis for stress.* It seems to be in vogue to have stress management seminars. Without knowing why individuals are experiencing stress, there is little that can be done to solve the problem. A typical stress management seminar deals with symptoms and teaches individuals how to cope with stress through the use of stress reduction techniques. The assumption frequently is that the problem is the individual's: "You let yourself be stressed." Of course, there is some truth to this assumption, but the major reason may not be due to the individual's personality and coping skills but due to the work environment. Therefore, the first step in a good stress management program would be to diagnose the basis for stress. It may well be that the employee is experiencing work overload, boredom, or role conflict or has ambigious goals and these are causing the problem.

2. *Take actions to reduce or manage stress.* It is unlikely that stress-reducing techniques will have a significant impact that is sustained over time if the problems causing stress are from the job environment. If the primary stressor is a job that is boring and low in terms of job enrichment, then enrichment of the job to motivate the employee would be appropriate. If the goals are ambiguous, then a goal-setting program should help reduce stress by clarifying the employees' job goals. However, if the employees experiencing stress are those who tend to over-respond to stressful events or there are events that cannot be changed, then a stress management program that teaches coping skills would be helpful in managing stress. The point is to tailor actions to the needs established during diagnosis.

3. *Follow-up evaluation.* A good evaluation program will help establish if the effects of stress reduction and management actions are being effective. It is a fact of life that all programs cost time and money, and we should see if our efforts are accomplishing their goals. Evaluation can be accomplished using measurement devices such as comprehensive health and stress evaluation surveys and sick leave rates. By using a pretest-posttest control group design, the impact of management's actions can be more firmly established.

4. *Consider a comprehensive health promotion and wellness program.* Stress is but one reaction of employees to their job environment. Data are accumulating that suggest that healthy organizations tend to have healthy people. A comprehensive health promotion or wellness program that evaluates the work environment and the characteristics of the employees will have stress management as a part of it. A truly comprehensive program will not be limited to medical screening but will include assessment of job factors, supervision, external factors (external to the job), personal characteristics (e.g., Type A behavior, exercise, smoking), stress, and consequences of health-related factors and stress. These consequences would include measures of job satisfaction, emotional exhaustion, illness rates, commitment, absenteeism, and productivity. Through the use of such a program, not only should stress be better managed, but the overall effectiveness of the organization should be improved.

REFERENCES

Albrecht, K. (1979). *Stress and the manager: Making it work for you*. Englewood Cliffs, NJ: Prentice-Hall.

Anderson, C.R. (1977). Locus of control, coping behaviors, and performance in a stress setting: A longitudinal study. *Journal of Applied Psychology, 62*, 446–451.

Bammer, K., & Newberry, B.H. (Eds.) (1981). *Stress and cancer*. Toronto: C.J. Hogrefe.

Bennett, A.W., & Cambor, C.G. (1961). Clinical study of hyperthyroidism. *Archives of General Psychiatry, 4*, 160–165.

Bettelheim, B. (1958). Individual and mass behavior in extreme situations. In E.E. Maccoby et al., *Readings in Social Psychology* (3d ed) (300–310). New York: Holt, Rinehart, & Winston.

Bunney, W., Jr., et al. (1982). Panel report on stress and illness. In G.R. Elliott & C. Eisdorfer (Eds.), *Stress and human health: Analysis and implications for research* (255–320). New York: Springer.

Chadwick, J.H., Chesney, M.A., Black, G.W., Rosenman, R.H., & Sevelius, G.G. (1979). *Psychological job stress and coronary heart disease* (Report No. CDC-99-74-42). Cincinnati, OH: National Institute for Occupational Safety and Health, Robert A. Taft Laboratories. (NTIS No. PB81-223588).

Chesney, M.A., & Rosenman, R.H. (1980). Type A behavior in the work setting. In C.L. Cooper & R. Payne (eds.), *Current concerns in occupational stress*, New York: John Wiley & Sons.

Cooper, C.L., & Marshall, J. (1976). Occupational sources of stress: A review of the literature relating to coronary heart disease and mental health. *Journal of Occupational Psychology, 49*, 11–28.

Crabtree, G.R., Gillis, S., Smith, K.A., & Munch, A. (1980). Mechanisms of glucocorticoid-induced immunosuppression: Inhibitory effects on expression of Fc receptors and production of T-cell growth factor. *Journal of Steroid and Biochemistry, 12*, 445–449.

Friedman, M., & Rosenman, R.H. (1974). *Type A behavior and your heart*. New York: Knopf.

Gillis, S., Crabtree, G.R., & Smith, K.A. (1979). Glucocorticoid-induced inhibition of T-cell growth factor production: The effect on mitogen-induced lymphocyte proliferation. *Journal of Immunology, 123*, 1624–1631.

Greenfield, N.S., Roessler, R., & Crosley, A.P., Jr. (1959). Ego strength and length of recovery from infectious mononucleosis. *Journal of Nervous and Mental Disorders, 128*, 125–128.

Guyre, P.M., Bodwell, J.E., & Munck, A. (1984). Glucocorticoid actions on lympoid tissue and the immune system: Physiologic and therapeutic implications. In E. Gurpie, R. Calandra, C. Levy, & R.J. Soto (Eds.), *Hormones and cancer: Progress in clinical and biological research* (vol. 142, 181–194). New York: A.R. Liss.

Haw, M.A. (1982). Women, work and stress: A review and agenda for the future. *Journal of Health and Social Behavior, 23*, 132–144.

Hendrix, W.H. (1985). Factors predictive of stress, organizational effectiveness, and coronary heart disease potential. *Aviation, Space, and Environment Medicine, 56*, 654–659.

Hendrix, W.H., Leap, T.L., & Steel, R.P. (1986). A health promotion model for organizations: The effect of health promotion on organizational effectiveness and absenteeism. In O. Brown, Jr., and H.W. Hendrick (Eds.), *Human factors in organizational design and management—II* (407–412). New York: North-Holland.

Hendrix, W.H., Ovalle, N.K., II & Troxler, R.G. (1985). Behavioral and physiological consequences of stress and its antecedent factors. *Journal of Applied Psychology, 70*(1), 188–201.

House, J. (1972). *The relationship of intrinsic and extrinsic work motivation to occupational stress and coronary heart disease risk*. Ph.D. dissertation, University of Michigan.

House, J.S. (1974a). Occupational stress and coronary heart disease: A review and theoretical integration. *Journal of Health and Social Behavior, 15*, 12–27.

House, J.S. (1974b). Occupational stress and physical health. In J. O'Toole (Ed.), *Work and the quality of life: Resource papers for work in America* (145–170). Cambridge: MIT Press.

House, J.S., & Jackman, M.F. (1979). Occupational stress and health. In P. Ahmed and G. Coelho (Eds.), *Toward a New Definition of Health* (135–158). New York: Plenum.

House, J.S., Strecher, V., Metzner, H.L., & Robbins, C.A. (1986). Occupational stress and health among men and women in the Tecumseh community health study. *Journal of Health and Social Behavior, 27*, 62–77.

Imboden, J.B., Canter, A., & Cluff, L.E. (1961). Convalescence from influenza: A study of the psychological and clinical determinants. *Archives of Internal Medicine, 108*, 393–399.

Ivancevich, J.M., & Matteson, M.T. (1980). *Stress and work: A managerial perspective*. Glenview, IL: Scott-Foresman.

Jacobs, M.H., Spelkin, A.Z., Norman, M.M., & Anderson, L.S. (1970). Life stress and respiratory illness. *Psychosomatic Medicine, 32*, 233–242.

Jenkins, C.D. (1971). Psychologic and social precursors of coronary disease. *New England Journal of Medicine, 284*, 244–255, 307–317.

Jenkins, C.D. (1976). Recent evidence supporting psychologic and social risk factors for coronary disease (parts I and II). *New England Journal of Medicine, 294*, 987–994, 1033–1038.

Kahn, R.L. (1981). *Work and health.* New York: Wiley.

Kasl, S., & Cobb, S. (1970). Blood pressure changes in men undergoing job loss: A preliminary report. *Psychosomatic Medicine, 32,* 19–38.

Luparello, T., Lyon, H.A., Bleeker, E.R., & McFadden, E.R., Jr. (1968). Influence of suggestion on airway reactivity in asthmatic subjects, *Psychosomatic Medicine, 30,* 819–825.

McClelland, D.C. (1979). Inhibited power motivation and high blood pressure in men. *Journal of Abnormal Psychology, 88,* 182–190.

McClelland, D.C., Alexander, C., & Marks, E. (1982). The need for power, stress, immune functions, and illness among male prisoners. *Journal of Abnormal Psychology, 91* (1), 61–70.

McClelland, D.C., Davidson, R.J., Floor, E., & Saron, C. (1980). Stressed power motivation, sympathetic activation, immune function and illness. *Journal of Human Stress, 6* (2), 11–19.

Malaspina, J.P., Bussiere, H., & LeCalve, G. (1981). The total cholesterol/HDL cholesterol ratio: A suitable atherogenesis index. *Atherosclerosis, 40,* 373–375.

Meyer, R.J., & Haggerty, R.J. (1962). Streptococcal infections in families: Factors altering individual susceptibility. *Pediatrics, 29,* 539–549.

Morse, D.R. (1982). Stress and bruxism: A critical review and report of cases. *Journal of Human Stress, 8* (1), 43–54.

Mueller, E.F. (1965). *Psychological and physiological correlates of work overload among university professors.* Ph.D. dissertation, University of Michigan.

Newberry, B.H., & Gerstenberger, T.J. (1986). Pituitary-neurohormonal immunoregulation in cancer. In I. Berczi (Ed.), *Pituitary function and imunity* (303–311). Boca Raton, FL: CRC Press.

Ornish, D. (1982). *Stress, diet, and your heart.* New York: Signet.

Quick, J.C., & Quick, J.D. (1984). *Organizational stress and preventive management.* New York: McGraw-Hill.

Riley, V. (1978). Stress and cancer: Fresh perspectives. In H.E. Nieburgs (Ed.), *Prevention and detection of cancer* (1769–1776). New York: Marcel Dekker.

Selye, H. (1976). *Stress in health and disease.* Boston: Butterworths.

Stoll, B.A. (Ed.) (1979). *Mind and cancer prognosis.* New York: Wiley.

Sturedevant, R.A.L. (1976). Epidemiology of peptic ulcer. *American Journal of Epidemiology, 104,* 9–14.

Tranin, N., Small, M., & Gabizon, A. (1978). Combined effects of immune depression and carcinogenesis. In H.E. Niebergs (Ed.), *Prevention and detection of cancer* (pt. 1, vol. 2, 1621–1630). New York: Marcel Dekker.

Troxler, R.G., & Wetzler, H.P. (1981). Executive stress: The symptoms, the cause, and the cure. *Air University Review* (March–April), 43–52.

Uhl, G.S., Troxler, R.G., Hickman, J.R., & Clark, D. (1978). Relation between high density lipoprotein cholesterol and coronary artery disease in asymptomatic men. *American Journal of Cardiology, 48,* 903–910.

U.S. Department of Health and Human Services, Public Health Service, Center for Disease Control (1980). *Ten leading causes of death in the United States, 1977.* Atlanta, GA.

Weiner, H. (1978). Emotional factors. In S.C. Werner, and S.H. Ingbar (Eds.), *The thyroid* (627–632). New York: Harper & Row.

73 NEW LEGAL RIGHTS RELATED TO EMOTIONAL STRESS IN THE WORKPLACE

Donald T. DeCarlo

A secretary suffers a nervous breakdown upon viewing the grisly office suicide scene of her supervisor. A metal worker fears further exposure to workplace chemicals upon reading that workers in another factory contacted cancer after exposure to the same chemicals. The sole male employee in a library feels harassed and belittled by his female supervisor and coworkers. A jet engine assembler is unable to cope with new duties after a transfer from the night shift to the day shift. A truck driver cannot emotionally function on the job when his routes are changed. An assembly line worker breaks down when unable to keep up with the pace of the job. A training specialist suffers an emotional collapse after a layoff and subsequent rehiring with a transfer to a new department. A white sanitation supervisor suffers a nervous breakdown because he is forced to work with blacks.

All of these factual scenarios are the actual subjects of recent workers' compensation claims from around the nation.[1] These claims alleging that mental stress on the job caused a mental disability bear little resemblance to the more traditional settings for workers' compensation claims—traumatic physical injuries caused by accidents at work and occupational diseases caused by exposure to toxic substances in the workplace.

THE INCREASE IN CLAIMS

In January 1985; the National Council on Compensation Insurance (NCCI) issued its legal monograph, *Emotional Stress in the Workplace—New Legal Rights in the Eighties*. Included in the monograph were NCCI-detailed claim information results showing that workers' compensation claims for mental disability caused by mental stress represented about 11 percent of all occupational disease claims.

More recent NCCI statistics show stress claims accounting for about 11.9 percent of all occupational disease claims, with the percentage of stress claims nearly tripling between 1979 and 1983. The most recent results also confirm earlier studies suggesting that stress claimants are younger and more likely to be female occupational disease claimants generally. The average age for stress claimants is 38.5 years (as opposed to 44.6 years for all other occupational disease claimants), and 45 percent of all stress claimants are women (as opposed to 24 percent of occupational disease claimants generally).

In states that have been particularly liberal in compensating mental stress claims, these claims now are becoming a significant percentage of all compensation claims, as demonstrated by the following chart showing the results in California.[2]

Mental Stress Injuries	Percentage of Total Injuries
1980: 1,282	0.3
1981: 1,844	0.5
1982: 2,644	0.8
1983: 3,785	1.1
1984: 4,236	1.1

REASONS FOR THE INCREASE

Publicity

It has often been suggested that highly publicized workers' compensation recoveries spur similar claims. This may be important in mental stress claims because of the universality of the exposure—mental stress. The claim of a construction worker who fell off a roof or a firefighter injured in a blaze may be highly publicized, but such claims are not likely to strike a chord with sendentary office workers. However, most workers can identify with an employee experiencing emotional stress from such job pressures as a change in duties or a conflict with supervisors. Indeed, in a recent survey conducted by the Canadian Mental Health Association, approximately 60 percent of the respondents reported experiencing "negative stress" on the job. Frequently cited sources of stress included work load and time pressures, quality of management, relationships with supervisors and coworkers, contact with the public or customers and, among men in blue-collar and farming occupations, the threat of job loss or change due to economic conditions or technological innovations.[3] Accordingly, a claim based on such pressures is likely to draw the attention of a large number of workers who feel that they are no less entitled to compensation.

Economic Conditions

Since dissatisfaction with working conditions commonly underlies mental stress claims, some of the increase may be related to increases in unemployment, plant closings, and relocations. Indeed, it now appears that a workers' compensation claim is sought as a potential remedy in many disputes between management and employees that, until recently, would be considered exclusively within the realm of labor relations.

Legal Recognition of Mental Impairment. A portion of the increase in mental stress claims may simply reflect the increasing legal recognition of compensation for mental injuries in contexts other than workers' compensation. An increasing tendency in the law allows tort recovery for both the intentional and negligent infliction of emotional distress. While such tort recoveries were previously limited to narrow and extreme situations (e.g., a parent who witnessed the wrongful killing of his or her child), recovery is now commonly permitted to compensate for fear and anxiety in a variety of contexts. A family in Hawaii was successful in obtaining a tort recovery for the emotional distress suffered when they witnessed the negligent killing of their dog. Recently, some courts have allowed substantial recovery to the survivors of airplane crash victims who suffered, albeit briefly, prior to the impact that killed them instantaneously. It is not surprising that this increased recognition of mental injury in tort would also spill over into workers' compensation, replacing the employee's tort remedy against an employer for injuries arising out of employment.

Less Social Sigma

Part of the increase may reflect the fact that emotional problems in society today are more likely to be acknowledged than in past generations. As these problems have come to be viewed like any other infirmity or handicap and visits to psychologists and psychiatrists have become less of an embarrassment or admission of weakness, the social stigma workers would have felt upon admitting an ability to cope in the past has become less of a deterrent.

Will the Increase Continue?

Whatever the cause, the increase in mental stress claims will probably continue. Statistics indicate a higher than expected percentage of claims by younger workers, which in time could indicate a new generation of workers who are more prone to stress or at least more willing to view their emotional problems as compensable injuries. The recent study of the Canadian Mental Health Association, which surveyed workers' perceptions rather than actual claims, also found that younger workers, particularly those between the ages of twenty-five and forty-four, were more likely to feel affected by negative stress in the workplace.[4]

The higher than expected percentage of claims by women could indicate that the "newer" white-collar and service industry jobs that have accommodated a significant portion of the increased number of women in the work force are more likely to produce mental stress claims than the "older" blue-collar and manufacturing jobs. For example, while it appears that there is no significant difference between the percentage of men and women who experience negative stress in the workplace, clerical workers, who are primarily women, are the most likely to report physical problems caused by the work stress. In this regard, it has been suggested that many women may be prone to job dissatisfaction where unequal job opportunities confine them to jobs with lower pay or less responsibility and independence than similarly qualified male counterparts.[5]

However, the most persuasive indicator that mental stress claims will be an increasingly significant workers' compensation subject comes not from demographic distinctions but from the size of the potential pool of claimants. It has frequently been suggested that between 15 and 30 percent of the overall population suffer impairments due to mental programs.[6] A recent study conducted by the National Institute of Mental Health concludes that about 19 percent of all adults, evenly distributed among men and women, have at least one psychiatric disorder during any six-month period.[7] The Canadian study suggests that the potential pool is even larger when workers evaluate their own reactions to stress; approximately 60 percent of workers felt negative stress in the workplace, with over 80 percent of this group responding that the stress affected either job performance, psychological well-being, or physical well-being.[8]

Finally, the American Institute of Stress has estimated that the total cost of stress to American business, including not only the more obvious occupational and nonoccupational medical and disability costs but also more subtle factors like reduced productivity, increase absenteeism and sick leave, high turnover, damage to and waste of materials, may exceed $100 billion per year.

In the light of the broad exposure and potential costs, the current direct cost of workers' compensation claims, estimated to be between $30 and $50 million per year, could be the tip of an iceberg.

MENTAL INJURIES AND WORKERS' COMPENSATION: BACKGROUND

Workers' compensation statutes, in effect in all fifty states, provide compensation on a no-fault basis for the loss of the ability to earn wages due to an accidental injury or disease arising out of and in the course of employment. The allowance of compensation, even where the employer is not to blame for the injury, is the result of a historic compromise, a quid pro quo in which employees gave up the right to bring lawsuits for workplace injuries, with the possibility of large, albeit uncertain, recoveries, in exchange for the certainty of statutory benefits. Employers, for their part, agree to provide these benefits without regard to fault but limit their potential liability to the predictable amounts scheduled by statute, generally a fixed percentage of the employee's lost wages for the duration of disability, subject to overall minimums and maximums, which vary by state.

Workers' compensation claims involving either mental stress or mental disability are often divided into three categories:

1. *Mental-physical* claims involve mental stress that results in a physical disability, for example, a stress-induced heart attack.

2. *Physical-mental* claims involve a physical injury that leads to a mental disability, for example, a conversation neurosis following a traumatic injury.

3. *Mental-mental* claims refer to mental stress that results in a mental disability, for example, a nervous breakdown brought on by job harassment.

Mental-physical claims and physical-mental claims are controversial in their own right. These claims have increased as a result of greater acceptance of the premise that stress may trigger a physical reaction or a physical infirmity may have psychological side effects. In all states, these claims are now potentially compensable if causation—the relationship between events or exposures in the workplace and the disability that ultimately results—can be established.

But in both mental-physical and physical-mental claims, there is at least some physical corroboration in support of a claim. In the example of a heart attack allegedly caused by workplace stress, the stress may be difficult to measure or even confirm, but there is physical evidence that an injury, a heart attack, did in fact occur. Similarly, in the case of a conversion neurosis, the resulting psychological problems may be amorphous, but the underlying traumatic injury can at least be confirmed and investigated.

It is the mental-mental claims that have shown the dramatic claims increase discussed earlier, and characteristically, there is no physical corroboration for either the stimulus (mental stress), the result (mental disability), or the casual relationship between the stress and the disability (work relatedness).

Not surprisingly, it is the mental-mental claims that are the most controversial kind of claims, and the states have adopted varying views as to allowance of such claims. Generally, the states can be divided into four categories of potential compensability:

1. Those states in which mental-mental claims are not compensable under any circumstances.

2. Those states in which mental-mental claims may be potentially compensable if the stress is a sudden, frightening, or shocking event, for example, witnessing the death of a coworker.

3. Those states in which mental-mental claims involving gradual stress may be compensable if the stress is unusual, for example, supervisory harassment or an increase in job duties.

4. Those states in which mental-mental claims may

be compensable even without unusual stress.

With few exceptions, the category where a state is found is determined by case law, not by explicit statutory definition or limitation. Few state statutes were written with any contemplation of purely mental injuries. While a comprehensive legal breakdown of the fifty states is beyond the scope of this chapter and available elsewhere,[9] suffice it to say that there is a definite legal trend in the case law under which most states are now in, or moving towards, one of the two more liberal categories: allowing mental-mental claims if the workplace stress is unusual, usually defined to mean greater than the stress of everyday life or employment, or allowing mental-mental claims even without unusual stress, in effect treating mental-mental claims no differently from physical injuries.

HOW HAVE THE STATES RESPONDED TO THIS NEW BREED OF CLAIM?

Case Law

Regardless of the standard adopted, most state courts have given some recognition to fears that mental-mental claims, with no physical corroboration for either the stress or the disability, create an opportunity for fraudulent claims or successful claims by malingerers. In commenting on the ability of psychiatry to evaluate and determine the origins of obsessive-compulsive neurosis, one court recently stated that

> great care must be taken in order to avoid the creation of voluntary "retirement" programs that may be seized upon by an employee at an early age if he or she is willing or, indeed, even eager to give up active employment and assert a neurotic inability to continue.
>
> It is all very well to say that the adversary system will expose the difference between the genuine neurotic and the malingerer. We have great fears that neither the science of psychiatry nor the adversary judicial process is equal to this task on the type of claim here presented.[10]

In states requiring unusual stress, the "unusual" requirement is no doubt premised on a belief that unusual events are more likely to be susceptible to proof.

States that do not require that stress be unusual

seem to be seeking similar assurances. In Pennsylvania, the case law has now clearly established that in a mental-mental claim, causation must be established by unequivocal evidence. New Jersey case law has emphasized that there must be objective medical proof of mental disability.

Perhaps the most widespread limitation that has been placed on the scope of compensable mental-mental claims is the near-universal rejection of the purely subjective standard in which there need be no stress in the workplace at all. That is, if a claimant with a preexisting emotional imbalance "misperceives" a source of stress in the workplace and suffers disability as a result, the injury is compensable.

A classic example of this kind of claim was a recent Oregon case involving a telephone repairman with a paranoid personality who could not cope with the stress of being supervised by younger and female supervisors. The claim was rejected because the source of stress was misperceived. In fact, the claimant was not subject to significant supervision by women or younger workers. Under the subjective standard, such a claim would be compensable notwithstanding that the disability is related solely to an emotional problem rooted outside the workplace. Fortunately, this illusory standard has now, with the possible exception of California, been rejected by every state court that has considered it and was abolished by statute in Michigan.

Statutory Changes

Case law, unfortunately, can never be static or entirely predictable. For example, in a case involving a worker who suffers a breakdown after witnessing a serious injury to a coworker, a court may allow compensation because the cause is a sudden, frightening, and shocking event. That, however, does not foreclose the possibility that in a future case involving less dramatic, albeit still "unusual," stress (e.g., an increase in job duties), the court will not move on to the next level of liberality, allowing the claim because the stress is in excess of the usual stress of everyday life or employment.

Particularly in the past few years, as mental-mental claims have begun to receive a great deal of publicity, a few states have attempted to define the class of potential claims by statute.

The approaches differ from state to state. Recent amendments in Ohio elect to exclude mental-mental claims altogether by providing that only mental disabilities resulting from a physical injury or an occupational disease may be compensable.[11]

A recent amendment in New Mexico excludes from the scope of permanent total disability "conditions solely due to stress."[12] On the one hand, this exclusion seems very broad (applicable to all stress-related conditions, not just mental-mental claims); on the other hand, it is not clear that the exclusion will apply to temporary total disability, and this is where most mental-mental claims seem to fall.

Massachusetts recently enacted a bill providing that mental or emotional disabilities are compensable only "where a contributing cause . . . is an event or series of events occurring within the employment."[13] This provision hardly seems to do more than restate the causation requirement applicable to any worker's compensation claim; more notable is the fact that appointment of an impartial examiner is authorized in claims involving mental disability.

UNCERTAINTY OF PSYCHIATRY

An issue that arises in all states, regardless of case law or statutory guidance, is concern over the reliability of psychiatric testimony in legal contexts. This problem takes on particular importance in mental-mental cases where expert psychiatric (or psychological) testimony is generally relied upon to identify the source of mental stress and to evaluate the extent and character of the disability, as well as to establish the causal relationship between the stress and the disability. Causal relationship presents a difficult problem in mental-mental claims because every nonwork aspect of a claimant's life can present an alternate source of the worker's mental problems. Indeed, the recent study by the Canadian Mental Health Association found that of workers reporting negative stress at work, 81 percent felt that personal problems at home, which were brought to the workplace, were a major source of stress. The most common problems specified were marital, financial, and family crises.[14]

Numerous commentators have suggested that well-intended pyschiatrists cannot even answer the most fundamental question of whether a patient suffers from a mental disability, let alone evaluate the source of extent of that disability with the "more probable than not" level of certainty generally required by the law.[15] Studies have suggested that psychiatrists have a greater tendency to err by diagnosing sickness in healthy people than to err by diagnosing wellness in sick people.[16] This tendency may come into play particularly in a workers' compensation claim where a psychiatrist will, understandably, be reluctant to label an apparently healthy claimant as a malingerer. Other studies have concluded that two psychiatrists, examining the same patient, will concur in choosing among the four possible diagnoses of psychosis, neurosis, personality disorder, and normality only between one-third and one-half of the time.[17] Finally, the diagnostic standards used by psychiatrists have often been criticized as too vague and unreliable to be the basis for legal judgments.[18]

Of course, these problems may not indict psychiatry as a form of treatment; there may be no harm in treating the well along with the sick. But in the light of the recognized fine line between the legal extremes of malingering and disabling neurosis and the fact that "psychiatry has not advanced to the point where it is an exact science in the same sense that physical medicine is an exact science,"[19] it is evident that safeguards are required to ensure that psychiatric evidence is used, and not abused, in the context of workers' compensation claims.

RECOMMENDATIONS: A LAWYER'S PERSPECTIVE

It has been suggested that this is a fruitful area for employer prevention, particularly since many of the options are also intended to boost morale, increase efficiency, and reduce the frequency of physical injuries. The preventative programs that can be used by employers include:

- Workplace wellness programs as well as more specific self-improvement opportunities for employees (e.g., employer-sponsored smoking cessation clinics and exercise classes).
- Programs that identify employees with the most stressful occupations and provide education on stress management techniques.
- Counseling for employees with personal problems (e.g., drugs, marital, and financial).
- Prehiring screening for susceptible employees and ongoing monitoring of employees for adverse stress reactions.

Of course, with or without prevention, some claims will occur. Accordingly, it would be beneficial if the workers' compensation system provided assistance to employers seeking to distinguish between claims that should be paid and those that are not meritorious.

Administration of Workers' Compensation

As to the day-to-day administration of the compensation system, I suggest that there is a great deal to be learned from the 1985 Report of the Subcommittee on Current Laws and Proposals of the National Association of Insurance Commissioners Advisory Committee on Occupational Disease. This report recommends that all states establish a panel of impartial experts in occupational medicine, industrial science, industrial hygiene, and epidemiology to determine the compensability of individual occupational disease claims. The NAIC subcommittee further suggests that administrative guidelines be developed addressing causation and diagnostic criteria and that central depositories for the latest medical, scientific, and epidemiological data relating to occupational disease be established. The NAIC subcommittee report also supports further development of courses to educate and train administrators in deciding occupational disease cases.

All of these suggestions seem particularly relevant to mental-mental claims. Since much of the controversy in mental-mental claims focuses on the uncertainty of psychiatry's ability to provide probative answers to legal inquiries, panels of impartial experts might lend greater credence to the reliability of the medical determinations. Administrative standards are more sorely needed in mental-mental claims than in other occupational disease claims because the diagnostic standards currently relied upon are not responsive to the issues that arise in workers' compensation claims. For example, the American Psychiatric Association's *Diagnostic and Statistical Manual of Mental Disorders,* used by most psychiatrists for diagnostic purposes, includes a caveat that the manual was not developed for nonclinical uses such as determinations of legal responsibility.[20] As a general rule, the manual does not attempt to address the etiology of mental disorders categorized within.[21]

Uniform diagnostic standards that are developed for determinations of legal responsibility, as applied by impartial panels of medical experts, might, at the very least, remove some doubts as to the genuineness of mental-mental claims, including doubts as to the frequency of fraud or malingering. Since these doubts have often been the source of the variety of special legal standards for potential compensability developed with broad disparity among the states, removal of these doubts might encourage a state-by-state uniformity, eliminating much of the uncertainty as to the potential compensability of mental-mental claims. Such uniformity certainly does not exist now.

Recommendations suggesting creation of central information depositories and educational programs also apply with particular relevance to mental-mental claims since so little information is currently available. Statistical monitoring and continuous educational updates will be necessary to ensure that the administration of standards that are developed and the standards themselves remain consonant with the current understanding of mental disorders.

Statutory Changes

Where statutory guidance is deemed necessary, it is desirable that there be provision for legitimate work-related claims to enter the system because workers' compensation, and not the tort system, is, after all, the intended remedy for all disabling bodily injuries and diseases that are work related. On the other hand, the desire to accommodate legitimate claims must be balanced against the need to address the peculiar problems that arise in this area: the lack of corroborating physical evidence, the uncertainty of psychiatry, and the need to ensure that the workers' compensation system is not burdened with the cost of providing a remedy for the myriad of personal problems employees bring to the workplace.

I would propose the following language as a starting point for a statute attempting to balance these competing concerns:

> A mental injury, illness, condition or disease shall not be considered an injury arising out of and in the course of employment or an injury caused by occupational disease, and is not compensable, unless it is established by clear and convincing objective medical evidence that:
>
> (i) some unexpected and identifiable stressful event, or series of stressful events, related to the employment and involving stress greater than the usual stress encountered in occupational and nonoccupational life; or
>
> (ii) some physical injury related to the employment was a substantial contributing cause of the mental injury, illness, condition or disease.

This definition incorporates the emerging majority view that stress should be "usual" and, in the light of the absence of physical corroboration for either the stress or the disability, causation should be clearly established. In addition, the "clear and convincing objective medical evidence" requirement addresses concerns over the reliability of psychiatric testimony.

Of course, physical-mental claims (e.g., traumatic neuroses) are accommodated by subparagraph ii.

Defense of a Claim

Once a claim does arise, this is an area in which claims investigation and case preparation take on particular significance.

Because every aspect of a claimant's nonwork life presents a potential alternate source of the alleged emotional problems, some inquiry into a claimant's personal life will often be necessary. For example, marital problems, financial problems, recent deaths in the family, and a host of other events could be the real cause of the worker's problems.

Possible physical causes originating outside the workplace must also be investigated—drug abuse, alcohol abuse, insomnia, eating disorders, a traumatic injury at home or suffered in an automobile accident—all could be the source of an emotional problem brought into the workplace.

It is also important to be aware of any preexisting emotional problems the worker may have. Investigation is more important than in a case involving a preexisting physical injury because there are not likely to be symptoms obvious to the lay person. A worker with a preexisting emotional disability may be reacting to "misperceived" stress in the workplace where in fact there is no harmful work-related stress. Such a claim is generally not compensable.

Finally, the expert opinions in support of the claim must be carefully evaluated; given the uncertainty inherent in even the most qualified psychiatrist's opinion, a claim that is supported only by the opinion of a general practitioner or other physician with questionable qualifications in this context should be viewed with a healthy skepticism.

CONCLUSIONS

Workers' compensation has for three-quarters of a century served American employers and employees well in providing a remedy for work-related injuries. While mental-mental claims are a new breed of claim, presenting some new problems, the system can accommodate the deserving claims no less than any other injury. The system may need a little help in distinguishing between the meritorious and less deserving claims, but the refinements that are needed are attainable.

NOTES

1. *Wolfe v. Sibley, Lindsay, & Curr Co.*, 330 N.E. 2d 603 (N.Y. 1975); *McMahon v. Anaconda Co.*, 678 P.2d 661 (Mont. 1984); *Taquino v. Sears, Roebuck & Co.*, 438 So. 2d 625 (La. Ct. App. 1983); *Candelaria v. General Electric Co.*, N.M. (1986); *Consolidated Freightways v. Drake*, 678 P.2d 874 (Wyo. 1984); *Kelly's Case*, 477 N.E.2d 582 (Mass. 1984); Claim of Gary Pearl before the Kentucky Workers' Compensation Board (1985).

2. California Workers' Compensation Institute, Bulletin No. 84-7 (September 4, 1985).

3. *Canadian Mental Health Association, Work and Well-Being* 45–49 (1984) (hereinafter cited as *Work and well being*).

4. Id. at 46, 49.

5. Id. at 46, 124, 131.

6. See, e.g., Fleming, Industry looks at the emotionally troubled employee, in *The emotionally troubled employee: A challenge to industry* 57 (1976).

7. *Newsday,* October 3, 1984, at 11, col. 3–4.

8. *Work and well being,* at 46–47.

9. National Council on Compensation Insurance, Emotional stress in the workplace—New legal rights in the eighties (1985).

10. *Seitz v. L & R Industries, Inc.,* 437 A.2d. 1345, 1349–350 (R.I. 1981) (footnote omitted).

11. S.B. 307.

12. S.B. 100.

13. H. 6850.

14. *Work and well being,* at 51–52.

15. See, e.g., Psychiatry and the presumption of expertise: Flipping coins in the courtroom, 62 *Calif. L. Rev.* 693 (1974); Almy, Psychiatric testimony: Controlling the "ultimate wizardry" in personal injury actions, 19 *Forum* 233, 242–262 (1984).

16. Id. at 251–52.

17. Id. at 245–46, nn. 63–64.

18. Id. at 247–250.

19. Smith, Problems in proof in psychic injury cases, 14 *Syracuse L. Rev.* 586, 633 n. 138 (1963).

20. American Psychiatric Association, *Diagnostic and statistical manual of mental disorders* 7 (3d ed. 1980).

21. Id. at 12.

74 ASSESSING STRESS IN THE WORKPLACE

John W. Jones

A REVIEW OF ORGANIZATIONAL STRESS ASSESSMENT INSTRUMENTS

Legal researchers are concluding that managers can no longer choose to recognize and deal with the sources and symptoms of stress on the job; it has become a legal obligation (Ivancevich, Matteson & Richards, 1985). Organizational stress surveys can be used to provide management with information on both the levels and sources of employee stress.

Stress surveys that can be employed in organizational settings are reviewed in this chapter. The review is not intended to be comprehensive. Instead, this chapter focuses on a few key stress inventories that were specifically designed for work settings and that have ample evidence of validity. It is geared toward practitioners who want to gain a better perspective on how to select, administer, score, and interpret organizational stress surveys. In addition, all of the instruments reviewed have been successfully tested in many companies.

The Cost of Occupational Stress

Stress is a costly business expense, affecting both employee health and company profits. However, companies can reduce stress and its effects through comprehensive worksite stress management programs.

Consider these stress facts gleaned from various safety and insurance industry research (Jones, 1985):

- In 1982, the total cost of work-related accidents in the United States alone was $32 billion.
- The causes of about 75–85 percent of all industrial accidents are accident susceptibility factors (e.g., fatigue, poor concentration, inattentiveness).
- Psychological or psychosomatic problems contribute to over 60 percent of long-term employee disability cases.

- About 11 percent of all occupational disease claims are for workplace stress.

With regard to the last statistic, three forms of work stress claims have been delineated (National Council on Compensation Insurance, 1985). *Physical-mental* claims occur when a physical injury results in a mental disability, such as phobic fear of heights after falling from a scaffold and breaking a leg. *Mental-physical* claims happen if mental stress results in a physical injury, such as when constant deadline pressures, coupled with overwork, culminate in a heart attack. Last, *mental-mental* claims occur when mental stress causes mental disability. An example would be sexual harassment that leads an office worker to have anxiety attacks.

Legal suits for job-related stress likely will increase in the future because:

- Research suggests a relationship between stress and injury or illness.
- Many state workers' compensation laws specify compensation for both physical and mental injuries resulting from job stress.
- More employees are prompted to file stress claims because they believe in the stress-loss connection and know that fellow employees have received workers' compensation for it.
- Lawyers, judges, and physicians are becoming more familiar with this type of claim. It is more easily diagnosed and more often used to receive legal and monetary restitution.

Hence, it becomes imperative that companies begin to understand, assess, and remedy excessive levels of occupational stress.

But what is stress? By definition stress is the

adverse emotional and physical reactions employees have to any source of pressure in their environment. These stress reactions negatively affect personal health and organizational effectiveness and often create losses. Among the personal effects of stress are the following:

Alcohol abuse
Drug abuse
Emotional instability
Lack of self-control
Fatigue
Marital problems
Depression
Insomnia
Violence
Insecurity
Frustration
Anxiety
Psychosomatic diseases
Eating disorders
Boredom
Mental illness
Suicide
Health breakdowns (cardiovascular, etc.)
Irresponsibility

The following effects are organizational:

Accidents
Thefts
Reduced productivity
High turnover
Increased errors
Absenteeism
Disability payments
Sabotage
Damage and waste
Replacement costs
Inflated health care costs
Unpreparedness
Lack of creativity
Increased sick leave
Premature retirement
Organizational breakdown
Disloyalty
Job dissatisfaction
Poor decisions
Antagonistic group action

Employees continually confront various pressures or "stressors." They experience stress if unable to cope effectively with such stressors as poor management, lack of job security, work overload, unclear communications, excessive deadline pressure, unrealistic expectations, insufficient pay, and uncertainty about job duties and responsibilities.

BREAKING THE DISTRESS CYCLE

The major goal of worksite stress managment programs is to help companies interrupt what is called the *distress cycle*. Figure 74–1 illustrates how this damaging cycle evolves. Research has shown that there are two basic approaches to breaking the distress cycle. One approach is to identify and modify the stressors. The other is to increase an employee's ability to cope with stress. Both methods can be used individually or in combination.

For example, organizational stressors can be identified and corrected. Consider one production unit with a very high stress level, a high number of accidents, and low productivity. Results of an organizational stress survey showed that poorly defined job responsibilities caused employee stress. After each person's job was analyzed and defined, production increased and accidents were reduced. The stress survey also revealed other stressors that needed controlling, including poor communications, undefined pay raise systems, and employee drug abuse (Jones, 1985).

The second way to break the distress cycle—increasing the ability to cope—consists of the more commonly known stress management techniques. These include physical fitness programs, relaxation techniques, assertiveness training, biofeedback, weight loss, drug and/or alcohol rehabiliation, and periodic physical examinations. These techniques are not intended to alter stressors but to increase an individual's ability to cope with stressors in his or her environment.

The Assessment of Organizational Stress

To control stress-related losses in industry better, companies must periodically use organizational stress surveys, which assess: employees' physical, mental, and emotional reactions to a stressful work environment; the corporate stressors that cause stressful,

Figure 74–1. The Distress Cycle

Employees are exposed to many stressors. Those who have coping deficiencies rather than coping skills become distressed. Chronic distress, in turn, leads to social and financial costs — accidents, injuries, turnover, and poor productivity. But it doesn't stop there. These symptoms of distress become, themselves, stressors, and the distress cycle develops.

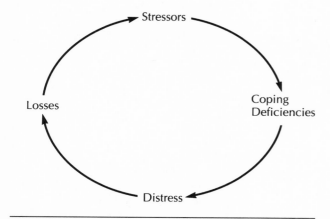

pressured work environments; and the corporate and employee coping skills and resources that can serve as "stress buffers."

Research at the St. Paul Insurance Company (Burdick & Jones, 1985) indicates that companies are more likely to use worksite stress management programs once they learn, through an organizational stress assessment, that their employees are indeed experiencing exceptionally high levels of occupational stress. Ideally, the stress assessment can pinpoint the overall level of company stress, levels of stress in selected work groups (e.g., departments, job types), and the major organizational stressors that are causing the employee stress. Four different assessment tools are reviewed.

Human Factors Inventory (HFI) The Human Factors Inventory (HFI) is a 162-item organizational climate survey (Jones, 1983; Jones & DuBois, 1985) used by businesses to assess various forms of occupational stress.

The following six scales make up the HFI: Job Stress, Job Dissatisfaction, Organizational Stress, Stressful Life Events, Life and Health Risks, and Accident Risks. Test-retest reliability coefficients (one-week interval) for these six scales are .91, .90, .89, .89, .88, and .87, respectively. Each of these scales is briefly described below. A distortion scale is also described. Norms exist based on over 100,000 employees representing hundreds of different companies and job types.

Job Stress. This scale identifies the average level of job stress employees are experiencing at an individual level. General signs of job stress include feelings of frustration, boredom, irritability, nervousness and burn-out at work. Physical signs of job stress include headaches, stomach upset, backaches, chest pains, chronic fatigue, and sleep difficulties. Employees scoring in the higher-risk ranges are also less productive, have higher rates of illness and absenteeism, and often think about leaving the company. Finally, they feel that work-related pressure contributes to tension in their family. Sample items include "I experience too much pressure on my job," "I have lost efficiency on my job," and "I feel burned out on my job."

Job Dissatisfaction. This scale assesses how dissatisfied employees are with various aspects of their job. Dissatisfaction with the following areas is assessed: job, pay, promotional opportunities, co-worker relationships, and overall management effectiveness. Sample items include "I am very satisfied with my job," "This company is well managed," "I am paid adequately for what I do," and "We have a good team relationship in my department."

Organizational Stress. This scale assesses employees' perceptions of organizational stress. It identifies if departments have unacceptable levels of organizational tension. Some general signs of organizational stress measured by this scale include poor productivity, interpersonal conflicts, departmental tension, excessive absenteeism, accidents and mistakes, and a perception that employees are distressed. Employee dishonesty, waste, and on-the-job alcohol and drug misuse are also assessed. Sample items include "My department is understaffed," "There is more absenteeism and tardiness in my department than usual," and "Staff turnover is high in my department."

Stressful Life Changes. This scale measures the amount of stressful life changes that employees have experienced in the past twelve months. Examples of stressful life changes that are assessed include taking on debts; an illness, injury, or death of a loved one; and major changes in job duties at work. This scale provides a measure of personal stress. Most companies request a stress survey that can differentiate between job stress and personal stress.

Life and Health Risks. This scale measures lifestyles and health habits that increase the risk for unnecessary injuries, illnesses, and premature deaths among employees. Examples of such risks include lack of exercise and relaxation, unsafe driving practices, poor nutrition and weight control, smoking, alcohol abuse, and so on. Sample items include "I get a thorough physical examination each year," "I try to prevent work stress by exercising and participating in recreational activities," and "I get approximately eight hours sleep at least four nights a week."

Accidents Risks. This scale measures four human factors that contribute to accidents and errors: (1) an inability to cope with stress, (2) poor safety attitudes, (3) a tendency to worry about job performance, and (4) an inability to manage time. Sample items include "Are you always safety conscious?" "Do you feel hurried or rushed to complete deadlines at work?" and "Do you feel fatigued during the workday?"

Distortion. This scale identifies the percentage of employees who are truthful with their responses. It identifies the number of employees who attempt to "fake good" or "fake bad" on the Human Factors Inventory.

Interpreting HFI Scale Scores. The HFI takes approximately 30 minutes to complete. Participation is both anonymous and voluntary. Results are computer scored and compared to the national norm. An organizational "stress quotient" is computed for each company. This comparison allows companies to determine if their employees are above or below a national average in terms of their stress reactions and coping skills. The inventory also indicates in which jobs or departments employees are experiencing the most stress.

The major findings of the Human Factors Inventory are derived from analyzing the survey data on three levels: (1) overall results for each scale for all company employees combined, (2) analyses by employee subgroups (e.g., job titles, departments, locations, demographic variables), and (3) response frequencies for individual items. HFI percentile scores ranging from 0 to 100 are plotted for each subscale. Higher scores mean greater risk. The following guidelines are used when interpreting all subscales:

Percentile Range	Description
0–20	*Very Low Risk.* The average employee is coping better than 80 percent or more of the employees represented in the norms. This is probably due to better coping skills and less exposure to stressful situations.
21–40	*Low Risk.* The typical employee is coping better than 60 to 79 percent of the employees in the normative sample.
41–60	*Average Risk.* The average employee is coping just as good as the average employee representeed in the norms. The typical employee in this group is no worse or no better than the typical employee from the normative sample. That is, scores in this range mean that employees have both coping skills and coping deficiencies.
61–80	*High Risk.* Scores in this range mean that there are opportunities to reduce stressors and improve coping skills. That is, the typical employee is coping worse than 61 percent to 80 percent of the normative sample employees. Interventions are needed for these employee groups.
81–100	*Very High Risk.* Active interventions are definitely needed for these employee groups. The average employee is coping worse than 81 percent to 100 percent of the employees represented in the norms. This is probably due to poorer coping skills and more exposure to stressful situations.

In brief, work groups with percentile scores greater than 50 are experiencing above-average levels of stress. Groups with percentile scores less than 50 are experiencing below-average levels of stress. A score of 80 or more indicates critically higher levels of stress and should serve as a warning to companies that worksite stress management programs are definitely needed.

Validity. A test or survey is valid when it predicts those behaviors and outcomes that it was designed to predict. A number of validation studies have been conducted with the HFI (Jones & Dubois, 1985). A selection of three validation studies is presented. The validity of the HFI has been established in a series of studies (of., Jones, Barge, Steffy, Fay, Kunz & Wuebker, 1988).

In one study, 150 employed college students completed the HFI and made anonymous admissions of accidents, injuries, and illnesses. Results showed that higher scores on the HFI (higher scores mean more stress and poorer coping skills) significantly correlated ($p < .05$) with higher rates of on-the-job accidents, minor injuries, major injuries, minor illnesses, major illnesses, and days of work missed due to injury and/or illness. Higher HFI scores were also associated with more frequent use of medical facilities. Finally, higher HFI scores were associated with poorer productivity and tendencies to look for a new job. This study has been replicated with over 6,000 employees representing hundreds of different job titles in many different corporations.

Forty-two employees who reported on-the-job injuries to an occupational nurse participated in another validity study. All employees worked for the same company. Reported injuries typically fell into one of four categories: falls and trips, lifting strains, lacerations, and miscellaneous (e.g., smashed finger, infection of unknown origin, hematoma from dropping cabinet on foot.). All injuries required medical care and time off from work. All of these occupationally injured employees completed the HFI to test the hypothesis that employees who get injured at work experience more job stress and dissatisfaction than their coworkers.

Obtained results supported the hypothesis. Statistical analyses showed that the injured employees, on the average, experienced higher levels of job stress, job dissatisfaction, and organizational stress compared to a control group of over 1,000 coworkers ($p < .01$). In addition, the injured employees encountered more stressful life changes during the past twelve months compared to the control group ($p < .01$). These findings support the hypothesis that employee stress is related to more on-the-job accidents and injuries.

Finally, the relationship between HFI scores and levels of chronic back pain was assessed with 518 hospital employees in another validity study. Employees indicated how often they experience distressing backaches and pains. Back pain and injury is a leading cause of workers' compensation claims. The following results were obtained:

Daily Pain Frequency	Sample Size	Percentage of Total
Never	69	13.3
Rarely	181	34.9
Sometimes	161	31.1
Often	83	16.0
Always	24	4.6
Total	518	100.0

Obtained results show that approximately 21 percent of all employees experience high rates of backaches and pains. Only 13 percent of employees reported that they "never" experienced back pain.

The relationship of HFI job stress scores to frequency of back pain was established. That is, employees who report higher levels of job stress also report significantly more back pain. In fact, the employees ($N = 24$) who report that they "always"

experience back pain also suffer from critically high levels of job stress.

The results of these validity studies indicate that companies using the HFI to assess corporate stress can be assured that higher HFI scores indicate a higher risk for loss due to accidents, injuries, illnesses, medical claims, poor productivity, turnover, and acts of negligence. Stress management training, at both the level of the individual employee and the organization, should lead to lower rates of stress-related accidents and losses.

Case Study. This case study describes how the HFI was used to control losses in the hospital industry. Approximately 1,500 employees from a southeastern hospital anonymously completed the HFI on company time. These employees represented over forty hospital departments. Analyses revealed that three clinical medicine departments (surgical nursing, anesthesia, and pharmacy) exhibited critically high levels of stress on the HFI Job Stress, Job Dissatisfaction, and Organizational Stress scales. Analysis of these departments' insurance loss statistics revealed that a number of malpractice claims ranging from $50,000 to over $100,000 had recently been filed. Item analyses of the HFI stress scales helped to identify a number of organizational stressors (e.g., poor communications, ineffective management, understaffing) that the administration was willing to correct now that a connection between high departmental stress and risk for medical malpractice was established. Moreover, the hospital administrators admitted that they had "suspicions" about these high-risk departments, yet they did not know where to begin to remedy the situation. Administration was now receptive to a number of different worksite stress management programs.

Another finding showed that employees in the general services department at the hospital (housekeeping, laundry, maintenance) had extremely high personal stress scores, as measured by the HFI Stressful Life changes scale. This same department also had nearly $100,000 in workers' compensation losses for the year preceding the stress assessment. This finding prompted the hospital to implement an employee assistance program (EAP) that provides opportunities for professional counseling to chronically distressed employees and their families. This case study documents how the HFI can be used to control losses. A summary of some of the other ways in which stress surveys like the HFI have been used in industry is provided below:

1. Focus efforts. Employee groups at greatest risk to have stress-related accidents, injuries, or illnesses

are identified. Some possible solutions to their situation are provided. Companies can then direct their training and development dollars to where the need is greatest.

2. Pinpoint strengths and weaknesses. Companies get a clear picture of how well the employees and managers are coping with stress compared to a national norm group. Companies can determine whether certain jobs or departments experience more or less stress than others. They can see if important human factors, such as job stress and employee wellness, cause their employees to be more susceptible to accidents, illness, poor productivity, and premature death.

3. Create awareness. Just by administering the HFI, employees feel management is interested in improving the quality of their work life. In turn, employees become more motivated to manage stress and seek wellness in their lives.

4. Employee involvement. The HFI opens an invaluable communication channel between all levels of employees and management. Such employee involvement leads to improved morale, especially when employees see that their input helped to facilitate the use of worksite stress management training programs.

5. Evaluate progress. Results presented in one year's HFI profile can be compared with the results of future employee profiles to develop a clear measurement of progress. Study after study indicates that a reduction in employee and corporate stress, followed by an increase in both job satisfaction and employee wellness, should lead to a decrease in medical claims and accidents, illness, turnover and absenteeism, theft, sabotage, and poor productivity. Such decreases should be reflected in improved employee morale, better organizational efficiency, and higher corporate gains.

6. Prevention. The HFI can be used to identify potential stress-related loss areas before they cause any significant level of loss.

Work Environment Scale (WES)

Dr. Rudolf Moos developed the Work Environment Scale to assess the quality of work life and stress levels in many types of work units. The WES is described in depth elsewhere (e.g., Moos, 1981). However, some key features of this organizational climate survey are described below.

The standard WES consists of ninety items that make up ten subscales. Normative data have been collected for over 1,400 employees from general work groups and over 1,600 employees from a variety of health care work groups. Test-retest reliability coefficients (one-month interval) are all in an acceptable range, varying from a low of .69 to a high of .83, depending on the subscale.

WES Subscales and Dimensions Descriptions. The ten WES subscales assess three underlying dimensions of organizational functioning: the Relationships dimension, the Personal Growth dimension, and the System Maintenance and System Change dimensions. The subscales that comprise each dimension follow:

1. Involvement: The extent to which employees are concerned about and committed to their jobs. (Relationship)

2. Peer cohesion: The extent to which employees are friendly and supportive of one another. (Relationship)

3. Supervisor: The extent to which management is supportive of employees and encourages employees to be supportive of one another. (Relationship)

4. Autonomy: The extent to which employees are encouraged to be self-sufficient and to make their own decisions. (Personal Growth)

5. Task Orientation: The degree of emphasis on good planning, efficiency, and getting the job done. (Personal Growth)

6. Work pressure: The degree to which the press of work and time urgency dominate the job milieu. (Personal Growth)

7. Clarity: The extent to which employees know what to expect in their daily routine and how explicit rules and policies are communicated. (System Maintenance and System Change)

8. Control: The extent to which management uses rules and pressures to keep employees under control. (System Maintenance and System Change)

9. Innovation: The degree of emphasis on variety, change, and new approaches. (System Maintenance and System Change)

10. Physical Comfort: The extent to which the physical surroundings contribute to a pleasant work environment. (System Maintenance and System Change)

The Involvement subscale is also an excellent measure of employee stress. This subscale determines if employees are concerned about and committed to their jobs (low stress) or if workers are apathetic about and uncommitted to their jobs (high stress). (Examples of items on this subscale include "There's not much group spirit," "A lot of people seem to be just putting in time," "It's hard to get people to do any extra work" and "Few people ever volunteer.")

The previous list reveals that the WES subscales can be used to assess organizational stress levels and major organizational stressors. For example, the Work Pressure subscale assesses the experience of workplace stress and tension. Examples of questions on this subscale include "There is constant pressure to keep working," "People cannot afford to relax" "It is very hard to keep up with your work load" and "There always seems to be an urgency about everything."

The WES also can be used to assess organizational stressors and stress buffers. For example, management can be considered a stress buffer if favorable scores are obtained on the Supervisor Support subscale and as a stressor if unfavorable scores are obtained on this subscale. Similar interpretations can be made with the Peer Cohesion, Task Oreintation, Clarity, Control, and Physical Comfort subscales.

Validity. Moos (1981) reviews a number of validity studies conducted on the WES. Holahan and Moos (1981a, 1981b) found that a number of WES subscales were related to complaints of depression and psychosomatic symptoms in a representative sample of workers. Brady, Kinnaird, and Friedrich (1980) found a relationship between perceived work environment, as measured by the WES, and job satisfaction among staff members of a mental health center. More specifically, employees who saw their work settings as more oriented toward involvement, cohesion, support, autonomy, and innovation showed greater satisfaction with their jobs.

Case Study. A number of practical applications for the WES are described by Moos (1981). A major use is to compare various subgroups of employees in order to assess their stress levels and determine some of the possible sources of their stress.

In this case study, the WES profile of thirty-five staff members in a residential care setting for older people (work group A) was compared to the profile of forty-two staff members in a community mental health center (work group B). Work group A was known to be relatively satisfied with their jobs, as evidenced by turnover rates that were much lower than that of other long-term care settings. Work group B was known to have a morale problem.

Analysis of WES profiles revealed that work group A differed from work group B on a number of different dimensions. Work group A, the low-stress

staff, felt committed to their jobs, were friendly and supportive of one another, and thought that the facility management was supportive and helpful. Group A staff felt there was a strong emphasis on good planning and efficiency and little work pressure. The group A staff reported that they knew what to expect in their daily routine and that rules and policies were clearly communicated. Finally, this staff perceived a better-than-average degree of autonomy and self-sufficiency in their jobs, and they reported that their facility was above average in physical attractiveness and convenience.

Conversely, work group B staff perceived a significantly different work environment as revealed by the WES. They reported low involvement, poor communications, and a lack of peer cohesion and supervisor support. This staff perceived an emphasis on autonomy and self-sufficiency, yet Work Pressure scores revealed excessive pressure to keep up with an ever-increasing work load. Furthermore, the staff perceived their workplace as being poorly organized and inefficient, and they were unclear about expectations, rules, and procedures. Comparing and contrasting the WES profiles in this case study indicates that improving the work environment of work group B may be an effective first step toward improving employee morale.

Maslach Burnout Inventory (MBI)

The Maslach Burnout Inventory (MBI) measures staff "burn-out," a syndrome of emotional exhaustion and cynicism that occurs frequently among chronically distressed "people workers" (Maslach, 1982). Hence, the MBI is appropriate for use with police officers, counselors, teachers, nurses, social workers, psychiatrists, psychologists, attorneys, physicians, and agency administrators. The MBI is thoroughly described elsewhere (e.g., Maslach and Jackson, 1981).

The MBI consists of three regular subscales and a fourth optional subscale:

1. The nine-item Emotional Exhaustion subscale (e.g., "I feel emotionally drained from my work".

2. The five-item Depersonalization subscale (e.g., "I feel I treat some recipients as if they were impersonal objects".

3. The eight-item Personal Accomplishment subscale (e.g., "I feel I'm positively influencing other people's lives through my work".

4. The three-item, optional, Personal Involvement

subscale (e.g., I feel I'm personally involved with my recipients' problems").

These four subscales are scored separately. They are highly reliable and have been validated against numerous criteria under a variety of validation strategies (Maslach & Jackson, 1981). For instance, Barad (1979) found that larger case loads were significantly correlated with more intense feeling of burn-out among social security employees.

Case Study. The MBI was administered to 130 police families in order to understand better the impact of job stress on family life (Maslach & Jackson, 1979). Both police officers and their spouses completed the MBI. Analyses showed that high burn-out scores were associated with more domestic strain. The ability to link job stress to marital problems provided the justification to use a variety of worksite stress management programs.

Indirect Measures

Some companies might not have access to organizational stress surveys for a number of reasons, one being financial. For these companies, a number of indirect measures of stress can be used to identify high-risk work groups.

Insurance claims data are often related to organizational stress (Jones & DuBois, 1985). Companies can analyze workers' compensation costs, medical costs, and the frequency and severity of accidents in order to determine if there are more losses than usual or more losses compared to similar types of companies. Other indirect measures include turnover and productivity data. Ideally, these data can be analyzed across time and by different work groups to identify an aberrant pattern of losses that can be linked back to job stress. Corrective actions could then be taken.

CONCLUSION

This chapter described a number of instruments used to assess organizational stress. These instruments are cost-efficient, brief, and can be used in nearly any type of work setting. They can be administered and scored by nonprofessional personnel, who, with training, can also deliver basic interpretive information to key decision makers within a company.

Other stress inventories like the Stress Map (Jaffe & Scott, 1985), the Stress Audit (Miller & Smith, 1983), and the Stress Management Questionnaire (Peterson & Lawrence, 1983) exist, but too little validity data have accumulated to warrant detailed descriptions in this chapter. By the same token, inventories like the Job Descriptive Index (Smith, Kendall & Hulin, 1969) have a proved track record, yet their focus is on employee satisfaction, not organizational stress. Still other instruments like those developed by the Institute for Social Research at the University of Michigan (Caplan, Cobb, French, Van Harrison &

Pinneau, 1975) and used in many studies of occupational stress do not lend themselves to use by those unfamiliar with psychometric theory. The Occupational Stress Inventory (Osipow & Spokane, 1987) is a very promising instrument for organizational stress assessment.

The purpose of this chapter was to describe a few key stress inventories that are valid and that have a history of successful business applications. Readers must be warned that accurately assessing employees' stress reactions and organizational stressors is the first step in controlling stress-related losses. The critical step is the implementation of comprehensive worksite stress management programs to control or actually prevent stress-related losses. Such programs should teach management how to correct organizational stressors and employees how to improve their stress coping skills.

REFERENCES

Barad, C. (1979). *Study of burnout among social security administration field contact workers* (Technical Report). Washington, DC: Social Security Administration.

Brady, C., Kinnaird, K., & Friedrich, W. (1980). *Job satis-*

faction and perception of social climate in a mental health facility. Houston: Texas Research Institute of Mental Sciences.

Brornot, E., & Moos, R. (1977). Environment resources

and the posttreatment functioning of alcoholic patients. *Journal of Health and Social Behavior, 18,* 326–335.

Burdick, C., & Jones, J.W. (1985). *The impact of stress surveys on the implementation of corporate stress management programs.* St. Paul, MN: St. Paul Insurance Companies.

Caplan, R.D., Cobbs, S., French, J.R.P., Jr, Van Harrison, R., & Pinneau, S.R. (1975). *Job demands and worker health* (DHHS [NIOSH] Publication No. 75–160). Washington, DC: U.S. Government Printing Office.

Holahan, C.J., & Moos, R. (1981a). *Development and validation of qualitative indices of social support.* Social Ecology Laboratory, Stanford University, and the Veterans Administration Medical Center, Palo, Alto, CA.

Holahan, C.J., & Moos, R. (1981b). *Social support and adjustment: Predictive benefits of social climate indices.* Social Ecology Laboratory, Stanford University, and the Veterans Administration Medical Center, Palo, Alto, CA.

Ivancevitch, J.M., Matteson, M.T. & Richards III, E.P. (1985). Who's liable for stress on the job? *Harvard Business Review* (March–April), 60–65.

Jaffe, D., & Scott, C.D. (1985). *The Stress Map: A comprehensive self-scoring stress assessment and action planning guide.* San Francisco: ESSI Systems.

Jones, J.W. (1983). *The Human Factors Inventory.* St. Paul, MN: St. Paul Insurance Companies.

Jones, J.W. (1985). Corporate stress management. *Risk Report, 7,* 1–8.

Jones, J.W., & DuBois, D. (1985). *The Human Factors Surveys: Background and interpretation guide.* St. Paul, MN: St. Paul Insurance Companies.

Jones, J.W., Barge, B.N., Steffy, B.D., Fay, L.M., Kunz, L.K., & Wuebker, L.J. (1988). Stress and medical mal-

practice: Organizational risk assessment and intervention. *Journal of Applied Psychology, 73*(4), 727–735.

Maslach, C. (1982). *Burnout: The cost of caring.* Englewood Cliffs, NJ: Prentice-Hall.

Maslach, C., & Jackson, S.E. (1979). Burned-out cops and their families. *Psychology Today, 12*(12), 59–62.

Maslach, C., and Jackson, S.E. (1981). *The Maslach Burnout Inventory.* Palo Alto, CA: Consulting Psychologist Press.

Maslach, C., and Pines, A. (1977). The burnout syndrome in the day care setting. *Child Care Quarterly, 6,* 100–113.

Miller, L.H., & Smith, A.D. (1983). *Stress Audit.* Boston: Biobehavioral Associates.

Moos, R.H. (1981). *Work Environment Scale: Manual.* Palo Alto, CA: Consulting Psychologist Press, Inc.

National Council on Compensation Insurance (1985). *Emotional stress in the workplace: New legal rights in the eighties.* New York: National Council on Compensation Insurance.

Osipow, S.H., & Spokane, A.R. (1987). *Occupational Stress Inventory: Research Version.* Odessa, FL: Psychological Assessment Resources, Inc.

Peterson, J.C., & Lawrence, H. (1983). *Stress Management Questionnaire.* Tucson, AZ: James J. Peterson, 1983.

Smith, P.C., Kendall, L.M., & Hulin, C.L. (1969). *The measurement of satisfaction in work and retirement.* Chicago: Rand-McNally.

Wetzel, J. (1976). *Dependence upon unsustaining environments as an antecedent variable of depression.* Ph.D. dissertation, Washington University. *Dissertation Abstracts International, 37,* 5361.

Wetzel, J. (1978). Depression and dependence upon unsustaining environments. *Clinical Social Work Journal, 6,* 75–89.

Rodney L. Lowman

This chapter addresses issues important in selecting, developing and managing an employee assistance program (EAP) for companies wishing to contract such services to mental health service providers outside the company. What the manager needs to consider in establishing such programs, how to assess competing proposals, and how to know if the program is working successfully are the major themes of this chapter. Despite an ever-increasing literature on EAPs, the promulgation of recommended practices has regrettably greatly surpassed the available research base (see, for example, Cairo, 1983; Weiss, 1987), and so much of this chapter's approach and recommendations must be based on clinical rather than research-grounded findings.

Today, employee assistance programs constitute

a buyer's market, one in which employers have a tremendous variety of choices, at least in major metropolitan areas. Employers therefore can and should be fussy about the services they expect to have included in an EAP and in deciding who will provide mental health care to their employees and family members. In addition, there are a number of potential pitfalls in establishing outside contracts with which managers need to be familiar. A company in California, for example, provided employee assistance program services at no direct charge to employers. This program was run by a hospital that used the EAP to funnel patients into its own inpatient programs. The so-called free program resulted in costly interventions that saved no money in the long run.

IDENTIFYING GOALS FOR THE EAP

The effectiveness of an EAP must be judged in relationship to the purposes for which it was established. Goals will vary depending on the identified needs of the employer. If, for example, the company wishes to contain rocketing mental health costs paid for by its insurance plan, then it may place much more emphasis on evaluating potential contractors' expertise in mental health cost containment. However, if the company is putting in a program just to provide a morale boost for employees, as an added benefit, or because other employers in its geographic area provide an EAP and the company wants to have competitive personnel practices, the decision about which firm to utilize may be influenced by other factors. The latter employer may focus less on cost-containment features and more on such issues as the number of companies a provider has worked with, satisfaction of other customers, or similar criteria. Not unexpectedly, many corporate officials will have limited knowledge about mental health services and therefore may not know the "right" questions to ask of a potential contractor or may make decisions on tangential factors.

An organization may have differing goals for an EAP. These aims may influence program development in several ways.

Early Case Identification

Because many mental health problems, especially substance abuse, can probably be treated more effectively and cheaper when intervention occurs earlier in the cycle (Trice & Roman, 1978; Walsh & Kelleher, 1987), EAPs can assist in identification of at-risk employees through such mechanisms as supervisory training and employee educational efforts. A company developing an EAP to assist in this early identification process needs to know what expertise they specifically have in increasing what is called "case finding" (early identification of employees with particular, defined problems).

In considering the effectiveness of early intervention strategies, the employer should have some familiarity with the number of workers who, in a "typical" work force, would be expected to have psychological problems needing assistance (Colligan, Smith & Harrell, 1977). Although Myers (1984b) maintains that 20 percent of workers are, on average, emotionally impaired and Jansen (1986) and Shain, Suurvali, and Boutilier (1986) also suggest widespread emotional dysfunction, the underlying literature to support these views is more equivocal. Unfortunately, we do not yet have good mental health epidemiological statistics (that is, data about the pervasiveness of mental health problems) specific to the workplace to know how many employees in a given work organization would be expected to be affected by particular mental health problems (Shain & Groeneveld, 1980). There are enormous difficulties in sampling at the organizational level, which will influence the representativeness of studies that are based on a small number of organizations.

The best data on employee population estimates of mental health problems available concern employee substance abuse. Many researchers and providers of EAP services have estimated that, on average, about 5 to 8 percent of any employed population will experience a problem with alcohol abuse significant enough to cause impairment (Cahalan, 1970; Parker, Kaelber, Harford & Brody, 1983; Walsh & Kelleher, 1987), though the reliability of such figures is currently disputed (Weiss, 1987). Franco's (1960) longitudinal study of alcoholic employees, for example, estimated that 2 to 3 percent of the work force was alcoholic. The extent of substance abuse among workers has also been asserted to be higher as the work force is more male than female, younger and more blue collar than white collar.

Drug abuse accounts for additional dysfunction (Axel, 1986; Flax, 1985; Shahandeh, 1985), though the extent of this problem among workers cannot reliably be estimated. Epidemiological statistics from general population samples indicate that about 2.4 percent of the population sampled was either drug abusing or drug dependent (National Institute of Mental Health, 1985), so presumably employed populations would have somewhat fewer drug-impaired individuals, on average, since the more severely impaired drug addicts would not be able to work. A self-report study by New York State indicates rather widespread usage of various illicit and prescription drugs (Chambers & Heckman, 1972), including abuse of such drugs on the job, but these findings have not been replicated and there are obvious problems with such methodologies. Nevertheless, many companies believe that drugs on the job constitute a significant problem and have begun such defensive measures as preemployment screening for drugs (*Drug Abuse*, 1987), despite the many problems associated with such an approach (e.g., Jackson, 1986).

Even in the rather widely explored area of employee alcohol abusers, it has been suggested that there may be less validity to the figures cited above than is commonly assumed (Weiss, 1987). Studies of the general population (including persons who work and those who do not), for example, report that persons who are alcohol abusers and/or alcohol dependent constitute from 5.8 to 7.2 percent of the population (Locke & Regier, 1985). Since the more severely incapacitated alcoholics would be expected not to be able to work, it is possible that the commonly cited statistics about the number of alcohol-impaired employees may be overestimates. Nevertheless, most organizations can expect that they will have a small but important group of employees whose work is affected by alcohol dysfunction. Moreover, these workers will often account for inordinately large costs in terms of absenteeism, low productivity, and health care costs (Foote, Erfurt, Strauch & Guzzando, 1978; Walsh & Kelleher, 1987).

It should also be noted that alcohol abuse is only one type of personal problem that may contribute to worker dysfunction. It has been estimated on the basis of careful research studies that about 19 percent of the general population has a psychological difficulty of sufficient magnitude to warrant a formal psychiatric diagnosis (National Institute of Mental Health, 1985). However, employed populations will vary from this figure, presumably downward, because persons with very serious mental impairment such as psychoses would often not be able to obtain or maintain employment. As noted above, we do not yet reliably know the number or percentage of workers in a given employment setting who would be expected to have psychological difficulties. Moreover, formal psychiatric diagnoses may not capture the employee with family or marital concerns or the worker preoccupied with an aging parent or dealing with normal variants of parent-teenager conflicts.

As an employer's EAP grows and develops and is successful in case identification and intervention, the number of employees untreated would presumably lessen (assuming the work force composition remains relatively constant). In evaluating an EAP contractor when a primary goal is case finding, the institution should inquire of potential providers about the methods they use to foster early referral and the specific results the firm has had in dealing with other, similar types of employers. Most important, the reported rate of success in case finding should be documented by data. The employer might ask to see (with company identity appropriately concealed) reports summarizing utilization by type of problem of companies with which the firm has previously done business. Employers should also inquire about the utilization experience the provider has had in working with other companies. On average, in a given year, how many employees (and, if covered, family members) made use of the service)? Again, the employer should strive to get specific, documented reports rather than vague generalities that the potential EAP contractor is not willing to put in writing.

Mental Health Cost Containment

Today there is substantial concern by self-insured employers about the costs they are paying for mental health insurance benefits (Bender, 1986; Lee & Schwartz, 1984; Lowman, 1987b; Sullivan, Flynn & Lewin, 1987; Psychiatric, Chemical Dependency Care, 1986; Tsai, Bernacki & Reedy, 1987). If the EAP is being installed to assist in lowering costs the company is paying for mental health care through its benefit plan, then the contractor's experience in mental health cost containment becomes an important area to evaluate. Although many EAPs give lip-service to cost containment and provide estimates (often unsubstantiated) of cost savings expected to be made by installing an EAP, most providers appear not to have data to support their claims. The employer should obtain specific information about the methodologies the EAP uses that are directed to cost containment and the successes it has had with other organizations in so doing.

Perhaps the major ways by which mental health benefit costs will be curtailed through the EAP occur when employees or family members get into treatment earlier than they otherwise would or when the EAP lessens the cost of help seeking by providing the care through the EAP or by referring the case to a cost-effective mental health care provider. When cost reduction is a goal of the employer, therefore, inquiry should be directed to the experience the EAP has had in cost control, including the specific methodologies it employs for this purpose. Of special importance to lowering referral costs is the ability to contain the costs of inpatient care (Lowman, 1987b).

Boosting Workplace Effectiveness

EAPs are typically presented by their proponents as significantly improving workplace productivity. There is evidence suggesting that EAPs can be effec-

tive in increasing the effectiveness of individual workers' productivity, but the specific relationship between productivity and mental disturbance is not well established (Foote, Erfurt, Strauch & Guzzando, 1978; Lowman, 1987a; Weiss, 1987). The company should be aware that the number of employees in direct need of EAP services will almost inevitably constitute a distinct minority of the work force, there may be little data available to address whether the EAP is indeed boosting workplace effectiveness among affected workers, and productivity increments are almost always multidetermined and it will therefore be very difficult to know how much credit for improvement should be assigned to the EAP.

The fact that only a few employees may benefit directly from the EAP service should not be a deterrent to developing such a program, particularly if the "right" employees (the most troubled and troublesome) are reached. It is also likely that problems with absenteeism and inefficiency are also caused by a few employees but that improvement in the effectiveness of these individuals will make a substantial difference in the organization as a whole.

If the primary goal of the EAP is to boost workplace efficiency, the EAP service provider should be able to demonstrate special expertise in case finding, supervisor training, and ability to handle complicated cases in which the employee's job may be contingent on improvement in the personal problems negatively affecting work performance. Most EAP service providers claim to have expertise in such areas, but it may be difficult to evaluate relative degrees of competence.

A Morale Booster

Some companies put in an EAP simply because other firms have one and they feel they must do so also in order to be competitive with their employee benefits package. Even if this is the primary motivation and there is no particular investment in the program, it is still important to attempt to define some relevant goals so that the company will know if services of appropriate quality are being provided. For example, the employer should still determine whether the EAP is intended to be a screening-and-referral service or also a provider of treatment. The former may require somewhat less attention to the clinical expertise of the providers, though the overall costs are likely to be higher.

WHAT TO LOOK FOR IN EVALUATING EAP PROGRAMS AND PROPOSALS

Not inappropriately, many managers have very little expertise in evaluating mental health programs and providers since such services are far removed from their day-to-day concerns and from their background and training. Accordingly, they may make contracting decisions on inappropriate bases such as who the dominant provider is within a particular geographic region or the satisfaction their colleagues at other companies express with the provider they have been using. Unfortunately, such information may be severely limiting, and a lower-quality program may result. There are some specific factors the manager should consider in evaluating alternative programs.

Quality of Staff

Managers should ask to see a listing of the names and credentials of all providers employed by or otherwise affiliated with the EAP program and to identify specifically those who will be seeing their own employees. The manager should review the list of mental health service providers to help determine the depth and breadth of service providers. Types of mental health professionals include:

Psychiatrist: M.D. plus internship plus residency in psychiatry. Especially appropriate for inpatient admissions and medications. Rarely included in EAP programs due to high cost. May be board certified in area of specialty.

Psychologist: Ph.D. in clinical or counseling psychology plus internship plus supervised experience. Must be licensed or certified to practice psychology. Sometimes are included in EAP programs but less frequently than social workers due to higher costs.

Social worker: Bachelor's degree plus two-year master's training program. Postmaster's supervised experience requirement. May or may not be licensed or certified depending on state of practice. May or may not be eligible to receive third party payments from insurance companies.

Psychiatric nurse: Usually a bachelor's degree in nursing and a master's degree in psychiatric nursing. Often have extensive experience in inpatient mental health settings. May be employed for utilization review as well as for providing counseling and/or assessment.

Certified alcoholism counselor: Often no specific degree or educational requirement. Must complete courses and supervised experience in substance abuse. In some states, a bachelor's degree may not even be required. If alcoholism certification is possessed in addition to a standard mental health degree and license or certification, it probably indicates specialty work in substance abuse. However, if this is the sole credential owned by a provider, the individual has training only in substance abuse and should generally not be utilized for nonsubstance abuse types of cases.

Other types of counselors may also be regulated in certain states. Qualifications may be highly variable, and the evaluator needs to check licensing or certification laws for such professionals in the states in which the practice will take place.

Managers evaluating the EAP staff presented should be wary of programs that rely on only one type of provider, particularly those with the least amount of training. Programs that have only substance abuse counselors (possibly recovering alcoholics) as their only staff should be especially carefully evaluated. The manager needs to be very clear on exactly which professionals will be available to see employees and/or family members. For example, a psychiatrist or psychologist may be listed as if on the staff of an EAP service provider yet be available only for consultation and may never actually see company employees or their family members. In general, the program that has ready access to a variety of types of mental health professionals and has specialized in occupational mental health is to be preferred. Note that there is a risk that the company may be held responsible and sued if the clinical services provided by the EAP are inadequate or inappropriate.

Experience in Doing EAP Work

The vendor should have experience with a wide variety of mental health problems and in doing employee assistance work. In general, more experience is better, especially if it is also combined with breadth of experience. However, experience is no substitute for adequacy of training and credentials. EAP providers should not be evaluated solely on the basis of the number of employees they already service. For one thing, the firm with the largest number of contracts may be spread too thin or may have gotten its business by low bidding at the possible sacrifice of quality. While serving a large number of clients can be a very valuable asset, it is also possible that the firm with the most experience in a particular geographic area may simply have gotten there first, whereas a newer provider may have the incentive to provider higher-quality, more extensive service.

Expertise in Cost Containment and Case Management

An EAP can save an employer a great deal of money, or it can be a net loss to the organization depending on the vendor's experience in cost containment and case management. By early intervention, short-term rather than inappropriately long-term treatment, and overseeing referrals made outside the EAP to ensure that treatment is not needlessly long or protracted, an EAP can assist in the process of cost containment. However, if an EAP has no experience or mandate for overseeing the referrals it makes outside the EAP, it may make too many referrals to overly costly mental health care providers or may refer too often to in-patient care when outpatient treatment would be equally effective.

Policies on Referring Outside the EAP

One way of evaluating an EAP's potential for mental health cost containment is to examine its policies on making referrals outside the EAP. If, for example, an EAP charges a very low rate per individual covered but then allows patients to continue in long-term therapy with its own providers at full-fee rates, it may cost rather than save money. Or, if the provider lacks expertise in evaluating the clinical appropriateness and effectiveness of outside referral sources, patients referred out of the EAP may get to the wrong provider for their type of problem or to one that uses excessively long or expensive therapy. The EAP vendor can be asked to provide written documentation of its referral policies, its experience in case management, and its specific expertise in mental health cost containment, especially of inpatient care. If the EAP is weak in this area or has built-in conflicts of interest, it may be an inappropriate choice, even if it is the low bidder.

To assist in evaluating this issue, potential EAP contractors can be asked to provide the employer with specific information on the referral resources it

has utilized in dealing with other clients over a given period of time. The employer should find out how many of the patients received all the help needed through the EAP and how many were referred outside the EAP. For those referred out, the vendor can be asked to provide a list of all referral sources utilized within a given period of time, say two years. Excessive reliance on a small number of referral sources chosen on the basis of friendships or other relationships with the EAP staff can be very problematic. In certain firms, for example, it is customary for mental health professionals to work for an EAP for a while and then leave the firm to start a practice, to which the EAP then makes referrals. In evaluating outside referral sources, concern should be raised when there are a large number of outside referrals or only a small number of different referral sources have been utilized in a geographic area that has many providers of mental health services.

The manager should also specifically ask whether the EAP allows self-referrals. For example, if an EAP contract provides for three sessions of treatment, is the employee or family member allowed to continue in treatment with the EAP provider at his or her own expense or using insurance coverage? While it can be argued that continuation in treatment with the same provider minimizes problems in making a transition to a new therapist, the potential for conflicts of interest is so great that a policy of forbidding such self-referrals is often to be recommended. This also helps prevent the EAP from becoming a funnel by which potential clients are obtained by the mental health service providers for longer-term treatment.

EAPs that charge on the basis of number of individuals using the service rather than on a prepaid basis should be carefully evaluated as to their self-referral policies. One such firm charged a relatively low rate per-session fee for seeing EAP referrals but then kept them in treatment for extended periods of time at the expense of the company's insurance policy. In so doing, inappropriately long dependencies were developed. Even though users of the service were very favorably inclined to it, they were unable to see that they had come to rely on its counselors excessively, with treatment often extending for inappropriately long periods of time.

Finally, the effectiveness of the EAP in avoiding excessive usage of inpatient care should be evaluated. Because inpatient care typically accounts for the vast majority of all mental health care costs in this country (Lowman, 1987b), EAPs can significantly affect the costs the employer is paying for mental health care by its success in avoiding inpatient care in favor of equally effective outpatient alternatives whenever clinically appropriate. Special attention on this issue should be directed to EAPs that are offered by in-patient facilities and permit self-referral.

Program Evaluation

In the long run, the effectiveness of an EAP needs to be evaluated on several criteria. How many people are making use of the service? How much is it costing when these employees are referred out? What is the short-term and long-term success of the EAP in assisting employees with their problems? The EAP vendor should be willing to provide written explanations of the procedures, if any, it uses to evaluate its own effectiveness. Routine follow-up of cases is desired and using a procedure that will get accurate and reliable information. Employers can ask to see the forms used by the EAP vendor to evaluate its programs and to see a sample feedback report evaluating a similar program offered by the EAP to another client (again, all identifying information should be concealed).

How Quickly Will the Company's Referrals Be Seen?

EAPs are sometimes undertaken by clinical practices to fill in unscheduled hours in their schedules. In such circumstances, there may be little incentive to see EAP clients quickly. Ideally, appointments should be made for within 24 to 48 hours after the appointment is requested. In any event, it should be clearly specified to the provider the length of time that there will be, on average, between calling in and receiving an appointment.

Fees

Most typically, EAPs are priced on a capitation basis; that is, a flat rate is charged per employee per year, in exchange for which the EAP agrees to provide services limited only by the terms of the agreement. Some EAP vendors charge on a per-usage basis.

The appropriate evaluation of fees charged for EAP services can be difficult and elusive. The components of an external EAP may vary considerably from one EAP to another, so it is important to make sure that similar services are being provided by EAPs that differ in price. Employers should be extremely cautious in comparing programs solely on the basis of price. While the cost can be important, the difference in a capitation rate of $20 per employee and $10 per employee can be trivial in the company's overall bud-

get. Yet the $20 program may include higher-quality providers or longer length of treatment, for example. Or the low bid may consist of a single provider, with no mental health credentials, such as a recovering alcoholic who is not also a mental health professional.

In comparing costs, the employer also needs to determine how much the EAP will be able to save in the referrals it makes to outside providers. Use of efficient providers and excellence in case management can more than make up for slightly higher capitation rates. On the other hand, if quality of services being offered is fairly similar and there are essentially minimal differences between providers, cost can then be an important differentiating factor. Most important, the EAP vendor should not raise any potential liability issues for the employer, such as by having inadequately trained mental health professionals who may raise later issues of tort liability.

Provisions of the EAP Contract

The formal agreement should clearly specify the services to be offered by the EAP. The following list covers most of the possible services that would be expected to be included in well-developed EAP programs. Not all vendors will include each of these items, however, and the price for the program would be expected to be higher as more of the services listed here are included:

Assistance in preparation of the company's policy statement on use of the EAP.

Introduction of the program to employees.

Training of supervisors.

Regularly scheduled (often, quarterly) on-site "brown bag" talks.

Assessment and up to a defined number of sessions of counseling.

Types of counseling to be provided (e.g., personal, financial, legal, aftercare).

Case management of referrals made out of the EAP.

Supervisor consultation on specific cases or organizational issues.

Coverage of family members included (verses employees only).

Program evaluation.

Articles for the in-house company newspaper.

Brochures (often printed by the company).

Twenty-four-hour emergency telephone access.

Reports (typically quarterly) on usage of the service.

In addition, the company should determine whether the contract includes a "hold-harmless" clause defining the mental health service provider as an independent contractor and ensuring that all claims for malpractice or damage will be directed against the service provider rather than the employer. (This does not totally immunize the company from legal action if malpractice is encountered but provides at least some protection.) As a minimal precaution, the contract should also require that the EAP vendor carry malpractice insurance at policy limits acceptable to the company. Typical minimum coverage is $1 million per occurrence.

The contract should specify the number of sessions of counseling to be included in the program and the confidentiality protections governing the mental health services provided. The contract should also indicate whether the EAP service provider is permitted to make referrals to itself. If this is prohibited, it should be formally stated in the contract. Also, the responsibility, if any, of the EAP for case management when a referral outside the EAP must be made should be specified.

Space does not permit elaboration of all issues relevant to installing, overseeing, and managing an effective external EAP program. Good practical guides are available in the literature (Dickman, Emener & Hutchinson, 1985; Egdahl & Walsh, 1980; Lewis & Lewis, 1986; Myers, 1984a; Masi, 1984; Shain, 1980). More technical works are also valuable (e.g., Schramm, Mandell & Archer, 1978; Shain & Groeneveld, 1980; Shain, Suurvali & Boutilier, 1986).

EVALUATING ONGOING EAP PROGRAMS

Even if a program is mature, it is important that systematic evaluation regularly be undertaken to ensure that the program is working effectively. The criteria for evaluation will depend on the specific goals of the program. At least every two to three years, the firm should consider a major evaluation of the program's effectiveness, linking the evaluation questions to the major purposes of having established the program. Below are listed some typical questions that can be asked in evaluating a mature external EAP program. Evaluations of EAPs can vary from a simple listing of the number of employees using the service to very sophisticated productivity analyses (Cairo, 1983; Dickman, Emener & Hutchinson, 1985; Foote, Erfurt, Strauch & Guzzardo, 1978; Myers, 1984b; Shain & Groeneveld, 1980; Schramm, 1977).

Are the users of the service satisfied with the care they receive? The EAP service provider should have a written procedure for evaluating the clinical effectiveness of the services it provides. At least a sample of those using the service (and, in a smaller covered population, all persons) should be sent rigorously designed surveys evaluating their experience with the service. This data should be aggregated and presented to company officials on a semiannual or annual basis at least. Alternatively, or in addition, the company may want to conduct its own anonymous evaluations periodically. Questions about the EAP may be added to existing surveys, or a special form can be developed to be sent to all or a sizable sample of the work force asking about awareness of the EAP, the extent to which it has been utilized, and, for those who have done so, their evaluation of its quality and effectiveness. Such surveys must, of course, be anonymous and any demographic data that might reveal individuals or small groups of employees (e.g., black female managers) kept to a minimum. Of course, not all individuals using the service will have been helped. However, a sizable majority of those making use of the EAP should report a favorable experience, and the majority should be aware that the service exists. If dependents are also eligible to utilize the service, it is desirable to sample their feedback as well.

How many supervisory referrals have been made? Especially in the area of substance abuse, the supervisor is a critical link in early problem identification and referral. Supervisors should be aware of the service, know how to make referrals to it, and at least some of them should be doing so. If they are not making such referrals, management needs to consider initiating refresher training and to make sure that a norm has not developed that a referral to the EAP means that the supervisor somehow is not managing his or her employees suitably.

Is the company's share of mental health insurance costs decreasing over time? If cost containment is a goal, then over the long run the company should be paying, per capita, less for its mental health costs covered by the company's insurance costs. Over the short term, mental health costs may actually rise because more people are, appropriately, getting the help that they need. Over time, however, the EAP should be effective in reducing the costs by intervening earlier in the process and, if it is within the EAP's area of competence, by its cost-containment referral strategies. In addressing this issue, the company should examine annual aggregated mental health claims experience, adjusted for current number of insured covered and calculated in dollar figures adjusted for inflation.

Where it is possible and funds have been allocated, it is desirable also to know the extent to which individuals making use of the service make use of mental health insurance benefits. The EAP should, over the long run, reduce the health insurance costs. If this can be examined without violating the confidentiality of persons using the service, it can provide an important component of the evaluation process.

Is the EAP referring only to appropriate, high-quality providers? Because EAP service providers control a large number of mental health referrals, the question of to whom they refer, especially in a program that is primarily an assessment and referral service, becomes very important. The EAP contractor can be asked to provide (typically annually) a list of all referral sources utilized. The better EAPs will in each case (or, in a very large company, on a sampling basis) also evaluate the effectiveness of the referral and have these data ready for audit. Those EAPs that make consistent use of a small number of referral sources without supporting data to demonstrate the effectiveness of such referrals must be carefully scrutinized.

SUMMARY

The externally contracted EAP has come considerable distance from the days of alcohol detection and referral services. While the potential for work force productivity improvements is very high, the firm contracting out EAP services today faces a tremendous assortment of would-be contractors, some of excellent quality and others highly inadequate. The purchaser of EAP services is well advised to identify the goals of the program before considering alternative providers. Assessment of competing proposals should be done on the basis of these goals, which should also serve as the basis for evaluating the program's effectiveness once it is in place. EAPs can be powerful vehicles not just for improving individual worker productivity but also for lowering the cost of mental health benefits, an increasing area of concern for many employers.

REFERENCES

Axel, H. (Ed.) (1986). *Corporate strategies for controlling substance abuse.* New York: Conference Board.

Bender, P. (1986). Controlling costs of outpatient mental health care. *Business and Health, 3,* 36–38.

Cahalan, D. (1970). *Problem drinkers: A national survey.* San Francisco: Jossey-Bass.

Cairo, P.C. (1983). Counseling in industry: A selected review of the literature. *Personnel Psychology, 36,* 1–18.

Chambers, C.D., & Heckman, R.D. (1972). *Employee drug abuse: A manager's guide for practice.* Boston: Cahners Books.

Colligan, M.J., Smith, M.J., & Harrell, J.J., Jr. (1977). Occupational incidence rates of mental health disorders. *Journal of Human Stress, 32,* 34–39.

Dickman, J.F., Emener, W.G. Jr., & Hutchinson, W.S., Jr. (1985). *Counseling the troubled person in industry: A guide to the organization, implementation, and evaluation of employee assistance programs.* Springfield, IL: Charles C. Thomas.

Drug abuse. The workplace issues (1987). New York: American Management Association, Publications Division.

Egdahl, R. H., & Walsh, D.C. (1980). *Mental wellness programs for employees.* New York: Springer-Verlag.

Flax, S. (1985). The executive addict. *Fortune* (June 24), 24–32.

Foote, A., Erfurt, J.C., Strauch, P.A., & G.A. Guzzando (1978). *Cost effectiveness of occupational employee assistance programs: Test of an evaluation method.* Ann Arbor: Institute for Labor and Industrial Relations, University of Michigan and Wayne State University.

Franco, S.C. (1960). A company program for problem drinking. *Journal of Occupational Medicine, 2,* 157–162.

Jackson, G.W. (Ed.). (1986). Substance abuse. *Seminars in Occupational Medicine, 1* (4).

Jansen, M.A. (1986). Emotional disorders and the labour force. Prevalence, costs, prevention and rehabiliation. *International Labour Review, 125* (5), 605–615.

Lee, F.C., & Schwartz, G. (1984). Paying for mental health

care in the private sector. *Business and Health, 1* (10), 12–16.

Lewis, J.A., & Lewis, M.D. (1986). *Counseling programs for employees in the workplace.* Monterrey, CA: Brooks Cole.

Locke, B.Z., & Regier, D.A. (1985). Prevalence of selected mental disorders. In C.A. Taube & S.A. Barrett (Eds.), *Mental health, United States, 1985.* Rockville, MD: U.S. Department of Health and Human Services.

Lowman, R.L. (1987a). *Ethical issues in psychological screening of nuclear power personnel.* Paper presented at the annual meeting of the American Nuclear Society, Dallas.

Lowman, R.L. (1987b). *Economic incentives in the delivery of alternative mental health services.* Paper presented at the annual meeting of the American Psychological Association, New York.

Masi, D.A. (1984). *Employee counseling services.* New York: American Management Association.

Myers, D.W. (1984a). *Establishing and building EAP's.* Westport, CT: Quorum.

Myers, D.W. (1984b). Measuring cost effectiveness of EAP's. *Risk Management, 31,* 56–61.

National Institute of Mental Health. (1985). *Mental Health, United States, 1985* (DHHS Pub. No. [ADM] 85-1378). C.A. Taube & S.A. Barrett (Eds.). Washington, DC: Superintendent of Documents, U.S. Government Printing Office.

Parker, D.A., Kaelber, C., Harford, T.C., & Brody, J.A. (1983). Alcohol problems among employed men and women in metropolitan Detroit. *Journal of Studies on Alcohol, 44,* 1026–1039.

Psychiatric, chemical dependency care big-ticket items for Los Angeles firms. (1986). *Benefits Today, 3,* 271.

Schramm, C. (1977). Measuring the return on program costs: Evaluation of a multi-employer alcoholism treatment program. *American Journal of Public Health, 67* (1), 50–53.

Schramm, C.J., & DeFillippi, R.J. (1975). Characteristics of successful alcoholism treatment programs for American workers. *British Journal of Addictions, 70,* 271–275.

Schramm, C.J., Mandell, M.W., & Archer, J. (1978). *Workers who drink.* Lexington, MA: Lexington Books.

Shain, M. (1980). *Employee assistance programs: Philosophy, theory and practice.* Lexington, MA: Lexington Books.

Shain, M., & Groeneveld, J. (1980). *Employee assistance programs.* Lexington, MA: Lexington Books.

Shain, M., Suurvalie, H., & Boutilier, M. (1986). *Healthier workers: Health promotion and employee assistance programs.* Lexington, MA: Lexington Books.

Shanadeh, B. (1985). Drug and alcohol abuse in the work place: Consequences and countermeasures. *International Labour Review, 124,* 207–234.

Sullivan, S., Flynn, T.J., & Lewin, M.E. (1987). The quest to manage mental health costs. *Business and Health, 4,* 24–28.

Trice, H.M., & Roman, P.M. (1978). *Spirits and demons at work: Alcohol and other drugs on the job* (2d ed.). Ithaca, NY: New York State School of Industrial and Labor Relations.

Tsai, S.P., Bernacki, E.J., & Reedy, S.M. (1987). Mental health care utilization and costs in a corporate setting. *Journal of Occupational Medicine, 29* (10), 812–816.

Walsh, D.C., & Kelleher, S.E. (1987). *Preventing alcohol and drug abuse through programs at the workplace.* Washington, DC: Washington Business Group on Health.

Weiss, R.M. (1987). Writing under the influence: Science versus fiction in the analysis of corporate alcoholism programs. *Personnel Psychology, 40,* 341–356.

76 DEVELOPING WORKPLACE SUBSTANCE ABUSE PROGRAMS: A STRATEGIC PLANNING APPROACH

Thomas E. Backer

Substance abuse among workers represents a significant challenge to public and private employers in the United States. According to the National Institute on Drug Abuse, 10 to 23 percent of all workers in the nation use drugs on the job, and perhaps 5 percent have a serious addiction problem. Add the number of workers who are alcoholic or have a significant work-related drinking problem, and the numbers become even larger.

The U.S. Chamber of Commerce reported that it costs over $7,000 to replace someone who leaves an organization because of alcohol or drug abuse (Backer, 1987c). A single accident caused by a worker under the influence can cost lives and/or millions of dollars in damages.

Studies conducted by the Research Triangle Institute in North Carolina indicate that in 1983 the total cost of drug abuse to employers was over $60 billion. That estimate was probably on the low side if such intangible factors as drug abuse's effect on motivation and creativity are considered. Adding in the incidence and economic costs of alcohol abuse expands the problem enormously. And no dollar amount can be placed on the human misery substance abuse causes.

Attempts to solve the specific problems of drug abuse in the worksite have generated much activity recently. Conferences have been organized specifi-

cally to deal with this challenge, the Anti-Drug Abuse Act was passed by Congress in 1986, and anti–drug abuse campaigns have been conducted by President Reagan and first lady Nancy Reagan as well as by corporate leaders. Drug abuse problems have been especially highlighted in the executive ranks (Backer, 1985; Braham, 1986; Flax, 1985; Olson, 1986) and in certain industries (Chapman, 1986; DiBlase, 1986; DuPont, 1986b; Sudo, 1986; Wagner, 1986).

Employers have gained considerable awareness recently about the challenges of workplace alcohol and drug abuse. Now many resources are becoming available that can help employers determine the nature and extent of their response to these challenges (Philips, 1986; Axel, 1986; AMA Research Study, 1987).

Most of what follows will concentrate on the particular issue of drugs in the workplace, including a discussion of the special problems presented by worker abuse of drugs like heroin and cocaine. Another list of the special problems of alcohol abuse, such as social tolerance for alcohol, also could be drawn up, of course. (Moreover, multiple addiction, where both alcohol and one or more drugs are abused, is extremely common today.) But the basic approach—strategic planning—to solving these problems seems to have equal value whether drugs, alcohol, or both together are the issue.

THE CRISIS RESPONSE: DRUGS IN THE WORKPLACE, 1986–1987

Many public and private organizations reexamined and restructured their activities during 1986 and 1987, both to assist workers with drug abuse problems and to reduce the costs associated with such problems. Corporate policies have been initiated or rewritten; management training has been provided; consultants and outside employee assistance programs (EAP) contractors have been hired; in-house

EAP staff have been trained in specific aspects of drug abuse (Taravella, 1986). Drug testing has become a growth industry, with estimates of its current size ranging from $100 million to $300 million a year (Backer, 1987b).

Numerous conferences, educational seminars, and special events by business and industry organizations have been conducted on drug abuse and in particular on issues surrounding drug testing. Coverage in business periodicals and business-oriented television and radio shows has proliferated (e.g., "Battling the Enemy Within," 1986).

Even workplaces that do not have a new program to fight drug abuse have often assigned a human resources or medical department staff person to look into the problem. Other employers have started an employee committee or task force.

The resulting situation is reminiscent of the ancient Chinese language symbol for crisis: it contains elements of both danger and opportunity. The opportunity comes from the energy and motivation to consider new programs and practices, some of which can result in genuine improvements in how workplaces deal with drugs. The danger is that this same energy comes in an atmosphere or urgency to act immediately, sometimes almost a panic response. Some of these crisis-driven responses include:

- Bringing in a consultant for a problem-focused dialogue with management, usually just for a few hours, or a few days at most, with no follow-up.

- Providing a top or middle management seminar, again usually led by an outside consultant, again usually brief, and again with no follow-up.

- Issuing a memo or policy paper identifying the problem and promising to solve it promptly.

- Adopting a technologically oriented solution, such as a drug testing program, without any other intervention set in place.

Such responses tend to have certain features in common, however they are shaped in terms of technical content or specific goals. First, they are usually implemented quickly, with little advance planning or needs assessment. Second, they are usually implemented by top management with little input from other levels of the organization. Third, they are not usually viewed as a part of management's overall plans or objectives but rather as a deliberately isolated solution to a problem seen only in isolation. And fourth, these responses are often selected because they promise quick solutions at a minimal price, often just a few thousand dollars for a consultant or a training package.

The track record of these crisis-driven responses is dismal; many, if not most of them, have little lasting impact. Many even create negative side effects—encouraging management to think they have solved the problem when they have not and thus lower their problem-solving efforts; producing a backlash ("we tried to solve the problem, and look at what happened") when they fail to produce immediate results; producing further backlash among workers smart enough to see that many of these so-called solutions were never intended to be anything more than "Band-aids" for cosmetic and public relations purposes.

Drug testing programs, adopted quickly and in isolation of any other organizational changes, are especially like to generate negative side effects. Even the most vigorous proponents of testing argue that a testing program needs to be combined with workplace education, changes in attitudes and structures in the organization, and some sort of treatment and rehabilitation alternatives for employees who are discovered to have a problem (Walsh & Hawks, 1986). Without these larger-scale components, drug testing programs can have a deadening effect on employee morale and trust for top management and can lead to legal actions as well. Yet many companies have been rushing to implement testing for new hires or for current employees, at least in certain categories, turning drug testing into a growth industry. These programs are not likely to be effective.

ANOTHER LEVEL OF SOLUTION

Now that the first wave of intense interest in workplace drug abuse programs has subsided, we can look more dispassionately at the problem and how to address it. Some employers already have moved on to "the next crisis" and have little interest in anything further to do with workplace drug abuse programs. For many others, however, the positive side of the media attention and crisis orientation is that enduring awareness has been created of how drugs in the workplace destroy both people and profits. Employers having this awareness are then able to consider programs that move beyond the crisis and the quick solution to this perplexing, multifaceted problem.

These more successful programs are likely to start from a very different set of operating assumptions:

1. A workplace drug abuse program involves *significant organizational change* and must be handled like any other change to be implemented effectively.

2. A commitment of *leadership*—top management

support—must be made for a program to be successful.

3. A commitment of *personnel and financial resources* for the program must be made.

4. A commitment to the use of *strategic planning principles* must be made, including *worker participation* in designing and implementing the program and activities that attempt changes in the *organizational culture*—for instance, worker values about drugs, or values about intervening with employee personal problems.

This approach fits with much of what has emerged from fifty years of management sciences research. Effective strategy is essential for an outstanding organization. Strategy is the single most important differentiating factor between successful and unsuccessful businesses and between corporate leaders and followers. A well-developed strategic plan, coupled with management commitment and deployment of adequate resources to implement the plan, is the single most important ingredient for a successful workplace drug abuse effort.

Moreover, few programs are really starting from ground zero. There are an estimated 10,000 EAPs in U.S. work organizations and many other kinds of programs that are intended to help workers deal with problems such as drug abuse. In research being done by the Human Interaction Research Institute under funding support from the National Institute on Drug Abuse, it has already become clear that most effective workplace drug abuse programs involve retooling and expanding programs already set in place. They also involve careful coordination with other innovative activities in the workplace, such as health promotion programs, health care cost containment procedures, and management development and education.

In our research, we are already beginning to document the limited success of many of the quick-fix solutions employers rushed to adopt in 1986 and early 1987. The more successful programs manifest the four key qualities just mentioned. Two specific examples are given here that may help clarify how to undertake the large-scale organizational change needed for an effective workplace drug abuse program. First, let us look at some of the special challenges presented by drugs in the workplace and at the principles of strategic planning that were applied in the two examples about to be examined.

WORKPLACE DRUG ABUSE: THE SPECIAL CONTEXT

Part of the complexity employers must deal with in developing or improving a workplace drug abuse program is the special nature of drugs of abuse.

Use of drugs, except for prescribed medical purposes, is illegal. Employees using drugs are subject to arrest and imprisonment. Moreover, drug-using workers often buy their drugs in the workplace, introducing further illegal activity and the criminals who engage in drug sales. This can create problems of safety and security and can increase the likelihood of other criminal behavior in the workplace (e.g., stealing from an employer in order to buy drugs). In worst-case scenarios, the whole social structure of the workplace can be jeopardized (e.g., a medical director fighting drugs on the job site who gets death threats, workers who are assaulted and robbed by other drug-addicted employees who "need a fix").

The shield of medical necessity often obstructs identifying and assisting workers with drug abuse problems. Prescription drugs are widely abused, but workers may be able to hide behind the claim, "My doctor told me to take these pills."

The toxicity of some drugs (e.g., cocaine, especially in crack form, and many "designer drugs") is much greater than that of alcohol in the doses generally taken and can lead to much more rapid and severe physical and psychological consequences. Drug abuse specialists note that it often takes twenty years for severe physical side effects to emerge from abuse of alcohol, as compared with six to twelve months for crack cocaine. Deaths from alcohol overdoses, while not unheard of, are rare (though the death rate from long-term complications of alcoholism is, of course, very high).

Drugs such as cocaine often present a detection difficulty. Excessive use of alcohol on the job leads to drunken behavior, which is usually hard to conceal, but workers on drugs like cocaine often can maintain an appearance of normality even while using heavily. As with alcohol, detection is made much more difficult by the worker's active efforts to conceal and deny his or her problem and by the frequent complicity of coworkers in shielding the person with the problem. Drugs such as marijuana may exert subtle, but significant, effects on perceptual-motor performance. Workers high on cocaine may seem energized and creative, but when evaluated more carefully their ideas are often thin and judgments weak. By the time supervisors recognize these more subtle signs, great damage may already have been done.

The traditional orientation of EAPs to alcoholism is still a problem in some workplaces because many employee assistance efforts were started by recovering alcoholics and most of their services are oriented in this direction. Some EAP staff have yet to receive specific professional training in drug abuse, and this may limit their effectiveness. Similarly, some supervisors may not identify performance problems as due to drug abuse, where the signs and symptoms can be somewhat different from alcohol abuse.

STRATEGIC PLANNING STEPS

An effective workplace drug abuse program can be developed by public or private employers using as a general template the following ten planning steps (described in more detail in Backer, 1987c):

1. *Establish a drug abuse policy.* An organization without a written policy on worker drug abuse should formulate one as part of overall human resources policy. Policies need to be written with input from all levels of the organization and with consideration for the special problem of a particular worksite (e.g., concerns for worker and public safety arising from the nature of the work done there).

2. *Develop a written program design.* Usually the result of research by a special employee task force, the written program design will serve as a tool for implementing the program successfully.

3. *Supervisory training.* It is not the purpose of a workplace drug abuse program to train supervisors to function as undercover police or drug abuse counselors. What is required is to train supervisors to recognize employees with performance problems that may be related to drug abuse and to know how to get them connected with treatment (the term *smart supervisors* is currently used to designate those who have received such training).

4. *Identification and outreach.* Many programs have floundered due to a lack of visibility. Notices in pay envelopes and posters are classic methods of program identification, along with seminars and audiovisual materials. In some organizations, a drug testing program also may be of value in identifying those workers who may have a problem (for more on the complex development and operation of a testing program see DuPont, 1986a; Hawks & Chaing, 1986; O'Keefe, 1987; Walsh & Hawks, 1986).

5. *Security.* Drugs are illegal. Having them in the workplace means that workers are committing illegal acts. Drug trafficking is also illegal and yet is on the rise in the workplace. With this in mind, policies and procedures need to be implemented for working with external law enforcement agencies and for internal security arrangements as needed.

6. *Assessment and referral.* Once a person with a drug problem has been identified, the organization needs to be able to assess the extent of the problem and provide appropriate referral for treatment and rehabilitation. These are the most common functions of the traditional EAP.

7. *Counseling and treatment.* Providing outpatient or inpatient services to workers with drug abuse problems can range from sending the worker to a hospital or drug treatment facility, to offering services directly in the workplace. Careful selection of treatment programs and attention to cost containment are among the issues employers must deal with. The concern does not end with completion of a treatment program; 60 to 90 percent of those treated for drug abuse return to drugs after treatment. Successful programs must include maintenance measures such as referrals to self-help organizations or changes in the nature of the employee's working conditions (e.g., to reduce job stress or frequent contacts with others who may be using drugs).

8. *Follow-up.* Particularly because of the high rates of recidivism, drug abuse cases must be followed up by employers to learn what other services may be needed.

9. *Record keeping and evaluation.* Good record keeping is essential to meet potential legal challenges, which are becoming more common. Also, well-kept records permit evaluation of the entire program so it can be improved and its cost justified to management.

10. *Prevention and family education.* The potential personal impact of programs that focus on the family is very great. More and more employers are developing prevention-oriented programs that emphasize both worker and family education (DeBernardo, 1987). These programs are founded on the assertion that the best way to reduce drug abuse at work is to educate people so they will not begin using drugs. Family education is also part of many workplace programs, and it can sometimes have positive side benefits. For instance, one of the best ways companies have found of getting their employees into assistance programs and into treatment is to have a brown-bag lunch seminar called "Are Your Kids on Drugs?"

TWO CASE EXAMPLES

Capital Cities/ABC

The crisis for the company that owns ABC Television actually started three years ago when an employee died of a cocaine overdose on the job. The shock waves that went through the company could have been classic triggers for a crisis-driven response, yet instead the company's top management took a very different direction ("Cap Cities/ABC Customizes Drug Program for Employees," 1987).

First came the commitment of leadership and resources. President Dan Burke and chairman Tom Murphy put their personal imprint of support on the development of a program and funded it sufficiently to make it company-wide and comprehensive. Then they issued a directive that employees from all levels of the company should be involved in formulating a response. A group of sixteen workers, called the Employee Advisory Committee, was formed to study the problem. While appropriate consultants have been used along the way, Capital Cities/ABC has vested most of the decision-making authority in this committee, which now is a permanent body and continues to supervise the program that resulted.

The committee heard from medical experts and from other firms with similar problems that were putting programs in place. It developed a policy statement that was sent to all employees over the signatures of Burke and Murphy. The committee then developed an in-house EAP, deliberately targeted only to employees with substance abuse difficulties. It includes a toll-free hot line with a referral service, a multimedia educational campaign that has been implemented company-wide, a supervisor's handbook that explains the moral and legal responsibilities of management, and a revised employee benefits package that is designed both to contain health care costs and provide effective treatment. Outpatient treatment, which has been established as essential for long-term rehabilitation and reducing recidivism, has been greatly increased in coverage under this new plan. Moreover, the costs of the new benefits plan are almost offset by the savings from changing the old plan in terms of reduced costs for employee hospitalizations.

Three years since its inception, the Capital Cities/ABC program is regarded as a model within the entertainment industry. Its potent combination of employee involvement and company-wide education have resulted in significant change in the organizational culture, as well as an effective workplace drug abuse program that treated 300 persons in its first year of operation alone.

A Second Example

A major manufacturing company, with more than 3,000 employees in twelve domestic sites, approached me, requesting consultation on expanding its EAP to deal better with drug abuse at its worksites. Rather than pile a partial solution onto what was already a long-existing EAP, the direction taken in improving this program was a months-long review process, involving management at several levels. An employee task force to implement the program also was recommended, although this has not yet been enacted.

Along the way, some interesting phenomena emerged. First, the company's review of its existing EAP led to management's realization that the program itself needed to be changed; dissatisfaction with the current outside EAP contractor had become pronounced. This operating problem might not have come into focus had it not been for the review. A new EAP consulting firm subsequently was selected.

Second, although drug testing was seriously considered as a possibility for an expanded program, the company recognized that there would be many technical and morale problems involved in implementing the program. Consultation was recommended with several companies in the organization's geographic area that had prior experience with drug testing programs. A special concern for testing and for treatment services was the company's smaller worksites throughout the country, some of them in remote areas. Ultimately, the decision was made not to implement drug testing.

Next the company began to explore how its benefits package needed to be altered in order to support the drug abuse program. Outpatient coverage (using Capital Cities/ABC as a model) was explored, as were mental health services for family members in need of support while a loved one undergoes treatment for chemical dependency. Another criticism of the existing EAP was that it had provided relatively little in the way of supervisory training. The current concepts of developing "smart supervisors" skilled at detecting early warning signs of possible substance abuse and acting on them were emphasized as necessary objectives of an improved training program. Moreover, company management began to look at general supervisory training on topical areas such as disciplinary actions and performance review. These, they concluded, also needed to be expanded as part of substance abuse training.

Management of this company is now exploring how to formulate an overall program incorporating the above components. Because this is an American subsidiary of a foreign conglomerate, progress has been slow, but the reliance on careful study and planning increases the chance for a successful outcome. Some improvements, such as the new EAP contractor, have already been made.

DEVELOPING RESOURCES

Both public and private resources have become more widely available in the last several years to help employers design effective programs. At the federal level, the Anti-Drug Abuse Act of 1986 greatly increased resources in agencies such as the National Institute on Drug Abuse, which established the Office of Workplace Initiatives (OWI). In addition to providing assistance to the private sector, OWI is setting standards and offering technical assistance to all thirty-seven federal government agencies that must implement drug abuse programs under the executive order for a drug-free federal workplace. OWI also sponsors research on various aspects of drug testing and workplace drug abuse treatment, education, and prevention.

Recognizing the need for a resource book to help employers understand and act on strategic planning approaches to the drug abuse problem, NIDA also funded the preparation of *Strategic Planning for Workplace Drug Abuse Programs* (Backer, 1987c). This book contains more detailed coverage of the principles and examples presented here. NIDA also maintains an Employer Helpline, a toll-free number employers can call for materials or technical assistance in establishing a workplace drug abuse program.

The private sector has undertaken a number of initiatives, with major seminars and conference programs and a number of publications. The U.S. Chamber of Commerce (DeBernardo, 1987), the American Management Association (AMA Research Study, 1987), and the Conference Board (Axel, 1986) are just a few of the business associations that have taken a leadership role in helping private businesses learn about drug testing, EAPs, education and prevention programs, and smart supervisors.

In January 1987, the Human Interaction Research Institute initiated the National Study of Workplace Drug Abuse Programs, which is supported both by the National Institute on Drug Abuse and by private grants from major corporations. This is the first comprehensive research and policy development study to be conducted on drug abuse in public and private workplaces. A survey questionnaire has been sent to 8,000 EAP coordinators and consultants across the country, and subsequent phases of the research include intensive telephone interviews and site visits. The project also has established a computer bulletin board on drugs in the workplace with national accessibility and an abstract database on the growing literature in this field. The national study is only one part of what is needed for understanding the complexities of workplace substance abuse. There are many issues that have yet to be researched and methodological problems to be solved (Godwin, Lieberman & Leukefeld, 1985).

THE FUTURE

With such resources set in place, employers needing to implement an improved program to fight drugs in the workplace have much to help them. Making the commitment to strategic planning and to more comprehensive—and costly—solutions takes courage on the part of management, but it is clearly the way to go.

Strengthening a workplace drug abuse program often brings to the surface long-standing deficits in management training in such areas as performance review. I was shocked to discover that one major corporation did not even have an up-to-date performance review form but rather continued to use one that even the lowest-level supervisors could see was outdated. Management must be helped to recognize that such deficits significantly impede the success of any drug abuse program.

Also, since 25 percent of all AIDS cases in the United States are drug abusers, developing a drug abuse program often is a backdoor way for companies to begin considering an AIDS policy and program. Most employers are not even aware of the real statistics about intravenous (IV) drug abuse—for example, that many IV drug users are not unemployed, inner-city minorities but often are blue- or white-collar workers of all races, thus placing many workers at risk for AIDS if they also share needles (and NIDA estimates that 95 percent of all IV drug users do share needles at least on occasion) (Backer, 1987a).

Finally, whether with drug abuse, AIDS, or other human issues, employers can mount programs that recognize their larger social responsibilities. There is certainly enough economic self-interest alone to warrant a response, but the context is even larger. As Richard Lesher, president of the U.S. Chamber of Commerce, has said, "It is imperative that business people take the lead in the campaign against drug abuse in our society. . . . Business people wield significant power and influence in their communities. They are looked to for leadership in setting standards of personal behavior and particularly in public affairs" (Lesher, 1986). The larger goals of managed change in American work organizations reflect such assumptions: that effective organizational change helps society at the same time it helps workers and employers.

REFERENCES

AMA Research Study (1987). *Drug abuse: The workplace issues.* Saranac Lake, NY: American Management Association.

Axel, H. (Ed.) (1986). *Corporate strategies for controlling substance abuse.* New York: The Conference Board, Inc.

Backer, T.E. (1985). *Substance abuse and the entertainment industry: A leadership challenge.* Los Angeles: Human Interaction Research Institute.

Backer, T.E. (1987a). *AIDS in the workplace: How employers can respond.* Presentation to Executive Seminar on Crisis Management, University of Southern California, Los Angeles, September.

Backer, T.E. (1987b). *Drug testing in the workplace: Whose right is it anyway?* Paper presented at Conference on Substance Abuse in the Workplace, California State University, Northridge, California, February.

Backer, T.E. (1987c). *Strategic planning for workplace drug abuse programs.* Rockville, MD: National Institute on Drug Abuse.

Battling the enemy within (1986). *Time* (March 17), 52–61.

Braham, J. (1986). Cocaine creeps toward the top. *Industry Week,* 34–37.

Cap Cities/ABC customizes drug program for employees. (1987). *Drugs in the Workplace* (June), 1–3.

Chapman, B. (1986). Drug abuse: Enemy in the workplace. *Graphic Arts Monthly* (October), 130–131.

DeBernardo, M. (1987). *Drug abuse in the workplace: An employer's guide for prevention.* Washington, DC: U.S. Chamber of Commerce.

DiBlase, D. (1986). Companies crack down on substance abuse. *Business Insurance* (October 27), 38–39.

Dupont, R.L. (1986a). Should drug testing in the workplace be mandatory? (Point). *U.S. Journal* (February), 16.

DuPont, R.L. (1986b). *Substance abuse in the construction industry: The problem and its identification.* Paper presented at the National Conference on Substance Abuse in Construction, Minneapolis.

Flax, S. (1985). The executive addict. *Fortune, 62,* 24–31.

Godwin, D.F., Lieberman, M.L., & Leukefeld, C.G. (Eds.) (1985). *The business of doing worksite research.* Washington, DC: Alcohol, Drug Abuse and Mental Health Administration, U.S. Department of Health and Human Services.

Hawks, R.L., & Chaing, N. (1986). *Urine testing for drugs of abuse.* Rockville, MD: National Institute on Drug Abuse, 1986.

Lesher, R.L. (1986). Business must lead the war on drugs. *Coalition Report, 5* (8), 1.

O'Keefe, A.M. (1987). The case against drug testing. *Psychology Today, 21* (6), 34–38.

Olson, L. (1986). Corporate America's hidden cocaine crisis. *Working Woman* (March), 122–145.

Philips, J. (1986). Enough talk! What can employers do about drug abuse? *Wall Street Journal* (November 17).

Sudo, P.T. (1986). Drug abuse in the workplace: How do banks deal with it? *Daily Financial Services Newspaper, 151* (195), 1.

Taravella, S. (1986). EAPs cope with growing cocaine use. *Business Insurance* (September 29).

Wagner, D. (1986). The drug dependency dilemma. *California Business, 21,* 30–37.

Walsh, J.M., & Hawks, R.L. (1986). *Q&A: Employee drug screening: Detection of drug use by urinalysis.* Rockville, MD: National Institute on Drug Abuse.

ADDITIONAL RESOURCES

In addition to the References, following are some resources that may be of value to employers seeking to develop a substance abuse program (the emphasis is on programs specific to drug abuse):

- Association of Labor Management Administrators and Consultants on Alcoholism (ALMACA), 1800 North Kent Street, Suite 907, Arlington, VA 22209. The largest professional-trade association for those involved in the EAP field. Sponsors national and regional conferences and has a clearinghouse for information and problem-solving consultation.

- *Drugs in the Workplace,* Business Research Publications, 817 Broadway, New York, NY 10003. A monthly newsletter summarizing developments of interest to employers, including updates on prevention, detection, treatment, and recent court rulings.

- Drugs in the Workplace (DAWP) Computer Bulletin Board, (213) 825-3736. A collaborative effort of the National Study and the UCLA Drug Abuse Information and Monitoring Project, DAWP is accessible to anyone with an IBM-compatible microcomputer and a telephone modem. It contains up-to-date listings of references, sample employer policies, sample training programs, audiovisual training media, and other resources.

- National Study of Workplace Drug Abuse Programs, Human Interaction Research Institute, 1849 Sawtelle Boulevard, Suite 102, Los Angeles, CA 90025. Conducts research and policy studies on drugs in the workplace and has available a number of publications targeted to both employers and professionals.

- National Institute on Drug Abuse Helpline, (800) 843-4971. Open from 8 A.M. to 8 P.M. weekdays, the Helpline is designed to provide information to employers on treatment and prevention programs, drug testing, policy, and available resources for program development.

77 IMPLEMENTING, MAINTAINING, AND EVALUATING COMPANY-SPONSORED PHYSICAL FITNESS PROGRAMS

Loren E. Falkenberg, Deborah F. Crown, Joseph G. Rosse

In the last ten years there has been a dramatic increase in the importance placed on fitness and overall wellness. Cognizant of this societal shift, numerous organizations have implemented company-sponsored physical fitness programs (CSPFPs). In Canada approximately 1,000 companies are involved in physical fitness, and in the United States it is estimated that 50,000 business firms promote physical activity (Cox, 1984; Driver & Ratliff, 1982). The scope of these programs ranges from aerobic classes offered during lunch to million-dollar in-house wellness centers providing weight lifting, running tracks, tennis courts, and swimming pools. Unfortunately, there is relatively little empirical research on the value of employee exercise programs; thus large investments are being made on limited knowledge.

Three lines of reasoning underlie the implementation of these programs. The first is that an increasing number of employees recognize the need to exercise and value the ability to do so during the workday. Organizations' support of employee exercise centers thus reflects their concern for employees' nonwork as well as work needs. A more pragmatic consideration is that an employee exercise program may act as a

mechanism for recruiting and retaining employees. Exercise programs are particularly valuable to young, well-educated individuals (Dishman, Sallis & Orenstein, 1985; Stephens, Jacobs & White, 1985) and so may play an important role in attracting individuals in the more competitive job markets.

A second rationale is that employee exercise programs may reduce the impact of stress. It is generally accepted that high stress levels result in reduced work performance and higher turnover, absenteeism, and accident rates. More physically fit individuals are perceived to have improved health and are thus better able to cope with work-related stress (Driver & Ratliff, 1982).

The third line of reasoning suggests that increasing the fitness level of employees should improve productivity. It is assumed that this improvement is achieved through reduced absenteeism and turnover, as well as improved capacity for mental work due to improved concentration and effort.

Because of the dearth of research, many exercise programs are based on erroneous assumptions, leading to poorly designed programs and a lower probability of achieving desired outcomes. The purpose of this chapter is to describe the outcomes that an organization and an individual can anticipate from support of and participation in exercise programs. These outcomes then provide the base for developing the components of an effective employee exercise program.

This chapter is the synthesis of two manuscripts, one submitted by the first author and the other by the second and third authors. Order of authorship reflects the order of these original manuscripts.

EXERCISE AND THE INDIVIDUAL

Relationship between Exercise and Stress

Exercise may assist in reducing the physiological impact of stress in three ways. First, long-term aerobic exercise may decrease the level of physiological arousal that occurs under stressful conditions. The physiological response to stressful situations involves increased muscle tension, increased respiration rate, sympathetic stimulation of sweating, increased heart rate, dilation of blood vessels, and release of glucose by the liver. Physically fit individuals demonstrate less muscular activity, slower respiration, a lower resting heart rate, and less accumulation of the acid by-products of exercise under stressful situations (Ledwidge, 1980). Thus, long-term aerobic exercise may help to reduce the physiological response of the body during stressful situations (Michael, 1957; Selye, 1975; Terjung, 1979).

Second, exercise may alleviate the physiological changes brought about by social and psychological stressors. The body responds to stress by rapidly mobilizing potential energy that in previous times allowed the individual to respond physically to threats. Today, however, very few stressful situations require or allow physical exertion. Thus an individual under stress mobilizes his or her system for rapid utilization of energy but is unable to expend the built-up energy. Physical exercise is a vehicle that can metabolize the fatty acids released into the blood and dissipate the physiological arousal built up in reactions to stressors (Everly & Rosenfield, 1981; Selye, 1975).

Finally, exercise may bring about a greater state of relaxation after or during a stressful experience. For example, deVries and Adams (1972) found that exercise produced a greater reduction in anxiety and tension than tranquilizers did.

Relationship between Exercise and Mental Health

The impact of exercise on mental health varies according to whether long-term or immediate consequences are considered. Long-term exercise is associated with more positive changes in personality traits. More physically fit men have demonstrated greater emotional stability and security than the less physically fit (Young & Ismail, 1976). Also, long-term exercise has been associated with decreases in trait depression and anxiety (Kavanagh & Shepard, 1973).

Jogging and other vigorous exercise can also have a short-term effect in reducing state anxiety (Dienstbier et al., 1981; Dishman, 1982; Lichtman & Poser, 1983). Interestingly, the actual act of engaging in physical activity may be more important for reducing state anxiety than an individual's overall level of physical fitness (Dishman, 1982; Heaps, 1978; Killip, 1985). Engaging in physical exercise can be perceived as an attempt to increase fitness and thus lead to positive feelings about one's self.

Relationships among Exercise, Cognitive Functioning, and Performance

The rationale for more physically fit individuals having higher performance levels stems from the interaction between the state of the physiological system and the specific task requirements. The physiological arousal of more physically fit individuals is lower for a given physical work load than that of less fit individuals. Generalizing this finding to mental work, the physiological arousal of a more fit individual should be substantially less for a given cognitive load. It is generally accepted that complex motor and/or cognitive tasks are best performed under low to moderate arousal levels. Thus a more physically fit person should be able to perform better on complex mental tasks, particularly when working under stressful conditions (Weingarten, 1973).

The most scientifically controlled research suggests that cognitive performance does not differ between fit and less fit individuals; however, higher levels of fitness are associated with faster recovery rates from cognitive work. In a review of relevant studies Falkenberg (1987) concluded that physical fitness should be a factor only under "more stressful" conditions; unfortunately there have been no studies that have manipulated the level of fitness and cognitive demands over a typical 8-hour work period.

EMPLOYEE FITNESS PROGRAMS AND WORK-RELATED FACTORS

Productivity

As noted in the introduction, organizations often expect an increase in productivity as a return for investing in employee exercise programs. Improvements in performance may develop because of an increased ability to cope with and recover from demanding cognitive work as discussed in the preceding section. Falkenberg (1987) found that in all the studies she reviewed, subjects claimed they could work harder mentally and that their work performance improved after participating in an employee fitness program. Unfortunately, all of the reviewed studies used subjective rather than objective measures to analyze productivity. However, Bernacki and Baun (1984) did find a strong association between the proportion of individuals with above-average performance and adherence to an exercise program.

Absenteeism

It is generally assumed that absenteeism rates will drop with increased levels of physical fitness because more physically fit individuals are healthier, and healthier employees are less likely to be absent. This explanation relates only to absence that is due to physical illness. Absenteeism may also be indirectly affected if the CSPFP increases job satisfaction or commitment to the organization. The presence of an on-site fitness facility may also affect absenteeism and lateness if it allows workers to schedule their exercise during working hours.

The only reviewed study that employed objective measures of absenteeism found that high-level participants of a fitness program had a significantly lower rate of absenteeism than either low-level participants or nonparticipants (Cox, Shepard & Corey, 1981). Unfortunately, no explanation as to why these differences in absenteeism occurred was provided.

Organization Commitment and Turnover

A negative relationship between commitment to the organization and turnover has consistently been reported (Clegg, 1983; Michaels & Spector, 1982; Porter, Steers, Mowday & Boulian, 1974; Steers, 1977). One factor that influences commitment is the extent to which the organization is perceived as dependable in carrying out its commitments to employees. An organization is more likely to be perceived as being concerned about the employees' welfare if it supports an identifiable activity related more directly to employee rather than company goals. By supporting an employee fitness program, a company can demonstrate concern for the employees' health and nonwork needs. A CSPFP may also affect turnover directly by providing an additional inducement for retaining (or attracting) employees who value such a facility. The only study that analyzed employee turnover found that participants of the employee fitness program had a significantly lower turnover rate than nonparticipants (Cox, Shephard & Corey, 1981).

A MODEL OF THE RELATIONSHIPS AMONG PHYSICAL FITNESS, PHYSICAL ACTIVITY, AND EMPLOYEE EXERCISE PROGRAMS

Falkenberg (1987) recently developed a model of the relationships among physical fitness, physical activity, and employee exercise programs for the individual and the organization. A critical feature of this model is the separate identification of the benefits of exercise programs to both the individual and the organization. The rationale for this distinction is that if an employee exercises on his or her own (outside an organization's facilities or without financial assis-

tance), both the organization and the individual derive the benefits of physical fitness.

An organization supporting an employee exercise program gains from the additional advantages arising from the short-term consequences of exercise and the long-term benefits arising from greater commitment and reduced turnover. In particular, the availability of exercise facilities at work could provide an opportunity for employees to take an exercise break during periods of demanding cognitive work that could result in a reduction in physiological stress symptoms. (This assumes that the organization allows such flexible timing of exercise periods.) An on-site program could also provide employees who want to exercise greater flexibility in scheduling their exercise activities, leading to reduced absenteeism and lateness. In addition, if employees perceive the organization is concerned about their welfare, they may develop more loyalty to the company, indirectly leading to reduced turnover.

Another important feature of the model, particularly for designing employee exercise programs, is the delineation of the short- and long-term consequences for individuals engaging in physical activity. The immediate consequences are an improved mobiliza-

tion of fatty acids generated during demanding cognitive work, better relaxation, and lower levels of anxiety and depression, which should lead to a reduction in stress symptoms. Exercise may also produce more appropriate arousal levels for cognitive work, thus improving productivity. The long-term consequences of aerobic exercise are greater emotional stability, greater feelings of security, lower levels of depression, and lower levels of anxiety. These consequences lead to more positive mental health. Also, physically fit individuals have demonstrated a more rapid dissipation of tension after demanding cognitive work, and they may have more appropriate arousal levels for complex mental activity. These conditions should produce a greater stress resistance and improved productivity.

EXAMPLES OF COMPANY-SPONSORED FITNESS PROGRAMS

To give a better understanding of the issues involved in developing a CSPFP, we will be using three organizations' programs as examples. These were selected from the firms that we studied to provide a sampling of the range of CSPFPs. The first, that of the Adolph Coors Company, exemplifies a program that has developed extensive physical facilities. Next, the Denver Police Department provides an unusual example of a fitness program in which participation is partly mandatory. The third, Daniels and Associates, provides a contrast of a less structured and resource-intensive program.

The Adolph Coors Company

The impetus for the construction of the Coors facility was Bill Coors, a fitness enthusiast, who wanted to give his employees the opportunity to work out at work. This multimillion dollar facility includes an indoor running track, aerobic floor, weight machines, free weights, rowing machines, and exercise bicycles. They also offer classes in stress management, pre- and postnatal exercise, dietary and nutritional needs, weight loss, smoking cessation, anger management, parenting skills, cardiac and orthopedic rehabilitation, alcohol and dental education, and screening for breast and skin cancer.

They estimate that 52 percent of their work force uses the facility, which is open 14 to 17 hours a day. Their staff includes a cardiologist, one individual with a Ph.D. and three with a master's degree in exercise science, and a social worker with an undergraduate degree in physical education. Each of these people

teaches at least one aerobics class a week, with the remainder of their instructors provided by an outside firm. Coors feels that contracting with this firm allows more continuity in class structure (because instructor training is standardized) and fewer scheduling problems.

The Denver Police Department

The Denver Police Department also has a fitness program, but participation is not entirely voluntary. All employees are required to attend a three-day workshop in which the importance of fitness is stressed with films and lectures on the dangers of smoking, unrestricted cholesterol, obesity, and drug and alcohol abuse. During this orientation, fitness measures are taken, which include measures of aerobic and dynamic strength, flexibility, body fat, and cholesterol and triglyceride levels. Each person is then given a goal for each of these measures and an exercise prescription to help meet those goals. After returning to their work duties, the employees are encouraged to use their district's exercise facility or to exercise on their own.

Adherence to the program is optional, although the department has established fitness standards that serve as criteria for hiring and promotion. As the department moves to the use of these standards for continued employment, the "voluntary" nature of participation becomes more tenuous.

The personnel for their program includes sixty trainers from all ranks who receive special instruction from the Institute for Aerobics Research in Houston,

Texas. Each trainer interacts on a one-to-one basis with the officers they instruct, which places the trainers in a key role.

Daniels and Associates

The third organization is unique in its flexibility. Daniels and Associates is a geographically diversified organization with its headquarters in Denver. This organization built a fitness facility at the suggestion of their chief executive officer (CEO), whose rationale was simply that employees would enjoy it. The facility includes two racquetball courts, weight machines, exercise bikes, a sauna and steam room, and shower facilities. Because of an informal flextime arrangement, employees can exercise before, during, or after work, at either the in-house facility or a neighboring health club. The only requirement of this arrangement is that employees finish their work on schedule. The fitness facility is not staffed, and employees exercise completely independently. At other sites lacking in-house fitness facilities, Daniels's employees are compensated for health club dues as long as they exercise at least six times per month. At all locations, Daniels and Associates offers free executive physicals, provides employees with complimentary fruit during their work breaks, and sponsors workshops on fitness-related topics.

MAKING THE DECISION TO HAVE A CSPFP

The first step in deciding whether to develop a CSPFP should be a thorough needs analysis. We have mentioned several reasons that a company may want to begin a fitness program, but the effectiveness of a CSPFP is likely to be increased by a clear understanding of its objectives in a specific setting. For one firm stress management may be a particular concern, whereas another may discover that nutritional counseling is a higher priority. Whether the goal is to meet an organizational need or to provide a program that employees will enjoy, it is critical that the specific objectives be agreed upon at the outset.

One objective any fitness program needs to address is participant involvement, that is, which employees the company wants to attract to the program. Sedentary employees who are uninterested in wellness may have the most potential for benefit but are considered the most difficult to attract to a CSPFP. The middle group, people who are not currently exercising but who are mildly interested in wellness and fitness, are easier to attract and can also benefit from the program. Actively exercising employees, who are the easiest to attract, are also the employees with the least potential for additional gains. Therefore, it appears that the environment where a CSPFP has maximum potential is one with a high percentage of employees who are not currently exercising but who are interested in fitness.

A survey of attitudes toward a CSPFP is often a useful way to determine (and possibly increase) employees' interest in a fitness program. In addition to assessing interest in the general concept, the survey should focus on specific activities that employees would like. Like most other organizational surveys, confidentiality is essential (particularly if asking sensitive questions about stress or fitness). For this reason, many organizations use consultants to collect this information. For example, Coors uses a consulting firm and one internal employee to collect both continuing needs analysis information and assessment data.

Another critically important factor to assess is the support of the CEO, president, or other influential member of the organization. In the majority of companies we studied, the CEO's support for the CSPFP was crucial. In the cases of Coors and Daniels & Associates, it was the CEO who initiated the idea of a company-sponsored program. Without the support of someone at the top level, a CSPFP is extremely difficult to implement and maintain, especially through its first years of existence.

Building Support

In situations where the chief executive is not already an advocate, it is critical to begin building commitment among supporters at the highest level possible. Mere appeals to cost savings often seem to meet with little success, probably for three reasons. First, the majority of proposed benefits are based on limited data, and the cause-and-effect linkage is yet to be established. Second, the effect may not be readily apparent, and an impatient administration may not be willing to wait for long-term effects. The most important factor, though, seems to be inertia. A number of our respondents suggested that intellectual acceptance alone is not enough; there must be a deeper commitment to wellness that is contagious.

Another strategy for building commitment is to

involve upper management directly in the proposed program. Managers who are personally affected by fitness or wellness changes tend to become enthusiastic supporters. At the Denver Police Department, for example, several members of the top administration participated in the wellness workshop and subsequently lost weight, quit smoking, and began exercising. They are now dedicated supporters of the program.

The climate of the organization is another factor to consider. If the climate is one that values wellness, a fitness or wellness program will be more readily accepted. While changing an organization's culture may be difficult, it can be done. Take, for example, Scherer Brother's Lumber Company (cited in Terborg, 1988). It took several health-related deaths to motivate this company to change its unhealthy work climate. They began with simple steps, such as unplugging the cigarette and candy machines, providing free fruit and nutritious lunches, and buying a blood pressure kit for employees to use. They also formed a wellness committee, offered seminars on weight loss and smoking cessation, distributed a newsletter, sponsored sports teams, and reduced the noise level in the lumberyard. They also began to pay for drug and alcohol treatment, initiated "well-pay" and on-the-job injury reduction programs, installed orthopedically designed seats in their trucks, and offered free checkups to employees over the age of fifty-five.

Resource Requirements

Company resources are an obvious consideration in deciding whether to establish a company-sponsored fitness program. Two resources that are often limited are space and financing. A consultant for the Coors Health Hazard Appraisal Program states that one of the unfortunate effects of people touring the Coors Wellness Center is that they leave feeling that they could not afford either the cost or space of such an elaborate facility. In most cases that is probably true, but the benefits of a CSPFP do not appear to be dependent on the cost or spaciousness of the facility. An organization committed to a CSPFP can work with limited financing and physical space and still have a successful program.

Nevertheless, there are costs to even basic programs. Not only does the exercise program itself cost money (either on-site costs or the expense of funding off-site programs), but there are costs involved in increasing acceptance and adherence to the program (such as education programs and workshops to instill

an understanding of the importance of wellness). Incentives may also be necessary to get people started in a program. In addition, time and money are needed to assess the employees' needs and level of wellness. Finally, liability insurance and legal costs must be assumed. Terborg (1988) has developed a model and Lotus 1-2-3 program for estimating the overall costs of a program.

Physical resource limitation can often be accommodated when designing a program, at least within limits. If on-site space is a problem, a company can often utilize community resources (e.g., parks and recreation or YMCA programs) or contract with private health clubs. Of course, the firm then loses some control over the type of facilities, availability, and quality control. On the other hand, the external programs may also relieve the firm of many direct and indirect costs associated with CSPFPs.

As a general rule, an adequate facility will require at least a large room, preferably with hard floors and a mirrored wall; weights (free weights are a necessary initial investment, but as participation increases a move to an isokinetic/variable resistance system should be anticipated); stationary bicycles, treadmills, and rowing machines (again starting with a small number and planning to increase as participation grows); smaller pieces of exercise equipment, such as exercise mats, skipping ropes, and heavy hands; bulletin boards; weight scales; and mens' and womens' showers and lockers. Further guidance can be obtained through exercise equipment suppliers, consultants, publications (e.g., *Corporate Fitness and Recreation, Employee Services Management*), and consulting with professional organizations.

The selection and training of program staff is a topic of considerable importance. The majority of CSPFP administrators we interviewed stressed the necessity of highly trained personnel, including an exercise physiologist. However, a survey conducted prior to 1984 showed that only 65 percent of CSPFPs actually employed an exercise physiologist (Kondrusak, 1984).

A basic question is whether to use internal or external employees to staff the CSPFP. While internal employees are often effective in building goodwill and support for the program, they may be less qualified and dependable than an outside staff. Generally, an external staff is preferable because quality of instruction is so vital to the success of the program. Of course there are exceptions, and the Denver Police Department appears to be such a case. They carefully choose their trainers from all ranks based on several criteria (such as a balanced life-style, a commitment to wellness, and abstinence from smoking) and train and update them based on a program developed by a nationally known consultant. They appear to have success with this approach since the trainers work one-on-one with the officers in their district, and consensus building is an important component.

DESIGNING AND RUNNING A CSPFP

The first prerequisite of a successful program is getting people in the door, which can be accomplished only if employees are aware of the program. Some direct methods of increasing awareness include offering in-service programs and workshops, publishing a newsletter describing wellness topics and specific offerings of the company's program, sponsoring wellness campaigns and events, and using the needs assessment to make employees aware of both their needs and how the CSPFP can address those needs.

Indirect methods for increasing awareness and promoting wellness can also be effective. These include such things as putting up posters, building shelters for bicycles to encourage bike riding to work, eliminating candy and cigarette machines, providing nutritious foods in vending machines and in the cafeteria, labeling food with nutritional information, and disseminating information through informal employee channels. An example of the latter is Coor's Talk to a Friend Program. The Wellness Center brought in one woman from each department and offered her a free mammogram along with education on its importance. Following their tests, these women were encouraged to "talk to friends" about the free service. This technique has been extremely successful, and at this point more than 80 percent of the female employees and 35 percent of spouses have participated in the program.

Another method for increasing program awareness is to identify informal leaders and encourage them to disseminate positive information about the program. This strategy can be helpful not only in increasing awareness but also in increasing participation. Ideally, spokespersons for the program should be credible, visible employees with a strong link to either upper management or the employee grapevine.

In addition to being familiar with the program, employees must also be aware of the benefits of wellness. The needs analysis process can be one means of building this awareness, particularly if it involves an assessment of employees' health and fitness. Ongoing assessments can also be used to tailor the program to employee needs and desires. For example, because the Coors facility was viewed as a health club for its first year of existence, it attracted only those who were already predisposed to attend such a facility. It was only after gearing their program more to the needs of their work force (e.g., offering back trauma prevention classes to a work force plagued with back injuries) that attendance and participation grew.

The importance of designing a CSPFP to the specific needs of employees cannot be overemphasized. "Canned" programs may have lower start-up costs, but the benefits of tailor-made versus prepackaged programs can outweigh the start-up costs. For example, if few employees smoke, a package including smoking cessation classes is not likely to be the most cost-effective strategy. Designing programs that cater to employee needs and wants also increases participation. Some specific program guidelines include offering classes at appropriate and convenient times (e.g., during lunch, starting classes 10 to 15 minutes after work ends, or completing classes 15 to 30 minutes before work begins), beginning with classes and exercise equipment for which employees have specified a desire and need, offering programs that help affect organizational goals, and making fitness appealing (e.g., purchasing equipment with features that allow employees to keep track of their progress, offering low-calorie gourmet cooking classes, keeping facilities looking new and clean, and maintaining high-quality equipment and instruction).

Another technique for increasing the likelihood that employees will participate in the CSPFP is the use of incentives. These can include free physical assessments, paying employees to attend workshops and seminars, reducing health care premiums or deductibles for participating employees, and rewarding employees for specific behavioral changes (e.g., weight loss or smoking cessation). Although few organizations use formal incentive programs, their implementation could increase participation levels. Unfortunately, we have uncovered no empirical data regarding what type or size of reward is most effective. There are examples of rewards ranging from $150 to $1,500 for employees who have abstained from smoking for a year, but there are no data as to which is more effective in eliciting or sustaining this behavior. The amount typically rewarded for weight loss ranges from $1 to $30 per pound, but again there is no basis for stating the optimum or minimum dollar amount to effect change (Terborg, 1988). Nonmonetary incentives, including competition among individuals or groups, may also be useful for increasing involvement.

While incentives and competition may increase participation, it is unlikely that their use alone will result in long-term behavioral changes. As such, the addition of response-cost programs may help to maintain adherence. In these programs, employees pay a certain amount of money to enter a weight loss or smoking cessation class and then receive a refund when they complete the class or maintain the desired behavior for a specified period of time. This technique is considered more effective than rewards in maintaining behavior because people are more sensitive to loss than to reinforcement (Terborg, 1988).

Terborg also discusses several possible detrimental effects associated with reinforcement and response-cost programs. These include the possibility that employees might increase or begin undesired behavior in order to participate in an incentive program, falsify self-report measures so that they can receive a reward, resent the company for rewarding employees who eliminated an undesired behavior but not those who previously exhibited the desired behavior, and the possibility that employees might become dependent on the availability of the reward.

DETERMINING THE EFFECTIVENESS OF A CSPFP

The final stage in the development of a CSPFP should be program evaluation. As is the case with most other training and development programs, there is a strong tendency to overlook this crucial step. As a result, the "evidence" in support of programs is usually anecdotal or, at best, characterized by extremely crude designs that allow little confidence in their conclusions.

Reluctance to evaluate a program is generally attributable to some combination of three factors: a belief that the benefits of a program are obvious, a feeling that evaluation is too difficult to do, or an inability to carry out good intentions due to a lack of resources. Let us consider each in turn.

The belief that the benefits of a program are so obvious that they do not need substantiation is widespread and is probably partly attributable to the value our society places on education and development. Unfortunately, it is also a result of viewing programs as either good or bad. Combined with a bit of enthusiasm and defensiveness, this naturally leads to the conclusion that evaluation is a waste of money (the head of one program we spoke to suggested that doing a "proper" evaluation would probably require doubling the budget). On the other hand, many of those we interviewed noted that the primary purpose of evaluation is not to determine if the program works but how to improve it. Especially when a program is adapted from one developed elsewhere, it may be very important to determine how well the program survived the translation and how it might be improved.

Program evaluation is not a simple endeavor, yet the conclusion that it is not worth trying because it is so difficult to do is probably an exaggeration. This belief is often the result of an overemphasis on traditional laboratory and clinical methods; Industrial-organizational psychologists in particular have made great strides in developing methods more suitable to organizational settings. In fact, the typical use of pre-program health assessments and follow-ups as a natural part of many wellness programs, as well as the availability of personnel records relating to health claims and illnesses, make suitable research strategies easier in this area than in many.

The issue of resources may be the least tractable. Many firms seem to have an emphasis on "doing something," so that staff, time, and rewards are not as available for evaluating programs as they are for developing and implementing them. The problem is exacerbated by the need for staff with specialized skills in developing evaluation programs. Our respondents noted the importance of designing in such activities at the outset, when pursestrings may be somewhat looser. The use of outside experts may also be of some help and brings the added advantage of an increased sense of confidentiality.

Despite the resistance, there are good reasons to devote the effort to evaluation. The most obvious is to make sure the program works. The fitness craze has brought with it its share of fanatics, and the credibility of CSPFPs is surely an issue in the minds of many decision makers. Even firms with successful programs noted that cynics' doubts have a way of recurring at the most awkward times and that a good evaluation is the surest way of silencing them. This need to justify program expenses is particularly acute during hard economic times and with highly visible programs, such as those in the public sector.

Moreover, there is the continual need to search for possible ways to improve the program. One example, already noted, is whether a program found to be effective elsewhere (or at a different time) is maximally effective in a new situation. In addition, as users grow more familiar with a program, they are likely to address more sophisticated questions. One useful example might be the relative effectiveness of two (or more) alternative programs. We have already mentioned that CSPFPs range from simple educational programs to sophisticated (and expensive) fitness facilities. One might wish to determine the marginal gain from more expensive components of a program or the relative effectiveness of off-site versus on-site programs. Another interesting set of questions deals with ways to increase participation rates, especially among those most in need but least likely to get involved. Managers of such programs would be well served with data on the effectiveness of competition, rewards or social support systems.

The first step in program evaluation is to determine the objectives of the program. Campbell (1978) has made the important point that the objectives are heavily value laden; in order to reach any consensus on the meaning of evaluation data, it is first critical that the key decision makers discuss and agree on the criteria they see as important. A number of respondents emphasized that for their firms, cost-effectiveness was not really the issue. Rather, key decision makers—often the CEO—viewed CSPFPs as a valuable employee benefit simply because workers appreciated them. The concern was even voiced that if workers felt that the programs were nothing more than a way for the company to save money, they would sabotage them. (However, it should be noted that some of these same companies had not conducted needs analyses or surveys to confirm their assumption that employees appreciated this "benefit.")

Based on the program's objectives, criteria typically may be developed in the areas of participants' reactions, learning, and behavioral changes, as well as organizational (and personal) results. *Reactions* refer simply to participants' feelings about a program and are the most frequently used criteria. Clearly, the effectiveness of a program, especially one designed to change life-style and habits, is heavily dependent on positive reactions by participants. Yet as our respondents told us, having a "good show" is not enough; behavioral change is also necessary.

Learning refers to the assimilation of knowledge or skills and may or may not be relevant to CSPFPs. Many programs place a heavy emphasis on education and feel that the development of an awareness of good nutrition and exercise is a key to behavior change. A change in attitudes may also be expected.

Changes in *behavior* are obviously of paramount importance. Precisely what behavior is relevant is likely to be a function of both program objectives and the particular activities that a program emphasizes. In many cases it is assessed in terms of participation, although others may focus on more specific indicators, such as the ability to do a certain number of push-ups or run a distance in a set time. Whether it is better to monitor effort or accomplishment is an unanswered question; it may be particularly relevant for programs that use incentives.

Results, the ultimate objectives of a program, are usually measured in terms of such organizationally relevant outcomes as reduced absenteeism and health care costs, improved performance, or greater job satisfaction. As suggested earlier, some expected outcomes may have little rational basis, and others (such as performance) may be more likely in some jobs than others. A second concern is accurate measurement; absence, performance, and other aspects of organizational effectiveness are notorious for their poor measurement in many organizations. Other outcomes, such as health factors and turnover, may not be measurable until after an extended period. One solution may be to measure a variety of variables representing various stages in a model of outcomes. Using health-risk measures rather than actual disease, for example, has the dual benefits of quick measurement and better statistical properties (a continuous and probably less skewed distribution); of course, long-term follow-up is also recommended.

The purpose of program evaluation is to ask four questions relative to the chosen criteria: Did a change occur? Can the change be attributed to the CSPFP? Can the change be expected to occur in future samples of employees? And was the change implemented in the most efficient manner? These questions may be asked at the reaction, learning, behavior, and results level.

The question of whether a change in reactions occurred is addressed fairly simply (see Kirkpatrick, 1976, for suggestions), but the others require more rigorous treatment. Generally assessing whether a change occurred involves the use of pre- and post-program measures or a time-series design. Determining whether a change was a result of the training program rather than some other factor is considerably trickier and usually involves control groups who do not receive the program. Because this may create antagonism, it may be advisable to form control groups from those who cannot be immediately scheduled into the program or to use subjects as their own controls in a time-series design.

The proper design of experimental or quasi-experimental studies is obviously beyond the scope of this chapter, and the reader is referred to Campbell and Stanley (1963) and Goldstein (1986) for useful guidelines. CSPFPs present some special problems requiring close attention, many of which pertain to the manner in which subjects are chosen (or volunteer). In many cases, evaluations are based on subjects who volunteer for a treatment; this violation of the principle of random assignment to treatments may create problems in interpreting results. If people who volunteer are unusual (either extremely fit or out of shape), pre-post comparisons are likely to be inaccurate because of the tendency of scores to regress toward the mean. On the other hand, Terborg (1988) has suggested that many factors traditionally believed to interfere with internal and external validity of experiments may in fact increase the effectiveness of CSPFP implementation. If so, the results of experiments may represent underestimates of true effectiveness.

Program evaluation is easily ignored or at least forgotten. It is not as glamorous as program design and implementation and can easily be viewed as unnecessary or even threatening. Yet it is necessary and can contribute to a program's long-term effectiveness and acceptance. Conducting a useful evaluation is not a trivial task, and at times the obstacles may seem insurmountable. What is necessary is to reach a compromise between the ideals of the methodologists and the reality of the work world. As Goldstein (1986) has noted, all programs are evaluated, either formally or informally. The question is not whether to evaluate; rather it is how to develop the most effective means of evaluation.

A final point is that organizational decision makers should not grow excessively disheartened by the generally poor quality of evidence regarding CSPFPs. As Newman and Beehr (1979) noted in the area of stress management, the issue of employee health is too important to sit back and wait for the final answer. Rather, the responsible strategy is to try what seems reasonable under conditions that will help determine if it is effective and how it might be improved.

REFERENCES

Bernacki, E.J., & Baun, W.B. (1984). The relationship of job performance to exercise adherence in a corporate fitness program. *Journal of Occupational Medicine, 26*, 529–531.

Campbell, D.T., & Stanley, J.C. (1963). *Experimental and quasi-experimental designs for research*. Chicago: Rand McNally.

Campbell, J.P. (1978). *What are we about: An inquiry into the self concept of industrial and organizational psychology*. Presidential address to the Division of Industrial and Organizational Psychology, 86th annual meeting of the American Psychological Association, Toronto.

Clegg, C.W. (1983). Psychology of employee lateness, absence and turn-over: A methodological critique and an empirical study. *Journal of Applied Psychology, 68*, 88–101.

Cox, M.H. (1984). Fitness and lifestyle programs for business and industry: Problems in recruitment and retention. *Journal of Cardiac Rehabilitation, 4*, 136–142.

Cox, M., Shephard, R., & Corey, P. (1981). Influence of an employee fitness programme upon fitness, productivity and absenteeism. *Ergonomics, 24*, 795–806.

deVries, H.G., & Adams, G.M. (1972) Electromyographic comparison of single doses of exercise and meprobamate as to effects on muscular relaxation. *American Journal of Physical Medicine, 51*, 130–141.

Dienstbier, R.A., Crabbe, J., Johnson, G.O., Thorland, W., Jorgensen, J.A., Sadar, M.M., & Lavells, D.C. (1981). Exercise and stress tolerance. In M.H. Sacks & M.L. Sachs (Eds.), *Psychology of running* (192–210). Champaign, IL: Human Kinetics.

Dishman, R.K. (1982). Contemporary sport psychology. In R.L. Terjung (Ed.), *Exercise and sport sciences reviews* (vol. 10, 120–159). New York: Franklin Institute Press.

Dishman, R.K., Sallis, J.F., & Orenstein, D.R. (1985). The determinants of physical activity and exercise. *Personnel Administrator, 28* (8), 21–26.

Driver, R.W., & Ratliff, R.A. (1982). Employers' perceptions of benefits accrued from physical fitness programs. *Personnel Administrator, 27* (8), 21–26.

Durbeck, D.C., Heinzelmann, F., Schacter, J., Haskell, W.L., Payne, G.H., Maxley, R.T., Nemiroff, J., Limoncelli, D.D., Arnoldi, L.B., & Fox, S.M. (1972). The National Aeronautics and Space Administration—US Public Health Service health evaluation and enhancement program. *American Journal of Cardiology, 30*, 784–790.

Everly, B.S., Jr., & Rosenfeld, R. (1981). *The nature and treatment of the stress response: A practical guide for clinicians*. New York: Plenum Press.

Falkenberg, L.E. (1987). Employee fitness programs: Their impact on the employee and the organization. *Academy of Management Review, 12*, 511–522.

Goldstein, I.L. (1986). *Training in organizations*. Monterey, CA: Brooks/Cole

Heaps, R.A. (1978). Relating physical and psychological fitness: A psychological point of view. *Journal of Sports Medicine and Physical Fitness, 18*, 399–408.

Kavanagh, T., & Shephard, R.J. (1973). The immediate antecedents of myocardial infarction in active men. *Canadian Mental Association Journal, 109*, 19–22.

Killip, S.M. (1985). *Aerobic fitness: Effects on stress and psychological well-being.* Ph.D. dissertation, University of Calgary.

Kirkpatrick, D.L. (1976). Evaluation of training. In R. Craig (Ed.), *Training and development handbook* (2d Ed.). New York: McGraw-Hill.

Kondrusak, J. (1984). Corporate physical fitness programs: The role of the personnel department. *Personnel Administrator, 75,* 78–80.

Ledwidge, R. (1980). Run for your mind: Aerobic exercise as a means of alleviating anxiety and depression. *Canadian Journal of Behavioral Sciences, 12* (2), 126–140.

Lichtman, S., & Poser, E.G. (1983). The effects of exercises on mood and cognitive functioning. *Journal of Psychosomatic Research, 27,* 43–52.

Michael, E.D. (1957). Stress adaptation through exercise. *Research Quarterly, 28,* 51–54.

Michaels, C.E., & Spector, P.E. (1982). Causes of employee turnovers: A test of the Mobley, Griffeth, Hand and Meglino model. *Journal of Applied Psychology, 67,* 53–59.

Newman, J.E., & Beehr, T.A. (1979). Personal and organizational strategies for handling job stress: A review of research and opinion. *Personnel Psychology, 32* (1), 1–43.

Porter, L.W., Steers, R.M., Mowday, R.T., & Boulian, P.V. (1974). Organizational commitment, job satisfaction, and turnover among psychiatric technicians. *Journal of Applied Psychology, 59,* 603–609.

Selye, H. (1975). *Stress without distress.* New York: Signet.

Steers, R.M. (1977). Antecedents and outcomes of organizational commitment. *Administrative Science Quarterly, 22,* 46–56.

Stephens, T., Jacobs, D.R., & White, C.C. (1985). A descriptive epidemiology of leisure-time physical activity. *Public Health Reports, 100,* 147–158.

Terborg, J.R. (1988). The organization as a context for health promotion. In S. Oskump and S. Spacapan (Eds.), *Social psychology and health: The Claremont symposium on applied social psychology.* Newbury Park, CA: Sage.

Terjung, R. (1979). Endocrine response to exercise. *Exercise and Sport Science Reviews, 7,* 153–180.

Weingarten, G. (1973). Mental performance during physical exertion: The benefit of being physically fit. *International Journal of Sport Psychology, 4,* 16–26.

Young, R.J., & Ismail, A.H. (1976). Personality differences of adult men before and after a physical fitness program. *Research Quarterly, 47,* 513–519.

Lisa Kunz

INCIDENCE

Business growth worldwide continues to expand due to new technologies. The newest wave of business expansion is growth both horizontally and vertically through acquisitions and mergers. Although the total number of mergers decreased in 1986, the trend continues, particularly in smaller transactions. The number of mergers in 1986 topped nearly 4,000, equaling over $175 billion worth of transactions (Weiss, Ellis & Levine, 1987). Schweiger and Ivancevich (1985) point out that the ten largest mergers in 1984, for

example, directly affected the lives of more than 250,000 employees.

The overall estimate of merger success and failure, as pointed out by Pritchett (1987), is "a 50-50 chance of achieving a successful merger, with the worst case findings showing up to 80% of all mergers being disappointments." Somewhere between half and two-thirds of mergers simply do not work (Prokesh & Carson, 1985).

DEFINITIONS AND PERSPECTIVES

From a psychological perspective, what is a merger? A merger is an upset in the work environment (imbalance) that requires adaptation of both the worker and environment to not only the situation at hand but, more important, to each other, as suggested by Dawis and Lofquist (1984). Mergers can involve drastic and intense interactions and situations, as asserted by Johnston (1986) in her book *Takeover*. Mergers create stress on both the individual and organization, requiring massive adaptation to change.

This change requires the work environment and the individual to readapt to one another. As described in the book *A Psychological Theory of Work Adjustment* (Dawis & Lofquist, 1984), correspondence between the work environment and an employee is necessary to create satisfaction for the employee and satisfactoriness of the employee to the work environment. When correspondence is achieved and maintained, improved commitment to the organization ensues. It is important to realize this interdependency of the work environment on the individual and the individual on the work environment. In a merger situation, the employee needs to fulfill the new or changed job requirements and complete certain tasks in order to make the merger work. However, it is often forgotten that the work environment must meet the workers' needs, too. If not, employee morale

and productivity can be negatively affected, and the worker may choose to leave the work environment. Increasing turnover, tardiness, and absenteeism may result. Ignoring the human side of the merger and not maintaining this correspondence between the work environment and individual may explain why some mergers fail or are not as profitable as predicted.

From another perspective, this interdependence between employer and employee is seen as a psychological contract (Baker, 1985; Tornow, 1987). These contracts include all written and unwritten expectations of employee and employer. Unwritten contracts are sometimes misunderstood and poorly explained. Generally the employer needs production, and the employee needs reinforcers such as pay and appreciation. Many expectations may be more subtle, however, yet are often considered just as important (e.g., a cooperative attitude, perceptions of fairness).

When employees enter the work environment, the employer accepts the employees' expectations, and the employees accept the organizations' expectations. During a merger, the employer may appear to be breaking the psychological contract because the work environment changes its expectations (needs) of employees. A merger typically requires more from an employee to be satisfactory to the work environment during the transition period. Yet in mergers, the employee is generally not involved in the negotiation of new expectations with the employer. Employees are swept into the merger and have often rendered little input in decisions about the merger that will affect them directly. For a period of time the employer cannot meet the employees' expectations. The contract appears to have been tabled with the expectation that later negotiation will be on the employer's terms.

Such violation of the psychological contract subjects the relationship to trauma where trust, good faith, and reciprocity are weakened (Rousseau, 1987). Correspondence has been upset because needs are met for neither employees nor employer. Employees may react to uncertainty and job insecurity by being counterproductive in meeting organizational needs.

LITERATURE

In the business literature, mergers are typically analyzed as financial successes or failures. Since corporate growth is typically the motive for mergers, financial considerations are the obvious variables to examine. However, many analysts ignore a key factor that affects the success of mergers: the employees behind the scenes. Employees' issues get lost in the organizational shuffle, and employees become estranged by confusion and new expectations created by the merger.

At present, little scientific literature exists regarding merger-personnel issues. However, three relevant studies on mergers and human factors were located.

In a study by Boland (1970), fifty chief executive officers (CEOs) were asked to rate in order of importance twenty-six factors that could be considered when investigating a company for a possible acquisition. Boland found only three of the top twelve factors rated by the CEOs to be related to the human resource function: to-be-acquired company's top management talent (ranked 5), depth of management talent (ranked 7), and compatibility of organization structures (ranked 11). After the merger, the CEOs made a second rating. Boland found that seven of the top twelve factors were now human resource oriented. This includes the aforementioned three plus capability of research and development staff, employee benefit programs, labor relations, and union contract. This suggests that top management does not initially realize the need to focus on the impact of mergers on employees and the need for more emphasis on personnel-related issues.

In a second study, Robino and DeMeuse (1985) sent questionnaires to personnel managers across the United States to identify problems they might have encountered during a merger. No statistical tests were performed because of the small sample size (N = 22). Human factors (competence of upper-level management, favorable labor-management relations, equitable wage structure, employee benefits program and delegation of significant decisions) were perceived as more important after the merger than before by both acquired and acquiring company personnel managers. The only exception to this trend was the employee benefits program, for which the acquiring company directors perceived benefit programs as less important than managers from the acquired companies. Personnel managers initially did not think human resource factors would have the biggest contribution to a successful merger. They also found that job satisfaction for the acquired company decreased on all eight facets (pay levels, employee benefits, job security, communication level, participation in the decision-making process, opportunity for professional growth development of personal job skills, promotion potential, and overall job satisfaction) after a merger. Job satisfaction decreased for acquiring firms for six of the eight facets. The only increase in job satisfaction was seen in the opportunity for professional growth and promotion potential for acquiring company employees. The results from job dissatisfaction are extensive. Robino and DeMeuse found that productivity decreased after the merger and stress increased.

Marks (1982), in an ongoing study, has drawn some general conclusions about mergers. His six-year study is revealing some trends that can be categorized in three areas: the management of the merger process, organizational issues in mergers, and personal issues in mergers. First, Marks observes that in management of the merger process, "employees in an acquired firm who are satisfied with how their management handles the acquisition—including communication and opportunity for participation—tend to feel more positive about the acquisition, that it will improve their organizational and personal work situation, than employees who do not feel adequately informed or involved." Second, in organizational issues, Marks found that a good fit between management styles and cultures in a corporate merger is very important. Last, Marks observes that in employee personal issues, "there can be varying degrees of loss of autonomy and control over one's situation, separation from friends and important work associates, and lost opportunity to realize intrinsic rewards."

Mergers can also offer new opportunities through relocation and additional training. However, it appears that the merger process can help or hinder this restoration process (depending on how it is carried out). Management can guide the merger process in either a positive or negative direction. The goal is to have employees believe in the merger and support it to make it work. Management needs to communicate openly and effectively about merger events to employees to get their input and support.

In various other studies, researchers have stressed additional human factors that affect merger success and need to be addressed. Pritchett (1987) asserts that many mergers fail due to the cost of lost talent, lost productivity, loss of competitive position, and union problems. Frantzreb (1983) suggests that personnel problems in general are one of the major reasons for merger failure. Prokesh and Carson (1985) observes that "corporate buyers spend little time considering the risks and management skills that are central to potential acquisition success." Manzini and Gridley (1986) say "human resources are dismissed as quickly and cost-effectively as legally possible." Newly merged organizations report dysfunctional changes in employee behavior, lost productivity, high turnover rates among senior management people in key positions, leadership struggles, mismatches in human resource skills and jobs that have not been anticipated, and hosts of other personnel problems. If a merger wishes to succeed, it must depend on the people involved (Hamilton, 1986).

In addition, literature on organizational change and stress also examines the effects change has on employees. Scott and Jaffe (1987) found that mergers increased stress and distress symptoms, which led to increased absenteeism for minor ailments, accidents, lower morale, and higher blood pressure. They conceptualize a merger as a process of change where employees first deny the merger, resist it, explore options created by it, and last, establish a commitment to the new environment. They assert that employees go through stages similar to what people go through when grieving a death. Organizational change creates stress and may help us realize the effects on employees resulting from an organizational change such as a merger.

Stress has been shown to affect negatively job satisfaction (Caplan, Cobb, French, Van Harrison & Pinneu, 1975; Cooper and Payne, 1978), job performance, absenteeism, and tardiness (Beehr & Newman, 1978). Job stress creates physiological, psychological, and behavioral problems (Selye, 1974). It can even induce suicide (Schweiger & Ivancevich, 1985). Employee stress adversely affects the bottom line. Job stress can lead to intolerable levels of tension, which can result in industrial accidents (Murphy, DuBois & Hurrel, 1986) and even medical malpractice (Jones, Steffy, Wuebker, Fay & Kunz, 1987). More focus needs to be centered on the balance of employee and employer needs in regard to mergers to prevent excessive stress from surfacing and causing business losses (Jones, 1985). All of these studies emphasize the need for attention to human factors in mergers because of the debilitating effects on not only the organization but on employees and their health.

ASSESSING MERGER STRESS

How can we make mergers more successful in protecting human resources? First, problems and sources of stress in the organization and those particular to the merger situation need to be identified. Stress is created by imbalance. Dawis and Lofquist (1984) suggest that psychological stress is a measure of the imbalance or absence of correspondence between employee and employer. They define psychological stress as "an intervening psychological state inferred from an antecedent condition of discorrespondence (imbalance) and consequent behavior directed toward reducing the discorrespondence establishing balance." Many assert that merger management issues should be handled through the human resource department (Hamilton, 1986). Assessment should

include both employer and employee needs and problems. To measure stress levels along with employee perceptions of the merger could be ideal in order to assess the intensity of the imbalance.

What do the employees perceive to be imbalanced? What do they see as the psychological stressors? Questions such as these can be assessed by a questionnaire or audit. Kunz and Jones (1987) designed a questionnaire to help identify these "merger stressors"—the creators of psychological imbalance. This questionnaire assesses employee perceptions and attitudes toward personal issues related to the merger: job issues, organizational issues, and training needs. (A sample of questionnaire items foor each area is shown in table 78–1). Each of these areas

Table 78-1
Sample Merger Attitude Questionnaire

Job satisfaction
  Have you been questioning your future with this company since the merger?
  Do you have more work to do now than before the merger?
  Do you feel management is strongly committed to employee development?

General merger stress
  Has it been difficult to concentrate on your work since the merger because of job-related uncertainties?
  Has the merger adversely affected your personal and family life?
  Do you think that most employees believe that the merger will be beneficial to them?

Coping skills and resources
  Do you feel you are a participant in deciding changes that directly affect you and your job assignments?
  Since the merger, has effort been put forth to build or rebuild teams?
  Have planning and goal-setting meetings been held since the merger?

serves to assess individual perceptions of the imbalance and what is going on in the organization. The power of this assessment tool is that it is used in conjunction with a valid and reliable stress inventory (Jones, 1983; Jones & DuBois, 1985), which is given at the same time as the merger questionnaire. The combined administration not only identifies merger stress but the intensity and scope of the stress connected with these problem areas. Others have suggested a merger audit to be a critical element in diagnosing problem areas (Schweiger & Ivancevich, 1985). These assessment instruments permit management to identify areas of dissatisfaction (imbalance), where discorrespondence is evident, and where opportunities for improvement exist. A case study illustrates the importance of this questionnaire.

CASE STUDY

Method

A large electronics merger was examined. A smaller electronics company acquired a larger electronics company six months earlier. The focus of analysis is on postmerger attitudes and stress levels of the acquired employees.

Table 78-2
Questionnaire Results

HFI Overall Results	Percentile Score[a]
Job stress	56
Job dissatisfaction	56
Organizational stress	52
Stressful life changes	62
Life and health risks	45
Accident risks	49
Distortion	69

Note: MAO key findings: *Strengths* —75 percent do not plan to transfer or relocate; 75 percent, health has not been negatively affected; and 75 percent well informed about job expectations. *Weaknesses* —81 percent question future with company; 57 percent have had difficulty concentrating since merge; and 53 percent have not been educated about the acquiring company.
[a]Scores range from 0 to 100. 0 to 20 indicates a very low stress level, 20 to 40 low level, 40 to 60 moderate, 60 to 70 high, 80 to 100 very high.

Employees were assessed with the Merger Attitude Questionnaire (MAQ) (Kunz & Jones, 1987) and the Human Factors Inventory (HFI) (Jones, 1983). Approximately 1,300 acquired employees at all job levels were surveyed. Questions on the MAQ involved three merger-related areas: job stress, general merger stress, and merger coping skills. The HFI is a valid and reliable stress inventory that assesses employee stress on six different dimensions (Jones, 1983; Jones & DuBois, 1985). The HFI was used to determine the relationship between merger events and issues, and employee stress. Both the MAQ and HFI are self-administered, paper-and-pencil surveys. It takes about 30 minutes to complete both surveys. Results were computer scored.

Findings

Results of the MAQ revealed areas of both strengths and weaknesses of the acquired company employees. Overall, stress levels were moderate. A summary of key findings is listed in table 78-2. Most salient were the needs for more merger-stress coping skills, as well as the need for more education and communication in regards to the merger.

When MAQ questions and responses were related to job stress levels, a trend was evident: employees who replied in a negative manner on a MAQ question tended to also report higher stress levels (See figure 78–1, 78–2, and 78–3).

Integration Strategies

After the HFI and MAQ results were analyzed, twelve prioritized integration strategies were recommended to the client. The overarching goal was to help employees cope with the merger. The focus was on postmerger strategies as the merger had occurred six months prior.

1. *Put the right people in the right places.* Know the key players of the acquired company and do everything in your power to keep them. Court them. Keep them. Choose people carefully for leadership roles. Require that the key leaders are very visible and that they communicate courage, purpose, commitment and trust.

2. *Managers must become very action oriented.* Move fast in an informed, purposeful fashion. Require and review key business plans and strategies. Hold more meetings, help employees remain "focused" on business, hold employees accountable for high levels of production, manage by walking around (MBWA), and praise and reprimand employees as needed. Integrate, consolidate, terminate, and reorganize or redirect as quickly as possible. Keep things moving. The tendency is to get caught in "analysis paralysis." A good plan acted on today can be better than a perfect plan acted on later.

3. *Continually promote and sell the merger.* This should be a well-planned, formalized strategy. Give employees good reasons for wanting the merger to work and show them how. Positive motivation is continually needed.

4. *Get the complete story out about the merger as quickly as possible.* The message should clearly set forth goals, policies, and reporting relationships. Try to eliminate discrepancies between merged organizations' compensation systems and other personnel policies such as vacation and sick-day policies. Also, establish reporting relationships early and do not change unless absolutely necessary. Never mislead employees.

5. *Keep communication honest, open, and flowing.* Establish some formalized communication strategies (e.g., special newsletters on merger happenings, regularly scheduled briefings) where employees can expect clear, truthful updates on the merger integra-

Figure 78–1. Job Stress & Perceptions of Merger

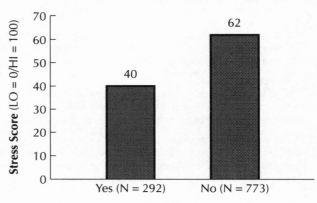

Employees Believe the Merger is Beneficial

Figure 78–2. Job Stress & Participation in Decisions

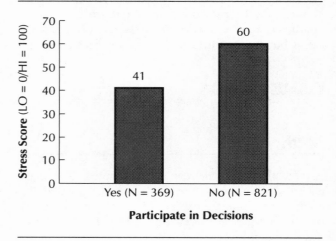

Participate in Decisions

Figure 78–3. Job Stress & Informed of Changes

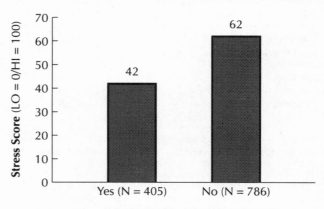

Informed of Changes Regarding the Merger

tion process. A written communication strategy is essential. Explain things better. Communicate a balanced story; emphasize both the "good" and "bad" news. If employees ask and you do not know, tell them you do not know. You want to reassure employees that there is purpose and direction to the merger, as well as try to eliminate some of the insecurity employees feel.

6. *Reward people who both identify and report breakdowns.* Establish an "open line" system where people can register both complaints and compliments. Use suggestion boxes and set up a toll-free telephone number where employees can anonymously report problems. Encourage input from all levels of personnel. Legitimize employees' feelings. Especially encourage managers to point out merger problems and do not perceive them as being resistive.

7. *Use problem-solving groups.* When employees spot problems, use their help in finding solutions. It is important to move quickly on problems. Merger-integration teams can be established. They can be comprised of all levels of personnel. Their findings should be forwarded to a central committee.

8. *Educate employees about the merger and the "new" company.* Present videotaped discussions between key executives who are discussing critical aspects of the merger. Have executives address differences and similarities between the two corporate cultures, along with the steps needed to integrate the two cultures. Emphasize the need to accept and adapt to management styles and corporate cultures.

Educate employees about the merger process. A merger is not an event but a process that takes many years to complete. Management should discuss the stages employees go through when involved in a merger situation. This will also help employees identify with others. Employees are first shocked and numbed by merger changes—struck with uncertainty and insecurity. Next, they enter a suffering stage where they become angry with merger events. Finally,

employees enter a resolution stage where they become more accepting of the situation and calm down.

9. *Let employees go through the merger integration stages.* Let employees vent their anger, frustration, and insecurity through communication channels. Do not turn a deaf ear. Let them mourn the loss of their old company—have a going-away party. As humans, we need to go through stages in order to resolve inner conflict (e.g., grieving a death of a loved one). Employees need to adapt, and that takes time. However, if employees do not get the time and support they need from management, they will leave the company or, at worst, become counterproductive.

10. *Encourage team building.* Mergers tend to break up coworker groups and cliques. Employee teams are important to employee morale and productivity. Employees need support from one another. The tendency in a merger situation is for employees to go head to head. Team building is best accomplished during the resolution stage of the merger process.

11. *Provide a stress management program.* Many suggest stress management training in order to help employees deal more effectively with stress the merger has created (Pritchett, 1987; Schweiger & Ivancevich, 1985). Stress management programs can help employees reduce tension and better control the negative impacts of stress on health through relaxation, regular exercise, and balanced diet.

12. *Be preventative.* Expect problems, and aggressively look for trouble. Continually monitor the merger process. Involve an outside consultant to maintain objectivity.

In conclusion, management has to be strong and directive yet establish an environment of caring and understanding. Management needs to reduce employee uncertainty and insecurity before it affects productivity and employee health. All strategies suggested may require additional training programs (e.g., communication training).

CONCLUSION

There is a lack of relevant literature on the identification and study of the interdependence of employees and employer to meet each other's needs in the merger situation. More methodological research is needed to help identify personnel problems and

improve employee-employer relations in the merger situation. Ways to address the issues uncovered are also needed. More focus needs to be placed on employees—the key players in the success of an organization in order to prevent merger failures.

REFERENCES

Baker, H. (1985). The unwritten contract. *Personnel Journal,* (July), 37–41.

Beehr, T.A., & Newman, J.E. (1978). Job stress, employee health and organizational effectiveness: A facet analysis, model and literature review. *Personnel Psychology, 31,* 665–699.

Boland, R.J. (1970). Merger planning: How much weight do personnel factors carry? *Personnel, 47* (2) (March–April), 8–13.

Caplan, R.D., Cobb, S., French, J. R. P., Jr., Van Harrison R., & Pinneu, S. R. (1975). *Job demands and worker health: Main effects and occupational differences.* Washington, DC: U.S. Government Printing Office.

Cooper, C.L., and Payne R. (1978) *Stress at work.* New York: John Wiley and Sons.

Dawis R., & Lofquist L. (1984). *A psychological theory of work adjustment: An individual-differences model and its application.* Minneapolis: University of Minnesota Press.

Frantzreb, Richard B. (1983). *HRPlanning Newsletter, 5* (1).

Gall, Adrienne L. (1986). What is the role of HRD in a merger? *Training and Development Journal, 40* (April), 18–23.

Hamilton, R. (1986). HRD value in mergers and acquisitions. *Training and Development Journal, 40* (June), 31–33.

Jemison, D., & Sitkin, S. (1986). Acquisitions: The process can be a problem. *Harvard Business Review* (March–April), 107–116.

Johnston, M. (1986). *Takeover.* New York: Arbor House.

Jones, J.W. (1983). *The human factors inventory survey.* Saint Paul, MN: Risk Management Division, Saint Paul Companies.

Jones, J.W. (1984). A cost evaluation for stress management. *EAP Digest* (November–December).

Jones, J.W., and DuBois, D. (1985). *The human factors surveys: Background and interpretation guide.* Saint Paul, MN: Risk Management Division, Saint Paul Companies.

Jones, J.W., Steffy B.D., Wuebker, L.W., Fay L.M., & Kunz, L.K. (1987). *Stress and medical malpractice: An organizational assessment of risk and intervention.* Presented at the 2d Annual Conference of the Society for Industrial and Organizational Psychologists Incorporated, Atlanta, Georgia, April 4–6.

Kunz, L.K., & Jones, J.W. (1987). *Merger Attitude Questionnaire.* St. Paul, MN: Risk Management Division, St. Paul Companies.

Manzini, A., & Gridley, J. (1986). Human resource planning for mergers and acquisitions: Preparing for the "people issues" that can prevent merger synergies. *Human Resource Planning, 9* (2).

Marks, M.L. (1982). Merging human resources: A review of current research. *Mergers and Acquistions, 17* (2), 38–44.

Murphy, L.R., DuBois, D., & Hurrell, J.J. (1986). Accident reduction through stress management." *Journal of Business and Psychology 1.*

Pritchett, P. (1987). *Making mergers work.* Park Ridge, IL: Dow Jones-Irwin.

Prokesch, S., & Carson, T. (1985). Do mergers really work? *Business Week,* (June 3), 88–89.

Robino D., & DeMeuse K. (1985). Corporate mergers and acquistions: Their impact on HRM. *Personnel Administrator* (November), 33–44.

Rousseau, D.M. (1987). The impact of psychological and implied contracts on behavior in organizations. Kellogg Graduate School of Management, Northwestern University, Evanston, Ill.

Schweiger, D., & Ivancevich, J. (1985). Human resources: The forgotten factor in mergers and acquisitions. *Personnel Administrator* (November), 47–61.

Scott, C., & Jaffe, D. (1987). How you and your organization can survive and thrive in times of change: Phases of personal and organizational transition. *Vision/Action,* 10–13.

Selye, H. (1974). *Stress without distress.* New York: New American Library.

Tornow, W.W. (1987). *Psychological perspectives on the changing employee contract.* Presented at the 95th Annual American Psychological Association: New York, New York, August 31.

Weiss, G., Ellis J., & Levine J. (1987). *The top 200 deals. Business Week* (April 17), 273–292.

PART IX

MANAGING SAFETY AND SECURITY

79 PHYSICAL AND PSYCHOLOGICAL ASSESSMENTS TO REDUCE WORKERS' COMPENSATION CLAIMS

Joyce Hogan, Steven Arneson

Idaho State School and Hospital (ISSH) provides treatment and training to approximately 300 developmentally disabled residents. The hospital's direct care staff (habilitation therapists) sustain a number of injuries and disabilities resulting from the physical demands of caring for the residents. A careful analysis of the habilitation therapist job indicated that therapists must regularly lift and lower residents who may weigh as much as 200 pounds and who may be unable to assist the therapist in this process. Moreover, state insurance costs for compensating employees who sustain injuries is substantial. Records for the years 1980–1986 show that employees at ISSH comprised about 5 percent of the state work force but were responsible for about 20 percent of state insurance costs. During this period, workers' compensation claims and medical payments for ISSH habilitation therapists were $1,599,247.

Workers' compensation is designed to protect employees from financial consequences of work-related injuries, illnesses, or disabilities. At last report, 79 million workers in the United States were covered by workers' compensation, and employers, were paying $17.5 billion annually in premiums (U.S. Social Security Administration, 1984). These staggering costs are likely to increase in the future because recent court decisions have granted awards to mentally troubled employees who suffer stress-related conditions acquired at work. However, the vast majority of worker compensation claims are still filed by individuals who are physically injured on the job. Because premiums generally increase with higher accident experience, employers must take steps to reduce the possibility of on-the-job injuries. Some immediate solutions may include safety or employee awareness programs. However, a particularly effective strategy to reduce injuries involves hiring individuals who are both physically and psychologically suited for the work.

We believe that there are two employee characteristics that, if present, will reduce the likelihood of workers' compensation claims due to injury. First, the employee must be physically capable of performing the work. Although accidents can result in injuries to even the most able of employees, frequently injuries occur because the employee is simply unable to perform the work. Employers whose jobs require physical labor recognize the consequences of filling these jobs with physically unqualified personnel; there is a probability of injury to self or others when an individual is unable to perform the assigned work.

Second, we suspect that there are workers who file illegitimate claims. Research over the years suggests that, in a typical organization, 10 percent of the work force will account for 90 percent of the medical absences. Although these numbers may not reflect the degree to which employees file illegitimate workers' compensation claims, it is reasonable to expect that a certain amount of on-the-job injury claims are bogus. Injuries can be faked, and there may be a substantial economic gain to the individual as a result of filing a workers' compensation claim. Therefore, one of the best ways to reduce costs due to injuries is to select individuals who are physically qualified to perform the work and good organizational citizens. This chapter describes a case in which a physical abilities test and a personality inventory were used to hire qualified personnel to reduce the costs associated with on-the-job injuries.

OBJECTIVE

Because we were concerned with reduction of both legitimate and illegitimate claims for workers' compensation benefits at ISSH, we used two parallel sets of procedures. To reduce the legitimate claims, our primary concern was to evaluate the actual physical requirements of the job and validate tests to ensure that future personnel could meet these job demands. To reduce the illegitimate claims, we needed to evaluate the personal qualities associated, on one hand, with organizational citizenship and, on the other hand, with organizational delinquency. By definition, filing a bogus insurance claim is a delinquent act. Our procedures were designed to validate personnel selection tests using a concurrent strategy that would reduce all claims for workers' compensation, regardless of their legitimacy. Specifically, we sought to validate a physical test and a personality measure that could be use to select personnel who meet the job-related physical demands and who do not engage in counterproductive behaviors.

METHOD

The research required a job analysis as the basis for specifying an experimental test battery and for developing job performance criteria. The methodology used a construct validation approach with a concurrent strategy. The research was conducted over a six-month time period with approximately three months dedicated to the job analysis.

Job Analysis

The job analysis proceeded through four phases. First, we reviewed available job descriptions, training manuals, and other documents containing information about performance required by habilitation therapists. Next, we observed habilitation therapists performing their normal duties in each of the residential units where they were assigned. Third, individual interviews and panel discussions provided information about specific job tasks; workshops held with supervisors indicated task information and performance standards. The final step involved compiling this information from the various phases into a job analysis questionnaire consisting of evaluations for (1) importance and frequency of job tasks, (2) importance of knowledge, skills, and abilities, and (3) personal characteristics of the ideal worker.

Results of the job analysis questionnaire are based on responses from 182 habilitation therapists and 40 supervisors. This sample represents nearly all persons employed in these positions. There was significant agreement between habilitation therapists and their supervisors on all portions of the job analysis questionnaire. Using ratings for frequency and importance in combination, forty-one of the ninety job tasks were identified as critical to job performance. Analysis of the knowledge, skills, and abilities

importance ratings indicated that most of the critical knowledge and skills are learned in preservice training, while the abilities are not. The critical abilities involved physical abilities or interpersonal competencies, which are not readily acquired in a training environment. Data from the endorsements of personal characteristics of the ideal habilation therapist describe these workers as calm, responsible, sociable, tactful, hardworking, cooperative, not hostile, not irritable, not unreliable, not rebellious, and not tense.

Additional analyses were conducted using the forty-one tasks identified as critical for job performance; these analyses were designed to reveal the specific abilities underlying performance of the critical tasks. Seven physical ability dimensions and ten psychological constructs were identified, defined, and scaled using five-point ratings with bipolar anchors. These seventeen scales appear in figure 79–1. A panel of six job incumbents was trained to use the physical ability constructs and asked to rate the importance of the abilities for performing the critical tasks. The ratings were made independently, and then after discussion, a consensus was formed. A similar procedure was used by a second panel to evaluate the psychological requirements of the critical tasks. Independently, thirty-two job incumbents rated the importance of these constructs for task performance; no consensus procedures were used.

Results of these analyses link abilities to the critical tasks. The physical abilities muscular strength, flexibility, and balance were important for performing the physically demanding tasks. Examples of these tasks included:

Lifts resident onto and off the toilet.

Lifts resident onto and off bathing tables and tubs.

Lifts and transfers resident from bed to wheelchair.

Restrains aggressive resident.

Protects resident during seizure.

All of these tasks require the habilitation therapist to use muscular strength for lifting or resisting forces in body positions where the joint must be flexed. Resisting forces and moving body mass also require maintaining one's equilibrium. Physical tests that assess the ability to generate muscular force with the body balanced and the limbs flexed are appropriate experimental predictors. For the psychological constructs, the raters indicated that adjustment, prudence, reliability, service orientation, stress tolerance, and likability were the most important dimensions for successful performance of the critical tasks.

Predictors

Based on job analysis results, two types of tests were chosen as independent variables in a concurrent validation strategy. First, a static lift test, designed to assess physical strength using a leg lift posture, was chosen as a predictor because it (1) conforms to the construct definition of muscular strength and simulates the activity of lifting, (2) can be administered easily and safely, and (3) has face validity for jobs where lifting is critical. Perhaps the overriding consideration for use of the lift test in our research is its demonstrated validity in other empirical studies (Hogan & Pederson, 1984; Wunder, 1981; Denning 1984). This test usually results in lesser adverse impact against females than other strength tests (e.g., hand grip, upper body lift).

The second type of test investigated was the Hogan Personality Inventory (HPI) (R. Hogan, 1986). The HPI is a 310-item true-false, self-report personality inventory that contains six primary scales. These scales consist of 43 Homogenous Item Composites (HICs), short scales that reflect facets or aspects of the primary scales. The advantage of this test construction structure is that correlational analyses for validation research can be computed at the scale and the HIC level, allowing for both general and specific prediction of job behavior.

We chose the HPI to assess the noncognitive, psychological constructs associated, on the one hand, with organizational citizenship and, on the other, delinquent behavior. These personal characteristics are implicit in behavior identified as effective job performance. The HPI has the advantage of bringing together personality theory and personality measurement in a way that is defensible both conceptually and psychometrically. The primary scales of the HPI represent the state-of-the-art personality scale structure, and they capitalize on the "Big Five" dimensions many personality psychologists consider fundamental to understanding interpersonal competence (Digman & Takemoto-Chock, 1981; McCrae & Costa, 1985; Wiggins, 1973). The six primary HPI scales are Intellectance (bright versus dull), Adjustment (self-confident versus neurotic), Prudence (compliant versus impulsive), Ambition (ascendent versus anergic), Sociability (extraverted versus introverted), and Likeability (agreeable versus aloof). Research evidence for the development of the HPI can be found in R. Hogan (1983), and documentation of scale psychometrics, including factor structure and construct validity, appears in R. Hogan (1986).

Criterion Measures

Based on the job analysis interviews, results of the job analysis questionnaire, and inspection of data maintained in personnel record files, we determined that both subjective and objective criterion data could be collected. We were interested in gathering data reflecting physical inability to perform the job safely, and we specifically sought to identify areas of performance reflecting employee dependability and conscientiousness and, conversely, organizational unreliablity.

Subjective Criteria. Four types of subjective criterion data were collected. The first, supervisory ratings of employee performance, was based on critical incidents (Flanagan, 1954) of excellent and unacceptable job performance collected during job analysis interviews. Unit managers provided examples of forty-four "positive" and forty-two "negative" incidents of employee behavior. Three raters sorted the incidents independently and classified them into seven categories; these categories represent dimensions of a therapist's performance. Definitions and behavioral anchors for each category were placed on a five-point rating scale and used for performance evaluation (see figure 79–2). Then, first-line supervisors and unit managers were trained in the use of the rating instrument, as well as the detection and avoidance of standard rating errors. Supervisors were asked to rate their immediate subordinate therapists; unit managers evaluated all therapists in their respective units. We requested two independent evaluations of each therapist, and we received dual ratings for 80 percent of those therapists evaluated. To determine the reliability of these ratings, twelve pairs of supervisor-unit manager ratings, representing evaluations of 120

Figure 79–1. Physical Ability Construct Rating Scales

1. Muscular Strength: exerting muscular force against objects.

1	2	3	4	5
Task requires little or no muscular strength		Task requires some degree of muscular strength		Task requires a high degree of muscular strength

2. Muscular Power: exerting muscular force quickly or in bursts.

1	2	3	4	5
Task requires little or no muscular power		Task requires some degree of muscular power		Task requires a high degree of muscular power

3. Muscular Endurance: muscular exertion over extended periods of time; resistance to muscular fatigue.

1	2	3	4	5
Task requires little or no muscular endurance		Task requires some degree of muscular endurance		Task requires a high degree of muscular endurance

4. Cardiovascular Endurance: sustaining effort with increased heart rate; resistance to overall fatigue when body systems (heart, lungs, muscle, etc.) are under stress.

1	2	3	4	5
Task requires little or no cardiovascular endurance		Task requires some degree of cardiovascular endurance		Task requires a high degree of cardiovascular endurance

5. Flexibility: bending, stretching, or twisting the body or limbs.

1	2	3	4	5
Task requires little or no flexibility		Task requires some degree of flexibility		Task requires a high degree of flexibility

6. Intellectance: the degree to which a person is seen as intelligent, well-educated, creative, and interested in ideas and knowledge for their own sake.

Low		Average		High
1	2	3	4	5
Conventional Practical Few Interests				Creative Imaginative Curious

7. Adjustment: the degree to which a person seems free from the everyday symptoms of maladjustment.

Low		Average		High
1	2	3	4	5
Nervous Moody Irritable				Calm Consistent Optimistic

8. Prudence: the degree to which a person seems dependable, conscientious, and reliable.

Low		Average		High
1	2	3	4	5
Impulsive Nonconforming Delinquent				Careful Conforming Planful

9. Ambition: the degree to which a person seems hardworking, energetic, and leaderlike.

Low		Average		High
1	2	3	4	5
Contented Unassertive Follower				Competitive A leader Assertive

10. Sociability: the degree to which a person seems gregarious and affiliative.

Low		Average		High
1	2	3	4	5
Quiet Shy One who likes to work alone				Extraverted Talkative One who likes to work with others

11. Likeability: the degree to which a person seems agreeable and pleasant.

Low		Average		High
1	2	3	4	5
Unfriendly Aloof Blunt				Friendly Warm Tactful

12. Service Orientation: the degree to which a person is pleasant, courteous, tactful, and cooperative in dealing with customers, clients (patients), and co-workers.

Low		Average		High
1	2	3	4	5
Rude Insensitive Moody				Pleasant Courteous Likeable

continued on next page

Figure 79–1 *continued*

---

13. Reliability: the degree to which a person is conscientious, rule-abiding, honest, dependable and responds well to supervision.

Low		*Average*		*High*
1	2	3	4	5

Impulsive
Hostile
Insubordinate

Mature
Self-controlled
Dependable

14. Stress Tolerance: the degree to which a person misses work due to illness, suffers on the job accidents, or complains about health problems.

Low		*Average*		*High*
1	2	3	4	5

Complaining
Moody
Inconsistent

Dependable
Sensitive to Others
Positive

15. Verbal Comprehension: the degree to which a person understands the meaning of words.

Low		*Average*		*High*
1	2	3	4	5

Has difficulty
reading and grasp-
ing the meaning of
written materials

Quickly reads
and grasps the
meaning of
written materials

16. Balance: maintaining the body in a stable position.

1	2	3	4	5

Task requires
little or no
balance

Task requires
some degree
of balance

Task requires
a high degree
of balance

17. Coordination: precision in sequencing and/or simultaneously moving arms, legs, and/or entire body.

1	2	3	4	5

Task requires
little or no
coordination

Task requires
some degree
of coordination

Task requires
a high degree
of coordination

---

therapists, were randomly selected. Correlations of unit manager and supervisor ratings exceeded .67 for eight of the twelve pairs of raters, indicating an adequate degree of agreement regarding therapist performance.

The second and third types of subjective criteria, employee nominations and estimates of employee malingering, were also generated specifically for this study. For the nomination criterion, unit managers were asked to nominate ten employees they would recruit if they were starting a new hospital and, conversely, ten employees they would not recruit. Thus, a total of thirty nominations were received for both the best and worst categories. For the malingering criterion, the same raters were asked to respond yes or no (for each employee) to the following question: "Do you suspect that this employee has used more time off than necessary for injuries received?" Finally, the fourth subjective criterion consisted of performance appraisals routinely kept by the hospital. The supervisory rating received by each employee on the most recent performance appraisal was extracted from personnel files and recorded. This final rating proved subsequently to be redundant with the other supervisory rating variables and was not used in further analyses.

Objective Criteria. In addition to the four subjective criterion measures, several sources of objective data

routinely kept by ISSH were available for each therapist. First, the total hours of sick leave used by each therapist from January 1, 1985, to March 1, 1986, were recorded; these two figures were summed to form an overall indication of sick leave used during these fifteen months. Second, the number of hours lost due to injuries received on the job was recorded. Other objective criteria included the number of disciplinary notations accumulated over fifteen months, the number of complimentary notations received in that time period, and the number of times late reporting for work over the fifteen-month period. Finally, records of each therapist's worker compensation claims were provided by the Idaho state insurance fund. Records were reviewed for a six-year period (1980–1986); these data included the number of injuries compensated, number of days compensated for injury, total compensation paid, total medical payments, and the total reserve held for each outstanding claim. A complete list and description of the subjective and objective criterion measures appear in table 79–1.

Sample

The research sample consisted of all of the incumbents who reported for work during a one-week test

Figure 79–2. ISSH Habilitation Therapist Job Evaluation

Directions: This job evaluation form contains seven rating scales that are to be used to evaluate performance of employees you supervise. Read the description of each rating scale. Next, read the description of superior performance and then read the description of performance below standard. Finally, decide where the person you are evaluating is on this performance dimension and circle the number corresponding to your rating. A score of "1" indicates the worst possible performance on that dimension. Please be sure to evaluate all seven dimensions. Do NOT omit any ratings.

1. Citizenship: The degree to which an individual's attitudes, values, and behaviors reflect, on the one hand, enthusiastic commitment, motivation, and "going the extra mile" or, on the other hand, a detrimental attitude and delinquent behavior.

Below Standard		Adequate		Superior
1	2	3	4	5

Difficult to work with; creates trouble; loafs on job

Builds department morale by working enthusiastically and serving as a good example for other employees

2. Concern with Residents' Hygiene: The degree to which the employee attends to the full range of residents' hygiene needs. This includes grooming, dressing, feeding, and medical care.

Below Standard		Adequate		Superior
1	2	3	4	5

Allows residents to live in untidy and unsanitary conditions

Consistently and carefully cleans residents and maintains high standards of hygiene.

3. Respect for Residents: The degree to which the employee treats the residents with sensitivity, empathy, and humanity.

Below Standard		Adequate		Superior
1	2	3	4	5

Physically and verbally abuses residents

Consistently respects the rights and emotional needs of residents

4. Judgment and Attention to Detail: The degree to which the employee exercises good judgment in carrying out duties and attends to the essential details. Attending to details (e.g., tying shoes, buttoning clothes) is more than a positive attitude toward the job.

Below Standard		Adequate		Superior
1	2	3	4	5

Shows poor judgment or is inattentive to residents' needs as other aspects of the job

Always anticipates and prepares for potential problems and residents' needs; performs work thoroughly

5. Physical Technique: The degree to which the employee has mastered and uses proper procedures for handling and restraining residents.

Below Standard		Adequate		Superior
1	2	3	4	5

Uses improper techniques thereby risking injury to self and others

Always uses proper technique thereby minimizing chances of injury

6. Physical Ability: The degree to which the employee is capable of performing physically demanding tasks using sufficient muscular strength, endurance, and coordination.

Below Standard		Adequate		Superior
1	2	3	4	5

Has difficulty lifting, maneuvering, and restraining residents; has difficulty performing routine physical tasks and needs assistance

Physically well-suited for the work. Displays no difficulty handling residents. Physical skill enhances job performance.

7. Empathic Involvement: The degree to which the employee is concerned about and involved in the welfare of the residents.

Below Standard		Adequate		Superior
1	2	3	4	5

Indifferent to or uncaring about the welfare and safety of residents

Concerned about and involved in the welfare of residents

Table 79–1
Descriptions of Subjective and Objective Criterion Measures

Measure	Description
Subjective	
Supervisory ratings of job performance	From critical incidents, seven dimensions of job performance were conceptualized; two independent ratings were gathered from unit managers and supervisor
Employee nominations	Unit managers nominated thirty employees in both "best" and "worst" categories.
Estimates of employee malingering	Raters estimated whether workers took more time off than others.
Objective	
Sick leave	Total hours of sick leave used
Hours lost due to job injuries	Total number of hours lost due to injuries received on the job
Disciplinary notations	Total number of disciplinary notations received
Complimentary notations	Total number of complimentary notations received
Time late	Number to times reporting late for work
Compensable injuries	Total number of job injuries compensated by the state
Days compensated for Injuries	Number of days for which compensation was received as a result of a job injury
Compensation for injuries	Total compensation paid (in dollars)
Medical payments	Total medical payments paid to treat job injuries
Reserve total	Total amount of dollars held in reserve for each therapists' outstanding claim

period; the sample totaled 175 therapists. Of these, 128 were females, and 47 were male; 166 were white, 6 were Hispanic, 2 were native American, and 1 was black. The average length of service with ISSH was 4.26 years. Validity coefficients were calculated for the total sample. Subgroups other than white females and white males contained insufficient numbers for meaningful separate analysis.

Procedure

Criterion data were collected for all habilitation therapists prior to testing. This procedure attempted to minimize criterion contamination arising from knowledge of test scores.

All habilitation therapists completed the HPI, which required approximately 40 minutes. Subjects were told that they could omit any items they wished not to answer. The research subjects then engaged in a set of warm-up exercises prior to the strength test. They were given instructions for completing the strength test, and two trials were administered and recorded. Each trial required approximately 30 seconds to administer and record. Each lift test resulted in a score for maximum force exerted and a score for the average force exerted over the five. Subjects were given their scores after the final trial.

RESULTS

We proceeded through five steps to evaluate the test results and their usefulness. First, we examined the relationship between the physical lift test and the criterion measures and determined the empirical suitability of this test for selection purposes. Second, we examined the HPI HIC predictors for some consistent pattern of association with the criterion measures. Third, we identified a preliminary set of HICs on the basis of both empirical and conceptual relationship to critical criteria of the job performance structure. Next we assembled these HICs into a single scale, with each HIC contributing equally to the total scale score; this scale was then correlated with all criterion measures. Finally, we evaluated the fairness of these measures through archival analyses of race, sex, and age differences.

Table 79–2
Correlations between Lift Test Scores and Subjective and Objective Criteria

	Males	Females	<40	>40	Total Sample
Ratings of physical technique	.19 (p<.11)	.12 (p<.10)	.20 (p<.02)	.42 (p<.00)	.26 (p<.00)
Ratings of physical activity	.19 (p<.10)	.19 (p<.02)	.38 (p<.00)	.62 (p<.00)	.49 (p<.00)
Supervisor ratings of job performance	.15 (p<.17)	.14 (p<.07)	.15 (p<.06)	.32 (p<.02)	.18 (p<.01)
Employee nominations					.16
Estimates of employee malingering					−.11
Sick leave					−.18*
Hours lost due to job injuries					−.02
Disciplinary notations					−.03
Complimentary notations					.01
Time late					−.04
Compensable injuries					−.09
Days compensated for injuries					−.05
Compensation for injuries					−.08
Medical payments					−.05
Reserve total					−.05

*p<.01.

Predictor-Criterion Relationships

Physical Lift Test. Predictor-criterion relationships were examined for the physical lift test. Two trials of the lift test were administered, and each trial yielded two scores. A maximum force exerted and an average force exerted over 5 seconds were recorded for each trial. Table 79–2 presents Pearson product-moment correlations between the physical lift test scores and the criterion measures. Test scores representing the average force exerted during trial 2 was the best predictor of supervisor ratings of physical ability ($r = .26$), physical technique ($r = .49$), overall job performance ($r = .18$), and sick leave totals ($r = −.18$). This lift test variable is the only score used for subsequent analyses. The test correlations with supervisory ratings were corrected for attenuation using procedures specified by Nunnally (1970, p. 116–117), and these corrections are .34, .62, and .23 for ratings of physical ability, physical technique, and overall job performance, respectively. The test-retest reliability of the lift test calculated from the two trials administered to the research sample was .92.

Personality Inventory. Pearson product-moment correlations were computed between the HPI variables and criterion variables, and these appear in table 79–3. There are a number of significant correlations; we hypothesized, however, that aspects of Prudence, Adjustment, and Likeability, in the positive direction, as well as limited facets of Intellectance, Ambition, and Sociability, in the negative direction, would be most highly associated with good performance of habilitation therapists. For example, Prudence will be associated with rule compliance and maturity; Adjustment will be associated with positive psychological health and absence of anxiety and self-doubt; Likeability will be associated with friendliness, being pleasant, affability, tolerance, and personal warmth. Intellectance, in the negative direction, will be associated with a lack of curiosity and a narrow range of interests; Ambition, in the negative direction, will be associated with complacency, conformity, and unassertiveness; Sociability, in the negative direction, will be associated with quiet and reserved behavior.

Because of the number of possible predicators (43 HICs) and the relatively small sample size ($N = 175$), certain precautions were taken to minimize the effects of chance in the data analysis. First, HICs that comprised the final selection instrument were identified on conceptual grounds rather than simply choosing the HICs with the greatest empirical validity in this sample. Second, HICs were also chosen for their statistical association with multiple criteria. Several experimental scales were composed from selected HICs, and these were then correlated with the criterion variables across male, female, and total samples.

Table 79–3
Correlations between HPI HICs and Criteria (N=174)

HIC Description	HPI Scale											
	1	2	3	4	5	6	7	8	9	10	11	12*
Intellectance												
Good Memory	−.06	−.05	−.04	.07	−.08	−.08	−.09	.03	.04	.06	−.00	.05
School Success	.14	−.06	−.04	−.00	−.19	−.10	−.05	−.05	−.11	−.11	−.14	.23
Math Ability	.04	−.13	−.12	.01	−.11	−.10	−.01	−.05	−.02	−.06	−.07	.03
Science Ability	.16	−.11	.01	−.03	−.00	.08	.14	−.03	−.02	−.05	−.08	.02
Reading	−.01	.03	.12	−.00	.02	.10	.04	.02	.10	.05	.03	.12
Cultural Taste	.09	−.10	.08	−.13	−.05	.10	.06	−.08	−.03	−.08	−.12	.17
Curiosity	.22	−.12	−.04	−.02	−.03	.11	.12	.04	.02	−.04	−.02	.18
Intellectual Games	.19	−.09	−.07	−.05	−.08	.01	−.03	−.03	−.03	.01	−.05	.18
Adjustment												
Not Anxious	−.01	−.08	.00	−.09	−.10	−.06	−.07	−.02	.02	−.15	−.18	.01
No Social Anxiety	.10	−.13	−.06	−.05	−.08	.02	−.05	.01	−.02	−.03	−.03	−.01
No Guilt	.09	−.10	.01	−.10	−.11	−.05	−.08	.02	−.02	−.07	−.12	.19
Not Depressed	.04	−.15	.04	.07	−.07	−.03	−.02	.06	−.00	.01	−.12	−.01
No Somatic Complaint	.09	−.06	−.14	−.01	−.20	−.18	−.17	.06	−.02	−.09	−.15	.06
Calmness	.00	−.00	.00	.01	−.04	−.07	−.06	.03	−.07	−.05	−.17	−.01
Self Confidence	−.05	−.03	.07	.08	−.05	−.08	.05	.04	.05	.02	.01	−.11
Identity	−.01	−.03	−.02	.04	−.10	−.03	−.05	.14	.09	.12	.01	.03
Self-focus	.05	−.03	.05	−.02	−.03	.04	−.14	.07	.04	.00	.03	−.02
Prudence												
Good Attachment	−.08	−.08	−.02	−.14	−.03	.01	.02	−.09	−.21	−.05	−.08	−.15
Planfulness	−.03	.05	−.01	.02	−.03	.05	−.11	.05	.02	.05	.08	−.01
Appearance	−.01	−.05	−.10	−.04	−.12	−.08	−.03	−.04	−.07	−.04	−.11	.22
Mastery	.01	−.15	.00	.04	−.09	−.02	−.09	−.05	−.04	.02	.04	.20
Perfect	−.02	−.11	−.02	.03	−.02	−.05	−.10	−.01	−.11	.05	−.03	−.05
Impulse Control	−.10	−.08	−.03	−.18	−.09	−.06	−.02	−.03	−.11	−.05	−.08	.03
Avoids Trouble	−.02	−.10	.11	−.12	−.09	.12	−.03	−.05	−.20	.02	−.03	.04
Not Experience Seeking	−.06	.08	.03	−.04	−.03	−.10	−.11	.04	−.05	.04	−.02	.13
Not Thrill Seeking	−.06	−.12	.01	−.12	−.05	.04	−.12	−.07	.03	−.01	.01	−.15
Not Spontaneous	.01	−.11	−.16	−.10	−.14	.02	−.01	−.10	−.26	−.19	−.21	.13
Ambition												
Generates Ideas	.20	−.03	.03	.14	−.05	.01	−.06	.12	.06	.04	.02	.17
Leadership	.02	−.07	−.09	.12	−.15	−.08	−.02	.12	.02	.05	.01	.05
Competitive	.02	−.06	−.16	−.01	−.18	−.05	−.07	.04	−.07	.04	.03	−.03
Status Seeking	.00	.04	−.05	.07	−.03	−.06	.13	.03	−.12	.00	.04	.07
Impression Management	−.10	.06	−.03	.04	.12	.19	.16	−.00	.00	.10	.11	.08
Sociability												
Entertaining	.03	−.04	.07	.23	−.05	−.01	−.07	.11	−.02	.12	.10	.02
Exhibitionistic	.17	−.06	.01	.12	.09	.11	.13	.05	.08	−.08	−.02	.11
Likes Crowds	−.03	.03	−.03	.03	−.04	−.01	−.00	−.00	−.04	.09	.07	−.01
Likes Parties	−.09	.00	.01	.13	.12	−.06	.05	.01	.02	.04	.00	−.24
Expressive	.04	−.02	−.11	.09	.02	−.03	−.11	.01	−.07	.05	.02	−.06
Likeability												
Easy to Live With	−.07	−.13	−.00	.04	−.11	−.13	−.01	−.03	.03	−.00	−.04	−.19
Even Tempered	.06	−.17	−.03	−.13	−.17	−.13	−.06	−.09	−.15	−.15	−.30	.02
Caring	.03	−.09	.06	.04	−.12	−.14	−.01	−.00	.06	.03	.02	.02
Trusting	−.02	−.10	−.03	−.07	−.18	−.14	−.17	−.12	−.05	−.14	−.19	−.09
Likes People	−.14	.01	.20	.06	.02	−.00	−.04	−.04	.01	.09	.09	−.22
Autonomy	−.07	−.09	−.03	−.09	−.13	−.04	−.13	−.26	−.16	−.04	−.11	−.11

Note: 1 = Supervisor Ratings; 2 = Estimates of Malingering; 3 = Total Sick Leave; 4 = Hours Lost to Job Injury; 5 = Disciplinary Notations; 6 = Complementary Notations; 7 = Time Late; 8 = Compensation Total; 9 = Medical Payment Total; 10 = Days Compensated for Injury; 11 = No. of Compensable Injuries; 12 = Nominations (N = 58).

$p < .05$ at r= ± .13.
$p < .01$ at r= ± .18.
*$p < .05$ at r= ± .22.
*$p < .01$ at r= ± .38.

Table 79-4
Correlations between the Therapist Selection
Inventory and the Criterion Measures

	Correlation with the TSI
Supervisor ratings of job performance	−.03
Employee nominations	.05
Estimates of malingering	−.13*
Sick leave	−.07
Hours lost due to job injuries	−.18**
Disciplinary notations	−.22**
Complimentary notations	−.17**
Time late	−.10
Compensable injuries	−.28**
Days compensated for injuries	−.20**
Compensation for injuries	−.08
Medical payments	−.14*
Reserve total	−.09

* $p < .05$.
** $p < .01$.

The best pattern of prediction for both males and females was obtained with the scale consisting of HICs for School Success, Not Anxious, No Somatic Complaint, Impulse Control, Generates Ideas, Even-Tempered, and Autonomy. The correlations between this scale and all objective and subjective criteria appear in table 79-4.

The seven HICs contain thirty-four items, and these were unit weighted as a final scale, called the Therapist Selection Inventory (TSI). Of the correlations presented in table 79-4, seven of the thirteen were significant ($p < .05$). The best pattern of prediction was achieved for the objective criteria—number of compensable injuries ($r = -.28$), disciplinary notations ($r = -.22$), and days compensated for injury ($r = -.20$). Test-retest reliability of the TSI was evaluated by scoring HPI protocols in an archival sample ($N = 36$ employed adults; see J. Hogan & R. Hogan, 1986) for the TSI. The resulting reliability coefficient was .77.

Test Fairness

Descriptive statistics, including means and standard deviations for the Therapist Selection Inventory, physical lift test, and the criterion measures are presented in table 79-5. Because the research sample contained insufficient numbers for the analysis of race differences, the TSI was used to score HPI protocols in our archival sample (J. Hogan & R. Hogan, 1986) This sample does provide sufficient numbers for analysis of race (black versus white) differences. Sex differences were analyzed using both the research

and archival samples. The various individual samples included in the overall archival sample are described in J. Hogan and R. Hogan (1986). In lieu of an actual applicant sample from ISSH, it appeared that this archival sample could reasonably approximate an unselected applicant pool.

The results of scoring the HPI archival sample also appear by subgroups in table 79-5. No mean differences of practical significance were found, except that individuals 40 years or older tend to score higher on the TSI than those who are younger. These results indicate that the operational use of the TSI should not result in either adverse impact or unfair denial of employment opportunities on the basis of sex, race, or age.

Issues of test fairness are of considerable concern when physical strength tests are used for employment because females, as a group, always score lower than males. Several published studies have indicated that strength test score differences from male and female subgroups are also reflected in proportional differences in job performance (Arnold, Rauschenberger, Soubel & Guion, 1982; Reilly, Zedeck & Tenopyr, 1979). Within the context of the Uniform Guidelines on Employee Selection Procedures (1978), physical tests in these studies resulted in adverse impact but were also shown to be valid and fair. Unlike the two examples described above, the ISSH validation study was conducted using an incumbent sample where white females represent the majority group. If analyzed using definitions provided in the Uniform Guidelines, ISSH evaluations of adverse impact should compare selection ratios of "minority" subgroups to the majority group or the group with the highest selection ratio. In this case, the majority group is white female. Concern for adverse impact of physical tests used at ISSH should be for selection of any race, sex, or ethnic group that is less than four-fifths of the rate for the group with the highest selection rate. Under this definition, use of the lift test will not result in adverse impact for the minority group of white males, since the average score ($M = 217$) for males significantly ($t = 13.98$, $p < .00$) exceeds the average score ($M = 104$) for females. Data to evaluate race differences were insufficient for meaningful subgroup analyses.

However, if the selection ratios for employment at ISSH should change in the future and females become a "minority" group, adverse impact using the physical lift test could very possibly occur, and evidence of validity and fairness would need to be produced. Such evidence is presented in table 79-2 with the total group correlations using supervisory ratings and sick leave criteria. The lift test correlations for the female subgroup with supervisor ratings of physical

Table 79–5
Descriptive Statistics for Predictor and Criterion Measures

	Mean	SD	N	Min	Max
Predictors (Tests)					
Physical lift test (Mean 2)	136.56	0.00	167	33	346
Therapist selection inventory (max. possible = 34)	17.43	4.57	169	4	28
Sample subgroups					
Sex					
Male	18.77	4.88	47	9	28
Female	20.03	4.98	118	5	30
Race[a]					
White					
Black					
Age					
Under 40	19.20	5.03	114	5	30
40 or Over	21.12	4.56	43	9	30
Archival subgroups					
Sex					
Male	20.57	4.58	603	6	33
Female	20.40	4.66	605	6	32
Race					
White	21.04	4.42	149	6	33
Black	21.53	4.75	236	8	30
Age					
Under 40	19.54	4.65	215	6	31
40 or Over	21.93	4.38	207	7	33
Criterion measures					
Supervisor Ratings (max. = 70)	50.28	7.37	175	30	67
Employee nominations	.47	.50	59	0	1
Estimates of malingering	.08	.27	168	0	1
Sick leave	77.50	0.21	174	0	461
Hours lost to job injuries	24.23	2.08	174	0	640
Disciplinary notations	.98	1.58	174	0	8
Complementary notations	2.87	2.28	174	0	11
Time late	3.98	9.54	174	0	51
Compensation paid	160.24	617.24	175	0	3,880.84
Medical payments	475.96	1,387.20	175	0	10,188.02
Number of compensable injuries	1.18	1.79	175	0	10
Days compensated for injury	10.87	22.06	175	0	102

[a]Insufficient number for subgroup analysis.

ability for job performance were significant, and correlations for ratings of physical technique and overall supervisory ratings approached significance. These results indicate higher test scores are associated with higher ratings of job performance.

Analyses of age effects for the lift test indicated that individuals younger than forty years of age ($N = 113$) scored significantly higher than individuals forty years or older ($N = 42$). The correlation between the age variable (dichotomized using the subgroup under forty years and the subgroup forty years and older) and lift test performance was $-.13$ ($p < .05$), indicating that older persons, as a group, will tend to score lower than younger persons. However, subgroup analyses by age indicate the relationship between the lift test and the criterion ratings are significant and provide no evidence of test unfairness. This suggests that the actual use of the lift test for future selection should be monitored to determine if these general age differences are reflected in hiring decisions.

These considerations are not meant to dissuade use of the lift test for personnel decisions. As the ISSH work force is currently selected and composed, no adverse impact against the "minority" male group will result. Even in the event of adverse impact, the lift test has demonstrated validity in terms of supervisory ratings and also is fair in that test validity exists for sex and age subgroups.

Utility Analysis

A utility analysis, using procedures described by Casio (1982), was calculated to estimate the total dollar gain in improved performance. The utility of a selection device is the degree to which its use improves the quality of the individuals selected beyond what would have occurred had the device not been used (Blum & Naylor, 1968). Data used to determine the utility index include the number of applicants selected, the validity of the selection procedure (concurrent validity coefficient), the criterion standard deviation estimated in dollars, and the cost of putting one person through the testing process.

Utilities were computed for the ISSH's previous selection procedure, the personality measure, the physical lift test, and the personality and physical test in conjunction with using the following equation (Cronbach & Gleser, 1965):

$$U = N_s \, r_{xy} \, SD_y \, \lambda/\phi - N_s \, C_y /\phi,$$

where U = total gain in utility from use of the hiring procedure over random selection; N_s = number of applicants selected; r_{xy} = validity of the selection procedure; SD_y = standard deviation of the dollar-valued job performance criterion; λ = ordinate of the normal curve at the cutting score of the test procedure (Z score); ϕ = the selection ratio; and C_y = the cost of putting one person through the selection procedure.

Results of these computations are presented in table 79–6. The data for all equations are based on the 1985 hiring year. We used the 40 percent statistic to calculate the standard deviation of dollar-valued job performance (Hunter & Schmidt, 1983). Because the ISSH's previous selection procedure basically consisted of interviewing applicants, an accepted validity coefficient for interviews ($r = .13$; Hunter & Hunter, 1984) was used for this statistic. For the physical lift test, the correlation between the test and supervisor's ratings of overall job performance ($r = .18$) was used as the validity coefficient. For the personality measure, the correlation between the TSI and the number of compensable injuries ($r = .28$) was chosen. Finally, to estimate the overall utility of the two predictors used in conjunction, the multiple correlation of the physical lift test and the TSI with disciplinary notations ($r = .33$) was chosen.

As seen in table 79–6, the expected gain to ISSH from the use of either the physical lift test or the personality measure is substantial. Use of the physical test over random selection is estimated at $67,444.71 per year; for the personality measure, the job performance dollar improvement over random selection is estimated at $117,416.91 per year. When both of the tests are used in conjunction, the estimated gain in dollar-valued job performance is $141,940.51 a year; the total utility of the two selection procedures over the interview previously used by the ISSH is $99,019.40 per year.

In addition to utility analysis, we can use archival insurance data from the state of Idaho to estimate insurance savings that might have occurred had the personality and physical lift tests been used to hire the current group of habilitation therapists at ISSH. During the past six years, workers' compensation

Table 79–6
Utility of the Current Selection Procedure, the Therapist Selection Inventory, and the Physical Lift Test over Random Selection

Terms	Current Procedure	Lift Test	TSI	Lift Test and TSI
N_s	74	74	74	74
R_{xy}	.13	.18	.28	.33
SD_y	$4,502.00	$4,502.00	$4,502.00	$4,502.00
λ	.24	.24	.24	.24
ϕ	.16	.16	.16	.16
C_y	$47.66	$48.66	$48.66	$49.66

Cost Comparison of Alternative Selection Methods

Method	Validity	Total Cost	Per Hiree Utility	Total Utility	Per Hiree Gain	Total Gain
Interview	.13	47.66	$580.11	$42,921.11		
Lift test	.18	48.66	$911.42	$67,444.71	$331.31	$24,523.60
TSI	.28	48.66	$1586.72	$117,416.91	$1,006.61	$74,495.80
Lift test and TSI	.33	49.66	$1918.12	$141,940.51	$1,338.01	$99,019.40

Note: Equation components for the selection methods: $\Delta\mu = N_s r_{xy} SD_y \lambda/\phi - N_s C_y/\phi$.

claims and medical payments for ISSH therapists totaled $1,599,247. There were 175 therapists in our research sample, and they accrued $112,406 (7 percent) in compensation claims and medical payments. There was also a 25 percent to 30 percent turnover at ISSH during those six years; presumably the persons who left account for the difference between the total costs and the costs for which we can account. Because claims from the research sample comprise only 7 percent of the total and assuming this research sample is representative of ISSH employees over the preceding six years, a more accurate estimate of costs-savings should include the residual 93 percent of claims.

As an example to estimate costs, assume we use a cutting score on the TSI of 21—which is the average score for the research sample. Among the ISSH therapists, there were .81 incident per person for those with scores of 21 or greater versus 1.5 incidents per person for those with scores below 21. In the above-twenty-one group, the average cost per incident was $710; in the below-twenty-one group, the average cost per incident was $1037. There were 59 incidents in the above-twenty-one group, for a total cost of $41,890; there were 144 incidents in the below-twenty-one group for a cost of $149,328. If the TSI had been developed and used earlier, ISSH would have yielded a net savings of $107,438 in state work-

ers' compensation claims. This is based only on the 7 percent of the total sample who were available for testing, which is a severe financial underestimate considering the attrition in personnel at ISSH over the six-year period. If these results are applied to the residual 93 percent of the claims, the state would have yielded an estimated $1,427,390 in net savings for workers' compensation claims.

Similar estimates can be made for the physical lift test. Using a cutting score of 100 (the mean for females) and applying this cutoff to the majority group, there were 1.08 incidents per person for those with scores of 100 or greater and 1.36 incidents per person with scores below 100. In the above-100 group, the average cost per incident was $480.50; in the below-100 group, the average cost per incident was $743.08. There were 64 incidents in the above-100 group, for a total cost of $59,446.40. Again, these figures underestimate actual dollars due to employee turnover.

Both the utility analyses and the cost accounting analyses of workers compensation claims paid indicate substantial financial benefits associated with the use of valid tests for personnel selection. Moreover, these figures corroborate Casio's (1982) claim that even tests with modest validities result in more than modest economic gains to the organization.

SUMMARY

Private enterprise has realized for over eighty years that attention to the process of personnel selection pays significant dividends in terms of productivity and, ultimately, profitability. Government, perhaps because it is less profit oriented, has tended to be less self-conscious about the hiring process. Nonetheless, a moment's reflection suggests that incorrect hiring decisions translate into large and unnecessary costs for local, state, and federal government. This case study, which focuses on a single job category, habilitation therapist, at Idaho State School and Hospital (ISSH), rather dramatically documents this point.

Research over the years suggests that, in a typical organization, 10 percent of the people in an organization will account for 90 percent of the medical absences; this means, in turn, that medical absences are a reliable and therefore predictable problem. In addition to the medical costs accrued by the staff at ISSH, other records show an annual turnover in the 25 percent range. This translates into substantial expenses in training costs.

A careful analysis of the habilitation therapist job indicated that it was physically demanding;

employees must regularly lift and lower residents who may weigh as much as 200 pounds and who may be unable to assist the employee in this process. The job analysis also indicated that the best employees were perceived as well adjusted, conscientious, and empathic. Results from the job analysis dictated the choice of experimental tests; we chose a lift test and a measure of normal personality for investigation.

As indexes of competent performance in the habilitation therapist job, we developed (from the job analysis) a performance appraisal form. We also chose, from personnel files, a number of objective criterion data as indicators of performance. We tested 175 habilitation therapists at ISSH (about 95 percent of the incumbents) during the spring of 1986 with our tests. We recorded supervisors' ratings for these people, and we recorded job performance data for each case. We computed correlations between our tests and these indeves of competent (and incompetent) performance. Results indicated that the physical lift test was a valid predictor of performance defined in terms of various supervisory ratings and amount of sick leave taken.

From the personality measure we developed the Therapist Selection Inventory (TSI). In the incumbent sample, scores on the TSI were significantly and substantially correlated with the number of on-the-job injuries for each employee. Blacks, whites, men, and women all receive comparable scores on the TSI, which means that it should not discriminate against women or blacks. More important, however, is the fact that, over a six-year period, persons in the research sample with scores of 21 (the average for the sample) or higher have significantly fewer accidents than those with scores below 21 (59 versus 144), they miss much less work (611 days versus 1248), they have fewer worker compensation claims ($5207 versus $23,316), lower medical costs ($23,269 versus $60,614), and total costs ($47,100 versus $172,583).

The TSI will save the state substantial dollars per year in costs from a variety of sources, including fewer insurance claims, greater efficiency of the hiring process, reduced turnover, reduced shrinkage, lower absenteeism, and increased productivity. Although the financial savings will be appreciable, there will also be significant gains in the effectiveness of ISSH as an organization. These will be seen in terms of increased morale, improved staff interactions, and better-quality care for the residents.

REFERENCES

Arnold, J.D., Rauschenberger, J.M., Soubel, W.G. & Guion, R.M. (1982). Validation and utility of a strength test for selecting steelworkers. *Journal of Applied Psychology, 67,* 588–604.

Blum, M.L., & Naylor, J.C. (1968). *Industrial psychology: Its theoretical and social foundations* (rev. ed.). New York: Harper & Row.

Casio, W.F. (1982). *Costing human resources: The financial impact of behavior in organizations.* Boston: Kent Publishing Co.

Cronbach, L., & Gleser, G. (1965). *Psychological tests and personnel decisions.* Carbondale: University of Illinois Press.

Denning, D.L. (1984). *Applying the Hogan model of physical performance of occupational tesks.* Paper presented at American Psychological Association Convention Symposium, Toronto, Canada.

Digman, J.M., & Takemoto-Chock, N.R. (1981). Factors in the natural language of personality: Reanalysis, comparison, and interpretation of six major studies. *Multivariate Behavioral Research, 16,* 149–170.

Flanagan, J.C. (1954). The critical incident technique. *Psychological Bulletin, 51,* 327–358.

Hogan, J., & Pederson, K. (1984). Validity of physical tests for selecting petrochemical workers. Unpublished manuscript.

Hogan, J., & Quigley, A.M. (1986). *Physical standards for employment and the courts.* Tulsa: University of Tulsa.

Hogan, R. (1983). A socioanalytic theory of personality. In M. Page (Ed.), *Nebraska symposium on motivation* (55–89). Lincoln: University of Nebraska Press.

Hogan, R. (1986a). *Hogan Personality Inventory Manual.* Minneapolis, MN: National Computer Systems.

Hogan, R. (1986b). *User's manual for the Hogan Personality Inventory.* Minneapolis, MN: National Computer Systems.

Hogan, J., & Hogan, R. (1986). *Manual for the Hogan Personnel Selection Series.* Minneapolis, MN: National Computer Services.

Hunter, J.E., & Hunter, R.F. (1984). Validity and utility of employment tests by race: A comprehensive review and analysis. *Psychological Bulletin, 96,* 72–98.

Hunter, J.E., & Schmidt, F. (1983). Quantifying the effects of psychological interventions on employee job performance and work-force productivity. *American Psychologist, 38,* 473–478.

McCrae, R.R., & Costa, P.T., Jr. (1985). Validation of the big five factor model of personality across instruments and observers. *Journal of Personality and Social Psychology, 56,* 931–939.

Nunnally, J.C. (1970). *Introduction to psychological measurement.* New York: McGraw-Hill.

Reilly, R.R., Zedeck, S., & Tenopyr, M.L. (1979). Validity and fairness of physical ability tests for predicting craft jobs. *Journal of Applied Psychology, 64,* 262–274.

U.S. Social Security Administration. (1984). *Annual Statistical Supplement to the Social Security Bulletin* December.

Wiggins, J.C. (1973). *Personality and prediction.* Reading, MA: Addison-Wesley.

Wunder, R.S. (1981). *Predictive validity of a physical abilities testing program for process apprentices.* Houston, TX: Personnel Research, Employee Relations Department, Exxon, U.S.A.

80 PERSONALITY CHARACTERISTICS OF THE ACCIDENT-INVOLVED EMPLOYEE

Curtiss P. Hansen

A major concern of every industrial business in the world is the avoidance of accidents. Employee accidents threaten the integrity of a company by the personal injuries, lost production time, costly lawsuits, disability payments, damaged equipment, and wasted materials that often result. According to the National Safety Council, 1 million productive-person hours are lost each year due to work-related accidents. In addition, yearly accident costs are estimated to be $31.4 billion in lost wages, medical and insurance expenses, and property damage (National Safety Council, 1983). During 1984, 3,740 employees were killed in work-related accidents in the United States, while almost 2 million workers were injured in industrial accidents (Cotter, 1986).

Many companies have dealt with this problem by creating strong safety departments that have much influence in determining how the work should be carried out. In recognizing that 90 percent of all accidents can be attributed to human error (McKenna, 1983), a typical concern of a safety department is to design the work so that the possibility of error is held to a minimum. Related to this function is the training of personnel in proper procedures and safety regulations (Denton, 1982).

While these efforts are commendable and have certainly had a positive impact on the accident problem, there is another approach to reducing human error that is often neglected. That method is the "personnel selection" approach. This strategy seeks to identify those worker characteristics that differentiate between employees involved in accidents and those not involved in accidents. If personal differences are discovered that are associated with accident occurrences, then future job applicants with those traits may not be hired or will be placed in low-risk positions (Landy & Trumbo, 1980). These "personal differences" may be physical (weight, height, strength, agility), background (education, marital status, home adjustment), perceptual (visual and auditory acuity), or personality characteristics (introverted versus extroverted, calm versus nervous, optimistic versus depressed, passive versus aggressive, careful versus impulsive, etc.). This chapter will focus on the personality traits that have been associated with accident occurrences over sixty-five years of research.

HISTORICAL PERSPECTIVE

The personnel selection method of understanding the individual's personal contribution to the accident process evolved from the decades-long debate over the concept of accident proneness. The first researcher to use this term, Vernon (1918), proposed that workers involved in accidents have an "accident-prone personality," and that is why they have accidents. Although this idea was eventually recognized to be a useless tautology and heuristic dead end in that it tells nothing about how these workers differ from workers without accidents, the basic notion recurs throughout the accident literature even to the present day (Pannain, Correra, Starace & D'Alessio, 1983; Wellman, 1982; Wilson, 1980).

The following are two of the better-known definitions of accident proneness, the first being the original formal statement of the concept, while the second is a more recent formulation. "Accident proneness is a personal idiosyncrasy of relative permanence predisposing the individual to a higher rate of accidents" (Farmer & Chambers, 1926, p. 3). "Accident proneness implies that even when exposed to the same conditions some people are more likely to have accidents than others, or that people differ fundamentally in their innate propensity for accidents" (Shaw & Sichel, 1971, p. 14).

What are the critical requirements of the concept of accident proneness? This is difficult to specify, for, as Cameron (1963) emphasizes, there are many strikingly different versions of the theory. What most of the versions have in common are as follows:

1. Accident proneness is a personality trait or syndrome. Most proponents regard it as a unitary trait.
2. Accident proneness is innate or inherent.
3. Accident proneness is stable across time.
4. The accident proneness trait will "cause" workers to be involved in accidents.
5. Workers with the accident proneness trait will be involved in repeated accidents.

Hundreds of studies have been conducted and published on accident proneness. In evaluating this research, it is clear that the key criteria are not supported. One, the determinents of an accident are multiple, with only a part attributable to personality. Two, a number of personality traits, some unrelated to each other, have been associated with accidents. Three, people rarely, if ever, consistently have repeated accidents throughout their lives (Haddon, Suchman & Klein, 1964; Hale & Hale, 1972).

Although the concept of accident proneness was discredited, the associated research did discover that certain personality traits were strongly related to the occurrence of accidents. Rather than searching for an underlying accident-proneness trait, the focus gradually shifted to the description of how accident-having individuals are different from those without accidents. The remainder of this chapter will review this research.

LOCUS OF CONTROL AND ACCIDENTS

The locus of control construct was developed and operationalized by Rotter (1966). The theory defines an "external" locus of control as the belief that one's efforts to effect change are useless, that events occur "as they will," and that one cannot have an influence over life happenings. Conversely, an "internal" locus of control is defined as the belief that one has the power to achieve mastery over life events. Locus of control is usually measured by Rotter's original scale.

Theoretically, locus of control should be strongly related to accident occurrences. A worker who believes that he or she has little control over involvement in an accident should have a higher probability of incurring an accident (Suchman, 1965). Similarly, the worker who feels in control of events occurring in the workplace would be less likely to have an accident. The latter worker should be more active in preventing the occurrence of an accident, whereas the former will not expend much energy in this regard as it would seem futile from his point of view.

Many studies have supplied indirect evidence establishing a connection between locus of control and accidents. Bridge (1971) and Hoyt (1973) found that internals used seatbelts more often than externals. Wichman and Ball (1983) demonstrated that internality-externality scores could be used to predict safety clinic attendance among general aviation pilots, with internals attending significantly more often than externals. Related to this last finding, Denning (1983) has shown that industrial workers who attend safety clinics have fewer accidents than workers who do not attend. Thus, from the previous two studies, we can logically conclude that internals will have fewer accidents than externals.

The research that is discussed in the remainder of this section are true empirical tests of the locus of control-accident relationship. The most convincing evidence to date has been generated by Jones and his associates. Jones has refined the Rotter Locus of Control Scale by developing questions measuring locus of control for a specific area of concern. This area is employee attitudes toward accidents and safety behaviors. The product of this venture was the Safety Locus of Control Scale (SLCS) (Jones, 1984). In the same vein, Dahlhauser (1982) constructed a Football Locus of Control Scale and discovered that players with an internal locus of control suffered fewer injuries than did externally oriented players.

The SLCS was validated in a study of 120 hotel employees (Wuebker, Jones & Dubois, 1985). Workers were assigned to one of four criterion groups: no accidents, minor accidents, major accidents, and terminations for unsafe behavior. The no-accident and minor-accident groups scored significantly different on the SLCS from the major-accident group. However, there was no difference between the no-accident and minor-accident groups. Thus, the SLCS appears to differentiate among workers on the basis of severity and presence of an accident, with the major-accident group endorsing an external locus of control and the minor/no-accident groups an internal locus of control.

Another study with the SLCS used 283 hospital employees (Jones & Wuebker, 1985a). Using self-reported work injuries for the preceding twelve months as the outcome variable, employees were placed in one of three groups based upon the level of their SLCS scores. The group with the most external SLCS scores had significantly more reported accidents than either the group with the most internal SLCS scores or the group scoring in the middle range of SLCS scores.

A third study validated the SLCS on bus driver applicants (Jones & Foreman, 1984). Twenty-one applicants were classified as high accident risks due to having two or more moving violations on their driving records. The remaining twenty-five applicants were judged to be low risks because they had either one or no moving violations. The results lent further support to the validity of locus of control as a differentiating personal trait in that 79 percent of those "failing" on the SLCS were in the high-risk group, whereas only 31 percent of those "passing" on the scale were in the high-risk category. Two minor studies that lend further support to the validity of the SLCS and the locus of control concept are Jones and Wuebker (1984, 1985b).

Other researchers have conducted empirical studies relating general locus of control to the occurrence of accidents. In one of the best recent studies, Denning (1983) used multiple predictors (e.g., biographical information, psychological tests) and multiple criteria (e.g., number of injuries, severity of injuries, supervisor's rating of safety behavior) in comparing a large sample of injured and noninjured workers at Du Pont Chemical Company. Her results include significant correlations between locus of control scores (Rotter scale) and both self-rated measures of safety performance and supervisor's ratings of safety behavior. More direct evidence was obtained from a cluster analysis, from which it was discovered that workers with high accident and injury rates are comprised of two distinct groups, one of which was characterized by an external locus of control.

In research on automobile drivers, Bridge (1971) found that subjects reporting one or more accidents in the last two years were significantly more external on the Rotter scale than were drivers reporting no accidents. Mayer and Treat (1977) found that locus of control (Rotter scale) was more external for young drivers with three or more accidents in a three-year period than for those without any accidents. Finally, Clement and Jonah (1984) and Mozdzierz, Macchitelli, Planek, and Lottman (1975) reported similar results.

Two recent studies in industrial settings, however, did not find any differences in Rotter locus of control scores among groups with different accident rates (Janzen, 1983; Sims, Graves & Simpson, 1984). Janzen (1983) interpreted these negative findings as due to the inappropriateness of the Rotter scale for some blue-collar workers. The mineworkers and sawmill employees in these two studies probably had difficulty with the language and concepts in the questionnaire, Janzen would suggest. If this explanation is correct, then the need for a situation-specific, industrially related locus of control scale with appropriate language, such as the Safety Locus of Control Scale, is clearly underlined. Overall, though, it appears that locus of control is associated with the occurrence of accidents. Theoretically, the link is strong, and empirical research has lent strong support to the theory.

INTROVERSION-EXTRAVERSION AND ACCIDENTS

The bipolar personality dimension of introversion-extraversion (I-E) as proposed by Eysenck (1947) has been investigated in relation to accidents more than any other personality dimension. I-E is a continuum, with introversion defined as a "person's preference for attending to his inner world of experience, with an emphasis on reflective, introspective thinking" (Morris, 1979, p. 6). Extroversion, conversely, refers to the "preference for attending to the outer world of objective events with an emphasis upon active involvement in the environment" (Morris, 1979, p. 6). The introverted person is described as quiet, intellectual, organized, and emotionally controlled. In contrast, the extrovert is sociable, lively, novelty seeking, carefree, and emotionally expressive.

Eysenck (1962, 1965, 1970) and Keehn (1961) proposed that higher accident rates would be associated more with extroversion than with introversion. This would be expected due to the extrovert's "lower level of vigilance" (Eysenck, 1962). In other words, although the extrovert is more actively involved with the environment, the introvert places a greater value upon being in control of his or her interactions with the world. Thus, the introvert would tend to be more "vigilant" or careful when doing things. Balken (1969), who demonstrated in an experimental study that introverts performed better than extroverts on a vigilance task, concluded that this result was obtained because introverts are more alert and attentive when the environmental situation demands such abilities.

Most of the research relating I-E to accidents has supported Eysenck's prediction. Perhaps the most widely cited study relating I-E to accidents to that of Fine (1963). He found extroverts to have had more traffic accidents and safety violations than introverts. In a recent, yet similar study of 113 twenty- to twenty-three-year-old males, Smith and Kirkham (1981) corroborated Fine's finding that extroversion significantly correlated with both number of accidents and violations. In an industrial setting, Craske (1968) found a high positive correlation between number of accidents and extroversion for males but not for females. In a West German study (Schenk & Rausche, 1979), level of extroversion discriminated among three groups: no accident, one accident, and more than one accident. Finally, Powell, Hale, Martin, and Simon (1971) discovered that extroversion and accident rates were positively correlated for minor accidents in a wide variety of industrial settings. Many other studies have been done that support the extroversion-accident link (Fernandez, 1978; Keehn, 1961; MacKay, DeFonseka, Blair & Clayton, 1969; Mozdzierz et al., 1975; Shaw & Sichel, 1961; Suchman, 1970).

Not all of the research have supported the above conclusions. Cleland, Robinson, and Simon (1971) found no difference between high-accident and no-accident groups on their average I-E scores. Some studies have even found the opposite association, as in Kunda's (1957) study of 100 Indian factory workers. In a more recent study involving Indians, Pestonjee and Singh (1980) found that the no-accident group was more extroverted than the multiple-accident group. In the light of these two studies, it would appear that the association between high accident rates and extroversion does not translate to the Indian culture for unknown reasons.

In conclusion, the majority of the research has shown that extroversion is strongly related to accident occurrences. In their brief review of four I-E studies, Hale and Hale (1972) concluded that "the general agreement is that there is a positive correlation between extroversion and accidents and violations of safety rules" (p. 51).

AGGRESSION AND ACCIDENTS

Aggression is a broad characteristic and ranges from the hostility of a social argument to an assault and battery. The common factor underlying this range of behaviors is most likely the tendency to act out one's anger and frustration to some degree. Many studies have shown that aggression appears to be part of a constellation of traits (see next section for detailed discussion) that are consistently associated with accidents and injuries (Shaw & Sichel, 1971). In an attitude study on accident-incurring drivers, Goldstein and Mosel (1958) discovered that their distinguishing characteristic was an aggressive attitude toward others. Several studies have reported that a high level of general aggression as measured by interviews and personality tests correlated highly with the occurrence of traffic accidents and clearly distinguished accident groups from nonaccident groups (Conger, Gaskill, Glad, Rainey, Sawrey & Turrell, 1957; Davids & Mahoney, 1957; Jimenez, 1977; McGuire, 1972; Schenk & Rausche, 1979; Selzer & Vinokur, 1974; Shaffer, Towns, Schmidt, Fisher & Zlotowitz, 1974; Stewart, 1958; Zelhart, 1972).

Some research has demonstrated that violent acting out of aggressive feelings characterized the lives of people with high rates of accidents (Pandey, Kishore & Jha, 1981; Norali-Daninos, Aubrey & Cerf, 1961; Shaw, 1965), particularly those involved in fatal accidents (Selzer, Rogers & Kern, 1968).

It would appear, then, that aggression is solidly linked to accidents. A more in-depth understanding of the context of aggression in the personality structure of the accident haver will be gained from the next section.

GENERAL SOCIAL MALADJUSTMENT AND ACCIDENTS

Social maladjustment is a general category of behaviors and personality characteristics that have usually been found in combination with each other and have been consistently associated with high accident rates. These have included the following: sociopathic attitudes and past behaviors, delinquency and law breaking, marital or familial strife, disregard for other people, immaturity, emphasis upon exaggerated masculinity (for males), hostility and anger, irresponsibility, superficial social relationships, self-centeredness, problem drinking, and authority problems (Barmack & Payne, 1961; Chambers, 1939; Davids & Mahoney, 1957; McFarland & Moseley, 1954; McGuire, 1956a; Mozdzierz et al. 1975; Pandey et al. 1981; Rommel, 1959; Sarmany, 1975; Schulzinger, 1954; Schwenk, 1967; Selling, 1945; Stewart, 1958; Shaw, 1965; Suchman, 1970; Viney, 1971; Willett, 1964; Wilson, 1980; Wong & Hobbs, 1949; Zelhart, 1972).

The various facets of social maladjustment have been assessed and measured by many different methods such as objective personality inventories, projective tests, biographical information, interviews, and observations. Several of the better-designed and executed studies will be reviewed in the following paragraphs.

The earliest study to link social maladjustment with accidents was that of Tillman and Hobbs (1949). They compared twenty taxi drivers with poor accident records (more than four accidents in the past fifteen years) to a group of twenty taxi drivers with low accident rates on the basis of interview information elicited while riding with each driver. Their findings characterized the high-accident group as having histories of domestic problems (i.e., infidelity, violence), delinquency, frequent job changes due to firings, immaturity, a macho-type grandiosity, and a general lack of responsibility. In a related study of industrial workers, Wong and Hobbs (1949) concluded that a similar list of factors differentiated brewery workers with poor accident records from those with no accidents. In the light of the characterological nature of social maladjustment, the authors conclude that this "accident tendency was a life-long characteristic, and that it appears to invade all aspects of life" (p. 293).

Two of the best studies in this area were conducted on automobile drivers by McGuire (1956b, 1972). Two groups of sixty-seven drivers were carefully matched on the basis of age, driving experience, miles driven, education, and marital status. One group was composed of drivers with at least one accident in the past three months, while the drivers in the other group were without traffic accidents at any time. The several personality tests given described the accident haver as being less mature, experiencing negative attitudes toward laws and authority, and generally having a poor social adjustment. In a follow-up study, McGuire (1972) replicated these findings. In addition, he found the accident haver to be more traditionally "masculine," frequently express hostile feelings, have chaotic family relationships, and prefer nonpersonal contacts with others.

A study by Conger, Gaskill, Glad, Rainey, Sawrey, and Hassell (1959) looked at personality differences between ten military subjects with the worst accident records and the ten with the best records. In the resulting analyses, the high-accident group was clearly more self-centered and indifferent to the rights of others, angrier and more resentful, inappropriately assertive (to the point of belligerence), and generally unable to tolerate frustration without acting out.

Kaestner (1964) compared biographical data on 904 drivers involved in fatal car accidents over a two-year period with those of a comparable control group. He found that the accident group was much more immature and prone to sociopathic acting out. The author felt that the latter point was reflected in this group's many nontraffic-related convictions. Thus, as few as one accident (albeit a fatal one) is sufficient to differentiate people who are socially maladjusted from those with a normal adjustment.

In a series of studies on South African bus drivers (Shaw, 1965; Shaw & Sichel, 1961, 1971), Shaw and Sichel identified two main personality factors that described the drivers with repeated accidents. The primary factor was described as an extreme extroversion with sociopathic features. This personality type was further portrayed as being selfish and self-centered, overconfident and overassertive, resentful and bitter, intolerant and impatient, with pronounced antisocial attitudes or criminal tendencies, and a marked antagonism toward authority.

Hansen's (1989) research with production and maintenance workers in a large, industrial facility supported the existence of a social maladjustment factor as key in accident causation. His results describe one type of accident haver as being resentful, hostile, immature, antisocial, and with a history of delinquency.

In a study of injuries among state police, Wellman (1982) compared 144 officers with and without injury-causing accidents in the past ten years. It was discovered that officers with less than ten years' experience who had sustained injuries were more dominant and belligerent in social interactions and had greater mood fluctuations than similar colleagues with no injuries. Injury-receiving officers with more than ten years' experience tended to avoid social interactions, had fewer friends, and were more superior or macho acting than similar officers with no injuries.

In summary, the evidence is overwhelming in its implication of social maladjustment characteristics in accident causation. That each study has not identified all of these traits does not invalidate the existence of the social maladjustment factor but only points to the limitations of the different personality measurement instruments used in each study.

NEUROSIS AND ACCIDENTS

Eysenck's proposal that extroversion would be associated with accidents was also accompanied by the hypothesis that neuroticism would be correlated with accident occurrences (Eysenck, 1970). Others have echoed his belief in this regard (McFarland, 1957; Tillman & Hobbs, 1949). Neurosis is distinct from social maladjustment by virtue of the subjective emotional distress felt by the individual with the neurotic condition. This distress is usually accompanied by lower self-esteem and confidence. In contrast to neurotic characteristics, the social maladjustment traits are generally more troubling to other people than to the afflicted individual.

The connection between accidents and neurosis should be fairly evident if the intervening variable of "attention to the task" is inserted. Contrary to psychoanalytic thinking, wherein accidents are unconsciously willed as self-punishment by the neurotic person, it is more likely that a neurotic condition causes one's attention to be diverted from the task being done to the person's unpleasant physical or psychic symptoms. For example, the anxious person struggles to control his or her internal anxiety and panic, giving less attention to the details of safe performance. The depressed person is preoccupied with the internal world of ruminations, not with the exigencies of the external world. Hakkinen (1958), in his analysis of a large number of psychological and sensorimotor test data, found that an attention factor had the strongest association with accident occurrences.

The research investigating neurotic aspects of behavior and affect in relation to accidents has either focused on a specific neurotic symptom such as anxiety, depression, or psychosomatic tendency or has simply assessed the overall degree of neurosis in the person. Many studies have related the general neurosis variable to accidents. As a whole, this research is contradictory and confusing. Several studies have found that drivers with accidents were more neurotic than drivers without accidents (Schenk & Rausche, 1979; Smiley, 1955; Suchman, 1970). The strongest evidence for the neurotic component is the factor analytic work of Shaw and Sichel (1971). Their analysis generated an important secondary personality factor, which they termed "neurotic-anxious." This factor was significantly associated with accidents. A person high on this dimension would tend to be anxious, tension ridden, panicky, unduly sensitive to criticism, indecisive, easily intimidated or influenced, and with feelings of inadequacy.

Hansen (1989) developed a measure of general neurosis, which he termed "distractibility." In an industrial setting, this measure clearly distinguished one type of accident haver. These workers were described as tense, nervous, easily fatigued, melancholic, and unable to sustain concentration.

Several studies, however, have found no relationship between accidents and neuroticism (Cleland, Robinson, & Simon 1971; Kainuma, 1965; Pestonjee & Singh, 1980). Smith and Kirkham (1981), though, found that extremely neurotic subjects had a higher accident rate than other groups, even though the "average" neurotic did not. To complicate matters further, two studies have reported an inverse relationship between accidents and neuroticism. That is, neurotic drivers tended to have better safety records than nonneurotic drivers (Alexander, 1953; Andersson, Nilsson & Henriksson, 1970).

The problem in this area of research is that neurosis is a multidimensional phenomenon. Perhaps only a part of neurosis is related to accidents, and perhaps our measures of neurosis are capturing several of its component parts. In some studies the parts correspond; in other studies the parts do not match up. What is needed, then, is for the dimensions of neurosis to be separately measured and related to accidents. Some research has done so by assessing level of depression, anxiety, or psychosomatic tendency.

Several studies have reported that depression and guilt were implicated in accident causation, or at least discriminated among drivers and workers with and without accidents (Craske, 1968; Fernandez, 1978; Paffenbarger, King, & Wing, 1969; Selzer, Rogers & Kern, 1968; Tiffin & McCormick, 1962). The Selzer et al. study dealt with fatal accidents and indicated that the victims had been clinically depressed with suicidal thoughts for some time prior to the accidents. Although anxiety and nervousness are often mentioned in the popular works on accident proneness as being causally implicated with accidents, there are few studies investigating the role of anxiety. Perhaps this is due to the temporary or "state" nature of most anxiety. Whether measured before or after the accident, if the measurement interval is long enough, there will most likely be little evidence of state anxiety. The existing research dealing with anxiety and accidents appears to have measured a long-term or "trait" anxiety.

Shaw and Sichel (1971) identified anxiety as part of their second factor characterizing high-accident-risk drivers. Jenkins (1956) found in his study of industrial workers that those with accidents were easily distracted and had limited attention spans. Their psychological tests revealed a greater degree of anxiety than was shown in the accident-free group's tests. Other studies have corroborated these results (Feaicht, 1972; Paffenbarger, King & Wing, 1969; Rivera Frutos, 1983).

Psychosomatic tendency, or the development of physical illness in response to stress, is related to accidents in that it is often the outcome of chronic anxiety (Rapaport & Schafer, 1968). Smart and Schmidt (1960) report that a group of stomach ulcer patients had a higher accident rate than a group of nonulcer patients. The authors conclude that anxiety is responsible for both the ulcers and the accidents. In a study of police officers, Wilson (1980) found that a group of officers with accidents had an "exaggerated preoccupation" with somatic signs of physical illness.

IMPULSIVITY AND ACCIDENTS

Impulsivity has been implicated in the occurrence of accidents in several ways. One, it is quite logical to assume that a person who acts quickly and without adequate forethought will be at a higher risk for error and, presumably, accidents. Most important, impulsivity has been linked to accidents in many empirical studies. On the basis of observational and interview data from air force pilots who had been in accidents, Biesheuvel and White (1949) concluded that this group was more "emotionally variable and impulsive" than a control group. Schuman, Pelz, Ehrlich, and Selzer (1967) found that young male drivers scoring high on a measure of "impulsive expression" also had more traffic accidents and violations than those scoring low. Selling (1945) found his sample of industrial accident havers to be "reckless."

Barthe (1967) discovered that younger accident repeaters in an industrial work setting were characterized by "impulsive actions," which were judged to be a cause of their accidents. In Denning's (1983) study at Du Pont, impulsivity was a trait that was characteristic of one group of injured workers. Many other studies have demonstrated a relationship between accidents and impulsivity (Craske, 1968; Kunce & Reeder, 1974; Kunce & Worley, 1966; Mayer & Treat, 1977; Mozdzierz et al. 1975; Suchman, 1970 Wilson, 1980; Zelhart, 1972). Overall, the current state of research suggests that impulsivity is a human trait consistently associated with accidents.

RISK TAKING AND ACCIDENTS

It is a common belief that many people who have accidents do so because they take greater risks than people who do not have accidents. However the validity of this popular conclusion is difficult to test. One study that attempted to test this belief was done by Evans and Wasielewski (1982). They observed 2,576 drivers' rush-hour driving behaviors and rated each driver as to the degree of risk exhibited (tailgating, speeding, dangerous lane changes or passes). Using license plate numbers, records of accident involvement and moving violations were obtained for each driver. The authors discovered that the drivers exhibiting risky behaviors also had a significantly greater number of both accidents and tickets than the "safe" drivers.

An interesting laboratory study was conducted using a "risk simulator" by Rockwell (1967). The specific findings of this study are as follows: (1) workers with poor accident records took greater risks than those with good accident histories; (2) skilled workers took fewer risks than did unskilled workers; (3) younger workers took more risks than older workers; (4) females took fewer risks than males; (5) in general, the high-risk taker was more anxious, sociable, and less emotionally stable.

Several other studies have linked risky driving behaviors with accidents (Cohen, Dearnaley & Hansel, 1956; Jonah, 1986; Risser, 1985). While risk taking would seem to relate logically to safety behavior and accidents, however, there has not been enough direct research on this relationship to conclude with a strong degree of confidence that high-risk takers are also high accident risks.

CONCLUSIONS FROM PERSONALITY-ACCIDENT RESEARCH

The previous sections have reviewed the research investigating the relationship between personality-related variables and accident occurrences. Conclusions that appear to be fairly well established are as follows.

1. There is ample evidence that locus of control is related to accidents, specifically that an external orientation is associated with higher accident rates.

2. Extroversion has been strongly related to high accident rates.

3. Aggression has been strongly and repeatedly associated with accidents.

4. There is overwhelming evidence that social maladjustment is not only related to accidents but is probably a primary factor in accident causation.

5. There appears to be a relationship between general neurosis and accidents.

6. Specific neurotic conditions such as anxiety and depression have been associated with accidents in the few studies done on these topics.

7. There is consistent and moderately strong evidence to link impulsivity with accident occurrences.

8. The research is too sparse to conclude anything about risk taking and accidents.

DIRECTIONS FOR FUTURE RESEARCH

The most significant contribution of past research has been to identify the large, multifaceted personality type that is reflected in the concept of social maladjustment. In fact, while treated separately in this review, external locus of control, aggression, extroversion, impulsivity, and risk taking are all theoretically congruent with the socially maladjusted personality style. For the future, it is necessary to continue investigating the other individual components of social maladjustment such as sociopathy, immaturity, authority problems, hostility, irresponsibility, and so forth. If better measures can be developed to assess these characteristics, then our ability to identify the person at high risk to have an accident will be multiplied.

DIFFERENTIAL ACCIDENT LIABILITY

Although there have been many studies on personality and accidents in the past twenty years, there is not an overwhelming interest in the subject among psychologists and managers involved in accident prevention. This relative dormancy is largely due to the past confusion concerning the concept of accident proneness and the seemingly identical issue of personality-accident involvement. When accident-proneness theory was disproved, many researchers also rejected the idea that personality was related to accident behaviors in any manner (Arbous & Kerrich, 1951; Goldstein, 1964; Mintz & Blum, 1949; Whitlock, Clouse & Spencer, 1963). The research reviewed in this chapter should emphasize the potential value of this area of study in understanding the dynamics of the human error component in the occurrence of accidents. Several authors have noted this potential (Hale & Hale, 1972; McGuire, 1976; McKenna, 1983).

In place of the discredited accident-proneness theory, it is proposed here that the concept of "differential accident liability" be used to guide future research and the application of the personnel selection approach to reducing industrial accidents. This concept recognizes that the small number of people responsible for a large number of accidents is a temporally shifting population. Differential accident liability attempts to define the personality parameters of this population at any point in time. It assumes that the same traits are causally implicated in accidents but not that certain people will possess these characteristics consistently over long periods of time. The old accident-proneness theory did not allow for the fact that people change over time. Thus, a person could be quite immature at age twenty-two but later have experiences causing him to "grow up" by age twenty-six. His accident rate at age twenty-two would therefore not correlate with his rate four years later because he is no longer the same type of person.

One might question the value of continued research or employee selection programs based on the differential accident liability concept. The implication is that long-term prediction of an individual's accident liability would not be possible. While this is true, it is also true that long-term prediction of anything involving human behavior is usually quite inaccurate. More realistically, our goal should be the identification of current high-accident risks and the short-term assessment of their accident potential (several years). Obviously, short-term prediction will be most accurate when the differentiating traits are relatively stable. For example, sociopathy is known to be very stable over time (Barlow, 1985) and would be a better predictor than anxiety, which is often a relatively transient state (Rapaport & Schafer, 1978), all else being equal. Yet at one point in time, both may have equal capacity to differentiate on the basis of the accident criterion. Thus, in addition to the worthwhile goal of identifying short-term, high-accident risks (from a business and social viewpoint), the heuristic goal of further understanding the dynamics of the accident liable employee will also have been gained.

Related to the issue of predicting accident occurrences, McGuire (1970) proposed two types of accident tendency: long term and short term, with the former spanning several years and the latter constituting a matter of hours, days, or weeks. In the short-term category, he included the transient situational disturbances brought on by stressful conditions and characterized by brief episodes of anxiety and depression. In the long-term category, he included "character conditions," which are equivalent to the social maladjustment traits detailed in this chapter, as well as clinical neuroses and psychoses. He proposed that the short-term conditions will "clear up" on their own accord. It is the long-term problems that should be the concern of accident researchers, as they are more enduring with outcomes that are more reliable and predictable (relative to a time frame of several years). Sampson (1971) proposed a similar model of long-term and short-term accident liability, while Viney (1971) described long-term accident repeaters as discussed above.

PRACTICAL IMPLICATIONS OF THE STUDY OF PERSONALITY AND ACCIDENTS

What is the value of the research reviewed in this chapter to business? Given the loss statistics cited earlier, it would seem to be of great potential value. If only a fraction of these accidents could be avoided, hundreds of thousands of dollars would be saved, to say nothing of the deaths and injuries that would not occur. How can this potential be realized?

A first step would be to use the available information from accident research to guide the construction and validation of selection tests. McGuire's Safe Driver Scale (McGuire, 1961) is an example of a potent test that was developed by correlating present personality characteristics with future accident and safety behaviors. The Safety Locus of Control Scale has been cited as a powerful instrument that can identify high-accident risks yet only assesses one of the personality characteristics reviewed in this chapter. If industry-related tests could be developed to assess the traits of extroversion, aggression, impulsivity, neuro-sis, and the various facets of social maladjustment, then a comprehensive battery of tests could be assembled that should prove quite powerful in identifying the accident liable worker or job applicant. Once such a job applicant is identified, the person could be assigned to a less hazardous work area or be given intensive safety training and supervision if he or she is hired. For employees who are revealed to be in a state of high-accident liability, the same remedies would be appropriate. However, to be in accord with legal guidelines, applicant data on the discussed variables should not be used as sole determinants of the selection decision but are best used when combined with other validated applicant variables. Finally, Yanowitch, Mohler, and Nichols (1972) discussed the possibility of training employees to recognize when they are most susceptible to accidents. In sum, the field of applied personality-accident research is a worthwhile area for management to invest its money and efforts.

REFERENCES

Alexander, C. (1953). Psychological tests for drivers at the McClean Trucking Company. *Traffic Quarterly, 7,* 186–197.

Andersson, A.L., Nilsson, A., & Henriksson, N. (1970). Personality differences between accident-loaded and accident-free young car drivers. *British Journal of Psychology, 61,* 409–421.

Arbous, A.G., & Kerrich, J.E. (1951). Accident statistics and the concept of accident proneness. *Biometrics, 7,* 340–432.

Balken, P. (1969). Extroversion-introversion and decrement in an auditory-vigilance task. In *Vigilance: A symposium,* D.N. Bucker & I.I. McGrath (Eds.). New York: McGraw-Hill.

Barlow, D.H. (1985). *Clinical handbook of psychological disorders.* New York: Guilford Press.

Barmack, E., & Payne, D.E. (1961). The Lackland accident countermeasure experiment. *Highway Research Board Proceedings, 40,* 513–522.

Barthe, A. (1967). *The study of a group of accident repeaters* (CIS Card 784). Geneva: International Labour Office.

Biesheuvel, S., & White, M.E. (1949). The human factor in flying accidents. *South African Air Force Journal, 1,* 25–36.

Bridge, R.G. (1971). *Internal-external control and seat-belt use.* Paper presented at the meeting of the Western Psychological Association, San Fransisco.

Cameron, N. (1963). *Personality development and psychopathology.* Boston: Houghton Mifflin.

Chambers, E.G. (1939). A preliminary inquiry into the part played by character and temperament in accidents. *British Journal of Psychiatry, 85,* 115–118.

Cleland, E.A., Robinson, C.D., & Simon, J.G. (1971). *Personality and social variables in unsafe driving.* Paper presented at the 6th Annual Conference of the Australian Psychological Society, Melbourne, Australia.

Clement, R., & Jonah, B.A. (1984). Field dependency, sensation seeking, and driving behavior. *Personality and Individual Differences, 5,* 87–93.

Cohen, J., Dearnaley, E.J., & Hansel, C.E.M. (1956). Risk and hazard. *Opinion Research Quarterly, 73,* 67–82.

Conger, J.J., Gaskill, H.S., Glad, D.D., Rainey, R.V., Sawrey, W.L., & Hassell, L. (1955). Psychological and psychophysical factors in motor vehicle accidents. *Journal of the American Medical Association, 169,* 1581–1587.

Conger, J.J., Gaskill, H.S., Glad, D.D., Rainey, R.V., Sawrey, W.L., & Turrell, E.S. (1957). Personal and interpersonal factors in motor vehicle accidents. *American Journal of Psychiatry, 113,* 1069–1074.

Cotter, D.M. (1986). Work-related deaths in 1984: BLS survey findings. *Monthly Labor Review, 109,* 42–45.

Craske, S. (1968). A study of the relation between personality and accident history. *British Journal of Medical Psychology, 41,* 399–404.

Dahlhauser, M. (1982). Visual disembedding and locus of control as variables associated with college football injuries. *Dissertation Abstracts International, 42,* 4985A.

Davids, A., & Mohoney, J.T. (1957). Personality dynamics and accident proneness in an industrial setting. *Journal of Applied Psychology, 41,* 303–309.

Denning, D.L. (1983). *Correlates of employee safety performance.* Paper presented at the Southeastern I/O Psychology Association Meeting, Atlanta, Georgia.

Denton, K. (1982). *Safety management: Improving performance.* New York: McGraw-Hill.

Evans, L., & Wasielewski, P. (1982). Do accident involved drivers exhibit riskier everyday driving behaviors? *Accident Analysis and Prevention, 14,* 57–64.

Eysenck, H.J. (1947). *Dimensions of personality.* London: Routledge & Kegan Paul.

Eysenck, H.J. (1962). The personality of drivers and pedestrians. *Medicine, Science, and the Law, 3,* 416–423.

Eysenck, H.J. (1965). *Fact and fiction in psychology.* Harmondsworth, England: Penguin.

Eysenck, H.J. (1970). *The structure of human personality* (3d ed.). London: Methuen.

Farmer, E., & Chambers, E.G. (1926). *A psychological study of individual differences in accident rates* (Tech. Rep. No. 38). British Industrial Fatique Research Board.

Feaicht, B. (1972). Statistical and clinical studies on accident proneness. In A.R. Hale & M. Hale, *A Review of the industrial accident literature.* London: Her Majesty's Stationery Office.

Fernandez, J.L.S. (1978). Psychology of the automobile driver: Personality factors of drivers with multiple accidents. *Revista De Psicologia General Y Aplicada, 33,* 217–228.

Fine, B.J. (1963). Introversion-extroversion and motor vehicle driver behavior. *Perceptual and Motor Skills, 16,* 95–100.

Goldstein, L.G. (1964). Human variables in traffic accidents: A digest of research. *Traffic Safety Research Review, 8,* 26–31.

Goldstein, L.G., & Mosel, J.N. (1958). A factor study of driver's attitudes with further study on driver aggression. *Highway Research Board Bulletin, 172,* 9–29.

Haddon, W., Suchman, E.A., & Klein, D. (Eds.) (1964). *Accident proneness.* New York: Harper & Row.

Hakkinen, S. (1958). *Traffic accidents and driver characteristics: A statistical and psychological study* (Tech. Rep. No. 13). Helsinki: Finland Institute of Technology, Scientific Research.

Hale, A.R., & Hale, M. (1972). *A review of the industrial accident literature.* London: Her Majesty's Stationery Office.

Hansen, C.P. (1989). A causal model of the relationship among accidents, biodata, personality, and cognitive factors. *Journal of Applied Psychology, 74,* 81–90.

Hoyt, M.F. (1973). Internal-external control and beliefs about automobile travel. *Journal of Research in Personality, 7,* 288–293.

Janzen, J.M. (1983). A study of the relationship of locus of control, age, and work experience variables used to discriminate individuals susceptible to industrial accidents in the sawmill industry. *Dissertation Abstracts International, 44,* 438A.

Jimenez, P.P. (1977). Aggressiveness as a cause of accidents. *Revista De Psicologia Genral Y Aplicada, 32,* 573–579.

Jonah, B.A. (1986). Accident risk and risk taking behavior among young drivers. *Accident Analysis and Prevention, 18,* 255–271.

Jones, J.W. (1984). *The safety locus of control scale.* St. Paul, MN.: St. Paul Companies.

Jones, J.W., & Foreman, R.J. (1984). *Relationship of the HFPSI safety scale scores to motor vehicle reports* (Technical Report). St. Paul, MN: St. Paul Companies.

Jones, J.W., & Wuebker, L.J. (1984). *The HFPSI scores of a fatally injured construction worker.* Research paper presented at the Fourth Annual Construction Insurance Conference, Westin Hotel, Galleria, Dallas, November 13–16.

Jones, J.W., & Wuebker, L. (1985a). Development and validation of the Safety Locus of Control (SLC) Scale. *Perceptual and Motor Skills, 61,* 151–161.

Jones, J.W., & Wuebker, L.J. (1985b). *Psychometric properties of the Safety Locus of Control Scale.* Paper presented at the 27th Annual Conference of the Military Testing Association, San Diego, October 21–25.

Kaestner, N.F. (1964). The similarity of traffic involvement records of young drivers and drivers in fatal accidents. *Traffic Safety Research Review, 8,* 34–39.

Kainuma, Y. (1965). Studies on the personal characteristics of motor vehicle accident repeaters in Japan. *Traffic Safety Report, 1,* 35–46.

Keehn, J.D. (1961). Accident tendency, avoidance learning, and perceptual defense. *Australian Journal of Psychology, 13,* 157–169.

Kunce, J.T., & Reeder, C.W. (1974). SVIB scores and accident proneness. *Measurement and Evaluation in Guidance, 7,* 118–121.

Kunce, J.T., & Worley, B. (1966). Interest patterns, accidents, and disability. *Journal of Clinical Psychology, 22,* 195–207.

Kunda, S.R. (1957). A psychological study of accidents in a factory. *Education Psychology, 4,* 17–28.

Landy, F.J., & Trumbo, D.A. (1980). *Psychology of work behavior* (rev. ed.). Homewood, Il: Dorsey Press.

McFarland, R.A. (1957). Psychological and psychiatric aspects of highway safety. *Journal of the American Medical Association, 163,* 233–237.

McFarland, R.A., & Moseley, L.A. (1954). *Human factors in highway transport.* Cambridge, Ma: Harvard School of Public Health.

McGuire, F.L. (1956a). Rosenweig Picture Frustration study for selecting safe drivers. *USAF Medical Journal, 7,* 200–207.

McGuire, F.L. (1956b). Psychological comparison of automobile drivers. *USAF Medical Journal, 7,* 1741–1748.

McGuire, F.L. (1961). *The McGuire Safe Driver Scale.* Beverly Hills, CA: Western Psychological Services.

McGuire, F.L. (1972). The understanding and prediction of accident producing behavior. *North Carolina Symposium On Highway Safety, 1,* 116–118.

McGuire, F.L. (1976). Personality factors in highway accidents. *Human Factors, 18,* 433–442.

MacKay, G.M., DeFonseka, C.P., Blair, I., & Clayton, A.B. (1969). *Causes and effects of road accidents.* Department of Transportation, University of Birmingham.

McKenna, F.P. (1983). Accident proneness: A conceptual analysis. *Accident Analysis and Prevention, 15,* 65–71.

Mayer, R.E., & Treat, J.R. (1977). Psychological, social, and cognitive characteristics of high-risk drivers: A pilot study. *Accident Analysis and Prevention, 9,* 1–8.

Mintz, A., & Blum, M.L. (1949). A reexamination of the accident proneness concept. *Journal of Applied Psychology, 33,* 195–211.

Morris, L.W. (1979). *Extroversion and introversion: An interactional perspective.* New York: Halstead Press.

Mozdzierz, G.J., Macchitelli, F.J., Planek, T.W., & Lottman, T.J. (1975). Personality and temperament differences between alcoholics with high and low records of traffic accidents and violations. *Journal of Studies on Alcohol, 36,* 395–399.

National Safety Council (1983). *Accident facts, 1983 edition.* Chicago: National Safety Council.

Norali-Daninos, A., Aubrey, J., & Cerf, F. (1961). Psychosomatics and trauma. In N. Aboulker, P. Chertok, & J. Sapir, *Psychology of accidents.* Paris.

Paffenbarger, R.S., King, S.H., & Wing, A.L. (1969). Chronic disease in former college students: Characteristics in youth that predispose to suicide and accidental death in later life. *American Journal of Public Health, 59,* 900–908.

Pandey, R.P., Kishore, G.S., & Jha, S. (1981). Some attitudinal correlates of traffic accidents. *Asian Journal of Psychology and Education, 7,* 44–48.

Pannain, B., Correra, M., Starace, A., & D'Alessio, G. (1983). Victimological aspects of involuntary crimes, with particular reference to road accidents and Italion law. *Victimology: An International Journal, 8,* 53–67.

Pestonjee, D.M., & Singh, U.B. (1980). Neuroticism-extroversion as correlates of accident occurrence. *Accident Analysis and Prevention, 12,* 201–204.

Powell, P.I., Hale, M., Martin, J., & Simon, M. (1971). *2,000 Accidents.* London: National Institute of Industrial Psychology.

Rapaport, D., & Schafer, R. (1968). *Diagnostic psychological testing* (2d ed.). New York: International University Press.

Risser, R. (1985). Behavior in traffic conflict situations. *Accident Analysis and Prevention. 17,* 179–197.

Rivera Frutos, O. (1983). Causes of accident propensity. *Boletin de Psicologia. 6,* 16–24.

Rockwell, T.H. (1967). Some exploratory research on risk acceptance in man/machine settings. *Journal of the American Society of Safety Engineers. 13,* 6–19.

Rommel, R.C.S. (1959). Personality characteristics and attitudes of youthful accident repeating drivers. *Traffic Safety Research Review. 3,* 13–14.

Rotter, J.B. (1966). Generalized expectancies for internal versus external control of reinforcement. *Psychological Monographs. 80* (1, Whole No. 609).

Sampson, A.A. (1971). The myth of accident proneness. *Medical Journal of Australia. 2,* 913–916.

Sarmany, I. (1975). Traumatic affinity and some personality traits. *Psychologie V Ekonomicke Praxi. 10,* 155–160.

Schenk, J., & Rausche, A. (1979). The personality of accident-prone drivers. *Psychologie Und Praxis, 23,* 179–186.

Schulzinger, M.S. (1954). Accident proneness. *Industrial Medicine and Surgery. 6,* 151–152.

Schuman, S.H., Pelz, D.C., Ehrlich, N.J., & Selzer, M.L. (1967). Young male drivers: Impulse expression, accidents and violations. *Journal of the American Medical Association. 200,* 1026–1030.

Schwenk, L.C. (1967). Personality correlates of accident involvement among young male drivers. *Dissertation Abstracts International. 27,* 3734A.

Selling, L.S. (1945). Psychiatry in industrial accidents. *Advanced Management. 10.*

Selzer, M.L., Rogers, J.E., & Kern, S. (1968). Fatal accidents: The role of psychopathology, social stress, and acute disturbance. *American Journal of Psychiatry. 124,* 8–19.

Selzer, M.L., & Vinokur, A. (1974). Life events, subjective stress, and traffic accidents. *American Journal of Psychiatry. 131,* 903–906.

Shaffer, J.W., Towns, W., Schmidt, C.W., Fisher, R.S., & Zlotowitz, H.J. (1974). Social adjustment file of fatally injured drivers: A replication and extension. *Archives of General Psychiatry. 30,* 508–511.

Shaw, L. (1965). The practical use of projective personality tests as accident predictors. *Traffic Safety Research Review. 9,* 34–72.

Shaw, L., & Sichel, H.S. (1961). The reduction of traffic accidents in a transport company by the determination of the accident liability of individual drivers. *Traffic Safety Research Review. 5,* 2–12.

Shaw, L., & Sichel, H.S. (1971). *Accident proneness.* Oxford: Pergamon Press.

Sims, M.T., Graves, R.J., & Simpson, G.C. (1984). Mineworkers' scores for the Rotter Internal-External Locus of Control Scale. *Journal of Occupational Psychology. 57,* 327–329.

Smart, R.G., & Schmidt, W.S. (1960). Psychosomatic disorders and traffic accidents. *Journal of Psychosomatic Research. 6,* 38–42.

Smiley, J.A. (1955). A clinical study of group of accident prone workers. *British Journal of Industrial Medicine. 12,* 263–267.

Smith, D.I., & Kirkham, R.W. (1981). Relationship between some personality characteristics and driving record. *British Journal of Social Psychology. 20,* 229–231.

Stewart, R.G. (1958). Can psychologists measure driving attitudes? *Educational and Psychological Measurement. 13,* 63–73.

Suchman, E.A. (1965). Cultural and social factors in accident occurrences and control. *Journal of Occupational Medicine. 7,* 487–492.

Suchman, E.A. (1970). Accidents and social deviance. *Journal of Health and Social Behavior. 11,* 4–15.

Tiffin, J., & McCormick, E.J. (1962). *Industrial psychology.* London: George Allen and Unwin.

Tillman, W.A., & Hobbs, G.R. (1949). The accident-prone automobile driver: A study of the psychiatric and social background. *American Journal of Psychiatry. 106,* 321–331.

Vernon, H.M. (1918). *An investigation of the factors concerned in the causation of industrial accidents.* Health of Munitions Workers Committee, Memo No. 21.

Viney, L. (1971). Accident proneness: Some psychological research. *Medical Journal of Australia. 2,* 916–918.

Wellman, R.J. (1982). Accident proneness in police officers: Personality factors and problem drinking as predictors of injury claims of state troopers. *Dissertation Abstracts International. 43,* 538B.

Whitlock, G.H., Clouse, R.J., & Spencer, W.F. (1963). Predicting accident proneness. *Personnel Psychology. 16,* 33–34.

Wichman, H., & Ball, J. (1983). Locus of control, self-serving biases, and attitudes toward safety in general aviation pilots. *Aviation, Space, and Environmental Medicine. 54,* 507–510.

Willett, T.C. (1964). *Criminal on the road.* London: Tavistock Publishers.

Wilson, A.W. (1980). Reported accidental injuries in a metropolitan police department. *Dissertation Abstracts International. 41,* 1936B.

Wong, W.A., & Hobbs, G.E. (1949). Personal factors in industrial accidents. *Industrial Medicine and Surgery. 18,* 291–294.

Wuebker, L.J., Jones, J.W., & Dubois, D. (1985). *Safety locus of control and employee accidents* (Technical Report). St. Paul, MN: The St. Paul Companies.

Yanowitch, R.E., Mohler, S.R., & Nichols, E.A. (1972). Psychosocial reconstruction inventory: A postdictal instrument in aircraft accident investigation. *Aerospace Medicine. 43,* 551–554.

Zelhart, P.F. (1972). Types of alcoholics and their relationship to traffic violations. *Quarterly Journal of Studies on Alcoholism. 33,* 811–813.

81 A BEHAVIOR-BASED SAFETY MANAGEMENT PROCESS

Thomas R. Krause

Accidents get a lot of attention, and it is easy to understand why. An accident is a dramatic event that involves both human suffering and considerable expense. Insofar as each accident signals a failure of existing safety systems, safety professionals quite naturally have thought of the accident as their primary item of interest.

At the same time, most managers recognize the fact that accidents are caused by unsafe acts—the behaviors of employees. The question is, What strategy will be most effective in changing the safety-related behavior of employees?

Traditional safety efforts have focused on employee attitudes. This approach has left many managers unsure of their effectiveness because of the difficulties of measurement: How do we know whether our safety effort worked—or failed? Employee attitude is of importance to effective safety management, of course, but only because of its relationship to behavior. A technology now exists that allows the manager to measure safety-related behaviors directly and thus to manage them.

Subsequent to measurement, the key factor to successful management of safety-related behaviors is the proper use of consequences. Two types of consequences are discussed here: charting and verbal feedback.

Finally, four representative case histories are discussed.

FOUNDATIONS OF SAFETY-RELATED BEHAVIORAL CHANGE

According to behavioral science research, the three most significant factors determining a worker's behavior are organizational culture, individual attitudes, and the consequences of the behavior. In order to bring home the importance for safety management of this cluster of factors, let us imagine for a moment that we work for a large manufacturing company where our job is to drive a forklift in a warehouse. As the finished product comes off the assembly line, our responsibility is to move it to the warehouse where we must stack it neatly.

Good performance is defined by how much product we move to the warehouse and how neatly we stack it. There is also an unwritten plant law saying that the best drivers are the ones who drive fast and move a lot of product. However, we also know that we must drive carefully and safely in order to avoid accidents. Even just one spillage of product could mean negative consequences. In short, we are faced with a dilemma: should we drive too fast in order to move a lot of product and be regarded as a "good driver," or should we slow down a bit in order to avoid spilling the product and possibly causing an accident, and risk being regarded as a slow worker?

In this example there are several factors that will influence worker behavior. In order to understand, predict, and manage safety-related behavior, we need to address two questions:

1. How will a worker behave under a given set of circumstances?
2. What will determine or control this behavior?

A thorough grasp of the interplay of the three factors mentioned above lays the foundation for managing behavioral change. In this section we discuss how these three factors—organizational culture, individual attitudes, and the consequences of the behavior—contribute to the way that workers finally behave.

Organizational Culture

Organizational culture is a broad concept used to describe the general practices, procedures, shared values, and climate of an organization. People who work in an organization become aware of its values, climate, and so forth by seeing how others behave as well as by awareness of how things are supposed to be done—in short, what goes and does not go in the organization. This awareness affects the workers' behavior.

For example, take the company that has no explicit dress code for its professional workers. In most cases, without ever asking or being instructed, it is clear to these workers what they may or may not wear to work. This is the organizational culture affecting their behavior.

The same is true for the forklift driver. He knows what behavior is acceptable to the organization because he is aware of the organization's culture. In his case, the unwritten law is that it is "O.K. to speed." He will therefore adjust his behavior according to whatever the organization is willing to tolerate.

Culture has an important impact on safety. It can be particularly detrimental if it encourages unsafe behavior or if it fosters beliefs that are opposed to safety—for example, the belief that safety and production are opposed, that concern for safety problems is the responsibility of only certain, specialized groups of individuals, or that "serious accidents can't happen here." These are all cultural beliefs that affect safety-related behaviors.

Attitudes

Individual attitudes are a second factor that can affect behavior. Attitudes are mental processes. Unlike behaviors, attitudes occur in a person's mind. They are enduring, positive and negative feelings and thoughts that affect our outlook and perceptions of the environment.

What is the relationship between attitudes and behavior? This question is of interest to us in safety because it is commonly assumed that attitudes cause accidents, that is, "This worker broke his arm because of his "bad attitude' toward safety, his boss, or his coworkers." This assumed relationship between attitudes and accidents is common in organizations. We post safety signs, hold "safety awareness" meetings, and talk about safety because we hope that by changing worker attitudes in pro-safe directions, we will cause workers to act more safely.

Considerable research, however, shows that this is not usually what happens. Attitudes are very difficult to change. What is the effect of telling a worker or supervisor to "change your attitude about safety"? Usually this approach is ineffective. In addition, the relationship between attitudes and behavior is not as direct as we would like to believe.

There are better ways to understand and explain why behaviors, and therefore accidents, occur. These explanations center around the consequences of behavior.

Behavioral Consequences

If we are to understand why people choose particular courses of action, we must examine the consequences of their behavior. Consequences control behavior. The focus of this approach is on identifying the specific consequences that control essential or critical safety-related behaviors.

For example, for a forklift driver, one consequence of his speeding behavior could be positive reinforcement such as praise from coworkers (e.g., "what a guy") or from supervisors (e.g., "what a hustler"). He might even get off work early as a consequence of working faster. Certainly these are powerful motivators.

Interestingly, we know from research that consequences such as these are the most powerful motivators that determine behavior. Thus, if we are to change unsafe behavior, we must identify what consequences are motivating (controlling) our workers. Once these consequences are identified, we are then in a position to alter them or add additional ones to change behavior. The remainder of this section will outline methods to identify and control behavioral consequences.

Applied Behavior Management

Applied behavior management is simply a way to analyze human behavior, a way to determine systematically why people behave in certain ways. The model has three components: antecedents, behavior, and consequences. Things or events that come before behaviors are referred to as antecedents, and those that come after behavior are referred to as consequences. The behavior itself is the observable act (e.g., speeding on a forklift).

Antecedents serve as triggers to get behavior going. Examples include training programs, supervisors' instructions, policies, and seeing how others behave. They are what come before behavior and therefore can stimulate workers to behave in certain ways.

Consequences are things that follow or come after behavior. If they are positive and meaningful to the person, they serve to keep the behavior going. Examples include supervisor praise, money, social approval from coworkers, and tangible rewards. If consequences are negative, they serve to suppress behavior. Examples include formal discipline for wrong behavior (e.g., unsafe behavior), ridicule from

Table 81–1
Examples Using Applied Behavior Management

Antecedents	Behavior	Consequences
1. Telephone rings	Pick up phone	Conversation
2. Sign Says "wear personal protective equipment (PPE)	Worker wears PPE	Discomfort, inconvenience, protection
3. Passed by another driver traveling at 70 mph	Drive at 70 mph	Accident, arrive faster, etc.

coworkers, traffic citations, and supervisor disapproval.

Taken together, antecedents, behavior, and consequences combine to form a model of behavior. Table 81–1 shows examples of how the three relate to each other.

In most organizations, the focus of the safety effort is on the antecedents, or those things that go on before a behavior occurs. For example, when a supervisor tells a crew to be careful, holds a safety tailgate meeting, or gives workers a safety manual, he or she is relying on antecedents to make workers safe. Behavioral science research shows us that relying on antecedents to change behavior is often an ineffective approach.

In order to be effective, antecedents must be associated with consequences. For example, an employee will follow a supervisor's instructions to "work safely" only if he or she knows for a fact that consequences will follow upon either safe or unsafe work practices. The consequences in this case could be either punishment for unsafe behavior or praise for safe behavior. If a consequence from the supervisor (either positive or negative) does not follow the worker's behavior, then he or she is far less motivated to follow the supervisor's instructions.

In other words, antecedents are effective in controlling behavior only if they predict a consequence. Taken by themselves, antecedents are virtually ineffective. Simply altering antecedents without consideration of the behavioral consequences will have little effect on behavior. This means that in order to change behavior, one must make some adjustment in consequences.

Performance-Related Feedback

Adjusting consequences in order to control behavior can easily be done via performance-related feedback to workers for safe and unsafe acts. Figure 81–1 illustrates this.

Performance-related feedback can take several forms. One form involves showing workers control

charts that represent the workers' safety-related behavioral performance (i.e., percentage of safe behaviors performed relative to unsafe behaviors). This can be accomplished by an observation and feedback process that involves systematic observation of behavior, feedback charts in the workplace, and verbal feedback from other people.

The type of feedback the worker receives about a behavior determines whether he or she will produce more or less of that behavior in the future. Figure 81–2 demonstrates this principle. Consider a behavior X, which produces feedback to the worker. If the feedback produces an increase in the frequency of behavior X, the event is defined as a reinforcement. For instance, if a worker is praised for cleaning up an oil spill and her oil spill-cleaning-behavior increases, then the praise is a reinforcer.

If the feedback produces a decrease in the frequency of the behavior, it is defined as a punishment. If a worker is criticized by supervisors for leaving tools in the traffic aisle, the criticism would be considered a punishment only if leaving tools in the aisle decreased.

Thus, if we want to increase the frequency of a behavior, it is necessary to provide reinforcement

Figure 81–1. Behavior Feedback Loop

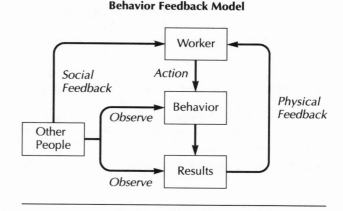

Behavior Feedback Model

Figure 81–2. Types of Feedback

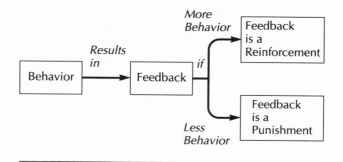

after the behavior is performed. If we want to decrease a behavior's frequency, we follow that behavior with a punishment. This process is called conditioning.

When conditioning is just starting, it is important that either reinforcement or punishment be contingent on behavioral performance. Once conditioning is established, it can be maintained with only an occasional reinforcement. The temporal sequence of behaviors and reinforcements (or punishments) is called a schedule of feedback.

Operationally Defined Behavior

The principles of behavior management sketched here can be effectively applied on only *operationally defined* behaviors. An operationally defined behavior is one that several independent observers would recognize as the same behavior. For example, "working safely" is not an operationally defined behavior. Different people could see it very differently. "Wearing safety glasses and shield while grinding" and, "cleaning up oil spills as they occur" *are* operationally defined safe behaviors.

Once behaviors are operationally defined, it is easy to provide appropriate feedback to increase or decrease their frequency. Without operational definitions, it is difficult to determine when feedback should be provided. This difficulty *always* results in an inconsistent—and therefore unpredictable—schedule of feedback. Since the frequency of behavior can be changed only with a consistent, predictable schedule of feedback, it is easy to see that successful conditioning is possible only with operationally defined behaviors.

This is one of the problems with incentive programs. Incentive programs increase awareness and motivation but do nothing to punish unsafe behavior or to *reinforce* safe behaviors.

Behavioral Consequences in the Workplace

Even though we do not always recognize it, the principles of behavior management are continually operating to change our own behaviors. Consider a worker who reaches in to clear a jammed production line without first stopping it. His or her supervisor may be inadvertently reinforcing this behavior by praising him or her for being concerned with productivity. Further, this type of reinforcement does not have to come from other people. The worker can self-reinforce for maintaining "the unwritten law of the shop" or "being a hustler."

This type of feedback—called social feedback—is very powerful (see figure 81–1). In fact, social reinforcers are the single greatest force shaping behavior. Against this, the occasional punishment of an observed safety infraction cannot help very much. It may have a small temporary effect, but because it leaves the network of social reinforcement intact, unsafe behavior will return as soon as the heat is off. This results in the phenomenon that is frequently seen in safety programs that are in trouble: unsafe behaviors and accidents drop for a while but then increase when the crisis passes and management's attention is directed elsewhere.

Punishment could help if it were contingent on the performance of every, or almost all, unsafe behavior. However, the overwhelming majority of unsafe behaviors go unnoticed. The worker knows that the chance of getting caught is slim, and the risk is preferable to acting differently from the other workers and thereby losing social reinforcement. Thus, the punishment of unsafe behaviors, while a potentially valid approach, cannot be effectively implemented in an industrial setting. It would be monumentally expensive. Since reprisal for unsafe behavior is the heart of many traditional safety programs, it is easy to see why many of these programs take on a negative tone and thus fail to reduce the incidence of unsafe behavior and accidents.

The secondary strategies of traditional safety programs (e.g., toolbox meetings, contests, propagandizing, and education) do very little to modify worker behavior effectively. These programs rely too much on antecedents. Even more critical, they do almost nothing to counter the effects of social reinforcement for unsafe behavior, and they can even indirectly increase such reinforcement.

A more effective strategy is to provide feedback (consequences) to workers for both the safe and unsafe behaviors that they perform. Before this can be done, however, a list of behaviors to observe must be developed. Determining what these behaviors are is our next topic.

MEASURING BEHAVIOR

Critical Behaviors

In order to manage safety behavior, we must have a schedule of reinforcement. This in turn requires the development of a list, or inventory, of behaviors that are critical to safety. For our purposes, critical behaviors are those behaviors that can serve one of two contrary functions: they can make a job safer and thereby decrease the chances of an accident, or they can make a job less safe and thereby increase the chances of an accident.

Before we can change safety-related behavior, we must first have a clear idea of what these behaviors are. Examples of safe and unsafe critical behaviors are as follows:

1. Unsafe: Not wearing full protective equipment.
   Safe: Wearing protective equipment.
2. Unsafe: Failing to follow lock-out procedures.
   Safe: Following lock-out procedures.
3. Unsafe: Moving a drum without a drum truck.
   Safe: Moving a drum with a drum truck.

This section provides instruction on how to arrive at an inventory of behaviors like those above, as well as how to write the behavioral descriptions (operational definitions) that allow for the systematic observation of these behaviors. Later I present the actual procedures necessary to change unsafe behavior to safe behavior.

The Critical Behaviors Inventory (CBI)

The CBI is a list of operationally defined, observable behaviors that are common to any workplace or task at a given facility. The core of the CBI, then, covers such things as housekeeping, personal protective equipment, body use, and position behaviors—areas of behavior that are critical to most organizations. The best method for developing a CBI combines two procedures:

1. Systematic examination of the organization's safety records.
2. Careful interviews of a representative cross-section of its workers.

A careful analysis of a company's safety records for the past several years is a good way of discovering items that should be included in its CBI. The reviewers study each accident with an eye to identifying the behaviors associated with it. The guiding questions of this careful scrutiny are: "What behavior or behaviors *caused* this accident?" and "What must a worker *do* in order to prevent this accident?" The reviewer then adds it to the inventory, taking special care to formulate it in observable, operational terms.

The people charged with developing their company's CBI should also talk with employees—both in order to get them involved in the program and to listen to their concerns about potential hazards, accidents, or injuries in the workplace. The interviewers should plan to talk with 5 to 10 percent of hourly employees and with as many of the supervisors as possible. The interviewers talk with them in small groups and ask them to identify the three kinds of accidents or injuries that they see most often. The most fruitful questions are, "What is unsafe in your work area?" and "What observable acts are you most concerned with for safety's sake?"

Observing Behavior with the CBI

Once an organization's reviewers have developed their Critical Behaviors Inventory, trained observers can take a *dependable measure* of the amount of accident exposure that is present in the workplace. This method of measuring consists of observing critical behaviors and calculating exposure based on these observations. Guided by the results of these behavioral observations, management and supervisors provide *feedback* to workers on how safely or unsafely they are performing their work.

Behavioral observation means going out into the workplace and watching people work. The behavioral observer uses the CBI as a standard against which to score whether the item is being performed safely or unsafely. These observations are conducted on a frequent, but random, basis.

Successful behavioral observations—which means accurate, valid, dependable observations—follow certain procedural guidelines. Before an observation, the workers are told why the observer is there and what he or she will be doing. Being honest with employees about CBI observations is an important way of enlisting their cooperation, a crucial element in any truly sustained safety management program. They must be assured that safety observations are to help them and will not be used against them. It helps to show them the CBI score sheet that the company's reviewers have developed.

A CBI score sheet typically has several categories of behavior (e.g., housekeeping, personal protective equipment [PPE]) The best observational technique is first to observe those categories that are easily seen—housekeeping and PPE are examples—then to take a little more time to observe the more difficult items such as the workers' body use, tool use, compliance with policy and procedure, and so forth.

The following is a complete list of the observation procedure:

1. Observe at a random time of day.

2. Determine a schedule for conducting your observations, usually from once daily to once weekly—more at first, less later.

3. Observe a total of twenty to thirty critical behaviors during each observation period.

4. Observe for about 30 minutes at a stretch.

5. Inform workers of your purpose.

6. Observe housekeeping, PPE, or some other behavior initially.

7. Then observe the other behavioral items in more detail.

Scoring Behavior: Computing Percentage of Safe Behavior

An introductory article such as this is not the place for a detailed presentation of the CBI scoring and computation procedures. The general point is that unsafe behavior is scored differently from safe. For instance, in the case of a particular workstation, if a behavior—wearing gloves, say—is unsafe, then each instance of that behavior is counted, and none of the safe behavior is counted. In other words, during a given observation using the CBI, all instances of an operationally defined behavior must be safe before it is considered safe. Scoring this way makes the measure very sensitive to any change in the unsafe behavior. It can thus reflect small improvements or deteriorations in safety performance—a very important matter when it comes to producing accurate feedback charts.

After an observer has completed the observation of a work site using the CBI, he or she computes the percentage of safe behaviors observed. The percentage of safe behavior is an index of the safety of the observed workplace. On the basis of this ongoing quantitative assessment of the workplace, management can develop baselines (figure 81–3) and provide effective feedback in order to improve the safe behavior percentage.

PROVIDING CONSEQUENCES

We come, once again, to a consideration of consequences. In the opening section of this chapter, I pointed out that consequences are the critical factors effective in changing worker behavior. There are two forms of behavioral consequences that have been useful in changing safety-related behaviors: feedback via the CBI scoreboard (safe behavior percentage graphs and charts) and feedback via verbal reinforcement.

Feedback through Graphs

After behavioral observations have been conducted, worker feedback is provided by plotting the safe behavior percentage on a CBI scoreboard. This Scoreboard is a performance chart (control chart) that indicates to employees their percentage of safe behaviors. The chart plots the percentage of safe behaviors against individual observations.

Figure 81–3 shows a sample feedback chart. On the vertical axis is the percentage of safe behaviors ranging from 0 to 100. On the horizontal axis is the number of observations. The first observation is number 1 on the horizontal axis, the second is number 2, and so on. The chart in the figure shows the results from the first three observations of a workplace. During observation 1, the observer scored the workers at 55 percent safe. Observation 2 produced a score of 65 percent safe, and the resultant score of observation 3 is 55 percent safe—the same as observation 1. This particular chart has room for twenty-one observation scores.

After five observations have been completed, there are enough data to establish baseline levels. A baseline level is simply an index of how safe the workplace is *before* any kind of intervention, training, or feedback occurs. It serves as a yardstick from which to measure subsequent improvement.

For instance, as shown in figure 81–3, the first observation yielded a percentage of 55 percent, and the next two were 65 percent and 55 percent, respectively. For the last two observations, let us say that

Figure 81–3. Plotting Percentage Safe Behaviors

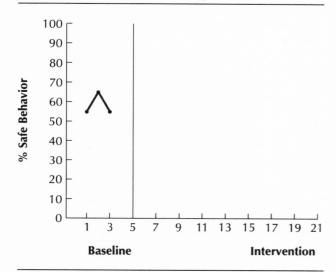

the observer obtained scores of 50 percent and 60 percent. These five percentage scores would then serve as the baseline level of safety performance for our hypothetical workplace.

Changing Behavior with Feedback Charts

The CBI scoreboard is posted in the workplace where everyone can see and inspect it. Supervisors explain what behaviors are reflected on the chart and how to read the chart. This is an opportunity to outline the safety-related behaviors that management and workers want to emphasize (often done with slides) and to say why they are important. The worker group's baseline level is discussed, and they then set a safety performance goal. It is explained to them that when their safety performance line begins to rise, this means that the workplace is becoming safer. When the line goes down, they are more at risk, and the chances of their having an accident are greater. The rise and fall of the line provide the work group with positive *and* negative feedback—remember, positive feedback *increases safe* behavior, and negative feedback *decreases unsafe* behavior—so these qualities of graphic feedback serve to help workers change their behavior.

Feedback through Verbal Reinforcement

Graphic feedback is powerful in changing behavior; another powerful form of feedback to workers are

those things that are said to them by their supervisors and peers while they are working. This is called *social reinforcement,* and it is probably the single most powerful force shaping worker behavior.

While they are conducting their observations, behavioral observers will be providing feedback to workers regarding the safe and unsafe behaviors that they see. Supervisors will also provide verbal feedback.

The following is a review some of the salient points of this very powerful form of feedback. The four statements below spell out the qualities of feedback that are most effective in changing a person's behavior:

1. Feedback is better if it is positive (versus negative).
2. Feedback should be delivered soon after the behavior occurs (versus later).
3. Feedback should occur predictably and consistently after the behavior (versus unpredictably).
4. Feedback must be is contingent on specific, concrete behaviors.

Once a person has learned the behavior, the schedule of reinforcement (feedback) should be made unpredictable and less frequent. This makes the learned behavior resistant to change. This process is called "thinning." Thinning reinforcement too fast or too much causes behavior to revert towards baseline.

Errors to Avoid

There are some areas to consider when reinforcement does not seem to be working.

Not Doing What You Intend. The first thing that can go wrong in providing verbal feedback is failing to provide the intended consequence. This can happen in several ways. People are often unsure of the difference between antecedents and consequences. To give an antecedent all the while thinking that one is giving a consequence is a formula for frustration. For instance, consider this statement: "If I catch you without your hard hat one more time, you're in big trouble." Is this statement an antecedent or a consequence? It is an antecedent and therefore, in and of itself, not terribly effective as a control of whether a worker wears a hard hat. On the other hand, if the statement comes to signal a consequence, then it will become effective. That is, if it is consistently followed up with a consequence, then such a statement has teeth. The employee will know that the consequence actually follows the antecedent. He or she comes to treat the antecedent as though it were the consequence. This is the only way that an antecedent has some power over the behavior.

Using Outmoded Reinforcers. Another way to fail to give a proper consequence is to use an outmoded reinforcer. An outmoded reinforcer is one that the person has had enough of. Reinforcers are related to needs. A person will find things that meet his or her needs to be reinforcing. Often, once a need is met, the thing that met it ceases to be reinforcing. When we are hungry, food is a reinforcer. Once we are full, however, it loses its appeal. Thus, when a supervisor first starts using a reinforcer, it may be powerful; later, it may not be. The alert supervisor does not fall into the trap of using a reinforcer past the point that it is valuable. He or she gives it a rest and uses something else until the need for the first reinforcer grows again.

Sandwiching. Another way in which reinforcement fails is when it is given with one hand and taken away with ther other. A common example of this is known as sandwiching punishment. It has been frequently recommended that criticism or punishment should be preceded and followed by praise or some other positive consequence. This technique of sandwiching the negative between two positives actually undermines the benefit of both praise and criticism. Another common form of taking and giving at the same time happens when goal setting and consequences are combined—for example, "Glad to see you with that glove on, Joe. I hope next time you can manage to wear both of them."

Insincerity. Another and very serious way that reinforcement fails to work is when it becomes insincere and mechanical. The supervisor must not fail to appreciate good performance, nor can he or she afford to feel that it is his or her due. For the same reason it is important that the supervisor express appreciation in a variety of ways. Insincerity is detected easily and is the keynote of manipulation. Related to this is the mistake of being a "nice guy" or an "s.o.b." A "nice guy" is someone who gives rewards habitually, not as consequences. This may make a supervisor popular, but it certainly will not make him or her effective at controlling behavior. An "s.o.b." is someone who habitually gives punishment regardless of whether it is deserved. This makes the punishment ineffective. An employee who has a "nice guy" or an "s.o.b." for a boss learns to use, ignore, or avoid him or her.

Injustice. Ideally, reinforcement or punishment is given always and only as it is deserved. Reinforcement should not be given just when the supervisor feels like it, or when he or she happens to have the time. It must be given as something earned. Reinforcement and punishment are not self-expression; they are something owed to another person because of performance.

Nonsense. So far I have mentioned several ways that feedback can go wrong. All of these mistakes boil down to either not actually giving proper consequences or giving them on an improper schedule. There is another way in which the power of reinforcement is undermined, and that is giving it in ways that do not make sense. This means that the performance-related information that is communicated along with the reward or punishment just does not add up. For example, if a supervisor blows up equally regardless of the size of the offense, there is something that does not make sense about what is being communicated. The same thing goes for someone who responds with the same excitement and enthusiastic praise regardless of the accomplishment. Another example is the supervisor who feels guilty or afraid after he or she has punished someone and so tries to be reinforcing to make up for it. This communicates a mixed message to the person and thereby undermines the value of the consequence.

Summary. The moral of all this is that reinforcement must be given on the proper schedule and that the best guarantee of this is a finely honed sense of justice. This means that the best guide to giving proper consequences is to give a person what he or she deserves, right away. To be good at this requires that the supervisor not assume that good performance is his or her due. He or she must genuinely appreciate it. The other moral is that when a supervisor means to reinforce, he or she must make sure that he or she is indeed giving a genuine, bona-fide, good-as-gold reinforcement.

Verbal Feedback

Skillful verbal feedback has several important characteristics: it must be clear, it must elicit commitment, and it must provide guidelines. Verbal feedback is a two-way process, and to be completed it requires that the person who is listening communicate back.

Personal contact mediates effective communication. Skillful communicators do the following things. They take the initiative and make contact with the person they want or need to talk to. They do this explicitly by informing the person that they want to talk to him or her. They set up a time and a place. They let the other person know what the subject matter is. They touch the other person to get his or her attention, address the person by name or title, and look the other in the eye.

Effective communication gathers in the other person's attention; therefore, it should be interesting and relevant. The expression of job-related concerns often accomplishes this. Skillful communication is clear, specific, and to the point. It does not take a bite too large to be digested in the time alloted.

In effective communication, what is communicated nonverbally must match with what is communicated verbally. A supervisor who is saying something important must not look bored or apathetic. The content of what is said must be reasoned and logical. It must convey objective necessity in terms that are relevant to the person being communicated with. This means that the communicator should think through what to say. It is often necessary to demonstrate what is being talked about or to step through it. This is because words alone are frequently not enough to convey the complete meaning in the time alloted.

Finally, for communication to be effective, the feedback loop must be completed. The other person must communicate back his or her understanding and commitment to the supervisor. If this step is omitted, the supervisor has lost control of the communication process because he or she does not really know what was accomplished.

The principles of effective verbal communication indicate the following about giving verbal feedback. The supervisor must take the initiative, pick the time and place, and make solid contact. Thinking through what he or she wants to say means considering what he or she knows about the things that reinforce the person he or she will be talking with. Being clear means that the supervisor identifies precisely which behavior he or she is reinforcing and why it needs to be reinforced. Completing the feedback loop means that the supervisor makes sure that he or she said was actually reinforcing.

FOUR CASE HISTORIES

The following are case histories of companies using a behavioral approach to safety management. These four cases are drawn from a broad spectrum of industries. The human side of the data shows up in various ways—in the positive effect the process has on employee morale and involvement and in the enthusiasm it fosters in supervisors. The key to using the behavioral process successfully is employee involvement. Fortunately, this coincides with other goals that most companies already have, goals such as improving quality, getting hourly employees more involved, and improving supervisory skills. Safety performance is an ideal target to focus on in order to get results in all of these areas.

Company 1 is a manufacturer of specialty chemicals with 700 employees. This company had achieved record-holding safety performance for the preceding several years, but during that time improvement had leveled off, with very slight increases. In an effort to change this, behavioral observation and feedback were used extensively to develop and apply an inventory of behaviors that were critical for the improvement of the safety performance of this company. This inventory is the Critical Behaviors Inventory. First-line supervisors each received a 20-hour training course in behavioral methods. Observers were drawn from all levels of the company. Safe behavior was charted and displayed extensively, and tracked by department using a specialized computer software program. The results were that safe behavior

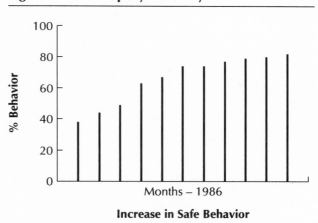

Figure 81–4. Company 1's Safety Record

Increase in Safe Behavior

Decrease in Accident Frequency

increased plantwide from 39 percent to 81 percent over one year, and during that same period, total injuries decreased by 45 percent (figure 81–4).

Company 2 is an oil Drilling company with 250 employees. This company had a safety record well above average for the industry, but for the years 1976–1981 safety performance had leveled off. The safety manager, who was strongly committed to improving the company's record, was frustrated by the performance plateau.

Over one year, each foreman received a 20-hour training course in behavioral methods, and hourly employees each received a 2-hour training course. An extensive CBI was developed for the company's operations, and behavioral observations were conducted with charted feedback of safe behavior (figure 81–5). The results were that overall safe behavior increased from 79 percent to 94 percent in the first year, and recordable injury frequency rate decreased 20 percent in the first year and 35 percent in the second year.

Company 3 is a heavy equipment manufacturer with 1,100 employees, acquired just prior to the year

in question by an international company with a strong safety record. Traditional safety program efforts at this manufacturing plant had failed to reduce the high incidence rate of on-the-job injuries.

The process of change began with the foremen, who were central to the approach. Each received a 20-hour training course in behavioral methods for accident prevention. Behavioral observation and feedback were used extensively to develop a CBI, and unsafe behavior percentages were charted. The results were that unsafe behavior decreased 60 to 80 percent over one year, and lost-time accident frequency decreased 41 percent over one year, with further decreases in subsequent years (figure 81–6).

Company 4 is a transit authority with 6,000 employees. Though the accident rates for this municipal transit authority were low for the industry, they still produced staggering workers' compensation costs.

To change this, bus operators were involved in the process of developing the company CBI. Supervisors

Figure 81–5. Company 2's Safety Record

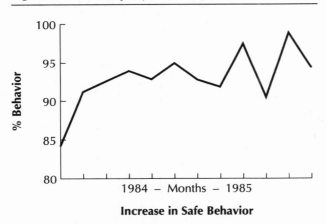

Increase in Safe Behavior

Figure 81-6. Company 3's Safety Record

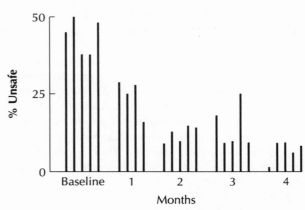

Decrease in Unsafe Behavior

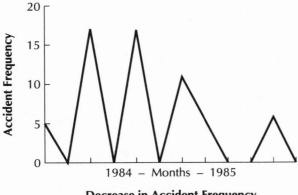

Decrease in Accident Frequency

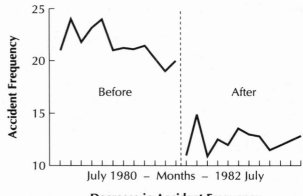

Decrease in Accident Frequency

and operators each received an 8-hour course in behavioral methods. Operators were taught to observe and chart their own critical behaviors daily. Supervisors were taught how to observe each operator two times a month. A feedback graph was developed for each bus operator that charted both the supervisor's ratings of the operator and the operator's self-observed ratings. Following each bimonthly supervisor observation of an operator, there was a discussion of any discrepancy between the operator and supervisor ratings.

Though operators admitted that they were reluctant to rate themselves unsafe, they nonetheless said they learned from the CBI procedure and were very enthusiastic about it. Greater operator objectivity was reflected in their self-observations. At the beginning of the CBI process, most operators rated themselves 95 to 100 percent safe, but within a few months, their own ratings declined to more accurate levels (figure 81–7). Supervisor observations of operators typically started at the 50 to 60 percent level of safe behavior. Within a few months supervisors rated

Figure 81–7. Company 4's Safety Record

Increase in Safe Behavior

the operators at 80 to 90 percent safe. Accident rates declined 66 percent during the four-month period following the training.

ADDITIONAL SOURCES

Chhokar, S.J., & Wallin, J.A. (1984). Improving safety through applied behavior analysis. *Journal of Safety Research, 15* (4), 141–151.

Cleveland R. et al. (1979). *Safety program practices in record-holding plants* (National Institute for Occupational Safety and Health, Publication No. 79–136). Morgantown, WV.

Cohen, H.H., & Jensen, R.C. (1984). Measuring the effectiveness of an industrial lift truck safety training program. *Journal of Safety Research, 15* (3), 125–135.

Fellner, D.J., & Sulzer-Azaroff, B. (1984). Increasing industrial safety practices and conditions through posted feedback. *Journal of Safety Research, 15* (1), 7–21.

Geller, E.S. (1984). A delayed reward strategy for large-scale motivation of safety belt use: A test of long-term impact. *Accident Analysis and Prevention, 16* (5/6), 457–463.

Haddon W., Jr., & Baker S. (1980). Injury control. In D. Clark & B. MacMahon (Eds.), *Preventive and community medicine,* (2d ed.). Boston: Little, Brown.

Haynes, R.S., Pine, R.G., & Fitch, H.G. (1982). Reducing accident rates with organizational behavior modification. *Academy of Management Journal, 25* (2), 407–416.

Kim J., & Hamner C. (1976). Effect of performance feedback and goal setting on productivity and satisfaction in an organizational setting. *Journal of Applied Psychology, 61,* 48–57.

Komaki J., Barwick K.D., & Scott L.R. (1978). Behavioral approach to occupational safety: Pinpointing and reinforcing safe performance in a food manufacturing plant. *Journal of Applied Psychology, 4,* 434–445.

Komaki, L.J., Collins, R.L., & Penn, P. (1982). The role of performance antecedents and consequences in work motivation. *Journal of Applied Psychology, 67* (3), 334–340.

Komaki J., Heinzmann A.T., & Lawson L. (1980). Effect of training and feedback: Component analysis of a behavioral safety program. *Journal of Applied Psychology, 65* (3), 261–270.

Krause T.R., Hidley J.H., & Lareau W. (1984). Behavioral science applied to industrial accident prevention. *Professional Safety* (July).

Levensen, H. et al. (1979). Industrial accidents and recent life events. *Journal of Occupational Medicine, 21,* 26–31.

Levi, L. (1979). Occupational mental health: Its monitoring, protection, and promotion. *Journal of Occupational Medicine, 21,* 26–32.

McIntire R.W., & White J. (1975). Behavior modification. In B. Margolis & W. Kroes, eds. the *human side of accident prevention.* Springfield, Ill: Charles C. Thomas, 1975.

Peterson, D. (1981). *Human error reduction and safety management.* New York: Garland Press.

Peterson, D. (1984). An experiment in positive reinforcement. *Professional Safety, 29* (4), 30–35.

Reber, R.A., & Wallin, J.A. (1983). Validation of behavioural measure of occupational safety. *Journal of Organizational Behaviour Management, 5*(2), 69–77.

Reber, R.A., Wallin, J.A., & Chhokar, J.S. (1984). Reducing industrial accidents: A behavioural experiment. *Industrial Relations, 23*(1), 119–125.

Rhoton, W.W. (1980). A procedure to improve compliance with coal mine safety regulations. *Journal of Organizational Behaviour Management, 2*(4), 243–249.

Schaeffer M. (1976). An evaluation of epidemiologic studies related to accident prevention. *Journal of Safety Research, 8,* 19–22.

Smith, M.J., Anger, W.K., & Uslan, S.S. (1978). Behavioral modification applied to occupational safety. *Journal of Safety Research, 10*(2), 87–88.

Sulzer-Azaroff, Beth, & de Santa Maria, M.C. (1980). Industrial safety reduction through performance feedback. *Journal of Applied Behavior Analysis, 13,* 287–295.

Sulzer-Azaroff, B., & Fellner, D. (1984). Searching for performance targets in the behavioral analysis of occupational health and safety: An assessment strategy. *Journal of Organizational Behaviour Management, 6*(2), 53–65.

Zohar, D. (1980). Promoting the use of personal protective equipment by behavior modification techniques. *Journal of Safety Research, 12*(2), 78–85.

Zohar, D., & Nussfeld, N. (1981). Modifying earplug wearing behaviour by modification techniques: An empirical evaluation. *Journal of Organizational Behaviour Management, 3*(2), 41–52.

82 PROVIDING DISABILITY MANAGEMENT AND REHABILITATION COUNSELING SERVICES IN THE WORKPLACE

Rochelle V. Habeck, Stephen J. O'Connor, Michael J. Leahy

Nationally, the problem of disability has become too significant to ignore. A profile of the disability costs was offered by Carbine and Schwartz (1987) in summarizing the outcome of a recent national conference. For example, in the past twenty-five years, there has been a 400 percent increase in the number of severely disabled people, predominantly male, between the ages of seventeen and forty-four, representing an important segment of the work force in its most productive years. In 1986 alone, approximately $140 billion in disability claims were paid out by business and government. On average, short-term disability costs comprise 2 to 4 percent of an employer's total payroll, and long-term disability costs add on another 1/2 to 1 percent. Employers can expect the total costs of an average work injury to be $19,000. And companies that have 1,000 employees can expect twenty-seven lost work-day injuries per year. Given a 4 or 5 percent profit margin, it would take $11.3 million in sales for a company to offset these costs (Carbine & Schwartz, 1987). In the area of workers' compensation disabilities alone, from 1980 to 1985 the cost of wage loss payments increased 57 percent, the cost of medical benefits 88 percent, and the cost of premiums 67 percent. Low back pain makes up almost half of these cases (Abraham, 1988).

The growing magnitude of the economic and human costs of the disability problem for employers and employees has provided a compelling reason for companies to provide effective disability management and rehabilitation practice as a critical business and human resource strategy. As Carbine and Schwartz (1987) pointed out, in most companies disability benefits, medical benefits, and workers' compensation activities are usually not integrated in their administration, financing, data tracking, plan design, or case management.

In a 1986 survey of disability policies and practices among 400 major employers, Schwartz found that fewer than one-third of the responding employers reimburse for vocational rehabilitation services, and roughly one-third have a designated person responsible for coordinating and managing disability benefits. Although only a few of the respondents employ full-time rehabilitation consultants to work with employees who have disabilities, nearly half the companies have developed case management programs, and many more intend to adopt this approach. A small minority of these employers provides rehabilitation in their long-term disability policies.

Now, many leaders in the business and labor community have begun to experiment with proactive intervention strategies—prevention and health promotion, early identification of employees at risk, placement specialists for light duty, modified, or transitional work, expanded use of employee assistance programs (EAP) and referrals, claims and case management—to prevent or reduce the impact of disability (Galvin, 1986). An increasingly broad range of companies are implementing various approaches to manage disability and have demonstrated that carefully planned and coordinated disability and rehabilitation services can be cost beneficial (Carbine & Schwartz, 1987). This evolution of the concept and practice of disability management has been thoroughly summarized elsewhere (Galvin, 1986; Tate, Habeck & Galvin, 1986; Schwartz, 1986; Mitchell & Shrey, 1985).

The importance of prompt provision of rehabilitation services cannot be overstated. As Levitan and Taggart (1982) have pointed out and numerous subsequent studies have supported, "the key to continued labor force participation is the ability to remain in the same job after the onset of the disabling condition" (p. 129). They argue that the evidence supports the notion that once the tie to the labor force is severed, it is common for individuals to adapt to income transfer payments, and other obstacles evolve that create substantial barriers to returning to the labor force. They propose that the goal should be to reach individuals while they are still on the job and to prevent them from transferring to disability benefits at all.

Thus, Ed Eckenhoff, president of the National Rehabilitation Hospital, has observed that the concept of employer-based disability management and rehabilitation provides a unique fit between humanitarian and utilitarian values, social and economic benefits, and qualitative and quantitative potential (Galvin, 1986).

THE CONCEPT OF DISABILITY MANAGEMENT

The aim of disability management, then, is to prevent human and economic loss from disability by minimizing the occurrence and impact of disability on the individual worker and the work force as a whole. The intended results are interrelated: to improve employees' security and quality of life, to improve the productivity of the work force, and reduce the costs of injury and illness for the company. Three specific objectives for achieving these results are:

1. *Prevent* or avoid disabilities from occurring in the workplace through safety, ergonomic, and health promotion.
2. *Early intervention* for health risks and management of illness and injuries when they first occur to minimize disability and absence from work.
3. *Restore* working capacity and facilitate a timely return to work *through* early and aggressive *rehabilitation* for those whose conditions require accommodation in usual routines.

The specific focus of employer programs often depends on the perspective of the persons involved and where it took root in the company. As an evolving approach, there is no "recipe" that defines the precise ingredients for such a program or a set formula for putting the ingredients together in such a way that guarantees its success. There are, however, elements that have been repeatedly identified in the successful corporate programs to date (Evert, 1982). Most important, these efforts are a comprehensive, systematic, and coordinated activity that is part of the company's total operation; they have active support from an informed top management and are rooted in a genuine corporate philosophy of commitment to employees. These elements can be summarized as follows:

1. Corporate leadership (e.g. public statements, written policy, management behavior).

2. Administrative capacity (e.g., automated and integrated disability claims function, data analysis and review of safety, medical, benefit experience).
3. Managed organization process (e.g. identified responsibilities and decision making, interdepartmental systems).
4. Supportive policies and programs (e.g., return-to-work incentives and accountability for supervisors and employees, rehabilitation-orientation benefits and controls in benefit design, vendor selection and evaluation)
5. Specific services and procedures (e.g., safety training, wellness, screening, case management, transitional/modified duty placement procedures; in-house or contracted rehabilitation services).
6. External linkages (e.g., education of community medical providers, relationships with local community resources).

As noted earlier, an array of program models and strategies has been successfully implemented and described A few are briefly presented here to illustrate different aspects of these approaches and the outcomes achieved.

Administrative Approach

The Honeywell Corporation implemented a decentralized system for workers' compensation, with claims management and cost control functions taking place at the divisional level to maximize results. They estimate that costs decreased by 80 percent from 1979 to 1986. The program achieved informed participation of top management, unions, managers and supervisors, and local medical providers. A comprehensive system of claims administration and documentation was developed to prevent fraud, effectively manage claims, and achieve return to work through a committee of the administrator, union, employee, and supervisor (Carbine & Schwartz, 1987). Honeywell also provides an extensive prevention program and a light-duty program for return to work.

Preventive Approach

The Walbro Corporation implemented an athletic training model in a new, on-site wellness facility to strengthen "industrial athletes" so as to prevent the most frequent injuries due to sprains and strains and to provide on-site restorative treatment for minor injuries that do occur. In less than one year, the full costs for start-up of the center and its sophisticated training and treatment equipment, expected to take several years to recapture, were offset due to cost savings. Costs due to sickness and accidents have dropped, and recovery time for work and nonwork-related disabilities have decreased.

Transitional Work Approach

The Herman Miller Corporation began its Transitional Work Center in 1982 to reduce loss time from injuries, provide productive work for employees with physical restrictions, and demonstrate its values toward its employees. Described as a program rather than a place, the center attempts to match the recovery needs of employees with existing work opportunities throughout the company in order to promote reintegration and avoid the negative aspects of sheltered work. Over 400 employees have been served by the program to date, which includes coordination with company medical services, local medical providers, benefits representatives, and external vocational rehabilitation providers. The proportion of cases resulting in days away from work and the number of days away has decreased, and the program is highly rated by employees, supervisors, and managers as having essentially achieved its major objectives.

THE PROVISION OF REHABILITATION COUNSELING SERVICES

Rehabilitation counseling services are an important feature of the return-to-work aspect of employer-based disability management and rehabilitation programs. Depending on the size and focus of the program, rehabilitation counseling services may be provided by hiring an internal, full-time employee in the company or by contracting services from an external vendor. A brief introduction to the profession of rehabilitation counseling and its application to disability management are summarized here.

General Features of the Profession

Rehabilitation counseling is a dynamic professional discipline that has consistently responded to change, expansion, and the evolution of its professional roles in providing needed services to individuals with disabilities. The discipline began as the result of federal legislation in 1920 (Smith Fess Act, P.L. 66–236), which authorized specific employment-related services to a limited population of individuals with physical disabilities under state-federal sponsorship. Now, vocational rehabilitation services in this country can be viewed as three distinct efforts: public, private nonprofit, and private for profit. As a result of tremendous growth over the past seventy years, the

field of rehabilitation counseling has broadened to include a wide range of clientele, services, goals, sponsors, and settings (Danek, Wright, Leahy & Shapson, 1987), and it has acquired the status of a profession with associated graduate preparation, a body of literature and research, ethical codes, professional associations, and requirements for credentialing. The emergence of the rehabilitation counseling role within employer organizations currently represents one of the newest settings for professional practice.

In general, rehabilitation counseling can be described as a facilitative process that assists clients with disabilities to understand existing problems and potentials and to help make effective use of personal and environmental resources for the best possible vocational, personal, and social adjustment following injury or illness (Jacques, 1970). The effective role of the rehabilitation counselor, who is the central professional person in the postmedical phase of rehabilitation, is as a problem solver who perceives the problems of each individual client as they relate to vocational adjustment within specific environments and to help plan and implement appropriate intervention strategies (Maki, McCraken, Pape & Scofield, 1978). In applied practice, rehabilitation counseling draws upon several fields of psychology, including counseling, clinical, industrial and personnel, measurement, and rehabilitation psychology (Wright, 1980).

In response to disability-related problems, the rehabilitation counselor operates as a vocational expert from a psychological base, functions as part of a psychosocial and health-related team, and provides a broad range of services for individuals with disabilities (Jacques, 1970). Thus, rehabilitation counselors play a multifaceted role in the provision of services to individuals with disabilities, which includes effective case identification, intake and diagnosis, plan development, service provision, placement, and follow-up (Rubin & Roessler, 1987). Counselors must be able to assess the functional impact of disability (e.g., medical, psychosocial, and vocational aspects) and have the knowledge and skills to utilize all environmental resources available to effect appropriate employment outcomes. The fundamental competencies of rehabilitation counselors include client assessment, vocational counseling, personal adjustment counseling, individual and group job placement services, job development, and case management.

The trend toward private sector practice in recent years has emphasized other competencies as important for these practitioners and introduced new knowledge and skill areas. Practitioners in the proprietary sector are usually highly skilled in short-term evaluations of transferable occupational skills, job placement, and knowledge of workers' compensation legislation. They usually have special skills in job analysis, labor market surveying, job restructuring consultation, and medical case management (Matkin, 1985). The "return-to-work" philosophy of private rehabilitation tends to be the predominant focus of services provided, using counseling and case management skills to effect appropriate internal and external relationships, services, and outcomes for injured workers and employer organizations.

Special Features of Employer-Based Practice

The exact nature of the competencies required by the practitioner will vary greatly, depending on the extent to which a program has developed within the employer organization, the type of program, and the specific characteristics of the organization. According to Habeck and Munrowd (1987) three levels of practice roles may be required of rehabilitation counselors within employer organizations: (1) the clinical and direct service role, (2) the administrative and program development role, and (3) organizational change agent role. Depending on the level of sophistication of the employer organization in dealing with effects of disability on the work force, the rehabilitation counselor may be required to perform

supplemental functions not typically associated with the role (Habeck & Munrowd, 1987). These might include corporate disability analysis, program development, coordination and evaluation, training and consultation, and referral and vendor selection.

In order to perform these functions effectively, counselors in these settings must be knowledgeable about organizational behavior and development, legislation, insurance and benefit systems, corporate and union agreements, prevention and wellness approaches, and the collective bargaining process. Additional skills that may be emphasized within this environment include needs assessment, policy analysis, communication, and management. Given the complexity of these tasks and the need for expanded knowledge and skills, rehabilitation counselors who will effectively enter this area of practice need to be experienced individuals with appropriate professional training and a high degree of knowledge and skill.

As with any other emerging area of practice, there are a number of different approaches to providing rehabilitation services within employer-based settings. This lack of crystalization in the roles and required competencies is partially a function of the newness of the sector and the diverse setting characteristics and needs of employer organizations. Examples of a few divergent approaches are presented to provide an illustration of a number of models in practice today.

Corporate Examples of Rehabilitation Counseling Services

At the Buick, Oldsmobile, Cadillac (BOC), Lansing Product Team, Division of General Motors (Tate, Habeck & Munrowd, 1987) an in-house rehabilitation program was developed in conjunction with the Rehabilitation Counseling Program at Michigan State University. A team approach was implemented including medical, benefit, and rehabilitation specialists and external rehabilitation providers. Departments were brought together to facilitate a coordinated rehabilitation service approach. A rehabilitation specialist position, staffed by a rehabilitation counselor, was created to monitor the system, implement an organized system for selecting and evaluating external service providers, identify and screen appropriate referrals to these providers, provide liaison with departments, coordinate team meetings, and develop monthly cost tracking and reporting mechanisms. Critical to the success of the approach was support from management and unions, along with extensive and ongoing inservice education.

At the Xerox Corporation (Hoeffel, 1987) the rehabilitation counselor's position is referred to as the rehabilitation coordinator. The rehabilitation coordinator has a background that combines medical training and rehabilitation counseling, bringing unique and necessary qualities to the team in the areas of medical information, case management, job analysis, evaluation, placement, and psychology. At Xerox, the rehabilitation professional's role is one of teacher, trainer, consultant, and counselor and has continued to expand as program effectiveness is demonstrated. The coordinator is part of the company's clinical and disability services staff and provides an array of preventive, rehabilitative, and placement services to disabled employees. This direct service role is contrasted with that of the rehabilitation specialist at BOC where the focus is on referral and coordination of services provided by external providers.

Another notable approach to the provision of rehabilitation counseling services is one operated for several years by the 3M Corporation. At 3M, a coordinated disability management program was implemented by centralizing staff responsibility for long-term disability benefits, workers' compensation, and rehabilitation (Beaudway, 1986). Within this coordinated program, specific rehabilitation services may be provided by its own rehabilitation staff, by contracting services from external private rehabilitation providers, or by referral to state vocational rehabilitation agencies. Services most often used include case assessment, job analysis, medical coordination, and job placement.

Effective Use of Services

Few companies have hired full-time rehabilitation counselors to provide services. Rather, most services are obtained from external providers of vocational rehabilitation and case management services on a contractual basis. In the past, these services were primarily available only from public agencies. Since 1970, changes in workers' compensation and insurance laws and the growing recognition by employers of the need for and value of rehabilitation services have contributed to dramatic growth of the private rehabilitation sector as providers of services to insurance sponsors and employer programs. Gardner (1987) outlines the differences between public and private sector vocational rehabilitation programs and makes the case that in the area of workers' compensation, rehabilitation private for-profit and nonprofit providers have been able to be more flexible and responsive and to have achieved more desirable outcomes than traditional public rehabilitation agencies, by virtue of their distinct mandates, philosophies, and operations. While the benefits of these services have been stressed, the costs of private sector rehabilitation services to third-party sponsors have grown at 30 percent each year, from less than $250,000 in 1972 to over $450 million in 1982 (Schwartz, 1986). Thus, employers and their insurers have begun to include rehabilitation services among the many costs of disability that require strategies for effective management.

In the case of BOC General Motors, 3M, the Michigan Hospital Association, and many other employers, the rehabilitation counselors hired by these companies have taken on the combined roles of program, case manager, and, to varying degrees, direct providers of clinical services. Several advantages accrue when rehabilitation counselors are hired as internal employees of the company: (1) they can more easily ensure that early intervention occurs in a timely way; (2) they are more familiar with the inner workings of the company and can establish relationships that improve access to suitable job opportunities for restricted workers; and (3) they are more available for supportive and follow-up services after return to work. In-house, they often take on the functions of facilitating the overall disability management effort, assisting the education and awareness of managers, employees, and unions, ensuring communication across departments, selecting and monitoring external providers of contracted rehabilitation services, and coordinating services for individual return-to-work programs.

Whether a company should consider hiring a rehabilitation counselor on staff will depend on the size of the company, the number of disabled employers in a given location, whether the type of industry is likely to experience a high incidence of disability, how adequate and cost-effective the rehabilitation services available in the local community have been, and the availability of other resources within the company that could take on these coordinating functions (Schwartz, 1987). Regardless of the program model, it is likely that most companies or their insurance carriers are purchasing specific rehabilitation services. Accordingly, companies should develop specific criteria for selecting, using, and evaluating vendors of rehabilitation counseling services. The Institute for Rehabilitation and Disability Management (IRDM) of the Washington Business Group on Health has identified several principles to assist employers in this process (Schwartz, 1986; Carbine & Schwartz, 1987).

Companies that have been successful in using rehabilitation counselor services have incorporated these services and the providers in the company's overall strategy for disability management (which includes the essential elements and human resource philosophy outlined earlier). These companies stay involved in cases referred out for service through case management, regular monitoring, and communication with all parties (Carbine & Schwartz, 1987). Effective use also requires the creation of criteria for the following aspects of vendor use:

1. Selecting cases that are appropriate candidates for referral (e.g., age, length of time off work, severity of disability).

2. Selecting desirable vendors (e.g., familiarity with the jobs and the workplace, effective relations with the company and its employees, stable business history, credentials of staff, ethical standards of professional practice, evidence of cost-effective interventions).

3. Monitoring performance of vendors (e.g., timely action on referrals, comprehensive initial assessment, regular, written progress reports, specific and feasible plans for rehabilitation and return to work, detailed vouchers in compliance with service guidelines).

4. Evaluating service outcomes (e.g., closure outcomes, costs and documentation; employer feedback; follow-up services) (Schwartz, 1987).

THE MICHIGAN HOSPITAL ASSOCIATION: A CASE STUDY

In order to provide a more thorough description of disability management and rehabilitation services provided in employer-based settings, this extended case study is presented as an example of their evolution and operation in a service industry. The problem of disability in the health services industry has become a major concern as the number of workers' compensation claims due to patient care and management of client behavior has dramatically increased. For example, in 1985, 2.4 percent of the 260,000 people employed in the health services industry in Michigan had workers' compensation claims that involved lost workdays. The average number of lost workdays for this group was seventeen days per lost day claim, totaling 104,000 days.

The Michigan Hospital Association (MHA) is the primary state health care trade association, representing the interests of Michigan's 194 hospitals. In addition to advocacy and educational services, MHA has created a service corporation to provide consulting expertise to health care facilities. This corporation is wholly owned by the MHA and assists the members with a wide variety of administrative functions, from insurance to staffing to compliance with regulatory requirements. The MHA Service Corporation is the third-party administrator for a group workers' compensation fund for 113 hospitals, representing an annual premium of $9 million. This program also provides services (loss prevention, claims management and rehabilitation) to 18 free-standing, self-insured facilities, totaling 131 hospitals and approximately 45,000 employees.

About 1,650 claims are made per year, with 750 of these resulting in lost time. Approximately 20 per-

cent of lost time claims involve over four months' time off work. The corporation recognized that it was purchasing larger volumes of medical management and return-to-work services from external rehabilitation vendors to contain workers' compensation costs and to comply with statutory mandates. Thus, in 1985, an in-house worker rehabilitation service was established to provide more control over costs and timeliness of rehabilitation service and to ensure provision of rehabilitation and reasonable accommodation of workers with disabilities. The focus of the MHA program was to develop a systematic return-to-work approach that could be implemented by each of its member institutions.

The association recognized that the rehabilitation program must be autonomous and placed within the organization in a location free from direct control by the claims department. This was done both to avoid the perception of a conflict of interest (biased rehabilitation recommendations) and to allow the rehabilitation staff to operate within the guidelines of ethical, professional rehabilitation practice. Therefore, the rehabilitation program was placed in the MHA Service Corporation separate from and on an equal plane with the Loss Prevention and Claims departments, preserving the capacity for objectivity, injured worker advocacy, and credibility of the rehabilitation consultant role.

MHA has endorsed the concept of disability management, which has led to the adoption of a return-to-work model. The MHA has developed a written guide and provides education and technical assistance to its members in adopting this model. The critical parties identified in their program include the injured worker, the facility administrator-employer, the risk manager or personnel officer, the claims representative (on a compensable disability), the employee health physician, the rehabilitation specialist, the departmental manager, and the union representative (where applicable). The injured worker is involved early and continuously as an active member of the team, whose rights and responsibilities are incorporated in the plans and goals. Rehabilitation counseling services are an inherent aspect of the program operation.

The administrator writes and enforces the policy statement, the risk manager or personnel officer develops the procedures to implement policy, the claims person authorizes early, preventative re-

habilitation cost services, and employee health staff support increased physical activity recommendations (sports medicine). The rehabilitation specialist serves as the liaison among these parties, helps modify work requirements to accommodate restrictions, and provides counseling in support of these goals. The department manager supervises coworkers in support of the return-to-work effort, and the union representative negotiates contract language that will facilitate a disability management program. Aspects of the written guide are summarized in figure 82–1.

MHA encourages its members to have one identified person as responsible for disability management cases. This individual maintains supportive communication with the injured worker during the acute

Figure 82–1. The Michigan Hospital Association's Guide for Returning Injured Employees to Work

Reasons for Implementing a Return-to-Work Program

- Financially benefits the organization
- Accountability of the injured employee
- Builds trust with employees
- Reconditions employee for work via increased activity level

Procedures

- Give a caring response when illness or injury occurs
- Provide prompt medical attention to keep injury from getting worse
- Develop a follow-up system to keep informed of employee's progress
- Encourage return to restricted work if doctor permits
- Make job accommodations

Vital Components for a Successful Program

- Try all ways to accommodate employee in original department
- Centrally fund the program so that restricted workers provide extra help to other departments in the organization
- Provide job that meets individual skills
- Provide job that is similar to original job, duties, pay, hours
- Conduct a job analysis of each position to match requirements with physical restrictions of the injured employee

Employee Health Care Management

- Employee Health Services is only authorized agent
- Referral policy is referenced in employee accident report
- Provide specialists for specific injuries
- Communicate with attending physician regarding status
- Educate physicians about the organization's problem area of workers' compensation
- Meet any restrictions prescribed (reasonable amount)
- Inform physicians about physical requirements of original job when requesting return to work

Responsibilities of the Participating Department

- Use the services of the restricted employee in a productive manner
- Assign duties to the restricted employee in accord with any restrictions specified by the attending physician
- Supervise the restricted employee without discrimination
- Schedule the restricted employee
- Verify and approve time card
- Insure that performance meets standards of the assigned position

phase, before the medical condition is stable, and throughout the return-to-work process. The sequential steps to return restricted employers to work are as follows:

Step 1. Medical stability with fixed restrictions identified on Physical Capacity Evaluation Form.

Step 2. Assessment interview with employee to identify return to work needs and attitude.

Step 3. Job analysis to determine need for accommodations to original job.

Step 4. Job analysis of alternate positions to determine compatibility with physical restrictions.

Step 5. Determine need for short-term training, if any, and identify financial resources.

Step 6. Secure medical approval of job requirements, as specified by job analysis.

Step 7. Employment offer made to employee in writing (registered mail) specifying starting date, wage, medical approval, hours scheduled, status of fringe benefits upon return to work (with copies to claim representative, department supervisor, attorney and physician).

Step 8. Timely follow-up to determine the adequacy of accommodations and to deal with adjustment problems to avoid additional loss time.

Step 9. Reevaluation of injured employee's job to determine that it continues to be a good match with restrictions (i.e., should transitional [restricted] job continue? Should employee return to original job? Should new, unrestricted job be provided?).

Step 10. Obtain feedback from all parties. Evaluate final outcomes.

Employee input in the selection of the job is urged in order to contribute to successful placement. Member institutions are urged to develop a systematic procedure for cross-checking all job openings against the list of disabled employees with stable medical conditions who could return to work in alternative placements that accommodate their restrictions. They also recommend that these employees be given priority over new hires for job vacancies and new jobs that meet their physical restrictions and for which they are otherwise qualified.

Each organization is also encouraged to develop a functional job analysis that describes the behavioral and physical requirements of each job classification, in addition to their standard job descriptions. These functional job descriptions are used to help the physician determine realistic limitations for return to work. They are used by the rehabilitation specialist and other personnel in providing reasonable accommodation and to determine the need for specific modifications. These functional job analyses reduce subjectivity and improve safe, responsible judgments regarding the feasibility of return to work.

MHA recommends to member programs that they develop reinforcers and incentives to secure participation and cooperation from department managers and supervisors in providing light-duty work and implementing procedural and structural modifications to jobs. Three budgetary incentives they use are: (1) charging back to the original department budget the dollars spent on workers' compensation benefits that could have been saved by a return to work; (2) crediting those dollars saved as a result of a return to light duty from workers' compensation or other wage loss benefits to the department budget for providing reasonable accommodation; and (3) budgeting the restricted work dollars from a separate account or a line item on a central budget (e.g., human resources), thereby offering "free labor" to the receiving department. Disability management works best when it has both policy and budget support.

The outcomes of the program to date have been positive. In 1987, eight individuals successfully returned to work through the rehabilitation program. They ranged in age from thirty-five to fifty-nine years (the mean was forty-six) and had been off work from thirteen to forty-eight months (the mean was twenty-four). Their total annual indemnity rates cost were $59,194, compared to the total annual vocational rehabilitation costs of $11,191 for a total indemnity cost savings of $48,003 in the first year.

As further inducements to participation, in 1988 the MHA approved the application of discount points in the calculation of workers' compensation premiums for member institutions that implement the model return-to-work program and established systematic methods of referring claimants from their employee health services to the program. In addition, on-the-job training funds may be spent from the workers' compensation fund to encourage other employers in the community to retrain and hire displaced hospital employees. And finally, a rehabilitation nurse has been added to the program staff to improve liaison to physicians and other treatment providers.

SUMMARY

The provision of rehabilitation counseling services in the context of a return-to-work program for disability management in the workplace offers significant potential as a resource to managers, employers, and employees. Selection of the particular program model should be based on realistic consideration of the characteristics of the organization (e.g., management philosophy, nature of the work, size and makeup of the work force, incidence of disability, benefits use and costs), analysis of external factors influencing the organization (e.g., business and labor market conditions, state legislation affecting disability benefits and programs) and available resources and opportunities to assist the program (e.g., graduate internship programs from area universities, consultation from public agencies, assistance from voluntary disability organizations).

To be successful, in-house disability management and rehabilitation programs must be justified in terms of both cost containment and human relations. Control mechanisms must be developed to assume efficient and effective decisions at each stage in the disability management program. Policy and funding support from upper management must be obtained and communicated. The goals and purpose of the program must be understood by all employees and by community health care and rehabilitation providers. The program must continue to adapt to changing needs and try innovative approaches. Although systematic procedures are necessary, the program must be flexible in meeting the individual needs of people who may be dealing with fear of reinjury, pain management, or psychological adjustment as they return to the workplace and their former jobs.

The success of an organizational attempt to provide productive work routinely for restricted employees and to prevent the development of chronic, costly, long-term claims with psychological overlay will be determined largely by the degree of trust the employer can develop with employees. This trust must begin with ongoing, positive communication with the injured or ill worker when he or she is still recuperating from the acute phase of the injury. The disability management program should be presented to the work force in its policies and its actions as both a fringe benefit and a clear indication of individual job security, even in the face of disability. It is difficult in any organization to implement a program that is comprehensive and requires extensive interdepartmental cooperation such as on-site management of disabled workers. It may be useful to begin this effort by selecting a few pilot cases of injured workers who have not returned to work in order to demonstrate the economic benefits, feasibility, and intrinsic satisfaction of the rehabilitation approach to employee disability.

Workplace rehabilitation programs provide an effective and responsible solution to the problem of unnecessary lost work time or premature retirement from chronic disability. Employees are discouraged from taking more time off than is medically necessary, knowing their employer guarantees the opportunity to work within restrictions specified by the treating physician and the employee health department. In this way, stabilized but restricted employees are more likely to choose the psychological benefits of employment and avoid the disincentives of the disability system. In turn, the employer has a means for managing the economic and productivity costs of employee disability. Creative and commonsense programs that utilize the skills of rehabilitation professionals to accommodate injured employees at the work site give managers a framework within which to structure a productive and caring response to problems of disability. This response communicates to employees that they are a valuable asset to the organization and that they are expected and needed to make a productive contribution in accordance with their abilities.

REFERENCES

Abraham, L. (1988). Occupational health clinics help curb employee injuries. *American Medical News* (April), 2, 33–34.

Beaudway, D.L. (1986). 3M: A disability management approach. *Journal of Applied Rehabilitation Counseling*, 17 (3), 20–22.

Carbine, M.E., & Schwartz, G.E. (1987). *Strategies for managing disability costs*. Washington, DC: Washington Business Group on Health/Institute for Rehabilitation and Disability Management.

Danek, M.M., Wright, G.N., Leahy, M.J., & Shapson, P.R. (1987). Introduction to rehabilitation competency studies. *Rehabilitation Counseling Bulletin, 31*(2), 84–93.

Evert, D. (1982). What is the role of private enterprise? In G. Athelstan (Ed.), *The disabled worker: Overcoming the system's barriers.* Minneapolis: University of Minnesota.

Galvin, D.E. (1986). Employer-based disability management and rehabilitation programs. In E.L. Pan, S.S. Newman, T.E. Backer, & C.L. Vash (Eds.), *Annual review of Rehabilitation* (vol. 5). New York: Springer Publishing Company

Gardner, J.A. (1987). Vocational rehabilitation: Lessons for employers. *Business and Health, 4*(5), 20–21,24.

Habeck, R.V., & Munrowd, D.C. (1987). Employer-based rehabilitation practice: An educational perspective. *Rehabilitation Education, 1* (2–3), 95–107.

Habeck, R.V., Williams, C., Dugan, K.E., & Ewing, M.E. (1988). Balancing human and economic costs in disability management. Manuscript submitted for publication.

Hoeffel, J.Z. (1987). In-house rehabilitation. *Rehabilitation Education, 1* (2–3), 111–114.

Jacques, M. (1970). *Rehabilitation counseling: Scope and services.* Boston: Houghton Mifflin.

Levitan, S., & Taggart, R. (1982). Rehabilitation employment and the disabled. In J. Rubin (Ed.), *Alternatives in rehabilitating the handicapped: A policy analysis.* New York: Human Sciences Press.

Lynch, R.K., & Beck, R.J. (1987). Rehabilitation counseling in the private sector. In R.M. Parker (Ed.), *Rehabilitation counseling: Basics and beyond.* Austin: Pro-Ed.

Maki, D.R., McCracken, N., Pape, D.A., & Scofield, M.E.

(1978). The theoretical model of vocational rehabilitation. *Journal of Rehabilitation, 44*(4), 26–28.

Maktin, R.E. (1985). *Insurance rehabilitation.* Austin, TX: Pro-ed.

Mitchell, K., & Shrey, D. (1985). The risk manager's guide to disability management. *Risk Management, 32*(9), 42–44,46.

Rubin, S.E., & Roessler, R.T. (1987). *Foundations of the vocational rehabilitation process* (3d ed.). Austin, TX: Pro-ed.

Schwartz, G.E. (1986). *State of the art; Corporate behavior in disability management survey results.* Washington, DC: Washington Business Group on Health/Institute for Disability Management.

Schwartz, G.E., & Carbine, M.E. (1987). *Using private rehabilitation vendors: Selection criteria and performance standards to ensure quality.* Washington, DC: Washington Business Group on Health/Institute for Rehabilitation and Disability Management.

Staff. (1988). Critical condition. *Time* (February 1), 42–43.

Tate, D.G., Habeck, R.V., & Galvin, D.E. (1986). Disability management: Origins, concepts and principles for practice. *Journal of Applied Rehabilitation Counseling, 17*(3), 5–11.

Tate, D.G., Habeck, R.V., & Munrowd, D.C. (1987). Building a better rehabilitation program. *Business and Health, 4*(9), 32, 33–34.

Tonti, D., Trudeau, T., & Daniel, M. (1987). The fitness-rehabilitation link. *Business and Health, 4*(11), 23, 26–27.

Wright, G.N. (1980). *Total rehabilitation.* Boston: Little, Brown.

83 SCREENING FOR PSYCHOPATHOLOGY: INDUSTRIAL APPLICATIONS OF THE MINNESOTA MULTIPHASIC PERSONALITY INVENTORY

James N. Butcher

Psychological problems can have a significant effect upon job motivation and performance, work morale, and even safety of operation in some settings. Increasingly in contemporary business and industry, corporations are employing psychologists or contracting with psychological consultants to assist in the identification and assessment of problem employees. Personnel managers and other corporate executives have become aware of the importance of personality assessment for psychological problems in industry in recent years. Two major areas in which psychological assessment procedures are being applied in the workplace are assessment and intervention with problem employees and screening for potential psychological maladjustment in some sensitive or highly responsible occupations in preemployment evaluations. These two major assessment activities will be illustrated in this chapter.

RATIONALE FOR PERSONALITY TESTING IN INDUSTRY

The rationale for each of these two psychological test applications in industry is somewhat different and will be addressed separately below.

Preemployment Personality Screening

Personality adjustment is not necessarily a relevant job performance variable in all occupations. Few occupations require preemployment screening for psychopathology or warrant employing clinical-personality tests in the psychological evaluation of applicants. Most jobs in business and industry can be performed effectively by a wide range of "personality types," even by persons with psychological problems. For example, many jobs can be performed by individuals who vary in effectiveness as a result of their personal problems, such as depression, tension, and so forth. A case can even be made that some jobs are better performed by individuals with certain types of personality problems. There may be more than a grain of truth in the oft-heard statement, "You've gotta be a little crazy to do this job!" There are several criteria for determining whether a particular position warrants the cost and the necessary invasion of privacy that personality evaluation entails. In general, psychological screening is particularly important when an occupation involves a high degree of public trust or when great public harm could result from a failed job performance due to an individual's emotional instability or immaturity. Screening out emotionally unstable individuals or those with a history of irresponsibility is considered desirable. For example, an individual who works as a police officer should be free from personal insecurity and immaturity, which make him or her vulnerable to misbehavior such as threatening or abusing people. Similarly, jobs in which a high degree of critical judgment, responsibility, and a well-balanced life-style are required, such as that of airline flight crew members, should be filled with individuals who are stable and responsible.

Another important reason for justifying psychological screening of applicants is that some positions, such as firefighter or air traffic controller, are inherently stressful; individuals selected for such positions should be as free from disabling psychological conflicts or emotional frailties as possible.

Psychological Referral and Assessment of Problem Employees

Several reasons can be found for employing psychological assessment procedures with current employees can be found.

One of the most frequent referral reasons for current employees is to provide psychological help for them if they are experiencing problems at work.

In recent years, many referrals for psychological evaluation have been motivated by the need for providing an alternative to employment termination in situations where employees are creating serious morale or work problems for others. For example, one company recently referred a male engineer with seventeen years of very productive employment with the company for evaluation because he was reportedly harassing a young female employee at work by writing love notes to her. The company management's goal was to determine if the employee could be "rehabilitated" to continue his employment in addition to ceasing his unacceptable behavior.

A third frequent reason for referring current employees for psychological evaluation is to evaluate the extent to which alleged psychological impairment has result from work-related injury or problems (Butcher & Cross, 1985).

THE MMPI AS A CLINICAL ASSESSMENT INSTRUMENT IN INDUSTRY

The Minnesota Multiphasic Personality Inventory (MMPI) is an objective personality assessment instrument that was developed for screening individuals for psychopathology in psychiatric and medical settings. Developed in the 1940s, the MMPI has become the most widely used and researched clinical test for assessing and describing psychological problems (Lubin, Larsen & Matarazzo, 1984). There have been over 10,000 books and articles and over 115 translations supporting the MMPI's application. The instrument is used in over forty-six other countries (Butcher, 1985).

The MMPI was developed originally using an empirical scale construction strategy. Hathaway and McKinley (1940) used a method of contrasted group discrimination to develop item clusters into scales that empirically separate persons with clinical problems, such as depression, from "normals." Over the years research in clinical settings has documented the effectiveness of the MMPI in assessing behavioral and personality characteristics. (Graham, 1987; Marks, Seeman & Haller, 1975; Gilberstadt & Duker, 1965). A summary of well-established correlates for clinical scale elevations is given in table 83–1. Hypotheses related to MMPI scale elevations in normal range samples are given in table 83–2.

Table 83–1
Personality Characteristics Associated with Elevations on the Basic MMPI Scales

Scale	Characteristics
? Cannot Say	A validity score that, if high, may indicate evasiveness. Attenuated clinical scales are suspected if ? raw score is greater than 30 in the first 400 items.
L Life Scale	A validity scale that measures the tendency to claim excessive virtue or place oneself in an overly favorable light. Elevated scores suggest the need to see or present oneself in a "saintly" manner, suggesting an unrealistically positive self-image or life circumstance.
F Fake Bad Scale	A validity scale composed of highly infrequent items. A high score suggests carelessness, confusion, or claiming an inordinate amount of symptoms or "faking illness." Random responding also will result in an elevated F score.
K Subtle Defensiveness	A validity scale that measures defensiveness and a willingness to discuss personal matters. Scores are related to intelligence, education, and social class. Thus, these factors must be considered in scale interpretation. For example, middle-class clients with low K may be viewed as overly frank, complaining, and masochistic while low scores are considered

continued on next page

Table 83–1 *continued*

typical in low-socioeconomic status (SES) clients. Scores of 55–65 are considered modal for middle- and upper-SES clients. Scores over $T = 70$ reflect uncooperativeness or unwillingness to discuss problems.

1 (Hs) Hypochondriasis	High scorers present numerous physical problems of a vague nature. Their problems tend to be chronic, and they do not respond well to psychological treatments. High scorers are generally unhappy, self-centered, whiney, complaining, hostile, demanding, and command attention.
2 (D) Depression	Elevations reflect depressed mood, low self-esteem, and feelings of inadequacy. This scale is one of the most frequently elevated in clinical patients. High scoreres are described as moody, shy, despondent, pessimistic, distressed, high strung, lethargic, overcontrolled, and guilt prone. Elevations may reflect great discomfort and need for change or symptomatic relief.
3 (Hy) Hysteria	High scorers tend to rely on neurotic defenses—denial and repression to deal with stress. They tend to be dependent, naive, outgoing, infantile, and narcissistic. Their interpersonal relations are often disrupted, and they show little insight into problems. Higher levels of stress are accompanied by development of physical symptoms in high-3 people. Scale 3 is the peak score among female medical patients who have negative medical findings. High scorers often respond to suggestion, however, they resist insight oriented treatment. They show low psychological mindedness and interpret psychological problems as phony.
4 (Pd) Psychopathic Deviate	Associated with antisocial behavior—rebelliousness, disrupted family relations; impulsiveness; school, work, or legal difficulties; alcohol or drug abuse, etc. Personality trait disorder likely among high scorers—they are outgoing, sociable, likeable but deceptive, manipulative, hedonistic, exhibitionistic, show poor judgment, unreliable, immature, hostile, aggressive. They often have difficulty in marital or family relations and trouble with the law. High scores usually reflect long-standing character problem, which are highly resistant to treatment. High scorers may enter treatment but usually terminate quickly.
5 (MF) Masculinity-Femininity	High-scoring males are described as sensitive, aesthetic, passive, or feminine. They may show conflicts over sexual identity and low heterosexual drive. Low-scoring males are viewed as masculine, aggressive, crude, adventurous, reckless, practical, and having narrow interests.
	High-scoring females are seen as masculine, rough, aggressive, self-confident, unemotional, insensitive. Low-scoring females are viewed as passive, yielding, complaining, fault finding, idealistic, sensitive.
6 (Pa) Paranoia	High elevations on this scale are often associated with being suspicious, aloof, shrewd, guarded, worrisome, and overly sensitive. High scorers may project or externalize blame and harbor grudges against others. High scores are generally hostile and argumentative and are not very amenable to psychotherapy.
	Low scorers (below $T = 45$) may show guarded, evasive, and paranoid behavior.
7 (Pt) Psychasthenia	High scorers are tense, anxious, ruminative, preoccupied, obsessional, phobic, rigid. They frequently are self-condemning, guilt prone, and feel interior and inadequate. Clients with spike 7 elevations overintellectualize, ruminate, rationalize, and resist psychological interpretation in treatment.
8 (Sc) Schizophrenia	High scorers ($T = 70–80$) show unconventional or schizoid life-style. They are withdrawn, shy, feel inadequate, tense, confused, and moody. May have unusual or strange thoughts, poor judgment, and erratic mood. Very high scorers (T over 80) may show poor reality contact, bizarre sensory experiences, delusions, and hallucinations. High scorers may have difficulty relating in therapy; they tend to lack information and have poor problem-solving skills.
9 (Ma) Mania	High scorers ($T = 70–75$) are viewed as sociable, outgoing, impulsive, overly energetic, optimistic, and have liberal moral views, flighty, drink excessively, grandiose, irritable, unqualified optimism, and unrealistic planning. They overvalue self-worth and are manipulative. They show impatience and irritability. Very high scorers (T over 75) may show affective disorder, bizarre behavior, erratic mood, very poor and impulsive behavior, and delusions possible.
O (Si) Social Introversion-Extroversion	High scorers are introverted, shy, withdrawn, socially reserved, submissive, overcontrolled, lethargic, conventional, tense, inflexible, and show guilt.
	Low scorers are extroverted, outgoing, gregarious, expressive, aggressive, talkative, impulsive, uninhibited, spontaneous, manipulative, opportunistic, and insincere in social relations.

Table 83-2
Applicant Personality Characteristics from High Point MMPI Scale Elevations: Subclinical Interpretive Hypotheses

MMPI Scale	T-Score Range	Hypotheses
Validity Scales		
L Scale	$T > 65$ $T < 69$	Overly virtuous self-presentation; claiming of excessive; overly idealized self-image; desire to be viewed in a favorable way; naive attributions of positive qualities
F Scale	$T > 65$ $T < 69$	Unusual symptom reporting; errors in response format or pattern; unusual and unconventional life-style; possible reading difficulties
K Scale	$T > 65$ $T < 74$	Overly defensive; extremely self-protective; rigid self-view as "perfect"
Clinical Scales		
1 (Hs)	$T > 65$ $T < 69$	Overly concerned with health; vulnerable to "sickness"; prone to unnecessary doctor visits under stress; pessimistic and cynical approach to life; whiny and complaining approach to others; rigid in supervision; resentful; self-preoccupied
2 (D)	$T > 65$ $T < 69$	Tendency toward low moods; low self-esteem; defeatist attitude; low energy level; feelings of insecurity and inadequacy; conventional; nonadventurous; quiet; passive; timid; dissatisfied with life; socially retiring
Hy	$T > 65$ $T < 69$	Denying problems; overly optimistic; avoids conflict; suggestible; overreacts to stress; socially responsive; presents self in an overly favorably way; concerned with social image
Pd	$T > 65$ $T < 69$	Assertive; self-confident; venturesome; socially adept; manipulative and persuasive in social relationships; tends toward aggressiveness; impulsive; quick and possibly careless judgments at times; self-centered; pleasure oriented; irritable
Mf (Males)	$T > 65$ $T < 75$	Shows gender role flexibility; broad interests; interested in intellectual or artistic activities; interpersonally sensitive
(Males)	$T < 45$	Narrow pattern of interests; interests characteristically and stereotypically masculine; interpersonally insensitive; prefers action to reflection
Mf (Females)	$T < 45$	Interested in traditional female role activities; strong role identification; interpersonally sensitive
	$T > 65$	Broad pattern of interests; dominant in interpersonal relationships; aggressive in interpersonal situations
Pa	$T > 65$ $T < 69$	Oversensitive in interpersonal relationships; moralistic; mistrustful of others; prone toward suspiciousness; questioning; autocratic; authoritarian; prone to rigid thinking; distrustful; opinionated
Pt	$T > 65$ $T < 69$	Perfectionistic; efficient; resentful; slow; methodical; touchy; indecisive; lacking in self-confidence; prone to feeling guilty; tendency toward feeling anxious; feels unaccepted
Sc	$T > 65$ $T < 69$	Unconventional; informal; low self-confidence; lacks poise; alienated; socially withdrawn or isolated; disorganized; confused; aloof
Ma	$T > 65$ $T < 74$	Energetic; active, possibly overactive; high initiative; high self-confidence; possibly overly self-confident; unrealistic self-appraisal; rebellious; aggressive; moody; irritable; touchy; daring; high risk taker; verbal; talkative; dislikes detail work; careless in detail activities; lacks direction; enjoys taking risks
Si	$T > 60$ $T < 69$	Introverted; shy; timid; lacks self-confidence; submissive; compliant in relationships; quiet; not easy-going; inhibited; low energy; listless in activity; lacks enthusiasm; distant from others

Sources: Graham & McCord, 1981; Kunce & Anderson (1976).

REVISED VERSION OF THE MMPI: IMPLICATIONS FOR FUTURE APPLICATIONS IN INDUSTRY

In 1982, the University of Minnesota Press, the MMPI copyright holder, initiated a project to revise, extend, and restandardize the MMPI on a current national sample. The original MMPI items that were linguistically archaic were rewritten, and the item pool was expanded to incorporate several additional content dimensions. The MMPI-2 item pool has been modified to make the items less objectionable to subjects taking the test, particularly those in personnel selection situations. Butcher and Tellegen (1966) pointed out a number of items, such as the religion item and bowel and bladder functioning, which produced high rates of objectionability. These offensive items have been deleted in the revised version of the instrument.

A modern sample of normal subjects ($N = 2,600$) were tested with the MMPI-2 item pool to establish the new Minnesota normative population for the instrument. In addition, a number of other studies were completed to evaluate the MMPI with contemporary normal and clinical populations such as military personnel, elderly individuals, college students, airline pilot applicants, and several clinical groups, including alcoholics, psychiatric inpatients, chronic pain patients, and other problems.

The goal of the MMPI-2 project has been to refine many of the MMPI clinical scales in order to improve discrimination in contemporary samples. In addition, several new MMPI scales have been developed to evaluate MMPI content themes (see Butcher, Graham, Williams, & Ben-Porath, in press). One new content scale, the Negative Work Attitudes Scale, appears to have promise in detecting personal attitudes and motivations that would negatively affect job performance. Butcher (1988) found that the Work Interference Scale (WRK) significantly differentiated groups of individuals with clearly different work histories and work problems. Airline pilot applicants obtained significantly low scores as compared with the new Minnesota Normative Sample and a group of active-duty military personnel, while groups of alcoholics and psychiatric inpatients (with significant employment problems) obtained significantly higher scores than the two "normal" groups.

UTILITY OF USING THE MMPI IN ASSESSING INDIVIDUALS IN NONCLINICAL SETTINGS

Can a psychological test, which was developed initially for use in clinical and medical assessment, be effectively employed with "normal-range" individuals in industrial settings? An affirmative answer to this question is supported by several sources of research information on the MMPI.

The MMPI was originally developed on a large sample of "normals." Most of the early normative studies for the MMPI scales were based on responses of individuals who were defined as normal, that is, were not under a doctor's care at the time. The normal reference group (referred to as the Minnesota normals) provided the basis for the empirical comparisons in the original scale development. Continu-

ing in the MMPI tradition, the MMPI-2 has been based on an extensive study of individuals without psychological problems.

Extensive research on the MMPI with normal-range populations has been published. Following the initial studies on the MMPI, the instrument was used extensively to screen possible individuals with psychological problems in the military and industry.

The sensitivity of the MMPI to psychological problems in normal-range populations has been demonstrated. The MMPI has been shown to have validity in discriminating personality and emotional problems in groups of applicants (Butcher, 1979).

TEST DEFENSIVENESS AMONG JOB APPLICANTS

Individuals seeking high-paying positions are likely to approach psychological testing, as they do their personnel interviews, with the mind-set to make the most favorable impression possible. The MMPI-2, made up of true and false statements, is open to response sets to proclaim excessive virtue or, as in some clinical settings, to present a pattern of psychological problems. Can an individual distort his or her response to

the MMPI-2 items in order to present an overly favorable self-image? Yes; however, the MMPI contains several scales to assess these deviant test-taking attitudes. The validity scales that are most relevant to personnel screening are the L Scale (Lie) and K Scale (Subtle Defensiveness Scale) since these measures detect the presence of willful and unconscious efforts to claim excessive virtue in response to the test items.

QUALIFICATIONS FOR APPROPRIATE USE: EXPERIENCE REQUIREMENTS

The American Psychological Association has established criteria for using clinical tests like the MMPI-2, and most test publishers and distributors follow these guidelines in deciding who is eligible for purchasing and using psychological tests. The following procedures were developed by National Computer Systems, official distributors of the MMPI, to establish the qualifications of MMPI system users.

> The Professional Assessment Services of National Computer Systems, Inc. (NCS) has developed guidelines for the distribution of materials and services that are available through NCS. Given the potential for misuse—including well-intentioned, inadvertent use—of psychological assessment materials, the purpose of these guidelines is to ensure as much as is possible, that the products and services listed in NCS catalogs are available only to those who are competent in their use. . . .
>
> All test materials and computer-based test scoring services offered by NCS have been classified into one of five levels according to the level of training and/or skill that NCS has determined to be necessary for their use. The classification level for these materials and services is indicated in the pricing grid for each instrument. (National Computer Systems, 1987)

The MMPI is considered to be a Level A test. Level A tests are automatically available to fellows, members, and associate members (not student affiliates) of the American Psychological Association (APA) and psychologists licensed to practice psychology on an independent basis by a state board of psychology. These materials and services are also available to individuals with a graduate degree in applied psychology or a closely related field who can document that he or she has had appropriate graduate coursework and the equivalent of one year of experience in the interpretation of desired Level A tests under the supervision of a licensed psychologist (National Computer Systems, 1987).

In addition to the APA standards for test usage, the use of clinical tests in industrial screening requires further consideration. For example, the use of a clinical instrument like the MMPI with normal-range populations also requires that the assessment psychologist understand and have experience in evaluating personality profiles of nonpatients as well as having clinical experience with the instrument.

PREEMPLOYMENT SCREENING USING THE MMPI: AN ILLUSTRATION

The MMPI-2 profile shown in figure 83–1 was generated by a 38-year-old engineer who was applying for a position as a nuclear power plant control room technician. His MMPI-2 profile suggests that he is experiencing a great deal of depression, low self-esteem, ruminative self-doubt, and decreased efficiency. It is likely that his current maladjustment results in emotional instability that could interfere with work functioning.

In follow-up interviews, he reported that he had been experiencing some psychological problems over the past two years for which he sought psychological treatment. He was divorced about a year ago and became despondent to the point of attempting suicide about nine months ago. He continued to have problems and has been unemployed for the part six months.

ASSESSMENT OF PSYCHOPATHOLOGY IN CURRENT EMPLOYEES: AN ILLUSTRATION

The MMPI-2 profile shown in figure 83–2 was produced by an applicant for FAA recertification as an air traffic controller. He had lost his medical certification following his acknowledged alcohol and drug abuse problems. He reportedly had completed an alcohol treatment program a few months before and was seeking medical recertification. His MMPI-2 profile shows a great likelihood of continued problems in

Figure 83–1. MMPI Profile of an Applicant for a Position with a Nuclear Power Company

Profile for Basic Scales

Name _____ Address _____

Occupation _____ Date Tested __/__/__ Education _____ Age ___ Marital Status ____

Referred By _____ MMPI-2 Code _____ Scorer's Initials ____

MALE

	L	F	K	Hs+5K 1	D 2	Hy 3	Pd+4K 4	Mf 5	Pa 6	Pt+1K 7	Sc+1K 8	Ma+2K 9	Si 0	

Fractions of K

K	5	4	2
30	15	12	6
29	15	12	6
28	14	11	6
27	14	11	5
26	13	10	5
25	13	10	5
24	12	10	5
23	12	9	5
22	11	9	4
21	11	8	4
20	10	8	4
19	10	8	4
18	9	7	4
17	9	7	3
16	8	6	3
15	8	6	3
14	7	6	3
13	7	5	3
12	6	5	2
11	6	4	2
10	5	4	2
9	5	4	2
8	4	3	2
7	4	3	1
6	3	2	1
5	3	2	1
4	2	2	1
3	2	1	1
2	1	1	0
1	1	0	0
0	0	0	0

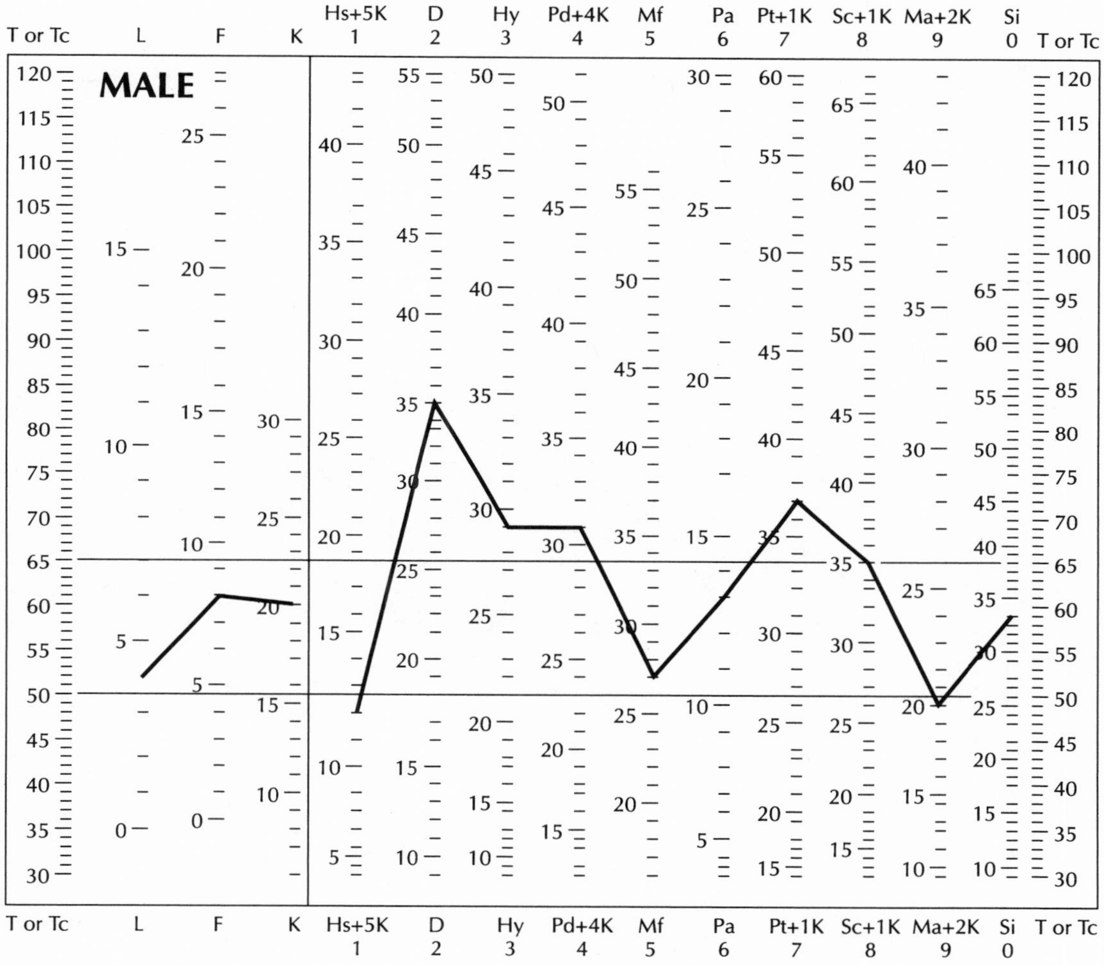

	L	F	K	Hs+5K 1	D 2	Hy 3	Pd+4K 4	Mf 5	Pa 6	Pt+1K 7	Sc+1K 8	Ma+2K 9	Si 0
Raw Score	4	8	20	8	35	29	23	27	13	17	15	16	34
K to be Added				10			8			20	20	4	
Raw Score with K				18			31			37	35	20	

? Raw Score ____

Figure 83–2. MMPI Profile of an Applicant for Recertification as an Air Traffic Control Operator

Profile for Basic Scales

Name _____ Address _____

Occupation _____ Date Tested _/_/_ Education _____ Age ___ Marital Status _____

Referred By _____ MMPI-2 Code _____ Scorer's Initials ____

MALE

Fractions of K

K	5	4	2
30	15	12	6
29	15	12	6
28	14	11	6
27	14	11	5
26	13	10	5
25	13	10	5
24	12	10	5
23	12	9	5
22	11	9	4
21	11	8	4
20	10	8	4
19	10	8	4
18	9	7	4
17	9	7	3
16	8	6	3
15	8	6	3
14	7	6	3
13	7	5	3
12	6	5	2
11	6	4	2
10	5	4	2
9	5	4	2
8	4	3	2
7	4	3	1
6	3	2	1
5	3	2	1
4	2	2	1
3	2	1	1
2	1	1	0
1	1	0	0
0	0	0	0

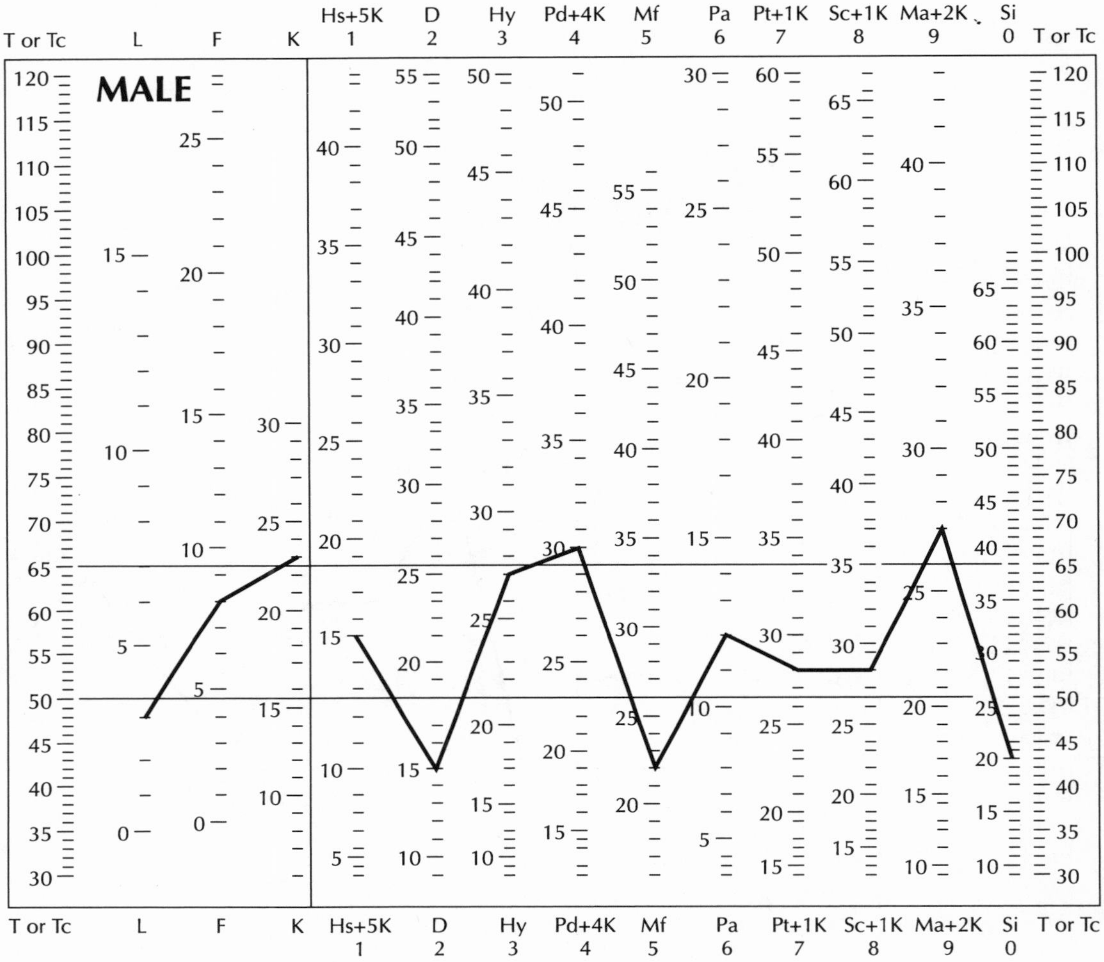

Scale columns: T or Tc | L | F | K | Hs+5K 1 | D 2 | Hy 3 | Pd+4K 4 | Mf 5 | Pa 6 | Pt+1K 7 | Sc+1K 8 | Ma+2K 9 | Si 0 | T or Tc

	L	F	K	Hs+5K 1	D 2	Hy 3	Pd+4K 4	Mf 5	Pa 6	Pt+1K 7	Sc+1K 8	Ma+2K 9	Si 0	
Raw Score	2	8	23	3	15	27	21	22	12	5	5	22	20	
K to be Added				12			9			23	23	5		
Raw Score with K				15			30			28	28	27		

? Raw Score _____

acting-out behavior and interpersonal relationships. His personality profile is associated with hedonistic, irresponsible behavior and a strong possibility of poor judgment and authority conflicts. His uncontrolled behavioral history and present pattern of impulsivity suggest that he is likely to be a poor risk for reemployment in a responsible position of public trust at this time.

Interestingly, his poor judgment and manipulative behavior were also found in the clinical situation as well. When he was given a break from the testing, he was observed to go quickly behind the nurse's station and read through his chart. Moreover, his documentation of sobriety was suspect. In order to document his abstinence from alcohol, he had brought to the clinic three notes from other people documenting his sobriety (from his wife, from his cousin, and from someone named "Willie"). All were written in the same, seemingly hurried handwriting.

AFFIRMATIVE ACTION CONSIDERATIONS

In order to comply with guidelines for ensuring equal economic opportunity it is important for corporate psychologists to ascertain that personnel screening procedures do not unfairly disadvantage minority group job applicants. Does the MMPI unfairly depict minority group members as pathological, thereby making them less attractive job candidates? This question has been raised by Gynther (1972) who called for using special norms for the MMPI with blacks since, in his view, they responded to MMPI items in a deviant manner because of their minority group status. This view has not been supported in the research literature, especially in studies of industrial settings. Several studies relevant to black and Hispanic MMPI performance in industry have been published. Recently, Bernstein, Teng, Grannemann, and Garbin (1987) demonstrated that the factor structure of MMPI scales of blacks and white applicants is invariant. They conclude that any scale elevations differences obtained between the two groups probably represent valid variance. Their study does not support the notion that the test measures different psychological qualities in the two groups.

Empirical research studies in industrial settings that compared blacks with whites on the MMPI have not reported meaningful differences. King, Carroll, and Fuller (1977) reported no group mean MMPI differences between blacks and whites in the chemical industry; Wennerholm and Lopez-Roig (1983) found that Puerto Rican executives produced similar MMPI profiles as white executives; and Butcher (1987a) found that "blind" clinical ratings of MMPI profiles of airline pilot applicants did not result in a greater classification of minorities as disturbed. Muller and Bruno (1988), in one of the best-controlled research comparisons to date, found no significant differences among black, white, and Hispanic police applicants from similar educational backgrounds. The relative accuracy of computer-based psychological test interpretations with blacks and whites was recently examined by Eyde, Kowal, and Fishburne (1987). They found that MMPI-based computerized personality reports were equally accurate for minority group patients as for whites.

Recent comprehensive reviews of minority group influences on MMPI responses have been published by Dahlstrom, Lachar, and Dahlstrom (1986) and Greene (1987). The book by Dahlstrom, Lachar, and Dahlstrom (1986) surveys all of the published literature on minority group membership and MMPI profiles. The authors concluded that MMPI profiles of minority group members can be interpreted in a similar manner as those of white, middle-class subjects with accuracy. The authors note:

> At this stage in the development of the knowledge of how to use the MMPI in personnel and psychiatric assessment with various minority group subjects or clients, the best procedure would seem to be to accept the pattern of results generated by the standard scales on the basic MMPI profile, male or female, and, when the pattern is markedly deviant, to take special pains to explore in detail the life circumstances of that individual in order to understand as fully as possible the nature and degree of his or her problems and demands. (p. 204)

Greene's (1987) view of the black-white MMPI research literature supports the conclusions made by Dahlstrom, Lachar, and Dahlstrom that ethnic minority differences on MMPI responses are minimal sources of variance on the test.

USE OF COMPUTERS IN PERSONNEL SCREENING

Electronic computers have been used in scoring and interpretation of psychological assessment procedures for over twenty-five years. Early efforts to computerize psychological tests primarily involved the MMPI since its objective format and well-established empirical correlates lent itself particularly well to computer programming. Over the past two decades, computer-based scoring and interpretation programs for the MMPI have gained broad acceptance in clinical settings (Butcher, 1987). In 1982, National Computer Systems published an extensive MMPI scoring and interpretation system for the MMPI in personnel selection situations. This program, developed by Butcher (National Computer Systems, 1982), incorporates MMPI scores and empirical data from normal-range, usually employment selection settings.

Two types of computer-based assessment programs are available to psychologists employing the MMPI in preemployment screening: the Minnesota Personnel Interpretive for the MMPI-2 and the MMPI-2 Screening Report. Both interpretive outputs are illustrated on the following applicant (see figures 83–3 and 83–4).

The applicant, a forty-three-year-old pilot who is currently employed as a captain by a small regional commuter air charter company, was applying for a position as a flight crew member with a major air carrier. Although he had the requisite educational background and extensive flying background, most of his experience was in small, single engine and twin propeller aircraft. His actual performance in the 727 flight simulator was marginal though technically in the passable range. He made a good impression on the employment interviewers since he tends to present himself very well in interpersonal situations. His performance on the MMPI, as reflected in his elevated score on the deviance and masculinity scales, suggests the presence of a long-standing personality problem which could interfere with relationships at work. A careful background check showed that he had a number of problems with past employers because of his overly aggressive interpersonal behavior and his social poor judgment at times. He was quite forward with females who worked for the company and on some occasions shocked them with his sexual comments.

EFFECTIVENESS OF COMPUTER-BASED PSYCHOLOGICAL ASSESSMENT

The wide availability of personal computers makes automated psychological assessment a practical reality (Butcher, 1987b). On-line test administration and test interpretation can provide the psychologist with immediate results for practical decisions. Moreover, the cost of psychological assessment is considerably reduced by using computer-based scoring and interpretation. How effective are computer interpretation programs for the MMPI? The congruence between computer-based adjustment ratings and clinician rating of adjustment was recently demonstrated by Butcher (1988). He compared the congruence between computer-based MMPI classification rules (Minnesota Personnel Report, NCS) with ratings of clinicians interpreting profiles. Clinicians rated 262 airline pilot applicants in terms of their overall level of emotional adjustment on a three-point scale of Adequate, Problems Possible, and Problems Likely (see table 83–3). The clinicians had access to the pilot applicants' MMPI profiles, special scale scores, and other MMPI interpretative information. They did not have access to the computer-based MMPI decisions from the applicant's MMPI profile.

The comparison of the computer-rated MMPIs with the clinician ratings of adjustment is informative. Overall, the Pearson product moment correlation between the clinician ratings and computer ratings is high (.68). However, the classification analysis shown in table 83–3 is more informative. The results show that when the clinician rated an applicant as Adequate, the computer-based ratings also classified 98.5 percent of these cases as adequate. Similarly, when the clinicians rate an applicant as likely to have problems, the computer-based rules agree on 88 percent of the cases and consider only 3 percent of these Problems Likely cases as having good adjustment.

Figure 83–3. Minnesota Personnel Interpretive Report for the MMPI for an Airline Pilot Applicant

MMPI – 2™
MINNESOTA MULTIPHASIC PERSONALITY INVENTORY – 2™
by Starke R. Hathaway and J. Charnley McKinley

THE MINNESOTA REPORT:™ PERSONNEL SELECTION SYSTEM SCREENING REPORT
By James N. Butcher

| Client ID: | 3171 | Report Date: | 23-AUG-X9 | Age: | 43 |
| Sex: | Male | Occupation: | Flight Crew | Education: | 16 |

Openness to Evaluation

Overly Frank	Quite Open	Adequate	Overly Cautious	Guarded	Indeterminate
X					

Social Facility

Excellent	Good	Adequate	Problems Possible	Poor	Indeterminate
				X	

Addiction Potential (Standard Level)

Low	No Apparent Problem	Problems Possible	Moderate	High	Indeterminate
				X	

This index is associated with Addiction Potential; it does not confirm existing abuse.

Stress Tolerance

High	Good	Adequate	Problems Possible	Low	Indeterminate
				X	

Overall Adjustment

Excellent	Good	Adequate	Problems Possible	Poor	Indeterminate
				X	

His MMPI-2 responses indicate that his psychological adjustment is likely to be poor.

Individuals with this pattern of scores tend to encounter problems as a result of their poor judgment, impulsivity, and interpersonal aggressiveness. He may have difficulty in a position requiring consistent and sustained performance, conscientiousness, or attention to detail.

This applicant should be evaluated further to determine if he has adjustment problems.

Note: This MMPI-2 report can serve as a useful guide for employment decisions in which personality adjustment is considered important for success on the job. The decision rules on which these classifications are based were developed through a review of the empirical literature on the MMPI-2 with "normal-range" individuals (including job applicants) and the author's practical experience using the test in employment selection. The report can assist psychologists and physicians involved in personnel selection by providing an "outside opinion" about the applicant's adjustment. The MMPI-2 should *not* be used as the *sole* means of determining the applicant's suitability for employment. The information in this report should be used by qualified test interpretation specialists *only*.

Content Themes

The following content themes may serve as a source of hypotheses for further investigation. These content themes summarize similar item responses that appear with greater frequency with this applicant than with most people.

May be overly sensitive in interpersonal relationships.
May be overly self-centered and excessively motivated by self-interest.
May be overly rigid and inflexible in his thinking.
May have feelings of alienation.
May have temper-control problems.
May have antisocial attitudes and behavior.
May have engaged in behavior that runs counter to societal norms.
May have some unconventional beliefs or attitudes that affect the way he gets along with supervisors.
May show irresponsible attitudes.
May sometimes disregard rules when it suits him.

Figure 83–3. Cont.

May have problems with authority.
May tend to question supervisory decisions.
May be experiencing family discord that interferes with his functioning.
May show some disregard for the feelings of others.

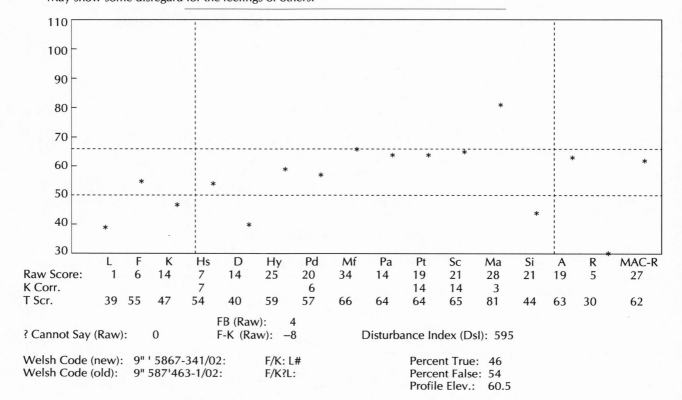

	L	F	K	Hs	D	Hy	Pd	Mf	Pa	Pt	Sc	Ma	Si	A	R	MAC-R
Raw Score:	1	6	14	7	14	25	20	34	14	19	21	28	21	19	5	27
K Corr.				7			6			14	14	3				
T Scr.	39	55	47	54	40	59	57	66	64	64	65	81	44	63	30	62

FB (Raw):   4

? Cannot Say (Raw):   0   F-K (Raw): −8   Disturbance Index (DsI): 595

Welsh Code (new): 9" ' 5867-341/02:   F/K: L#   Percent True: 46
Welsh Code (old): 9" 587'463-1/02:   F/K?L: Percent False: 54
                                                          Profile Elev.: 60.5

Content Scales Profile
Butcher, Graham, Williams, and Ben-Porath (1989)

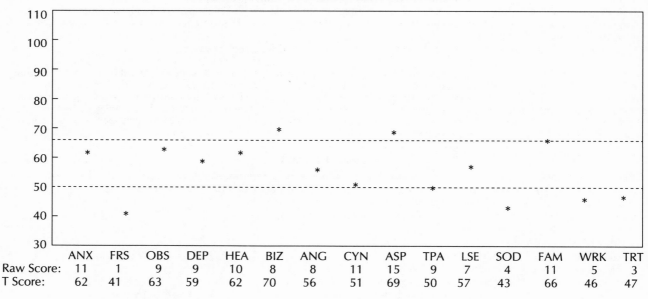

	ANX	FRS	OBS	DEP	HEA	BIZ	ANG	CYN	ASP	TPA	LSE	SOD	FAM	WRK	TRT
Raw Score:	11	1	9	9	10	8	8	11	15	9	7	4	11	5	3
T Score:	62	41	63	59	62	70	56	51	69	50	57	43	66	46	47

continued on next page

Figure 83–3 *continued*

Supplementary Score Report

	Raw Score	*T Score*
Ego Strength (Es)	37	49
Dominance (Do)	17	51
Social Responsibility (Re)	14	34
Overcontrolled Hostility (O-H)	11	45
True Response Inconsistency (TRIN)	8	57F
Variable Response Inconsistency (VRIN)	5	50

Depression Subscales (Harris-Lingoes):

Subjective Depression (D1)	6	48
Psychomotor Retardation (D2)	2	32
Physical Malfunctioning (D3)	1	35
Mental Dullness (D4)	2	48
Brooding (D5)	2	51

Hysteria Subscales (Harris-Lingoes):

Denial of Social Anxiety (Hy1)	3	45
Need for Affection (Hy2)	9	59
Lassitude-Malaise (Hy3)	3	52
Somatic Complaints (Hy4)	5	62
Inhibition of Aggression (Hy5)	3	48

Psychopathic Deviate Subscales (Harris-Lingoes):

Familial Discord (Pd1)	3	58
Authority Problems (Pd2)	5	61
Social Imperturbability (Pd3)	4	52
Social Alienation (Pd4)	4	51
Self-Alienation (Pd5)	3	48

Paranoia Subscales (Harris-Lingoes):

Persecutory Ideas (Pa1)	2	52
Poignancy (Pa2)	4	62
Naivete (Pa3)	6	56

Schizophrenia Subscales (Harris-Lingoes):

Social Alienation (Sc1)	4	55
Emotional Alienation (Sc2)	2	59
Lack of Ego Mastery, Cognitive (Sc3)	2	54
Lack of Ego Mastery, Conative (Sc4)	2	49
Lack of Ego Mastery, Def. Inhib. (Sc5)	4	68
Bizarre Sensory Experiences (Sc6)	7	75

Hypomania Subscales (Harris-Lingoes):

Amorality (Ma1)	3	58
Psychomotor Acceleration (Ma2)	10	73
Imperturbability (Ma3)	6	65
Ego Inflation (Ma4)	5	63

Social Introversion Subscales (Ben-Porath, Hostetler, Butcher, and Graham):

Shyness/Self-Consciousness (Si1)	6	53
Social Avoidance (Si2)	1	41
Alienation — Self and Others (Si3)	5	50

Uniform T scores are used for Hs, D, Hy, Pd, Pa, Pt, Sc, Ma, and the Content Scales; all other MMPI-2 scales use linear T scores.

Figure 83–4. Minnesota Report Personnel Screening Rules for the MMPI for the Airline Pilot Applicant

MMPI – 2™

MINNESOTA MULTIPHASIC PERSONALITY INVENTORY – 2™
by Starke R. Hathaway and J. Charnley McKinley

THE MINNESOTA REPORT:™ PERSONNEL SELECTION SYSTEM INTERPRETIVE REPORT
By James N. Butcher

Client ID:	3171	Report Date:	25-AUG-X9	Age:	43
Sex:	Male	Occupation:	Flight Crew	Education:	16

Profile Validity

This is a valid MMPI-2 profile. The applicant appeared to cooperate in describing his personality characteristics. His frank and open response to the items can be viewed as a positive indication of his involvement with the evaluation. The MMPI-2 profile is probably a good indication of his present personality functioning.

Personal Adjustment

The applicant's performance on the MMPI-2 suggests that he is outgoing and considers himself to have few psychological problems. However, his overuse of denial and tendency to overextend himself may occasionally cause him difficulties. He tends to be very aggressive, overconfident, and somewhat self-centered, with an unrealistic view of his capabilities. At times he is likely to be overly optimistic, fails to recognize his own limitations, and is insensitive to the needs of others. He tends to be an expressive, spontaneous person who might act or make decisions without careful consideration of consequences. Without apparent cause he may become somewhat elated, and at other times be moody and irritable.

He seems to have a wide range of interests, and appears to enjoy aesthetic and cultural activities. He appears to have no sex-role conflict.

In addition, the following description is suggested by the content of this applicant's responses. He may view the world as a jungle and sees others as hypercritical and dishonest. He shows some disrespect for authority and believes that a person should get away with everything he can. He believes it is acceptable to violate rules as long as "you don't get caught." He reports experiencing bizarre sensations, experiences, and/or hallucinations. His thinking may be quite confused, and he feels that others do not understand him and are trying to control him. He is also tending toward withdrawal into a world of fantasy. He seems quite hyperactive, impulsive, and excitable. He becomes easily bored and seeks stimulation. He is experiencing periods of excitement and unexplained elated mood. He appears to be tense, agitated, and restless, and is likely to become bored and frustrated easily. Individuals with these reported behaviors tend to act out impulsively, creating problems for themselves and others.

Interpersonal Relations

He appears to be a very outgoing person, forward and aggressive in relationships and able to influence others easily. Although he makes a good first impression, his relationships tend to be rather superficial.

He is outgoing and sociable and has a strong need to be around others. He shows little social anxiety, is probably effective in social situations and tends to be persuasive in dealing with others.

The content of this applicant's MMPI-2 responses suggests the following additional information concerning his interpersonal relations. He reported a moderate degree of family conflict at this time. He feels that his family life is not as pleasant as that of other people. He indicated that he has some troublesome family issues which might create problems at times.

Behavioral Stability

His behavior may be somewhat variable. He may appear quite outgoing and elated but may be susceptible to mood changes and irritability.

Possible Employment Problems

Flight crew applicants with this MMPI-2 profile should be carefully evaluated for possible impulsive behavior. Some individuals with this profile show careless judgment at times. They may engage in actions that are inappropriate or irresponsible because they are driven to seek pleasure. At times they may be thoughtless in their actions toward others.

While the applicant generally appears to be hard driving and expansive, he may become over-extended and have difficulty completing projects. He is frequently overconfident and may make promises that are difficult to keep. He also tends to dislike practical matters, preferring to be rather vague and superficial. There is some possibility that his interpersonal style may be a bit overbearing and might create strained relationships.

Table 83-3

Comparison of Overall Adjustment Ratings of Airline Pilots (N=262) Made by Experienced Clinicians and by Computer-Based Decision Rules

	Adequate	Problems Possible	Problems Likely	Row Total
Excellent (1)	2.4			1.9
Good (2)	42.5	20.0		35.9
Adequate (3)	53.6	43.3	3.0	48.5
Problems possible (4)	1.4	26.7	24.0	6.5
Poor (5)		10.0	64.0	7.3
Total	79.0	11.5	9.5	100.0

Clearly, the computer-based decision rules can provide both reliable and clinically congruent classifi- cations. The Minnesota Report Classification Deci- sion Rules were recently validated in police selection.

SUMMARY

Business and government managers have been employing psychologists to conduct psychological evaluations on both current and prospective employ- ees with greater frequency in recent years. Psycholog- ical tests, like the MMPI-2, that assess personality adjustment have been particularly valuable in evalu- ating applicants for jobs in highly sensitive, responsi- ble, or stressful occupations such as police, nuclear power plant operation, airline flight crews, and air traffic control. The MMPI-2 has been shown to be an effective instrument for objectively appraising per- sonality. Several examples of MMPI-2 use with employees and applicants were included.

Issues concerning the appropriateness of using psychological tests in business were discussed. The question of possible adverse impact upon minority group applicants was discussed. It was concluded, particularly with regard to the MMPI-2, that research has shown that minority group applicants are not adversely affected by the test. The efficiency and validity of the computerized MMPI-2 was discussed. One important value of using computer-based scor- ing and interpretive approaches in the area of per- sonnel screening is that the test interpretation procedures are objective and not open to the criti- cisms of selection bias as are other, more impression- istic approaches such as interview or projective tests.

REFERENCES

Bernstein, I., Teng, G., Grannemann, B.D., & Garbin, C.P. (1987). Invariance in the MMPI's component struc- ture. *Journal of Personality Assessment, 51,* 522–531.

Butcher, J.N. (1979). Use of the MMPI in industry. In J.N. Butcher (Ed.). *New developments in the use of the MMPI.* Minneapolis: University of Minnesota Press.

Butcher, J.N. (1985). Perspectives on International MMPI use. In J.N. Butcher & C.D. Spielberger (Eds.), *Advances in personality assessment* (vol. 4). Hillsdale, NJ: Lawrence Erlbaum Press.

Butcher, J.N. (1987a). *Use of the MMPI in personnel screening.* Paper given at the 22d Annual Symposium on Recent Developments in the Use of the MMPI, Seat- tle, Washington.

Butcher, J.N. (Ed.). (1987b). *Computerized psychological assessment.* New York: Basic Books.

Butcher, J.N. (1988). *Use of the MMPI in personnel screen- ing.* Paper given at the 23rd Annual Symposium on Recent Developments in the Use of the MMPI, St. Petersburg, Florida.

Butcher, J.N., & Cross, T. (1985). Psychological assessment in personal injury cases. In A. Hess & I. Weiner (Eds), *Handbook of forensic psychology.* New York: John Wiley & Sons.

Butcher, J.N., Graham, J.R., Williams, C.L., & Ben-Porath (In preparation). *Content scales for the MMPI-2.* Min- neapolis, Minnesota: University of Minnesota Press.

Butcher, J.N., & Tellegen, A.M. (1966). Objections to MMPI items. *Journal of Consulting Psychology, 30,* 527–534.

Dahlstrom, W.G., Lachar, D., & Dahlstrom, L. (1986). *MMPI patterns of American minorities.* Minneapolis: University of Minnesota Press.

Eyde, L., Kowal, D.M., & Fishburne, J.E. (1987). *Clinical implications of validity research on computer-based test interpretations of the MMPI.* Paper given at the annual meetings of the American Psychological Association, New York.

Gilberstadt, H., & Duker, J. (1965). *A handbook for clinical and actuarial MMPI interpretation.* Philadelphia: Saunders.

Graham, J.R. (1987). *The MMPI: A practical guide (2d ed.).* New York: Oxford University Press.

Greene, R. (1987). Ethnicity and MMPI performance: A review. *Journal of Consulting and Clinical Psychology, 55,* 497–512.

Gynther, M. (1972). White norms and black MMPIs: A prescription for discrimination? *Psychological Bulletin, 78,* 386–402.

Hathaway, S.R., & McKinley, J.C. (1940). A multiphasic personality schedule (Minnesota) I: Construction of the schedule. *Journal of Psychology, 10,* 249–254.

King, H.F., Carroll, J.L., & Fuller, G.B. (1977). Comparison of non-psychiatric blacks and whites on the MMPI. *Journal of Clinical Psychology, 33,* 725–728.

Kunce, J.T., & Anderson, W.P. (1976). Normalizing the MMPI. *Journal of Clinical Psychology, 32,* 776–780.

Lubin, B., Larsen, R.M., & Matarazzo, J. (1984). Patterns of psychological test usage in the United States, 1935–1982. *American Psychologist, 39,* 451–454.

Marks, P.A., Seeman, W., & Haller, D. (1975). *The actuarial use of the MMPI with adults and adolescents.* Baltimore: Williams & Wilkins.

Muller, B. (1988). *Use of the MMPI in police selection.* Paper given at the 23d Annual Symposium on Recent Developments in the Use of the MMPI, St. Petersburg, Florida.

Muller, B., & Bruno, L. (1988). *Ethnic differences in personality assessment of police candidates.* Paper given at the 23d Annual Symposium on Recent Developments in the Use of the MMPI, St. Petersburg, Florida.

National Computer Systems (1987). *Test users qualifications form: Qualifications to purchase assessment instruments.* Minneapolis.

University of Minnesota Press (1982). *User's guide for the Minnesota Report.* Minneapolis: National Computer Systems.

University of Minnesota Press (1984). *User's guide for the Minnesota Personnel Report.* Minneapolis: National Computer Systems.

Wennerholm, M., & Lopez-Roig, L. (1983). *Use of the MMPI with executives in Puerto Rico.* Paper given at the Eighth International Conference on Personality Assessment, Copenhagen, Denmark, August.

84 PERSONNEL SELECTION TO CONTROL EMPLOYEE THEFT AND COUNTERPRODUCTIVITY

John W. Jones, William Terris

The main purpose of preemployment polygraph examinations was to screen job applicants with a propensity for employee theft and other counterproductivity. Employee theft is widespread, difficult to detect, and the most costly crime against business (American Management Association, 1977). Hollinger and Clark (1983) surveyed thousands of employees to establish the base rate of employee theft. They found that the average percentage of people who admitted to theft was 42 percent for retail sector employees, 32 percent for hospital employees, and 26 percent for manufacturing personnel. Slora (1988) conducted an anonymous survey among fast food employees and found that 62 percent admitted to theft of company property or cash, and 78 percent admitted to "time theft" (e.g., faking illness and calling in sick; leaving work early without permission). These findings are consistent with Hefter's (1986) claim that one in three employees steals at work. Moreover, Meinsma's (1985) research suggests that anywhere from 10 percent to 30 percent of all business bankruptcies can be attributable in part to employee theft problems. These researchers are beginning to quantify both the total frequency and cost of employee theft. The existence of significant theft in the workplace is widely accepted by security researchers and professionals.

Two general approaches have been used by businesses to reduce theft losses. The first has been to alter the work environment so as to preclude the possibility of theft. This strategy is primarily aimed at shoplifters. It includes the use of undercover security officers, closed-circuit televisions, special sensor tags on each inventory article, and other methods of control. Though these systems may be effective in reducing theft by shoplifters, employee thieves often circumvent them.

A second approach has been to concentrate upon the preemployment screening process to minimize the selection of job applicants who are likely to engage in theft-related behaviors. This approach is aimed at employee theft. Preemployment screening appears to be one of the methods of choice for retail organizations in their efforts to control employee theft as a source of inventory shrinkage and profit drain (Sackett & Harris, 1984). Theft rates are typically lower in those organizations that conduct careful and extensive preemployment screening (Baumer & Rosenbaum, 1984; Jones, 1989).

Among the most popular selection methods used to determine the integrity of prospective employees has been the preemployment polygraph exam. The use of "lie detectors" to test job applicants became a normal business practice. Yet employers have needed to find alternatives to the preemployment polygraph since the passing of the federal Employee Polygraph Protection Act of 1988.

THE EMPLOYEE POLYGRAPH PROTECTION ACT OF 1988

The Employee Polygraph Protection Act became effective December 27, 1988 (Frierson, 1988; House of Representatives, 1988). It outlawed most business uses of polygraphs, especially preemployment polygraph exams to screen out job applicants with a history of theft. In fact, the act outlaws any type of physiologically based "lie detectors," including polygraphs, deceptographs, and voice stress analyzers. Businesses may be assessed a civil penalty of not more than $10,000 if they violate this provision. Moreover, employers may be liable to prospective employees affected by such a violation. Equitable relief to the applicant of both an offer of employment and the payment of lost wages and benefits can be deemed appropriate by the courts.

Polygraphs were outlawed for three major reasons. First, there was no scientifically acceptable research that showed that job applicants' polygraph results were accurate predictors of their past or future theft. That is, the preemployment polygraph exam was never thoroughly and scientifically validated with job applicants.

Second, the accuracy, fairness, and consistency of the polygraph exam appeared to be a function of the skill of the examiner. For example, more reliable admissions were obtained by licensed, highly trained examiners as opposed to less skilled examiners. The polygraph industry never established and enforced universal standards of competence that had to be met by all polygraphers. Examples of abuse were common.

Finally, the preemployment polygraph examination has been criticized as being unpleasant and stressful to applicants. Polygraphers were often skilled at interrogation and getting theft admissions from applicants. Unfortunately, this process tended to provoke strong negative feelings from applicants (e.g., Lykken, 1981).

Employee theft is still a very serious and costly problem for businesses to grapple with. In many jobs, employees know that they can easily steal cash or valuable merchandise or equipment. They can do so without any serious possibility of being caught. Hence, the federal ban on preemployment polygraph exams will lead employers to seek other methods to determine the honesty of job applicants.

The purpose of this chapter is to describe screening methods that companies use to hire a dependable work force (cf., Jones & Terris, 1989). Special emphasis will be given to preemployment integrity tests. These psychological Inventories are easy to administer and have scientific studies documenting their ability to screen out applicants who are likely to engage in on-the-job theft. Advantages and limitations of each selection procedure are summarized in table 84–1.

THEFT REDUCTION THROUGH PERSONNEL SELECTION

Preemployment Polygraph Examinations

There are a few exceptions to the Polygraph Protection Act. Hence, the preemployment polygraph examination is reviewed first. The act does allow governmental units—federal, state, or local—to continue the use of polygraphs except as limited by state laws. Some companies with nuclear power–related contracts with the Department of Energy may also be allowed to use the polygraph. Finally, businesses will be allowed to use polygraphs for selection in two situations: the hiring of certain private security firm employees and the hiring of persons with access to specified drugs (Schedule I, II, III, or IV drugs as defined in the Federal Control Substances Act).

The purpose of a preemployment polygraph examination is to uncover all undetected dishonest acts committed by a job applicant during a certain period of time. The underlying theory is that past behavior predicts future behavior. The preemployment examination typically covers many different areas of dishonest behavior. For instance, in a typical preemployment examination, the examiner will try to uncover the following information:

1. Prior convictions.
2. Prior undetected thefts of money from the job.
3. Prior undetected thefts of property and merchandise from the job.

4. Various types of undetected theft off the job.
5. Illegal drug use.
6. Selling of illegal drugs.
7. Other information requested by the employer.

The preemployment polygraph examination yields the following two types of information: *admissions* and *signs of deception*. Thus, the applicant may either make or not make an admission to any question and either show or not show signs of deception. Admissions have an obvious type of face validity. The applicant who admits taking $200 in merchandise from a previous employer had probably taken that much at the very least. The validity (accuracy) of the polygrapher's interpretation of deception is much more controversial (e.g., Sackett & Decker, 1979).

Employment Interviews

The traditional interview is an important part of almost every company's personnel selection procedures. Unfortunately, while there have been many studies investigating the various types of validity of the employment interview (e.g., Schmitt, 1976), there has been no published research investigating the effectiveness of the employment interview as a method to predict and reduce employee theft. The general validity of the interview apparently depends upon the interviewer's having accurate and complete information about the job and worker requirements

Table 84–1
Summary of Main Screening Methods Used to Reduce Employee Theft

Screening Method	Convenience Issues	Main Problems	Main Advantages
Preemployment polygraph	Requires additional time if exam is off-site	Illegal for most business uses May offend job applicants Validity is questioned Difficulty in obtaining well-trained examiners	May discourage dishonest applicants from even applying Often results in actual admissions from applicants
Selection interview	Usually part of hiring procedure	No evidence of validity Difficult to determine truthfulness in discussing theft and counterproductivity	Inexpensive (already part of hiring procedures) Structured integrity interviews show promise
Reference checks	Often time-consuming	Little evidence of validity Most misconduct is undetected Company reluctant to give negative information	May increase truthfulness of applicants Verifies information provided on application form and resumes
Credit checks	Quick but somewhat costly	Relevance to theft not clear May not meet EEOC guidelines	Obtains information relevant to financial need and fiscal responsibility
Honesty tests	Can easily be made part of the usual screening procedure	Test scores can be misinterpreted Not all honesty tests are thoroughly validated	More validity data than other selection methods Inexpensive Not offensive No adverse impact (meets EEOC guidelines) May discourage dishonest applicants from even applying

(e.g., Landy, 1976). However, interviewers are not likely to have accurate or complete information regarding valid predictors of employee theft since relatively little is known about this subject. Interviewers are likely to rely upon certain stereotypes when making a judgment regarding honesty (e.g., firm handshake, shifty eyes, type and style of clothes). Finally, the employment interview is very likely to cause problems in the areas related to equal employment opportunities (e.g., Arvey, 1979). Traditional employment interviews need to be validated against theft criteria before they can be seen as viable alternatives to preemployment polygraph exams.

Wilson (1988) is pioneering a new approach to employment interviewing called "structured integrity interviewing." This type of interview can be used to identify job applicants who are at risk for dishonest behavior in the workplace. Structured interviews are a new breed of interviews that have much higher levels of validity than traditional, open-ended interviews (McDaniel, 1988).

Structured integrity interview questions are based on a thorough analysis of both the job and the opportunities to steal at work. Structured interviewers typically ask job applicants to describe their past job behavior. Past behavior is highly predictive of how a person will perform in a new job (cf., Janz, 1982). Some structured questions are phrased to ask applicants how they would respond to hypothetical scenarios related to employee theft in the workplace. Finally, all structured questions are written in advance and presented in a structured interview guide. Answers to each structured question are rated on five-point, behaviorally anchored rating scale to improve the overall accuracy of this selection procedure.

Wilson's structured integrity questions ask applicants to describe situations where they were particularly honest or dishonest at another job. In addition, she recommends a series of probing questions in case applicants are resistant to answer questions truthfully and comprehensively related to their levels of integrity and dependability. Interviewers are also taught how to ask these types of sensitive questions in order to put applicants at ease when answering them. Structured integrity interviewing is one of the most promising new strategies in the field of personnel interviewing.

Reference Checks

Perhaps the major purpose of the reference check is to verify information which the applicants have previously supplied to the company. Moreover, applicants expecting reference checks are thought to be more truthful in the information they supply to the company. Usually reference checks are costly and time-consuming when one considers the amount of information that is produced. Perhaps this is the reason that most companies do not perform complete reference checks on most applicants. There is little, if any, direct evidence that the use of reference checks actually reduces employee theft (cf. Terris, 1986).

While reference checks are probably desirable, they do have major limitations in terms of obtaining information relevant to employee theft. One problem is that employers are often reluctant to give negative information concerning past employees because of possible lawsuits. In fact, dishonest employees caught stealing sometimes make a deal with their employers. The employee agrees to resign and return the money or property in return for a good or at least neutral reference. A more important problem is that in most companies the employer is not really aware of which employees are stealing. Another problem is that there is little evidence as to the validity or accuracy of data obtained from reference checks. Finally, job applicants can usually easily omit from the reference list the names of any companies where they are known to have stolen money or merchandise.

Criminal Background Checks

Criminal background checks and investigations can vary from little more than a reference check to a complete investigation of an individual's entire life. Usually the background check is limited to a check on a person's past criminal history. Arrest records, while probably valid, are seldom used to make a hiring decision because of possible legal ramifications. Several states ban employers outright from either asking about or using arrest information to make a hiring decision. While federal laws apparently do not absolutely forbid using arrest information, using arrest records to make hiring decisions would probably result in adverse impact against blacks and some other minority groups.

Convictions, on the other hand, can be considered when making a hiring decision. However, one possible requirement is that only relevant or job-related criminal histories be considered. For example, an applicant with a prior conviction for theft could be denied employment where the opportunity for on-the-job theft is great (e.g., clerks in a jewelry store). It is not yet certain if a company can use irrelevant convictions. Actually, the question of relevant versus irrelevant convictions is essentially an empirical question, and research is needed to show whether a certain type of conviction is predictive of future employee theft.

There are a number of problems with criminal checks. First, legal and practical obstacles make it time-consuming and difficult to obtain criminal records. Any information obtained is likely to be incomplete or misleading. For example, most crimes are never detected. Most detected crimes never lead to actual arrest, and apparently many arrests do not lead to a conviction. Furthermore, many convictions are based upon plea bargaining or some other type of reduced sentencing. It should also be remembered that employee thieves are almost never caught or convicted.

Credit Checks

Some employers use credit checks to make a hiring decision. The rationale is that applicants with either a great need for money to pay bills or a history of irresponsible financial management are thought to be greater risks for positions of trust. While there apparently is no empirical evidence to support this belief, it does seem likely that individuals who really need a great deal of money would be more tempted to steal than those without a great need. Credit checks would seem to have a high probability of producing adverse impact against racial minorities.

Employment Application Forms

While weighted employment application forms and similar biographical data have been found to be valid predictors of job success in many different occupations (cf., England, 1971), only one study has been published related to employee theft (Rosenbaum, 1976). The main predictors in this study were essentially racial in nature, and the validity coefficients were low. Hence, current research suggests that this procedure does not accurately predict theft and in fact may lead to discrimination against racial minorities. Much more research is needed to determine the viability of the employment application form as an alternative to preemployment polygraphs.

Psychological Assessment

Historically, attempts to predict criminal behavior with personality tests have not been successful (cf., Schuessler & Cressey, 1950). Commonly used personality tests such as the Sixteen Personality Factor Questionnaire (16PF) (Cattell, Ebert & Tatsuoka, 1970) and the Minnesota Multiphasic Personality Inventory (MMPI) (Dahlstrom & Welsh, 1980) have not been found to predict employee theft consistently.

More recently, an extensive amount of research has been conducted with paper-and-pencil integrity tests (Sackett, Burris & Callahan, 1989). Integrity tests are psychological tests designed to predict job applicants' proneness for theft and other forms of counterproductivity. Most integrity tests are designed to measure job applicants' attitudes toward, perceptions of, and opinions about theft. Validation research that complies with test development guidelines of the American Psychological Association has been published for a number of integrity tests (e.g., London House, 1980). Although all integrity tests differ from one another in important ways, leading overt integrity tests measure attitudes related to one or more of the following psychological constructs:

1. Tolerance of others who steal.
2. Projection about the extent of theft by others.
3. Acceptance of rationalizations for theft.
4. Antisocial beliefs and behaviors.
5. Admissions of theft-related activities.

Unlike general personality testing and other types of personnel screening procedures, there has been a great deal of validity research where integrity test scores have predicted theft behavior. Most of the current research with integrity tests has been conducted with the Personnel Selection Inventory (PSI), McDaniel & Jones, 1988; Sackett & Harris, 1984). Terris (1979a) found that the PSI accurately predicted theft admissions made in preemployment polygraph examinations. Ash (1970, 1971, 1972, 1976) was able to obtain a similar pattern of results with another preemployment integrity test. Yet the validity of the PSI is not limited to polygraph admissions.

The PSI has also been found to predict the following theft criteria: (1) supervisors' ratings of employees' dishonesty (Jones & Terris, 1983a), (2) applicants who are likely to get caught stealing once hired (Jones & Terris, 1981), (3) applicants who have a criminal history (Jones & Terris, 1985), and (4) applicants who are likely to make theft admissions in an anonymous testing situation (Terris, 1979b; Jones, 1980, 1981).

Other longitudinal studies have shown that a group of convenience stores using the PSI experienced a 50 percent reduction in shrinkage over a period of approximately eighteen months (Terris & Jones, 1982). This impact-on-losses study was replicated in the home improvement center industry (Brown, Jones, Terris & Steffy, 1987). Several other studies (Jones & Terris, 1984; Terris & Jones 1982) have shown that applicants and employees from high-theft stores score more poorly on integrity tests than do applicants and employees from low-theft stores.

Employees Thief Profile

The following psychological profile emerges from the empirical research on integrity tests. Employee thieves tend to:

1. Rate themselves lower in honesty and in other related areas of integrity (e.g., illicit drug abuse).
2. Believe or suspect that most employees steal.
3. Accept the many common rationalizations for theft.
4. Often fantasize about successful theft.
5. Obsessively think and ruminate about theft.
6. Make many more theft-related admissions.
7. Are more deviant in other areas of life (e.g., illegal drug use, violence, unsafe behavior).

Hence, employee thieves have a definite psychological profile that is different from honest employees. Paper-and-pencil integrity tests can accurately measure the various dimensions of this profile. Yet even though integrity tests can predict employees' theft proneness, they must be fair to all minority groups, and they must be nonoffensive to applicants.

Adverse Impact Analysis

Personnel selection methods, including integrity tests, cannot adversely discriminate against any race or sex groups (EEOC, 1979). All of the integrity tests report a lack of adverse impact against protected groups (cf., Terris, 1979a; O'Bannon, Goldinger & Appleby, 1989; Sackett, Burris & Callahan, 1989). Female applicants do as well as or better than males (more honest) in all of the studies, and no racial differences have been found. Hence, integrity tests appear to be fair to all minority groups. Adverse impact studies should routinely be conducted for any selection method that a company chooses to control employee theft.

Test Takers' Reactions

Unlike preemployment polygraphs, the majority of job applicants are not offended when they take a paper-and-pencil integrity test. Jones and Joy (1988) found that 82 percent of the applicants who took the PSI had no objections to the test. The few applicants who did object to the test were reliably more likely to score below standards (in the "dishonest" direction). Similar results were found by Ryan and Sackett (1987). It appears that employment applicants with both tolerant attitudes toward theft and a history of dishonest activities are most likely to get defensive about and object to taking preemployment integrity tests.

Privacy Issues

Jones, Ash, and Soto (1990) concluded that preemployment integrity tests do not seem to infringe upon the workplace privacy rights of job applicants if professionally developed tests are selected, implemented, and interpreted. These researchers reviewed a large number of privacy issues that must be considered when using preemployment integrity tests. For example, companies should use integrity tests only if they have an obvious business exposure to employee theft and other counterproductivity. In this situation, integrity tests are one of the most effective approaches to a very real business problem. The integrity test selected should meet all professional and legal standards for test development, implementation, and general use. The test should include only questions that are permissible according to federal and state laws. Applicants should sign informed consent forms where applicable, and all applicants should be administered the test in a quiet, comfortable test-taking environment. Only properly trained company representatives should have access to applicants' test scores on a need-to-know basis, and public disclosure of test scores should be avoided at all costs. Finally, completed test booklets and scoring keys should be locked up at all times.

Candid Responses

Some people falsely assume that smarter job applicants might deduce the purpose of the preemployment integrity tests and skew their answers to reflect, falsely, a more honest disposition. Yet Jones and Terris (1983b) found that job applicants' intelligence test scores are not related to their honesty scores. Smarter people did not score better on the integrity test.

Also, integrity tests typically contain a separate Distortion Scale to determine if job applicants are being candid with their answers. Applicants are also discouraged from trying to "fake good" or distort their answers on integrity tests since the instructions state that any attempts to provide inaccurate answers can be detected and could invalidate the test results. Paper-and-pencil integrity tests appear to be valid, fair, and useable.

Alternate Explanations

Psychological integrity tests are effective because they screen out theft-prone individuals and screen in more honest, productive employees. However, there are other explanations that could further explain the reduction in theft. One such explanation is that the use of a valid selection procedure creates an organizational climate that is unfavorable to theft. Employees prone to steal may be less likely to consider the possibility of theft if their fellow employees obviously disapprove of theft (cf., Hollinger & Clark, 1983).

Another possibility is that using an integrity test sends a message to all applicants and employees that the company cares about preventing theft and will do something about it. Perhaps this serves as a warning signal to all employees. This is the deterrent effect.

A third possible explanation is that a selection system sensitizes the entire work force to these issues. Using a psychological test to screen out theft-prone applicants usually generates a great deal of discussion about theft in all levels of the organization. It is possible that values and opinions may be changed somewhat in the process.

A fourth possible explanation is that the implementation of a personnel selection procedure creates system changes of one type or another within the organization. For example, interviewers may begin to do a better job interviewing, perhaps security personnel will become more vigilant, and so on. From the point of view of the organization, the reasons that something works may be less important than the fact that it works. However, from the point of view of the personnel researcher, the reasons are important. Certainly when we understand why something works, we can also maximize the effectiveness of the procedure.

Negligent Hiring

Companies should have the right to use integrity tests to avoid negligent hiring lawsuits. Companies have a legal responsibility to provide a safe and crime-free workplace. Employers maybe held liable for negligently hiring employees who prove to be dangerous or dishonest workers. Employers who negligently employ a counterproductive individual may be liable to third parties whose injury or loss is proximately caused by the employer's negligence.

The tort of negligent hiring addresses the risk created by exposing members of the public to a potentially dangerous or dishonest individual. The doctrine of *respondeat superior* is based on the theory that the employee is the agent of the employer. Case law has concluded that liability is predicated on the negligence of an employer in placing an applicant with known propensities that should have been discovered by reasonable investigation in an employment position in which, because of circumstances of employment, it should have been foreseeable that the hired individual posed a threat of injury to others.

Many companies use preemployment integrity tests to prevent negligent hiring claims. For example, security guard companies want to avoid hiring dishonest guards who might plan and execute a theft of cash or property at the location they are guarding. Such an activity, with or without a weapon (e.g., an armed robbery), could put the company that provided the guard services at risk for a lawsuit.

A manufacturer of gold sunglass frames for the U.S. government recently recovered over $300,000 against a security firm on the theory of negligent hir-

ing. A guard from a national security firm was involved in three thefts of gold used in the making of sunglass frames. The security firm was found liable for negligent hiring. In upholding the jury verdict, the court also stated that an employer had a continuing duty to retain in its service only those employees who are fit and competent (*Welsh Manufacturing v. Pinkerton,* 1984).

Negligent hiring cases are becoming more popular. Another case cited in the *Wall Street Journal* (April 5, 1985, p. 1) is summarized below:

> Careless hiring leads to costly lawsuits when employers are found negligent. . . .An Arizona appeals court upheld a $184,000 award against a realty firm that hired a [dishonest] saleswoman it knew had committed forgery. . . .The saleswoman forged signatures on a sales contract; the seller sued and won. . . .In North Carolina, a court recently held an employment agency negligent for referring a bookkeeper who embezzled from her new employer. (*Pruitt v. Pavelin,* 1984)

Preemployment integrity tests can help companies better control this type of legal exposure. Companies that use valid integrity tests to screen job applicants carefully will reduce their exposure to negligent hiring claims.

MODEL GUIDELINES FOR INTEGRITY TESTS

The Association of Personnel Test Publishers (APTP, 1989) published the *Model Guidelines for Preemployment Integrity Testing Programs.* These guidelines are to be used in conjuction with other professional and legal standards on the proper use of personnel tests. APTP developed these guidelines to ensure that both test publishers and test users adhere

to effective ethical and legal integrity testing practices in the following areas: (1) test development and selection, (2) test administration, (3) scoring, (4) test fairness and confidentiality, and (5) public statements and test marketing practices. Companies would benefit from guidelines that help them to select and use preemployment integrity tests properly.

NEW DIRECTIONS IN PERSONNEL SELECTION

The preemployment polygraph examinations typically provided companies with additional information besides applicants' likelihood to steal. Preemployment polygraphs were also used to assess applicants' history of illicit drug use, their tendency to quit work over work-related conflicts and their feigning worker compensation injuries when no true injury exists. Companies need information in these areas to control better drug-related accidents, turnover costs, and escalating insurance premiums, respectively.

Many integrity tests, including the PSI, have been designed to provide companies with important supplemental information, too. For example, tables 84–2 and 84–3 highlight the different supplemental areas measured by the PSI. The Drug Avoidance Scale can be used by companies that want to control drug-related crimes and accidents. The Customer Relations Scale identifies applicants who will provide high-quality service to customers. The Safety Scale is used by businesses that are concerned about controlling

Table 84–2
Personnel Selection Inventory Subscale Descriptions

Honesty
  Measures an applicant's attitudes toward theft, as well as the likelihood that the individual will not engage in theft-related behavior on the job.

Responsibility
  Measures an applicant's tendencies to perform job duties in a dependable, responsible and trustworthy manner. The version with this scale is designated with an "R."

Tenure
  Measures the likelihood that an applicant will stay with a company once hired. Versions of the PSI with this scale are designated with a "T."

Drug Avoidance
  Measures the likelihood that the applicant will not use or sell illicit drugs on the job. The drug opinion inquiry, an unscored section available only on the PSI-2, includes additional items about on-the-job use or sale of illegal drugs.

Nonviolence
  Measures the likelihood that an applicant is not prone to abusive or hostile behavior.

Employee/customer relations
  Measures an applicant's tendencies toward courtesy, cooperation, and customer service.

Emotional Stability
  Measures whether an applicant is likely to have emotional problems that could disrupt work performance and safety practices.

Safety
  Measures an applicant's attitudes toward safety and how it may cause or prevent on-the-job accidents. Versions of the PSI with this scale are designated with an "S."

Work Values
  Measures an applicant's attitudes toward work and positive work habits.

Supervision attitudes
  Measures the likelihood that an applicant will respond appropriately to supervision and follow company policy.

Validity/distortion
  Indicates the extent to which the individual responds to the inventory in a socially desirable manner. Low scores indicate a tendency to exaggerate positive traits and minimize negative qualities.

Validity/accuracy
  Indicates the degree to which the applicant understood and carefully completed the inventory.

Employability index
  A composite scale to determine the applicant's overall suitability for hire.

Detailed personal and behavioral history (not scored)
  Enables the employer to gather other applicant background information as well as information on specific job skills and experience.

Note: Each version of the PSI contains one or more of the scales listed in this table.

escalating insurance costs. The Work Values and Supervision scales tell companies if applicants will be productive workers and follow their supervisors' orders, respectively. The Tenure Scale informs management if an applicant is likely to quit a job prematurely, thus wasting training dollars and leaving a company understaffed. These additional scales are valid and reliable predictors of the job-related behaviors they purport to predict. Supplemental scales can help companies better contain costs and increase profits in areas other than just theft reduction.

Also, Sackett, Burris, and Callahan (1989) have documented the emergence of personality-oriented measures of integrity. While this type of assessment system appears to be a weaker predictor of on-the-job theft (Frost & Rafilson, 1989), it does appear to yield useful levels of validity when predicting more general forms of employee counterproductivity (Rafilson, 1988).

CONCLUSIONS

There are no simple solutions to controlling employee theft and other forms of counterproductivity. However, theft reduction through personnel selection appears to be an effective strategy for protecting bottom-line profits. Research is always needed to determine the extent to which any personnel selection

Table 84–3
Personnel Selection Inventory Version Titles

PSI Scales	PSI Version Titles														
	1	2	3	3S	3T	3R	3ST	4	5	5S	7	7S	7T	7ST	7RS
Honesty Scale	*	*	*	*	*		*	*	*	*	*	*	*	*	
Responsibility Scale						*									*
Tenure Scale					*		*						*	*	*
Drug Avoidance Scale			*	*	*	*	*	*	*	*	*	*	*	*	*
Nonviolence Scale			*	*	*	*	*	*	*	*					
Employee/Customer Relations Scale									*	*					
Emotional Stability Scale															
Safety Scale				*			*				*	*	*	*	*
Work Values Scale											*	*	*	*	*
Supervision Scale											*	*	*	*	*
Validity Scale—Distortion	*	*	*	*	*	*	*	*	*	*	*	*	*	*	*
Validity Scale—Accuracy	*	*	*	*	*	*	*	*	*	*	*	*	*	*	*
Employability Index							*				*	*	*	*	*
Detailed personal and behavioral history								*	*						
Drug opinion inquiry		*													
French editions			*												
Spanish editions			*	*							*	*			

procedure is a valid measurement of job applicants' propensity for on-the-job counterproductivity. Companies should consider the following issues before choosing and implementing any selection strategy designed to control employee theft and counterproductivity:

1. Companies should use only selection procedures that have been adequately validated. Ideally, the validation strategy would include a series of studies in which the selection procedure is validated in many different ways against many different types of counterproductivity. Since each validation approach has different strengths and weaknesses, a multimethod validation approach is best.

2. An adverse impact analysis should be conducted for any selection procedure being considered. This analysis should be performed in accordance with the Equal Employment Opportunity Commission guidelines.

3. Nearly all the existing validation research has been conducted with psychological integrity tests. Companies should attempt to validate any personnel selection procedure that does not have sufficient validation research.

4. The integrity test should be used as only one part of a more comprehensive assessment program. The test should be used in accordance with professional and legal standards.

REFERENCES

American Management Association (1977). *Crimes against business project: Background and recommendations.* New York: American Management Association.

Arvey, R. (1979). Unfair discrimination in the employment interview: Legal and psychological aspects. *Psychological Bulletin, 86,* 736–765.

Ash, P. (1970). The validation of an instrument to predict the likelihood of employee theft. *Proceedings of the 78th Annual Convention of the American Psychological Association.* Washington, DC: The Association.

Ash, P. (1971). Screening employment applicants for attitudes toward theft. *Journal of Applied Psychology, 55,* 161–164.

Ash, P. (1972). Attitudes of work applicants toward theft. *Proceedings of the 17th International Congress of Applied Psychology.* Liège, Belgium.

Ash, P. (1976). The assessment of honesty in employment. *South African Journal of Psychology, 6.* 68–79

Ash, P. (1989). *The legality of preemployment inquiries.* Park Ridge, IL: London House; Inc.

Association of Personnel Test Publishers (1989). *Model guidelines for preemployment integrity testing programs.* Washington, D.C.: Author.

Baumer, T.L., & Rosenbaum, D.P. (1984). *Combatting retail theft: Programs and strategies.* Boston: Butterworth Publishers.

Brown, T.S., Jones, J.W., Terris, W., & Steffy, B.D. (1987). The impact of preemployment integrity testing on employee turnover and inventory shrinkage losses. *Journal of Business and Psychology, 2,* 136–149.

Campbell, D., & Stanley, J. (1963). *Experimental and quasi-experimental designs for research.* Chicago: Rand McNally.

Cattel, R.B., Ebert, H.W., & Tatsuoka, M.M. (1970). *Handbook for the Sixteen Personality Factor Questionnaire (16PF).* Champaign, IL: Institute for Personality and Ability Testing.

Dahistrom, W.G., & Welsh, G.S. (1980). *An MMPI Handbook.* Minneapolis: University of Minnesota Press.

England, G.W. (1971). *Development and use of weighted application blanks* (rev. ed). Minneapolis: University of Minnesota Industrial Relations Center.

Equal Employment Opportunity Commission (EEOC) (1979). Adoption of questions and answers to clarify and provide a common interpretation of the Uniform Guidelines on Employee Selection Procedures. *Federal Register, 44,* 11996–12009.

Frierson, J.G. (1988). The new federal polygraph law's impact on business. *Commerce* (Fall), 70–71.

Frost, A.G., & Rafilson, F.M. (1989). Overt integrity tests versus personality-based measures of delinquency: An emperical comparison. *Journal of Business and Psychology, 3* (3), 269–277.

Hefter, R. (1986). The crippling crime. *Security World, 23,* 36–38.

Hollinger, R., & Clark, J. (1983). *Theft by employees.* Lexington, MA: Lexington Books.

House of Representatives (1988). *Employee Polygraph Protection Act of 1988.* 100th Congress, 2d Session, Report 100–659.

Janz, T. (1982). Initial comparisons of patterned behavior description interviews versus unstructured interviews. *Journal of Applied Psychology, 67,* 577–580.

Jones, J.W. (1980). Attitudinal correlates of employees' deviance: Theft, alcohol use, and nonprescribed drug use. *Psychological Reports, 47,* 71–77.

Jones, J.W. (1981). Attitudinal correlates of employee theft of drugs and hospital supplies among nursing personnel. *Nursing Research, 30,* 351–359.

Jones, J.W. (1989). Measure for measure. Is your testing program paying off? *Journal of Staffing and Recruitment* (Fall), 57–62.

Jones, J.W., & Joy, D. (1988). Emperical investigation of job applicants' reactions to taking a preemployment honesty test. Manuscript submitted for publication.

Jones, J.W., & Terris, W. (1981). *Predictive validation of a dishonesty test that measures theft proneness.* Paper presented at the 18th Interamerican Congress of Psychology, Santo Domingo, Dominican Republic.

Jones, J.W., & Terris, W. (1983a). Predicting employees' theft in home improvement centers. *Psychological Reports, 52,* 187–201.

Jones, J.W., & Terris, W. (1983b). Personality correlates of theft and drug abuse among job applicants. *Proceedings of the Third International Conference on the 16PF test.* Champaign, IL: IPAT Press.

Jones, J.W., & Terris, W. (1984). *The organizational climate of honesty: empirical investigation* (Technical report No. 27). Park Ridge, IL: London House Press.

Jones, J.W., & Terris, W. (1985). Screening employment applicants for attitudes toward theft: Three quasi-experiments. *International Journal of Management, 2,* 62–72.

Jones, J.W., & Terris, W. (1989). After the polygraph ban. *Recruitment Today* (May–June), 25–31.

Jones, J.W., Ash, P., & Soto, C. (in press). Selecting honest employees while protecting job applicants' privacy rights. *Employee Relations Law Journal.*

Landy, F.J. (1976). The validity of the interview in police officer selection. *Journal of Applied Psychology, 61,* 193–198.

London House, Inc. (1980). *Personnel Selection Inventory (PSI).* Park Ridge, IL: London House Press.

Lykken, D.T. (1981). *A tremor in the blood.* New York: McGraw-Hill.

McDaniel, M.A. (1988). *Employment interviews: Structure, validity, and unanswered questions.* Paper presented at the Third Annual Convention of the Society for Industrial and Organizational Psychology, April.

McDaniel, M.A., & Jones, J.W. (1988). Predicting employee theft: A quantitative review of a standardized measure of honesty. *Journal of Business and Psychology, 2,* 327–345.

Meinsma, G. (1985). Thou shalt not steal. *Security Management, 29,* 35–37.

O'Bannon, R.M., Goldinger, L.A., & Appleby, G.S. (1989). *Honesty and integrity testing: A practical guide.* Atlanta, GA: Applied Information Resources.

Pruitt v. Pavelin (1984). 685 P. 2d 1347 (Ariz. App.).

Rafilson, F.M. (1988). Development of a standardized measure to predict employee productivity. *Journal of Business and Psychology, 3* (2), 199–213.

Rosenbaum, R.W. (1976). Predictability of employee theft using weighted application blanks. *Journal of Applied Psychology, 61,* 94–98.

Ryan, A.M., & Sackett, P.R. (1987). Preemployment honesty testing: Fakability, reactions of test takers, and company image. *Journal of Business and Psychology, 1,* 248–256.

Sackett, P.R., Burris, L.R., & Callahan, C. (1989). Integrity testing for personel selection: An update. *Personnel Psychology, 41,* 421–429.

Sackett, P., & Decker, P. (1979). Detection of deception in the employment context: A review and critical analysis. *Personnel Psychology, 32,* 487–506.

Sackett, P.R., & Harris, M.E. (1984). Honesty testing for personel selection: a review and critique. *Personnel Psychology, 37,* 221–246.

Schmitt, N. (1976). Social and situational determinants of interview decisions: Implications for the employment interview. *Personnel Psychology, 29,* 79–101.

Schuessier, K., & Cressey, D. (1950). Personality characteristics of criminals. *American Journal of Sociology, 55,* 476–484.

Slora, K. (1988). *Employee theft in the fast food industry* (Technical Research Report No. 2). Park Ridge, IL: London House Press.

Terris, W. (1979a). Attitudinal correlates of employee integrity: Theft-related admissions made in preemployment polygraph examinations. *Journal of Security Administration, 2,* 30–39.

Terris, W. (1979b). *Attitudinal correlates of theft, violence and drug use.* Paper presented at the 17th Interamerican Congress of Psychology, Lima, Peru.

Terris, W. (1986). *Employee theft: Research, theory, and applications.* Park Ridge, IL: London House Press.

Terris, W., & Jones, J.W. (1982). Psychological factors related to employee theft in the convenience store industry. *Psychological Reports, 51,* 1219–1238.

Welsh Manufacturing v. Pinkerton's Inc. (1984). 474 A.2d 436 (R.I.).

Wilson, C. (1988). *New developments in selection interviewing.* Paper presented at the Training '88 Conference for Human Resource Professionals, New York, December 12–16.

Stephen G. Glasscock, C. William Deckner, Thomas F. Mahan

Consumer and employee theft are difficult problems for a wide range of businesses, and both types of theft usually result in higher prices for consumers. There are numerous estimates regarding how costly these problems may be. For example, Wright (1972) has suggested that shoplifting accounts for an annual loss of $2 billion to $3.5 billion to consumers in terms of increases in the cost of consumer services and products. Similarly, Lykken (1974) has suggested that $6 billion is lost annually to employee theft. Other estimates exist, both higher and lower; however, it is prudent to assume that the true incidence and economic cost of consumer and employee theft are unknown.

In part, the difficulty is that these estimates are obscured by the lack of technology to measure these types of theft accurately. Further, even to the extent that there are ways of measuring these losses, there is no standard method of measurement that permits comparisons of losses in different business settings (McNees, Gilliam, Schnelle & Risley, 1979). In fact, this "ordinary crime" (see Arboleda-Florez, Durie &

Costello, 1977) may benefit and thrive on management's lack of measurement specificity in accounting for shrinkage.

Consumer theft has been treated in two major fashions. First, shoplifters have been given psychotherapeutic treatment for shoplifting, thus implying that consumer theft is a psychological problem (cf. Kellam, 1969; Henderson, 1981; Gauthier & Pellerin, 1982). Also, shoplifting has been handled in a more global fashion, wherein all consumers are subjected to interventions designed to prevent consumer theft in the setting where it occurs. Many of the latter interventions are commonly in major department stores and include strategies such as convex mirrors, closed-circuit television, and security guards. Most employers attempt to minimize employee theft through preventive methods. These interventions include developing and publishing employee antitheft policies, implementing inventory and financial control systems, screening job applicants, and installing security systems.

REVIEW OF THE LITERATURE

Unevaluated Techniques

Numerous popular press articles provide, at most, brief descriptions of various theft-prevention techniques. These include hanger locks, signs indicating that someone may enter a fitting room at any time to check merchandise, circulating inspectors, crisscrossing hangers, rewards (up to $2,500 at Macy's) to employees who report other employees, conspicuous

arrests, transferring merchandise in locked containers to lessen the chance of inside jobs, advertising that prosecution will follow all arrests for theft, and undercover security people posing as stockpersons and housekeeping staff. Unfortunately, few, if any, of the popular press articles offer any basis for evaluating the efficacy of these techniques. Articles from the popular press, clinical studies, and analogue studies will not be reviewed. Our assumption in making this decision is that the reader of this book are primarily businesspersons who are interested in interventions that have been documented to have global preventive impact in specific business settings. Accordingly, attention will be given to studies offering a functional evaluation of various interventions' effectiveness.

Preparation of this manuscript was partially supported by grants from NICHD to George Peabody College of Vanderbilt University and Vanderbilt Medical Center. The authors gratefully acknowledge Bette Reilly for her assistance in the preparation of this manuscript.

With this focus, practical, research-validated strategies may be considered by the reader pertinent to preventing consumer and employee theft.

It is clearly regrettable that so few studies provide evaluations of intervention effectiveness since there is an evident need for a means of assessing which procedures are best for one's particular business. This is not intended to imply that security firms or other organizations (e.g., National Retail Merchants' Association) that provide consumer and employee theft programs are offering ineffective programs. Rather, our point is that either systematic evaluations of the efficacy of those programs have not been conducted, or, if such evaluations have been done, there has been no dissemination of their findings in the business and behavioral science literature. We recommend utilization of theft prevention programs that have been validated by research as opposed to seemingly effective

and often expensive programs for which there are no data to evaluate purported effectiveness.

Evaluated Techniques

The following studies are presented as models of research that document an intervention's impact in actual business settings. In each of the presented studies, the investigators conducted an analysis of the degree of theft reduction achieved, disseminated their findings, and provided sufficient procedural detail that the intervention could be replicated in similar business settings. These studies demonstrate that visual feedback, in the form of a written message such as a sign or the public posting of a graph, is effective in reducing theft. Various forms of visual feedback have been used alone and in conjunction with other interventions to reduce consumer and employee theft.

SIGNS AND CONSUMER THEFT

McNees, Kennon, Schnelle, Kirchner, and Thomas (1980) devised an intervention that entailed public posting of signs designed to reduce retail theft by elementary school–aged youth. These investigators noted that over 50 percent of all shoplifters are youth (Heinstein, 1974) and that increasing losses to shoplifters each year were estimated to total over 13 million per day ("To Catch a Thief," 1974). Additionally, they noted that shoplifting may seriously affect the direction of youths' lives by limiting educational, employment, and professional opportunities.

The setting of McNees et al.'s (1980) research was a convenience food market. They found that during a six-week preintervention phase, approximately thirty-two items were stolen per week. A program that consisted of providing tokens exchangeable for special prizes, visual feedback (the sign), and rewards for reducing merchandise loss was designed for the children who came into the market. During a six-week period in which the program was implemented, the average number of items stolen dropped from the thirty-two during preintervention to about fifteen items stolen per week. Confirming that this reduction was attributable to the intervention, the average number of items stolen per week rose to forty-four when the intervention was withdrawn. When the intervention was in effect, stealing of merchandise was 58 percent less than during the period just prior to intervention.

McNees, Egli, Marshall, Schnelle, and Risley (1976) evaluated the effects of general antishoplifting signs in one experiment and the effects of signs and

symbols that specifically identified merchandise frequently found to be missing in a second experiment. The setting of both experiments was a young women's clothing department of a large store; management had indicated that shoplifting was particularly problematic in that part of the store. In order to ensure that the interventions did not have adverse impact on sales, McNees et al. monitored daily sales volume throughout the two studies.

The first experiment evaluated the effect of four antishoplifting signs that presented the following messages: (1) shoplifting is stealing, (2) shoplifting is a crime, (3) shoplifting is not uplifting, (4) shoplifting increases inflation. The four signs were placed in the young women's clothing department.

During the preintervention period of twenty-six days, the mean number of items missing was 1.30, and the mean number of items sold was 1.04. During an intervention period of twenty days, the number of missing items per day fell to 0.88 while sales remained at approximately the same level, 1.00 per day. When the signs were removed, the number of missing items increased to 1.40 per day and sales to 2.0 per day. Thus, the placement of the general antishoplifting signs reduced but did not eliminate shoplifting.

The second experiment of McNees et al. (1976) evaluated the effect of specifically identifying items that were frequently stolen. During the intervention phase, signs (17.5 by 27.5 centimeters) were placed on clothing racks and walls in the young women's clothing department. These signs stated: "Attention Shoppers and Shoplifters: The items you see marked with a red star are items that shoplifters frequently take!" Red stars, approximately 12.5 centimeters from point to point, were mounted on racks that contained target merchandise. Six such signs and stars were placed in the department after thirty-four days of preintervention observation and were directed only at pants. After a preintervention period of forty-eight observation days, six more stars were placed in the department to designate frequently taken tops.

There was a dramatic reduction in items missing with the introduction of the signs and stars: a pre-intervention mean of 0.66 versus an intervention mean of 0.06 tops taken per day and a preintervention mean of 0.50 versus an intervention mean of 0.03 pants per day.

Comparing the results of the two experiments by McNees et al. (1976) suggests that publicly identifying specific merchandise that shoplifters most often take is more effective than general antishoplifting signs. Although specific identification of merchandise is a slightly more complicated intervention than the placement of general signs, managers of many stores may find that both procedures are economically justifiable.

In a replication and extension of the second experiment by McNees et al. (1976), Carter, Hansson, Holmberg, and Melin (1979) implemented a procedure that involved publicly identifying frequently stolen items. Carter et al. (1979) noted that the low cost and demonstrated effectiveness of the public identification procedure make it extremely attractive as a means of preventing shoplifting.

Carter et al. (1979) suggested that including a variety of target merchandise in studies of shoplifting prevention is important in assessing the generality of a procedure's effect. Besides type of merchandise, size of items may influence a procedure's utility since size affects the ease with which an item can be concealed and stolen. Additionally, the price of merchandise may influence the effectiveness of an intervention. Inexpensive items may be the object of impulse shoplifters, while expensive merchandise may attract the attention of professional shoplifters. The highly frequent theft of inexpensive items may make their loss equally costly to that of less frequently stolen expensive items. This makes it important to develop a procedure to prevent the loss of both types of merchandise.

Carter et al. (1979) learned from the management of a department store that a variety of items were frequently being stolen. Gross sales for the store in 1976 were about $21 million, with disappearances comprising 1.9 percent ($411,600).

In appropriate departments, Carter et al. (1979) placed signs that stated: "Attention! Consumers! The items marked with red circles are frequently stolen by shoplifters!" Red circles were taped to the displays directly above and behind the target merchandise. Carter et al. (1979) found that the number of missing items was reduced following the introduction of the signs and circles, while there were moderate to marked increases in sales during the period of intervention. Their measure was percentage shoplifting, defined as the number of missing items divided by the sum of missing items and items sold multiplied by 100.

In terms of this measure, they found the following:

1. Missing Elvis Presley records decreased from 9 percent during preintervention to 3 percent during intervention.
2. The loss of halogen lightbulbs was reduced from 31 percent during preintervention to 10 percent during intervention.
3. Lip gloss shortage decreased from 18 percent during preintervention to 9 percent during intervention.

It will be recalled that McNees et al. (1976) achieved almost complete elimination of the theft of targeted clothing items. The most similar item in Carter et al.'s (1979) study was leather coats. They found that disappearances of leather coats were reduced from 18 percent during preintervention to 0 percent during intervention.

An analysis of Carter et al.'s (1979) graphic data indicates there was some tendency for the theft of lip gloss and halogen bulbs to increase to preintervention levels during the final phase of intervention. This suggests the intervention's initial effect was attributable simply to its novelty. Interestingly, however, no such regression to preintervention levels was graphically indicated with respect to the Elvis Presley records and leather coats. Moreover, McNees et al.'s (1976) study reported no regression to preintervention levels during intervention with respect to the clothing items they targeted.

In a manner that can be usefully emulated in other studies, Carter et al. (1979) translated their intervention's effect into economic impact—money saved by means of the theft reduction. The item for which the intervention was most effective in reducing theft, leather coats, was also the most costly item targeted. The positive results obtained with a greater number and variety of target items than were included in the McNees et al. (1976) study imply that the procedure can be effectively extended. However, the relatively modest results obtained with the smaller, cheaper items indicate that the procedure is differentially effective depending upon the specific target item.

A subsequent study by Thurber and Snow (1980) further indicates the importance of evaluating intervention effects in particular settings. Thurber and Snow obtained results that indicate strategies to combat shoplifting may interact with and be moderated by two factors: characteristics of the target merchandise and attributes of shoplifters themselves.

Based on McNees et al.'s (1976) study, Thurber and Snow (1980) focused on the theft of cigarette packages in a retail supermarket. They conducted their research over four consecutive periods of one week each. Period 1 was a preintervention stage; during period 4 the intervention was withdrawn. During periods 2 and 3, specific and general antishoplifting signs were compared. Both the specific and general antishoplifing signs were positioned above the cigarette carton display. The specific signs (period 2 intervention) read: "Cigarettes are the items most often shoplifted in this store." The general signs (period 3 intervention) read, "Everyone pays for shoplifting."

A very disturbing result was obtained: the antishoplifting signs were associated with increases in shoplifting rates when compared to preintervention. Shoplifting frequencies of packages of cigarettes across the four periods were: 372 (preintervention), 637 (specific signs), 532 (general signs), 376 (withdrawal of intervention). The ratio of shoplifting frequency to sales was the same in periods 1 and 4, (3 percent), but increased to 5 percent with specific signs and 4 percent when the general signs were displayed.

Thurber and Snow (1980) suggested that these unanticipated results may be unique to merchandise that has high demand characteristics, that is comparatively easy to shoplift, and that is a likely object of theft for older children and adolescents who may gain peer recognition from breaking minor legal codes and outwitting security systems. This interpretation implies that the antishoplifting signs made the theft of cigarettes more challenging and attractive to certain adolescent and preadolescent subgroups that frequented that particular supermarket.

Prevention of Consumer Theft: Procedures

A. Preintervention stage
    1. Identify products suspected of theft.
    2. Take inventory of the volume of sales, the frequency of items taken, and the volume of shoppers visiting the store.
    3. Design specific signs for the suspected shoplifted merchandise similar to McNees et al. (1976), Carter et al. (1979), and Thurber and Snow (1980).
B. Intervention stage
    4. Place the signs next to the targeted merchandise being studied.
    5. Repeat step 2 during intervention.
    6. Document and record results.
C. Evaluation stage
    7. Evaluate outcomes and determine whether to maintain the program:
       a. If sales and volume of shoppers during preintervention and intervention are grossly unequal, results are likely to be difficult to interpret. In this event, reimplement the procedures in order to achieve a more reliable comparison.
       b. If sales and volume of shoppers are approximately equal during preintervention and intervention, then comparisons of items stolen during the two periods may be made. Only with such unambiguous data can a rational decision be made as to whether to maintain an intervention or replace it with a potentially more effective one.

SIGNS AND EMPLOYEE THEFT OF MERCHANDISE

McNees, Gilliam, Schnelle, and Risley (1979), noting that employee theft constitutes 75 percent of all retail theft and costs consumers and business $3.6 billion annually, studied the effects of signs in reducing theft committed by employees. Specifically, McNees et al. (1979) assessed the amount of missing merchandise, food items, during business hours when only employees were present (prior to opening and during clean-up after business hours). This intervention consisted of posting signs that specified the food item(s) taken, the time the particular item was taken, and the quantity of the item that was taken. The specific identification of stolen items appeared to be effective in reducing theft rates with respect to each targeted food item. For purpose of experimental evaluation, there were different preintervention periods regarding each food item, whereas the intervention period regarding each item was five days.

Ten days of preintervention observation regarding potato chips indicated theft rates averaged 2.1 bags stolen per day. During intervention, the rates decreased to 0.20 bag stolen per day. Fifteen days of preintervention observation regarding milk indicated theft rates averaged 3.0 cartons stolen per day. During intervention, the rate was 0.20 carton per day. Twenty days of preintervention observation regarding ice cream bars indicated theft rates averaged 3.25 ice cream bars stolen per day. During intervention, the rate was 0.20 ice cream bar. Twenty days of preintervention observation regarding cold sandwiches indicated theft rates averaged 2.0 sandwiches stolen per day. During intervention the rate was zero sandwiches stolen.

The effect of the signs in reducing theft was immediate when each food item was identified. When the sign specifying employee theft of a new food item (e.g., milk) was introduced, the previous sign (i.e., specifying potato chip theft) was removed. There was no resumption of high theft rates of previously treated items even when the sign specifying it was removed, indicating that this type of intervention can produce durable effects. Theft rates remained low for as long as three weeks following the withdrawal of intervention.

McNees et al. (1979) suggested two possible explanations for their intervention's effectiveness. First, it is possible that for the first time employees were provided with explicit feedback on a behavior that could result in dismissal and prosecution. More probably, the level of feedback specifically served to increase the threat of detection. The authors concluded that, whatever the reason for the effects, pub-licly and specifically identifying what, when, and how much employees were stealing was clearly effective and may therefore be a viable theft prevention strategy in other situations.

Prevention of Employee Theft of Merchandise: Procedures

A. Preintervention stage
   1. Identify products suspected of employee theft.
   2. Measure shrinkage by taking careful inventories.
      a. Note sales of the suspected item as compared to the initial inventory during business hours.
      b. Take inventories during pre- and postbusiness hours and compare them against daytime sales and inventories.
B. Intervention stage
   3. Post the signs identifying which product is being lost due to suspected employee theft during pre- and postbusiness hours. For example, inventories may be publicly posted on large poster boards during these hours.
   4. Repeat step 2.
   5. Document and record results.
C. Evaluation stage
   6. Evaluate outcomes and determine whether to maintain the program:
      a. If pre- and postbusiness hours show a reduction in employee theft, continue using the program.
      b. If pre- and postbusiness hours do not show any difference from preintervention, replace the program.
      c. If employee theft is difficult to differentiate from consumer theft, implement a sign program for both consumer and employee theft.

SIGNS AND EMPLOYEE THEFT OF CASH

Gaetani and Johnson (1983) evaluated the effects of signs, praise, and tangible reinforcement in decreasing cash shortages when provided to store managers in a retail beverage chain. They demonstrated that the public posting of data, praise, and the two in combination all produced decreases in cash shortages. Additionally, they demonstrated that supplementary tangible reinforcement, lottery tickets contingent upon performance by the store manager, reduced cash shortages further.

In this study, Gaetani and Johnson employed a measure of cash shortages, termed an efficiency estimate (EE). The efficiency estimate (EE) equaled the total sales divided by the cash shortages. An advantage of this ratio is that it enables direct comparisons of stores of lower sales volume with stores of higher sales volume. Gaetani and Johnson found that only minimal expenditure of time and organizational funds was necessary to maintain even the most effective of the interventions, the intervention that entailed provision of lottery tickets. The investigators state that the cost to the company "was less than $100.00, while examination of the data suggested that savings were nearly $10,000.00!" Comments by employees also indicated that, in replacing the company's previous policy of aversive feedback to store managers contingent upon poor performance, more positive channels of communication were established between upper management and store managers.

The reductions in cash shortages obtained may have been due either to reductions in theft by customers and employees or to reductions in errors related to employee carelessness in change calculations. While Gaetani and Johnson's study does not permit analysis of the relative contributions of these factors, the decreases in cash shortages reported are clearly attributable to the experimental intervention.

Prevention of Employee Theft of Cash: Procedures

A. Preintervention stage
  1. Obtain measures on total sales. Obtain measures on cash shortages.
  2. Use these data to compute an efficiency estimate (EE) per week: (EE) = total sales / cash shortages.
B. Intervention stage
  3. Publicly post an EE graph near the cash register.
  4. Use the graphs to praise employees for EEs above the preintervention EE means. In order to increase the effectiveness of this program further, it may be beneficial to add incentives for keeping EEs above the preintervention mean. As noted, Gaetani and Johnson (1983) used lottery tickets to increase and then maintain the treatments' effectiveness. Other incentives may include increased time off for lunch, permitting employees to leave work early, and providing small monetary bonuses or other relatively inexpensive rewards.
C. Evaluation stage
  5. Evaluate outcomes and determine whether to maintain the program:
    a. If cash shortages decrease, continue using the program.
    b. If cash shortages do not change, discontinue and seek another program.

SIGNS AND EMPLOYEE THEFT OF CASH: GROUP INTERVENTION

Marholin and Gray (1976) designed a group procedure to decrease cash shortages in a family-style restaurant. Fifteen full- and part-time people were employed by a small business that operated seven days a week from 9 A.M. to 1 A.M. With this procedure, cash shortages were subtracted from the salaries of employees on duty during shifts in which shortages exceeded 1 percent of total daily sales. Employees were alerted to the contingencies in effect by a small sign next to the cash register.

Initial preintervention data revealed a mean daily shortage of 4.02 percent of total daily receipts. Shortages ranged from a low of 1.13 percent to a high of 8.97 percent. Implementing the group procedure resulted in an immediate drop from the mean pretreatment shortage of 4.02 percent to a mean of 0.43 percent. In the first group response-cost condition, lasting twelve days, the 1 percent criterion level was exceeded only twice. Removing the intervention for three days resulted in an immediate increase in cash shortages per day to 3.58 percent, 6.10 percent, and 2.81 percent. Reinstating the group contingency again resulted in a reduction in cash shortages to 0.04

percent. During the twenty-one days of the group contingency reinstatement, the 1 percent criterion was never exceeded.

A practical problem identified by Marholin and Gray was observed cash overages on a number of the days during which the group contingency was in effect. It is possible, therefore, that the victim of theft became the customer instead of the employer; that is, the employees may have resorted to shortchanging the customer rather than taking money directly from the cash register. Another possibility is that cashiers may have begun underringing sales. These possibilities might be addressed by conducting unobtrusive observations of cashier-customer interaction (e.g., frequency of customer complaints) and of other cashier behaviors (e.g., register ringing accuracy).

Marholin and Gray (1976) present a thorough discussion of potential legal difficulties in utilizing group-cost contingencies. Although discussion of the rights of employees and constitutional responsibilities of employers is beyond the scope of this chapter, readers should consider the cautionary notes and pertinent literature discussed by Marholin and Gray.

Prevention of Employee Theft of Cash, Group Intervention: Procedures

A. Preintervention stage
1. Take measures on all cashiers' cash register balances. Compare these balances to the cumulative sales.
2. Note and record discrepancies in sales and cash. It is recommended that a minimum preintervention record of one week be collected for each cashier so that a trend may be established. If major discrepancies in sales and cash exist, implement the intervention stage.
3. Set criteria for the group response-cost procedure. (In taking this step, it is important to comply with federal laws regarding the amount of money subtracted from an employee's gross wage as established by the minimum wage clause of the Fair Labor Standards Act.)
B. Intervention stage
4. Inform each cashier of the contingency in effect and place a small sign stating the group-response cost. Note any cash shortages per day. If criterion is met, deduct the designated amount from each employee's salary.
5. Compare cashiers' balances over a one-week intervention period with balances over a one-week preintervention period.
C. Evaluation Stage
6. Evaluate outcomes and determine whether to maintain the program:
   a. If cashiers' balances improve, continue the program.
   b. If cashiers' balances do not improve, replace the program.

SUMMARY AND DISCUSSION

A primary objective of a business manager is to improve the bottom line. This objective is dependent on several specific managerial tasks associated with reducing expenditures, increasing sales and revenues, reducing production and delivery costs, increasing productivity, and reducing overhead, including inventory loss. The manager's compensation is often determined by improvements in these areas and consequent increases in company profits.

The purpose of this chapter was to describe how signs can be used to control consumer and employee theft. The reviewed research demonstrates that signs, when systematically applied and evaluated, can be effective interventions in reducing consumer and employee theft. Figure 85–1 illustrates the studies employing public postings directed at consumer theft. Figure 85–1 illustrates the studies employing public postings directed at consumer theft. Of the relatively small number of studies that meet our criteria for review, three of the four directed at consumer theft were effective: McNees et al. (1976), Carter at al. (1979), and McNees et al. (1980). Thurber & Snow (1980), the fourth consumer study reviewed, found that shoplifting signs were not effective in reducing or

Figure 85–1. Studies Employing Public Posting of Signs: Consumer Theft

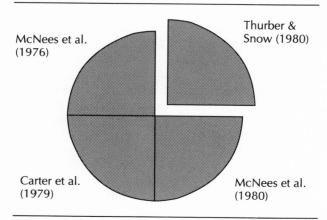

Figure 85–2. Studies Employing Public Posting of Signs: Employee Theft

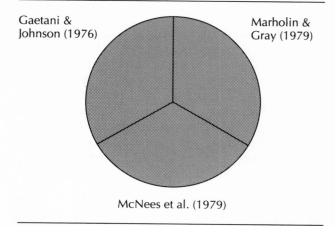

controlling consumer theft. Instead, it was found that antishoplifting signs may, in fact, increase consumer theft.

Three studies met our criteria for review regarding the use of signs to decrease employee theft: Marholin and Gray, 1976; McNees et al. 1979; and Gaetani and Johnson, 1983. Each of these studies demonstrated that signs are effective in reducing or eliminating employee theft. See figure 85–2.

It is evident that additional research is necessary to determine when an intervention will reduce shoplifting and when an intervention may actually exacerbate the problem. Some interventions may be both relatively simple to implement and highly beneficial to an organization. For example, the intervention of McNees et al. (1976) was effective in eliminating womens' clothing theft, and that of Carter et al. (1979) was effective in eliminating the theft of leather coats. Thurber and Snow's findings indicate, however, that it would be risky to implement an intervention without frequent evaluations of its effects, even though someone may have found it to be highly effective in a different setting. Also, the type of shoplifter that may be attracted to expensive as opposed to inexpensive merchandise is potentially important with respect to the design of interventions.

The cautions regarding the use of group interventions, suggested by Marholin & Gray (1980), illustrate the issues a manager must consider when intervening with employee compensation. There is little sense in having rules designed to govern employee behavior unless contingent consequences can be implemented. Therefore, it is not advisable to implement a group contingency system without establishing whether there is compliance with union or individual contracts and without prior consideration of such issues as minimum wage laws and laws pertinent to discipline policy and disparate treatment.

Just as there is little sense in having rules without legally enforceable consequences, so too is there little sense in having a rule without its being communicated. Putting the contingency in writing (the sign), distributing it to employees or consumers (the public posting), and verifying that employees and representatives of consumer groups understand the procedure is a way to ensure that employees and consumers are informed of rules and consequences. Clearly, the objective is not to terminate employees or to lock up consumers who are stealing; the objective is to eliminate stealing.

While good practice is directed by good research, it is not always in the manager's purview to implement and evaluate studies measuring interventions' effectiveness. Similarly, it is not always within the manager's domain to enforce rules and regulations. This is especially true for store or department managers who report to an active superior. While the studies reviewed provide the reader with general procedures to follow in an attempt to control business loss, these procedures could not be implemented successfully without supportive management practices with respect to both inventory monitoring and consequences to be applied once the occurrence of theft has been established.

Essential to a decision to implement any program is knowing how accountable upper management expects middle managers and employees to be for the business' resources. If upper management expects middle managers and employees to be accountable, then upper management must follow through with consequences for those who steal. Rules without follow-through are not rules. Additionally, prior to implementing any procedure, it is advisable to conduct an analysis of the cost of monitoring the system as compared to the cost due to consumer and employee theft. If one is going to implement a procedure, it should be done with accurate information as to the bottom-line impact on the organization. Clearly, the cost of the intervention cannot outweigh the cost of preintervention losses.

Finally, it is important to have inventory systems that monitor transactions and inventory in reference to establish norms and to communicate discrepancies from norms to employees. This communication is another form of public posting. The studies reviewed indicate there is a high probability that public posting interventions, when properly implemented, will reduce or eliminate shoplifting and employee theft.

REFERENCES

Arboleda-Florez, J., Durie, H., & Costello, J. (1977). Shoplifting—an ordinary crime? *International Journal of Offender Therapy and Comparative Criminology, 21,* 201–207.

Carter, N., Hansson, L., Holmberg, B., & Melin, L. (1979). Shoplifting reduction through the use of specific signs.

Journal of Organizational Behavior Management, 2, 78–84.

Gaetani, J.J., & Johnson, C.M. (1983). The effect of data plotting, praise, and state lottery tickets on decreasing cash shortages in a retail beverage chain. *Journal of Organizational Behavior Management, 5,* 5–15.

Gauthier, J., & Pellerin, D. (1982). Management of compulsive shoplifting through covert sensitization. *Journal of Behavior Therapy and Experimental Psychiatry, 13*, 73–75.

Heinstein, G.H. (1974). The truth about teen-age shoplifting. *Parents Magazine, 49*, 42–43, 60–61.

Henderson, J.Q. (1981). A behavioral approach to stealing: A proposal for treatment based on ten cases. *Journal of Behavior Therapy and Experimental Psychiatry, 12*, 231–236.

Kellam, A.M.P. (1969). Shoplifting treated by aversion to a film. *Behavior Research and Therapy, 7*, 125–127.

Lykken, D.T. (1974). Psychology and the lie detector industry. *American Psychologist, 29*, 725–739.

McNees, M.P., Egli, D.S., Marshall, R.S., Schnelle, J.F., & Risley, T.R. (1976). Shoplifting prevention: Providing information through signs. *Journal of Applied Behavior Analysis, 9*, 399–405.

McNees, M.R., Gilliam, S.W., Schnelle, J.F., & Risley, T.R. (1979). Controlling employee theft through time and product identification. *Journal of Organizational Behavior Management, 2*, 113–119.

McNees, M.P., Kennon, M., Schnelle, J.F., Kirchner, R.E., & Thomas, M.M. (1980). An experimental analysis of a program to reduce retail theft. *American Journal of Community Psychology, 8*, 379–385.

Marholin, D., & Gray, D. (1976). Effects of group-response procedures on cash shortages in a small business. *Journal of Applied Behavior Analysis, 9*, 25–30.

To catch a thief. (1974). *Newsweek*, (September), 79–80.

Thurber, S., & Snow, M. (1980). Signs may prompt antisocial behavior. *Journal of Social Psychology, 112*, 309–310

Wright, R.A. (1972). Nation's retail merchants mobilize security systems to combat fast-growing shoplifting trend. *New York Times*, (May 21), p. 51N.

INDEX

ABOUT THE EDITORS

John W. Jones, Ph.D., is vice president of research and development for London House, Inc., Park Ridge, Illinois. London House is an organization of human resource professionals who develop and implement psychological testing and evaluation systems for business and industry.

Well-known for his work in risk management, especially in the areas of substance abuse, industrial safety, and burnout, Dr. Jones has had extensive experience in industrial/organizational psychology. Most recently, he was chief industrial/organizational psychologist at the St. Paul Fire and Marine Insurance Company, a subsidiary of the St. Paul Insurance Companies. He was founder and director of the International Human Factors Institute for Loss Control, the St. Paul Insurance Companies.

Dr. Jones is the founder and editor-in-chief of the *Journal of Business and Psychology,* a scholarly periodical devoted to articles on all aspects of psychology that apply to business settings. In addition, he is associate editor of *The American Journal of Health Promotion.* He is the author or co-author of 15 psychological tests and surveys, as well as 5 books. He is senior editor of *Applying Psychology in Business: The Handbook for Managers and Human Resource Professionals* (Lexington Books, 1990). He has published over 80 articles and has frequently presented papers at scholarly and professional conferences.

Dr. Jones has broad clinical experience, specializing in employee health psychology. He has been awarded Diplomat status by the American Board of Medical Psychotherapists. He is a certified clinical mental health counselor and a licensed clinical psychologist in the state of Illinois. He has served as consulting psychologist at the Salvation Army Tom Seay Service Center. He was also staff psychologist at the Lutheran Center for Substance Abuse, Lutheran General Hospital, Park Ridge, Illinois.

He is a member of the American Psychological Association (APA), the Society of Industrial and Organizational Psychologists (APA Division 14), the Society of Psychologists in Management, the American Management Association, the Association of Personnel Test Publishers, and the American Mental Health Counselors Association.

Dr. Jones holds a B.A. in psychology from the University of Cincinnati; an M.A. in applied experimental psychology from DePaul University, Chicago; and a Ph.D. in psychology, specializing in industrial/organizational psychology, applied research and counseling psychology, also from DePaul University.

Brian D. Steffy currently teaches at Franklin and Marshall College, Lancaster, PA. Previously he taught at the University of Minnesota's Industrial Relations Center and at the University of Kentucky. Prior to teaching he worked as a psychiatric social worker. Dr. Steffy is co-founder of Human Factors Systems, a personnel consulting firm.

Dr. Steffy's research work is quite broad and he has contributed numerous articles to publications such as *Journal of Applied Psychology, Organizational Behavior and Human Decision Processes, Personnel Psychology, Academy of Management Review, Academy of Management Journal, Journal of Vocational Behavior,* and *Journal of Occupational Psychology.*

He is associate editor of the *Journal of Business and Psychology* and permanent reviewer for the *American Journal of Health Promotion.* His current research deals with the conceptualization and measurement of human economic productivity and the impact of personnel investments on the value of the firm. Past research dealt with such topics as physiological correlates of job stress, stess and medical malpractice, employment discrimination in selection, job search, and problems in dual-career families.

Dr. Steffy received his Ph.D. in human resource management from the University of Georgia. Other graduate work was done at Duke University and the State University of New York-Binghamton.

Douglas W. Bray is chairman of the board of Development Dimensions International, a leading human resources development firm which he co-founded with William C. Byham in 1970. Overlapping with this activity was his twenty-eight year career with AT&T from which he retired in 1983 as director of basic human resources research.

While at AT&T, Dr. Bray initiated and conducted ambitious longitudinal studies of managerial careers, one product of which was his award winning book, co-authored with Ann Howard, *Managerial Lives in Transition: Advancing Age and Changing Times.* As part of this research, Dr. Bray designed and applied the first management assessment center in 1956. He has been involved in assessment center research and development ever since.

Dr. Bray has been president of the Division of Industrial and Organizational Psychology of the American Psychological Association, president of the American Board of Professional Psychology, and chair of the American Psychological Association Task Force on the Practice of Psychology in Industry.

Dr. Bray has received awards for Distinguished Contributions to Applied Psychology from the American Psychological Association, the Society for Industrial and Organizational Psychology, the American Board of Professional Psychology, the Society of Psychologists in Management, the APA Division of Consulting Psychology, and Hofstra University.

His Ph.D. in psychology is from Yale University.